D0559368

"[A] simultaneous submission is simply bad manners and one more symptom of our national obsession with speed."
—John Daniel, **Wilderness**

"No simultaneous submissions please. Poems are often selected because they complement other work, so when a poem is withdrawn, the effect is often more than the loss of that individual work."
—**Douglas DeMars, Nightsun**

"Simultaneous submissions? Why not? Life is short! But honesty dictates divulging same."
—**Don D. Wilson, Singular Speech Press**

"We are giving some thought to abandoning our policy of reading/accepting simultaneous submissions because a few authors have abused this policy by withdrawing accepted work just prior to publication. One or two have had the audacity to send a substitute, usually inferior. For the moment, we are continuing this courtesy, but we may soon rather not read simultaneous submissions."
—**Anonymous**

"Writers should submit and publish their work whenever and wherever they can. The only time an editor/publisher should ask/demand unpublished/nonsimultaneous work is when he pays enough to deserve that."
—**Troxey Kemper, Tucumcari Literary Review**

1996
Poet's Market

Where & how to publish your poetry

Edited by
Christine Martin

Assisted by
Chantelle Bentley

WRITER'S DIGEST BOOKS
Cincinnati, Ohio

If you are a poetry publisher and would like to be considered for a listing in the next edition of Poet's Market, *please request a questionnaire from* Poet's Market—*QR, 1507 Dana Ave.,* Cincinnati, Ohio 45207. Questionnaires received after March 15, 1996, will be held for the 1998 edition.

Distributed in Canada by McGraw-Hill Ryerson, 300 Water Street
Whitby Ontario L1N 9B6.
Also distributed in Australia by Kirby Books, Private Bag No. 19, P.O. Alexandria NSW 2015.

Managing Editor, Market Books Department: Constance J. Achabal;
Supervising Editor: Michael Willins.

This 1996 hardcover edition of Poet's Market features a "self-jacket" that eliminates the need for a separate dust jacket. It provides sturdy protection for your book while it saves paper, trees and energy.

International Standard Serial Number 0883-5470
International Standard Book Number 0-89879-712-8

Cover Illustration: Mercedes McDonald

Attention Booksellers: This is an annual directory of F&W Publications. Return deadline for this edition is December 31, 1996.

Contents

The Markets

Resources

Indexes

From the Editor

Drive down to your favorite bookstore and you're sure to find new poetry collections—and new journals seeking poetry for publication—just waiting to be devoured. Call on your local café for a cup of coffee and you'll probably catch word about an upcoming poetry reading. Turn on your television and you can tune in to well-known poets reading their work and sharing their views about poetry on PBS.

Today, opportunities to get involved in the world of poetry are everywhere. And you can bring them even closer to home with this directory. In fact, this edition of *Poet's Market*—the largest ever—provides you with opportunities to see your work in print, read your work aloud, and hear different poetic voices—all in one package.

First, *Poet's Market* includes listings of 1,700 poetry publishers—300 of which are new to this edition. You'll find small publications solely devoted to poetry, literary journals with space for both poetry and fiction, and larger magazines that use one or two poems in each issue. You'll also discover listings for numerous chapbook and book publishers. And if you're not sure what a "chapbook" is, you can learn all about this manner of publication by reading our interview with **Laurence F. Hawkins**, editor and publisher of Trout Creek Press.

Second, this edition features a special article about poetry readings, including how to read your work in front of an audience, how to locate information about readings in your area, and how to organize readings if you're unable to find any venues in your neighborhood. Besides the general places mentioned as sources of information, you'll also find a list of specific organizations and publications to contact. And, in a separate interview with **Patrick McKinnon**, director of Poetry Harbor, you'll learn how a successful reading spawned an entire organization promoting poetry.

Third, as in years past, we include interviews with a variety of poets who not only talk about their work but also offer advice on writing and submitting poetry. In our in-depth interviews, which now feature full-length poetry selections, you can discover the diverse voices of poets **Ayanna Black**, **Chrystos**, **William Greenway**, and **Lola Haskins**. You'll also hear from **Paul B. Janeczko**, who writes poetry—and compiles anthologies—for young adults, as well as well-known cowboy poet **Wallace McRae**.

In addition, this year you'll hear directly from editors and publishers about the "business aspects" of submitting poetry. Many have detailed their preferences within their listings, and you'll find a sampling of their general opinions on the endleaves of this edition. As always, we provide a comprehensive, step-by-step article about the submission process. And be sure to read the interview with **Timothy Hodor**, a poet who has successfully followed our procedures.

Finally, *Poet's Market* not only includes information about publishers of poetry, but you'll also find updated listings for conferences and workshops, writing colonies, useful organizations and publications, and contests and awards. In fact, turn the page and you'll find details about our own poetry contest. With this directory in your possession, opportunities are truly at your fingertips!

Christine Martin

A Call for Entries

Would you like to see your work in the next edition of *Poet's Market*? All you need to do is write a great poem(s) about writing or submitting poetry—any aspect of the process—and enter your work in our poetry contest. The best three poems will be published in the *1997 Poet's Market*. And the three winners will receive a free copy of our annual directory and a cash prize of $100, $75 or $50, respectively. Read the following rules for details.

1. All poems must be original, unpublished, and not under consideration by any other publisher or in any other contest.

2. *Poet's Market* retains first publication rights to the three winning poems, which will be published in the 1997 edition (to be released in September 1996). All other rights will be returned.

3. Each poem must relate to the writing or submitting of poetry. Poems may be in any form, rhymed or unrhymed, but no poem can exceed 32 lines in length.

4. You may enter as many poems as you like, but each poem counts as one entry and must be accompanied by a $3 handling fee. (Make checks or money orders payable to Writer's Digest Books.)

5. Poems must be clearly typed (single-spaced with double-spacing between stanzas) on one side of $8\frac{1}{2} \times 11$ white paper.

6. You must submit two copies of each entry. On one copy, include your name, address and telephone number in the upper left corner. The second copy must only contain the poem. Entries will be separated on arrival to allow for blind judging.

7. All entries must be postmarked by midnight, January 31, 1996. Note that manuscripts cannot be acknowledged or returned.

8. Every entry will be read and judged by the staff of *Poet's Market*. In the event of a tie, an outside judge will be consulted.

9. Winning poets will be notified by phone on or before March 15, 1996. To receive the names of the winning poets (after March 15, 1996), you must enclose a self-addressed, stamped envelope with your entry.

10. The three winning poets will receive $100, $75 or $50, respectively, and a copy of the *1997 Poet's Market*.

11. Employees of F&W Publications, Inc. and their immediate family members are not eligible.

12. *Poet's Market* reserves the right to forego publication of any winning entry. In such cases, first rights will be returned.

Note: Failure to comply with these guidelines will result in disqualification.

Send entries to: *1997 Poet's Market* Poetry Contest
1507 Dana Ave.
Cincinnati, OH 45207

Deadline: January 31, 1996

How to Use Your *Poet's Market*

To reap the benefits of *Poet's Market*, you need to know how to use it. After all, this directory not only provides listings of poetry publishers, but it is also designed to help you determine which ones are the best markets for your work.

The first step, however, is to examine your poetry. Do you write poetry that makes a political statement? Poetry about wildlife? religious symbols? other poets? Do you write sonnets? prose poems? About a certain area? In a language other than English?

Maybe you don't write any specific type of poetry. Maybe the answer depends on which one of your works we're talking about. No matter. If you've put craft into your poems, you'll find places for them.

Start with the indexes

All Publishers of Poetry listings are coded as to the category of poetry they are seeking. Publishers that desire poetry within certain realms—on certain subjects, in certain forms, or by certain folks—can be quickly identified by a **IV** and terms denoting the specialization(s). For example, *The Leading Edge* is coded **IV-Science fiction/ fantasy** because it seeks material related to those genres.

Once you've defined your own poetry, you don't have to comb each page for compatible listings. Turn to the Subject Index (where you will find all publishers with **IV** codes divided according to their specializations) and scan the boldface headings to locate the specialization that matches your work. If you write haiku, for instance, check under **Form/Style**. If you're an older adult who writes about the woods near your home, check under both **Senior Citizen** and **Nature/Rural/Ecology** and write down the names of those publishers that sound interesting.

Publishers may classify themselves as **Regional** in the Subject Index, but checking the Geographical Index is also helpful. There you'll discover the publishers located in your state or country. While some don't consider themselves "regional" in terms of the poetry they accept, they are often more open to writers from their own areas.

Also useful, particularly if you're trying to publish a small collection of poems, is the Chapbook Publishers Index, which lists publishers who consider chapbook manuscripts (typically 20-25 pages of poetry connected by a theme). For a closer look at a chapbook publisher, read the interview with Laurence F. Hawkins on pages 404-405. You'll also find information about both chapbook and book publishing in Charting Your Path to Poetry Publication, beginning on page 11.

Check market codes

Once you have a list of possible markets for your work—because of specialization or location or an interest in chapbooks—look up each listing and check the market category code(s) following the title to discover how open it is to submissions.

Besides a **IV** code, a publisher can also have **I**, **II**, **III** or **V**. Those with **I** are open to beginners' submissions, so if you're just starting out, try sending to them. Publishers with **II** codes are general markets which expect you to be familiar with literary journals and magazines. Those coded **III** are limited as to the number of submissions they accept, so your chances of publishing with these folks are limited too. Finally, those with **V** are not accepting unsolicited manuscripts. Although you may have picked such a publisher out of the Geographical Index, you can't submit your poetry to it at this time. That's okay. Cross it off your list and move on to the next one.

When you discover publishers with more than one code, read their listings to determine if they're still possible markets for your work. For instance, a publisher may be **I, IV-Religious**, which means it either wants religious material as well as poetry from beginners or religious material only, including poetry from beginners. To learn more about market category codes, see the Publishers of Poetry introduction.

Also, as you read the listings based on the indexes, others will attract your eye. Don't feel limited by those on your list. Many publications don't want to be noted for a specialization and are open to ALL types of work.

Read carefully

When you've refined your list of possible markets by checking market categories, study each listing *carefully*. Look for the general purpose of the publisher and statements about its interests in poetry. For example, *Hellas* accepts any kind of poetry but especially welcomes poems in meter. In their listing, they say, "We prize elegance and formality in verse, but specifically encourage poetry of the utmost boldness and innovation, so long as it is not willfully obscurantist."

Also, the names of recently published poets and sample lines of poetry will indicate what level of writing an editor is seeking and provide insight into editorial tastes.

Consider the date a publisher was founded as well. Older publishers have more stability, and sometimes more prestige. However, newer publishers, especially those new to this edition (designated by a ‡), are often more receptive to submissions.

Carefully reading the description of a publication's format will help you visualize how your poetry will appear in its pages. Better yet, review sample copies. This is the best way to determine whether your poetry is right for a publication. Sample copies can be ordered from publishers or often found in your library or local bookstore.

However, don't just locate a sample copy, decide your work is appropriate, and submit to that market without knowing submission procedures. Inappropriate submissions will not only leave a bad impression of your work, but they can also affect a publisher's willingness to accept unsolicited manuscripts from others as well.

If you haven't already done so, read Charting Your Path to Poetry Publication. It offers a step-by-step approach to every aspect of the submission process. Most publishers also include specific submission procedures in their listings. And many offer guidelines for a self-addressed, stamped envelope (SASE). Send for them. The goal, after all, is to increase—not decrease—your chances of acceptance.

Other resources

As you develop your craft, take advantage of the various resources for poets. For support services and feedback from others, for example, join one of the groups listed in Organizations Useful to Poets. If you're searching for a place to get away and write, check Writing Colonies. Or, if you're seeking instruction and marketing tips, attend one of the events in Conferences and Workshops or consult one of the magazines listed in Publications Useful to Poets.

Finally, if you don't recognize a symbol or an abbreviation being used, refer to the Key to Symbols on page 18 or the Glossary on page 513. And, for easy reference, you will find a list of U.S. and Canadian Postal Codes on page 17.

Meet the Poetry Community Through Open Readings

by Carolyn Peyser

Standing just inside the door of New York City's Nuyorican Poets Cafe, I had barely adjusted to the darkness of the room when the guy making announcements at the mike stopped mid-sentence, smiled at me and said, "Hi, do you want to read?"

I froze. I'd never been to a reading before (wasn't even sure what one *was*), had never written a poem on my own, and for no apparent reason had elected to visit the café for an "open room" which I'd heard about on the radio. By now, the ten other people in the room had turned in their seats and were looking at me. "Can I just listen?" I asked.

That was September 1991, when I first stumbled into the poetry scene—discovering there an empathy that quickly became a molten desire to read and hear other people's poetry and to write and read my own poems. That's what this article is about: getting out there, getting into it, getting your voice raised and your words heard.

Open readings, in which anyone can participate, introduce you and your work to the community of poets. Each reading is a time and place to share your poetic voice, try new ideas, hear different ways to write and perform poetry, keep your mind open and your heart flexible. And if you're lucky, you'll get to hear someone haltingly, delicately read a poem to an audience for the first time. That gives me incredible chills.

Nervous about reading aloud?

Of course, when you first want to read your work, getting up in front of an audience is half the battle. Yes, most people's knees have knocked at some early point when faced with performance. But that's okay. From all the readings I've listened to and participated in, here are some suggestions to ease the fears of new readers:

• Try poems out on yourself, full voice, first. Then corral one or two friends and read to them. If they happen to have performing experience of any kind, that's a plus, but it's not necessary. While your friends will most likely be honored to hear your poems, what's most important is to get feedback on volume and whether you're reading too fast, so your words will have the vocal clarity they deserve. Microphones are tools toward this end. Most need readers to be not more than two inches away. Practice with a mike if you can.

• Memorize only if you want to. There's nothing wrong with reading from the page in an open reading—or in a featured guest reading, for that matter. Letting the audience see your face as you see them, and being unencumbered by paper, however, can be a powerful experience for listeners *and* readers.

*Carolyn Peyser is the public relations director for Poets House, New York City's 30,000-volume poetry library and literary resource center. Co-producer of the spoken-word CD **Nuyorican Symphony** (Knitting Factory Works, 1994), she also worked on project development and fundraising for the five-part PBS series **The United States of Poetry** (Washington Square Films/ITVS, 1995). The series, which airs early in 1996, presents the words of more than 60 contemporary poets—ages 6 to 88—speaking from and about all walks of life.*

If you are reading from the page, maybe you can occasionally finish a line from memory as you look at your audience. If you're uneasy about meeting people's eyes, skim the tops of their heads as you scan the room; the listeners will think you're looking right at them.

• Worried about your hands shaking noticeably? Try placing your poems in a light-weight vinyl binder that can fold back on itself—so you can hold it with one hand as you read. It can be fun to have one hand free . . . and unsupported paper really *does* show the shakes.

• Remember to be as supportive and attentive to other poets as you'd like them to be for you. And follow the "house rules." Sometimes it's one poem per reader, or the time limit might be three to five minutes (more in less populated situations). Know how long your work takes to read—you get this from timing your poems as you read them aloud—and be respectful of the other poets in the room. We all want to be heard, and the good news is there are a lot of us. Be fair to the others who want to read, and keep "your time" in mind.

Just want to listen? That's great, too. Poets eager to read their poems and people hungry to hear them feed each other. But try not to talk during readings. Listen. These are words that have not gone through a juried selection process, nor have they been approved by corporate sponsors. This is fresh air—in the midst of ever-intensifying pollution. If you want to leave before the reading is finished, though, try to wait until a poem has ended so you don't interrupt the focus of the poet and listeners. Also, don't be shy about telling a poet you like the work once a reading is over. That can mean as much as, or much more than, applause levels. That said, don't hesitate to clap!

Where o where

Yet, before you can decide if readings are right for you, you must first discover where they are held in your area. While open-mike readings, or open mikes as they're often called, are in urban centers and suburban areas across the country, sometimes it takes a little work to find them. Following this article is a list of specific places and publications that have such information, but here are some general ideas.

Check with your state's arts council. Some—including Alaska, Hawaii, Illinois, Ohio and Wyoming—are very tapped in to this information. For addresses and phone numbers of arts councils in both the United States and Canada, see the State and Provincial Grants section in this directory.

Any colleges or universities in your area? English departments and student activities lines are good prospects for information about readings. Also contact the public library, adult education centers and bookstores—particularly those with a literary bent.

Weekend arts sections in your daily paper—and smaller weeklies—will often carry listings of poetry events. Other possibilities can be found in Organizations Useful to Poets beginning on page 498. And looking in the business section of the white pages in the phone book under "poetry," "writer," etc., *might* bear some fruit, too.

In addition, contact one of the literary centers springing up around the country. The National Association of Independent Literary Centers is in formation and seeks "to establish a greater understanding of and appreciation for contemporary literature and a broader interaction between writers and the wider community by offering a range of services to writers at all stages of their development, presenting programs to the general public, and providing a space that creates a permanent, year-round presence for literature in the community." If these centers don't know where local open mikes are, they are bound to know where to direct you for information.

You might also learn that independent literary centers—like my "home base," Poets House in New York City—are presenting poetic events not necessarily geared to poets reading their own work but, for example, poets reading and discussing the work of poets who have influenced them. Support these nonprofit centers. They are yet another way to keep the wide world of poetry open and accessible to all.

And then there was the slam!

In your search for open mikes, by the way, you may run across information about slams. A slam is an age-old contest which began its 20th-century incarnation as a poet/performer-controlled show in Chicago in the early 1970s. It is often a three- or four-round mock poetic competition among three or more poets who are scored Olympic-style by judges chosen from the audience. At the Nuyorican Poets Cafe, it's preceded by a poet performing in a 20-minute Spotlite and followed by an early morning Open Room where anyone may read *one* poem.

Today, slams—like open mikes—are popping up across the country. The slamming poets are usually booked ahead of time, and prize money often isn't much—and needn't be. Slam Opens, where anyone who walks in can compete, are often crowded with participating poets so there might be fewer rounds. They are chances to put your toes in the waters before jumping headlong into a regular slam.

If winning is the highest priority among the participating poets and hosts, if poets write and perform work whose *raison d'être* is to score well, or if *anybody* takes the whimsically chosen judges' scores too seriously, people are missing the point. A slam at its usual best is challenging, energized, poetic entertainment that sharpens your mind and tunes your ears as you experience a great deal of poetry. I've participated in (and lost!) several full-length slams—and have heard *many* more during the past four years. I've had a great time, learned a lot, and my exposure hasn't been fatal—or even damaging.

Want to start an open mike?

Above all, know that there are no hard-and-fast rules as to how to organize an open-mike reading. If it's in a living room or a fairly small public space, you don't even need the mike. It can be as freewheeling and informal as Our Unorganized Reading Series, held in the basement of ABC No Rio (a rock club in Manhattan's Lower East Side) on quiet Sunday afternoons when there's "no time limit, list, features, b.s." . . . and no regular host. Biblio's Bookstore and Cafe in New York's neighboring Tribeca is the softly lit, snug home for various reading series each week, including Matthew Courtney's open mike every Thursday night.

The times I've been at No Rio the proprietor was not present and food and drink had to be purchased outside; most of the time there was heat when needed. At Biblio's the owners are in rapt, supportive attendance, offering (for sale) a variety of beverages and other treats. And, at the heart of the East Village/Lower East Side poetry scene, at The Poetry Project at St. Mark's Church-in-the-Bowery, there have been several weekly, nighttime feature and open-mike reading series held in the landmark church since 1966. My point is readings can be held anywhere, anytime.

When you're looking for a presenting space in which to start an open-mike reading, check public libraries, local colleges and bookstores (which often have free space available for public use), coffee shops and cafés (which are more apt to ask for some kind of fee) and bars (which most likely will demand one). Often weeknights, normally quiet weekend afternoons, or early evenings are good times to try at first.

Whatever the case, be sure to find out what the owner's ideas are about poetry. I recently heard a story where an open mike became an ongoing platform for derisive speeches (with line breaks, presumably) about people in town *and* in the room. The disgruntled proprietor—who had been expecting a more conventional kind of verse—soon silenced the series. I've heard similar stories before.

The emcee (or organizer, if they're different) may need to use a sense of humor, humanity, and strength of conviction to defuse possible problems so a series can continue. The lesson here is mainly to keep in touch with the hosting staff. It doesn't need to be much, but you'll get a lot more leeway—and have much more fun—if things stay open and friendly. The fact that things poetic usually aren't major money-makers, a current reality we all live with, is another reason to keep your host on your side. However, bend only as much as you can bear. And remember to publicize, publicize, publicize!

A few notes for emcees

First, be sure to use a mike if the room size demands it, if you expect an audience of more than 15 people, or if you want to record the reading. Remember to test all equipment *before* the reading begins; obvious, maybe, but it often gets overlooked.

Know that serving hungry poets, the audience, and the word is a true responsibility—and a noble task. It behooves you to set an example by paying attention to the poet reading—and to be fair. Let poets know if they're running over their time limits. Use your judgment, though; sometimes "rules" can be bent when an earnest poet *needs* to read. Just be ready afterwards to deal with other poets who want equal time.

Many emcees begin open-mike readings by booking a reader to give a 10- to 15-minute featured reading to warm up the room or set a mood. These poets might (rightfully) expect a piece of the door receipts, so settle that *before* the evening's over.

If you're working with a nonprofit group that wants to sponsor an open mike (with features or not) and can budget for it, good suggestions are found in *Author & Audience: A Readings and Workshops Guide*, a terrific resource for writers and presenters which also lists national venues. It is available from Poets & Writers, Inc.; see their listing in Publications Useful to Poets.

Finally, as emcee you're running the show, but that doesn't mean it's *your* show. Warming up the room with a poem of your own (or that of another poet) is a great thing to do, but it's my opinion that a five- to ten-minute emcee feature is out of line. So is peppering the reading with your own poems. Be generous, and give the mike to the poets supporting the reading.

While open mikes are not for everyone, I've lived in and loved the reading scene for a number of years, and I encourage everyone of any age to get involved. Try out different venues, and find a situation that is comfortable for you. Not only will you have the opportunity as a poet to share your work with other poets and lovers of language, but as part of the audience you will hear what other people are thinking about and how they fashion their thoughts into the gorgeous variety of verse that is poetry today.

Looking for information on readings?

Here are some of the organizations and publications in the United States and Canada that have information on open-mike readings (and often much more). Be sure to check with the arts council in your area for additional opportunities (see State and Provincial Grants on pages 473-475). And read Meet the Poetry Community Through Open Readings for other resources as well as tips about organizing readings in your area.

United States

●**ALABAMA:** *Where Poets Speak*, 1516 S. 16th Ave., Birmingham 35205.

●**ARIZONA:** *South Ash Press*, 2311 E. Indian School Rd., Phoenix 85016; also see the listing in the Publishers of Poetry section.

The Writer's Voice, Scottsdale/Paradise Valley YMCA, 6869 E. Shea Blvd., Scottsdale 85254.

●**ARKANSAS:** Ozark Poets and Writers Collective, P.O. Box 3717, Fayetteville 72721-3717.

●**CALIFORNIA:** *Caffeine*, P.O. Box 4231-306, Woodland Hills 91365; e-mail: poetrymag@aol.com.

Cups, 1101 Clay St., San Francisco 94108; e-mail: cupsmag@aol.com.

NEXT . . . , P.O. Box 13019, Long Beach 90803; e-mail: NEXTmag@aol.com.

Out/Spoken, 4773 Harmony Lane, Orcutt 93455.

Poetry Conspiracy, P.O. Box 3762, San Diego 92163-1762.

Poetry Flash: A Poetry Review and Literary Calendar for the West, P.O. Box 4172, Berkeley 94704. Includes nationwide listings; found free in selected sites, $15 subscription.

The Shire Post, 940 E. Colorado Blvd., #412, Pasadena 91106; e-mail: BernieZfan@aol.com.

●**CONNECTICUT:** The Writer's Voice, Greater Bridgeport/Fairfield YMCA, 841 Old Post Rd., Fairfield 06430.

●**DISTRICT OF COLUMBIA:** Husain Naqvi, Box 578707, Room LXRG106, Georgetown University, Washington 20057.

●**FLORIDA:** The Writer's Voice, c/o Tampa Metropolitan Area YMCA, 110 E. Oak Ave., Tampa 33602.

●**GEORGIA:** *The Shaky Table*, c/o Cafe Diem, 640 N. Highland Ave., Atlanta 30306.

Atlanta Writing Resource Center, 750 Kalb St., Atlanta 30312.

●**ILLINOIS:** *Letter eX*, P.O. Box 476920, Chicago 60647-6920.

The Writer's Voice, Duncan YMCA, 1001 W. Roosevelt Rd., Chicago 60608.

●**INDIANA:** Writers' Center, P.O. Box 88386, Indianapolis 46208; also see the listing for the Writers' Center Press in Publishers of Poetry.

●**KENTUCKY:** The Writer's Voice, The YMCA of Central Kentucky, The Carnegie Center, 251 W. Second St., Lexington 40507.

●**MARYLAND:** The Writer's Center, Attn: Jane Fox, 4508 Walsh St., Bethesda 20815; has modem bulletin board. Also see the listing in Organizations Useful to Poets.

●**MASSACHUSETTS:** *Slam*, 24 Arlington St., Medford 02155; e-mail: BosSlam@aol.com.

●**MICHIGAN:** Poetry Resource Center of Michigan, Attn: M.L. Liebler, Dept. of English, Wayne State University, Detroit 48202; also see the listing in Organizations Useful to Poets.

●**MINNESOTA:** *Art Forum*, P.O. Box 423, Moorehead 56560; covers western Minnesota and eastern North Dakota.

The Corresponder, Mankato State University, Box 13, P.O. Box 8400, Mankato 56002; covers southern/southeastern Minnesota.

Minnesota Literature, 1 Nord Circle, St. Paul 55127.

Poetry Harbor, P.O. Box 103, Duluth 55801-0103; also see the listing in Publishers of Poetry and the interview with Patrick McKinnon.

●**MISSOURI:** The Writer's Voice, West County YMCA, P.O. Box 4038, Chesterfield 63006.

●**MONTANA:** Hellgate Writers, P.O. Box 7131, Missoula 59807.

The Writer's Voice, Billings Family YMCA, 402 N. 32nd St., Billings 59101.

●**NEW JERSEY:** *New Jersey Poetry Calendar*, Attn: Maria Mazziotti Gillan, Poetry Center, Passaic County Community College, Paterson 07505; also see the listing for *Footwork: The Paterson Literary Review* in the Publishers of Poetry section.

Walt Whitman Cultural Arts Center, 2nd and Cooper St., Camden 08102; also see the listing in Organizations Useful to Poets.

●**NEW YORK:** *New York City Poetry Calendar*, 611 Broadway, Suite 905, New York 10012; found free around New York City, $15 subscription.

The Writer's Voice, Silver Bay Association YMCA, Silver Bay 12874.

●**NORTH CAROLINA:** Poetry Alive!, Attn: Bob Falls, P.O. Box 9643, Asheville 28815.

North Carolina Writers' Network, P.O. Box 954, Carrboro 27510; also see the listing in Organizations Useful to Poets.

●**OHIO:** *Ohio Writer*, Poets' League of Greater Cleveland, P.O. Box 91801, Cleveland 44101 or P.O. Box 528, Willoughby 44094; also see the listing in Publications Useful to Poets.

Poetry Fly, P.O. Box 10259, Columbus 43201.

●**OREGON:** Mountain Writers Series, 2812 SE 22nd Ave., Portland 97202.

●**PENNSYLVANIA:** Painted Bride Arts Center, Attn: Aaren Perry, 230 Vine St., Philadelphia 19106; also see the listing for *Painted Bride Quarterly* in the Publishers of Poetry section.

●**TENNESSEE:** Beatlicks, 1016 Kipling Dr., Nashville 37217; e-mail: kameleo n2@aol.com.

●**TEXAS:** Austin Writers' League, 1501 W. Fifth St., Suite E2, Austin 78703; has numerous resources. Also see the listing for their spring and fall workshops in the Conferences and Workshops section.

●**VIRGINIA:** *Musings*, 217 Nottoway St. SE, Leesburg 22075-4002.

●**WASHINGTON:** *Poetry Exchange*, P.O. Box 85477, Seattle 98145-1477; also see the listing in Publications Useful to Poets.

●**WISCONSIN:** The Writer's Place, 122 State St., Madison 53705.

Woodland Pattern Book Center, 720 E. Locust, Milwaukee 53212; also see the listing in Organizations Useful to Poets.

Canada

●**BRITISH COLUMBIA:** Tom Snyder, 1067 Granville St., Suite 201, Vancouver V6Z 1C4.

●**ONTARIO:** *Bywords*, c/o English Dept., University of Ottawa, 175 Wallor St., Ottawa K1N 6N5.

League of Canadian Poets, 54 Wolseley St., Third Floor, Toronto M5T 1A5; serves members. Also see the listing in Organizations Useful to Poets.

Word, 378 Delaware Ave., Second Floor, Toronto M6H 2T8.

Charting Your Path to Poetry Publication

by Christine Martin

For many, true joy comes not only from writing poetry but also from sharing it with others—be they family and friends, members of the audience at a poetry reading, or readers of local, regional or national publications. Whether you've just spent the last few months writing (and polishing) your first poems and are anxious to start sending them to editors and publishers or whether you've been writing poetry for years and have just been convinced by your spouse, sibling or best friend that your poetry deserves a wider audience, you probably have a number of questions about how to properly submit your work.

Let's even say your first question is quite basic, more basic than, for example, whether you should engage in simultaneous submissions (which we'll get to later). Perhaps you're really wondering: "Where do I begin?" Well, in many ways, you've come to the right place. Here we'll answer, with up-to-date, detailed information, the most often asked questions about submitting poetry. And you'll find related quotes from editors and publishers on the endleaves of this edition.

Where to begin

So, where *do* you begin to look for editors and publishers who might be interested in your work? The easiest answer of course is in this directory. Included along with listings for contests and awards and resources such as organizations and publications, you'll find about 1,700 publishers of poetry from around the world. And most of these magazine and book publishers specifically indicate what they do and do not want to see in the way of poetry for their pages. The biggest challenge you'll have here is narrowing down our list of markets. (For help on this matter, read How to Use Your *Poet's Market* on page 3.)

Yet, if you're just beginning, don't overlook the publications you have right on your living room coffee table. Those small (and often specialized) publications, such as your local church bulletin, the weekly neighborhood newspaper, your inhouse company magazine and the regional garden club gazette, are probably not listed within these pages. That's okay. Unless you're strictly out for literary fame, they're considered viable options. After all, the best way to determine whether your poetry is appropriate for a publication is to read several sample issues, and you've been reading these magazines for months, perhaps even years. You're already familiar with their contents and you probably have much in common with their other readers. So even if your weekly newspaper does not have a poetry page, the editor might publish an occasional poem—particularly if it relates to life in your neighborhood.

We should also add that new magazines are established all the time—even as you're reading these pages. To keep up with new literary journals and small presses, read publications such as *Poets & Writers Magazine* or *Writer's Digest*, both which regularly contain information about new markets. On a more local level, check the notices posted on the bulletin board at your library or nearest bookstore. There you may discover a new publication particularly interested in the work of regional writers.

Appearance is everything

When preparing to submit your work to any publication, however, remember that neatness counts. Use a typewriter or personal computer with a letter-quality (or at least near letter-quality) printer to type or print your poems on good, white, standard-size (generally 8½×11) bond paper. Do not handwrite your poems and do not use onion skin or erasable bond. Make sure your equipment has a good dark ribbon so each word of your poem is clear. And proofread your work carefully. Sloppy manuscripts with spelling or typographical errors are likely to be returned without comment.

Except for haiku, no matter how short your work, editors prefer that you submit each poem on a separate page with the title centered above it and your name, address and telephone number (typically) in the upper right or left corner. Some editors want poems double-spaced. Others prefer single spacing (with double spacing between stanzas) to give them an idea of how your poem will appear on their pages. If your poem carries over to a second sheet, note whether the lines at the top are a continuation of the same stanza or the start of a new one. Don't leave an editor wondering about such details. In all aspects, submit your work exactly as you would like it printed.

What to send

How many poems should you submit? In general, send only three to five poems to any editor at any given time. A few editors, particularly those who like to "feature" poets, prefer to receive seven or eight poems in a submission. But this is rare. Many of the listings in this directory now note exactly how many poems an editor will consider. You can also avoid irritating an editor with too many (or too few) poems by requesting a copy of the publication's submission guidelines (which may indicate how many poems you should send *and* exactly how they should be typed).

As many editors and publishers have very specific submission policies, it is always a good idea to send a self-addressed, stamped envelope (SASE) to receive a copy of a publisher's guidelines before submitting any work. If you're interested in a magazine or book publisher outside of your own country, send a self-addressed envelope (SAE) and International Reply Coupons (IRCs), which can be purchased from most post offices. If a publisher does not have guidelines or if the guidelines do not indicate the number of poems you should submit, don't worry. Sending three to five poems is considered standard.

Choosing which poems to send—and their arrangement—is up to you. More than anything else, an editor wants to see your best work. Of course, you also want to send work that is appropriate for the publication in question. And in arranging your poetry, your goal is simply to entice an editor to continue reading.

To copyright or not to copyright

Before you send off the poems you have spent months perfecting, however, you may be wondering about copyright protection. The good news is that you own the copyright to your work from the moment of creation. And, you can, if you wish, put the copyright symbol (©) on your poetry, followed by the year of creation and your name. Yet, copyright notices are typically considered unnecessary as most editors know you own the copyright to your work and few, if any, will steal your ideas. For some, in fact, copyright notices signal the work of amateurs who are distrustful of editors and publishers.

While the decision is certainly yours, it is important to note that most magazines are copyrighted and book publishers will usually register copyrights in your name. In addition, those who are inclined to "borrow" your ideas will do so whether or not the copyright notice is attached. If you wish to register your copyright, however, or if you would like more information, write to the Copyright Office, Library of Congress, Washington DC 20559.

On a more serious note, anyone who *does* steal someone else's work is subject to prosecution for plagiarism. While it would be nice to believe plagiarism does not exist, poet Neal Bowers's unfortunate experience—reported in *The New York Times* (October 25, 1994)—has shown otherwise. In short, after Bowers's work was published, it was slightly altered and submitted to other magazines by an individual who claimed the work was his own.

Keep in mind that plagiarism not only injures the poet whose work is stolen, but it also affects all poets, particularly beginners. Kimberly A. Willardson, editor of *The Vincent Brothers Review*, explains it well: "A few years ago, we were informed that we'd published a plagiarized poem. I felt like I'd been kicked in the stomach. . . . I've never felt the same about unsolicited poetry submissions since then and we're very cautious about working with poets whose work is new or unfamiliar to us from our outside reading of other litmags." That said, know that many editors are still taking work from new poets. Some have simply instituted policies where poets must sign statements saying the work is their own.

Cover letters

Another issue poets have had to grapple with—though one of a far less serious nature—is whether to include cover letters with their submissions. In the past, most editors and publishers did not state their preferences, so poets had to decide for themselves. Now, however, many editors are specifically indicating a desire for cover letters in their market listings and submission guidelines.

Overall, a cover letter allows you to personally present yourself—and your work— to specific editors. To do so graciously, you'll not only want to list the titles of the poems you are submitting, but you'll also want to demonstrate some familiarity with the publication in question. Editors, of course, like to know their contributors are among their readers. Include a few of your most recent publishing credits as well. And what if you haven't published a poem yet? Then note that. Some editors are particularly interested in new writers and have special sections for beginners' work.

Before you compose your cover letter, though, check to see if the editor has requested biographical information for the magazine's contributors' page. If so, add a few lines about your job or hobbies, particularly if either relates to the enclosed poems. Above all, refrain from praising your work. Let your poems speak for themselves. And, no matter how much information is requested, keep your cover letter to one page.

Finally, address your letter to the person listed as the poetry editor (or the editor if the publication is small). Most of the publications in this directory have a particular individual to whom you should direct your submissions. If no one is listed, however, check the publication's guidelines or the masthead of a recent copy. If you are still unable to locate a specific name, simply address your letter to "Poetry Editor." Of course, use an acceptable business-style format and make sure your letter is free of misspellings and grammatical errors.

Sign, seal and deliver

Once you have decided which poems you are going to submit, place them together and fold them into thirds. Do not fold your poems individually as the hassle of having to unfold and read each poem is apt to annoy editors, many of whom are already overworked. If you have elected (or are required) to also enclose a cover letter, fold the letter into thirds and place it on top of your batch of poems. Then put all of this material into a business-size (#10, 4⅛×9½) envelope.

To ensure a response from the editor or publisher in question, you must also include a SASE. You can use either a #9 (4×9) envelope or a #10 envelope folded into thirds. If you're submitting your poetry to a publication outside of your own country, include a SAE and IRCs. One IRC, by the way, is usually enough for one ounce by surface mail. For airmail return, you need one IRC for each half-ounce. In either case, make sure your reply envelope contains enough postage to cover the cost of returning your submission. And make sure your outside envelope has enough postage attached to get your poetry to the editor in the first place. (In general, three pages of poetry, a cover letter and a SASE can be mailed for one first-class stamp.)

Keeping records

But don't just send the only copy of your poems winging its way through the wild blue yonder. Always keep extra copies for yourself. In fact, you may want to keep the original typewritten or computer-printed version of your work and submit good, clean photocopies to editors and publishers. After all, you never know when your poetry will end up lost in the mail or somewhere in the heap of other submissions at a publisher's office. If you submit your one-and-only copy of your work and it gets lost in the process, you're simply out of luck.

It's also important to keep a record of which poems you have submitted, where and when. You can record such information on 3×5 cards arranged alphabetically (by poem title) in a metal storage container. Or you can use sheets of paper arranged in file folders (in which you can also keep the original copy of each poem). Or you can create a database on your personal computer. In any case, list the title of each poem, the name of the magazine to which it was submitted, and the date your work was mailed. Also note the date of each editor's reply, the outcome of your efforts, and any comments that may prove useful when you're next submitting to that market (such as changes in editors, reading periods or frequency of publication).

Tracking responses

By keeping detailed records of when and where you are submitting your work— and the date of the editor's reply—you are also tracking response times. Most editors and publishers indicate (in their market listings and submission guidelines) approximately how long you must wait before you can expect to receive a reply. If an editor does not specify when you will receive a report, it is generally expected to be within three months. Many times, however, the approximate date (or three-month benchmark) will come and go without a word from the editor or publisher.

What should you do when you haven't heard from an editor within the specified time period? Wait another month, then send a note inquiring about the status of your submission. Note the titles of your poems and the date sent. Ask when the editor anticipates making a decision. And enclose a SASE or self-addressed, stamped postcard for the editor's response. If you still do not hear from the market, send a postcard withdrawing your poems from consideration. Then submit your work elsewhere.

By all means, do *not* call editors with questions about submissions. Phone calls are only likely to irritate those who must divide their time between publishing a small press magazine and maintaining a fulltime job and family obligations. And you stand little chance of accomplishing your goal anyway as many editors simply cannot supply such answers over the phone. Why risk having your poems completely dropped from consideration?

Previously published poems

When you submit your poetry to magazine editors and publishers, by the way, they not only assume the work is original (that it is yours and nobody else's), but they also assume the work has not been previously published and is not being simultaneously submitted. Nothing is wrong with sending an editor a poem that has already been published. Some editors, however, are simply not open to such submissions. These folks want to be the first to publish new work—not the second. They are looking to acquire first rights to your poetry—not reprint rights. So before you send any previously published material, check market listings or submission guidelines to see if the editor or publisher in question is willing to consider such work. If so, note (in your cover letter) where the particular poem(s) first appeared.

. . . and simultaneous submissions

As many editors and publishers take months to reply to submitted work, poets in recent years have responded by sending the same package of poems to several editors at the same time. This is considered simultaneously submitting. And most who engage in this practice believe that a batch of three to five poems submitted to two or more editors has a better chance of resulting in an acceptance. However, if you submit your work simultaneously and an editor accepts one of your poems, you must contact the other editor(s) immediately and withdraw your work from consideration. This is likely to annoy (or even anger) the other editor(s) still in the process of making a decision. And future submissions to these markets may no longer be welcome.

To lessen the risks involved with this practice, you need to tell editors up front (in your cover letter) that you are simultaneously submitting your work. This is not only a way of forewarning them, but it may also prompt an editor to make a more timely decision. However, if you're going to tell editors that you're simultaneously submitting your material, make sure they are actually open to such submissions. If not, it is unlikely they will even consider your work. In addition, simultaneously submitting your work only to those publications open to the practice greatly decreases your chances of irritating any editors in the process. Again, check market listings or submission guidelines for specific information.

Yet the question still remains whether you should simultaneously submit your work in the first place. Why rush the process? You certainly don't try to take shortcuts in writing your poems. Why take shortcuts in submitting? After all, if you're just beginning or are still perfecting your craft, you're likely to quickly collect rejections. That can be discouraging. And if you're already regularly publishing, you're more likely to garner two acceptances at once—which puts you back at the point of having to contact editors and withdraw your work. The final decision, of course, is yours.

Chapbooks and others

Book publishers, by the way, expect some of the poems in your manuscript to be previously published. And, knowing the difficulty poets face in placing a collection, they are more accepting of the practice of simultaneous submissions. Yet you should only begin to think about book publication once you have gathered a fair number of publication credits in literary or small press magazines. Often, publishing a chapbook is a good middle step.

A chapbook is a small volume of 20-25 pages (or less). As such a volume is less expensive to produce than a full-length book collection (which may range from 48 to 80 pages), a chapbook is a safe way for a publisher to take a chance on a lesser-known poet. Most chapbooks are saddle-stapled with card covers. Some are photocopied publications. Others contain professionally printed pages. While chapbooks are seldom noted by reviewers or carried by bookstores, they are good items to sell after readings or through the mail. You'll discover that, in addition to some book publishers, a number of magazine publishers also publish chapbooks (for a complete list, refer to the Chapbook Publishers Index). For a closer look at a chapbook publisher, read the interview with Laurence F. Hawkins in the Publishers of Poetry section.

Whether you're planning to submit your work to either chapbook or book publishers, however, you should always examine sample copies of their previously published collections. This is not only the best way to familiarize yourself with the press' offerings, but it is also a good way to determine the quality of the product. To solicit a publisher's interest in your work, the standard procedure is to first query. Send a sampling of your poems (three to five, unless a publisher has noted otherwise), with a cover letter including brief biographical information and a few of your more noteworthy publication credits. Also let the publisher know that you are familiar with their other collections. And don't forget to include a SASE (or SAE and IRCs) for the publisher's reply.

Book publishing options

Once you develop an interest in having a collection of your work published, you'll soon discover that publishing arrangements vary. Some, in fact, are more beneficial to poets than others. Consider the following options carefully.

• **Standard publishing.** In a standard publishing contract, the publisher usually agrees to assume all production and promotion costs for your book. You receive a 10% royalty on the retail (or sometimes wholesale) price, though with some small presses you are paid with a percentage of the press run instead. Such publishers only release a small number of poetry volumes each year.

• **Cooperative publishing.** This arrangement is exactly that: cooperative. Although the details of such contracts vary, they require some type of investment of either time or money on your part. Some, for instance, require involvement in marketing. Others specify money for production costs. In any case, know what you're signing. While cooperative publishing is respected in the literary and small press world (and many such publishers can bring your work the attention it deserves), some vanity/subsidy presses try to label themselves as "cooperative." True cooperative publishing, however, shares both the risks and the profits.

• **Self-publishing.** This option may be most appealing if your primary goal is to publish a small collection of your work to give to family and friends. It is also a good choice for those who prefer complete control over the creative process. In this scenario, you work hand-in-hand with a local printer and invent a name for your "press." Most important is that you pay all the costs but own all the books and net all the proceeds from any sales (which you, of course, must generate). For more information, read *The Complete Guide To Self-Publishing* by Tom and Marilyn Ross.

• **Vanity/subsidy presses.** This is probably the least desirable option. Companies in this category usually advertise for manuscripts, lavishly praise your work, and ask for fees far in excess of costs (compare their figures to those of your local printer for a book of similar size, format and binding). These companies also make a habit of collectively advertising their books, that is, your work will simply receive a line along with 20 or so other books in an ad placed in the general media rather than a specific market. Worse yet, sometimes you own all copies of your book; sometimes you don't. Note that some anthology publications also fall under "vanity" publishing as you must pay a tidy sum to purchase the volume containing your work. If you have concerns about such a publisher, call the Poets & Writers Information Center at (212)226-3586. Calls are welcome weekdays from 11 a.m. to 3 p.m. (EST).

U.S. and Canadian Postal Codes

United States

AL	Alabama
AK	Alaska
AZ	Arizona
AR	Arkansas
CA	California
CO	Colorado
CT	Connecticut
DE	Delaware
DC	District of Columbia
FL	Florida
GA	Georgia
GU	Guam
HI	Hawaii
ID	Idaho
IL	Illinois
IN	Indiana
IA	Iowa
KS	Kansas
KY	Kentucky
LA	Louisiana
ME	Maine
MD	Maryland
MA	Massachusetts
MI	Michigan
MN	Minnesota
MS	Mississippi
MO	Missouri
MT	Montana
NE	Nebraska
NV	Nevada
NH	New Hampshire
NJ	New Jersey
NM	New Mexico
NY	New York
NC	North Carolina
ND	North Dakota
OH	Ohio
OK	Oklahoma
OR	Oregon
PA	Pennsylvania
PR	Puerto Rico
RI	Rhode Island
SC	South Carolina
SD	South Dakota
TN	Tennessee
TX	Texas
UT	Utah
VT	Vermont
VI	Virgin Islands
VA	Virginia
WA	Washington
WV	West Virginia
WI	Wisconsin
WY	Wyoming

Canada

AB	Alberta
BC	British Columbia
LB	Labrador
MB	Manitoba
NB	New Brunswick
NF	Newfoundland
NT	Northwest Territories
NS	Nova Scotia
ON	Ontario
PEI	Prince Edward Island
PQ	Quebec
SK	Sasketchewan
YT	Yukon

ALWAYS include a self-addressed, stamped envelope (SASE) when sending a ms or query to a publisher within your own country. When sending material to other countries, include a self-addressed envelope and International Reply Coupons (IRCs), available for purchase at most post offices.

Key to Symbols and Abbreviations

‡—*New listing*
ms—*manuscript;* **mss**—*manuscripts*
b&w—*black & white (photo or illustration)*
p&h—*postage & handling*
SASE—*self-addressed, stamped envelope*
SAE—*self-addressed envelope*
IRC—*International Reply Coupon (IRCs should be sent with SAEs for replies from countries outside your own)*

Important Market Listing Information

● *Listings are based on questionnaires and verified copy. They are not advertisements* nor *are markets necessarily endorsed by the editors of this book.*
● *Information in the listings comes directly from the publishers and is as accurate as possible, but publications and editors come and go, and poetry needs fluctuate between the publication date of this directory and the time you use it.*
● *If you are a poetry publisher and would like to be considered for a listing in the next edition, please request a questionnaire from* **Poet's Market**—*QR, 1507 Dana Ave., Cincinnati OH 45207. Questionnaires received after March 15, 1996, will be held for the 1998 edition.*
● **Poet's Market** reserves the right to exclude any listing that does not meet its requirements.

The Markets

Publishers of Poetry

If you're like most of our readers, this section, Publishers of Poetry, is the very reason you have our book in your hands. After all, it's this section that includes page after page of listings for all types of poetry publishers—hundreds of folks who may want *your* work for *their* pages.

Here you'll find listings for everything from small, stapled newsletters published by one or two dedicated individuals to larger, perfect-bound journals produced by volunteers at colleges and universities to slick magazines with paid staffs. You'll also discover listings for chapbook publishers and publishing houses that release perfect-bound, paperback collections.

But there's even more! Blue Mountain Arts, Inc. (one of approximately 300 listings new to this edition) is seeking poetry for publication on greeting cards and in anthologies. *The Blowfish Catalog* (also new this year) is a mail-order catalog of erotic products that includes short, erotic poems in its pages. And *The Blue Penny Quarterly* (another new listing) is an electronic magazine whose pages must be printed by home computer.

All told, this section contains about 1,700 poetry publishing markets, includes nine in-depth interviews with folks in the field, and showcases the covers of 11 different publications. And if we had to describe it in one word, that word would be "diverse!"

Locating specific markets

Given the number of listings (and the number of pages), how do you find information about a particular publisher, say one you've heard about at a writer's conference? Simple. Check the General Index for the page number. Although we list all publishers of poetry in this section alphabetically, information about related markets is grouped together in one listing to provide an overview of a publisher's entire operation. Yet all titles are included in the General Index.

The listing for *Amelia* is a classic example. If you look up our entry for *Amelia*, you'll also find information about *Cicada* and *SPSM&H*, as well as the numerous awards offered by the same publisher. When all of these activities are noted in one listing, it's easy to understand why the publisher's response to your submission may take a bit longer than expected. Nevertheless, if you were specifically looking for *Cicada*, you would find it listed in the General Index with a cross-reference to *Amelia* and the appropriate page number.

This also applies to publications that have changed names (often as the result of changing hands). For instance, *Infinity Limited* was acquired by John Hart and is now called *Prairie Dog*. And *Flyway* has succeeded *Poet & Critic* as the literary publication at Iowa State University. You will find all four of these titles in the General Index with cross-references where necessary.

Welcome new listings!

If you want to know which listings are new to this edition, look for the double dagger (‡) preceding the listing titles. As in years past, some new listings are publications that were in earlier editions of *Poet's Market* but not the previous one. We're happy to welcome back, for example, *The Carolina Quarterly*, *Gulf Coast*, *Oxford Magazine*, *Philomel*, *The Poetry Miscellany* and *Sonoma Mandala*.

Other listings new to this edition are actually "new," that is, they are magazines or presses that began publishing in the last few years. These include *Atlanta Review*, *Cripes!*, *Fledgling*, *Liberty Hill Poetry Review*, *Nerve* and *Smellfeast*, all of which were founded in 1994. Sarabande Books, Inc., by the way, is a new press which is open to queries (in September only) and sponsors an annual contest.

We are also delighted to have a number of new listings from outside the United States, including *Afterthoughts* and *McGill Street Magazine*, both published in Canada; *Redoubt*, based in Australia; and *The Plaza*, a bilingual publication located in Tokyo, Japan.

Every one has a mission

What prompts an individual, or group, to undertake publishing a magazine or developing a press? Of course, it's primarily a love of poetry. But it's also something else. In the introduction to the first issue of his publication, *Damaged Wine*, Daniel Scurek writes, "The question is relevant: do we really need another poetry magazine? Probably not. Publications come and go, many with a briefer shelf life than bananas. It would be more than a little naive to believe that the world of poetry would suffer in any way if *Damaged Wine* didn't exist. Yet, I feel it is important. . . ."

Much of what Scurek says is true. Many publications do not continue. In fact, you will find a list of those publishers from the 1995 edition who are not included in this edition under Publishers of Poetry/'95-'96 Changes at the end of this section. But what's more important is that Scurek, who wants to publish "the finest free verse poetry received," has a mission—as do all the publishers in this section.

As you make your way through the listings—and we encourage you to review them all—you will discover missions as diverse as the names of the publications and presses themselves. Some editors, like Scurek, publish magazines solely devoted to certain types of poetry. Others produce publications open to both poetry and fiction. And still others, particularly editors of very specialized publications, welcome poetry on specific topics but have space for only a few poems each issue. Discovering each publisher's mission will help you determine if your work is appropriate for his or her pages.

Watch submission details

Besides uncovering a publisher's mission (however loosely it may be defined), you must pay attention to submission details if you want your work to be given serious consideration. While a number of practices are considered standard, more and more editors are opting for variations. Thus, each year we ask editors and publishers to not only update the general information within their listings but to also clarify specific submission details.

For instance, this year we wanted to know how many poems poets should submit at one time. Though many editors said three to five (which is considered standard), others permit poets to submit as many as ten and a few want no more than three. Watch for this information as you read through the listings. It is better to stay within the editors' stated parameters rather than risk annoying them by sending too many (or too few) poems.

It is also important to note if, and when, editors publish theme issues. While some editors develop all of their issues around themes, others only publish one or two theme issues a year (or even every few years). Of course, whenever an editor is reading for a theme issue, that's the type of work he or she wants to receive. If you send unrelated work, even if the editor does not normally publish theme-based material, your work will probably not be considered.

Once again we specifically asked editors to supply details about their upcoming themes and related deadlines. Though a number of editors were able to provide this information for 1996, quite a few had not yet finalized their plans when we contacted them. To be sure that your submission will be welcome, it is always best to send a self-addressed, stamped envelope (SASE) to receive up-to-date information about themes, deadlines, and other submission guidelines.

By the way, as you read the listings in this section, you will also notice a number of e-mail addresses. Be careful when contacting editors in this manner. While some actually encourage submissions via computer, others simply supply their e-mail addresses to facilitate requests for guidelines or other additional information.

Include reply envelopes!

Although we didn't specifically ask editors and publishers if they had complaints about submissions, a large number of them said they still receive submissions without SASEs (or without sufficient return postage on SASEs). This is discouraging. Throughout this book, readers are repeatedly instructed to include a SASE or a SAE (self-addressed envelope) and IRCs (International Reply Coupons—for replies from countries outside your own) with all submissions, queries or requests for information.

It's really very simple: If you want to know if an editor accepts or rejects your material, you must include a vehicle for a reply. And it only makes sense that if it takes you two stamps to mail material, it will take two stamps for the material to be returned—unless you are sending a disposable manuscript. But if you do not want your poems returned to you (i.e., the manuscript can be discarded), the editor needs to be told that the SASE is only for his or her response.

It's not surprising that frustrated editors are creating policies about submissions lacking SASEs. As one editor wrote last year (and it's well worth repeating): "In the past two years, I have been receiving more and more submissions without SASEs. This gets to be a terrible drain on a budget that runs in the red as it is. As it stands now, the problem has gotten so bad that I feel I have to include a disclaimer regarding SASEs with my notice."

His disclaimer? "Submissions without a SASE cannot be acknowledged." Some editors are not so kind; they are discarding submissions without SASEs before the material is even read. Although we have started noting these policies within the listings, your safest bet is to make a habit of sending a SASE (or SAE and IRCs) with all your correspondence. Also, to make sure you're following other expected submission procedures, read (or reread) Charting Your Path to Poetry Publication, beginning on page 5.

Evaluating publishers

Other types of information within listings are editorial comments designed to help you evaluate the quality of various publications and the interests of various publishers. Such comments include a detailed description of a publication's physical appearance and notes about its content.

Of course, the best way to evaluate any publication is to actually review a sample copy. However, our descriptions provide you with general ideas about what publications look like and how much space they have for poetry. Although it's tempting to aim only for very high-profile, attractive magazines, some of the smaller, more simply produced publications are the most receptive to as-yet-unpublished poets. (Note: A number of printing and production terms, such as saddle-stapled and perfect-bound, are defined in the Glossary on page 513.)

As another way of helping you evaluate publishers, we have also included information about awards and honors that have been bestowed on editors and publishers or their magazines and books. For instance, we continue to note which publications have had poetry selected for inclusion in recent volumes of *The Best American Poetry*, an annual anthology highlighting the best poetry published in periodicals during the previous year.

Once again, thanks to David Lehman, who edits *The Best American Poetry* series, and his assistant, Maggie Nelson, we were able to obtain an advance list of those publications that have work included in the 1995 volume, guest edited by Richard Howard. As a different guest editor compiles the anthology every year, knowing which publications have work included, especially in all of the most recent volumes, can provide insight into the type and quality of material used.

In addition, *The Best American Poetry* (published by Scribner, 866 Third Ave., New York NY 10022) can help you develop a sense for trends in the field. The 1995 volume, by the way, is published at the same time as this edition of *Poet's Market*. So, when you're ready to read the poetry that has been selected from the publications listed here, check your nearest library or bookstore.

Understanding market categories

Finally, all the listings in this section include one or more Roman numerals in their headings. These "codes," selected by editors and publishers, can help you determine the most appropriate markets for your poetry. (For more information, see How to Use Your *Poet's Market* on page 3.) The market category codes and their explanations are as follows:

 I. **Publishers very open to beginners' submissions.** For consideration, some may require fees, purchase of the publication or membership in an organization, but they are not, so far as we can determine, exploitative of poets. They publish much of the material received and frequently respond with criticism and suggestions.

 II. **The general market to which most poets familiar with literary journals and magazines should submit.** Typically they accept 10% or less of poems received and usually reject others without comment. They pay at least one copy. A poet developing a list of publication credits will find many of these to be respected names in the literary world.

III. **Limited markets,** typically overstocked. This code is often used by many prestigious magazines and publishers to discourage widespread submissions from poets who have not published elsewhere—although many do on occasion publish relatively new or little-known poets.

IV. **Specialized publications** encourage contributors from a specific geographical area, age-group, sex, sexual orientation or ethnic background or accept poems in specific forms or on specific themes. In most **IV** listings we also state the specialty (e.g., **IV-Political**). Often a listing emphasizes more than one subject area; these listings are marked with two codes. To quickly locate such markets, refer to the Subject Index which lists publishers according to their specialties.

 V. **Listings which do not accept unsolicited manuscripts.** You cannot submit to these without specific permission to do so. If the press or magazine for some reason seems especially appropriate for you, query with a SASE. But, in general, these folks prefer to locate poets themselves. Sometimes they are just temporarily overstocked; other times they have projects lined up for several years.

We have included these listings because it is important to know not only where to send your poetry but also where NOT to send it. In addition, many are interesting publishers, and this book is widely used as a reference by librarians, researchers, publishers, suppliers and others who need to have as complete a listing of poetry publishers as possible.

ABBEY; ABBEY CHEAPOCHAPBOOKS (II), 5360 Fallriver Row Court, Columbia MD 21044, e-mail greisman@aol.com, founded 1970, editor David Greisman. **They want "poetry that does for the mind what that first sip of Molson Ale does for the palate. No pornography or politics."** They have recently published poetry and artwork by Richard Peabody, Vera Bergstrom, D.E. Steward, Carol Hamilton, Harry Calhoun, Wayne Hogan and Cheryl Townsend. *Abbey*, a quarterly, aims "to be a journal but to do it so informally that one wonders about my intent." It is magazine-sized, 20-26 pgs., photocopied. They publish about 150 of 1,000 poems received/year. Press run is 200. Subscription: $2. **Sample postpaid: 50¢. Guidelines available for SASE. Reports in 1 month. Pays 1-2 copies.** *Abbey Cheapochapbooks* come out 1-2 times a year averaging 10-15 pgs. **For chapbook consideration query with 4-6 samples, bio and list of publications. Reports in 2 months. Pays 25-50 copies.** The editor says he is "definitely seeing poetry from two schools—the nit'n'grit school and the textured/reflective school. I much prefer the latter."

ABIKO QUARTERLY (II, IV-Translations), 8-1-8 Namiki, Abiko, Chiba Japan 270-11, phone 011-81-471-84-7904, founded 1988, founding editor Laurel Sicks, poetry editor Jesse Glass, is a literary-style quarterly journal **"heavily influenced by James Joyce's *Finnegan's Wake*. We publish all kinds, with an emphasis on the innovative and eclectic. We sometimes include originals and translations. However, we no longer consider unsolicited poetry and fiction. All of our new work comes from our annual international poetry and fiction contest. See *Writer's Digest, Poets & Writers* and *AWP Chronicle* for details."** Contest runs from September 1 to December 31 and is judged by a well-known poet. They have published poetry by Kenji Miyazawa, Jon Silkin, Cid Corman, Lew Turco, William Bronk and Edith Shiffert. It is magazine-sized, desktop-published with Macintosh laser printer. Press run is 350 for 150 subscribers of which 10 are libraries, 100 shelf sales. **Sample postpaid: 900 yen.** Open to unsolicited reviews. Poets may also send books for review consideration. The editor says, "Poets are in a hurry to publish. Poets, educate yourselves! Read contemporary poetry. In fact, read all poetry! Work at your craft before you attempt to publish. Please remember U.S. postage does not work in Japan with SAEs!"

ABORIGINAL SF (IV-Science fiction), Box 2449, Woburn MA 01888-0849, founded 1986, editor Charles C. Ryan, appears quarterly. **"Poetry should be 1-2 pgs., double-spaced. Subject matter must be science fiction, science or space-related. No long poems, no fantasy."** The magazine is 116 pgs., with 12 illustrations. Press run is 23,000, mostly subscriptions. Subscriptions for "special" writer's rate: $12/4 issues. **Sample postpaid: $4.95. No simultaneous submissions. Send SASE for guidelines. Reports in 2-3 months, no backlog. Always sends prepublication galleys. Pays $25/poem and 2 copies. Buys first North American serial rights.** Reviews related books of poetry in 100-300 words.

ABRAXAS MAGAZINE (V); GHOST PONY PRESS (III), 2518 Gregory St., Madison WI 53711, *Abraxas* founded 1968, Ghost Pony Press in 1980, by editor/publisher Ingrid Swanberg, who says "Ghost Pony Press is a small press publisher of poetry books; *Abraxas* is a literary journal publishing contemporary poetry, criticism, translations and reviews of small press books. *Do not confuse these separate presses!"* *Abraxas* no longer considers unsolicited material, except as announced as projects arise. The editor is interested in poetry that is **"contemporary lyric, concrete, experimental, narrative." Does not want to see "political posing; academic regurgitations."** They have published poetry by William Stafford, Ivan Argüelles, Denise Levertov, César Vallejo and Andrea Moorhead. As a sample the editor selected the final lines of an untitled poem by próspero saíz:

> *the beautiful grief of the moon is my beam of silence*
> *Dawn*
> *the splendor of the moon dies*
> *my lips open to a gentle breeze*
> *she rides a silken yellow scarf into the vanishing clouds*
> *i am still here.*

The magazine is up to 80 pgs. (160 pgs., double issues), 6×9, flat-spined (saddle-stitched with smaller issues), litho offset, with original art on its matte card cover, using "unusual graphics in text, original art and collages, concrete poetry, exchange ads only, letters from contributors, essays." It appears "irregularly, 4- to 9-month intervals." Press run is 600, 550 circulation, 300 subscribers of which 150 are libraries. Subscription: $16/4 issues, $20/4 issues Canada, Mexico and overseas. **Sample postpaid: $4 ($6 double issues). Submit 5 poems at a time.** *Abraxas* **will announce submission guidelines as projects arise. Publishes theme issues. Themes for 1995-96 include contemporary avant-garde; concrete poetry; and lyric poetry. Send SASE for details. Pays 1 copy plus 40% discount on additional copies. To submit to Ghost Pony Press, inquire with SASE plus 5-10 poems and cover letter. Previously published material OK for book publication by Ghost Pony Press. Editor sometimes comments briefly on rejections. Reports on queries in 1-3 months, mss in 3 months. Payment varies per project. Send SASE for catalog to buy samples.** They have published *zen concrete & etc.*, a "definitive collection" of poetry by d.a. levy. That book is a 245-page, 8½×11, perfect-bound paperback available for $27.50. They have also published *the bird of nothing & other poems* by próspero saíz. It is a 168-page, 7×10, perfect-bound paperback available for $20 (signed and numbered edition is $35). For either book, add $2 p&h.

ACM (ANOTHER CHICAGO MAGAZINE) (II); LEFT FIELD PRESS (V), 3709 N. Kenmore, Chicago IL 60613, founded 1976, poetry editor Barry Silesky. *ACM* is a literary biannual, **emphasis on quality, experimental, politically aware** prose, fiction, poetry, reviews, cross-genre work and essays. The editor wants **no religious verse**. They have published prose and poetry by Albert Goldbarth, Michael McClure, Jack Anderson, Jerome Sala, Nance VanWinkel, Nadja Tesich, Wanda Coleman, Charles Simic and Diane Wakoski. As a sample, the editor selected these lines by Dean Shavit:

> Just the facts. Forgotten on purpose.
> This is our land. Yes, you said, "ours."
> A gang of teenagers, too young for the army, too stupid for respect.

Silesky says *ACM* is 220 pgs., digest-sized, offset with b&w art and ads. Editors appreciate traditional to experimental verse with an emphasis on message, especially poems with strong voices articulating social or political concerns. Circulation is 1,500, for 500 subscribers of which 100 are libraries. **Sample postpaid: $7. Submit 3-4 typed poems at a time. No previously published poems; simultaneous submissions OK. Reports in 2-3 months, has 3- to 6-month backlog. Sometimes sends prepublication galleys. Pays $5/page and 1 copy. Buys first serial rights.** Reviews books of poetry in 250-500 words. Open to unsolicited reviews. Poets may also send books for review consideration. **They do not accept unsolicited submissions for chapbook publication.** Work published in *ACM* has been included in *The Best American Poetry* (1992, 1994 and 1995) and *Pushcart Prize* anthologies. The editor says, "Buy a copy—subscribe and support your own work."

THE ACORN; EL DORADO WRITERS' GUILD (II, IV-Regional), P.O. Box 1266, El Dorado CA 95623, phone (916)621-1833, founded 1993, poetry consultant Hatch Graham, is a quarterly journal of the Western Sierra, published by the El Dorado Writers' Guild, a nonprofit literary organization. It includes "history and reminiscence, story and legend, and poetry." **They want poetry "up to 30 lines long, though we prefer shorter. Focus must be on western slope Sierra Nevada. No erotica, pornography or religious poetry."** They have recently published poetry by Taylor Graham, Michael Meinhoff and Michael Spring. As a sample the poetry consultant selected these lines from "Yard Elegies for August" by Edward C. Lynskey:

> Let the straggler gherkin mellow
> to umber rot on the vine for zinc-
> topped mason jars jam the cellar,
> pickled like saintly relics held
> in worship to weather the worst.

The poetry consultant says *the Acorn* is 44 pgs., 5⅛×8½, desktop-published on quality paper and saddle-stapled. They receive about 250 poems a year, use approximately 15% (10-12/issue). Press run is 200 for 25 subscribers, 100 shelf sales. Single copy: $3.50; subscription: $12. **Sample postpaid: $4. Submit 3-7 poems, neatly typed or printed, at a time. Previously published poems OK; simultaneous submissions discouraged. Cover letter with short (75-word) bio required. Deadlines are February 1, May 1, August 1 and November 1.** Time between acceptance and publication is 1 month. **"Five editors each score poems for content, form and suitability. Poetry consultant selects top group. Graphics editor selects to fit space available." Often comments on rejections.   Reports within 3 weeks after deadline. Pays 1 copy. All rights revert to author on publication.** The editor says, "If your poetry is about nature, be accurate with the species' names, colors, etc. If you describe a landscape, be sure it fits our region. Metered rhyming verse had better be precise (we have an editor with an internal metronome!). Slant rhyme and free verse are welcome. Avoid trite phrases."

‡ACORN WHISTLE (II), 907 Brewster Ave., Beloit WI 53511, founded 1994, first issue published in spring 1995, editor Fred Burwell, appears twice yearly. "We seek writing that moves both heart and mind. **We seek accessible poetry: narrative, lyrical, prose poem. No length requirements. We are not interested in experimental, religious, erotic or New Age work.** We also publish fiction, memoir and personal essay." Their first issue included poetry by Thom Ward and G. Mark Jodon. As a sample the editor selected the first stanza of "Out on the Water" by Denise Pendleton:

> *Lights blaze and I can feel*
> *how lit up it is inside. Either hand I reach*
> *will touch them from any spot I stand in. My mother*
> *stirs soup simmering at my elbow while my father's*
> *bushy arms crowd the table I set. All day*
> *we have sailed with the wind behind, lifting*
> *us toward sky and at last we are held*
> *where we are, drinking iceless drinks*
> *while breathing in the small cabin's air.*

The editor says *AC* is 75 pgs., 8½×11, staple-bound, using b&w photos and art, no ads. Press run is 500. Subscription: $10. **Sample postpaid: $5. No previously published poems; simultaneous submissions OK. Often comments on rejections. Send SASE for guidelines. Reports in 1-8 weeks. Pays 2 copies. Acquires first North American serial rights.** The editor says, "We publish no reviews, although we plan to mention publications by our past authors. We wish that more writers would focus on material that matters to them, rather than trying to impress an audience of editors and teachers. We seek accessible writing for an audience that reads for pleasure and edification. We encourage a friendly, working relationship between editors and writers."

ACUMEN MAGAZINE; EMBER PRESS (I, II), 6 The Mount, Higher Furzeham, Brixham, South Devon TQ5 8QY England, phone (01803)851098, press founded 1971, *Acumen* founded 1984, poetry editor Patricia Oxley, is a "small press publisher of a general literary magazine with emphasis on good poetry." **They want "well-crafted, high quality, imaginative poems showing a sense of form. No experimental verse of an obscene type."** They have published poetry by Elizabeth Jennings, William Oxley, Gavin Ewart, D.J. Enright, Peter Porter, Kathleen Raine and R.S. Thomas. As a sample Mrs. Oxley selected this poem, "Northbound Train," by Ken Smith:

> *Birds rising. These flecks*
> *white on the brown ploughland*
> *flakes of fine snow, they are birds,*
> *they are gulls suddenly flying.*

Acumen appears 3 times a year (in January, May and September) and is 100 pgs., A5, perfect-bound. "We aim to publish 120 poems out of 12,000 received." Press run is 650 for 400 subscribers (20 libraries). **Sample copy: $15. Submit 5-6 poems at a time. No previously published poems; simultaneous submissions OK, if not to UK magazines. Reports in 1 month. Pays "by negotiation" and 1 copy.** Staff reviews books of poetry in up to 300 words, single format or 600 words, multi-book. Send books for review consideration to Glyn Pursglove, 25 St. Albans Rd., Brynmill, Swansea, West Glamorgan SA2 0BD Wales. Patricia Oxley advises, "Read *Acumen* carefully to see what kind of poetry we publish. Also read widely in many poetry magazines, and don't forget the poets of the past— they can still teach us a great deal."

ADASTRA PRESS (II), 101 Strong St., Easthampton MA 01027, founded 1980 by Gary Metras, who says, "I publish poetry because I love poetry. I produce the books on antique equipment using antique methods because I own the equipment and because it's cheaper—I don't pay myself a salary—it's a hobby—it's **a love affair with poetry and printing of fine editions**. I literally sweat making these books and I want the manuscript to show me the author also sweated." All his books and chapbooks are **limited editions, handset, letterpress**, printed with handsewn signatures. "Chances of acceptance are slim. About 1 in 200 submissions is accepted, which means I only take 1 or 2 unsolicited mss a year." The chapbooks are in flat-spine paper wrappers, cloth editions also handcrafted. He wants **"no rhyme, no religious. Poetry is communication first, although it is art. Long poems and thematic groups are nice for chapbooks. No subjects are tabu, but topics should be drawn from real life experiences. I include accurate dreams as real life."** Poets recently published include Thomas Lux, W.D. Ehrhart, Jim Daniels and Miriam Sagan. As a sample the editor selected these lines from "Things We Leave Go" by Greg Joly:

> *tubers of bearded iris*
> *swim dark into the clouded lawn*
> *seed heavy weeds*
> *come the full solstice moon*
> *grackles wire feet dance*
> *on empty metal silos*

1-4 chapbooks are brought out each year. **Author is paid in copies, usually 10% of the print run. "I only read chapbook manuscripts in the month of February, picking one or two for the following year. Queries, with a sample of 3-5 poems from a chapbook manuscript, are read throughout the year and if I like what I see in the sample, I'll ask you to submit the ms in February. I prefer a cover letter and a) samples from a completed chapbook ms or b) a completed chapbook ms. Do** not submit or query about full-length collections. I will only be accepting chapbook manuscripts of 12-18 double-spaced pages. Any longer collections would be a special invitation to a poet. **If you want to see a typical handcrafted Adastra chapbook, send $5 and I'll mail a current title**. If you'd like a fuller look at what, how and why I do what I do, send check for $11.50 ($10 plus $1.50 p&h) and I'll mail a copy of *The Adastra Reader: Being the Collected Chapbooks in Facsimile with Author Notes, Bibliography and Comments on Hand Bookmaking*, published in 1987. This is a 247-page anthology covering Adastra publishing from 1979-1986."

ADRIFT (II, IV-Ethnic), 46 E. First St., #3D, New York NY 10003, founded 1980, editor Thomas McGonigle, who says, "**The orientation of the magazine is Irish, Irish-American. I expect reader-writer knows and goes beyond Yeats, Kavanagh, Joyce, O'Brien.**" The literary magazine is open to all kinds of submissions, but does not want to see "junk." They have published poetry by James Liddy, Thomas McCarthy, Francis Stuart and Gilbert Sorrentino. *Adrift* appears twice a year and is 32 pgs., magazine-sized, offset on heavy stock, matte card cover, saddle-stapled. Circulation is 1,000 with 200 subscriptions, 50 of which go to libraries. Single copy: $4; subscription: $8. **Sample postpaid: $5 (checks payable to T. McGonigle). Simultaneous submissions OK. Magazine pays, rate varies; contributors receive 1 copy.** Reviews books of poetry. Open to unsolicited reviews. Poets may also send books for review consideration.

ADVOCACY PRESS (V, IV-Children), P.O. Box 236, Santa Barbara CA 93102, founded 1983, contact William Sheehan, publishes children's books. "**Must have rhythm and rhyme.**" They have published 3 books of rhymes for children: *Father Gander Nursery Rhymes* (nonsexist, nonviolent, nonracist version of *Mother Goose*), *Mother Nature Nursery Rhymes* and *Nature's Wonderful World in Rhyme*. Their books are 32-48 pgs., illustrated in full color. "**No present plans for additional books in the Children's series. Publish no other poetry at this time.**" **Query with description of concept and sample. SASE required for reply.** "All Advocacy Press books have gender equity, self-esteem themes."

THE ADVOCATE (I), 301A Rolling Hills Park, Prattsville NY 12468, phone (518)299-3103, founded 1987, editor Remington Wright, is a bimonthly advertiser-supported tabloid, 12,000 copies distributed free, **using "original, previously unpublished works,** such as feature stories, essays, 'think' pieces, letters to the editor, profiles, humor, fiction, poetry, puzzles, cartoons or line drawings." **They want "nearly any kind of poetry, any length, but not religious or pornographic. Poetry ought to speak to people and not be so oblique as to have meaning only to the poet. If I had to be there to understand the poem, don't send it."** As a sample the editor selected the opening lines from "You Brought Me Lilacs" by Tilitha Waicekauskas:

> *I was young and slender, and in your eyes*
> *I was more beautiful than morning skies.*
> *My hair was as black as a raven's wing*
> *And the love in your eyes made my spirit sing.*
> *For I adored you and on my hand*
> *Was your diamond of promise—a platinum band*
> *   —And you brought me lilacs.*

They accept approximately 25% of poems received. **Sample postpaid: $4. No previously published poems or simultaneous submissions.** Time between acceptance and publication is an average of 4-6 months. **Editor "occasionally" comments on rejections. Reports in 6-8 weeks. Pays 2 copies. Acquires first rights only.** Reviews books of poetry. Open to unsolicited reviews. Poets may also send books to the attention of J.B. Samuels for review consideration. Offers occasional contests. The editor says, "All submissions and correspondence must be accompanied by a self-addressed, stamped envelope with sufficient postage."

AEGINA PRESS, INC.; UNIVERSITY EDITIONS (I, II), 59 Oak Lane, Spring Valley, Huntington WV 25704, founded 1983, publisher Ira Herman, is **primarily subsidy for poetry,** strongly committed to publishing new or established poets. Publishes subsidy titles under the University Editions imprint. They have also published non-subsidized poetry as well. **Authors of books accepted on a non-subsidized basis receive a 15% royalty.** "We try to provide a way for talented poets to have their collections published, which otherwise might go unpublished because of commercial, bottom-line considerations. We will publish quality poetry that the large publishers will not handle because it is not commercially viable. We believe it is unfair that a poet has to have a 'name' or a following in order to have a book of poems accepted by a publisher. Poetry is the purest form of literary art, and it should be made available to those who appreciate it." They have recently published *Soundings* by Sally Gibbs and *Poems for the Christian Year* by Thomas Waldron Philips. As a sample the editor selected these lines from "Chaos" in *Clinging to a Ray* by Dr. Riyad Y. Hamzah:

> *The roar of the crowd was quieted. The lights were lowered.*
> *And I walked out onto the stage, raised my arms,*

And brought them crashing down,
Here to conduct the music of my mind.

"Most poetry books we accept are subsidized by the author. In return, the author receives all sales proceeds from the book, and any unsold copies left from the print run belong to the author. Minimum print run is 500 copies. We can do larger runs as well. Our marketing program includes submission to distributors, agents, other publishers, bookstores and libraries." **Mss should be typed and no shorter than 40 pages. There is no upper length limit. For a query, submit 3 or more poems. Simultaneous submissions OK. Reporting time is 1 month for full mss, 7-10 days for queries. Always sends prepublication galleys.** They publish perfect-bound (flat-spined) paperbacks with glossy covers. **Sample books are available for $5 each plus $1.50 p&h.**

AERIAL (V), P.O. Box 25642, Washington DC 20007, phone (202)244-6258, founded 1984, editor Rod Smith, editorial assistants Gretchen Johnsen and Wayne Kline, is an occasional publication. Issue #8 (published in May 1995) was the Barrett Watten issue (available for $15). They have published work by Jackson MacLow, Melanie Neilson, Steve Benson, Phyllis Rosenzweig and Charles Bernstein. A special issue is in the works, on Bruce Andrews, therefore **they're not looking for new work at this time.** As a sample the editor selected these lines from "subtracted words" by P. Inman:

still dollar in its pale
mice sight. Parts of knock
in a river of propellor blade.
Wage sand gist. Keyhole
college, its brink on. An
ash stelm of mind ball

The magazine is 6×9, offset, varies from 180 to 280 pgs. Circulation is 1,000. **Sample postpaid: $7.50.** Also publishes critical/political/philosophical writing.

AETHLON: THE JOURNAL OF SPORT LITERATURE (IV-Sports), Dept. PM, English Dept., East Tennessee State University, Box 70683, Johnson City TN 37614-0683, phone (615)929-4339, founded 1983, general editor Don Johnson, Professor of English, ETSU, **poetry editor Robert W. Hamblin, Professor of English, Southeast Missouri State University, Cape Girardeau MO 63701.** (Submit poetry to this address.) *Aethlon* publishes a variety of sport-related literature, including scholarly articles, fiction, poetry, personal essays and reviews; 6-10 poems/issue; two issues annually, fall and spring. **Subject matter must be sports-related; no restrictions regarding form, length, style or purpose. They do not want to see "doggerel, cliché-ridden or oversentimental" poems.** Poets published include Neal Bowers, Joseph Duemer, Robert Fink, Jan Mordenski, H.R. Stonebeck, Jim Thomas, Stephen Tudor and Don Welch. The magazine is digest-sized, offset printed, flat-spined, with illustrations and some ads, 200 pgs./issue. Circulation is 1,000 of which 750 are subscriptions, 250 to libraries. Subscription is included with membership ($30) in the Sport Literature Association. **Sample postpaid: $12.50. "Only typed mss with SASE considered." Will accept simultaneous submissions. Submissions are reported on in 6-8 weeks and the backlog time is 6-12 months. Contributors receive 5 offprints and a copy of the issue in which their poem appears.**

AFRICA WORLD PRESS (V, IV-Ethnic), Box 1892, Trenton NJ 08607, founded 1983, editor Kassahun Checole, publishes **poetry books by Africans, African-Americans, Caribbean and Latin Americans**. They have published *Under A Soprano Sky* by Sonia Sanchez, *From the Pyramid to the Projects* by Askia Muhammad Toure and, most recently, *The Time: Poems and Photographs* by Esther Iverem. However, they are currently not accepting poetry submissions. Send SASE for catalog.

AFRICAN AMERICAN REVIEW (IV-Ethnic), Dept. of English, Indiana State University, Terre Haute IN 47809, phone (812)237-2968, founded 1967, poetry editors Sterling Plumpp, Thadious M. Davis, Pinkie Gordon Lane and E. Ethelbert Miller, is a "magazine primarily devoted to the analysis of African American literature, **although one issue per year focuses on poetry by African Americans." No specifications as to form, length, style, subject matter or purpose.** They have published poems by Amiri Baraka, Gwendolyn Brooks, Dudley Randall and Owen Dodson. *AAR* is 6×9, 200 pgs. with photo on the cover. They receive about 500 submissions/year, use 50. Individual subscriptions: $24 USA, $31 foreign. **Sample postpaid: $10. Submit maximum of 6 poems to editor Joe Weixlmann. The editors sometimes comment on rejections. Publishes theme issues. Send SASE for guidelines. Reports in 3-4 months. Always sends prepublication galleys. Pays in copies.**

‡AFRICAN VOICES (I, II, IV-Ethnic), 270 W. 96th St., New York NY 10025, phone (212)865-2982, founded 1992, contact poetry editor, is a bimonthly "art and literary publication that **highlights the work of people of color. We publish ethnic literature and poetry on any subject. We do not wish to limit the reader or author."** They have recently published poetry by Reg E. Gaines, Maya Angelou, Tony Medina and Louis Reyes Rivera. As a sample we selected these lines from "Which patent leather shoe belong to which found leg" by Letta Simone-Nefertari Neely (which also appears in *Gawd and alluh huh sistahs*, published by the Collective Effort Coalition Press):

> *30 years later and ahm bout to start a funeral dirge cuz they*
> *wuz*
> *sittin at the 16th street baptist church swingin too short legs*
> *back and forth in pews and giglin like kids do if they ain't*
> *thinkin bout death*
> *they wuz*
> *thinkin bout what they wuz gonna do after sunday school/how*
> *they wuz gonna sang in the choir/bout who they thought wuz*
> *cute*
> *thinkin bout everything but being bombed outta they skins*

African Voices is a newsprint tabloid. They receive about 100 submissions a year, accept approximately 30%. Press run is 20,000 for 5,000 subscribers of which 30 are libraries, 40% shelf sales. Single copy: $1; subscription: $10. **Sample postpaid: $1.50. Previously published poems and simultaneous submissions OK. Cover letter and SASE required. Three poetry editors make final selections. Seldom comments on rejections. Send SASE for guidelines. Reports in 6-8 weeks. Pays 5 copies. Acquires first or one-time rights.** Reviews books of poetry in 500-1,000 words. Open to unsolicited reviews. Poets may also send books for review consideration, attn. Layding Kaliba. Sponsors periodic poetry contests. Send SASE for details. The editor says, "We strongly encourage new writers/poets to send in their work and not give up if their work is not accepted the first time. And accepted contributors are encouraged to subscribe."

AFRO-HISPANIC REVIEW (IV-Ethnic), Romance Languages, #143 Arts & Sciences, University of Missouri, Columbia MO 65211, founded 1982, editors Marvin A. Lewis and Edward J. Mullen, appears twice a year, in the fall and spring, using some **poetry related to Afro-Hispanic life and issues.** They have published poetry by Manuel Zapata Olivella, Melvin E. Lewis and Antar Al Basir. **Sample copy: $5. Submit 2 poems at a time. "Prefer clean copy with accents." Reports in 6 weeks. Pays 5 copies.** Reviews books of poetry in "about 500 words." Their Fall 1995 issue was set to focus on Afro-Hispanic women.

‡AFTERTHOUGHTS; LAKEWOOD PRESS (I, II), 4380 Wellington Rd. S., Box 42069, London, Ontario N6E 3V1 Canada, founded 1994, editor J.K. Andromeda, is a quarterly "independent periodical of poetic thought and observation." **They want "poems that are a raw upsurge of emotion from the unexplored depths of the writer's soul. Poets are welcome to express themselves as freely as possible, but in a spirit of mutual understanding and respect for others. Be as negative and cynical as you wish, but it would be nice if somewhere in your work there is a glimmer of hope for a better tomorrow. We'd like to see poems dealing with emotional conflict, sexual experience, nature, vegetarianism, and the exposure of hypocrisy—but we're open to all topics and themes. We publish free verse, rhyme (well metered and unforced), haiku, avant-garde and any other form or style, as long as the workmanship is good."** They have recently published poetry by Beryl Baigent, Doug Muir, Shannon Foskett, Gregory Wm. Gunn, Vic Elias, Carol Ann Weston and Amy Evans. As a sample the editor selected "Driftwood" by Ross Sinclair:

> *One gentle wave,*
> *one rolling sea—driftwood washed*
> *of symmetry;*
> *that washing back might rob the lee*
> *of soft and sudden harmony.*
> *So when I quit this port, go free,*
> *though sands stay,*
> *driftwood goes with me.*

Afterthoughts is 72 pgs., digest-sized, copied from laser printed originals and perfect-bound with textured card stock cover and b&w illustrations throughout. Press run is 400-500 of which 80 are sent to the largest public libraries across Canada, the US, Great Britain, Australia and a dozen other countries. Subscription: $10. **Sample postpaid: $3. Money orders should be in Canadian funds and made payable to Lakewood Press. Simultaneous submissions OK. Brief bio required. Reports in 3 weeks. Pays 1 copy. "We reserve the right to reprint accepted poetry in future issues. Other than that, all rights revert back to the poet after publication."** The editor says, "Make sure your work is honest and accessible to readers from all walks of life. Write with your heart *and* with your head—but mostly with your heart."

AGENDA EDITIONS; AGENDA (II), 5 Cranbourne Ct., Albert Bridge Rd., London SW11 4PE England, founded 1959, poetry editors William Cookson and Peter Dale. *Agenda* is a quarterly magazine (1 double, 2 single issues/year). **"We seek poetry of 'more than usual emotion, more than usual order' (Coleridge).** We publish special issues on particular authors such as T.S. Eliot, Ezra Pound,

David Jones, Stanley Burnshaw, Thomas Hardy, etc." Some of the poets who have appeared in *Agenda* are Geoffrey Hill, Seamus Heaney, C.H. Sisson, Patricia McCarthy and W.S. Milne. As a sample the editors selected these lines (poet unidentified):

> *How will you want the snowy impermanence of ash,*
> *your dust, like grass-seed, flighted over heathland,*
> *drifting in spinneys where the boughs clash,*
> *with matted needles laying waste beneath them.*

Agenda is 80 pgs. (of which half are devoted to poetry), 5×7. They receive some 2,000 submissions/year, use 40, have a 5-month backlog. Circulation 1,500-3,000, 1,500 subscriptions of which 450 are libraries. Subscription: individuals US $44, libraries and institutions US $54. **Sample: £4 ($8 surface mail). Submit around 6 poems at a time. Reports in 1 month. Sometimes offers a small payment for poetry.** Reviews books of poetry. Open to unsolicited reviews. Poets may also send books for review consideration. **To submit book ms, no query necessary, "as little as possible" in cover letter. SAE and IRCs for return. Reports within a month. Pays copies.** The editors say poets "should write only if there is an intense desire to express something. They should not worry about fashion."

AGNI (II), Boston University, 236 Bay State Rd., Boston MA 02215, phone (617)353-5389, founded 1972, editors Askold Melnyczuk and Erin Belieu. *AGNI* is a biannual journal of poetry, fiction and essays "by both emerging and established writers. **We publish quite a bit of poetry in forms as well as 'language' poetry, but we don't begin to try and place parameters on the 'kind of work' that** *AGNI* **selects."** Editors seem to select readable, intelligent poetry—mostly lyric free verse (with some narrative and dramatic, too)—that somehow communicates tension or risk. They have published poetry by Derek Walcott, Patricia Traxler, Thom Gunn, Maxine Scates, Mark Halliday and Ha Jin. As a sample the editor selected these lines from "The Owl" by Joe Osterhaus:

> *So Hegel's Owl of Minerva spreads*
> *its wings at dusk, beginning its long flight*
> *when depth and outline are the most obscure—*
> *how true the image is, yet how unclear,*
> *as if the thinker wanted both the night*
> *and the raptor's shadow gliding over the dry beds.*

AGNI is typeset, offset-printed and perfect-bound with about 40 poems featured in each issue. Circulation is 1,500 by subscription, mail order and bookstore sales. Subscription: $12. **Sample: $7. Submit 3 poems at a time. "No fancy fonts, gimmicks or preformatted reply cards. Brief, sincere cover letters." They will consider simultaneous submissions but not previously published poems. Reads submissions October 1 through April 30 only. Mss received at other times will be returned unread. Reports in 2-5 months. Pays $10/page, $150 maximum, plus 2 copies and one-year subscription. Buys first serial rights.** Work published in *AGNI* has been included in *The Best American Poetry* (1992, 1993, 1994 and 1995) and *Pushcart Prize* anthologies.

AG-PILOT INTERNATIONAL MAGAZINE (IV-Specialized), P.O. Box 1607, Mt. Vernon WA 98273, phone (206)336-9737, publisher Tom Wood, "is intended to be a fun-to-read, technical, as well as humorous and serious publication for the ag pilot and operator. Interested in **agricultural aviation (crop dusting) and aerial fire suppression (air tanker pilots) related poetry ONLY—something that rhymes and has a cadence.**" As a sample we selected these lines from "Freedom" by Jack B. Harvey:

> *So now I dress in faded jeans*
> *And beat up cowboy boots.*
> *My flying's done on veg'tables,*
> *The row crops, and the fruits.*
>
> *My wife now drives the flaggin' truck*
> *And marks off all my fields.*
> *She tells me all about the crops*
> *And talks about the yields.*

It appears monthly, 48-64 pgs., circulation 8,400. **Buys 1 poem/issue. Pays $10-50**.

✚ **The double dagger before a listing indicates that the listing is new in this edition. New markets are often the most receptive to submissions.**

THE AGUILAR EXPRESSION (I, II), P.O. Box 304, Webster PA 15087, phone (412)379-8019, founded 1986, editor/publisher Xavier F. Aguilar, appears 2 times/year, and is **"open to all types of poetry, including erotica that is well written. We insist that all writers send a SASE for writer's guidelines before submitting."** They have recently published poetry by Kimberly Harwell and Dann Ward. As a sample the editor selected the poem "Unnoticed" by Kathleen Lee Mendel:

> *I am blank paper*
> *kept in the back*
> *of your black leather*
> *address book.*

The editor describes it as 6-12 pgs., magazine-sized, circulation 200. **Sample postpaid: $6. Submit 3 poems at a time. "Send copies; mss will not be returned." Cover letter, including writing background, and SASE for contact purposes, required with submissions. Reports in 2 months. Pays 1 copy.** Open to unsolicited reviews. **"We are also now seeking poetry manuscripts as we wish to publish 1 or 2 chapbooks in 1995-1996. Send SASE for details."** The editor says, "In publishing poetry, I try to exhibit the unique reality that we too often take for granted and acquaint as mediocre. We encourage poetics that deal with *now*, which our readers can relate to. We also offer a cash prize for an essay relating to the writing of poetics (four typed pages). Guidelines for SASE."

AHSAHTA PRESS; COLD-DRILL; COLD-DRILL BOOKS; POETRY IN PUBLIC PLACES (IV-Regional), English Dept., Boise State University, Boise ID 83725, phone (208)385-1999. Ahsahta Press is a project to publish **contemporary poetry of the American West**. But, say editors Tom Trusky, Orv Burmaster and Dale Boyer, **"Spare us paens to the pommel, Jesus in the sagebrush, haiku about the Eiffel Tower, 'nice' or 'sweet' poems."** The work should **"draw on the cultures, history, ecologies of the American West."** They publish collections (45+ pgs.) of individual poets in handsome flat-spined paperbacks with plain matte covers, with an appreciative introduction, at most 3/year. Occasionally they bring out an anthology of their authors on cassette. And they have published *Women Poets of the West*, an anthology (94 pgs.) with an introduction by Ann Stanford. Some of their poets are Susan Deal, Leo Romero, David Baker, Linda Bierds, Philip St. Clair and Gretel Ehrlich. As a sample here are lines from Gerrye Payne's "Machines," in the collection *The Year-God*:

> *Machines sit to hand, vortices of possibility.*
> *Under their blank gaze biological life*
> *Flares and dies, is ashamed.*
> *The neighbor's tractor hums, clearing brush,*
> *inventing geometry in random chaparral.*

You may submit only during their January 1 through March 31 reading period each year—a sample of 15 of your poems with SASE. Multiple and simultaneous submissions OK. They will report in about 2 months. If they like the sample, they'll ask for a book ms. If it is accepted, **you get 25 copies of the 1st and 2nd printings and a 25% royalty commencing with the 3rd. They seldom comment on the samples, frequently on the mss**. Send SASE for their catalog and order a few books, if you don't find them in your library. "Old advice but true: Read what we publish before submitting. **75% of the submissions we receive should never have been sent to us. Save stamps, spirit and sweat."** *cold-drill* publishes **"primarily Boise State University students, faculty and staff, but will consider writings by Idahoans—or writing about Idaho by 'furriners.' "** They do some of the most creative publishing in this country today, and it is worth buying a **sample of *cold-drill* for $9** just to see what they're up to. This annual "has been selected as top undergraduate literary magazine in the U.S. by such important acronyms as CSPA, CCLM and UCDA." It comes in a box stuffed with various pamphlets, postcards, posters, a newspaper, even 3-D comics with glasses to read them by. **No restrictions on types of poetry**. As yet they have published no poets of national note, but Tom Trusky offers these lines as a sample, from Patrick Flanagan, "Postcard From a Freshman":

> *The girls here are gorgeous, studying hard,*
> *many new friends, roommate*
> *never showers, tried to*
> *kill myself, doctor says*
> *i'm getting better*

Circulation is 400, including 100 subscribers, of which 20 are libraries. **"We read material throughout the year, notifying only those whose work we've accepted December 15 through January 1. Manuscripts should be photocopies with author's name and address on separate sheet. Simultaneous submissions OK. Payment: 1 copy."** They also publish two 24-page chapbooks and one 75-page flat-spined paperback/year. **Query about book publication**. "We want to publish a literary magazine that is exciting to read. We want more readers than just our contributors and their mothers. Our format and our content have allowed us to achieve those goals, so far." Poetry in Public Places is a series of 8 monthly posters/year "presenting the poets in Boise State University's creative students series and poets in BSU's Ahsahta Press poetry series." The posters are on coated stock. These, like all publications emanating from BSU, are elegantly done, with striking art.

‡**AILERON PRESS; AILERON: A LITERARY JOURNAL; VOWEL MOVEMENT (II)**, P.O. Box 891, Austin TX 78767-0891, founded 1980, editor Lyman Grant. *Aileron* is an annual periodical consisting of poetry and occasional short fiction, with some art. They want **"poetry that moves us, that makes us want to read it again and again. We are especially keen on innovative uses of language—the unexpected word and the unusual cadence. We would like to see more poetic craft displayed, and, though not inimical to rhymed work, feel that few contemporary poets handle rhyme well."** They have published poetry by Anselm Hollo, Simon Perchik, Hal J. Daniel III and Tomaz Salamun. As a sample the editor selected these lines by Elkion Tumbalé:

> *Blue cup modal gorges*
> *Lurk frondly on*
> *Orchid Zontal*
> *Obsidian felines*

Aileron is digest-sized, saddle-stapled, typeset (in small type), with b&w original line art and stiff cover with art. Each issue contains 40-60 pages of poetry garnered from 400-600 submissions each year of which 60-100 are used, 6-month backlog. Circulation is 350, with 25 subscriptions. Subscription: $20 for 4 issues. **Sample postpaid: $6. All formats acceptable; must have name and address on each page; no limitations on form, length or subject matter. Send SASE for guidelines. Reports in 6 weeks. Pays 1 copy.** *Vowel Movement*, "a 'pataphysical journal,' is published occasionally as a special issue of *Aileron*. It contains **avant-garde humor, satire, and work that is outrageous or experimental in nature.**"

AIM MAGAZINE (IV-Social issues, ethnic), 7308 S. Eberhart Ave., Chicago IL 60619, phone (312)874-6184, founded 1974, poetry editor Henry Blakely, is a magazine-sized quarterly, circulation 10,000, glossy cover, **"dedicated to racial harmony and peace." They use 3-4 poems ("poetry with social significance mainly"—average 32 lines) in each issue.** They have published poetry by J. Douglas Studer, Wayne Dowdy and Maria DeGuzman. They receive about 30 submissions a year, use half. They have 3,000 subscribers of which 15 are libraries. Subscription: $10. **Sample postpaid: $4. Simultaneous submissions OK. Reports in 3-6 weeks. Pays $3/poem. You will not receive an acceptance slip: "We simply send payment and magazine copy."** The editor's advice: "Read the work of published poets."

‡**AIREINGS (II, IV-Women)**, Brudenell Rd., #24, Leeds, West Yorkshire LS6 1BD United Kingdom, phone 01532-785893, founded 1980, editor Jean Barker, appears twice a year. "Poems acceptable from all over the world. **Primarily like women's work** as we are a Women's Co-op running the mag and like to redress the balance a bit, but we are **happy to receive work by men also. Poetry on all subjects. We do draw a line on sexist/racist stuff, but we like a broad spectrum of work as long as it is not too long, as we only run to 40 pgs."** They have published poetry by Geoffrey Holloway, Pauline Kirk, Jane Legge, Mary Sheepshanks, C.A. de Lomallini and Linda Marshall. As a sample the editor selected these lines (poet unidentified):

> *For what's so indestructible as names,*
> *Though so haphazard, like those seeds, en masse,*
> *blown out across the graves; and some are lost.*
> *Yet, see the golden harvest in the grass,*
> *each seed a planting and each plant a word.*

Aireings is 40 pgs., digest-sized, saddle-stapled, photocopied from typescript with matte b&w card cover, "illustrated by our own artist. No ads yet, but we may have to later, if we are under extreme financial pressure." They publish about 5% of the poetry received. Their press run is 300-350 for 100 subscribers (10 libraries) and shelf sales. It costs £1.50/copy, which includes UK postage (overseas: Payment in sterling £5. Other currencies: check equivalent of £10 or in notes equivalent of £6.50.). **Submit 4 poems at a time. "Work should be typed if possible—just legible if not." Simultaneous submissions and previously published poems (if not in the North of England) OK, "if declared." Reports "after our editorial deadlines, which are the 1st of January and July." Pays 2 copies.** Staff reviews books of poetry in 500 words.

ALABAMA LITERARY REVIEW (II), English Dept., Troy State University, Troy AL 36082, phone (205)670-3286, fax (205)670-3519, poetry editor Ed Hicks, a biannual, **wants contemporary poetry that is "imagistic—*but* in motion." Will look at anything, but does not want to see "lyrics sent as poetry. We want serious craft."** They have published poetry by R.T. Smith, Ed Peaco, Joanne M. Riley, Martha Payne, Edward Byrne and Katherine McCanless. As a sample the editor selected these lines from "Late Fall" by Diane Swan:

> *It's hard to tell birds*
> *from wind-rushed leaves*
> *as they skirl up in the funnels*
> *of blinking October light*

The beautifully printed 100-page, 6×9 magazine, matte cover with art, b&w art and some colored pages inside, receives 300 submissions/year, uses 30, has a 2-month backlog. **Sample postpaid: $4.50. Submit 2-5 poems at a time. "SASE with appropriate postage is paramount." Will consider simultaneous submissions. Reads submissions September 1 through July 31 only. Sometimes comments on rejections. Reports in 2-3 months. Sometimes sends prepublication galleys. Pays copies, sometimes honorarium. Acquires first rights.** Open to unsolicited reviews. Poets may also send books for review consideration.

ALASKA QUARTERLY REVIEW (II), College of Arts and Sciences, University of Alaska Anchorage, 3211 Providence Dr., Anchorage AK 99508, phone (907)786-4775, founded 1981, executive editor Ronald Spatz. "A journal devoted to contemporary literary art. **We publish both traditional and experimental fiction, poetry, essays and criticism on contemporary writing, literature and philosophy of literature.**" Editors seem to welcome all styles and forms of poetry with the most emphasis perhaps on voice and content that displays "risk," or intriguing ideas or situations. They publish two double-issues a year, **each using between 18-25 pgs. of poetry**. They receive up to 2,000 submissions each year, accept about 40. They have a circulation of 1,300; 250 subscribers, of which 32 are libraries. Subscription: $8. **Sample postpaid: $5. Manuscripts are *not* read from May 15 through August 15. They take up to 4 months to report, sometimes longer during peak periods in late winter. Pay depends on funding. Acquires first North American serial rights.**

ALBATROSS; THE ANABIOSIS PRESS (II, IV-Nature), P.O. Box 7787, North Port FL 34287-0787, phone (813)426-7019, founded 1985, editors Richard Smyth and Richard Brobst. *Albatross* appears once a year. **"We consider the albatross to be a metaphor for an environment that must survive. This is not to say that we publish only environmental or nature poetry, but that we are biased toward such subject matters. We publish mostly free verse, 200 lines/poem maximum, and we prefer a narrative style, but again, this is not necessary. We do not want trite rhyming poetry which doesn't convey a deeply felt experience in a mature expression with words."** They have published poetry by Simon Perchik, Michael Jennings, Karen Volkman and Elizabeth Rees. As a sample, the editors selected these lines by Polly Buckingham:

> *Many white birds scatter like*
> *doves in a sand dollar,*
> *and I receive you, my body*
> *a murex, whelk, moonshell.*

The magazine is 28-36 pgs., 5½×8½, laser typeset with linen cover, some b&w drawings, and, in addition to the poetry, has an interview with a poet in each issue. Circulation 400 to 75 subscribers of which 10 are libraries. Many complimentary copies are sent out to bookstores, poets and libraries. Subscription: $5/2 issues. **Sample postpaid: $3. Submit 3-5 poems at a time. "Poems should be typed single-spaced, with name and address in left corner and length in lines in right corner." No simultaneous submissions. Cover letter not required; "We do, however, need bio notes if published." Send SASE for guidelines. Reports in 4-6 months, has 6- to 12-month backlog. Pays 2 copies. Acquires all rights. Returns rights provided that "previous publication in *Albatross* is mentioned in all subsequent reprintings."** Staff reviews books of poetry. Also holds a chapbook contest. **Submit 16-20 pgs. of poetry, any theme, any style. Deadline is March 31 of each year. Include name, address and phone number on the title page. Charges $6 reading fee (check payable to *Albatross*). Winner receives $50 and 25 copies of his/her published chapbook. All entering receive a free copy of the winning chapbook.** "The Anabiosis Press is now a nonprofit organization. Membership fee is $20/year." Comments? "We expect a poet to read as much contemporary poetry as possible."

ALDEBARAN (II), Roger Williams University, 1 Old Ferry Rd., Bristol RI 02809, phone (401)254-3503, managing editor Kym Jones, publishes a spring and a fall issue. *"Aldebaran* publishes both poetry and fiction in **traditional, contemporary and experimental forms; we are receptive to nearly all styles and topics. Accept poems up to 3 pages in length** and fiction up to 2,500 words. We would like to see more diversity in our magazine and encourage submissions from writers of all genres, from fantasy to dark fiction, science fiction, comedy, horror and drama, as well as classical and contemporary poetry and fiction. We also want to encourage more work from students." The magazine is 50-100 pgs., side-stapled or perfect-bound, digest-sized. Press run is 300. Subscription: $10 for 2 issues. **Sample postpaid: $5. Submit no more than 5 poems at a time. Reads submissions February 1 through April 1 and September 1 through November 1. Student-run publication. Seldom comments on rejections. Send SASE for guidelines. Reports in 6-12 weeks. Sometimes sends prepublication galleys.**

ALICEJAMESBOOKS; BEATRICE HAWLEY AWARD (IV-Regional, women, ethnic), University of Maine at Farmington, 98 Main St., Farmington ME 04938, phone (207)778-7071, founded 1973, is "an author's collective which only publishes **poetry. Authors are primarily from the New England Area**. We strongly encourage submissions by poets of color." They publish flat-spined paperbacks of high quality, both in production and contents, no children's poetry, and their books have won numerous awards and been very respectably reviewed. "Each poet becomes a working member of the co-op with a two-year work commitment." That is, you have to live close enough to **attend meetings and participate in the editorial and publishing process**. They publish about 4 books, 72 pgs., each year in editions of 1,000, paperbacks—no hardbacks. **Query first, but no need for samples: simply ask for dates of reading period, which is in early fall and winter. Send 2 copies of the ms. Simultaneous submissions OK, but "we would like to know when a manuscript is being submitted elsewhere." Reports in 2-3 months. Pays authors 100 paperback copies.** Offers Beatrice Hawley Award for poets who cannot meet the work requirement due to geographical restraints.

ALIVE NOW (IV-Spirituality, themes); POCKETS (IV-Religious, children, themes); WEAVINGS; THE UPPER ROOM (V), 1908 Grand Ave., P.O. Box 189, Nashville TN 37202, phone (615)340-7200. This publishing company brings out about 20 books a year and four magazines: *The Upper Room, Alive Now, Pockets* and *Weavings*. Of these, two use unsolicited poetry. *Pockets, Devotional Magazine for Children*, which comes out 11 times a year, circulation 68,000-70,000, is for children 6-12, "offers stories, activities, prayers, poems—all **geared to giving children a better understanding of themselves as children of God. Some of the material is not overtly religious but deals with situations, special seasons and holidays, and ecological concerns from a Christian perspective."** It uses 3-4 pgs. of poetry/issue. **Sample free with 7½ × 10½ SAE and 4 first-class stamps. Ordinarily 24-line limit on poetry. Send SASE for themes and guidelines. Pays $25-50.** The other magazine which uses poetry is *Alive Now*, a bimonthly, circulation 75,000, for a general Christian audience interested in reflection and meditation. **They buy 30 poems a year, avant-garde and free verse. Submit 5 poems, 10-45 lines. Send SASE for themes and guidelines. Pays $10-25.** *The Upper Room* **magazine does not accept poetry.**

ALLARDYCE, BARNETT, PUBLISHERS (V), 14 Mount St., Lewes, East Sussex BN7 1HL England, founded 1982, editorial director Anthony Barnett. Allardyce, Barnett publishes "literature, music, art. **We cannot consider unsolicited manuscripts."** They have recently published books of poetry by J.H. Prynne, Douglas Oliver, Veronica Forrest-Thomson, Anne-Marie Albiach and César Vallejo. In the US, their books can be obtained through Small Press Distribution in Berkeley, CA.

ALLEGHENY REVIEW (I, IV-Undergraduate students), Dept. PM, Box 32, Allegheny College, Meadville PA 16335, founded 1983. "Each year *Allegheny Review* compiles and publishes a review of the nation's best **undergraduate literature.** It is entirely composed of and by college undergraduates and is nationally distributed both as a review and as a classroom text, particularly suited to creative writing courses." In the Fall of 1995, they added a section of essays on poetry and literature. (Submit 10-15 typed pgs., double-spaced.) "We will print **poetry of appreciable literary merit on any topic, submitted by college undergraduates. No limitations except excessive length (2-3 pgs.)** as we wish to represent as many authors as possible, although exceptions are made in areas of great quality and interest." They have published poetry by Eric Sanborn, Cheryl Connor, Rick Alley and Kristi Coulter. The *Review* appears in a 6 × 9, flat-spined, professionally-printed format, b&w photo on glossy card cover. Single copy: $5. **Sample: $3.50 and 11 × 18 SASE (back issue: $3). Submit 3 to 5 poems, typed.** Submissions should be accompanied by a letter "telling the college poet is attending, year of graduation, any background, goals and philosophies that the author feels are pertinent to the work submitted." Reports 1-2 months following deadline. Poem judged best in the collection earns $50-75 honorarium.** "Ezra Pound gave the best advice: 'Make it new.' We're seeing far too much imitation; there's already been a Sylvia Plath, a Galway Kinnell. Don't be afraid to try new things. Be innovative. Also, traditional forms are coming 'back in style,' or so we hear. Experiment with them; write a villanelle, a sestina or a sonnet. And when you submit, please take enough pride in your work to do so professionally. Handwritten or poorly typed and proofed submissions definitely convey an impression—a negative one."

ALLY PRESS CENTER (V), Dept. PM, 524 Orleans St., St. Paul MN 55107, founded 1973, owner Paul Feroe, **publishes and distributes work by Robert Bly, Michael Meade, James Hillman and Robert Moore, including books, cassette tapes and videotapes.** Two to three times a year a complete catalog is mailed out along with information about Bly's reading and workshop schedule. **The press is not accepting unsolicited mss at this time.** Book catalog is free on request.

ALMS HOUSE PRESS (I), P.O. Box 217, Pearl River NY 10965-0217, founded 1985, poetry editors Lorraine De Gennaro and Alana Sherman, holds an **annual poetry competition with $9 entry fee (contestants receive a copy of a chapbook). "We have no preferences with regard to style as long as the poetry is high caliber. We like to see previous publication in the small press, but we are open to new writers. We look for variety and excellence and are open to experimental forms as well as traditional forms. Any topics as long as the poems are not whiny or too depressing, pornographic**

or religious." They have recently published chapbooks by Lenore Balliro and William Vernon. As a sample they selected these lines by Stephen R. Roberts:

> Silence reaches to clap the mouth shut.
> Waves from the wake of the last boat
> reach these eroded hills, touch soundlessly
> as a friend would tap your shoulder in a crowd
> to say to you in a fingertip of contact,
> it is time to go now, to be alone.

Submit 16- to 24-page chapbook including all front matter, title page and table of contents, between March 1 and July 1. Simultaneous submissions OK, "if we know about them." Name, address and phone number should appear on cover page only. Winner receives 15 copies. Send SASE for current rules. Sample copy postpaid: $4. They offer a critical and editorial service for $50. The editors say, "We treat every poem, every manuscript and every author with respect. We believe poetry should be well presented."

ALOHA, THE MAGAZINE OF HAWAII AND THE PACIFIC (IV-Regional), 1240 Ala Moana Blvd., Suite 320, Honolulu HI 96814, phone (808)593-1191, fax (808)593-1327, editorial director Cheryl Chee Tsutsumi, is a bimonthly (every 2 months) "consumer magazine with Hawaii and Pacific focus. **Not interested in lengthy poetry. Poems should be limited to 100 words or less. Subject should be focused on Hawaii."** As a sample the editorial director selected these lines by Sheri Rice:

> Sea touching sand
> Licks the silent shore
> Footsteps melting into smoothness
> Erasing ridges, indentations
> As each slap and pull of the ocean
> Planned by tides and moonlit nights
> Delivers one more day.

Aloha is 64 pgs., magazine-sized, flat-spined, elegantly printed on glossy stock with many full-color pages, glossy card cover in color. They publish 6 of more than 50 poems received/year. Circulation 65,000. **Sample: $2.95 plus $2.62 p&h. Ms should be typed, double-spaced, with name, address and phone number included.** Poems are matched to color photos, so it is "difficult to say" how long it will be between acceptance and publication. **Send SASE for guidelines. Reports within 2 months. Pays $30 plus 1 copy (and up to 10 at discount).**

ALPHA BEAT SOUP; ALPHA BEAT PRESS (I, IV-Form/style), 31 Waterloo St., New Hope PA 18938, phone (215)862-0299, founded 1987, poetry editor David Christy, appears irregularly **emulating the Beat literary tradition.** *Alpha Beat Soup* is "an international poetry and arts journal featuring Beat, 'post-Beat independent' and modern writing." Christy says that **25% of each issue is devoted to little known or previously unpublished poets.** They have recently published works by Pradip Choudhuri, Erling Friis-Baastad, Jack Micheline, Haynes/elliott and A.D. Winans. As a sample the editor selected these lines by Ana Christy:

> the alley in its
> complacency surrenders
> to
> morning scavenger birds
> squawking an Ornette
> Coleman sax.

ABS is 50-75 pgs., 7 × 8½, photocopied from IBM laser printer, card cover offset, graphics included. They use 50% of poetry received. Press run is 600 for 400 subscribers (11 of them libraries). Single copy: $8; subscription: $15. **Sample postpaid: $10. Submit 3-6 poems at a time. Simultaneous submissions and previously published poems OK. Cover letter, including "an introduction to the poet's work," required. Editor comments on rejections "only on request." Sometimes sends prepublication galleys. Pays 1 copy.** Reviews books of poetry in approximately 700 words, multi-book format. Open to unsolicited reviews. Poets may also send books for review consideration. **Alpha Beat Press publishes chapbooks and supplements as well as a monthly broadside series featuring unknown poets. They offer cooperative publishing of chapbooks, "as a way to fund our press and also showcase the unknown poet." Write for details.** Also see listings for *Bouillabaisse* and *Cokefish*.

ALTERNATIVE ARTS & LITERATURE MAGAZINE (II), (formerly *Alternative Press Magazine*), P.O. Box 205, Hatboro PA 19040, founded 1989, poetry editor Bob Lennon, co-editor Lynne Budnick-Lennon, appears quarterly using **"experimental, philosophical poetry; open to many subjects and styles. No traditional, religious, or worn-out love poems."** They have published poetry by Thomas Kretz, Rod Farmer, Robb Allan, Michael Estabrook, Tracy Lyn Rottkamp and Cheryl A. Townsend. As a sample we selected these lines from "The Easy Window Out" by Steven Booth:

> *if there is no way in,*
> *show me the easy window out*
> *the cold humorless blade*
> *or the*
> *warm hungry silk*
> *the gold-plated derringer*
> *and the hyenas*
> *laughing hysterically*

AALM is photocopied from typescript, digest-sized, 36 pgs. with matte card cover, saddle-stapled. Press run is 500 for about 100 subscribers, and growing. Some shelf sales. Subscription: $10 for 4 issues. **Sample postpaid: $3. Inquire about reduced rates for back issues. "Poets from Canada and overseas should include $1 extra for each issue ordered." Make all checks payable to Bob Lennon. "*Alternative Arts & Literature* will attempt to print many poems submitted unlike some magazines that print trash and reject most poems. Submit up to 5 poems—remember that we publish a digest-sized mag and longer pieces have a harder time finding a place."** Simultaneous submissions and previously published poems OK. Publishes theme issues occasionally. **Guidelines available for SASE. Reports within 2 weeks to 2 months. Pays 1-3 copies and "occasionally small sums." Editor comments on submissions "sometimes."** They are "now doing reviews of 'zines, books, chapbooks and music." Open to unsolicited reviews. Poets may also send books for review consideration. "*AALM* is currently not accepting unsolicited mss for our chopbook (that's no typo) series but they are available for $3 postage paid." The editor says, "We like to publish new poets, but they should read at least one copy to see what the magazine is about. Send poetry that comes from inside, not works that conform to outdated modes of writing. Response to this listing has been outstanding, but everyone who submits stands a fair chance at being published. This includes our friends in Europe, Australia and Canada too. We are trying to lose our sanity at *AALM*. The amount of poetry that we receive adds to this but a lot of normal, bland and unfeeling poetry is no help. Remember, no SASE—no reply! Creative people should avoid creative writing courses. I want to see the '90s on fire. Write poetry that will burn in my fingers when I read it."

AMATEUR WRITERS JOURNAL/FOUR SEASONS POETRY CLUB MAGAZINE (V), 3653 Harrison St., Bellaire OH 43906, phone (614)676-0881, founded 1967, editor/publisher Rosalind Gill, appears quarterly. Though **you have to buy a copy to see your work in print**, *AWJ* "accepts all types of articles, essays, short stories and **poetry of any theme. However, we currently have enough material to last through 1996."** They have published poetry by Robert Lowery, Eleanore M. Barker, Elsie Watkins and Remelda Gibson. As a sample the editor selected the first stanza of "Inspiration" by Donna Dietrich:

> *In the darkness, words come*
> *prancing across my pillow,*
> *clogging my veins and synapses*
> *tap-dancing across my brain.*
> *I quickly reach for the light switch*
> *blinding my bleary eyes.*

AWJ is 38 pgs., magazine-sized, photocopied from typescript, side-stapled with colored paper cover. Press run is 500. Subscription: $9. **Sample postpaid: $2.50.**

AMBER; MARSH & MAPLE (III), 40 Rose St., #404, Dartmouth, Nova Scotia B3A 2T6 Canada, phone (902)461-4934, founded 1967, editor Hazel F. Goddard, appears 4 times/year (in January, April, July and October). "*Amber* and its one-page supplement, *Marsh & Maple*, promote and distribute current work. *Amber* is nonprofit, entirely subscription-supported." **They want "free verse, half page, regular line lengths (not over 56 characters preferred), also haiku and occasional sonnet. Any subject, but must be in good taste, *not vulgar*. Original, bright content. No religious verse. Prefer poems to be seasonal, if on nature."** They have published poetry by John D. Engle, Jr., Diana K. Rubin and Tony Cosier. As a sample the editor selected these lines (poet unidentified):

> *i am a symphony*
> *blazing syllables of light*
> *across each phrase*
> *lengthening like eighth notes*
> *from a phantom violin*
> *to touch the inner ear*

Amber is 28 pgs., digest-sized, photocopied on colored paper and saddle-stapled with paper cover. They receive about 500 poems a year, use roughly 70%. Press run is 100 for 90 subscribers of which 3 are libraries. Single copy: $2.50; subscription: $10. **Sample postpaid: $1. Submit 2 poems at a time. Every sheet should bear the poet's name. Previously published poems OK; no simultaneous submissions.** Time between acceptance and publication is 1-6 months. **Seldom comments on rejections. "First acceptance paid for with 1 free copy; continuing submissions expected to be covered**

by a subscription." The editor says, "I receive many books of poets' poems. If up to an average standard I select from them for publication in my magazine. Most poems are from well-crafted poets, a few new writers. Need not be professional but *must* be good work. When space allows, I list contests poets may like to enter, comment on books poets send and devote centrefold to personal chatting, poets' successes, etc."

‡AMBIT (III), 17 Priory Gardens, Highgate, London N6 5QY England, phone 0181-340-3566, editor Martin Bax; poetry editors Edwin Brock, Carol Ann Duffy and Henry Graham; prose editor J.G. Ballard; and art editor Mike Foreman. *Ambit* is a 96-page quarterly of **avant-garde, contemporary and experimental work.** As a sample the editor selected these excerpts from "Two Poems For Two Suicides" by Henry Graham:

> *1*
> *All right then*
> *who would fardels bare?*
> *Or the world away out of earshot*
> *careless of your one foot in too many graves*
> *every waking hour.*
>
> *2*
> *It got to seem like a war,*
> *casualties*
> *I used to say,*
> *though no one was shooting at us.*
> *Or were they?*

Subscription: £22 individuals, £33 institutions (UK); £24 ($48) individuals, £35 ($70) institutions (overseas). **Sample: £6. Submit 6 poems at a time, typed double-spaced. No previously published poems or simultaneous submissions. Pay is "variable plus 2 free copies."** Staff reviews books of poetry. Send books for review consideration, attn. review editor.

AMELIA; CICADA; SPSM&H; THE AMELIA AWARDS (II, IV-Form), 329 "E" St., Bakersfield CA 93304 or P.O. Box 2385, Bakersfield CA 93303, phone (805)323-4064. *Amelia*, founded 1983, poetry editor Frederick A. Raborg, Jr., is a quarterly magazine that publishes chapbooks as well. Central to its operations is a series of contests, most with entry fees, spaced evenly throughout the year, awarding more than $3,500 annually, but they publish many poets who have not entered the contests as well. Among poets published are Pattiann Rogers, Stuart Friebert, John Millett, David Ray, Larry Rubin, Charles Bukowski, Maxine Kumin, Charles Edward Eaton and Shuntaro Tanikawa. As a sample the editor selected these lines by Robert Gibb:

> *Yours is not the whole handprint*
> *Left palmed on the walls of a cave*
> *Or the bright sides of a pony.*
> *This darkness is yours which rolls*
> *From beneath the nails, prints*
> *Gleaming like the back of fist,*
> *Freshly gutted and spread flat.*
> *They are boxy as Mayan glyphs, ten*
> *Small likenesses, ten little mirrors*
> *which flash as black as obsidian. . . .*

They are **"receptive to all forms to 100 lines. We do not want to see the patently-religious or overtly-political. Erotica is fine; pornography, no."** The digest-sized, flat-spined magazine is offset on high-quality paper and sometimes features an original four-color cover; its circulation is about 1,556, with 612 subscribers, of which 28 are libraries. Subscription: $25/year. **Sample postpaid: $8.95. Submit 3-5 poems at a time. No simultaneous submissions except for entries to the annual Amelia Chapbook Award. Reports in 2-12 weeks, the latter if under serious consideration. Pays $2-25/ poem plus 2 copies. "Almost always I try to comment."** The editor says, "*Amelia* is not afraid of strong themes, but we do look for professional, polished work even in handwritten submissions. Poets should have something to say about matters other than the moon. We like to see strong **traditional pieces as well as the contemporary and experimental. And neatness *does* count**." Fred Raborg has done more than most other editors to ensure a wide range of styles and forms, from traditional European to Asian, from lyric to narrative. Typically he is swamped with submissions and so response time can exceed stated parameters. *Amelia* continues to place in outside surveys as a top market, because of editorial openness. Brief reviews are also featured. As for Raborg's other publications, *Cicada* is a quarterly magazine that publishes **haiku, senryu and other Japanese forms**, plus essays on the form— techniques and history—as well as fiction which in some way incorporates haiku or Japanese poetry in its plot, and reviews of books pertaining to Japan and its poetry or collections of haiku. Among poets published are Roger Ishii, H.F. Noyes, Knute Skinner, Katherine Machan Aal, Ryah Tumarkin Goodman and Ryokufu Ishizaki. These sample lines are by Elizabeth St. Jacques:

> *shrinking*
> *the small garden plot*
> *a silver-striped melon*

> *the quiet search over rocks*
> *of a thin green vine*

They are **receptive to experimental forms as well as the traditional. "Try to avoid still-life as haiku; strive for the** *whole* **of an emotion, whether minuscule or panoramic. Erotica is fine; the Japanese are great lovers of the erotic."** The magazine is offset on high quality paper. Circulation 600, with 432 subscribers of which 26 are libraries. Subscription: $14/year. **Sample postpaid: $4.95. Submit 3-10 haiku or poems. No simultaneous submissions. Reports in 2 weeks. No payment, except three "best of issue" poets each receive $10 on publication plus copy. "I try to make some comment on returned poems always."** *SPSM&H* is a quarterly magazine that publishes **only sonnets, sonnet sequences**, essays on the form—both technique and history—as well as romantic or Gothic fiction which, in some way, incorporates the form, and reviews of sonnet collections or collections containing a substantial number of sonnets. They are **"receptive to experimental forms as well as the traditional, and appreciate wit when very good."** Among poets published are Margaret Ryan, Harold Witt, Sharon E. Martin, Rhina P. Espaillat and Robert Wolfkill. These sample lines are by Michael J. Bugeja:

> *She knew the steps, the key. The cadence*
> *When she came to him with another minuet,*
> *Sheeted music in her satchel like a poem:*
> *Heavy, black. But even she could dance*
> *Later as he taught her, timing the duet*
> *With the indifference of a metronome.*

Perhaps it may help to know the editor's favorite Shakespearean sonnet is #29, and he feels John Updike clarified the limits of experimentation with the form in his "Love Sonnet" from *Midpoint*. The magazine is offset on high quality paper. Circulation 600, for 432 subscribers and 26 libraries. Subscription: $14/year. **Sample postpaid: $4.95. Submit 3-5 poems at a time. No simultaneous submissions. Reports in 2 weeks. No payment, except two "best of issue" poets each receive $14 on publication plus copy. "I always try to comment on returns."** The following annual contests have various entry fees: The Amelia Awards (six prizes of $200, $100, $50 plus three honorable mentions of $10 each); The Anna B. Janzen Prize for Romantic Poetry ($100, annual deadline January 2); The Bernice Jennings Traditional Poetry Award ($100, annual deadline January 2); The Georgie Starbuck Galbraith Light/Humorous Verse Prizes (six awards of $100, $50, $25 plus three honorable mentions of $5 each, annual deadline March 1); The Charles William Duke Longpoem Award ($100, annual deadline April 1); The Lucille Sandberg Haiku Awards (six awards of $100, $50, $25 plus three honorable mentions of $5 each, annual deadline April 1); The Grace Hines Narrative Poetry Award ($100, annual deadline May 1); The Amelia Chapbook Award ($250, book publication and 50 copies, annual deadline July 1); The Johanna B. Bourgoyne Poetry Prizes (six awards of $100, $50, $25, plus three honorable mentions of $5 each); The Douglas Manning Smith Epic/Heroic Poetry Prize ($100, annual deadline August 1); The Hildegarde Janzen Prize for Oriental Forms of Poetry (six awards of $50, $30, $20 and three honorable mentions of $5 each, annual deadline September 1); The Eugene Smith Prize for Sonnets (six awards of $140, $50, $25 and three honorable mentions of $5 each); The A&C Limerick Prizes (six awards of $50, $30, $20 and three honorable mentions of $5 each); The Montegue Wade Lyric Poetry Prize ($100, annual deadline November 1).

AMERICA; FOLEY POETRY CONTEST (II), 106 W. 56th St., New York NY 10019, phone (212)581-4640, founded 1909, poetry editor Patrick Samway, S.J., is a weekly journal of opinion published by the Jesuits of North America. They primarily publish articles on religious, social, political and cultural themes. **They are "looking for imaginative poetry of all kinds. We have no restrictions on form or subject matter, though we prefer to receive poems of 35 lines or less."** They have published poetry by Howard Nemerov, Fred Chappell, William Heyen and Eve Shelnutt. *America* is 24 pgs., magazine-sized, professionally printed on thin stock with thin paper cover. Circulation 35,000. Subscription: $33. **Sample postpaid: $1.25. Send SASE for excellent guidelines. Reports in 2 weeks. Pays $1.40/line plus 2 copies.** The annual Foley Poetry Contest offers a prize of $500, usually in late winter. Send SASE for rules. "Poems for the Foley Contest should be submitted between January and April. Poems submitted for the Foley Contest between July and December will normally be returned unread." The editor says, "*America* is committed to publishing quality poetry as it has done for the past 86 years. We would encourage beginning and established poets to submit their poems to us."

AMERICAN ATHEIST PRESS; GUSTAV BROUKAL PRESS; AMERICAN ATHEIST (IV-Specialized), P.O. Box 2117, Austin TX 78768-2117, phone (512)458-1244, founded 1958, editor R. Murray-O'Hair, publishes the quarterly magazine with 30,000 circulation, *American Atheist*, and under various imprints some dozen books a year reflecting "concerns of atheists, such as separation of state and church, civil liberties and atheist news." **Poetry is used primarily in the poetry section of the magazine. It must have "a particular slant to atheism, dealing with subjects such as the atheist lifestyle. Anticlerical poems and puns are more than liable to be rejected. Any form or style is acceptable. Preferred length is under 40 lines."** They have published poetry by Julia Rhodes Pozonzycki, Allan Case and Thomas A. Easton. The magazine-sized format is professionally printed, with art and photos, glossy, color cover. They receive over 20-30 poetry submissions/week, use about 12/year. Of their 17,000 subscriptions, 1,000 are libraries. Single copy: $2.95; subscription: $25. **Sample free. Submit 6-8 poems at a time, typed and double-spaced. Simultaneous submissions OK. Time-dependent poems (such as winter) should be submitted 4 months in advance. Guidelines and upcoming themes available for SASE, but a label is preferred to an envelope. Reports within 3-4 months. Pays "first-timers" 10 copies or 6-month subscription or $12 credit voucher for AAP products. Thereafter, $15/poem plus 10 copies. Buys one-time rights. Sometimes comments on rejected mss.** Reviews related books of poetry in 500-1,000 words. They do not normally publish poetry in book form but will consider it.

THE AMERICAN COWBOY POET MAGAZINE (I, IV-Cowboy), Dept. PM, P.O. Box 326, Eagle ID 83616, phone (208)888-9838, founded 1988 as *The American Cowboy Poet Newspaper,* magazine format in January 1991, publisher Rudy Gonzales, editor Rose Fitzgerald. *ACPM* is a quarterly "about real cowboys" using **"authentic cowboy poetry. Must be clean—entertaining. Submissions should avoid 'like topics.' We will not publish any more poems about Old Blackie dying, This old hat, if this pair of Boots could talk, etc. We do not publish free verse poetry. Only traditional cowboy with rhyme and meter."** They also publish articles including a "Featured Poet," stories of cowboy poetry gatherings and news of coming events. Subscription: $12/year, $15 Canada, $20 overseas. **Sample: $3 plus $1.25 p&h. Cover letter required with submissions. Send SASE for guidelines. Editor always comments on rejections.** Staff reviews related books and tapes of poetry. Send books and cowboy music tapes for review consideration.

AMERICAN LITERARY REVIEW (II), University of North Texas, P.O. Box 13827, Denton TX 76203, phone (817)565-4670, editor Barbara Rodman, is a biannual publishing **all forms and modes of poetry, but "less interested in poetry in the personal mode."** They have published poetry by Penelope Austin, Wendy Barker, Bruce Bond, Kevin Cantwell, David Citino, Wyn Cooper, Elizabeth Dodd, Joseph Duemer, Pattiann Rogers, William Stafford, Lee Upton and Ralph Wilson. As a sample the editor selected these lines from "Double or Nothing" by Jack Myers:

> And, now, like an amnesiac trying to feel special on his birthday,
> I've decided that death must be what it's like before we're born.
> Have I finally broken through? Unafraid of the nothing that's eternal
> in favor of the nothing that will pass?

Sample postpaid: $8. Submit up to 5 poems at a time. Reports in 2 months. Sometimes sends prepublication galleys. Pays copies.

AMERICAN POETRY REVIEW (III), Dept. PM, 1721 Walnut St., Philadelphia PA 19103, phone (215)496-0439, founded 1972, is probably the **most widely circulated (18,000 copies bimonthly) and best-known periodical devoted to poetry in the world**. Poetry editors are Stephen Berg, David Bonanno and Arthur Vogelsang, and they have **published most of the leading poets writing in English and many translations**. The poets include Gerald Stern, Brenda Hillman, John Ashbery, Norman Dubie, Marvin Bell, Galway Kinnell, James Dickey, Lucille Clifton and Tess Gallagher. *APR* is a newsprint tabloid with 13,000 subscriptions, of which 1,000 are libraries. The editors receive about 8,000 submissions/year, use 200. This popular publication contains mostly free verse (some leaning to the avant-garde) with flashes of brilliance in every issue. Editors seem to put an emphasis on language and voice. Because *APR* is a tabloid, it can feature long poems (or ones with long line lengths) in an attractive format. Translations are also welcome. In all, this is a difficult market to crack because of the volume of submissions. **Sample and price per issue: $3.50. No simultaneous submissions. Reports in 3 months, has 1- to 3-year backlog. Always sends prepublication galleys. Pays $2/line.** The magazine is also a major resource for opinion, reviews, theory, news and ads pertaining to poetry. Each year the editors award the Jerome J. Shestack Prizes of $1,000, $500 and $250 for the best poems, in their judgment, published in *APR*. Poetry published here has also been included in the 1992, 1993, 1994 and 1995 volumes of *The Best American Poetry*.

THE AMERICAN SCHOLAR (III), 1811 Q St. NW, Washington DC 20009, phone (202)265-3808, founded 1932, associate editor Sandra Costich, is an academic quarterly which **uses about 5 poems/ issue. "We would like to see poetry that develops an image, a thought or event, without the use of a single cliché or contrived archaism. The most hackneyed subject matter is self-conscious love; the most tired verse is iambic pentameter with rhyming endings. The usual length of our poems is 30 lines. From 1-4 poems may be submitted at one time;** *no more* **for a careful reading."** They have published poetry by Robert Pack, Alan Shapiro and Gregory Djanikian. What little poetry is used in this high-prestige magazine is accomplished, intelligent and open (in terms of style and form). Study before submitting (**sample: $6.50, guidelines available for SASE). Reports in 2 months. Always sends prepublication galleys. Pays $50/poem. Buys first rights only.**

AMERICAN TOLKIEN SOCIETY; MINAS TIRITH EVENING-STAR; W.W. PUBLICATIONS (IV-Specialized, themes), P.O. Box 373, Highland MI 48357-0373, founded 1967, editor Philip W. Helms. There are special poetry issues. Membership in the ATS is open to all, regardless of country of residence, and entitles one to receive the quarterly journal. Dues are $7.50 per annum to addresses in US, $12.50 in Canada and $15 elsewhere. Their journal and chapbooks use **poetry of fantasy about Middle-Earth and Tolkien.** They have published poetry by Thomas M. Egan, Anne Etkin, Nancy Pope and Martha Benedict. *Minas Tirith Evening-Star* is magazine-sized, offset from typescript with cartoon-like b&w graphics. They have a press run of 400 for 350 subscribers of which 10% are libraries. Single copy: $3.50; subscription: $7.50. **Sample postpaid: $1.50.** "Please make checks payable to American Tolkien Society." **No simultaneous submissions; previously published poems "maybe." Cover letter preferred. Editor sometimes comments on rejections. Publishes theme issues occasionally. Send SASE for guidelines. Reports in 2 weeks. Sometimes sends prepublication galleys. Pays contributor's copies.** Reviews related books of poetry; length depends on the volume, "a sentence to several pages." Open to unsolicited reviews. Poets may also send books to Paul Ritz, Reviews, P.O. Box 901, Clearwater FL 34617 for review consideration. Under imprint of W.W. Publications they publish collections of poetry 50-100 pgs. **For book or chapbook consideration, submit sample poems. Publishes 2 chapbooks/year.** They sometimes sponsor contests.

AMERICAN WRITING: A MAGAZINE; NIERIKA EDITIONS (IV-Form/style), 4343 Manayunk Ave., Philadelphia PA 19128, founded 1990, editor Alexandra Grilikhes, appears twice a year using **poetry that is "experimental and the voice of the loner, writing that takes risks with form, interested in the powers of intuition and states of being. No cerebral, academic poetry. Poets often try to make an experience 'literary' through language, instead of going back to the original experience and finding the original images. That is what we are interested in: the voice that speaks those images."** They have published poetry by Ivan Argüelles, Antler, Eleanor Wilner, Diane Glancy and Margaret Holley. As a sample the editor selected these lines from "Coyote" by Shelley M. Miller:

> *There is pain, Coyote, that you have not known yet.*
> *It is good your legs still carry you*
> > *tirelessly away from peace;*
> *that your grin still frightens away false caretakers,*
> *that you long ago ate your own heart to survive.*
>
> *There is pain ahead, Coyote.*
> *Muscle, cunning, speed? These will never set you free.*

AW is 80 pgs., digest-sized, flat-spined, professionally printed, with matte card cover. Press run is 2,000 for 350 subscribers. Subscription: $10. **Sample postpaid: $6. Submit 8 poems at a time. No previously published poems; simultaneous submissions OK. Guidelines on subscription form. Reporting time varies. "If it's a 'possible,' we may keep it 4 months." Pays 2 copies/accepted submission group.** Since *American Writing* began in 1990, 15 of the authors they have published won national awards after publication in the magazine. The editor says, "Many magazines print the work of the same authors [the big names] who often publish 'lesser' works that way. *AW* is interested in the work itself, its particular strength, energy and voice, not necessarily in the 'status' of the authors. We like to know *something* about the authors, however."

‡THE AMHERST REVIEW (II), Box 1811, Amherst College, P.O. Box 5000, Amherst MA 01002-5000, editor Molly Lyons, is an annual literary magazine seeking quality submissions in fiction, poetry, nonfiction and photography/artwork. **"All kinds of poetry welcome."** The editor says the review is 50 pgs., 5 × 8, soft cover with photography, art and graphics. They receive 300-500 poems a year, accept around 10. Most copies are distributed free to Amherst students. **Sample postpaid: $6. No previously**

published poems; simultaneous submissions OK. Reads submissions from October to February only. Magazine staff makes democratic decision. Seldom comments on rejections. Send SASE for guidelines. Reports in late March. Pays 1 copy.

THE AMICUS JOURNAL (IV-Nature/rural/ecology), 40 W. 20th St., New York NY 10011, is the quarterly journal of the Natural Resources Defense Council. *Amicus* **publishes about 15 poems a year and asks that submitted poetry be "rooted in nature."** They have published poetry by some of the best known poets in the country, including Mary Oliver, Gary Snyder, Denise Levertov, Marvin Bell and the late William Stafford. As a sample, the editors selected these lines from "In the Labyrinth of Elements" by Duane Niatum:

> The painter descends into the world
> like the morning sun
> on madrona branch, azalea and peony,
> follows the gold thread passing stem,
> leaf, petal, moss, mushroom and trunk,
> twig and stone. . . .

The Amicus Journal is finely-printed, saddle-stapled, on high quality paper with glossy cover, using much art, photography and cartoons. Circulation 170,000. **Sample postpaid: $4. Pays $50/poem plus a year's subscription.**

ANACONDA PRESS; FUEL (II), P.O. Box 146640, Chicago IL 60614, e-mail alowry@spagmumps. com, editor-in-chief Andy Lowry. Currently publishes *fuel*, "a wiry, highly energized mini-magazine using lots of cool poetry, art and fiction." Also publishes **3-4 poetry chapbooks/year. "We're looking for daring, eccentric works. No academia allowed!" Submit up to 6 poems at a time. "Previously published poems are OK if not too terribly recent. Simultaneous submissions are frowned upon. We appreciate cover letters." Send SASE for most recent guidelines. Sometimes sends prepublication galleys. Pays 1-2 copies if published in 'zine. Chapbook payment is negotiable. Rights revert to authors. Sample copy postpaid: $3.**

ANALECTA (IV-Students), Dept. PM, Liberal Arts Council, FAC 17, University of Texas, Austin TX 78712, phone (512)471-6563, founded 1974, contact Marc Faletti and Jennifer Conwell, is an annual of literary works and art by **college/university students and graduate students chosen in an annual contest. No restrictions on type; limited to 5 poems/submission. Submissions cannot be returned.** "Our purpose is to provide a forum for excellent student writing. **Works must be previously unpublished.**" As a sample, the editor selected this excerpt from "Jitterbug Puppet" by Alex Travgott:

> She dances in the garden
> with tiger lilies in her white arm
> like a swarm of clouds before a storm.
>
> Her legs pound down the dirt in time. . .

It is a 150-page magazine, glossy plates for interior artwork in b&w, 7 × 10, flat-spined, soft cover. Of about 800 submissions received, they publish about 40. Press run is 800 for 700 subscribers, 100 shelf sales. **Sample postpaid: $7.50. Entries must be typed; name should appear on cover sheet only. Send SASE for guidelines. Deadline is in mid-October. Prizes in each category. Pays 2 copies and various monetary prizes.**

ANATHEMA REVIEW (II), P.O. Box 891, Bowling Green OH 43402, founded 1993, editors Edward A. Gore and Matthew David Gengler, appears approximately 4 times/year. **They want "poetry that is not only well crafted but also *says* something. No poetry without thought, purpose or meaning. Nothing overly sentimental."** They have recently published poetry by Simon Perchik, Gary Whitehead and Barbara Van Noord. As a sample we selected these lines from "Lambis Reads My Palm" by David Hassler:

> When I return to Greece, I'll say to my friends
> I drove a cadillac in America.
> Already he has a contract to record,
>
> His life running a course, sure
> as the music he played this evening.
> Truth of silence! he warns his students
>
> before they touch the keys.
> In my country, we sing our poetry.
> That's how we know it's good.

AR is 30-40 pgs., 5½ × 8½, professionally printed and saddle-stapled with card cover, b&w art and photos. They accept less than 5% of poetry received. Press run is 150, 50% shelf sales. Subscription:

$10. **Sample postpaid: $3. Submit 5 poems at a time. No previously published poems; simultane-ous submissions OK. Cover letter required.** Time between acceptance and publication is up to 5 months. **Send SASE for guidelines. Reports in 2-5 weeks. Pays 1 copy.**

ANHINGA PRESS; ANHINGA PRIZE (II), P.O. Box 10595, Tallahassee FL 32302-0595, phone (904)575-5592, fax (904)442-4146, founded 1972, poetry editors Rick Campbell and Van Brock, publishes **"books and anthologies of poetry. We also offer the Anhinga Prize for poetry—$1,000 and publication—for a book-length manuscript each year. We want to see contemporary poetry which respects language. We're inclined toward poetry that is not obscure, that can be understood by any literate audience."** They have recently published poetry by Yvonne Sapia, Judith Kitchen, Ricardo Pau-Llosa, Michael Mott, Frank X. Gaspar, Gary Corseri, Nick Bozanic, Jean Monahan, Earl S. Braggs and Janet Holmes. As a sample the editors selected these lines from *The Secret Life of Moles* by P.V. LeForge:

> The sun migrates across whatever scenes
> death can spare:
> and we have many of these small reprieves
> living within us.
> When we die, will life stop again?
> And for whom?

Considers simultaneous submissions. Send SASE for catalog. Also send SASE for rules (submissions accepted in January and February) of the Anhinga Prize for poetry, which requires a $15 entry fee. The contest has been judged by such distinguished poets as William Stafford, Louis Simpson, Henry Taylor, Hayden Carruth, Denise Levertov, Marvin Bell and Donald Hall. For the next three years the judge will be Joy Harjo.

ANJOU (V), P.O. Box 322 Station P., Toronto, Ontario M5S 2S8 Canada, founded 1980, edited by Richard Lush and Roger Greenwald, publishes broadsides of poetry. **"We do not wish to receive submissions because we publish only by solicitation."**

ANSUDA PUBLICATIONS; ANSUDA MAGAZINE (II), P.O. Box 158JA, Harris IA 51345, founded 1978, editor/publisher Daniel Betz, "is a small press operation, publishing independently of outside influences, such as grants, donations, awards, etc. Our operating capital comes from magazine and book sales only." Their magazine, *Ansuda*, "uses some poetry. **We prefer poems with a social slant and originality—we do** *not* **want love poems, personal poems that can only be understood by the poet, or anything from the haiku family of poem styles. No limits on length, though very short poems lack the depth we seek—no limits on form or style, but rhyme and meter must make sense. Too many poets write senseless rhymes using the first words to pop into their heads. As a result, we prefer blank and free verse."** They have published poetry by Ian Lawrence, Paul M. Lamb, Anthony Constantino and Terry Everton. They offer no sample because "most of our poems are at least 25-30 lines long and every line complements all other lines, so it is hard to pick out lines to illustrate." *Ansuda*, which appears irregularly (1-3 times a year), is a low-budget publication, digest-sized, mimeo-graphed on inexpensive paper, making it possible to print 80 or more pages and sell copies for **$4 (the price of a sample)**. Press run is 200 for 100 subscribers, of which 7 are libraries. Each issue has 3-12 pages of poetry, but **"we would publish more if we had it; our readers would like more poetry."** Everything accepted goes into the next issue, so there is no backlog. **Reports immediately to 1 month. Pays 2 copies. Acquires first rights.** "We are *not* interested in past credits, who you studied under, etc. Names mean nothing to us and we have found that the small press is so large that big names in one circle are unknown in another circle. In fact, **we get better material from the unknowns who have nothing to brag about (usually)."** Daniel Betz adds, "About all I have left to say is to tell the novice to keep sending his work out. It won't get published in a desk drawer. There are so many little mags out there that eventually you'll find homes for your poems. Yes, some poets get published on their first few tries, but I've made first acceptances to some who have been submitting for 5 to 10 years with no luck, until their poem and my mag just seemed to click. It just takes time and lots of patience."

ANTERIOR POETRY MONTHLY; ANTERIOR BITEWING LTD. (I), 993 Allspice Ave., Fenton MO 63026-4901, e-mail 72247.1405@compuserve.com, founded 1988, editor Tom Bergeron, appears 12 times a year using **"poems of excellence. We prefer articulate, logical writing that follows tradi-tional poetic practices. Submissions welcome from everyone; however, there is a $1 reading fee per poem submitted unless you are a subscriber. The top four poems in each issue receive awards of $25, $15, $10 and $5 respectively. Other poems may be published with no payment to the author. Entries received after the 15th, extra submissions and poems more suited to later seasons are automatically entered in future month's contest."** They have recently published poetry by J. Alvin Speers, Pearl Bloch Segall, Katherine Brooks and Marian Ford Park. As a sample the editor selected these lines from "The Light" by Barbara N. Paul-Best:

> *Cold are the winds that blow,*
> *Cold as December ice and January snow;*
> *Soothing as a blanket of snow-starred down;*
> *Peaceful as the absence of every sound.*

It is 20 pgs., digest-sized, desktop-published and saddle-stapled with colored paper cover. Press run is 200-300 for 110 subscribers. Subscription: $20. **Sample postpaid: $1. Make checks payable to Anterior Bitewing Ltd. Submit 5 poems at a time. Name and address on each page. "We like cover letters." Include sufficient first-class postage to cover returns. Send SASE for guidelines. Buys one-time rights.** The editor says, "Always resubmit. There's some editor out there somewhere who will love your work. Take advice, make changes accordingly and keep on resubmitting."

ANTHOLOGY OF MAGAZINE VERSE & YEARBOOK OF AMERICAN POETRY (III, IV-Anthology), % Monitor Book Company, P.O. Box 9078, Palm Springs CA 92263, phone (619)323-2270, founded 1950, editor Alan F. Pater. The annual *Anthology* is a selection of the **best poems published in American magazines during the year and is also a basic reference work for poets.** Alan F. Pater says, "We want poetry that is 'readable' and in any poetic form; we also want translations. **All material must first have appeared in magazines.** Any subject matter will be considered; we also would like to see some rhyme and meter, preferably sonnets." They have published poetry by Margaret Atwood, Stanley Kunitz, Robert Penn Warren, Richard Wilbur, Maxine Kumin and John Updike. Indeed, the anthology is a good annual guide to the best poets actively publishing in any given year. For the most part selections are made by the editor from magazines, but some poets are solicited for their work which has been in magazines in a given year. **Cover letters should include name and date or issue number of magazine in which the poem was originally published.**

ANTIETAM REVIEW (IV-Regional), Washington County Arts Council, 7 W. Franklin St., Hagerstown MD 21740, phone (301)791-3132, an annual founded 1982, poetry editors Crystal Brown and Ann Knox, looks for **"well-crafted literary quality poems. We discourage inspirational verse, haiku, doggerel." Uses poets (natives or residents) from the states of Maryland, Pennsylvania, Virginia, West Virginia, Delaware and District of Columbia. Needs 22 poems/issue, up to 30 lines each.** Poets they have published include Roberta Bevington, Naomi Thiers and Ed Zahniser. As a sample the editor selected these lines from "Fireflies" by Barbara Hurd:

> *Perhaps we were all once luminescent like that,*
> *could summon with light whatever we longed for,*
> *until something, consciousness maybe,*
>
> *needed the light inside, drew it into our bodies,*
> *left us opaque on the outside, desire raking the sky*
> *like a dark searchlight.*

AR is 48 pgs., 8½×11, saddle-stapled, glossy paper with glossy card cover and b&w photos throughout. Press run is 1,000. **Sample postpaid: $3.15 back issue, $5.25 current. Submit 5 typed poems at a time. "We prefer a cover letter stating other publications, although we encourage new and emerging writers. We do not accept previously published poems and reluctantly take simultaneous submissions." Do not submit mss from February through August. "We read from September 1 through February 1 annually." Send SASE for guidelines. Sends prepublication galleys, if requested. Pays $20/poem, depending on funding, plus 2 copies. Buys first North American serial rights.** The editors seem open to all styles of poetry, free and formal, as long as the author is from the designated region. Overall, a good read; but poems have to compete with prose. Ones used, however, are featured in attractive boxes on the page. Work published in *Antietam Review* has been included in a *Pushcart Prize* anthology, and *Antietam Review* received first runner-up for editorial content as part of the 1993-1994 American Literary Magazine Awards.

THE ANTIGONISH REVIEW (II), St. Francis Xavier University, P.O. Box 5000, Antigonish, Nova Scotia B2G 2W5 Canada, phone (902)867-3962, fax (902)867-5153, e-mail tar@stfx.juliet.ca, founded 1970, editor George Sanderson, poetry editor Peter Sanger. This high-quality quarterly "tries to produce the kind of literary and visual mosaic that the modern sensibility requires or would respond to." They want poetry **not over "80 lines, i.e., 2 pgs.; subject matter can be anything, the style is traditional, modern or post-modern limited by typographic resources. Purpose is not an issue."** No **"erotica, scatalogical verse, excessive propaganda toward a certain subject."** They have recently published poetry by Andy Wainwright, W.J. Keith, Michael Hulse, Jean McNeil, M. Travis Lane and Douglas Lochhead. *TAR* is flat-spined, 6×9, 150 pgs. with glossy card cover, offset printing, using "in-house graphics and cover art, no ads." They accept about 10% of some 2,500 submissions/year. Press run is 850 for 700 subscriptions. Subscription: $20. **Sample postpaid: $3. Submit 5-10 poems at a time. No simultaneous submissions or previously published poems. Include SASE or SAE and IRCs if outside Canada. Editor "sometimes" comments on rejections. Pays 2 copies.**

THE ANTIOCH REVIEW (III), P.O. Box 148, Yellow Springs OH 45387, phone (513)767-6389, founded 1941, poetry editor David St. John, "is an independent quarterly of critical and creative thought ... **For over 50 years, creative authors, poets and thinkers have found a friendly reception ... regardless of formal reputation**. We get far more poetry than we can possibly accept, and the competition is keen. Here, where form and content are so inseparable and reaction is so personal, it is difficult to state requirements or limitations. Studying recent issues of *The Review* should be helpful. **No 'light' or inspirational verse**." They have recently published poetry by Ralph Angel, Jorie Graham, Mark Strand, Kathleen Peirce, Gillian Conoley and Adrian C. Louis. They receive about 3,000 submissions/ year, publish 20 pages of poetry in each issue, have about a 6-month backlog. Circulation is 5,000, of which 70% is through bookstores and newsstands. Large percentage of subscribers are libraries. Subscription: $35. **Sample: $6. Submit 1-10 poems at a time. No previously published poems. Reads submissions September 1 through May 15 only. General guidelines for contributors available for SASE. Reports in 6-8 weeks. Pays $10/published page plus 2 copies.** Reviews books of poetry in 300 words, single format. This is a beautiful journal featuring some of the best poems being written by new and well-known writers. Work published in this review has been included in *The Best American Poetry 1995* and *Pushcart Prize* anthologies. As David St. John says, "I have a policy of publishing a poet only once during my tenure as poetry editor. It may be a dumb policy, but it's one way to help keep the magazine open to new folks. I'd like to think that there's at least one place where new poets feel they have a shot." Consequently, voices here are varied and exciting.

ANTIPODES (IV-Regional), 8 Big Island, Warwick NY 10990, e-mail pakane@vassar.edu, founded 1987, poetry editor Paul Kane, is a biannual of Australian poetry and fiction and criticism and reviews of Australian writing. They want **work from Australian poets only. No restrictions as to form, length, subject matter or style.** They have published poetry by A.D. Hope, Judith Wright and John Tranter. As a sample the editor selected these lines from "Poetry and Religion" by Les Murray:

> *Religions are poems. They concert*
> *our daylight and dreaming mind, our*
> *emotions, instinct, breath and native gesture*
> *into the only whole thinking: poetry*

The editor says *Antipodes* is 180 pgs., 8½ × 11, perfect-bound, with graphics, ads and photos. They receive about 500 submissions a year, accept approximately 10%. Press run is 500 for 200 subscribers. Subscription: $20. **Sample postpaid: $17. Submit 3-5 poems at a time. No previously published poems or simultaneous submissions. Cover letter with bio note required. The editor says they "prefer submission of photocopies which do not have to be returned." Seldom comments on rejections. Reports in 2 months. Pays $20/poem plus 1 copy. Acquires first North American serial rights.** Staff reviews books of poetry in 500-1,500 words. Send books for review consideration.

ANYTHING THAT MOVES: BEYOND THE MYTHS OF BISEXUALITY (IV-Bisexual, themes), 2404 California St., #24, San Francisco CA 94115, phone (415)703-7977, founded 1991, attention fiction/poetry editor. This quarterly uses **"material only from those who consider themselves bisexual, whether they identify as such or not. Pen names are permissible with written notification, however author's real name and address must accompany submission (not to be published). Include name(s), address and phone number on each page. Submissions need not address bisexuality specifically, but may be on topics/themes/subjects of interest to bisexuals. Special consideration given to people of color, those differently abled, those living with HIV disease or AIDS, and those whose work has been denied/censored/erased in mainstream literary communities and publications."** As a sample the editor selected these lines from "Feminine" by Chocolate Waters:

> *The word has become hateful.*
> *It reminds you of little girl voices,*
> *clutch purses, ankle bracelets,*
> *clean underwear in case you get hit*
> *by a truck.*

It is 64 pgs., professionally printed, magazine-sized with glossy paper cover, saddle-stapled. Press run is 5,000 for 1,000 subscribers of which 100 are libraries, 3,000 shelf sales. Subscription: $25. **Sample: $6. Cover letter required. "Include titles of submission(s) and short (under 30 words) bio." No comments on rejections. Publishes theme issues. Send SASE for upcoming themes. "Accepted material cannot be returned. Do not send original copy. Shorter poems are more likely to be accepted. Notification of use will be in the form of 2-copy payment, although notification of acceptance will be given 6-8 weeks upon receipt of submission.** *ATM* is published by the Bay Area Bisexual Network (BABN), a nonprofit institution, and is distributed nationally, with a small international distribution." Open to unsolicited reviews. Poets may also send books for review consideration.

APALACHEE QUARTERLY; APALACHEE PRESS (II, IV-Themes), P.O. Box 10469, Tallahassee FL 32302, founded 1971, editors Barbara Hamby, Mary Jane Ryals and Kim MacQueen. They have

AQ 42

"This cover doesn't specifically represent our philosophy except in that we are always looking for something a little offbeat. And, we liked its looks," says Barbara Hamby, one of the editors of the Tallahassee, Florida-based Apalachee Quarterly. Every third issue is organized around a theme and the cover is often chosen to reflect that theme, Hamby says. While they publish both poetry and fiction, AQ is primarily a poetry magazine. "We publish more poems than we do stories, but because of the long-windedness of fiction writers we are forced to devote more pages to fiction—but not that many more." The cover art is by Kathleen Connolly, a New York City-based visual artist.

recently published poetry by David Kirby, Peter Meinke, Alfred Corn and Virgil Suarez. *Apalachee Quarterly* is 160 pgs., 6×9, professionally printed and perfect-bound with card cover. There are 55-95 pgs. of poetry in each issue. "Every year we do an issue on a special topic. Past issues include Dental, Revenge, Cocktail Party and Noir issues." Circulation 700, with 350 subscribers of which 75 are libraries. Subscription: $15. **Sample postpaid: $5. Submit clear copies of up to 5 poems, name and address on each. Simultaneous submissions OK. "We don't read during the summer (June 1 through August 31)." Sometimes comments on rejections. Send SASE for guidelines. Pays 2 copies.** Staff reviews books of poetry. Send books for review consideration.

‡APHRODITE GONE BERSERK: A JOURNAL OF EROTIC ART (IV-Erotica), 233 Guyon Ave., Staten Island NY 10306, founded 1995 (first issue due out early 1996), editor C. Esposito, is a semiannual journal of erotic art, including poetry, fiction, memoirs and photography. **They want "poetry that deals with the erotic or sexuality in any form and from any orientation or perspective."** The editor says *AGB* will be 50 pgs., 8½×11. They expect to receive about 200 submissions a year and accept approximately 10%. Press run will be 1,000. Single copy: $6; subscription: $10. **Previously published poems and simultaneous submissions OK.** Time between acceptance and publication is 6-12 months. **Send SASE for guidelines. Reports in 1 month. Pays 1 copy. Acquires one-time rights.** "We accept books, chapbooks, magazines and videos that deal with the erotic and sexuality for possible review in *AGB*." Also open to unsolicited reviews. The editor says, "Especially when writing erotic poetry, stay away from the cliché and write honestly."

APPALACHIA; THE APPALACHIA POETRY PRIZE (II, IV-Nature), 5 Joy St., Boston MA 02108, phone (617)523-0636, founded 1876, poetry editor Parkman Howe, editor-in-chief Sandy Stott, is a "semiannual journal of mountaineering and conservation which describes activities outdoors and asks questions of an ecological nature." **They want poetry relating to the outdoors and nature—specifically weather, mountains, rivers, lakes, woods and animals. "No conquerors' odes."** They have published poetry by Reg Saner, Warren Woessner, Susan Lier, Mary Oliver and Thomas Reiter. The editor says it is 160 pgs., 6×9, professionally printed with color cover, using photos, graphics and a few ads. They receive about 200 poems a year, use 10-15. Press run is 10,000. Subscription: $10/year. **Sample postpaid: $5. Submit maximum of 6 poems. "We favor shorter poems—maximum of 36 lines usually." No previously published poems or simultaneous submissions. Cover letter required.** Time between acceptance and publication is 1 year. **Seldom comments on rejections. Send SASE for guidelines. Reports in 4-6 weeks. Pays 1 copy. Acquires first rights.** Staff reviews "some" books of poetry in 200-400 words, usually single format. Offers an annual award, The Appalachia Poetry Prize, given since 1972. The editor says, "Our readership is very well versed in the outdoors— mountains, rivers, lakes, animals. We look for poetry that helps readers see the natural world in fresh ways. No generalized accounts of the great outdoors."

APPALACHIAN HERITAGE; DENNY C. PLATTNER AWARDS (IV-Regional), Hutchins Library, Berea College, Berea KY 40404, phone (606)986-9341, ext. 5260, fax (606)986-9494, founded 1973, editor Sidney Saylor Farr, a literary quarterly with Southern Appalachian emphasis. The journal publishes several poems in each issue, and the editor wants to see **"poems about people, places, the human condition, etc., with Southern Appalachian settings. No style restrictions but poems should have a maximum of 14 lines, prefer 8-10 lines." She does not want "blood and gore, hellfire and damnation, or biased poetry about race or religion."** She has published poetry by Jim Wayne Miller, James Still, George Ella Lyon and Robert Morgan. The flat-spined magazine is 6×9, professionally printed on white stock with b&w line drawings and photos, glossy white card cover with 4-color illustration. Issues we have scanned tended toward lyric free verse, emphasizing nature or situations set in nature, but the editor says they will use good poems of any subject and form. **Sample copy: $6. Submit 2-4 poems at a time, typed one to a page. No previously published poems; simultaneous submissions OK. Requires cover letter giving information about previous publications where poets have appeared. Publishes theme issues occasionally. Send SASE for upcoming themes. Reports on mss in 2-4 weeks. Sometimes sends prepublication galleys. Pays 3 copies. Acquires first rights.** Reviews books of poetry. Open to unsolicited reviews. Poets may also send books for review consideration. The Denny C. Plattner Awards go to the authors of the best poetry, article or essay, or short fiction published in the four issues released within the preceding year. The award amount in each category is $200.

APPLEZABA PRESS (III), P.O. Box 4134, Long Beach CA 90804, founded 1977, poetry editor D.H. Lloyd, is "dedicated to publishing modern poetry and distributing to the national market." They publish both chapbooks and flat-spined collections of individual poets and occasional anthologies, about 3 titles/year. **"As a rule we like 'accessible' poetry, some experimental. We do not want to see traditional."** They have published poetry by Leo Mailman, Gerald Locklin, John Yamrus, Toby Lurie and Nichola Manning. These sample lines are from Lyn Lifshin's "Kent State 1970":

The ROTC building
still smoking
the Guard moved in, feet on the
grass. By
Monday just
after noon sirens Blood sinking into warm
ground. Parents picking up phones
that burned
their hands

The books are digest-sized, flat-spined paperbacks with glossy covers, sometimes with cartoon art, attractively printed. **No query. Submit book ms with brief cover letter mentioning other publications and bio. Simultaneous submissions OK. Reports in 3 months. Always sends prepublication galleys. Pays 6-12% royalties and 10 author's copies. Buys all rights, does not return them. Send SASE for catalog to order samples.**

APROPOS (I, IV-Subscribers), RD 4, Ashley Manor, Easton PA 18042, founded 1989, editor Ashley C. Anders, appears 6 times/year, and **publishes all poetry submitted by subscribers (subscription: $25/year) except that judged by the editor to be pornographic or in poor taste. Maximum length 40 lines— 50 characters/line.** As a sample, the editor selected her own "Simple Poem":

If I can write a simple poem
that makes somebody smile,
or wipes away a teardrop,
then my poem will be worthwhile.

It need not win a trophy,
for that would not mean as much,
as knowing that my simple poem
and someone's heart will touch.

It is 90 pgs., digest-sized, plastic ring bound, with heavy stock cover, desktop-published. **Sample postpaid: $3. Submit 6 poems at a time. Simultaneous submissions and previously published poems OK. Send SASE for guidelines. All poems are judged by subscribers.** Special contests for subscribers are also offered throughout the year at no additional fee. Prizes are $25, $10 and $5.

AQUARIUS (II), Flat 10, Room A, 116 Sutherland Ave., Maida-Vale, London W9 England, poetry editor Eddie Linden, is a literary biannual publishing quality poetry. Issue 19/20, guest edited by Hilary Davies, contains poetry, fictional prose, essays, interviews and reviews. The latest issue is on the English poet Roy Fuller and contains prose and poetry. Single copy: $10. Subscription in US: $50. **Payment is by arrangement.**

ARARAT (IV-Ethnic), Dept. PM, 585 Saddle River Rd., Saddle Brook NJ 07662, phone (201)797-7600, editor-in-chief Leo Hamalian, is a quarterly magazine **emphasizing Armenian life and culture**

for Americans of Armenian descent and Armenian immigrants. **They use about 6 poems/issue and want any verse that is Armenian in theme. They do not want to see traditional, sentimental love poetry.** Their circulation is 2,400. **Sample copy: $7 plus 4 first-class stamps. Previously published submissions OK. Submit seasonal/holiday material at least 3 months in advance.** Publishes ms an average of 1 year after acceptance. **Reports in 6 weeks. Pays $10. Buys first North American serial rights and second (reprint) rights to material originally published elsewhere.**

ARGONAUT (V,IV-Science fiction/fantasy), P.O. Box 4201, Austin TX 78765, founded 1972, editor/publisher Michael Ambrose, is a **"semiannual magazine anthology of science fiction and weird fantasy, illustrated."** They publish "speculative, weird, fantastic poetry with vivid imagery or theme, up to 30 lines. Prefer traditional forms. Nothing ultramodernistic, non-fantastic." They have recently published poetry by John Grey, David Lunde, William John Watkins and Joey Froehlich. The editor describes it as 64 pgs., digest-sized, typeset. They accept 5-8 of 100-200 poems received. Press run is 800 for 50 subscribers of which 3 are libraries. Subscription: $8. **Sample postpaid: $4.95.** *Argonaut* was closed to submissions in 1995. Query for 1996. If open, submit no more than 5 poems at a time. No previously published poems or simultaneous submissions. Editor comments on submissions "occasionally." Send SASE for guidelines. Reports in 1-2 months. Sometimes sends prepublication galleys. Pays 1 copy. The editor says, "Too much of what I see is limited in scope or language, and inappropriate for the themes of *Argonaut*. Poets should know what the particular market to which they submit is looking for and not simply shotgun their submissions."

ARIEL, A REVIEW OF INTERNATIONAL ENGLISH LITERATURE (III), English Dept., University of Calgary, Calgary, Alberta T2N 1N4 Canada, phone (403)220-4657, founded 1970, is a "critical, scholarly quarterly with about 5-8 pgs. of poetry in each issue." Though subject matter is open, editors here seem to prefer mostly lyric free verse with attention to form—line, stanza and voice. As a sample here are lines from "Ecstasy!" by Fritz Hamilton:

> being the
> Jackson Pollock of
> poetry I
>
> dance over the paper in
> the street with
> my pen poised to
>
> pour my words of
> poetry onto
> the world . . .

Ariel is 100 pgs., digest-sized, professionally printed, flat-spined, with glossy card cover. They receive about 300 submissions of poetry/year, use 20-30. Circulation 850, almost all subscriptions of which 650 are libraries. Subscription: $27 institutions; $18 individuals. **Sample postpaid: $6. Submit 4-8 poems at a time. No long poems. No simultaneous submissions. Cover letter required. Pays 10 offprints plus 1 copy. Editor comments on rejections, "only occasionally and not by request." Canadian postage (or IRCs) required with SAE for return of submissions.**

ARJUNA LIBRARY PRESS; JOURNAL OF REGIONAL CRITICISM (I, II), 1025 Garner St. D, Space 18, Colorado Springs CO 80905, library founded 1963, press founded 1979, editor Prof. Joseph A. Uphoff, Jr. "The Arjuna Library Press is avant-garde, designed to endure the transient quarters and marginal funding of the literary phenomenon (as a tradition) while presenting a context for the development of current mathematical ideas in regard to theories of art, literature and performance; photocopy printing allows for very limited editions and irregular format. Quality is maintained as an artistic materialist practice." He wants to see **"surrealist prose poetry, visual poetry, dreamlike, short and long works; not obscene, profane (will criticize but not publish), unpolished work."** He is currently publishing work by Rick Still and Lisa Kucharski. As a sample the editor selected these lines from "She Said I Used To Like" by Lyn Lifshin:

> the fragrance
> of her hair. I
> never figured out
> what it was
> jasmine, magnolia
> I used to love
> to sleep curled
> close to her,
> my nose in
> her hair, drift in the
> garden of her

JRC is published on loose photocopied pages of collage, writing and criticism, appearing frequently in a varied format. Press run: 1 copy each. **Submit 1 or more poems at a time. Previously published poems and simultaneous submissions OK. Cover letter preferred; include "biography, intent, discourse (theories, ethics, history). I like ingenuity, legibility, convenience, polish. I expect some sympathy for mathematical, logical and philosophical exposition and criticism. These arguments remain our central ambition." Pays "notification."** Reviews books of poetry "occasionally." Open to unsolicited reviews. Poets may also send books for review consideration. "Upon request will treat material as submitted for reprint, one-time rights." Arjuna Library Press publishes 6-12 chapbooks/year, averaging 50 pgs. **To submit to the press, send complete ms, cover letter including bio, publications, "any information the author feels is of value." The press pays royalties "by agreement, if we ever make a profit" and copies. Send $1 for sample.** The editor says, "At a point where the writer has achieved a level of attainment the disparagement of detractors will convince competitors that success is very easy. However, it is too late to defeat the victorious author in regard to the realization of a cherished dream; it will be impossibly difficult to surpass a full scale career from a lax beginning. One should practice every day not to fight or argue but simply to entertain an audience."

THE ARK (V), Dept. PM, 35 Highland Ave., Cambridge MA 02139, phone (617)547-0852, founded 1970 (as BLEB), poetry editor Geoffrey Gardner, publishes books of poetry. **"We are unable to take on new projects at this time."** They have published poetry by David Budbill, John Haines, Joseph Bruchac, Elsa Gidlow, W.S. Merwin, Eliot Weinberger, Kathy Acker, George Woodcock, Kathleen Raine, Marge Piercy and Linda Hogan. The editor selected these lines by Kenneth Rexroth (a translation from the Sanskrit) as a sample:

> *You think this is a time of Shiva's waking*
> *You are wrong*
> *You are Shiva*
> *But you dream*

THE UNIVERSITY OF ARKANSAS PRESS (V); ARKANSAS POETRY AWARD (I, II), 201 Ozark, Fayetteville AR 72701, founded 1980, acquisitions editor Kevin Brock, publishes flat-spined paperbacks and hardback collections of individual poets. Miller Williams, director of the press, says, **"We are not interested in poetry that is obscure or private or self-consciously erudite."** They have published poetry by Frank Stanford, Henri Coulette, Enid Shomer and John Ciardi. As a sample, here is a stanza from "Joy" by William Dickey:

> *Now I am driving in my small car up the Coast Highway.*
> *The motor is regular, the headlights are dipped and raised*
> *to accommodate other travellers. I am warm and alone*
> *between the dark vigorous sea and the dark mountains.*
> *This is contentment, surely, but it is not joy.*

That's from his book *In The Dreaming*, 106 pgs., digest-sized, flat-spined, elegantly printed on eggshell stock with matte 2-color card cover. **Query with 5-10 sample poems. Replies to queries in 2 weeks, to submissions (if invited) in 2-4 weeks. No replies without SASE. Always sends prepublication galleys. Offers 10% royalty contract plus 10 author's copies. Send SASE for catalog to buy samples.** First-book mss are not considered except as submissions for the Arkansas Poetry Award. The Arkansas Poetry Award competition is open to any original ms by a living American poet whose work has not been previously published or accepted for publication in book form. Chapbooks, self-published books, and books produced with the author's subsidy are not considered previously published books. No translations. Submit 50-80 pgs., not more than one poem/page, counting title page in page count. An acknowledgments page listing poems previously published should accompany ms. Author's name should appear on the title page only. $15 reading fee. Postmark no later than May 1. Publication the following spring. A $500 cash advance is part of the award.

ARNAZELLA (II), Bellevue Community College, 3000 Landerholm Circle SE, Bellevue WA 98007-6484, phone (206)649-3084, established 1979, advisor Jeffrey White, is a literary annual, published in spring, using **well-crafted poetry, no "jingles or greeting card" poetry**. They have published poetry by William Stafford, Judith Skillman and Colleen McElroy. The editor describes this student publication (which uses work from off campus) as 75 pgs., 6 × 8, offset, using photos and drawings. **They are currently accepting submissions only from poets in Washington, Oregon, Idaho, Alaska and British Columbia.** Of 150-200 poems received/year they use about 30. Press run is 500 for 3 subscriptions, one of which is a library. **Sample postpaid: $5. Submit up to 3 poems. Deadline is usually at the end of December. Send SASE for guidelines. Reports in 1-4 months. Pays 1 copy.**

ARROWSMITH (I, II), P.O. Box 2148, Bellaire TX 77402, founded 1993, editor Keddy Ann Outlaw, is a biannual publication of poetry, short short fiction, b&w photos and collages. **"All styles of poetry considered, as long as well crafted. Length no more than 2 pages per poem. No greeting card doggerel, clichéd statements of self pity or Sunday school verse."** They have recently published poetry by Sharron Crowson, John Gorman, James Michael Robbins, Chocolate Waters and Holly Hildebrand. As a sample the editor selected these lines from "The Astronaut's Ex-Wife" by Sandra Reiff:

> The wife began to sharpen her scissors
> her brushes   her wits   and cut
> off her organdy shadow   leave it on the bed
> with her obedient iron shoes and other
> empty rockets

Arrowsmith is 36-44 pgs., digest-sized, laser printed and saddle-stapled. They currently accept about 1 out of 100 poems received. Press run is 350 for 50 subscribers. Subscription: $8. **Sample postpaid: $4. Submit up to 5 poems at a time. Previously published poems OK by invitation only. Simultaneous submissions OK, if indicated. Cover letter with brief bio preferred.** "Indicate if a yes-or-no reply is sufficient in lieu of poems being returned. **May comment on strong points of poems that almost made it, if time allows." Send SASE for guidelines. Reports in 2-8 weeks. Pays 1 copy. Acquires first-time rights only.** The editor says, "When a poem is finished, sharp and true, it is ready to fly, to pierce its readers with all its singleness, authenticity and intensity. *Arrowsmith* is the place such ammunition is gathered, a literary quiver let loose on the world."

ARSENAL PULP PRESS (V), 100-1062 Homer St., Vancouver, British Columbia V6B 2W9 Canada, founded 1980, publishes 1 paperback book of poetry/year. They only publish the work of Canadian poets and are **currently not accepting any unsolicited mss.**

‡**ARSHILE (III)**, P.O. Box 3749, Los Angeles CA 90078, founded 1993, editor Mark Salerno. *Arshile* is a biannual "Magazine of the Arts," including poetry, fiction, drama, essays on art and interviews. **They want poetry "leaning toward experimental."** They have recently published poetry by Creeley, Bronk, Sorrentino and Angeline. The editor says *Arshile* is 5½ × 8½, professionally printed and perfect-bound with 4-color cover and b&w art and ads inside. Press run is 1,000 for 100 subscribers of which 25% are libraries, 30% shelf sales. Subscription: $18 for 2 issues. **Sample postpaid: $8-10. No previously published poems or simultaneous submissions. Reports in 1-2 months. Pays 2 copies. Rights revert to authors/artists.**

ART TIMES: A LITERARY JOURNAL AND RESOURCE FOR ALL THE ARTS (II), P.O. Box 730, Mount Marion NY 12456-0730, phone (914)246-6944, poetry editor Cheryl A. Rice, is a monthly tabloid newspaper devoted to the arts. *Art Times* focuses on cultural and creative articles and essays, but also publishes some poetry and fiction. The editor wants to see **"poetry that strives to express genuine observation in unique language; poems no longer than 20 lines each."** As a sample she selected these lines from "E = MC2" by Marea Needle:

> No, I'm not talkin' 'bout Einstein
> I'm talkin' 'bout you baby!
> Everything means crazy doubled twice
> or Excellent my cute one, cute one.
> Eddie meets Charlie and it's a duo.
> Ecstasy equals us at the corner of 2nd.

Art Times is 16-24 pgs., newsprint, with reproductions of artwork, some photos, advertisement-supported. They receive 700-1,000 poems/month, use only 40-50/year. Circulation is 15,000, of which 5,000 are by request and subscriptions; most distribution is free through galleries, theatres, etc. Subscription: $15/year. **Sample: $1 postage cost. Submit 4-5 typed poems at a time. Simultaneous submissions OK. Criticism of mss is provided "at times but rarely." They have a 2-year backlog. Guidelines available for SASE. Reports in 6 months. Pays 6 copies plus 1-year subscription.** This publication celebrated its tenth anniversary in 1994 and was recognized as a "valuable resource" in a citation from then-Governor Mario Cuomo.

ART-CORE! (I, IV-Themes); APEX (I, IV-Erotica), P.O. Box 49324, Austin TX 78765, founded 1988, publisher/editor Patty Puke, is published 3 times/year **using poems of "one page or less, alternative, underground, off-beat, avant-garde, uncensored—typed or visual layout. No mainstream or lengthy poems."** The editor describes *Art-Core!* as 24 pgs., magazine-sized, offset. Subscription: $10. **Sample postpaid: $4. Cover letter required with submissions. Publishes theme issues. However, they are moving away from publishing poetry and are concentrating on art. Send SASE for guidelines, upcoming themes and product list. Responds within 3 months. Sometimes sends pre-publication galleys. Pays 1 copy.** *APEX* is a poetry publication sponsored by Art-Core and Electric Lord Productions. The premier issue was a book of erotic poetry. Publication is planned annually. "We are searching for a select group of poets and artists to participate. Interested parties should submit a short sample of their work and SASE." **Sample postpaid: $5.** The editor says: "Caution! Everything we print is uncensored. We support anarchy in art. We advise contributors to view a sample copy before submitting. **You must include age statement to participate."**

ARTFUL DODGE (II, IV-Translations), Dept. of English, College of Wooster, Wooster OH 44691, founded 1979, poetry editor Daniel Bourne, is an annual literary magazine that "takes a strong interest in poets who are continually testing what they can get away with successfully in regard to subject, perspective, language, etc., but who also show mastery of current American poetic techniques—its varied textures and its achievement in the illumination of the particular. What all this boils down to is that we require high craftsmanship as well as a vision that goes beyond *one's own* storm windows, grandmothers or sexual fantasies—to paraphrase Hayden Carruth. **Poems can be on any subject, of any length, from any perspective, in any voice, but we don't want anything that does not connect with both the human and the aesthetic. Thus, we don't want cute, rococo surrealism, someone's warmed-up, left-over notion of an avant-garde that existed 10-100 years ago, or any last bastions of rhymed verse in the civilized world.** On the other hand, we are interested in poems that utilize stylistic persuasions both old and new to good effect. We are not afraid of poems which try to deal with large social, political, historical, and even philosophical questions—especially if the poem emerges from one's own life experience and is not the result of armchair pontificating. We often offer encouragement to writers whose work we find promising, but *Artful Dodge* **is more a journal for the already emerging writer than for the beginner looking for an easy place to publish. We also have a sustained commitment to translation, especially from Polish and other East European literatures,** and we feel the interchange between the American and foreign works on our pages is of great interest to our readers. We also feature interviews with such outstanding literary figures as Jorge Luis Borges, W.S. Merwin, Nathalie Sarraute, Stanislaw Baranczak, Omar Pound, Gwendolyn Brooks, John Giorno, William Least Heat-Moon, Cynthia Macdonald, Tim O'Brien, Lee Smith and William Matthews. Recent and forthcoming poets include Naomi Shihab Nye, Julia Kasdorf, Charles Simic, Denise Duhamel, Walter McDonald, Lola Haskins, Ron Wallace, Alberta Turner, David Ignatow, Jim Daniels, Peter Wild, William Stafford, Karl Krolow (German), Tomasz Jastrun (Polish), Jorge Luis Borges (Spanish), U Sam Oeur (Khmer), Laureano Alban (Spanish), Mahmud Darwish (Palestinian) and Tibor Zalan (Hungarian)." The digest-sized, perfect-bound format is professionally printed, glossy cover, with art, ads. There are about 60-80 pgs. of poetry in each issue. They receive at least 2,000 poems/year, use 60, and the backlog is 1-12 months between acceptance and publication. Press run is 1,000 for 100 subscribers of which 30 are libraries. **Sample: $5 for recent issues, $3 for others. "No simultaneous submissions. Please limit submissions to 6 poems. Long poems may be of any length, but send only one at a time. We encourage translations, but we ask as well for original text and statement from translator that he/she has copyright clearance and permission of author." Reports in up to 5 months. Pays 2 copies, plus, currently, $5/page honorarium because of grants from Ohio Arts Council.** Open to unsolicited reviews; "query first." Poets may also send books for review consideration; however, "there is no guarantee we can review them!"

ARTS END BOOKS; NOSTOC MAGAZINE (II), P.O. Box 162, Newton MA 02168, founded 1978, poetry editor Marshall Brooks. **"We publish good contemporary writing. Our interests are broad and so are our tastes.** People considering sending work to us should examine a copy of our magazine and/or our catalog; check your library for the former, send us a SASE for the latter." Their publications are distinguished by excellent presswork and art in a variety of formats: postcard series, posters, pamphlets, flat-spined paperbacks and hardbacks. As a sample the editor selected the poem "Mr. Green Again" by Bill Costley:

after I got out of jail	—	*cold*	—	*grey*	—	*steel*
by way of the courthouse	—	*hot*	—	*red*	—	*brick*
& picked up my pay	—	*check*	—	*double*	—	*check*

I went down to the Public Gardens
& rode on the Swanboats

to feel how it was to be back
                                                    in the green again.

The magazine appears irregularly in print runs of 300-500, about 30 pgs. of poetry in each, 100 subscriptions of which half are libraries. They receive a few hundred submissions/year, use 25-30. **Sample postpaid: $4. Submit 5-6 poems at a time with name and address on each page. "SASE essential."** They offer **"modest payment plus contributor's copies. A cover letter is a very good idea for any kind of submission;** we receive *very* few good, intelligent cover letters. What to include? That's up to the writer, whatever he/she feels important in terms of the work, in terms of establishing a meeting." **Discourages simultaneous submissions. Frequently comments on rejected mss. Tries to report within a few weeks. Always sends prepublication galleys.** Reviews books of poetry "on occasion, length varies." Brooks says, "We try to respond warmly to writers interested in making genuine contact with us and our audience."

ARUNDEL PRESS; MERCER & AITCHISON (V), 8380 Beverly Blvd., Los Angeles CA 90048, phone (213)852-9852, founded 1984, managing editor Phillip Bevis. Arundel Press "publishes only major texts (as we see them) in limited editions printed letterpress. **We no longer consider unsolicited manuscripts.** Most work is illustrated with original graphics. Mercer & Aitchison publishes definitive editions of major (as we see them) works of poetry, literature and literary criticism."

ASCENT (II), P.O. Box 967, Urbana IL 61801, founded 1975, editor Audrey Curley, appears 3 times/year, using **poetry that is "eclectic, shorter rather than longer."** They have recently published poetry by Thomas Reiter, Michael Bugeja and Kathleen Lynch. As a sample the editor selected these lines from "The Poems Escape" by Dan Campion:

> Suppose all sense drained from their stricken hands,
> All light chased from their eyes, their tongues a gag.
> That's how it was inside, and where they're bound.
> Once mad to climb the wall and leap the fence,
> Though, they skin out. Then hounds can't match their stride.

The editor describes *Ascent* as 64 pgs., 6×9, perfect-bound, professionally printed with matte card cover. They accept about 5% of 750 poems received/year. Press run is 900 copies for 250 subscribers of which 90 are libraries. Subscription: $9/year. **Sample postpaid: $3.50. Submit 3-6 poems at a time. Always sends prepublication galleys. Pays 3 copies.** This continues as one of the "best buys" in the literary world for its low price, openness to all forms and styles, and relatively quick and encouraging response times. The editor says, "I am usually the sole reader. Poems are rejected or accepted from 2-8 weeks, usually closer to 2 weeks. Acceptances are usually published within the year." In 1994, *Ascent* received an Illinois Arts Council Literary Award for "Lessons in Cartography," a poem by Lynne Kuderko. Poetry published here has also been included in *The Best American Poetry 1994*.

THE ASHLAND POETRY PRESS (V, IV-Anthologies, themes), Ashland University, Ashland OH 44805, founded 1969, editor Robert McGovern, publishes anthologies on specific themes and occasional collections. He has recently published the collection *American Lit* (a sonnet sequence) by Harold Witt and the anthology *Scarecrow Poetry: The Museum Post-Middle Age*. As a sample he selected lines from "Jacqueline Du Pré" by Leonard Trawick:

> Jacqueline du Pré, when your muscles came untuned,
> wasn't the music still there, all those silent years——
> just as, after the last note, when players poise their bows
> triumphant for one still moment before the applause,
> the whole quartet hangs perfect in the air?

That poem appears in *80 on the 80's: A Decade's History in Verse* edited by Robert McGovern and Joan Baranow. **"Watch publications such as *Poets & Writers* for calls for mss, but don't submit otherwise. We do not read unsolicited mss; anthology readings take quite a bit of time."** Considers simultaneous submissions. On collections, poet gets 10% royalty; anthologies, poets are paid stipulated price when sufficient copies are sold. Write for catalog.

ASIAN PACIFIC AMERICAN JOURNAL; ASIAN AMERICAN WRITERS' WORKSHOP (I, IV-Ethnic/nationality, gay/lesbian/bisexual, themes), 37 St. Mark's Place, #B, New York NY 10003, phone (212)228-6718, fax (212)228-7718, e-mail aaww@panix.com, founded 1992. The *APA Journal* is a biannual published by the AAWW, a not-for-profit organization. It is **"dedicated to the best of contemporary Asian-American writing."** They have published poetry by Amy Uyematsu and R. Zamora Linmark. As a sample the editor selected these lines from "Sound among Sounds" by Koon Woon:

> And so because the leaves flutter, we know wind from their gaps.
> While the thought of wind is tame, yet by it,
> One room inflates, another deflates; one world inflates, another deflates.

APA Journal is 140-190 pgs., digest-sized, typeset and perfect-bound with 2-color cover and ads. They receive submissions from about 80 poets/year, accept about 30%. Press run is 1,500 for 150 subscribers of which 5 are libraries, 800 shelf sales. Single copy: $10; subscription: $20. **Sample postpaid: $12. Submit 4-6 poems at a time. Previously published poems and simultaneous submissions OK. Cover letter with phone and fax numbers and 1- to 4-sentence biographical statement required. Submissions on 3.5 Macintosh disk (or IBM, if necessary) welcome. Deadlines are usually May 15 and December 15 for October 1 and April 1 issues, respectively. Often comments on rejections. "We will work with authors who are promising." Send SASE for guidelines and upcoming themes. Reports in 3 months. Pays 2 copies. Acquires one-time rights.** The AAWW offers creative

---

Market categories: (I) Beginning; (II) General; (III) Limited; (IV) Specialized; (V) Closed.

writing workshops, a newsletter, a bookselling service, readings and fellowships to young Asian-American writers. Write for details.

ATHENA INCOGNITO MAGAZINE (I), 1442 Judah St., San Francisco CA 94122, founded 1980, editor Ronn Rosen, is an annual of experimental writing and other arts. **They want poetry that is "experimental, surrealist, Dada, etc. 3 pgs. max. No greeting card verse, overly religious poetry or epics."** They have published poetry by Greg Wallace, Michael McClellan and Steven Saxonberg. As a sample the editor selected these lines (poet unidentified):

> *Arrow strikes*
> *Swims out*
> *Narrow gap lapped up that vulture*
> *Heron heron heron*
> *Of summer brambled.*

The editor says the magazine is usually 20-30 photocopied pgs. They receive about 50 poems a year, use approximately 15%. Press run is 200 for 50 subscribers of which 2 are libraries, 50 shelf sales. **"All people submitting poetry *must* buy a sample copy—$5 postpaid."** Previously published poems and simultaneous submissions OK. **"Name and address required on all pages. SASE also required." Often comments on rejections. Reports in 1-2 months. Pays 1 copy.** The editor says, "Be well read in world poetry, surrealism and Dada, and get inspired."

‡ATLANTA REVIEW; POETRY ATLANTA, INC. (II), P.O. Box 8248, Atlanta GA 30306, founded 1994, contact poetry editor, is a semiannual primarily devoted to poetry, but also featuring fiction, interviews, essays and fine art. **They want "quality poetry of genuine human appeal."** They have recently published poetry by Charles Simic, Linda Pastan, Maxine Kumin, Josephine Jacobsen and Mark Jarman. As a sample the editor selected these lines from "Mother at 75" by Derek Economy:

> *An ocean, wild and vast*
> *is now my mother's mind.*
> *The pelicans glide in loose*
> *formation out of her eyes.*
> *I sit quietly and trawl*
> *gather in nets and try*
> *to read the random tides.*

AR is 112 pgs., 6×9, flat-spined, professionally printed on acid-free paper, with glossy cover and b&w artwork. They receive about 10,000 poems a year, use about 1%. Press run is 4,000 for 300 subscribers of which 15 are libraries, 2,500 shelf sales. Single copy: $6; subscription: $10. **Sample postpaid: $5. No previously published poems. "Issue deadlines are April 1 and October 1. Publishable manuscripts received shortly after these dates may have a long wait."** Time between acceptance and publication is 2 months. **All publishable poems are read by three editors. Editors alternate as final issue editor. Seldom comments on rejections. Each Spring issue has an International Feature Section: Ireland 1996, the Caribbean 1997. Send SASE for guidelines. Reports in 1 month. Pays 2 copies plus 1 subsequent issue. Acquires first North American serial rights.** They say, "We are making a serious effort to give today's poets the wider audience they truly deserve."

THE ATLANTEAN PRESS REVIEW; THE ATLANTEAN PRESS (II, IV-Specialized: Romantic poetry, translations), P.O. Box 7336, Crescent Branch, Golden CO 80403, e-mail 0004889616@mcimail.com, founded 1990, publisher Patricia LeChevalier. The Atlantean Press was founded to publish Romantic fiction, drama and poetry. *The Atlantean Press Review*, published quarterly, includes a small amount of poetry as well as fiction, drama and essays. **"We are looking for intelligent, thoughtful poetry that addresses human values and aspirations. We publish rhyming poetry almost exclusively, usually in traditional forms."** As a sample the publisher selected these lines from "Icarus" by Moira Russell:

> *I still refuse to believe that he ever fell: the gold*
> *which ran down his bronze shoulders was gold,*
> *not wax. Why else should it be told*
> *and told again, how he flew, and be told*
> *so often that the story is swallowed in his name,*
> *Icarus and foolish flight the same?*

Submit up to 6 poems at a time. Previously published poems OK. Often comments on rejections. Send SASE for guidelines. Reports in 2 months. Always sends prepublication galleys. Pays up to $2/line plus copies. Buys one-time rights. The publisher says, "We'd also be very interested in competent translations of Victor Hugo's poetry."

THE ATLANTIC (II), Dept. PM, 745 Boylston St., Boston MA 02116, phone (617)536-9500, founded 1857, poetry editor Peter Davison, assistant poetry editor David Barber, publishes 1-5 poems monthly. **Some of the most distinguished poetry in American literature** has been published by this magazine, including work by William Matthews, Mary Oliver, Stanley Kunitz, Rodney Jones, May Swenson, Galway Kinnell, Philip Levine, Red Hawk, Tess Gallagher, Donald Hall and W.S. Merwin. The magazine has a circulation of 500,000, of which 5,800 are libraries. They receive some 75,000 poems/year, of which they use 35-40 and have a backlog of 6-12 months. **Sample postpaid: $3. Submit 3-5 poems with SASE. No simultaneous submissions. Publishes theme issues. Always sends prepublication galleys. Pays about $3/line. Buys first North American serial rights only.** Wants "to see poetry of the highest order; we do *not* want to see workshop rejects. **Watch out for workshop uniformity. Beware of the present indicative. Be yourself.**" Poetry published here has been included in the 1992, 1993 and 1995 volumes of *The Best American Poetry*.

‡**ATLANTIS: A WOMEN'S STUDIES JOURNAL (IV-Feminist)**, Dept. PM, Institute for the Study of Women, Mount Saint Vincent University, Halifax, Nova Scotia B3M 2J6 Canada, phone (902)457-6319, fax (902)443-1352, founded 1975, appears twice a year using **poetry "certainly no longer than 5 ms pgs.; should have a feminist perspective, preferably academic."** They have published poetry by Liliane Welch. The editor describes it as 150 pgs., magazine-sized, flat-spined with card cover They accept about 5-10% of submissions. Press run is 1,000 with 600 subscribers of which 55% are libraries. Subscription: Canada $25; US $40 (Canadian). **Sample postpaid: $7.50 Canadian. Reports in 6-12 weeks. Pays 1 copy.**

ATOM MIND (II); MOTHER ROAD PUBLICATIONS (V), P.O. Box 22068, Albuquerque NM 87154, first founded 1968-70, reestablished 1992, editor Gregory Smith. *Atom Mind* is a quarterly journal of "alternative literature, mostly influenced by the Beats, Steinbeck, John Fante and Bukowski. **Narrative, free verse, 20-80 lines preferred, although length restrictions are not set in stone. No light verse, inspirational poetry, doggerel, 'moon-spoon-June' rhyming verse."** They have published poetry by Lawrence Ferlinghetti, Charles Plymell and Wilma Elizabeth McDaniel. As a sample we selected these lines from "good stuff" by Charles Bukowski:

> *beer from China.*
> *think of it.*
> *this is some a.m.*
> *Caesar and Plato hulk in the*
> *shadows and I love you all*
> *for just a*
> *moment.*

The editor says *AM* is 120 pgs., 8½×11, offset, with illustrations and photographs. They receive approximately 2,000 submissions annually, publish perhaps 5%. Press run is 1,000 for 750 subscribers of which 25 are libraries. Subscription: $16. **Sample postpaid: $5. Prefers to consider submissions of 5-8 poems at a time, rather than 1 or 2 poems. Previously published poems OK; no simultaneous submissions.** Time between acceptance and publication is 8-12 months. **"*Atom Mind* is very much a one-man operation; therefore, submissions are subject to the whims and personal biases of the editor only."** Often comments on rejections. Send SASE for guidelines. **Reports in 1-2 months. Pays copies, number varies. Acquires first or one-time rights.** Mother Road Publications also publishes 2 paperback and 2 hardback collections of poetry/year. **"Book-length poetry manuscripts considered by invitation only."** Send SASE for catalog.

‡**AURA LITERARY/ARTS REVIEW (II)**, Dept. PM, Box 76, Hill University Center, University of Alabama at Birmingham, Birmingham AL 35294-1150, phone (205)934-3216, founded 1974, editor Steve Mullen, is a semiannual magazine that publishes "fiction and art though majority of acceptances are poetry—90-100 per year. **Length open, style open, subject matter open. We are looking for quality poetry. Both first-time and often published poets are published here."** *Aura* has published work by Lyn Lifshin, Adrian C. Louis and William Miller. The 6×9 magazine is 100-140 pgs., perfect-bound, printed on white matte with b&w photos, lithography and line art. Circulation is 500, of which 40-50 are subscriptions; other sales are to students and Birmingham residents. Subscription: $6. **Sample postpaid: $2.50. Writers should submit "3-5 poems, with SASE, no simultaneous submissions, will take even neatly hand-written."** Send SASE for guidelines. **Reports in 2-3 months. Pays 2 copies.**

THE AVANT-GARDEN (II), P.O. Box 1342, Interlachen FL 32148, phone (904)481-0020, founded 1993, "avant-gardian" James Valvis, is a biannual publication designed "to breathe life into a dying art." **They are open to all forms, lengths, subject matter and styles of poetry, but they do not want to see "rhymed, nonsense, academia."** They have published poetry by Shannon Frach, Robert W. Howington, C.F. Roberts, Cheryl Townsend and Lyn Lifshin. As a sample the editor selected these lines by Ron Androla:

> *ah fuck. who i suppose is the manager comes*
> *in behind the bar with a bagful of zucchini*
> *shakes one like a big, green cock at the amused*
> *barmaid. "in yr dreams!" she yells.*

The editor says **The Avant-Garden** is 30-40 pgs., 8½ × 11, side-stapled. They accept about 5% of the poetry received. Press run is 100-250 for 15 subscribers, 50 shelf sales. Single copy: $5; subscription: $10. "It should go without saying: Always make the check out to the editor not to the magazine." **No previously published poems or simultaneous submissions. Cover letter required. Seldom comments on rejections. Reports in 1 week to 2 months. Pays 1 copy. Acquires first-time rights.** Valvis reviews a few chapbooks and other magazines very briefly. Poets may send books for review consideration. He also hopes to begin publishing 1-2 chapbooks/year. The editor adds, "I don't care who you are until you show me that you can write poetry. There are so few left. Let your words be my thoughts."

‡THE BABY CONNECTION NEWS JOURNAL (V), Drawer 13320, San Antonio TX 78213-0320, founded 1986, Ms. Gina G. Morris Boyd, C.I.D.I./editor, is "a monthly news journal **to support, educate, move and inspire new and expectant parents** in their role of rearing babies and preschoolers up to 5 years of age. Parenting is such a tough job—our publication strives to reward and motivate positive and nurturing parenting skills." **They publish "poetry only on the subjects of mothering, fathering, birthing, pregnancy, child rearing, the power, the love, the passion and momentum, fertility." However, they are currently not accepting poetry submissions: "We have received over 17,500 pieces and are overwhelmed."** They have published poetry by Alex Grayton, Barbara Kane, E.K. Alasky, Jim McConnell and Laura Rodley. As a sample the editor selected these lines from "Night Music" by Marc Swan:

> *The moon casts a mosaic of light and dark*
> *against her bedroom wall. I lean low to*
> *tuck her in & kiss her goodnight. Dad,*
> *she whispers, look at Peter Pan's shadow. I hug*
> *her tightly, close to my chest. If it gets lost*
> *you can sew it back on. Yes, she says,*
> > *I will.*

The tabloid-sized newsprint publication is 24 pgs. Press run is 30,000 for 1,700 subscribers of which 10% are libraries. Subscription: $9/year. **Sample postpaid: $3 for 2 different issues. "We also offer a reduced rate subscription of $4.75 for 6 months so we can be assured the poet knows our context and cares enough to follow us for a term." Cover letter with brief personal bio required. Pays 5 copies.** Reviews books of poetry. They also publish 5-8 chapbooks and flat-spined paperbacks/year averaging 16-72 pgs. **Pays 6 copies and honorarium averaging $25.**

BABY SUE (I), P.O. Box 1111, Decatur GA 30031-1111, founded 1985, editor/publisher Don W. Seven, appears twice a year publishing harsh, rude humor for the extremely open-minded and not easily offended. **"We are open to all styles, but prefer short poems."** No restrictions. They have published poetry by Edward Mycue, Susan Andrews, Stephen Fievet and Barry Bishop. The editor says **baby sue** is 32 pgs., offset. "We print prose, poems and cartoons. We usually accept about 5% of what we receive." Single copy: $3; subscription: $12 for 4 issues. **Sample postpaid: $2. Previously published poems and simultaneous submissions OK. Deadlines are March 30 and September 30 of each year. Seldom comments on rejections. Reports "immediately, if we are interested." Pays 1 copy.** "We do occasionally review other magazines." The editor adds, "We have received no awards, but we are very popular on the underground press circuit and sell our magazine all over the world."

THE BACON PRESS (V), 4228 Rt. 212, #2, Lake Hill NY 12448, founded 1990, editor T.S. Paul, is a "sporadic" journal of poetry and art, usually appearing 2-3 times/year. **Due to "overwhelming response," they are *not* accepting unsolicited mss at this time.** They have recently published poetry by Mikhail Horowitz and George Montgomery. As a sample the editor selected these lines from his own poem, "Building The House":

> *Her old lovers stir in their beds*
> *Like iron filings*
> *They will shift and gather in moonlight*
> *To stalk this dream of building*
> *Stalk it with beams and sweat and money*
> *While she sleeps.*

The Bacon Press is 16 pgs., 5½ × 8½, saddle-stapled with occasional graphics/b&w art. They receive 1,000 poems a year, accept approximately 24. Press run is 100 for shelf sales in local bookstores. **Sample postpaid: $2.** The editor says, "I find the current 'scene' to be very uplifting for poets. I would encourage beginners to read in public as often as possible, and submit as widely as possible."

THE BAD HENRY REVIEW; 44 Press (III), Box 831, Hudson NY 12534, founded 1981, poetry editors Evelyn Horowitz, Michael Malinowitz and Mary du Passage. They have published poetry by John Ashbery, Gilbert Sorrentino, Stephen Sandy and William Matthews. *The Bad Henry Review* is an annual publishing quality poetry and is 64 pgs., digest-sized. Press run is 500-1,000 for 200 subscriptions of which 15 are for libraries; 200-300 for shelf sales. Single copy: $6; subscription: $12/2 issues. **Sample: $5. Submit 2-5 poems with SASE. No simultaneous submissions or previously published poems. Cover letter preferred. Rarely comments on rejected mss. Publishes theme issues. Pays 1 copy with half price discount for contributors.** The editor comments, ''We've done one issue of long poems and we are doing an issue on collaboration in 1996.''

BAGMAN PRESS (I), P.O. Box 81166, Chicago IL 60681-0166, founded 1989, publisher Bill Falloon, publishes 1 paperback/year—**"emphasis is on 'new' writers who can create powerful first impressions."** They have published *Joe the Dream*, poetry by J.J. Tindall, and *Playing Soldiers in the Dark*, fiction by Stephen Dueweke. **Submit complete ms with SASE. Previously published poems OK; no simultaneous submissions. Cover letter required. Seldom comments on rejections. Replies to queries in 2 weeks, to submitted mss in 6 months or less. Pays 5-10% royalties and 30 author's copies.** ''Inland Book Co. and Small Press Distribution are our primary distributors.'' The publisher says, ''Our aim is to publish writers whose voices have not yet had the opportunity to be heard. We want to publish writing that is consistently strong from beginning to end, writing that will challenge readers to respond to the nuance of a writer's imagination.''

BAKUNIN (II), P.O. Box 1853, Simi Valley CA 93062-1853, founded 1990, editor Jordan Jones, is an annual publication. **"We are looking for poems that challenge accepted pieties and norms. We are also interested in powerful personal poems."** They want **"avant-garde, surrealist, Beat, visceral and mainstream poetry of humor, pathos and social comment. No trite or hackneyed verse; no poem that uses but does not earn the word love."** They have published poetry by Sandra McPherson, Dennis Schmitz, Benjamin Saltman and William Stafford. As a sample the editor selected the opening lines of ''The Aqueduct'' by Dorianne Laux:

> *We played there on hot L.A. summers, kids poking through*
> *the slick algae and bloated tires, the delicate rafts*
> *of mosquito eggs. Open boxcars pulled gray squares*
> *of sky overhead as we took apples and crackers*
> *from our pockets and ate, watched the cursing workers*
> *from the can factory gathering at the silver lunch truck*

Bakunin is 200 pgs., 6×9, offset on acid-free recycled paper, perfect-bound, with laminated cover, b&w artwork and some ads. They receive about 500 submissions a year, publish approximately 5%. The free verse is mostly lyric, and the poems tend to be one-page. Press run is 1,000 for 100 subscribers, 450 shelf sales. Subscription: $10, $12 foreign, $20 institutional. **Sample postpaid: $10; back issue: $5. Submit 1-5 poems at a time. No previously published poems; simultaneous submissions OK, "if the author indicates they are such." Cover letter required.** Time between acceptance and publication is 1-2 years. **Seldom comments on rejections. Send SASE for guidelines. Reports in 3-6 months. Pays 2 copies. Acquires first North American serial rights.** ''We publish 250- to 750-word reviews of single books, magazines or whole presses.'' The editor says, ''*Bakunin* is a magazine for the dead Russian anarchist in all of us.''

BANGTALE INTERNATIONAL (II), P.O. Box 83984, Phoenix AZ 85071-3984, founded 1989, editor William Dudley, appears twice a year. **They want "contemporary poetry of any form and subject, quality in language & imagery, unique presentation & style—Experimental High Energy/Beat Culture/Avant-Garde Poetry."** They have published poetry by B.Z. Niditch, Rod Farmer, Lyn Lifshin and John M. Bennett. As a sample the editor selected this complete poem, ''Unheard Lights,'' by Timothy Hodor:

> *Moths of stars*
> *Eat their way*
> *Into black wool.*
> *They nibble on darkness,*
> *Leaving a hole big enough*
> *For the dawn to crawl through.*

Bangtale is 44 pgs., digest-sized, offset and saddle-stapled, glossy card cover with b&w art. Press run is 500. Subscription: $8. **Sample: $4. Sometimes sends prepublication galleys. Pays 1 copy.** The editor says, ''We would like to see some humorous poetry and also any b&w artwork.''

THE BANK STREET PRESS; THE PORT AUTHORITY POETRY REVIEW (V), 24 Bank St., New York NY 10014, phone (212)255-0692, founded 1985, poetry editor Mary Bertschmann. A small group of poets meet at the Bank Street home of Mary Bertschmann and publish their poetry annually in a series of flat-spined paperbacks called *The Port Authority Poetry Review*. **Sample postpaid: $7.** The

Bank Street Press also publishes solo collections of poetry. They have published *Goslings on the Tundra* ($20 including postage and handling) and *52 Sonnets* ($12 including postage and handling), both limited, fine print volumes by Mary York Sampson. Their most recent title is *The Golden Falcon*, a make-believe story for children of all ages, set at the time of King Arthur. Also written by Mary York Sampson, with illustrations by Harry Bertschmann, the book has 48 cantos and 112 pages ($22.50, including postage and handling). As a sample the editor selected these lines:

> As they ascended, the moon bathed them in pale, milky light,
> Then the boy and the hippogriff plunged into the night.
> The land rushed away beneath them for many an hour,
> They strode that vault of heaven and tasted of its power.
> The snorting of the beast and the wind against its wings
> Made a mighty music like a universe that sings.

BANTAM DOUBLEDAY DELL PUBLISHING GROUP (V), 1540 Broadway, New York NY 10036, phone (212)354-6500, **accepts mss only from agents**.

BAPTIST SUNDAY SCHOOL BOARD; CHRISTIAN SINGLE (IV-Religious, themes); HOME LIFE (IV-Religious); MATURE LIVING (IV-Religious, senior citizen), 127 Ninth Ave. N., Nashville TN 37234, the publishing agency for Southern Baptists. "We publish magazines, monthlies, quarterlies, books, filmstrips, films, church supplies, etc., for Southern Baptist churches. **We want poetry with a message to inspire, uplift, motivate, amuse."** *Christian Single*, founded in 1979, managing editor Ivey Harrington, is a monthly magazine for single adults, ages 25-45. **"We need inspirational poetry targeted to single adults. Poetry that is happy, positive and shows people living single successfully. This will be thought-provoking, spiritual poetry to tie in with monthly themes."** *Christian Single* is 50 pgs., magazine-sized, with a circulation of 70,000. Uses 12-20 poems/year. **Previously published poems OK; prefers not to receive simultaneous submissions. For sample, send 9 × 12 SAE with 4 first-class stamps.** Publishes 6-12 months after acceptance. **Reports in 2 months. Pays upon acceptance; payment varies.** The biggest of the monthlies is *Home Life*, which began in 1947. Circulation 600,000; 20,000 subscribers. It is a magazine-sized, saddle-stapled, slick magazine, 60 pgs., illustrated (no ads). Its editor, Charlie Warren, says he wants **"religious poetry; poetry treating marriage, family life and life in general from a Christian perspective. We rarely publish anything of more than 25 lines." Sample: $1 to authors with 9 × 12 SASE. Submit 5 poems at a time. Query unnecessary. Send SASE for guidelines. Reports in 6-8 weeks. Pays $25-50.** *Mature Living: A Christian Magazine for Senior Adults*, founded in 1977, is a monthly mass circulation (360,000) magazine providing **"leisure reading for senior adults. All material used is compatible with a Christian life-style." The poetry they use is of Christian content, inspirational, about "nature/ God," rhymed, 8-24 lines. You do not have to be a senior citizen to submit.** *Mature Living* is 52 pgs., magazine-sized, saddle-stapled, using large print with color art. They "receive hundreds" of poems/year, use 50-100. Most of their distribution is through churches who buy the magazine in bulk for their senior adult members. **For sample, send 9 × 12 SAE and 4 first-class stamps. Reports in 6-8 weeks, but there might be a 3-year delay before publication. Pays $13-25.**

E.W. BARHAM PUBLISHING (III), P.O. Box 5, Bowling Green OH 43402, founded 1992, editor Wayne Barham, plans to publish 1-3 paperbacks, 0-1 hardbacks and **1-3 chapbooks/year**. He wants **"poetry that uses evocative imagery, has a sense of the music of words, has a consistent voice and presents the reader with the world renewed. No so-called L-A-N-G-U-A-G-E poetry."** The first book of poetry he published was "the complete works of a completely unknown poet named Mahlon F. Scott" (released in June 1993), though he says it isn't characteristic of what he expects to be publishing in the future. **Query first with list of magazine (and book) publications and a sample of 10-12 pages of poetry. Previously published poems and simultaneous submissions OK. Replies to queries in 2-3 weeks, to mss in 1-3 months.** "All final decisions will be made by the poetry contact person in consultation with other local poets." **Seldom comments on rejections. Pays 12½ to 15% royalties, $150 honorarium and 10 author's copies. Query regarding availability of sample books or chapbooks.** The editor says, "While we're told (mostly by big commercial publishers) that there is no market (i.e. audience) for poetry, we need to be careful that we are not making that claim a self-fulfilling prophesy. There is an audience, but poets have to create it. Give readings at every opportunity. Listen to your listeners; learn from them what still stirs the human soul." **NOTE: At press time we discovered that Mr. Barham had moved and left no forwarding address.**

‡BARNWOOD PRESS; BARNWOOD PRESS COOPERATIVE (III), P.O. Box 146, Selma IN 47383, phone (317)288-0145, founded 1978, editors Tom Koontz, Haven Koontz and Thom Tammaro, publishes collections of poetry on occasion. They have published poetry by Bly, Friman, Goedicke and Stafford. As a sample the editors selected these lines from "Light Casualties" by Robert Francis:

> Did the guns whisper when they spoke
> That day? Did death tiptoe his business?

> *And afterwards in another world*
> *Did mourners put on light mourning,*
> *Casual as rain, as snow, as leaves?*
> *Did a few tears fall?*

Query first for book publication. Replies to queries in 1 month, to mss (if invited) in 1-6 months. Pays 100 author's copies (10% of press run). Send SASE for further information.

WILLIAM L. BAUHAN, PUBLISHER (V, IV-Regional), P.O. Box 443, Old County Rd., Dublin NH 03444, phone (603)563-8020, founded 1959, editor William L. Bauhan, publishes poetry and art, especially New England regional books. **Currently accepts no unsolicited poetry.** They have published books of poetry by Sarah Singer, Anne Marx, Phoebe Barnes Driver and May Sarton.

BAY AREA POETS COALITION (BAPC); POETALK (I), P.O. Box 11435, Berkeley CA 94712-2435, founded 1974, direct submissions to Editorial Committee. Coalition sends bimonthly poetry letter, *Poetalk*, to over 300 people. They also publish an annual anthology (16th—144 pgs., out in February 1995), giving one page to each member of BAPC (minimum 6 months) who has had work published in *Poetalk* during the previous year. *Poetalk* publishes approximately 75 poets each issue. BAPC has 160 members, 70 subscribers, but *Poetalk* is open to all. **No particular genre. Short poems (under 30 lines). "Rhyme must be well done."** Membership: $15 for 12 months of *Poetalk*, copy of anthology and other privileges; extra outside US. Also offers a $50 patronage, which includes a subscription and anthology for another individual of your choice, and a $25 beneficiary/memorial, which includes membership plus subscription for friend. Subscriptions: $6/year. As a sample the editors selected this complete poem, "Coinage," by Doris Straus:

> *presidents*
> *goddesses*
> *good folks go grey*
> *with tarnish.*

Poetalk is 6 legal-sized pgs., photocopied and folded in half to make 24 pgs. total. **Send SASE with 64¢ postage for a free complimentary copy. Each poem should be 3×4 maximum, 4 to a page. Typewritten, single-spaced OK. Simultaneous and previously published work OK, but must be noted. "All subject matter should be in good taste." Send 4 poems (on 1 page) with SASE every 6 months. Response time is 2 weeks to 4 months. You'll get copy of *Poetalk* in which your work appears.** BAPC holds monthly readings, yearly contest, etc.; has mailing list open to local members. People from many states and countries have contributed to *Poetalk* or entered their annual contests. Send SASE in early September for contest guidelines. The editors say, "We differ from many publishers in that we are very actively involved in working with the poets to make their poems publishable. We try to help people get to the point where we can publish their work, i.e., we make editorial comments on almost everything we reject. If you don't want suggested revisions you need to say so clearly in your cover letter."

BAY WINDOWS (IV-Gay/lesbian), 1523 Washington St., Boston MA 02118, fax (617)266-5973, founded 1983, poetry editor Rudy Kikel. *Bay Windows* is a weekly gay and lesbian newspaper published for the New England community, regularly using **"short poems of interest to lesbians and gay men. Poetry that is 'experiential' seems to have a good chance with us, but we don't want poetry that just 'tells it like it is.' Our readership doesn't read poetry all the time. A primary consideration is giving *pleasure*. We'll overlook the poem's (and the poet's) tendency not to be informed by the latest poetic theory, if it *does* this: pleases. Pleases, in particular, by articulating common gay or lesbian experience, and by doing that with some attention to form. I've found that a lot of our choices were made because of a strong image strand. Humor is *always* welcome—and hard to provide with craft. Obliquity, obscurity? Probably not for us. We won't presume on our audience."** They have recently published poetry by John Briggs, May Kerr, Robert K. Martin, David Milley and Judith Saunders. As a sample Rudy Kikel selected this complete poem, "The Accusation," by David A. Bolduc:

> *You said you love me.*
> *You said you'd stick around, no matter what.*
> *You said we didn't need rubbers.*
>
> *You lied.*

"We try to run four poems each month." They receive about 300 submissions/year, use 1 in 6, have a 3-month backlog. Press run is 13,000 for 700 subscribers of which 15 are libraries. Single copy: 50¢; subscription: $40. **Sample postpaid: $2. Submit 3-5 poems at a time, "5-25 lines are ideal; include short biographical blurb." All poems should now be sent care of Rudy Kikel, *Bay Windows*, at the address above. Reports in 2-3 months. Pays copies. Acquires first rights. Editor "often" comments on rejections.** They review books of poetry in about 750 words—"Both single and omnibus reviews (the latter are longer)."

BEACH HOLME PUBLISHERS; PORCÉPIC BOOKS (II, IV-Regional), 4252 Commerce Circle, Victoria, British Columbia V8Z 4M2 Canada, phone (604)727-6514, fax (604)727-6418, founded 1971, editor Antonia Banyard, publishes 3-4 paperback books of poetry each year under the imprint Porcépic Books. They want **"excellent quality writing—all subjects, cultures, etc.—by Canadian authors."** They have published *Wrestling the Angel* by Robin Skelton, *Oedipal Dreams* by Evelyn Lau, *Cocktails at the Mausoleum* by Susan Musgrave and *Love As It Is* by Marilyn Bowering. **Query first, with sample poems and cover letter with brief bio and publication credits. Previously published poems and simultaneous submissions OK, if indicated.** Time between acceptance and publication is 12-18 months. **Seldom comments on rejections. Replies to queries in 3-4 weeks, to mss (if invited) in 3-4 months. Pays 10% royalties and 5-10 author's copies. Samples may be ordered directly from Beach Holme Publishers or through a bookstore.** The editor says, "We are open to new authors, although we are most interested in poets who have had individual poems published in magazines, etc., or who have some familiarity with the literary scene. We appreciate authors who are familiar with our recent or backlist titles and our company."

BEACON (IV-Regional), Southwestern Oregon Community College, 1988 Newmark Ave., Coos Bay OR 97420, phone (503)888-7335, editor changes yearly. *Beacon* is a small, college literary magazine that appears twice a year and publishes the work of local writers and artists. **They want poetry only from those who have had their beginnings or currently reside in Southwestern Oregon. No specifications as to form, length, subject matter or style. "Submissions limited to five poems per term, prefer non-saga poems; one story per term, maximum 3,000 words."** The editor says *Beacon* is 50-70 pgs., 5½ × 8, professionally printed with color cover and b&w art within; no ads. They receive about 400 poems a year, accept approximately 25%. Press run is 300, all shelf sales. Single copy: $3. **Sample postpaid: $3.50. No previously published poems or simultaneous submissions. Cover letter required. Reads submissions December 1 to January 15 and March 1 to April 15.** Time between acceptance and publication is 2 months. **Seldom comments on rejections. Reports "on publication." Pays 1 copy. Acquires first rights.** The editor says, "We encourage poets to visit for readings and bring works to offer for sale. We do not compensate in any way for these readings. The purpose of our magazine is to heighten the value of literature in our community."

BEDLAM PRESS (V), Church Green House, Old Church Lane, Pateley Bridge, N. Yorkshire HG3 5LZ England, phone 01423 711508, founded 1982, is a "small press publisher of poetry books, specializing in **long poems or sequences, mainly concerned with public affairs." Not accepting mss.**

‡**BEER & PUB POETRY (I, IV-Specialized)**, %Creative Adventures, 2574 PGA Blvd., Suite 811, Palm Beach Gardens, FL 33410, founded 1992, editor Edwin Riley, is an annual anthology. **"The theme of the poem should relate to beers and pubs of the world. Point-of-view is totally subjective. Judges seek submissions ranging from ridiculous to sublime." Poems should be no longer than 5 double-spaced pages.** As a sample the editor selected these lines from "Closing Time" by C.J. Houghtaling:

> *As I leave there's a smile that crosses my face;*
> *And though I am tired, there's a spring in my pace.*
> *Because this ol' bar where I feel so safe*
> *Makes me proud when I say that I own the place.*

The 1992 anthology is 42 pgs., 5¾ × 8¼, professionally printed and saddle-stapled with card cover. It includes 30 poems and a brief introduction by Alan D. Eames, "internationally known beer historian" and author. **Sample postpaid: $7.95. Previously published poems and simultaneous submissions OK. Each poem must be accompanied by a $5 reading fee. Submission deadline: October 31 postmark. Reports November 30. Pays 1 copy. Acquires all rights.**

BEGINNER'S MIND PRESS (II), 1059 27th St., Apt. 2, Des Moines IA 50311, founded 1992, editor Christien Gholson, publishes both chapbooks (2/year) and broadsides. **"I want to see poetry that has depth, ideas, music; that can be read out loud. No rhyme (unless blues oriented); no vague introspection; no poetry from the world of TV, suburbia; no academic verse (poetry with the poetry edited out of it)."** They have recently published poetry by Kevin Bezner, Christopher Conlon, Andrew Gettler and Louis McKee. As a sample the editor selected these lines from "Candelabra, for Pablo Nervoa" by Maia:

> *between us, oceanic*
> *murmur of the sheets*
>
> *where we lie together*
> *under the long bells*
>
> *the green gaze*
> *of time*

The chapbooks are generally 16 pgs., digest-sized, printed on plain white paper and saddle-stapled with b&w graphic on paper cover. **"I encourage poets to send the entire manuscript. My chapbooks are, at the most, 16 pages long, so there's no reason to just send samples. I want to see the whole." For broadsides, submit 6 poems at a time. Previously published poems and simultaneous submissions OK, if indicated as such. "A cover letter is sometimes helpful, but never necessary." Does not read mss in December or June through August. Seldom comments on rejections. Reports in 1 month. Pays copies.** The editor says, "All chaps and broadsides are given away free-for-postage (55¢ for a chap, 32¢ for a couple B'sides). Price can never define the worth of Art. Art has very little to do with being published—it's a way of life."

BELHUE PRESS (III, IV-Gay), 2501 Palisade Ave., Suite A1, Riverdale, Bronx NY 10463, founded 1990, editor Tom Laine, is a small press **specializing in gay male poetry**, publishing 3 paperbacks/year—no chapbooks. **"We are especially interested in anthologies, in thematic books, in books that get out of the stock poetry market."** They want **"hard-edged, well-crafted, fun and often sexy poetry. No mushy, self pitying, confessional, boring, indulgent, teary or unrequited love poems— yuck!"** As a sample the editor selected these lines from "Thoth" in the book *Sex-charge* by Perry Brass:

> *How I lie*
> *in your winding sheet, sleeping*
> > *past the wake*
> *of our small end,*
> *a whiter corner in your light,*
> *curled toe to toe*
> *against your parts.*

"Poets must be willing to promote book through readings, mailers, etc." Query first with 6 pgs. of poetry and cover letter. Previously published poems and simultaneous submissions OK. Time between acceptance and publication is 1 year. **Often comments on rejections. Will request criticism fees "if necessary." Replies to queries and submitted mss "fast." No payment information provided. Sample: $7.95.** "The only things we find offensive are stupid, dashed off, 'fortune cookie' poems that show no depth or awareness of poetry. We like poetry that, like good journalism, tells a story."

BELLOWING ARK PRESS; BELLOWING ARK (II), P.O. Box 45637, Seattle WA 98145, phone (206)545-8302, founded 1984, editor Robert R. Ward. *Bellowing Ark* is a bimonthly literary tabloid that **"publishes only poetry which demonstrates in some way the proposition that existence has meaning or, to put it another way, that life is worth living. We have no strictures as to length, form or style; only that the work we publish is to our judgment life-affirming."** They do not want **"academic poetry, in any of its manifold forms."** They have recently published poetry by Jon Jech, Irene Culver, Peter Russell, Hannah B. Adams, Muriel Karr, Teresa Noelle Roberts and Mark Allan Johnson. As a sample the editor selected these lines from "*A Small Sweet Moment At Breakfast*" by Jim Bernhard:

> *He closes his eyes*
> *As a small sweet moment passes through him.*
> *Then, through a sliver of flat cool gaze,*
> *He surveys his surroundings*
> *And enjoys the bitter pleasure*
> *Of being left slightly hungry most of the time.*

The paper is 32 pgs., tabloid-sized, printed on electrobright stock with b&w photos and line drawings. It is a lively publication. Almost every poem is accessible, enjoyable and stimulating. All styles seem to be welcome—even long, sequence poems and formal verse. Circulation is 1,000, of which 200 are subscriptions and 600 are sold on newsstands. Subscription: $15/year. **Sample postpaid: $3. Submit 3-6 poems at a time. The editors say, "absolutely *no* simultaneous submissions." They reply to submissions in 2-6 weeks and publish within the next 1 or 2 issues. Occasionally they will criticize a ms if it seems to "display potential to become the kind of work we want." Sometimes sends prepublication galleys. Pays 2 copies.** Reviews books of poetry. Send books for review consideration. Bellowing Ark Press publishes collections of poetry by invitation only.

BELL'S LETTERS POET (I, IV-Subscribers), P.O. Box 2187, Gulfport MS 39505, founded 1956, publisher and editor Jim Bell, is a quarterly which **you must buy ($5/issue, $20 subscription) to be included.** The editor says "many say they stop everything the day it arrives," and judging by the many letters from readers, that seems to be the case. **Though there is no payment for poetry accepted, many patrons send awards of $5-20 to the poets whose work they especially like. Subscription "guarantees them a byline each issue." Poems are "4 to 20 lines in good taste."** They have recently published poetry by Marie White, Jaye Giammarino, Richard Diem and Violet Tackett. As a sample of the spirit of *BL* poetry the editor selected these lines by Maria Veronica Bakkum:

> *Accept my love. It is a gift.*
> *Yet, like your fine collectibles,*
>   *let it rest upon the shelf of memory,*
>   *to steep*
>   *and grow familiar,*
>   *or sequester it*
>   *within the cluttered desk*
>   *of vast preoccupations.*

BL is 64 pgs., digest-sized, offset from typescript on plain bond paper (including cover). **Sample with guidelines: $5. Submit 4 poems a year. Ms may be typed or even hand-written. No simultaneous submissions. Previously published poems OK "if cleared by author with prior publisher." Accepted poems by subscribers go immediately into the next issue. Deadline for poetry submissions is 3 months prior to publication.** Reviews books of poetry by subscribers in "one abbreviated paragraph." "The Ratings" is a competition in each issue. Readers are asked to vote on their favorite poems, and the ratings are announced in the next issue, along with awards sent to the poets by patrons. *BL* also features a telephone exchange among poets.

THE BELOIT POETRY JOURNAL; CHAD WALSH POETRY PRIZE (II), Box 154, RFD 2, Ellsworth ME 04605, phone (207)667-5598, founded 1950, editor Marion K. Stocking, is a well-known, long-standing quarterly of quality poetry and reviews. **"We publish the best poems we receive, without bias as to length, school, subject or form**. It is our hope to discover the growing tip of poetry and to introduce new poets alongside established writers. **We publish occasional chapbooks on special themes to diversify our offerings."** They want **"fresh, imaginative poetry, with a distinctive voice. We tend to prefer poems that make the reader share an experience rather than just read about it, and these we keep for up to 3 months**, circulating them among our readers, and continuing to winnow out the best. At the quarterly meetings of the Editorial Board we read aloud all the surviving poems and put together an issue of the best we have." They have published poetry by Sherman Alexie, Hillel Schwartz, Jane Mead, Albert Goldbarth and Ursula K. Le Guin. As a sample the editor selected these lines from "I Want" by J. Cordary:

> *I want*
> *something wicked:*
> *black pigroast wanton with juice,*
> *royal-colored raspberries swooning in cream,*
> *opals to twine their fiery light*
> *like knives,*
> *ah, you*
> *here, now.*

The journal is 48 pgs., digest-sized, saddle-stapled, and attractively printed with tasteful art on the card covers. All styles of verse—providing they articulate ideas or emotions intelligently and concisely—are featured. The editor is also keen on providing as much space as possible for poems and so does not include contributors' notes. They have a circulation of 1,700 for 575 subscribers of which 325 are libraries. **Sample copy: $4, including guidelines. SASE for guidelines alone. Submit any time, without query, any legible form.** *"No previously published poems or simultaneous submissions. Any length of ms, but most poets send what will go in a business envelope for one stamp. Don't send your life's work."* No backlog: **"We clear the desk at each issue." Pays 3 copies. Acquires first serial rights.** Staff reviews books of poetry in an average of 500 words, usually single format. Send books for review consideration. The journal awards a $3,000 Chad Walsh Poetry Prize to a poem or group of poems published in the calendar year. "Every poem published in 1996 will be considered for the 1996 prize." Poetry published in *The Beloit Poetry Journal* has also been included in *The Best American Poetry 1994* and *Pushcart Prize* anthologies. The editor says, "We'd like to see more strong, imaginative, experimental poetry; more poetry with a global vision; and more poetry with fresh, vigorous language."

BENEATH THE SURFACE (II), % The Dept. of English, Chester New Hall, McMaster University, Hamilton, Ontario L8S 4L9 Canada, founded 1911, editor changes yearly, is a biannual using **"top quality poetry/prose that achieves universality through individual expression."** They want **"qual-**

Use the General Index to find the page number of a specific publisher. If the publisher you are seeking is not listed, check the " '95-'96 Changes" list at the end of this section.

ity poetry; any form; no restrictions." Also interested in short stories. Science fiction and medical
themes are most welcome. They have published poetry by Dorothy Livesky and John Barlow. As a
sample the editor selected these lines from "War Monument" by tristanne j. connolly:

> *a soldier's soul*
> *ascending, but concrete*
> *is heavy to lift*
> *war monument, the cross on top*
> *forgotten til the very last minute*

It is 30-50 pgs., professionally printed, saddle-stapled, with cover art, drawings and b&w photographs.
They receive about 250 submissions/year, use approximately 10%. Press run is 150 for 8 subscribers of
which 3 are libraries, 92 shelf sales. Subscription: $8/year. **Sample postpaid: $4. No previously
published poems or simultaneous submissions. Submit 4-6 poems with cover letter, including
short bio and summary of previous publications, if any. Reads submissions September through
April only. Often comments on rejections. Reports in 4-6 weeks. Sometimes sends prepublication
galleys. Pays nothing—not even copies. Acquires first North American serial rights.** Rarely reviews books of poetry, "though we do include literary essays when submitted." The editor says, "Do
not get discouraged. Getting work in respectable literary journals takes much love and even more hard
work. Be patient and allow your work to evolve and mature."

BENNETT & KITCHEL (IV-Form), P.O. Box 4422, East Lansing MI 48826, phone (517)355-1707,
founded 1989, editor William Whallon, publishes 1-3 hardbacks/year of **"poetry of form and meaning. No free verse or blank verse, no sestinas or haiku."** As an example of what he admires, the editor
selected these lines by Troxey Kemper:

> *I think what Jeremiah said,*
> *And add my woes in quiet sums.*
> *A cup of broth, a plate of crumbs,*
> *Are all my meat when mirth is fled:*
> *What does it mean?*

Bennett & Kitchel has also published *Lapsing into Grace*, by Rhina P. Espaillat. **Sample postpaid: $8.
Simultaneous submissions and previously published poems OK if copyright is clear. Minimum
volume for a book "might be 750 lines." If a book is accepted, publication is within 9 months.
Editor seldom comments on submissions. Reports in 2 weeks. Terms are "variable, negotiable."**
He remarks, "To make a bad rhyme not from incompetence but willfully is like stubbing your toe on
purpose."

BERKELEY POETRY REVIEW (II), 700 Eshleman Hall, University of California, Berkeley CA 94720,
founded 1973, is an annual review "which publishes poems and translations of local as well as national
and international interest. **We are open to a broad range of poetry but are always looking for
innovation."** They have recently published poetry by Bob Hass, Lyn Hejinian, Albert Goldbarth,
Ishmael Reed and Thom Gunn. The editors describe it as a flat-spined paperback, averaging 150 pgs.
Circulation 500. Subscription: $10/year. **Submit 4 poems at a time *with SASE*. No previously pub-
lished poems or simultaneous submissions. Reads submissions September through March only.
Reports in 1-3 months. Pays 1 copy.**

**BILINGUAL REVIEW PRESS; BILINGUAL REVIEW/REVISTA BILINGÜE (IV-Ethnic/Hispanic,
bilingual/Spanish)**, Hispanic Research Center, Arizona State University, Box 872702, Tempe AZ
85287-2702, phone (602)965-3867, journal founded 1974, press in 1976. Managing editor Karen Van
Hooft says they are "a small press publisher of U.S. Hispanic creative literature and of a journal
containing poetry and short fiction in addition to scholarship." The journal contains some poetry in
each issue; they also publish flat-spined paperback collections of poetry. **"We publish poetry by and/
or about U.S. Hispanics and U.S. Hispanic themes. We do not publish translations in our journal
or literature about the experiences of Anglo Americans in Latin America. We have published a
couple of poetry volumes in bilingual format (Spanish/English) of important Mexican poets."**
They have published poetry by Alberto Ríos, Demetria Martínez, Pablo Medina, Marjorie Agosin and
Alma Villanueva. The editor says the journal, which appears 3 times a year, is 7×10, 96 pgs., flat-
spined, offset, with 2-color cover. They use less than 10% of hundreds of submissions received each
year. Press run is 2,000 for 1,200 subscriptions. Subscriptions are $16 for individuals, $30 for institutions. **Sample postpaid: $6 individuals/$10 institutions. Submit "2 copies, including ribbon original if possible, with loose stamps for return postage." Cover letter required. Pays 2 copies.
Acquires all rights.** Reviews books of US Hispanic literature only. Send books, Attn: Editor, for
review consideration. **For book submissions, inquire first with 4-5 sample poems, bio, publications.
Pays $200 advance, 10% royalties and 10 copies.** Over the years, books by this press have won five
American Book Awards and two Western States Book Awards.

BIRMINGHAM POETRY REVIEW (II, IV-Translations), English Dept., University of Alabama at Birmingham, Birmingham AL 35294, phone (205)934-8573, founded 1988, co-editors Robert Collins and Randy Blythe. The review appears twice a year using poetry of **"any style, form, length or subject. We are biased toward exploring the cutting edge of contemporary poetry. Style is secondary to the energy, the *fire* the poem possesses. We don't want poetry with cliché-bound, worn-out language."** They have published poetry by Hague, Hopes, McDonald, Richards, Call and Miltner. As a sample the editors selected these lines from "Charisma Revisited" by Brendan Galvin:

> Still, there was something to be said
> for their peasant reticence, though
> it leaves us confounded as to why
> the country has been empty
> these hundred years.

They describe their magazine as 50 pgs., 6×9, offset, with b&w cover. Their press run is 600 for Fall Issue, 500 for Spring Issue; 275 subscriptions. Subscription: $3. **Sample postpaid: $2. Submit 3-5 poems, "no more. No cover letters. We are impressed by good writing; we are unimpressed by publication credits. It should go without saying, but we receive more and more manuscripts with insufficient return postage. If it costs you fifty-two cents to mail your manuscript, it will cost us that much to return it if it is rejected. Manuscripts with insufficient return postage will be discarded."** No simultaneous or multiple submissions, and previously published poems only if they are translations. Editor sometimes comments on rejections. Send SASE for guidelines. Reports in 1-4 months. Pays 2 copies and one-year subscription. They say, "Advice to beginners: Read as much good contemporary poetry, national and international, as you can get your hands on. Then be persistent in finding your own voice."

BISHOP PUBLISHING CO. (IV-Themes), 2131 Trimble Way, Sacramento CA 95825, phone (916)971-4987, professor Roland Dickison, is a "small press publisher of **folklore in paperbacks, including contemporary** and out-of-print."

BITS PRESS (III, IV-Humor), English Dept., Case Western Reserve University, Cleveland OH 44106, phone (216)795-2810, founded 1974, poetry editor Robert Wallace. **"Bits Press is devoted to poetry. We publish chapbooks (and sometimes limited editions) by young as well as well-known poets. Our main attention at present is given to light verse and funny poems."** The chapbooks are distinguished by an elegant but inexpensive format. They have published chapbooks by David R. Slavitt, John Updike and Gerald Costanzo. These sample lines are from Ted Kooser's *Etudes*:

> ...five small black birds as quick
> as quarter notes touched down at once, striking
> a perfect chord at the cold, high end of the keyboard,
> and it frightened them, and off they flew together.

The few chapbooks they publish are mostly solicited. Send $3 for a sample chapbook. Sometimes sends prepublication galleys. Pays poet in copies (over 10% of run). Acquires one-time rights.

BLACK BEAR PUBLICATIONS; BLACK BEAR REVIEW; POETS ELEVEN ... AUDIBLE (II, IV-Political, social issues), 1916 Lincoln St., Croydon PA 19021-8026, founded 1984, poetry and art editor Ave Jeanne, review and audio editor Ron Zettlemoyer. *Black Bear Review* is a semiannual international literary and fine arts magazine that also publishes chapbooks and holds an annual poetry competition. **"We like well crafted poetry that mirrors real life—void of camouflage, energetic poetry, avant-garde, free verse and haiku which relate to the world today. We seldom publish the beginner, but will assist when time allows. No traditional poetry is used. The underlying theme of *BBR* is social and political, but the review is interested also in environmental, war/peace, ecological and minorities themes. We would like to receive more ideas on AIDS awareness, life styles and current political topics."** Poets recently published in *BBR* include Kyle Laws, John Sullivan, Allan Winans, Elliot Richman, Sean Brendan-Brown and Marc Swan. *Poets Eleven ... Audible* has released poetry on tape by A.D. Winans, Tony Moffeit, Kevin Zepper and Mike Maggio. As a sample from *BBR*, the editor selected the poem "Condensation" by Robert S. King:

> The grave dirties all,
> rich and poor in the same pocket
> the earth getting them mixed up.
>
> In socialist wealth
> they break new ground as flowers,
> the royal and ragged hair
> woven in common web of dew,
> their silver souls shining together through.

BBR is 64 pgs., digest-sized, perfect-bound, offset from typed copy on white stock, with line drawings, collages and woodcuts. Circulation is 500, of which 300 are subscriptions; 15 libraries. Price: $5/issue;

subscription: $10, $15 overseas. **A sample of *BBR* postpaid: $5; back copies when available are $4. Submit 5 poems at a time, one to a page. "Please have name and address on each page of your submissions." Simultaneous submissions are not considered. "Submissions without SASE will be held one month, then discarded." Guidelines available for SASE. Reports in 2 weeks, publication is in 6 months. Pays contributor's copy. Acquires first North American serial rights.** Considers reviews of books of poetry and recent issues of literary magazines, maximum 250 words. Send books for review consideration. The editors explain that *Poets Eleven ... Audible* is now by invitation only. **They also publish 2 chapbooks/year.** Most recently published: *Rubato Jitter* by John Sullivan. **Chapbook series requires a reading fee of $5, complete ms and cover letter. Send SASE for guidelines.** For book publication, they would prefer that *"BBR* has published the poet and is familiar with his/her work, but we will read anyone who thinks they have something to say." **Author receives one-half print run.** They say, "We appreciate a friendly, brief cover letter. Tell us about the poet; omit degrees or any other pretentious dribble. All submissions are handled with objectivity and quite often rejected material is directed to another market. If you've not been published before—mention it. We are always interested in aiding those who support small press. We frequently suggest poets keep up with the current edition of *Poet's Market* and read the listings and reviews in issues of *Black Bear*. Most recent issues of *BBR* include reviews on small press markets—current releases of chapbooks and the latest literary magazines. We make an effort to keep our readers informed and on top of the small press scene. Camera-ready ads are printed free of charge as a support to small press publishers. We do suggest reading issues before submitting to absorb the flavor and save on wasted postage. Send your best! Our yearly poetry competition offers cash awards to poets." Deadline: November 1. Guidelines available for SASE. The editors add, "We receive too many submissions with the right topic but the wrong style. We do not have time for poems with 'dirty' words where no poetry surrounds them. In 1994, we celebrated our tenth year in publication, and we are proud to have been supported by our readers."

BLACK BOOKS BULLETIN: WORDSWORK; THIRD WORLD PRESS (IV-Ethnic), 7822 S. Dobson, P.O. Box 19730, Chicago IL 60619, phone (312)651-0700, fax (312)651-7286. *BBB* is a periodic journal of Black culture, including **"Black literature and current issues facing the African-American community."** They have published poetry by Gil Scott Heron, Brian Gilmore, Sonia Sanchez, Keorapetse Kgositsile and Amiri Baraka. They also publish book reviews, essays, interviews, short stories and literary criticism. **Write, fax or call for further information.**

BLACK BOUGH (II, IV-Form), 7 Park Ave., Flemington NJ 08822, founded 1991, editor Charles Easter, associate editor Kevin Walker, is a triannual that publishes "haiku and related forms which demonstrate the distinctiveness of haiku as well as its connection to western traditions in poetry." **They want "haiku, senryu, tanka, haibun (in particular) and sequences. No renga, academic essays or extremely long poems."** They have published work by Jean Jorgensen, Francine Porad and Stuart Dybeck. As a sample the editors selected this haiku by Michael Ketchek:

> *pausing to gaze at*
> *the storm damaged tree*
> *boxer doing road work*

bb is 30 pgs., digest-sized, professionally printed, saddle-stitched, with cover art, no ads. Every third issue is a chapbook of a single author's work. They receive about 5,200 poems a year, use 5-10%. Press run is 200 for 100 subscribers. Subscription: $13.50. **Sample postpaid: $5. "Submit no more than 20 haiku; prefer several haiku/page."** No previously published poems or simultaneous submissions. Time between acceptance and publication is 3-6 months. **Comments on rejections "if requested." Reports in 3-6 weeks. Pays $1/verse, up to $4 for a long poem or haiku sequence. Acquires first rights.**

BLACK BUZZARD PRESS; BLACK BUZZARD REVIEW; VISIONS—INTERNATIONAL, THE WORLD JOURNAL OF ILLUSTRATED POETRY; THE BLACK BUZZARD ILLUSTRATED POETRY CHAPBOOK SERIES; INTERNATIONAL—VISIONS POETRY SERIES (II), 1110 Seaton Lane, Falls Church VA 22046, founded 1979, poetry editor Bradley R. Strahan, associate editor Shirley G. Sullivan. "We are an independent nonsubsidized press dedicated to publishing fine accessible poetry and transla tion (particularly from lesser known languages such as Armenian, Gaelic, Urdu, Vietnamese, etc.) accompanied by original illustrations of high quality in an attractive format. **We want to see work that is carefully crafted and exciting work that transfigures everyday experience or gives us a taste of something totally new; all styles except concrete and typographical 'poems.' Nothing purely sentimental. No self-indulgent breast beating. No sadism, sexism or bigotry. No unemotional pap. No copies of Robert Service or the like. Usually under 80 lines but will consider longer."** They have published poetry by Ted Hughes, Louis Simpson, Marilyn Hacker, James Dickey, Naomi Shihab Nye and Lawrence Ferlinghetti. Bradley Strahan says that "no 4 lines can possibly do even minimal justice to our taste or interest!" *Visions*, a digest-sized, saddle-stapled magazine finely printed on high-quality paper, appears 3 times a year, uses 56 pages of poetry in each issue. Circulation 750 with 300 subscribers of which 50 are libraries. **Sample postpaid: $3.50. Current issue: $4.50.** They receive *well* over a thousand submissions each year, use 150, have a 3- to 18-month backlog. *"Visions* is international in both scope and content, publishing poets from all over the world and having readers in 48 U.S. states, Canada and 24 other countries." *Black Buzzard Review* is a "more or less annual informal journal, dedicated mostly to North American poets and entirely to original English-language poems. In *BBR*, we are taking a more wide-open stance on what we accept (including the slightly outrageous)." **Sample postpaid: $3.50. Current issue: $4.50.** It is 36 pgs., magazine-sized, side-stapled, with matte card cover. **Submit 3-6 poems at a time. "Poems must be readable (not faded or smudged) and *not* handwritten. We resent having to pay postage due, so use adequate postage! No more than 8 pages, please." No previously published poems or simultaneous submissions. Publishes theme issues. Send SASE for upcoming themes. Theme for Winter 1996 issue is Translations from Celtic tongues. Deadline: December 15, 1995. Reports in 3 days to 3 weeks. Pays copies or $5-10 "if we get a grant." Buys first North American serial rights.** Staff reviews books of poetry in "up to 2 paragraphs." Send books for review consideration. **To submit for the chapbook series, send samples (5-10 poems) and a *brief* cover letter "pertinent to artistic accomplishments." Reports in 3 days to 3 weeks. Pays in copies. Usually provides criticism. Send $4 for sample chapbook.** They have also recently initiated the International-Visions Poetry Series. Send SASE for flyer describing titles and order information. Bradley Strahan adds that in *Visions* "We sometimes publish helpful advice about 'getting published' and the art and craft of poetry, and often discuss poets and the world of poetry on our editorial page."

THE BLACK SCHOLAR; THE BLACK SCHOLAR PRESS (IV-Ethnic), P.O. Box 2869, Oakland CA 94609, founded 1969, publisher Robert Chrisman, uses **poetry "relating to/from/of the black American and other 'Third World' experience."** The quarterly magazine is basically scholarly and re-search-oriented. They have published poetry by Ntozake Shange, Jayne Cortez, Andrew Salkey and D.L. Smith. The editor says it is 64 pgs., 7×10, with 10,000 subscribers of which 60% are libraries, 15% shelf sales. "We only publish one issue every year containing poetry." Subscription: $30. **Sample issue: $6. Enclose "letter & bio or curriculum vita, SASE, phone number, no originals." Send SASE for guidelines. Pays 10 copies and subscription.** Reviews books of poetry. They also publish 1-2 books a year, average 100 pgs., flat-spined. **Send query letter. For sample books, send $8½ \times 11$ SASE for catalog, average cost $10.95 including p&h.** The publisher says, "Please be advised—it is against our policy to discuss submissions via telephone. Also, we get a lot of mss, but read *every single one,* thus patience is appreciated."

‡BLACK SHEETS (I, IV-Erotica, themes), P.O. Box 31155, San Francisco CA 94131, fax (415)431-0172, founded 1993, appears 3-4 times a year. *Black Sheets* is "a kinky, queer, intelligent, and irrever-ent zine of sex and popular culture." **They want "erotic poetry that is sexy, thought-provoking and funny. We are a sex zine, so don't send any non-erotic poetry. Work pertaining to any sexual orientation or gender is fine. We strongly advise buying a sample *before* sending submissions. Also, each issue has a specific theme and poets have a better chance if their themes conform to ours. A schedule is sent with the purchase of a sample."** They have recently published poetry by Simon Sheppard, Trebor Healey, Mark Hallman, Bill Brent and Keith Hennessy. *Black Sheets* is 48 pgs., $8½ \times 11$, offset and saddle-stitched with a 2- to 3-color glossy cover and cartoons and illustrations. Much of the content—from graphics to writing to ads—is sexually explicit. They accept about 10% of the poetry received and publish 3-8 poems each issue. Press run is 2,500 for 150 subscribers, 600 shelf sales and 250 additional single copy sales. Subscription: $20 for 4 issues. **Sample postpaid: $6. Previously published poems and simultaneous submissions OK. IBM-compatible disk submissions OK.** Time between acceptance and publication is 6 months to 1 year. **Often comments on rejections. Reports anywhere from 1 week to 6 months. Pays $5/poem and 1 copy (2 more with 9×12 SASE). Requires signed agreement before publication. Prefers to retain anthology rights for possible "best of" collections.** Reviews related books of poetry in less than 200 words, single format. Open to unsolicited reviews. Poets may also send erotic poetry books for review consideration. The editor says, "Truth is brief. The best work is sexy, thought-provoking and funny. We prefer graphic to romantic, terse to verbose."

BLACK TIE PRESS (III), P.O. Box 440004, Houston TX 77244-0004, phone (713)789-5119, founded 1986, publisher and editor Peter Gravis. "Black Tie Press is committed to publishing innovative, distinctive and engaging writing. We publish books; we are not a magazine or literary journal. We are not like the major Eastern presses, university presses or other small presses in poetic disposition. To get a feel for our publishing attitude, we urge you to buy one or more of our publications before submit-ting." He is **"only interested in imaginative, provocative, at risk writing. *No rhyme."*** Published poets include Steve Wilson, Guy Beining, Sekou Karanja, Craig Cotter, Donald Rawley, Dieter Wes-lowski, Laura Ryder, Toni Ortner and Jenny Kelly. As a sample the editor selected these lines from "Blue Mirror" from *A Game of Rules,* by Harry Burrus:

> *He thought the white glove*
> *Of her memory would suffocate*

> *By its own flame,*
> *Burning itself out like a suicide,*
> *And she would forget*
> *The amber memories their time imbued.*

Sample postpaid: $8. "We have work we want to publish, hence, unsolicited material is not encouraged. However, we will read and consider material from committed, serious writers as time permits. Query with 4 sample poems. Write, do not call about material. *No reply without SASE.***" Cover letter with bio preferred. Reports in 2-6 weeks. Always sends prepublication galleys. Author receives percent of press run.** Peter Gravis says, "Too many writers are only interested in getting published and not interested in reading or supporting good writing. Black Tie hesitates to endorse a writer who does not, in turn, promote and patronize (by actual purchases) small press publications. Once Black Tie publishes a writer, we intend to remain with that artist."

THE BLACK WARRIOR REVIEW (II), P.O. Box 2936, Tuscaloosa AL 35486-2936, phone (205)348-4518, founded 1974, is a semiannual review. They have recently published poetry by Lee Upton, David Wojahn, Christopher Buckley, Ricardo Pau-Llosa, Sherod Santos and Linda Gregg. As a sample the editor selected these lines from "Coleman Valley Road" by Gerald Stern:

> *The strings are stretched across the sky; one note*
> *is almost endless—pitiless I'd say*
> *except for the slight sagging; one note is*
> *like a voice, it almost has words, it sings*
> *and sighs, it cracks with desire, it sobs with fatigue.*
> *It is the loudest sound of all. A shrieking.*

BWR is 144 pgs., 6×9. Circulation 2,000. **Sample postpaid: $6. Address submissions to Poetry Editor. Submit 3-6 poems at a time. Simultaneous (say so) submissions OK. Send SASE for guidelines. Reports in 1-3 months. Pays $15-30/poem plus 2 copies. Buys first rights.** Awards one $500 prize annually. Reviews books of poetry in single or multi-book format. Open to unsolicited reviews. Poets may also send books for review consideration to Mark S. Drew, editor. Poetry published in *BWR* has been included in *The Best American Poetry 1993*. The editor says, "We solicit a nationally-known poet for a chapbook section. The remainder of the issue is chosen from unsolicited submissions. Many of our poets have substantial publication credits, but our decision is based simply on the quality of the work submitted."

BLANK GUN SILENCER; BGS PRESS (II), 1240 William St., Racine WI 53402, phone (414)639-2406, founded 1991, editor Dan Nielsen, is "an independent art/lit mag" which appears twice a year "publishing Buk-heads, post Dada freaks and everything in between." **They want poetry that is "tight, concise, startling, funny, honest, causing leaps of recognition—a good solid kick in the head. Nothing flowery, overly 'poetic,' too academic, rhyming or blatantly pointless."** They have published poetry by Charles Bukowski, Gerald Locklin, Fred Voss and Ron Androla. As a sample the editor selected these lines from "Edge" by Mark Weber:

> *where are my John Coltrane records?*
> *o, i sold them when*
> *i was a junkie*
> *they sold good*
> *but now i want to hear them*
> *need to hear the cycle of 5ths played backwards*
> *on "Giant Steps"*
> *one of the purest musicians ever*

The editor says *BGS* is 60-80 pgs., digest-sized, photocopied and saddle-stapled with card stock cover and b&w art. They accept approximately 200 poems a year. Press run is 300 for 50 subscribers of which 7 are libraries. Single copy: $4; subscription: $8. **Sample postpaid: $3. Submit 6 poems at a time. Fresh copies preferred. Previously published poems OK, if notified. No simultaneous submissions. Cover letter required.** Time between acceptance and publication is up to 1 year. **Often comments on rejections. Send SASE for guidelines. Reports within 3 months. Pays up to 3 copies. Acquires first or one-time rights.** Reviews books of poetry in up to 3 pages. Open to unsolicited reviews. Poets may also send books for review consideration. BGS Press **publishes 4 chapbooks/year. Query first with sample poems and cover letter with bio and publication credits. Replies to queries in 1 week, to mss within 1 month. Sometimes sends prepublication galleys. Pays 30 copies. For sample chapbook, send $2.**

BLIND BEGGAR PRESS; LAMPLIGHT EDITIONS; NEW RAIN (IV-Ethnic, anthology, children), P.O. Box 437, Williamsbridge Station, Bronx NY 10467, phone/fax (914)683-6792, founded 1976, literary editor Gary Johnston, business manager C.D. Grant, publishes **work "relevant to Black and Third World people, especially women."** *New Rain* is an annual anthology of such work. Lamplight Editions is a subsidiary which publishes "educational materials such as children's books, manuals, greeting cards with educational material in them, etc." They want to see **"quality work that shows a concern for the human condition and the condition of the world—arts for people sake."** They have published work by Judy D. Simmons, A.H. Reynolds, Mariah Britton, Kurt Lampkin, Rashidah Ismaili, Jose L. Garza and Carletta Wilson. As a sample the editor selected the opening lines of Brenda Connor-Bey's "Crossroad of the Serpent":

> *Like a serpent*
> *splitting open fields*
> *this road always brings me back*
> *to this magical place of healing*
> *to this place of hidden waters*

New Rain is a digest-sized, saddle-stapled or perfect-bound, 60- to 200-page chapbook, finely printed, with simple art, card covers. **Sample postpaid: $5.** They also publish about 3 collections of poetry by individuals each year, 60-100 pgs., flat-spined paperback, glossy, color cover, good printing on good paper. **Sample: $5.95. For either the anthology or book publication, first send sample of 5-10 poems with cover letter including biographical background, philosophy and poetic principles. Considers simultaneous submissions. Reads submissions January 15 through September 1 only. Replies to queries in 3-4 weeks, to submissions in 2-3 months. Pays copies (the number depending on the print run). Acquires all rights. Returns them "unconditionally."** Willing to work out individual terms for subsidy publication. Catalog available for SASE.

BLOCK'S POETRY COLLECTION; ALAN J. BLOCK PUBLICATIONS (II), 1419 Chapin St., Beloit WI 53511-5601, founded 1993, editor Alan J. Block, is a quarterly. **"Poems of shorter length (two pages or less), high quality and unique perspective have a home here."** They do not want erotica or religious verse. They have published poetry by Spencer Wright, Ginger Tait, Joyce Frazeur and Steven Duplij. As a sample the editor selected these lines from "Intervention" by Corrine DeWinter:

> *Clio lingers over Ambrosia,*
> *Licking the tips of her fingers*
> *As she contemplates*
> *The casualty of time.*
> *The sand convenes*
> *Around her toes.*

The editor says *BPC* is 25 pgs., $5\frac{1}{2} \times 8\frac{1}{2}$, offset, saddle-stapled, with cover art and ads. Press run is 500 for 50 subscribers. Subscription: $18. **Sample postpaid: $5. Submit 5 poems at a time. No previously published poems or simultaneous submissions.** Time between acceptance and publication is 6-8 months. **Always comments on rejections. Reports in 1-3 months. Pays copies.** They plan to also publish *Poetic Community News*, a newsletter of poetry events and articles. The editor says, "I am open to most kinds of poetry. I see too much trite verse and not enough skillful rhyme. If you submit, be prepared to receive critical comments with returned poems."

BLOODREAMS: A MAGAZINE OF VAMPIRES & WEREWOLVES (I, IV-Specialized), 1312 W. 43rd St., North Little Rock AR 72118, phone (501)771-2047, founded 1991, editor Kelly Gunter Atlas, is an annual appearing in October. They primarily publish short fiction, with poetry and artwork used as fillers. **"All styles of poetry (including traditional) are considered, but all poetry *must* relate to vampires or werewolves. We prefer poetry that is 25 lines or less, but will consider longer works if especially well-written. However, we do not accept poems which are longer than one typewritten page, single-spaced, unless solicited by the editor."** They have published poetry by Dirk Roaché and Lisa S. Laurencot. As a sample the editor selected these lines from Laurencot's "Mender of the Wounded Spring":

> *Wolf and Red Man, their mother, Dawn,*
> *shared earth with seasons' wonders.*
> *Ever round spring's pristine coils,*
> *mirrored esteem thrust symbolic nexus.*

Bloodreams is 40-50 pgs., $8\frac{1}{2} \times 11$, computer typeset and photocopied on 20 lb. paper, bound by plastic spiral, with 60 lb. colored paper cover, b&w drawings and 3-5 pgs. of ads. They receive about 60 poems/ year, use 4-5/issue. Press run is 100 for 75 subscribers. **Sample postpaid: $4. Make check or money order payable to Kelly Atlas. Submit 1-4 poems at a time. Previously published poems OK, if author includes name and date of publication. Cover letter required. Reads submissions February-July. "Poems are accepted or rejected depending on availability of space in the issue and on the impact the poem has on the editor." Seldom comments on rejections. Reports in 1-2 weeks. Pays 1 copy. Acquires one-time rights.** "We have a review column, 'Fang and Claw,' where books, comics and vampire/werewolf-related poetry chapbooks are reviewed. It varies from issue to issue." The editor says, "We look for poetry that has mood, atmosphere and description. Make us feel that we are not merely reading it, but experiencing it."

CLOSE-UP

Telling Life's Stories Through Poetry

William Greenway's poetry has a wonderful quality; it's like a close friend who is always full of
surprises. One explanation for this is Greenway's
use of "story," taken from his own life experiences.
Raised in Atlanta, Georgia, where it was hoped he
would become a Baptist preacher like his father,
and a football hero, Greenway's first exposure to
poetry was actually through hymns and sermons,
and through folk music, which he says "dovetailed
perfectly" with his adolescence. "I tried to be a
folk singer and started writing my own songs, but
I wasn't very good with tunes—I thought it was a

William Greenway

lot of fun to write the lyrics, though, and eventually moved out of the music and
just started writing words. Then, by accident, I ran into some poets—poets on
the page—and knew that was the kind of thing I would like to do."

Greenway, who has published five books of poetry, including ***Pressure Under
Grace*** (Breitenbush Books, 1982), ***Where We've Been*** (Breitenbush Books,
1987), and ***How the Dead Bury the Dead*** (University of Akron Press, 1994), is
very much a self-taught poet. "I was never in a creative writing course, so I was
free to develop my own voice. Nobody was pressuring me to do one thing or
the other. For this same reason, I am very nondirective in the way I teach creative
writing," says Greenway, a professor of English at Youngstown State University
in Youngstown, Ohio.

"One of the important things you do learn in a creative writing class is that
taking criticism is a skill. When Ezra Pound showed his poems to Ford Madox
Ford, Ford rolled on the floor with laughter. Later, Pound said that roll saved
him two years. I think sensibility can be accelerated by a creative writing class,
although you need a lot of life experience too."

For Greenway, life experience is what it's all about. "There are many different
kinds of poetry. The poets that I tend to like, write about themselves. The trick
is writing about yourself so that you're writing about the reader too," says
Greenway, who places a lot of importance on the "story" of the poem. "I think
not enough poems are stories—the stories that happen in your life. The thing
that happens is as high as it can be. What brings it down is when you start
applying language to it. Then you try to pull it back up to the original feeling
you had. That's what you've lost—that immediacy—the thing that happened. If
you can tell the story with an awareness of its significance, then that significance
will be there."

Sometimes, these stories can come from sources other than oneself. Many of

"Anniversary"

Soon I'll be the age you are
forever, the day you pulled
off the interstate, your heart
boiling like a cracked block,
to die in a phonebooth
while everyone passed you by.

We'll be twins—
I see us coming in the amber of store windows.
The next day I'll be
the eldest, you
tagging along to some
place you've already been.

Already you could be my mother's son.
Someday, you could be mine.
Maybe then you'd listen
when I told you to stay
off the fatty foods and the interstates,
to slow down and stay well.
To grow old. To call.

(from *How the Dead Bury the Dead*, 1994, reprinted by permission of University of Akron Press)

the stories Greenway writes about are those he heard growing up. "My family was big on storytelling, and a lot of my poems just try to recount those stories, with perspective, and are given irony now by the fact that a lot of these people are dead. Stories like my mother telling me that they used to tie me to a tree so that I wouldn't run off seem not only funny and interesting, but full of meaning.

"I care as much about how people say things as about what they say. I try to catch this realistic, perhaps regional tone in my poems. My family had a very quaint way of telling stories. As a kid, I used to love to listen to them talk. If you can just catch the tone, then a lot of the work is done. It's who's telling the story, how they're telling it, and what their feelings are about it that you bounce off of your own. I guess it seems to me that what people starting out don't trust enough is reality. They are always looking for something else. For me, the thing is to trust people's perceptions of what really happened as indicated by the sound of their voices, because what happened doesn't really matter. What matters is how it has been internalized and turned around into a myth, a story."

Greenway did not recognize the importance of "story" in his early work. He describes his first poems as "cerebral and cold-blooded" in his attempt to "find something to write about that would sound poetical." It was not until his father died that Greenway's poetry began to change. "I got very angry and bitter, and that gave me juice. Not only did I have something to write about, but I found my own voice. I sounded like me for a change. Sounding poetical didn't matter anymore, I just wanted to get this out.

"On a conscious level, it was a feeling that my father's life was wasted, so how could it be given value now? Well, I thought, I could preserve it. If it was going to have meaning, I was going to have to give meaning to it. There was nobody else to do it—somebody had to tell the story. That was a very strong impulse: Tell the story—somebody's got to know."

Eventually, you become the mythologizer, he says. "Sometimes when I write a poem, there's this voice telling the story and it's me, but different. The story has already moved onto the level of myth or legend. When that happens, certain things recede and certain things come forward and become the icons or the images in the story that are luminous, as Pound says. Part of making the story a myth is to tell as many people as possible; that's where publishing your work comes in. Writing is something of a 'life or death struggle' because you are saving something—the story—from oblivion.

"I've kept every rejection slip I've ever had," Greenway adds, "which tells me that, in a funny kind of way, I like rejection. I never like anything that's easy. One of my first responses to getting rejected is to write something. I used to think that I hated rejection, but there are two things I hate more—complacency and boredom—and I never feel bored when I get rejected. Sending your work out, getting published, keeping track of where your poems are—that's fun. You know, you can't write poetry all the time, but you can be a poet all the time."

—*Michelle Moore*

❝The trick is writing about yourself so that you're writing about the reader too. ❞

—**William Greenway**

‡**THE BLOWFISH CATALOG (IV-Erotica)**, 2261 Market St., #284, San Francisco CA 94114, fax (415)864-1858, e-mail blowfish@blowfish.com, founded 1994, appears 3 times/year. *"The Blowfish Catalog* is a catalog of mail-order erotic products. **We include fiction and poetry as well and are interested in short, erotic pieces of any format. All material must be on the general subject of sex, sexuality, gender or related matters."** As a sample we selected these lines from "Hit and Run" by James E. Myers:

> *I ran over a myth last night*
> *I think it might have been true love*
> *It wasn't really my fault*
> *It's always so dark out*
> *And the headlights don't help much*
> *Not really . . .*

The Blowfish Catalog is 48 pgs. (including cover), 8½ × 11, web offset and saddle-stapled with a few b&w photos and graphics. The issue we received contained 2 poems. Press run is 4,000. **Sample postpaid: $3. Previously published poems and simultaneous submissions OK.** Time between acceptance and publication is 2 months. **Send SASE for guidelines. Reports in approximately 1 month. Pays $25-75. "We will also pay 25% additional in merchandise credit, if desired."** Buys one-time rights.

BLUE LIGHT PRESS (V), P.O. Box 642, Fairfield IA 52556, phone (515)472-7882, founded 1988, partner Diane Frank, publishes 3 paperbacks, 3 chapbooks/year. **"We like poems that are imagistic, emotionally honest and uplifting. Women, Visionary Poets, Iowa Poets, San Francisco Poets. No rhymed poetry or dark poetry." They are currently accepting work by invitation only. Interested poets should query.** They have published poetry by Rustin Larson, Nancy Berg, Viktor Tichy, Tom Centolella and Meg Fitz-Randolph. As a sample the editor selected these lines from *The Houses Are Covered in Sound* by Louise Nayer:

> *There was something*
> *moving in a garbage can,*
> *a white light glowing in a spiral.*
> *I thought it was a child,*
> *no the wind, no the part*
> *of myself that glowed.*

That book is 60 pgs., digest-sized, flat-spined, professionally printed, with elegant matte card cover: $10. They have also published two anthologies of Iowa poets. They have an editorial board, and "work in person with local poets, have an ongoing poetry workshop, give classes, and will edit/critique poems by mail—$30 for 4-5 poems."

‡**BLUE MESA REVIEW (II, IV-Themes)**, Dept. of English, Humanities Bldg. #217, University of New Mexico, Albuquerque NM 87131-1106, phone (505)277-6347, fax (505)277-5573, founded 1989 by Rudolfo Anaya, managing editor Patricia Lynn Sprott, faculty editor Dr. David Johnson, is an annual review of poetry, short fiction, creative essays and book reviews. **They want "all kinds of free, organic verse; poems of place encouraged. No length limits; no greeting card verse."** They have recently published poetry by Adrian Louis, Peter Wild, Janice Gould and Alexis Rotella. As a sample we selected these lines from "You Could See It In Missoula" by Martha Elizabeth:

> *The man walking his fish in the Clark Fork*
> *smokes a pipe in baroque puffs, moustache*
> *curving up in waxed points, catching silver.*
> *No pole, just a loop of line held loose.*
> *His boots are tied on around the middle,*
> *ankle belts, leather flaring like waistlines.*

BMR is about 200 pgs., 6 × 9, professionally printed and flat-spined with glossy cover, photos and graphics. This hefty publication includes a number of long poems—several spanning three pages. They receive about 1,000 poems a year, accept 10% or less. Press run is 1,600 for 600 shelf sales. Single copy: $10. **Sample postpaid: $12. No previously published poems or simultaneous submissions. Cover letter required. Accepts mss from May 15 through September 30 only. Poems are then passed among readers and voted on. Seldom comments on rejections. Publishes theme issues. Theme for the Spring 1996 issue is "Approaching the Millennium." Send SASE for upcoming themes. Reports on mss by mid-December. Pays 2 copies.** Reviews books of poetry. Open to unsolicited reviews. Poets may also send books to Patricia Sprott for review consideration.

‡**BLUE MOUNTAIN ARTS, INC. (IV-Specialized: greeting cards)**, Dept. PM, P.O. Box 1007, Boulder CO 80306-1007, founded 1971, contact editorial staff. Blue Mountain Arts is a publisher of greeting cards, calendars, prints and mugs. They are looking for poems, prose and lyrics (**"usually nonrhyming"**) appropriate for publication on greeting cards and in poetry anthologies. "Poems should reflect a message, feeling or sentiment that one person would want to share with another. We'd like to

receive **sensitive, original submissions about love relationships, family members, friendships, philosophies and any other aspect of life. Poems and writings for specific holidays (Christmas, Valentine's Day, etc.) and special occasions, such as graduation, anniversary and get well, are also considered.** Only a small portion of the material we receive is selected each year and the review process can be lengthy, but be assured every manuscript is given serious consideration." **Submissions must be typewritten, one poem/page. Prefers original material. Simultaneous submissions OK, "if notified of acceptance elsewhere." Submit seasonal material at least 4 months in advance. Send SASE for guidelines. Reports in 3-6 months. Pays $200/poem for the worldwide, exclusive right to publish on a greeting card; $25/poem for one-time use in a book.** They advise, "We strongly suggest that you familiarize yourself with our products before submitting material, although we caution you not to study them too hard. We do not need more poems that sound like something we've already published. Overall, we're looking for poetry that expresses real emotions and feelings."

‡BLUE PENNY QUARTERLY (II), 1212 Wertland St., Apt. 6, Charlottesville VA 22903, e-mail dlawson@ebbs.english.vt.edu (best way to contact), founded 1994, editor Doug Lawson, poetry editor Leigh Palmer, is a quarterly designed to promote fine literature in the electronic communities. **"We welcome a variety of forms and themes—except inspirational verse, randomness jury-rigged to back up literary theory, and therapeutic journalism. We value the wild and the well-made."** They have recently published poetry by Ioana Ieronim (in translation), Eva Shaderowfsky and Robert Klein Engler. *BPQ* is an electronic publication, more than 100 pgs., using full-color artwork. It is printable by the reader's home computer and readers are encouraged to pass the software along to others. They accept 10-20% of the poetry received. **No previously published poems; simultaneous submissions OK. Cover letter required. Submissions via e-mail welcome.** Time between acceptance and publication is 1 month to 1 year. **Send SASE for guidelines or inquire via e-mail. Reports in up to 3 months. Acquires first North American or one-time rights and electronic rights. Electronic rights returned upon request.** Reviews books of poetry in about 1,000 words. Open to unsolicited reviews. Poets may also send books for review consideration, attn: Doug Lawson.

BLUE UNICORN, A TRIQUARTERLY OF POETRY; BLUE UNICORN POETRY CONTEST (II, IV-Translations), 22 Avon Rd., Kensington CA 94707, phone (510)526-8439, founded 1977, poetry editors Ruth G. Iodice, Harold Witt and Daniel J. Langton, wants **"well-crafted poetry of all kinds, in form or free verse, as well as expert translations on any subject matter. We shun the trite or inane, the soft-centered, the contrived poem. Shorter poems have more chance with us because of limited space."** They have published poetry by James Applewhite, Kim Cushman, Charles Edward Eaton, Patrick Worth Gray, Joan LaBombard, James Schevill, John Tagliabue and Gail White. As a sample the editors selected these lines from "Sonnet #45" by Harold Grier McCurdy:

> Doen in the poor, Boeotian, beaten South,
> By wagon-tracks, by stubble fields, I've gone
> With rumbling bees into the golden mouth
> Of trumpeting daylilies, and have flown
>
> With herons over canebrakes to the river
> And in its moving surface read the clouds,
> And have imagined I could live forever
> In that lone contemplation, far from crowds.

The magazine is **"distinguished by its fastidious editing, both with regard to contents and format."** It is 56 pgs., narrow digest-sized, saddle-stapled, finely printed, with some art. It features 40-50 poems in each issue, all styles, with the focus on excellence and accessibility. They receive over 35,000 submissions a year, use about 200, have a year's backlog. **Sample postpaid: $5. Submit 3-5 typed poems on 8½×11 paper. No simultaneous submissions or previously published poems. "Cover letter OK, but will not affect our selection." Send SASE for guidelines. Reports in 1-3 months (generally within 6 weeks), sometimes with personal comment. Pays 1 copy.** They sponsor an annual contest with small entry fee to help support the magazine, with prizes of $100, $75, $50 and sometimes special awards, distinguished poets as judges, publication of 3 top poems and 6 honorable mentions in the magazine. Entry fee: $4 for first poem, $3 for others to a maximum of 5. Write for current guidelines. **Criticism occasionally offered**. The editors add, "We would advise beginning poets to read and study poetry—both poets of the past and of the present; concentrate on technique; and **discipline yourself by learning forms before trying to do without them**. When your poem is crafted and ready for publication, study your markets and then send whatever of your work seems to be compatible with the magazine you are submitting to."

BLUELINE (IV-Regional), Dept. PM, English Dept., Potsdam College, Potsdam NY 13676, fax (315)267-3256, e-mail tylerao@potsdam.edu, founded 1979, editor-in-chief Anthony Tyler, and an editorial board, "is an annual literary magazine dedicated to prose and **poetry about the Adirondacks and other regions similar in geography and spirit."** They want **"clear, concrete poetry pertinent**

to the countryside and its people. It must go beyond mere description, however. **We prefer a realistic to a romantic view. We do not want to see sentimental or extremely experimental poetry.** **They usually use poems of 75 lines or fewer, though "occasionally we publish longer poems" on "nature in general, Adirondack Mountains in particular. Form may vary, can be traditional or contemporary."** They have published poetry by Phillip Booth, George Drew, Eric Ormsby, L.M. Rosenberg, John Unterecker, Lloyd Van Brunt, Laurence Josephs, Maurice Kenny and Nancy L. Nielsen. It's a handsomely printed, 112-page, 6×9 magazine with 40-45 pgs. of poetry in each issue. Circulation 400. **Sample copies: $4 for back issues. Submit 5 poems at a time. Include short bio. No simultaneous submissions. Submit September 1 through November 30.** They have a 3- to 11-month backlog. **Occasionally comments on rejections. Guidelines available for SASE. Reports in 2-10 weeks. Pays copies. Acquires first North American serial rights.** Reviews books of poetry in 500-750 words, single and multi-book format. "We are interested in both beginning and established poets whose poems evoke universal themes in nature and show human interaction with the natural world. We look for **thoughtful craftsmanship rather than stylistic trickery."**

‡**BLUFF CITY (II)**, P.O. Box 7697, Elgin IL 60121, founded 1990, poetry editor Aaron Anstett, is an annual that aims "to fill the void between the academic press and the popular press." **They want "poetry that takes a risk—anything from traditional to dangerously experimental. No didactic or religious poetry."** They have recently published poetry by Richard Jones, Stuart Freibert, Ruth Daigon, Todd Moore, Martha Vertreace and John Bradley. They say offering a sample would be "too limiting." The editor describes *BC* as 100 pgs., laser printed and perfect-bound with glossy b&w photos, some small press ads. They accept approximately 5% of the poetry received. Press run is 500. **Sample postpaid: $4. "We prefer 3-5 tightly crafted poems per submission." No previously published poems; simultaneous submissions OK. Reads submissions August-October. Send SASE for guidelines. Reports in 3 months or less. Pays 1 copy. Acquires first rights.** The editor says, "Read back copies before submitting to any publication. Purchase sample copies and read guidelines. Familiarize yourself with the literary press."

BOA EDITIONS, LTD. (V), 92 Park Ave., Brockport NY 14420, phone (716)637-3844 or (716)473-1896, founded 1976, poetry editor A. Poulin, Jr. **"We regret that we cannot consider unsolicited manuscripts for publication. Due to restricted funds, our annual publishing schedule is very limited."** They have published some of the major American poets, such as W.D. Snodgrass, John Logan, Isabella Gardner, Richard Wilbur and Lucille Clifton, and they publish introductions by major poets of those less well-known. For example, Gerald Stern wrote the foreword for Li-Young Lee's *Rose*.

BOGG PUBLICATIONS; BOGG (II), 422 N. Cleveland St., Arlington VA 22201, founded 1968, poetry editors John Elsberg (USA), George Cairncross (UK: 31 Belle Vue St., Filey, N. Yorkshire YO 14 9HU England), Sheila Martindale (Canada: P.O. Box 23148, 380 Wellington St., London, Ontario NGA 5N9 Canada) and Robert Boyce (Australia/New Zealand: 48 Academy Ave., Mulgrave, Victoria 3170 Australia). "We publish *Bogg* magazine and occasional free-for-postage pamphlets." The magazine uses a great deal of poetry in each issue (with several featured poets)—**"poetry in all styles, with a healthy leavening of shorts (under 10 lines). Prefer original voices. Our emphasis is on good work per se and Anglo-American cross-fertilization. We are currently looking for American work with British/Commonwealth themes/references."** This is one of the liveliest small press magazines published today. It started in England and in 1975 began including a supplement of American work; it now is published in the US and mixes US, Canadian, Australian and UK work with reviews of small press publications from all of those areas. It's thick (68 pgs.), typeset, saddle-stitched, in a 6×9 format that leaves enough white space to let each poem stand and breathe alone. They have published work by Jon Silkin, John Millett, Robert Cooperman, Ann Menebroker, Charles Bukowski, Janine Pommy Vega and Laurel Speer. As a sample the editors selected these lines from "Wallace Stevens and I try 'Oh Susannah' " by New Zealand poet Bernard Gadd:

> *we image only too lucidly,*
> *wallace and i, ourselves among*
> *israel's elders spying spying*
> *from the branchy screens*
> *bright nipples loosing*
> *lucent drops upon the brown flesh*

The Subject Index, located before the General Index, can help you narrow down markets for your work. It lists those publishers whose poetry interests are specialized.

They accept all styles, all subject matter. "Some have even found the magazine's sense of play offensive. Overt religious and political poems have to have strong poetical merits—statement alone is not sufficient. Submit 6 poems at a time. Prefer typewritten manuscripts, with author's name and address on each sheet. We will reprint previously published material, but with a credit line to a previous publisher." No simultaneous submissions. Cover letters preferred. "They can help us get a 'feel' for the writer's intentions/slant." SASE required for return of ms. There are about 50 pgs. of poetry/issue. Press run is 850 for 400 subscribers of which 20 are libraries. Subscription: $12 for 3 issues. **Sample postpaid: $3.50.** They receive over 10,000 American poems/year, use 100-150. "We try to accept only for next 2 issues. SASE required or material discarded (no exceptions)." **Send SASE for guidelines. Reports in 1 week. Pays 2 copies. Acquires one-time rights.** Reviews books and chapbooks of poetry in 250 words, single format. Open to unsolicited reviews. Poets may also send books to relevant editor (by region) for review consideration. Their occasional pamphlets and chapbooks are by invitation only, the author receiving 25% of the print run, and you can get **chapbook samples free for 6 × 9 SASE.** Better make it at least 2 ounces worth of postage. John Elsberg advises, "Become familiar with a magazine before submitting to it. Long lists of previous credits irritate me. Short notes about how the writer has heard about *Bogg* or what he or she finds interesting or annoying in the magazine I read with some interest."

BOHEMIAN CHRONICLE (I), P.O. Box 387, Largo FL 34649-0387, founded 1991, editor/publisher Emily Skinner, is a monthly publication "promoting sensitivity in the arts." **They want experimental poetry no longer than one page. No rhyming poetry.** They have published poetry by Holly Day and Pamela Portwood. The editor simply describes it as 12 pgs., stapled. They receive about 100 poems a year, use 24. Press run is 500 for 100 subscribers, 400 sent abroad free. Subscription: $12. **Sample: $1 and #10 SASE. Submit 4 poems maximum. No previously published poems; simultaneous submissions OK. Reads submissions January through September only.** Time between acceptance and publication is 6-8 months. **Always comments on rejections. Send SASE for guidelines. Reports in 1-2 months. Pays $2 and 2 copies. Buys all rights or first rights. If all rights, does not return them.** "We select the year's best for our anniversary issue each May and award Bohos (framed certificates) to the best in each category." The editor says, "We are not formula-oriented. We only buy what we like, good or bad."

BOMB MAGAZINE (III), 594 Broadway, Suite 1002 A, New York NY 10012, founded 1981, managing editor Lawrence Chua, is a quarterly magazine that "encourages a dialogue among artists of various media. **Experiments with form and language are encouraged. No limericks, inspirational verse, clever or greeting card styles.**" They have published poetry by David Mamet, Harold Pinter and A.C. Purcell. As a sample the editors selected these lines by Agha Shahid Ali:

> *Cries Majnoon:*
> *Those in tatters*
> *May now demand love:*
> *I've declared a fashion*
> *of ripped collars.*
> *The breezes are lost*
> *travellers today,*
> *knocking, asking*
> *for a place to stay.*
> *I tell them*
> *to go away.*

Bomb is 96 pgs., saddle-stitched with 4-color cover. "We receive about 100 manuscripts a month; we accept 2 or 3 every 4 months." Press run is 12,000 for 2,000 subscribers of which 600 are libraries. Single copy: $4; subscription: $18/year. **Sample postpaid: $5. No previously published poems; simultaneous submissions OK. Cover letter including name, address, telephone number and previous publications required. "Poetry should be legibly typed."** Time between acceptance and publication is 4-6 months. **Reports in 4 months. Pays $50. Buys first North American serial rights.**

BONE & FLESH PUBLICATIONS (II), P.O. Box 349, Concord NH 03302-0349, phone (603)225-0521, founded 1988, editors Lester Hirsh, Frederick Moe and Amy Shea, managing editor Monica A. Cruickshank-Nagle, phone (603)293-8466. In 1996, there will be one main issue of *Bone & Flesh* literary journal and one chapbook featuring the works of a selected poet or prose writer and artist. "We are looking for **quality work from seasoned writers/artists: prose, poems, fiction, essays, reviews and art. Themes vary and tend to focus on the substance of our lives and the links with other lives and times.**" They have recently published works by Lyn Lifshin, Mara Attina, Tim Hoppey, Mary Winters and Arthur Kagle. As a sample the editors selected these lines from "Raking Leaves" by Bruce MacMahon:

> *All day the gathering*
> *these cupped hands full*

> *of sky to a ground*
> *rasped into piles*
>
> *taking a select few*
> *I burn them in silence*
> *to an aged night wind. . .*

Bone & Flesh is 50-75 pgs. Subscription: $14. **Sample postpaid: $6. Submissions are accepted February through May only. Editors will comment on work "when appropriate." Reports in 1-3 months. Pays 1 copy. Acquires first North American serial rights.** *Bone & Flesh* recently published *Bone & Flesh #13, Shadowdance*, which includes stories, poems and artwork.

‡BONG (I, II), 6745 Greenway-New London Rd., Verona NY 13478, phone (315)336-1439, founded 1993, editor Dale R. Millson, is a quarterly of poetry and some art. "Purpose is to go beyond the disease of writing poetry and just have fun." The editor says it is devoted to "sex, drugs and personal freedom." **They want "experimental poetry, 40 lines max. No rhyme, no religion, no shiny-happy poetry."** They have recently published poetry by Ana Christy, Élliott, and Mike Costanzo. The editor says *Bong* is 10 pgs., 8½ × 11, photocopied and stapled in the corner with paper cover and cover art. They receive about 150 poems a year, accept about 35. Press run is 25. Subscription: $6. **Sample postpaid: $2. Make checks payable to Dale R. Millson. Previously published poems OK; no simultaneous submissions. Cover letter and SASE required.** Time between acceptance and publication is 3-12 months. **"I read submissions three times and accept whatever grabs me by the throat." Always comments on rejections. Send SASE for guidelines. Reports in 2 months. Pays 1 copy. Acquires first or one-time rights.** As for reviewing books of poetry, the editor says he will read anything sent, but can't guarantee a review. His advice? "Have fun! It's usually the little garbage zines that are the best places to hang out in. So grab a beer at the door, take your clothes off and jump in! And remember, poetry is more a curse than anything else."

BOOG LITERATURE; MA! (I, II), P.O. Box 221, Oceanside NY 11572-0221, founded 1991, editor/publisher David Kirschenbaum. BOOG Literature publishes *MA!*, a quarterly zine of poetry, prose and arts reviews, as well as 5-10 chapbooks/year and occasional broadsides. The editor says he **would like to see more "heartfelt, non-manufactured political poetry."** They have published poetry by Eileen Myles, Bernadette Mayer, Elliot Richman and Anne Waldman. As a sample the editor selected these lines from "keeping up with the joneses" by Kent Taylor, published in *MA!*:

> *I wait stunned*
> *in Jammin' Java*
> *for the first shudder*
>   *of deliverance*
> *as Caroline*
> *of the fine*
>   *bones*
> *dispenses hit*
>   *after hit*

MA! is 40 pgs., digest-sized, offset printed and saddle-stitched, with card stock cover, art, graphics and small press ads. "We accept 10-15 poems per issue, sometimes more, never less." Press run is 500 for 10 subscribers, 200 shelf sales. Single copy: $2.50; subscription: $9. **Sample postpaid: $3. Make all checks payable to David Kirschenbaum. Submit up to 5 poems; 6 short poems can count as 1 poem or page of poetry. Previously published poems and simultaneous submissions OK. "A friendly cover letter is always appreciated. Most small presses have low circulations, so if your piece was (or may be) published elsewhere, but you think it deserves/needs to be read by more people, send it along (but please tell us when and where it was or will be published)."** Time between acceptance and publication is "usually no more than 3 months." **Often comments on rejections. Send SASE for guidelines. Reports in 6-12 weeks. Pays 1 copy. Acquires first North American serial or reprint rights.** "We welcome and will write reviews of either chaps or mags in 250-1,000 words, single or multi-book format." **For chapbook or broadside publication, query with sample poems and cover letter including brief bio and publication credits. Replies to queries within 2 months, to mss within 3 months. Pays 10% of press run; first printing is 100-200 copies.** Recent chapbooks include *Models* by Pat McKinnon and *a museme* by Lee Ann Brown. For sample chapbook, "send check or money order for $1.50 to $4.50, and we will select a chap to send in return." The press also publishes occasional spoken word cassette compilations. Query before sending tapes. The editor says, "The job of the small press is to get the word out. If it's solid, we will publish it. It's quality, not résumé."

BOOTS: FOR FOLKS WITH THEIR BOOTS ON! (I, IV-Cowboy, themes), P.O. Box 766, Challis ID 83226, phone (208)879-4475, founded 1990, editor Ethie Corrigan, is a biannual magazine using **"well-crafted cowboy poetry and historical pieces (Western Americana). No modernistic mumbo-jumbo." They look for poetry with humor as well as nature/rural/ecology, regional (Western)**

and/or inspirational themes. They have published poetry by Wallace McRae, Gwen Peterson, Sandy Seaton and Mike Logan. As a sample we selected these lines from "The Quilted History Book" by Marilyn Diamond:

> And see this piece of pale pink
> With flecks of green and rose
> It's from the dress I wore, the night
> Your daddy, he proposed.
> And them squares of creamy ivory
> There must be ten or more,
> They're bits saved from my daddy's shirt
> He died when I was four.

Boots is 60 pgs., web press printed, saddle-stitched, with glossy cover, photos and ads. Press run is 2,500 for 1,500 subscribers of which 8 are libraries. Single copy: $4.50; subscription: $8. **Sample postpaid: $2.50. Submit up to 3 poems at a time. Previously published poems OK; no simultaneous submissions. Submit typed poems January through March for fall issue; April through September for spring. Always comments on rejections. Publishes theme issues. Send SASE for upcoming themes. The September 1995 issue celebrates their 5th anniversary and focuses on grandmas and old barns. Reports "immediately." Pays copies, "exact number depends on length."** Reviews related books of poetry "now and then." Open to unsolicited reviews. Poets may also send books for review consideration. The editor says poets should be careful when "trying to write about the West if they don't know the background, vocabulary, etc."

BORDERLANDS: TEXAS POETRY REVIEW (II), P.O. Box 49818, Austin TX 78765, founded 1992, appears twice a year publishing "high-quality, outward-looking poetry by new and established poets, as well as brief reviews of poetry books and critical essays. Cosmopolitan in content, but particularly welcomes Texas and Southwest writers." **They want "outward-looking poems that exhibit social, political, geographical, historical or spiritual awareness coupled with concise artistry. We also want poems in two languages (one of which must be English), where the poet has written both versions. Please, no introspective work about the speaker's psyche, childhood or intimate relationships."** They have recently published poetry by Wendy Barker, John Knoepfle, Laurel Speer, James Ulmer and Ronald Wallace. As a sample the editors selected these lines from "Gold in the Black Hills" by Robert James Tillett:

> You could hear their women's children crying
> within the circled-wagon barricades.
> But still those copper voices clicked and thrummed
> that metal language—and later, explosions
> in the hills, a new war sounding in the canyons
> and men raging underground.

Borderlands is 80-120 pgs., 5½×8½, offset, perfect-bound, with 4-color cover, art by local artists. They receive about 2,000 poems a year, use approximately 120. Press run is 800. Subscription: $17/year; $33/2 years. **Sample postpaid: $8.50. Submit 3-6 typed poems at a time. No previously published poems; simultaneous submissions OK. Include SASE (or SAE and IRCs) with sufficient postage to return poems and a response. Seldom comments on rejections. Reports in 4-6 months. Pays 1 copy. Acquires first rights.** Reviews books of poetry in one page. Also uses 3- to 6-page essays on single poets and longer essays (3,500-word maximum) on contemporary poetry in some larger context (query first). Sponsors a poetry and essay contest awarding one $500 prize in poetry and five $100 prizes for essays. Entry fee: $10 for poems, $5 for essays. Postmark deadline: March 1 through April 30, 1996. Send SASE for details. They say, "We believe it's possible—though not easy—for poetry to be both involved with the world and high-quality."

BOREALIS PRESS; TECUMSEH PRESS LTD.; JOURNAL OF CANADIAN POETRY (V), Dept. PM, 9 Ashburn Dr., Nepean, Ontario K2E 6N4 Canada, founded 1972. Borealis and Tecumseh are imprints for books, including **collections of poetry, by Canadian writers only, and they are presently not considering unsolicited submissions.** Send SASE (or SAE with IRCs) for catalog to buy samples. Poets published include John Ferns and Russell Thornton. These sample lines are by Fred Cogswell:

> Often in dreams, when powerless to wake
> Or move and thereby ease my pounding heart,
> I have felt like a mouse that cannot squeal
> When the sprung trap pins its broken spine or
> Like a rabbit mesmerized by a snake's
> Unchanging otherness of lidless eyes.

The *Journal* is an annual that publishes articles, reviews and criticism, not poetry. **Sample postpaid: $15.95.**

THE BOSTON PHOENIX: PHOENIX LITERARY SECTION (PLS) (III), 126 Brookline Ave., Boston MA 02215, phone (617)536-5390, founded 1966, poetry editor Lloyd Schwartz, is a monthly book review with one poem in almost every issue. Press run is 150,000. Single copy: $1.50. **Submit 1-3 poems at a time, under 50 lines each. "Please include cover letter and SASE." Reports in 1 month. Pays $50.** Open to unsolicited reviews. Poets may also send books for review consideration to Robert Sullivan, supplements editor. Poems published in this review appear in the 1992 and 1995 volumes of *The Best American Poetry*.

BOSTON REVIEW (II), 33 Harrison Ave., Boston MA 02111, founded 1975, poetry editor Kim Cooper, is a bimonthly magazine of arts, culture and politics which uses about **three pages of poetry/issue, or 25 poems a year**, for which they receive about 700 submissions. Poems in select issues seem to echo or somehow complement the prose, which concerns social or literary affairs. The poetry features lyric and narrative verse with an emphasis on voice, often plaintive-sounding or dream-like in tone. They have a 4- to 6-month backlog. Circulation is 20,000 nationally including subscriptions and newsstand sales. **Sample postpaid: $4. Submit no more than 6 poems at a time. Simultaneous submissions discouraged. Cover letter listing recent publications encouraged. Reports in 2-4 months "if you include SASE." Always sends prepublication galleys. Pay varies. Buys first serial rights.** Reviews books of poetry. Only using *solicited* reviews. Poets may send books for review consideration. Poetry published by this review has been included in *The Best American Poetry 1993*. The editor advises, "To save the time of all those involved, poets should be sure to send only *appropriate* poems to particular magazines. This means that a poet should not submit to a magazine that he/she has not read. Poets should also avoid lengthy cover letters and allow the poems to speak for themselves."

BOTTOMFISH (II), Creative Writing Program, De Anza College, 21250 Stevens Creek Blvd., Cupertino CA 95014, editor Robert Scott. This college-produced magazine appears annually. **"Spare us the pat, generic greeting card phrases. We want sharp, sensory images that carry a strong theme."** They have published poetry by Chitra Divakaruni and Edward Kleinschmidt. As a sample here are lines from "Blowout" by Walter Griffin:

> *Suddenly you are there, out by the highway, arm*
> *wrestling the dark with the wheel in your hands*
> *gauging the distance between odometers and stars*
> *that shimmer like ghosts in the falling air*
> *as the wheel comes loose from the column and*
> *your brakeless car rolls toward the cliff*

Bottomfish is 60 pgs., 7 × 8¼, well-printed on heavy stock with b&w graphics, perfect-bound. Circulation is 500, free to libraries, schools, etc., but **$4/copy to individual requests. "Before submitting, writers are strongly urged to purchase a sample copy; subject matter is at the writer's discretion, as long as the poem is skillfully and professionally crafted." Best submission times: September through February 1. Deadline: February 1 each year. Reports in 2-6 months, depending on backlog. Pays 2 copies.** The editor adds, "Nobody likes the stock rejection letter, but no other response is possible. We do make specific requests for changes, however, if we really want to publish something and it has only minor problems."

BOUILLABAISSE (I, IV-Form/style), % Alpha Beat Press, 31 Waterloo St., New Hope PA 18938, phone (215)862-0299, founded 1991, editors Dave Christy and Ana Christy, is a biannual using **"poetry that reflects life and its ups and downs."** They want **"modern, Beat poetry; poetry from the streets of life—no limit. No rhythm, Christian or sweet poetry."** They have recently published poetry by Jan Kerouac, Allen Ginsberg, William Haynes/elliott and Erling Friis-Baastad. As a sample the editors selected these lines by Janine Pommy Vega:

> *Archangel Mary falls into the water*
> *killing the bridges, the Tappanzee and*
> *railroad tresks. Her backside against the pier, they promenade*
> *across her, River Edge to Harlem*
> *and time runs out*

The editors say *Bouillabaisse* is 160 pgs., 8½ × 11, offset, saddle-stitched, with graphics. They receive 200 submissions a year, accept 40%. Press run is 500 for 350 subscribers of which 9 are libraries. Subscription: $15. **Sample postpaid: $10. Submit 5 poems at a time. Previously published poems and simultaneous submissions OK. Cover letter required. Always comments on rejections. Send SASE for guidelines. Reports "immediately." Pays 1 copy.** Reviews books of poetry in 250-500 words. Open to unsolicited reviews. Poets may also send books for review consideration. They also publish 2 paperbacks and 7 chapbooks/year. "We work with each individual on their project." **Replies to queries "immediately," to mss within 3 weeks. Always sends prepublication galleys for chapbooks. Pays author's copies.** Also see listings for *Alpha Beat Soup* and *Cokefish*.

BOULEVARD (II), % editor Richard Burgin, P.O. Box 30386, Philadelphia PA 19103, phone (215)568-7062, founded 1985, appears 3 times a year. **"We've published everything from John Ashbery to Howard Moss to a wide variety of styles from new or lesser known poets. We're eclectic. Do not want to see poetry that is uninspired, formulaic, self-conscious, unoriginal, insipid."** They have published poetry by Amy Clampitt, Molly Peacock, Jorie Graham and Mark Strand. As a sample, editor Richard Burgin selected these lines from "Three Soundings of January Snow" by Stuart Lishan:

> *Snow arias the ground tonight. It quilts*
> > *the house; it sounds like a samba of whispers,*
> > *Muffled, like a mitten slipped over love, like guilt.*

Boulevard is 200 pgs., digest-sized, flat-spined, professionally printed, with glossy card cover. Poetry herein—mostly free verse but wide-ranging in content, length and tone—is accessible and exciting. Poems have one thing in common: careful attention to craft (particularly line, stanza and voice). Their press run is 3,000 with 700 subscribers of which 200 are libraries. Subscription: $12. **Sample postpaid: $7. "Prefer name and number on each page with SASE. Encourage cover letters but don't require them. Will consider simultaneous submissions but not previously published poems." Reads submissions October 1 through May 1 only. Editor sometimes comments on rejections. Pays $25-250/ poem, depending on length, plus 1 copy. Buys first-time publication and anthology rights.** Open to unsolicited reviews. Poetry published in *Boulevard* has also been included in the 1992, 1993, 1994 and 1995 volumes of *The Best American Poetry*. Richard Burgin says, "We believe the grants we have won from the National Endowment for the Arts, etc., as well as the anthologies that continue to recognize us, have rewarded our commitment. My advice to poets: 'Write from your heart as well as your head.' "

GEORGE BRAZILLER, INC. (II), 60 Madison Ave., New York NY 10010, phone (212)889-0909, founded 1955, editor Adrienne Baxter, is a major literary publisher. In 1980 they published *Classic Ballroom Dances* by Charles Simic, from which this sample poem, "Bedtime Story," was selected:

> *When a tree falls in a forest*
> *And there's no one around*
> *To hear the sound, the poor owls*
> *Have to do all the thinking.*
>
> *They think so hard they fall off*
> *Their perch and are eaten by ants,*
> *Who, as you already know, all look like*
> *Little Black Riding Hoods.*

It is 64 pgs., digest-sized, professionally printed, flat-spined, with glossy card cover, $3.95. **"We consider reprints of books of poetry as well as new poems. If submitting a book for reprint, *all* reviews of the book should be submitted as well. Submit sample of work, never *entire* original pgs." Reports in 1 month or less. Payment varies in each case. Buys all rights.** The editor says, "We are a small publishing house that publishes few books (in general) each year. Still, we have published many well-known authors and are always receptive to new writers of every kind—and from all parts of the world."

‡THE BRIAR CLIFF REVIEW (II, IV-Regional), Briar Cliff College, 3303 Rebecca St., Sioux City IA 51104, founded 1989, poetry editor Jeanne Emmons, is an attractive annual "eclectic literary and cultural magazine focusing on (but not limited to) Siouxland writers and subjects." **They want "quality poetry with strong imagery; especially interested in regional, Midwestern content with tight, direct, well-wrought language. No suicide notes, anguished teen-aged reflections or allegorical emotional landscapes."** They have recently published poetry by Karen Jobst, James Autry, Ken McCullough and Ann Struthers. As a sample the editor selected these lines from "Custer Nat'l Park" by Diane Glancy:

> *There are times I think*
> *how the wilderness is a wool sweater dried on high*
> *when cleaners are called for in the label*
> *at the back of the neck.*
> *Even the sky comes around with a sack.*

BCR is 64 pgs., 8½×11, professionally printed on 70 lb. matte paper, saddle-stapled, four-color cover on 10 pt. coated stock, b&w photos inside. They receive about 100 poems a year, accept 12. Press run is 500, all shelf sales. Single copy: $4. **Sample postpaid: $5. No previously published poems; simultaneous submissions OK. "We will assume that submissions are not simultaneous unless notified." Cover letter with short bio required. "No manuscripts returned without SASE." Reads submissions August 1 through November 1.** Time between acceptance and publication is 5-6 months. **Seldom comments on rejections. Reports in 6 months. Pays 2 copies. Acquires first serial rights.** *Briar Cliff Review*'s 1994 issue was awarded the Gold Crown Award from Columbia Scholastic Press Association and the All American (with five marks of Distinction) by the National Scholastic Press Association at the University of Minnesota.

THE BRIDGE: A JOURNAL OF FICTION AND POETRY (II), 14050 Vernon St., Oak Park MI 48237, founded 1990, editor Jack Zucker, appears twice a year using **"exciting, largely mainstream poetry."** They have published poetry by Ruth Whitman and Daniel Hughes. It is 192 pgs., digest-sized, perfect-bound. Press run is 700. Subscription: $8. **Sample postpaid: $5.** An editorial board of 3 considers mss; decision made by editor and 1 special editor. **Editor rarely comments on submissions. Pays 2 copies. Acquires first rights.** Reviews books of poetry and prose in 1-10 pgs. Poetry published in *The Bridge* has been selected for inclusion in *The Best American Poetry 1994*.

BROADSHEET MAGAZINE (IV-Feminist, regional), P.O. Box 56147, Auckland, Aotearoa, New Zealand, phone 09-3764857, founded 1972, is a quarterly appearing in March, June, September and December. "We are now run as a voluntary concern and **publish limited poetry at present, all by New Zealand women poets and written from a feminist perspective."** They have published poetry by Margaret Berry and Sue Rifelelt. It is 64 pgs., newsprint. Subscription: $27.50 NZ; overseas: $45 NZ (airmail). **Sample postpaid: $9 NZ. Pays 1 copy.**

BROKEN STREETS (I, IV-Religious), 57 Morningside Dr. E., Bristol CT 06010, founded 1979, editor Ron Grossman, is a **"Christian-centered outreach ministry to poets."** The editor wants **"Christian-centered poetry, feelings, etc., usually 5-15 lines, but also haiku. No more than 3 poems at a time. Not necessary to query, but helpful."** He has published Bettye K. Wray and Naomi Rhoads. The magazine, which appears twice a year, is 40-50 pgs., digest-sized, photocopied typescript with card cover. Uses about 300 of the 500 poems submitted/year—by folks of all ages, including children and senior citizens. Press run is 1,000. Subscription: $10 (includes "all mailings and current chapbook"). **Sample postpaid: $4. No previously published poems. Cover letter required. Reports in 1 week. No pay but copies.** Reviews books of poetry. Open to unsolicited reviews. Poets may also send books for review consideration.

BROOKLYN REVIEW (II), 2900 Bedford Ave., Brooklyn College, Brooklyn NY 11210, founded 1974, editors change each year, address correspondence to poetry editor. They have published such poets as Allen Ginsberg, Elaine Equi, Amy Gerstler, Eileen Myles, Alice Notley, Honor Moore, Ron Padgett and David Trinidad. *BR* is an annual, 128 pgs., digest-sized, flat-spined, professionally printed with glossy color cover and art. Circulation 750. **Sample postpaid: $6. "Please send no more than four poems." Cover letter with brief history required. Reads submissions September 1 through December 1 only. Reports in 6 weeks to 6 months. Pays copies.** Poetry published in *BR* has also been selected for inclusion in *The Best American Poetry 1992*.

BRUNSWICK PUBLISHING CORPORATION (I), 1386 Lawrenceville Plank Rd., Lawrenceville VA 23868, phone (804)848-3865, founded 1978, poetry editor Dr. Walter J. Raymond, is a **partial subsidy publisher. Query with 3-5 samples. Response in 2 weeks with SASE. If invited, submit double-spaced, typed ms. Reports in 3-4 weeks, reading fee only if you request written evaluation. Always sends prepublication galleys. Poet pays 50-80% of cost, gets same percentage of profits for market-tester edition of 500, advertised by leaflets mailed to reviewers, libraries, book buyers and bookstores**. As a sample we selected these lines from " 'Round And 'Round We'd Twirl" by Dee Brown:

> *I remember when I was just a little girl*
> *You would pick me up and 'round and 'round we'd twirl*
>
> *You'd stop to catch your breath*
> *All the while, I begged for more*
> *Now, as I reminisce of those days so long ago*
> *I close my eyes, to watch us twirl across the floor*

That's from her book *Beyond What You See*, 54 pgs., digest-sized, flat-spined, neatly printed, glossy cover with photo. Cost: $9.95. **Send SASE for catalog to order samples and "Statement of Philosophy and Purpose," which explains terms**. That Statement says: "We publish books because that is what we like to do. Every new book published is like a new baby, an object of joy! We do not attempt to unduly influence the reading public as to the value of our publications, but we simply let the readers decide that themselves. We refrain from the artificial beefing up of values that are not there. . . . We are not competitors in the publishing world, but offer what we believe is a needed service. We strongly believe that in an open society every person who has something of value to say and wants to say it should have the chance and opportunity to do so."

BUFFALO SPREE MAGAZINE (II), 4511 Harlem Rd., Buffalo NY 14226, founded 1967, poetry editor Janet Goldenberg, is the quarterly regional magazine of western New York. It has a controlled circulation (21,000) in the Buffalo area, mostly distributed free (with 3,000 subscriptions, of which 25 are libraries). Its glossy pages feature general-interest articles about local culture, plus book reviews, fiction and poetry contributed nationally. It receives about 300 poetry submissions/year and uses about 25, which have ranged from work by Robert Hass and Carl Dennis to first publications by younger poets. As a sample the editor selected these lines from "Alien in Spring" by Martha Bosworth:

> *I am a tall pale animal in boots*
> *trampling forget-me-nots and scaring birds*
> *from the lemon tree: with my long-handled claw*
> *I pull down lemons—tear-shaped, dimpled, round,*
> *bouncing they vanish into vines and weeds.*

They use 5-7 poems/issue, **these are selected 3-6 months prior to publication. Sample postpaid: $3.75. Submit 1-6 poems at a time. Considers simultaneous submissions, "but we must be advised that poems have been or are being submitted elsewhere." Pays $25/poem.**

‡BUTTON MAGAZINE; THIMBLE PRESS (I, II), P.O. Box 876, Lunenburg MA 01462, founded 1993, poetry editor Mark P. Timms, "is New England's tiniest quarterly of fiction, poetry and gracious living." **They want poetry about the quiet surprises in life, not sentimental.** They have recently published poetry by William Corbett, David Barber, Emerson Sargent Foster and John Grey. As a sample we selected these lines from "love" by Christopher P. Mulholland:

> *It's on the 82nd floor*
> *in the janitor's closet*
> *behind the mop and bucket*
> *in the corner*
> *that hasn't been swept for years. . . .*

Button is 26 pgs., 4¼ × 5½, saddle-stitched, card stock cover with illustrations that incorporate one or more buttons (our favorite shows the Statue of Liberty holding needle and thread). *The Boston Globe* called it charmingly homemade in feel and and liked "its lack of pretension and its quirky humor." Press run is 1,200 for more than 300 subscribers; 300 shelf sales. Single copy: $1; subscription: $6/year. **Sample postpaid: $1. Submit up to 4 poems at a time. No previously published poems; simultaneous submissions OK. Cover letter required.** Time between acceptance and publication is 3-6 months. **Poems are circulated to an editorial board. Often comments on rejections. Send SASE for guidelines. Reports in 4-7 weeks. Pays 2 year subscription and authors copies. Acquires first North American serial rights.** Thimble Press **publishes 2 chapbooks/year. Query first, with sample poems and cover letter with brief bio and publication credits. Replies to queries in 6 weeks. Pays half net profit and 30 author's copies. For sample, send $1 "and request '*The Reluctant Butterfly*,' our first publication."** The editor says, "We walk a fine line between positive thinking and realism. We hate self-pity and braggadocio. Please wait three months between submissions and be aware there is a difference between writing to write and writing to publish."

BYLINE MAGAZINE (IV-Writing), P.O. Box 130596, Edmond OK 73013, founded 1981, editor Marcia Preston, poetry editor Betty Shipley, is a **magazine for the encouragement of writers and poets, using 8-10 poems/issue about writers or writing.** As a sample the editor selected these lines from "A Prayer for Words" by John D. Engle, Jr.:

> *I have had enough*
> *of words that sigh*
> *their meekness*
> *on the margins of the mind.*
> *I want the centered word*
> *that holds a high*
> *degree of mystery*
> *no one can find*
> *explained in any*
> *common dictionary.*

Byline is professionally printed, magazine-sized, with illustrations, cartoons and ads. They have about 3,000 subscriptions and receive about 2,500 poetry submissions/year, of which they use 144. **Sample postpaid: $4. No more than 4 poems/submission, no reprints. Send SASE for guidelines. Reports within 6 weeks. Pays $5-10/poem. Buys first North American serial rights.** Sponsors monthly poetry contests. Send #10 SASE for details. Marcia Preston advises, "We are happy to work with new writers, but please read a few samples to get an idea of our style. We would like to see more serious poetry about the creative experience (as it concerns writing)."

BYRON POETRY WORKS (I, IV-Regional), P.O. Box 221, Yellow Springs OH 45387, founded 1993, editor J.L. Preston, is "a journal of regional poetry" appearing twice a year. **"*BPW* features poetry from Ohio and its bordering states—Indiana, Kentucky, Michigan, Pennsylvania and West Virginia. We are open to all types of poetry. Poems about our region welcome! No extremely long poems (100 lines maximum) or foreign language poems."** They have recently published poetry by Robert Miltner, Kenneth Leonhardt and Mary Weems. As a sample the editor selected these lines from "Jackhammer Writing" by Pamela Steed Hill:

> *The poet sits down to dance to the rhythm*
> *to think to the rhythm of the black*
> *and the bright. He sits down under*
> *a strobe light. Shudders without moving*
> *a bone. Dreams the big dream: to hum*
> *to the music of the jack.*

BPW is 28 pgs., 5½×8½, photocopied and saddle-stapled with card cover, b&w graphics and a few ads. They accept approximately 30% of submissions. Press run is 70 for 20 subscribers. Subscription: $5/year. **Sample postpaid: $2. Make checks payable to Terri Howard-Preston, associate editor. Submit 3 poems at a time. No previously published poems or simultaneous submissions. Cover letter not required, "but certainly welcomed and encouraged." Submissions from outside Ohio, Indiana, Kentucky, Michigan, Pennsylvania and West Virginia are not considered, but will be returned. Reads submissions January 1 through April 30 for spring issue and June 1 through September 30 for fall. Often comments on rejections. Send SASE for guidelines. Reports in about 2 months. Pays 1 copy. Acquires one-time rights.** The editor says, "Enjoy expressing yourself with poetry. Don't worry so much about being published. Write your best and be true to your vision. Publication will come. There are many 'little magazines' like ours all over the country. It is encouraging to know that publishing is never very far from the average person. Poetry is alive and well in the U.S."

C.L.A.S.S. MAGAZINE (IV-Regional), Dept. PM, 900 Broadway, Eighth Floor, New York NY 10003, phone (212)677-3055, editor Denolyn Carroll, is a monthly magazine, covering **Caribbean/American/ African Third World** news and views. It has a slick full-sized format with full-color glossy paper cover. Circulation 250,000. Subscription: $12.95, $18 overseas. **Sample: $2.95. Publishes 10-20 poems a year, 22-30 lines, on appropriate themes. Submit maximum of 10 poems. Pays maximum of $10.**

‡CADMUS EDITIONS (III), P.O. Box 687, Tiburon CA 94920, founded 1979, editor Jeffrey Miller, publishes hardback and paperback editions of poetry: **"only that which is distinguished."** They have published poetry by Federico García Lorca, Tom Clark, Bradford Morrow and Carol Tinker. These sample lines are by Ed Dorn:

> *The common duty of the poet*
> *in this era of massive disfunction*
> *& generalized onslaught upon alertness*
> *is to maintain the plant*
> *to the end that the mumbling horde*
> *bestirs its pruned tongue.*

Query first, no samples, with "an intelligent literate letter accompanied by a SASE." Replies to queries in 1 month, to mss (if invited to submit) in 1-2 months. Contracts are for 5-10% royalties. Comments "occasionally but not often in that most unsolicited submissions do not warrant same."

THE CAFÉ REVIEW (II), c/o Yes Books, 20 Danforth St., Portland ME 04101, phone (207)775-3233, founded 1989, editors Steve Luttrell and Wayne Atherton, is a quarterly which has grown out of open poetry readings held at a Portland cafe. The editors say they aim "to print the best work we can!" **They want "free verse, 'beat' inspired and fresh. Nothing rhyming or clichéd."** They have published poetry by Denise Levertov, Gerard Malanga and Anne Waldman. As a sample the editor selected these lines from "Cream Hidden" by Michael McClure, beginning with lines by Rumi:

> *"LIKE CREAM HIDDEN IN THE SOUL OF MILK*
> *no-place keeps coming into place."*
> *No-place is where I am at.*
> *My soil is where no toil*
> *will upearth it.*

The Review is 50-60 pgs., 5½×8½, professionally printed and perfect-bound with card cover, b&w art, no ads. They receive over 300 submissions a year, accept approximately 25%. Press run is 200 for 50 subscribers of which 8 are libraries, 50-75 shelf sales. Subscription: $16. **Sample postpaid: $4. No previously published poems or simultaneous submissions. Cover letter with brief bio required. "We usually respond with a form letter indicating acceptance or rejection of work, seldom with additional comments." Reports in 2-4 months. Pays 1 copy.** They also publish 1-2 chapbooks/year. For those interested, poetry readings are still held on second Tuesday evenings, September through May. Write for information.

CALAPOOYA COLLAGE; $1,000 CAROLYN KIZER POETRY AWARDS (V), P.O. Box 309, Monmouth OR 97361, phone (503)838-6292, founded 1981, editor Thomas L. Ferte. *CC* is a literary annual using **"all kinds" of poetry. However, the annual will not be published again until August 1997. Submissions welcome beginning January 1997.** They have published poetry by Robert Bly, Joseph

Bruchac, Octavio Paz, Marge Piercy, Etheridge Knight, Vassar Miller, William Stafford, Ursula K. LeGuin, Patricia Goedicke, David Wagoner and David Ray. It is 48 pgs., tabloid-sized. Press run is 1,500 for 250 subscribers of which 16 are libraries. They accept about 6% of 6,000 poems received annually. **Sample postpaid: $5. Reads submissions September 1 through June 1 only. Best times for submissions are January and February. Reports in 1-2 months. Pays 2 copies.** Reviews books of poetry in 600-1,000 words. Open to unsolicited reviews. Poets may also send books for review consideration. All poems accepted for publication are eligible for annual $1,000 Carolyn Kizer Poetry Awards.

CALDER PUBLICATIONS LTD.; RIVERRUN PRESS INC.; ASSOCIATION CALDER (V), 179 Kings Cross Rd., London WC1X 9BZ England, phone 0171-833-1300, publisher John Calder, is a literary book publisher. On their list are Samuel Beckett, Breyten Breytenbach, Erich Fried, Paul Eluard, Pier Paolo Passolini and Howard Barker. **"We do not read for the public,"** says John Calder, and he wants **no unsolicited mss.** "Any communication which requires a response should be sent with a SAE."

CALLALOO (IV-Ethnic), Dept. PM, Dept. of English, University of Virginia, Charlottesville VA 22093, phone (804)924-6616, founded 1976, editor Charles H. Rowell. Devoted to **poetry dealing with North America, Europe, Africa, Latin and Central America, South America and the Caribbean**. They have published poetry by Rita Dove, Jay Wright, Alice Walker, Yusef Komunyakaa, Aimé Césaire, Nicolás Guillén and Jimmy Santiago Baca. Visually beautiful and well-edited with thematic, powerful poems in all forms and styles, this thick quarterly journal features about 15-20 poems in each issue (along with concise and scholarly book reviews). Circulation is 1,400, with 1,400 subscriptions of which half are libraries. Subscription: $27, $54 for institutions. **"We have no specifications for submitting poetry except authors should include SASE." Reports in 6 months. Pays copies.** Poetry published in *Callaloo* has been included in the 1992, 1994 and 1995 volumes of *The Best American Poetry*.

CALYX, A JOURNAL OF ART & LITERATURE BY WOMEN (IV-Women, lesbian), P.O. Box B, Corvallis OR 97339, phone (503)753-9384, founded 1976, managing editor M. Donnelly, is a journal edited by a collective editorial board, **publishes poetry, prose, art, book reviews and interviews by and about women.** They want **"excellently crafted poetry that also has excellent content."** They have published poetry by Diane Glancy, Robin Morgan, Lyn Lifshin, Kathleen Crown and Eleanor Wilner. As a sample the editor selected these lines from "Surviving" by Gail Tremblay:

> I dream of dancing naked under stars,
> the dew on grass dampening my ankles,
> the moon, sensuous ancestor, calling
> to my blood. I dream the impossible
> moment when tongues touch, try to forget
> how much I've lost.

Each issue is 7 × 8, handsomely printed on heavy paper, flat-spined, glossy color cover, 125-200 pgs., of which 50-60 are poetry. Poems tend to be lyric free verse that makes strong use of image and symbol melding unobtrusively with voice and theme. **Sample for the single copy price: $8 plus $1.50 postage. In 1996, *Calyx* is open to submissions October 1 through November 15 only. Mss received when not open to reading will be returned unread. Send up to 6 poems with SASE and short bio. "We accept copies in good condition and clearly readable. We focus on new writing, but occasionally publish a previously published piece." Simultaneous submissions OK, "if kept up-to-date on publication." Guidelines available for SASE. Reports in 2-6 months. Pays cash and copies.** Open to unsolicited reviews. Poets may also send books for review consideration. *Calyx* has received the 1993-1994 American Literary Magazine Award for best cover design and an honorable mention for editorial content. They say, "Read the publication and be familiar with what we have published."

CAMELLIA; CAMELLIA PRESS INC. (II), P.O. Box 417, Village Station, New York NY 10014-0417, editor Tomer Inbar, associate editor Beth Stevens. *Camellia* is a biannual poetry magazine "currently available for free in the San Francisco/Oakland Bay area, Madison, Seattle, Ithaca and D.C., or by sending a 55¢ SASE. **We publish poetry in the W.C. Williams tradition. The poetry of things, moment and sharpness. We encourage young writers and like to work with the writers who**

Market conditions are constantly changing! If you're still using this book and it is 1997 or later, buy the newest edition of Poet's Market *at your favorite bookstore or order directly from* Writer's Digest Books.

publish with us. Our main goal is to get the poetry out. We do not want to see poetry where the poem is subordinate to the poet or poetry where the noise of the poetic overshadows the voice. We look for poetry that is honest and sharp and unburdened." As a sample the editor selected this poem, "Dear Bill," by Jeff Vetock:

> *These bees matter*
> *for a day, from the door*
> *in summer he moves*
> *willingly often enough*
> *outside to tree*
> *no longer weather*
> *like a page turns*
> *to notice in time*
> *some sunlit sparrow*
> *for now, this*

Camellia is 20-24 pgs., digest-sized, desktop-published. The first thing that catches your eye is the design. The editors make up for this modest-looking, stapled publication with creative typesetting inside, featuring lively avant-garde or imagistic free verse with titles in large points and varied fonts. "We receive approximately 300-350 poems/issue and publish about 20." Press run is 500-900. Subscription: $5/year, $7 overseas. **Sample: 55¢ SASE. Submit 8 poems at a time. Simultaneous submissions and previously published poems OK. "Cover letters are helpful, but shouldn't go overboard. Sometimes the cover letters are more interesting than the poetry received." Reports "ASAP." Pays 2 copies. Editor comments on submissions "if asked for or if I want to see more but am not satisfied with the poems sent.** We currently publish two regular issues per year and are instituting a series of special project issues. The first, a chapbook of poems by Jerry Mirskin entitled *Picture A Gate Hanging Open And Let That Gate Be The Sun*, is now available for $5 from Camellia Press Inc. The second is a poster of poetry, photographs and design using poems from the first 6 years of *Camellia*." **They send prepublication galleys only for chapbooks.**

CANADIAN AUTHOR; CANADIAN AUTHORS ASSOCIATION (III), 275 Slater St., Suite 500, Ottawa, Ontario K1P 5H9 Canada, poetry editor Sheila Martindale. *Canadian Author*, a quarterly, is magazine-sized, 28 pgs., professionally printed, with paper cover in 2 colors. It contains articles useful to writers at all levels of experience. **Sample postpaid: $4.50. Buys 40 poems a year. "The trend is toward thematic issues and profiles of featured poets, so query letters are recommended." Pays $15 plus one copy.** (See also Canadian Authors Association Literary Awards in the Contests and Awards section.)

CANADIAN DIMENSION: THE MAGAZINE FOR PEOPLE WHO WANT TO CHANGE THE WORLD (III, IV-Political), 401-228 Notre Dame Ave., Winnipeg, Manitoba R3B 1N7 Canada, phone (204)957-1519, fax (204)943-4617, e-mail info@canadiandimension.mb.ca, founded 1964, editorial contact Brenda Austin-Smith, appears 6 times/year, using **"short poems on labour, women, native, gay/lesbian and other issues. Nothing more than one page."** They have published poetry by Tom Wayman and Milton Acorn. It is 48-56 pgs., magazine-sized, slick, professionally printed, with glossy paper cover. Press run is 3,500 for 2,600 subscribers of which 800 are libraries, 1,000 shelf sales. Subscription: $30.50 US ($24.50 Canadian). **Sample postpaid: $2. Submit 1-5 poems at a time. Simultaneous submissions OK, if notified. Previously published poems are unlikely to be accepted. Editor comments on submissions "rarely." Publishes theme issues. Send SASE (or SAE and IRC) for upcoming themes.** Reviews books of poetry in 750-1,200 words, single or multi-book format. "We are broadly political—that is, not narrowly sloganeering, but profoundly sensitive to the connections between words and the state of the world. Topics can be personal as well as political. Also, American writers are reminded to include Canadian return postage or its equivalent in reply coupons, etc."

CANADIAN LITERATURE (IV-Regional), 2029 West Mall, University of British Columbia, Vancouver, British Columbia V6T 1Z2 Canada, phone (604)822-2780, founded 1959, editor W.H. New, is a quarterly review which publishes **poetry by Canadian poets. "No limits on form. Less room for long poems."** They have published poetry by Atwood, Ondaatje, Layton and Bringhurst. As a sample the editor selected these lines from "Subtexts" by Susan Ioannou:

> *Imagine words are snow we crawl under*
> *and scratch at matted ice for crocuses.*
>
> *Or, flattened on our backs in white,*
> *that words fan angel wings.*
>
> *And how could we forget*
> *that clouds are words too?*

Each issue is professionally printed, digest-sized, flat-spined, with 176 pgs., of which about 10 are poetry. They receive 100-300 submissions/year, use 10-12. Circulation 1,500, two-thirds of which are libraries. **Sample for the cover price: $15 Canadian plus postage and GST. No simultaneous submissions or reprints. Cover letter and SASE required. Reports within the month. "Accepted poems must be available on diskette." Pays $10/poem plus 1 copy. Buys first rights.** Reviews books of poetry in 500-1,000 words, depending on the number of books.

CANADIAN WRITER'S JOURNAL (IV-Writing); WIND SONGS (IV-Form/style), Gordon M. Smart Publications, P.O. Box 6618, Depot 1, Victoria, British Columbia V8P 5N7 Canada, is a small quarterly, publishing mainly short "how-to" articles of interest to writers at all levels. They use a few **"short poems or portions thereof as part of 'how-to' articles relating to the writing of poetry and occasional short poems with tie-in to the writing theme."** The Wind Songs column of *CWJ* accepts **unpublished poems including haiku, senryu, tanka, sijo, one-liner renga and sequences. Maximum 15 lines. Submit 5 poems or less (identify each form)** to Elizabeth St. Jacques, Poetry Editor, 406 Elizabeth St., Sault Ste. Marie, Ontario P6B 3H4 Canada. **Include SASE ("U.S. postage accepted; do not affix to envelope"). Token payment.** Subscription: $15 for 1 year, $25 for 2 years. **Sample: $4.** The magazine runs an annual poetry competition with closing date June 30. Send SASE for current rules.

CANDLESTONES (V), P.O. Box 10703, St. Petersburg FL 33733, founded 1990, editor Ann Blain, is a biannual literary arts magazine. "The purpose is to encourage artists and poets who have not been published and share creativity with people who usually do not buy poetry." They publish poetry, b&w art and photos, and short stories. **"I want poetry the poet is proud of. Some long poems are accepted and I always need short poems. No poems containing profanity. No pornographic poetry."** As a sample the editor selected these lines by Holly Blain:

> *Sun-dappled kisses*
> *Echo off my skin to you*
> *Caught in the web of our love.*
> *We stare*
> *and understand.*

"We accept simultaneous submissions and previously published works. We like cover letters just because they are interesting reading. However, at this time we are overstocked." Seldom comments on rejections. Reports in 3 months or longer. Pays 3 copies. The editor says, "*Candlestones* is an outgrowth of a monthly coffee house held in my home. Most contributors are under 30. Its twofold purpose is to give people a chance to have their creative efforts viewed by others and show the general populace (people who would never buy a book of poetry) the artistic achievement around them. It has been distributed in gas stations, factories, bookstores, record stores and beauty parlors. My advice is to submit. If one place rejects it, submit somewhere else. One poet I know wrote a poem in 1922. When it was submitted in 1990, it was printed. Don't wait so long. But be patient with the small press."

THE CAPE ROCK (II), Department of English, Southeast Missouri State University, Cape Girardeau MO 63701, phone (314)651-2500, founded 1964, editor Dr. Harvey Hecht, appears twice yearly and consists of **64 pgs. of poetry and photography, with a $200 prize for the best poem in each issue and $100 for featured photography. "No restrictions on subjects or forms. Our criterion for selection is the quality of the work. We prefer poems under 70 lines; no long poems or books, no sentimental, didactic or cute poems."** They have published poetry by Stephen Dunning, Joyce Odam, Judith Phillips Neeld, Lyn Lifshin, Virginia Brady Young, Gary Pacernik and Laurel Speer. As a sample the editor selected these lines from "At The Rodin Museum, Stanford" by Fred D. White:

> *The lovers unleash their passion on the hot*
> *summer grass of the sculpture garden,*
> *surrounded by metal longing.*
>
> *They drop wild desires into each other's mouths*
> *like mother birds.*

It's a handsomely printed, flat-spined, digest-sized magazine. Their circulation is about 500, with 200 subscribers, of whom half are libraries. Single copy: $5; subscription: $7/year. **Sample: $3. Submit 3-7 poems at a time. Guidelines available for SASE.** They have a 2- to 8-month backlog and **report in 1-3 months. Do not submit mss in May, June or July. Pays 2 copies.** This is a solid publication that features a wide selection of forms and styles, leaning in recent years toward free verse that establishes a mood or milieu.

CAPERS AWEIGH MAGAZINE (I, IV-Regional), P.O. Box 96, Sydney, Nova Scotia B1P 6G9 Canada, founded 1992, publisher John MacNeil, is a quarterly of **poetry and short fiction "of, by and for Cape Bretoners at home and away." They want work by Cape Bretoners only. Nothing profane.** The publisher says it is 50-60 pgs., 5×8, desktop-published, stapled, including computer graphics and trade ads. Press run is 500. Subscription: $20. **Sample postpaid: $5. No simultaneous submissions. Cover letter required. Seldom comments on rejections. Pays 1 copy.**

THE CAPILANO REVIEW (III), 2055 Purcell Way, North Vancouver, British Columbia V7J 3H5 Canada, phone (604)984-1712, fax (604)983-7520, founded 1972, editor Robert Sherrin, is a literary and visual media review appearing 3 times/year. **They want avant-garde, experimental, previously unpublished work, "poetry of sustained intelligence and imagination."** *TCR* comes in a handsome digest-sized format, 150 pgs., flat-spined, finely printed, semi-glossy stock with a glossy full-color card cover. Circulation: 1,000. **Sample: $9 prepaid. Do not submit mss during June and July. No simultaneous submissions. Reports in up to 6 months. Pays an honorarium plus 2 copies.**

CAPPER'S (I, IV-Nature, inspirational, religious, humor), 1503 SW 42nd St., Topeka KS 66609-1265, founded 1879, editor Nancy Peavler, is a biweekly tabloid (newsprint) going to **370,000 mail subscribers, mostly small-town and farm people. Uses 6-8 poems in each issue. They want short poems (4-10 lines preferred, lines of one-column width) "relating to everyday situations, nature, inspirational, humorous."** They have published poetry by Helen Harrington, Emma Walker, Sheryl Nelms, Alice Mackenzie Swaim, Ralph W. Seager and Ida Fasel. As a sample we selected these lines from "Out West" by Jeannine Thyreen:

> *I want to see mountains etched in*
> *the distance,*
> *where God stretches the land and*
> *stars,*
> *holding the ends with His*
> *fingertips, arms opened wide.*

Send $1 for sample. Not available on newsstand. "Most poems used in *Capper's* **are upbeat in tone and offer the reader a bit of humor, joy, enthusiasm or encouragement. Short poems of this type fit our format best." Submit 4-6 poems at a time. No simultaneous submissions. Now returns mss with SASE. Reports within 4-5 months. Pays $10-15/poem. Buys one-time rights.** The editor says "Poems chosen are upbeat, sometimes humorous, always easily understood."

THE CARIBBEAN WRITER; THE DAILY NEWS PRIZE; THE PAIEWONSKY PRIZE (IV-Regional), University of the Virgin Islands, RR 02, P.O. Box 10,000, Kingshill, St. Croix, USVI 00850, phone (809)692-4152, founded 1987, editor Dr. Erika Waters, is an annual literary magazine **with a Caribbean focus. The Caribbean must be central to the literary work or the work must reflect a Caribbean heritage, experience or perspective.** They have published poetry by Derek Walcott, Phillis Gershator and Ian McDonald. As a sample the editor selected the opening lines of "Nineteen Ninety-Two" by Howard Fergus:

> *Dawns 1992 a magic landfall*
> *on a brand new world of gold*
> *in Europe. Columbus makes a second*
> *coming after five hundred years*
> *not to violate virgin peoples*
> *but to carnival God for earlier conquests*

The magazine is 190 pgs., 6×9, handsomely printed on heavy pebbled stock, flat-spined, with glossy card cover, using advertising and b&w art by Caribbean artists. Press run is 1,000. Single copy: $9 plus $1.50 postage; subscription: $18 for 2 years. **Sample: $5 plus $1.50 postage. Send SASE for guidelines. (Note: Postage to and from the Virgin Islands is the same as within the US.) Simultaneous submissions OK. Blind submissions only: name, address, phone number and title of ms should appear in cover letter along with brief bio. Title only on ms. Deadline is September 30 of each year.** The annual appears in the spring. **Pays 2 copies. Acquires first North American serial rights.** Reviews books of poetry and fiction in 500 words. Open to unsolicited reviews. Poets may also send books for review consideration. The magazine annually awards The Daily News Prize of $300 for the best poem or poems and The Paiewonsky Prize of $100 for first-time publication.

‡CARN; THE CELTIC LEAGUE (IV-Ethnic), 11 Hilltop View, Braddan, Isle of Man, founded 1973, general secretary Bernard Moffatt, is a magazine-sized quarterly, circulation 2,000. "The aim of our quarterly is to contribute to a **fostering of cooperation between the Celtic peoples,** developing the consciousness of the special relationship which exists between them and making their achievements and their struggle for cultural and political freedom better known abroad. Contributions to *Carn* come **through invitation to people whom we know as qualified to write more or less in accordance with that aim. We would welcome poems** *in the Celtic languages* **if they are relating to that aim.** If I had to put it briefly, we have a political commitment, or, in other words, *Carn* **is not a literary magazine."** Reviews books of poetry only if in the Celtic languages.

CARNEGIE MELLON MAGAZINE (II, IV-Specialized: university affiliation), Carnegie Mellon University, Pittsburgh PA 15213, phone (412)268-2132, editor Ann Curran, is the **alumni magazine** for

the university and **limits selections to writers connected with the university.** As a sample the editor
selected these lines from "Raw October" by Jim Daniels, associate professor of English:

> We toss eggs
> at cars, houses,
> Crazy Eddie chases
> us down the street
> Larry rips
> his shirt on a fence . . .

**Submit 3 poems at a time (typed, double-spaced, with SASE) to Gerald Costanzo, poetry editor.
No payment.** Only uses staff-written reviews.

‡THE CAROLINA QUARTERLY; THE CHARLES B. WOOD AWARD (II), Greenlaw Hall, CB
#3520, University of North Carolina, Chapel Hill NC 27599-3520, founded 1948, poetry editor Carrie
Blackstock, appears 3 times a year primarily publishing fiction and poetry. **They have no specifications
regarding form, length, subject matter or style of poetry.** They have recently published poetry by
Stephen Dunn, Mark Doty, Denise Levertov and X.J. Kennedy. As a sample the editor selected these
lines from "Jacob" by George Garrett:

> Came then in the dark
> Out of the dark a dark
> Man without name or number
> > a brute fact
> > a sweet dream
> labor of love and death

TCQ is about 90 pgs., 6 × 9, professionally printed and perfect-bound with one-color matte card cover,
a few graphics and ads. They receive about 6,000 poems a year, accept less than 1%. Press run is 1,500
for 200 library subscriptions and various shelf sales. Single copy: $4; subscription: $10. **Sample
postpaid: $5. No previously published poems or simultaneous submissions. "Every manuscript is
read by at least two people. Manuscripts that make it to the meeting of the full poetry staff are
discussed by all. Any poem with strong support of one or more people is accepted."** Seldom
comments on rejections. **Send SASE for guidelines. Reports in 2 months. Pays 4 copies. Acquires
first rights.** Reviews books of poetry. Open to unsolicited reviews. Poets may also send books for
review consideration (attn: Editor). The Charles B. Wood Award for Distinguished Writing is given to
the author of the best poem or short story published in each volume of *The Carolina Quarterly*. Only
those writers *without* major publications are considered and the winner receives $500.

CAROLINA WREN PRESS (II, IV-Women, ethnic, gay/lesbian, social issues), 120 Morris St.,
Durham NC 27701, phone (919)560-2738, founded 1976, publishes 1 book/year, **"primarily women
and minorities, though men and majorities also welcome."** They have published poetry by Jaki
Shelton Green, Mary Kratt and Steven Blaski. **Send book-length mss only. Reports in 2-4 months.
Pays 10% of print run in copies. Send 9½ × 12 SASE for catalog and guidelines (include postage
for 3 ounces).**

CAT FANCY (IV-Specialized, children), P.O. Box 6050, Mission Viejo CA 92690, phone (714)855-
8822, founded 1965, editor Debbie Phillips-Donaldson. *Cat Fancy* is a magazine-sized monthly that
uses **poems on the subject of cats. "No more than 30 short lines; open on style and form, but a
conservative approach is recommended. In our children's department we occasionally use longer,
rhyming verse that tells a story about cats. No eulogies for pets that have passed away."** They have
published poetry by Lola Sneyd and Edythe G. Tornow. Press run is 368,575 for 303,328 subscribers,
37,502 shelf sales. Subscription: $23.97. **Sample postpaid: $5.50. Submit ms with name and address
"in upper left-hand corner." Editor sometimes comments on submissions, "especially if the ms is
appealing but just misses the mark for our audience." Reports in 6-8 weeks. Pays $20/poem plus 2
copies.** She says, "We have an audience that very much appreciates sensitive and touching work about
cats. As for advice—get input from knowledgeable sources as to the marketability of your work, and be
open to learning how your work might be improved. Then send it out, and hang on. Rejection may not
mean your work is bad. We are able to accept very few submissions, and the competition is fierce.
Timing and luck have a lot to do with acceptance, so keep trying!"

CATAMOUNT PRESS (II, IV-Anthology), 2519 Roland Rd. SW, Huntsville AL 35805, founded
1992, editor Georgette Perry, publishes 1-2 chapbooks and 1 anthology/year. **During 1996, the philosophy at Catamount will be "Think small." Plans include a mini-anthology of short nature poems,
12 lines or less, and several micro-size (4½ × 5½) Monad Chapbooks, each containing 10-12 poems
by one author. "Before submitting a chapbook ms, send 3 unattached 32¢ stamps for guidelines
and sample, so that your submission will fit the format."** Poets recently published include June
Owens and Richard Davignon. As a sample the editor selected these lines from "Poem for the Earth"
by Jeanne Shannon:

> *Earth, frail as a rose in hailstone weather,*
> *accept our meditations for your healing.*

> *Accept our thanks for*
> *a flood-scoured gorge on the Gauley River,*

> *the cry of loons,*
> *the dolphins' play,*

> *the boat-billed heron's cloudy wings.*

The editor says, **"The best chance for publication is to submit 3-5 brief poems, with SASE and cover note.** I publish more free verse but do not rule out formal verse. **The poems that appeal to me tend to be subtle and understated, but I want a variety to choose from."** Previously published poems OK if author holds copyright. Often comments on rejections. Reports in 1 month. Pays copies.

THE CATHARTIC (II), P.O. Box 1391, Ft. Lauderdale FL 33302, phone (305)967-9378, founded 1974, edited by Patrick M. Ellingham, "is a **small biannual poetry magazine devoted to the unknown poet** with the understanding that most poets are unknown in America." He says, "While there is no specific type of poem I look for, **rhyme for the sake of rhyme is discouraged. Any subject matter except where material is racist or sexist in nature. Long poems, over 60 lines, are not right for this magazine normally. I would like to see some poems that take chances with both form and language.** I would like to see poems that get out of and forget about self ['I'] and look at the larger world and the people in it with an intensity that causes a reader to react or want to react to it. I am gravitating toward work that looks at the darker side of life, is intense and uses words sparingly." **Considers sexually explicit material.** Recently published poets include Joy Walsh, Alice Olds-Ellingson, Paul Dilsaver and Errol Miller. It's a modest, 28-page pamphlet, offset printed from computer-generated text, MSWord and Pagemaker, consisting mostly of poems and b&w drawings and photos. He receives over 1,000 submissions/year, uses about 60. No backlog. **Sample postpaid: $3. Submit 5-10 typed poems at a time. No previously published poems; simultaneous submissions OK. "Submissions without SASE are not considered or returned." Send SASE for guidelines. Reports in 1 month. Contributors receive 1 copy.** The editor advises, "The only way for poets to know whether their work will get published or not is to submit. It is also essential to read as much poetry as possible—both old and new. Spend time with the classics as well as the new poets. Support the presses that support you—the survival of both is essential to the life of poetry."

CATS MAGAZINE (IV-Specialized), P.O. Box 290037, Port Orange FL 32129, phone (904)788-2770, fax (904)788-2710, editor Tracey Copeland, is a monthly magazine **about cats, including light verse about cats in a column called "Few Lines 'Bout Felines,"** for cat enthusiasts of all types. They have recently published poetry by Helen Peppe, Elizabeth McClung, Simon Teakettle and Marilyn Helmer. As a sample we selected this complete poem, "Nobody's Fool," by Misty Gregory:

> *A cat's not fooled by all his toys,*
> *for these are naught but clever ploys*
> *to cunning skill distract.*

> *His hunt will his attention hold,*
> *though what he stalks cannot be told,*
> *nor when he might attack.*

Sample copy and writer's guidelines for $4 (including p&h). All submissions must have SASE. Publishes theme issues. Send SASE for upcoming themes. Reports in 3-4 months. Pays $5-30/ poem on publication.

CAVEAT LECTOR (III), 400 Hyde St., Apt. 606, San Francisco CA 94109, founded 1989, editors Christopher Bernard, James Bybee, Gordon Phipps and Andrew Towne, appears 3 times/year. "*Caveat Lector* is devoted to the arts and to cultural and philosophical commentary. We publish visual art and music as well as literary and theoretical texts." **They want poetry that is "technically polished and deeply felt—if humorous, actually funny. Classical to experimental. 200-line limit."** They have recently published poetry by Lyn Lifshin, Errol Miller, Voz de Fronz, Li Min Hua and Alfred Robinson. As a sample the editors selected these lines from "Matthew, do you ride?" by Zoon:

> *How can you rule a god*
> *who doesn't speak your language?*
> *Why? When the shadow of god's passage touches you*
> *you don't deny the awful unanticipated call —*
> *you rise.*

The editors say *CL* is 28-32 pgs., 6½ × 8½, offset and saddle-stitched. They receive about 100 poems a year, accept less than 10%. Press run is 500 for 100 subscribers of which 20 are libraries, 350 shelf sales. Single copy: $2.50; subscription: $10 for 4 issues. **Sample postpaid: $3. "Due to overstock, we are not encouraging submissions until the latter part of 1996." Simultaneous submissions OK.** Time between acceptance and publication is 6 months. **Often comments on rejections. Reports in 1 month. Pays 5 copies. Acquires first publication rights.** Christopher Bernard says, "The two rules of writing are: 1. Rewrite it again. 2. Rewrite it again. The writing level of most of our submissions is pleasingly high. A rejection by us is not always a criticism of the work, and we try to provide comments to our more promising submitters."

WM CAXTON LTD. (I, IV-Regional), 12037 Hwy. 42, Ellison Bay WI 54210, phone (414)854-2955, founded 1986, publisher K. Luchterhand. **"About 50% of our books involve an author's subvention of production costs with enhanced royalties and/or free copies in return," and the publisher acquires all rights.** They want **"any serious poetry, not children's or doggerel." Poetry must have Northern Midwest author or subject.** They have published books of poetry by David Koenig (*Green Whistle*), Marilyn Taylor (*Shadows Like These*), William Olson (*North of Death's Door*) and Caroline Sibr (*Moon Gold*). Write or call to purchase sample copies.

THE CENTENNIAL REVIEW (II), 312 Linton Hall, Michigan State University, East Lansing MI 48824-1044, phone (517)355-1905, e-mail cenrev@msu.edu, founded 1957, editor R.K. Meiners, appears 3 times/year. **They want "that sort of poem which, however personal, bears implications for communal experience."** They have published poetry by David Citino and Dimitris Tsaloumas. As a sample the editor selected these lines from "Those Who Claimed We Hated Them" by Sherri Szeman:

> . . . *We clicked tongues in sympathy*
> *at the blue-black scratchings on their forearms.*
>
> *But we had all suffered during the war.*
> *We suffered, as they did. We had only*
>
> *feigned gaiety at their misfortunes, to*
> *convince our oppressors to spare our homes.*

It is 240 pgs., 6×9, desktop-published, perfect-bound, with 3-color cover, art, graphics and ads. They receive about 500 poems a year, accept about 2%. Press run is 1,000 for 800 subscribers. Subscription: $12/year. **Sample postpaid: $6. Submit 5 poems at a time. No previously published poems or simultaneous submissions. Seldom comments on rejections. Publishes theme issues. Send SASE for guidelines and upcoming themes. Reports in about 2 months. Pays 2 copies plus 1-year subscription. Acquires all rights. Returns rights "when asked by authors for reprinting."**

CENTER PRESS; MASTERS AWARD (III), Box 16452, Encino CA 91416-6452, founded 1980, editor Gabriella Stone. Center Press is "a small press presently publishing approximately 6-7 works per year including poetry, photojournals, calendars, novels, etc. We look for quality, freshness and that touch of genius." In poetry, **"we want to see verve, natural rhythms, discipline, impact**, etc. We are flexible but **verbosity, triteness and saccharine make us cringe. We now read and publish only mss accepted from the Masters Award."** They have published books by Bebe Oberon, Walter Calder, Exene Vida, Carlos Castenada, Claire Bloome and G.G. Henke. Their tastes are for poets such as Charles Bukowski, Sylvia Plath, Erica Jong and Bob Dylan. **"We have strong liaisons with the entertainment industry and like to see material that is media-oriented and au courant." Sample postpaid: $8.** "We sponsor the Masters Awards, established in 1981, including a poetry award with a $1,000 grand prize annually plus each winner (and the five runners up in poetry) will be published in a clothbound edition and distributed to selected university and public libraries, news mediums, etc. There is a one-time only $15 administration and reading fee per entrant. Further application and details available with a #10 SASE." The editor says, "Please study what we publish before you consider submitting."

UNIVERSITY OF CENTRAL FLORIDA CONTEMPORARY POETRY SERIES (II), % English Dept., University of Central Florida, Orlando FL 32816-1346, phone (407)823-2212, founded 1968, poetry editor Judith Hemschemeyer, publishes **two 50- to 75-page hardback or paperback collections each year.** "Strong poetry on any theme in the lyric-narrative tradition." They have recently published poetry by Robert Cooperman, Katherine Soniat and John Woods. As a sample the editor selected these lines from "The Everly Brothers" in *Music Appreciation* by Floyd Skloot:

> *My brother thought they were freaks*
> *of nature, voices fitting together*
> *through some fluke of chemistry.*
> *He said they might just as well*
> *have been Siamese twins sharing*
> *a heart, or the Everly humpbacks.*

Submit complete paginated ms with table of contents and acknowledgement of previously published poems. Simultaneous submissions OK. "Please send a reading fee of $7, a SASE for return of ms and a self-addressed postcard for acknowledgment of receipt of ms." Reads submissions September through April. Reports in 3 months. Time between acceptance and publication is 1 year.

‡CHAMINADE LITERARY REVIEW (II, IV-Regional), 3140 Waialae Ave., Honolulu HI 96816, founded 1986, editor Loretta Petrie, appears twice yearly giving special consideration to Hawaii's writers or Hawaii subject matter. "No jingles or pop poetry." They have recently published poetry by Eleanor Wilner, William Heyen and Rob Wilson. As a sample the editor selected these lines from "The Waking Stone" by Michael McPherson:

> *The sharks here cannot be trusted.*
> *Poisons in their meat make them crazy,*
> *they feel no bond of loyalty or kinship*
> *nor any longer honor the ancient ways.*
> *Living seas near shore are stained*
> *with runoff from the burning fields,*
> *effluents open like brown dark flowers*
> *and coax the grey swimmers to frenzy.*
> *Spirit warriors are returning to land,*
> *they stand and cast a spectral gaze*
> *over plains now littered with debris.*

CLR features the work of many well-known creative writers and thus, at first blush, seems like a mainstream literary magazine. But poems, prose and artwork play off each other for added effect and unify such themes as ecology, love, nature, etc. The handsomely printed magazine averages 175 pgs., 6×9, flat-spined with glossy card cover. They accept about 25% of 500 poems received/year. Press run is 500 for 350 subscribers of which 6 are libraries. Subscription: $10/year, $18/2 years. Sample postpaid: $4. Submit at least 3 poems at a time. Previously published poems OK. Pays year's subscription. Open to unsolicited reviews.

CHAMPION BOOKS, INC.; NEW SHOES SERIES (II), P.O. Box 636, Lemont IL 60439, phone (800)230-1135, fax (800)827-7415, founded 1993, president Rebecca Rush, publishes 3-12 flat-spined paperback books of poetry/year through their New Shoes Series. They say, "In their prime, Kerouac and Ginsberg were never literary stars; they were the unknown and the unheard, speaking their minds and breaking new literary ground. But, now, decades after their heyday, they have become the pantheon for the mainstream of today's youth. Combined with the crossover between music and literature by such artists as Henry Rollins, William Burroughs and Jim Morrison, this has created a new era of readers with an appreciation for the great authors of the past as well as an interest in the direction of writing in the future. Champion Books seeks obscure and unrenowned authors interested not in following in the footsteps of others, but in creating their own new shoes to walk in." As a sample the editor selected "Untitled" from *My Gradual Demise & honeysuckle* by Douglas A. Martin:

> *licking wounds like a deranged dog,*
> *I fall to the altar of a desk,*
> *drink communion from a fountain pen,*
> *and bleed onto an empty page of redemption.*
> *I will come again.*

Query first, with 5-10 sample poems, cover letter with brief bio. Previously published poems and simultaneous submissions OK. Replies to queries in 1-3 months. Pays 7-10% royalties and about 4 author's copies. Write for catalog to order samples. Rebecca Rush says, "As an editor I am more interested in the content and tone of the poetry rather than the number of periodicals in which the poems have previously appeared. I am also impressed with authors who take initiative to promote their own works through self-published chapbooks and readings; it's always helpful if an author is willing to extend their own time and effort in order to get their works out to the public."

CHANTRY PRESS (III), P.O. Box 144, Midland Park NJ 07432, founded 1981, poetry editor D. Patrick, publishes perfect-bound paperbacks of "high quality" poetry. No other specifications. They have published work by Laura Boss, Anne Bailie, Ruth Lisa Schechter, Susan Clements and Joanne Riley. These sample lines are from *Winter Light* by Maria Gillan:

> *Remember me, Ladies,*
> *the silent one?*
> *I have found my voice*
> *and my rage will blow*
> *your house down.*

That's from an 80-page book (usually books from this press are 72 pgs.), flat-spined, glossy cover, good printing on heavy paper, author's photo on back, $5.95. Send SASE for catalog to order sample. Don't send complete ms. Query first, with 5 sample poems, no cover letter necessary. Submission period October through April. Replies in 4 months. Simultaneous submissions OK. Always sends prepublication galleys. Pays 15% royalties after costs are met and 10 author's copies. Very short comment "sometimes" on rejected mss. The editor advises: "Do not be rude in inquiring about the status of your manuscript."

CHANTS (II, IV-Translations), Dept. of English, Kennesaw State College, P.O. Box 444, Marietta GA 30061, founded 1988, editors Austin Hummell and Michael Fournier, appears twice a year. The editors "publish the **best translations and the most ambitious lyric poetry we can find. We encourage all poets, particularly younger ones, for whom poetry is a ruling passion.**" They have recently published poetry by Jorie Graham, Ron Rash and Ricardo Pau-Llosa. As a sample the editors selected the following lines from "Rerun" by Pamela McClure:

> Rivervalley, unusual eddy
> And cerulean's the seizure above
> So in the daylight noise the road ahead
> Drops us back to the house and its cover
> Of shadow, hollyhock limbs limbering
> Up the rerun of vine-braid and ivy.

Chants is 64 pgs., digest-sized, professionally printed, flat-spined, with photo or graphic on cover but no inside art. They accept about 5% of poems received. Single copy: $4. **Sample: $4 plus $1 postage. No previously published poems or simultaneous submissions.** Time between acceptance and publication is up to 6 months—occasionally longer. **Sometimes comments on rejections. Reports in 1-3 months. Pays 2 copies.** The editor says, "We favor the lyric above other modes, but will publish any poem, formal or informal, that has heart and imagination. We discourage timid and anecdotal verse, and bloodless experiment. We publish poetry exclusively, and are fond of translation. We feature one poet per issue, and try to include a brief essay to accompany each feature."

CHAPMAN (IV-Ethnic); CHAPMAN PRESS (V), 4 Broughton Place, Edinburgh EH1 3RX Scotland, phone (0131)557-2207, fax (0131)556-9565, founded 1970, editor Joy Hendry, "provides an outlet for new work by **established Scottish writers and for new, up-and-coming writers also,** for the discussion and criticism of this work and for reflection on current trends in Scottish life and literature. But *Chapman* is not content to follow old, well-worn paths; it throws open its pages to new writers, new ideas and new approaches. In the international tradition revived by MacDiarmid, *Chapman* also features **the work of foreign writers and broadens the range of Scottish cultural life.**" They have published poetry and fiction by Alasdair Gray, Liz Lochhead, Sorley MacLean, T.S. Law, Edwin Morgan, Willa Muir, Tom Scott and Una Flett. As a sample the editor selected these lines from Judy Steel's poem "For Nicole Boulanger" who, Steel says, "was born in the same year as my daughter and died in the Lockerbie air disaster of 1988":

> You died amongst these rolling Border hills:
> The same our daughters played and rode and walked in -
> They make a nursery fit to shape and mould
> A spirit swift as water, free as air.
>
> But you, west-winging through the Christmas dark
> Found them no playground but a mortuary -
> Your young life poised for flight to woman's years
> Destroyed as wantonly as moorland game.

Chapman appears 4 times a year in a 6×9, perfect-bound format, 104 pgs., professionally printed in small type on matte stock with glossy card cover, art in 2 colors. Press run is 2,000 for 900 subscribers of which 200 are libraries. They receive "thousands" of poetry submissions/year, use about 200, **have a 4- to 6-month backlog. Sample: £3.50 (overseas). Cover letter required. No simultaneous submissions. Reports "as soon as possible." Always sends prepublication galleys. Pays £8/page.** Staff reviews books of poetry. Send books for review consideration. **Chapman Press is not interested in unsolicited mss.** The editor says poets should not "try to court approval by writing poems especially to suit what they perceive as the nature of the magazine. They usually get it wrong and write badly." Also, they are interested in receiving poetry dealing with women's issues and feminism.

THE CHARITON REVIEW PRESS; THE CHARITON REVIEW (II), Northeast Missouri State University, Kirksville MO 63501, phone (816)785-4499, founded 1975, editor Jim Barnes. *The Chariton Review* began in 1975 as a twice yearly literary magazine and in 1978 added the activities of the press, producing "limited editions (not chapbooks!) of **full-length collections . . . for the purpose of introducing solid, contemporary poetry to readers**. The books go free to the regular subscribers of *The Chariton Review*; others are sold to help meet printing costs." The poetry published in both books and the magazine is, according to the editor, **"open and closed forms—traditional, experimental, mainstream. We do not consider verse, only poetry in its highest sense, whatever that may be. The sentimental and the inspirational are not poetry for us. Also, no more 'relativism': short stories**

and poetry centered around relatives." They have published poets such as Michael Spence, Neil Myers, Sam Maio, Andrea Budy, Charles Edward Eaton, Wayne Dodd and Harold Witt. There are 40-50 pages of poetry in each issue of the *Review*, a 6×9, flat-spined magazine of over a hundred pages, professionally printed, glossy cover with photographs, circulation about 600 with 400 subscribers of which 100 are libraries. They receive 7,000-8,000 submissions/year, of which they use 35-50, with never more than a 6-month backlog. Subscription: $9 for 1 year, $15 for 2 years. **Sample postpaid: $5. Submit 5-7 poems, typescript single-spaced. No simultaneous submissions. Do *not* write for guidelines. Always sends prepublication galleys. Pays $5/printed page. Buys first North American serial rights. Contributors are expected to subscribe or buy copies.** Open to unsolicited reviews. Poets may also send books for review consideration. *The Chariton Review* continues to be a lively magazine open to all styles and forms with only one criterion: excellence. Moreover, response times here are quick, and accepted poems often appear within a few issues of notification. **To be considered for book publication, query first—samples of books $3 and $5. Payment for book publication: $500 with 20 or more copies. Usually no criticism is supplied.**

THE CHATTAHOOCHEE REVIEW (II), DeKalb College, 2101 Womack Rd., Dunwoody GA 30338, phone (404)551-3166, founded 1980, editor-in-chief Lamar York, poetry editor (Mr.) Collie Owens, is a quarterly of poetry, short fiction, essays, reviews and interviews, published by DeKalb College. **"We publish a number of Southern writers, but *CR* is not by design a regional magazine. In poetry we look for vivid imagery, unique point of view and voice, freshness of figurative language, and attention to craft. All themes, forms and styles are considered as long as they impact the whole person: heart, mind, intuition and imagination."** They have published poetry by Peter Meinke, David Kirby, Allan Peterson, Bin Ramke, Peter Wild and Cory Brown. As a sample the editors selected these lines from "A Good Date" by David Staudt:

> *We walked onto the ice dams after supper,*
> *cool floors powdered for a two-step.*
> *Snowfall we couldn't see hissed like sparks*
> *doused on our wet faces. Under the cliffs,*
> *reliefers from Packerton drank and howled,*
> *and domes of visible flakes, thick as glitter*
> *in souvenirs from the Poconos,*
> *flickered over cans of sterno or sticks*
> *where fishermen hunkered in lawnchairs*
> *over blue slots routered in the ice.*

The Review is 90 pgs., 6×9, professionally printed on white stock with b&w reproductions of artwork, flat-spined, with one-color card cover. Its reputation as a premiere literary magazine continues to grow. Recent issues feature a wide range of forms and styles augmenting prose selections. Circulation is 1,250, of which 300 are complimentary copies sent to editors and "miscellaneous VIP's." Subscription: $15/year. **Sample postpaid: $5. Writers should send 1 copy of each poem and a cover letter with bio material. No simultaneous submissions. Publishes theme issues. Send SASE for guidelines. Queries will be answered in 1-2 weeks. Reports in 3 months and time to publication is 3-4 months. Pays 2 copies. Acquires first rights.** Staff reviews books of poetry and short fiction in 1,500 words, single or multi-book format. Send books for review consideration.

CHELSEA; CHELSEA AWARD COMPETITION (III, IV-Translations), P.O. Box 773, Cooper Station, New York NY 10276, founded 1958, editor Richard Foerster, associate editors Alfredo de Palchi and Andrea Lockett, is a long-established, high-quality literary biannual aiming to promote intercultural communication. **"We look for intelligence and sophisticated technique in both experimental and traditional forms. We are also interested in translations of contemporary poets. Length: 5-7 pgs. per submission. Although our tastes are eclectic, we lean toward the cosmopolitan avant-garde. We would like to see more poetry by writers of color. Do not want to see 'inspirational' verse, pornography or poems that rhyme merely for the sake of rhyme."** They have recently published poetry by Mei-mei Berssenbrugge, Kathleen Fraser, Alvin Greenberg, Ann Lauterbach and C.D. Wright. The editors say *Chelsea* is "128-144 pgs., flat-spined, 6×9, offset, cover art varies, occasional use of photographs, ads." Circulation: 1,300, 700 subscriptions of which 200 are libraries. Subscription: $13 domestic, $17 foreign. **Sample: $7. 5-7 pgs. of poetry are ideal; long poems should not exceed 10 pgs.; must be typed; include brief bio. No previously published poems or simultaneous submissions. "We try to comment favorably on above-average mss; otherwise, we do not have time to provide critiques." Reports within 3 months. Always sends prepublication galleys. Pays $10/page and 2 copies. Buys first North American serial rights and one-time nonexclusive reprint rights.** Guidelines for their annual Chelsea Award Competition (deadline December 15), $500 for poetry, available for SASE to P.O. Box 1040, York Beach ME 03910. Work published in *Chelsea* has been included in the 1993, 1994 and 1995 volumes of *The Best American Poetry*. Richard Foerster, editor, comments: "Beginners should realize that a rejection often has more to do with the magazine's production schedule and special editorial plans than with the quality of the submission. They should also realize that editors of little magazines are always overworked (and in our case unpaid) and that it is necessary haste and not a lack of concern or compassion that makes rejections seem coldly impersonal."

CHICAGO REVIEW (III, IV-Themes, translations), 5801 S. Kenwood, Chicago IL 60637, founded 1946, poetry editor Angela Sorby. **"We publish high quality poetry. About 50% of the work we select is unsolicited; the remainder is solicited from poets whose work we admire. Translations are welcome, but please include a statement of permission from the original publisher if work is not in the public domain."** They have published poets as diverse as Alice Fulton, Billy Collins, Yusef Komunyakaa, Turner Cassity, Michael Donaghy, Meena Alexander and Adrian C. Louis. "Out of the 1,500 submissions we receive each year, we accept around 50." Editors seem to prefer lyric free verse—some of it leaning toward avant-garde and some quite accessible—with emphasis on voice and content (depicting tense or intriguing topics or situations). Circulation 2,500. **Sample postpaid: $5. New submissions read year-round. Publishes theme issues. Send SASE for upcoming themes. Reports in 3 months, longer in some cases. Sometimes sends prepublication galleys. Pays in copies and one-volume subscription.** Occasionally reviews books of poetry. Open to unsolicited reviews.

CHICKADEE MAGAZINE; THE YOUNG NATURALIST FOUNDATION (IV-Children, nature), 179 John St., Suite 500, Toronto, Ontario M5T 3G5 Canada, founded 1979, editor Lizann Flatt, is a magazine **for children 3-9 about science and nature** appearing 10 times/year. **They want "evocative poetry; poems that play with words; humorous poetry; no longer than 50 lines. Nothing religious, anthropomorphic; no formal language; no poetry that is difficult to understand."** As a sample the editor selected this complete poem, "Snow Stars," by Goldie Olszynko Gryn:

> *I'm stepping on snow stars,*
> *small glittery glow stars.*
> *I'm stepping on snow stars*
> *that fall from the sky.*
>
> *I'm stepping on snow stars,*
> *cold crystally pole stars,*
> *but now there are no stars*
> *where I have walked by.*

Chickadee is 32 pgs., magazine-sized, professionally printed in full-color, with paper cover. They accept 1-2% of every 500 poems received. Circulation: 25,800 within US and 100,000 within Canada. Subscription: $14.95 US. **Sample postpaid: $3.75. Submit up to 10 poems at a time. Simultaneous submissions considered. Send SASE (or SAE and IRC) for writers' guidelines. Pays $10-75/poem plus 2 copies. Buys all rights.** "*Chickadee* is a 'hands-on' science and nature publication designed to entertain and educate 3- to 9-year-olds. Each issue contains photos, illustrations, an easy-to-read animal story, a craft project, puzzles, a science experiment and a pullout poster." The magazine received the 1994 EDPress Golden Lamp Honor Award and 1994 Parents' Choice Gold Seal Award.

‡CHICORY BLUE PRESS (IV-Women, senior citizens), 795 East St. N., Goshen CT 06756, phone (203)491-2271, founded 1988, publisher Sondra Zeidenstein, **publishes 2-3 chapbooks/year. She is currently open to receiving queries for chapbooks by women poets over age 60. Submit 5-7 poems and cover letter with only "a line or two of introduction of self and work." Replies to queries and mss (if invited) in 3 months. Seldom comments on rejections. Pays royalties, honorarium or 10 author's copies.** She has published poetry by Honor Moore and Pattiann Rogers. **Samples can be ordered from the press.**

CHILDREN'S BETTER HEALTH INSTITUTE; BENJAMIN FRANKLIN LITERARY AND MEDICAL SOCIETY, INC.; HUMPTY DUMPTY'S MAGAZINE; TURTLE MAGAZINE FOR PRESCHOOL KIDS; CHILDREN'S DIGEST; CHILDREN'S PLAYMATE; JACK AND JILL; CHILD LIFE (IV-Children), 1100 Waterway Blvd., P.O Box 567, Indianapolis IN 46206-0567. This publisher of magazines stressing health for children has a **variety of needs for mostly short, simple poems.** For example, *Humpty Dumpty* is for ages 4-6; *Turtle* is for preschoolers, similar emphasis, uses many stories in rhyme—and action rhymes, etc.; *Children's Digest* is for preteens (10-13); *Jack and Jill* is for ages **7-10.** *Child Life* is for ages 9-11. *Children's Playmate* is for ages 6-8. All appear 8 times a year in a 6½×9, 48-page format, slick paper with cartoon art, very colorful. **Sample postpaid: $1.25. Send**

✚ *The double dagger before a listing indicates that the listing is new in this edition. New markets are often the most receptive to submissions.*

SASE for guidelines. Reports in 8-10 weeks. Pays $15 minimum. Staff reviews books of poetry. Send books for review consideration. The editors suggest that writers who wish to appear in their publications **study current issues carefully.** "We receive too many poetry submissions that are about kids, not for kids. Or, the subject matter is one that adults think children would or should like. We'd like to see more humorous verse."

CHIRON REVIEW; CHIRON BOOKS; CHIRON REVIEW POETRY CONTEST (I, II), 522 E. South Ave., St. John KS 67576-2212, phone (316)549-3933, founded 1982 as *Kindred Spirit*, editor Michael Hathaway, assistant editor Jane Hathaway, contributing editor (poetry) Gerald Locklin, is a quarterly tabloid using photographs of featured writers. **No taboos.** They have published poetry by Charles Bukowski, Marge Piercy, Antler, Wilma Elizabeth McDaniel and Will Inman. As a sample the editor selected "R.S.V.P.," by CAConrad, which won the 1994 *CR* Poetry Contest:

> *he wrote "I have AIDS and kissed this wall"*
> *X marked the spot.*
>
> *I wrote "I'm not afraid" and kissed him back*
> *wherever he is*

Each issue is 24-32 pgs. and "contains dozens of poems." Their press run is about 1,000. **Sample postpaid: $3 ($6 overseas or institutions). Submit 3-6 poems at a time, "typed or printed legibly." No simultaneous submissions or previously published poems. Very seldom publishes theme issues. Send SASE for guidelines and any upcoming themes. Reports in 2-4 weeks. Pays 1 copy. Acquires first-time rights.** Reviews books of poetry in 500-900 words. Open to unsolicited reviews. Poets may also send books for review consideration. **For book publication submit complete ms.** They publish 1-3 books/year, flat-spined, professionally printed, **paying 25% of press run of 100-200 copies.** Their annual poetry contest offers awards of $100 plus 1-page feature in Winter issue, $50, and 5 free subscriptions and a Chiron Press book. Entry fee: $5/poet.

THE CHRISTIAN CENTURY (II, IV-Religious, social issues), Dept. PM, 407 S. Dearborn St., Chicago IL 60605, phone (312)427-5380, founded 1884, named *The Christian Century* 1900, founded again 1908, joined by *New Christian* 1970, poetry editor Dean Peerman. This "ecumenical weekly" is a liberal, sophisticated journal of news, articles of opinion and reviews from a generally Christian point-of-view, **using approximately one poem/issue, not necessarily on religious themes but in keeping with the literate tone of the magazine. "No pietistic or sentimental doggerel, please."** They have published poetry by Robert Beum, Joan Rohr Myers, Ida Fasel, Jill Baumgaertner, David Abrams, Catherine Shaw, J. Barrie Shepherd and Wendell Berry. As a sample the editor selected this poem, "Grain Silos," by James Worley:

> *Cathedrals of the oldest preached religion,*
> *towers erected to the oldest useful god*
> *(the one now worshiped three times every day*
> *by those who can, invoked by those who can't)*
> *these cylinders of homage (oblong praise)*
> *project a plenty that is its own reward,*
> *a yearning that has grown its own response:*
> *the deity whom these raised prayers rise to laud*
> *resides (when crops are good) in grateful guts.*

The journal is magazine-sized, printed on quality newsprint, using b&w art, cartoons and ads, about 30 pgs., saddle-stapled. **Sample postpaid: $2. No simultaneous submissions. Submissions without SASE or SAE and IRCs will not be returned. Pays usually $20/poem plus 1 copy and discount on additional copies. Acquires all rights. Inquire about reprint permission.** Reviews books of poetry in 300-400 words, single format; 400-500 words, multi-book.

CHRISTIAN POET; REDWOOD FAMILY CHAPEL PUBLICATIONS (I, II, IV-Religious), 2745 Monterey Hwy. #76, San Jose CA 95111-3129, founded as Realities Library in 1975, as CCR Publications in 1987, now Redwood Family Chapel Publications, editor and publisher Ric Soos. He has published books of poetry by Ruth Daigon and Ella Blanche Salmi. "Because of economic conditions, we have discontinued our book series. To replace the book series we have started *Christian Poet*. It will be published as often as we have time, poetry and finances. Seven issues appeared in 1992, 15 issues in 1993 and 32 in 1994." As a sample the editor selected this poem, "The Test," by Pete Green:

> *Lugging wood from yard to stove*
> *I come to the kitchen step and door;*
> *The Test, with arms loaded numb,*
> *groping, groping,   never grasping that*
> *Christ is a door nailed open.*

Christian Poet is one 8½ × 11 page of colored paper, neatly printed and tri-folded. Subscription: $5 for 12 issues. **Sample: $1 for 2 copies. Poets may submit up to 15 poems for consideration. Include**

CLOSE-UP

Listen to the Voice of Your Own Spirit

It's not necessary to have lived a "hard life" to create great art, says Chrystos, but those who wish to create such art must be ready to sacrifice some emotional as well as physical comfort. "I'm not saying you have to be a starving artist to be a great writer, but when the creation of literature is the foremost goal in your life it doesn't make for a comfortable existence.

"Being a creative person is an extremely difficult journey and requires great courage. I think a part of what great art is all about is revealing that deep pain, deep joy and deep anger—all the powerful emotions a person feels living on this earth."

©Photo by Chick Rice

Chrystos

Life for Chrystos, a poet whose work often reflects the suffering she's witnessed or experienced while growing up a Native American female in urban America, has been far from comfortable. Abuse; addiction; homelessness; poverty; the mistreatment of women, children and the earth; and the effects of colonialism on native peoples are all subjects which appear in her work, and have touched her in some way.

"I've been through the usual drinking and drugging kinds of ways of surviving a difficult life," she says. "But, after my first book was published, I realized the only thing that was going to keep me alive was my writing. When I write, I can 'contain' the toxic waste of what has happened to me and make it possible for me to think about something else."

Her first book, *Not Vanishing*, published by Press Gang Publishers in 1988, was partly a response to the reference to Native Americans as the "Vanishing Americans." In the introduction, she says, "My purpose is to make it as clear and as inescapable as possible, what the actual, material conditions of our lives are.... Despite the books which still appear ... we are not Vanishing Americans."

Chrystos's commitment to exposing and exploring the abuse of native peoples at the hands of colonial governments has led her to become active on a variety of Native American causes, including respect for land and treaty rights. She is also a feminist and a "proud lesbian for 25 years" and these things, too, have led her to speak out on a variety of issues at gatherings across the country.

Yet, she says, a writer must have time out of the spotlight, to be alone to reflect. Between speaking engagements, readings and teaching workshops, Chrystos "escapes" to her little house on Bainbridge Island off the coast of Washington state. She tries to write daily, at least in her journal, the place in which she feels free to "rant and rave and get through the day...."

"Winter Count"

By their own report america has killed
forty million of us in the last century
The names of those who murdered us are remembered
in towns, islands, bays, rivers, mountains, prairies, forests
our own names
We have died as children, as old men & women without defenses
We have been raped, mutilated, we have been starved
experimented on, we have been given gifts that kill
we've been imprisoned, we've been fed the poison of alcohol
until our children are born deformed
We have been killed on purpose, by accident, in drunken rage
As I speak with each breath
another Indian is dying   Someone part of our Holocaust
which they have renamed civilization
Our women are routinely sterilized
without their consent during operations for other reasons
I have seen the scars
We are the butt of jokes, the gimmicks for ad campaigns
romanticized into oblivion   So carefully obscured
that many think we are all dead
For every person who came here to find freedom
there are bones rattling in our Mother
The ravage of suburbia covers our burial grounds
our spiritual places, our homes
Now we are rare & occasionally cherished as Eagles
though not by farmers who still potshot us for sport
Suddenly we have religions they want & they'll pay
Down the long tunnel of death my grandmothers cry   No
Give no solace to our destroyers
Into the cold night I send these burning words
Never forget
america is our hitler

(from **Dream On**, 1991, reprinted by permission of Press Gang Publishers)

She says it's hard to pinpoint exactly where ideas come from, but it's important to recognize a good idea when it occurs. "Poems come to you just as birds who flit by you when you're walking on a path in the woods—just ZIP!—and that's it. If you don't stop when the moment touches you, then that poem never gets written. I think good writing comes from learning to be attentive to those birds who skim across your mind."

While she often does extensive rewrites, Chrystos warns writers to avoid editing themselves early in the writing process. "I tell people in my workshops to just scribble it down any ol' way. You can always go back later and change it, but it's important to get that first impulse down as clearly as you can. To some extent, writing is listening to a voice outside yourself speaking to you, and trying to control that voice will kill it."

To write, she says, people must give themselves permission to listen to the voices of their own spirits. "We have to peel away all the brainwashing and all the false ego. We have to be able to lay aside all the nonsense in our lives." For women, this is especially true. "We have to write from our real spirit and not as a Barbie doll whose intent is to please the rest of the world. It's not that you can't be civil, but when you believe you have to be nice you can't write."

Chrystos has published two more books with Press Gang, *Dream On* in 1991, which contains more political poems as well as love poems and other themes, and *In Her I Am* in 1993, a book of poetry celebrating lesbian eroticism. As a result of winning the Audre Lorde Poetry Competition for Lesbians of Color in 1994, her fourth book, *Fugitive Colors*, was published by the Cleveland State University Poetry Center in 1995.

Despite the variety of themes and subjects in her work, a structural familiarity exists in many of her poems. Among her early influences were e.e. cummings and Walter Benton, who wrote "a very erotic and sensual meditation on the body of the woman he loved." She admits this was an odd combination. "Yet my poetic sensibility was formed by these two men, especially in the way in which both blew up structure. I was quite taken by the puns in cummings's work and the ways he would play with spelling and push line structure to the utmost extent."

It's important to read widely and internationally, says Chrystos, who is currently trying to find translated work by Chinese and Arab women. "It really angers me that in the U.S. we have all this access to incredible publication technology, yet there's so much valuable literature from the rest of the world we don't have easy access to. The whole issue of the unavailability of women's voices and nonwhite voices is extremely important to me."

Poetry as a whole does not get the respect it deserves in this country, she says. "It's kind of strange that something that is revered in so many other countries as sacred and spiritual is considered something to line your garbage pail with here." She adds that poetry has the potential to make people aware of things they tend to put out of their minds because those things may be too painful, and this is one of the true functions of the craft.

The beat of the powwow drum can be heard in Chrystos's writing and there's good reason. Most people are asleep in this country, she says, watching soap operas, working at mindless jobs, trying not to think about life in America in the 1990s. "I think of good poems as alarm clocks or as drums. You have to beat a drum to wake people up, and that's what I'm trying to do with my work."

—Robin Gee

short bio and SASE with submission. Previously published poems OK. Seldom comments on rejections. Send SASE for guidelines. Pays 25 copies. The editor says, "Please keep in mind when you contact me that I believe in Jesus Christ, and that anything I publish will be to help further the Gospel if it is for that purpose. In poetry, I look for items that will not hinder the spread of the Gospel. In other words, the poet need not be Christian, does not need to mention Christ by name, but I will no longer be publishing for shock value." He publishes those "who support me in some respect . . . Support is not always financial."

THE CHRISTIAN SCIENCE MONITOR (II), The Home Forum Page, 1 Norway St., Boston MA 02115, phone (617)450-2474, founded 1908, is an international daily newspaper. **Poetry used regularly in The Home Forum, editor Elizabeth Lund. They want "finely crafted poems that celebrate the extraordinary in the ordinary. Seasonal material always needed. Especially interested in poems about life in the city. No violence, sensuality or racism. Short poems preferred."** They have published work by William Stafford, Diana der-Hovanessian, Steven Ratiner and Lyn Lifshin. As a sample the editor selected these lines from "Working in the Rain" by Robert Morgan:

> *My father loved more than anything to*
> *work outside in wet weather. Beginning*
> *at daylight he'd go out in dripping brush*
> *to mow or pull weeds for hog and chickens.*

Submit no more than 5 poems at a time, single-spaced. SASE must be included. "Please do not fold each page individually." No previously published poems or simultaneous submissions. Usually reports within 1-2 months. Pays varying rates, upon publication.

THE CHRISTOPHER PUBLISHING HOUSE (II), 24 Rockland St., Commerce Green, Hanover MA 02339, phone (617)826-7474, fax (617)826-5556, founded 1910, managing editor Nancy Lucas, who says **"We will review all forms of poetry."** They have recently published *Heartbeats* by Ron J. Flemming, *My Love, My Friend, and My Dreams* by Gabriela Freitas and *Poems 1942-1992* by I. Lesley Briggs. **Submit complete ms of at least 65 poems. Enclose SASE for return of ms. Always sends prepublication galleys.**

THE CHRONICLE OF THE HORSE (IV-Specialized), P.O. Box 46, Middleburg VA 22117, phone (703)687-6341, founded 1937, assistant editor Tricia Booker, is a weekly magazine using **short poetry related to horses "the shorter the better. No free verse."** The magazine is devoted to English horse sports, such as horse shows and steeplechasing. It averages 68 pgs., magazine-sized. Subscription: $42. **Sample postpaid: $2. No simultaneous submissions. Summer "is not a good time" to submit. 1-3 editors read poems. Reports in 4-6 weeks. Pays $20/poem. Buys first North American rights.** "We review books submitted to us but do not accept reviews for publication."

THE CHRYSALIS READER (II, IV-Spirituality, themes), Rt. 1 Box 184, Dillwyn VA 23936, founded 1985, editor Carol Lawson, poetry editor Robert Lawson. *Chrysalis Reader* is published by the Swedenborg Foundation as a "contribution to the search for spiritual wisdom." It appears intermittently and is now a "series that draws upon diverse traditions to engage thought on questions that challenge inquiring minds. Each issue addresses a topic from varied perspectives using literate and scholarly fiction, essays and poetry dealing with spiritual aspects of a particular theme." **They want poetry that is "spiritually related and focused on the particular issue's theme. Nothing overly religious or sophomoric."** They have recently published poetry by Kate Cheney Chappell and Robert Bly. As a sample the editor selected these lines from "Burning the Long Boat" by Robert F. Lawson:

> *We stand on the flagstones.*
> *Such a small opening for a big man to disappear into.*
> *Alone in the dark, he broke down the coffee table,*
> *in his haste to save his heart;*
> *the vial of pills showed its teeth*
> *just out of reach at the top of the chest.*

TCR is 150 pgs., 6×9, professionally printed on archival paper and perfect-bound with coated cover stock, illustrations, photos and ads for other literary publications. They receive about 150 poems a year, use 8-10%. Press run is 3,500. **Sample postpaid: $6. No previously published poems or simultaneous submissions. Submit no more than 6 poems at one time.** Time between acceptance and publication is 18 months maximum. **Seldom comments on rejections. Send SASE for themes and guidelines. Themes for Summer 1995 and Autumn 1995 issues were Play and The Good Life, respectively. Reports in 2 months. Always sends prepublication galleys. Pays $25 and 5 copies. Buys first-time rights.** "We like to be credited for reprints."

THE CHURCH-WELLESLEY REVIEW; XTRA! (IV-Gay/lesbian), 491 Church St., Suite 200, Toronto, Ontario M4Y 2C6 Canada. *The Church-Wellesley Review* is the annual supplement for *XTRA!* (Canada's largest gay/lesbian newspaper.) **"We want wild humour, fast-paced drama, new takes**

on old themes, gays and lesbians in other contexts. **Our aim is always quality, not style. Although we prefer non-traditional poetry,** we have in the past published a contemporary 30-line 'up-dating' of Chaucer called 'Provincetown Tales.' **Amaze us or amuse us, but just don't bore us.''** They have published Patrick Roscoe, Jane Rule, Timothy Findley, Chocolate Waters and David Watmough. The magazine receives over 1,000 submissions/year. Press run is 37,000 in Toronto plus 22,000 in Vancouver and is distributed free. **Poetry can be any length ("no epics, please"), but no more than 10 poems per writer per year. Mss should include 8 poems with name on every page, daytime phone number and 50-word bio. Submissions are accepted March 1 through July 1.** "We do not respond at other times. We report as soon as possible, definitely by publication in early fall." **Payment is made in Canadian funds within one month of publication.** Staff reviews books of poetry. Send books for review consideration to the attention of Fiction Editor. *Xtra*, the review's parent magazine, has received several community awards as well as a journalism award for a column on Living with AIDS.

CIMARRON REVIEW (II), 205 Morrill Hall, Oklahoma State University, Stillwater OK 74078-0135, founded 1967, poetry editors Thomas Reiter, Sharon Gerald, Doug Martin, Hugh Tribbey and Sally Shigley, is a quarterly literary journal. **"We emphasize quality and style. We like clear, evocative poetry (lyric or narrative) controlled by a strong voice. No obscure poetry. No sing-song verse. No quaint prairie verse. No restrictions as to subject matter, although we tend to publish more structured poetry (attention to line and stanza).** Also, we are conscious of our academic readership (mostly other writers) and attempt to accept poems that everyone will admire." Among poets they have published are Robert Cooperman, James McKean, David Citino, Tess Gallagher and Albert Goldbarth. This magazine, 6×9, 100-150 pgs., perfect-bound, boasts a handsome design, including a color cover and attractive printing. Poems lean toward free verse, lyric and narrative, although all forms and styles seem welcome. There are 15-25 pages of poetry in each issue, circulation 500, mostly libraries. Subscription rates: $3/issue, $12/year ($15 Canada), $30 for 3 years ($40 Canada), plus $2.50 for all international subscriptions. **Submit to Poetry Editor, anytime, 3-5 poems, name and address on each, typed single- or double-spaced. No simultaneous submissions. Reports within 3 months. Pays $15 for each poem published. Buys all rights. "Permission for a reprinting is granted upon request."** Reviews books of poetry in 500-900 words, single-book format, occasionally multi-book. All reviews are assigned.

CINCINNATI POETRY REVIEW; CINCINNATI WRITERS' PROJECT (II, IV-Regional), Humanities Dept., College of Mount St. Joseph, 5701 Delhi Rd., Cincinnati OH 45233, founded 1975, editor Jeffrey Hillard, "attempts to set local poets in a national context. Each issue includes **a quarter to a third of work by local poets (within about 100 miles of Cincinnati)**, but most are from all over." They use **"all kinds" of poetry** and have published such poets as Enid Shomer, Lynne Hugo deCourcy, Pat Mora, Eve Shelnutt, David Citino, Jeff Worley, Harry Humes, Walter Pavlich and Yusef Komunyakaa. They publish one issue/year, usually a fall/winter issue. *CPR* is 80 pgs., digest-sized, handsomely printed and flat-spined, all poems with art on the glossy card cover. They use about 40-60 of 2,000 submissions/year. Circulation is about 1,000, with 130 subscriptions, 30 of which are libraries. Subscription: $9 for 4 issues. **Sample: $2. Submit typed mss with address on each poem. "Occasionally" publishes theme issues.** Theme for a special section of *CPR* #25 was Cuban poetry and it included an interview with Cuban poet Julia Calzadilla. **Note, however, that the editor solicits material for special sections. Reports in 1-3 months. Pays 2 copies.** Each issue offers a poetry contest for poems of all types. The poems judged best and second in each issue receive cash awards of $150 and $50. *CPR* is published by the Cincinnati Writers' Project. Other publications include *The Shadow Family* by Jeffrey Hillard, *The Kansas Poems* by Dallas Wiebe, *Dismal Man* by Jon Christopher Hughes, *River Dwellers—Poems on the Settling of the Ohio River* by Jeffrey Hillard and *Down the River—A Collection of Fiction & Poetry on the Ohio River Valley*, edited by Dallas Wiebe.

THE CINCINNATI POETS' COLLECTIVE (II), 716 Maple Ave., Newport KY 41071, founded 1988, editor Rebecca M. Weigold, is an annual poetry magazine. **"I am looking for fresh poetry that takes risks. I would like to see more poetry written about current issues from a conservative or politically incorrect point of view, however no subject is taboo. I do not want overly-didactic or ambiguous poetry; no soapbox material professing to be a poem. I am open to extensively published poets and to those who deserve to be but are not."** Poets published include Claire Donohue Roof, Richard Stansberger and J. Patrick Kelly. As a sample the editor selected these lines from "Coup de Grace" by Mg:

> You gave me your darkness
> that I have now enshrined
> in the Crypt of Most Cherished Memory,
> the heathen crypt,
> where nothing dead ever rises.

TCPC is digest-sized, saddle-stapled. Circulation is approximately 150 through bookstore sales and subscriptions. **Submit up to 5 poems at a time. No previously published poems. Simultaneous** submissions OK, if noted. Submit mss October 1 through April 1 only. Send SASE for guidelines. Reports in 4-6 months. Pays 1 copy.

CITY LIGHTS BOOKS (III), 261 Columbus Ave., San Francisco CA 94133, phone (415)362-1901, founded 1955, edited by Lawrence Ferlinghetti and Nancy J. Peters, is a paperback house that achieved prominence with the publication of Allen Ginsberg's *Howl* and other **poetry of the "Beat" school.** They publish **"poetry, fiction, philosophy, political and social history."** Simultaneous submissions OK. **"All submissions must include SASE." Reports in 6-8 weeks. Payment varies.**

‡THE CLAREMONT REVIEW (I, IV-Teens/Young Adults), 4980 Wesley Rd., Victoria, British Columbia V8Y 1Y9 Canada, phone (604)658-5221, fax (604)658-5387, founded 1993, is a biannual review which publishes poetry and fiction **written by those ages 13 to 19.** Each fall issue also includes an interview with a prominent Canadian writer. **They want "vital, modern poetry with a strong voice and living language. We prefer works that reveal something of the human condition. No clichéd language nor copies of 18th and 19th century work."** They have recently published poetry by Gillian Roberts, Lori Acker and Erin Baade. As a sample the editors selected these lines from "These Days Like Prayers Between Us" by Julie Lambert:

> *When I was 12 my body*
> *opened up soaked through*
> *my underwear to stain*
> *new jeans and I wept*
> *to see my childhood run*
> *between my legs.*

The Claremont Review is 110 pgs., 6×9, professionally printed and perfect-bound with an attractive color cover. They receive 600-800 poems a year, publish 120. Press run is 700 for 200 subscribers of which 50 are libraries, 250 shelf sales. Subscription: $12/year, $20/2 years. **Sample postpaid: $6. Submit poems typed one to a page with author's name at the top of each. No previously published poems; simultaneous submissions OK. Cover letter with brief bio required. Reads submissions September through June. Always comments on rejections. Send SASE (or SAE and IRCs) for guidelines. Reports in 2-6 weeks (excluding July and August). Pays 1 copy and funds when grants allow it. Acquires first North American serial rights.** The editors add "We strongly urge potential contributors to read back issues of *The Claremont Review*. That is the best way for you to learn what we are looking for."

THE CLASSICAL OUTLOOK (IV-Specialized, translations), Classics Dept., Park Hall, University of Georgia, Athens GA 30602, founded 1924, poetry editors Prof. David Middleton (original English verse) and Prof. Jane Phillips (translations and original Latin verse), "is an internationally circulated quarterly journal (4,000 subscriptions, of which 250 are libraries) for high school and college Latin and Classics teachers, published by the American Classical League." **They invite submissions of "original poems in English on classical themes, verse translations from Greek and Roman authors, and original Latin poems. Submissions should, as a rule, be written in traditional poetic forms and should demonstrate skill in the use of meter, diction and rhyme if rhyme is employed. Original poems should be more than mere exercise pieces or the poetry of nostalgia. Translations should be accompanied by a photocopy of the original Greek or Latin text. Latin originals should be accompanied by a literal English rendering of the text. Submissions should not exceed 50 lines."** They have recently published work by X.J. Kennedy and Timothy Steele. As a sample we selected these lines from "Consolation for Tamar On the Occasion of Her Breaking an Ancient Pot" by A.E. Stallings:

> *You know I am no archaeologist, Tamar,*
> *And that to me it is all one dust or another.*
> *Still, it must mean something to survive the weather*
> *Of the Ages—earthquake, flood, and war—*
>
> *Only to shatter in your very hands. . . .*

There are 2-3 magazine-sized pgs. of poetry in each issue, and they use 30% of the approximately 250 submissions they receive each year. They have a 6- to 12-month backlog, 4-month lead time. **Submit 2 anonymous copies, double-spaced, no more than 5 poems at a time. Receipt is acknowledged by letter. Poetry is refereed by poetry editors. Send SASE for guidelines. Reports in 3-6 months. Pays 2 complimentary copies. Sample copies are available from the American Classical League, Miami University, Oxford OH 45056 for $7.50.** Reviews books of poetry "if the poetry is sufficiently classical in nature." The editors add, "Since our policy is to have poetry evaluated anonymously, cover letters, names and addresses on poems, etc., just make work at this end. Also, we never knowingly publish any works which have been or will be published elsewhere."

CLEANING BUSINESS MAGAZINE; CLEANING CONSULTANT SERVICES, INC. (IV-Specialized), P.O. Box 1273, Seattle WA 98111, phone (206)622-4241, fax (206)622-6876, founded 1976, poetry editor William R. Griffin. *CBM* is "a quarterly magazine **for cleaning and maintenance professionals" and uses some poetry relating to their interests. "To be considered for publication in** *Cleaning Business*, **submit poetry that relates to our specific audience—cleaning and self-employment."** He has published poetry by Don Wilson, Phoebe Bosche, Trudie Mercer and Joe Keppler. The editor says it is 100 pgs., 8½×11, offset litho, using ads, art and graphics. Of 50 poems received, he uses about 10. Press run is 5,000 for 3,000 subscriptions (100 of them libraries), 500 shelf sales. Single copy: $5; subscription: $20. **Sample postpaid: $3. Send SASE and $3 for guidelines. Simultaneous submissions OK; no previously published poems. Pays $5-10 plus 1 copy.** William Griffin suggests "poets identify a specific market and work to build a readership that can be tapped again and again over a period of years with new books. Also write to a specific audience that has a mutual interest. We buy poetry about cleaning, but seldom receive anything our subscribers would want to read."

CLEVELAND STATE UNIVERSITY POETRY CENTER; CSU POETRY SERIES (II); CLEVELAND POETS SERIES (IV-Regional), Cleveland State University, Cleveland OH 44115, fax (216)687-6943, coordinator Rita Grabowski, editors Leonard Trawick, David Evett and Ted Lardner. The Poetry Center was founded in 1962, first publications in 1971. **The Poetry Center publishes the CSU Poetry Series for poets in general and the Cleveland Poets Series for Ohio poets. "Open to many kinds of form, length, subject matter, style and purpose. Should be well-crafted, clearly of professional quality, ultimately serious (even when humorous). No light verse, devotional verse or verse in which rhyme and meter seem to be of major importance."** They have recently published poetry by Jared Carter, Richard Jackson, Jan Freeman and Susan Firer. As a sample Leonard Trawick selected these lines from *Hurdy-Gurdy* by Tim Seibles:

> When a man is killed
> the wind doesn't cool his face
> and the sky is like an urn, like
> a painted bowl turned over on him.
> He's so weak lying there—his hand
> is like a starfish too far from the sea.

Books are chosen for publication from the entries to the CSU Poetry Center Prize contest. (Write for free catalog and sampler of some 65 Poetry Center books.) Deadline: March 1. Entry fee: $15. The winner receives $1,000 and publication. They publish some other entrants in the Poetry Series, providing 50 copies (of press run of 1,000) and 10% royalty contract. The Cleveland Poets Series (for Ohio poets) offers 100 copies of a press run of 600. To submit for all series, send ms between December 1 and March 1. Reports on all submissions for the year by the end of July. Mss should be for books of 50-100 pgs., pages numbered, poet's name, address and phone number on cover sheet, clearly typed. Poems may have been previously published (listed on an acknowledgement page). Simultaneous submissions OK, if notified and "poet keeps us informed of change in status." Send SASE for guidelines. The Center also publishes other volumes of poetry, including chapbooks (20-30 pgs.), with a **$10 reading fee for each submission (except for Ohio residents).**

THE CLIMBING ART (IV-Specialized: mountaineering), Fairfield Communications, P.O. Box 1378, Laporte CO 80535, phone (303)221-9210, founded 1986, editor Scott Titterington, is a quarterly journal **"read mainly by mountain enthusiasts who appreciate good writing about mountains and mountaineering. We are open to all forms and lengths. The only requirement is that the work be fresh, well-written and in some way of interest to those who love the mountains. If in doubt, submit it."** They have recently published poetry by Terry Gifford, Allison Hunter, Paul Willis, Denise K. Simon and Barry Govenor. As a sample we selected "Our Mission" by John Grey:

> The mountain has size on its side,
> the sense that things that big
> need not have opinions
> or make peace with the world.
> We, on the other hand,
> are at the bottom,
> suburbs, impossible affairs,
> promotions missed.

It is 160 pgs., digest-sized, professionally printed on heavy stock with glossy card cover. They use 8-10 poems/issue of 100-200 submissions received/year. Press run is 1,500 for 700 subscribers of which 10 are libraries, 500 shelf sales. Subscription: $18. **Sample postpaid: $4. Simultaneous submissions and previously published poems OK. Reports in 2 months. Sometimes sends prepublication galleys. Pays 3 copies and subscription. Acquires one-time rights.** Reviews books of poetry only if they concern mountains. Open to unsolicited reviews. They also sponsor an annual poetry contest; first prize: $100.

CLOCKWATCH REVIEW (I, II), Dept. of English, Illinois Wesleyan University, Bloomington IL 61702, phone (309)556-3352, founded 1983, editor James Plath, associate editors Lynn Devore, James McGowan and Pamela Muirhead. "We publish a variety of styles, leaning toward poetry which goes beyond the experience of self in an attempt to SAY something, without sounding pedantic or strained. **We like a strong, natural voice, and lively, unusual combinations in language.** *Something fresh, and that includes subject matter as well.* **It has been our experience that extremely short/long poems are hard to pull off.** Though we'll publish exceptions, we prefer to see poems that can fit on one published page (digest-sized) which runs **about 32 lines or less.**" They have published Peter Wild, Martha Vertreace, John Knoepfle, Rita Dove and Peter Meinke. Asked for a sample, the editors say "trying to pick only four lines seems like telling people what detail we'd like to see in a brick, when what we're more interested in is the design of the *house*." The 80-page, semiannual *CR* is printed on glossy paper with colored, glossy cover. They receive 2,080 submissions/year, use 20-30. They use 7-10 unsolicited poems in each issue, with 1 featured poet. Circulation is 1,400, with 150 subscribers, of which 25 are libraries. They send out 300 complimentary copies and "the balance is wholesale distribution and single-copy sales." **Sample postpaid: $4. Submit 5-6 poems at a time. "We are not bowled over by large lists of previous publications, but brief letters of introduction or sparse mini-vitas are read out of curiosity. One poem per page, typed, single-spacing OK."** No backlog. **Comments on rejections "if asked, and if time permits." Reports in 2-3 months. Pays 3 copies, and, when possible, small cash awards—currently $5/poem.** Only uses staff-written or solicited reviews. Send books for review consideration if not self-published.

CLOUD RIDGE PRESS (V), 815 13th St., Boulder CO 80302, founded 1985, editor Elaine Kohler, is a "literary small press for unique works in poetry and prose." They publish letterpress and offset books in both paperback and hardcover editions. In poetry, they publish **"strong images of the numinous qualities in authentic experience grounded in a landscape and its people."** The first book, published in 1985, was *Ondina: A Narrative Poem* by John Roberts. The book is 6×9¼, handsomely printed on buff stock, cloth bound in black with silver decoration and spine lettering, 131 pgs. 800 copies were bound in Curtis Flannel and 200 copies bound in cloth over boards, numbered and signed by the poet and artist. This letterpress edition, priced at $18/cloth and $12/paper, is not available in bookstores but only by mail from the press. The trade edition was photo-offset from the original, in both cloth and paper bindings, and is sold in bookstores. The press plans to publish 1-2 books/year. **Since they are not accepting unsolicited mss, writers should query first. Queries will be answered in 2 weeks and mss reported on in 1 month. Simultaneous submissions are acceptable. Royalties are 10% plus a negotiable number of author's copies. A brochure is free on request; send #10 SASE.**

CLUBHOUSE; YOUR STORY HOUR (I, IV-Children, teens), Dept. PM, P.O. Box 15, Berrien Springs MI 49103, poetry editor Elaine Trumbo. The publication is printed in conjunction with the **Your Story Hour** radio program, founded 1949, which is designed to teach the Bible and moral life to children. The magazine, *Clubhouse*, started with that title in 1982, but as *Good Deeder*, its original name, it has been published since 1951. Elaine Trumbo says, **"We do like humor or mood pieces. Don't like mushy-sweet 'Christian' poetry. We don't have space for long poems. Best—16 lines or under."** They have published poetry by Lillian M. Fisher, Audrey Osofsky, Sharon K. Motzko, Bruce Bash and Craig Peters. As a sample the editor selected these lines from "Nurses Office" by Eileen Spinelli:

> *And it hurts behind my ear,*
> *And I've got a cut right here,*
> *And a rash between my toes,*
> *And a pimple on my nose.*
> *Ouch, my knee feels sore and tender-*
> *Bumped it on my bike's back fender.*
> *I can't tell you all I've got.*
> *Where's the aspirin?*
> *Bring the cot!*
> *I need T.L.C. and rest.*

> *Too bad I'll miss that spelling test!*

"*Clubhouse* has been downscaled to 8 pages from 32—to make it possible to print on inhouse equipment. However, the number of issues per year has increased to 12." The magazine has a circulation of 6,000, with 6,000 subscriptions of which maybe 5 are libraries. Subscription: $5 for 12 issues/year. **Sample cost: 3 oz. postage. Submit mss in March and April. Simultaneous submissions OK. The "evaluation sheet" for returned mss gives reasons for acceptance or rejection. Writer's guidelines available for SASE. Pays about $12 for poems under 24 lines plus 2 contributor's copies. Negotiates rights.** The editor advises, "Give us poetry with freshness and imagination. We most often use mood pieces and humorous poems that appeal to children."

CLUTCH (II), 132 Clinton Park, #4, San Francisco CA 94103, founded 1991, editors Dan Hodge and Lawrence Oberc, is an irregular (1 or 2 issues/year) "alternative/underground literary review." **They want "poetry which explores or reveals an edge, societal edges especially.** *Take chances.* **Academic, overly studied poems are not considered."** They have published poetry by Charles Bukowski, Lorri Jackson, Todd Moore and Robert Peters. As a sample the editors selected these lines from "1492" by Mitchel Cohen:

> *and the syringe is the size of a lover, O yes!*
> *and the kisses, and the bodies,*
> *and the fleshy zipless hallucinations*
> *that pass for lovers*
> *are no cure, no cure at all . . .*

The editors describe *Clutch* as 60-70 pgs., approximately 5½×8½. "Printing, binding and graphics vary with each issue. We receive approximately 300 unsolicited submissions a year, but we accept less than 10% of unsolicited material. The majority of material is solicited." Press run is 500 for 35 subscribers of which 4 are libraries, approximately 70 shelf sales. Subscription: $5/issue for as many future issues as specified. **Sample postpaid: $5. Make checks payable to Dan Hodge. Previously published poems and simultaneous submissions OK. Cover letter required. Seldom comments on rejections. Reports in 1-4 months. Pays 1 copy. Rights revert to authors.** "Open to publishing reviews of books/magazines from underground press." Poets may also send books for review consideration. The editors say, "We advise obtaining a sample copy or otherwise becoming familiar with the kind of poetry we've previously published before considering a submission."

COACH HOUSE PRESS (V, IV-Regional), 50 Prince Arthur Ave., Suite 107, Toronto, Ontario M5R 1B5 Canada, phone (416)921-3910, fax (416)921-4403, founded 1964, poetry editors Michael Ondaatje, Christopher Dewdney, Frank Davey, Lynn Crosbie and Michael Redhill, publishes **"mostly living Canadian writers of poetry and fiction, drama and literary criticism."** They have published finely-printed flat-spined paperback collections by such poets as Phyllis Webb, Michael Ondaatje, Robin Blaser, Diana Hartog and Dionne Brand. They **"lean toward experimental." However, they are currently not accepting unsolicited mss.** Catalog sent on request. **"We expect poets to be familiar with the Coach House flavor and to have a few journal publication credits to their name.** You don't have to be famous, but you do have to be good. Make the effort to do a little research on us, and save yourself time and postage. No SASE, no reply . . . and Canada Post does not accept American postage."

‡COASTAL FOREST REVIEW; AFTERIMAGE (II), 6900 Ventnor Garden Plaza, Ventnor NJ 08406, founded 1992, is an annual literary magazine "dedicated to promoting literary talent." It publishes poetry, fiction, essays, reviews and profiles by artists throughout New Jersey and the surrounding areas. **They have no restrictions in form, length, subject matter or style of poetry. "We want to see quality. Don't want pornographic material, 'suffering as a writer' poems, or flat language that lacks courage or imagination."** They have recently published poetry by Stephen Dunn, Donald Lawder, Shirley Warren and BJ Ward. As a sample the editor selected these lines from "Pinto Beans" by N.F. Ingram:

> *No world has seemed right.*
> *My left cheek is still scarred*
> *from my attempt to shave*
> *when I was three years old.*
> *There's no use*
> *knowing what it means.*

CFR is 80 pgs., 7½×10½, perfect-bound with glossy b&w cover and b&w photography and art. "Of the approximately 300 manuscripts received, we publish approximately 15%." Press run is 550, 80% shelf sales. **Sample postpaid: $5. Previously published poems and simultaneous submissions OK. Brief cover letter preferred. Reads submissions December 1 to April 1 only. "Poetry is chosen by an editorial staff of four to five people. Final decisions are made by the poetry editor." Seldom comments on rejections. Send SASE for guidelines. Reports in 2-3 months. Pays 1 copy. Acquires one-time rights.** Reviews books of poetry and fiction by New Jersey writers in up to 4,000 words. Open to unsolicited reviews ("academic criticism"). AfterImage is a South Jersey-based arts organization which sponsors poetry and fiction readings and writing workshops in addition to publishing *Coastal Forest Review*. The editor says, "Send only pieces that you feel very strongly about; be imaginative, write from your own experience."

‡COCHRAN'S CORNER (I, IV-Subscribers), 1003 Tyler Court, Waldorf MD 20602, phone (301)870-1664, founded 1985, poetry editor Billye Keene, is a **"family type" quarterly open to beginners, preferring poems of 20 lines or less. You have to be a subscriber to submit. "Any subject or style (except porn)."** She has published poetry by J. Alvin Speers, Becky Knight and Francesco BiVone. *CC* is 58 pgs., saddle-stapled, desktop-published, with matte card cover. Press run is 500. Subscription: $20.

Sample: $5 plus SASE. Submit 5 poems at a time. Simultaneous submissions and previously published poems OK. Cover letter welcome. Send SASE for guidelines. Reports in average of 3 months. Pays 2 copies. Acquires first or one-time rights. Reviews books of poetry. Send books for review consideration. Contests in March and July; $3 entry fee for 2 poems. "We provide criticism if requested at the rate of $1 per page." The editor says, "Write from the heart, but don't forget your readers. You must work to find the exact words that mirror your feelings, so the reader can share your feelings."

THE COE REVIEW (II), Coe College, 1220 First Ave. NE, Cedar Rapids IA 52402, phone (319)399-8660, founded 1972, editor Amanda Moore, is "an annual little literary magazine with **emphasis on innovative and unselfconscious** poetry and fiction. We are **open to virtually any and all subject matter.**" They have published poetry by James Galvin and Jan Weissmiller. The annual is 100-150 pgs., flat-spined, digest-sized with matte card cover. "Each issue includes 4-8 reproductions of works of art, usually photographs, lithography and etched prints." Circulation is about 500. **Sample postpaid: $4. Submit 3-5 poems at a time. No simultaneous submissions. Accepted work appears in the next issue, published in Spring. Include "brief cover letter with biographical information. One of the fun things about *The Coe Review* is the Contributor's Notes at the end. We only accept submissions from August 31 through March 15 due to the academic school year." Send SASE for guidelines. Pays 1 copy.** The editor says, "We are supportive in the endeavors of poets whose material is original and tasteful. We are eclectic in our publication choices in that variety of subject matter and style make *The Coe Review* exciting."

COFFEE HOUSE PRESS (III), Dept. PM, 27 N. Fourth St., Suite 400, Minneapolis MN 55401, phone (612)338-0125, founded 1984, editorial assistant Cheri Hickman, publishes 15 paperbacks/year, 6 of which are poetry. **They want poetry that is "challenging and lively; influenced by the Beats, the NY School or Black Mountain."** They have published poetry collections by Victor Hernandez Cruz, Anne Waldman, Andrei Codrescu and Linda Hogan. As a sample the editor selected these lines from "Heading North" by Steve Levine:

> The family that eats together
> eats together and eats together, rides a
> tiny Honda together, two of them, huge
> matching bellies heading north

Submit 8-12 poems at a time. Previously published poems OK; no simultaneous submissions. Cover letter required. "Please include a SASE for our reply and/or the return of your ms." Seldom comments on rejections. Replies to queries in 1 month, to mss in 6 months. Always sends prepublication galleys. Pays 8% royalties, $500 honorarium and 15 author's copies. Send SASE for catalog to order sample. Coffee House Press books have won numerous honors and awards. As an example, *The Book of Medicines* by Linda Hogan won the Colorado Book Award for Poetry and the Lannan Foundation Literary Fellowship. The editor says, "We'd like to see more books by writers of color."

COFFEEHOUSE (I, II), P.O. Box 77, Berthoud CO 80513, founded 1990, editor Ray Foreman, is a quarterly that focuses exclusively on **"free verse narrative poetry, prose poems and short shorts that are imaginative and clear with opening lines that hook the reader."** They have recently published poetry by Michael Estabrook, Albert Huffstickler and Richard Dixon. As a sample the editor selected these lines from "The Banana Railroad Blues" by Ray Clark Dickson:

> He sits behind the coal car on the old banana railroad
> watching snowy cattle egrets drop morning breakfasts
> of golden doughnuts steaming in the sun; flapping back
> in a blur of feathers to the stumpy shade of cahoun palms.

Coffeehouse is now 20 pgs. (instead of 40). They accept about 5% of 3,000 poems submitted/year. Press run is 400-500 for 170 subscribers. Subscription: **$4 for 2 years (8 issues). Sample postpaid: $1. Submit up to 5 poems at a time. Previously published poems and simultaneous submissions OK. "However, please send SASE for guidelines *before* submitting." Reports in about 2 weeks.** The editor has changed his "payment" policy as follows: **"Poets whose work is accepted are required to purchase a contributor's pack of 14 copies for $5 (postpaid) and expected to give, send or distribute these copies to people they know,** thus insuring their work will be read by someone other than other poets in the same magazine." He adds, "All I want to do is select prime material, publish it, and send it out to the poets. Frankly, my criteria of good work is that people other than poets enjoy it. We look for work with three qualities: It must be interesting, must be entertaining and must be well-written. Why would anyone want to read it if it doesn't have these qualities?"

COKEFISH; COKEFISH PRESS (I), 31 Waterloo St., New Hope PA 18938, phone (215)862-0299, founded 1990, editor Ana Christy, is an irregular journal **with an entry fee of $1/3 poems. "I want to see work that has passion behind it. From the traditional to the avant-garde, provocative to**

discreet, trivial to the significant. Am interested in social issues, alternative, avant-garde, erotica and humor for people with nothing to hide." They have recently published poetry by Kurt Nimmo, Herschel Silverman, Dale Russell, Dave Christy and Mike Costanzo. As a sample the editor selected these lines from "Contortionist" by Albert Huffstickler:

> The hardest parts the recovery
> Unkinking limbs locked into place
> Till distortions become the truer way
> There's pain and exposure in realignment . . .
> And a blood-deep sorrow you can't account for

The format is 60 pgs., side-stapled on heavy paper with a cover printed on both sides on colored photocopy paper. Press run is 300 for 150 subscribers. Subscription: $15. **Sample postpaid: $4. Submit 5-7 poems at a time. Accepts 30% of mss received. Note entry fee: $1/3 poems, additional $1 for additional poems. Simultaneous submissions and previously published poems OK. Cover letter "explaining why the poet chose *Cokefish*" required. Send SASE for guidelines. Reports in 1 week. Sometimes sends prepublication galleys. Pays 1 copy.** "We publish a mostly poetry broadside and will work with poets on publishing their chapbooks and audiotapes through Cokefish Press. Manuscript length up to 40 pages—$5 reading fee." Cokefish Press also publishes cooperative chapbooks. Write for details. The editor advises, "Spread the word; don't let your poems sit and vegetate in a drawer. Send me stuff that will make my hair stand up on end." Also see listings for *Alpha Beat Soup* and *Bouillabaisse*.

‡COLD MOUNTAIN REVIEW (II), English Dept., Appalachian State University, Boone NC 28608, editors Kathy Henson and Wanda Lloyd. *CMR* is published twice a year by students in the English Department at Appalachian State University and features poetry, short fiction, b&w line drawings and photographs. **They have no specifications regarding form, length, subject matter or style of poetry.** They have recently published poetry by Errol Miller, Yvonne V. Sapia and Scott Owens. As a sample we selected these lines from "The Aunts, November Morning" by Jennifer Hubbard:

> They rise to kitchen time
> the last clouds of
> classical music floating into news of wars and famines.
> They halfhear with coffee warmth
> filling the grooves of their lifelaced hands
> greyed and purpled like the dappled drifting into sleep.

CMR is about 60 pgs., 6×9, neatly printed with 1 poem/page (or 2-page spread), saddle-stitched, with light card stock cover. They publish about 10% of the submissions received. **For sample, send SASE or make donation to ASU Visiting Artist Series. Previously published poems and simultaneous submissions OK.** "Please include short biographical description." **Reads submissions September 1 through November 20 and January 10 through March 15. Send SASE for guidelines. Reports within 6 weeks. Pays 3 copies.**

COLLAGES & BRICOLAGES, THE JOURNAL OF INTERNATIONAL WRITING (II, IV-Transla-tions, feminist, political, social issues, themes), P.O. Box 86, Clarion PA 16214, founded in 1986, editor Marie-José Fortis. *C&B* is a "small literary magazine with **a strong penchant for literary, feminist, avant-garde work.** Strongly encourages poets and fiction writers, as well as essayists, whether English-speaking or foreign. (**Note: Writers sending their work in a foreign language must have their ms accompanied with an English translation.**) We are presently looking for **poetry that is socially aware—politically engaged. No sexism, racism or glorification of war. We are going towards focus-oriented issues.**" As a sample the editor selected these lines by Anne Blonstein:

> on Sunday   even the devil
> must rest   let us
> plant provisionally   paradise in our heads

The annual is 100 pgs., magazine-sized, flat-spined, with card cover. They accept 5% of 500 poetry submissions/year. Press run is 800. **Sample postpaid: $7.50, 50% off for back issue. Submit 1-5 poems at a time, no more. Reads submissions August 15 through November 30 only. Publishes theme issues. They were accepting material on Samuel Beckett and/or Eugene Ionesco until December 15, 1995. Send SASE for upcoming themes. Reports in 1-3 months. Always sends prepublication galleys. Pays 2 copies. Acquires first rights.** "It is recommended that potential contributors order a copy, so as to know what kind of work is desirable. We understand that nobody's budget is unlimited, but remember that most lit mags' back issues are half price. *C&B*'s are only $3. Be considerate to editors, as many of them work on a voluntary basis and sacrifice much time and energy to encourage writers. And please, do not send a tiny SASE in which we will have to fold material a zillion times—use at least a 9½×4 envelope." Marie-José Fortis says, "Show me that you write as if nothing else mattered."

COLLEGE & CAREER PUBLISHING; CALIFORNIA WORK WORLD (I, II, IV-Children/teen/ young adult, students), P.O. Box 900, Ontario CA 91762, fax (909)465-0313, founded 1989. *California Work World* is a "monthly newsletter/workbook to help junior high and high school students learn about college and jobs as well as how to be a good citizen in our world and cope with problems encountered along the way." **They want "rhyming poems with messages for teenagers; 5-40 lines. Particularly interested in humorous poems, social issues and poems about life on the job. No non-rhyming, free-form verse."** As a sample the editor selected these lines by Anita Elam:

> *Don't quit a job in anger*
> *for someday you may find,*
> *yourself in an even worse place—*
> *the unemployment line.*

CWW is 16 pgs., glue bound, with puzzles and illustrations. Press run is 10,000. **Sample postpaid: $1. Submit 3 poems at a time. Previously published poems and simultaneous submissions OK.** Time between acceptance and publication is 3-4 months. "Poems are tested with groups of teenagers, and they choose favorites." **Often comments on rejections. "If comments are desired, poet must include SASE." Send SASE for guidelines. Reports in 2-3 months. Pays $35 and 20 copies.**

COLLEGE ENGLISH; NATIONAL COUNCIL OF TEACHERS OF ENGLISH (II), Dept. of English, University of Massachusetts-Boston, 100 Morrissey Blvd., Boston MA 02125-3393, phone (617)287-6733, editor Louise Z. Smith, poetry editors Helene Davis and Lloyd Schwartz. This journal, which is sent 8 times/year to members of the National Council of Teachers of English (membership: $40, includes subscription to *CE*), is a scholarly journal for the English discipline, but includes poetry by such poets as Beth Kalikoff, Peter R. Stillman and E.M. Schorb. It is 100 pgs., perfect-bound, with matte card cover, $7\frac{1}{2} \times 9\frac{1}{2}$, circulation 18,000. Poems tend to be wide-ranging in style, form and content. **Sample postpaid: $6.25, from NCTE, 1111 W. Kenyon Rd., Urbana IL 61801-1096. Submit a "letter-quality copy" of each poem with cover letter including titles of poems submitted. Reports in 4 months maximum, except for summer submissions. Pays 2 copies.**

COLOR WHEEL; MINK HILLS JOURNAL; 700 ELVES PRESS (II, IV-Nature/ecology, spiritual), 36 West Main St., Warner NH 03278, founded 1990, editor Frederick Moe, associate editor Carol Edson, appears approximately 2 times/year. **"*Color Wheel* uses high quality prose and poetry related to spiritual, ecological and mythological themes. We want poetry that explores more deeply and intensely our relationships with the earth and one another. All forms of poetry are welcome, including longer poems (2-4 pages). No rhymed verse."** They have recently published poetry by R.D. Savage, Lynn Kozma, David Sparenberg, Jeanne Shannon and Walt Franklin. The editor says it is 32-40 pgs., 8×11, flat-spined, with heavy cover stock, cover art, graphics and line drawings. They receive about 300 submissions a year, use an average of 5%. Press run is 300 for 30 subscribers of which 4 are libraries, more than 100 shelf sales. Single copy: $6; subscription: $15 (3 issues). **Sample back issue postpaid: $5. Make checks payable to Frederick Moe. Submit 5 poems at a time. No simultaneous submissions. Cover letter required—include "something that does not keep the writer 'anonymous'!" Reads submissions September through May only. Comments on "close" rejections. Publishes theme issues. Send SASE for guidelines, publication list and upcoming themes. Reports in up to 1 month. Pays copies. Retains one-time reprint rights for special editions.** Staff reviews books of poetry. Send books for review consideration to Frederick Moe at the above address. Send Northwest area submissions to Carol Edson at 1804 NE 50th, Seattle WA 98105. 700 Elves Press also publishes an annual titled *Mink Hills Journal* which publishes poetry and creative nonfiction **"with a focus on the Northeast region. Submissions to *Color Wheel* may also be considered for *Mink Hills Journal.*"** The premier issue was scheduled for autumn 1995. Frederick Moe says, "*Color Wheel* is esoteric yet focused in content. Poets should be familiar with the evolution of the magazine and type of material we publish before sending work. I encourage 'new' voices and appreciate creative approaches to the material. I am annoyed by poets who enclose postcards for response rather than a SASE and expect me to recycle their manuscript. I do not respond to such submissions. Inclusion of a SASE allows me to return press information with response and demonstrates concern on the part of the writer for their work. It is worth the extra expense! I would also like to note that we would appreciate audio submissions of poetry/music/performance/creative work for a potential audio tape issue or anthology. 700 Elves Press is known for publishing deeply ecological poetry, with intricate in-depth exploration of self in relation to nature. We have published several challenging long poems and are not afraid to take risks."

COLORADO REVIEW (II, IV-Translations, themes), Dept. of English, 359 Eddy Bldg., Colorado State University, Ft. Collins CO 80523, phone (303)491-5449, fax (303)491-5601, founded 1955 as *Colorado State Review*, resurrected 1977 under "New Series" rubric, renamed *Colorado Review* 1985, editor David Milofsky, poetry editor Jorie Graham. *Colorado Review* is a journal of contemporary literature which appears twice annually; it combines short fiction, poetry, interviews with or articles about significant contemporary poets and writers, articles on literature, culture and the arts, translations of poetry from around the world and reviews of recent works of the literary imagination. **"We're**

interested in poetry that explores experience in deeply felt new ways; merely descriptive or observational language doesn't move us. Poetry that enters into and focuses on the full range of experience, weaving sharp imagery, original figures and surprising though apt insight together in compressed precise language and compelling rhythm is what triggers an acceptance here." They have published poetry by Tess Gallagher, James Galvin and Brendan Galvin. They have a circulation of 1,500, 300 subscriptions of which 100 are libraries. They use about 10% of the 500-1,000 submissions they receive/year. Subscription: $15/year. **Sample postpaid: $8. Submit about 5 poems at a time. Reads submissions September 1 through May 1 only. "When work is a near-miss, we will provide brief comment and encouragement." Publishes theme issues. Send SASE for upcoming themes. Reports in 3-6 months. Always sends prepublication galleys. Pays $10/printed page for poetry. Buys first North American serial rights.** Reviews books of poetry, both single and multi-book format. Open to unsolicited reviews. Poets may also send books for review consideration. Poetry published in *Colorado Review* has been included in the 1993, 1994 and 1995 volumes of *The Best American Poetry*. They say, "Our attitude is that we will publish the best work that comes across the editorial desk. We see poetry as a vehicle for exploring states of feeling, but we aren't interested in sentimentality (especially metaphysical)."

COLUMBIA: A MAGAZINE OF POETRY & PROSE (II), Dept. PM, 404 Dodge Hall, Columbia University, New York NY 10027, phone (212)854-4391, founded 1977, poetry editors Jennifer Franklin and Elizabeth Stein, is a literary semiannual using "quality short stories, novel excerpts, translations, interviews, nonfiction and **poetry.**" They have recently published poetry by April Bernard, Torie Dent, Charles Wright and Brenda Hillman. As a sample the editors selected these lines from "November" by Sophie Cabot Black:

> *Hoarse crows keen through unalterable sky.*
> *Leaves sink and wheel,*
> *Braiding themselves to ground.*
>
> *Haybale, scarecrow, frozen lamb: the saved*
> *Break down, restless. I gather what remains*
> *For the witness of a warm wind, that vital day.*

It is a digest-sized, approximately 180 pgs., with coated cover stock. They publish about 12 poets each issue from 400 submissions. **Sample postpaid: $7. Submit double-spaced mss. "Very brief comments at editor's discretion." Send SASE for guidelines. Reports in 1-3 months. Pays up to 2 copies.**

‡COMMON LIVES/LESBIAN LIVES (I, IV-Lesbian), P.O. Box 1553, Iowa City IA 52244, founded 1980, contact poetry editor, is a quarterly publication that "seeks to document the experiences and thoughts of lesbians as we claim our past, name our present conditions, and envision our evolving futures. *CL/LL* will reflect the complexity and richness of those experiences and thoughts by describing the lives of ordinary lesbians—women who have always struggled to survive and create a culture for ourselves. **The magazine is a forum for developing and clarifying our lesbian-defined social and political relationships.**" It features stories, journals, graphics, essays, humor and **poetry by lesbians.** They have recently published poetry by Libré Cory, Pamela Gray, Ellen Grove and Cassidy Sims. As a sample we selected this poem, "Trust," by Patricia Victour:

> *Before love must come trust,*
> *and I begin, slowly,*
> *to trust her with raw pieces of myself*
> *no one ever touched before—*
> *stretch marks on my belly,*
> *old nightmares,*
> *echos in my heart*
> *that whisper, "Not so fast. . .*
> *pain goes there."*

CL/LL is 127 pgs., digest-sized, attractively printed, flat-spined, glossy cover with b&w photo, contain-

---

ALWAYS include a self-addressed, stamped envelope (SASE) when sending a ms or query to a publisher within your own country. When sending material to other countries, include a self-addressed envelope and International Reply Coupons (IRCs), available for purchase at most post offices.

ing b&w photos, some illustrations and ads. "We receive a lot of poetry and publish 10 or so poems each issue." Press run is 2,000 for 1,000 subscribers, 700 shelf sales. "Free back issues to lesbians in prisons, mental institutions and old-age homes." Single copy: $5; subscription: $15/year. **Sample postpaid: $4.50. Submit 3 poems or 5 pages ("whichever is shorter") at a time. No previously published poems or simultaneous submissions. Cover letter with brief description of work and 2 copies of a short personal bio required. Mail submissions flat, not folded. Poems are circulated to an editorial board. Often comments on rejections. Send SASE for guidelines. Pays 2 copies.** "Unless an author requests otherwise, **all copyable manuscripts submitted to** *CL/LL* **become a part of the** *Common Lives/Lesbian Lives* **Special Collection at the Lesbian Herstory Archives**. In this way the voices of all the lesbians we hear are preserved and accessible." They say, *CL/LL* feels a strong responsibility to insure access to women whose lives have traditionally been denied visibility and to encourage lesbians who have never before thought of publishing to do so."

COMMONWEAL (III, IV-Religious), 15 Dutch St., New York NY 10038, phone (212)732-0800, poetry editor Rosemary Deen, appears every 2 weeks, circulation 20,000, is a general-interest magazine for college-educated readers **by Catholics. Prefers serious, witty, well-written poems of up to 75 lines. Does not publish inspirational poems.** As a sample the editor selected these lines from "One is One," a sonnet by Marie Ponsot:

> *Heart, you bully, you punk, I'm wrecked, I'm shocked*
> *stiff. You? you still try to rule the world—though*
> *I've got you: identified, starving, locked*
> *in a cage you will not leave alive . . .*

In the issues we reviewed, editors seemed to favor free verse, much of it open with regard to style and content, appealing as much to the intellect as to the emotions. **Sample: $3. Considers simultaneous submissions. Reads submissions September 1 through June 30 only. Pays 50¢ a line. Buys all rights. Returns rights when requested by the author.** Reviews books of poetry in 750-1,000 words, single or multi-book format.

COMMUNICATIONS PUBLISHING GROUP; COLLEGE PREVIEW, A GUIDE FOR COLLEGE-BOUND STUDENTS; DIRECT AIM; A GUIDE TO CAREER ALTERNATIVES; JOURNEY, A SUCCESS GUIDE FOR COLLEGE AND CAREER-BOUND STUDENTS; VISIONS, A SUCCESS GUIDE FOR NATIVE AMERICAN STUDENTS; FIRST OPPORTUNITY, A GUIDE FOR VOCATIONAL TECHNICAL STUDENTS (IV-Youth, themes, ethnic), Dept. PM, 106 W. 11th St., #250, Kansas City MO 64105-1806, phone (816)221-4404, editor Georgia Clark. These five publications are 40% freelance written. All are designed to inform and motivate their readers in regard to college preparation, career planning and life survival skills. All except *First Opportunity*, which is quarterly, appear in spring and fall. *College Preview* **is for Black and Hispanic young adults, ages 16-21.** Circ. 600,000. *Direct Aim* **is for Black and Hispanic young adults, ages 18-25.** Circ. 500,000. *Journey* **is for Asian-American high school and college students, ages 16-25.** Circ. 200,000. *Visions* **is for Native American students and young adults, ages 16-25.** Circ. 100,000. *First Opportunity* **is for Black and Hispanic young adults, ages 16-21.** Circ. 500,000. **Sample copy of any for 9 × 12 SAE with 4 first class stamps. Simultaneous and previously published submissions OK. Submit seasonal/holiday material 6 months in advance.** "Include on manuscript your name, address, phone and Social Security numbers." **They use free verse. Each magazine buys 5 poems/year. Submit up to 5 poems at one time. Length: 10-25 lines. Writer's guidelines for #10 SASE. Reports in 2 months. Pays $10-25/poem. All these magazines pay on acceptance.**

COMMUNITIES: JOURNAL OF COOPERATIVE LIVING (IV-Specialized), 1118 Round Butte Dr., Fort Collins CO 80524, phone (303)224-9080, founded 1972, managing editor Diana Christian, is a "quarterly publication on **intentional communities and cooperative living,**" occasionally using poetry relevant to those topics. It is magazine-sized, professionally printed on recycled white stock with 2-color glossy paper cover, 76 pgs., saddle-stapled. **Submit 3-4 poems at a time. SASE required. Previously published poems and simultaneous submissions OK. No comment on rejections. Publishes theme issues. Send SASE for upcoming themes. Pays 1 copy.** They also publish the *Communities Directory*.

A COMPANION IN ZEOR (IV-Science fiction/fantasy), 307 Ashland Ave., McKee City, Egg Harbor Township NJ 08234, phone (609)645-6938, founded 1978, editor Karen Litman, is a **science fiction, fantasy fanzine appearing** *very* **irregularly (last published issue November 1994; hopes to publish again this year).** "Material used is now limited to creations based solely on works (universes) of Jacqueline Lichtenberg. No other submission types considered. Prefer nothing obscene. Homosexuality not acceptable unless very relevant to the piece. Prefer a 'clean' publication image." As a sample, we selected these lines from "Song of the Captive" by Gail Ray Barton:

> *Nerves burning, blood drying,*
> *Can't you hear me or care?*

You're deafened by legend,
The bars are made of air.
I am caged inside your fear,
With attrition torment here;
And the sun says, it's too late;
And the bars are made of hate.

It is magazine-sized, photocopied from typescript. Press run is 100. **Send SASE for guidelines. Cover letter preferred with submissions; note whether to return or dispose of rejected mss. Sometimes sends prepublication galleys. Pays copies. Acquires first rights. "Always willing to work with authors or poets to help in improving their work."** Reviews books of poetry. Open to unsolicited reviews. Poets may also send books for review consideration.

COMPENIONS; THE WRITER'S CLUB OF STRATFORD (I), P.O. Box 2511, St. Marys, Ontario N4X 1A3 Canada, founded 1983, contact Marco Balestrin, is a quarterly publication of The Writer's Club of Stratford. "We print works by the members of the W.C.S. but would like to expand our mandate to include poetry and short fiction by other writers." **They want "original, sincerely-written poetry of any form, 30 lines maximum. No clichéd or trite poetry. No pornography."** They have recently published poetry by Patrick Seguin, Jim Cherry and Stuart C. Nottingham. As a sample Marco Balestrin selected these lines from "A Dark Day in Emmittsville" by Sara Holt:

Alas, there was tea, baked apples and
roundbread
to staple these people
together, like pages of a universal script
to be read to children
in times of desperate measures.

Compenions is 14-20 pgs., 8½ × 11, photocopied, side-stapled, with computer graphics. They receive about 40 poems a year, use approximately 90%. Press run is 30 ("will increase after further submissions are received"). **Sample postpaid: $4. Submit up to 6 poems at a time *with $3.50 reading fee*. (Make cheques or money orders payable to The Writer's Club of Stratford.) Previously published poems and simultaneous submissions OK. Cover letter required. "Please include a SASE (if within Canada) or SAE and 2 IRCs (if outside Canada)." Reads submissions September 1 through June 30 only. "Two to three members read over submissions and choose suitable poems." Often comments on rejections. Publishes theme issues. Send SASE for upcoming themes. Themes for September 1995, December 1995, March 1996, June 1996 and September 1996 are fire, water, east, west and north, respectively. Reports in 1-2 months. Pays 2 copies.** Balestrin says, "We would like to be a forum providing writers (especially beginners) the opportunity to get published, thereby also exposing ourselves to what is going on 'out there,' in other words, to have a literary relationship beneficial to both parties!"

CONCHO RIVER REVIEW; FORT CONCHO MUSEUM PRESS (IV-Regional), 213 E. Ave. D, San Angelo TX 76903, phone (915)942-2281, fax (915)942-2229, founded 1984, poetry editor Gerald M. Lacy. "The Fort Concho Museum Press is entering another year of publishing *Concho River Review*, a literary journal published twice a year. **Work by Texas writers, writers with a Texas connection and writers living in the Southwest preferred. Prefer shorter poems, few long poems accepted; particularly looking for poems with distinctive imagery and imaginative forms and rhythms. The first test of a poem will be its imagery."** Short reviews of new volumes of poetry are also published. *CRR* is 120-138 pgs., digest-sized, flat-spined, with matte card cover, professionally printed. They use 35-40 of 600-800 poems received/year. Press run is 300 for about 200 subscribers of which 10 are libraries. Subscription: $12. **Sample postpaid: $4. "Please submit 3-5 poems at a time. Use regular legal-sized envelopes—no big brown envelopes; no replies without SASE. Type must be letter-perfect, sharp enough to be computer scanned." Publishes theme issues. Send SASE for upcoming themes. Reports in 1-2 months. Pays 1 copy. Acquires first rights.** The editor says, "We're always looking for good, strong work—from both well-known poets and those who have never been published before."

CONFLUENCE; OHIO VALLEY LITERARY GROUP (II), P.O. Box 336, Belpre OH 45714, phone (614)373-2999, founded 1983 as *Gambit*, 1989 as *Confluence*, editor Barbara McCullough-Cress. *Confluence* is an annual "credible platform for outstanding student work complemented by established/emerging authors. This literary magazine is published at Marietta College, Marietta, Ohio, and was named to represent the merging of the Ohio and Muskingum Rivers as well as the collaboration of the Ohio Valley Literary Group with Marietta College." **As for poetry, they want "truths retold in vital, economical language. Nothing cliché, sentimental, same old ax to grind."** They have recently published poetry by Lyn Lifshin, Denise Duhamel, Margaret Gibson and Louis Phillips. As a sample the editor selected these lines from "The breathtaking indigo of their clothes" by Brigitte Oleschinski, translated by Gary Sea:

> *Fissures, footprint, shingles.*
> *On the stones spreads a topography of weather*
> *of time, Thirst*
> *and questions. You*
> *wonder over torrent-scarred rock onto*
> *rivers of sand, sun-blanched clefts, stumbling—hear*
> *the barometer's dispatch like*
> *a saxophone and all things blue*
> *are oceans in your head.*

Confluence is 96-112 pgs., digest-sized, professionally printed and perfect-bound with 2-color matte card cover and b&w graphics. They receive 800-1,000 submissions a year, accept approximately 2%. Press run is 500 for 300 subscribers of which 10 are libraries, about 150 shelf sales. Single copy: $5. **Sample: $3 plus $1.25 postage. No previously published poems or simultaneous submissions. Cover letter with brief bio required. Reads submissions January 1 to March 1 only.** Time between acceptance and publication is 6 months. **Always comments on rejections. Send SASE for guidelines. Reports in 3 months. Pays 1-3 copies. Returns rights upon publication.**

CONFLUENCE PRESS (II, IV-Regional), Lewis-Clark State College, Lewiston ID 83501, phone (208)799-2336, founded 1975, poetry editor James R. Hepworth, is an "independent publisher of fiction, poetry, creative nonfiction and literary scholarship. **We are open to formal poetry as well as free verse. No rhymed doggerel, 'light verse,' 'performance poetry,' 'street poetry,' etc. We prefer to publish work by poets who live and work in the northwestern United States."** They have published poetry by John Daniel, Greg Keeler, Nancy Mairs and Sherry Rind. They print about 2 books a year. **"Please query *before* submitting manuscript." Query with 6 sample poems, bio, list of publications. Replies to queries in 6 weeks. Pays $100-500 advance and 10% royalties plus copies. Buys all rights. Returns rights if book goes out of print. Send SASE for catalog to order samples.**

CONFRONTATION MAGAZINE (II), English Dept., C.W. Post Campus of Long Island University, Brookville NY 11548-0570, phone (516)299-2391, fax (516)299-2735, founded 1968, editor-in-chief Martin Tucker, is "a semiannual literary journal with **interest in all forms. Our only criterion is high literary merit.** We think of our audience as an educated, lay group of intelligent readers. **We prefer lyric poems. Length generally should be kept to 2 pages. No sentimental verse."** They have published poetry by Karl Shapiro, T. Alan Broughton, David Ignatow, Philip Appleman, Jane Mayhall and Joseph Brodsky. As a sample the editor selected these lines from "Imagination" by Scott Thomas:

> *He builds things in my cellar. He fashions things*
> *From wood and glass, flesh and bone, green eyes*
> *And dirt. One day while I was down there washing*
> *Bedclothes, he was at his workbench tinkering*
> *With a small electric motor. "Rewiring*
> *A soul," he said.*

Confrontation is 190 pgs., digest-sized, professionally printed, flat-spined, with a circulation of about 2,000. A visually beautiful journal, and well-edited, each issue features about 30-40 poems of varying lengths. The magazine is recommended not only for its "showcase" appeal, but also for the wide range of formal and free styles, displaying craft and insight. They receive about 1,200 submissions/year, publish 150, have a 6- to 12-month backlog. **Sample postpaid: $3. Submit no more than 10 pgs., clear copy. No previously published poems. Do not submit mss June through August. "Prefer single submissions." Publishes theme issues. Send SASE for upcoming themes. Reports in 6-8 weeks. Sometimes sends prepublication galleys. Pays $5-50 and copy of magazine**. Staff reviews books of poetry. Send books for review consideration. Basically a magazine, they do on occasion publish "book" issues or "anthologies." Their most recent "occasional book" is *Phantom Pain*, story and drawings by Alfred Van Loen.

CONJUNCTIONS (III), Dept. PM, Bard College, Annandale-on-Hudson NY 12504, founded 1981, managing editor Dale Cotton, editor Bradford Morrow, is an elegant journal appearing twice a year, using work that is **"stylistically innovative. Potential contributors should be familiar with the poetry published in the journal."** They have published poetry by John Ashbery, Robert Kelly, Charles Stein, Michael Palmer, Ann Lauterbach and Fanny Howe. As a sample here are lines from "Paulownia" by Barbara Guest:

> *ravenous the still dark a fishnet—*
> *robber walk near formidable plaits*
> *a glaze—the domino overcast—*
> *violet. shoulder.*

This publication is distributed by Consortium. It is 350 pgs., 6×9, flat-spined, professionally printed. Issues reviewed feature mostly lyric free verse with occasional sequences and stanza patterns (some leaning toward the avant-garde). Poems compete with prose, with more pages devoted to the latter.

Press run is 5,500 for 600 subscribers of which 200 are libraries. Subscription: $18. **Sample postpaid: $12. Pays $100-175.**

THE CONNECTICUT POETRY REVIEW (II), P.O. Box 818, Stonington CT 06378, founded 1981, poetry editors J. Claire White and Harley More, is a "small press that puts out an annual magazine. **We look for poetry of quality which is both genuine and original in content. No specifications except length: 10-40 lines.**" The magazine has won high praise from the literary world; they have recently published such poets as John Updike, Robert Peters, Diane Wakoski and Marge Piercy. Each issue seems to feature a poet. As a sample the editors selected these lines by Odysseus Elytis (translated by Jeffrey Carson):

> *Maybe I'm still in the state of a medicinal*
> *herb or of a cold Friday's snake*
> *Or perhaps of one of those sacred beasts*
> *with its big ear full of heavy sounds*
> *and metallic noise from censers.*

The flat-spined, large digest-sized journal is "printed letterpress by hand on a Hacker Hand Press from Monotype Bembo." Most of the 45-60 pgs. are poetry, but they also have reviews. Editors seem to favor free verse with strong emphasis on voice (and judicious use of image and symbol). They receive over 1,200 submissions a year, use about 20, have a 3-month backlog. Press run is 400 for 80 subscribers of which 35 are libraries. **Sample postpaid: $3.50. Reports in 3 months. Pays $5/poem plus 1 copy.** The editors advise, "Study traditional and modern styles. Study poets of the past. Attend poetry readings. And write. Practice on your own."

CONNECTICUT RIVER REVIEW; BRODINE CONTEST; CONNECTICUT POETRY SOCIETY (II), 35 Lindsley Place, Stratford CT 06497, founded 1978, appears twice yearly, editor Norah Christianson. They are looking for **"original, honest, diverse, vital, well-crafted poetry. Translations and long-poems accepted."** They have recently published poetry by Rennie McQuilkin, Paul Petrie, Cortney Davis and Dick Allen. Each of the attractively printed, digest-sized issues contains about 40 pgs. of poetry, has a circulation of about 500 with 175 subscriptions of which 5% are libraries. They receive about 2,000 submissions/year, use about 80. Subscription: $12. **Sample postpaid: $6. Submit no more than 3 poems. No previously published poems or simultaneous submissions. Guidelines available with SASE. Pays 1 copy.** The Brodine Contest has a $2 entry fee/poem and three cash awards plus publication in the *Connecticut River Review*. Entries must be postmarked between May 1 and July 31.

CONSCIENCE (II), CFFC, 1436 U St. NW, Suite 301, Washington DC 20009-3997, founded 1980, poetry editor Andrew Merton, is a quarterly newsjournal of prochoice Catholic opinion, published by Catholics for a Free Choice. **They want poetry up to 45 lines maximum. "We're topically broad and broadminded. However, no polemics (about abortion/choice/religion) nor poems in conflict with a prochoice—albeit not stiflingly politically correct—organization."** They have published poetry by Mekeel McBride and Romana Huk. As a sample the editor selected these lines from "The Cyclops" by Gwen Strauss:

> *I would not mock the man*
> *for his blindness;*
> *Don't lovers grant us*
> *the permissions of their blindness—*
> *so that we may invent ourselves.*

Conscience is 48 pgs., $8 \times 10\frac{1}{2}$, web press newsprint, saddle-stitched with some b&w art, photos and ads. They accept less than 10% of poetry received. Press run is 15,000. Single copy: $3.50; subscription: $10/year. **Sample free for 9×12 SASE with $1.01 postage. Submit 3-5 poems at a time. No previously published poems; simultaneous submissions OK, if noted.** Time between acceptance and publication is 1-8 months. **Seldom comments on rejections. Reports in 2 months. Pays $10 and 5 copies. Buys first serial rights.** Interested poets are strongly urged to read a few issues of this publication before submitting. The editor says, "*Conscience* explores ethical and social policy dimensions of sexuality and reproductive health and decision-making, church-state dynamics and related topics. CFFC is a nonprofit educational organization that shapes and advances sexual and reproductive ethics that are based on justice, reflect a commitment to women's well-being, and respect and affirm the moral capacity of women and men to make sound and responsible decisions about their lives."

CONSERVATIVE REVIEW (II), 1307 Dolley Madison Blvd., Room #203, McLean VA 22101, phone (703)893-7302, fax (703)893-7273, founded January 1990, poetry editor Mattie F. Quesenberry, is a bimonthly magazine that includes "political articles, political statistics, political cartoons and especially strong articles on foreign affairs. **We want to see poetry of any form exploring our relationship to the natural world, especially poems exploring the impact of 20th century science and technology on traditional values. We do not want to see any political poetry. Poetry transcends political divisions because it captures universal experiences."** They have recently published poetry by Eric

Trethewey, Barbara N. Ewell, Linda Jenkins and Filemann Waitts. As a sample the editor selected these lines from "Let There Be" by Leslie Woolf Hedley:

> *Let there be a writer of silences*
> *who can design a thousand ideas*
> *without one noisy word*
> *made thick with second-hand sweat.*
> *Yet do so with utmost softness,*
> *etched like an opening leaf.*

CR is 40 pgs., 8½ × 11, offset printed and saddle-stitched with glossy card cover. They use one page of poetry in each issue. Press run is 950 for 810 subscribers of which 170 are libraries. Subscription: $28/year. **Sample postpaid: $5. Submit 3 poems at a time. Previously published poems and simultaneous submissions OK.** "Unsolicited manuscripts must be accompanied by a letter certifying the material is the original work of the author and involves no contravention of copyright or unauthorized use of another author's material." Time between acceptance and publication is up to a year. **Often comments on rejections. Reports in 1-2 months. Pays 3 copies. Acquires all rights. Returns rights upon request.** "We will review books and chapbooks, and print short critical essays." Open to unsolicited reviews. Poets may also send books for review consideration. The editor says, "There is no real division between poetry and our twentieth century science and technology. Even the most specialized specialists live their lives with consciences housed in flesh and blood. Even our most unscientific writers and poets must live and react in the modern world."

CONTEXT SOUTH (III), 2100 Memorial Blvd., #4504, Kerrville TX 78028, founded 1988, editor/publisher David Breeden, appears twice a year using **"any form, length, subject matter. Looking for strong rhythms, clear vision. Nothing sentimental."** They have published poetry by Andrea Hollander Budy, Simon Perchik and Peter Drizhal. As a sample the editor selected these lines by Dean Taciuch:

> *The myth remains with us even after the land*
> *has emptied itself into shallow basins our faces*
> *stare back through waves and fields where*
> *the water ran and covered our heads in song.*

It is 65 pgs., digest-sized, saddle-stapled, using fiction, criticism and book reviews as well as poetry. They accept less than 1% of poems received. Press run is 500 for 60 subscribers of which 6 are libraries. **Sample: $5. Simultaneous submissions OK. Reads submissions January 1 through March 31 only. Publishes theme issues. Pays 1 copy. Acquires first serial rights.** Reviews books of poetry in 500 words maximum. Open to unsolicited reviews. Poets may also send books for review consideration. The editor advises, "Read every poem you can find from the beginning of time. Every poem encapsulates the tradition."

COPPER BEECH PRESS (III), P.O. Box 1852, English Dept., Brown University, Providence RI 02912, phone (401)863-3744, founded 1973, poetry editor Randy Blasing, publishes **books of all kinds of poetry**, about three 64-page, flat-spined paperbacks a year. They have recently published Phillis Levin, Margaret Holley, Robert B. Shaw and Kay Ryan. **Query with 5 poems, biographical information and publications. Considers simultaneous submissions. Do not submit queries from Memorial Day to Labor Day. Replies to queries in 1 month, to mss in 3 months. Always sends prepublication galleys. Pays 5% royalties. For sample books, call or write for free catalog.**

COPPER CANYON PRESS (III), P.O. Box 271, Port Townsend WA 98368, founded 1972, editor Sam Hamill, publishes 10 paperback books of poetry/year, one of which is through the National Poetry Series Annual Open Competition (for details, write National Poetry Series at P.O. Box G, Hopewell NJ 08525). They have published books of poetry by Lucille Clifton, Hayden Carruth, Carolyn Kizer and Olga Broumas. **Query first with sample poems and cover letter with brief bio and publication credits. Replies to queries and mss (if invited) in 1 month.** Time between acceptance and publication is 2 years. **Write for catalog to order samples.**

CORNERSTONE (IV-Religious), Jesus People USA, 939 W. Wilson, Chicago IL 60640, phone (312)561-2450 ext. 2080, poetry editor Tammy Boyd, is a mass-circulation (50,000), low-cost ($2.50/copy) publication appearing 2-4 times/year, **directed at young adults (20-35)**, covering **"contemporary issues in the light of Evangelical Christianity."** They use avant-garde, free verse, haiku, light verse, rarely traditional—**"no limits except for epic poetry. (We've not got the room.)"** As a sample the editor selected these lines from "Mary" by Tina Quinn Durham:

> *But I bear no Christ-child for kings to welcome*
> *and men to pierce. Mine is the baby your son died for,*
> *and his conception was an act of the flesh,*
> *unsanctioned by the Spirit, heralded by tears,*
> *not angels.*

Do you understand?

Buys 10-50 poems/year, uses 1-2 pgs./issue, has a 2- to 3-month backlog. **Sample: $2.50. Submit maximum of 5 poems at a time. Cover letter required. Send SASE for guidelines. Pays $10 for poems having 1-15 lines, $25 for poems having 16 lines or more. Buys first or one-time rights.** Open to unsolicited reviews. Poets may also send books for review consideration. In past years, *Cornerstone* has received numerous awards from the Evangelical Press Association (including second place for poetry) as well as a Medal of Distinctive Merit from the Society of Publication Designers and a Certificate of Design Excellence from *Print* magazine.

CORONA (II), Dept. of History and Philosophy, Montana State University, Bozeman MT 59717, phone (406)994-5200, founded 1979, poetry editors Lynda and Michael Sexson, "is an interdisciplinary occasional journal bringing together reflections from those who stand on the edges of their disciplines; those who sense that insight is located not in things but in relationships; those who have deep sense of playfulness; and those who believe that the imagination is involved in what we know." In regard to poetry they want **"no sentimental greeting cards; no slap-dash."** They have published poems by Wendy Battin, William Irwin Thompson, Frederick Turner and James Dickey. In the spring of 1996 the editors are planning a special issue on the subject of the "book." The journal is 125-140 pgs., perfect-bound, professionally printed. They use about 20-25 pgs. of poetry/issue. Press run is 2,000. **Sample postpaid: $7. Submit any number of pages. No simultaneous submissions. Reports in 1 week to 9 months. Payment is "nominal" plus 2 contributor's copies.** The editors advise, "Today's poet survives only by the generous spirits of small press publishers. Read and support the publishers of contemporary artists by subscribing to the journals and magazines you admire."

COSMIC TREND; PARA*phrase (I, IV-Themes, love/romance/erotica), Sheridan Mall Box 47014, Mississauga, Ontario L5K 2R2 Canada, founded 1984, Cosmic Trend poetry editor George Le Grand, *PARA*phrase* editor Tedy Asponsen. Cosmic Trend annually publishes 1 chapbook anthology and 1 special project with narrated music cassettes of **"New Age, and Post-New-Age, sensual and mind-expanding short material of any style, but preferably unrhymed; also: humorous, unusual or zany entries (incl. graphics) with deeper meaning. We ignore epics, run-of-a-mill romantic and political material. Would like to publish more free verse."** They have recently published poetry by Jay Bradford Fowler, Jr., Iris Litt and Charles David Rice. As a sample the editor selected these lines by Susan Benischek:

> *Beyond—*
> > *where time stands still*
> > > *a river runs forever*
> > > > *backwards*
> > > *into reality*
> > > *and fantasy*
> > *of the mind!*

PARA*phrase—Newsletter of Cosmic Trend (irregular: 2-3 times a year)—publishes "poetry related to our major anthologies advertised there." **Submit up to 10 poems at a time with name and address on each sheet. Submission fee: $1 for each two poems submitted, plus $1 for postage. Minimum fee is $2 plus postage. ("No US postal stamps, please.") They will consider simultaneous submissions and previously published poems "with accompanied disclosure and references." Publishes theme issues. Themes for Summer 1996 and Spring 1997 are "Tornados of Calm" (deadline: April 15, 1996) and "Gardens from Beyond" (deadline: September 30, 1996), respectively. Send $1 for guidelines and upcoming themes or $6 for sample publication, guidelines and upcoming themes. Response time is usually less than 3 weeks. Editor "often" comments on submissions. Poets purchase a copy of the publication in which their work appears for the "discounted price" of $6. Rights revert to authors upon publication.** Reviews books of poetry. Open to unsolicited reviews. Poets may also send books for review consideration, attn. Tedy Asponsen. Cosmic Trend publishes electronic music cassette tapes in addition to their poetry/music anthology accompaniments. They say, "Share your adventure of poetry beyond the usual presentation! Cosmic Trend can choose your poems for narration with music and inclusion into our cassette accompaniments to our illustrated anthologies."

COSMOPOLITAN (IV-Women), 224 W. 57th St., New York NY 10019, founded 1886, is a monthly magazine "aimed at a female audience 18-34," part of the Hearst conglomerate, though it functions independently editorially. They want **"freshly-written free verse, not more than 25 lines, either light or serious, which addresses the concerns of young women. Prefer shorter poems, use 1-4 poems each issue. Poems shouldn't be too abstract. The poem should convey an image, feeling or emotion that our reader could perhaps identify with. We do publish mostly free verse, although we're also open to well-crafted rhyme poems. We cannot return submissions without SASE."** They have a circulation of 2,987,970. **Buy sample at newsstand. Reports in 3-5 weeks. Pays $25.** "Please do not phone; query by letter if at all, though queries are unnecessary before submitting."

COTEAU BOOKS; THUNDER CREEK PUBLISHING CO-OP; WOOD MOUNTAIN SERIES (II, IV-Regional, children), 401-2206 Dewdney Ave., Regina, Saskatchewan S4R 1H3 Canada, phone (306)777-0170, fax (306)522-5152, founded 1975, managing editor Shelley Sopher, is a "small literary press that publishes poetry, fiction, drama, anthologies, criticism, young adult novels—**only by Canadian writers.**" They have published poetry by Nancy Mattson, Kim Morrissey, Anne Szumigalski, Patrick Lane, Louise Halfe, Paul Wilson, Judith Krause, Barbara Klar and Dennis Cooley and 2 anthologies of Saskatchewan poetry. **"We publish theme anthologies occasionally." However, writers should submit 30-50 poems "and indication of whole ms," typed; simultaneous and American submissions not accepted. Cover letter required; include publishing credits and bio and SASE or SAE with IRC if necessary. Queries will be answered in 2-3 weeks and mss reported on in 2-4 months. Always sends prepublication galleys. Authors receive 12.5% royalty; 10 copies.** Their attractive catalog is free for 9×12 SASE, or SAE with IRC, and sample copies can be ordered from it. The editor says: "Membership has changed through the years in the Thunder Creek Publishing Co-op, but now stands at eight. Each member has a strong interest in Canadian writing and culture. Generally, poets would have published a number of poems and series of poems in literary magazines and anthologies before submitting a manuscript." However, the imprint Wood Mountain Series is for first collections, reflecting their commitment to publishing new writers. Coteau Books published *The Night You Called Me A Shadow*, by Barbara Klar, which won the 1994 Lampert Memorial Award.

COTTONWOOD; COTTONWOOD PRESS (II, IV-Regional), Box J, 400 Kansas Union, University of Kansas, Lawrence KS 66045, phone (913)748-0853, founded 1965, poetry editor Philip Wedge. **The press "is auxiliary to** *Cottonwood Magazine* **and publishes material by authors in the region. Material is usually solicited." For the magazine they are looking for "strong narrative or sensory impact, non-derivative, not 'literary,' not 'academic.' Emphasis on Midwest, but publishes the best poetry received regardless of region. Poems should be 60 lines or less, on daily experience,** *perception.*" They have published poetry by Rita Dove, Allen Ginsberg, Walter McDonald, Patricia Traxler and Ron Schreiber. The magazine, published 3 times/year, is 112 pgs., 6×9, flat-spined, printed from computer offset, with photos, using 15-20 pages of poetry in each issue. They receive about 2,000 submissions/year, use about 30, have a maximum of 1-year backlog. They have a circulation of 500-600, with 150 subscribers of which 75 are libraries. Single copy: $6.50. **Sample postpaid: $4. Submit up to 5 pgs. of poetry at a time. No simultaneous submissions. Sometimes provides criticism on rejected mss. Reports in 2-5 months. Pays 1 copy.** The editors advise, "Read the little magazines and send to ones you like."

COUNTRY JOURNAL (II), 4 High Ridge Park, Stanford CT 06905, phone (203)321-1778, fax (203)322-1966, editor Peter V. Fossel, is a bimonthly magazine featuring country living **for people who live in rural areas or who are thinking about moving there. They use free verse and traditional.** Average issue includes 6-8 feature articles and 10 departments. They have published poetry by Mary Oliver and Wendell Berry. As a sample the editor selected these lines from "The Springs Under the Lake" by Kate Barnes:

> The rest of the way
> I didn't talk. I could almost hear the words
> combining in her mind, the lines gathering
> inside her head like butter when it suddenly
> starts to come, when it clumps up thick in the churn.

Of 1,000 poems received each year, they accept 10-12. Circulation 200,000. Subscription: $24. **Sample postpaid: $4. Submit seasonal material 1 year in advance. Editor seldom comments on submissions. Reports in 1-2 months. Pays $50/poem on acceptance. Buys first North American serial rights.**

COUNTRY WOMAN; REIMAN PUBLICATIONS (IV-Women, humor), P.O. Box 643, Milwaukee WI 53201, founded 1970, managing editor Kathy Pohl. *Country Woman* "is a bimonthly magazine dedicated to the lives and interests of country women. Those who are both involved in farming and ranching and those who love country life. In some ways, it is very similar to many women's general interest magazines, and yet its subject matter is closely tied in with rural living and the very unique lives of country women. **We like short (4-5 stanzas, 16-20 lines) traditional rhyming poems that reflect on a season or comment humorously or seriously on a particular rural experience. Also limericks and humorous 4- to 8-line filler rhymes. No experimental poetry or free verse. Poetry will not be considered unless it rhymes. Always looking for poems that focus on the seasons. We don't want rural putdowns, poems that stereotype country women, etc. All poetry must be positive and upbeat. Our poems are fairly simple, yet elegant. They often accompany a high-quality photograph.**" They have published poetry by Hilda Sanderson, Edith E. Cutting and Ericka Northrop. *CW* is 68 pgs., magazine-sized, glossy paper with much color photography. They receive about 1,200 submissions of poetry/year, use 40-50 (unless they publish an anthology). Their backlog is 1 month to 3 years. Subscription: $16.98/year. **Sample postpaid: $2. Submit maximum of 6 poems. Photocopy OK if**

stated not a simultaneous submission. **Reports in 2-3 months. Pays $10-25/poem plus copy. Buys first rights (generally) or reprint rights (sometimes).** They hold various contests for subscribers only. One of their anthologies, *Cattails and Meadowlarks: Poems from the Country*, is 90 pgs., saddle-stapled with high-quality color photography on the glossy card cover, poems in large, professional type with many b&w photo illustrations. The editor says, "We're always welcoming submissions, but any poem that does not have traditional rhythm and rhyme is automatically passed over."

THE COUNTRYMAN (IV-Rural), Sheep St., Burford, Oxon OX18 4LH England, phone 0993 (Burford) 822258, founded 1927, editor Christopher Hall, is a bimonthly magazine "on rural matters." The editor wants **poetry on rural themes, "accessible to general readership but not jingles."** As a sample the editor selected this complete poem, "Crows, Cedar Springs Farm," by Don Russ:

> *Their softened raucousness, calling across*
> *from wood to wood—in the hugeness of morning,*
> *muted, almost music: before us,*
> *gathered fields, and in some distant field*
> *and the balers still baling, barns half-filled—*
> *and even with you here I hear it,*
> *winter's empty musings in the wind.*

It is a handsome, flat-spined, digest-sized magazine, 200 pgs., using popular articles and ads. **Submit 2-3 poems at a time. Submissions should be short. No previously published poems or simultaneous submissions. Reporting time is "within a week usually,"** longer if from outside the country. **Time to publication is "3 months to 3 years." Pays a maximum of £20/poem. Buys all rights "but we stipulate never to refuse permission to reprint at author's wish."** Staff reviews books of poetry in "25 words upwards." Send books for review consideration. The editor says, "Not all our poems are *about* birds or flowers or animals. Personal reaction to rural experience is valued if it comes in a form to which our readers (high-income, quiet not violently green, British for the most part) can relate. We get quite a few American submissions which I always read with much interest, not least because of my own love of the few American landscapes I know. Too often these submissions are too obviously American (because of tell-tale species or phrases) and I generally rule these out because 95% of my readers expect a British mag."

THE COVENANT COMPANION; COVENANT PUBLICATIONS (II, IV-Religious), 5101 N. Francisco Ave., Chicago IL 60625, phone (312)784-3000, founded 1923, executive secretary of publications John E. Phelan Jr., is a monthly designed to "gather, stimulate and enlighten the church it serves—The Evangelical Covenant Church—on the way to promoting Christ's mission in the world." **They want brief poems with Christian viewpoint. Nothing sing-songy.** The editor says it is 40 pgs., 8 × 10, some 4-color, some 2-color, some b&w, with self cover, pictures, graphics and ads. They receive about 200 poems a year, use 5-10. Press run is 21,000 for about that many subscribers. Subscription: $26. **Sample postpaid: $2.25. Submit 3-6 poems at a time. Previously published poems and simultaneous submissions OK.** Time between acceptance and publication is 3 months. **Seldom comments on rejections. Reports on submissions "as we get around to them." Pays $10-15 and 3 author's copies. Buys first or one-time rights.**

COVER MAGAZINE (II), P.O. Box 1215, Cooper Station, New York NY 10276, phone (212)673-1152, founded 1986, contact editor/publisher Jeffrey C. Wright, poetry editor Joe DiMattio, is a "broad-based arts monthly covering all the arts in every issue, a 40-page tabloid sold on newsstands and in select bookstores nationwide." **They want "shorter poems—2-24 lines generally, modern, favoring new romantic work. Nothing stodgy or simplistic."** They have published poetry by John Ashbery, Lawrence Ferlinghetti, Allen Ginsberg, Robert Creeley and Molly Peacock. As a sample we selected these lines from "Notes From My Pockets" by Ira Cohen:

> *"I Left three days ago*
> *but no one seems to know*
>   *I'm gone."*
> popular song
>
> *Having left yet still here*
> *perhaps the poem can sustain me*
> *still yearning for your touch*
> *I'm afraid it will burn me. . .*

Cover tries "to reach a cutting edge/front-line audience in touch with the creative fields." They receive about 1,000 poems a year, accept approximately 50. Entirely supported by subscriptions, sales and ads. Press run is 20,000 for 3,400 subscribers (20 of them libraries), 4,000 shelf sales. Two-year subscription: $15. **Sample postpaid: $5. Submit 4 poems with cover letter.** Time between acceptance and publication is 4-6 months. **Editor often comments on submissions. Send SASE for upcoming themes. Reports in 4 months. Pays nothing, not even a copy.** Open to unsolicited reviews. Poets may also send books for review consideration. Offers annual poetry contest, for subscribers only.

COYOTE CHRONICLES: NOTES FROM THE SOUTHWEST (I, II, IV-Political, regional), 222 W. Brown Rd., Suite #9, Mesa AZ 85201, founded 1993, editor Jody Namio, is a "small press publisher of fiction, poetry, nonfiction and scholarly publications, publishing a biannual literary journal. Limited subsidy publishing services offered to selected authors." She wants **"poetry with emphasis on progressive political themes and ideas, ecology etc. No religious, fantasy or 'scenery' poetry."** They have published poetry by Norman German, John Grey, Mark Maire and Richard Davignon. As a sample she selected these lines (poet unidentified):

> *Last night I went to bed intoxicated again. You watched*
> *"Ghandi," repressing violence.*
> *Today, I am drinking too much coffee,*
> *smoking too many cigarettes.*
> *You say you'll be late . . .*

CC is 80 pgs., 8½ × 11, professionally printed on recycled paper, saddle-stitched. They accept 10-15% of 1,000 poems received a year. Subscription: $12. **Sample postpaid: $4. Guidelines available for SASE. They consider simultaneous submissions and previously published poems. Submit with cover letter and bio.** "Backlog of submissions at this time." **Editor sometimes comments on rejections, "more substantial critiques on request." Reports in 6-8 weeks. Pays 5 copies. "Contributors encouraged to buy additional copies."** Publishes several chapbooks a year averaging 64 pgs. **For chapbook consideration either query or send ms with cover letter and bio. Reports in 12-14 weeks. "Large backlog at this time, but we welcome all submissions." Payment "varies with author."** Send SASE for catalog to buy samples.

‡CQ (CALIFORNIA STATE POETRY QUARTERLY); CALIFORNIA STATE POETRY SOCIETY (II), P.O. Box 7126, Orange CA 92613, founded 1972. *CQ* is the official publication of the California State Poetry Society (an affiliate of the National Federation of State Poetry Societies) and is designed "to encourage the writing and dissemination of poetry." **They want poetry on any subject, 60 lines maximum. "No geographical limitations. Quality is all that matters."** They have recently published poetry by Michael L. Johnson, Lyn Lifshin and Robert Cooperman. As a sample they selected "The Fading" by Anne Marple:

> *I dream you back again*
> *but after waking*
> *I must strain to remember*
> *as though peering at a faded snapshot*
> *where the knitted hat and muffler*
> *are still distinct*
> *but the face has disappeared.*

CQ is 50-60 pgs., 5½ × 8½, offset and perfect-bound, heavy paper cover with art. They receive 3,000-4,000 poems a year, accept approximately 5%. Press run is 500 for 300 subscribers of which 24 are libraries, 20-30 shelf sales. Membership in CSPS is $12/year and includes a subscription to *CQ*. **Sample of *CQ* postpaid: $4 (guidelines contained within). Send SASE for guidelines alone. Submit up to 6 "relatively brief" poems at a time; name and address on each sheet. Generally no previously published poems or simultaneous submissions. Seldom comments on rejections. Reports in 1-4 months. Pays one copy. Acquires first rights.** CSPS also sponsors an annual poetry contest. Awards vary. All entries considered for *CQ*. They say, "Since our editor changes with each issue, we encourage poets to resubmit. Also, we are not opposed to rhyme, but it should be used with great discretion."

CRAB CREEK REVIEW (V, IV-Anthology, themes), 4462 Whitman Ave. N., Seattle WA 98103, phone (206)633-1090, founded 1983, editor Linda J. Clifton. Previously a biannual publication, *CCR* now appears approximately once every 2 years as a theme-based anthology. *Crab Creek Review: Anniversary Anthology*, currently available, highlights the "Best of our Past," and "New Work." They publish **poetry which is "free or formal, expresses complex notions through clear imagery, has wit and a voice that is interesting, energetic and gives a strong sense of the individual; accessible to the general reader rather than full of very private imagery and obscure literary allusion."** They have recently published poetry by Laurel Speer, Olga Popova, Diane Glancy, Michael Lassell, David Romtvedt and Eastern European, Japanese, Chinese and Latin American writers. As a sample the editor selected these lines from "Listening at Little Lake Elkhart" by William Stafford:

> *What signal brought us, following the faintest of trails?*
> *Is there bread for this hunger, this long exile from earth?*
> *Listening as well as we can, we hear the loon cry—*
> *from a dark shore it echoes; it tells how far*
> *the northland goes, one gray lake then another*
> *all the way to the edge of the wind.*

The editor says *CCR* is a 160-page, perfect-bound paperback. **Sample postpaid: $10. They are cur-**

rently not accepting unsolicited submissions. Poets can check *Poets & Writers* or send SASE for upcoming themes and reading periods. Back issues of the biannual publication are available for $3.

CRAZYHORSE (II), Dept. PM, Dept. of English, University of Arkansas at Little Rock, Little Rock AR 72204, phone (501)569-3161, founded 1960, managing editor Zabelle Stodola, poetry editor Ralph Burns, fiction editor Judy Troy, is a highly respected literary magazine appearing twice a year. They have recently published poetry by Alberto Rios, Mark Jarman, Bill Matthews, Yusef Komunyakaa and Lynda Hull. As a sample we selected these lines from "Freshman English Poetry Anthology (University of Minnesota, 1964)" by Maura Stanton:

> *I looked at the two lyres*
> *Printed across the cover*
> *Of my thick green anthology,*
> *I knew the lyre was the symbol*
> *For Poetry, but I wondered*
> *Why there were two, not one.*
> *I opened the brand new book*
> *And wrote my name in pencil*
> *Across the white front page.*

Crazyhorse is 145-180 pgs., 6×9, offset, color cover. Press run is 1,000. Subscription: $10. **Sample postpaid: $5. Prefers submissions of 1-2 poems at a time. No previously published poems or simultaneous submissions. Always enclose SASE. Brief, professional cover letter preferred. No submissions May through August. Reports in 1-2 months. Pays $10/printed page plus 2 copies. Offers two $500 awards for best poem and best story.** Reviews books of poetry. To get a sense of the quality of the magazine, the editors suggest poets purchase a sample copy.

CRAZYQUILT QUARTERLY (II), P.O. Box 632729, San Diego CA 92163-2729, phone/fax (619)688-1023, founded 1986, editor Jackie Ball, is a literary quarterly which has published poetry by B.Z. Niditch, Charles B. Dickson and Alan Seaburg. As a sample the editor selected these lines from "Road with Cypress and Star" by Charles Fishman:

> *Earlier, the trees are earth,*
> *then water and flame—but here*
> *they are smoke, dark green smoke*
> *. . . turrets of blue wind.*

CQ is 90 pgs., digest-sized, saddle-stapled, professionally printed on good stock with matte card cover. Circulation 200. Subscription: $19 (2 years for $32). **Sample: $5 plus $1 postage; back issue: $3. Submit 1-5 poems at a time, one poem to a page. Previously published poems and simultaneous submissions OK. Reports in 10-12 weeks, time to publication is 12-18 months. Pays 2 copies. Acquires first or one-time rights.**

CREAM CITY REVIEW (II), P.O. Box 413, Dept. of English, University of Wisconsin at Milwaukee, Milwaukee WI 53201, phone (414)229-4708, editors-in-chief Mark Drechsler and Andrew Rivera, poetry editors Kristin Terwelp and Cynthia Belmont, is a nationally distributed literary magazine published twice a year by the Creative Writing Program. The editors will consider **any poem that is well-crafted and especially those poems that "have a voice, have place or play with the conventions of what poetry is. We get very little humor or parody, and would enjoy getting more."** They have published poetry by Albert Goldbarth, Audre Lorde, Marge Piercy, May Sarton, Philip Dacey, Amiri Baraka, Tess Gallagher, Cathy Song, Mary Oliver and Philip Levine. They do not include sample lines of poetry; "We prefer not to bias our contributors. We strive for variety—vitality!" *CCR* is 5½×8½, perfect-bound, averaging 300 pgs., with full-color cover on 70 lb. paper. This journal is fast becoming a leader in the literary world. It's lovely to look at—one of the most attractive designs around—with generous space devoted to poems, all styles (but favoring free verse). Press run is 2,000, 450 subscriptions of which 40 are libraries. **Sample postpaid: $5. "Include SASE when submitting and please submit no more than 5 poems at a time."** Simultaneous submissions OK when notified. **"We have had a strange string of problems with simultaneous submissions. We will continue to look at them, but authors need to be more responsible in notifying us that work has been accepted elsewhere."** Editors sometimes comment on rejections. Send SASE for guidelines. **Reports in 2 months, longer in summer. Payment varies with funding and includes choice of 2 copies or 1-year subscription. Buys first rights.** Reviews books of poetry in 1-2 pgs. Open to unsolicited reviews. Poets may also send books to the poetry editors for review consideration. **"We give an award of $100 to the best poem published in *Cream City Review* each year."**

Market categories: (I) Beginning; (II) General; (III) Limited; (IV) Specialized; (V) Closed.

CREATIVE WITH WORDS PUBLICATIONS (C.W.W.); SPOOFING (IV-Themes); WE ARE WRIT-ERS, TOO (I, IV-Children, seniors), P.O. Box 223226, Carmel CA 93922, founded 1975, poetry editor Brigitta Geltrich, **offers criticism for a fee**. It focuses "on furthering **folkloristic tall tales** and such; creative writing abilities in **children** (poetry, prose, language-art); creative writing in **senior citizens** (poetry and prose)." The editors publish on a wide range of themes relating to human studies and the environment that influence human behaviors. **$5 reading fee/poem, includes a critical analysis.** The publications are anthologies of children's poetry, prose and language art; anthologies of special-interest groups such as senior citizen poetry and prose; and *Spoofing: An Anthology of Folkloristic Yarns and Such*, which has an announced theme for each issue. **"Want to see: folkloristic themes; poetry for and by children; poetry by senior citizens; special topic (inquire). Do not want to see: too mushy; too religious; too didactic; expressing dislike for fellowmen; political; pornographic; death and murder poetry." Guidelines and upcoming themes available for SASE.** *Spoofing!* and *We are Writers, Too!* are low-budget publications, photocopied from typescript, saddle-stapled, card covers with cartoon-like art. **Submit 20-line, 40 spaces wide maximum, poems geared to specific audience and subject matter.** They have recently published poetry by Erin Jaco, John Buechnet and Max Douglas. As a sample the editor selected these lines by Walter Kamens:

> . . . *The man in the moon winks down at me*
> *He says, "Sleep well, sleep tight.*
> *Say your prayers and let your cares*
> *Float away on the wings of the night . . .*

"Query with sample poems (one poem/page, name and address on each), short personal biography, other publications, poetic goals, where you read about us, for what publication and/or event you are submitting." They have "no conditions for publication, but C.W.W. is dependent on author/poet support by purchase of a copy or copies of publication." They offer a 20% reduction on any copy purchased. The editor advises, "Trend is proficiency. Poets should research topic; know audience for whom they write; check topic for appeal to specific audience; should not write for the sake of rhyme, rather for the sake of imagery and being creative with the language. Feeling should be expressed (but no mushiness). Topic and words should be chosen carefully; brevity should be employed. We would like to receive more positive and clean, family-type poetry."

THE CREATIVE WOMAN (IV-Women, feminist, themes), 126 E. Wing, Suite 288, Arlington Hts. IL 60004, phone (708)255-1232, founded 1977, editor Margaret Choudhury, is a quarterly publishing nonfiction articles, fiction, poetry and book reviews. **"We focus on a special topic in each issue, presented from a feminist perspective."** They want poetry **"recognizing, validating, celebrating women's experience, especially fresh and original style."** They have published poetry by Marge Piercy and Larissa Vasilyeva. As a sample the editor selected these lines from "Custom as a Veil" by Carol Ciavonne:

> *Women do not cry at weddings,*
> *they grieve with open ears.*
> *Let there be compensation they say,*
> *let it be beautifully phrased.*

The Creative Woman is 52 pgs., magazine-sized, saddle-stapled, professionally printed with b&w photos, graphics and ads. They use about 5% of several hundred poems received each year. Press run is 2,000 for 600 subscriptions (65 libraries). Subscription: $16, $26 outside US. **Sample postpaid: $5. Mss should be double-spaced, name and address on each page. No simultaneous submissions or previously published poetry. Cover letter required. Send SASE for upcoming themes. Theme for Winter 1995 issue: "Cartoonists," for Spring 1996: "Women and Violence," for Summer 1996: "Astronomy" and for Autumn 1996: "Style versus Society: Women & Fashion." Reports in up to 1 year. Pays 3 copies and opportunity to purchase more at half price.** Staff reviews related books of poetry. Send books for review consideration.

CREATIVITY UNLIMITED PRESS; ANNUAL CREATIVITY UNLIMITED PRESS POETRY COMPE-TITION (I), 30819 Casilina, Rancho Palos Verdes CA 90274, phone (213)541-4844, founded 1989, editor Shelley Stockwell, publishes annually a collection of poetry submitted to their **contest, $5 fee for 1-5 poems; prizes of $300, $150 and $75 in addition to publication. Deadline: December 31. "Clever spontaneous overflows of rich emotion, humor and delightful language encouraged. No inaccessible, verbose, esoteric, obscure poetry. Limit 3 pgs. per poem, double-spaced, one side of page."** As a sample the editor selected her own "Freeway Dilemma":

> *Of all enduring questions*
> *A big one I can't answer;*
> *How come, whenever I change lanes,*
> *The other lane goes faster?*

They also accept submissions for book publication. Query first. "Poems previously published will be accepted provided writer has maintained copyright and notifies us." Editor comments on submissions "always. Keep it simple and accessible." Publishes theme issues. Send SASE for

upcoming themes. **Sometimes sends prepublication galleys.** The editor says, "We are interested in receiving more humorous poetry."

CRESCENT MOON PUBLISHING; PASSION (II, IV-Anthology, gay/lesbian, love/romance/ erotica, occult, religious, spirituality, women/feminism), 18 Chaddesley Rd., Kidderminster, Worcestershire DY10 3AD England, founded 1988, editor Jeremy Robinson, publishes about 25 books and chapbooks/year **on arrangements subsidized by the poet.** He wants **"poetry that is passionate and authentic. Any form or length."** Not **"the trivial, insincere or derivative.** We are publishing a new quarterly magazine, *Passion* ($4 each, $17 subscription). It features poetry, fiction, reviews and essays on feminism, art, philosophy and the media. Many American poets are featured, as well as British poets such as Jeremy Reed, Penelope Shuttle, Alan Bold, D.J. Enright and Peter Redgrove. **Contributions welcome. We are also publishing two anthologies of new American poetry each year entitled *Pagan America*."** They have also published studies of Rimbaud, Rilke, Cavafy, Shakespeare, Beckett, German Romantic poetry and D.H. Lawrence. As a sample the editor selected these lines from Peter Redgrove's poem "Starlight":

> *Her menstruation has a most beautiful*
> *Smell of warm ripe apples that are red,*
> *And an odour of chocolate, a touch of poppy,*
> *And bed-opiums roll from her limbs*
> *Like the smokes of innumerable addicts between the sheets . . .*

The above is from the book ***Sex-Magic-Poetry-Cornwall: A Flood of Poems***, by Peter Redgrove, 76 pgs., flat-spined, digest-sized. Anthologies now available ($8.99 or $17 for 2 issues of *Pagan America*) include: *Pagan America: An Anthology of New American Poetry, Love in America: An Anthology of Women's Love Poetry, Mythic America: An Anthology of New American Poetry* and *Religious America: An Anthology of New American Poetry*. **Submit 5-10 poems at a time. Cover letter with brief bio and publishing credits required ("and please print your address in capitals"). Send SASE (or SAE and IRCs) for upcoming anthology themes. Replies to queries in 1 month, to mss in 2 months. Sometimes sends prepublication galleys.** The editor says, "Generally, we prefer free verse to rhymed poetry."

CRICKET; SPIDER, THE MAGAZINE FOR CHILDREN; LADYBUG, THE MAGAZINE FOR YOUNG CHILDREN; BABYBUG, THE LISTENING AND LOOKING MAGAZINE FOR INFANTS AND TODDLERS (IV-Children), P.O. Box 300, Peru IL 61354-0300, *Cricket* founded 1973, *Ladybug* founded 1990, *Spider* founded 1994, *Babybug* founded 1994, editor-in-chief Marianne Carus. *Cricket* (for ages 9-14) is a monthly, circulation 90,000, **using "serious, humorous, nonsense rhymes" for children and young adults. They do not want "forced or trite rhyming or imagery that doesn't hang together to create a unified whole." They sometimes use previously published work.** The attractive 8 × 10 magazine is 64 pgs., saddle-stapled, with color cover and full-color illustrations inside. *Ladybug*, also monthly, circulation 143,000, is similar in format and requirements but is aimed at younger children (ages 2-6). *Spider*, also monthly, circulation 80,000, is for children ages 6-9. Format and requirements similar to *Cricket* and *Ladybug*. *Babybug*, published at 6-week intervals, circulation 28,000, is a read-aloud magazine for ages 6 months to 2 years; premier issue published November 1994. It is 24 pgs., 6¼ × 7, printed on cardstock with nontoxic glued spine and full-color illustrations. The magazines receive over 1,200 submissions/month, use 25-30, and have up to a 2-year backlog. **Do not query. Submit no more than 5 poems—up to 50 lines (2 pgs. max.) for *Cricket*; up to 20 lines for *Spider* and *Ladybug*, up to 8 lines for *Babybug*, no restrictions on form. Sample of *Cricket*, *Ladybug* or *Spider*: $4; sample of *Babybug*: $5. Guidelines available for SASE. Reports in 3-4 months. Payment for all is up to $3/line and 2 copies. "All submissions are automatically considered for all four magazines."** *Cricket* and *Spider* hold poetry contests every third month. *Cricket* accepts entries from readers of all ages; *Spider* from readers ages 10 and under. Current contest themes and rules appear in each issue. *Cricket* has received Parents' Choice Awards every year since 1986. *Ladybug*, launched in 1990, has received Parents' Choice Awards every year since 1991 and the EdPress Golden Lamp Award in 1994.

‡CRIPES! (II), 514½ E. University Ave., Lafayette LA 70503, fax (318)482-2506, founded 1994, co-editor Jim Tolan, is a biannual publication of poetry, prose and artwork. **They want "the well made, the eccentric, the imaginatively precise, the evocative and provocative." They do not want to see "formal exercises, sensationalism, the shoddily crafted or the soulless."** They have recently published poetry by Joel Dailey, Dennis Formento, Tom MacLean and Jill Wicknick. As a sample the editor selected these lines from "Preservation" by A.D. Fallon:

> *With thin wooden tongs*
> *we slowly pull our brains out*
> *our noses, placing each chunk in*
> *a hand-thrown jar. They surround*
> *our skulls in clay mosaic halos—*

> *We are the angels of dust.*

Cripes! is 36-48 pgs., digest-sized, offset and saddle-stitched with 2-color card cover, artwork and graphics; no ads. They accept about 10% of submissions. Press run is 300 for 20 subscribers, 10% shelf sales. Subscription: $8 for 3 issues. **Sample postpaid: $3. Make checks payable to Jim Tolan. No previously published poems; simultaneous submissions OK. "Though we don't require a cover letter, we do like to know how a person has come to know about** *Cripes!***" Seldom comments on rejections. Send SASE for guidelines. Reports within a month. Pays 1 copy.** "We plan to publish reviews of books, chaps and other zines in no more than two to three pages." Open to unsolicited reviews. Poets may also send books for review consideration. Jim Tolan says, "We see *Cripes!* as a carefully gnawed niche between the formally competent but soulless verse of academic and avant-garde journals and the emotionally charged but poorly crafted poeming of the zines. And we encourage others who acknowledge the possibility of such a place to submit to our magazine."

THE CRITIC (II), 205 W. Monroe St., Sixth Floor, Chicago IL 60606, phone (312)609-8880, e-mail critictma@aol.com, founded 1940, is a Catholic literary and cultural quarterly. **"Poetry is a minor aspect of the publication. No word games, doggerel, light verse or haiku."** They have published poetry by Samuel Hazo and Martha Vertreace. The editor says *The Critic* is 128 pgs., 7×10, perfect-bound, no ads. Press run is 2,500 for 2,000 subscribers of which about 200 are libraries. Subscription: $20/year, $32/2 years. **Sample postpaid: $6. No previously published poems or simultaneous submissions. Cover letter required. Seldom comments on rejections. Reports in 1-3 months. Pays $25-50. Buys first serial rights.**

‡**CROSS ROADS: A JOURNAL OF SOUTHERN CULTURE (IV-Regional)**, P.O. Box 726, University MS 38677, founded 1992, founding editor Ted Olson, is biannual. "*Cross Roads* serves as a forum for a wide range of responses to the South from creative, academic, popular and folk perspectives; one fourth to one half of each issue is creative writing (poetry, fiction, drama and nonfiction essays)." **They want "poetry by Southerners and poetry (by anyone) about the South. We would like to see high-quality poetry about any aspect of Southern culture (Southern history, Southern folkways, Southern identity, Southern art/music, etc.—in short, any aspect of the Southern experience). Nothing overly sentimental, stereotyping or awkwardly rhyming. Also no 'local color' poetry."** They have recently published poetry by Jim Wayne Miller, Walter McDonald, Patricia Spears Jones and Charlie Braxton. As a sample the editor selected these lines from "The Crater, Vicksburg" by Franz K. Baskett:

> *Standing on the lip of The Crater*
> *I think about what it feels like*
> *To hold a gun and shoot.*
> *The heft of two and a half pounds*
> *Of blue steel. To shoot. To feel*
> *The kick. To aim and squeeze off.*
> *But not like it was done here.*
> *No Sir.*

Cross Roads is 112 pgs., digest-sized, perfect-bound, with artwork, b&w photographs, music notation, and several ads. They receive 200 poems a year, use 20. Press run is 800 for 70 subscribers of which 25 are libraries. Subscription: $9 for individuals, $12 for institutions. **Sample postpaid: $4.50. No previously published poems or simultaneous submissions. Cover letter required. Include "a short biographical statement explaining background and connection with the South or interest in the study of Southern culture. One paragraph is enough." Seldom comments on rejections. Reports within 3 months. Pays 1 copy. Acquires first North American serial rights.** The editor says, "We would consider reviewing extraordinary books by Southerners and/or about the South, though reviewing is not one of our primary goals."

CROSS-CULTURAL COMMUNICATIONS; CROSS-CULTURAL REVIEW OF WORLD LITERATURE AND ART IN SOUND, PRINT, AND MOTION; CROSS-CULTURAL MONTHLY; CROSS-CULTURAL REVIEW CHAPBOOK ANTHOLOGY; INTERNATIONAL WRITERS SERIES (II, IV-Translations, bilingual), Dept. PM, 239 Wynsum Ave., Merrick NY 11566-4725, phone (516)868-5635, fax (516)379-1901, founded 1971, Stanley H. and Bebe Barkan. Stanley Barkan began CCC as an educational venture, a program in 27 languages at Long Island University, but soon began publishing collections of poetry translated into English from various languages—some of them (such as Estonian) quite "neglected"—in bilingual editions. During the 70s he became aware of Antigruppo (a group against groups), a movement with similar international focus in Sicily, and the two joined forces. **CCR** began as a series of chapbooks (6-12 a year) of collections of poetry translated from various languages and continues as the **Holocaust, Women Writers, Latin American Writers, African Heritage, Asian Heritage, Italian Heritage, International Artists, Art & Poetry, Jewish, Israeli, Cajun, Dutch, Turkish,** and **Long Island** and **Brooklyn Writers Chapbook Series** (with a number of other permutations in the offing)—issued simultaneously in palm-sized and regular paperback and cloth-binding

CLOSE-UP

Children's Poet Says: "Write for Yourself First"

When Paul Janeczko visits schools, teachers want him to tell students an inspirational story about how he began writing. They want to point to him and say, "Here's a guy who started writing when he was four, and look where he's gone!" But it just wasn't that way.

Janeczko, who makes his home in Hebron, Maine, actually spent more than 20 years teaching high school English, and it was this career that eventually lead him to publish poetry. Ironically, the first book he published was not a volume of his own work; it was an anthology of poetry written by others that he compiled for young readers.

©Photo by Nadine Edris

Paul B. Janeczko

"When I started teaching, the poetry I was expected to use with the kids was from a nine-pound anthology," Janeczko says. "And I found the kids really weren't taking to it." So he started bringing in mimeographed sheets of poetry he believed the kids could relate to. When that worked, he augmented the collection of poems he was using in the classroom, and, in 1977, his first anthology, *The Crystal Image*, was published by Dell.

Since then Janeczko has published more than a dozen anthologies marketed for young adults, including *Strings: A Gathering of Family Poems* (Bradbury Press, 1984), *The Music of What Happens: Poems That Tell Stories* (Orchard Books, 1988), and *Preposterous: Poems of Youth* (Orchard Books, 1991). He's also published an anthology, with writing exercises, for middle readers, entitled *Poetry from A to Z: A Guide for Young Writers* (Bradbury Press, 1994). And more projects are in the works.

"I had no idea it was going to grow to the extent it has," Janeczko says. "I mean, I keep finding more poems and new approaches and angles for collections. And I keep trying to do something different, but, at the same time, provide good quality poetry that is more accessible to kids than much of the stuff available in some of the other books."

What is it that attracts kids to his anthologies? It's the themes and the language, he says. Many of the poems are also ones that speak of things kids are concerned about or to which they can relate. And all have some element of surprise. "Any poem that is in one of my books is a poem that has gotten a reaction from me, and usually the reaction is 'I have to show this to somebody.'" What results then are not only collections of poetry by both new and established voices, but also books that can be enjoyed by anyone, young or old.

In many ways, for Janeczko, anthologies were the entrée into the publishing field. By constantly reading and compiling the work of others, his sense of quality improved, he says. He learned a lot from seeing how different poets approached particular subjects or writing poetry in general. And these things carried over into his own writing.

In fact, in 1989 Orchard Books published **Brickyard Summer**, a collection of Janeczko's own poems about the activities of a young boy and his best friend during the summer between eighth grade and high school. That book was later followed by **Stardust otel** (Orchard Books, 1993), poems about a teenage boy and the people who stay at the Stardust, the hotel owned by the boy's '60s-generation parents.

"History: Stardust otel"

My parents —
flower children,
Woodstock lovers —
named me Leary
after their hero

insisted I call them Nick and Lucy

bought a house:
three floors,
tired brown clapboards,
a long front porch
hanging like a pouting lower lip

named it
after powdering their faces with stardust
in a psychedelic vision.

The H fell nearly 15 years ago:
the day I was born
Nick swung on it in joy
until it snapped off in his hands.
He never replaced it,
saying he liked to be reminded
of how he felt that day.

Though the poems in either of Janeczko's collections could stand on their own, when the poems are taken together they tell larger stories. And it's the characters and their situations in those stories that young readers, particularly boys, find appealing. "I always try to create interesting characters, because if I can do that, then they're going to do interesting things," he says.

"What I generally do when I'm working on a poem like the ones in **Brickyard** and **Stardust** is that I will sit at my desk; I'll get my legal pad; I'll get my fountain pen. I'll write the name of a character at the top of the first page and then I'll just spend time writing down anything at all that comes to mind for that character. Then, after I've done that for a while, I try to find the hook for the character and start building the poem."

While many times ideas will come from the characters themselves, ideas can also come from things you see and mark down, says Janeczko. One day he saw a man driving down the street with a full trash bag on the trunk of the car. It was such an unusual sight that later that day Janeczko found himself wondering where the man was going and what was in the bag. If you play with different scenarios, you develop ideas for poems.

That's why, when he visits schools, Janeczko tells kids to watch, to listen, and to save their ideas. You never know when the ideas are going to come, so you just have to be ready for them. And you have to record them and work with them. Just write and see what comes of it.

As for any adult who wants to write for children, he says, "Don't write for children, but write for yourself. And when you write for yourself, you may find things that are suitable for children. But, if you don't write for yourself first, you tend to write down to kids, and then you're in trouble." In addition, he encourages aspiring children's poets to read the work of other children's poets as it's important to be aware of the material that already exists.

"I'm also a firm believer in hanging in there," he says. "I mean, talent is one thing, and you need talent, but you really need perseverance. If rejection is going to stop you, then you need to do something else, because your work is always going to get rejected. You just have to keep plugging away at it."

Finally, to all poets seeking publication, Janeczko offers a typical teacher admonition: "Do your homework! Don't try to sell a science fiction poem to a fundamentalist religious magazine. Know the market. Know who buys what and who doesn't, and keep current on that."

—*Christine Martin*

❝I always try to create interesting characters, because if I can do that, then they're going to do interesting things. ❞
—Paul B. Janeczko

editions and boxed and canned, as well as audiocassette and videocassette. **All submissions should be preceded by a query letter with SASE. The Holocaust series is for survivors. Send SASE for guidelines. Pays 10% of print run.** In addition to publications in these series, CCC has published anthologies, translations and collections by dozens of poets from many countries. As a sample the editor selected the beginning of a poem by Pablo Neruda, as translated by Maria Jacketti:

> *Quartz opens its eyes in the snow*
> *and covers itself with thorns,*
> *slides into whiteness,*
> *becomes its own whiteness:*

That's from the bilingual collection *Heaven Stones*, the second in the **Cross-Cultural Review International Writers Series** published in 1992. It is 80 pgs., digest-sized, smythe-sewn paper and cloth, professionally printed 10pt. chromecoat cover, photo of the Chilean poet on the back—$15 (paperback), $25 (cloth). **Sample chapbook postpaid: $7.50.** *Cross-Cultural Monthly* focuses on bilingual poetry and prose. Subscription: $36. **Sample postpaid: $5. Pays 1 copy.** CCC continues to produce the International Festival of Poetry, Writing and Translation with the International Poets and Writers Literary Arts Week in New York and recently co-produced the 1993-1994 Multicultural Poetry Series at the Barnes & Noble flagship superstore in NYC, currently (1994-) at Borders Books & Music in Westbury, Long Island.

CRUCIBLE; SAM RAGAN PRIZE (I, II), Barton College, College Station, Wilson NC 27893, phone (919)399-6456, founded 1964, editor Terrence L. Grimes, is an annual using **"poetry that demonstrates originality and integrity of craftsmanship as well as thought. Traditional metrical and rhyming poems are difficult to bring off in modern poetry. The best poetry is written out of deeply felt experience which has been crafted into pleasing form. No very long narratives."** They have published poetry by Robert Grey, R.T. Smith and Anthony S. Abbott. As a sample the editor selected these lines from "Toward Short Off Mountain" by Mary C. Snotherly:

> *So dense the fog, each man trudged alone,*
> *accompanied only by a stumble of boots,*
> *slap of laurel, by his own separate breathing,*
> *and like thunder roll, the barks resounding.*

It is 100 pgs., 6×9, professionally printed on high-quality paper with matte card cover. Good type selection and point sizes highlight bylines and titles of poems. Press run is 500 for 300 subscribers of which 100 are libraries, 200 shelf sales. **Sample postpaid: $6. Send SASE for guidelines for contests (prizes of $150 and $100), and the Sam Ragan Prize ($150) in honor of the Poet Laureate of North Carolina. Submit 5 poems at a time between Christmas and mid-April. No previously published poems or simultaneous submissions. Reports in 3 months or less. "We require 3 unsigned copies of the manuscript and a short biography including a list of publications, in case we decide to publish the work."** Editor leans toward free verse with attention paid particularly to image, line, stanza and voice. However, he does not want to see poetry that is "forced."

CUMBERLAND POETRY REVIEW; THE ROBERT PENN WARREN POETRY PRIZE (II, IV-Translations), Dept. PM, P.O. Box 120128, Acklen Station, Nashville TN 37212, founded 1981, is a biannual journal presenting poets of diverse origins to a widespread audience. "Our aim is to support the poet's effort to keep up the language. We accept special responsibility for reminding American readers that not all excellent poems in English are being written by U.S. citizens. We have recently published such poets as Debra Marquart, Richard Tillinghast and Rachel Hadas." As a sample the editorial board selected these lines from "Gesualdo" by Arthur Gregor:

> *Although the father of two boys, he talked*
> *as the child in him still might,*
> *of the happiness he felt in the music,*
>
> *the happiness of being one with all that is*
> *outside yourself, vast as the clear autumn sky,*
> *tall as the poplars already turned yellow.*

CPR is 75-100 pgs., 6×9, flat-spined. Circulation 500. **Sample postpaid: $7. Send poetry, translations or poetry criticism with SASE or SAE with IRC. Submit up to 6 poems at a time. No previously published poems. "We accept, but do not like to receive simultaneous submissions." Cover letter with brief bio required. Reports in 6 months. Acquires first rights. Returns rights "on request of author providing he acknowledges original publication in our magazine."** They award The Robert Penn Warren Poetry Prize annually. Winners receive $500, $300 and $200. For contest guidelines, send SASE.

CURMUDGEON; BUT(T) UGLY PRESS (I, II), 2921 Alpine Rd., #112, Columbia SC 29223, phone (803)736-1449, founded 1991, editor Erik C. McKelvey, assistant editor Lori Ann Larkin, is a biannual of "reality." **As for poetry, they want "reality. Stuff that can be seen. All forms. No surrealism. I'm**

not a big fan of reading for the way the words are on the page. I like a meaning to grab me." They have recently published poetry by James Michael Ward, Kevin Keck, Bruce Williams and Diane Robertson. As a sample the editor selected these lines from "Karma dances a Zen movement" by elliott:

> at the foot of my brass bed
> My past lives devour my false guilt
> I pin the spider beneath my weight
> Her taut web drawing me to her
> My juices, her venom, sing
> We recreate Eden.

The editor says *Curmudgeon* is 40-60 pgs., 8½ × 11, folded, photocopied with color cover, art and ads. They receive about 200 poems a year, accept approximately 25%. Press run is 100 for 20 subscribers. Subscription: $6. **Sample postpaid: $3. Submit 5 poems at a time. Previously published poems and simultaneous submissions OK. Cover letter, "telling us where the poet found our name," required.** Time between acceptance and publication is 6 months. **Seldom comments on rejections. Offers criticism for a fee. "A short, critical spiel is free; but if there needs to be more, terms can be worked out between the individual and the editors." Send SASE for guidelines. Reports in 2-3 weeks. Pays 1 copy.** Reviews books and chapbooks of poetry in 500 words. Open to unsolicited reviews. Poets may also send books for review consideration. The editor adds, "I want reality. I frown on surrealism. We like new poets for every issue of the magazine."

CUTBANK; THE RICHARD HUGO MEMORIAL POETRY AWARD (II), English Dept., University of Montana, Missoula MT 59812, phone (406)243-5231, founded 1973, has revolving editors. *Cutbank* is a biannual literary magazine which publishes regional, national and international poetry, fiction, reviews, interviews and artwork. Also offers 2 annual awards for best poem and piece of fiction, The Richard Hugo Memorial Poetry Award and The A.B. Guthrie, Jr. Short Fiction Award. Winners announced in spring issue. They have recently published poetry by Seamus Heaney, Norman Dubie, James Tate, Amiri Baraka and Gerald Stern. As a sample the editors selected these lines from "Faces" by Mark Levine:

> We can't make the faces go away
> The bodies are not such a problem
> We pull them apart with chemicals and stretch them out
> Along the cracked surface of the old freeway.

There are about 100 pgs. in each issue, 50 pgs. of poetry. Circulation of 400 for 250 subscribers of which 30% are libraries. Single copy: $6.95; subscription: $12/two issues. **Sample postpaid: $4. Submission guidelines for SASE. Submit 3-5 poems at a time, single-spaced. Simultaneous submissions discouraged but accepted with notification. "We accept submissions from August 15 through March 15. Deadlines: Fall issue, November 15; Spring issue, March 15. Reports in 2 months. Pays copies. All rights return to author upon publication.** Staff reviews books of poetry in 500 words, single or multi-book format.

CWM (II, IV-Themes), % Ge(of Huth), 875 Central Pkwy., Schenectady NY 12309-6005, (or % David Kopaska-Merkel, 1300 Kicker Rd., Tuscaloosa AL 35414, phone (205)553-2284), founded 1990, co-geologians Ge(of Huth) and David Kopaska-Merkel. (These "geologians" also edit dbqp press publications and *Dreams and Nightmares*, but *CWM* has no relation to their other imprints.) This magazine, published annually **on set themes, is "not tied down by ideas of proper style, form or substance, and presents work for the person of divergent tastes. The only considerations will be length and quality (as we see it). Extremely long poems will be at a disadvantage. Poems must be on the theme of the issue. The theme for the 1996 issue is 'Archaeology of the Soul.'** Unusual pieces of any kind are welcome, and should be submitted in whatever form the author deems most suitable." As a sample the geologians chose these lines from "The Drowned" by Jonathan Brannen:

> Once boatloads of pilgrims
> arrived to worship
> the drowned children
> whose bodies miraculously whole
> and uncorrupted were on display

Press run is 100. **Submit 5 poems at a time. No previously published poems; simultaneous submissions OK, if notified. Send SASE for guidelines and upcoming themes. Reports within 6 weeks. Pays "at least one copy."** Staff reviews books of poetry and poetry journals. Send books for review consideration.

DAGGER OF THE MIND; K'YI-LIH PRODUCTIONS; SMART PRODUCTIONS (IV-Science fiction/fantasy, horror), 1317 Hookridge Dr., El Paso TX 79925, phone (915)591-0541, founded 1989, executive editor Arthur William Lloyd Breach, assistant editor Sam Lopez, wants **"poetry that stirs the senses and emotions. Make the words dance and sing, bring out the fire in the human soul. Show flair and fashion. No four-letter words, nothing pornographic, vulgar, blasphemous,**

obscene and nothing generally in bad taste." They have published poetry by Jessica Amanda Salmonson. The quarterly *DOTM* is magazine-sized, saddle-stapled, with high glossy covers. They use about 50 of 100-150 poems received/year. Press run is 4,000-5,000 with 100 subscribers. Subscription: $8/half year, $16/year. **Sample postpaid: $3.50. "Send in batches of 10. I will consider simultaneous submissions only if told in advance that they are such. Include cover letter with published credits, a very brief bio and kinds of styles written. Length is open as is style. Be creative and try to reflect something about the human condition. Show me something that reflects what is going on in the world. Be sensitive but not mushy. Be intelligent not sophomoric. Don't try to carbon copy any famous poet. You lead the way—don't follow. I don't like the trend toward blood and gore and obscenity. Report back in 6 weeks tops." Pays $1-5/poem plus 1 copy. Buys first North American serial rights and reprint rights. "*DOTM* is devoted to** *quality* **horror. The key word is quality.** *DOTM* is a publication under the division of K'yi-Lih Productions." The editor will evaluate work and review books of poetry for a fee, depending on length and quantity. Send books for review consideration. He says, "I'm planning an anthology of Lovecraftian related material. The paperback will be predominantly Cthulhu Mythos fiction, but I do intend to publish some poetry."

DAILY MEDITATION (V), Box 2710, San Antonio TX 78299, editor Ruth S. Paterson, is a **nonsectarian** religious quarterly that publishes **inspirational poems up to 14 lines, but is currently not accepting poetry submissions. Sample postpaid: $2.**

THE DALHOUSIE REVIEW (II), Sir James Dunn Bldg., Suite 314, Halifax, Nova Scotia B3H 3J5 Canada, phone (902)494-2541, e-mail DALREV@AC.DAL.CA, founded 1921, is **a prestige literary quarterly preferring poems of 40 lines or less.** As a sample the editor selected these lines from "A place with your past held" by Rhonda Batchelor:

> *like motionless swings on the beach,*
> *footprints lead away, towards the water.*
> *Beyond, the town waves in heat.*
> *Gesturing to a street, you say*
> See that bunch of houses? That's where
>   we used to live. . . .

The review is 144 pgs., 6×9, professionally printed on heavy stock with matte card cover. Relatively few poems are featured in each issue, but ones that are tend to be free verse with emphasis on image and voice. Individual copies range in cost from $8.50-25. Subscription: $21/year within Canada and US, $28/year outside (both in Canadian dollars). **Submit 6-10 poems at a time. No previously published poems; simultaneous submissions OK. Cover letter welcome. Contributors receive $3 for a first poem, and for each poem after (in the same issue) he or she will receive $2/poem; 2 complimentary copies of issue and 15 offprints.**

DAMAGED WINE (II, IV-Form), P.O. Box 722, Palos Park IL 60464-0722, founded 1993 (first issue fall/winter 1994), editor-in-chief Daniel A. Scurek, appears irregularly. "*Damaged Wine*'s purpose is to publish the finest free verse poetry received and to help give greater definition and respect to the much (and often deservedly) maligned form. **We seek only high-quality free verse. We like poetry that takes a more traditional approach; poetry with meaning, attention to detail and clarity, a sense of structure. Length, subject matter, style and content are open, though we encourage poets to stay clear of self-indulgent writing, a problem typical in free verse. No metered poetry, overtly experimental poetry, poems that extend obviously into prose."** They have published poetry by Richard Calisch, Effie Mihopoulos and John Dickson. *DW* is approximately 50 pgs., $4\frac{1}{4} \times 11$, laser typeset, saddle-stapled with card cover and artwork (mostly line drawings). They receive about 1,500 poems a year, accept approximately 10%. Press run is about 300. Single copy: $4; subscription: $12 for 3 issues. **Sample postpaid: $5. "All submissions must be typed; only one poem per page; name and address on each. Send no fewer than 2 poems and no more than 6. Please include a short bio note listing previous credits."** Previously published poems and simultaneous submissions OK, if **notified upon submission. Cover letter welcome but not required.** Time between acceptance and publication is 6 months. **Seldom comments on rejections ("unless requested"). Send SASE for guidelines or order a sample copy as guidelines are printed in each issue. Reports in 4 months. Pays 2 copies. Acquires one-time rights.** "We do accept books and chapbooks for review, provided they are books of free verse poetry. Reviews run from 5-10 pages and are typically but not exclusively in single-book format. We are not open to unsolicited reviews, but poets may send books for review consideration." The editor adds, "Free verse has defined modern poetry, not always in the most flattering way. We look to give free verse a stronger distinction and more defined quality. We feel that strongly experimental and prose poetry, for example, are fine stylistically, and may even define the poetry of the future, but are, in form, different from free verse. Free verse doesn't necessarily mean absence of meter, absence of logic or absence of internal flow. Poets should concentrate on the strengths of quality free verse: strong visual imagery and a sense of rhythm. Remember, good free verse is actually more difficult to write than metered poetry. We'd even suggest that poets analyze some of the masters of meter (be it Pope or Frost) as well as the masters of free verse (from Williams to Plath)."

DANCE CONNECTION (IV-Specialized), 815 First St. SW, #603, Calgary, Alberta T2P 1N3 Canada, phone/fax (403)237-7327, e-mail eltonh@cuvg.ab.ca, founded 1983, editor Heather Elton, appears 5 times a year and uses **poems about dance—"contemporary poetry dealing with 'issues' rather than lyrical poetry about young ballerinas. Something tough/challenging that deals with the body in a postmodern context."** It is 60 pgs., magazine-sized, desktop-published and saddle-stapled. Press run is 5,000 for 3,000 subscribers of which 35 are libraries, 1,500 newsstand sales. Subscription: $21 individuals, $33 institutions. **Sample postpaid: $5. Reports in 3 months. Sometimes sends prepublication galleys. Pays 3 copies and "occasional honorarium." Acquires all rights. Returns rights.** The editor says they "very occasionally publish poetry. When we get larger we will publish more, but now space is a precious commodity for review/calendars/news/columns and feature departments."

DANCING SHADOW PRESS; DANCING SHADOW REVIEW (I, II), P.O. Box 28423, Baltimore MD 21234, phone (410)557-0110, founded 1992, editors Alan C. Reese and Bernard J. Wenker. *Dancing Shadow Review* is a biannual "dedicated to publishing outstanding poetry and fiction without regard for political, ideological, social or stylistic constraints." **They want "poetry in which the form and language hammer home the poet's vision. We want to see it all, but tend to shy away from preachy or sentimental claptrap."** They have recently published poetry by Harvey Lillywhite and Richard Peabody. As a sample the editors selected these lines from Harvey Lillywhite's poem "Finding the Mother-Country":

> *No myth illuminates the all-night driving*
> *That is our poverty, except how memory is*
> *A country of myth—the road curves over*
> *The planet, seems to start at the beginning*
> *And to end in kingdom come—*

DSR is 80-100 pgs., digest-sized and perfect-bound with glossy card cover and b&w artwork. Press run is 500 for 100 subscribers, 50 shelf sales. Single copy: $6.95; subscription: $14. **Sample postpaid: $8. Submit 3-5 poems at a time with a biographical sketch. Previously published poems OK; no simultaneous submissions. Reads submissions September 1 through June 30 only. Often comments on rejections. Pays 1 copy.** Dancing Shadow Press also publishes 2-4 chapbooks/year. **Query first with sample poems and cover letter with brief bio and publication credits. Replies to queries in 4-6 weeks, to mss in 2-4 months. Pays author's copies, 10% of the press run.** They have recently published *The Algebra of Hooves*, stories and poems by Nora Myers. It is 32 pgs., digest-sized and saddle-stapled with light card stock cover. Sample postpaid: $6.

DANDELION (II); BLUE BUFFALO (IV-Regional), The Alexandra Centre, 922-9th Ave. SE, Calgary, Alberta T2G 0S4 Canada, phone (403)265-0524, founded 1975, poetry editor Jenine Werner-King, managing editor Bonnie Benoit, appears twice a year. They want **"quality—We are open to any form, style, length. No greeting card verse."** They have published poetry by Claire Harris, Susan Ioannou and Robert Hilles. As a sample the editor selected these lines by Roger Nash:

> *On Sabbath evenings, a slow hand*
> *tuned the guitar. A fast hand*
> *moved the shifting stars. And, somewhere,*
> *while we were growing up, there was a street still*
> *made of gold of tin of slush*

Dandelion is 102 pgs., 6×9, with full-color cover, professionally printed and bound. They accept about 10% of 600 mss received. Press run is 750. **Sample postpaid: $7. Submit 4-7 poems at a time. No previously published poems or simultaneous submissions. Cover letter with brief bio "appreciated." Reads submissions January through March and July through September for issues in June and December. Cover letter with bio required. Send SASE for a short statement of their needs. Reports in 4-6 weeks. Pays honorarium plus 1 copy. Acquires one-time rights.** Reviews books of poetry in 500-1,200 words; preference is for books by Alberta writers. Open to unsolicited reviews. Poets may also send books for review consideration to Reviews Editor. *blue buffalo* is a magazine which falls under the Dandelion Magazine Society umbrella. *blue buffalo* is also published twice yearly, but **submissions are accepted *only* from Alberta writers.**

JOHN DANIEL AND COMPANY, PUBLISHER; FITHIAN PRESS (II), a division of Daniel & Daniel, Publishers, Inc., P.O. Box 21922, Santa Barbara CA 93121, phone (805)962-1780, founded 1980, reestablished 1985. John Daniel, a general small press publisher, specializes in literature, both prose and poetry. Fithian Press is a subsidy imprint open to all subjects. **"Book-length mss of any form or subject matter will be considered, but we do not want to see pornographic, libelous, illegal or sloppily written poetry."** He has recently published *After Images*, the collected poems of Kingsley Tufts; *The Burning Place*, by Judith Bishop; and *Ornaments of Fire—The World's Best 101 Short Poems and Fragments*, edited by Edd Wheeler. As a sample John Daniel selected "John Keats Takes

His Leave" from the book *Gold of a Certain Kind*, by Annemarie Ewing Towner:

> *Sodden with fever, as death*
> *Chokes the breath in the throat, so*
> *I must go, now as always*
> *Awkward at making a bow.*

He publishes 10 flat-spined paperbacks, averaging 64 pgs., each year. **For free catalog of either imprint, send #10 SASE. To submit material send 12 sample poems and bio. Reports on queries in 2 weeks, on mss in 2 months. Simultaneous submissions and disks compatible with Macintosh OK. Always sends prepublication galleys. Pays 10-75% of net receipts royalties. Buys English-language book rights. Returns rights upon termination of contract. Fithian Press books (50% of his publishing) are subsidized, the author paying production costs and receiving royalties of 50-75% of net receipts. Books and rights are the property of the author, but publisher agrees to warehouse and distribute for one year if desired.** John Daniel advises, "Poetry does not make money, alas. It is a labor of love for both publisher and writer. But if the love is there, the rewards are great."

DAUGHTERS OF SARAH (IV-Feminist, religious, social issues, themes), 2121 Sheridan Rd., Evanston IL 60201, phone (708)866-3882, founded 1974, editor Elizabeth Anderson, is a quarterly magazine "integrating feminist philosophy with biblical/Christian theology and making connections with social issues." The magazine includes 1-3 pieces of poetry. The editor says, **"Please no rhymed couplets; must be short enough for one (or two) 5½ × 8½ page, but prefer less than 20 lines. Topics must relate to Christian feminist issues, but prefer specific to abstract terminology." She does not want "greeting card type verse or modern poetry so obscure one can't figure out what it means."** As a sample the editor selected these lines by Ann Bailey:

> *Who would lay her head on stone,*
> *Would crush the dark to dust?*
> *What dreamstruck one will hurl herself toward holiness*
> *and fight for her own blessings?*
> *Who here would risk her life to wrestle with the Lord?*

The magazine is 64 pgs., digest-sized, with photos and graphics, web offset. Its circulation is 4,500, of which 4,400 are subscriptions, including about 250 libraries; bookstore sales are 50. Single copy: $4.50; subscription: $18/year. Back issues available for $4. **Prefers shorter poems. Submit no more than two at once to Cathi Falsani, associate editor.** Time to publication is 3-18 months. **Publishes theme issues. Send SASE for guidelines and upcoming themes. Themes for 1995-96 include: Contemplative Life (Fall '95) and Women and Money (Winter '96). Send SASE for upcoming themes. Reports in 2-3 months.** *Daughters of Sarah* pays $15-30/poem plus 2-3 copies. Buys one-time rights. *Daughters of Sarah* recently received the Associated Church Press Honorable Mention for Poetry and Chicago Women in Publishing's 2nd Place Award for Literature. The editor says, **"Write first for list of upcoming themes, since we usually choose poetry to fit with a particular theme."**

DBQP; ALABAMA DOGSHOE MOUSTACHE; A VOICE WITHOUT SIDES; &; HIT BROAD-SIDES; THE SUBTLE JOURNAL OF RAW COINAGE; DBQPRESCARDS (IV-Form), 875 Central Pkwy., Schenectady NY 12309-6005, founded 1987, poetry editor Ge(of Huth). "dbqp is the name of the overall press. *Alabama Dogshoe Moustache* publishes **language poetry (usually very short) & visual poetry.** *A Voice Without Sides* is an occasional magazine in very small runs (about 24 copies) and in strange formats (in jars, as earrings, etc.); it uses the same type of poetry as *ADM.* **&** is a series of leaflets each featuring a single poem. *Hit Broadsides* is a broadside series. *The Subtle Journal of Raw Coinage* is a monthly that publishes coined words but occasionally will publish an issue of *pwoermds* (one-word poems such as Aram Saroyan's 'eyeye') or poems written *completely* with neologisms. *dbqprescards* is a postcard series publishing mostly poetry. These publications are generally handmade magazines, leaflets, broadsides and objects of very small size. **I am interested only in short language poetry and visual poetry. No traditional verse or mainstream poetry."** They have published poetry by John M. Bennett, Bob Grumman and Jonathan Brannen. As a sample the editor selected this complete poem by damian lopes:

> *the small boy walks*
> *like turning pages*
> *& runs like an alphabet*
> *without vowels*

Their major poetry magazine is *Alabama Dogshoe Moustache*, which appears in various formats up to 15 pgs., magazine-sized, held together with thread, staples, fasteners, or packaged inside containers. Its press run is 100-125 with 10 subscriptions. Single copy: 40¢-$2.50. **Sample postpaid: $1-2. Make checks payable to Geof Huth. Catalog available for SASE. Reports within 2 weeks. Pays "at least 2 copies."** Staff occasionally reviews books of poetry. Send books for review consideration. The editor says, "Most of the poetry I reject is from people who know little about the kind of poetry I publish. I don't mind reading these submissions, but it's usually a waste of time for the submitters. If you are familiar with the work of the poets I publish, you'll have a much better idea about whether or not I'll be interested in your work."

DE YOUNG PRESS; THE NEW CRUCIBLE (I), Rt. 1 Box 76, Stark KS 66775, founded 1964, publisher Mary De Young. *The New Crucible* is an environmental magazine appearing 8 times/year. They publish environmental, political, free-thought, health, rural farm/garden and general interest articles. **They are open to all forms and styles of poetry but nothing epic-length. Also, no religious poetry, explicit sex or obscene language.** They have published poetry by Alan Rickard and Branley Branson. As a sample the editor selected these lines from Branson's "Ruminations on Raking Leaves":

> What color windrows itself in the lurch
> Of cycles on the sleepy grass I've wooed
> All summer to grow. The leaves cannot lie
> Where they fall for their inner stuff will taint
> The soil and next year's hairy rootlets will die
> (All this comes by way of word of mouth) . . .

The editor says *The New Crucible* is approximately 30 pgs., 8½ × 11, perfect-bound, with b&w cover. Subscription: $50/12 issues. **Sample postpaid: $5. No previously published poems; simultaneous submissions OK. Cover letter and SASE required.** Time between acceptance and publication is 6 months. **Pays 1 copy. Rights remain with author.** De Young Press **is a subsidy publisher. "Authors should write for particulars. Can be flexible with arrangements."**

‡DEAD OF NIGHT PUBLICATIONS; DEAD OF NIGHT MAGAZINE (IV-Horror, science fiction/ fantasy, mystery), 916 Shaker Rd., Suite 228, Longmeadow MA 01106-2416, founded 1989, editor Lin Stein. *Dead of Night* is a quarterly magazine that primarily publishes horror, fantasy, mystery and science fiction stories as well as reviews, interviews and an average of 2-3 poems per issue. **They want "genre poetry only: horror/fantasy/mystery/science fiction. All forms acceptable, including haiku. Works 32 lines or under preferred. No poetry which is outside these genres or of a 'general' theme."** They have recently published poetry by John Grey, Ann K. Schwader, S.G. Johnson and Jacie Ragan. As a sample we selected "Cycles" by Vance Reed:

> Full-moon winter night
> freedom's cycle now complete
> I run on wolf's feet.

Dead of Night is 84 pgs., magazine-sized, newsprint, saddle-stapled with slick one-color cover; b&w art and ads inside. Press run is 3,000 for 700 subscribers, various shelf sales. Single copy: $4; subscription: $15. **Sample postpaid: $2.50 (back issue). "No multiple submissions, please, unless the poems are VERY short (6-8 lines). In that case, 2-3 poems at one time are OK." No previously published poems or simultaneous submissions. Cover letter required. Reads submissions September 1 through May 31 only.** Time between acceptance and publication is 6-18 months. **Seldom comments on rejections. Send SASE for guidelines. Reports in 4-6 weeks. Pays $7/poem plus 1 copy. Buys first North American serial rights.** The editor says, "We advise poets to study our guidelines and/or a sample issue or back issue before submitting."

DEATHREALM (IV-Horror, fantasy), 2210 Wilcox Dr., Greensboro NC 27405-2845, e-mail s.raine y@geis.com, founded 1987, editor Mark Rainey, is a quarterly using **"mostly tales of horror/dark fantasy. Small amount of poetry in each issue. No poetry reviews. Poems may be any style or length, though epic-scale pieces are *not* recommended. Rhyme or freestyle OK."** They have published poetry by Ardath Mayhar, Jessica Amanda Salmonson, Michael Arnzen and Chad Hensley. It is 64-72 pgs., magazine-sized, saddle-stapled, color covers. They accept 10-12 of 200-300 poems received/year. Press run is 3,000 for 500 subscribers, 2,500 shelf sales. Subscription: $15.95. **Sample postpaid: $4.95. Submit no more than 4 poems at a time. No simultaneous submissions. "Cover letters welcome, but limit to brief bio information, how writer found out about *Deathrealm*, et. al. Do not put cover letter with poetry excerpts." Closed to submissions annually January 1 through March 1. Send SASE for guidelines. Reports in 6-9 weeks. Pays $4-8 plus 1 copy. Buys first North American serial rights.** In 1994, *Deathrealm* received the Best Magazine and Best Editor awards from the Small Press Genre Association.

DEFINED PROVIDENCE; DEFINED PROVIDENCE PRESS (II), P.O. Box 16143, Rumford RI 02916, founded 1992, editor Gary J. Whitehead. *Defined Providence* is an annual which aims to publish "new and unknown poets alongside some of those poets considered to be the best in America." They want **"well-crafted lyrical or narrative poems grounded in experience, up to 3 pages long. No overly abstract, surreal or 'language' poetry. No overly religious or pornographic; singsong or conspicuous rhyme. Nothing long."** They have recently published poetry by Fred Chappell, Mark Doty, Sean Thomas Dougherty, X.J. Kennedy, Jack Myers and Gary Soto. As a sample the editor selected these lines from "Evening Walk" by Eric Trethewey:

> The stars, haphazard in their swarming,

> *blink on—remote, precise in themselves,*
> *as though to pinpoint anew the aim*
> *of each impossible longing.*

DP is an average of 72 pgs., digest-sized, offset from laserprint, perfect-bound with color card cover and exchange ads. "We receive about 1,500 poems per year and accept about 60 of them." Press run is 400 for 50 subscribers of which 2 are libraries, 30 shelf sales. Subscription: $4, $7 for 2 years. **Sample postpaid: $3. Submit no more than 4 poems at a time, single-spaced. No previously published poems or simultaneous submissions. Cover letter required. Often comments on rejections. Send SASE for guidelines. Reports in 1-6 weeks. Pays 1 copy. Acquires first rights.** The magazine also includes essays, interviews with well-known poets and book reviews (in both single and multi-book format). Defined Providence Press publishes 1 chapbook each even-numbered year through a contest. Winner receives $50 and 50 copies of a perfect-bound book, 40-56 pgs. $10 reading fee required. The 1994 selection was *Road Against Wind*, by Ronald J. Goba, 54 pgs., available for $5. In odd-numbered years they hold an individual poem contest (send up to 10 poems, $3/poem fee, 3 prizes). The editor says, "I see too much poetry that is hurried and uninteresting. I like to see poems that are surprising in their use of language, that are not predictable, that have closure. Those submitting are encouraged to read a copy prior to submitting. I also remind poets that small mags stay alive through subscriptions."

DELAWARE VALLEY POETS, INC. (IV-Membership, anthology), P.O. Box 6203, Lawrenceville NJ 08648, publications director Donna Gelagotis. "We publish contemporary anthologies and broadsides of **poetry by invitation to submit and books or chapbooks by members who are ready to publish.**" They have published poetry by Maxine Kumin, Theodore Weiss and Geraldine C. Little. As a sample, they selected these lines from "Mr. Kurtz, I Presume" by John Falk:

> *and a blue mantle of water unclasps,*
> *Slides down from the clouds and reclothes*
> *The worn and broken armature of stones.*

Members submit 6 samples, bio, publications. Reports in 6 months. "For anthologies, poets must have some connection with the basic organization. Anthologies are paid for by DPV, Inc., and all sales go to the organization. Individual authors pay printing costs; individual editorial services and distribution are provided by DVP. All sales go to the author." They add, "Poets serious about their work need to read all the poetry they can find, write poetry, attend poetry readings and find someone to trade poetry and criticism with. If there is no workshop available, start one."

DENVER QUARTERLY; LYNDA HULL POETRY AWARD (II), Dept. of English, University of Denver, Denver CO 80208, phone (303)871-2892, founded 1965, editor Bin Ramke, is a quarterly literary journal that publishes fiction, poems, book reviews and essays. **There are no restrictions on the type of poetry wanted.** Poems here focus on language and lean toward the avant-garde. Length is open, with some long poems and sequences also featured. They have published poetry by John Ashbery, Ann Lauterbach and Marjorie Welish. *Denver Quarterly* is 130 pgs. average, 6×9, handsomely printed on buff stock, flat-spined with two-color matte card cover. Press run is 1,000 for 600 subscribers (300 to libraries) and approximately 300 shelf sales. Subscription: $15/year to individuals and $18 to institutions. **Samples of all issues after Spring 1985 are available for $5 postpaid. Submit 3-5 poems at a time. Simultaneous submissions discouraged. No submissions read between May 15 and September 15 each year. Publishes theme issues. Send SASE for guidelines and upcoming themes. Reports in 2-3 months. "Will request diskette upon acceptance." Pays 2 copies and $5/page.** Reviews books of poetry. The Lynda Hull Poetry Award is awarded annually for the best poem published in a volume year. All poems published in the *Denver Quarterly* are automatically entered. Poetry published here has also been included in *The Best American Poetry 1992*.

‡DEPTH CHARGE; JOURNAL OF EXPERIMENTAL FICTION (II), P.O. Box 7037, Evanston IL 60201, phone (708)733-9554, founded 1986, editor Eckhard Gerdes. The *Journal of Experimental Fiction*, which appears irregularly (approximately twice a year), is a "literary and scholarly journal focusing on the limits of fiction, especially areas where it interfaces other art forms, including poetry, visual art and music." **They want "poetry from the interface zone, where it meets experimental fiction and the avant-garde."** They have recently published poetry by Richard Kostelanetz, Arthur W. Knight and Tim W. Brown. The editor says it is 100 pgs., 5½×8½, perfect-bound with a 2-color cover (occasionally 4-color), some b&w artwork and ads. They receive 100-200 submissions a year, accept 5-10. Press run is 500 for 250 subscribers of which 100 are libraries, 100 shelf sales. **Sample postpaid: $9. No previously published poems or simultaneous submissions. Cover letter required.** Time between acceptance and publication is 2 months to 1 year. **Always comments on rejections. Send SASE for guidelines. Reports in 2 weeks to 2 months. Pays 3-5 copies. Acquires first North American serial rights.** Reviews books of poetry in 100-200 words. Open to unsolicited reviews. Poets may also send books for review consideration. Depth Charge also publishes 2-4 paperback books of poetry a year. **Query first, with sample poems and cover letter with brief bio and publication credits. Replies to queries and mss (if invited) in 2 weeks to 2 months. Pays 10% royalties and 20**

author's copies. The editor says, "Please familiarize yourself with our publications before submitting."

DESCANT (III, IV-Regional), Box 314, Station P, Toronto, Ontario M5S 2S8 Canada, founded 1970, editor-in-chief Karen Mulhallen, is "a quarterly journal of the arts committed to being the finest in Canada. **While our focus is primarily on Canadian writing we have published writers from around the world.**" Some of the poets they have published are Lorna Crozier, Stephen Pender and Libby Scheier. As a sample the editor selected these lines from "Isla Grande" by Lake Sagaris:

> *I had caught children in my womb like clams*
> *watched them pried open and consumed and tossed away*
> *and still I was young.*

Descant is an elegantly printed and illustrated flat-spined publication with colored, glossy cover, oversized digest format, 140 pgs., heavy paper. They receive 1,200 unsolicited submissions/year, of which they use less than 10, with a 2-year backlog. Circulation is 1,200 (800 subscribers of which 20% are libraries). **Sample postpaid: $8. Guidelines available for SASE. Submit typed ms of no more than 6 poems at a time, unpublished work not in submission elsewhere, name and address on first page and last name on each subsequent page. Include SASE with Canadian stamps or SAE and IRCs. Reports within 4 months. Pays "approximately $100." Buys first-time rights.** Karen Mulhallen says, "Best advice is to know the magazine you are submitting to. Choose your markets carefully."

DESCANT: TEXAS CHRISTIAN UNIVERSITY LITERARY JOURNAL (II), English Dept., Box 32872, Texas Christian University, Fort Worth TX 76129, phone (817)921-7240, founded 1956, editors Betsy Colquitt, Stan Trachtenberg, Harry Opperman and Steve Sherwood, appears twice a year. **They want "well-crafted poems of interest. No restrictions as to subject matter or forms. We usually accept poems 40 lines or fewer but sometimes longer poems."** It is 92 pgs., 6×9, saddle-stapled, professionally printed, with matte card cover. Poems in issues we read tended to be lyric free verse under 50 lines with short line lengths (for added tension). "We publish 30-40 pgs. of poetry per year. We receive probably 4,000-5,000 poems annually." Their press run is 500 for 350 subscribers. Single copy: $6; volume: $12, $18 foreign. **Sample postpaid: $4. No simultaneous submissions. Pays 2 copies.**

THE DEVIL'S MILLHOPPER PRESS; THE DEVIL'S MILLHOPPER; KUDZU POETRY CONTEST; SAND RIVER POETRY CONTEST (II), University of South Carolina at Aiken, 171 University Parkway, Aiken SC 29801, phone/fax (803)641-3239, e-mail gardner@univscum.csd.scarolina.edu, founded 1976, editor Stephen Gardner, publishes one magazine issue of *The Devil's Millhopper* each year and one chapbook, winner of an annual competition. **They want to see any kind of poetry, except pornography or political propaganda, up to 100 lines.** Some of the poets they have published are Susan Ludvigson, Ann Darr, Lynne H. deCourcy, Ricardo Pau-Llosa, Katherine Soniat, Walt McDonald, R.T. Smith, Dorothy Barresi and Richard Frost. The magazine is 32-40 pgs., digest-sized, saddle-stapled, printed on good stock with card cover and using beautiful b&w original drawings inside and on the cover. The print run of *Devil's Millhopper* is 500. The annual chapbook has a print run of 600, going to 375 subscribers of which 20 are libraries. **Sample postpaid: $4. Submit 5-6 poems at a time. Send regular, non-contest submissions September and October only. They want name and address on every page of submissions; simultaneous submissions acceptable. Sometimes the editor comments on rejected mss. Reports usually in 2 months. Sometimes sends prepublication galleys. Pays copies. Acquires first North American serial and reprint rights. Rights automatically revert to author upon publication.** Send SASE for their annual Kudzu Poetry Contest rules (prizes of $50, $100 and $150, $3/poem entry fee), annual Sand River Contest for poetry in traditional fixed forms (prizes of $250, $150 and $50, $3/poem entry fee), chapbook competition rules, and guidelines for magazine submissions. Send Kudzu Contest submissions September 1 to October 31; Sand River Contest submissions June 1 to July 31; chapbook contest submissions January 1 to February 28. Chapbook competition requires $10 reading fee. Pays $50 plus 50 copies. The editor advises, "There is no substitute for reading a lot and writing a lot or for seeking out tough criticism from others who are doing the same."

‡DIALOGUE: A JOURNAL OF MORMON THOUGHT; MARGARET RAMPTON MUNK POETRY AWARD (IV-Religious), P.O. Box 658, Salt Lake City UT 84110, founded 1966, poetry editor Susan Elizabeth Howe, "is an independent quarterly established to express Mormon culture and to examine the relevance of religion to secular life. It is edited by Latter-Day Saints who wish to bring their faith

---

Use the General Index to find the page number of a specific publisher. If the publisher you are seeking is not listed, check the " '95-'96 Changes" list at the end of this section.

into dialogue with the larger stream of Judeo-Christian thought and with human experience as a whole and to foster artistic and scholarly achievement based on their cultural heritage. The views expressed are those of the individual authors and are not necessarily those of the Mormon Church or of the editors." **They publish 6-8 poems in each issue, "humorous and serious treatments of Mormon topics or universal themes from a Mormon perspective. Under 40 lines preferred. Must communicate with a well-educated audience but not necessarily sophisticated in poetic criticism. Free verse OK but only if carefully crafted."** They have published poetry by Michael Collins, R.A. Christmas, May Swenson and Linda Sillitoe. As a sample the editor selected these lines from "You Heal" by Emma Lou Thayne:

> *After things happen, under the scarring*
> *you heal. It takes its jagged course*
> *upward and then . . .*

The journal has an elegant 6×9 format, 170 pgs., with color, artistically decorated cover and tasteful b&w drawings within. They receive about 200 submissions/year, use 35-40. They have a circulation of 4,000-4,500 subscriptions of which 150 are libraries. **Sample postpaid: $7. Submit 3-5 poems at a time, typed, 1 poem/page with name, address and telephone number on each sheet. No previously published poems or simultaneous submissions. Acknowledges in 10 days, reports in 3 months. Payment is 10 offprints plus one contributor's copy. Acquires first publication rights.** Reviews "books by Mormon poets or about Mormon themes and/or culture." Open to unsolicited reviews. Poets may also send books to Book Review Editor for review consideration. They sponsor the Margaret Rampton Munk Poetry Award annually; three prizes: first, $100; second, $75; third, $50.

JAMES DICKEY NEWSLETTER (III), DeKalb College, 2101 Womack Rd., Dunwoody GA 30338, founded 1984, editor Joyce M. Pair, a biannual newsletter devoted to critical articles/studies of James Dickey's works/biography and bibliography. They **"publish a few poems of *high* quality. No poems lacking form or meter or grammatical correctness."** As a sample here are the opening lines from "Haft Blossom" by R.T. Smith:

> *Long-sleeping, I rose in the morning*
> *and opened the door to sunlight.*
> *Trough water woke me with sunlight,*
> *dark and the other stars having*
> *yielded their power . . .*

It is 30 pgs. of ordinary paper, neatly offset (back and front), with a card back-cover, stapled top left corner. The newsletter is published in the fall and spring. Subscription to individuals: $12/year (includes membership in the James Dickey Society), $14 to institutions. **Sample available for $3.50 postage. Contributors should follow MLA style and standard ms form, sending 1 copy, double-spaced. Cover letter required. Pays 5 copies. Acquires first rights.** Reviews "only works on Dickey or that include Dickey." Open to unsolicited reviews. The editor's advice is: "Acquire more knowledge of literary history, metaphor, symbolism and grammar, and, to be safe, the poet should read a couple of our issues."

THE DIDACTIC (II), 11702 Webercrest, Houston TX 77048, founded 1993, editor Charlie Mainze, is a monthly publishing **"only, only didactic poetry. That is the only specification. Some satire might be acceptable as long as it is didactic in spirit."** The editor is still experimenting with the format of the magazine. **Previously published poems and simultaneous submissions OK.** Time between acceptance and publication is about a year. "Once it is determined that the piece is of self-evident quality and is also didactic, it is grouped with similar or contrasting pieces. This may cause a lag time for publication." **Reports "as quickly as possible." Pay is "nominal." Buys one-time rights.** Considering a general review section, only using staff-written reviews. Poets may send books for review consideration.

THE DISABILITY RAG & RESOURCE (IV-Specialized), P.O. Box 145, Louisville KY 40201, founded 1980, fiction/poetry editor Anne Finger, appears 6 times a year and "is the nation's leading disability rights magazine." **The editors have no restrictions as to form, length or style of poetry. "We are interested in vivid material by disabled writers or about the disability experience. Nothing sappy, sentimental, stereotyped or clichéd."** They have recently published poetry by Kenny Fries, Margaret Robison, Bill Abrams and Barbara Seaman. As a sample we selected the opening lines of "A Quiet Heard" by Nancy Bigelow Clark:

> *In the silence of an old growth forest*
> *She speaks in layers, a fluency*
> *of flesh and air where even swear words*
> *Are a litany of fern, wild grape*
> *Growing undisturbed because few take*
> *The time to learn her language.*

The editor says *DR* is approximately 48 pgs., 8×10⅝, b&w graphics on newsprint, some advertising.

They receive about 100 poems a year, accept approximately 15%. Press run is 5,000 for 4,500 subscribers of which approximately 10% are libraries, 350 shelf sales. Single copy: $3.95; subscription: $17.50 individuals, $35 institutions, $42 international. **Sample postpaid: $4.50. Previously published poems OK, "provided they have not appeared in a publication that circulates to the disabled community." No simultaneous submissions. Cover letter required.** Time between acceptance and publication is 6-12 months. **Often comments on rejections. Send SASE for guidelines and upcoming themes. Reports within 1 month. Pays $25/poem plus 2 copies. Buys first North American serial rights.** "We do publish reviews of disability-related poetry collections; our reviews run approximately 250-500 words." In 1994, they also published *The Ragged Edge*, an anthology of essays and poems from *The Rag*'s first 15 years.

DOC(K)S; EDITIONS NEPE; ZERROSCOPIZ; ANTHOLOGIES DE L 'AN 2.000; LES ANARTISTES (II, IV-Bilingual/foreign language), Le Moulin de Ventabren, 13122 Ventabren, France 13122, uses **"concrete, visual, sound poetry; performance; mail-art; metaphysical poetry," not "poesie à la queue-leu-leu" . . . whatever that means.** They have published work by J.F. Bory, Nani Balestrini, Bernard Heidsieck, James Koller, Julien Blaine and Franco Beltrametti. The magazine *Doc(k)s* is published 4 times a year and has a circulation of 1,100, of which 150 are subscriptions. It is an elegantly produced volume, 7×10, over 300 pgs., flat-spined, using heavy paper and glossy full-color card covers. Most of it is in French. "We cannot quote a sample, because concrete poetry, a cross between poetry and graphic art, requires the visual image to be reproduced." **There are no specifications for submissions. Pay for poetry is 5 copies.** Nepe Editions publishes collections of poetry, mostly in French.

DOLPHIN LOG (IV-Children, themes), 870 Greenbrier Circle, Suite 402, Chesapeake VA 23320, phone (804)523-9335, founded 1981, editor Elizabeth Foley, is a bimonthly educational publication for children offered by The Cousteau Society. "Encompasses all areas of science, ecology and the environment as they relate to our global water system. Philosophy of magazine is to delight, instruct and instill an environmental ethic and understanding of the interconnectedness of living organisms, including people." They want to see **"poetry related to the marine environment, marine ecology or any water-related subject matter to suit the readership of 7- to 13-year-olds and which will fit the concept of our magazine. Short, witty poems, thought-provoking poems encouraged. No dark or lengthy ones (more than 20 lines). No talking animals."** The editor excerpted these sample lines from "Garbage Pirates" by Marianne Dyson:

> *Their treasure bags ready*
> *The garbage pirates three,*
> *Set sail in a wagon boat*
> *Upon the Sidewalk Sea.*
>
> *They steer around bottle fish*
> *With broken, jagged teeth,*
> *And pinch their noses at the smell*
> *Of trash on Driveway Beach.*

It is 20 pgs., magazine-sized, saddle-stapled, offset, using full-color photographs widely throughout, sometimes art, no advertising. It circulates to 80,000 members, approximately 860 library subscriptions. Membership: $35/year for a Cousteau Society family membership, $15/year for *Dolphin Log* only. **Sample: $2.50 plus 9×12 SAE with 3 first-class stamps. Prefers double-spaced submissions. Publishes theme issues. Reports within 4 months. Always sends prepublication galleys. Pays $25-100 on publication and 3 copies. Rights include one-time use in *Dolphin Log*, the right to grant reprints for use in other publications, and worldwide translation rights for use in other Cousteau Society publications.** The editor advises, "Become familiar with our magazine by requesting a sample copy and our guidelines. We are committed to a particular style and concept to which we strictly adhere and review submissions consistently. We publish only a very limited amount of poetry each year. We are looking for longer poetry about entire ecosystems rather than one specific animal. For example, a poem about the wetlands or tidepools would be great."

DOLPHIN-MOON PRESS; SIGNATURES (II, IV-Regional), P.O. Box 22262, Baltimore MD 21203, founded 1973, president James Taylor, is **"a limited edition (500-1,000 copies) press which emphasizes quality work (regardless of style), often published in unusual/'radical' format."** The writer is usually allowed a strong voice in the look/feel of the final piece. "We've published magazines, anthologies, chapbooks, pamphlets, perfect-bound paperbacks, records, audio cassettes and comic books. **All styles are read and considered, but the work should show a strong spirit and voice. Although we like the feel of 'well-crafted' work, craft for its own sake won't meet our standards either."** They have published work by Michael Weaver, John Strausbaugh, Josephine Jacobsen and William Burroughs. They have also previously published a collection by the late Judson Jerome, *The Village: New and Selected Poems*, $10.95 paperback, $15.95 hardcover. **Send SASE for catalog and purchase**

samples or send $10 for their 'sampler' (which they guarantee to be up to $20 worth of their publications). To submit, first send sample of 6-10 pgs. of poetry and a brief cover letter. Replies to query in 2-4 weeks, to submission of whole work (if invited) in 2-4 weeks. Always sends prepublication galleys. Pays in author's copies. Acquires first edition rights. Three of the books published by this press have been nominated for the Pulitzer Prize and another for a National Book Award. "Our future plans are to continue as we have since 1973, publishing the best work we can by local, up-and-coming and nationally recognized writers—in a quality package."

THE DOMINION REVIEW (II), Bal 220, English Dept., Old Dominion University, Norfolk VA 23529-0078, phone (804)683-3991, founded 1982, faculty advisor Janet Peery, Creative Writing, says, **"There are no specifications as to subject matter or style, but we are dedicated to the free verse tradition and will continue to support it."** They have published poetry by Donald Morrill, Ioanna-Veronika Warwick and Peter Spiro. *TDR* is 80 pgs., digest-sized, flat-spined, professionally printed, and appears each spring. They have 300 subscriptions. **Sample: $5. They will not consider previously published poems. Cover letter and brief bio requested. Submissions read from September 1 through December 7; allow to March 15 for replies. Sometimes sends prepublication galleys. No pay. Acquires first North American serial rights.**

DOUBLE-ENTENDRE (II), P.O. Box 781408, Wichita KS 67278-1408, founded 1993, editor Joshua Friend, is a biannual which contains poetry, short fiction and b&w line art. In regard to poetry, **they are open to all forms, lengths, subjects, etc. However, they do not want "that which is melodramatic, overly abstract or propagandizing."** They have recently published poetry by Peter Huggins, Michael Trammell, Jennifer Wheelock, Joyce Frazeur and Daniel Spees. As a sample the editor selected these lines from "Fruit" by Shara McCallum:

> What a good girl I was, cleaning
> And keeping house and caring for the picknies.
> You liked showing me off to your men.
> What a special mango baby doll I was, peeling
> Off my skin, revealing the fruit. I saved
> The dried-out seed to paint my smiling face onto.

The editor says it is 50-60 pgs., $5\frac{1}{2} \times 8\frac{1}{2}$, desktop-published and staple bound, no ads. Press run is 100. Single copy: $4; subscription: $8. **Submit 4-7 poems at a time. Previously published poems and simultaneous submissions OK. "Work that is submitted without SASE cannot be returned."** Time between acceptance and publication is up to 8 months. **Seldom comments on rejections. Reports in 2-3 months. Pays 2 copies. Rights remain with authors.** The editor says, "Believe in your work. Sometimes great works get rejected many times, and the only things that will keep the possibility of publication alive are your continued faith in yourself and your persistence in submitting."

DRAGON'S TEETH PRESS; LIVING POETS SERIES (III), El Dorado National Forest, 7700 Wentworth Springs Rd., Georgetown CA 95634, founded 1970, poetry editor Cornel Lengyel. Published poets include Francis Weaver, Marcia Lee Masters and Stanley Mason. As a sample, the editor selected the beginning lines of "Not Just By Word of Mouth Alone" from *The Thirteenth Labor* by Ronald Belluomini:

> My sole being elliptic
> I have now and anciently dreamt in
> the treasuries of hope about
> a scheme to elude delusion's wrath,
> but I have broken
> my egg-shaped dream with collusion's fact.

Dragon's Teeth Press **"subsidy publishes 25% of books** if book has high literary merit, but very limited market"—which no doubt applies to books of poetry. They publish other books on 10% royalty contract. **Simultaneous submissions OK. Reports in 2 weeks on queries, 1 month on mss.**

DREAM INTERNATIONAL QUARTERLY (I, IV-Specialized), % Tim Scott, 4147 N. Kedvale Ave., Apt. 2B, Chicago IL 60641, founded 1981, senior poetry editor Tim Scott. **"Poetry must be dream-inspired and/or dream-related. This can be interpreted loosely, even to the extent of dealing with the transitory as a theme. Nothing written expressly or primarily to advance a political or religious ideology. We have published everything from neo-Romantic sonnets to stream-of-consciousness, ala 'the Beat Generation.' "** They have recently published poetry by Kimberly Anne Brittingham, Lyn Lifshin and Allen Foster. As a sample the editor selected these lines from "Epistle to Dracula" by Linda Yen:

> Now they hang like miniature stalactites
> those calcified fangs
> that made you in certain circles
> a fashionable lover.

DIQ is 150-180 pgs., 8½ × 11, with vellum cover and drawings. They receive about 150 poems a year, accept about 20. Press run is 300 for 200 subscribers of which 4 are libraries. Subscription: $30 for 1 year. **Sample postpaid: $8. Submit 1-5 typed poems at a time. Previously published poems and simultaneous submissions OK. Disk submissions welcome (details available in guidelines). Cover letter including publication history, if any, and philosophy of creation required. "As poetry submissions go through the hands of two readers, poets should enclose one additional first-class stamp, along with the standard SASE." Do not submit mss October through December.** Time between acceptance and publication is 1 year. **Comments on rejections if requested. Send SASE for guidelines. Reports in 1-4 weeks. Sometimes sends prepublication galleys. Pays 1 copy, "less postage."** Also, from time to time, "exceptionally fine work has been deemed to merit a compli-mentary subscription." **Acquires first North American serial or reprint rights.** Staff considers reviewing books of poetry "if the poet is a former contributor to *DIQ*. Such reviews usually run to about 500 words." Tim Scott says, "Don't get discouraged. Discouragement is the beginning writer's biggest enemy. If you are good at your craft, you will eventually find an outlet for it. Know your literary predecessors and the tradition in which you are working. Read everything from Shakespeare and Donne to Baudelaire and Rimbaud, from Crane and Hopkins to Plath and Sexton."

THE DREAM SHOP; VERSE WRITERS' GUILD OF OHIO; OHIO HIGH SCHOOL POETRY CON-TESTS (IV-Membership, students), 233 E. North St., Medina OH 44256, founded 1928, editor J.A. Totts. The Verse Writers' Guild of Ohio (Amy Jo Zook, treasurer, 3520 St. Rte. 56, Mechanicsburg OH 43044) is a state poetry society open to members from outside the state, an affiliate of the National Federation of State Poetry Societies. *The Dream Shop* is their poetry magazine, appearing twice a year. **Only members of VWG may submit poems. They do not want to see poetry which is highly sentimental, overly morbid or porn—and nothing over 40 lines. "We use beginners' poetry, but would like it to be good, tight, revised. In short, not first drafts. Too much is sentimental or prosy when it could be passionate or lyric. We'd like poems to make us think as well as feel something."** They have published poetry by Yvonne Hardenbrook, Frankie Paino and Bonnie Jacobson. The editor selected these sample lines from "Portrait of Daruma (Hakuin Ekaku, 1685-1768)" by Jim Brooks:

> *How is it the word "tango"*
> *follows me into this corner*
> *of shaped light, follows me*
> *among sacred statues—wooden,*
> *bronze and sandstone eyes*
> *closed or half-closed on faces*
> *full of quiet, full of almost*
> *too remote tranquility? . . .*

The magazine is 52 pgs., computer typeset, digest-sized, with matte card cover. "Ours is a forum for our members, and we do use reprints, so new members can get a look at what is going well in more general magazines." Annual dues including *The Dream Shop*: $15. Senior (over 65): $12. Single copies: $2. **Previously published poems and simultaneous submissions OK, if "author is upfront about both. Cover letters should be brief. All rights revert to poet after publication."** The Verse Writers' Guild sponsors an annual contest for unpublished poems written by high school students in Ohio with categories of traditional, modern, and several other categories. March deadline, with 3 money awards in each category. For contest information write Verse Writers' Guild of Ohio, 1798 Sawgrass Dr., Reynoldsburg OH 43068.

THE DREAMBUILDING CRUSADE; THE IDEA CO. (I, IV-Spirituality/inspirational), P.O. Box 995, La Mirada CA 90637, founded fall 1992, editor and publisher Art Garcia. *The Dreambuilding Crusade* is a bimonthly newsletter promoting spiritual growth through motivation and inspiration. **They want "short, simple poems relating to spirituality, motivation and inspiration. No sad or negative poetry."** They have recently published poetry by Judy Jones, Javier Cervantes, Mary Green and Dolores Thompson. As a sample the editor selected this poem, "Emergence," by Alicen Boyer:

> *As we clear away old branches of hurt,*
> *new blooms of love form.*
> *After the rain, sunlight shines.*
> *Away from the darkness, radiance flows.*
> *Love and prosperity are released as we unlock our hearts*
> *to see the beauty of our souls.*

The newsletter is 4 double-sided, 8½ × 11 pages, corner-stapled. It includes announcements and "rec-ognitions," poetry, and information on pen pal networking and networking newsletters. "We accept 80% of submitted poetry." Press run is 100 for 50 subscribers. Single copy: $2; subscription: $12. **Sample postpaid: $3. Submit 1-5 poems at a time. Include name and address on all submissions. Previously published poems and simultaneous submissions OK. "We like to receive cover letters explaining a little bit about the poet and the reasons for publication."** Time between acceptance and publication is 2-6 months. **No reply or return of rejections. Rather, the authors of the accepted** poems simply receive the issues in which their poems are included. **Pays 1 copy, "more only on request."** The editor adds, "We would appreciate any donation of monies or stamps to help defer cost. Make checks payable to The Idea Co."

DREAMGIRLS WITH SHAMAN; COMIC UPDATE (I, IV-Erotica, science fiction), (formerly listed as *Naughty Naked Dreamgirls*), 5960 S. Land Park Dr., Suite 253, Sacramento CA 95822, phone (916)429-8522, founded 1986, publisher Andrew L. Roller, editor William Dockery **(and submissions should be sent directly to him at P.O. Box 3663, Phenix City AL 36868).** These newsletters appear "approximately monthly." **They want experimental and/or erotic poetry.** Also willing to look at **"occult or science fiction poetry (political or comics related)."** They have recently published poetry by Rick Howe, G.J. Sulzbach, P.D. Wilson, Kathy Strickland and Jim Corrigan. As a sample the publisher selected these lines by William Dockery:

> Sassanna was painting the back porch,
> in the early afternoon.
> I opened the window, hot air flowed in.
> Carried the smell of both soup
>   and nearby garbage.
> Singing and pissing on a bluebricked wall,
> Lit by moonlight.

The newsletters are 8 pgs., saddle-stitched. Press run is 500 for 20 subscribers. **Sample postpaid: $1 US or free for SASE from William Dockery at his address above ("greeting card SASE preferred"), $2 Canada, $3 foreign. Submit 2-4 poems at a time. "Poems should be well typed for camera ready reproduction." Reports "at once." Pays 4 copies. Acquires first North American serial rights.** Reviews loose poetry, books of poetry and zines in *Comic Update*. Open to unsolicited reviews. Poets may also send chapbooks for review consideration to William Dockery. Send loose poetry for review consideration to Joe Harbuck, 425 Third Ave., Columbus GA 31901. The editor says, "As for poetry submissions, I'm getting more poems than I can handle right now. I prefer to send 'rejected' poems on to other potential publishers and respond with an informative letter on self-publishing."

DREAMS AND NIGHTMARES (IV-Science fiction/fantasy), 1300 Kicker Rd., Tuscaloosa AL 35404, phone (205)553-2284, e-mail d.kopasks-me@genie.geis.com, founded 1986, editor David C. Kopaska-Merkel, is published twice a year. The editor says, **"I want to see intriguing poems in any form or style under about 60 lines (but will consider longer poems). All submissions must be either science fiction, fantasy or horror (I prefer supernatural horror to gory horror). Nothing trite or sappy, no very long poems, no poems without fantastic content, no excessive violence or pointless erotica. Sex and/or violence is OK if there is a good reason."** He has recently published poetry by Lisa Kucharski, Charlee Jacob, Herb Kauderer, D.F. Lewis, Wendy Rathbone and Thomas Wiloch. As a sample the editor selected these lines from "Wolf" by Karen Oyerly:

> The night sized wolf
> howls, sinks his teeth
> into a house of snow.

Dreams and Nightmares is 20 pgs., digest-sized, photocopied from typescript, saddle-stapled, with a colored card stock cover and b&w illustrations. They accept about 80 of 1,000-1,500 poems received. Press run is 250 for 90 subscriptions. Subscription: $10/6 issues. Lifetime subscription: $50 (includes available back issues). **Samples: $2. Submit 5 poems at a time. "Rarely" uses previously published poems. No simultaneous submissions. Send SASE for guidelines. Reports in 2-10 weeks. Pays $3/poem plus 2 copies. Buys first North American serial rights.** The editor reviews books of poetry "for other magazines; I do not publish reviews in *DN*." Send books for review consideration. *Dreams and Nightmares* received an award from the Professional Book Center for "advancing the field of speculative poetry." The editor says, "There are more magazines publishing fantastic poetry than ever before, and more good fantastic poetry is being written, sold for good money and published. The field is doing very well."

DROP FORGE; JONESTOWN PRESS (I, IV-Form/style), P.O. Box 7237, Reno NV 89510, founded 1992, editor Sean Winchester, appears 3-4 times/year. *Drop Forge* is a "forum of individual forays into two-dimensional forms of divinity. **Experimental, visual, otherstream poetry. I want results from a series of personal discoveries in creativity. I do not want to see most established and widely accepted formats, in fact, anything that would fit a format developed by another."** They have published poetry by Chris Dew and David Starkey. As a sample the editor selected these lines by Jake Berry:

> (tertiary sheath) disclosed:
> 36.639 xPE. (or) fisile infraquark
>   vault perenially violated

The editor says the format of *Drop Forge* varies. The issue we received is 24 pgs., 7×8½, saddle-stapled with paper cover, hand-drawn and rubber-stamped cartoons and art, and ads. They accept 10-15% of the poetry received. Press run is 200-500; most distributed free. Subscription: $8. **Sample postpaid: $2.50. "Purchase of sample copy is advised, but by no means required." No previously published poems or simultaneous submissions. Cover letter encouraged. "Please include explanation of motive for the less perspicacious, if necessary."** Time between acceptance and publication varies. **Often comments on rejections. Reports in 2 weeks to 2 months. Pays 1-3 copies. Acquires first rights. Rights revert to author upon publication.** The editor says his editorial process is "extremely whimsical, though I always look for integrity, personality, dedication to and exploration of language—and its realities. As for the current literary scene, pay it little attention."

‡THE DRY CREEK REVIEW (II), Aims Community College, Loveland Center, 104 E. Fourth, Loveland CO 80537, founded 1990, faculty advisor Tony Park, is an annual. "We accept creative nonfiction, fiction, translations, and quality poetry." **They are open to all forms/styles. "We want poems built around vivid imagery, rich language and risk. We do not want to see the abstract based on the insignificant."** They have recently published poetry by Evan Oakley, Greg Grummer, Linda Aldrich and Deanna Kern Ludwin. As a sample the editor selected these lines from "When I was Blond" by Veronica Patterson:

> *When I was blond*
> *I played with the amber monkeys in pines*
> *and none could tell us*
> *from the night. I grew*
> *morning glories from an apple. All said*
> *the blossoms were the color of my eyes.*

The Dry Creek Review is 95-105 pgs., 6×9, professionally printed and flat-spined with 4-color light card cover with art and b&w art and photos inside. They receive 300-400 poems a year, accept 10-15%. Press run is 750, all distributed free. **No previously published poems; simultaneous submissions OK. Reads submissions September 15 through April 30 only. Poems are circulated to an editorial board. Seldom comments on rejections. Reports in 3-6 months. Rights revert to author on publication.** Open to unsolicited reviews. Poets may also send books for review consideration.

DRY CRIK REVIEW; DRY CRIK PRESS (IV-Cowboy, nature/rural/ecology), P.O. Box 44320, Lemon Cove CA 93244, phone (209)597-3512, fax (209)597-2103, founded 1991, editor John C. Dofflemyer, is a quarterly **of contemporary cowboy poetry.** "The function of *Dry Crik Review* is to inspire and communicate not only within the range livestock culture but to enhance an understanding of the people and dilemmas facing this livelihood with the urban majority, honestly. **Well-crafted expression must demonstrate insight gained from experience within this rural culture. Topics range from pastoral to political, humorous to serious. Poetry should be purposeful and accessible. No slapstick doggerel or barnyard-pet poetry, please! Prefer shorter unpublished works."** They have recently published poetry by Wilma Elizabeth McDaniels, Keith Wilson, William Studebaker, Errol Miller, Annette Le Box and Linda Hussa. As a sample the editor selected this poem, "Baby of the Dustbowl," by Barbara Shirk Parish:

> *Daughter—*
> *stillborn—*
> *1938—*
> *buried in the ravaged earth*
> *of this weary state:*
> *her stone reads simply, BABY—*
> *(She was our first.)—*
> *because we dared not*
> *give our grief*
> *a name.*

DCR is 60 pgs., digest-sized, photocopied from typescript on quality textured paper with matte card cover and perfect-bound. It features free and formal verse with a distinct Western flavor. This magazine is lively and engaging with a sense of humor and social commitment to the land and environment—a rare combination. Press run is 800 for 400 subscribers of which 25 are libraries, 20% shelf sales. Subscription: $20. **Sample postpaid: $7, some back issues more. Submit 5 poems at a time. No simultaneous submissions. Cover letter preferred with first submission. Publishes theme issues. Send SASE for guidelines and upcoming themes. Reports within 3 months. Always sends prepublication galleys. Pays 2 copies. Acquires one-time rights.** Staff reviews books of poetry in 350-400 words, single format. Send books for review consideration. Dry Crik Press **also publishes chapbooks. However, all material is solicited by the editor.** The editor says, "I am looking for an individualistic perspective that creatively dares contemporary subject matter that may not only serve a function today, but might possibly last as an art/tool."

DUST (FROM THE EGO TRIP); CAMEL PRESS (IV-Specialized), HC 80, Box 160, Big Cove Tannery PA 17212, phone (717)573-4526, founded 1981, poetry consultant Katharyn Howd Machan, publisher James Hedges, who describes himself as "editor/printer of scholarly and scientific journals, does occasional poetry postcards and chapbooks for fun." *Dust (From the Ego Trip)* is "an intermittent journal of personal reminiscences." For it he wants **"autobiographical material (can address any subject, but written from the viewpoint of an active participant in the events described). Mss should be between 1,000 and 2,500 words and can be one long poem or a collection of related shorter poems. Any style OK, including haiku, and any language using the roman alphabet. No religious (evangelizing) material or other material written primarily to advance a point of view. Any topic is OK, and coarse language is OK, but only if used artistically."** As a sample James Hedges selected these lines from "Wanderin" by Maura Gage:

> *Cats meowing in alley*
> *keep me up all night.*
> *Cats keep wailin' at moon,*
> *their cries come into my room*
> *keepin' me up all night.*
> *Where have you gone, Tramp?*

He publishes 1-2 chapbooks a year under the Camel Press imprint, average 20 pgs. **Query with "a few sample poems." Cover letter not required, "but I like the personal contact and the show of sincere interest." No bio or publications necessary because, "we judge on material only, status of poet is irrelevant." Simultaneous submissions and previously published material OK. Reports in 10 days. Always sends prepublication galleys. Pays 50 copies plus half of net after production costs are recovered.** He is open to subsidy publishing poetry of "artistic merit." To buy samples, request catalog. He says, "I always write a cover letter, but I'm not a poetry critic, just a considerate publisher. I do a bit of poetry because I want to encourage the art and broaden my catalog. Everything I publish is handset in metal type and letterpress printed on fine paper. The authors are expected to do most of the promotion. Press run is normally 500, and I give away about 400 copies to friends, plus 50 for the author. The author can order more copies in advance if he expects to sell a large number. Financial arrangements are negotiable."

DWAN (I, IV-Gay/lesbian, translations), Box 411, Bellefonte PA 16823, founded 1993, editor Donny Smith, appears every 2 to 3 months. *Dwan* is a "queer poetry zine; some prose; some issues devoted to a single poet or a single theme ('Jesus' or ' Mom and Dad,' for instance)." The editor wants **"poetry exploring gender, sexuality, sex roles, identity, queer politics, etc. If you think Charles Manson is cool—or even Charles Bukowski—you might not feel welcome at *Dwan*."** They have recently published poetry by B.Z. Niditch, Vytautas Pliura and Stephanie Weckler. As a sample the editor selected these lines from "Art Imitates Life at the Throbbing Opera" by C. Payne Brunty:

> *I place my mouth upon a womans*
> *and discover one thousand small birds*
> *set free in a secret season.*

Dwan is 16 pgs., 5½ × 8½, photocopied on plain white paper, and unstapled. They receive 400-500 pgs. of poetry/year ("that's no exaggeration!"), accept less than 10%. Press run is 75. **Sample available for 64¢ in stamps. Submit 5-15 poems typed "in black on white please, no colored paper, no blue ink." Previously published poems and simultaneous submissions OK. Cover letter required.** Time between acceptance and publication is 6-18 months. **Often comments on rejections. Send SASE for upcoming themes. Reports in 1-3 months. Pays copies.** The editor reviews books, chapbooks and magazines usually in 25-150 words. Send books for review consideration. "Heterosexuals always welcome."

EAGLE'S FLIGHT; EAGLE'S FLIGHT BOOKS (I, IV-Translations), P.O. Box 465, Granite OK 73547, phone (405)535-2452, founded 1989, editor and publisher Shyamkant Kulkarni, is a quarterly "platform for poets and short story writers—new and struggling to come forward." **They want "well-crafted literary quality poetry, any subject, any form, including translations. Translations should have permission of original poets."** They have recently published poetry by Mary Foucalt, Thomas Bynes and Diane Krugger. As a sample the editor selected these lines from "Life" by Susan K. Behm:

> *Universe so grand, reaches*
> *beyond man. Planet so fragile*
> *Containing life so delicate,*
> *Nature so cycling, brings*
> *Everything back to its origin,*
> *Animals so bonding, working for*
> *Survival, man so selfish, ignores*
> *All until its destruction.*

Eagle's Flight is 8-12 pgs., 7 × 8½, printed on colored paper and saddle-stapled, including simple art, few ads. They receive about 50 poems/year, accept 10%. Press run is 200 for 100 subscribers. Subscription: $5. **Sample postpaid: $1. Submit 1-5 poems at a time. No previously published poems or simultaneous submissions. Cover letter required. Reads submissions January 1 to June 30.** Time between acceptance and publication is 1 year. **Seldom comments on rejections. Send SASE for guidelines. Reports in 2-3 months. Pays 2 copies. Acquires first publication rights.** Reviews books of poetry in 250-750 words, single format. Under Eagle's Flight Books, they publish 1 paperback/year. "Up to now we have been publishing our own books, but **if somebody wants to share publishing cost, we can help or undertake publishing a book/anthology. We don't have selling organizations. Anybody interested in this may enquire." Replies to queries in 1 month.** "We also plan to organize a contest and publish anthologies of poetry. Award depends on our enthusiasm at that time and availability of funds." The editor says, "We expect poets to be familiar with our publication and our expectations and our limitations. To be a subscriber is one way of doing this. Everybody wants to write poems and, in his heart, is a poet. Success lies in getting ahead of commonplace poetry. To do this one has to read, to be honest, unashamed and cherish decent values of life in his heart. Then success is just on the corner of the next block."

EARTH'S DAUGHTERS: A FEMINIST ARTS PERIODICAL (IV-Women/feminism, themes), P.O. Box 41, Central Park Station, Buffalo NY 14215, founded 1971. The "literary periodical **with strong feminist emphasis**" appears 3 times a year, irregularly spaced. Its "format varies. Most issues are flat-spined, digest-sized issues of approximately 60 pgs. We also publish chapbooks, magazine-sized and tabloid-sized issues. Past issues have included broadsheets, calendars, scrolls and one which could be assembled into a box." **Poetry can be "up to 40 lines (rare exceptions for exceptional work), free form, experimental—we like unusual work. All must be strong, supportive of women in all their diversity. We like work by new writers, but expect it to be well-crafted. We want to see work of technical skill and artistic intensity. We rarely publish work in classical form, and we never publish rhyme or greeting card verse."** They have published poetry by Christine Cassidy, Rose Romano, Lyn Lifshin, Helen Ruggieri, Joan Murray, Susan Fantl Spivack, "and many fine 'unknown' poets, writers and artists." They publish poetry by men if it is supportive of women. As a sample the editor selected "On Saving Letters From Friends" by Jean LeBlanc from *#43/44 The Girlfriends Issue*:

> . . . *Time, folded deliberately into thirds—*
> *past, present, future—*
> *can, for an instant, be held fast between our fingers,*
> *replayed, reviewed, remembered,*
>
> *understood, accepted, forgiven,*
> *then refolded and neatly ordered in a drawer. . . .*

"Our purpose is to publish primarily work that otherwise might never be printed, either because it is unusual, or because the writer is not well known." Subscription: $14/3 issues for individuals; $22 for institutions. **Sample postpaid: $5. Simultaneous submissions OK. "Per each issue, authors are limited to a total of 150 lines of poetry, prose or a combination of the two. Submissions in excess of these limits will be returned unread. Business-size envelope is preferred, and use sufficient postage—we do not accept mail with postage due." Send SASE for guidelines. Some issues have themes, which are available for SASE after April of each year. Length of reporting time is atrociously long if ms is being seriously considered for publication, otherwise within 3 weeks. Pays 2 copies and reduced prices on further copies. Editor comments "whenever we have time to do so—we want to encourage new writers."** The collective says: "Once you have submitted work, please be patient. We only hold work we are seriously considering for publications, and it can be up to a year between acceptance and publication. If you must contact us (change of address, notification that a simultaneous submission has been accepted elsewhere), be sure to state the issue theme, the title(s) of your work and enclose SASE."

EASTERN CARIBBEAN INSTITUTE (I, IV-Regional), P.O. Box 1338, Frederiksted, U.S. Virgin Islands 00841, phone (809)772-1011, fax (809)772-3463, founded 1982, editor S.B. Jones-Hendrickson, editorial contact Cora Christian, is a "small press publisher with plans to expand," **especially interested in poetry of the Caribbean and Eastern Caribbean.** As a sample the editor selected these lines from "The AIDS Watch" in *Of Mask and Mysteries* by Lillian Sutherland:

> *Today I watched a mother*
> *   just sitting there and crying*
> *Today I watched a mother*
> *   just sitting there and dying*
> *Today I watched a mother*
> *   put her husband in his grave*

Their books are softcover, averaging 60 pgs. Sample copies available for purchase. **Submit 5 sample poems and cover letter with bio and previous publications. Simultaneous submissions and previously published poems OK. Reads submissions January to May only. Reports in 1 month. Pays 50 copies.** The editor says, "In our part of the world, poetry is moving on a new level. People who are interested in regional poetry should keep an eye on the Caribbean region. There is a new focus in the Virgin Islands."

‡**ECHOES MAGAZINE (I, II)**, P.O. Box 3622, Allentown PA 18106-0622, fax (610)776-1634, e-mail echoesmag@aol.com or 73200.1446@compuserve.com, founded 1993, is a bimonthly designed to "provide a forum for people in all walks of life to share their experiences and perspectives in creative ways—poetry, stories, plays, drawings. **We want poems that speak to the reader, sharing the writer's unique perspective and inspiring new insights or understanding. We look for imaginative use of imagery, metaphor, and language that is meaningful to the average reader. We avoid poetry whose language or construction make it difficult."** They have published poetry by both well-known poets and talented newcomers. As a sample we selected the first stanza of "Joyful Restraint" by Robert F. Vitalos:

> *It was 5:32 in the morning,*
> *And the first feet*
> *Of dawn sneakered in.*
> *I was watching your lips*
> *Pursue breathing,*
> *And the feather tick*
> *Nestling your chin.*

Echoes is 64 pgs., 6×9, offset printed and perfect-bound with card stock cover and original drawings and artwork. They receive about 1,000 poems a year, accept approximately 10%. Press run is 1,200. Subscription: $23 for 6 issues. **Sample postpaid: $5. Submit 4-6 poems at a time, name and address on each page. Previously published poems OK, "if publication was to a limited audience." No simultaneous submissions. Cover letter required; include brief description of background and writing experience. "We also accept ASCII text files on 3.5 computer disks, Mac or DOS."** Time between acceptance and publication is 2-5 months. **Poems are circulated to 2-3 members of an editorial review panel and to each editor. Often comments on rejections. Send SASE for guidelines. Reports in 3-6 weeks. Pays 6 copies. "We ask all writers of accepted work to authorize the Library of Congress to include their work in its programs of Braille and sound recordings for the handicapped. We also request exclusive magazine, reprint, and anthology rights for one year, including the right to publish audio or electronic issues, and nonexclusive rights thereafter. All negotiable to fit author's situation."** They are also planning to hold a contest and a conference in 1996. Interested poets should send SASE for information. The editor says, "We believe that the current scene suffers from too much poetry that is barren of vital images or meaning, or is overwrought with arcane language and references, that it is not accessible to the average reader."

EDICIONES UNIVERSAL (IV-Ethnic, foreign language, regional), 3090 SW Eighth St., Miami FL 33135, phone (305)642-3234, founded 1964, general manager Marta Salvat-Golik, is a small press subsidy publisher of **Spanish language books. "We specialize in Cuban authors and themes."** They have published books of poetry by Olga Rosalo and Amelia del Castillo. Poets **"must be able to purchase in advance 75% of the copies, due to the fact that poetry does not sell well."** Poets receive the copies they paid for. Submit sample, bio, publications. Reports in 1 month.

EDINBURGH REVIEW (II, IV-Translations), 22 George Sq., Edinburgh EH8 9LF Scotland, phone 0131 650 4218, founded 1969, is a literary biannual, which uses **quality poetry. Especially interested in non-metropolitan work, translations, aphorisms, philosophy for the generalist and interviews with lesser known writers. Also interested in poetry with ethnic/nationality, gay/lesbian, political and women/feminism themes.** The *Review* is a 160-page paperback. Circulation 2,500. **Sample: £4.95 for back issues, £6.95 for current issues, plus 50p. p&h. Submit 3-6 poems at a time. Publishes theme issues. Always sends prepublication galleys. Pays.** Reviews books of poetry.

EIDOS MAGAZINE: SEXUAL FREEDOM & EROTIC ENTERTAINMENT FOR WOMEN, MEN & COUPLES (IV-Erotica, women), P.O. Box 96, Boston MA 02137-0096, phone (617)262-0096, fax (617)364-0096, founded 1982, poetry editor Brenda Loew Tatelbaum. "Our press publishes erotic literature, photography and artwork. Our purpose is to provide an alternative to women's images and male images and sexuality depicted in mainstream publications like *Playboy, Penthouse, Playgirl*, etc. We provide a forum for the discussion and examination of two highly personalized dimensions of **human sexuality: desire and satisfaction. We do not want to see angry poetry or poetry that is demeaning to either men or women. We like experimental, avant-garde material that makes a personal, political, cultural statement about sensu-sexuality."** They have published poetry by Pamela Hughes, Tracy Henley, Connie Meredith, Sara White and Pete Lee. As a sample we selected these lines from "Byron 12" by Michael Dmytryk:

> *Sex is a moment I can trust.*
> *Whether it becomes a cornfield of grace*
> *Or a grim rockfield of pain,*

> *It is a moment of ecstasy—*
> *Like the blooming dawn,*
> > *quietly smiling its welcome,*
> *Or the lasting storm,*
> > *huge in its confusion,*
> *Or the music of winding tree limbs,*
> > *playing with the thick wind.*

Eidos is a professionally printed, newsprint tabloid, with photography and art, **number of poems/issue varies.** They receive hundreds of poems/year, use about 100. No backlog right now. Press run is 10,000 for over 7,000 subscribers. **Sample postpaid: $15. Only accepts sexually explicit material. 1 page limit on length, format flexible. Camera-ready, "scannable" poems preferred, but not required. No previously published poems; simultaneous submissions OK. Do not send computer disks. Publishes bio information as space permits. Comment or criticism provided as often as possible. Send SASE for guidelines. Reports in 1 month. Pays 1 copy. Acquires first North American serial rights.** Open to unsolicited reviews. Poets may also send books for review consideration. The editor advises, "There is so much poetry submitted for consideration that a rejection can sometimes mean a poet's timing was poor. We let poets know if the submission was appropriate for our publication and suggest they resubmit at a later date. Keep writing, keep submitting, keep a positive attitude."

1812 (III), Box 1812, Amherst NY 14226, founded 1993, editors Dan Schwartz and Richard Lynch, is an annual literary arts publication **"looking for material with a *bang*."** The editor says *1812* is 100 pgs., 6×9, with glossy cover and b&w art. They receive about 1,000 poems a year, accept 1-3%. **Previously published poems OK; no simultaneous submissions. Cover letter required.** Time between acceptance and publication is 6-12 months. **Sometimes comments on rejections. Send SASE for guidelines. Payment is "arranged." Buys one-time rights.** Open to unsolicited reviews. Sponsors the Overture Award for poetry. Reading fee is $5 for first poem, $2 for each additional entry. Award is $100 and publication. Send SASE for guidelines.

THE EIGHTH MOUNTAIN PRESS; EIGHTH MOUNTAIN POETRY PRIZE (IV-Women, feminist), 624 SE 29th Ave., Portland OR 97214, founded 1985, editor Ruth Gundle, is a "small press publisher of **feminist literary works by women."** They have published poetry by Karen Mitchell, Irena Klepfisz, Maureen Seaton and Lori Anderson. They publish 1 book of poetry averaging 128 pgs., every other year. **"We now publish poetry *only* through the Eighth Mountain Poetry Prize." Pays 8-10% royalties. Buys all rights. Returns rights if book goes out of print.** The Eighth Mountain Poetry Prize is a biennial award of a $1,000 advance and publication for a ms of 50-120 pgs. written by a woman; no restrictions as to subject matter. Send SASE for rules. **Submit during January in even-numbered years; postmark deadline: February 1.** Entry fee: $15. "The selection will be made anonymously. Therefore, the ms must have a cover sheet giving all pertinent information (title, name, address, phone number). No identifying information except the title should appear on any other ms page. The contest will be judged by a different feminist poet each year, whose name will be announced after the winning ms has been chosen." Previous judges have included Andre Lorde, Linda Hogan, Marilyn Hacker, Judy Grahn and Lucille Clifton.

‡EKSTASIS EDITIONS (II), Box 8474, Main Postal Outlet, Victoria, British Columbia V8W 3S1 Canada, phone/fax (604)385-3378, founded 1982, publisher Richard Olafson, annually publishes 12 paperbacks, 2 hardbacks and 10 chapbooks of "well crafted" poetry. **They have no specifications regarding form, length, subject matter or style of work.** They have recently published collections of poetry by Robin Skelton, Michael Bullock, Pierre Reverdy and Richard Stevenson. **Query first, with sample poems and cover letter with brief bio and publication credits. Previously published poems and simultaneous submissions OK. Replies to queries and mss (if invited) in 4 months. Pays 5-10% royalties and author's copies.**

EL BARRIO; CASA DE UNIDAD (V, IV-Ethnic, regional), 1920 Scotten, Detroit MI 48209-1648, phone (313)843-9598, founded 1981, poetry editor Marta Lagos. They publish **poetry from Latino residents of the SW Detroit area concerning life, family, politics, repression, etc., but do not normally accept unsolicited material. Query first.** They have published poetry by Lolita Hernandez, Gloria House and Jose Garza. As a sample the editor selected these lines from "Let Us Stop This Madness" by Trinidad Sanchez, Jr.:

> *Let us destroy the factories*
> *that make the guns*
> *that shoot the bullets*
> *that kill our children.*
> *Let us take a stand*
> *to share life,*
> *to break bread*

with each other.

El Barrio is published "to keep the Latino people of the SW Detroit area informed, to give them an opportunity to speak to the community." It appears 3-4 times a year, is about 28 pgs., magazine-sized, professionally printed with commissioned art on the matte card cover, using up to 3 poems/issue. Their press run is 5,000, $3/issue, $12 for a subscription. **"Please call for a sample copy." They sometimes use previously published poems. Sometimes publishes theme issues.** The press has published 2 anthologies: *Detroit: La Onda Latina en Poesía—Latin Sounds in Poetry*, Vols. I and II ($6 each).

‡**EL TECOLOTE (IV-Ethnic)**, 25-14th St., Suite 210-A, San Francisco CA 94103, phone (415)252-5957, fax (415)252-5701, founded 1970, is a monthly "community newspaper with **subject matter primarily about the Latino/Chicano community in America**. Much cultural coverage in general, but not a lot of poetry." They want **"short (1 page or less) poems inspired by life in U.S. Latino communities or in Latin America. Would like to see poetry that acknowledges the struggle of Latino/Latinas who must live in a culture different from their own.** The struggle both uncovers our history and creates a positive role model for the future. Open to poetry by either sex, sexual preference, and all ages." They have published poetry by Manilio Argueta from El Salvador. *El Tecolote* (The Owl) is a tabloid, l6 pgs., using art, graphics and ads. Press run 10,000. They accept about 1 out of 10 pages of poetry submitted. **Submit 3-5 poems at a time, double-spaced, with name and address on each sheet. Simultaneous submissions and previously published poems OK. Cover letter preferred. Send SASE for guidelines and upcoming themes.** Open to unsolicited reviews. Poets may also send books for review consideration, attn. L. Gutierrez.

‡**ELECTRIC CONSUMER (III)**, P.O. Box 24517, Indianapolis IN 46214, founded 1951, editor Emily Born, is a monthly publication for rural electric consumers in Indiana including electrical/energy information and general interest features. **"We very rarely publish poetry and prefer contributors to be rural electric members from Indiana."** The editor says *EC* is a 24-page, stitched and trimmed tabloid. They receive 30-50 poems a year, "may run 6." Press run is 280,000 for 279,000 subscribers. Subscription: $7/year. **No previously published poems or simultaneous submissions. On *rare* occasions poems are published as needed to fill space. However, they have a 3-year backlog, do not generally report on submissions, and do not pay.**

11TH ST. RUSE; BIG FISH (I), 322 E. 11th St., #23, New York NY 10003, phone (212)475-5312, founded 1987, editor Lucid. *11th St. Ruse* appears every 3 months, 4 pgs. mimeo, wants **poems "short, without subterfuge, preferably written very quickly. Especially interested in angry, obscure, humorous, religious, primitive or mysterious poetry and minority poets."** They have recently published poetry by Teres d' Compagnie, Richard Kostelanetz, Trifon Trifonopoulos and Tomàs Mac-Phaidin. As a sample the editor selected these lines from "Bad Karma" by John Hulse:

> they made a movie
> about his life
> ten years after
> he died
> and all during
> his second
> and third
> reincarnations
> he never got
> around to
> seeing it.

Press run is 250. Single copy: 33¢. **Sample postpaid: 50¢. Make checks payable to Ellen Carter. Submit 5 poems at a time. Simultaneous submissions OK. Reports in 1 day to 3 months. Pays 1 copy.** Open to unsolicited reviews. Poets may also send books for review consideration. The editor says, "I have another magazine, *Big Fish*, and I am currently seeking poems in foreign languages without translations."

ELF: ECLECTIC LITERARY FORUM (ELF Magazine) (II), P.O. Box 392, Tonawanda NY 14150, phone/fax (716)693-7006, founded 1990, editor C.K. Erbes, is a quarterly. **"Subject matter and form are open, but we are looking for well-crafted poetry. We prefer poems of 30 lines or less, but will**

The Subject Index, located before the General Index, can help you narrow down markets for your work. It lists those publishers whose poetry interests are specialized.

consider longer poems. No trite, hackneyed, ill-crafted effluvia." They have published poetry by Gwendolyn Brooks, Joyce Carol Oates, John Dickson, Daniel Berrigan, X.J. Kennedy, Nikki Giovanni, John Tagliabue, William Stafford, Michael Bugeja and R.T. Smith. As a sample the editor selected these lines from "Even After" by Gloria Glickstein Brame:

> Even after I've stopped loving you I still
> love you, because the mind isn't an obedient witness.
> The subconscious refreshes its surreal screen
> with tableaux-vivants that catch one off guard.

Elf is 52-56 pgs., magazine-sized, with semi-gloss cover, professionally printed, saddle-stapled. They use approximately 140 poems/year. Circulation 6,000. Subscription: $16. **Sample postpaid: $5.50. Submit 3 poems at a time. Send SASE for guidelines. "Accepted writers are asked to submit a bio of 25 words or less." Poems are circulated to an editorial board of professional poets and writers. Editor comments when possible. Reports in 4-6 weeks. Sometimes sends prepublication galleys. Pays 2 copies. Acquires first North American serial rights.** Staff reviews books of poetry. Publishers only may send books for review consideration. They also sponsor the Ruth Cable Memorial Prize for Poetry (annual deadline March 31). Send SASE for guidelines.

ELK RIVER REVIEW (V), 606 Coleman Ave., Athens AL 35611-3216, founded 1991, editor John Chambers, is an annual "devoted only to poetry and associated reviews, articles, essays and interviews. **Open to all types of poetry, no line limit. We want poems that are well-crafted, musical, provocative. However, we are currently overstocked through 1996."** They have recently published poetry by Vivian Shipley, Dan Leidig, Charles Clifton, Carolyn Moore, Kennette Wilkes, Joanne Lowery and Greg Ling. As a sample we selected these lines from "Snowflakes and Satellites" by Bettye Cannizzo:

> One delights the eye like a baby's smile,
> tickles the tongue like a Margarita.
> The other jolts the imagination like poetry,
> stimulates the mind like philosophy.

The editor says *ERR* is approximately 128 pgs., 6×9, professionally printed, perfect-bound with glossy cover and b&w drawings inside. Press run is 600 of which 25 go to libraries. Subscription: $12. **Sample postpaid: $6.50. Submit 3-5 poems at a time; name, address and phone number on each page. No previously published poems. Cover letter required. Include "succinct biographical facts and publishing credits (if any)."** Often comments on rejections. Send SASE for guidelines. **Reports in 2-4 months. Always sends prepublication galleys. Pays 1 copy. Acquires first rights.** Reviews poetry collections (including chapbooks) of regional interest. Open to unsolicited reviews; query first. Poets may also send books for review consideration. Sponsors Marjorie Lees Linn Poetry Award, an annual contest that awards a $750 grand prize and a $250 prize split by second and third places. "All winners will be published in an issue of *ERR*, receive 3 copies of the issue and receive a free book of poetry by Marjorie Lees Linn." Submit 2 copies each of as many poems as desired; open length, poem and subject matter. Entry fee: $10 for 1-3 poems; $2 each additional. "Those submitting 5 or more poems will receive a free subscription." Judge changes every year. Send SASE for details.

ELLIPSE (V, IV-Translations, bilingual), C.P. 10, FLSH Université de Sherbrooke, Sherbrooke, Quebec J1K 2R1 Canada, phone (819)821-7000, founded 1969, editors M. Grandmangin and C. Bouchara, **publishes Canadian poetry in translation.** That is, on facing pages appear either poems in English and a French translation or poems in French and an English translation. **Currently they are not accepting unsolicited mss.** They have recently published poetry by Patrick Lone, Gwen McEwen and Anne Hébert. As a sample, the editors selected these lines from "La Malemer" by Rina Lasnier:

> Malemer, mer stable et fermée à la foudre comme à l'aile—
> mer prégnante et aveugle à ce que tu enfantes,
>
> emporte-moi loin du courant de la mémoire—et de la longue flottaison des souvenirs;

translated by D.G. Jones:

> Malemer, firm sea impervious to the lightning as to the
> whispering wing—pregnant and oblivious to your generation,
>
> bear me far away from the currents of memory—and the long
> hulls cargoed with recollection;

The magazine appears twice yearly in an elegant, flat-spined, 6×9 format, professionally printed, 120 pgs. Subscription: $12. **Sample postpaid: $5.**

ELLIPSIS MAGAZINE (II), Westminster College of Salt Lake City, 1840 S. 1300 East, Salt Lake City UT 84105, phone (801)488-4158, founded 1967, appears twice a year using **"all kinds of good poetry. Limited on space."** They have published work by William Stafford, William Kloefkorn, Lyn Lifshin and Ron Carlson. The editor describes it as 80-112 pgs., digest-sized, flat-spined. Subscription: $18/

year. **Sample postpaid: $10. Send ms with SASE and contributor notes. Responds within 6 months. Pays $10/poem, $20/story, plus 1 copy.**

EMBERS (II), P.O. Box 404, Guilford CT 06437, phone (203)453-2328, founded 1979, poetry editors Katrina Van Tassel, Charlotte Garrett and Mark Johnson, is a "poetry journal of talented new and occasional well-known poets." The editors say, **"no specifications as to length, form or content. We want excellent craftsmanship. Interested in new poets with talent; not interested in lighter way-out verse, porn, or poetry that is non-comprehensible."** As a sample, the editors selected these lines from "The Time Change: April" by Lynne deCourcy:

> *Soon the time will change*
> *and change ahead, advancing*
> *into summer's wild and heady growth,*
> *but tonight this cold rain is ringing*
> *through my skull, the tension*
> *of straining rivers rising in me. . .*

Embers is 52 pgs., digest-sized, nicely printed on white stock with an occasional b&w photograph or drawing, 52 pgs., flat-spined with one-color matte card cover handsomely printed in black; it appears twice a year—spring/summer and fall/winter. Single copy: $6; subscription: $12/year. **Sample postpaid: $3. Submit up to 5 poems at a time. Submissions must be typed, previously unpublished, with name, address and brief bio of poet. Deadlines: "basically March 15 and October 15, but we read continuously." Cover letter preferred. Pay for acceptance is 2 copies. Rights revert to author after publication.** They sponsor a chapbook contest. Deadline: January 15. Winner is reported by March 15. Write for details. Editors' advice is "Send for sample copies of any publication you are interested in. Be patient. Most editors read as quickly as they can and report likewise. If a poet sends in work at the beginning of a reading time, or long before a deadline, he/she will have to wait longer for answers. *Embers* editors are interested in the poet's voice and would like to read up to five submissions showing variety of subject, form, etc."

EMERALD COAST REVIEW; WEST FLORIDA LITERARY FEDERATION; FRANCIS P. CASSIDY LITERARY CENTER; THE LEGEND; BACK DOOR POETS; WISE (WRITERS IN SERVICE TO EDUCATION) (IV-Regional), 400 S. Jefferson St., Pensacola Cultural Center, Pensacola FL 32501. The WFLF was founded in 1987 and began the Cassidy Literary Center, a regional writers' resource and special collection library. One of their programs is WISE, which provides over 50 area writers who volunteer their time to share their writing and writing experiences with local students. They sponsor a Student Writers Network for students in grades 9-12 and scholarships for area college student writers. WFLF also sponsors a PEN-WISE poetry contest for grades 1-12. The contest awards publication in a chapbook. They publish *The Legend*, a newsletter bringing literary arts news to 800-1,000 area writers and their supporters. Back Door Poets, one of their subgroups, conducts open microphone poetry readings the third Saturday of each month. Also, WFLF hosts a writing workshop the first Sunday of every month. Membership in WFLF ranges from $10/year for students to $500 and up for life-time memberships. The *Emerald Coast Review* is an **annual limited to Gulf Coast regional writers. Sample postpaid: $12. Send SASE for guidelines. Submit with required form (included in guidelines) May 1 to July 31. Pays copies.**

‡EMRYS JOURNAL (II), P.O. Box 8813, Greenville SC 29604, founded 1982, editor Jeanine Halva-Neubauer, an annual, wants **"all kinds of poetry, though we don't publish poems of more than 2-3 pgs."** They have published poetry by Jan Bailey, Gil Allen and Cecile Goding. As a sample, here are lines from "A Beauty" by Kathi Morrison:

> *Late harvest; nothing sour remains*
> *in this strawberry field. I pick,*
> *wary of rot and small bites rabbits make*
> *when evening settles on U-Pick acres*
> *and forest spreads its shadows thick as jam.*

It is handsomely printed, 6×9, flat-spined, up to 120 pgs. "For our 1995 issue we received about 1,200 poems from 300 people. We printed 15." Press run is 400 for 250 subscribers of which 10 are libraries. **Sample postpaid: $10. Submit 5 poems maximum. Editor sometimes comments on rejections. Send SASE for guidelines. Pays 5 copies.** They say, "We try to report within 6 weeks of receipt. We read from August 15-December 1."

THE EMSHOCK LETTER (IV-Subscribers), P.O. Box 411, Troy ID 83871-0411, phone (208)835-4902, founded 1977, editor Steve Erickson, appears 3-12 times a year, occasionally with **poetry and other writings by subscribers.** It is **"a philosophical, metaphysical, sometimes poetic expression of ideas and events. It covers a wide range of subjects and represents a free-style form of expressive relation. It is a newsletter quite unlike any other."** The editor describes it as 5-7 pgs., magazine-sized, photocopied from typescript on colored paper. Subscription: $25. **"Poets (who are subscribers)**

should submit poetry which contains some meaning, preferably centering on a philosophic theme and preferably 50 lines or less. Any good poetry (submitted by a subscriber) will be considered for inclusion and will receive a personal reply by the editor, whether or not submitted material is published in *The Emshock Letter*. Editor will promptly discard any and all material submitted by nonsubscribers. Poets must become subscribers prior to submitting any material!" Reviews books of poetry only if written by subscribers.

EN PLEIN AIR (I, II, IV-Translations), Gerbegasse 18, 3210 Kerzes, Switzerland, founded 1993, editor Aida Ghanim, appears 3 times/year. *En Plein Air* is a poetry journal "emphasizing imagery and timely insight and accepting material in all languages, with English translations." **They want "surrealist prose and English translations of contemporary, timely, significant poetry with dreamlike imagery and insight. Nothing sentimental or biased. No unnecessary raw language."** As a sample the editor selected these lines by Carol Gunther:

> *mapping out the void*
> *where dolphins of mercy break*
> *and phosphorescent*
> *say to him, "Reveal, reveal."*

The editor says *En Plein Air* is offset with linen card cover, art and photos, "ecologically friendly but economically limited." Press run is 300 for 200 subscribers. **Sample: $5 plus $4 (in US cash) for airmail. Submit 4 poems at a time. No previously published poems or simultaneous submissions. Cover letter required. Send SAE plus $4 (in US) cash for return postage and comments. Reports in 6 weeks. Pays 2 copies.** Sponsors an annual contest. "Send SAE and postage money for details."

ENCODINGS: A FEMINIST LITERARY JOURNAL (IV-Women/feminism), P.O. Box 6793, Houston TX 77265, founded 1989, co-editors Jacsun Shah and Lazette Jackson. *Encodings* appears "randomly, twice a year," using **"high quality poetry with a feminist perspective; especially interested in women's ways of knowing, women's invention and use of language."** As a sample the editor selected these lines from "The Anthropologist" by Jill Hammer:

> *Her scarf,*
> *the color of tea leaves and faded buttercups,*
> *becomes the mantle of an archer,*
> *a hunter of generalizations.*
> *Garnets hang from her ears,*
> *and girls hang from her words . . .*

Encodings is 40-60 pgs., $7 \times 8\frac{1}{2}$, photocopied from typescript and saddle-stapled with glossy card cover. Press run is 300 for 60 subscribers of which 1 is a library. Subscription: $9. **Sample postpaid: $4.50. Submit up to 5 poems at a time. Cover letter with brief bio preferred. Send SASE for guidelines.** Editor "occasionally" comments on rejections. Reports in 2-3 months. Pays 2 copies.

ENITHARMON PRESS (V), 36 St. George's Ave., London N7 0HD England, phone (0171)607-7194, fax (0171)607-8694, founded 1969, poetry editor Stephen Stuart-Smith, is a publisher of fine editions of poetry and literary criticism in paperback and some hardback editions, about 15 volumes/year averaging 100 pages. They have published books of poetry by John Heath-Stubbs, Phoebe Hesketh, David Gascoyne, Jeremy Hooker, Frances Horovitz, Ruth Pitter, Edwin Brock and Jeremy Reed. **"Substantial backlog of titles to produce, so no submissions possible before 1997." Interested poets should query.**

ENVOI (II), 44 Rudyard Rd., Biddulph Moor, Stoke-on-Trent, Staffs ST8 7JN United Kingdom, founded 1957, editor Roger Elkin, appears 3 times/year using poetry, articles about poetry and poets, and reviews. "1) *Envoi* does not subscribe to any one particular stable, school or style of contemporary poetry writing and has catholic tastes; 2) To be selected, **poetry must be sincere in its emotional and intellectual content, strongly integrated in form and contemporary in its subject matter—while a poem may be set in classical times or depend heavily on mythic archetypes, its overall 'texture' must have contemporary relevance; 3) *Envoi* requires writing that is daring in its subject matter and challenging in its expressive techniques— in short, work that takes risks with the form, the language and the reader; 4) *Envoi* is, however, still interested in traditional verse structures (the villanelle, pantoum, sonnet) but these must subscribe to the points listed in 2); and 5) *Envoi* is** looking for writing that sustains its creative strengths over a body of poems, or sequence. These criteria are prescriptive, rather than proscriptive; gates rather than hurdles. The over-riding concern is the creation of access for writers and readers to as wide a variety of contemporary poetry as space will allow." *Envoi* is 176 pgs., digest-sized, perfect-bound, professionally printed with matte card cover. "The emphasis is on giving space to writers so that the reader can begin to assess the cumulative strengths of any one author over a body of work. This means that competition for space is very keen. I handle between 250 and 300 poems per week and can only feature the equivalent of 100 poems three times a year!" Press run is 1,000 including 20 library subscriptions. Subscription: £10 or $25 ("preferably in bills rather than checks because of the high cost of conversion rates") or equivalent number of IRCs. Single copy: £3 ($7). **Sample: £2 ($5 bills). Submit no more than 6 poems, or a long poem of up to 6 sides; each poem on a separate page, bearing name and address; an accompanying SAE with 3 IRCs for return. Reports in 1-2 months. Pays 2 copies.** Roger Elkin says "*Envoi* presents the work of any one poet by a group of poems, up to six. Space is given to long(er) poems and short sequences, or extracts from longer sequences. We have a First Publication Feature for writers who have not appeared in national publications previously, and each issue contains a 'reading' of a modern poem or an article on poetic style. The Review section has been expanded in length to feature more comprehensive articles. Each issue also features a competition with prizes totalling £200; prize-winning poems are published along with a full adjudicator's report. We also feature poems in collaboration, as well as translations."

‡**EPICENTER (I)**, P.O. Box 367, Riverside CA 92502, founded 1994, is a quarterly poetry and short story forum **open to all styles.** They have recently published poetry by Mike Cluff, Max Berkovitz, Stan Nemeth and Vicki Solheid. As a sample the editors selected this poem by Todd Raboy:

> talking
> i accidentally
> sipped your coffee
>> 4 years later
> someone asked me
> if i had ever kissed
>> you
> i answered
>> yes
> honestly believing
> i had

Epicenter is 24 pgs., digest-sized and saddle-stapled with semi-glossy paper cover and b&w graphics. They receive about 300 submissions a year, use approximately 15%. Press run is 400 for 250 shelf sales. Single copy: $3. **Sample postpaid: $3.50. Previously published poems and simultaneous submissions OK. Six editors consider every submission. Seldom comments on rejections. Send SASE for guidelines. Pays 1 copy. Acquires one-time rights.** The editors add, "*Epicenter* is looking for ground-breaking poetry and short stories from new and established writers. No angst-ridden, sentimental or earthquake poetry."

THE EPIGRAMMATIST (II, IV-Form, translations), P.O. Box 828, Davis CA 95617-0828, e-mail 72330.3175@cis.com or epigram@aol.com, founded 1990, editor Nancy Winters. *The Epigrammatist* appears 3 times a year, in April, August and December. ("The August issue has traditionally been devoted to a single author by invitation.") **"We publish exclusively epigrams as understood by the tradition, which is not to say that innovation and variation are not permissible. Writers should be very familiar with the genre. There is no restriction as to subject. Translations, especially with original texts, are welcome."** They have recently published epigrams by Timothy Steele, Turner Cassity, Richard Wilbur and Katherine McAlpine. As a sample the editor selected "Essay on Certain Species of Epigram" by Fred Chappell:

> A grief
> in brief
>
> is the wit
> of it.

The Epigrammatist is 24 pgs., 4¼ × 5½, offset and saddle-stitched with card cover. They receive approximately 500 submissions a year, accept about 25%. Press run is 300 for 80-100 subscribers of which 10-15 are libraries. Single copy: $4; subscription: $11 individuals, $18 institutions. **Sample postpaid: $3.50. Submit no more than 6-8 poems at a time. Poems should be submitted on 8½ × 11 sheets with poet's name and address on each. No previously published poems or simultaneous submissions. Electronic submissions welcome.** Time between acceptance and publication is 6-12 months. **Send SASE for guidelines. Reports "depend on when submissions are made. I try to be reasonably prompt, but sometimes need to hold work for some weeks." Pays 5 copies. Rights remain with the writer.** Includes occasional quotes from collections of related interest. "Review copies may be sent, but will not necessarily be used." The editor says, "*The Epigrammatist* continues the long tradition of the epigram, which, according to David Middleton, 'is a distillation of much complex experience into a little wisdom.' It may be humorous or witty, but is emphatically not simply a quip, a cartoon caption, or a wisecrack."

EPOCH; BAXTER HATHAWAY PRIZE (III), 251 Goldwin Smith, Cornell University, Ithaca NY 14853, phone (607)255-3385, founded 1947, has a distinguished and long record of publishing **exceptionally fine poetry** and fiction. They have published work by such poets as Ashbery, Ammons,

Eshleman, Wanda Coleman, Molly Peacock, Robert Vander Molen and Alvin Aubert. The magazine appears 3 times a year in a 6×9, professionally printed, flat-spined format with glossy color cover, 100 pgs., which goes to 1,000 subscribers. They use less than 1% of the many submissions they receive each year, have a 2- to 12-month backlog. Mostly lyric free verse, with emphasis on voice and varying content and length, appears here (and, occasionally, avant-garde or "open" styles)—some of it quite powerful. **Sample postpaid: $5. "We** *don't read* **unsolicited mss between April 15 and September 15." Reports in 2 months. Occasionally provides criticism on mss. Pays $5-10/page. Buys first serial rights.** The annual Baxter Hathaway prize of $1,000 is awarded for a long poem or, in alternate years, a novella. Write for details. Poetry published in *Epoch* has also been included in the 1992 and 1993 volumes of *The Best American Poetry*. The editor advises, "I think it's extremely important for poets to read other poets. I think it's also very important for poets to read the magazines that they want to publish in. Directories are not enough."

EQUINOX PRESS (V); BRITISH HAIKU SOCIETY; BLITHE SPIRIT (IV-Form/style, translations), Sinodun, Shalford, Braintree Essex CM7 5HN England, phone 01371-851097, founded 1990, c/o Mr. David Cobb. Equinox publishes poetry (mainly haiku and senryu), 1-2 volumes/year. **They have a waiting list at present and are unable to consider submissions.** BHS publishes a quarterly journal, *Blithe Spirit*, a quarterly newsletter and other occasional publications (pamphlets, folios). *Blithe Spirit* **publishes mainly haiku, senryu and tanka sent in by society members,** but one section, "The Pathway," accepts **originals in any language plus a translation in one of English, French or German, and is open to non-members.** As a sample the Equinox editor selected this haiku (poet unidentified):

> *a cloudless sky*
> *painters stretch ladders*
> *to their farthest rungs*

Staff reviews books of poetry. Send books for review consideration. The Museum of Haiku Literature, Tokyo, gives a quarterly best-of-issue award (£50). In addition, BHS administers the annual James W. Hackett Haiku Award (currently £100). Rules of entry are available annually in the spring. Send SASE (or SAE and IRC from outside England).

ESSENCE (V, IV-Women, ethnic), 1500 Broadway, New York NY 10036, phone (212)642-0647, founded 1970, poetry editor Angela Kinamore. "*Essence* caters to the **needs of today's Black women." They publish poetry with humor or poetry dealing with love/romance, politics, religion, social issues or spirituality.** They have published poetry by Margaret Walker Alexander and Pinkie Gordon Lane. As a sample the editor selected these lines from "Ode to My Sons" by Mari Evans:

> *I am the vessel from whence you came*
> *the lode filled with imaginings*
> *aside from dreams my longing cannot*
> *touch your reaching nor can I direct*
> *your quest . . .*

Essence is a mass-circulation consumer magazine with an upscale tone. It is 140 pgs., slick stock with full-color art, photos and ads. **They are currently not accepting poetry submissions.**

EUROPEAN JUDAISM (IV-Religious, ethnic), Kent House, Rutland Gardens, London SW7 1BX England, founded 1966, poetry editor Ruth Fainlight, is a "twice-yearly magazine with emphasis on European Jewish theology/philosophy/literature/history, with **some poetry in every issue. It should preferably be short and have some relevance to matters of Jewish interest."** They have recently published poetry by Linda Pastan, Elaine Feinstein, George Szirtes and Dannie Abse. As a sample the editor selected these lines from a poem by Micheline Wandor:

> *we scions of the wooden spoon*
> *must spit the coal dust*
> *and the tailor's chalk*
> *and wipe*
> *the black and the white*
> *from the corners*
> *of our mouths.*

It is a glossy, elegant, 6×9, flat-spined magazine, rarely art or graphics, 110 pgs. They have a press run of 950, about 50% of which goes to subscribers (few libraries). Subscription: $27. **Sample can be obtained gratis from Carfax Publishing Co., P.O. Box 25, Abingdon, Oxfordshire OX14 3VE United Kingdom. Submit 3-4 poems at a time. "I prefer unpublished poems, but poems from published books acceptable." Cover letter required. Pays 1 copy.**

EVENT (II, IV-Themes), Douglas College, P.O. Box 2503, New Westminster, British Columbia V3L 5B2 Canada, founded 1971, editor David Zieroth, is "a literary magazine publishing **high-quality contemporary poetry**, short stories and reviews. **In poetry, we tend to appreciate the narrative and**

sometimes the confessional modes. In any case, we are eclectic and always open to content that invites involvement. We publish mostly Canadian writers." They have published poetry by Tom Wayman, Elisabeth Harvor and Richard Lemm. These sample lines are from "Poetry" by Don Domanski:

> is it a side street or a cat's jaw?
> cerecloth or the body's flesh?
> I've named it the heart's pillow
> wind in a mirror   cloud-rope
> lighthouse on the edge of a wound
> beadwork   the mote's halo   wolf-ladder

Event appears three times a year. It is 140 pgs., 6×9, flat-spined, glossy-covered and finely printed with a circulation of 1,000 for 700 subscribers, of which 50 are libraries. **Sample postpaid: $6. Submit 5 poems at a time. No previously published poems. Brief cover letter with publication credits required. Include SASE or SAE and IRCs. "Tell us if you'd prefer your manuscript to be recycled rather than returned."** Time between acceptance and publication is within 1 year. **Comments on some rejections. Reports in 3-4 months. Pays honorarium. Buys first North American serial rights. Sometimes they have special thematic issues, such as: work, feminism, peace and war, coming of age.**

‡**THE EVER DANCING MUSE; WHO WHO WHO PUBLISHING (II)**, P.O. Box 7751, East Rutherford NJ 07073, founded 1993, editor John Chorazy, is a "semiannual attempt to publish fine work in a small press format." **The editor wants "thinking, feeling poetry; all kinds, under three pages. I like short, tight poems but I'll look at anything."** They have recently published poetry by Lyn Lifshin, Sparrow and Duane Locke. As a sample the editor selected these lines from "Heading South: Green Pine Concerto" by Alan Britt:

> An angel
>   walks
>   along the back of my hand;
>   her voice
>   vibrates inside
>   rusted railroad tracks

The Ever Dancing Muse is 20 pgs., 5½ × 8½, saddle-stapled with light card cover. Press run is 100 for 25 subscribers. Subscription: $8 for 3 issues, 1 back issue free. **Sample postpaid: $3. Previously published poems and simultaneous submissions OK, if stated as such. "Cover letters are interesting and appreciated but not required." Seldom comments on rejections. Reports in 1 day to 1 month. Pays 2 copies. Acquires one-time rights.** The editor reminds poets, "This magazine, and all small press publications, need the support of poets and poetry readers to continue. Read a sample issue!"

THE EVERGREEN CHRONICLES (IV-Gay/lesbian), P.O. Box 8939, Minneapolis MN 55408, phone (612)649-4982, e-mail bzsura@aol.com, is "a semiannual journal of arts and cultures dedicated to presenting the best of lesbian and gay literary and visual artists. **The artistry presented is not limited to 'gay' or 'lesbian' themes, but extends to life, in all its dimensions."** Subscription: $15. **Sample: $7.95 plus $1 postage. "Send 4 copies of your work, up to 10 pgs. of poetry. Please include cover letter with short biographical paragraph describing yourself and your work. Deadlines: July 1 and January 1." Send SASE for upcoming themes. Pays 1 copy and honorarium. Acquires first-time rights.** Staff reviews books of poetry in 500 words, single format. Send books for review consideration.

EVIL DOG (II), 331 Ludlow Ave., Cincinnati OH 45220, founded 1992, editor-in-chief Jeff Wilson, is a quarterly of strange, offbeat fiction, poetry, narrative art and photography. **They want "offbeat, grotesque, wild, weird, wonderful poetry. No mainstream, conventional poetry."** They have published poetry by Aralee Strange, Ken Ehrman, David Siders and Ashu Misingi. The editor says *ED* is 40-50 pgs., digest-sized, newsprint, matte cover. Circulation 2,000, mostly shelf sales. Single copy: $1; subscription: $10. **Sample postpaid: $2.25. "Please send no more than five poems at a time." No previously published poems; simultaneous submissions OK. Cover letter required.** Time between acceptance and publication is 1-3 months. **Send SASE for guidelines. Reports in 1-2 months. Pays 2 copies. Acquires first North American serial rights.** Reviews books of poetry. Poets may also send books for review consideration. The editor says, "*Evil Dog* is drawn to the strange and offbeat. We are open to all formats of poetry, but the individual work must stand on its own. We welcome art along with poetry submissions."

‡**EXCURSUS LITERARY ARTS JOURNAL (II)**, P.O. Box 1056, Knickerbocker Station, New York NY 10002, founded 1994, publisher Giancarlo Malchiodi, is an annual "eclectic collection of quality work from both new and established poets. **All literary excursions are welcome . . . from the idyllic to the**

rebellious, formal and traditional to free form and avant-garde, imagistic to concrete to narrative to 'language' to Beat, to everything in between and beyond." However, they do not want "religious poetry nor any romantic pablum." As a sample the publisher selected these lines from "Watching Willy Wonka Alone on a Saturday Night" by Meredith Schuman:

> *And fantasy floats through my 12-inch set*
> *up a broken antenna as I spoon gummy pink*
> *Amoxil into my flushed cheeks like Violet*
> *chewing an illicit blueberry Gobstopper.*
> *Solitude sticks like static to the screen, its dusty knobs*
> *decaying like a tootsie roll in my fevered mouth.*

The publisher says *Excursus* is about 80 pgs., 8½ × 11, offset printed and "square-bound," with glossy card stock cover and b&w art and photos. They receive upwards of 2,500 submissions a year, accept 5-10%. Press run is 1,000. **Sample postpaid: $5 (available November 1995). Submit up to 3 poems at a time, "not to exceed 170 lines total," addressed "Attn: Poetry." Simultaneous submissions and previously published poems OK, "if notified of previous placement." Personalized cover letter required. Reads submissions September 1 through June 30 only. "Publisher initially screens all submissions and forwards quality work to Editorial Collective." Seldom comments on rejections. Send SASE for guidelines. Reports within 5 months. Pays 1 copy. Acquires one-time rights.** They sponsor an annual contest. Entry fee: $5 for 5 poems, addressed "Attn: Contest." Deadline: June 30. The winner receives $200, 4 pages of dedicated space in the magazine, 5 copies, and an invitation to join the Editorial Collective. The publisher says "Don't be concerned with 'fads' in poetry, whether 'formal,' 'performance,' or whatever . . . write from your instincts. Assimilate what you read and enjoy, but don't copy."

EXIT 13 (IV-Specialized: geography/travel), % Tom Plante, 22 Oakwood Ct., Fanwood NJ 07023, phone (908)889-5298, founded 1987, editor Tom Plante, is a "contemporary poetry annual" using **poetry that is "short, to the point, with a sense of geography."** They have recently published poetry by Ruth Moon Kempher, Gerard Coulombe, Robert Cooperman, Ray Mizer and Madeline Hoffer. As a sample the editor selected these lines by Jennifer A. Zogott:

> *in this land dominated by*
> *memory, ghosts, skeletons*
>
> *presiding, ex-officio,*
> *the Parachute Jump*
> *silently observes the sturdy inaugural turn*
> *of the Wonder Wheel*

Exit 13, #7, was 60 pgs. Press run is 300. **Sample postpaid: $6,** *payable to Tom Plante.* **They accept simultaneous submissions and previously published poems. Send SASE for guidelines. Reports in 3 months. Pays 1 copy. Acquires one-time and possible anthology rights.** Staff reviews books of poetry and magazines in a "Publications Received" column, using 25-30 words/listing. Send books for review consideration. The editor advises, "Write about what you know. Study geography. *Exit 13* looks for adventure. Every state and region is welcome. Send a snapshot of an 'Exit 13' road sign and receive a free copy of the issue in which it appears."

EXPEDITION PRESS (III, IV-Love, religious), 105 E. Walnut St., #2306, Kalamazoo MI 49007-5253, publisher Bruce W. White, publishes chapbooks of **love poems and religious poems. "I dislike violence."** He likes to see **"experimental, fresh new approaches, interesting spatial relationships, as well as quality artwork. I dislike political diatribes."** He has published poetry by J. Kline Hobbs, Jim DeWitt, Martin Cohen and C. VanAllsburg. As a sample the publisher selected this haiku of his own:

> *a tree by a lake.*
> *the same tree in winter.*
> *a harvest moon over the lake.*

Submit typed ms of 20-30 pgs. and cover letter with brief bio. No previously published poems or simultaneous submissions. Ms on cassette OK. Reports in 1 month. Sometimes sends prepublication galleys. Pays 100 copies. Bruce White provides "much" criticism on rejected mss.

EXPLORATIONS (II), UAS, 11120 Glacier Highway, Juneau AK 99801-8761, phone (907)465-6418, fax (907)465-6406, founded 1980, editor Professor Art Petersen, is the annual literary magazine of the University of Alaska, Southeast. **"The editors respond favorably to 'language really spoken by men and women.' Standard form and innovation are encouraged as well as appropriate and fresh aspects of imagery (allusion, metaphor, simile, symbol . . .)."** As a sample the editor selected these lines from "Seven come eleven" by Charles Bukowski:

> *I've never ever quite met*
> *anybody*

"We found the composition and detail of this work well conceived and executed," says Editor Art Petersen, of the zinc etching which appears on the cover of Explorations' 1994 edition. "Our philosophy is to reward, with publication, those artists who succeed in breathing life into a work of art and to honor this life by sharing it with others." The annual magazine is a publication of the University of Alaska Southeast and accepts poetry, prose fiction and graphic art. "We look for poetry that explores the human condition, that successfully recreates inner human experience, that employs traditional poetic frameworks and explores new ones," says Petersen. The cover art, entitled "Heron Magic," is by Dianne R. Anderson, Juneau resident and University of Alaska Southeast adjunct instructor.

> like myself—
> living with deadly calm
> inside this hurricane of hell.

Explorations is digest-sized, nicely printed, with front and back cover illustration in one color, saddle-stapled. The editors tend to go for smaller-length poems (with small line breaks for tension) and often print two on a page—mostly lyric free verse with a focus on voice. **Sample postpaid: $4.** In 1995, they offered first prizes of $500 for poetry and prose and published the best of the submissions received. Each year a prominent poet or writer serves as judge (1995: Nancy Lord). **An entry/reading fee is required: $2/poem (up to 5, each 60 lines maximum), $4/story (up to 2, each 3,500 words maximum); those paying reader/contest entry fees of $4 or more will receive a copy of the publication. Checks should be made payable to "VAS Explorations." Mss must be typed with name, address, and 3- or 4-line biography on the back of each first page. Simultaneous submissions OK. Submit January through March. Mss are not returned. Send SASE for guidelines. Submissions are reported on in May or June, publication is annual, out in May or June. Pays 2 contributor copies. Acquires one-time rights.**

EXPLORER MAGAZINE; FLORY LITERARY FOUNDATION (I, IV-Inspirational, nature, love), P.O. Box 210, Notre Dame IN 46556, phone (219)277-3465, founded 1960, editor and publisher Raymond Flory, is a semiannual magazine that contains **short inspirational, nature and love poetry** as well as prose. The editor wants **"poetry of all styles and types; should have an inspirational slant but not necessary. Short poems preferred—up to 20 lines—the shorter the better. Good 'family' type poetry always needed. Seasonal material also welcome. No real long poetry or long lines; no sexually explicit poetry or porno."** He has recently published poetry by Glenn J. Amorosia, Joanna M. Weston, M.L. Moeller and Kristen Hinkle. As a sample the editor selected "My Secret Garden" by Jo Ann Starr Harrelson:

> There is a place inside of me
> A place where flowers grow,
> A secret garden with a well
> From which pure waters flow.

Explorer is 44 pgs., digest-sized, photocopied from typed copy in a variety of fonts (some of it dot-matrix) and saddle-stapled with card cover. Their most recent issue contains the work of 60 authors from 8 different countries. Circulation is 300. Subscription: $6/year. **Sample available for $3, guidelines for SASE. Subscribers vote for the poems or stories they like best and prizes are awarded; four prizes each issue: $25, $20, $15 and $10; first-prize winner in each issue receives a plaque along with the cash prize. In addition to the regular cash prizes, there is also an editor's choice award, the Joseph Flory Memorial Award, named after the editor's late father. Award is $10 and a plaque.** Recent winner: Martin Caskey. The editor awards the new Angel Light Award, given to the author whose prose or poetry most emphasizes the "spiritual." Award is $10 and a plaque. The first award winner is Glenda

Wojcik for "The Only Light We Have." **Writers should submit 3-4 poems, typed, camera-ready. Material must be previously unpublished; simultaneous submissions OK. Reporting time is 1 week and time to publication 1-2 years. Pays 1 copy only to those appearing in the magazine for the first time.** The editor says, "Over 90% of the poets submitting poetry to *Explorer* have not seen a copy of the magazine. Order a copy first—then submit. This will save poets stamps, frustration, etc. This should hold true for whatever market a writer is aiming for!"

EXPRESSIONS (I, IV-Specialized: people with disabilities/ongoing health problems), P.O. Box 16294, St. Paul MN 55116-0294, phone (612)451-1208, fax (612)552-1209, founded 1993, editor Sefra Kobrin Pitzele, is a nonprofit semiannual, subtitled "Literature and Art by People with Disabilities and Ongoing Health Problems," designed "to provide a place for talented people to be published." **They are open to any topic provided entry is written by people with disabilities and/or ongoing health problems.** They have published poetry by James Syndal, Tara Allen and Geoffrey Cook. As a sample the editor selected these lines from "Montana Wind" by Sheryl L. Nelms:

> *it rushes up*
> *through dry grass*
> *pushes the antelope*
> *over the ridge*
>
> *drops off*
> *the limestone cliff . . .*

Expressions is 56-72 pgs., 5½×8½, perfect-bound with 60 lb. glossy card cover. They publish about 25% of the poetry received. Press run is 650 for 120 subscribers. Subscription: $10 US, $15 foreign and institutions. **Sample postpaid: $6. Submit 5 poems at a time. Previously published poems and simultaneous submissions OK. Cover letter with 4- to 5-line bio and statement of ownership required. Do not submit mss from December 15 to January 15.** "Five others read each submission and grade it—independently—from 1 to 5. Most 5's are published." **Often comments on rejections. Send SASE for guidelines and upcoming themes. Reports in 3-5 months. Pays 2 copies. Acquires one-time rights.** They sponsor an annual poetry contest. Deadline: December 15. Write for details. "At the end of each issue, we print book reviews appropriate to our audience. We only review informational books on disability or illness." However, they are open to unsolicited reviews of such materials.

EXPRESSIONS FORUM REVIEW (I), 2837 Blue Spruce Lane, Wheaton MD 20906, founded 1991, is a semiannual of poetry, **"any kind, any form, 20 lines maximum. No sex-related matters, no obscenity." They are currently looking to receive more traditional forms of poetry.** Single copy: $3; subscription: $12. **Submit 1-4 poems with $3 reading fee. Previously published poems and simultaneous submissions OK. Typewritten poems preferred; do not send original copies. Seldom comments on rejections. Send SASE for guidelines. Reports in 4 months. Pays 1 copy.** Open to unsolicited reviews. Poets may also send books for review consideration. Reading fee includes entry into spring and fall poetry contests. 1st prize: $100; 2nd: $50; 3rd: $25 (and 25 honorable mentions). The editor says, "Speak from the heart and soul."

EXQUISITE CORPSE (II), P.O. Box 25051, Baton Rouge LA 70894, founded 1983, editor Andrei Codrescu (whom you can often hear in commentary segments of "All Things Considered," The National Public Radio news program). This curious and delightful monthly ($20/year), when you unfold it, is 6″ wide and 16″ long, 20 pgs., saddle-stapled, professionally printed in 2 columns on quality stock. The flavor of Codrescu's comments (and some clues about your prospects in submitting here) may be judged by this note: "A while ago, alarmed by the number of poems aimed at the office—a number only the currency inflation and Big Macs can hold candles to—we issued an edict against them. Still they came, and some even came live. They came in the mail and under the door. We have no poetry insurance. If we are found one day smothered under photocopy paper, who will pay for the burial? The *Corpse* wants a jazz funeral. Rejections make poets happy. Having, in many cases, made their poems out of original, primal, momentary rejections, the rejection of these rejections affirms the beings forced to such deviousness." He has published poetry by Carol Bergé, Charles Plymell, Lawrence Ferlinghetti, Alice Notley and many others. You'll find all styles and forms here, even short light verse. Most examples are freestyle, leaning toward expressionism (effective use of symbol), and accessible, too. Translations also seem welcome. **Payment: "Zilch/Nada." You take your chances inserting work into this wit machine. As of 1990 this is their policy: ". . . we are abolishing the SASE-based privacy system . . . Your submissions will be answered directly in the pages of our publication. Look for your name and for our response to your work in the next *Corpse*. We will continue returning your submissions by SASE if you wish, but as to what we think of your *écriture*, please check 'Body Bag,' our new editorial column. Please rest assured that your work will receive the same malevolently passionate attention as before. Only now we are going to do it in public."** Here's an example: "We were excited by 'The Wind Got Excited' until the puppy-hero got too excited and leapt off the 13th floor. That was cruel . . . " Comments you want, comments you get! Poetry published in this magazine has been included in *The Best American Poetry 1992*.

FABER AND FABER, INC. (V), 50 Cross St., Winchester MA 01890, phone (617)721-1427, editor Betsy Uhrig, has a distinguished list of poetry publications but is **not accepting mss.**

‡FAR GONE (II), P.O. Box 43745, Lafayette LA 70504-3745, founded 1995, editor/publisher Todd Brendan Fahey, is an annual journal "stalking the giants of tomorrow." It includes fiction, poetry and interviews. **They want "a sure voice in any style of poetry. Nothing not accomplished."** They have recently published poetry by Skip Fox, Minal Hajratwala and Juliet Rodeman. *Far Gone* is 42-48 pgs., 11 × 8½ (landscape format), offset and handsewn. The cover is professionally printed on 64 lb. fine-laid paper with halftone reproduction of classic art. It's a striking package. They accept 3-8 poems/issue. Press run is 100 for 20 subscribers of which 10 are libraries, 20 shelf sales. **Sample postpaid: $7. No previously published poems; simultaneous submissions OK ("though they may cause one heartache"). Cover letter required. Seldom comments on rejections. Pays 1 copy. Rights returned to contributors upon written request.** Staff reviews small press books of poetry (no chapbooks) in 250 words. Send books for review consideration. They offer $50 and publication to the Best Interview-of-Year ("of literary persons of note"). Entry fee: $5. (The inaugural issue features interviews with Ken Kesey and Timothy Leary.) The editor says, "Each issue of *Far Gone* will be a piece of art (check out #1). Poetry selected will meet such a standard."

FARMER'S MARKET; MIDWEST FARMER'S MARKET, INC. (II), Elgin Community College, 1700 Spartan Dr., Elgin IL 60123-7193, founded 1981, editors Patrick Parks, Rachael Tecza and Joanne Lowery, is a biannual seeking **poems that are "tightly structured, with concrete imagery, reflective of the clarity, depth and strength of Midwestern life. Not interested in highly abstract work or light verse."** They have published poetry by Larry Starzec, Melanie Richards, Philip Dacey, Edward C. Lynskey and Marjorie Maddox. As a sample, they offer these lines from "Everything Changes to Beauty" by Kathryn Burt Winogrod:

> The clear skimming line of my father's fishing pole
> rides its twinned self off the brightening pond,
> a lifting rain of light returning to light,
> and beneath, where fish round their mouths
> like moons to swallow it, the lure
> tiny and shimmering, make-believe.

FM is 100-200 pgs., digest-sized, perfect-bound with card cover, handsomely printed with graphics and photos. The poems are almost always accessible . . . clear, crafted lyric free verse. All in all, this is an enjoyable read. They receive about 1,500 submissions/year, of which they use 50-60, have a 6-month backlog. Circulation 700 for 200 subscribers, of which 25 are libraries. **Sample: $4.50 plus $1 p&h. Submit 4-6 poems at a time, typed. Would rather not have simultaneous submissions. Comments on rejections, "only if we think the work is good." Send SASE for upcoming themes. Reports in 6-8 weeks (summer replies take longer). Pays 2 copies. Acquires one-time rights.** This publication has received numerous Illinois Arts Council Literary Awards.

FARRAR, STRAUS & GIROUX/BOOKS FOR YOUNG READERS (II, IV-Children), 19 Union Square W., New York NY 10003, phone (212)741-6900, founded 1946, contact Editorial Dept./Books for Young Readers. They publish one book of children's poetry "every once in awhile," in both hardcover and paperback editions. **They are open to book-length submissions of children's poetry only.** They have published collections of poetry by Valerie Worth and Deborah Chandra. As a sample the editor selected "Suspense" from Chandra's book *Balloons*:

> Wide-eyed
> the sunflowers
> stare and catch their summer
> breath, while I pause, holding basket
> and shears.

Query first with sample poems and cover letter with brief bio and publication credits. Poems previously published in magazines and simultaneous submissions OK. Seldom comments on rejections. Send SASE for reply. Replies to queries in 1-2 months, to mss in 1-4 months. "We pay an advance against royalties; the amount depends on whether or not the poems are illustrated, etc." Also pays 10 author's copies.

FAT TUESDAY (II), RD2 Box 4220, Manada Gap Rd., Grantville PA 17028, phone (717)469-7159, founded 1981, editor-in-chief F.M. Cotolo, other editors Kristen von Oehrke, B. Lyle Tabor, Thom Savion and Lionel Stevroid, is an annual which calls itself "**a Mardi Gras of literary and visual treats featuring many voices, singing, shouting, sighing and shining, expressing the relevant to irreverent.** On Fat Tuesday (the Tuesday before Ash Wednesday, when Lent begins) the editors hold The Fat Tuesday Symposium. In over ten years no one has shown up." **They want "prose poems,**

poems of irreverence, gems from the gut. Usually shorter, hit-the-mark, personal stuff inseparable from the voice of the artist. Form doesn't matter, but no rhyming greeting-card stuff. Also particularly interested in hard-hitting 'autofiction.' " They have published poetry by Mark Cramer, Mary Lee Gowland, Chuck Taylor, Patrick Kelly, Charles Bukowski, Gerald Locklin and Kilgore Rimpau. As a sample they offer these lines by John Quinnett:

> It is enough to be alive,
> To be here drinking this cheap red wine
> While the chili simmers on the stove
> & the refrigerator hums deep into the night.

The digest-sized magazine is typeset (large type, heavy paper), 36-50 pgs., saddle-stapled, card covers, (sometimes magazine-sized, unbound) with cartoons, art and ads. Circulation 200 with 20-25 pgs. of poetry in each issue. They receive hundreds of submissions each year, use 3-5%, have a 3- to 5- month backlog. **Sample postpaid: $5. Submit 4 poems at a time. "Handwritten OK; we'll read anything." No previously published poems or simultaneous submissions. "Cover letters are fine, the more amusing the better." Reads submissions June through December. Reports in 1-2 weeks. Pays 1 copy. Rights revert to author after publication.** The editors say, "Our tip for authors is simply to be themselves. Poets should use their own voice to be heard. Publishing poetry is as lonely as writing it. We have no idea about current trends, and care less. We encourage all to buy a sample issue to see what they have which best fits our style and format, and also to help support the continuation of our publication. We rely on no other means but sales to subsidize our magazine, and writers should be sensitive to this hard fact which burdens many small presses."

‡FAUQUIER POETRY JOURNAL (I), P.O. Box 68, Bealeton VA 22712, founded 1994, managing editor D. Clement, is a quarterly that contains poetry and poetry comment; "purpose is to encourage new and developing poets with talent." **They want "fresh, creative, well-crafted poetry, any style. Due to format, longer poems over 40 lines are not often used. Do not want overly sentimental or religious themes, overdone subjects, or overly obscure work. We are turned off by poets who disguise a lack of talent by being too cute and clever."** They have recently published poetry by Marylin Faith Rumph, R.G. Ribble, J.L. Seger and Michael Musante. As a sample the editor selected these lines from "Fog Riders" by Nancy Ryan:

> Fog rolls in jagged streaks
> linking granite sky
> to rockbound seas.
> Even the cold is gray.
> Iron-willed fishermen
> hunker down in yellow slickers . . .

FPJ is 30-40 pgs., digest-sized, photocopied from laser-printed originals on plain white paper and saddle-stapled with bright colored paper cover. Press run is more than 100 for 50 subscribers. Subscription: $20. **Sample postpaid: $5. The editor encourages subscriptions by requiring a reading fee for nonsubscribers ($5 for 1-5 poems); no reading fee for subscribers. Submit poetry with name and address in the upper left corner of each page and include SASE. Simultaneous submissions OK. Rarely accepts previously published poems. Often comments on rejections. Send SASE for guidelines. Reports in 2-6 weeks. Offers Editor's Choice Awards of $5-25 for the best entries in each issue. Pays 1 copy to remainder of published poets. Acquires one-time rights.** They also sponsor quarterly poetry contests, explained in the journal. Entry fee: $5. Prizes range from $5-50, and winners are published in the following issue. The editor says, "Let us see a variety in your submission; what one editor likes, another won't. Send a range of work that illustrates the breadth and depth of your talent; this helps us decide if there's something we like. As we are new, we encourage submissions from anyone who is writing mature, well-crafted poetry."

FEELINGS: AMERICA'S BEAUTIFUL POETRY MAGAZINE; ANDERIE POETRY PRESS; QUARTERLY EDITOR'S CHOICE AWARDS (I, II), P.O. Box 85, Easton PA 18044-0085, phone (610)559-9287, founded 1989, editors Carl and Carole Heffley, a quarterly magazine, uses **"high-quality poetry favoring traditional form, no more than 40 lines. No theme is taboo though pornography will be returned unread."** They have recently published poetry by Frances Fabiani, Harvey Stanbrough and Ann Gasser. As a sample here are the opening lines from "Sudden Storm" by M.H. Mitchell:

> The sudden storm raged on and on—
> our boat was swept out to the sea.
> The waves were king—we were the pawn.
> The sudden storm raged on and on.

Feelings is magazine-sized, saddle-stapled with heavy paper cover, professionally printed on lightweight paper, using "photography appropriate to the season or subject." Subscription: $24. **Sample postpaid: $6.50. Cover letter with background, credits ("something about the writer") required with submissions. "SASE must accompany all correspondence." Send SASE for guidelines. Reports in 6 weeks. Pays $10 for 3 Editor's Choice Awards in each issue. Acquires first rights.** Also runs several contests throughout the year with prizes ranging from $25 to $100. **"We publish chapbooks, info/price list upon request with SASE."** Mss on "how-to" write/publish poetry welcome. Payment for articles varies.

FEH! A JOURNAL OF ODIOUS POETRY (IV-Humor), 200 E. Tenth St., #603, New York NY 10003, founded 1986, editor Simeon Stylites, appears twice a year, using **"silliness and nonsense, but *good* silliness and nonsense; humor, satire, irreverence, eccentricity, fanaticism, etc.; rhyming and non."** They have recently published poetry by Jerm Boor and Blaster Al Ackerman. As a sample the editors selected these lines by Ferdinand "Skeet" Giaclepousse:

> *I believe in God and Bigfoot*
> *and the right to worship as I please.*
> *I've seen angels, demons and the Virgin Mama*
> *in the midst of my D.T.'s*

It is 36 pgs., 8½ × 11, with photocopied paper cover. Their press run is 200 with about 35 subscriptions, and sales through bookstores. **Sample postpaid: $2. Submit up to 6 poems at a time. Considers simultaneous submissions and previously published poems. Editor sometimes comments on rejections, if asked. Send SASE for guidelines. Reports within 2 months. Pays 1 copy. Acquires one-time rights.**

‡FELLOWSHIP IN PRAYER (IV-Religious), 291 Witherspoon St., Princeton NJ 08542, phone (609)924-6863, fax (609)924-6910, founded 1950, editor M. Ford-Grabowsky, is an interfaith bimonthly **"concerned with prayer, meditation and spiritual life"** using short poetry **"with deep religious (or spiritual) feeling."** It is 48 pgs., digest-sized, professionally printed, saddle-stapled with glossy card cover. They accept about 2% of submissions received. Press run is 10,000. Subscription: $16. **Sample free. Submit 5 poems at a time, double-spaced. Simultaneous submissions and "sometimes" previously published poems OK. Cover letter preferred. Reports in 1 month. Pays 5 copies.** Staff reviews books of poetry in 75 words, single format.

FEMINIST STUDIES (IV-Women/feminism), %Women's Studies Program, University of Maryland, College Park MD 20742, phone (301)405-7415, fax (301)314-9190, founded 1969, poetry editor Alicia Ostriker, **"welcomes a variety of work that focuses on women's experience, on gender as a category of analysis, and that furthers feminist theory and consciousness."** They have published poetry by Janice Mirikitani, Paula Gunn Allen, Cherrie Moraga, Audre Lorde, Judith Small, Milana Marsenich, Lynda Schraufnagel, Valerie Fox and Diane Glancy. The elegantly-printed, flat-spined, 250-page paperback appears 3 times a year in an edition of 8,000, goes to 7,000 subscribers, of which 1,500 are libraries. There are **4-10 pgs. of poetry in each issue. Sample postpaid: $12. No simultaneous submissions; will only consider previously published poems under special circumstances. Manuscripts are reviewed twice a year, in May and December. Deadlines are May 1 and December 1. Authors will receive notice of the board's decision by June 30 and January 30. Always sends prepublication galleys. No pay.** Commissions reviews of books of poetry. Poets may send books to Claire G. Moses for review consideration.

THE FIDDLEHEAD (I, II, IV-Regional, students), Campus House, University of New Brunswick, P.O. Box 4400, Fredericton, New Brunswick E3B 5A3 Canada, founded 1945, poetry editors Robert Gibbs, Robert Hawkes and Don MacKay. From its beginning in 1945 as a local little magazine devoted mainly to student writers, **the magazine retains an interest in poets of the Atlantic region and in young poets** but prints poetry from everywhere. It is **open to excellent work of every kind, looking always for vitality, freshness and surprise.** Among the poets whose work they have recently published are Brett Hursey and Ruth Warat. As a sample, we selected these lines from "A Little Poem About Commitment" by Kim Roberts:

> *Truth to the spirit of the event in this narrative takes precedence*
> *over a strict adherence to history.*
> *Due to the earth's curvature, the map plates in this book cannot*
> *conform to borders.*
> *If you are not fully satisfied, a refund will be provided.*
> *We cannot be responsible for loss or damage of personal property.*

> *I have not hesitated to invent wherever it seemed fictionally right*
> *to do so.*
> *If swallowed, drink a glass of water to dilute.*

The Fiddlehead is a handsomely printed, 6×9, flat-spined paperback (120 pgs.) with b&w graphics, colored cover, paintings by New Brunswick artists. They use less than 10% of submissions. Circulation is 1,000. Subscription: $18/year plus $6 postage (US). **Sample: $7 (US). Submit 3-10 poems at a time. No simultaneous submissions. For reply or return of ms, send SAE with Canadian stamps, IRCs or cash. Reporting time is 2-6 months, backlog 6-18 months. Pay is $10-12/printed page.** Reviews books by Canadian authors only.

FIELD; FIELD TRANSLATION SERIES; CONTEMPORARY AMERICAN POETRY SERIES; O.C. PRESS (II, IV-Translations), Rice Hall, Oberlin College, Oberlin OH 44074, phone (216)775-8408, founded 1969, editors Stuart Friebert, David Young, Alberta Turner and David Walker, is a literary journal appearing twice a year with "emphasis on poetry, translations and essays by poets." **They want the "best possible" poetry.** They have published poetry by Thylias Moss, Seamus Heaney, Charles Simic and Sharon Olds. The handsomely printed, digest-sized journal is flat-spined, has 100 pgs., rag stock with glossy card color cover. Although most poems fall under the lyrical free verse category, you'll find narratives and formal work here on occasion, much of it sensual, visually appealing and resonant. Circulation 2,500, with 800 library subscriptions. Subscription: $12/year, $20/2 years. **Sample postpaid: $6. Reports in 2 weeks, has a 3- to 6-month backlog. Always sends prepublication galleys. Pays $20-30/page plus 2 copies.** They publish books of translations in the Field Translation Series, averaging 150 pgs., flat-spined and hardcover editions. **Query regarding translations. Pays 7½-10% royalties with some advance and 10 author's copies.** They have also inaugurated a Contemporary American Poetry Series with the publication of a collection of new and selected poems by Dennis Schmitz. This series is by invitation only. Write for catalog to buy samples. Work published in *Field* has also been included in the 1992, 1993, 1994 and 1995 volumes of *The Best American Poetry*. Stuart Friebert says they would like to see more poetry from "minority" poets "of any and all cultures."

‡5TH GEAR (I, II), PV 24-7, 4505 Patriots Circle, Fairfax VA 22030, phone (703)993-6016, founded 1994, first issue August 1995, editor Andy Fogle, who says, "*5th Gear* is an annual outlet for lesser-known writers that I know, as well as anyone else who wants to come along for the ride. . . ." **As for poetry, "I'm wide open—energetic, sad, surreal, imagist, prose poems, original verse—it's fine. I'll look at everything, but am not too fond of laziness."** They have recently published poetry by Cindy Goff, Jeffrey McKinney and Ana Christy. The editor says *5th Gear* is 30 pgs., digest-sized and saddle-stapled with b&w art inside and on the cover. They receive about 150 poems a year, accept 20-25. Press run is 100 for 10 subscribers. Subscription: $3 **Sample postpaid: $3. Submissions must be typed. No previously published poems; simultaneous submissions OK. Cover letter welcome. "Please, no poems folded separately."** Time between acceptance and publication is up to a year. **Often comments on rejections. Send SASE for guidelines. Reports in 1 month. Pays 1 copy. Acquires first rights and requests mention "if poem later appears somewhere else."** The editor says, "In replies, I'm gonna be nice to you, but I'm also gonna be blunt. I'm in love with my life. There is no 'literary scene,' just literature, and out of that literature that is submitted to me, I publish what I like best. I have fairly wide tastes, but I also have my biases. I won't lie to you."

‡FIFTY SOMETHING MAGAZINE (I, IV-Seniors), 8250 Tyler Blvd., Mentor OH 44060, phone (216)951-2468, founded 1989, editor Linda L. Lindeman, is a quarterly, "for those fifty or better," that serves Northeast Ohio. **They want "short, lighthearted poems related to issues on aging. Nothing too long or depressing."** As a sample the editor selected these lines from "The 'Known' Soldier" by Peggy Fleming (which was published in the magazine several years ago):

> *Richard's wife leaves him a rose,*
> *And tries hard to be brave;*
> *And a mother sheds her pent up tears,*
> *Over her beloved Dave.*
> *No, it isn't an Unknown Soldier,*
> *It's just a mismarked grave;*
> *For Tom or Dick or Harry,*
> *Or Mom's beloved Dave.*

Fifty Something is 48 pgs., 8½×11, printed 4-color on semiglossy paper and saddle-stitched, with photos, art and ads throughout. Press run is 25,000 for 15,000 shelf sales. Single copy: $1.95; subscription: $12.95. **Sample free. Previously published poems and simultaneous submissions OK.** Time between acceptance and publication is 1 year. Poems are circulated to an editorial board. **Reports in 3 months. Pay is negotiable. Buys one-time rights.**

FIGHTING WOMAN NEWS (IV-Women, specialized: martial arts), 6741 Tung Ave. W., Theodore AL 36582, founded 1975, poetry editor Debra Pettis, provides "a communications medium for women in martial arts, self-defense, combative sports." They want **poetry "relevant to our subject matter and nothing else."** They have published poetry by Dana Ridgeway. As a sample the editor selected these lines from "Practice" by Cathy Drinkwater Better:

> become
> the moment
> concentrate
> be one
> with the impact
> timing
> is all

Fighting Woman News appears quarterly in a magazine-sized, saddle-stapled format, 24 pgs. or more, finely printed, with graphics and b&w photos. Circulation 3,500. **Sample postpaid: $4.50, "and if you say you're a poet, we'll be sure to send a sample with poetry in it." Uses only 1 or 2 poems in each issue. "If your poem *really* requires an audience of martial artists to be appreciated, then send it." Simultaneous submissions OK. Cover letter required; poets should include "who they are and possibly why submitting to** *FWN*.**" Replies "ASAP." Sometimes sends prepublication galleys. Pays copies. Acquires one-time rights.** Open to unsolicited reviews. Poets may also send books for review consideration. "Because our field is so specialized, most interested women subscribe. It is not a requirement for publication, but **we seldom publish a nonsubscriber.**" The editor advises, "Read first; write later. To guarantee publication of your poem(s), submit a hard-core martial arts nonfiction article. Those are what we really need! Fighters who are also writers can have **priority access to our very limited poetry space by doing articles**. Please do not send any poems if you have not read any issues of *FWN*."

THE FIGURES (V), 5 Castle Hill Ave., Great Barrington MA 01230-1552, phone (413)528-2552, founded 1975, publisher/editor Geoffrey Young, is a small press publishing poetry and fiction. They have published poetry by Lyn Hejinian, Clark Coolidge, Ron Padgett and Christopher Dewdney. **They pay 10% of press run. However, they currently do not accept unsolicited poetry.**

FILLING STATION (II), P.O. Box 22135, Bankers Hall, Calgary, Alberta T2P 4J5 Canada, founded 1993, appears 3 times/year (January, May and September). *Filling Station* is a magazine of contemporary writing featuring poetry, fiction, interviews, reviews and other literary news. **"We are looking for all forms of contemporary writing. No specific objections to any style."** They have published poetry by George Bowering, Fred Wah, Nicole Markatic and Su Croll and say, "as an editorial collective, to pick one specific example goes against our objective of representing many different voices." *FS* is 48 pgs., 8½ × 11, saddle-stapled with card cover and includes photos, artwork and ads. They receive about 100 submissions for each issue, accept approximately 10%. Press run is 500 for 50 subscribers, 150 shelf sales. Subscription: $15/1 year, $25/2 years. **Sample postpaid: $6. Submit typed poems with name and address on each page. No previously published poems; simultaneous submissions OK. Cover letter required. Deadlines are November 15, March 15 and July 15. Seldom comments on rejections. Send SASE (or SAE with IRC) for guidelines. Reports in 3 months. Pays 2 copies. Acquires first North American and second reprint rights.** Reviews books of poetry in both single and multi-book format. Open to unsolicited reviews. Poets may also send books for review consideration. Here's what the collective has to say about *Filling Station* and the philosophy behind this publication: "You stop between these 'fixed' points on the map to get an injection of something new, something fresh that's going to get you from point to point. . . . We want to be a kind of connection between polarities: a link. We'll publish any poem or story that offers a challenge: to the mind, to the page, to writers and readers."

FINE MADNESS (II), P.O. Box 31138, Seattle WA 98103-1138, founded 1982, president Louis Bergsagel. *Fine Madness* publishes 3 issues every 2 years (a new issue roughly every 8 months). **They want "contemporary poetry of any form and subject. We look for highest quality of thought, language and imagery. We look for the mark of the individual: unique ideas and presentation; careful, humorous, sympathetic. No careless poetry, greeting card poetry, poetry that 10,000 other people could have written."** They have published poetry by Tess Gallagher, David Young and Caroline Knox. As a sample the editor selected these lines from "Natural History of an Idea" by Melinda Mueller:

> *Ice is over with quickly, while a knife, say, keeps happening,*
> *long after skin has healed. And the mind that thinks this—*
> *this is strangely consoling—is another event among the rest.*
>
> *Not that that's the end of it. There's the phone*
> *that rings, the avalanche of lights on that suburban hill*
> *across the lake, the incessant evening . . .*

Fine Madness is 64 pgs., digest-sized, perfect-bound, offset with color card cover. They accept about 40 of 1,000 poems received. Their press run is 1,000 for 100 subscribers of which 10 are libraries.

Subscription: $9. **Sample postpaid: $4. Guidelines available for SASE. Submit 2-5 poems, prefera-bly originals, not photocopy, 1 poem/page. No previously published poems or simultaneous sub-missions. Reports in 1-4 months. Pays 1 copy plus subscription.** Open to unsolicited reviews. Poets may also send books for review consideration to John Malek. They give 2 annual awards of $50 each to editors' choice. *Fine Madness* has had poetry selected for inclusion in the 1990, 1991, 1992, 1993 and 1994 volumes of *The Best American Poetry*. Coeditor Sean Bentley says, "If you don't read poetry, don't send us any."

FIREBRAND BOOKS (IV-Feminist, lesbian, ethnic), 141 The Commons, Ithaca NY 14850, phone (607)272-0000, founded 1984, editor and publisher Nancy K. Bereano, "is a **feminist and lesbian** publishing company committed to producing quality work in multiple genres by ethnically diverse women." They publish both quality trade paperbacks and hardbacks. As a sample, here is a stanza of a sestina, "great expectations," from the book *Living As A Lesbian* by Cheryl Clarke:

> *dreaming the encounter intense as engines*
> *first me then you oh what a night*
> *of rapture and risk and dolphin*
> *acrobatics after years of intend-*
> *ing to find my lesbian sources in the window*
> *of longing wide open in me*

The book is 94 pgs., flat-spined, elegantly printed on heavy stock with a glossy color card cover, a photo of the author on the back, $7.95. **Simultaneous submissions acceptable with notification. Replies to queries within 2 weeks, to mss within 1 month. Pays royalties.** Send for catalog to buy samples.

FIREWEED: A FEMINIST QUARTERLY (IV-Women), P.O. Box 279, Station B, Toronto, Ontario M5T 2W2 Canada, phone (416)504-1339, founded 1978, edited by the Fireweed Collective, is a feminist journal of writing, politics, art and culture that **"especially welcomes contributions by women of color, working-class women, native women, lesbians and women with disabilities."** As a sample we selected the opening lines of "These Military Men" by Joy Hewitt Mann:

> *My husband was*
> *a military man.*
> *Dinner*
> *5:30*
> *sharp.*
> *No give.   No take.*

Fireweed is 88 pgs., 6¾×9¾, flat-spined, with 3- or 4-color cover. Poems tend to be freestyle lyrics leaning toward avant-garde, with some room for rhymed verse and stanza patterns. Press run is 2,000. Subscription: $18 individuals, $27 institutions in Canada; $24 individuals, $36 institutions in US. **Sample postpaid: $6 in Canada, $7 in US. Simultaneous submissions OK. Editor comments on submissions "occasionally." Reports in 6-12 months. "Please include SAE and IRC for reply." Pays $30 for first printed page, $5-10 for remaining full or partial printed page.**

FIREWEED: POETRY OF WESTERN OREGON (IV-Regional), 1330 E. 25th Ave., Eugene OR 97403, founded 1989, is a quarterly publishing the work of **poets living in Western Oregon or having close connections to the region. However, poems need not be regional in subject; any theme, subject, length or form is acceptable.** They have published poetry by Vern Rutsala, Barbara Drake, Lisa Steinmann and Lex Runciman. As a sample they selected these lines from "Fault" by Barbara La Morticella:

> *Quick hold me;*
> *for once, let me hold you.*
>
> *Our children's suitcases are packed,*
> *and even the hills move in waves.*

Fireweed is 44 pgs., digest-sized, laser printed and saddle-stapled with card cover. "We receive several hundred poems and publish about ¼ or ⅕ of them." Press run is 250 for 180 subscribers of which 20 are libraries, 25 shelf sales. Subscription: $10. **Sample postpaid: $2.50. Submit 3-5 poems at a time, name and address on each page. No previously published poems; simultaneous submissions OK. Cover letter with brief bio required. Often comments on rejections. They do not publish guide-lines for poets but will answer inquiries with SASE. Reports in 2-4 months. Pays 1 copy. Acquires first North American serial rights.** Reviews books of poetry by Oregon poets in 500-750 words, single format. Open to unsolicited reviews. Oregon poets may also send books for review consideration. They add, "We occasionally have special issues organized by theme, compiled by a guest editor or focused on newcomers to *Fireweed*. Support your local magazines by sending work and buying subscriptions! Submit to the smaller little publications *first*!"

1ST & HOPE (V), P.O. Box 36A27, Los Angeles CA 90036, founded 1994 (first issue initially sched-uled for December 1994 or January 1995, postponed until September 1995), editor Mike Bucell, is an annual designed to publish "the highest quality work we receive. It is also our wish to publish new and emerging talent that gets 'crowded out' of the 'prestige' markets. **We want poetry that is crisp, concise, vivid and carefully, thoughtfully written. Any subject and style is welcomed. Poets should send us the poems that made them sweat blood as they worked on them. Poems should be neither too obscure nor too obvious.** The editor says *1st & hope* will be 60-80 pgs., 6×9, professionally printed from laser-printed camera-ready copy and perfect-bound. Estimated press run is 500. **No previously published poems or simultaneous submissions. Cover letter required. Often comments on rejections. Send SASE for guidelines. Reports in 3-4 months. Pays 1 copy/poem published. Acquires first or one-time rights.** The editor says, "We are currently unable to accept more submissions due to the delay in printing our first issue." Interested poets should query.

FIRST HAND (IV-Gay, subscribers), Box 1314, Teaneck NJ 07666, phone (201)836-9177, founded 1980, poetry editor Bob Harris, is a **"gay erotic publication written mostly by its readers."** The digest-sized monthly has a circulation of 70,000 with 3,000 subscribers of which 3 are libraries and uses 1-2 pgs. of poetry in each issue. They have published poetry by Michael Swift and Robert Patrick. As a sample the editor selected these lines from "Hustler" by Christopher Thomas:

> *We celebrate the skin—*
> *I, for the joy of unzipping,*
> *he, for the thirty-five dollars cash—*
> *our mouths wet and wonderful around it all.*

Submit poems no longer than 1 typed page. No queries. Editor Bob Harris sometimes comments on rejected mss. Reports in 6 weeks. Pays $25/poem. Reviews books of poetry. The editor advises, "Make sure what you're writing about is obvious to future readers. **Poems need not be explicitly sexual, but must deal overtly with gay situations and subject matter."**

5 AM (III), 1109 Milton Ave., Pittsburgh PA 15218, founded 1987, editors Patricia Dobler, Lynn Emanuel, Ed Ochester and Judith Vollmer, is a poetry publication that appears twice a year. They are **open in regard to form, length, subject matter and style. However, they do not want poetry that is "religious or naive rhymes."** They have published poetry by Rita Dove, Elton Glaser, Alicia Ostriker and Alberto Rios. The editors describe *5 AM* as a 24-page, offset tabloid. They receive about 3,000 poems a year, use approximately 2%. Press run is 1,000 for 550 subscribers of which 22 are libraries, about 300 shelf sales. Subscription: $10 for 4 issues. **Sample postpaid: $3. No previously published poems or simultaneous submissions. Each editor chooses 25% of the magazine. Seldom comments on rejections. Reports within 3 months. Pays 2 copies. Acquires first rights.**

‡**FLEDGLING (I)**, 137 Gore Rd., Revere MA 02151, founded 1994, editor/publisher Mary-Margaret Mulligan, appears twice a year. "*Fledgling* is dedicated to publishing poetry, short fiction and commentary by new and emerging writers." **They want to see "descriptive, tactile poetry, with tastes and smells and sounds. Two pages maximum, any form. No rhyming for no reason, no sickly-sweet poems, no love poems, no poor-me poems."** They have recently published poetry by Charles Carroll, Mark DeCarteret and Tamson Weston. As a sample the editor selected these lines from "The Cafe Venus" by Ricia Anne Chansky:

> *each tooth shines*
> *the purest cane*
> *pushed into delicate cubes*
> *and man*
> *she stirs me*
> *like a coffee queen should.*

Fledgling is 32 pgs., 5½×8½, photocopied and saddle-stapled, card stock cover with b&w illustrations of a bird. They publish 10-12 poems each issue. Press run is 100 for 28 subscribers, more than 30 shelf sales. Single copy: $3; subscription: $5 (2 issues). **Sample postpaid: $2. Submit no more than 5 poems at a time. No previously published poems; simultaneous submissions OK. Often comments on rejections (when asked or when the work is close to what she's looking for). Reports within 3 months. Pays 1 copy.** Reviews books of poetry. "We print one review each issue, either staff-written or guest. No maximum length." Open to unsolicited reviews. Poets may also send books for review consideration. *Fledgling* also sponsors a reading to celebrate each issue. Poets published in that issue are invited to read.

‡**FLEETING MONOLITH ENTERPRISES (II); VERTICAL IMAGES (IV-Regional)**, 62 Langdon Park Rd., London N6 5QG England, phone (0181)340-5807, founded 1986, editor Mike Diss. Fleeting Monolith publishes about 3 chapbooks/year. *Vertical Images* is an annual using primarily poets connected with the Vertical Images poetry group: "All those submitting work are given equal representation in the magazine, which grows largely out of consistent workshop practice every two weeks. We suggest moving to London, joining the group and taking it from there." For their chapbooks, Fleeting Monolith wants **"inspired/delirious/challenging/manic/radical/subversive work—who cares about**

form! Nothing dead/academic/po-faced/sensitive stuff." They have published poetry by Slaughter District, Chris Brown, Jondi Keane and the editor, who selected the following complete poem (poet unidentified) as a sample:

> Logic
> Bombs

Their chapbooks are in a variety of formats and **payment depends "entirely on the format and scope of each work." All rights remain with author. Sample postpaid: £2.** "Series of free poetry broadsheets available on request—IRC preferred." The editor says, "*L'art, c'est un connerie-*. Artaud said that, but we wish we had. Poetry can be a garden shed: Michaux said that (who cares about form! count this, count that!) and he wasn't English either—in fact, not many poets are, now that Keats and Lewis Carroll are dead. Buster Keaton was a poet and Jean Tinguely is a poet. At Fleeting Monolith, only a small part of the living process of poetry gets crystallized into books. Write us a letter, send us something, join the network of creative discontent."

FLIPSIDE (II), 109 Dixon Hall, California University of Pennsylvania, California PA 15419, founded 1987, poetry editors Cindy Speer and Derek C.F. Pegritz, is a literary tabloid appearing twice a year. **"We publish highly imageable poetry about concrete people, places and things. We tend to publish poems that deal with a darker, more unusual side of life. We don't publish melodramatic love poems or mushy ballads, nor do we publish bitter poetry."** They have published poetry by Charles Bukowski and Arthur Winfield Knight. As a sample the editor selected the poem "Mother Lover" by Michael Bagamery:

> Make-up on that face
> Like rubble.
> Ivy won't run up a building
> Unless it stands.

The tabloid is 48 pgs., professionally printed on newsprint with b&w photos and line drawings inside, some ads. They accept less than 5% of hundreds of poems submitted. Press run is 5,000, distributed free to the public, libraries, writing schools, colleges, advertisers, poets, etc. **Sample postpaid: $2. Send SASE for guidelines. Reports in 2 months. Pays as many copies as you want.**

THE FLORIDA REVIEW (II), Dept. of English, University of Central Florida, Orlando FL 32816, phone (407)823-2038, founded 1972, editor Russ Kesler, is a "literary biannual with emphasis on short fiction and poetry." **They want "poems filled with real things, real people and emotions, poems that might conceivably advance our knowledge of the human heart."** They have recently published poetry by Knute Skinner, Elton Glaser, Silvia Curbelo and Walter McDonald. It is 128 pgs., flat-spined, professionally printed, with glossy card cover. Press run is 1,000 for 500 subscribers of which 50 are libraries, 150 shelf sales. **Sample postpaid: $4.50. Submit no more than 6 poems at a time. Simultaneous submissions OK. Editor comments on submissions "occasionally." Send SASE for guidelines. Reports in 1-3 months. Always sends prepublication galleys. Pays 3 copies, small honorarium occasionally available. Acquires all rights. Returns rights "upon publication, when requested."** Reviews books of poetry in 1,500 words, single format; 2,500-3,000 words, multi-book. Send books for review consideration. The editor says they would like more formal verse.

FLUME PRESS (II), 773 Sierra View, Chico CA 95926, phone (916)342-1583, founded 1984, poetry editors Casey Huff and Elizabeth Renfro, publishes poetry chapbooks. **"We have few biases about form, although we appreciate control and crafting, and we tend to favor a concise, understated style, with emphasis on metaphor rather than editorial commentary."** They have recently published chapbooks by Tina Barr, Randall Freisinger, Leonard Kress, Carol Gordon, Gayle Kaune, Luis Omar Salinas, Judy Lindberg, Ava Leavell Haymon and Martha M. Vertreace. As a sample, the editors selected these lines from "Touch Pool" by Pamela Uschuk:

> Around and around
> the holding pool, rays soar
> like squadrons of angels, now and then lifting
> a wing to test the edge
> as if they would swim through the glass to the sea

Chapbooks are chosen from an annual competition, March 1 through June 30. $6 entry fee. Submit 20-24 pgs., including title, contents and acknowledgments. Considers simultaneous submissions. Brief cover letter preferred. "Flume Press editors read and respond to every entry." Sometimes sends prepublication galleys. Winner receives $100 and 25 copies. **Sample: $5 plus $1.50 p&h.**

FLYWAY (II), (formerly *Poet & Critic*), 203 Ross Hall, Iowa State University, Ames IA 50011, phone (515)294-2180, fax (515)294-6814, founded 1961, editor Stephen Pett, appears 3 times a year. This reformulation of *Poet & Critic* "is one of the best literary magazines for the money; it is packed with some of the most readable poems being published today—all styles and forms, lengths and subjects.

The editor shuns elite-sounding free verse with obscure meanings and pretty-sounding formal verse with obvious meanings." *Flyway* is 6×9, 48 pgs., professionally printed and perfect-bound with matte card cover with color. Circulation is 400 for 300 subscribers of which 100 are libraries. Subscription: $18. **Sample postpaid: $8. Submit 4-6 poems at a time. Cover letter preferred. "We do not read mss between the end of May and mid-August." Reports in 2 weeks (often sooner). Pays 1 copy. Acquires first rights.** The magazine also includes review-essays usually focusing on the works of one poet. "We assign reviews following a query." Poets may also send books for review consideration.

FOLIO: A LITERARY JOURNAL (II), Dept. of Literature, Gray Hall, The American University, Washington DC 20016, founded 1984, is a biannual. Editors change annually. They have published poetry by Jean Valentine, Henry Taylor and William Stafford. There are 12-20 poems published in each issue. *Folio* is 64-72 pgs., 6×9, perfect-bound, neatly printed from typeset. **Sample postpaid: $5. Submit up to 6 pgs. with brief bio/contributor's note from August to March 1. Considers simultaneous submissions. Reads submissions September 1 through March 1 only. Pays 2 copies. Acquires first rights.** They also sponsor a contest open to all contributors with a $75 prize for the best poem of the fall and spring issue. A poem published by this journal was selected for inclusion in *Editor's Choice III*.

FOOLSCAP (I, II), 78 Friars Rd., East Ham, London E6 1LL England, founded 1987, editor Judi Benson, appears twice yearly (summer and winter). **"We are looking for poetry which surprises as well as informs. We look for confidence and a sense of humor, though veer away from flippancy and trite over-used rhyme. We like our poetry to reflect today's world and the issues that concern us all without laborious political banner waving. In other words, we are looking for craft as much as statement."** They have published poetry by Ian Duhig, Frances Wilson and Sal Salasin. As a sample the editor selected "Filmclip: Leningrad, October, 1935" by Ken Smith:

> Dark comes early, and wet snow.
> The citizens hurry from work,
> scarfed, buttoned, thinking of supper,
> the tram clanking and squealing
> in whose glass an arm has wiped
> a V of lit space wherein smoke,
> old and young wrapped for winter,
> eyes focussed somewhere ahead,
> dreaming perhaps of a sausage,
> of bread, coffee, a warm bed,
> a bullet in the back of the brain.
> Then they're gone. Next comes
> the future. It looks like the past.

The editor describes *Foolscap* as approximately 80 pgs., A4, camera-ready photocopying, with b&w illustrations. "No ads, no reviews, no frills, though we do include short prose pieces and welcome good translations." They accept about 120 of 1,200 poems received/year. Press run is between 150-200 for 150 subscribers. "Copies also sold at poetry readings, bookshops, libraries and to universities." Subscription: $16/£6. **Submit "no more than 6 poems at a time. No previously published poems, as a general rule, and do not appreciate simultaneous submissions. Cover letter indicating whether or not to return ms required. Best if overseas not to have to return. Allow ample IRCs and 1-2 months for response. If IRCs are not included, material will be thrown away. Publication could take as long as a year due to backlog of accepted material." Pays 1 copy.** The editor says, "We accept a wide range of styles from both unpublished poets as well as well-known poets from all geographical locations. We advise people to get a copy of *Foolscap* before submitting and suggest 'new' poets share their work with others before submitting."

FOOTWORK: THE PATERSON LITERARY REVIEW; HORIZONTES; ALLEN GINSBERG POETRY AWARDS; THE PATERSON POETRY PRIZE; PASSAIC COUNTY COMMUNITY COLLEGE POETRY CENTER LIBRARY (II, IV-Regional, bilingual/foreign language), Poetry Center, Passaic County Community College, Cultural Affairs Dept., 1 College Blvd., Paterson NJ 07505-1179, phone (201)684-6555. A wide range of activities pertaining to poetry are conducted by the Passaic County Community College Poetry Center, including the annual literary magazine *Footwork*, founded 1979, editor and director Maria Mazziotti Gillan, using **poetry of "high quality" under 100 lines; "clear, direct, powerful work."** They have published poetry by David Ray, Diane Wakoski, William Stafford, Sonia Sanchez, Laura Boss and Marge Piercy. *Footwork: The Paterson Literary Review* is 160 pgs., magazine-sized, saddle-stapled, professionally printed with glossy card 2-color cover, using b&w art and photos. Circulation 1,000 with 100 subscribers of which 50 are libraries. **Sample postpaid: $10. Send no more than 5 poems/submission. Simultaneous submissions OK. Reads submissions September through January only. Reports in 1 year. Pays 1 copy. Acquires first rights.** *Horizontes*, founded in 1983, editor José Villalongo, is an annual Spanish language literary magazine using **poetry of high quality no longer than 20 lines. Will accept English translations, but Spanish**

version must be included. They have published poetry by Nelson Calderon, Jose Kozer and Julio Cesar Mosches. *Horizontes* is 120 pgs., magazine-sized, saddle-stapled, professionally printed with full color matte cover, using b&w graphics and photos. Circulation 800 with 100 subscribers of which 20 are libraries. **Sample postpaid: $4. Accepts simultaneous submissions. "On occasion we do consider published works but prefer unpublished works." Reads submissions September through January only. Reports in 3-4 months. Pays 2 copies. Acquires first rights.** Staff reviews books of poetry. Send books for review consideration. The Poetry Center of the college conducts The Allen Ginsberg Poetry Awards Competition each year. Entry fee: $12. Prizes of $300, $150 and $100. Deadline: March 1. Send SASE for rules. They also publish a *New Jersey Poetry Resources* book, the *PCC Poetry Contest Anthology* and the *New Jersey Poetry Calendar*. The Paterson Poetry Prize of $1,000 is awarded each year (split between poet and publisher) to a book of poems published in the previous year. Publishers should write with SASE for application form to be submitted by February 1. Passaic County Community College Poetry Center Library has an extensive collection of contemporary poetry and seeks small press contributions to help keep it abreast. The Distinguished Poetry Series offers readings by poets of international, national and regional reputation. Poetryworks/USA is a series of programs produced for UA Columbia-Cablevision.

FOREST BOOKS (V, IV-Translations), 20 Forest View, Chingford, London E4 7AY United Kingdom, phone 081-529-8470, founded 1984, director Brenda Walker, publishes 15-20 paperbacks/year. They have published *Enchanting Beasts: An Anthology of Modern Women Poets in Finland*, a handsomely printed flat-spined book of 126 pgs., **but their list is full for the next 2 years.** Samples may be purchased through Dufour Editions, P.O. Box 449, Chester Springs PA 19425.

‡FOREVER ALIVE (IV-Specialized: physical immortality), P.O. Box 12305, Scottsdale AZ 85267-2305, phone (602)922-0300, fax (602)922-0800, founded 1989, editor Herb Bowie, is a quarterly, published by People Forever International, which includes news, articles, essays, fiction and poetry on the subjects of health, aliveness and physical immortality. **They want "poems expressing a positive attitude toward living forever."** As a sample the editor selected the opening lines of "A Prayer Spontaneous" by Joe Bardin:

> *There is a poetry of us,*
> *a prayer spontaneous:*
> *driving the car,*
> *or in the sudden stillness of parking*
> *sunshine warming the steering wheel,*
> *or in the shower*
> *hot water washing the muscle, the flesh.*

FA is 52 pgs., 8½×11, web press printed and saddle-stapled with glossy 4-color paper cover and b&w inside. They publish one poem each issue. Press run is 2,000 for 400 subscribers, 300 shelf sales. Single copy: $6; subscription: $24. **Sample postpaid: $3. No previously published poems or simultaneous submissions. Cover letter required. Seldom comments on rejections. Reports in 3 months. Pays 10 copies. "All published submissions become the property of People Forever International, unless specific rights are reserved by the author."**

THE FORMALIST; HOWARD NEMEROV SONNET AWARD (II, IV-Form, translations), 320 Hunter Dr., Evansville IN 47711, founded 1990, editor William Baer, appears twice a year, **"dedicated to contemporary *metrical* poetry written in the great tradition of English-language verse."** This is one of a handful of magazines that publish formal (metered, rhymed) poetry *exclusively*. The poems here are among the best in the genre—a joy to read—tastefully edited so that each verse plays off the other. They have published poetry by Richard Wilbur, Donald Justice, Mona Van Duyn, Derek Walcott, John Updike, Maxine Kumin, James Merrill, Karl Shapiro, X.J. Kennedy, May Swenson, W.S. Merwin, W.D. Snodgrass and Louis Simpson. As a sample the editor chose the opening stanza from "The Amateurs of Heaven" by Howard Nemerov:

> *Two lovers to a midnight meadow came*
> *High in the hills, to lie there hand in hand*
> *Like effigies and look up at the stars,*
> *The never-setting ones set in the North*
> *To circle the Pole in idiot majesty,*
> *And wonder what was given them to wonder.*

"We are interested in metrical poetry written in the **traditional forms, including ballads, sonnets, couplets, blank verse, the Greek forms, the French forms, etc. We will also consider metrical translations of major formalist non-English poets—from the Ancient Greeks to the present. We are not, however, interested in haiku (or syllabic verse of any kind) or sestinas. Only rarely do we accept a poem over 2 pages, and we have no interest in any type of erotica, blasphemy, vulgarity or racism.** Finally, like all editors, we suggest that those wishing to submit to *The Formalist* become thoroughly familiar with the journal beforehand." Subscription: $12/year; $22/2 years. **Sample post-**

paid: **$6.50.** *The Formalist* considers submissions throughout the year, 3-5 poems at one time. No simultaneous submissions, previously published work, or disk submissions. A brief cover letter is recommended and a SASE is necessary for a reply and return of ms. **Reports within 2 months. Pays 2 copies. Acquires first North American serial rights.** The Howard Nemerov Sonnet Award offers $1,000 and publication in *The Formalist* for the best unpublished *sonnet*. The final judge for 1995 was Mona Van Duyn. Entry fee: $2/sonnet. Postmark deadline: May 15. Send SASE for guidelines. See also the contest listing for the World Order of Narrative and Formalist Poets. Contestants must subscribe to *The Formalist* to enter. Work published in *The Formalist* also appears in *The Best American Poetry 1992.*

THE FOUR DIRECTIONS; SNOWBIRD PUBLISHING COMPANY (IV-Ethnic), P.O. Box 729, Tellico Plains TN 37385, phone (615)253-3680, founded 1991, publisher William Meyer. *The Four Directions* is an American Indian literary journal designed to further American Indian literature. **All authors must be of American Indian heritage, and they want poetry that reflects or touches commom/uncommon American Indian concerns.** They have published poetry by Susan Clements and Shirley Hill Witt. The editor says it is 60-68 pgs. with approximately 54 pgs. of poetry, short stories, articles and reviews. They receive about 200 poems a year, use approximately 48. Press run is 2,000 for 180 subscribers of which 90 are libraries, 1,800 shelf sales. Subscription: $21, $25 institutions. **Sample postpaid: $7. Previously published poems and simultaneous submissions OK. Cover letter required. Often comments on rejections. Publishes theme issues. Send SASE for upcoming themes. Reports in 6-9 weeks. Sometimes sends prepublication galleys. Pays $10 for full-page of poetry. Buys one-time rights.** Accepts reviews of all media, including books of poetry. Reviews range from 200 to 2,000 words. Snowbird Publishing Company publishes books but "so far we have not published any books of poetry." **Query first with sample poems and cover letter with brief bio and publication credits. "Poetry may be previously published or not, but must be of professional quality." Replies to queries and mss in 6-9 weeks. Pays 10-18% royalties and 10 author's copies.** The editor says, "The field of American Indian literature is the fastest growing literary effort in North America. We tend to seek writing that furthers the growth of the Indian spirit. We would like to see more traditional American Indian poetry and poetry in bilingual (American Indian and English or Spanish and English) forms."

FOX CRY (II), University of Wisconsin Fox Valley, 1478 Midway Rd., P.O. Box 8002, Mcnasha WI 54952-8002, phone (414)832-2662, founded 1973, editor Professor Don Hrubesky, is a literary annual using **poems up to 50 lines long, deadline February 15.** They have published poetry by Shirley Anders, Ellen Kort, David Graham, Clifford Wood and Laurel Mills. As a sample, the editor selected these lines (poet unidentified):

> *She was out there with the leaves*
> *the old woman bent but broad of back*
> *In long even pulls, she collected*
> *the detritus of the sun's decline.*

Their press run is 400. **Sample postpaid: $5. Submit maximum of 3 poems from September 1 through February 15 only. Simultaneous submissions considered. Send SASE for guidelines. Pays 1 copy.**

FRANK: AN INTERNATIONAL JOURNAL OF CONTEMPORARY WRITING AND ART (II, IV-Form, translations), 104 rue Edouard Vaillant, 93100 Montreuil France, founded 1983, editor David Applefield. *Frank* is a literary semiannual that **"encourages work of seriousness and high quality which falls often between existing genres. Looks favorably at true internationalism and stands firm against ethnocentric values. Likes translations. Publishes foreign dossier in each issue. Very eclectic."** There are no subject specifications, but the magazine "discourages sentimentalism and easy, false surrealism. Although we're in Paris, most Paris-poems are too thin for us. Length is open." They have published poetry by Rita Dove, Derek Walcott, Duo Duo, Raymond Carver, Tomas Tranströmer, James Laughlin, Breytenbach, Michaux, Gennadi Aigi, W.S. Merwin, Edmond Jabes, John Berger, and many lesser known poets. The journal is 224 pgs., digest-sized, flat-spined, offset in b&w with color cover and photos, drawings and ads. Circulation is 4,000, of which 2,000 are bookstore sales and subscriptions. Subscription: $30 (individuals), $60 (institutions) for 4 issues. **Sample postpaid: $9 airmail from Paris. Guidelines available for SAE and IRCs. Poems must be previously unpublished. The editor often provides some criticism on rejected mss. Submissions are reported on in 3 months, publication is in 3-6 months. Pay is $5/printed page and 2 copies.** Editor organizes readings in US and Europe for *Frank* contributors. He says, "Send only what you feel is fresh, original, and provocative in either theme or form. Work of craft that also has political and social impact is encouraged."

FREE FOCUS (I, IV-Women/feminist); OSTENTATIOUS MIND (I, IV-Form/style), P.O. Box 7415, JAF Station, New York NY 10116, *Free Focus* founded 1985, *Ostentatious Mind* founded 1987, poetry editor Patricia D. Coscia. *Free Focus* "is a literary magazine **only for creative women, who reflect their ideas of love, nature, beauty and men and also express the pain, sorrow, joy and enchantment that their lives generate. *Free Focus* needs poems of all types on the subject matters above. Nothing x-rated, please. The poems can be as short as 2 lines or as long as 2 pages.** The objective of this magazine is to give women poets a chance to be fullfilled in the art of poetry, for freedom of expression for women is seldom described in society." They have published poetry by Helen Tzagoloff, Elizabeth Hahn Ph.D., Patricia A. Pierkowski, D.R. Middleton, Crystal Beckner, Elaine F. Powell, Kris Anderson, Carol L. Clark and Mary Anderson. As a sample the editor selected these lines from "A Woman I Once Knew" by Maura Schroeder:

> She sleeps in the desert alone,
> Carving ancestral bone,
> from waking mountains.
> She sleeps in the desert alone,
> Wading in salt-soaked rivers,
> with wounds unfolded.

Ostentatious Mind "is a co-ed literary magazine **for material of stream of consciousness and experimental poems. The poets deal with the political, social and psychological.**" They have published poetry by Paul Weinman, Rod Farmer, L. Mason, Dr. John J. Soldo, Carl A. Winderl, James W. Penha and Joe Lackey. As a sample the editor selected this poem, "Poetic Wax," by Sheryl L. Nelms:

> comes in 1.5 liter
>
> bottles
>
> at Majestic
> Liquors

Both magazines are printed on 8 × 14 paper, folded in the middle and stapled to make a 10-page (including cover) format, with simple b&w drawings on the cover and inside. The two magazines appear every 6-8 months. **Sample of either is $3.50 postpaid. Submit only 3 poems at a time. Poems should be typed neatly and clearly on white typing paper. Simultaneous submissions and previously published poems OK. Publishes theme issues. Send SASE for guidelines and upcoming themes. Reports "as soon as possible." Sometimes sends prepublication galleys. Pays 1-2 copies.** The editor says, "I think that anyone can write a poem who can freely express intense feelings about their experiences. A dominant thought should be ruled and expressed in writing, not by the spoken word, but the written word."

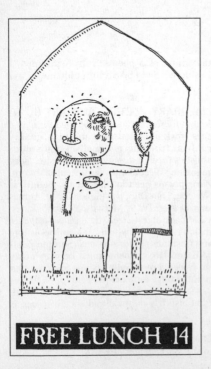

FREE LUNCH 14

"This cover was chosen because it projects a mixture of whimsy and mystery I find appealing," says Ron Offen, editor of the California-based Free Lunch. *"The figure holds and contemplates a strange object, which lights the candle of his imagination and fills the cup of his heart. The wittiness of the artwork underscores my feeling that the greatest poetry (and art), no matter how serious, has an element of humor in it." The journal appears approximately three times a year and publishes only poetry and information about poetry. FL is interested in experimental work and work by unestablished poets. Unfortunately, a large backlog is forcing the editor to be a bit more selective. The cover art is by Larry Tomoyasu, freelance artist/illustrator and poet.*

FREE LUNCH (II), P.O. Box 7647, Laguna Niguel CA 92607-7647, founded 1988, editor Ron Offen, is a **"poetry journal interested in publishing whole spectrum of what is currently being produced by American poets. Occasionally offers a 'Reprise Series' in which an overlooked American poet is reexamined and presented. Among those that have been featured are Kenneth Patchen, Maxwell Bodenheim, Stephen Vincent Benet and Kenneth Fearing.** Also features a 'Mentor Series,' in which an established poet introduces a new, unestablished poet. Mentors have included Maxine Kumin, James Dickey, Lucille Clifton, Kenneth Koch, Stephen Dunn and Diane Wakoski. **Especially interested in experimental work and work by unestablished poets. Hope to provide all serious poets living in the US with a free subscription. For details on free subscription send SASE. No restriction on form, length, subject matter, style, purpose. Don't want cutsie, syrupy, sentimental, preachy religious or aggressively 'uplifting' verse. No aversion to form, rhyme."** Poets recently published include Sherman Alexie, Dave Etter, Phyllis Janowitz, Glenna Luschei and Barry Spacks. As a sample the editor selected these lines from "These Heart Hammers, These Small Xylophone Joys" by Peter Bakowski:

> *These hearthammers, these small xylophone joys,*
> *Keep the taste of fire*
> *burning in my mouth*
> *and my hands fill with*
> *rubies, wise sparrows, the moth's dizzy haunting*
> *of candles and schemes,*
> *and I sit here eating corn off the cob*
> *as if I were tasting*
> *the petals of the sun.*

FL is published 2-3 times a year. It is 32-40 pgs., digest-sized, saddle-stapled, attractively printed and designed, featuring free verse that shows attention to craft with well-knowns and newcomers alongside each other. Press run is 1,200 with 200 subscribers of which 15 are libraries. Subscription: $12 ($15 foreign). **Sample postpaid: $5 ($6 foreign). "Submissions must be limited to 3 poems and are considered only between September 1 and May 31. Submissions sent at other times will be returned unread. Although a cover letter is not mandatory, we like them. We especially want to know if a poet is previously unpublished, as we like to work with new poets."** They will consider simultaneous submissions. Editor usually comments on rejections and tries to return submissions in 2 months. Send SASE for guidelines. Pays 1 copy plus subscription. Work published in *Free Lunch* has been included in *The Best American Poetry 1993*. He quotes Archibald MacLeish, " 'A poem should not mean/ But be.' Poetry is concerned primarily with language, rhythm and sound; fashions and trends are transitory and to be eschewed; perfecting one's work is often more important than publishing it."

‡FREEDOM RAG MAGAZINE (I, IV-Ethnic), 858 W. Armitage, Box 151, Chicago IL 60614, phone (312)654-8042, fax (312)654-0729, founded 1993, poetry editor Sherrie Brock-Parker, publisher Kelli Curry, is a quarterly magazine with bases in Chicago and New York. "Created by and for a youth culture restless with quickly fading trends and fads, *Freedom Rag* highlights the best underground and established poets, essayists and critical theorists in the country. On these pages they grapple with the issues that shape our conscience and control our cultures." **They have no specifications regarding form, length, subject matter or style of poetry, but are particularly open to the work of Latin American, Hispanic and African-American poets. They do not want to see "personal, unimaginative or cliché poetry."** They have recently published poetry by Sterling Plumpp and Greg Tate. As a sample the editor selected these lines from Plumpp's "Be-Bop," which also appears in the book *Horn Man* published by Third World Press:

> *Be-Bop is precise clumsiness.*
> *Awkward lyricism*
> *Under a feather's control.*
> *A world in a crack.*
> *Seen by ears.*

They do not offer a description of the publication, but say they accept 15-20% of the poetry received. Press run is 15,000 for 200 subscribers of which 15 are libraries. Single copy: $3; subscription: $12. **Sample postpaid: $2. Submit poems double-spaced, with name, address and phone number on every page. IBM 3.5 or 5.25 disk submissions (in WordPerfect, Word, WinWrite) welcome. Previously published poems and simultaneous submissions OK. Often comments on rejections. Send SASE for guidelines. Reports in 1 month. Pays 5 copies plus a *Freedom Rag* shirt.** Open to unsolicited reviews. Poets may also send books for review consideration. The magazine also holds an annual contest, usually in August. Send SASE for details. The editor says, "*Freedom Rag* is the opportunity to stay steps ahead by connecting to the grassroots of world culture. Send us your best work, which is achieved by studying the work of others and using workshops to clarify your voice."

FRENCH BROAD PRESS (III), Dept. PM, The Asheville School, Asheville NC 28806, phone (704)255-7909, founded 1989, publishers Jessica Bayer and J.W. Bonner, publishes 20- to 40-page chapbooks. **"Any style or form welcome. Considers sexually explicit material."** They have recently published poetry by Thomas Meyer, Jeffrey Beam, Jonathan Williams, Jonathan Greene and Wallace Fowlie. **"We're slow. May take 6 months to respond to a ms and up to 2 years before publication. Always sends prepublication galleys. Many of our poets have paid 'in kind': typesetting mss and covers on disks or pasting up the book for printing." Pays 10% of press run.** Write to buy samples or order from The Captain's Bookshelf, 31 Page Ave., Asheville NC 28801.

FRIENDS JOURNAL (II, IV-Specialized: Quakerism), 1501 Cherry St., Philadelphia PA 19102, phone (215)241-7277, founded 1827 as *The Friend*, 1844 as *Friends Intelligencer,* 1955 as *Friends Journal,* appears monthly, magazine-sized, circulation 9,500. Subscription: $21/year. **"We seek poetry that resonates with Quakerism and Quaker concerns, such as peace, nonviolence and spiritual seeking." No multiple or simultaneous submissions. Pays 2 copies/poem.**

FRITZ (V), P.O. Box 170694, San Francisco CA 94117, founded 1991, editor Lisa McElroy, is a biannual publishing new writers/artists "that is accessible and soulful. **I publish all kinds of poetry. However, because of limited space we are currently not accepting poetry submissions."** They have published poetry by Rane Arroyo and Nancy Bonnell-Kangas. *Fritz* is 24 pgs., 8½ × 11, offset, saddle-stitched, with line drawings and b&w photos. They receive under 150 poems a year, use approximately 5%. Press run is 300 for 100 shelf sales. Single copy: $2. **Sample postpaid: $3.**

FROGMORE PAPERS; FROGMORE POETRY PRIZE (III), 42 Morehall Ave., Folkestone, Kent CT19 4EF England, founded 1983, poetry editor Jeremy Page, is a biannual literary magazine with emphasis on new poetry and short stories. **"Quality is generally the only criterion, although pressure of space means very long work (over 100 lines) is unlikely to be published."** They have published poetry by Geoffrey Holloway, Myra Schneider, Frances Wilson, Linda France, Pauline Stainer, R. Nikolas Macioci and John Latham. As a sample the editor selected these lines by Elizabeth Garrett:

> I rock on my heels and test
> My breath's spillage on the air.
> I shall fold it with the weather
> For safe keeping, in a camphor chest.

The magazine is 38 pgs., saddle-stapled with matte card cover, photocopied in photoreduced typescript. They accept 5% of poetry received. Their press run is 250 with 100 subscriptions. Subscription: £5 ($10). **Sample postpaid: £1 ($3). (US payments should be made in cash, not check.) Submit 5-6 poems at a time. Considers simultaneous submissions. Editor rarely comments on rejections. Reports in 3-6 months. Pays 1 copy.** Staff reviews books of poetry in 2-3 sentences, single format. Send books for review consideration to Sophie Hannah, reviews editor, 127 Horton Rd., Manchester M14 7QD England. They also publish *Crabflower* pamphlets and have published collections by Geoffrey Holloway, Robert Etty, David Lightfoot and Sophie Hannah as well as several anthologies. Write for information about the annual Frogmore Poetry Prize. The editor says, "My advice to people starting to write poetry would be: Read as many recognized modern poets as you can and don't be afraid to experiment."

FROGPOND: QUARTERLY HAIKU JOURNAL; HAIKU SOCIETY OF AMERICA; HAIKU SOCIETY OF AMERICA AWARDS/CONTESTS (IV-Form, translation), % Japan Society, 333 E. 47th St., New York NY 10017, has been publishing *Frogpond* since 1978, now edited by Kenneth C. Leibman, PhD., and **submissions should go directly to him** at P.O. Box 767, Archer FL 32618-0767. *Frogpond* is a saddle-stapled quarterly of 48 pgs., 5½ × 8½, of haiku, senryu, sequences, linked poems (renga/renku), haibun, tanka and haiku translations. It also contains essays and articles, book reviews, some news of the Society, contests, awards, publications and other editorial matter—a dignified, handsome little magazine. Poets should be familiar with modern developments in English-language haiku as well as the tradition. **Haiku should be brief, fresh, using clear images and non-poetic language. Focus should be on a moment keenly perceived. Dr. Leibman hopes contributors will be familiar with contemporary haiku and senryu as presented in** *The Haiku Handbook* **(William J. Higginson) and** *The Haiku Anthology* **(Cor van den Heuvel, Ed.).** Recent contributors include Kenneth Tanemura, Lenard D. Moore, Michael Dylan Welch, Bruce Ross, Ion Codrescu and Patricia Neubauer. Consid-

---

✚ *The double dagger before a listing indicates that the listing is new in this edition. New markets are often the most receptive to submissions.*

erable variety is possible, as these two examples from the magazine illustrate:

I climb the mountain with my eyes never ending snow
—Pamela A. Babuski

Sardine clouds—
the salty breath
of the fisherman
—Margaret Chula

Each issue has between 25 and 30 pages of poetry. They receive about 8,000 submissions/year and use about 400-450. The magazine goes to about 600 subscribers, of which 15 are libraries, as well as to over a dozen foreign countries. **Sample back issues postpaid: $10 (biannual issues of 1992, 1993); $5 (quarterly issues). Make checks payable to Haiku Society of America. They are flexible on submission format, but Dr. Leibman prefers 5-20 poems on 1 or 2, 8½ × 11 sheets. No single poems. No simultaneous submissions. Seasonal material should be submitted 3-4 months before seasonal issue is due; non-seasonal material read anytime. Reports within 6 weeks. They hope contributors will become HSA members, but it is not necessary, and all contributors receive a copy of the magazine in payment. Send SASE for Information Sheet on the HSA and submission guidelines.** Poetry reviews usually 1,000 words or less. Open to unsolicited reviews. Poets may also send books for review consideration. Four "best-of-issue" prizes are given "through a gift from the Museum of Haiku Literature, Tokyo." The Society also sponsors The Harold G. Henderson Haiku Award Contest, The Gerald Brady Senryu Award Contest, The Haiku Society of America Renku Contest, The Nicholas A. Virgilio Memorial Haiku Competition for High School Students and gives Merit Book Awards for books in the haiku field.

FRONTIERS: A JOURNAL OF WOMEN STUDIES (IV-Feminist), %Susan Armitage, Women Studies Program, Washington State University, Pullman WA 99164-4032, founded 1975, is published 3 times a year and **uses poetry on feminist themes.** They have published work by Audré Lorde, Janice Mirikitani, Carol Wolfe Konek and Opal Palmer Adisa. The journal is 200-208 pgs., 6 × 9, flat-spined. Circulation 1,000. **Sample: $8. No simultaneous submissions. Reports in 3-5 months. Pays 2 copies.** "We are not currently publishing reviews of books, poetry or otherwise. However, we consider review essays, if from a clear theoretical perspective."

THE FUDGE CAKE (I, IV-Children/teens), P.O. Box 197, Citrus Heights CA 95611-0197, founded 1994, editor/publisher Jancarl Campi, is a bimonthly children's newsletter designed to showcase the work of young writers. **They want poetry and short stories written by children ages 6-17. "Any form is fine. Open to any style or subject matter. Poetry: 30 lines or less. Short stories: 200 words."** As a sample we selected this poem, "Super Hero," by Ben Wade, age 9:

I know a super hero.
He has more friends than zero.
Lasers come out of his hands.
He can bury people in the sand.
He's stronger than titanium.
He can speed through a gymnasium.
He doesn't need a bed.
All he says is, "Nuff said!"

The Fudge Cake is 20 pgs., 5½ × 8½, desktop-published and saddle-stapled with colored paper cover and computer-generated graphics. Press run is 200 for 25 subscribers; 150 distributed free to libraries and bookstores. Subscription: $10 US, $12 Canada. **Sample postpaid: $2.50. Submit 1-4 poems at a time. "Submissions should be typed or neatly printed on 8½ × 11 white paper." Previously published poems and simultaneous submissions OK. Cover letter required. Often comments on rejections or suggests revisions. Send SASE for guidelines. Reports in 1 month. Pays 1 copy. Authors retain all rights.** Holds bimonthly contests. Winners are published in the winners' section of the next edition. The editor adds, "We value the work of today's children and feel they need an outlet to express themselves."

FUGUE (I), Room 200, Brink Hall, University of Idaho, Moscow ID 83844, founded 1991, is a biannual literary digest of the University of Idaho. **They have "no limits" on type of poetry. "We're not interested in trite or quaint verse. Nothing self-indulgent or overly metaphoric to the point of being obscure."** They have published poetry by Ricardo Sanchez and Maria Theresa Maggi. As a sample the editor selected these lines from Maggi's "The Appointment":

. . . the conceptual warble of arms and legs
caught me in cold waves
at the isinglass window, slicing
its heavy and not quite
willing prisoners, my parents
and all parents, in a tide

of dulled longing and shadows.

The editor says *Fugue* is 42 pgs., digest-sized, saddle-stapled. They receive approximately 400 poems/ semester, use 10 poems/issue. Press run is 200 plus an electronic version on Internet World Wide Web. **Sample postpaid: $3. No previously published poems or simultaneous submissions. Reads submissions September 15 through April 15 only. Send SASE for guidelines. Reports in 1-3 months. Pays roughly $5-10 plus one copy. Buys first North American serial rights.** The editor says, "Proper manuscript format and submission etiquette is expected; submissions without proper SASE will not be read or held on file."

‡**FULL-TIME DADS (IV-Specialized)**, P.O. Box 577, Cumberland ME 04021, phone (207)829-5260, founded 1991, editor/publisher Stephen Harris, is a bimonthly journal that seeks "to encourage and support men in their work as fathers." **They want material about fathers, fatherhood, and parenting from a father's perspective. As for poetry, "short is better. Not overly sentimental, but must come from the heart. Humor a plus. Absolutely no violence or anti-child, anti-male attitudes."** As a sample we selected these lines from "Becoming A Father" by Gary H. Stern:

> *You are crying at night.*
> *Soon you will stay up later than I do,*
> *and you will turn off the TV for me.*
> *While I read the morning paper you will ask questions,*
> *And I am supposed to know all the answers. . . .*

Full-Time Dads is 24 pgs., 8½ × 11, attractively designed, printed on white paper and saddle-stapled, including occasional graphics. They accept about 10 poetry submissions a year. Press run is 400 for 325 subscribers. Subscription: $26. **Sample postpaid: $5. Previously published poems OK; no simultaneous submissions. Always comments on rejections. Send SASE for general writer's guidelines. Reports in 2 weeks. Pays 1 copy. Acquires one-time rights.** Reviews books, etc., that deal with fatherhood. Open to unsolicited reviews. Poets may also send related books for review consideration.

FURRY CHICLETS: A LAWPOETS CREATION (I, IV-Themes), 269 Nepal Rd., Ashland OR 97520, e-mail lawpoet@mind.net, founded 1990, editor Charles Carreon, an annual, wants **"poetry that cares enough about meaning to be brief, cares enough about being read to be interesting, and yet is utterly unconcerned with how it is classified. Poems: 1 page."** As a sample the editors selected these lines from "those who abide (cybernetic foreskin)" by Robert O'Neal Schultz:

> *he drives himself hard.*
> *those who abide drive him*
> *   to the breaking point.*
> *before he can hold the truth,*
> *know it is good,*
> *clocks ring midnight down.*
> *he is crushed under the hour.*
> *neurons misfire.*
> *his typewriter grunts.*

FC consists of approximately 75 photocopied pages stapled at the top to a blue matte backing. **Back issues available for $5. Make checks payable to Charles Carreon.** "*FC* tends to pick up the odd poems that other publications overlook. Too much angst, chaos or exuberance? We can help." Editors often comment on submissions. They try to respond in 3 months.

FUTURIFIC MAGAZINE (IV-Specialized), Foundation for Optimism, 150 Haven Ave., Terrace 3, New York NY 10032, phone (212)297-0502, founded 1976, publisher Balint Szent-Miklosy, is a monthly newsmagazine dealing with **current affairs and their probable outcomes. "We pride ourselves on the accuracy of our forecasting. No other limits than that the poet try to be accurate in predicting the future." They want to see "positive upbeat poetry glorifying humanity and human achievements."** *Futurific* is 32 pgs., magazine-sized, saddle-stapled, on glossy stock, with b&w photos, art and ads. Circulation 10,000. Subscription: $140; for students and individuals: $70. **Sample postpaid: $10. Pays 5 copies.** The editor says, "*Futurific* is made up of the words Future-Terrific. Poets should seek out and enjoy the future if they want to see their work in *Futurific*."

G.W. REVIEW (II), Marvin Center Box 20B, 800 21st St. NW, Washington DC 20052, phone (202)994-7288, founded 1980, editor Merrell K. Maschino, appears twice a year publishing **unconventional, solid work and some translations**. "The magazine is published for distribution to the George Washington University community, the Washington, D.C. metropolitan area and an increasing number of national subscribers." They have published poetry by William Stafford, Jean Valentine, Carol Muske, Jeffrey Harrison and Richard Peabody. It is 64 pgs., perfect-bound with b&w illustration or photo on the cover. They receive about 3,300 poems a year and accept 50-60. Their annual press run averages 4,000 copies. Subscription: $5/year, $8/2 years. **Sample postpaid: $3. Submit 1-5 poems at a time. They**

consider simultaneous submissions but not previously published poems. Cover letter, including list of enclosed poems, present career, recent publications and phone number, required. The staff does not read manuscripts from May 15 through August 15. Editor sometimes comments on rejections when the staff likes the work but thinks it needs to be revised. Reports in 1-3 months. Pays 5 copies.

GAIRM; GAIRM PUBLICATIONS (IV-Ethnic, foreign language), 29 Waterloo St., Glasgow G2 6BZ Scotland, phone/fax (0141)221-1971, editor Derick Thomson, founded 1952. *Gairm* is a quarterly, circulation 2,000, which uses **modern/cosmopolitan and traditional/folk verse in Scottish Gaelic only.** It has published the work of all significant Scottish Gaelic poets, and much poetry translated from European languages. An anthology of such translations, *European Poetry in Gaelic*, is available for £7.50 or $15. *Gairm* is 96 pgs., digest-sized, flat-spined with coated card cover. **Sample: $3.50. Submit 3-4 poems at a time. Reads submissions October 1 through July 31 only.** Staff reviews books of poetry in 500-700 words, single format; 100 words, multi-book format. Occasionally invites reviews. Send books for review consideration. **All of the publications of the press are in Scottish Gaelic.** Spring 1995 publications include *A' Gabhail Ris* by Maoilios Caimbeul and *Meall Garbh/Rugged Mountain* by Derick Thomson. Catalog available.

GAZELLE PUBLICATIONS (V), 1906 Niles-Buchanan Rd., Niles MI 49120, phone (616)465-4004, founded 1976, editor Ted Wade, is a publisher for home schools and compatible markets including **books of verse for children but is not currently considering unsolicited manuscripts.**

GENERATOR; GENERATOR PRESS (V), 8139 Midland Rd., Mentor OH 44060, founded 1987, poetry editor John Byrum, is an annual magazine "devoted to the presentation of **all types of experimental poetry, focussing on language poetry and 'concrete' or visual poetic modes.**" They have published poetry by Susan Smith Nash, Jessica Grim, Jane Reavill Ransom, Deborah Meadows, Liz Waldner and Carla Bertola. As a sample the editor selected these lines by W.B. Keckler:

> or char ds of
> st one or cha
> r ds of st one
> who looks through sad pylons
> roasted in belief. ripe river lotus. lotioned.
>   flax seed asphalt in a constant mash
> bee technology, ham radio, cream pink feet
>   crocodile colors in eyes in silky glass

Generator is magazine-sized, photocopied, side-stapled, using b&w graphics, with matte card cover. Press run is 200 copies for 25 subscribers of which 20 are libraries. **Sample postpaid: $8.** Generator Press also publishes the **Generator Press chapbook series. Approximately 2-4 new titles/year. They are currently not accepting unsolicited manuscripts for either the magazine or chapbook publication.** Together with Score (see listing in this section), Generator Press has published *CORE: A Symposium on Contemporary Visual Poetry*, described as "an international survey of the methods, opinions and work of over 75 contemporary visual poets" ($7 postpaid individuals, $11 institutions). The editor adds, "Worthwhile writers do not need advice and should not heed any but their own."

THE GENTLE SURVIVALIST (I, IV-Ethnic, nature, inspirational), Box 4004, St. George UT 84770, founded 1991, editor/publisher Laura Martin-Bühler, publishes "11 issues over a 13-month period" (not published in February and August). *The Gentle Survivalist* is a newsletter of "harmony— timeless truths and wisdom balanced with scientific developments. For Native Americans and all those who believe in the Great Creator." **They want poetry that is "positive, inspirational, on survival of body and spirit, also man's interconnectedness with God and all His creations. Nothing sexually oriented, occult, negative or depressing."** They have published poetry by Keith Moore and C.S. Churchman. As a sample the editor selected these lines from Moore's poem, "A Line in Motion":

> Little else pleases like
> Seven-o'clock downing sun
> On the faces and flanks of beasts,
> An hour of crisp clarity and
> The highest flattery in nature

TGS is 8 pgs. (two 11 × 17 sheets folded in half). The issues we have received warn readers about the dangers of aluminum and formaldehyde and the deficiency of magnesium in US diets. They also offer natural remedies for winter colds as well as money-saving tips and ideas on writing a personal history. "We print three poems average per issue." Press run is 200. Subscription: $20. **Sample postpaid: $2. Submit 4 poems at a time. Previously published poems and simultaneous submissions OK. Cover letter required; "just a note would be fine. I find noteless submissions too impersonal."** Time between acceptance and publication is 3-4 months. **Often comments on rejections. Send SASE for guidelines. Reports within 2 months. Pays 2 copies.** Sponsors a contest for readers of *Poet's Market*.

Awards a 1-year subscription to the winner. Entrants must mention *Poet's Market* to be eligible. Winner will be chosen one year after release of the 1996 edition. The editor says, "To succeed, one must not seek supporters, but seek to know whom to support."

GEORGETOWN REVIEW (II), 400 E. College St., Box 227, Georgetown KY 40324, founded 1992 (first issue Spring 1993), is a biannual literary journal publishing fiction and poetry—no criticism or reviews. **They want "honest, quality work; not interested in tricks."** They have published poetry by Fred Chappell, John Tagliabue, William Greenway, Elton Glaser, X.J. Kennedy, Peter Wild, Michael Cadnum and Alan Feldman. *GR* is 100-120 pgs., 5½ × 8½, perfect-bound, with heavy stock cover with art. They receive about 1,000 submissions a year, "take maybe 10%." Press run is 1,000. Subscription: $10/year. **Sample postpaid: $5. Submit no more than 5 poems at a time, name and address on each page. No previously published poems; simultaneous submissions OK. Reads submissions September 1 through May 1 only. Poems are read by at least 3 readers. Sometimes comments on rejections. Reports in 2-4 months. Always sends prepublication galleys. Pays 2 copies. Acquires all rights. Returns rights provided "our name is mentioned in any reprint."** Sponsors annual poetry contest. $150 1st prize; runners-up receive publication and subscription. Entry fee: $2.50/poem. Deadline: August 1. Winner and runners-up announced in fall issue each year. 1994 winner: "Disco in China" by Jianqing Zheng.

GEORGIA JOURNAL (IV-Regional), P.O. Box 1604, Decatur GA 30031-1604, phone (404)377-4275, poetry editor Janice Moore. *Georgia Journal* is a quarterly magazine, circulation 15,000, covering the state of Georgia. **They use poetry "from Georgia writers or poetry about Georgia. It should be suitable for the general reader."** They have recently published poems by former President Jimmy Carter, Stephen Corey, Blanche Farley and Adrienne Bond. As a sample Janice Moore selected these lines from "Next Door" by John Stone:

> *of a sudden*
> *with no fanfare*
> *but much finesse*
>
> *the gingko that*
> *has blazed all month*
> *has acquiesced*

Georgia Journal is 80 pgs., 8½ × 11, saddle-stapled and professionally printed on glossy paper with color cover. Recent issues feature accessible narrative and lyric free verse. Content is genuinely open and varied, from nature and personal poems to war and meditative verse. About 4-6 poems appear in each issue. **Sample: $3. Submit maximum of 3-4 poems, maximum length 30 lines. "A brief cover letter with previous publications is fine, but keep it brief." Send SASE for guidelines. Reports in 2-3 months. Pays copies. Acquires first rights.** Staff selects books by Georgia authors to review.

UNIVERSITY OF GEORGIA PRESS; CONTEMPORARY POETRY SERIES (II), 330 Research Dr., Suite B100, University of Georgia, Athens GA 30602-4901, phone (706)369-6140, press founded 1938, series founded 1980, series editor Bin Ramke, publishes four collections of poetry/year, **two of which are by poets who have not had a book published,** in paperback editions. They have published poetry by Martha Collins, Marjorie Welish, Arthur Vogelsang and C.D. Wright. As a sample the editor selected these lines from "The Sciences Sing a Lullabye" by Albert Goldbarth:

> *Physics says: go to sleep. Of course*
> *you're tired. Every atom in you*
> *has been dancing the shimmy in silver shoes*
> *nonstop from mitosis to now.*
> *Quit tapping your feet. They'll dance*
> *inside themselves without you. Go to sleep.*

That is from the book *Heaven and Earth: A Cosmology* for which Goldbarth won the 1992 National Book Critics Circle Award. **"Writers should query first for guidelines and submission periods. Please enclose SASE." There are no restrictions on the type of poetry submitted,** but "familiarity with our previously published books in the series may be helpful." **$10 submission fee required.** Manuscripts are *not* returned after the judging is completed. **Always sends prepublication galleys.** The book *Bag 'o' Diamonds* by Susan Wheeler won the Norma Farber First Book Award from the Poetry Society of America.

THE GEORGIA REVIEW (II), The University of Georgia, Athens GA 30602-9009, phone (706)542-3481, founded 1947, editor Stanley W. Lindberg, associate editor Stephen Corey. They have published poetry by Galway Kinnell, Yusef Komunyakaa, Pattiann Rogers, Gerald Stern, Lisel Mueller, Seamus Heaney, Linda Pastan, Albert Goldbarth, Rita Dove and Charles Simic. "Also have featured first-ever publications by many new voices over the years, but encourage all potential contributors to become familiar with past offerings before submitting." As a sample, Stephen Corey selected "Wave and Particle" by Laura Fargas:

> *Herons hunt at the marsh edge,*
> *lacking the mind to desire abstractions.*
> *What I take boating in the bright fog*
> *is my need to be seen by them, to feel*
> *the ice of the moon melting on my palms.*
> *Round as a kiss, sharp as a bullet,*
> *light soaks the slow event.*

This is a distinguished, professionally printed, flat-spined quarterly, 200 pgs., 7 × 10, glossy card cover. They use 60-70 poems a year, less than one-half of one percent of those received. Circulation: 7,000. Subscription: $18/year. **Sample postpaid: $6. Submit 3-5 poems at a time. No simultaneous submissions. Rarely uses translations. No submissions accepted during June, July and August. Publishes theme issues occasionally. Reports in 1-3 months. Always sends prepublication galleys. Pays $3/ line. Buys first North American serial rights.** Reviews books of poetry. "Our poetry reviews range from 500-word 'Book Briefs' on single volumes to 5,000-word essay reviews on multiple volumes." *The Georgia Review* is one of the best literary journals around. It respects its audience, edits intelligently and has won or been nominated for awards in competition with such slicks as *The Atlantic*, *The New Yorker* and *Esquire*. Work appearing here has also been included in the 1992 and 1995 volumes of *The Best American Poetry*. Needless to say, competition is extremely tough. All styles and forms are welcome, but response times can be slow during peak periods in the fall and late spring. Yet the editor says they would like to receive, "the very best work from an even wider slate of poets."

GEPPO HAIKU WORKSHEET; YUKI TEIKEI HAIKU SOCIETY ANNUAL MEMBERS' ANTHOLOGY; KIYOSHI TOKUTOMI MEMORIAL HAIKU CONTEST (I, IV-Form, membership), 20711 Garden Place Court, Cupertino CA 95014, *Geppo* founded 1977, published by the Yuki Teikei Haiku Society, editor Jean Hale. *Geppo* is a bimonthly offset newsletter for members-only. **Traditionally structured haiku are encouraged: "a poem illuminating the perception of nature (humans included) focused at a moment in time, of 17 syllables in 3 lines of 5, 7, and 5 syllables, and having one season word or *kigo*."** *Geppo* also publishes poems from the society's workshops, retreats, readings, and contest, as well as short invited articles on haiku form and practice by established haiku poets. As a sample we selected the following haiku by Alice Benedict:

> *cry of a night bird—*
> *paleness of the hazy moon*
> *sifts into the dunes*

Press run is 200. The new *Annual Member's Anthology* contains haiku in traditional form submitted by members and selected by an editorial board. It is about 40 pgs., 5½ × 8½, printed on heavy paper with card stock cover. Press run is about 300. Members who submit poems receive a copy for a mailing fee of $2; nonmembers can order it from the society for $5/copy. Membership in the Yuki Teikei Haiku Society is $15/year and includes 6 issues of *Geppo*. **Sample of** *Geppo* **available for SASE.** The Kiyoshi Tokutomi Memorial Haiku Contest is open to anyone. First prize is $100. Deadline: April 15. For guidelines, send SASE to Haiku Contest Coordinator, 782 Del Mar, Livermore, CA 94550.

THE GETTYSBURG REVIEW (II), Gettysburg College, Gettysburg PA 17325, phone (717)337-6770, founded 1988, editor Peter Stitt, is a multidisciplinary literary quarterly considering **"well-written poems of all kinds."** They have recently published poetry by Marilyn Nelson Waniek, Donald Hall, Denise Levertov, James Tate, Nancy Vieira Couto, Charles Simic and Linda Pastan. As a sample the editor selected these lines by Frankie Paino:

> *If each bone of the body is holy*
> *it is because it gives shape to*
> *mortal love—bowl of the pelvis*
> *like a cradle, sickles of the*
> *hips like two moons, every angle*
> *open as the mouth to a kiss—*

They accept 1-2% of submissions received. Press run is 4,500 for 2,700 subscriptions. **Sample postpaid: $7. Submit 3 poems at a time, with SASE. No previously published poems or simultaneous submissions. Cover letter preferred. Publishes theme issues occasionally. Pays $2/line.** Essay-reviews are featured in each issue. Open to unsolicited essay-reviews. Poets may also send books for review consideration. Editor Peter Stitt, a leading literary critic and reviewer, has created a well-edited and -respected journal that features a tantalizing lineup of poems in all styles and forms. Competition is keen, and response times can be slow during heavy submission periods, especially in the late fall. Work appearing in *The Gettysburg Review* has been included in *The Best American Poetry* (1993, 1994 and 1995) and *Pushcart Prize* anthologies. As for the editor, Peter Stitt won the first PEN/Nora Magid Award for Editorial Excellence.

GINGER HILL (II), c/o English Dept., Room 314, Spotts World Cultures Building, Slippery Rock University, Slippery Rock PA 16057, phone (412)738-2043, founded 1963, is an annual literary magazine using **"academic poetry, with preference for excellent free verse, but all forms considered. 27-line limit. No greeting card verse, no sentimentality, no self-serving or didactic verse."** They have published poetry by Elizabeth R. Curry, B.Z. Niditch and Robert Cooperman. It is digest-sized, "varies in format and layout every year," perfect-bound, with 2,000 distributed free. **Submit 3 poems at a time. No previously published poems. Submissions must be postmarked on or before December 1 of each year. Send SASE for guidelines. Pays 2 copies.** They say, "We choose about 5-10% of all submissions. Excellence is stressed."

‡THE GLASS CHERRY PRESS; THE GLASS CHERRY (II), 901 Europe Bay Rd., Ellison Bay WI 54210-9643, phone (414)854-9042, founded 1994, editor Judith Hirschmiller. *The Glass Cherry* is a quarterly literary magazine composed primarily of contemporary poetry. **They want "original poetry that is stunning; poetry that clings, leaves a scar. Any form, length, style or subject matter, except pornographic."** They have recently published poetry by Lyn Lifshin, Duane Locke, Simon Perchik and James Liddy. As a sample the editor selected these lines from "Snowing" by Martin J. Rosenblum:

> *sleep uncovered*
> *by windows letting*
> *lite in from snow*
> *skies backlit*

> *it is like looking*
> *thru an eggshell cracked*

The Glass Cherry is 40-60 pgs., 5½×8½, saddle-stapled with card stock cover. Each issue has a featured poet whose work comprises approximately 40% of the issue, and a photo of the featured poet appears on the back cover. They receive about 2,000 poems a year, accept less than 10%. Press run is 500 for 25 subscribers ("and growing"), 5% shelf sales. Single copy: $5; subscription: $15. **Sample postpaid: $6. Make checks payable to Judith Hirschmiller. Submit up to 5 poems at a time, name and address on each page. Previously published poems OK, "only if requested." No simultaneous submissions. Cover letter with brief bio required. Seldom comments on rejections. Send SASE for guidelines. Reports in 1 month. Pays 1 copy. Acquires first or one-time rights. Requests acknowledgement and notification from author when work is reprinted elsewhere.** Reviews books of poetry. Open to unsolicited reviews. Poets may also send books for review consideration. They also sponsor contests related to specific themes or occasions. Rules vary, but reading fees are required. Winning poems are published on the back covers of special issues. The Glass Cherry Press also plans to publish 3 books of poetry a year. **Poems included in book-length mss need not be previously published. The editor reads book-length submissions (20-60 pgs.) from January through April only. Send SASE for guidelines. Reports in 1-4 months. Samples are available from the press for $10 and a SASE.** The editor says, "Writers are encouraged to read back issues of *The Glass Cherry* prior to submitting."

GLB PUBLISHERS (III, IV-Gay/lesbian/bisexual), P.O. Box 78212, San Francisco CA 94107, phone (415)621-8307, founded 1990, associate editor John Hanley. **"We are cooperative publishers. Founded for gay, lesbian and bisexual writers. Authors share cost of printing and promotion but have much control over cover design, typefaces, general appearance."** They publish 2-4 paperbacks and 1-2 hardbacks/year. **They want "book-length collections from gay, lesbian or bisexual writers. Nothing antagonistic to gay, lesbian or bisexual life-styles."** They have published poetry by Robert Peters, Paul Genega and Thomas Cashet. **Previously published poems OK; no simultaneous submissions. Cover letter required. "Author should explain intention for poems and expectations for sales of books." Often comments on rejections. Replies to queries in 10 days, to mss in 1 month. Always sends prepublication galleys. Pays 15-25% royalties and 20 author's copies. Check bookstores for samples.**

GLOBAL TAPESTRY JOURNAL; BB BOOKS (II), Spring Bank, Longsight Rd., Copster Green, Blackburn, Lancs, BB1 9EU United Kingdom, founded 1963, poetry editor Dave Cunliffe. **"Experimental, avant-garde—specializing in exciting high-energy new writing. Mainly for a bohemian and counter-culture audience. Poetry in the Beat tradition. Don't want contrived, traditional, pompous and academic or pretentious mainstream."** Also considers sexually explicit material. In addition to the magazine, *Global Tapestry Journal*, BB Books publishes chapbooks. "We want honest, uncontrived writing, strong in form and content. We don't want 'weekend hobby verse' and poetry without energy." They have recently published poetry by George Montgomery, Madeline Tiger, Ana Christy, George Dowden and Chris Challis. As a sample the editor selected these lines by Tina Morris:

> *and the hedges stand*
> *as sharp and spiky*
> *as the death poking its way*

> *into what should have been*
> *the rest of our lives.*

GTJ is 72 pgs., 9×6, saddle-stapled, typeset in a variety of mostly small sizes of type, rather crowded format, casual pasteup, with b&w drawings, photos, collages, display and classified ads, with a 2-color matte card cover. Circulation 1,150 with 450 subscribers of which 50 are libraries. Subscription: £8 sterling for 4 issues mailed seamail to USA. **Sample postpaid: $3. Considers previously published poems. Cover letter, with clear address, telephone number and short publishing history, required. Send SASE (or SAE and IRC) for guidelines. Responds "soon," has an 18-month backlog. Pays 1 copy.** Open to unsolicited reviews. Poets may also send books for review consideration. **BB Books publishes about 4 chapbooks of poetry/year. To submit for chapbook publication send 6 samples and cover letter giving publication credits. Pays 10% of press run in copies. Send SASE (SAE with IRCs if foreign) for catalog to buy samples.** David Cunliffe comments, "The United Kingdom has a limited number of magazines and small press ventures publishing poetry from unknowns. Many little mags are self-publishing cliques or small-time vanity operations. Simultaneous submissions and simultaneous publication are often resented. There is much readership crossover among the non-poet subscribers and they resent seeing the same work in many magazines over a short period. We typeset for a few United Kingdom mags and publishers and we see this in the setting jobs we do every week. Many of the editors circulate poet blacklists to help prevent this tendency from spreading."

DAVID R. GODINE, PUBLISHER (V), P.O. Box 9103, Lincoln MA 01773. They say, **"Our poetry program is completely filled through 1996, so we are not accepting any unsolicited materials at this time."**

‡GOING DOWN SWINGING (II), P.O. Box 24, Clifton Hill, Victoria 3068 Australia, founded 1980, editors Lyn Boughton and Louise Craig is an annual using **"poetry that's tackling contemporary literary, social, political issues. No racist or sexist poetry."** They have recently published poetry by Emma Lew, Ouyang Yu, B.R. Dionysius and Lauren Williams. As a sample the editors selected these lines from "The Sound of the woman's voice" by Kerry Scuffins:

> *The sound of the woman's voice*
> *was once sweet and low*
> *like Shakespeare's most excellent*
> *of women*
> *but in time*
> *and under pressure from mighty forces*
> *the sound of the woman's voice*
> *began like molested earth's to crack and change*

It is flat-spined, digest-sized. Press run 1,000 for 300 subscribers of which 30 are libraries, 700 shelf sales. **Sample postpaid: $10 (A). Submit 3 poems at a time. No previously published poems. Reports in 3 months. Pays 1 copy and a "small fee."** They say, "We are primarily an Australian magazine, but we are open to new and outstanding writing from overseas. Our aim is to publish the work of new, young and generally unknown writers whose work excites and interests us. We review small press books." Open to unsolicited reviews. Poets may also send books for review consideration.

GOLDEN ISIS MAGAZINE; AGE OF AQUARIUS; GOLDEN ISIS PRESS; POEM OF THE YEAR CONTEST (I, IV-Mystical/Occult), P.O. Box 525, Fort Covington NY 12937, founded 1980, editor Gerina Dunwich. "*Golden Isis* is a mystical literary magazine of poetry, magick, pagan/Egyptian artwork, Wiccan news, occult fiction, letters, book reviews and classified ads. **Occult, Egyptian, cosmic, euphonic and Goddess-inspired poems, mystical haiku and magickal chants are published. We are also interested in New Age spiritual poetry, astrological verses and poems dealing with peace, love and ecology. All styles considered; under 60 lines preferred. We do not want to see pornographic, Satanic, sexist or racist material."** They have published poetry by H.L. Prosser, Eileen Kernaghan and Timothy Kevin Perry. As a sample the editor selected these lines from "Full Circle" by Mary Shifman:

> *The Goddess steps inside my heart*
> *To share me with Her dance*
> *The Horned God plies his minstrel art*
> *And all the world enchants*

The magazine is 15-20 pgs., digest-sized, desktop-published, saddle-stapled with paper cover. International circulation is 5,000. Single copy: $3; subscription: $10/year. "No postal money orders, please." **Submit 1 poem/page, typed single-spaced, name and address on upper left corner and the number of lines on upper right corner. No limit on number of poems submitted. Previously published poems and simultaneous submissions OK. Occasionally comments on rejected material. Reports within 2-3 weeks. No payment or free copies. "We can no longer afford it." All rights revert to author upon publication.** Reviews books of poetry, "length varies." Open to unsolicited reviews. Poets may also send books for review consideration. *Age of Aquarius* is a digest-sized "psychedelic journal of 60s counter-culture in the 90s." Sample: $3. Circulation: 3,600. Golden Isis Press **currently accepts mss for chapbook publication. Send complete ms and $5 reading fee. "Please make checks payable to Golden Isis. We offer a small advance, 10 free copies of the published work, and 10% royalty on every copy sold for as long as the book remains in print." Sample chapbook** (*Circle of Shadows* by Gerina Dunwich): **$3.95.** The magazine sponsors an annual "Poem of the Year" contest that offers cash prizes. Entry fee: $1/poem. Deadline: December 1. No limit on number of poems entered. Poems should be up to 60 lines, any form, with author's name and address on upper left corner of each page. Free guidelines and contest rules for SASE. *Golden Isis* is a member of W.P.P.A. (Wiccan/Pagan Press Alliance).

GOLDEN QUILL PRESS (I), P.O. Box 2327, Manchester Center VT 05255, phone (802)362-5066, publishes a great deal of poetry on a "cooperative" basis. **"Funds returned when guarantees are met." Call or write for detailed brochure before submitting complete ms. Reports in 2 weeks on queries, 1 month on submissions. Pays maximum 20% royalties.**

GOOSE LANE EDITIONS (V, IV-Regional), 469 King St., Fredericton, New Brunswick E3B 1E5 Canada, phone (506)450-4251, fax (506)459-4991, managing editor S. Alexander, founded 1956, is a small press publishing Canadian fiction, poetry and literary history. **Writers should be advised that Goose Lane considers mss by Canadian poets only.** They receive approximately 400 mss/year, publish 10-15 books yearly, 3 of these being poetry collections. Writers published include Claire Harris and Eric Trethewey. As a sample the editor selected these lines from "Thomas," published in *Resisting the Anomie* (1994) by Kwame Dawes:

> He sat there and broke bread
> his feet stirring the dust,
> his wine spilling through his beard
> soaked up by the boards
> rusty brown where the nails twisted.
>
> The wine softened the crumbs
> like flesh broken
>
> The stool is empty now.

They are not reading submissions before January 1996. After that date, unsolicited Canadian mss considered if individual poems have been previously published in literary journals. Cover letter required; include name and address and where work was previously published. SASE essential (IRCs or Canadian postage stamps only). Reports in 3-4 months. Always sends prepublication galleys. Authors may receive royalty of up to 10% of retail sale price on all copies sold. Copies available to author at 40% discount.

GOSPEL PUBLISHING HOUSE (IV-Religious); PENTECOSTAL EVANGEL (V); LIVE (IV-Religious); TEEN LIFE (V); TAKE FIVE; JUNIOR TRAILS (IV-Religious, children/teens), The General Council of the Assemblies of God, 1445 Boonville Ave., Springfield MO 65802, phone (417)831-8000 ext. 4276, fax (417)862-7566. **Gospel Publishing House produces the Spirit of Praise Bulletin Series. Poems accepted for back cover of bulletins. For more information, call or write to Promotions.** *Pentecostal Evangel* is a weekly magazine containing **inspirational articles and news of the Assemblies of God for members of the Assemblies and other Pentecostal and charismatic Christians**, circulation 250,000. **"Presently, the** *Pentecostal Evangel* **is not accepting poetry."** *Live* is a weekly **for adults in Assemblies of God Sunday schools**, circulation 200,000. **Traditional free and blank verse, 12-20 lines. "Please do not send large numbers of poems at one time." Submit seasonal material 1 year in advance; do not mention Santa Claus, Halloween or Easter bunnies. Sample copy and writer's guidelines for 7×10 SAE and 2 first-class stamps. Letters without SASE will not be answered. Pays 25¢/line on acceptance. Buys first and/or second rights.** *Teen Life* is a weekly magazine of **Christian fiction and articles for teenagers, 12-17,** circulation 78,000. *Take Five* is a youth devotional accepting poetry written by teens. **Poetry should be typed, double-spaced, and must include the teen's name, complete address, church and age. Pays $15 upon acceptance.** *Junior Trails* is a weekly tabloid covering **religious fiction and biographical, historical and scientific articles with a spiritual emphasis for boys and girls ages 10-11,** circulation 75,000. **Buys 10-15 poems/year. Free verse and light verse. Submit seasonal/holiday material 15 months in advance. Simultaneous and previously published submissions OK. Sample copy and writer's guidelines for 9×12 SAE and 2 first-class stamps. Reports in 2-4 weeks. Pays 20¢/line on acceptance. Buys first and/or second rights.** "We like poems showing contemporary children positively facing today's world. **For all our publications, submit 1-2 poems at a time."**

GOTTA WRITE NETWORK LITMAG; MAREN PUBLICATIONS (I, II, IV-Science fiction/fantasy, subscription), 612 Cobblestone Circle, Glenview IL 60025, phone/fax (708)296-7631, founded

1988, editor/publisher Denise Fleischer, is a desktop-published, semiannual, saddle-stapled, 76-page magazine featuring "contemporary poetry, articles, short stories and market listings. *GWN* now spans 40 states, Canada and England. Half of the magazine is devoted to science fiction and fantasy in a section called 'Sci-Fi Galleria.' **A short checklist of what I look for in all poems and stories would be: drawing the reader into the protagonist's life from the beginning; presenting a poem's message through powerful imagery and sensory details; and language that is fresh and dynamic. I prefer free verse. Would also like to receive experimental, multicultural, feminist, humor, contemporary and translations. The poetry we publish expresses today's society openly and honestly. Our contributors dive into the subjects where others turn away. They speak of moments before the bomb hit the Japanese, life in prison, anorexia, suicide attempts, and life in a nursing home."** She has recently published poetry by Jim DeWitt, Lyn Lifshin, Taylor Graham, Mary Winters and J. Blaine Hudson. As a sample the editor selected these lines from "Peri's Song" by Ilie Ruby:

> When lilies bloomed outside the stone house,
> yellow bursts like viruses through a blue body
> choking and frothing at the mouth, the sin of what was left
> Peri shivered in the room by the door and the grey floor,
> floured in dust and ruin, the concubine quarters, locked
> in for thirteen months through the icy heat of screaming
> fires and a man whose blond wisps licked her sweating face

"*Gotta Write Network* subscribers receive more than a magazine. In subscribing, they become part of a support group of both beginners and established poets. Readers are from all walks of life. I'm striving to give beginners a positive starting point (as well as promote the work of established writers and editors) and to encourage them to venture beyond rejection slips and writer's block. Publication can be a reality if you have determination and talent. There are over a thousand U.S. litmags waiting for submissions. So take your manuscripts out of your desk and submit them today!" Subscription: $12.75. **Sample postpaid: $5. Submit 1-5 poems at a time. Name and address on each page. No previously published poems or simultaneous submissions. Include a cover letter and SASE. Reports in 2-4 months. Sometimes sends prepublication galleys. Pays 1 copy. Acquires first North American serial rights.** Pays $5 for assigned by-mail interviews with established paperback authors and small press editors. Maren Publications now offers both typesetting, distribution and a "news service." She adds, "Write the way you feel the words. Don't let others mold you into another poet's style. Poetry is about personal imagery that needs to be shared with others."

GRAFFITI OFF THE ASYLUM WALLS (IV-Humor, erotica, fetishes), P.O. Box 1603, Nashville AR 71852-1603, e-mail bryan.westbrook@panda.org, founded 1991, "curator" BrYan Westbrook, is an "illiterary journal published whenever I receive enough suitable material." He wants **"stuff you would be afraid to show your mother, priest and/or shrink; also anything that can make me laugh. No formal poetry; no pro-religious or animal rights poetry; nothing boring."** They have published poetry by Cheryl Townsend, Belinda Subraman, harland ristau and Scott C. Holstad. As a sample the editor selected these lines from "Cheap Date" by Richard Cody:

> His hands played over her fine young body,
> seeking to unleash forbidden pleasures.
> "You better enjoy this . . ." he whispered.
> "You're going back to the graveyard tomorrow."

Press run and format vary. Subscription: $10 for 4 issues. **Sample postpaid: "$3 (checks made out to BrYan Westbrook) or will trade copies with other editors." Submit 5 poems at a time. Previously published poems and simultaneous submissions OK. Cover letter and SASE required. "I do not want to just see a list of previous publications. I want to know who you are more than where you've been." Often comments on rejections. Reports "usually next day, rarely more than 3 months." No payment, but offers contributors unlimited copies at discount price of $2. Acquires one-time rights.** Staff will review "*anything* someone wants to send me. Length varies with how much I think needs to be said." BrYan Westbrook says, "Throughout history the preserved literature of any period has mainly been what the people of that time actually enjoyed. Scholars have placed these works upon lofty pedestals and declared them the only true art. It's time we stop trying to imitate what others have considered entertainment and get on with creating the art we really want for ourselves. *GOTAW* is my contribution to this endeavor."

GRAHAM HOUSE REVIEW (II, IV-Translations), Box 5000, Colgate University, Hamilton NY 13346, phone (315)824-1000 ext. 262, founded 1976, poetry editors Peter Balakian and Bruce Smith, appears yearly. "We publish contemporary poetry, poetry in translation, essays and interviews. **No preferences for styles or schools, just good poetry.**" They have published poems by Seamus Heaney, Marilyn Hacker, Maxine Kumin, Michael Harper and Carolyn Forché. *GHR* is 120 pgs., digest-sized, flat-spined, professionally printed on heavy stock, matte color card cover with logo, using 150 pgs. of poetry in each issue. They receive about 2,000 submissions of poetry/year, use 20-50. One of the best "reads" in the literary world, this publication features well-crafted free verse depicting emotionally tense or intellectually stimulating ideas and themes. It welcomes translations and has an "international" flavor. Circulation 500, with 300 subscriptions of which 50 are libraries. **Sample postpaid: $7.50. Reports in 2 months or less. Pays 2 copies.**

GRAIN; SHORT GRAIN CONTEST (II), Box 1154, Regina, Saskatchewan S4P 3B4 Canada, phone (306)791-7747, founded 1971, is a literary quarterly. "*Grain* strives for artistic excellence and seeks material that is accessible as well as challenging to our readers. Ideally, a *Grain* poem should be well-crafted, imaginatively stimulating, distinctly original."** They have published poetry by Evelyn Lau and Jay Meek. The editor selected as a sample the opening of "The Children" by Patrick Lane:

> *The children are singing.*
> *Hear them as they rise out of the deep hollows,*
> *the tangles of wildwood and wandering vines.*
> *They are lifting from the shadows*
> *where the black creek water flows*
> *over mud and stones. They have left behind*
> *the green whip of a snake*
> *thrown like a thin necklace into the trees . . .*

Grain is digest-sized, professionally printed with chrome-coated cover, 144 pgs., circulation 1,500, with 1,100 subscriptions of which 100 are libraries. They receive about 700 submissions of poetry/year, use 80-140 poems. Subscription: $19.95 (Canadian), $23.95 for US, $25.95 for other foreign destinations. **Sample: $6.95 plus IRC (or 80¢ Canadian postage). They want "no poetry that has no substance." Submit maximum of 8 poems, typed on 8½ × 11 paper, single-spaced, one side only. No previously published poems or simultaneous submissions. Cover letter required. Include "the number of poems submitted, address (with postal or zip code) and phone number." Send SASE (or SAE and IRC) for guidelines. Reports in 4-6 months. Pays $30+/poem. Buys first North American serial rights.** Holds an annual Short Grain Contest. Entries are either prose poems (a lyric poem written as a prose paragraph or paragraphs in 500 words or less) or postcard stories (also 500 words or less). Prizes in each category, $500 first, $300 second, $200 third and honorable mentions. All winners and honorable mentions receive regular payment for publication in *Grain*. Entry fee of $20 (Canadian) allows up to two entries in the same category, and includes a one-year subscription. Additional entries are $5 each. Entries are normally accepted between January 1 and April 30. The editor comments, "Only work of the highest literary quality is accepted. Read several back issues."

GRAND STREET (III), 131 Varick St., Room 906, New York NY 10013, is a quarterly magazine publishing poetry, fiction, nonfiction and art. **"We have no writer's guidelines, but publish the most original poetry we can find—encompassing quality writing from all schools."** They have recently published poetry by John Ashbery, Nicholas Christopher, Fanny Howe, Robert Kelly, August Kleinzahler, Hilda Morley, Michael Palmer and Charles Simic. **Sample postpaid: $15. Submit 5 poems at a time. Occasionally publishes theme issues. Reports in 2 months. Pays approximately $3/line.** Work published in *Grand Street* has been included in the 1992, 1993, 1994 and 1995 volumes of *The Best America Poetry*.

GRASSLANDS REVIEW (I, II), Dept. of English, P.O. Box 13827, Denton TX 76203-3827, phone (817)565-2126, founded 1989, editor Laura B. Kennelly, is a magazine **"to encourage beginning writers and to give creative writing students experience in editing fiction and poetry; using any type of poetry; shorter poems stand best chance."** They have recently published poetry by Edward Byrne, Adrie S. Kusserow, John Dufresne, Peggy Little, Frances Treviño and John David Christensen. As a sample the editor selected these lines from "Bagpipe Music" by Frank K. Baskett:

> *Can pigs hear the wild bagpipe music of life?*
> *Leaning here on the rail, I don't think so.*
> *Not there in that stuff—this way, caught up,*
> *Busy being regulated as peoples pigs.*
> *As they are in this muddy November sty*
> *Their coy, fleshy ears hiding their cloudy eyes.*

ALWAYS include a self-addressed, stamped envelope (SASE) when sending a ms or query to a publisher within your own country. When sending material to other countries, include a self-addressed envelope and International Reply Coupons (IRCs), available for purchase at most post offices.

GR is 80 pgs., digest-sized, professionally printed, photocopied, saddle-stapled with card cover. They accept 60-70 of 500 submissions received. Press run is 300. Subscription (2 issues): $8 for individuals, $20 institutions. **Sample postpaid: $3. Submit only during October and March, no more than 5 poems at a time. No previously published poems or simultaneous submissions. Short cover letter preferred. Send #10 SASE for response. Editor comments on submissions "sometimes." Reports in 10-12 weeks. Sometimes sends prepublication galleys. Pays 2 copies.**

GRAYWOLF PRESS (V), 2402 University Ave., Suite 203, Saint Paul MN 55114, phone (612)641-0077, founded 1975, poetry editor Scott Walker, **does not read unsolicited mss.** They have published poetry by Tess Gallagher, Linda Gregg, Jack Gilbert, Chris Gilbert, John Haines, D. Nurkse and William Stafford. **Sometimes sends prepublication galleys. Pays 7½-10% royalties, 10 author's copies, advance negotiated.**

GREEN FUSE (III, IV-Political, ecology, social issues), 3365 Holland Dr., Santa Rosa CA 95404, phone (707)544-8303, founded 1984, editor Brian Boldt, is published each spring and fall. **"We seek accessible free verse—with strong concrete details and images—concerned with witness, ecology and dissent, poems that give voice to those who have been silenced and poems that celebrate the astonishing natural beauty and mystery of the planet. Send us work that offers poetic truth and sanity in an age of prosaic lies and madness. Sentimental or institutionally religious poems and work submitted without SASE or stinking of nicotine will be folded into origami. No Republicans."** They have recently published poetry by Antler, David Chorlton, Donald Hall, Dorianne Laux, Denise Levertov, Elliot Richman and Laurel Speer. As a sample the editor selected these lines from "Immemorial Celts Dreaming" by Carol Tufts:

> *. . . Then that other*
> *landscape breaks through . . .*
> *and all that is knows itself*
> *whole in the sweet air of that green world*
> *where phantoms of possibility take their ease*
> *in simple peace, before the dusty pigments*
> *deepen once more and we are left,*
> *like gazers through smoked glass,*
> *blinkered in the darkening moment.*

Green Fuse is 64 pgs., digest-sized, offset, perfect-bound, with b&w illustrations on the cover and throughout. They receive about 4,000 poems a year, accept approximately 100. Press run is 750 for subscription, bookstore and reading sales. Subscriptions: $14 for 3 issues, $18 for 4. **Sample postpaid: $4. "Please submit no more than three poems—of 70 or fewer lines. We discourage simultaneous submissions and don't consider previously published work (unless, of course, you've written the perfect *Green Fuse* poem). We often comment on submissions but take a break from reading manuscripts during February and March and August and September." Send SASE for guidelines. Reports within 3 months, "probably sooner." Pays 2 copies. Acquires first rights.**

GREEN MOUNTAINS REVIEW (II), Johnson State College, Johnson VT 05656, phone (802)635-2356 ext. 350, founded 1975, poetry editor Neil Shepard, appears twice a year and includes poetry (and other writing) by well-known authors and promising newcomers. **"We publish quality work; formal or free verse, realistic or surrealistic, narrative-based or language poetry."** They have recently published poetry by Galway Kinnell, Derek Walcott, Maxine Kumin, Stephen Dunn, David Mura, Larry Lewis and David St. John. *GMR* is digest-sized, flat-spined, 150-200 pgs. Of 600 submissions they publish 30 authors. Press run is 1,200 for 200 subscribers of which 30 are libraries. Subscription: $12/year. **Sample postpaid: $7. Submit no more than 5 poems at a time. No simultaneous submissions. Reads submissions September 1 through May 15 only. Editor sometimes comments on rejection slip. Publishes theme issues. Send SASE for guidelines and upcoming themes. Reports in 2-3 months. Pays 1 copy plus 1-year subscription. Acquires first North American serial rights.** Send books for review consideration. *GMR* received a 1994-95 grant from the Vermont Council on the Arts. Poetry published in *GMR* has been selected for inclusion in *The Best American Poetry 1994* and *Pushcart Prize* anthologies.

GREENHOUSE REVIEW PRESS (V), 3965 Bonny Doon Rd., Santa Cruz CA 95060, founded 1975, publishes a series of poetry chapbooks and broadsides. **"Unsolicited mss are not accepted."** Send SASE for catalog to buy samples.

GREEN'S MAGAZINE (II); CLOVER PRESS (V), P.O. Box 3236, Regina, Saskatchewan S4P 3H1 Canada, founded 1972, editor David Green. *Green's Magazine* is a literary quarterly with a balanced diet of short fiction and poetry; Clover Press publishes chapbooks. They publish **"free/blank verse examining emotions or situations." They do not want greeting card jingles or pale imitations of the masters.** They have recently published poetry by Mary Balazs, Robert L. Tener, Ruth Moon

Kempher, Geoff Stevens and Kit Knight. As a sample the editor selected these lines from "The Gossipmonger" by Janice Soderling:

> *Like a giant anteater*
> *she hovers over the scandal,*
> *her long, sticky tongue*
> *greedily prying into the deepest recesses,*
> *gobbling the fear, the pain,*
> *the despair.*

The magazine is 100 pgs., digest-sized, with line drawings. A sample chapbook is also digest-sized, 60 pgs., typeset on buff stock with line drawings, matte card cover, saddle-stapled. Circulation is 400. Subscription: $12. **Sample postpaid: $4. Submit 4-6 poems at a time. The editor prefers typescript, complete originals. No simultaneous submissions. "If © used, poet must give permission to use and state clearly the work is unpublished."** Time between acceptance and publication is 3 months. **Send SASE for guidelines. (IRCs for US queries and/or mss.) Reports in 2 months. Pays 2 copies. Acquires first North American serial rights.** Occasionally reviews books of poetry in "up to 150-200 words." Send books for review consideration. **Unsolicited submissions are accepted for the magazine but not for books; query first on latter. Comments are usually provided on rejected mss.** "Would-be contributors are urged to study the magazine first."

THE GREENSBORO REVIEW; GREENSBORO REVIEW LITERARY AWARDS; AMON LINER POETRY AWARD (II), English Dept., University of North Carolina, Greensboro NC 27412, phone (910)334-5459, fax (910)339-3281, e-mail clarkj@fagan.uncg.edu, founded 1966, editor Jim Clark. *TGR* appears twice yearly and showcases well-made verse in all styles and forms, though shorter poems (under 50 lines) seem preferred. They have recently published poetry by Stephen Dobyns, Askold Melnyczuk, Steven Cramer and Gail Mazur. As a sample the poetry editor selected these lines from "Leaving Fargo" by Michael Evans:

> *. . . and you count your steps away*
> *through waves of red dust*
>
> *knowing how quickly cramps will come*
> *on the long ride home, her panicked eyes dark*
> *and searching for an open place to jump,*
> *ready to abandon every room she's ever known*
> *for anything as kind as disgrace.*

The digest-sized, flat-spined magazine, 120 pgs., colored matte cover, professional printing, uses about 25 pgs. of poetry in each issue, about 2.5% of the 2,000 submissions received each year. Circulation 500 for 300 subscribers of which 100 are libraries. **Sample postpaid: $4. "Submissions (of no more than 5 poems) must arrive by September 15 to be considered for the Winter issue (acceptances in December) and February 15 to be considered for the Summer issue (acceptances in May). Manuscripts arriving after those dates will be held for consideration with the next issue."** No simultaneous submissions. **Cover letter not required but helpful. Include number of poems submitted. Reports in 2-4 months. Always sends prepublication galleys. Pays 3 copies. Acquires first North American serial rights.** They offer the Amon Liner Poetry Award for the best poem appearing in the magazine. They also sponsor an open competition for the Greensboro Review Literary Awards, $250 for both poetry and fiction each year. Deadline: September 15. Send SASE for guidelines.

GROVE ATLANTIC (V), 841 Broadway, New York NY 10003. Grove Press and Atlantic Monthly Press merged in February 1993. **They currently do not accept unsolicited mss.**

GRUE MAGAZINE (IV-Horror), P.O. Box 370, New York NY 10108, founded 1985, editor Peggy Nadramia, is a horror fiction magazine "with emphasis on the experimental, offbeat, rude." The editor wants **"poems of any length, including prose poems, with macabre imagery and themes. Not interested in Poe rip-offs (although we'll look at rhyming poems if subject is weird enough), 'straight' vampire, ghost or werewolf poems."** She has published poetry by Robert Frazier, G. Sutton Breiding, Denise Dumars, Todd Mecklem, John Grey and Jonathan Yungkans. As a sample she selected these lines from "And Die In Her Eyes" by Wayne Allen Sallee:

> *the night is her world*
> *a heaving narcopolis,*
> *its lodgers cramped in the most distant*
> *of outposts, or trapped*
> *with a nuclear awareness*
> *in urban townhouse isolation*

The magazine is 96 pgs., digest-sized, offset, with a glossy b&w cover, "sharp" graphics, and "a centerfold that is unique." It appears 3 times a year and has a press run of 3,000, of which 500 are subscriptions and 1,000 are newsstand sales. Subscription: $13/year. **Sample postpaid: $4.50. Submit** up to 5 poems at a time. The editor usually provides criticism of rejected mss. Guidelines are available for SASE. Reports in 3-6 months. Time to publication is 12-18 months. **Poets receive 2 copies plus $5/poem upon publication to a maximum of $5/issue.** Her advice is: "We like poems that go for the throat, with strong, visceral controlling images. We're also interested in poems that comment upon, or challenge the conventions of, the horror genre itself."

GUERNICA EDITIONS INC.; ESSENTIAL POET SERIES, PROSE SERIES, DRAMA SERIES; INTER-NATIONAL WRITERS (IV-Regional, translations, ethnic/nationality), P.O. Box 117, Toronto, Ontario M5S 2S6 Canada, founded 1978, poetry editor Antonio D'Alfonso. "We wish to bring together the **different and often divergent voices that exist in Canada and the U.S. We are interested in translations. We are mostly interested right now in translated poetry and essays on pluricultural-ism.**" They have recently published work by Hélène Dorion, Yves Préfontaine and Suzanne Jacob (Quebec); Alda Merini and Maria Luisa Spaziani (Italy); Gianna Patriarca, Joseph Maviglia and Ray-mond Filip (Canada); and Maria Mazziotti Gillan, Rachel Guido de Vries and Peter Carravetta (USA). **Query with 1-2 pgs. of samples. Send SASE (Canadian stamps only) or SAE and IRCs for catalog.** The editor comments, "We are interested in promoting a pluricultural view of literature by bridging languages and cultures. Besides our specialization in international translation, we also focus on the work of Italian, Italian/Canadian and Italian/American writers."

GUILD PRESS; FULL CIRCLE SERIES (I, IV-Ethnic), Dept. PM, P.O. Box 22583, Robbinsdale MN 55422, founded 1978, senior editor Leon Knight, **"the leading publisher of minority authors in Minnesota," wants poems to 40 lines max., nothing sexually graphic.** They have published poetry by George Clabon, Hazel Clayton Harrison and Nancy Ellen Williams (Big Mama). As a sample the editor selected these lines (poet unidentified):

> *I thought poetry*
> *made a difference*
> *. . .*
> *But photography*
> *doesn't alter sunsets:*
> *poetry does not*
> *restrain the wind*

The Full Circle Series are **annual anthologies of 35-50 poets. Individual collections are published "by invitation only" to poets who have appeared in the "open-invitation" anthologies. Send SASE for guidelines. Pays copies.**

‡GULF COAST: A JOURNAL OF LITERATURE AND FINE ART (II), Dept. of English, University of Houston, Houston TX 77204-3012, founded 1986, is published twice a year in the winter and summer. While the journal features work by a number of established poets, editors are also interested in "provid-ing a forum for new and emerging writers who are producing well-crafted work that takes risks, intensifying the accepted conventions for poetry—whether formally inventive or focused on a form's inherent strengths—with an acute awareness of its own language." Each issue includes poetry, fiction, essays, interviews, and color reproductions of work by Houston artists. As a sample we selected these lines by Lisa Lewis:

> *She knows what's tethered underwater. Not*
> *Children's bodies, but their toys, their lost,*
> *Lawed-against pleasures. I'm not going to*
> *Take up with her the ways we were persuaded*
> *To throw our joys into dark water.*

The editor says *Gulf Coast* is 140 pgs., 6×9, offset, perfect-bound. Single copy: $7; subscription: $12 for 1 year, $22 for 2 years. **Submit 1-4 poems at a time. No previously published poems; simultane-ous submissions OK. Cover letter with previous publications, "if any," and a brief bio required. Does not read submissions May through July. Send SASE for guidelines. Reports in 2-6 months. Pays copies. Returns rights upon publication.**

GULF STREAM MAGAZINE (II), English Dept., Florida International University, North Miami Cam-pus, North Miami FL 33181, phone (305)940-5599, founded 1989, editors Lynne Barrett and John Duframe, associate editors Andrew Goldman and Blythe Nobleman, is the biannual literary magazine associated with the creative writing program at FIU. They want **"poetry of any style and subject matter as long as it is of high literary quality."** They have recently published poetry by Gerald Costanzo, Naomi Shihab Nye, Jill Bialosky and Catherine Bowman. The handsome magazine is 90 pgs., digest-sized, flat-spined, printed on quality stock with glossy card cover. They accept less than 10% of poetry received. Press run is 750. Subscription: $7.50. **Sample postpaid: $4. Submit no more than 5 poems. No simultaneous submissions. Reads submissions September 15 through April 30 only. Editor comments on submissions "if we feel we can be helpful." Publishes theme issues.**

Send SASE for guidelines. Reports in 2-3 months. Pays 2 free subscriptions. Acquires first North American serial rights.

GUT PUNCH PRESS (III), P.O. Box 105, Cabin John MD 20818, founded 1987, editor Derrick Hsu, publishes 1-2 paperbacks/year. **They want "free verse with an innovative edge and possibly a sense of humor. No language school or formal narrative style."** They have published poetry collections by Richard Peabody, Sunil Freeman and Rose Solari, and an anthology of African-American poetry edited by Alan Spears. No poems previously published in book form or simultaneous submissions. Time between acceptance and publication is 1 year. **Replies to mss (if invited) in 3 months. Pays royalties ("determined on an individual basis") and 50 author's copies. For sample books, send SASE for list and order form.** Most books are $7.95 postpaid.

HAIGHT ASHBURY LITERARY JOURNAL (II, IV-Social issues, themes), 558 Joost Ave., San Francisco CA 94127, phone (415)221-2017, founded 1979-1980, editors Joanne Hotchkiss, Alice Rogoff and Will Walker, is a newsprint tabloid that appears 1-3 times a year. They use **"all forms and lengths, including haiku. Subject matter sometimes political, but open to all subjects. Poems of background—prison, minority experience—often published, as well as poems of protest and of Central America. Few rhymes."** They have published poetry by Joyce Odam, Jack Micheline, Edgar Silex, Leticia Escamilla, Bill Shields and Ina Cumpiano. As a sample the editors selected these lines by Elliot Richman (which also appear in *Shrapnel in the Heart: Letters & Remembrances from the Vietnam Veterans Memorial*):

> I'd like to love you as I did in Nam
> holding your hand on the last evening
> of your life. Helping you die
> is more intimate than sex,
> more intimate than the children I bore.

The tabloid has a photo of its featured poet on the cover, uses graphics, ads, 16 pgs., circulation 2,000-3,000. $35 for a lifetime subscription, which includes 3 back issues. $12 for 4-issue subscription. **Sample postpaid: $3. Make checks payable to Alice Rogoff. Submit up to 6 poems or 8 pgs. of poetry at a time. "Please type one poem to a page, put name and address on every page and include SASE." No previously published poems. Each issue changes its theme and emphasis. Send SASE for guidelines and upcoming themes. Reports in 2-3 months. Pays 3 copies. Rights revert to author except for reprints in future anthologies.** An anthology of past issues, *This Far Together*, was scheduled to appear in 1995. Interested poets should write for order information.

HAIKU HEADLINES: A MONTHLY NEWSLETTER OF HAIKU AND SENRYU (IV-Form), 1347 W. 71st St., Los Angeles CA 90044, phone (213)778-5337, founded 1988, editor/publisher David Priebe, uses **haiku and senryu only. The editor prefers the 5/7/5 syllabic discipline, but accepts minimalist haiku which display pivotal contrast and appropriate imagery.** They have recently published haiku by Don Foster, George Knox, Mark Arvid White and Beatrice Brissman. As a sample here are two haiku by Rengé/David Priebe:

> whatever language   carnival balloon
> random objects speak: the rain   rising up . . . and up . . . fading
>   speaks it fluently   into the darkness

The newsletter is 8 pgs., 8½ × 11, corner-stapled and punched for a three-ring notebook. They accept about 10% of submissions. Their press run is 325 for 200 subscribers of which 3 are libraries. Subscription: $18. **Sample postpaid: $1.50. Haiku may be submitted with up to 10/single page, 12 maximum. Submissions are "answered with proof sheets of acceptances, suggested revisions sheets, with occasional notes on originals—within 4-6 weeks." Publishes seasonal theme issues. Pays 1 copy with SASE, or free extra copy to subscribers.** Monthly Readers' Choice Awards: The Awards Kitty (average $50—contributions of postage stamps by the voters) is divided half for the 1st place winner; two runners-up share the other half. *HH* sponsors an annual contest (prizes $100, $75, $50) and publishes the results in a calendar book, *Timepieces: Haiku Week At-A-Glance*, which the selected contributors can purchase at half the market price. The contest is open to the public and accepts entries from April 1 through July 31. Write for details. *Timepieces: Haiku Week At-A-Glance 1994* received Honorable Mention in the Haiku Society of America Merit Book Awards.

HALF TONES TO JUBILEE (II), English Dept., Pensacola Junior College, 1000 College Blvd., Pensacola FL 32504, phone (904)484-1418, founded 1986, faculty editor Walter Spara, is an annual literary journal featuring poetry and short fiction. They have published poetry by R.T. Smith, Sue Walker, Larry Rubin and Simon Perchik. As a sample we selected these lines from "Penpal Who Has Not Written" by Andrea Hollander Budy:

> You are the one I've never met who
> wrote so splendidly when I needed you
> and I am the one who, after awhile, let

> *years grow like a row of taverns*
> *between receiving and giving*
> *back. . .*

HTTJ is 100 pgs., digest-sized, perfect-bound with matte card cover, professionally printed. They receive 1,000 submissions/year, use 50-60. Press run is 500. Subscription: $4. **Sample: $4. Submit 5 poems at a time. No previously published work or simultaneous submissions. SASE mandatory. Cover letter with bio and/or publication history preferred. Reads submissions August 1 through May 15 only. Reports in 2-3 months, faster when possible. Pays 2 copies. Acquires first rights.** *HTTJ* sponsors an annual poetry competition, $300 first prize, $200 second, $100 third. Entry fee: $2/poem. Send SASE for rules, deadlines. In addition to numerous awards from the Florida Press Association, *Half Tones to Jubilee* has received two national awards, a first place with merit from the American Scholastic Press Association, and first place, Southern division, literary magazine competition, Community College Humanities Association.

HAMMERS; DOUBLESTAR PRESS (II), 1718 Sherman, #203, Evanston IL 60201, founded 1989, editor Nat David. *Hammers*, "an end of millennium irregular poetry magazine," appears at least twice a year. Many of the poets they have published are from the Chicago area, although each issue also includes the work of poets from a variety of other geographical regions. **They want "honest, well-written poetry from the depths of the poet's universe and experience, which is cognizant of our interconnectedness."** They have recently published poetry by Duffy Childress, John Dickson, Lucy Anderton, Albert Huffstickler and T. Kilgore Splake. As a sample we selected these lines from "At the Grocery" by Hal J. Daniel III:

> *Ninety or so,*
> *confused about the one-way direction*
> *of the check out lane,*
> *she pushes her cart east*
> *rather than with the slow westward flow.*

Hammers is 88 pgs., 6⅞ × 8½, professionally printed and saddle-stapled with matte card cover. Single copy: $5; subscription: $15 for 4 issues. **Sample postpaid: $6. Submit 5-10 poems at a time. Editor seldom comments on submissions. Reports ASAP. Pays 1 copy.** In 1999, the editor intends to publish in book form *The Best of Hammers*.

HANDSHAKE EDITIONS (V); CASSETTE GAZETTE (II), Atelier A2, 83 rue de la Tombe Issoire, Paris, France 75014, phone 33-1-4327-1767, fax 33-1-4320-4195, founded 1979. *Cassette Gazette* is an audiocassette issued "from time to time. We are interested in **poetry dealing with love/romance, political/social issues and women/feminism themes."** Poets published include Ted Joans, Yianna Katsoulos, Judith Malina, Elaine Cohen, Amanda Hoover, Jayne Cortez, Roy Williamson and Mary Guggenheim. **Pays in copies. Handshake Editions does not accept unsolicited mss for book publication.** Jim Haynes, publisher, says, "I prefer to deal face to face."

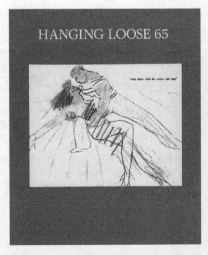

"I liked the movement and wit in the artwork," says Editor Robert Hershon, about this cover of Hanging Loose. *The art is from a series of working drawings originally created for an unrealized stage production of a ballad opera (San Francisco's Burning by Helen Adam) published by Hanging Loose Press. The Brooklyn, New York-based magazine appears three times a year and devotes 80 percent of its pages to poetry. It also features short fiction and concentrates on the work of new writers, including high school students. The cover art is by artist/translator/poet Norman MacAfee.*

HANGING LOOSE PRESS (V); HANGING LOOSE (I, II, IV-Teens/students), 231 Wyckoff St., Brooklyn NY 11217, founded 1966, poetry editors Robert Hershon, Dick Lourie, Mark Pawlak and Ron

Schreiber. **The press does not accept unsolicited book mss, but welcomes work for the magazine,** which appears 3 times/year. The magazine has published poetry by Paul Violi, Donna Brook, Kimiko Hahn, Ron Overton, Jack Anderson and Frances Phillips. *Hanging Loose* is 96 pgs., flat-spined, offset on heavy stock with a 2-color glossy card cover. One section contains **poems by high-school-age poets. The editor says it "concentrates on the work of new writers." Sample postpaid: $6.50. Submit 4-6 "excellent, energetic" poems. No simultaneous submissions. "Would-be contributors should read the magazine first." Reports in 1-12 weeks. Pays small fee and 3 copies.** Poetry published in *Hanging Loose* has been included in the 1993 and 1995 volumes of *The Best American Poetry*.

HARCOURT BRACE & COMPANY; HB CHILDREN'S BOOKS; GULLIVER BOOKS; BROWN-DEER PRESS; JANE YOLEN BOOKS (V, IV-Children), 525 B St., Suite 1900, San Diego CA 92101, phone (619)699-6810. HB Children's Books, Gulliver Books, Browndeer Press and Jane Yolen Books publish hardback and trade paperback books for children. They have published books of children's poetry by Jane Yolen, Arnold Adoff, James Dickey, e.e. cummings, Lee Bennett Hopkins and Carl Sandburg. **Unsolicited material is no longer accepted.**

HARD ROW TO HOE; MISTY HILL PRESS (I, IV-Nature/rural/ecology), P.O. Box 541-I, Healdsburg CA 95448, phone (707)433-9786. *Hard Row to Hoe,* taken over from Seven Buffaloes Press in 1987, editor Joe E. Armstrong, is a "book review newsletter of literature from rural America with a section reserved for short stories (about 2,000 words) and **poetry featuring unpublished authors. The subject matter must apply to rural America including nature and environmental subjects. Poems of 30 lines or less given preference, but no arbitrary limit. No style limits. Do not want any subject matter not related to rural subjects."** As a sample the editor selected "Foreclosure of Pride" by Ed Anderson:

> It's not an empty
> Pocket that makes
> A man die slowly
>
> It is hands
> Used to work
> That now only harvest
> A bitter crop
> Of time.

HRTH is 12 pgs., magazine-sized, side-stapled, appearing 3 times a year, 3 pgs. reserved for short stories and poetry. Press run is 300. Subscription: $7/year. **Sample postpaid: $2. Submit 3-4 poems at a time. No simultaneous submissions. Previously published poems OK only if published in local or university papers. Send SASE for guidelines. Editor comments on rejections "if I think the quality warrants." Pays 2 copies. Acquires one-time rights.** Reviews books of poetry in 600-700 words. Open to unsolicited reviews. Poets may also send books for review consideration. *Hard Row to Hoe* was selected by *Small Press Review* as one of the 10 best newsletters in the US.

HARP-STRINGS; EDNA ST. VINCENT MILLAY AWARD; ELIZABETH B. BROWNING SONNETS AWARD; ROBERT FROST BLANK VERSE AWARD (II), P.O. Box 640387, Beverly Hills FL 34464, founded 1989, editor Madelyn Eastlund, appears 3 times/year. **They want poems of "14-70 lines, narratives, lyrics, ballads, sestinas, rondeau, redouble, blank verse. Nothing 'dashed off,' trite, broken prose masquerading as poetry."** They have recently published poetry by Ralph Hammona, Robert Cooperman, Robin Shectman and Glenna Holloway. As a sample we selected these lines from "Standing on the South Rim of the Grand Canyon" by Lucille Morgan Wilson:

> The shuffle of my feet
> dislodges a pebble, sends it over the edge
> toward the turbulent river. From this distance
> I cannot tell if it breaks the water's surface,
> but I claim the instant of its descent.

Harp-Strings is 40 pgs., digest-sized, saddle-stapled, professionally printed on quality colored matte stock with matte card cover. She accepts 5-10% of poems received. Press run is 100 for 75 subscribers. Subscription: $12. **Sample postpaid: $5. Submit 3-5 poems at a time. Cover letters that provide information about poet or poem ("a few interesting lines to use in contributor's notes") welcome. Pays 1 copy. Acquires one-time rights. "I am interested in seeing poems that have won awards but have not been published."** Sponsors 3 contests each year: Elizabeth B. Browning Sonnets Award (Shakespearean or Petrarchan Sonnet, deadline March 15); Edna St. Vincent Millay Award (narrative from 36 to 80 lines, deadline July 15); Robert Frost Blank Verse Award (deadline November 15). Entry fee for each contest: $2/poem, $5/3 poems. Cash awards of $10-40 and publication. "Stanley Kunitz once said, 'Poetry today has become easier to write but harder to remember.' *Harp-Strings* wants poetry to remember, poetry that haunts, poetry the reader wants to read again and again."

THE HARTLAND POETRY QUARTERLY; HARTLAND PRESS (II, IV-Children, themes), Dept. PM, 168 Fremont, Romeo MI 48065, phone (313)752-5507, e-mail dtbock@aol.com, founded 1989, contact David Bock. **"Prefer 24 lines or less; no style restrictions; no pornography—none—nada—nil! Looking for serious poems by Viet Nam veterans and I mean serious—don't send the one-and-only angry poem—I got that stuff coming out of my ears. Very, very open to good children's poems written only by children under 15 for a special 'coming out' part of the magazine."** They have published poetry by Loriann Zimmer, T. Kilgore Splake and Laurence W. Thomas. Their quarterly is digest-sized, spine-stapled, 25-30 pgs. They accept about 15% of 300-500 poems received/year. Press run is 500 for 70 subscribers of which 15 are libraries, 300 shelf sales. Subscription: $8. **Sample postpaid: $1. Submit 3 poems at a time. Include bio with submission. Publishes theme issues occasionally. Reports in 8-10 weeks. Sometimes sends prepublication galleys. Pays 2 copies.** Reviews books of poetry. **They publish 2 chapbooks/year of poets already published in the quarterly. Pays 20 copies.** The editor says, "Write about what you have lived. Read, read, write, write—repeat cycle 'till death. Support as many small publications as you can afford."

THE HARVARD ADVOCATE (IV-Specialized: university affiliation), Dept. PM, 21 South St., Cambridge MA 02138, phone (617)495-0737, founded 1866, is a quarterly literary magazine, circulation 4,000, that publishes **poetry, fiction and art only by those affiliated with Harvard University; open to outside submissions of essays. Sample: $4. In submitting state your exact relationship to Harvard. Does not pay.** Reviews books, including poetry.

HAUNTS (IV-Science fiction/fantasy, horror), Nightshade Publications, P.O. Box 8068, Cranston RI 02926-0068, phone (401)781-9438, fax (401)943-0980, e-mail 76520.56@compuserve.com, is a "literary quarterly geared to those fans of the 'pulp' magazines of the 30s, 40s and 50s, with tales of **horror, the supernatural and the bizarre. We are trying to reach those in the 18-35 age-group."** They use free verse, light verse and traditional, about 12-16 poems a year. Circulation: 1,000. **Sample: $4.25 plus $1 postage. Send a maximum of 3 poems. Cover letter including "brief introduction of the writer and the work submitted" required. Send SASE for guidelines. Pays $3/poem.**

HAWAII PACIFIC REVIEW (II), 1060 Bishop St., Honolulu HI 96813, founded 1986, editor Elizabeth Fischel, is an annual literary journal "publishing quality poetry, short fiction and personal essays from writers worldwide. **Our journal seeks to promote a world view that celebrates a variety of cultural themes, beliefs, values and viewpoints. Although we do publish beginning poets on occasion, we do not publish amateurish poetry. We wish to further the growth of artistic vision and talent by encouraging sophisticated and innovative poetic and narrative techniques."** They have published poetry by Robert Cooperman and Mary Kay Rummel. As a sample the editor selected these lines from Rummel's "Stations of the Cross":

> *As I type through rivers of pulp*
> *The desktop meets me at the waist.*
> *I am the vertical shaft.*

> *We finish our crosses. A poor place*
> *to hang a life whether with yeasted strips*
> *of bread, cotton pieces or a plastic pen-*
> *to hang so long and miss the resurrection.*

HPR is 80-120 pgs., 6×9, professionally printed on quality paper, perfect-bound, with coated card cover; each issue features original artwork. Mostly free verse, poems here tend to be insightful, informative and well-made with an emphasis on cultural diversity. They receive 800-1,000 poems, accept 30-40. Press run is approximately 1,000 for 200 shelf sales. Single copy: $5-6. **Sample postpaid: $4. No previously published poems; simultaneous submissions OK. Cover letter with 5-line professional bio including prior publications required. Seldom comments on rejections. Send SASE for guidelines. Reports within 3 months. Pays 2 copies. Acquires first North American serial rights.** The editor says, "We'd like to receive more experimental verse. Many of the poems we receive are more personal therapy than true art. Good poetry is eye-opening; it investigates the unfamiliar or reveals the spectacular in the ordinary. Good poetry does more than simply express the poet's feelings; it provides both insight and unexpected beauty."

HAWAI'I REVIEW (I, II), % Dept. of English, University of Hawai'i, 1733 Donaghho Rd., Honolulu HI 96822, phone (808)956-3030, editor-in-chief Michelle Viray, poetry editors Sam Gonzalez and Ming Zhang. "We are interested in **all sorts of poetry, from free verse to formal lyricism, rhyme and meter; heroic narrative, haiku, light verse, satire and experimentation; we're also interested in poems translated from other languages; and while *Hawai'i Review* has published poets with established reputations like Eric Chock and W.S. Merwin, the beginner is also welcome."** They have published poetry by Lyn Lifshin, Lois-Ann Yamanaka and Tony Quagliano, and translations by

Carolyn Tipton and Alexis Levitin. As a sample the editors selected the poem "The Pearl" by Cai Qi-Jiao, translated by Edward Morin and Dennis Ding:

> The wound inside
> The oyster's tender body
> Expands into a hard, rough obstruction.
> Month by month, year after year,
> Wrapped in layer upon adhesive layer,
> It becomes mellow and smooth.
> Here you see crystaline grief and sea tears,
> Yet all humankind treasures it!
> I sense that it still wears the salt smell of the ocean,
> That its glistening teardrops bear
> The laments of sun, moon, stars, and clouds.

HR appears 3 times yearly and is 160 pgs., 6½ × 9½, flat-spined, professionally printed on heavy stock with b&w or color cover, 150 subscriptions of which 40 are libraries. Up to 1,800 are used by University of Hawai'i students. Subscription: $15/one year; $25/two years. **Sample: $5. Send SASE for guidelines. "Artwork to accompany poetry is welcomed." Editors rarely comment on rejections. Reports in 3-4 months.** Publication is 9-12 months thereafter. **Pays $10-60 plus 2 copies "to anyone with a Social Security number. Anyone without a Social Security number is paid in copies." Buys first North American serial rights.** Does not normally review books, but "authors can query" or send books for review consideration to Michelle Viray. The editorial staff rotates each year, so content varies. Sometimes one staff rejects work that has "come close" and suggests sending the same manuscript in the next year to see what the new editors think. The editors say, "Good poetry shows more than pseudo-literary erudition; it will, as Anthony Wallace says, *sing* and *mean*."

HAYDEN'S FERRY REVIEW (II), Box 871502, Arizona State University, Tempe AZ 85287-1502, phone (602)965-1243, founded 1986, managing editor Salima Keegan, is a handsome literary magazine appearing twice a year. They have published poetry by Dennis Schmitz, Maura Stanton, Ai, and David St. John. *HFR* is 6 × 9, 120 pgs., flat-spined with glossy card cover. Press run is 1,000 for 100 subscribers of which 30 are libraries, 500 shelf sales. They accept about 3% of 2,800 submissions annually. Subscription: $10. **Sample postpaid: $6. "No specifications other than limit in number (6) and no simultaneous submissions. We would like a brief bio for contributor's note included." Submissions circulated to two poetry editors. Editor comments on submissions "often." Send SASE for guidelines. Reports in 8-10 weeks of deadlines. Deadlines: February 28 for Spring/Summer issue; September 30 for Fall/Winter. Sends contributors galley proofs. Pays 2 copies.**

HEALING JOURNAL (III, IV-Specialized), 1050 Fulton Ave., Suite 150, Sacramento CA 95825, founded 1992, managing editor Marlene von Friederichs-Fitzwater, Ph.D., is an attractive quarterly magazine "about communication, providing a forum for healthcare professionals and patients to dialogue about the illness experience through art, poetry, interviews/profiles and personal essays." **They want "avant-garde, free verse or traditional poetry that is health related or 'healing' focused. Humor OK, but no limericks or puns."** As a sample the editor selected these lines from "After My Stroke" by Margaret Robison:

> My right side feels lonely for my left side.
> The two sides of my body
> are like husband and wife
> who stay together for the sake of the children.
> My left arm no longer listens
> to my brain. It has gone to sleep . . .

HJ is 36 pgs., 8½ × 11, professionally printed on matte-coated recycled paper and saddle-stapled with color cover, art and b&w photos. They publish 10-20 poems/year. Press run is 7,500. Single copy: $3; subscription: $30/year. **Submit no more than 5 poems at a time. Previously published poems OK; no simultaneous submissions.** Time between acceptance and publication is 4 months to 1 year. **Reports in 1 month. Pays 10 copies. Acquires one-time rights.**

‡THE HEARTLANDS TODAY (II, IV-Regional, themes), Firelands College, 901 Rye Beach Rd., Huron OH 44839, phone (419)433-5560, fax (419)433-9696, founded 1990, editors Deb Benko and David Shevin. *The Heartlands Today* is an annual publication of the Firelands Writing Center at Firelands College. They want work **by Midwestern writers about the Midwest Heartlands, "writing and photography that is set in the Midwest today and deals revealingly and creatively with the issues we face, good writing and art that documents our lives." Each issue has a specific theme.** They have recently published poetry by Alberta Turner, David Baker, Chris Llewellyn and James Bertolino. The editors describe it as 160 pgs., 6 × 9, perfect-bound with 30-40 b&w photos. They accept 10-20% of the poetry received. Press run is 850-900. Single copy: $8.50. **Sample postpaid: $5. Submit up to 5 poems at a time. Simultaneous submissions OK. Cover letter with brief bio required.**

Reads submissions January 1 to July 1 only. Often comments on rejections. Send SASE for guidelines and upcoming themes. Reports in 2 months once reading period begins. Pays $10 and 2 copies. Buys first or second rights. They also sponsor an annual chapbook contest. Send up to 10 poems ("a unified whole") with a $10 reading fee, which includes a critique and a copy of the magazine. Winner receives $100 and publication in *The Heartlands Today*.

HEAVEN BONE MAGAZINE; HEAVEN BONE PRESS; HEAVEN BONE PRESS INTERNATIONAL CHAPBOOK COMPETITION (II, IV-Spiritual, nature/rural/ecology), P.O. Box 486, Chester NY 10918, phone (914)469-9018, e-mail 71340.520@compuserve.com, founded 1986, poetry editor Steve Hirsch, publishes poetry, fiction, essays and reviews with **"an emphasis on spiritual, metaphysical, esoteric and ecological concerns."** They have recently published poetry and fiction by Charles Bukowski, Marge Piercy, Kirpal Gordon, Diane di Prima and Michael McClure. As a sample the editor chose "Five-Petaled Regular Corolla Rose" by Edward Mycue:

> *has surrounding fingers that play*
> *with your nose from the inner en-*
> *velope. This is not the Rose of*
> *Sharon. That spindling hollyhock*
> *is as near to a rose as a hemlock.*
> *The rosary has five sacred mysteries*
> *and five decades of Ave Marias, &*
> *each begins with a paternoster, ends*
> *with a Gloria, repeated in formula*
> *like a prayer or/and magic-mystic*
> *charm: more of a path than pastime.*
> *Rose, you single step, pilgrimage,*
> *you Rose, of colored hope, chafe.*
> *You are window, compass, pleasantly*
> *rote: I know you now, know you not.*

Heaven Bone is 96 pgs., magazine-sized, saddle-stapled, using b&w art, photos and ads, on recycled bond stock with glossy 4-color recycled card cover. Of 250-350 poems received they accept 18-30. They have a press run of 2,500. Subscription: $16.95. **Sample postpaid: $6. Submit 3-10 poems at a time. "I will not read submissions without SASEs." Simultaneous submissions and previously published poems OK "if notified." Occasionally publishes theme issues. Send SASE for upcoming themes. Reports in 2 weeks to 6 months, up to 8 months until publication. Sometimes sends prepublication galleys. Pays 2 copies. Acquires first North American serial rights.** Reviews books of poetry. Open to unsolicited reviews. Poets may also send books for review consideration. The press sponsors the annual Heaven Bone Press International Chapbook Competition which awards $100 plus publication to an original, unpublished poetry ms of 30 pgs. or less. Requires $10 reading fee. Send SASE for guidelines. Editor advises, "Please be familiar with the magazine before sending mss. We receive too much religious verse. Break free of common 'poetic' limitations and speak freely with no contrivances. No forced end-line rhyming please. Channel the muse and music without being an obstacle to the poem."

HELICON NINE EDITIONS (V); MARIANNE MOORE POETRY PRIZE (II), P.O. Box 22412, Kansas City MO 64113, phone (913)722-2999, founded 1977, editor Gloria Vando Hickok. Helicon Nine, formerly a literary magazine, is a publisher of books of poetry as well as fiction, creative nonfiction and anthologies. **"Our one requirement is excellence; nothing pedestrian."** They have published poetry by Joyce Carol Oates, Grace Paley, Ellen Gilchrist and James Dickey. As a sample the editor selected these lines from "The instruction of Clotilde" by Regina deCormier from her book, *Hoofbeats on the Door*:

> *Dragging his reluctant shadow, Francois*
> *leaves the stone paved courtyard of his house*
> *at dawn. His cloak lifts with the wind*
> *of his step, the long toes of his shoes*
> *curl, and point to Heaven. Light is*
> *just beginning to spool off the face*
> *of Our Lady of Paris and a bronze cock*
>
> *is crowing goodbye. Evening will find him*
> *fifteen kilometres southeast of Paris,*
> *a blue rug over his knees.*

"Payment varies, but we're in the publishing business to *help* poets and authors, not to hinder them or take advantage. We publish *beautiful* books and try to get them into the hands of readers. We have national distributors making sure our books are made available throughout the States. We also aggressively pursue new markets and book reviews and advertise in many trade publications as well as exhibit at the ABA, etc." **They are currently not accepting poetry submissions, other than annual contest entries.** The Marianne Moore Poetry Prize, $1,000 for an unpublished poetry ms of at least 50 pgs., is awarded each year and includes publication by Helicon Nine Editions. Send SASE for guidelines.

HELIKON PRESS (V), 120 W. 71st St., New York NY 10023, founded 1972, poetry editors Robin Prising and William Leo Coakley, **"tries to publish the best contemporary poetry in the tradition of English verse."** As a sample the editors selected these lines from *Selected Poems & Ballads* by Helen Adam:

> *Towers of atoms fall and rise*
> *Where gigantic Adam lies.*

"We read (and listen to) poetry and ask poets to build a collection around particular poems. We print fine editions illustrated by good artists. Unfortunately we cannot encourage submissions."

HELLAS: A JOURNAL OF POETRY AND THE HUMANITIES; THE HELLAS AWARD; THE AL-DINE PRESS, LTD.; THE NEW CLASSICISTS (II, IV-Form), 304 S. Tyson Ave., Glenside PA 19038, phone (215)884-1086, fax (215)884-3304, founded 1988, editor Gerald Harnett. *Hellas* is a semiannual published by Aldine Press that wants poetry of **"any kind but especially poems in meter. We prize elegance and formality in verse, but specifically encourage poetry of the utmost boldness and innovation, so long as it is not willfully obscurantist; no ignorant, illiterate, meaningless free verse or political poems."** They have published poetry by Hadas, Steele, Moore, Butler, Kessler, Gioia and many others. As a sample we selected these lines from "Seed" by Charley Custer:

> *Within the hard damp dark, marooned*
> *in rot between dead root and weed*
> *through every bitter winter wound*
> *and solstice, is the seed.*

Hellas is 172 pgs., 6×9, flat-spined, offset, using b&w art. Press run is 1,000. Subscription: $14. **Sample postpaid: $8.75. Submit 3-5 poems at a time. They will not consider simultaneous submissions or previously published poems. Editor comments on rejections "happily if requested. If I don't understand it, I don't print it. On the other hand, we don't want obvious, easy, clichéd or sentimental verse." Send SASE for guidelines. Reports in 3-4 months. Pays 1 copy. Acquires first North American serial rights.** The *Hellas* Award ($200) is open to *Hellas* subscribers only and is awarded annually to the finest poem entered in the contest. Poems may be submitted to both *Hellas* and the contest simultaneously at any time throughout the year, but the annual deadline is December 31. Winner is published in spring issue of *Hellas*. Enclose SASE if submission is to be returned. The New Classicists is a Society of friends of the Aldine Press that publishes a quarterly newsletter for members. In addition to *Hellas*, the press publishes Lyrica, an ongoing series of metrical poetry chapbooks, in conjunction with sponsoring The Lycidas Award offered to the best chapbook of that series. They also plan to publish The New Classicists, "the only permanent and ongoing series for new books of metrical poetry." In addition, they sponsor the *Hellas* readings, held at various locations in Philadelphia, New York and elsewhere. Send SASE for guidelines. Their flyer says, *"Hellas* is a lively and provocative assault on a century of modernist barbarism in the arts. A unique, Miltonic wedding of *paideia* and *poiesis*, engaging scholarship and original poetry, *Hellas* has become the forum of a remarkable new generation of poets, critics and theorists committed to the renovation of the art of our time . . . **Meter is especially welcome, as well as rhymed and stanzaic verse. We judge a poem by its verbal artifice and its truth. Lines should not end arbitrarily, diction should be precise: We suggest that such principles can appear 'limiting' only to an impoverished imagination. To the contrary: We encourage any conceivable boldness and innovation, so long as it is executed with discipline and is not a masquerade for self-indulgent obscurantism. . . . We do not print poems about Nicaragua, whales or an author's body parts. We do specifically welcome submissions from newer authors."**

HEN'S TEETH (V), P.O. Box 689, Brookings SD 57006, founded 1988, editor Janice H. Mikesell, expects to publish a book every 2 years but **will not be open for submissions. "I publish material that I have written or co-edited only. Unsolicited material, unless accompanied by a SASE, will not be returned."** She has published *Women Houses & Homes: an anthology of prose, poetry and photography,* $8 postage paid, a 52-page, saddle-stapled book, cut with a roof-line top, professionally printed with a cover photograph of a "painted lady" Victorian house and now in its fifth printing. As a sample the editor selected these lines from her second book, *A Survivor's Manual: a book of poems*:

> *I ask you this*
> *remember me*
> *I used to be your wife*
>
> *be sure that I'll remember you*
> *as the man who*
> *stole my life*

That book is a 52-page, perfect-bound paperback with an arresting cover photo (also $8 postage paid), now in its second printing.

HERSPECTIVES MAGAZINE (I, IV-Women, feminism), Box 2047, Squamish, British Columbia V0N 3G0 Canada, phone (604)892-5723, founded 1989, editor Mary Billy, uses **"poetry that expresses women's lives in a positive experiential way—open to almost anything by, for or about women. Nothing obscure. Short poems have a better chance. Will accept almost anything with intelligent humor."** As a sample the editor selected these lines by Gert Beadle:

> *When they have closed*
> *The windows where I fled*
> *And gave the empty house*
> *to fire*
> *Will they remember how*
> *I loved a mystery*

Herspectives appears quarterly in a 40- to 50-page stapled format. Uses 4-6 poems/issue. Press run is 250 for 125 subscribers of which 2 are libraries. Subscription: $22-35 ($35-45 US); $40-50 for businesses and organizations. **Sample postpaid: $6. "No checks from outside Canada; send cash or money order in Canadian funds, please." Simultaneous submissions and previously published poetry OK. Cover letter required. Publishes theme issues. Editor often comments on rejections. Pays 1 copy.** Reviews books of poetry in 500-750 words. Open to unsolicited reviews. Poets may also send books for review consideration. They also use short, short fiction and other writing. **"We are mainly interested in giving new writers exposure. I don't like poetry that is so obscure only the mentally defective can understand it. We are about openness and ideas, about women's creative expression, wherever that may lead them.** The name says it all: HER-spectives. We don't print material by men although they are welcome as subscribers."

HIGH PLAINS LITERARY REVIEW (III), 180 Adams St., Suite 250, Denver CO 80206, phone (303)320-6828, founded 1986, editor Robert O. Greer, associate poetry editor Ray Gonzalez, appears 3 times/year using **"high quality poetry, fiction, essays, book reviews and interviews."** The format is 135 pgs., 70 lb. paper, heavy cover stock. Subscription: $20. **Sample postpaid: $4. Pays $10/published page for poetry.**

HIGH PLAINS PRESS (IV-Regional), P.O. Box 123, Glendo WY 82213, phone (307)735-4370, founded 1985, poetry editor Nancy Curtis, considers books of **poetry "specifically relating to Wyoming and the West, particularly poetry based on historical people/events. We're mainly a publisher of historical nonfiction, but do publish one book of poetry every year."** They have published poetry by Peggy Simson Curry, Robert Roripaugh and Mary Alice Gunderson. As a sample she quoted these lines from the book *No Roof But Sky* by Jane Candia Coleman. The poem is "Geronimo photographed at Ft. Sill (1905)":

> *Bring me the elusive images*
> *of my life, and I will smile for you—*
> *over and over—an exchange of illusions*
> *like the dying change into light.*

Query first with 3 sample poems (from a 50-poem ms). Reports in 2 months, publication in 18-24 months. Always sends prepublication galleys. Pays 10% of sales. Buys first rights. Catalog available on request; sample books: $5. *No Roof But Sky* won the Wrangler Award for "accuracy and literary merit in portraying the West" in the poetry category from the National Cowboy Hall of Fame.

HIGH/COO PRESS; MAYFLY (IV-Form), 4634 Hale Dr., Decatur IL 62526, phone (217)877-2966, founded 1976, editors Randy and Shirley Brooks. High/Coo is a small press publishing nothing but **haiku in English.** "We publish haiku poemcards, minichapbooks, anthologies and a bibliography of haiku publications in addition to paperbacks and cloth editions and the magazine *Mayfly*, evoking emotions from contemporary experience. We are not interested in orientalism nor Japanese imitations." They previously published the *Midwest Haiku Anthology* which included the work of 54 haiku poets. **They publish no poetry except haiku.** They have published haiku by Virgil Hutton, Lee Gurga and Wally Swist. As a sample the editors selected this haiku by Bill Pauly:

> *country field—*
> *home run rolling*
> *past the headstones*

Mayfly is 16 pgs., 3 × 5, professionally printed on high-quality stock, saddle-stapled, one haiku/page. It appears in January and August. They publish 32 of an estimated 1,800 submissions. Subscription: $8. **Sample postpaid: $4. A Macintosh computer disk of haiku-related stacks is available for $10 postpaid. Submit no more than 5 haiku/issue. No simultaneous submissions or previously published poems. Send SASE for guidelines. Pays $5/poem; no copies.** High/Coo Press **considers mss "by invitation only."** Randy Brooks says, "Publishing poetry is a joyous work of love. We publish to share those moments of insight contained in evocative haiku. We aren't in it for fame, gain or name. We publish to serve an enthusiastic readership. **Please note that we have changed our policy of requiring contributors to be subscribers, so submissions are open from all writers."**

HIGHLIGHTS FOR CHILDREN (IV-Children), 803 Church St., Honesdale PA 18431, phone (717)253-1080, founded 1946, appears every month using **poetry for children ages 2-12. They want "meaningful and/or fun poems accessible to children of all ages. Welcome light, humorous verse. Rarely publish a poem longer than 16 lines, most are shorter. No poetry that is unintelligible to children, poems containing sex, violence or unmitigated pessimism."** They have published poetry by Nikki Giovanni, Aileen Fisher, John Ciardi, A.A. Milne, Myra Cohn Livingston and Langston Hughes. As a sample they selected these lines from "September" by Beverly McLoughland:

> When maple leaves
> Sport gold and green,
> You're in September
> Smack in between
> The summer's hot
> And the autumn's cool
> With a jump from the high-dive
> Back to school.

It is generally 42 pgs., magazine-sized, full-color throughout. They purchase 6-10 of 300 submissions/ year. Press run is 3.3 million for approximately 2.8 million subscribers. Subscription: $21.95 (one year; reduced rates for multiple years). **Submit typed ms with very brief cover letter. Please indicate if simultaneous submission. Editor comments on submissions "occasionally, if ms has merit or author seems to have potential for our market." Reports "generally within 1 month." Always sends prepublication galleys. Payment: "money varies" plus 2 copies. Buys all rights.** The editor says, "We are always open to submissions of poetry not previously published. However, we purchase a very limited amount of such material. We may use the verse as 'filler,' or illustrate the verse with a full-page piece of art. Please note that we do not buy material from anyone under 16 years old."

HILLTOP PRESS (V, IV-Science fiction), 4 Nowell Place, Almondbury, Huddersfield, West Yorkshire HD5 8PB England, founded 1966, editor Steve Sneyd, publishes **"mainly science fiction poetry nowadays," but does not accept unsolicited mss. Query with proposals for relevant projects.** Publications include *War of the Words*, humorous science fiction verse from the 30s to the 70s, including John Brunner, A. Vincent Clarke and C.S. Yond (John Christopher); and *The Fantastic Muse*, reprinting a 1938 article and 1939 poem by science fiction giant Arthur C. Clarke. As a sample the editor selected these lines from "AE—The Seven Wonders of the Universe," by Mike Johnson:

> between Zero and Eternity hearing a symphony within
> a new and subtle symphony and his knowledge gave itself
> back into the layers of space around him where he was
> an instrument and the never-never orchestra burned in
> star-harmony in which his gifts were stored.

The ongoing Data Dump series, up to #10 at the end of 1994, gives bibliographical information on science fiction poetry collections and anthologies. 4 pgs. A5 each. All but the latest issues are out of print, but photostat reprints can be supplied—#1-9 for $7.50 postpaid; #10 for $1.50 postpaid. (Checks payable to S. Sneyd. US orders: will also accept $ bills or small denomination, unused US stamps). "My advice for beginning poets is (a) persist—don't let any one editor discourage you. 'In poetry's house are many mansions,' what one publication hates another may love; (b) be prepared for the possibility of long delays between acceptance and appearance of work—the small press is mostly self-financed and part time, so don't expect it to be more efficient than commercial publishers; (c) *always* keep a copy of everything you send out, and put your name and address on *everything* you send."

HIPPOPOTAMUS PRESS (IV-Form); OUTPOSTS POETRY QUARTERLY; OUTPOSTS ANNUAL POETRY COMPETITION (II), 22 Whitewell Rd., Frome, Somerset BA11 4EL England, *Outposts* founded 1943, Hippopotamus Press founded 1974, poetry editor Roland John, who explains, "*Outposts* is a general poetry magazine that welcomes all work either from the recognized or the unknown poet. The Hippopotamus Press is specialized, with an affinity with Modernism. No Typewriter, Concrete, Surrealism. The press publishes 6 full collections per year." They have published in *OPQ* poetry by John Heath-Stubbs, Peter Dale and Elizabeth Jennings. *Outposts* is 70-100 pgs., digest-sized, flat-spined, litho, in professionally set small type, using ads. Of 60,000 poems received he uses about

---

Market categories: (I) Beginning; (II) General; (III) Limited; (IV) Specialized; (V) Closed.

300. Press run is 3,000 for 2,800 subscribers of which 10% are libraries, 2% of circulation through shelf sales. Subscription: $32. **Sample postpaid: $8. Submit 5 poems at a time. "IRCs must accompany US submissions." Simultaneous submissions and previously published poems OK. Cover letter required. Reports in 2 weeks plus post time. Sometimes sends prepublication galleys. Pays $8/ poem plus 1 copy. Copyright remains with author.** Staff reviews books of poetry in 200 words for "Books Received" page. Also uses full essays up to 4,000 words. Send books for review consideration, attn. M. Pargitter. The magazine also holds an annual poetry competition. Hippopotamus Press publishes 6 books a year, averaging 80 pgs. **For book publication query with sample poems. Simultaneous submissions and previously published poems OK. Reports in 6 weeks. Pays 10% royalties plus 20 paper copies, 6 cloth. Send for book catalog to buy samples.**

HIRAM POETRY REVIEW (I, II), P.O. Box 162, Hiram OH 44234, founded 1967, poetry editors Hale Chatfield and Carol Donley, is a semiannual with occasional special supplements. **"We favor new talent—and except for one issue in two years, read** *only* **unsolicited mss."** They are interested in **"all kinds of high quality poetry"** and have published poetry by Grace Butcher, David Citino, Michael Finley, Peter Wild, Jim Daniels, Peter Klappert and Harold Witt. As a sample they offer these lines from "Three Musics" by William Johnson:

> *Grief has a sound*
> *the way snow ticks*
> *and falls away*
> *from the metal light pole*

There are 30 pgs. of poetry in the professionally printed, digest-sized, saddle-stapled magazine (glossy cover with b&w photo). It has a circulation of 400, 300 subscriptions of which 150 are libraries. They receive about 7,500 submissions/year, use 50, have up to a 6-month backlog. Although most poems appearing here tend to be lyric and narrative free verse under 50 lines, exceptions occur (a few longer, sequence or formal works can be found in each issue). Single copy: $4; subscription: $8. **Sample: free! No simultaneous submissions. "Send 4-5 fresh, neat copies of your best poems." Reports in 2-6 months. Pays 2 copies plus year's subscription. Acquires first North American serial rights; returns rights upon publication.** Reviews books of poetry in single or multi-book format, no set length. Send books for review consideration.

HOB-NOB (I), 994 Nissley Rd., Lancaster PA 17601, phone (717)898-7807, founded 1969, poetry editor Mildred K. Henderson, is a small literary quarterly with certain "family" emphasis. About ¼ poetry, ¾ prose. **They publish "poetry preferably up to 16-line limit, light or humorous verse, serious poetry on vital current themes, people, nature, animals, etc. Religious poetry is also acceptable. No erotica, horror, suicide, excess violence, murder, overly depressing themes, especially utter hopelessness."** They have published poetry by Effie Mihopoulos, C. David Hay and Patrick J. Cauchi. As a sample Mildred Henderson selected these lines from "The Fence Post" by Cathryn Hoellworth:

> *Wrinkled and leaning,*
> *rails gone,*
> *still it stands*
> *Proud settler*
> *staking a claim*
> *to fertile dreams.*

Hob-Nob is 56 pgs., magazine-sized, saddle-stapled, offset, on 20 lb. bond and heavier cover, computer generated fonts. It offers free ads to subscribers and exchange publications. About 12 new poets are featured in each issue. Press run is 500. Subscription: $8/4 issues. **Sample postpaid: $3. Send SASE for guidelines. Pays 1 copy for first appearance only. After that you have to subscribe to be accepted. She accepts submissions from new contributors only in January and February of each year. Material received at other times will be returned unread. She prefers not to have simultaneous submissions. The editor comments on rejections "especially if I can think of a way a rejected item can be salvaged or made suitable to submit elsewhere." Reports in 2 months. Acquires first rights only.** The Readers Choice contest, every issue, pays $5 for first prize, lesser amount for other place (unless special prizes are offered by readers). Awards are on the basis of votes sent in by readers. The editor advises, "Poets and would-be poets should read contemporary poetry to see what others are doing. Most of what I receive does not seem to be rhymed and metered anymore, and unless a poet is extremely skilled with rhyme and meter (few are), he will find free verse much easier to deal with. I told one poet recently that the content is vital. Say something new, or if it's not new, say it in a new way. Nobody wants to see the same old 'June-moon-spoon' stuff. Patterns can be interesting, even without formal rhyme and meter. Take an unusual viewpoint. Notice the imagery in the poem quoted above, for an example. Let your imagination soar!"

‡HOBO STEW REVIEW (I, II), 1403 Stearns Hill Rd., Waltham MA 02154-3333, founded 1984, is a quarterly **seeking poetry that is "honest, evoking emotions—from multi-stanzas to single lines. No**

hateful or self-centered poetry. No limericks." *HSR* is 14 pgs., 8½×11, computer typeset and photocopied, side-stapled with 60 lb. card stock cover. They receive 100-200 poems/year, accept 30-40. Press run is 45, most distributed free to coffee shops, universities and clubs. Subscription: $5-10 sliding scale; "you pay what you can afford." **Submit 5-8 poems at a time. No previously published poems or simultaneous submissions. Always comments on rejections. Send SASE for guidelines. Reports in 2-4 weeks or more. Pays 1 copy.** Reviews books of poetry in up to 1,000 words. Open to unsolicited reviews. Poets may also send books for review consideration. "Hobo is terribly lazy. He is shocked at the backlog of manuscripts covering his desk. He does intend to read each one and return them all eventually. And he says, 'Keep it all honest, provoking and fun! Try reading out loud—alone and at public readings—to find your voice.' "

HOLIDAY HOUSE, INC. (V, IV-Children), Dept. PM, 425 Madison Ave., New York NY 10017, phone (212)688-0085, founded 1936, editor-in-chief Margery Cuyler, is a trade children's book house. They have published hardcover books for children by Myra Cohn Livingston. They publish 3 books a year averaging 32 pages. **However, they are currently not accepting poetry submissions.**

THE HOLLINS CRITIC (II), P.O. Box 9538, Hollins College, Roanoke VA 24020-1538, phone (703)362-6317, founded 1964, editor John Rees Moore, appears 5 times yearly, publishing critical essays, poetry and book reviews. **They use a few short poems in each issue, interesting in form, content or both.** They have recently published poetry by Peggy H. Lewis, Robert S. King, Charles E. Mann, Peggy A. Tartt and Robert Aaron Lobe. As a sample the editor selected these lines from "Cloud Nine" by Matthew J. Spireng:

> Know that I rose early one morning
> to count as they came over the horizon,
> big fluffy clouds soaring one by one
> like a fleet of hot air balloons, and
> when the ninth one slipped into view,
> I searched its edges for signs someone
> was there, riding cloud nine, happy
> as an angel, but saw nothing to distinguish
> cloud nine from cloud one or one hundred,
> and decided then, at a relatively tender
> age, any cloud would do to ride on.

The Hollins Critic is 20 pgs., magazine-sized. Circulation 500. **Sample: $1.50. Submit up to 5 poems, none over 35 lines, must be typewritten. Cover letter preferred. Reports in 6 weeks (slower in the summer). Pays $25/poem plus 5 copies.** Open to unsolicited reviews. Poets may also send books for review consideration. Traditionally, verse here has been open as to form and style with poems that please the mind, eye and senses. As the magazine is occasionally overstocked, your best bet is to send for a sample copy and inquire as to whether editors are reading unsolicited submissions.

HENRY HOLT & COMPANY (V), 115 W. 18th St., New York NY 10011, **accepts no unsolicited poetry.**

HOME PLANET NEWS (II), Dept. PM, P.O. Box 415, Stuyvesant Station, New York NY 10009, phone (718)769-2854, founded 1979, editors Enid Dame and Donald Lev, is a tabloid (newsprint) journal, appearing 3-4 times a year presenting a "lively, eclectic and comprehensive view of contemporary literature." **They want "honest, well-crafted poems, open or closed form, on any subject, but we will not publish any work which seems to us to be racist, sexist, ageist, anti-semitic or has undue emphasis on violence. Poems under 30 lines stand a better chance. We lean somewhat toward poetry with urban sensibility but are not rigid about this. Do not sacrifice craft for message."** They have published poetry by Alicia Ostriker, Tuli Kupferberg, Denise Duhamel, Will Inman, Andrew Glaze, Robert Peters, Carl Solomon and Rose Romano. As a sample the editors selected these lines from "Entered Collage" by Lorraine Schein:

> I am the ephemerist
> collecting myself, I disperse my thoughts.
> The wind blows this paper
> Out of my hand

They use approximately 13 full 11 × 16 pgs. of poetry in each 24-page issue. Circulation 1,000 with 400 subscribers of which 8 are libraries. Of 1,200 submissions/year, they use about 50-60. Publication could take one year from acceptance. Subscription: $8/year. **Sample postpaid: $3. Submit 3-5 poems, typed double-spaced, with SASE. No previously published poems or simultaneous submissions. Cover letter welcome. "We now only read poetry manuscripts between February 1 and May 31." Reports within 4 months. Pays 3 copies and year's subscription. All rights revert to author.** Reviews books of poetry. Open to unsolicited reviews. Poets may also send books for review consideration. "We cosponsor 'Day of the Poet,' a poetry festival and contest which takes place each October in

Ulster County, New York." Poetry by Daniel Berrigan published in *Home Planet News* appeared in the *Pushcart Prize* anthology.

HOPSCOTCH: THE MAGAZINE FOR GIRLS; BOYS' QUEST (IV-Children), P.O. Box 164, Bluffton OH 45817-0164, phone (419)358-4610, founded 1989, editor Marilyn B. Edwards. *Hopscotch* is a bimonthly magazine for **girls 6-12. "No length restrictions. In need of short traditional poems for various holidays and seasons. However, we do not want Halloween-related material. Nothing abstract, experimental."** They have published poetry by Lois Grambling, Judy Nichols, Leila Dornak, Judith Harkham Semas and Maggie McGee. As a sample we selected these lines from "First Frost" by Glenn DeTurk:

> *The sugary white glaze*
> *Glistens in the morning sun.*
> *The whole world seems to be waiting,*
> *For a new season has begun.*

The editor describes *Hopscotch* as "full-color cover, 50 pgs. of 2-color inside, 7×9, saddle-stapled." They use about 30-35 of some 2,000 poems received/year. Press run is 9,000 for 8,200 subscribers of which 7,000 are libraries, 200 to inquiring schools and libraries. Subscription: $15. **Sample postpaid: $3. Submit 3-6 poems/submission. Cover letter preferred; include experience and where published. Publishes theme issues. Send SASE for upcoming themes. Theme for December 1995/ January 1996 issue: Ballet, for February/March: Bears, for April/May: Pets, for June/July: Brothers, and for August/September: Inventions. Reports in 2-4 weeks. Pays $10-40. Buys first American serial rights.** The few poems in this children's magazine occasionally address the audience, challenging young girls to pursue their dreams. To see how, order a sample copy (or check one out at the library) because it is too easy for poets who write children's verse to forget that each magazine targets a specific audience . . . in a specific way. *Hopscotch* received the Parents Choice Gold Medal Award for 1992 and an EDPress Award for "Best in Educational Publishing for One Theme Issue," in June 1993 and 1994. They also publish *Boys' Quest*, a bimonthly magazine for **boys 6-13.** Similar in format to *Hopscotch*, the magazine premiered in June/July 1995. **Upcoming themes include: Cartoonists (October/November 1995), Winter (December 1995/January 1996), Money (February/March), Zoo Animals (April/May), and the Circus (June/July). Send SASE for details.**

HOUGHTON MIFFLIN CO. (V), 222 Berkeley St., Boston MA 02116, founded 1850, poetry editor Peter Davison. Houghton Mifflin is a high-prestige trade publisher that puts out both hardcover and paperback books, but **poetry submission is by invitation only and they are not seeking new poets at present.** They have issued poetry books by Donald Hall, May Swenson, Rodney Jones, Geoffrey Hill, Galway Kinnell, Thomas Lux, Erica Funkhouser, William Matthews, Margaret Atwood and Andrew Hudgins. **Always sends prepublication galleys. Authors are paid 10% royalties on hardcover books, 6% royalties on paperbacks (minimum), $1,000 advance and 12 author's copies.**

HOUSEWIFE-WRITER'S FORUM (IV-Women, humor), P.O. Box 780, Lyman WY 82937, phone (307)782-7003, founded 1988, editor/publisher Emma Bluemel, is a magazine of "prose, poetry, information and open forum communication for and by housewives or any woman or man who writes while juggling a busy schedule. **We have no specifications as to form, subject, style or purpose. Length maximum 30 lines. We publish both serious poetry and humorous. Nothing pornographic, but erudite expression is fine."** As a sample she selected these lines from "Off Limits" by Katherine H. Brooks:

> *I used to save a lot of stuff.*
> *Till Mother hollered "That's enough!"*
> *And made me have, all day, a fear*
> *That something nice would disappear.*
> *I hurried home from school, to see*
> *What damage had been done to me,*
> *And when I went to find the rocks*
> *I'd hidden underneath my socks,*
> *I saw it—almost in a flash—*
> *That all my things were in the trash.*

Emma Bluemel describes the magazine as "a small market for women who aspire to write for larger women's markets or support each other in the quest for finding time and energy to write." It is 48 pgs., desktop-published, using some art, graphics and ads, appearing bimonthly. Press run is 2,000. **Sample postpaid: $3. "Simultaneous submissions are OK." Send SASE for guidelines. Reports in 2 months. Pays 1 copy plus $1-2/poem. Buys first-time rights.** She holds an annual contest with $4/ poem fee, June 1 deadline. *Housewife-Writer's Forum* received a 1st place award for magazine editing from Wyoming Media Professionals. The editor adds, "I like to see poems that have a strong central purpose and use the language to express it beautifully, powerfully. I also like to see poems that make me laugh."

HOWLING DOG (II), 2913 Woodcock Court, Rochester MI 48306, founded 1985, poetry editor Wipee Zippie, is a literary journal of "letters, words and lines." **The editor likes "found poetry, graphically interesting pieces, humorous work, avant-garde, experimental, fun and crazy. All forms. All subjects, but we tend to have a light satirical attitude towards sex and politics."** He has published poetry by Keith Wilson, John Sinclair, Laurel Speer, Larry Goodell and M.L. Liebler. As a sample the editor selected these lines by Edwin Romond:

> *I knew I was in trouble*
> *when the census taker told me*
> *ours was the first house on the block*
> *without a moosehead in the living room.*

Howling Dog appears 2 times a year. It is 64 pgs., digest-sized, flat-spined, offset. They receive some 4,000 submissions/year, use maybe 150. Press run is 500 for 100 subscribers of which 3 are libraries. Subscription: $20/4 issues. **Sample postpaid: $4. Submit 3-4 poems at a time with name and address on each page. Use regular #10 business-size envelopes. "We don't use much rhyme or poems under 10 lines." Previously published poems and simultaneous submissions OK "but let us know." Send SASE for guidelines. Reports in 6-12 months, "longer if we like it." Pays with copies and discount. Acquires first or one-time rights.** Reviews books of poetry in 200 words, single format. Open to unsolicited reviews. Poets may also send books for review consideration. **They are not presently considering book mss.** Wipee says, "We produce an effect similar to the howl of a dog with its foot caught in the fence. Something that may not be pleasant or permanent, yet still heard by everyone in the neighborhood. We are very full and very slow to respond."

HQ: THE HAIKU QUARTERLY; THE DAY DREAM PRESS (II), 39 Exmouth St., Kingshill, Swindon, Wiltshire SN1 3PU England, phone 0793-523927, founded 1990, editor Kevin Bailey, is "a platform from which new and established poets can speak and/or experiment with new forms and ideas." They want **"any poetry of good quality."** They have published poetry by Peter Redgrove, Alan Brownjohn, James Kirkup and Cid Corman. As a sample the editor selected these lines from "Copenhagen" by Tom Lowenstein:

> *It was winter in Europe.*
> *I thump up the pillows and*
> *lay Rilke on the bedside table.*
> *The snow drifts at random*
> *through the aspen branches.*

The editor says *HQ* is 48-64 pgs., A5, perfect-bound with art, ads and reviews. They accept approximately 5% of poetry received. Press run is 500-600 for 500 subscribers of which 30 are libraries. Subscription: £8. **Sample postpaid: £2.40. No previously published poems or simultaneous submissions. Cover letter and SASE (or SAE and IRCs) required.** Time between acceptance and publication is 3-6 months. **Often comments on rejections. Reports "as time allows." Pays 1 copy.** Reviews books of poetry in about 1,000 words, single format. Open to unsolicited reviews. Poets may also send books for review consideration.

HRAFNHOH (IV-Form, religious), 32 Strŷd Ebeneser, Pontypridd, CF 37 5PB Wales via GB, founded 1987, editor Joseph Biddulph, is a small press magazine **seeking "metrical verse."** They use **"poetry in traditional verse forms with a Christian inspiration and purpose, with an active concern for metrical technique and conveying a serious message in an evocative and entertaining style."** They have published poetry by John Waddington-Feather, M.A.B. Jones, Joe Keysor and many others. The editor describes *Hrafnhoh* as 24 pgs., digest-sized, typeset, illustrated with carefully-researched heraldic illustrations and other sketches. He accepts about 1 of 6-10 poems received, but is not always able to publish even if accepted. Press run is 100-500. **Sample postpaid: £3 outside Europe. Submit up to 7 poems at a time. Simultaneous submissions and previously published poems OK. Publishes theme issues. Reports as soon as possible. Pays "in free copies as required."** The editor says, "Almost all unsolicited manuscripts are in one form—free verse—and without substance, i.e., without a definite purpose, message or conclusion. I am anxious to obtain verse with a strong technique, particularly on Pro-Life and Christian subjects."

HU (HONEST ULSTERMAN) (II, IV-Regional), 14 Shaw St., Belfast BT4 1PT United Kingdom, founded 1968, editor Tom Clyde, is a literary magazine appearing 3-4 times a year using **"technically competent poetry and prose and book reviews. Special reference to Northern Irish and Irish literature. Lively, humorous, adventurous, outspoken."** They have published poetry by Seamus Heaney, Paul Muldoon, Gavin Ewart, Craig Raine, Fleur Adcock and Medbh McGuckian. The editor describes it as "75-100 pgs., A5 (digest-sized), photolithographic, phototypeset, with photographs and line drawings. Occasionally color covers." Press run is 1,000 for 300 subscribers. Subscription: $28. **Sample postpaid: $7. "Potential contributors are strongly advised to read the magazine before submitting two copies of their work." Submit 6 poems at a time. Editor comments on submissions "occasionally." Publishes theme issues. Theme for February 1996 issue is "Writing from the**

(Ulster) Borders." Deadline: **November 1995. Send SASE (or SAE and IRCs) for upcoming themes. Pays "a nominal fee" plus 2 copies.** Reviews books of literary and cultural interest in 500-1,000 words, single or multi-book format. Open to unsolicited reviews. Poets may also send books for review consideration. They also publish occasional poetry pamphlets.

HUBBUB (II), 5344 SE 38th Ave., Portland OR 97202, founded 1983, editors L. Steinman and J. Shugrue, appears once a year. *Hubbub* is designed "to feature a multitude of voices from interesting contemporary American poets. **We look for poems that are well-crafted, with something to say. We have no single style, subject or length requirement and, in particular, will consider long poems. No light verse."** They have recently published poetry by Madeline DeFrees, William Matthews, Cecil Giscombe, Carolyn Kizer, Agha Shahid Ali and Alice Fulton. The editors describe *Hubbub* as 60-65 pgs., 5½ × 8½, offset, perfect-bound, cover art only, usually no ads. They receive about 1,200 submissions/year, use approximately 2%. Press run is 350 for 100 subscribers of which 12 are libraries, about 150 shelf sales. Subscription: $5/year. **Sample postpaid: $2.65 (volumes 1-8), $3.15 (volumes 9 and 11), $6.25 (volume 10, 12 and following). Submit 3-6 typed poems (no more than 6). No previously published poems or simultaneous submissions. Send SASE for guidelines. Reports in 2-4 months. Pays 2 copies. Acquires first North American serial rights.** "We review two to four poetry books a year in short (3-page) reviews; all reviews are solicited. We do, however, list books received/recommended." Send books for consideration. Outside judges choose poems from each volume for two awards: Vi Gale Award ($100) and Adrienne Lee Award ($50). There are no special submission procedures or entry fees involved. The editors add, "You can tell when people read and know something about poetry—contemporary poetry—as well as writing it; this bespeaks someone serious about their craft."

THE HUDSON REVIEW; THE BENNETT AWARD (III), 684 Park Ave., New York NY 10021. *The Hudson Review* is a high-quality, flat-spined quarterly, considered one of the most prestigious and influential journals in the nation. Editors welcome all styles and forms. However, competition is extraordinarily keen, especially since poems compete with prose. **Sample postpaid: $7. Non-subscribers may submit poems only between April 1 and September 30. "Simultaneous submissions are returned unread." Reports in 6-8 weeks. Always sends prepublication galleys. Pays 50¢ a line for poetry.** They also sponsor the Bennett Award, established in memory of Joseph Bennett, a founding editor of *HR*. Every other year $15,000 is given to honor a writer "of significant achievement, in any literary genre or genres, whose work has not received the full recognition it deserves, or who is at a critical stage in his or her career—a stage at which a substantial grant might be particularly beneficial in furthering creative development. There are no restrictions as to language or nationality. **The Bennett Award is not open to nominations, and *The Hudson Review* will not accept nominations or applications in any form."** Work published in this review has also been included in the 1993 and 1994 volumes of *The Best American Poetry*.

THE HUMAN QUEST (IV-Political), 1074 23rd Ave. N., St. Petersburg FL 33704, editor Edna Ruth Johnson, is a "humanistic bimonthly dealing with society's problems, especially peace. We use practically no poetry." It is magazine-sized, appears 6 times a year, circulation 10,000, of which 1,000 go for library subscriptions. **Send for free sample. Pays copies.**

THE HUNTED NEWS; THE SUBOURBON PRESS (I), P.O. Box 9101, Warwick RI 02889, founded 1990, editor Mike Wood. *The Hunted News* is a biannual "designed to find good writers and give them one more outlet to get their voices heard." As for poetry, the editor says, **"The poems that need to be written are those that need to be read." They do not want to see "the poetry that does not need to be written or which is written only to get a reaction or congratulate the poet."** As a sample the editor selected these lines (poet unidentified):

> *Birds who strike window panes with*
> *a heavy thud*
> *are misinformed.*
> *They've been sabotaged by outmoded*
> *weather charts*
> *In miniscule and mugging ways*
> *they resemble our finest actors*
> *Bury them in sand . . .*
> *and wait.*

The editor says *THN* is 25-30 pgs., 8½ × 11, photocopied, unstapled. "I receive over 200 poems per month and accept perhaps 10%." Press run is 150-200. **Sample free with SASE. Previously published poems OK; no simultaneous submissions. Always comments on rejections. Send SASE for guidelines. Reports in 1 month. Pays 1 copy, more on request.** "I review current chapbooks and other magazines and do other random reviews of books, music, etc. Word count varies." The Subourbon Press **publishes 2 chapbooks/year. Query first with a few sample poems and cover letter with brief** bio and publication credits. **Replies to both queries and mss in 1 month. Pays 15-20 author's copies. "No subsidies unless given voluntarily." Send SASE for information about samples.** The editor says, "I receive mostly beginner's poetry that attempts to be too philosophical, without much experience to back up statements, or self-impressed 'radical' poems by poets who assume that I will publish them because they are beyond criticism. I would like poets to send work whose point lies in language and economy and in experience, not in trite final lines, or worse, in the arrogant cover letter."

HURRICANE ALICE (IV-Feminist), 207 Lind Hall, 207 Church St. SE, Minneapolis MN 55455, founded 1983, acquisitions editor Toni McNaron, is a quarterly feminist review. Poems should be **"infused by a feminist sensibility (whether the poet is female or male)."** They have published poetry by Alice Walker, Ellen Bass, Patricia Hampl, Nellie Wong, Pauline Brunette Danforth and Marcella Taylor. The magazine is a "12-page folio with plenty of graphics." Circulation is 500-1,000, of which 350 are subscriptions and about 50 go to libraries. Single copy: $1.95; subscription: $12 (or $10 low-income). **Sample postpaid: $2.50. Considers simultaneous submissions. Reports in 3-4 months and time to publication is 3-6 months. Pays 5-10 copies.** Reviews books of poetry. The editor says, "Read what good poets have already written. If someone has already written your poem(s), listen to the message. Spare the trees."

HYACINTH HOUSE PUBLICATIONS; BROWNBAG PRESS; PSYCHOTRAIN; THE CROWBAIT REVIEW (II), P.O. Box 120, Fayetteville AR 72702-0120, founded 1989, contact Shannon Frach. *Brownbag Press*, *The Crowbait Review* and *PsychoTrain* are semiannual magazines. *Brownbag Press* seeks "forceful writing full of spark and vigor for a widely diverse, intelligent, fairly left-of-center audience." *PsychoTrain* uses "bizarre, avant-garde material with a delightfully psychotic edge. Heady and chaotic." *The Crowbait Review* is a poetry-only publication "using a wide stylistic mix, from the abrasive and gut-level to the deliciously surreal. It comes out more often than our other publications and is cheaper to produce, hence allowing us to publish far more poetry than we used to. This is a zine in the rawest sense of the word; do not expect to see a perfect-bound, coffee-table edition. **Please send camera-ready copy for this magazine.**" The editors want **poetry that is "avant-garde, confessional, contemporary, erotic, experimental, gay/lesbian, pagan/occult or punk. Also Dada, surrealism and decadent writing at its best. Stop sending us rhyming poetry, mainstream poetry, academic poetry. We are interested in free verse. Don't send traditional 'horror' or vampire poetry. We're looking for what would typically be considered 'underground' or 'alternative' writing. People who send us material that isn't in some way twisted, bizarre or weird are wasting both our time and theirs. We're seeing far too much 'straight' writing. Be bold. Morbid humor is always a plus here. We prefer two-fisted, dynamic, very intense poetry. Don't be afraid to show us street language from any culture."** They have recently published poetry by Tom Caufield, Marty Evans, Paul Grillo, Noelle Kocot, Kimberly J. Bright and C.F. Roberts. As a sample the editors selected these lines from "preserved, upon a cross of perseverance" by Raymond Tod Smith:

> . . . and all those unborn to be laid down
> hear me when I howl half the night again
> at nothing:
> watch closely where you put your heart—
> once broken it may as well be bone.

Brownbag is 24 pgs. and *PsychoTrain* is 20 pgs., magazine-sized. Both are photocopied and stapled with card covers. *The Crowbait Review* is 14 pgs., photocopied and stapled. Press run for each is 300 for 100 subscribers, 125 shelf sales. **Sample postpaid: $4 for *Brownbag*, $4 for *PsychoTrain*, $2 for *The Crowbait Review*. "Make checks out to Hyacinth House Publications. Cash is also OK." Submit 4-8 poems at a time. Previously published poems and simultaneous submissions OK.** Time between acceptance and publication is 1 year or more. **Often comments on rejections. Send SASE for guidelines. Reports in "2 weeks to 8 months—depends on the backlog. We do not pay." Acquires one-time rights.** "Please, *always* tell us whether or not your submissions are disposable. If you send 4-8 poems, we have a better overview of your material, but are not overwhelmed. We'd prefer to see each poem on a separate sheet. Don't send us long poems; if a poem runs over a single standard-sized page, the chances of its acceptance diminish dramatically. Finally, always include a SASE. We are getting an alarming number of submissions arriving without return postage—submissions which are promptly used for kindling, as are any queries or correspondence arriving without the courtesy of an enclosed SASE." Hyacinth House also has **a chapbook series. "Presently we're using solicited material only**—please don't send us unsolicited chapbook mss at this time. We will be doing approximately seven chapbooks this year, all from authors who have first appeared in our magazines. We don't take chapbook submissions 'out of the blue'—we like to know who we're working with." Hyacinth House Publications also sponsors the Richard A. Seffron Memorial Poetry Prize. "This is an ongoing competition with an annual deadline of May 1. Winners receive chapbook copies and a small cash prize. Send SASE for details and any queries concerning the Seffron Prize. Do not even *think* about submitting without first acquiring guidelines." The editors say, "We may end up having to reject your submissions, but we'll still respect you in the morning. We encourage both new and established 'name' writers to submit here. Anyone sending us material should be aware that we don't like pretentious, windy, overly-serious poetry; we also dislike smarmy, trite rhymes about God and family. Send those to your hometown newspaper, not us. Also, please be aware that when you submit to one Hyacinth House publication, you're submitting to them all. If you submit to *Brownbag*, but the piece would work better in *PsychoTrain* or *The Crowbait Review*, that's where it's going."

"The interview with Sandra Cisneros was the main feature in this issue and we felt that this picture, in particular, would do better at grabbing the attention of the newsstand or bookstore browser," says Hyphen Magazine *Editor Mark Ingebretsen.* **"This cover doesn't take itself too seriously, but looks at you directly and invites you in. That's Hyphen."** *Poetry is very important to the Chicago-based magazine which appears three times a year. They publish six to eight poems in each issue and look for poetry that is unconventional, but not abstract or obscure. Cover photo: Alexandro Galindo.*

‡**HYPHEN MAGAZINE (II)**, P.O. Box 10481, Chicago IL 60610-0481, phone/fax (312)465-5985 (but no faxed submissions), e-mail ingebret@interaccess.com, founded 1991, appears 3 times a year (in February, June and October). "*Hyphen* presents new fiction, poetry, art and ideas in an accessible and appealing format, subversively trying to infiltrate your mind." **As for poetry, the editors say they have "no formal or subject restrictions; usually limited to 1-2 pages in length. We usually publish 1 or 2 performance poems each issue—but performance poems should read as well on the page as on the stage.** *Hyphen* **looks for poems that have immediacy, accessibility and craft; poems that break your heart, take your breath away, and blow the top right off your head. Please don't submit sentimental or inspirational poems, light comic verse, bad rhyming verse, violent or demeaning erotica, or, generally speaking, bad poetry of any kind. To really get an idea of the kind of poetry we publish, take this publisher's advice and** *order a sample copy.* **It's a good idea; it works."** They have recently published poetry by Luis Rodriguez, Paul Hoover, Dwight Okita and Cin Salach. As a sample the editors selected these lines from "The Non-Stick Gospels, or Everything I Know I Learned Talking Out Of Church," by Jim Banks:

> *You're born a chunk of raw id in a kennel full of authority figures.*
> *God's cops use choke-holds to coerce your voluntary love.*
> *The market is an illusion, but you continue to buy and sell.*
> *You didn't ask yourself in, you can't kick yourself out.*
> *If you're not allergic to this, you're addicted to that.*
> *You keep forgetting to panic.*

Hyphen is 72 pgs., 8½ × 11, offset and saddle-stapled with 2-color slick paper cover with photo. The interior includes b&w art, photos, graphics and ads. They receive 500-600 poems a year, accept about 30. Press run is 1,500 for 250 subscribers. Single copy: $3.95; subscription: $12/year, $22/2 years. **Sample postpaid: $5. Guidelines are found in the magazine. Submit no more than 6 poems at a time, (name and address on each sheet) with brief bio (75 words or less). No previously published poems; simultaneous submissions OK ("but we're not crazy about them"). Poems are circulated to an editorial board. Seldom comments on rejections. Reports in 3-4 months. Pays 2 copies. Acquires first North American serial rights and retains rights to anthologize.** Reviews books and other media in the "Aftershock" section, in 200-300 words. Open to unsolicited reviews. Poets may also send books for review consideration. *Hyphen* changed hands in January of 1995. The new editors say they hope to continue the magazine's fresh, 'zine-like take on contemporary poetry and fiction. *Hyphen* also plans to have an electronic version on the Internet soon; e-mail editor for details.

ICE COLD WATERMELON (IV-Ethnic, erotica, gay/lesbian), 2394B Adina Dr., Atlanta GA 30324, founded 1990, editors M. Christopher Young and Simoné, is an annual journal of memory and prophecy. **"Interested solely in poignant, economical poetry with voice and character using**

innovative imagery. **Want to see brave poetry with an edge, that gives us a peek into the mystical experience of persons of color. Erotica/gay/lesbian writings especially encouraged. Do not want to see anything that tries too hard. No academic or 'selfish' personal poetry. Nothing trite or mundane.**" As a sample the editors selected the poem "Yes" by M. Christopher Young:

> hey man,
> yeah, you
>
> the brother over there
> yeah, him, the one with
> the empty, outstretched hand
>
> he is speaking to you
> right this very minute
>
> can you hear what he is saying?

The editors describe it as 50-65 pgs., digest-sized, professionally printed. They accept about 150 of 500 submissions received annually. Press run is 200 with 5 library subscriptions. "Most copies distributed free to other editors, publishers and writing institutions." Subscription: $10 for 2 years. **Submit 5 poems, typed. Send SASE for guidelines. Reports in 8-10 weeks, up to 18-month backlog. Pays 2 copies.** They say, "What we want is writing that is empowered by spirit, magic and secrets. In your writing, we want you to have no qualms about telling the cultural truths as you know them and allowing our readers to share those experiences with you."

THE ICONOCLAST (I, II), 1675 Amazon Rd., Mohegan Lake NY 10547, founded 1992, editor/publisher Phil Wagner, is a general interest literary publication appearing 8 times/year "for those who find life absurd and profound." **They want "poems that have something to say—the more levels the better. Nothing sentimental, religious, obscure or self-absorbed. Our poetry is accessible to a thoughtful reading public."** *The Iconoclast* is 24-28 pgs., 5½×8½, double-stapled, typeset and photocopied on 20 lb. white paper, with b&w art, graphics and ads. They receive about 1,000 poems a year, use 5%. Press run is 500 for 240 subscribers. Subscription: $12 for 8 issues. **Sample postpaid: $1.50. Submit 3-4 poems at a time. Previously published poems and simultaneous submissions OK, though they say "previously published and simultaneous submissions must be demonstrably better than others."** Time between acceptance and publication is 1-6 months. **"Poems are subject to the extremely fallible judgements of the editor-in-chief." Often comments on rejections. Reports in 2-4 weeks. Pays 1 copy, 40% discount on extras. Acquires one-time rights.** Reviews books of poetry in 250 words, single format.

‡THE IDIOT (IV-Humor), 40 Edgelea Dr., Chambersburg PA 17201, founded 1993, editor Sam Hayes, is a biannual humor magazine. "We mostly use fiction, articles and cartoons, but **will use anything funny, including poetry. Nothing pretentious.**" They have recently published poetry by Puntjak Djaja and Brian Campbell. As a sample the editor selected these lines from "The Waste Receptacle" by Joe Deasy:

> Cerebus, why do you prevent me from opening my mail?
> The cries of the debt
> 10 little monkeys jumpin' on the bed.
> One fell off. Oh, haven't we all.

The Idiot is 48 pgs., 5½×8½, professionally printed and staple-bound with glossy cover. They receive about 30 submissions a year, accept 3-4. Press run is 300. Single copy: $3. **Sample postpaid: $4. Previously published poems and simultaneous submissions OK. Seldom comments on rejections. Reports in 2-6 months. Pays 1 copy. Acquires one-time rights.** The editor says, "Dr. Seuss may have written children's books, but that doesn't mean only children enjoy them. Look at the popularity of *The Grinch Who Stole Christmas*. Poetry can be read, but it's usually more powerful heard. Go to poetry readings."

IHCUT (I), P.O. Box 612, Napavine WA 98565, phone (206)262-9784, founded 1989, contact Larry L. Randall, is an inexpensively produced newsletter appearing every other month. **"I would love to see some positive poetry, something with some answers and hope. I would rather not see rhyming poetry."** They have recently published poetry by Laurie Calhoun and Victor Salinas. As a sample the editor selected "Dust Off That Resume" by Robert Dunn:

> The minimum wage job vacancy
> Requires double PhDs, twenty years experience,
> Plus marriage to the Boss's daughter
> This they call . . . . equal opportunity.

Ihcut is 15-20 pgs., photocopied, side-stapled on ordinary paper. Press run is 20. **Sample postpaid: $2. Submit 4 poems at a time. Previously published poems and simultaneous submissions OK. Cover** letter including **"likes and dislikes, personal stuff" required.** "It annoys me when a poet does not include a cover letter, which to me is a poem in itself." **Publishes theme issues. Send SASE for guidelines and upcoming themes. Reports in 1 week. Pays 1 copy.**

UNIVERSITY OF ILLINOIS PRESS (III), 1325 S. Oak St., Champaign IL 61820, founded 1918, poetry editor Laurence Lieberman, publishes **collections of individual poets, 65-105 pgs. Submissions by invitation only.** They have published collections of poetry by Mark Doty, Debora Greger, Alice Fulton, Len Roberts, Michael Harper, Miller Williams, Lorna Goodison and Stephen Berg. **Offers royalty contract and 10 copies.** Mark Doty's *My Alexandria* was a 1993 National Book Award Finalist, winner of the Los Angeles Times 1993 Book Prize for a Work of Poetry and winner of the National Book Critics Circle Award.

THE ILLINOIS REVIEW; ILLINOIS WRITERS, INC. (II), 4240/English Dept., Illinois State University, Normal IL 61790-4240, phone (309)438-7705, founded 1992, first issue fall 1993, editor Jim Elledge. *The Illinois Review* appears twice a year and supersedes *Illinois Writers Review.* **"We're open to any 'school'—experimental to traditional, alternative to mainstream—by recognized, unknown and marginalized poets. Translations and prose poems are acceptable.** Selection for publication is based on excellence of poems not reputation of poets. **We look for poetry that reveals control of language and form, that engages the intellect and emotions simultaneously, and that is honest. No specifications as to length, etc. We do not want to see poetry that is sentimental, religious, filled with abstractions, or 'self-therapy.' "** They have published poetry by Gary Soto, Lisa Ress, Rochelle Ratner, David Trinidad, Kelly Cherry, Albert Goldbarth, Alison Stone and William Matthews. As a sample the editor selected these lines from "Nightfall" by Yusef Komunyakaa:

> *Every Saturday night someone new*
> *Is on his arm, her low-cut gown*
> *A school of angelfish.*

The editor says the review is 72 pgs., 5½×8½, perfect-bound, offset, with b&w cover art. Press run is 500 for 300 subscribers of which 10 are libraries. Subscription: $10. **Sample postpaid: $6. Submit up to 6 poems at a time. No previously published poems or simultaneous submissions. Reads submissions August 1 through May 1 only.** "Because we have a very large backlog of material and because we publish only twice a year, accepted work may not appear in print for a year or longer." **Seldom comments on rejections. Reports in 1-2 months. Pays 2 copies and year's subscription. Acquires all rights. Returns rights upon publication. "However, we ask contributors to notify us if they reprint their work from the *Review* and to acknowledge the *Review* when reprinting."** Reviews books of poetry "but only those of Illinois authors or presses." Query first. Individuals or institutions interested in becoming members of Illinois Writers, Inc., which includes a one-year subscription to both *The Illinois Review* and the *I.W.I. Newsletter,* may send SASE for membership rates. The editor says, "While *The Illinois Review* is published by Illinois Writers, Inc., an organization dedicated to supporting in-state writers, it is not a regional nor a 'members only' journal but publishes work by poets throughout the U.S. and elsewhere, as well as by Illinois residents. It is truly eclectic. Potential contributors are advised to buy a sample before submitting, but this is not a requirement."

IMAGO: NEW WRITING; CITY OF BRISBANE POETRY AWARD (II, IV-Regional), School of Communication and Organisational Studies, Q.U.T., GPO Box 2434, Brisbane 4001 Queensland, Australia, fax (07)864-1811, founded 1988, appears three times a year, publishing "the best **Australian writing, placing particular emphasis on Queensland writing and culture, but also welcoming submissions from overseas. Poems preferably short—up to about 50 lines, most from 12-25 lines. Our main criterion is good writing."** They have recently published poetry by Tom Shapcott, Nancy Cato and Chris Wallace-Crabbe. As a sample the editor selected these lines from "Far and Near" by David Malouf:

> *. . . We are held*
> *by this; the coins in our pockets, amalgam fillings,*
> *gold that laps a finger gravely compliant*
> *as the magnet tilts and tugs us*
> *down. A flair for technology and faith is what keeps us*
> *above earth's instant muddle, but never far and not for long.*

Imago is 108 pgs., digest-sized, with glossy card cover. They accept about 10% of 500 poems from

---

Use the General Index to find the page number of a specific publisher. If the publisher you are seeking is not listed, check the " '95-'96 Changes" list at the end of this section.

about 150 writers. Press run is 1,000 for 450 subscribers of which 36 are libraries. Subscription: $A21 in Australia; $A28, overseas (airmail). **Sample postpaid: $A9.50. Submit 6-8 poems at a time. "A brief biography (few lines) of the writer accompanying the submission saves time if the work is accepted. We have a Notes on Contributors column." Comments if requested. Reports in 1-6 months. Never sends prepublication galleys "unless specifically asked for by contributor." Pays $A30-40 plus 1 copy. Buys first Australian serial rights. They publish the winning poems of the City of Brisbane Poetry Award (annual).** Reviews books of poetry in 600 words—"usually commissioned. Unsolicited reviews would have to be of books relevant to *Imago* (Queensland or writing)." Send books for consideration.

THE IMPLODING TIE-DYED TOUPEE; BURNING LLAMA PRESS (II, IV-Form/style), 100 Courtland Dr., Columbia SC 29223-7148, e-mail higginbotham@mid.tec.sc.us, founded 1993, editors Keith Higginbotham and Tracey R. Combs, is a biannual outlet "for people who dare to take language to its outer limits. We prefer sounds and juxtapositions of images over 'meaning.' " **They want "Dada, surrealism, experimental, visual poetry, found poetry, collaborative poetry—anything unusual. No traditional poetry, light verse, blood and guts, academic, confessional or inspirational poetry."** They have published poetry by Guy R. Beining, Richard Kostelanetz, Sheila E. Murphy and Dan Raphael. As a sample the editors selected "Hilt" by John M. Bennett:

> *Better lamping's what I*
> *need   or your face*
> *pillowed   a conference of*
> *hair   like the phone's*
> *dust   my pants just billowed*

> *Lace hanging like my speech milk*

The Imploding Tie-Dyed Toupee is 40 pgs., digest-sized, photocopied and saddle-stapled with card stock cover and bizarre graphics coupled with intriguing visual poems. "On the average, we accept one poem per 200 received." Press run is 200 for 20 subscribers, various shelf sales. Subscription: $16 for 4 issues. **Sample postpaid: $4. Submit 3-10 poems at a time. No previously published poems or simultaneous submissions. "Everyone, no matter how 'well known,' should have the decency or professional courtesy to include a cover letter or some kind of personal communication. Otherwise, we consider the poet to be arrogant. Poets should also always include a SASE.** Time between acceptance and publication varies. **Seldom comments on rejections. Send SASE for guidelines. Reports within 2 months. Pays 1 copy. Acquires first North American serial rights.** "Open to short reviews of magazines; surreal reviews of TV shows." Poets may also send books for review consideration. The editors add, "Salvador Dali once said, 'So little of what could happen actually does happen. When I order lobster, why doesn't the waiter bring me a telephone book on fire?' Bring us that telephone book. Do the unexpected with language."

IMPLOSION PRESS; IMPETUS (I, II, IV-Erotica, women), 4975 Comanche Trail, Stow OH 44224, phone/fax (216)688-5210, e-mail impetus@aol.com, founded 1984, poetry editor Cheryl Townsend, publishes *Impetus*, a quarterly literary magazine, chapbooks, special issues. The editor would like to see **"strong social protest with raw emotion. No topic is taboo. Material should be straight from the gut, uncensored and real. Absolutely no nature poetry or rhyme for the sake of rhyme, oriental, or 'Kissy, kissy I love you' poems. Any length as long as it works. All subjects okay, providing it isn't too rank.** *Impetus* **is now publishing annual erotica and all female issues. Material should reflect these themes."** They have published poetry by Ron Androla, Kurt Nimmo and Lonnie Sherman. As a sample the editor selected these lines from "Gun-shy" by B. Arcus Shoenborn:

> *Instead,*
> *I hid in my bedroom.*
> *Soaked between blooded sheets,*
> *I explored immaculate concepts.*
> *Then my white heart severed;*
> *It gushed rivers of angry rapists.*
> *One flagged a revolver;*
> *he held it to my head and said,*
> *I'd live, but couldn't tell.*

The 7½ × 9 magazine is photocopied from typescript, saddle-stapled. Press run is about 1,000, with 300 subscriptions. Generally a 3-month backlog. **Sample postpaid: $4; make check payable to Cheryl Townsend. Submit 3-8 poems at a time. The editor says, "I prefer shorter, to-the-point work." Include name and address on each page. Previously published work OK if it is noted when and where. "I always like a cover letter that tells me how the poet found out about my magazine." Send SASE for guidelines. Usually reports within 3 months. Pays 1 copy. Acquires first or onetime rights.** In her comments on rejections, the editor usually refers poets to other magazines she feels would appreciate the work more. Reviews books of poetry. Open to unsolicited reviews. Poets may also send books for review consideration. Implosion Press now hosts "The Last Friday Poetry Readings" at Borders Books & Music in Fairlawn, Ohio and will be touring cities with Borders inviting local *Impetus* poets to read. They also host "Notes from the Underground" on WAPS 91.3 FM radio in Akron, Ohio. The editor says, "Bear with the small press. We're working as best as we can and usually harder. We can only do so much at a time. Support the small presses!"

IMPROVIJAZZATION NATION (I), HQ, 19th Supcom, Unit 15015, P.O. Box 2879, APO AP 96218-0171, phone 82-53-473-5259, fax 82-53-470-8583, e-mail dmetcalf@freenet.scri.fss.edu, founded 1991, editor Dick Metcalf, who is currently stationed in Korea. *Improvijazzation Nation* is a quarterly "devoted to networking; prime focus is tape/music reviews, includes quite a bit of poetry." **They want "experimental, visual impact and non-establishment poetry, no more than 15 lines. No hearts and flowers, shallow, epic."** They have published poetry by John M. Bennett, Joan Payne Kincaid and Anthony Lucero. The editor says *IN* is 20 pgs., 8½ × 11, photocopied, no binding. They receive 50-100 poems a year, use approximately 50%. Press run is 100. Single copy: $2.25; subscription: $8 for 4 issues. **Sample postpaid: $2.50. Submit 3 poems at a time. Previously published poems and simultaneous submissions OK. Often comments on rejections. Reports within a week or two. "No payment, no contributor's copies, no tearsheets; poets must buy the issue their work appears in. The one exception is that any contributor who furnishes a valid e-mail address will receive an ASCII copy of the entire magazine, if requested."** Reviews books of poetry. Also accepts short essays/commentary on the use of networking to void commercial music markets, as well as material of interest to musical/artist improvisors.

IN YOUR FACE! (I), P.O. Box 6872, Yorkville Station, New York NY 10128-0017, founded 1992, editor Gina Grega, is a quarterly that publishes art, poetry, essays and reviews, "whatever strikes my fancy and knocks the wind out of me." **They want "anything bold, confrontative, risky and/ or risqué, funny, political, personal, sexual, unpretentious, honest, real-life language. No PC multicultural whinings, phony pseudo-emotionalism, rhyming poems, unintelligible manifestos filled with 50-cent words. No women-hating spewage."** They have recently published poetry by Alfred Vitale, Harvey Goldner, Chriss-Spike Quatrone and Mary Panza. As a sample the editor selected this poem, "When She Went To Florida," by Brent Askari:

> When she went to Florida
> my soul wailed like
> a hammond organ
> played by an epileptic
> during a power surge

IYF! is 50 pgs., 5½ × 8½, saddle-stapled, with colored card cover, b&w art and ads. They receive about 1,500 pieces a year, accept 10-15%. Press run is 350 for 100 subscribers. Subscription: $12. **Sample postpaid: $3. Submit no more than 5 pgs. at a time. Previously published poems and simultaneous submissions OK. "Be friendly, drop me a note, not a pretentious bio! SASE with appropriate postage a must. Also, if you don't want your writings returned, let me know." Often comments on rejections. Send SASE for guidelines. Publishes an annual women's issue. Reports in 1-3 months. Pays 1-2 copies.** Reviews books, chapbooks, 'zines, "whatever else I can get my hands on," in roughly 75-100 words each. Open to unsolicited reviews. Poets may also send books for review consideration. The editor says, "*In Your Face!* isn't afraid to offend. I look for gut-punching work—not big names. I especially encourage beginners as they haven't been polished by the cold, impersonal 'name' magazines and are usually still humble enough to send a 'hi' with their submission. We *recommend* that contributors see a copy of our publication, but this is not a requirement."

‡INDEFINITE SPACE (II), P.O. Box 40101, Pasadena CA 91114, founded 1992, editors Marcia Arrieta and Kevin Joy, is a biannual poetry journal. **They want "experimental, minimalistic, imagistic, philosophical poetry not exceeding two pages. No rhyming poetry."** They have published poetry by Hugh Fox, Jeffery, John M. Bennett and Sheila E. Murphy. As a sample the editors selected these lines from "Latitude" by Spencer Selby:

> Does not know
> this ship sprung up on soil
> to verify delivery
> at the entrance
> of world ruins
> I have never reached.

Indefinite Space is 32-40 pgs., 5½ × 8½, neatly printed and saddle-stapled with matte card cover with b&w art, no ads, poems appearing one to a page. Press run is 125-150 for 20 subscribers of which 5 are libraries. Subscription: $7. **Sample postpaid: $4. "Please make checks payable to editors." No previously published poems; simultaneous submissions OK. Seldom comments on rejections. Send SASE for guidelines. Reports usually within a month. Pays 1 copy. Rights remain with poet.**

INDIA CURRENTS (IV-Ethnic, regional), P.O. Box 21285, San Jose CA 95151, phone (408)274-6966, founded 1987, editor Arvind Kumar, is a monthly magazine about Indian culture in the U.S. They want **"poetry that offers an insight into India, Indians, Indian Americans; very brief works stand a better chance of acceptance."** They do not want **"poetry that exploits mystery or exoticism about India or long poems (over 300 words). Readership is 70% Indian, 30% non-Indian."** They have published poetry by Chitra Divakaruni. It is 136 pgs., 8½ × 11, offset, newsprint, saddle-stitched. They receive 50-75 submissions a year, "accept fewer than 12." Press run is 24,000 for 4,000 subscribers. Rest distributed free at stores, restaurants and libraries. Single copy: $1.95; subscription: $19.95. **Sample postpaid: $3. Previously published poems and simultaneous submissions OK. Cover letter with brief bio and background required.** Time between acceptance and publication is 6-12 months. **Send SASE for guidelines. Reports in 3 months.** Reviews books of poetry in 300 words maximum. Open to unsolicited reviews. Poets may also send books for review consideration. The magazine received a Cultural Awareness through Journalism Award from the Federation of Indo-American Associations in 1991. The editor says, "*India Currents* has a heavy tilt in favor of arts. We feel that arts can contribute to global understanding and peace by bringing it about at a personal level. America needs to learn about India just as India needs to learn about America."

INDIANA REVIEW (II), Indian University, 316 N. Jordan Ave., Bloomington IN 47405, phone (812)855-3439, founded 1982, is a biannual of new fiction and poetry. **"In general the *Review* looks for fresh, original poems of insight, poems that are challenging without being obtuse. We'll consider all types of poems—free verse, traditional, experimental. Reading a sample issue is the best way to determine if *IR* is a potential home for your work. Any subject matter is acceptable if it is written well."** They have recently published poetry by Philip Levine, Taslimā Nāsreen, Belle Waring, Charles Simic and Alberto Rios. As a sample, the editor selected these lines from "Fathers" by Jennifer Snyder:

> *I will go to school for my father.*
> *I will do a science experiment about my father*
>
> *Where I cut him open and inside*
> *Is a wild city made of wheat.*
> *Our fathers will die, they are dead,*
> *And the cemetry's bad news finds them,*
> *And their fingers confuse flowers.*

The magazine uses about 50-70 pgs. of poetry in each issue (6 × 9, flat-spined, 200 pages, color matte cover, professional printing). They receive about 8,000 submissions/year of which they use about 60. The magazine has 1,000 subscriptions of which 120 are libraries. **Sample postpaid: $7. Submit 3-5 poems at a time. "Please indicate stanza breaks on poems over 1 page. Simultaneous submissions very strongly discouraged." Publishes theme issues. Send SASE for upcoming themes. Pays $5/ page ($10 minimum/poem), plus 2 copies and remainder of year's subscription. Buys first North American serial rights only. "We try to respond to manuscripts in two to three months. Reading time is often slower during summer months."** This magazine's reputation continues to grow in literary circles. It is generally accepted now as one of the best publications, featuring all styles, forms and lengths of poetry (much of it exciting or tense). Brief book reviews are also featured. Send books for review consideration.

‡INDIGO MAGAZINE: THE SPANISH-CANADIAN PRESENCE IN THE ARTS (IV-Foreign languages, translations, themes), Room 252, Atkinson College, York University, North York, Ontario M3T 1P3 Canada, phone (416)736-2100, ext. 6632, founded 1989, editor-in-chief Prof. Margarita Feliciano, appears twice a year using **"poetry to be thematically of Hispanic contents if written in French or English (not the case if written in Spanish)."** They have published poetry by Rafael Barreto-Rivera and Rosemary Sullivan. As a sample the editor selected these lines (poet unidentified):

> *I was born on this lip of stone*
> *Jutting out over the jungle*
> *I've never wanted to go down.*
> *As a child I would run to the edge to catch the birds*
> *or follow the lizards with my hand along the ledges.*

It is approximately 150 pgs., professionally printed, flat-spined, with glossy card cover. "I accept 50% of submissions (about 40)." Press run 300 for 50 subscribers. Subscription: $25. **Cover letter, including background on the poet, required with submissions. Price of sample, payment, reporting time not given. The editor says she always comments on rejections.** Open to unsolicited reviews.

INKSLINGER (I, IV-Subscription), 8661 Prairie Rd. NW, Washington Court House OH 43160, founded 1993, publisher/editor Nancy E. Martindale, appears 3 times/year (in March, July and November) to "provide an additional market for poets and to further the poetic arts." **They want poetry from subscribers only. Any subject, any format, no longer than 30 lines. "No porn or erotica. Also no**

translations or foreign language poetry." They have recently published poetry by Geraldine Zeigler and A.M. Roman. As a sample, the editor selected the poem "Relationship" by Scott Stolsenberg:

> *Fragments of a broken dream*
> *Fall through a shattered mind*
> *A thousand hopes and wishes*
> *A treasure lost to time*
> *I only wish we could have known*
> *If it was meant to be*
> *What could have been will never pass*
> *We drift the lonely sea*

Inkslinger is 20 pgs., digest-sized, saddle-stapled with 60 lb. colored paper cover. They receive 60-75 poems a year, accept 54 or more if short in length. Subscription: $10.60/year, $20.14/2 years. **Sample postpaid: $4. "Purchase of a 1-year subscription is required to submit at present time—hoping to change this policy soon." Send no more than 3 poems at a time. Previously published poems OK if author still owns copyright; no simultaneous submissions.** Time between acceptance and publication is 1 month. "Poems arriving too late for one issue will be held for the next issue's consideration. Poems are judged according to imagery, style, creativity, originality and sincerity (5 points each). Poems with most points are accepted. One(s) with the highest is named 'Editor's Choice' and poet receives $10." **Seldom comments on rejections. Send SASE for guidelines. Reports in 5 months maximum. Pays no money at present (except to "Editor's Choice"), "but hoping to pay soon." Poets retain all rights.** The editor says, "Novices and experienced poets welcome. We're small, but open. *Always read guidelines first.* Failure to meet even one will result in unread, returned manuscripts."

INKSTONE: A MAGAZINE OF HAIKU (IV-Form), P.O. Box 75009, Hudson Bay Ctr., 20 Bloor St. E., Toronto, Ontario M4W 3T3 Canada, phone (416)962-6051, fax (416)966-9646, founded 1982, poetry editors Keith Southward, Marshall Hryciuk and J. Louise Fletcher, "is a publication dedicated to the development of a distinctive English language haiku and to the craft of writing as it relates to haiku. Submissions reflecting these concerns are welcomed. We publish haiku and related forms, plus reviews and articles related to haiku. **Poems must be haiku or related but we use a very liberal definition of haiku."** They have published haiku by Carol Montgomery, Alexis Rotella, Akira Kowano and Guy Beining. There are roughly 20 pgs. of poetry and reviews/articles in the digest-sized format, 40 pgs., offset from typescript, matte card cover. They accept "perhaps 10%" of the poems submitted each year. Poems appear as space permits, usually in the next issue after acceptance. Circulation 100. **Sample postpaid: $5.50. Submit any number of poems, preferably 1 per 5½×8½ sheet, typewritten. Editor "occasionally" comments on rejections. Reports within 6 weeks. Pays 1 copy. Acquires first serial rights.** Reviews books of poetry in 1 to 3 pgs., single or multi-book format. Open to unsolicited reviews. Poets may also send books for review consideration "with an indication that it is a review copy."

INKY BLUE (I), 3200 North Rd., Greenport NY 11944, founded 1989 by Cat Spydell, editor (as of December 1992) Yvonne Gillispie, associate editor Joey MacLellan, appears semiannually. Yvonne Gillispie continues her predecessor's quest for **"thought-provoking poetry, with a tendency to avoid the mundane. No sexist, red-necked-beer-bellied-middle-American-women-are-only-good-if-they-have-flat-heads poetry."** She has recently published poetry by Lyn Lifshin, George Wallace, Daniel Langton and Gloria Good. As a sample the editor selected these lines from "Trying Godiva" by Mari Niescior:

> *. . . Bright TV-babies*
> *turn me on; got me stepping*
> *through flowerbeds to be with you. Wish*
> *my legs were made of slinky*
> *just to feel your second-story*
> *love . . .*

The magazine averages 150 pgs. and is digest-sized with matte card cover, photographs and pen & ink drawings. Each issue features an interview with a poet (previously interviewed poets include Nicholas Christopher and Richard Howard). Press run is 500-1,000 depending on funding. The editor accepts 30% of submissions. Subscription: $15/year. **Sample postpaid: $8. Submit 3 poems at a time. Previously published poems and simultaneous submissions OK. Poems without a SASE or without the poet's name and address on each page will not be considered. Pays 1 copy. Rights revert to poet after publication.** The editor says, "We received over 15,000 submissions between May 1993 and September 1994 and we're swamped. We might have dark circles under our eyes and be delirious from lack of sleep, but we're sticking to our original goal: No poet will receive a form letter rejection. We give poets feedback and that's what makes us tick. We're accepting less poetry, but it's being drawn from a wide base of new poets. My advice: Send 3 poems, a short cover letter and a SASE. While most editors would consider a 4-page bio, 100 pages of poetry and a photo of the poet *sans* pet octopus fodder for the verticle file, we still read everything so have pity on us."

INSECTS ARE PEOPLE TOO; PUFF 'N' STUFF PRODUCTIONS (I, IV-Specialized), P.O. Box 146486, Chicago IL 60614, phone (312)772-8686, founded 1989, publisher H.R. Felgenhauer, an infrequent publication focusing solely on **"poems about insects doing people things and people doing insect things."** The first issue was a collection of the publisher's own poems. The second edition contains "better than 50 poems by 40 poets, one short story and one novella." As a sample the publisher selected these lines from a poem of his own, "Resist and You Will be Destroyed":

> *Geometrical abstraction of space-vehicle-ness sprouts conquest.*
> *Inferior species succumb to superior weapons, transport and*
> *communication systems blistering through onion skinned civilizations.*
> *They were bigger and better and all around us; we expanded right*
> *into their hoary mouths, razor sharp venom spouting ruin . . .*

Insects is 8½ × 11, stapled down the side, with card cover, b&w art and graphics. Press run is 400. Single copy: $3. **Sample postpaid: $4. Previously published poems and simultaneous submissions OK. Often comments on rejections. Reports "immediately." Pay varies.** Open to unsolicited reviews. Poets may also send books for review consideration. **Puff 'N' Stuff Productions publishes 1 chapbook/year. Replies to queries and mss in 10 days. Pay is negotiable.** H.R. Felgenhauer says, "Hit me with your best shot. Never give up—editors have tunnel-vision. The *BEST* mags you almost *NEVER* even hear about. Don't believe reviews. Write for yourself. Prepare for failure, not success."

INSOMNIA & POETRY (I), P.O. Box 0431, Murrieta CA 92564-0431, founded 1991, publishes irregularly, "but at least four times a year. This publication was started to give poets more opportunity to express themselves without the pressures of editorial intimidation (cover letters, guidelines, etc.). **Please send us your most poignant poetry—as the publication's title suggests. We try not to discriminate."** As a sample the editor selected these lines by Norman Schiffman:

> *in*
> *your most*
> *gorgeous eyes*
> *serpents*
> *&*
> *ancient ones*
> *appear*
> *like*
> *worms*
> *in*
> *summer*
> *wood*

Insomnia & Poetry is 8 pgs., 8½ × 11, photocopied with occasional photographs accompanying poems. Press run is 250, all distributed free—left in libraries, bookstores and at colleges. **Sample postpaid: $1 (no checks). "Please type name, address and the number of lines on every poem submitted." Previously published poems and simultaneous submissions OK. Reports ASAP. Usually pays 1 copy.** The editor says, "We don't think poetic expression is some privilege to be 'crafted' by only a select bunch. We think of it as human expression that can be shown by anyone—a cathartic endeavor for all."

THE INTERCULTURAL WRITER'S REVIEW; THE INTERCULTURAL WRITER'S ASSOCIATION (I, IV-Membership); MERLANA'S MAGICKAL MESSAGES (I, IV-Spirituality/inspirational, psychic/occult); NAVARRO PUBLICATIONS (IV-Anthology), P.O. Box 1107, Dept. PM, Blythe CA 92226-1107, managing editor Marjorie E. Navarro, consultant and art director Richard LeJose Navarro. *The Intercultural Writer's Review*, first published in April 1995, is the official publication of The Intercultural Writer's Association and is published quarterly. **They welcome poetry on any subject, up to 45 lines in length.** Short stories and articles, up to 2,500 words, are also used. They have recently published work by Jack Bernier, Brett K. Fletcher, Elizabeth Felton and Elmer Roy Green. The editor describes *TIWR* as 8½ × 11, soft cover, perfect-bound. **"Membership is not necessary for publication; however, members will be considered first."** The membership fee is $34/year and includes "a subscription and no-fee members' contests, discounts on extra copies and independently published poetry chapbooks."**Sample postpaid: $8.50. Make checks or money orders payable to Navarro Publications. Payment is in contributor's copies for members, tearsheets for nonmembers.** Their other publication, *Merlana's Magickal Messages*, first published in March 1995, is "a metaphysical, spiritual, New Age publication" which appears in March, July and October. **"We prefer uplifting material with a magickal message for our reader's spirit from the spirit of the author. We want poetry up to 45 lines.** We also use short stories (up to 2,500 words) and articles (up to 1,500 words). **It is best to send for a sample issue before submitting. And there is a reading fee of $2 for six poems, $3 for each article or short story."** They have recently published work by Gurattan Khalsa, Cheryl L. Schuck, Dr. James McGarry and Nichole Stevens. As a sample the editor selected these lines from "Jamaican Magick Two" by Richard LeJose Navarro:

I arise today, from a night of no sleep,
With thoughts of lovin' you deeply I keep . . .
I scan my environment; nothing is the same,
My psyche waits for you to call my name . . .
The mirror will tell me I know this is true
As I look, I see the aura of you.

The editor says *MMM* is desktop-published and perfect-bound. **Sample postpaid: $7. Make checks or money orders payable to Navarro Publications. Reports "as soon as possible." Pays in copies.** Navarro Publications is also planning one poetry anthology and three poetry chapbooks in 1996. "We also offer short-run book publishing. Information is available for this and our literary services for a SASE." The editor says, "In all our endeavors we seek originality and conciseness. Read *Poet's Market* listings *carefully* and send for sample copies to avoid sending material not suitable for various markets. Doing so saves on postage and helps the already overworked and underpaid editors tremendously!"

INTERIM (II), Dept. of English, University of Nevada at Las Vegas, Las Vegas NV 89154, phone (702)895-3458, magazine, founded in Seattle, 1944-55, revived 1986. Editor and founder A. Wilber Stevens, associate editors James Hazen, Joseph B. McCullough and Timothy Erwin, English editor John Heath-Stubbs. Member CLMP, New York. Indexed in *Index of American Periodical Verse*. Appears twice a year, **publishing the best poetry and short fiction it can find, no specific demands in form, new and established writers.** They have published poetry by William Stafford, Richard Eberhart, Diane Wakoski, Stephen Stepanchev and Anca Vlasopolos. As a sample we selected these lines from "Winter's Tale" by Charlotte F. Otten:

Her voice is silent now,
sunk deep into the tap root of her brain.
A stroke that struck her throat
blizzarded all sound.
Words swirl around her like an early snow
clinging to unfallen leaves.

Interim is 48 pgs., 6×9, professionally printed and saddle-stapled with coated card cover. Press run is 600. Individual subscription: $8 one year, $13 two years, $16 three years; libraries: $14/year. **Sample copy: $5. Submit 4-6 poems at a time, SASE and brief biographical note. No simultaneous submissions. Decision in 3 months. Sometimes sends prepublication galleys. Pays 2 contributor's copies and a 2-year subscription.** *Interim* **acquires copyright. Poems may be reprinted elsewhere with a permission line noting publication in** *Interim*. Starting short poetry review. Send books for review consideration.

INTERNATIONAL BLACK WRITERS; BLACK WRITER MAGAZINE (I, IV-Ethnic), P.O. Box 1030, Chicago IL 60690, founded 1970, contact Mable Terrell, executive director. *BWM* is a "quarterly literary magazine to showcase new writers and poets and provide educational information for writers. **Open to all types of poetry.**" The editor describes it as 30 pgs., magazine-sized, offset printing, with glossy cover, circulation 1,000 for 200 subscriptions. Subscription: $19/year. **Sample postpaid: $1.50. Reports in 10 days, has 1 quarter backlog. Pays 10 copies. For chapbook publication (40 pgs.), submit 2 sample poems and cover letter with short bio. Simultaneous submissions OK. Pays copies. For sample chapbook send SASE with bookrate postage.** They offer awards of $100, $50 and $25 for the best poems published in the magazine and present them to winners at annual awards banquet. *IBW* is open to all writers.

INTERNATIONAL OLYMPIC LIFTER (IOL) (IV-Specialized), P.O. Box 65855, Los Angeles CA 90065, founded 1973, poetry editor Dale Rhoades, is a bimonthly "for the serious weight lifter, coach, administrator and enthusiast." **They want poetry about olympic-style weight lifting—occasionally use poetry about nature, the environment or health. "We prefer balanced meter rhyming, 10-16 lines."** Press run is 3,000 for 2,700 subscribers of which approximately 5% are libraries. Subscription: $25. **Sample postpaid: $4.50. No previously published poems; simultaneous submissions OK. Reports "immediately." Pays $10-25.** The editor says, "Know your market. Often we get poems on body building, power lifting, running or aerobics which are all foreign to olympic lifting. Purchase a copy to understand our requirements."

INTERNATIONAL POETRY REVIEW (II, IV-Translations), Dept. of Romance Languages, UNC-Greensboro, Greensboro NC 27412, phone (910)334-5655, fax (910)334-5404, founded 1975, editor Mark Smith-Soto, is a biannual primarily publishing **translations of contemporary poetry with corresponding originals (published on facing pages) as well as original poetry in English.** They have recently published work by Jasha Kessler, Lyn Lifshin, Pureza Canelo, Jaime Sabines and Fred Chappell. As a sample the editor selected these lines from "Poema de Invierno" by Chilean poet Jorge Teillier:

En la casa ha empezado la fiesta.

> *Pero el niño sabe que la fiesta está en otra parte,*
> *y mira por la ventana buscando a los desconocidos*
> *que pasará toda la vida tratando de encontrar.*

translated as "Winter Poem" by Mary Crow:

> *In the house the party has begun.*
> *But the child knows the party is somewhere else,*
> *and he looks out the window searching for the strangers*
> *he will spend his whole life trying to find.*

IPR is 100 pgs., 5½×8½, professionally printed and perfect-bound with 2-3 color cover. "We accept 10% of original poetry in English and about 80% of translations submitted." Press run is 500 for 250 subscribers of which 100 are libraries. Subscription: $10 individuals, $15 institutions. **Sample postpaid: $5. Submit no more than 5 pages of poetry. No previously published poems; simultaneous submissions OK. Seldom comments on rejections. Send SASE for guidelines. Reports in 3 months. Pays 1 copy. All rights revert to authors and translators.** Occasionally reviews book of poetry. Open to unsolicited reviews. Poets may also send books for review consideration. The editor says, "We strongly encourage contributors to subscribe. We get too much original poetry and not enough translation. We prefer poetry in English to have an international or cross-cultural theme."

INTERNATIONAL POETS ACADEMY; INTERNATIONAL POETS (I, IV-Membership), 5, Mohamed Hussain Khan Lane, Royapettah, Madras 600-014, India, founded 1981, poetry editor Prof. Syed Ameeruddin. The Academy publishes books by members (for a price) and brings out special numbers of *International Poets*, their quarterly journal publishing poetry by members, "highlighting the poems of selected poets with detailed bio-data and with a scholarly critical article focusing the main features of the selected poet's poetry to the world audience, with a photograph of the poet published on the front cover." **Membership is $40 a year. Life fellow membership is $100.** They have recently published poetry by Naomi F. Faust (USA), Hugh Aitken (England), David Moe (USA), Maria Do Carmo Gaspar De Oliveira (Brazil), Takashi Arima (Japan), Frances Hockney (Australia) and Osman Turkay (Turkey). The editor describes the quarterly as 5¼×8½, perfect-bound; printed in Madras. Reviews books of poetry. They also publish 3 chapbooks/year subsidized by the poets. For details contact the Academy.

INTERNATIONAL QUARTERLY (II, IV-Translations), P.O. Box 10521, Tallahassee FL 32302-0521, phone (904)224-5078, fax (904)224-5127, founded 1993, editor-in-chief Van K. Brock. **"We welcome outstanding writing in all genres, in original English and in translation, quality work that transcends cultural givens. No one-dimensional views of people or place, work that is amateurish or lacks complexity."** They have recently published work by Joy Harjo, Peter Meinke and Adonis. As a sample the editor selected these lines by Dionisio Martínez, translated by Sandra Teichmann:

> *I will tell you a story of rain.*
> *I can tell you so many stories of rain.*
> *There are people all over the world telling*
> *stories of rain. This is the last story*
> *of rain that I carry in my eyes. This time*
> *you are going to listen and believe me.*

IQ is 200 pgs., 7½×10, offset, perfect-bound, with full-cover artwork on the coated card cover and an 8-page, 4-color insert. They receive about 800 mss/year, accept a quarter. Press run is 5,000 for 1,000 shelf sales. Single copy: $8; subscription: $22/year. **Sample postpaid: $6. Submit no more than 8 poems, name on each. No previously published poems; simultaneous submissions OK. Cover letter welcomed.** Time between acceptance and publication is 3-9 months. Poems go from multiple readers to poetry editor to editorial board and editor-in-chief. **Often comments on rejections. Send SASE for upcoming themes. Reports within 4 months. Pays 2 copies. Acquires first serial rights.** Reviews books of poetry. Open to unsolicited reviews; query first. Poets may also send books for review consideration. The editor says, "Writers who have not published elsewhere are welcome to submit, but rarely have the polish necessary to be published in *IQ*."

INTERTEXT (V, IV-Translations), 2633 E. 17th Ave., Anchorage AK 99508-3207, founded 1982, editor Sharon Ann Jaeger, publishes "full-length collections by poets of demonstrated achievement" and is "devoted to producing lasting works in every sense. We specialize in poetry, translations and short works in the fine arts and literary criticism. **We publish work that is truly excellent—no restrictions on form, length or style. Cannot use religious verse. Like both surrealist and realist poetry, poetry with intensity, striking insight, vivid imagery, fresh metaphor, musical use of language in both word sounds and rhythm. Must make the world—in all its dimensions—come alive."** To give a sense of her taste she says, "I admire the work of Sarah Kirsch, William Stafford, António Ramos Rosa and Rainer Maria Rilke." Forthcoming: *Karasuyama Poems*, by Brenda Jaeger. As a sample the editor selected these lines by James Hanlen from *17 Toutle River Haiku*:

> *I would paint a black*

> *cloud tied to roots; river rock*
> *floating on sunlight.*

She says, **"Because we are 'booked up,' Intertext will not be looking at any unsolicited mss in the foreseeable future." Query first with 3-5 samples and SASE sent by first-class mail. Simultaneous queries OK. "Cover letter optional—the sample poems are always read first—but no form letters, please. If sample poems are promising, then the complete book ms will be requested." Always sends prepublication galleys. Pays 10% royalty after costs of production, promotion and distribution have been recovered.** The editor says, "We would like to receive higher-quality poetry than is usually sent to us. Please do not send a complete manuscript unless we specifically ask to see it. Intertext is not grant-supported, and each poet published represents a heavy investment of time, money and life moments on the part of the staff."

INTRO (IV-Students), AWP, Tallwood House, MS 1E3, George Mason University, Fairfax VA 22030, founded 1970, publications manager D.W. Fenza. See Associated Writing Programs in the Organizations Useful to Poets section of this book. **Students in college writing programs belonging to AWP may submit to this consortium of magazines publishing student poetry, fiction and plays. They are open as to the type of poetry submitted except they do not want "non-literary, haiku, etc."** As to poets they have published, they say, "In our history, we've introduced Dara Wier, Carolyn Forché, Greg Pope, Norman Dubie and others." Circulation 9,500. **All work must be submitted by the writing program. Programs nominate *Intro* works in the fall. Ask the director of your writing program for more information.**

INVERTED-A, INC.; INVERTED-A HORN (I), 401 Forrest Hill, Grand Prairie TX 75052, phone (214)264-0066, founded 1977, editors Amnon Katz and Aya Katz, is a very small press that evolved from publishing technical manuals for other products. "Our interests center on freedom, justice and honor." *Inverted-A Horn* is a periodical, magazine-sized, offset, usually 9 pages, which appears irregularly; circulation is 300. **Submissions of poetry for *Horn* and chapbooks are accepted. They publish 1 chapbook/year. The editors do not want to see anything "modern, formless, existentialist."** As a sample, they quote the following lines by Delta Zahner:

> *The auto cockpit represents a scene*
> *Of gauges and controls I lust to test.*
> *A map projects the missions in the West;*
> *Then signals for volition turn to green.*
> *My steed inhales its air with gasoline,*
> *And gallops with aggression on its quest.*

Queries are reported on in 1 month, mss in 4 months. Simultaneous submissions are OK. Pay is one free copy and a 40% discount on further copies. Samples: "A recent issue of the *Horn* can be had by merely sending a SASE with postage for 2 ounces (subject to availability)." The editor says "I strongly recommend that would-be contributors avail themselves of this opportunity to explore what we are looking for. Most of the submissions we receive do not come close."

IOTA (II), 67 Hady Crescent, Chesterfield, Derbyshire S41 0EB Great Britain, phone 01246-276532, founded 1988, editor David Holliday, is a quarterly wanting **"any style and subject; no specific limitations as to length, though, obviously, the shorter a poem is, the easier it is to get it in, which means that poems over 40 lines can still get in if they seem good enough. No concrete poetry (no facilities) or self-indulgent logorrhea."** They have recently published poetry by Carole Baldock, Carole Raney, Anne Keith, George Gott, Peter Russell and Thomas Land. As a sample the editor selected this complete poem, "Solo Travel," by Ronald Epstein:

> *You've lost your way,*
> *all by yourself.*
> *Your folly really shames you.*
> *You've got no one else to blame*
> *and no one else to blame you.*

Iota is 36 pgs., printed from typescript, saddle-stapled, with colored paper cover. They publish about 200 of 4,000 poems received. Their press run is 400 with 200 subscriptions of which 6 are libraries. Subscription: $8 (£5). **Sample postpaid: $2 (£1.25) "but sometimes sent free." Submit 4-6 poems at a time. The editor prefers name and address on each poem, typed, "but provided it's legible, am happy to accept anything." He considers simultaneous submissions, but previously published poems "only if outstanding." First report in 1-3 weeks (unless production of the next issue takes precedence) but final acceptance/rejection may take up to a year. Pays 2 copies. Acquires first British serial rights only. Editor usually comments on rejections, "but detailed comment only when time allows and the poem warrants it."** Reviews books of poetry in about 200 words, single or multi-book format. Open to unsolicited reviews. Poets may also send books for review consideration. He says, "I am after crafted verse that says something; self-indulgent word-spinning is out. All editors have their blind spots; the only advice I can offer a beginning poet is to find a sympathetic editor (and you will only do that by seeing their magazines) and not to be discouraged by initial lack of success. Keep plugging!"

UNIVERSITY OF IOWA PRESS; THE IOWA POETRY PRIZES (III), Iowa City IA 52242-1000. The University of Iowa Press offers annually The Iowa Poetry Prizes **for book-length mss (50-120 pgs.) by poets who have already published at least one full-length book in edition of at least 750 copies. Two awards are given each year of $1,000 plus publication with standard royalty contract.** (This competition is the only way in which this press accepts poetry.) **Mss are received annually in February and March only. Mss are screened by a panel of poets and final judging is done by the press's editorial staff. All writers of English are eligible, whether citizens of the US or not. Poems from previously published books may be included only in mss of selected or collected poems, submissions of which are encouraged. Simultaneous submissions OK if press is immediately notified if the book is accepted by another publisher. No reading fee is charged, but stamped, self-addressed packaging is required or mss will not be returned.** "These awards have been initiated to encourage poets who are beyond the first-book stage to submit their very best work."

THE IOWA REVIEW (II), Dept. PM, 308 EPB, University of Iowa, Iowa City IA 52242, phone (319)335-0462, founded 1970, editor David Hamilton (first readers for poetry and occasional guest editors vary), appears 3 times a year in a flat-spined, 200-page, professionally printed format. The editor says, "We simply look for poems that at the time we read and choose, we admire. **No specifications as to form, length, style, subject matter or purpose.** There are around 30-40 pgs. of poetry in each issue and currently we like to give several pages to a single poet. Though we print work from established writers, we're always delighted when we discover new talent." They receive about 5,000 submissions/ year, use about 100. Editors of this influential journal do seem open to all styles and lengths, with most poems falling into the lyric free verse category. Diction, for the most part, is accessible although some examples show degrees of experimentation with form. In all, poems evoke intriguing situations or ideas. Circulation 1,200-1,300 with 1,000 subscribers of which about half are libraries. Subscription: $18. **Sample postpaid: $6. Submit 3-6 poems at a time. Reads submissions September 1 through May 1 only. Their backlog is "around a year. Sometimes people hit at the right time and come out in a few months." Occasional comments on rejections or suggestions on accepted poems. Reports in 1-4 months. Pays $1 a line, 2-3 copies and a year's subscription. Buys first North American serial rights.** Poetry published in *The Iowa Review* has also been included in the 1992, 1993, 1994 and 1995 volumes of *The Best American Poetry* and the *Pushcart Prize* anthology for 1994. The editor advises, "That old advice of putting poems in a drawer for 9 years was rather nice; I'd at least like to believe the poems had endured with their author for 9 months."

IOWA WOMAN (IV-Women), P.O. Box 680, Iowa City IA 52244, founded 1979, poetry editor Sandra Adelmund. "We are a literary quarterly publishing fiction, essays and poetry of interest to women. This is a literary magazine that has received national recognition for editorial excellence. We are publishing work **by women, about women and for women. Prefer contemporary poetry that is clear and concise. Prefer narrative and lyric. No greeting card verse.**" They have published poetry by Lyn Lifshin, Alice Friman and Enid Shomer. As a sample the editor selected these lines by Maria S. Wickwire:

> She forgot and forgot, releasing
> small things with infinite patience and love
> gently pulling threads from the tapestry she had kept so long in place.

> As she forgot the foxes, they came out from the trees
> and leaned their soft noses into her palms.
> All the forgotten birds came down in a flock, returning their wordless songs.

Iowa Woman is elegantly printed, 48 pgs., magazine-sized, 4-color cover with "original cover art and illustrations." Of 2,000 poems received "I accept about 30." Press run is 2,500 for subscriptions and national newsstand sales. **Sample postpaid: $6. Submit 4-5 poems at a time. No simultaneous submissions. Guidelines available for SASE. Pays 2 copies and $5/poem. Buys first rights.** Reviews books of poetry in 500-1,000 words. Open to unsolicited reviews. Poets may also send books to Book Editor for review consideration. "No guarantee that books sent will be reviewed; this is at the discretion of our reviewers." They hold an annual poetry contest with first place prize of $100. $10 entry fee, 3 poems, for non-subscribers. Last year's judge was Diane Glancey. Contest guidelines available after May. Deadline: December 31. The editor says, "We would like to receive more poetry from minority women about their life experiences."

‡IRIS: A JOURNAL ABOUT WOMEN (II, IV-Translations, women), Women's Center, Box 323, HSC, University of Virginia, Charlottesville VA 22908, founded 1980, poetry editors Margo Andrea Figgins and Lisa Russ Spaar, is a semiannual magazine that **"focuses on issues concerning women worldwide. It also features quality poetry, prose and artwork—mainly by women, but will also**

**accept work by men if it illuminates some aspect of a woman's reality. It also publishes transla-
tions. Form and length are unspecified.** The poetry staff consists of experienced poets with a diversity
of tastes who are looking for new and original language in well-crafted poems." Poets who have
appeared in *Iris* include Sharon Olds, Gary Snyder, Mary Oliver, Lisel Mueller, Linda Pastan, Deborah
Nystrom and Gregory Orr. As a sample of poetry recently published, the editors selected these lines by
Kathleen M. Heideman:

> *My whole body is not as heavy as the word 'sad.'*
> *When I was lonely, my shadow was a blue whale*
> *and moved its tail like a ponderous "goodbye."*
> *Loneliness was constant weight, a cardiac darkness*
> *under which my skin thickened. Solitude was pressure,*
> *and each mouth of water I ate was a search for plankton.*
> *I sieved the dancing ocean water, I moved that glow*
> *through the fleshy folds of my mouth and killed it.*
> *I ate, my body was a cloud of ink in water and I sank.*

Iris is magazine-sized, professionally printed on heavy, glossy stock with a full-color glossy card cover,
72 pgs., saddle-stapled, using graphics, photos and cartoons. It has a circulation of more than 3,000,
with 50 library subscriptions, 1,000 shelf sales. Single copy: $4; subscription: $16 for 2 years. **Sample:
$5 postpaid. Submit 1-5 poems at a time. Simultaneous submissions are discouraged. Pays 1 copy.
Acquires first rights. Reports in 3-6 months. Name, address, phone number should be listed on
every poem. Cover letter should include list of poems submitted and a brief bio.** "Because *Iris* is a
feminist magazine, it receives a lot of poetry that tends to focus on the political experience of coming to
consciousness. The editors are interested in *all* aspects of the reality of women's lives and because many
poems are on similar topics, freshness of imagery and style become even more important."

‡IRON PRESS; IRON (II), 5 Marden Terrace, Cullercoats, North Shields, Tyne & Wear, NE30 4PD
England, phone (091)2531901, founded 1973, poetry editors Peter Mortimer, Rosemary Norman and
David Stephenson, "publishes contemporary writing both in magazine form (*Iron*) and in individual
books. Magazine concentrates on poetry, the books on prose and drama." They are **"open to many
influences, but no 19th century derivatives please, or work from people who seem unaware
anything has happened poetically since Wordsworth."** Peter Mortimer says, "Writing is accepted
and published because when I read it I feel the world should see it—if I don't feel that, it's no good.
What's the point of poetry nobody understands except the poet?" The poets they have published include
John Whitworth, Richard Kostelanetz and Sharon Olds. *Iron* is 8¼ × 7¾, flat-spined, professionally
printed in small type, 1-3 columns, using b&w photos and graphics, three-color glossy card cover, about
50 pgs. of poetry in each issue, circulation 1,000; 600 subscriptions of which 50 are libraries. **Sample:
$10 (bills only, no checks) postpaid, or £4. Submit a maximum of 5 poems. "Just the poems—no
need for long-winded backgrounds. The poems must stand by themselves. For return of poems, a
SAE with IRCs is essential." He reports in "2 weeks maximum." Pays £10/page. He always
comments on rejections "provided poets keep to our maximum of 5 poems per submission."** Staff
reviews books of poetry. Send books for review consideration % Val Laws, Reviews Editor. They do
not invite poetry submissions for books, which they commission themselves. The editor advises, "Don't
start submitting work too soon. It will only waste your own and editors' time. Many writers turn out a
few dozen poems, then rush them off before they've learnt much of the craft, never mind the art." And
about his occupation as editor, this journalist, poet, playwright and humorist says, "Small magazines
and presses contain some awful writing, which is inevitable. They also contain a kind of truth which the
large commercial organizations (over-burdened with marketing men, accountants and financial advisors) have long forgotten. And the good writing in small presses more than compensates for the awful."

ISRAEL HORIZONS (IV-Ethnic), 224 W. 35th St., Suite #403, New York NY 10001, founded 1952,
poetry consultants Rochelle Ratner and Jon Shevin. A quarterly Socialist-Zionist periodical which **uses
poetry reflecting Israeli and Jewish culture and concerns.** *Israel Horizons* reflects the Israeli left
and the Zionist peace camp in Israel, including but not exclusively *Mapam* and the National Kibbutz
(*Artzi*) Federation; it deals with current challenges to Israeli Society and the world Jewish community
from a Socialist-Zionist perspective and examines questions confronting democratic socialism in our
day. It includes editorial comments, regular columns on various topics and book and film reviews. It has
an international readership with readers in the U.S., Israel, Canada and 22 other countries. The publication is 8½ × 11, 32-40 pgs. Press run is 5,000. Subscription: $15/year. **Sample: $3 and SASE.**

ITALIAN AMERICANA (IV-Ethnic), URI/CCE, 199 Promenade St., Providence RI 02908-5090,
founded 1974, editor Carol Bonomo Albright, poetry editor Dana Gioia, appears twice a year using **8-
10 poems "on Italian-American subjects, no more than 3 pgs. No trite nostalgia; no poems about
grandparents."** As a sample the editor selected these lines from "Late Evening in Cheyenne" by Ned
Condini:

> *Nocturnal warmths of spring are in the air,*

> *echoing our eager youth, a rare*
> *marriage of constellations in the sky.*
> *This aged wine burns, and I want you to drink it*
> *with me, feel it rush down your thirsty throat,*
> *and thus bewitched, on tantalizing days*
> *of loss, forget for this glory your cross.*

It is 150-200 pgs., 6×9, professionally printed, flat-spined. Press run is 1,000 for 900 subscribers of which 175 are libraries, the rest individual adult subscribers. Subscription: $15. **Sample postpaid: $7.50. Submit 3 poems at a time. No previously published poems or simultaneous submissions. Cover letter not required "but helpful." Name on first page of ms only. Do not submit mss in July, August or September. Occasionally comments on rejections. Reports in 4-6 weeks. Acquires first rights.** Reviews books of poetry in 600 words, multi-book format. Poets may send books for review consideration to Prof. John Paul Russo, English Dept., University of Miami, Coral Gables FL 33124. The editor says, "Single copies of poems for submissions are sufficient."

ITALICA PRESS (IV-Bilingual/foreign language), 595 Main St., #605, New York NY 10044-0047, phone (212)935-4230, fax (212)838-7812, e-mail italica@aol.com, founded 1985, publishers Eileen Gardiner and Ronald G. Musto, is a small press publisher of **English translations of Italian works** in Smyth-sewn paperbacks, averaging 175 pgs. They have published *Guido Cavalcanti, The Complete Poems*, a dual language (English/Italian) book with English translation and introduction by Marc Cirigliano, and *Selected Poems* by Gaspara Stampa, a dual-language book edited and translated by Laura Anna Stortoni and Mary Prentice Lillie. Forthcoming: *Women Poets of the Italian Renaissance*, a dual-language anthology, edited and translated by Laura Anna Stortoni and Mary Prentice Lillie. **Query with 10 sample translations of medieval and Renaissance Italian poets. Include cover letter, bio and list of publications. Simultaneous submissions OK, but translation should not be "totally" previously published. Reports on queries in 3 weeks, on mss in 3 months. Always sends prepublication galleys. Pays 7-15% royalties plus 10 author's copies. Buys English language rights. Sometimes comments on rejections.**

‡JACKSON HARBOR PRESS (V), RR1, Box 107AA, Washington Island WI 54246, founded 1993, editor/publisher William Olson, was scheduled to publish 3 chapbooks in 1995. **They are currently unable to accept unsolicited submissions**, but say that "perhaps we will be able to open our door to regional poets in one or two years."

JACKSON'S ARM (III), % Sunk Island Publishing, Box 74, Lincoln LN1 1QG England, phone (01522)575660, fax (01522)568353, e-mail 100074.140@compuserve.com, founded 1985, editor Michael Blackburn, is a small press publisher of poetry chapbooks and translations. **"No specifications as to subject or style. The poetry I want to publish should be vigorous and imaginative, with a firm grasp of everyday realities. Nothing bland, safe or pretentious."** The press publishes occasional chapbooks, books, cards and cassettes. However, the editor says **he does not usually accept unsolicited submissions. Pays in copies: 10% of print run.** Also sponsors the annual Jackson's Arm Poetry Pamphlet Competition for 16 pgs. of poetry. Winning collection is published. Two runners-up receive £25 each. Send SASE (or SAE and IRCs) for details. Mr. Blackburn advises, "Read everything you can, in particular *contemporary* poets and writers. Get hold of all the 'small' poetry magazines you can, as well as the more commercial and prestigious."

‡JANUS, A JOURNAL OF LITERATURE; JANUS PRESS (I), P.O. Box 376, Collingswood NJ 08108, founded 1993, editor David Livewell, is currently an annual spring publication with plans to increase frequency as submissions increase. The editor describes *Janus* as "a unique forum for both new and established writers of well-crafted verse, where each can delight and inform the other. **We seek well-crafted verse in forms that are necessary to the content. Both metrical and free verse are considered. Poems by emerging writers are especially welcome. We frown upon works that exhibit solipsistic, pornographic, or meandering language."** They have recently published poetry by Paul Ramsey, Louis McKee and Joseph Meredith. As a sample the editor selected these lines from "Ruisdael and Constable in South Jersey" by Claude Koch:

> *Then resurrection's commonplace*
> *olls from the heart its blinding stone*
> *Carapace of casual dread,*
> *And Janus-eyed, and from the dead*
> *We take the common vision home.*

Janus is 28 pgs., 5½×8½, neatly printed and saddle-stapled, with colored card cover and b&w graphics. They receive approximately 800 poetry submissions a year, accept about 12. Press run is 500. **Submit 3-5 poems at a time. "Submissions cannot be returned." Include SASE for response. No previously published poems or simultaneous submissions. Cover letter required. Poems are circulated to an editorial board. Almost always comments on rejections. Reports in 2-3 months.**

Pays 2 copies. "We review books of poetry and other books of literary merit." Open to unsolicited reviews. Poets may also send books for review consideration (attn: Book Editor). Janus Press "will also publish chapbooks and/or singular works by authors who have impressed us on a regular basis." The editor says, "We are pleased to accept work from beginners and are encouraged by a general return to the intracacies of form and meter. Our kind of publication can serve as a springboard for literary careers. We are willing to give emerging writers the careful consideration they deserve."

JAPANOPHILE (IV-Form, ethnic), P.O. Box 223, Okemos MI 48864, phone (517)349-1795, founded 1974, poetry editor Earl R. Snodgrass, is a literary quarterly about Japanese culture (not just in Japan). Issues include articles, photos, art, a short story and **poetry. They want haiku or other Japanese forms ("they need not be about Japanese culture") or any form if the subject is about Japan, Japanese culture or American-Japanese relations. (Note: Karate and ikebana in the US are examples of Japanese culture.)** They have recently published poetry by Linda McFerrin, Elizabeth St. Jacques, Alexis Rotella, Nancy Corson Carter, David Carroll, Mimi Hinman and reprints of Basho. There are 10-15 pgs. of poetry in each issue (digest-sized, about 58 pgs., saddle-stapled). They have a circulation of 800 with 100 subscriptions of which 30 are libraries. They receive about 500 submissions a year, use 70, have a 2-month backlog. **Sample postpaid: $4. Summer is the best time to submit. Cover letter required; include brief bio and credits if any. Send SASE for guidelines. Reports in 2 months. Pays $1 for haiku and up to $15 for longer poems.** Open to unsolicited reviews. Poets may also send books for review consideration, attn. Vada L. Davis. They also publish books under the Japanophile imprint, but so far only one has been of poetry. Query with samples and cover letter (about 1 pg.) giving publishing credits, bio. The editor says, "This quarterly is out as each season begins. Poems that name or suggest a season, and are received two or three months before the season, get a good look."

JEWISH CURRENTS (II), 22 E. 17th St., Suite 601, New York NY 10003-1919, phone (212)924-5740, founded 1946, editor Morris U. Schappes, is a magazine appearing 11 times a year that publishes **poetry on Jewish subjects and themes, including translations from the Yiddish and Hebrew** (original texts should be submitted with translations). The editor says it is 48 pgs., 5×8, offset, saddle-stapled. Press run is 2,600 for 2,500 subscribers of which about 10% are libraries. Subscription: $20/year. **Sample postpaid: $2. Submit 1 poem at a time, typed, double-spaced, with SASE. No previously published poems or simultaneous submissions. Cover letter required. Publishes theme issues.** Time between acceptance and publication is 2 years. **Seldom comments on rejections. Send SASE for guidelines and upcoming themes. Reports in 6-12 months. Always sends prepublication galleys. Pays 6 copies plus 1-year subscription.** Reviews books of poetry. Open to unsolicited reviews. Publishers may also send books of poetry for review consideration.

JEWISH SPECTATOR (IV-Religious), 4391 Park Milano, Calabasas CA 91302, phone (818)591-7481, fax (818)591-7267, founded 1935, editor Robert Bleiweiss. *Jewish Spectator* is a 68-page Judaic scholarly quarterly that **welcomes poetry on Jewish themes.** Subscribers: 1,400. **No simultaneous submissions or previously published poems. Cover letter with brief bio (2-3 lines) required. Reports in 6 weeks. Returns mss only with SASE. Pays 2 copies.** Open to unsolicited reviews. Poets may also send books for review consideration.

JEWISH VEGETARIANS NEWSLETTER; JEWISH VEGETARIANS OF NORTH AMERICA (I, IV-Religious, specialized), 6938 Reliance Rd., Federalsburg MD 21632, phone (410)754-5550, founded 1983, editor Eva R. Mossman. *Jewish Vegetarians Newsletter* is a quarterly publication of the Jewish Vegetarians of North America, a nonprofit organization. It is designed to promote vegetarianism within the Judaic tradition and includes various articles, recipes and short book reviews. **They want poetry that is "Jewish related and/or about vegetarianism, veganism, animal rights and/or the environment."** As a sample the editor selected these lines from "The Festival of Fruit" by Louis Berman, in honor of the Jewish Holiday Tu B'Shevat. ("Tu B'Shevat is a kind of springtime Thanksgiving."):

> *When Springtime warms the earth*
> *And lengthens the daylight hours*
> *This is the sign of promise*
> *That the earth is awakening from its wintry sleep*
> *And will again become fruitful.*

The newsletter is 16 pgs., $8\frac{1}{2} \times 11$, printed on recycled paper and saddle-stapled. Press run is 1,200 for 700 subscribers. Subscription: $12/year. **Sample available free with #10 SAE and 2 first-class stamps. Submit 2 poems at a time. Previously published poems and simultaneous submissions OK. Cover letter required. "Please include permission to print." Often comments on rejections. Send SASE for upcoming themes. Reports in no more than 3 months. "We do not pay for literary contributions." However, copies are available free for the cost of postage and all poetry remains the property of the author.** The editor says, "We encourage everyone to obtain a sample issue."

‡JEWISH WOMEN'S LITERARY ANNUAL; JEWISH WOMEN'S RESOURCE CENTER (IV-Ethnic, women), 9 E. 69th St., New York NY 10021, phone (212)751-9223, fax (212)935-3523, founded 1994, editor Henny Wenkart, publishes poetry and fiction **by Jewish women. They want "poems by Jewish women on any topic, but of the highest literary quality."** They have recently published poetry by Alicia Ostriker, Enid Dame and Lesléa Newman. As a sample the editor selected these lines from "To The Tideline" by Madeline Tiger:

> . . . *my eyes full of sky, my bosom bedazzled in seaweed;*
> *if I take you with me in the arms of the sea*
> *and break the boundaries of breath, birth, age, and belief,*
> *will you forget?*
> *will you forget my past?*
> *will you forget your grief?*

The annual is 160 pgs., 6×9, perfect-bound with a laminated card cover, b&w art and photos inside. They receive about 500 poems a year, publish approximately 15%. Press run is 1,000. **Sample postpaid: $5. No previously published poems. Poems are circulated to an editorial board. Often comments on rejections. Reports in 3-5 months. Pays 3 copies. Rights remain with the poet.** The Jewish Women's Resource Center holds a monthly workshop, sponsors occasional readings and **also publishes a few books of poetry.** "We select only one or two manuscripts a year out of about 20 submitted. But although authors then receive editing help and publicity, they bear the cost of production. Members of the workshop we conduct and poets published in our annual receive first attention." The editor says, "It would be helpful, but not essential, if poets would send for a sample copy of our annual before submitting."

‡THE JOHNS HOPKINS UNIVERSITY PRESS (V), 2715 N. Charles St., Baltimore MD 21218, founded 1878, editor-in-chief Eric Halpern. "One of the largest American university presses, Johns Hopkins is a publisher mainly of scholarly books and journals. We do, however, publish short fiction and poetry in the series Johns Hopkins: Poetry and Fiction, edited by John Irwin on 10% royalty contracts. **Unsolicited submissions are not considered."**

THE JOURNAL (III), Dept. of English, Ohio State University, 164 W. 17th Ave., Columbus OH 43210, founded 1972, co-editors Kathy Fagan and Michelle Herman, appears twice yearly with reviews, essays, quality fiction and poetry. **"We're open to all forms; we tend to favor work that gives evidence of a mature and sophisticated sense of the language."** They have published poetry by David Baker, T.R. Hummer, Cynthia Ozick and Carol Frost. The following sample is from the poem "The Helmet of Mambrino" by Linda Bierds:

> *I would know that tumble often, that*
> *explorer's slide, belief to belief, conviction*
> *to its memory, to conviction. Once I placed*
> *my marker-coin on Mt. Whitney's double, lost in a mist,*
> *convinced I had climbed to the highest land. Once*
> *I charted a lake from opal air.*

The Journal is 6×9, professionally printed on heavy stock, 80-100 pgs., of which about 40 in each issue are devoted to poetry. They receive about 4,000 submissions/year, use 200, and have a 3- to 6-month backlog. Press run is 1,500. Subscription: $8. **Sample: $5. On occasion editor comments on rejections. Pays copies and an honorarium of $25-50 when funds are available. Acquires all rights. Returns rights on publication.** Reviews books of poetry. Contributing editor David Citino advises, "However else poets train or educate themselves, they must do what they can to know our language. Too much of the writing that we see indicates that poets do not in many cases develop a feel for the possibilities of language, and do not pay attention to craft. Poets should not be in a rush to publish—until they are ready." (Also see Ohio State University Press/*The Journal* Award in Poetry.)

JOURNAL OF ASIAN MARTIAL ARTS (IV-Specialized), 821 W. 24th St., Erie PA 16502, phone (814)455-9517, fax (814)838-7811, founded 1991, editor-in-chief Michael A. DeMarco, is a quarterly "comprehensive journal on Asian martial arts with high standards and academic approach." **They want poetry about Asian martial arts and Asian martial art history/culture. They have no restrictions provided the poet has a feel for, and good understanding of, the subject. They don't want poetry showing a narrow view. "We look for a variety of styles from an interdisciplinary approach."** As a

---

The Subject Index, located before the General Index, can help you narrow down markets for your work. It lists those publishers whose poetry interests are specialized.

sample we selected the opening lines from "Kensei" by Berrien C. Henderson:

> *He approaches last.*
> *A zephyr gusts and swirls about him.*
> *His **gi** flaps and pops in the wind.*
> *Brow furrowed and jet hair shining, he stands*
> *As tranquil as a distant mountain*
> *While his topknot swings ever so gently.*

The editor says the journal is 128 pgs., 8½ × 11, perfect-bound, with soft cover, b&w illustrations, computer and hand art and ads. Press run is 6,000 for 1,000 subscribers of which 50 are libraries, the rest mainly shelf sales. Single copy: $9.75; subscription: $32 for 1 year, $55 for 2 years. **Sample postpaid: $10. Previously published poems OK; no simultaneous submissions. Cover letter required. Often comments on rejections. Send SASE for guidelines. Reports in 1-2 months. Sometimes sends prepublication galleys. Pays $1-100 and/or 1-5 copies on publication. Buys first and reprint rights.** Reviews books of poetry "if they have some connection to Asian martial arts; length is open." Open to unsolicited reviews. Poets may also send books for review consideration. The editor adds, "We offer a unique medium for serious poetry dealing with Asian martial arts. Any style is welcome if there is quality in thought and writing."

JOURNAL OF NEW JERSEY POETS (II, IV-Regional), English Dept., County College of Morris, Randolph NJ 07869, phone (201)328-5471, founded 1976, editor Sander Zulauf. This biannual periodical uses poetry from **current or former residents of New Jersey. They want "serious work that is regional in origin but universal in scope." They do not want "sentimental, greeting card verse."** Poets published include Lesley Choyce, Alfred Starr Hamilton, Phebe Davidson and Joe Weil. As a sample, the editor selected the following excerpt from " 'For May Is the Month of Our Mother' " by Cat Doty:

> *Next, I played Nelson Eddy "Ave Maria." Her one inch of face*
> *held too much sadness to bear. To cheer her up,*
> *I played "Rum and Coca Cola" The Andrews Sisters, and our souls*
> *were so open from all that ave maria that we threw ourselves*
> *into the rhythm, and jumped on the bed, and I beat Mary*
> *like a maraca in my palm, her burden of black beads clacking*
> *thick and loud, until one slap too many cracked her right in half,*
> *and her beads flung themselves to the floor, where they lay*
> *like intestines.*

The journal is published in March (spring) and October (autumn), digest-sized, offset, with an average of 64 pgs. Press run is 900. Subscription: $7/year, $12/2 years. **Sample: $4. There are "no limitations" on submissions; SASE required. Reports in 3-6 months.** Time between acceptance and publication is within 1 year. **Pays 2 copies/published poem. Acquires first North American serial rights.** Only using solicited reviews. Send books for review consideration. "We plan to offer brief reviews of 100-150 words."

JOURNAL OF POETRY THERAPY (IV-Specialized), Dept. PM, Human Sciences Press, 233 Spring St., New York NY 10013-1578, phone (212)620-8000 or (800)221-9369, founded 1987. **Poetry mss should be sent to journal editor,** Dr. Nicholas Mazza, School of Social Work, Florida State University, Tallahassee FL 32306-2024. They use **"poems that could be useful in therapeutic settings, prefer relatively short poems; no sentimental, long poems."** They have published poetry by Ingrid Wendt and Virginia Bagliore. As a sample the editor selected these lines from "all too often, love " by Elaine Preston:

> *like our hunger*
> *in the house where we warmed our fingers*
> *and laughed against cracks in walls*
> *long since plastered shut against the cold*

"The *Journal* is devoted to the use of the poetic in health, mental health education and other human service settings." The quarterly is 64 pgs., digest-sized, flat-spined, using 3-6 pgs. for poetry. They accept approximately 10% of 100 poems received. There are 500 subscriptions. Subscription: $42 (US), $49 (international) for individuals; $155 (US), $180 (international) for institutions. **Write publisher for free sample. Submit maximum of 3 poems, 4 copies of each with name on only 1 of them. Include SASE. Editor "occasionally" comments on rejections. Pays 1 copy.**

JOURNAL OF THE AMERICAN MEDICAL ASSOCIATION (JAMA) (II, IV-Specialized, themes), 515 N. State, Chicago IL 60610, phone (312)464-2417, fax (312)464-5824, founded 1883, associate editor Charlene Breedlove, has a "Poetry and Medicine" column and publishes **poetry "in some way related to a medical experience, whether from the point-of-view of a health care worker or patient, or simply an observer. No unskilled poetry."** They have recently published poetry by Caryn

Russell and Jack Coulehan. As a sample the editor selected these lines from "Channel" by Floyd Skloot:

> In time the fork my life took as illness
> cut its course will have wandered to the main
> stream. There, far below the long waterfalls
> and cataracts I will begin my rush
> to the place I was going from the start.

JAMA, magazine-sized, flat-spined, with glossy paper cover, has 360,000 subscribers of which 369 are libraries. They accept about 7% of 550 poems received/year. Subscription: $66. **Sample free. No previously published poems; simultaneous submissions OK, if identified. "I always appreciate inclusion of a brief cover letter with, at minimum, the author's name and address clearly printed. Mention of other publications and special biographical notes are always of interest." Publishes theme issues. Theme issues in late 1995 and early 1996 will include medical education, imaging, human rights, emerging microbial threats and Olympics/sports medicine. Write for details. Pays up to 3 copies. "We ask for a signed copyright release, but publication elsewhere is always granted free of charge."**

JUGGLER'S WORLD (IV-Specialized), % Ken Letko, College of the Redwoods, 883 W. Washington Blvd., Crescent City CA 95531-8361, phone (707)464-7457, founded 1982, literary editor Ken Letko, is a quarterly magazine, **using poems about juggling. "Only restriction is that all content is focused on juggling."** They have published poetry by Robert Hill Long, Barbara Goldberg and Margo Wilding. As a sample the editor selected these lines from "Street Mime" by Ann B. Knox:

> . . . a girl
> smiles, the man bows to her, then
> spreads his hands wide and silver
> balls lift in an arc high
> over his head. Faces pivot

JW is 40 pgs., magazine-sized, saddle-stapled, professionally printed on glossy stock with 2-color glossy paper cover. They receive 50-100 poetry submissions/year, use 4-8 poems. Press run is 3,500, circulated to more than 3,000 jugglers in more than 20 countries. Subscription: $18. **Sample: "$2 or $3 depending on issue." They will consider previously published poems. Editor sometimes comments on rejections, suggesting some revision. Reports in 1-4 months. Pays 1 copy. Acquires first or one-time rights.** The editor urges poets to "provide insights."

JUNIPER PRESS; NORTHEAST; JUNIPER BOOKS; THE WILLIAM N. JUDSON SERIES OF CONTEMPORARY AMERICAN POETRY; CHICKADEE; INLAND SEA SERIES; GIFTS OF THE PRESS (III, IV-Form), 1310 Shorewood Dr., La Crosse WI 54601, founded 1962, poetry editors John Judson and Joanne Judson, is one of the oldest and most respected programs of publishing poetry in the country. *Northeast* is a semiannual little magazine, digest-sized, saddle-stapled. **"Poets published in our books have first appeared in *Northeast* and are invited to submit mss. Any other book mss sent will be returned without being read." Reports in 2-4 months.** A subscription to *Northeast/*Juniper Press is $33/year ($38 for institutions), which brings you 2 issues of the magazine and the Juniper Books, Chickadees, WNJ Books and some gifts of the press, a total of about 5-8 items. (Or send SASE for catalog to order individual items. **Sample postpaid: $2.50.**) The Juniper Books are perfect-bound books of poetry; the WNJ Books are letterpress poetry books by one author; Chickadees are 12-24 pgs. each, in wrappers; Inland Sea Series is for larger works; Gifts of the Press are usually given only to subscribers or friends of the press. "Please read us before sending mss. It will aid in your selection of materials to send. If you don't like what we do, please don't submit."

JUST ABOUT HORSES (I, IV-Specialized), 14 Industrial Rd., Pequannock NJ 07440, founded 1975, editor Stephanie Macejko, is a magazine which appears 6 times/year and provides information about both the model horse hobby and real horses. **"Our magazine deals with model horses and real horses. Any style of poetry will be read as long as the style suits the subject matter."** *Just About Horses* is 40 pgs., digest-sized, saddle-stapled, professionally printed on glossy paper with b&w and color photos. Press run is 14,000 for 12,500 subscribers. Subscription: $12. **Sample postpaid: $2.50.**

KAIMANA: LITERARY ARTS HAWAII; HAWAII LITERARY ARTS COUNCIL (III, IV-Regional), P.O. Box 11213, Honolulu HI 96828, founded 1974, editor Tony Quagliano. *Kaimana*, a semiannual, is the magazine of the Hawaii Literary Arts Council. **Poems with "some Pacific reference are preferred—Asia, Polynesia, Hawaii—but not exclusively."** They have published poetry by Howard Nemerov, John Yau, Reuben Tam, Reuel Denney, Tony Friedson, Joe Balaz, Ursule Molinaro, Lyn Lifshin, Haunani-Kay Trask, Anne Waldman and Joe Stanton. As a sample the editor selected the first stanza of "The Castle" by Robert Bly:

> What am I? A son
> Newly born or newly

> *Awakened, writhing*
> *On the bed like a slave,*
> *Who goes at night to a castle*
> *Made of black sticks.*

Kaimana is 64-76 pgs., 7½ × 10, saddle-stapled, with high-quality printing. Press run is 1,000 for 600 subscribers of which 200 are libraries. Subscription: $12. **Sample postpaid: $5. Cover letter with submissions preferred. Sometimes comments on rejections. Reports with "reasonable dispatch." Pays 2 copies.** The editor says, "Hawaii gets a lot of 'travelling regionalists,' visiting writers with inevitably superficial observations. We also get superb visiting observers who are careful craftsmen anywhere. *Kaimana* is interested in the latter, to complement our own best Hawaii writers."

KALEIDOSCOPE: INTERNATIONAL MAGAZINE OF LITERATURE, FINE ARTS, AND DISABILITY (IV-Specialized, themes), 326 Locust St., Akron OH 44302, phone (216)762-9755, fax (216)762-0912, founded 1979, editor-in-chief Dr. Darshan C. Perusek, consulting poetry editor Christopher Hewitt. *Kaleidoscope* is based at United Disability Services, a nonprofit agency. **Poetry should deal with the experience of disability but not limited to that when writer has a disability. "*Kaleidoscope* is interested in high-quality poetry with vivid, believable images and evocative language. Works should not use stereotyping, patronizing or offending language about disability."** They have recently published poetry by Margaret Robison, Maurice Kenny, Alden Nowlan and Cheryl Marie Wade. As a sample, they offer these lines from "Hang Gliding" by Sheryl L. Nelms:

> *five crows dance*
> *on the thermal*
> *above the Bedford State Bank.*
> *land on the tenth floor ledge*
> *then one*
> *by one*
> *they push off*

Circulation 1,500, including libraries, social service agencies, health-care professionals, universities and individual subscribers. Single copy: $5; subscription: $9 individual, $14 agency. **Sample: $4. Submit photocopies with SASE for return of work. Limit 5 poems/submission. Previously published poems and simultaneous submissions OK, "as long as we are notified in both instances." Cover letter required. All submissions must be accompanied by an autobiographical sketch. Deadlines: March and August 1. Publishes theme issues. Send SASE for upcoming themes. Themes for 1996 are as follows: "Disability and Travel"—January 1996 (deadline August 1995), and "Disability and Violence in the Family"—July 1996 (deadline March 1996). Reports back in 3 weeks, acceptance or rejection may take 6 months. Pays $10-125. Rights return to author upon publication.** Staff reviews books of poetry. Send books for review consideration to Gail Willmott, senior editor.

KALLIOPE, a journal of women's art (IV-Women, translations, themes), 3939 Roosevelt Blvd., Jacksonville FL 32205, phone (904)381-3511, founded 1978, editor Mary Sue Koeppel, is a literary/visual arts journal published by Florida Community College at Jacksonville; the emphasis is on women writers and artists. The editors say, **"We like the idea of poetry as a sort of artesian well— there's one meaning that's clear on the surface and another deeper meaning that comes welling up from underneath. We'd like to see more poetry from Black, Hispanic and Native American women. Nothing sexist, racist, conventionally sentimental. We will have one special theme issue each year. Write for specific guidelines."** Poets recently published include Elisavietta Ritchie, Marge Piercy, Martha M. Vertreace, Enid Shomer and Tess Gallager. As a sample, the editor selected the following lines by Ruth Moon Kempher:

> *But I sail hot, sail cold, depending*
> *not on externals, but on that queer greed*
> *driving, from sea to street*
> > *on to dark hedgerows*
> *shadowed alleys, like a creature*
> *chased, like Cinderella*
> *shoes in hand.*

Kalliope calls itself "a journal of women's art" and publishes fiction, interviews, drama and visual art in addition to poetry. The magazine, which appears 3 times a year, is 7¼ × 8¼, flat-spined, handsomely printed on white stock, glossy card cover and b&w photographs of works of art. Average number of pages is 80. Poems here are lively, celebratory and varied in form, style and length. The circulation is 1,250, of which 400-500 are subscriptions, including 100 library subscriptions, and 600 are copies sold on newsstands and in bookstores. Subscription: $12.50/year or $22/2 years. **Sample: $7. Poems should be submitted in batches of 3-5 with brief bio note, phone number and address. No previously published poems. SASE required. Because all submissions are read by several members of the editing staff, response time is usually 3-4 months. Publication will be within 6 months. Criticism is** provided "when time permits and the author has requested it." Send SASE for guidelines and upcoming themes. **Pays 3 copies. Acquires first publication rights.** Reviews books of poetry, "but we prefer groups of books in one review." Open to unsolicited reviews. Poets may also send books for review consideration. They sponsor the Sue Saniel Elkind Poetry Contest. 1995 judge was Joy Harjo. First prize: $1,000; runners up published in *Kalliope*. Deadline: October 15. Send SASE for details. The editor says, "*Kalliope* is a carefully stitched patchwork of how women feel, what they experience, and what they have come to know and understand about their lives . . . a collection of visions from or about women all over the world. Send for a sample copy, to see what appeals to us, or better yet, subscribe!"

KANGAROOS AND BEANS (V), P.O. Box 40231, Redford MI 48240, phone (313)537-9425, founded 1989, editor Gregg Nannini, appears twice a year. **They publish "poetry that excites or strikes a philosophical chord." However, they are currently overstocked and not accepting any poetry submissions.** They have published poetry by Jeanette Picardi and Kathleen Meade. As a sample the editor selected these lines from Meade's "Attempts to Enter a Pastoral Painting":

> *Her fingers press the oil,*
> *   extract lanolin from sheep.*
> *Her tongue searches the Italian Vale.*

It is 20 pgs., 8½ × 11, photocopied from typescript and corner-stapled. Press run is 500. Subscription: $4. **Sample postpaid: $2. Make check payable to Gregg Nannini.**

KANSAS QUARTERLY; KANSAS ART COMMISSION AWARDS; SEATON AWARDS (II, IV-Regional, themes), The English Dept., Kansas State University, Manhattan KS 66506, phone (913)532-6716, founded 1968 as an outgrowth of *Kansas Magazine*, editors Ben Nyberg, John Rees and G.W. Clift, is "a magazine devoted to the culture, history, art and writing of mid-Americans, but not restricted to this area." It publishes poetry in all issues. They say, **"We are interested in all kinds of modern poetry except limericks, extremely light verse or book-length mss."** They have published poetry by David Ray, Tom Hansen, Bruce Cutler, Deborah Pierce Nichols, F.D. Reeve, Harold Witt, Anthony Sobin, David Citino, Peter Cooley and David Kirby. There are an average of 80 pgs. of poetry in each creative issue. They receive 10,000 submissions/year, use 300-400. There is at least a 12- to 18-month backlog unless a poem fits into a special number—then it may go in rapidly. Circulation 1,150-1,350 with 721 subscriptions of which 50% are libraries. **Sample postpaid: $6 ($8 for double number). Submit "enough poems to show variety (or a single poem if author wishes), but no books. Typed, double-spaced, OK. No queries. We consider, reluctantly, simultaneous submissions." Reports in 1-3 months. Pays 2 copies and yearly awards of up to $200/poet for 6-10 poets.** The *Kansas Quarterly*/Kansas Art Commission Awards are $200 (1st prize), $150 (2nd), $100 (3rd), $75 (4th) and up to 5 honorable mentions ($50). There are also similar prizes in the Seaton Awards (to native-born or resident Kansas poets). The editors **often comment on rejections, even at times suggesting revision and return.** An excellent market, this magazine has been known on occasion to pack the work of more than 60 poets in its 200 pages/issue. All styles are welcome, but response times can be slow. Editors say, "Our only advice is for the poet to *know* the magazine he is sending to: consult in library or send for sample copy. Magazines need the support and their published copies should provide the best example of what the editors are looking for. We believe that we annually publish as much generally good poetry as nearly any other U.S. literary magazine—between 250 and 400 poems a year. Others will have to say how good it really is."

KARAMU (II), Dept. of English, Eastern Illinois University, Charleston IL 61920, phone (217)581-5614, founded 1966, editor Peggy Brayfield, is an annual whose "goal is to provide a forum for the best contemporary poetry and fiction that comes our way. We especially like to print the works of new writers. **We like to see poetry that shows a good sense of what's being done with poetry currently. We like poetry that builds around real experiences, real images and real characters and that avoids abstraction, overt philosophizing and fuzzy pontifications. In terms of form, we prefer well-structured free verse, poetry with an inner, sub-surface structure as opposed to, let's say, the surface structure of rhymed quatrains. We have definite preferences in terms of style and form, but no such preferences in terms of length or subject matter. Purpose, however, is another thing. We don't have much interest in the openly didactic poem. If the poet wants to preach against or for some political or religious viewpoint, the preaching shouldn't be so strident that it overwhelms the poem. The poem should first be a poem."** They have published poetry by David Bond, Mary McDaniel, Pamela Donald and Karen Subach. As a sample the editor selected these lines from "We Begin Here" by Steven Blaski:

> *Your death broke into you as if it were a door*
> *of glass that you smashed your body through.*
> *Still, each night I followed you to the rooms*
> *of my ravaged childhood, where you wore*
> *the hellish body that performed in the freak show*
> *of intensive care . . .*

The format is 120 pgs., 5 × 8, matte cover, handsomely printed (narrow margins), attractive b&w art. The most recent issue carries 60 pgs. of poetry. They receive submissions from about 300 poets each year, use 40-50 poems. Never more than a year—usually 6-7 months—between acceptance and publication. They have a circulation of 350 with 300 subscribers of which 15 are libraries. **Sample: $5; 2 recent issues: $6. Poems—in batches of no more than 4-6—may be submitted to Peggy Brayfield. "We don't much care for simultaneous submissions. We read September 1 through June 30 only, for fastest decision submit February through May. Poets should not bother to query. We critique a few of the better poems. We want the poet to consider our comments and then submit new work." Publishes theme issues occasionally. Submissions on the theme, "Humor," may be submitted between September and November, 1995, for publication Spring 1997. Pays 1 copy. Acquires first serial rights.** The editor says, "Follow the standard advice: Know your market. Read contemporary poetry and the magazines you want to be published in. Be patient."

KATYDID BOOKS (V), 1 Balsa Rd., Santa Fe NM 87505, founded 1973, editors/publishers Karen Hargreaves-Fitzsimmons and Thomas Fitzsimmons, publishes 3 paperbacks and 1 hardback/year. "We publish three series of poetry: Asian Poetry in Translation, European Writing in Translation, and American Poets." They have published poetry by Makoto Ooka, Shuntaro Tanikawa and Ryuichi Tamura. **However, they are currently not accepting submissions.**

KAWABATA PRESS; SEPIA POETRY MAGAZINE (I, II, IV-Anthology), Knill Cross House, Millbrook, Torpoint, Cornwall, United Kingdom, founded 1977, poetry editor Colin David Webb, publishes **"nontraditional poetry, prose and artwork (line only), open to all original and well thought-out work. I hate rhymes, traditional poems and dislike 'genre' stories. I want original and thought-provoking material."** *Sepia* is published 3 times a year in an inexpensively produced, digest-sized, 32-page, saddle-stapled format, photoreduced from typescript, with narrow margins and bizarre drawings. They receive 250 submissions/year, use 50-60. Press run is 150 for 75 subscribers of which 5-6 are libraries. Subscription: £2 ($5) a year. **Sample: 75p. ($2). Submit 6 poems at a time, typed. Prefers not to use previously published poems. Simultaneous submissions OK. "Letter with poems is polite." Reports in 10 days. Sometimes sends prepublication galleys. Pays free copy.** Reviews books of poetry in 50-100 words. Open to unsolicited reviews. Poets may also send books for review consideration. Under the imprint of Kawabata Press, Colin Webb also publishes anthologies and collections. **However publication of these has been temporarily suspended. Query with 6-10 poems and "maybe a brief outline of intent." Poet gets 50% of profits (after cost of printing is covered) and 4 copies.** A book catalog of Kawabata Press publications is on the back of *Sepia*, for ordering copies. The editor **always comments on rejections** and advises, "Strike out everything that sounds like a cliché. Don't try any tricks. Work at it, have a feeling for what you write, don't send 'exercise' pieces. Believe in what you send."

KELSEY REVIEW (IV-Regional), Mercer County Community College, P.O. Box B, Trenton NJ 08690, phone (609)586-4800, fax (609)586-2318, e-mail schore@mccc.edu, founded 1988, editor-in-chief Robin Schore, is an annual published by Mercer County Community College. It serves as "an outlet for literary talent **of people living and working in Mercer County, New Jersey only."** They have **no specifications as to form, length, subject matter or style, but do not want to see poetry about** "kittens and puppies." As a sample we selected these lines from "It's Illegal for Dogs to Mate on Princeton Streets" by June Z. Connerton:

> *The urge to merge will*
> *surge*
> *but don't let your pet*
> *forget*
> *a hitch with a bitch in a*
> *ditch*
> *IS AGAINST THE LAW IN PRINCETON!*

Kelsey Review is 64 glossy pgs., 7 × 11, with paper cover and line drawings; no ads. They receive about 50 submissions a year, accept 6-10. Press run is 1,500. All distributed free to contributors, area libraries and schools. **Submit no more than 6 poems at a time, typed, under 2,000 words. No previously published poems or simultaneous submissions. Deadline: May 1. Always comments on rejections. Reports in May of each year. All rights revert to authors.**

THE KENYON REVIEW (III), Dept. PM, Kenyon College, Gambier OH 43022, phone (614)427-3339, founded 1939, editor David Lynn, is a quarterly review containing poetry, fiction, criticism, reviews and memoirs. It is **one of the country's leading literary publications.** Under David Lynn's editorship, this magazine continues to blossom, featuring all styles and forms, lengths and subject matters—a real openness. But this market is more closed than others because of the volume of submissions typically received during each reading cycle. Issues contain work by such poets as Cyrus Cassells, Judith Ortiz Cofer, Joy Harjo, Richard Howard, Josephine Jacobsen, Alicia Ostriker, Sherod Santos and Quincy

Troupe. The elegantly printed, flat-spined, 7×10, 180-page review has a circulation of 4,000 with 3,200 subscriptions of which 1,100 are libraries. They receive about 3,000-4,000 submissions a year, use 50-60 (about 50 pgs. of poetry in each issue), have a 1-year backlog. The editor urges poets to read a few copies before submitting to find out what they are publishing. **Sample postpaid: $8. Unsolicited submissions are read from September 1 through March 31** *only*. **Reports in 3 months. Pays $15/ page for poetry, $10/page for prose. Buys first North American serial rights.** Reviews books of poetry in 2,500-7,000 words, single or multi-book format. "Reviews are primarily solicited—potential reviewers should inquire first." Poetry published in *The Kenyon Review* was also selected for inclusion in the 1992, 1993 and 1994 volumes of *The Best American Poetry* and *Pushcart Prize* anthologies.

KEYSTROKES; COMPUWRITE ANNUAL POETRY CONTEST; WRITERS ALLIANCE (IV-Writing), 12 Skylark Lane, Stony Brook NY 11790, founded 1981, executive director of Writers Alliance, Kiel Stuart. Writers Alliance sponsors, in addition to its triannual newsletter *Keystrokes*, workshops and other activities devoted to building a "dedicated arts community." Membership: $10. You needn't be a member to enter its annual poetry contest (poems about writing with a computer, prize of computer software with a retail value of at least $100, subscription to and publication in the newsletter, January 15 deadline) or to submit poetry to the newsletter **"up to 10 lines on the subject of writing or using a computer or word processing system. 4-6 lines works best. We don't want anything that strays from the subject matter of writers, writing and using computers for that task."** They have published poetry by Karen Elizabeth Rigley and Margaret Park Bridges. As a sample the editor selected this poem, "Dilemma," by Beatrice G. Davis:

> *Free-lancer—hyphenated*
> *Freelancer—compounded*
> *Free lancer—separated*
>
> *Which am I?*
> *That's a typesetter's decision*
> *It would seem.*

Keystrokes is 16 pgs., desktop-published (on folded sheets of 8½×11 paper). "Receive about a dozen poems a year; room for 8-10 but less than 50% accepted." Subscription: $15 (with membership). **Sample postpaid: $3.50. "All checks are payable to Kiel Stuart. This is essential." Previously published poems OK if they did not appear in a competing magazine or more recently than 6 months. Editor frequently comments on rejections. Send SASE for guidelines. Reports in 6-8 weeks. Pays 2 copies. Acquires one-time rights.** Reviews books of poetry in 250 words, single format. The editor says more "well-done humor" is needed. The editor also advises, "Treat your craft with respect. Learn the business aspects of being a poet and adhere to those rules. Sloppiness or failure to stick to standard ms format or (worst of all) failure to enclose SASE with ANY communication does NOT indicate an artistic soul."

‡KINESIS; IF IT MOVES . . . CONTEST (II), P.O. Box 4007, Whitefish MT 59937, founded 1992. *Kinesis* is a monthly that calls itself "the literary magazine for the rest of us" and includes fiction, poetry, essays and reviews. **They want any type of poetry—"as long as it moves."** They have recently published poetry by Lucy Shaw, John Leax, Ross Talarico, Simon Perchik and Rick Newby. As a sample the editor selected these lines from "Leaving the Hospital" by Pamela McClure:

> *. . . I notice that it is the middle of summer where I step out*
>
> *and the ambulance is announcing its arrival*
> *and the nurses are announcing their arrival*
> *and the flutter of my father's pulse*
>
> *announces its set of exercises*
> *in his wrist. . . .*

Kinesis is 48 pgs., 8½×11, printed on recycled paper and saddle-stitched with spot color and artwork, graphics and ads inside. They accept about 10% of the poetry received. Press run is 2,000 for 1,200 subscribers of which 10 are libraries, 500 shelf sales. Single copy: $3; subscription: $20. **Sample postpaid: $4. Previously published poems and simultaneous submissions OK. Send SASE for guidelines. Reports in 1 month. Pays 5 copies and a subscription. Acquires one-time rights.** Reviews books of all kinds in 1,000-2,000 words and offers a page of "Book Briefs" in addition. Poets may also send books for review consideration. They sponsor an annual "If It Moves . . . Contest" for both poetry and fiction. $10 reading fee covers 3 poems or 1 story. All entrants receive a year's subscription. Poetry winners receive prizes of $100, $50 and $25 (fiction: $250, $100 and $50) in addition to publication. Send SASE for details.

KIOSK (II), 306 Clemens Hall, SUNY, Buffalo NY 14260, founded 1985, editor Lia Vella, poetry editor Charlotte Pressler, is an annual literary magazine using **poetry of "any length, any style, especially**

experimental." They have recently published poetry by Raymond Federman, Sheila Murphy, Lyn Lifshin, Carl Dennis and Charles Bernstein. As a sample the editor selected these lines by Seth Frechie:

> The intent
> to say it without awkwardness,
> "I_____"
> A grave uttering,
> the gravity—

The editor describes *Kiosk* as flat-spined, digest-sized. Of 400 poems they accept 10-15. **Sample free (if available) with SAE and 6 first-class stamps. Submit poems in batches of three. Cover letter not required, "but we suggest one be included." Reads submissions September 1 through April 30 only. Reports within 4 months. Pays in copies.**

KITCHEN TABLE: WOMEN OF COLOR PRESS (V, IV-Women/feminism, lesbian, ethnic, political), P.O. Box 908, Latham NY 12110, phone (718)935-1082, fax (718)935-1107, founded 1981, is "the only publisher in North America committed to producing and distributing the **work of Third World women of all racial/cultural heritages, sexualities and classes**." They publish flat-spined paperback collections and anthologies. **"Unfortunately, because we are severely undercapitalized and understaffed, we receive far more manuscripts than we can respond to and cannot, at this time, give the manuscripts the attention they deserve."** They publish an average of one book of poetry every other year and have published three anthologies, two of which contain poetry. All books are published simultaneously in hardback for library sales. **Write for catalog to purchase samples.** The editors say, "We are particularly interested in publishing work by women of color which would generally be overlooked by other publishers, especially work by American Indian, Latina, Asian-American and African-American women who may be working class, lesbian, disabled or older writers."

ALFRED A. KNOPF (V), 201 E. 50th St., New York NY 10022, poetry editor Harry Ford. Over the years Knopf has been one of the most important and distinguished publishers of poetry in the United States. **"The list is closed to new submissions at this time."**

KRAX (II, IV-Humor); RUMP BOOKLETS (V), 63 Dixon Lane, Leeds, Yorkshire LS12 4RR England, founded 1971, poetry editors Andy Robson et al. *Krax* appears twice yearly, and they want poetry which is **"light-hearted and witty; original ideas. Undesired: haiku, religious or topical politics, $1,000 bills." 2,000 words maximum. All forms and styles considered.** As a sample the editor selected these lines from "Hair Care" by Alan Hester:

> I love being rugged
> And not combing my hair
> But how can I not comb
> What is no longer there?

Krax is 6×8, 48 pgs. of which 30 are poetry, saddle-stapled, offset with b&w cartoons and graphics. They receive up to 1,000 submissions/year of which they use 6%, have a 2- to 3-year backlog. Single copy: £1.75 ($3.50); subscription: £6 ($12). **Sample: $1 (75p). "Submit maximum of 6 pieces. Writer's name on same sheet as poem. SASE or SAE with IRC encouraged but not vital." No previously published poems or simultaneous submissions. Brief cover letter preferred. Reports within 2 months. Pays 1 copy.** Reviews books of poetry (brief, individual comments; no outside reviews). Send books for review consideration. *Rump Booklets* are miniature format, 3×4, 16-page collections. **They are not currently accepting work in this series. Send SASE for catalog.** The editor says, "Before sending your poems, always add your address to the piece—we can't always place everyone's pseudonym."

KUMQUAT MERINGUE; PENUMBRA PRESS (I, II), P.O. Box 5144, Rockford IL 61125, phone (815) 968-0713, e-mail moodyriver@aol.com, founded 1990, editor Christian Nelson, appears approximately 2 times/year using **"mostly shorter poetry (under 20 lines) about the small details of life, especially the quirky side of love and sex. Not interested in rhyming, meaning of life or high-flown poetry."** They have recently published works by Gina Bergamino, T. Kilgore Splake, Antler, Lynne Douglass and Ianthe Brautigan. As a sample the editor selected these lines from "Leaping Lizards" by Emile Luria:

> After we made love . . . Kate said,
> "You're so weird, really,
> Even weirder than I thought."
> And I thought, could she taste the salt,
> Feel the sea lapping on my back?
> I went to sleep wondering
> About dinosaurs and lungfish
> And the deepest reaches of the sea

It is digest-sized, 32-36 pgs., "professionally designed with professional typography and nicely printed." Press run is 500 for 250 subscribers. Subscription: $8 (3 issues). **Sample postpaid: $4. "We like cover letters but prefer to read things about who you are, rather than your long list of publishing credits. Previously published and simultaneous submissions are OK, but please let us know." Often comments on submissions. Send SASE for guidelines. Usually reports in 50 days. Pays 1 copy. Acquires one-time rights.** The magazine is "dedicated to the memory of Richard Brautigan." The editor advises, "Read *Kumquat Meringue* and anything by Richard Brautigan to get a feel for what we want, but don't copy Richard Brautigan, and don't copy those who have copied him. We just want that same feel. We also have a definite weakness for poems written 'to' or 'for' Richard Brautigan. Reviewers have called our publication iconoclastic, post-hip, post-beat, post-antipostmodern; and our poetry, carefully crafted imagery. When you get discouraged, write some more. Don't give up. Eventually your poems will find a home. We're very open to unpublished writers, and a high percentage of our writers had never been published anywhere before they submitted here."

KUUMBA (IV-Ethnic, gay/lesbian), Box 83912, Los Angeles CA 90083-0912, phone (310)410-0808, fax (310)410-9250, founded 1991, editors G. Winston James and Terri L. Jewell, is a biannual poetry journal of the black lesbian and gay community. **They want subject matter related to black lesbian and gay concerns.** "Among the experiences of interest are: coming out, interacting with family and/or community, substance abuse, political activism, oral histories, AIDS and intimate relationships." **They do not want to see "gay only subjects that have no black content, or black only subjects with no gay content."** They have published poetry by David Frechette, Assotto Saint, Sabrina Sojourner and Eric S. Booth. As a sample we selected these lines from "The Sweetest Taboo" (for Gene) by Richard D. Gore:

> *Forbidden,*
>> *But I loved you anyway*
> *Dark, smouldering, and sweet*
>> *Luminous Black skin and Sloe-eyes. . .*

Kuumba is 48 pgs., 8½×11, offset and saddle-stitched, with b&w cover drawing and ads. They accept about 25% of the poetry received. Press run is 1,000 for 100 subscribers, 500 shelf sales. Subscription: $7.50/year. **Sample postpaid: $4.50. No previously published poems; simultaneous submissions OK, if notified. Seldom comments on rejections. Send SASE for guidelines. Reports in 6 weeks. Pays 2 copies. Acquires first North American serial rights and right to anthologize.** The editors add, "Named for one of the Nguzo Saba (Seven Principles) which are celebrated at Kwanzaa, Kuumba means creativity." This poetry journal is not only dedicated to the celebration of the lives and experiences of black lesbians and gay men, but it is also intended to encourage new and experienced writers to develop their poetic craft.

KWIBIDI PUBLISHER; KID'S PLAYYARD; GREAT ADVENTURES FOR YOUNG PEOPLE; THE JOURNAL OF THE NATIONAL SOCIETY OF MINORITY WRITERS AND ARTISTS; THE WRITERS' AND ARTISTS' AID (I, IV-Ethnic, children, membership), P.O. Box 3424, Greensboro NC 27402-3424. Kwibidi founded 1979, *JNSMWA* 1981, *KP* 1986. Editor Dr. Doris B. Kwasikpui. Kwibidi Publisher **"needs poems, one-act plays, short stories, articles, art, jokes, book reports, research papers and how-to-do and make, for books, *Kid's Playyard* (a biannual magazine for kids of all ages), *GAYP* (a biannual containing short stories, poetry and articles about nature, travel, science and history) and *JNSMWA*." Publication limited to minorities.** As a sample the editor selected this poem (poet unidentified):

> *Poems are desperate screams of drowning thoughts*
>> *sinking faster with every word,*
> *Bellowing verses of pain and despair*
>> *to surface buoyantly and to be heard.*

Reads submissions January 1 through August 30 only. Publishes much of the material received and often responds with suggestions. Send SASE for guidelines. Reports in about 3 weeks. Upon acceptance, requires membership in the National Society of Minority Writers and Artists ($15/year). Pays in copies.

LACTUCA (II, IV-Translations), 159 Jewett Ave., Jersey City NJ 07304-2003, phone/fax (201)451-5411, e-mail Lactuca@aol.com, founded 1986, editor/publisher Mike Selender, appears 1-3 times a

Market conditions are constantly changing! If you're still using this book and it is 1997 or later, buy the newest edition of Poet's Market *at your favorite bookstore or order directly from* Writer's Digest Books.

year. **"Our bias is toward work with a strong sense of place, a strong sense of experience, a quiet dignity and an honest emotional depth. Dark and disturbing writings are preferred over safer material. No haiku, poems about writing poems, poems using the poem as an image, light poems or self-indulgent poems. Readability is crucial. We want poetry that readily transposes between the spoken word and printed page. First English language translations are welcome provided that the translator has obtained the approval of the author."** They have published poetry by Sherman Alexie, Joe Cardillo, Christy Beatty and Kathleen ten Haken. As a sample the editor selected these lines from "The Jaws of Factory" by Peter Bakowski:

> *In war or prison there is fear,*
> *here it is the slow death:*
> *Danny's lost an arm last week,*
> *David's got crow's feet under his eyes*
> *and he's only 24. . .*

Lactuca is 72 pgs., digest-sized, saddle-stapled, laser printed or offset on 24 lb. bond with matte card cover, no ads. They receive "a few thousand poems a year of which less than 5% are accepted." Circulation 500 for 100 subscriptions, 200 stores. Subscription: $10/3 issues, $17/6 issues. **Sample postpaid: $4.** *As this edition went to press, the editor informed us he would not be accepting submissions until sometime in 1996. Query before submitting work.* **Submit 4-5 poems at a time. "We do not print previously published material nor do we accept simultaneous submissions. We comment on rejections when we can. However the volume of mail we receive limits this." Reports within 3 months, "usually within one." Always sends prepublication galleys. Pays 2-5 copies "depending on length." Acquires first rights.** Reviews books of poetry. Open to unsolicited reviews. Poets may also send books for review consideration. He says, "The purpose of *Lactuca* is to be a small literary magazine publishing high-quality poetry, fiction and b&w drawings. Much of our circulation goes to contributors' copies and exchange copies with other literary magazines. *Lactuca* is not for poets expecting large circulation. Poets appearing here will find themselves in the company of other good writers."

‡LAKE SHORE PUBLISHING; SOUNDINGS (I, IV-Anthology), 373 Ramsay Rd., Deerfield IL 60015, phone (708)945-4324, founded 1983, poetry editor Carol Spelius, is an effort "to put out decent, economical volumes of poetry." **Reading fee: $1/page. They want poetry which is "understandable and *moving*, imaginative with a unique view, in any form. Make me laugh or cry or think. I'm not so keen on gutter language or political dogma—but I try to keep an open mind. No limitations in length."** They have recently published poetry by Bob Mills, Constance Vogel and Dona Goldman. The editor selected these sample lines from "Slow Miracle" by Christine Swanberg:

> *There were times when walking here*
> *would not have been enough, times*
> *my restless spirit needed an ocean,*
> *not this river, serene and simple.*

The first 253-page anthology, including over 100 poets, is a paperback, at $7.95 (add $1 mailing cost), which was published (in 1985) in an edition of 2,000. It is flat-spined, photocopied from typescript, with glossy, colored card cover with art. *Soundings II* is scheduled for early 1996. **Submit 5 poems at a time, with $1/page reading fee, and a cover letter telling about your other publications, biographical background, personal or aesthetic philosophy, poetic goals and principles. Simultaneous submissions OK. Any form or length. "Reads submissions anytime, but best in fall." Send SASE for upcoming themes. Reports within 8 months. Pays 1 copy and half-price for additional copies. "All rights return to poet after first printing." The editor will read chapbooks, or full-length collections, with the possibility of sharing costs** if Lake Shore Publishing likes the book ($1/page reading fee). "I split the cost if I like the book." She advises, "I'm gathering poems for a small anthology, *Love Gone Away*, and a collection of poems for children." **Sample copy of anthology or random choice of full-length collections to interested poets: $5.**

THE LAMP-POST (I, II, IV-Religious, form/style), 29562 Westmont Court, San Juan Capistrano CA 92675, founded 1977, editor James Prothero, is the quarterly publication of the Southern California C.S. Lewis Society and "echoes his thoughts in scholarly essays, informal essays, fiction and poetry as well as reviews. **We look for (1) formal, (2) literary quality poetry with (3) an orthodox Christian slant. Will look at free verse, but prefer formal."** They have published poetry by Paul Willis and Joe Christopher. As a sample the editor selected these lines from "Still, to Be Neat" by John J. Brugaletta:

> *The lion's muzzle is a mess of blood;*
> *The rain's a blessing here but there a flood:*
> *A faith that's based on neatness will not last.*
>
> *When God sees neatness, he begins to blast*
> *Away at it with rounds of circumstance,*
> *Demolishing our plans with gifts of chance . . .*

The Lamp-Post is 32 pgs., digest-sized, professionally printed and saddle-stapled with card cover and b&w line drawings. They receive 20 poems a year, use about 6. Press run is 300 for 250 subscribers of which 5 are libraries. Subscription: $12, $8 students, seniors and libraries. **Sample postpaid: $3. For subscriptions and sample back issues, write to Edie Dougherty, managing editor/secretary, 1212 W. 162nd St., Gardena CA 90247. Previously published poems accepted "cautiously." No simultaneous submissions. Cover letter not required, "but we like them." No SASE, no reply.** Time between acceptance and publication is about 6 months. **Sometimes comments on rejections. Send SASE for guidelines. Reports in 6-8 weeks. Pays 3 copies. Acquires first serial or reprint rights.** Reviews books of poetry "if the poet is a Lewis scholar or the poetry has some connection to C.S. Lewis." Open to unsolicited reviews. Poets may also send books for review consideration to M.J. Logsdon, book review editor, 119 Washington Dr., Salinas CA 93905. The editor says, "We exist to echo the thought of C.S. Lewis in contemporary writing. Quality, literary poetry only, please. Read John Donne, George Herbert, Gerard Manley Hopkins and Francis Thompson and give us that sort of formal, literary and Christian quality—no 'inspirational' please; inspire us with quality and depth."

PETER LANG PUBLISHING, INC. (IV-Translations), 62 W. 45th St., New York NY 10036, phone (212)302-6740, fax (212)302-7574, publishes primarily scholarly monographs in the humanities and social sciences. List includes **critical editions of great poets of the past. Submit descriptive cover letter and *curriculum vita*.**

LANGUAGE BRIDGES QUARTERLY (I, IV-Ethnic, foreign language), P.O. Box 850792, Richardson TX 75085, founded 1988, editor Eva Ziem, "is a **Polish-English bilingual forum for Polish matters. One of its purposes is to introduce the English-speaking reader to Polish culture. The subject is Poland and the Polish spirit:** a picture of life in Poland, mainly after World War II, with emphasis on the new and ponderous Polish emigration problems." **For more information send SASE.**

LATEST JOKES NEWSLETTER (IV-Humor), P.O. Box 23304, Brooklyn NY 11202-0066, phone (718)855-5057, editor Robert Makinson. *LJN* is a monthly newsletter of humor for TV and radio personalities, comedians and professional speakers. **They want "short humorous verse that can be used by a public speaker to liven up a speech.** Short jokes for speakers are even more needed. **Seasonal material is not needed. Standard literary verse, professorial type material, is not wanted. Sample: $3 and 1 first-class stamp. Submit maximum 3 poems at a time. Reports in 3 weeks. Pays $1-3.**

THE LAUREATE LETTER; WRITERS GAZETTE (I), 899 Williamson Trail, Eclectic AL 36024-9275, founded 1993, editor Brenda Williamson, is a sporadically published newsletter open to submissions of poetry. It will also periodically contain markets, contests, reviews and other items of interest to writers. **As for poetry, they want "simple, easy to understand poems which stretch the mind to remember their lives, the hopes of others and the dreams that exist amongst us. Any form, but prefer titled, 16 lines maximum. No jibberish or extremely mushy garbage."** As a sample the editor selected these lines by Charles T. Gradel Jr.:

> In a world with so many voices
> No one can stand alone, And alone
> We're all so meaningless, so insubstantial
> Like a whisper, In a noisy room.

They receive 1,500-2,000 poems a year, accept 25%. Press run is 250. Single copy: $2. **Sample postpaid: $2 plus #10 SASE. Submit 3 poems at a time. Previously published poems and simultaneous submissions OK.** Time between acceptance and publication is 1-2 months. **Send SASE for guidelines. Reports in 1-4 weeks "most of the time." No pay in cash or copies, but no fee required for publication. Acquires one-time rights.** They also publish *Writers Gazette*. Founded in 1980, the publication appears 3 times/year and is designed "for writers, by writers, about writing." It includes poetry, fiction, nonfiction, art, cartoons, occasional photos, and sometimes contains market listings, contest information and news on related writing subjects. **They want poems of "any style, subject or length, but prefer short verses of under 24 lines. Always looking for shorter poems of 4-12 lines. New writers are always encouraged and regularly published, even children."** They have recently published poetry by Deloris Selinsky, Rochelle Lynn Holt and John Binns. As a sample the editor selected these lines from "Starry Night" by Edward Mitchell:

> I heard the owl hoot
> and the cricket make its sound
> as I lay upon my back
> and watched the world go round. . .

The editor says *WG* is 8½×11, approximately 16 pgs., with some ads. They receive 1,200 poems a year, accept 10%. Press run is 500 for 250 subscribers. Subscription: $15. **Sample postpaid: $6. Previously published poems and simultaneous submissions OK. Seldom comments on rejections. Send SASE for guidelines. Reports in 1-2 months. No pay in cash or copies. Acquires one-time**

rights. Reviews books and chapbooks of poetry. Poets may also send books for review consideration. They hold an annual Halloween Poetry Contest for poems of 16-36 lines in length. Entry fee: $5/poem. Deadline: June 1. Send SASE for details. The editor says, "I read everything that crosses my desk and reply as soon as possible. Be creative and unusual. Don't query—send entire manuscripts. Also, we check for SASE before ever considering poems. If authors cannot consider sending SASE, we cannot consider their work."

LAUREL REVIEW (III); GREENTOWER PRESS (V), Dept. of English, Northwest Missouri State University, Maryville MO 64468, phone (816)562-1265, founded 1960, co-editors William Trowbridge, David Slater and Beth Richards. *LR* is a literary journal appearing twice a year using **"poetry of highest literary quality, nothing sentimental, greeting card, workshop, spit and whistle."** They have recently published poetry by Patricia Goedicke, Paul Zimmer, Miller Williams, Albert Goldbarth, David Citino and Nancy Willard. This handsome journal (128 pgs., 6 × 9) features excellent poems—usually more than 20 each issue—in all styles and forms. Press run is 800 for 400 subscribers of which 53 are libraries, 100 shelf sales. Subscription: $8/year. **Sample postpaid: $5. Submit 4 poems at a time. No previously published poems or simultaneous submissions. Reads submissions September 1 through May 31 only. Editor "does not usually" comment on submissions. Reports in 1 week to 4 months. Always sends prepublication galleys. Pays 2 copies plus 1-year subscription. Rights revert to author upon publication.** Greentower Press **does not accept unsolicited mss.**

THE LEADING EDGE (I, IV-Science fiction/fantasy), 3163 JKHB, Provo UT 84602, e-mail tle@yvax.byu.edu (correspondence only, no submissions), executive editor Alex Grover. *The Leading Edge* is a magazine appearing 2 times a year. They want **"high quality poetry related to science fiction and fantasy. We accept traditional science fiction and fantasy poetry, but we like innovative stuff. No graphic sex, violence or profanity."** They have recently published poetry by Michael Collings, Ann K. Schwader and Bruce Boston. As a sample the editor selected this poem, "The Spectra of Galaxies (A Zen Joke)," by Alyce Wilson:

> A man with a telescope
> reduces the universe
> to one red-shifted line
> on a piece of graph paper.
>
> Folds it in his pocket, forgets it.
>
> On laundry day, he cleans
> galaxies out of the lint filter.
> And at last, he understands.

The editor describes the magazine as 6 × 9, 140 pgs., using art. They accept about 15 out of 150 poems received/year. Press run is 500, going to 100 subscribers (10 of them libraries) and 300 shelf sales. Single copy: $3.95; subscription: $11.85. **Sample postpaid: $4.50. Submit 1 or more poems with name and address at the top of each page. No simultaneous submissions or previously published poems. Cover sheet with name, address, phone number, length of poem, title and type of poem preferred. Send SASE for guidelines. Reports in 3-4 months. Always sends prepublication galleys. Pays $10 for the first 1-4 typeset pages, $4.50 for each additional page; plus 2 contributor's copies. Buys first North American serial rights.** They say, "Poetry is given equal standing with fiction and is not treated as filler, but is treated as art."

THE LEDGE POETRY AND FICTION MAGAZINE (II), 64-65 Cooper Ave., Glendale NY 11385, founded 1988, editor-in-chief/publisher Timothy Monaghan, co-editor George Held, associate editor Laura M. Corrado, **"is open to all styles, slants and types of poetry. We publish provocative work by well-known poets."** Recent contributors include Robert Cooperman, Barbara Hamby, Stephanie Dickinson, Philip Miller, Al Maginnes, Sean Thomas Dougherty and Carole Bernstein. As a sample the editor selected the opening lines of "Grief" by Terri Brown-Davidson:

> It blinds me. It makes me sick.
> I can scarcely stand up each morning to teach,
> and yesterday, when we made love on this grass, I
>   cupped
> your buttocks to pull you in deeper as you stroked
> my shoulder and whispered my name and I saw her
> again and again and again, saw
>
> my mother die with a tube up her nose.

The Ledge is 128 pgs., digest-sized, typeset and perfect-bound with glossy cover. They accept 5% of poetry submissions. Circulation is 1,000, including 200 subscribers. Subscription: $15 for 2 years, $9 for 1 year. **Current issue postpaid: $5. Submit up to 5 poems at a time. No previously published**

Keep Faith, Not Score When Submitting Work

"To Play Pianissimo"

Does not mean silence.
The absence of moon in the day sky
for example.

Does not mean barely to speak,
the way a child's whisper
makes only warm air
on his mother's right ear.

©Photo by Mark Dolan

To play pianissimo
is to carry sweet words
to the old woman in the last dark row
who cannot hear anything else,
and to lay them across her lap like a shawl.

Lola Haskins

(from **Forty-four Ambitions for the Piano**, 1994, reprinted by permission of Lola Haskins/Betony Press)

When Lola Haskins reads her work, she doesn't read from her books or from notes. She memorizes her poems and actually performs them rather than giving a straight reading. "If you can look people in the eyes and say what you mean when you're telling a poem, then it has more person-to-person impact than it would if you were hiding behind a book," she says.

Haskins has performed her work for audiences worldwide both in person and on radio. She's also collaborated with a number of composers to set her work to music. At 37 she realized a lifelong dream and began to study the piano. Her book **Forty-four Ambitions for the Piano**, first published by the University of Central Florida Press in 1990 and self-published in 1994, was inspired by classical piano and is Haskins's attempt to capture, in words, the meaning behind various musical terms.

After performing some of the poems from her book, Haskins was approached by a pianist from the music faculty at The University of Florida where she teaches computer science. He was so touched by the work he wanted to perform it with her. Since then she's worked with a number of composers and performed with full symphony and dance accompaniment. **Forty-four Ambitions for the Piano** has also been used in music curricula.

For those poets shy about reading or performing work for an audience, Haskins says, "Reading poems is like giving presents to people. It's such a joy. You have to realize that, no matter what, there will be people in the audience who don't like what you do. There also will be people who love it, and I figure if you reach one person in 50, it's well worth it. One thing you might consider is that your poems are like your children—you love your children and you love your poems. You'd stand up for your children, so you'd stand up for your poems in the same way."

Although Haskins is inspired by sound and the musicality of words, she says where she gets her ideas remains a mystery. "Ideas come into your head and you know it's the germ of something. It's like an itch you have to scratch."

When searching for new ideas, it helps to learn new things all the time, she says. Haskins has a habit of researching topics that appeal to her and sometimes this leads to poems. For instance, her book *Castings*, first published by Country-man Press in 1984, was based on her research of Florida history. "I had lived in places where the landscape was spectacular—Greece, England, Mexico, California. When I moved to northern Florida it wasn't spectacular but it was beautiful. I wanted to learn to appreciate it more so I began to research the plants and birds of the area. I also wanted to find out what happened in the past in this place, so I studied historical materials such as old letters and books about the area."

From this research she began to write poetry in which she creates characters from history and looks at events through their eyes. In addition to *Castings*, these historical poems appear in her books *Planting the Children* (University of Central Florida, 1983) and *Hunger* (University of Iowa Press, 1993).

By writing poems from someone else's point of view, says Haskins, she's been able to explore the impact of history on a very personal level. "I've set poems in Iceland in the year 1000, in Argentina in the 19th Century . . . and I don't always write as a woman either. This allows me to explore a lot of different things."

One way to keep work fresh, she says, is to challenge yourself. Write from different perspectives or try new styles of writing. "I began to be able to crank out historical poems easily so I stopped doing it for awhile. I try to do things that are hard, because I want to explore, to keep learning.

"My advice is to write, revise and read. Read a lot of poetry. When you first start writing you tend, at least subconsciously, to draw from what you've heard before and if you know only a few other voices, you'll be limited in finding your own. And don't read just what you like. Sometimes, the people who open you up are people whose work you don't like or people who don't write anything like you. Look for people who have imagination even if it is a very different imagination than your own."

Haskins's belief in revision comes from her experience as an early editor of *The Devil's Millhopper* as well as her experience as a writer whose work has been published in such places as *Beloit Poetry Journal*, *California Quarterly*, *Georgia Review*, *Prairie Schooner*, *The Quarterly* and *The Southern Review*. "You should keep sending your work out, but, on the other hand, you should avoid just throwing things out you haven't really thought through. When you submit a poem, it should be one you've worked on quite awhile and are certain it is the way you want it. The danger in sending out just anything is that after awhile editors begin to recognize that and will stop looking at your things carefully."

Haskins has submitted to a number of poetry award programs and competitions. Her latest book, *Hunger*, received the 1992 Edwin Ford Piper Poetry Award which resulted in publication by the University of Iowa Press. Submitting to competitions, she says, is the same as submitting to journals—you have to keep at it and expect long waits.

"I think the difference between talented people who make it and talented people who don't is one word—persistence. There are lots of talented writers out there but so many of them give up."

One way to keep going, she says, is to avoid keeping score. "Remember that all the rejections don't count. Don't think 'I sent 33 submissions out and got one accepted, that's a terrible ratio.' Say, 'I got one accepted!' and forget the rest. No matter where you are in your career you'll get lots of rejections. It's just a part of what you do. It's always a matter of finding a match between your work and an editor who relates to it. If you have faith in your work, keep sending it out. In the end, you'll find a match. I really believe that."

—*Robin Gee*

❝Read a lot of poetry. When you first start writing you tend, at least subconsciously, to draw from what you've heard before and if you know only a few other voices, you'll be limited in finding your own. ❞

—Lola Haskins

work. "We require contributing authors to sign a 'Consent to Publish' form upon acceptance, stating that the accepted work is the author's own and that the work has not been previously published anywhere else." Simultaneous submissions OK. Cover letter preferred. Reports in 4-6 weeks. Pays 2 copies. Acquires one-time rights. *The Ledge* awards a $50 Readers Choice Award each issue to the writer receiving the most votes for a particular poem or story. Sponsors *The Ledge* Annual Poetry Chapbook Contest. Submit 20-24 pgs., including title page, bio and credits. Winner receives $50 and 100 copies of typeset, perfect-bound chapbook. $10 reading fee includes copy of winning chapbook. 1994 winner, *Rag Men* by Terri Brown-Davidson, available for $4.75 postpaid. Contest deadline: April 30, 1996. *The Ledge* also holds annual poetry and fiction contests. First prizes: $100 and publication. Second prizes: $50 and publication. Ten Third prizes: Subscription. Fees: $5 for up to 3 poems; $5/story. Subscription to *The Ledge* gains free entry to either contest. Deadline: January 31, 1996. Timothy Monoghan says: "Daring work that shows craft and heart stands best shot here."

LEFT CURVE (II, IV-Social issues), P.O. Box 472, Oakland CA 94604, phone (510)763-7193, founded 1974, editor Csaba Polony, appears "irregularly, about every 10 months." **They want poetry that is "critical culture, social, political, 'post-modern,' not purely formal, too self-centered, poetry that doesn't address in sufficient depth today's problems."** They have published poetry by Jack Hirschman, Sarah Menefee and Etel Adan. As a sample the editor selected these lines by HM:

> my unfriend the machine awakens me
> to a world one step removed
> from the dark, from the grave

The editor describes it as "about 120 pgs., offset, flat-spined, Durosheen cover." Press run is 1,200 for 150 subscribers of which 50 are libraries, 800 shelf sales. Subscription: $25/3 issues (individuals). **Sample postpaid: $8. Submit 1-5 poems at a time. Cover letter stating "why you are submitting" required. Publishes theme issues. Send SASE for guidelines and upcoming themes. Reports in 3-6 months. Pays 3 copies.** Open to unsolicited reviews. Poets may also send books for review consideration.

‡LIBERTY HILL POETRY REVIEW (II), P.O. Box 426967, San Francisco CA 94142-6967, founded 1994, editor Ken Butler, is a biannual designed to publish local and national poets, both experienced writers and talented newcomers. **They want "well-crafted free verse which exhibits a thorough knowledge of and love for language and content. Poetry that is carefully thought-out with proper punctuation, spelling and grammar. No subject matter is taboo, except those which promote racism, homophobia, and the humiliation of any race, gender or orientation. No prose poetry, no haiku; visual and verbal gymnastics are discouraged."** They have recently published poetry by Arthur Winfield Knight, Errol Miller, CB Follett and Rose Marie Hunold. As a sample the editor selected these lines from "To Garcia Lorca" by Maggie Schold:

> You, Garcia Lorca, I love the sound of your name
> I love the sound of watermelons, crunch and swish
> of biting into firm flesh, you have such firm
> flesh, Garcia Lorca, if that is truly your name.

LHPR is 40 pgs., digest-sized, attractively designed, saddle-stapled with matte card stock cover. They receive about 200 submissions a year, accept 10-15%. Press run is 200. Single copy: $3.50; subscription: $6. **Sample postpaid: $2.50. Submit up to 5 typed poems of no more than 60 lines in length. Include name and address on each page. SASE required. Simultaneous submissions and previously published poems OK, but prefers original, unpublished work. Cover letter always welcome. Reads submissions August through October (for Fall issue) and January through March (for Spring). Often comments on rejections. Send SASE for guidelines. Reports in 1-2 months. Pays 2 copies. Acquires one-time rights.** The editor says, "Above all, please support your local small presses and readings. Read as much poetry as you write. And always read a copy of the magazine to which you are submitting. Poetry publishers don't get rich from the revenue collected from samples, rather your chances for acceptance are increased when you know and understand the market."

LIBIDO: THE JOURNAL OF SEX AND SEXUALITY (I, IV-Erotica, humor, gay/lesbian/bisexual), P.O. Box 146721, Chicago IL 60614, phone (312)275-0842, founded 1988, editors Marianna Beck and Jack Hafferkamp, is a quarterly. **"Form, length and style are open. We want poetry of any and all styles as long as it is erotic and/or erotically humorous. We make a distinction between erotica and pornography. We want wit not dirty words."** They have published poetry by Stuart Silverman, Alan Isler, Lani Kaahumanu, Anne MacNaughton, Chocolate Waters, Robert Perchan, Bruce Lennard and Bill Vickers. As a sample the editors selected these lines by Ralph Tyler:

> 'Twas brillig in that cheap hotel
> The looking glass had cataracts
> All mimsey were the bureau drawrs
> The paper was a glimpse of hell
> "Come to my arms, my beamish boy"

Her scarlet mouth invited him.

Libido is 88 pgs., digest-sized, professionally printed, flat-spined, with 2-color varnished card cover. They accept about 5% of poetry received. Press run is 9,500 for 3,500 subscribers, 3,500 shelf sales and 1,500 single issues by mail. Subscription: $30 in US, $40 in Canada and Mexico (US funds), $50 in Europe and $60 elsewhere. **Sample postpaid: $8. Submit 2-3 poems at a time. Cover letter including "a one-sentence bio for contributors' page" required with submission. "Please, no handwritten mss." Reports in 4-6 months. Pays $0-25 plus 2 copies.** Send books for review consideration "only if the primary focus is love/eroticism."

LIBRA PUBLISHERS, INC. (I), 3089C Clairemont Dr., Suite 383, San Diego CA 92117, phone (619)571-1414, poetry editor William Kroll, publishes two professional journals, *Adolescence* and *Family Therapy*, plus books, primarily in the behaviorial sciences but also some general nonfiction, fiction and poetry. "At first we published books of poetry on a standard royalty basis, paying 10% of the retail price to the authors. Although at times we were successful in selling enough copies to at least break even, we found that we could no longer afford to publish poetry on this basis. Now, unless we fall madly in love with a particular collection, **we offer professional services to assist the author in self-publishing.**" They have published books of poetry by Martin Rosner, William Blackwell, John Travers Moore and C. Margaret Hall. **Prefers complete ms but accepts query with 6 sample poems, publishing credits and bio. Replies to query in 2 days, to submissions (if invited) in 2-3 weeks. Ms should be double-spaced. Sometimes sends prepublication galleys. Send 9 × 12 SASE for catalog. Sample books may be purchased on a returnable basis.**

‡LICKING RIVER REVIEW (II), University Center, Northern Kentucky University, Highland Heights KY 41099, founded 1991, is an annual designed "to showcase the best writing by Northern Kentucky University students alongside work by new or established writers from the region or elsewhere." **They have no specifications regarding form, length, subject matter or style of poetry.** They have recently published poetry by Paul Zimmer, Jack Meyers, Thomas Reiter, Allison Joseph, William Greenway and Cindy Duesing. As a sample we selected these lines from "She Wears Her Body" by Margaret Goshorn Johnson:

> *She wears her body like a hand-me-down,*
> *slack breasts, belly, buttocks scalloped by*
> *the melt of early padding. Thin and shrunken*
> *in the bath, the crepe back humps beneath*
> *my scrubbing. I help her out to dry, dripping*
> *in clouds of steam that cannot warm cold bones.*

The review is 96 pgs., 7 × 10, offset on recycled paper and perfect-bound with a 16-page artwork inset (all art solicited). They accept 5% of the poetry received. Press run is 1,500. Single copy and **sample postpaid: $5. Submit no more than 4 poems at a time. No previously published poems; simultaneous submissions OK. Reads submissions September 1 through February 28. Poems are circulated to an editorial board. Reports in up to 6 months. Pays 2 copies. Rights revert to author. Requests acknowledgement if poem is later reprinted.** Reviews chapbooks or books of poetry in 800 words. Open to unsolicited reviews. Poets may also send books for review consideration to Phil Paradis, Dept. of Literature and Language, Northern Kentucky University, Highland Heights KY 41099.

LIFTOUTS MAGAZINE; PRELUDIUM PUBLISHERS (V), Dept. PM, 1414 S. Third St., Suite 110, Minneapolis MN 55454, phone (612)321-9044, founded 1971, poetry editor Barry Casselman, is a "publisher of **experimental literary work and work of new writers in translation from other languages.**" **Currently not accepting unsolicited material.** *Liftouts* appears irregularly. It is 5½ × 8, offset, 50-150 pgs. Press run is 1,000. Reviews books of poetry.

LIGHT (II), Box 7500, Chicago IL 60680, founded 1992, editor John Mella, is a quarterly of **"light and occasional verse, satire, wordplay, puzzles, cartoons and line art."** They do not want "greeting card verse, cloying or sentimental verse." As a sample the editor selected "The Cow's Revenge" by X.J. Kennedy:

> *Obligingly, the mild cow lets us quaff*
> *The milk that she'd intended for her calf,*
> *But takes revenge: In every pint she packs*
> *A heavy cream to trigger heart attacks.*

The editor says *Light* is 32 pgs., stapled, including art and graphics. Single copy: $6; subscription: $16. **Sample postpaid: $4. Submit one poem on a page with name, address, poem title and page number on each page. No previously published poems or simultaneous submissions. Seldom comments on rejections. Publishes theme issues. Send SASE for guidelines and upcoming themes. Reports in 3 months or less. Sometimes sends prepublication galleys. Pays 2 copies to domestic contributors, 1 copy to foreign contributors.** Open to unsolicited reviews; query first. Poets may also send books for review consideration.

LIGHT AND LIFE MAGAZINE; EVANGEL (IV-Religious), Dept. PM, Free Methodist Church of North America, P.O. Box 535002, Indianapolis IN 46253-5002, phone (317)244-3660. *Light and Life*, editor Bob Haslam, is a religious monthly magazine. **"Poems are used only as they relate to an article in the magazine. No 'fillers' or descriptive poems are used. We are looking for short, well-written devotional or inspirational pieces and poetry . . . offering unique insights into the great themes of the Bible. Poems should rhyme and flow with a recognizable rhythm pattern. Avoid obscure allusions and unfamiliar language. Maximum length: 20 lines. Each submission should be typed on plain white paper, double-spaced, at least 1" margin on all sides, no erasable bond, name, address and telephone number on each ms, each submission on a separate sheet of paper, even if they are short pieces." Send SASE for guidelines. Reports in 4-6 weeks. Pays $10/poem, "even short ones."** They also conduct annual writing contests with varying rules and prizes (send SASE for rules December through March). *Evangel*, editor Carolyn Smith, **is a weekly 8-page paper for adults using nature and devotional poetry, 8-16 lines, "free verse or with rhyme scheme."** The circulation is 35,000; it is sold in bulk to Sunday schools. **Sample for 6 × 9 SASE. SASE required with submissions. Simultaneous submissions OK. Reports in 1 month. Pays $10.** The editor advises, "Do not write abstractions. Use concrete words to picture concept for reader."

‡LIGHTHOUSE PUBLICATIONS; LIGHTHOUSE FICTION COLLECTION (III), P.O. Box 1377, Auburn WA 98071-1377, founded 1986. The *Lighthouse Fiction Collection* is a quarterly designed for family reading. "Readers of all ages are presented with a delightful variety of fiction that maintains time-honored values." While *LFC* primarily publishes fiction (including a section for work by children), on occasion, it finds room for a little poetry. **They are open to poetry "from light-hearted to inspirational, free verse or traditional, four lines to fifty, on nature, family, friends and life. Nothing erotic nor any 'soapbox' material."** They have recently published poetry by Kathleen Y. Bergeron and Jennifer Anne Messing. As a sample the editor selected these lines from "Clouds" by Loren Ritz:

> *I think I know the reason*
> *Why clouds stay up so high . . .*
> *It's so that trees, all reaching up,*
> *Won't poke 'em in the eye.*

LFC is 56 pgs., 5½ × 8½, photocopied and saddle-stapled with colored paper cover and simple art. They receive about 50 poems a week and because "most do not meet our needs," accept only 1 or 2. Press run is 300 for 100 subscribers (average). Single copy: $1.75; subscription: $7.95 for 6 issues, $14.95 for 12. **Sample postpaid: $3. Submit no more than 5 poems at a time, typed one to a page. No previously published poems or simultaneous submissions.** Time between acceptance and publication is 1-2 years. **Seldom comments on rejections. Send SASE for guidelines. Reports in up to 3 months. Pays up to $5. Buys first North American serial rights.** It may help to know that the editor believes the current literary scene contains "too much sex, swearing, violence and gore."

LILITH MAGAZINE (IV-Women, ethnic), 250 W. 57th St., Suite 2432, New York NY 10107, phone (212)757-0818, e-mail lilithmag@aol.com, founded in 1976, editor-in-chief Susan Weidman Schneider, poetry editor Alicia Ostriker, "is an independent magazine with a Jewish feminist perspective" which uses **poetry by Jewish women "about the Jewish woman's experience. Generally we use short rather than long poems. Run 4 poems/year. Do not want to see poetry on other subjects."** They have published poetry by Irena Klepfisz, Lyn Lifshin, Yael Messinai, Sharon Neemani, Marcia Falk and Adrienne Rich. It is glossy, magazine-sized. "We use colors. Page count varies. Covers are very attractive and professional-looking (one has won an award). Generous amount of art. It appears 4 times a year, circulation about 10,000, about 5,000 subscriptions." Subscription: $16 for 4 issues. **Sample postpaid: $5. Send no more than 3 poems at a time; advise if simultaneous submission. Editor "sometimes" comments on rejections. Send SASE for guidelines. Reports in 2-3 months.** She advises: "(1) Read a copy of the publication before you submit your work. (2) Be realistic if you are a beginner. The competition is *severe*, so don't start to send out your work until you've written for a few years. (3) Short cover letters only. Copy should be neatly typed and proofread for typos and spelling errors."

LILLIPUT REVIEW (II, IV-Form), 207 S. Millvale Ave. #3, Pittsburgh PA 15224, founded 1989, editor Don Wentworth, is a tiny (4½ × 3.6 or 3½ × 4¼) 12- to 16-page magazine, appearing irregularly and **using poems in any style or form no longer than 10 lines.** They have recently published poetry by Albert Huffstickler, Lonnie Sherman, Lyn Lifshin, Antler, and charlie mehrhoff. As a sample the editor selected the following poem by Susanne Bowers:

> *He crept in*
> *like mildew.*

LR is laser-printed on colored paper and stapled. Press run is 250. **Sample: $1 or SASE. Submit no more than 3 poems at a time. Currently, every fourth issue is a broadside featuring the work of one particular poet. Send SASE for guidelines. Reports usually within 2 months. Pays 2 copies/**

poem. Acquires first rights. Editor comments on submissions "occasionally—always at least try to establish human contact." He started the Modest Proposal Chapbook series in 1994, publishing 1-2 chapbooks/year, 18-24 pgs. in length. **Chapbook submissions are by invitation only. Query with standard SASE. Sample chapbook: $2.50.** The editor says, "For a magazine that publishes only short poems, *LR* receives surprisingly little haiku. We are always open to this and any other short Eastern forms, traditional or otherwise."

LIMBERLOST PRESS (II), HC 33, Box 1113, Boise ID 83706, phone (208)344-2120, founded 1976, co-editors Richard and Rosemary Ardinger. Limberlost Press publishes poetry, fiction and memoirs in letterpressed chapbooks, flat-spined paperbacks and other formats. **"We want the best work by serious writers. No restrictions on style or form."** They have published poetry by William Stafford, Lawrence Ferlinghetti, Charles Bukowski, Allen Ginsberg, John Clellon Holmes, Margaret Ano, John Haines, Nancy Stringfellow, Robert Creeley and Gino Sky. Chapbooks are printed in limited editions and are typeset and sewn by hand. **Sample postpaid: $10. No simultaneous submissions. For chapbook submission, submit samples, bio and prior publications. Editor sometimes comments on rejections. Reports on queries in 1 week, on submissions in 1-2 months. Pays a varied number of author's copies.** "We like interested poets to be familiar with our press work."

LIMESTONE: A LITERARY JOURNAL (II), Dept. of English, 1215 Patterson Office Tower, University of Kentucky, Lexington KY 40506-0027, phone (606)257-6993, founded as *Fabbro* in 1979, as *Limestone* in 1986, editor Todd Rutland, is an annual seeking **"poetry that matters, poetry that shows attention to content and form. We're interested in all poetics, but we do watch for quality of thought and a use of language that will wake up the reader and resonate in his/her mind."** They have published poetry by Wendell Berry, Guy Davenport, Michael Cadnum, Noel M. Valis and James Baker Hall. It is 6×9, perfect-bound, offset. They accept 5-10 of 100-150 poems submitted annually. Press run is 500 for 30 subscriptions (20 of them libraries). **Sample postpaid: $3. Simultaneous submissions OK. Submit 1-10 pgs. at a time. Reports in 3-6 months. Pays 3 copies.** "If you're considering publication," the editor advises, "read as much poetry as possible. Listen carefully. Work over your poems till you're sick of them. The lack of such care shows up in many of the mss we receive."

LIMITED EDITIONS PRESS; ART: MAG (III), P.O. Box 70896, Las Vegas NV 89170, phone (702)734-8121, founded 1982, editor Peter Magliocco, "have become, due to economic and other factors, more limited to a select audience of poets as well as readers. We seek to expel the superficiality of our factitious culture, in all its drive-thru, junk-food-brain, commercial-ridden extravagance—and stylize a magazine of hard-line aesthetics, where truth and beauty meet on a vector not shallowly drawn. Conforming to this outlook is an operational policy of **seeking poetry from solicited poets primarily, though unsolicited submissions will be read, considered and perhaps used infrequently. Sought from the chosen is a creative use of poetic styles, systems and emotional morphologies other than banally constricting."** They have recently published poetry by John Grey, B.Z. Niditch, Alan Catlin, Ray Tod Smith, Matthew M. Sobrinski and others. As a sample the editor selected these lines from "Juggler of Sarajevo" by Gayle M. Petty:

> An error by the master juggler
> Brought the moon . . .
> Up, up, up around into orbit
> Suspended in perpetual orbs.
> The master juggler drops the
> World landing on Sarajevo.

ART: MAG, appearing in 1-2 large issues of 100 copies/year, is limited to a few poets. **Sample copies are the price of a regular issue, $3.50 or more, postpaid. Submit 5 poems at a time with SASE. "Submissions should be neat and use consistent style format (except experimental work). Cover letters are optional." No previously published poems; simultaneous submissions OK. Sometimes comments on rejections. Publishes theme issues. Send SASE for guidelines and upcoming themes. Reports within 3 months. Pays 1 copy. Acquires first rights.** Staff occasionally reviews books of poetry. Send books for review consideration. The press also occasionally publishes chapbooks (such as *The Phone Sex Lady in Her Own Words*, by Paula Weinman and Peter Magliocco), "along with other possibly 'aesthetic surprises' (such as original art sketchbooks for patrons, etc.), but these aren't strictly scheduled."

LINCOLN SPRINGS PRESS (II), P.O. Box 269, Franklin Lakes NJ 07417, founded 1987, editor M. Gabrielle, publishes 1 paperback and 1 hardback book of poetry each year. They have published poetry by Maria Mazziotti Gillan, Justin Vitiello and Abigail Stone. **Query first with sample poems and cover letter with brief bio and publication credits. No previously published poems; simultaneous submissions OK. Seldom comments on rejections. Replies to queries in 2-4 weeks, to mss in 2-3 months. Always sends prepublication galleys. Pays 15% royalties.**

LINES N' RHYMES (I), 5604 Harmeson Dr., Anderson IN 46013, phone (317)642-1239, founded 1989, editor Pearl Clark, appears every other month using **"some poetry to 40 lines—use some 4 lines, most between 12-20 lines. I like poems concerning life, belief in God's guidance. Nothing pornographic or occult."** They have published poetry by Ainsley Jo Phillips, Ruth E. Cunliffe, Rosina Clifford, Dr. Harry Snider and Kae Jaworski. As a sample the editor selected these lines from "The Wilding" by C. David Hay:

> *You bloom and die in solitude*
> *Beyond the touch of care.*
> *Your shining was not wasted—*
> *God surely put you there.*

It is photocopied on 6 legal-sized colored sheets, sometimes 5. Press run is 70, 3-5 shelf sales. Subscription: $7/6 issues. **Sample: $1. Submit 3 poems at a time. "A brief cover letter is OK but not essential. I receive 170 poems/year—accept 70%. I pay nothing for poetry used. I award 'Editor's Choice' to two poets/issue at $2. I give preference to subscribers. However, I also use poetry from non-subscribers."** Previously published poems and simultaneous submissions OK. Reviews books of poetry and comments in current issue. Open to unsolicited reviews. Poets may also send books for review consideration. She holds a contest for humorous poetry (4-6 lines) each September with 3 prizes of $5 each, open only to subscribers.

LINES REVIEW (III, IV-Regional), Edgefield Rd., Loanhead, Edinburgh EH20 9SY Scotland, founded 1952 ("the oldest continuing Scottish literary magazine"), editor Tessa Ransford. *LR* is a quarterly which **gives priority to poets living in Scotland** and, the editor says, "is generally receiving too much from elsewhere at present. **I like to accept from 4-6 poems in traditional page format, though with energy and intelligence in use of language, form and content. No unusual typography, concrete, sensation-seeking, nostalgic, dully descriptive or fanatically political poetry."** They have recently published poetry by David Grubb, Martin Bennett, Alan Riach, Stewart Conn and Robin Fulton. *LR* is known for well-written, thoughtful, lucid poetry that is intelligible to the educated reader. Press run is 750 for 500 subscribers of which 100 are libraries, 100 shelf sales. **Sample postpaid: £3 sterling. Submit 4-6 poems at a time. No previously published poems. Cover letter required; include information relevant to the work. "Double spacing helps, and clear indication whether a page break is or is not also a stanza break, and careful attention to punctuation—that it is as it will be printed." Reports in 2-3 weeks. Pays £10/page plus 1 copy.** Includes "good review section." *LR* often has special issues devoted, for example, to poetry from Glasgow, Japan, America, Canada and Italy. They also publish translations. Tessa Ransford is also director of Scottish Poetry Library (see listing under Organizations) and offers a School of Poets and Critical Service through the library.

LINQ (II), c/o English Dept., James Cook University, Townsville, Queensland 4811 Australia, phone (077)814336 or (077)755227, fax (077)814077, founded 1971, secretary Ms. M. Miles. *LiNQ* is a 100-page biannual which "aims to publish works of a high literary standard, encompassing a wide and varied range of interest." **They do not want to see "overtly naive and self-consciously subjective poetry."** They have recently published poetry by Sally Sleinis, Kevin Irie, Sue Moss, Alan Peter Kelly, Eugene Dubnov and D.J. Dowsett. As a sample they selected these lines from "Eleven Archaeologies" by Colin Campbell:

> *The pubs arm the streets*
> *sentryboxes to pleasure,*
> *wateringholes in tandem and triplicate*
> *homes of hormone enhancement.*

They receive about 250 poems a year, use approximately 25%. Press run is 350 for 160 subscribers of which 30 are libraries, 180 shelf sales. Single copy: $8; subscription: $20 individual (within Australia), $25 institution (within Australia), $30 overseas (for individual and institution). Since the journal is published in May and October, all subscriptions are due by April 30. **Sample back issue postpaid: $6 (Australian). No previously published poems; simultaneous submissions OK. Cover letter with brief bio required. Submission deadlines: September 30 (May edition) and April 30 (October edition). "*LiNQ* rotates its editors. Each volume is the responsibility of an individual editor, with occasional co-editorial advice." Often comments on rejections. Reports "ASAP." Pays $25/poem (Australian). Author retains copyright.** Staff reviews books of poetry in 1,000 words. Send books for review consideration. The editors say, "*LiNQ* aims for a broadly based sympathetic approach to creative work, particularly from new and young Australian writers." The secretary adds, "Attention to presentation is a very important criteria taken into consideration by editors. Intending contributors should take note of this."

LINTEL (II), P.O. Box 8609, Roanoke VA 24014, phone (703)982-2265, founded 1977, poetry editor Walter James Miller, who says, **"We publish poetry and innovative fiction of types ignored by commercial presses. We consider any poetry except conventional, traditional, cliché, greeting card types, i.e., we consider any artistic poetry."** They have published poetry by Sue Saniel Elkind,

Samuel Exler, Adrienne Wolfert and Edmund Pennant. As a sample the editor selected these lines by Nathan Teitel:

> *loneliness*
> *is a Mexican earring*
> *and fear*
> *a crushed cigarette*

The book from which this was taken, ***In Time of Tide***, is 64 pgs., digest-sized, flat-spined, professionally printed in bold type, hard cover stamped in gold, jacket with art and author's photo on back. Walter James Miller asks that you **query with 5 sample poems. Reads submissions January and August only. He replies to the query within a month, to the ms (if invited) in 2 months. "We consider simultaneous submissions if so marked and if the writer agrees to notify us of acceptance elsewhere." Ms should be typed. Always sends prepublication galleys. Pays royalties after all costs are met and 100 copies. Buys all rights. Offers usual subsidiary rights: 50%/50%. To see samples, send SASE for catalog and ask for "trial rate" (50%).** The editor says, "Form follows function! We accept any excellent poem whose form—be it sonnet or free verse—suits the content and the theme. We like our poets to have a good publishing record in literary magazines, before they begin to think of a book."

LITE MAGAZINE: THE JOURNAL OF SATIRE AND CREATIVITY; THE LITE CIRCLE, INC.; LITE CIRCLE BOOKS (I), P.O. Box 26162, Baltimore MD 21210, phone (410)719-7792, founded 1989, editor/publisher David W. Kriebel. *Lite*, Baltimore's literary bimonthly is a, "general literary publication including humorous columns, reviews and perspective pieces and one interview in each issue." **They want "creative, thoughtful, beautiful poetry, generally 1 page or less in length. No overly-erotic, exploitative or dogmatic poetry. Also, no political or preachy religious poems."** The editor says *Lite* is generally 40 pgs., 8×10, newsprint with b&w photos, original art and ads. They receive about 150 poems a year, accept 20-25%. Press run is 10,000 for 100 subscribers, the rest distributed free to colleges, writing groups and art galleries. Subscription: $13 (includes membership in Lite Circle, Inc.) **Sample free with SAE and 2 first-class stamps. Previously published poems and simultaneous submissions OK. Cover letter required. Seldom comments on rejections—"Only when authors ask for it." Send SASE for guidelines. Reports in 3-6 months. Pays 5 copies. Acquires one-time rights.** Reviews books of poetry. Lite Circle Books publishes 2 paperbacks/year. "We are just getting into book publishing. **Right now we operate as a subsidy press. Terms are settled on a contract-by-contract basis."** Their first two books, *The Laughing Ladies* and *Stations In a Dream*, are each available as a sample for $6.95 plus postage. The Lite Circle, Inc. sponsors poetry readings and offers an annual contest with $75 first prize, $45 second. Send SASE for information. The editor says, "Be persistent. The market is tight, but if you are willing to work with the small presses, they will work with you. *Lite* is very kind to new writers."

‡LITERAL LATTÉ; LITERAL LATTÉ POETRY AWARDS (II), 61 E. Eighth St., Suite 240, New York NY 10003, phone (212)260-5532, founded 1994, editor Jenine Gordon, is a bimonthly tabloid of "pure prose, poetry and art," distributed free in coffeehouses and bookstores in New York City, and by subscription. **They are "open to all styles of poetry—quality is the determining factor."** They have recently published poetry by Allen Ginsberg, Carol Muske and John Updike. As a sample we selected these lines from "O.R." by Roberta Swann:

> *I watched a boy so pale he disappeared*
> *into the sandbox. His name was Alexander.*
> *He was the Sisyphus of kids, scooping*
> *up dirt, climbing out and over to a step,*
> *dumping and tamping it down, tumbling back*
> *into the box and starting again.*

LL is 24-28 pgs., 11×17, neatly printed, newsprint, with b&w art, graphics and ads. They receive about 2,000 poems a year, accept approximately 2%. Press run is 20,000 for 200 subscribers. Subscription: $15. **Sample postpaid: $5. No previously published poems; simultaneous submissions OK. Cover letter with bio and SASE required.** Time between acceptance and publication is 6 months. **Often comments on rejections. Send SASE for guidelines. Reports in 2-3 months. Pays 5 copies and a subscription. All rights return to author upon publication.** They also sponsor the *Literal Latté* Poetry Awards, an annual contest for previously unpublished work. Entry fee: $10 for 3 poems (or buy a

---

✚ *The double dagger before a listing indicates that the listing is new in this edition. New markets are often the most receptive to submissions.*

subscription and the entry fee for 3 poems is included. Their 1995 contest was judged by Carol Muske and offered $500 in awards, and publication. Send SASE for current details.

LITERARY FRAGMENTS; SAUVIE ISLAND PRESS (I), P.O. Box 751, Beaverton OR 97075, e-mail SIP@NWCS.ORG, founded 1980, editor Susan Roberts, is a printed and electronic quarterly "contemporary authors showcase" **open to all forms, lengths, styles and subjects of poetry as well as short stories.** As a sample the editor selected this poem, "Essentials," by Diana Watanabe:

> *The pierced heart*
> *The pulsating pain*
> *The provoked waves of poignant feelings*
> *Mental polarity struggling for identity*
> *Searching for trust. . . a trust in the process.*

The editor says *LF* is 24-80 pgs., 5½ × 8, saddle-stitched, with b&w art/graphics and display ads. They receive approximately 1,500 poems a year. Press run is 3,500, largely distributed free to various distant points. **Sample postpaid: $5 for current issue and guidelines. Send SASE for guidelines alone. Submit 10 or more poems with $10 reading fee and SASE. Previously published poems and simultaneous submissions OK. Prefers electronic submissions.** Time between acceptance and publication is 6 months. **Usually comments on rejections. Reports in 3-6 months. Pays $5 and up. Acquires one-time rights. "Poems of notable merit are also published in 'Best of' anthology."** Reviews books of poetry in 350-1,200 words, single or multi-book format. Open to unsolicited reviews. Poets may also send books for review consideration. Sauvie Island Press publishes chapbooks in an electronic format. Send SASE for information.

THE LITERARY REVIEW: An International Journal of Contemporary Writing (III), Fairleigh Dickinson University, 285 Madison Ave., Madison NJ 07940, phone/fax (201)593-8564, e-mail tlr@fdu.edu, founded 1957, editor-in-chief Walter Cummins, a quarterly, seeks **"work by new and established poets which reflects a sensitivity to literary standards and the poetic form." No specifications as to form, length, style, subject matter or purpose.** They have recently published poetry by Robert Cooperman, Gary Fincke, R.S. Thomas, Victoria McCabe and Beth Houston. The magazine is 128 pgs., 6 × 9, flat-spined, professionally printed with glossy color cover, using 20-50 pgs. of poetry in each issue. Circulation is 2,500 with 900 subscriptions of which one-third are overseas. They receive about 1,200 submissions/year, use 100-150, have a 6- to 12-month backlog. Poems appearing here show careful attention to line, image and form—largely lyric free verse. Editors of recent issues also seem particularly open to translations. **Sample postpaid: $5, request a "general issue." Submit no more than 5 poems at a time, clear typed. Simultaneous submissions OK. At times the editor comments on rejections. Publishes theme issues. Send SASE for upcoming themes. An "Iranian Exile" issue is scheduled for Spring 1996. Reports in 2-3 months. Always sends prepublication galleys. Pays copies. Acquires first rights.** Reviews books of poetry in 500 words, single format. Open to unsolicited reviews. Poets may also send books for review consideration. Work published in this review has also been selected for inclusion in *Editor's Choice III*. They advise, "Read a general issue of the magazine carefully before submitting."

LITERATURE AND BELIEF (II, IV-Religious), 3076-E Jesse Knight Humanities Building, Brigham Young University, Provo UT 84602, phone (801)378-3073, founded 1981, editor Richard H. Cracroft, is the "biannual journal of the Center for the Study of Christian Values in Literature." **It uses "affirmation poetry in the Judeo-Christian tradition."** They have published poetry by Ted Hughes, Donnel Hunter, Leslie Norris and William Stafford. It is handsomely printed, flat-spined. Single copy: $5 US, $7 outside US. They conduct an annual contest with $150 first prize for poetry.

LITTLE RIVER PRESS (V), 10 Lowell Ave., Westfield MA 01085, phone (413)568-5598, founded 1976, editor Ronald Edwards, publishes **"limited editions of poetry collections, chapbooks and postcards of New England poets."** They have published poetry by Steven Sossaman, Wanda Cook and Frank Mello. **However, they currently do not accept unsolicited submissions.**

‡LIVINGSTON UNIVERSITY PRESS (V), Livingston University, Station 22, Livingston AL 35470, founded 1981, editor Joe Taylor, publishes 4-6 paperbacks and 4-6 hardbacks each year. They have published *Synchronized Swimming* by Stephen Corey, *Lizard Fever* by Eugene Walter, *Speaking in Tongues* by Charles Ghigna and *Flight from Valhalla* by Michael J. Bugeja. **However, they are currently not accepting unsolicited submissions. Interested poets should query. They pay 5% royalties and author's copies.** Send SASE for catalog.

LODESTAR BOOKS (V, IV-Children/teen), 375 Hudson St., New York NY 10014, phone (212)366-2627, fax (212)366-2011, affiliate of Dutton's Children's Books, a division of Penguin USA, founded 1980, editorial director Virginia Buckley, is a trade publisher of **juvenile and young adult nonfiction, fiction and picture books. "We are not currently accepting unsolicited submissions."**

LONDON REVIEW OF BOOKS (III), 28 Little Russell St., London WC1A 2HM England, fax (071)404-3337, founded 1979, editor Mary-Kay Wilmers, is published 24 times a year, mostly reviews and essays but some poems. They have published some of the most distinguished contemporary poets, such as Ted Hughes, Tony Harrison, James Fenton, Frederick Seidel and Thom Gunn. As a sample we selected the opening stanza of "The Metronomic Moon" by Michael Young:

> In other years I would say, how pretty they are,
> The cherries outside our house.
> This autumn I see the first leaves
> Writhe from the green into the yellow and
> From the yellow into what seems a frantic red
> Before they corkscrew to their conclusion
> When the morning wipers scrape them from the windscreens
> To drop them in the dog shit on the pavement
> Their beauty has not brought them mercy.

The paper has a circulation of 17,000 with 14,000 subscriptions. **Sample: £2.15 in UK, $2.95 in US and Canada—excluding postage. Submit 3 poems at a time. "Poems should be typed, double-spaced, on one side of the paper only. Please send cover letter and enclose SAE (and IRCs). No previously published poems. Considers simultaneous submissions. Always sends prepublication galleys. Pays £50/poem.**

‡LONE WILLOW PRESS (III), P.O. Box 31647, Omaha NE 68131-0647, founded 1993, editor Dale Champy, publishes 2-3 chapbooks a year. **"We publish chapbooks on single themes and we are open to all themes. The only requirement is excellence. However, we do not want to see doggerel or greeting card verse."** They have recently published collections of poetry by Fredrick Zydek and Brian Bengtson. As a sample the editor selected these lines from "Living in the Vows" in *The Abbey Poems* by Fredrick Zydek:

> You must learn to pile your temptations
> like coins saved for a rainy day.
> You must let the will go. Let it float
> like a wonderful balloon
> through the celestial machinery.

That book is 20 pgs., digest-sized, neatly printed on gray paper and saddle-stapled with a light, gray card stock cover. **Query first with 5 sample poems and cover letter with brief bio and publication credits. Previously published poems OK; no simultaneous submissions.** Time between acceptance and publication is 6 months. **Seldom comments on rejections. Send SASE for guidelines. Replies to queries in 1 month, to mss (if invited) in 2-3 months. Pays 25 author's copies. "We also pay a small royalty if the book goes into a second printing." For a sample chapbook, send $7.95 in check or money order.** The editor says, "If you don't know the work of Roethke, DeFrees and Hugo, don't bother sending work our way. We work with no more than two poets at a time."

LONG ISLAND QUARTERLY (IV-Regional), P.O. Box 114, Northport NY 11768, founded 1990, editor and publisher George Wallace, is a quarterly using **poetry by people on or from Long Island. "Surprise us with fresh language. No conventional imagery, self-indulgent confessionalism, compulsive article-droppers."** They have published poetry by Edmund Pennant, David Ignatow and William Heyen. As a sample here are lines from "Summer" by Claire Nicolas White:

> The wind on its great wings erases sound,
> wipes out all desire, all preconceived notion
> of pleasure with the music on the panes
> and the leafy branches sweeping out there,
> shaking their green hair.

LIQ is a handsome publication whose clean design (28 pgs., digest-sized, saddle-stapled, professionally printed on quality stock with matte card cover) enhances the image-based, mostly lyric free verse inside. Most contributions show attention to craft and structure. Press run is 250 for 150 subscribers of which 15 are libraries, 50-75 shelf sales. Subscription: $12. **Sample postpaid: $3. Submit 3 poems at a time. Name and address on each page. Cover letter including connection to Long Island region required. Submissions without SASE are not returned. Responds in 3 months. Sometimes sends prepublication galleys. Pays 1 copy.** Sponsors a semiannual open poetry competition with deadlines of March 31 and August 31. The winner and runners up are awarded cash prizes. Entrants may send up to 5 original, unpublished poems for consideration. No restrictions on theme or length. Entry fee: $5. No mss will be returned. Winners announced 2 months after closing date. For competition results, include SASE. Send submissions to: Long Island Quarterly Poetry Prize at the above address. The editor advises: "(1) Go beyond yourself; (2) Don't be afraid to fictionalize; (3) Don't write your autobiography—if you are worth it, maybe someone else will."

LONG ISLANDER; WALT'S CORNER (II), 322 Main St., Huntington NY 11743, phone (516)427-7000, fax (516)427-5820, founded 1838 by Walt Whitman, poetry editor George Wallace, is a weekly newspaper, 25,000 circulation, using **unrhymed poetry up to 20 lines "grounded in personal/social matrix; no haiku, inspirational."** They have published poetry by David Ignatow, David Axelrod and R.B. Weber. As a sample the editor selected these lines from "Sleepless at Christmas" by L. Dellarocca:

> *It's another kind of light that seethes here,*
> *this wreched wreched orphanage of hearts.*
> *Death touched men who've come to worship night,*
> *god of bottles and mouths.*

It is "48 pgs., newsprint." They use 52 of about 1,000 poems submitted each year. Subscription: $18. **Sample postpaid: $2.50. Submit 3 poems at a time. Simultaneous submissions OK. "Cover letter should be simple, not effusive. SASE missing? Then it's going in the garbage." Editor "normally" comments on rejections. Pays 1 copy.** Staff reviews books of poetry. Send books for review consideration.

LONG SHOT (III), P.O. Box 6238, Hoboken NJ 07030, founded 1982, edited by Danny Shot and Nancy Mercado, is, they say, "writing from the real world." They have recently published poetry by Archie Shepp, Gregory Corso, Miguel Algarin, Pedro Pietri, Allen Ginsberg, Amiri Baraka and June Jordan. It is 190 pgs., flat-spined, professionally printed with glossy card cover using b&w photos, drawings and cartoons. It comes out twice a year. Press run is 2,500. Subscription: $22 for 2 years (4 issues). **Sample: $7. No previously published poems; simultaneous submissions OK. Reports in 2 months. Pays 2 copies.** Unlike other publishers, Danny Shot says they receive "too many requests for writer's guidelines. Just send the poems."

LONGHOUSE (II); SCOUT (V); ORIGIN PRESS (V), Green River R.F.D., Brattleboro VT 05301, founded 1973, editor Bob Arnold. *Longhouse* is a literary annual using **poems "from the serious working poet" from any region in any style.** They have published poetry by Hayden Carruth, Janine Pommy-Vega, Bobby Byrd, Sharon Doubiago, George Evans, Lorine Niedecker, Tim McNulty and Alan Lau. Its format is unusual: a thick packet of looseleaf 8½ × 14 sheets, photocopied from typescript, in a handsomely printed matte cover. Press run 200. **Sample postpaid: $5. Pays 2 copies.** Reviews books of poetry. **They publish chapbooks and books (manuscripts solicited only) under the imprints of Longhouse and Scout.** "We are also a bookshop and mail-order business for modern first editions and modern poetry and small presses. We encourage poets and readers looking for collectible modern first editions and scarce—and not so scarce—books of poetry and small press magazines to send a donation for our catalog; whatever one can afford." Bob Arnold says, "Origin Press is best known as Cid Corman's press. One of the quiet giants in American poetry plus the wide scope of international work. Established in the early 1950s in Boston, it has moved around as Cid went with his life: France, Italy, Boston, for many years now in Kyoto, Japan. Cid has merged with Longhouse in that we now edit and publish a few items together. He continues to edit, translate and publish from Kyoto. His own books are heavily based in our bookshop and mail-order catalog."

LOOM PRESS (II), P.O. Box 1394, Lowell MA 01853, founded 1978, editor Paul Marion, is a small press publisher of books. Poets recently published include Christine Gebhard, Ed Croke and Joseph Donahue. Books are perfect-bound, 6 × 9, with an average page count of 64. **Writers should query first for book publication, sending cover letter, credits, 5 sample poems and bio. Queries will be answered in 1 month, mss reported on in 2 months. Simultaneous submissions will be considered.** Time to publication is 6-12 months. **The editor comments on mss "when time allows." Always sends prepublication galleys. Pays royalties of 10%, plus 5% of print run. Samples are available at $5 each.** He says, "Please support the small publishers who make poetry available."

LOONFEATHER; LOONFEATHER PRESS (I, IV-Regional), P.O. Box 1212, Bemidji MN 56601, phone (218)751-4869, founded 1979, poetry editors Betty Rossi, Elmo Heggie and Marshall Muirhead, is a small press publisher of the literary magazine *Loonfeather* appearing 2 times a year, **"primarily but not exclusively for Minnesota writers. Prefer short poems of not over 42 lines, accepts some traditional forms if well done, no generalizations on worn-out topics."** They have recently published poetry by Spencer Reece, Joyce Penchansky, Thom Ward and Mary Winters. As a sample the editors selected these lines from "In Evening" by Holland Groves:

> *It seems night always comes too soon,*
> *spreading and darkening in the deep throat*
> *beneath the hills,*
> *in the place we meant to go to*
> *in the first place.*

Loonfeather is 5½ × 8½, 48 pgs., saddle-stapled, professionally printed in small type with matte card cover, using b&w art and ads. Subscription: $7.50/year; single copy current issue: $5; back issues: $2.50. **Submission deadlines January 31 and July 31 for May and November publications. Pub-**

lishes theme issues occasionally. **Send SASE for upcoming themes. Pays 2 copies.** Loonfeather Press publishes a limited number of quality poetry books. **Query with 2-3 sample poems, cover letter and previous publications. "Please do not query until after January 1996." Replies to queries in 3 months.** Time between acceptance and publication is 1-1½ years. **Pays 10% royalties.**

LORIEN HOUSE (I), P.O. Box 1112, Black Mountain NC 28711-1112, phone (704)669-6211, founded 1969, editor David A. Wilson, is a small press publishing many books under the Lorien House imprint (poetry on a subsidy basis). **Query regarding subsidized book publication. Editor comments on submissions "occasionally," and offers "full analysis and marketing help" for $1/typed page of poetry.**

LOTHROP, LEE & SHEPARD BOOKS (V), 1350 Avenue of the Americas, New York NY 10019, founded 1894, editor-in-chief Susan Pearson. **"We do not accept unsolicited mss."**

LOTUS POETRY SERIES; MICHIGAN STATE UNIVERSITY PRESS (II); NAOMI LONG MADGETT POETRY AWARD (IV-Ethnic), P.O. Box 21607, Detroit MI 48221, phone (313)861-1280, fax (313)861-4740, founded 1993, editor Naomi Long Madgett. "With one exception of a textbook, we publish books of **poetry by individual authors,** although we have published three anthologies. We occasionally sponsor readings. **Most, but not all, of our authors are black."** Their most recent anthology is *Adam of Ifé: Black Women in Praise of Black Men.* They have recently published poetry by Adam David Miller, Robert Chrisman and Alvin Aubert. As a sample we selected these lines from "Thinking About Medusa" from *Walking North* by Beverly V. Head:

> she must have been lonely
> watching all those possible lovers
> turn into beautiful stone
> horror painted perfectly
> across their faces. . .

Submit 5-10 sample poems, typed. Poems previously published in magazines OK; no simultaneous submissions. Time between acceptance and publication is 12-18 months. **Poems are circulated to an editorial board. "Senior editor reads manuscripts first, then passes on the best with names removed to other editors." Seldom comments on rejections. Response is usually within 6 weeks. Pays 10% royalties plus author's copies. Poets are not expected to contribute to the cost of publication. "Copies may be ordered from our catalog, which is free upon request. We do not give samples."** They also sponsor the Naomi Long Madgett Poetry Award. The award goes to a manuscript by an African-American poet who is 60 years of age or older. Interested persons may write for details. The editor says, "Beginners should read a great deal of contemporary poetry and recognize what is and what is not usually being done. That does not rule out experimentation, but styles of bygone eras and imitation of other poets' styles are discouraged."

LOUISIANA LITERATURE; LOUISIANA LITERATURE PRIZE FOR POETRY (II, IV-Regional), SLU- 792, Southeastern Louisiana University, Hammond LA 70402, phone (504)549-5022, fax (504)549-5021, editor David Hanson, appears twice a year. They say they **"receive mss year round although we work through submissions more slowly in summer. We consider creative work from anyone though we strive to showcase our state's talent. We appreciate poetry that shows firm control and craft, is sophisticated yet accessible to a broad readership. We don't use highly experimental work."** They have recently published poetry by Sue Owen, Catharine Savage Brosman, Diane Wakoski, Claire Bateman, Kate Daniels, Elton Glaser, Sandra Nelson, Gray Jacobik, Al Maginnes and Judy Longley. The editor chose these sample lines from "Four Coffees" by Jody Bilyeu:

> In his grandparents' shallow, ancient pond
> he discovered among cattails
> and swamped Sudan grass a hundred baby
> fish and yanked some into a kitchen strainer,
> rapt by their slippery blackness,
> their writhing, the fact that some had legs.

The magazine is a large (6¾×9¾) format, 100 pgs., flat-spined, handsomely printed on heavy matte stock with matte card cover. Subscription: $10 for individuals, $12.50 for institutions. Single copies: $5 for individuals. **Submit 1-5 poems at a time. Send cover letter, including bio to use in the event of acceptance. No simultaneous submissions. Enclose SASE specifying whether work is to be returned or discarded. Publishes theme issues. Theme for fall 1995 is Louisiana Ghost Stories and Poetry. Send SASE for upcoming themes. Sometimes sends prepublication galleys.** Open to unsolicited reviews. Poets may also send books for review consideration; include cover letter. The Louisiana Literature Prize for Poetry offers a $400 award. Send SASE for guidelines. The editor says, "It's important to us that the poets we publish be in control of their creations. Too much of what we see seems arbitrary."

LOUISIANA STATE UNIVERSITY PRESS (V), P.O. Box 25053, Baton Rouge LA 70894-5053, phone (504)388-6294, founded 1935, poetry editor L.E. Phillabaum, is a highly respected publisher of collections by poets such as Lisel Mueller, Margaret Gibson, Fred Chappell and Henry Taylor. **Currently not accepting poetry submissions; "fully committed through 1996."**

THE LOUISVILLE REVIEW (II, IV-Children/teen), Dept. PM, 315 Bingham Humanities, University of Louisville, Louisville KY 40292, phone (502)852-6801, founded 1976, faculty editor Sena Jeter Naslund, appears twice a year. **They use any kind of poetry except translations, and they have a section of children's poetry (grades K-12).** They have published poetry by Richard Jackson, Jeffrey Skinner, Maura Stanton, Richard Cecil, Roger Weingarten and Greg Pape. *TLR* is 200 pgs., flat-spined, 6×8¾. They accept about 10% of some 700 pieces received a year. **Sample postpaid: $4. "Poetry by children must include permission of parent to publish if accepted. In all of our poetry we look for the striking metaphor, unusual imagery and fresh language. We do not read in summer. Poems are read by 3 readers; report time is 1-2 months and time to publication is 2-3 months." Pays 1 copy.**

LOW-TECH PRESS (V), 30-73 47th St., Long Island City NY 11103, founded 1981, editor Ron Kolm, has published work by Hal Sirowitz, John Yau and Jennifer Nostrand. As a sample the editor selected these lines (poet unidentified):

> *They firebombed*
> *the dinner table*
> *taking us completely*
> *by surprise.*

"I am only interested in short poems with clear images. Since almost nobody gets paid for their work, I believe in multiple submissions and multiple publishings. Even though we only publish solicited mss, I respond right away to any mail the press receives."

LUCIDITY; BEAR HOUSE PUBLISHING (I), Route 2, Box 94, Eureka Springs AR 72632-9505, phone (501)253-9351, founded 1985, editor Ted O. Badger. *Lucidity* is a quarterly of poetry. **Submission fee required—$1/poem for "juried" selection by a panel of judges or $2/poem to compete for cash awards of $15, $10 and $5.** Other winners paid in both cash and in copies. In addition, the editor invites a few guest contributors to submit to each issue. Contributors are encouraged to subscribe or buy a copy of the magazine. The magazine is called *Lucidity* because, the editor says, "I have felt that too many publications of verse lean to the abstract in content and the obscure in style." They are **"open as to form. 38-line limit due to format. No restriction on subject matter except that something definitive be given to the reader. We look for poetry that is life-related and has clarity and substance." Purpose: "to give a platform to poets who can impart their ideas with clarity."** He does not want "religious, nature or vulgar poems." Recently published poets include E.A. Henderson, Violette Newton, Martha C. Calloway, Lyn Lifshin and Elizabeth Bernstein. As a sample of the type of verse sought, the editor offers these lines by Nancy Levins:

> *Me, full to the brim.*
> *You, like a hollow dead tree,*
> *ready to crumble.*

The magazine is 76 pgs., photocopied from typescript, digest-sized, saddle-stapled, with matte card cover. It's a surprisingly lively small press magazine featuring accessible narrative and lyric poetry, with almost equal space given to free and formal verse. Press run is 350 for 190 subscribers. Subscription: $10. **Sample postpaid: $2.50. Submit 3-6 poems at a time. Simultaneous submissions OK. Send SASE for guidelines. Reports in 2-3 months, a 3-month delay before publication. Buys one-time rights.** Bear House Press is a self-publishing arrangement by which poets can pay to have booklets published in the same format as *Lucidity,* prices beginning at 50 copies of 32 pgs. for $140. Publishes 10 chapbooks/year. The editor says, "Small press journals offer the best opportunity to most poets for publication."

LULLWATER REVIEW; LULLWATER PRIZE FOR POETRY (II), Box 22036, Emory University, Atlanta GA 30322, phone (404)727-6184, founded 1989, editor revolves, appears 2 times/year. **They want "original, imaginative treatment of emotional and intellectual topics. No mere wordplay. Ideas and concepts should be emphasized."** They have published poetry by Turner Cassity, Colette Inez, Mark Svenvold, Eve Shelnutt and Ioanna-Veronika Warwick. As a sample the editor selected this poem, "Seven Lean Cows," by Aurel Răuu, translated by Adam J. Sorkin and Liviu Bleoca:

> *Every day becomes a gift to the wise man.*
> *O, if only these stupid days had traveled on,*
> *these seven lean cows. The man of wax*
> *and the woman of wax*
> *and the emperor of wax*
> *that gleam in the wax museum of all the capitals*

they knew they knew not

Lullwater Review is a handsome, 6×9, flat-spined magazine, 96 pgs. Press run is 2,000. Subscription: $12. **Sample postpaid: $5. Submit no more than 5 poems at a time. "Prefer author's name, address and phone number on every page." No previously published poems; simultaneous submissions OK. Submissions must include cover letter and SASE. Reads submissions August 1 through May 31 only. Send SASE for guidelines. Reports in 2 months or less. Pays 3 copies. All rights revert to author upon publication.** Sponsors the annual Lullwater Prize for Poetry ($500). Send SASE for guidelines. "*Lullwater* places no limits on theme or style; the sole criterion for judging submitted work is its excellence. While much of the poetry we publish is free verse, we hold in high regard well-crafted formal poems. We expect our contributors to be acquainted with the broad field of contemporary poetry and able to find within that field a voice uniquely their own."

LUNA BISONTE PRODS; LOST AND FOUND TIMES (IV-Style), 137 Leland Ave., Columbus OH 43214, founded 1967, poetry editor John M. Bennett, may be the zaniest phenomenon in central Ohio. John Bennett is a publisher (and practicioner) of **experimental and avant-garde writing**, sometimes sexually explicit, and art in a bewildering array of formats including the magazine, *Lost and Found Times*, postcard series, posters, chapbooks, pamphlets, labels and audiocassette tapes. You can get a **sampling of Luna Bisonte Prods for $5. Numerous reviewers have commented on the bizarre** *Lost and Found Times,* "reminiscent of several West Coast dada magazines"; "This exciting magazine is recommended only for the most daring souls"; "truly demented"; "Insults . . . the past 3,000 years of literature"; "revolution where it counts, in the dangerous depths of the imagination," etc. Bennett wants to see **"unusual poetry, naive poetry, surrealism, experimental, visual poetry, collaborations—*no* poetry workshop or academic pablum."** He has recently published poetry by I. Argüelles, G. Beining, B. Heman, R. Olson, J. Lipman, B. Porter, C.H. Ford, P. Weinman, E.N. Brookings, F.A. Nettelbeck, D. Raphael, R. Crozier, S. Sollfrey, M. Andre, N. Vassilakis, S.E. Murphy, T. Taylor, F. Doctorovich and A. Ackerman. As a sample, the editor selected "Baroque Signal Interior Going Home," a complete poem by Susan Smith Nash:

> *Roads in & out of my head go chugging, flaming Hobbesian*
> *scenes of meat-gone-bad—where the film burns*
> *my eyes focus not on curls & meanders of teeth—*
> *your slept-on retinas chatter on the legs & other material*
> *of a beautiful morning—this is the moment of perception:*
> *I'm pouring coffee into my toes, a tangle into my hair.*

The digest-sized, 52-page magazine, photoreduced typescript and wild graphics, matte card cover with graphics, has a circulation of 350 with 75 subscribers of which 30 are libraries. **Sample postpaid: $5. Submit anytime—preferably camera-ready (but this is not required). Reports in 1-2 days. Pays copies. All rights revert to authors upon publication.** Staff reviews books of poetry. Send books for review consideration. **Luna Bisonte also will consider book submissions: query with samples and cover letter (but "keep it brief"). Chapbook publishing usually depends on grants or other subsidies and is usually by solicitation.** He will also consider subsidy arrangements on negotiable terms. The editor says, "I would like to see more experimental and avant-garde material in Spanish and Portuguese, or in mixtures of languages."

LUNA NEGRA (I), Box 26, % Office of Campus Life/Student Activities or English Dept., Kent State University, Kent OH 44240, is a student-run, biannual literary and art magazine of the KSU main campus, **open to all forms of poetry and prose.** The editor says it is 40-50 pgs., 5½×8½, with art and photography throughout. They receive 400-450 poems a year, accept 40 or 50. Press run is 2,000, most distributed to KSU students. **Submit no more than 3 poems at a time. Simultaneous submissions OK. Reads submissions September 1 through March 30 only. Seldom comments on rejections. Reports in 1 month or so ("depending on school calendar"). Pays 1 copy. "All rights revert to author immediately after publication."** The editor adds, "We are also interested in any b&w reproducible artwork or photographs."

THE LUTHERAN JOURNAL (IV-Religious), Dept. PM, 7317 Cahill Rd., Edina MN 55439, phone (612)941-6830, editor The Rev. Armin U. Deye, is a family quarterly, 32 pgs., circulation 125,000, for Lutheran Church members, middle age and older. They use **poetry "related to subject matter," traditional, free verse, blank verse. Sample free for SASE. Simultaneous submissions OK. Pays.**

LYNX, A JOURNAL FOR LINKING POETS; AHA BOOKS; INTERNATIONAL TANKA SPLENDOR AWARD (IV-Form), P.O. Box 1250, Gualala CA 95445, phone (707)882-2226, founded as *APA-Renga* in 1986, later the name was changed to *Lynx* "to link an endangered species of poetry with an endangered animal and to inspire the traditional wit of renga," says editor Jane Reichhold. *Lynx,* published 3 times a year (February, June and October) "**is based on the ancient craft of renga, linked verse with origins in Zen and Japanese culture, and now publishes both renga and tanka.** A renga is a non-narrative series of linked images as a group effort. Tanka is the most popular poetry form in

Japan and the oldest continued form." As a sample the editor selected this renga excerpt by Jane Reichhold, T.B., Kenneth C. Leibman and Tundra Wind:

> *panty hose   as she crosses her legs   she whispers*
> *from the back room   a sigh*
> *on the table   her letter punctuated   with a teardrop*
> *from the apartment upstairs   a lullaby*

Lynx is 60-90 pgs., 4½×11, neatly printed and comb-bound with card cover. It also publishes essays, book reviews, articles, interviews, experimental linked forms, linked prose, art, commentaries and "whatever encourages poets to link ideas." They currently have 300 subscribers. Subscription: $15 US and Canada, $20 elsewhere. **Sample postpaid: $4, includes guidelines. Please make checks payable to AHA Books. Submit 1 rengo and/or 6-10 tanka at a time.** *Lynx* **encourages submissions by those experienced and experimenting with collaborative forms. Subscribers participate in ongoing rengas, start trends and otherwise determine the content. All submissions should include a brief bio with the title of the work. "Please send us copies that do not need to be returned." Include SASE for reply. Editor responds to all who submit. Reports in 1 week.** AHA Books also sponsors the International Tanka Splendor Award. Winning entries will be published in *Tanka Splendor*. Deadline: September 30. Send SASE for details.

‡LYNX EYE; SCRIBBLEFEST LITERARY GROUP (I), 1880 Hill Dr., Los Angeles CA 90041, phone (213)550-8522, founded 1994, co-editor Pam McCully. *Lynx Eye* is the quarterly publication of the ScribbleFest Literary Group, a new organization dedicated to the development and promotion of the literary arts. *Lynx Eye* is **"dedicated to showcasing visionary writers and artists, particularly new voices." Each issue contains a special feature called Presenting, in which an unpublished writer of prose or poetry makes his/her print debut. They have no specifications regarding form, subject matter or style of poetry, but poems should be 30 lines or less.** They have recently published poetry by A.D. Winans, Hal Sirowitz, Joanne Seltzer and Errol Miller. As a sample we selected these lines from "Quo Vadis" by Taylor Reese:

> *Man cannot wrest time from its path;*
> *Though silent, it is too relentless,*
> *Too permanent in movement.*
> *Nor can the ocean's tide be heard far inland,*
> *Despite its universal effect.*

Lynx Eye is about 90 pgs., 5½×8½, perfect-bound with card stock cover and b&w artwork. They receive about 500 poetry submissions a year and have space for about 40. Press run is 250-500 for 100 subscribers, 100 shelf sales. Single copy price varies from $5 to $7.50. Subscription: $20/year. **Sample postpaid: $5. No previously published poems; simultaneous submissions OK. Name, address and phone number on each piece. Always comments on rejections. Send SASE for guidelines. Reports in 2 months. Pays $10/piece and 5 copies. Buys first North American serial rights.**

THE LYRIC (II, IV-Form, students), 307 Dunton Dr. SW, Blacksburg VA 24060-5127, founded 1921 ("the oldest magazine in North America in continuous publication devoted to the publication of traditional poetry"), poetry editor Leslie Mellichamp, uses about 65 poems each quarterly issue. **"We use rhymed verse in traditional forms, for the most part, with an occasional piece of blank or free verse. 40 lines or so is usually our limit. Our themes are varied, ranging from religious ecstasy to humor to raw grief, but we feel no compulsion to shock, embitter or confound our readers. We also avoid poems about contemporary political or social problems—grief but not grievances, as Frost put it. Frost is helpful in other ways: If yours is more than a lover's quarrel with life, we're not your best market. And most of our poems are accessible on first or second reading. Frost again: Don't hide too far away."** They have recently published poetry by Anne Barlow, Tom Riley, Michael J. Bugeja, Rhina P. Espaillat, Richard Moore, Irene Warsaw, Alfred Dorn, Sharon Kourous, Gail White, Neill Megaw and Alice Mackenzie Swaim. The editor selected these sample lines from "Settling" by Gregory A. Jahn:

> *Though footing deep and brick laid true*
> *My little house will go;*
> *In wetted earth a rendezvous*
> *Is being kept below.*
>
> *What makes this mortar split and fall,*
> *What slow unhappiness,*
> *Can break so bravely raised a wall*
> *And tip this sad address?*

The Lyric is 36 pgs., digest-sized, professionally printed with varied typography, matte card cover, has a circulation of 850 with 800 subscriptions of which 290 are libraries. They receive about 5,000 submissions/year, use 250, have an average 3-month backlog. Subscription: $10 US, $12 Canada and other countries (in US funds only). **Sample postpaid: $3. Submit up to 5 poems at a time. No** previously published poems; simultaneous submissions OK. "Cover letters often helpful, but not required." Send SASE for guidelines. Reports in 1 month (average). Pays 1 copy, and all contributors are eligible for quarterly and annual prizes totaling over $800. Leslie Mellichamp comments, "Our *raison d'être* has been the encouragement of form, music, rhyme and accessibility in poetry. We detect a growing dissatisfaction with the modernist movement that ignores these things and a growing interest in the traditional wellsprings of the craft. Naturally, we are proud to have provided an alternative for 75 years that helped keep the true roots of poetry alive."

M.I.P. COMPANY (IV-Foreign language, erotica), P.O. Box 27484, Minneapolis MN 55427, phone (612)546-7578, founded 1984, contact Michael Peltsman, publishes 3 paperbacks/year. **They only publish Russian erotic poetry and prose written in Russian.** They have published poetry collections by Mikhail Armalinsky and Aleksey Shelvakh. **No previously published poems; No simultaneous submissions OK. Replies to queries in 1 month. Seldom comments on rejections.**

MACFADDEN WOMEN'S GROUP; TRUE CONFESSIONS; TRUE ROMANCES; TRUE LOVE; TRUE STORY; SECRETS; MODERN ROMANCES (I), Dept. PM, 233 Park Ave. S., New York NY 10003, phone (212)979-4800. **Address each magazine individually; do not submit to Macfadden Women's Group.** Each of these romance magazines uses poetry—usually no more than 1 poem/issue. **Their requirements vary; readers should study them individually and write for guidelines.** These mass-circulation magazines (available on newsstands) are a very limited market, yet a possible one for beginners—especially those who like the prose contents and are tuned in to their editorial tastes.

‡MCGILL STREET MAGAZINE (I, II), 193 Bellwoods Ave., Toronto, Ontario M6J 2P8 Canada, founded 1992, poetry editor Lisa Schmidt, is a quarterly, 70% fiction, 30% poetry (some interviews and reviews planned for future issues). **"Focus is on emerging writers and poets. Usually accept poems of no more than 2 pages, but will consider longer pieces on an individual basis. No limit on style or subject matter—focus is on diversity of voice."** They have recently published poetry by Janice Kulyk-Keefer and Esta Spalding. As a sample the editor selected these lines from "the space an embrace creates" by nathalie stephens:

> i will bleed into the wind
> 　　　i whisper
> find me in the kerosene rainbow
> hovering over heathrow
> look for me in the sun setting
> a deeper red over
> melbourne

McGill Street is 44-52 pgs., 8½×11, professionally printed and saddle-stitched, with coated paper cover, b&w art, photos and ads. They receive about 500 submissions a year, accept 10-15% of poems submitted. Press run is 1,500 for 300 subscribers of which 20 are libraries, 400-500 shelf sales. Subscription: $18 Canadian, $20 US. **Sample postpaid: $5 Canadian ("SASE appreciated"). No previously published poems; simultaneous submissions OK. Cover letter preferred. "Each poem is read by at least three people. Comments are made and the poetry editor decides to accept/ reject. Each submission then receives a personal letter." Almost always comments on rejections. Guidelines available for SASE but, they say, "Just send us your stuff!" Reports in 1-3 months."** Pays 2 copies. All rights remain with authors.

THE MACGUFFIN (II), Schoolcraft College, 18600 Haggerty Rd., Livonia MI 48152, phone (313)462-4400, ext. 5327, fax (313)462-4558, founded 1983, editor Arthur Lindenberg, who says, "*The MacGuffin* is a literary magazine which appears three times each year, in April, June and November. We publish the best poetry, fiction, nonfiction and artwork we find. We have no thematic or stylistic biases. **We look for well-crafted poetry. Long poems should not exceed 300 lines. Avoid pornography, trite and sloppy poetry. We do not publish haiku, concrete or light verse."** They have recently published poetry by Kathleen Ripley Leo, Stephen Dunning, Jim Daniels and Daniel James Sundahl. As a sample the editor selected these lines from "Neruda" by Peter Brett:

> The women pass like calendar days
> leaving in mind the aftertaste of
> mango, papaya days with high fore-
> heads and astonished eyes . . .

The MacGuffin is 144 pgs., digest-sized, professionally printed on heavy buff stock, with matte card cover, flat-spined, with b&w illustrations and photos. Circulation is 600, of which 140 are subscriptions and the rest are local newsstand sales, contributor copies and distribution to college offices. Single copy: $4.50; subscription: $12. **Sample postpaid: $4. "The editorial staff is grateful to consider unsolicited manuscripts and graphics."** Writers should submit no more than 5 poems of no more than 300 lines; poems should be typewritten. **"We discourage simultaneous submissions."** Publishes theme issues. Send SASE for upcoming themes. Mss are reported on in 8-10 weeks and the publication backlog is 6 months. Pays 2 copies, "occasional money or prizes." Poetry published in *The MacGuffin* has been selected for inclusion in *Pushcart Prize* anthologies. The editor says, "We will always comment on 'near misses.' Writing is a search, and it is a journey. Don't become side-tracked. Don't become discouraged. Keep looking. Keep traveling. Keep writing."

MACMILLAN PUBLISHING CO.; CHARLES SCRIBNER'S SONS; ATHENEUM; COLLIER, 866 Third Ave., New York NY 10022. Prefers not to share information.

MAD RIVER PRESS (V), State Road, Richmond MA 01254, phone (413)698-3184, founded 1986, editor Barry Sternlieb, publishes 3 broadsides and 1 chapbook/year, **"all types of poetry, no bias,"** but **none unsolicited.** They have published poetry by Gary Snyder, Hayden Carruth, W.S. Merwin, Louise Glück, Linda Gregg and Richard Wilbur. Call or write for information.

THE MADISON REVIEW; FELIX POLLAK PRIZE IN POETRY (II), Dept. of English, Helen C. White Hall, University of Wisconsin, 600 N. Park St., Madison WI 53706, phone (608)263-0566, founded 1978, poetry editors Christine Grimando and Joshua Moses, want **poems that are "smart and tight, that fulfill their own propositions. Spare us: love poems, religious or patriotic dogma, light verse. We'd like to see poetry in ethnic/nationality, form/style, gay/lesbian, humor (not light verse, though), political, social issues and women/feminism categories."** They have published work by Lise Goett, Lisa Steinman and Richard Tillinghast. As a sample the editors selected these lines from "Gulls" by Jerry Mirskin:

> *Now it's the sharp and damp smell of gasoline*
> *and now the sun, the full theater of the sun*
> *torching the town, so the windows*
> *of the houses along the shore burn like glasses of tea.*

The Madison Review is published in May and December, with 15-20 poems selected from a pool of 750. **Sample back issue postpaid: $2.50. Submit maximum of 6 poems. No simultaneous submissions. Usually reports in 4 months, may be longer in summer. Pays 2 copies. "We do appreciate a concise cover letter with short bio information."** The Felix Pollak Prize in Poetry is for $500 and publication in *TMR*, for "the best group of three unpublished poems submitted by a single author." Send SASE for rules before submitting for prize or see announcement for guidelines in *AWP* or *Poets & Writers* magazines. Submissions must arrive during September—winner announced December 15. The editors say, "Contributors: Know your market! Read before, during and after writing. Treat your poems *better* than job applications!"

THE MAGAZINE OF SPECULATIVE POETRY (IV-Science fiction), P.O. Box 564, Beloit WI 53512, founded 1984, editors Roger Dutcher and Mark Rich, is an irregularly published magazine that features **"the best new speculative poetry. We are especially interested in narrative form, but interested in variety of styles, open to any form, length (within reason), purpose. We're looking for the best of the new poetry utilizing the ideas, imagery and approaches developed by speculative fiction and will welcome experimental techniques as well as the fresh employment of traditional forms."** They have published poetry by Brian Aldiss, Jane Yolen, William Stafford, Ron Ellis and S.R. Compton. As a sample Roger Dutcher chose these lines from "Time Machines" by Steve Rasnic Tem:

> *The Big Bang tide sends us chasing*
> *each of our moments through space*
> *trying to escape the collapse*
> *and our own heat-death*
> *when all time runs backward*
> *and we leap from our graves*

The digest-sized magazine, 20-24 pgs., is offset from professional typesetting, saddle-stapled with matte card cover. They accept less than 10% of some 500 poems received/year. Press run is 100-200, going to nearly 100 subscribers of which 4 are libraries. Subscription: $11. **Sample postpaid: $3.50. Submit 3 poems at a time, double-spaced. No previously published poems or simultaneous submissions. "We like cover letters but they aren't necessary. We like to see where you heard of us; the name of the poems submitted; a statement if the poetry ms is disposable; a big enough SASE; and if you've been published, some recent places."** Editor comments on rejections "on occasion." Send SASE for guidelines. **Reports in 1-2 months. Pays 3¢/word, minimum $3, plus copy. Buys first North American serial rights.** Reviews books of speculative poetry. Query on unsolicited reviews. Send speculative poetry books for review consideration.

MAGIC CHANGES (IV-Themes), P.O. Box 658, Warrenville IL 60555-0658, phone (708)416-3111, founded 1978, poetry editor John Sennett, is published every 18 months, in an unusual format. Photocopied from typescript on many different weights and colors of paper, magazine-sized, stapled along the long side (you read it both vertically and horizontally), taped flat spine, full of fantasy drawings, pages packed with poems of all varieties, fiction, photos, drawings, odds and ends—including reviews of little magazines and other small press publications. It is **intended to make poetry (and literature) fun—and unpredictable. Each issue is on an announced theme.** *"Magic Changes* **is divided into sections such as 'The Order of the Celestial Otter,' 'State of the Arts,' 'Time,' 'Music' and 'Skyscraper Rats.' A magical musical theme pervades."** They have published poetry by Sue Standing, Caleb Bullen, Hugh Ogden, Brian Shaw, Chris Robbins, Kaela Sennett, Patricia A. Davey and Walt Curtis. As a sample the editor selected these lines from "Satchmo" by Roberta Gould:

> *Satchmo's teeth gleam*
> *like the diamond "LA"*
> *on his ring*
> *and his cheeks shine*
> *like the sun he*
> *lifts in his horn*

There are about 100 pgs. of poetry/issue, circulation 500, 28 subscriptions of which 10 are libraries. **Sample postpaid: $5. Submit 3-5 poems anytime. Send SASE for upcoming themes. The editor sometimes comments on rejections and offers criticism for $5/page of poetry. Reports in 2-4 months. Pays 1 or 2 copies. Acquires first North American serial rights.** Reviews books of poetry in "usually about 500 words." Open to unsolicited reviews. Poets may also send books for review consideration.

THE MAGIC MOUNTAIN, THE LITERARY JOURNAL OF INDIVIDUAL EXCELLENCE; A QUIET CUP (WITH FEET UP); CARTER AND COMPANY PRESS (III), P.O. Box 7161, Syracuse NY 13261, phone/fax (315)685-0434, e-mail candcprs@aol.com, founded 1993, editor Greg Carter, is a monthly electronic magazine for individual thought, available, free of charge, through America OnLine. They want to see **"the work of individuals, poetry related to individual growth and experience. Sample copies are available through e-mail or by sending one 3.5 diskette and two first-class stamps. Submit 1-5 poems at a time, either hardcopy or "preferably" 3.5 computer diskette (IBM-PC). Submissions may also be e-mailed to the above address. Previously published poems and simultaneous submissions OK. Reports in 2-4 weeks. Pays 1 contributor's copy through e-mail or 1 contributor's issue-diskette. Acquires one-time rights.** Carter and Company Press also publishes *A Quiet Cup (with feet up)*, a quarterly journal celebrating the art of Care—Nursing, and publishes electronic books through The Magic Mountain Arts Co-op. Write for details. The editor says, "As always, the criteria for acceptance is excellence. I want work—poetry, prose, graphic, whatever—that is expressed through a strong and pure individual voice. I am not interested in you as representative of various groups and affiliations; I want the you that is uniquely and wonderfully human."

THE MALAHAT REVIEW (II); LONG POEM PRIZES (II, IV-Form), P.O. Box 1700, MS 8524, University of Victoria, Victoria, British Columbia V8W 2Y2 Canada, phone (604)721-8524, founded 1967, editor Derk Wynand, is "a high quality, visually appealing literary quarterly which has earned the praise of notable literary figures throughout North America. Its purpose is to publish and promote poetry and fiction of a very high standard, both Canadian and international. **We are interested in various styles, lengths and themes. The criterion is excellence.**" They have recently published poetry by Erin Mouré, Susan Musgrave and Tom Wayman. As a sample the editor selected these lines from "How Were the People Made?" by Marilyn Bowering:

> *They were made from pictures that were altered,*
> *and altered again.*
> *They were made from paintings*
> *by a child with an imaginary friend.*
> *They were made from a single shoe in the middle of the road.*
> *They were made from expectations.*

They use 50 pgs. of poetry in each issue, have 1,500 subscribers of which 300 are libraries. They use about 100 of 2,000 submissions received/year, have no backlog. Topics and length in this handsome publication are particularly open, though editors show a distinct taste for free verse exhibiting craft and focus. Subscription: $20. **Sample postpaid: $7. Submit 5-10 poems, addressed to Editor Derk Wynand. The editors comment if they "feel the ms warrants some attention even though it is not accepted." Send SASE (or SAE and IRC) for guidelines. Reports within 3 months. Pays $25 per poem/page plus 2 copies and reduced rates on others.** Reviews books of poetry. The Long Poem Prizes of $400, plus publication and payment at their usual rates, entry fee $20 (which includes a year's subscription), is for a long poem or cycle 5-15 pgs. (flexible minimum and maximum), deadline March 1 of alternate years (1995, 1997, etc.).

‡MAÑANA (II), P.O. Box 4590, Austin TX 78765-4590, phone/fax (512)323-9350, e-mail sfeher@mail.utexas.edu, founded 1994, editor Sonya Fehér, is a bimonthly publication of poetry, prose and art. **"There is no theme restriction, no specific writing style that we're looking for. What we want is honest work that gives readers knowledge, feeling, something to take with them when they close the magazine. Free verse mainly, all subjects; no epics. No rhyming/form poetry, violent or**

dead end message/subject, or Hallmark poetry." They have recently published poetry by Lyn Lifshin, Miriam Sagan, Albert Huffstickler and Marlys West. As a sample the editor selected these lines from "The Horses" by Cindi J. Harrison:

> *From the ceiling we lie now,*
> *suspended in our painted bowl*
> *we are naked but not unclothed,*
> *we are silent, not without thought,*
> *we are strong, not without bearing. . .*

Mañana is 20 pgs., 8½×11, offset and saddle-stapled, card cover with b&w photo and b&w line drawings, photos (including some nudes), cartoons and ads inside. They receive about 2,000 poems a year, accept 10-20%. Press run is 1,000 for 150 subscribers of which 10 are libraries, 650 shelf sales. Single copy $3.50; subscription: $18. **Sample postpaid: $3.50. Make checks or money orders payable to** *Mañana.* **Previously published poems and simultaneous submissions OK. Name and address on each poem, "phone numbers are nice but not required. We also accept Mac MS Word disks 5.1 or below and e-mail submissions."** Time between acceptance and publication is 1-3 months. **Often comments on rejections using a rejection form with both general and specific comments. Send SASE for guidelines. Reports in 6-8 weeks. Pays 1 copy. Acquires one-time rights.** In addition to a variety of poetry selections, "we 'feature' one poet a month, usually using 6-10 poems, photo and bio." Featured author receives 3 copies. *Mañana* also sponsors poetry readings every other month for local contributors to the magazine and traveling contributors who happen to be in Austin. The editor says, "We like poetry that has taken some time and editing with logical line breaks. The most aggravating submissions are those without titles, punctuation or capitalization. That usage style is usually distracting unless a very good poet has taken a lot of time. Most often that style is laziness or trying to look cool."

THE MANDEVILLE PRESS (III), Old Hall, Norwich Rd., South Burlingham, Norfolk NR13 4EY England, phone 0493-750-804, founded 1972, editors Peter Scupham and John Mole, publishes handset pamphlets of the work of individual poets. **They want "formal poetry, intelligence guiding emotion. No formless poetry, emotion eliminating intelligence."** They have published poetry by Anthony Hecht, Patric Dickinson, Edward Lowbury and Bernard O'Donoghue. **Interested poets may query. Replies to queries in 1 week, to mss (if invited) in 1 month. Pays 10 author's copies. Send SASE for catalog to buy samples.**

MANDRAKE POETRY MAGAZINE; THE MANDRAKE PRESS (II), ul. Wielkiej Niedźwiedzicy 35/8, Gliwice 44-117 Poland, founded 1993 in New York, editor and publisher Leo Yankevich, appears twice a year, in April and October. The editor says, **"I'd like to see well-crafted poetry, broadly formalist, with the passion of John the Baptist and the insight of Pythagoras or Plotinus. I have a weakness for Italian sonnets. I prefer masculine rhymes as well as off-rhymes. I think that moon/spoon is much better than pretty/city, but moon/gryphon is even better. Anything with a metaphysical-existential slant, if well done, has a good chance of being accepted. I'm very open to Japanese forms as well as translations. I don't want to see poetry that's trite, hackneyed, banal, nor anything trendy and uninspired that reads like lines from a newspaper."** They have recently published poetry by Stephen Todd Booker, Leonard Cirino, Terence Hughes, M.L. McCarthy, M.A. Schaffner, Mary Rudbeck Stanko and David Rhine. As a sample the editor selected these lines from "Bloody moons hatch in a spectacle of innocence" by David Castleman:

> ——*For each, one's neighbor is the lesser martyr*
> *vaguely preliminary as was Christ,*
> *and each one is Judas, born to barter*
> *substance too real for a substance of mist.*

Mandrake Poetry Magazine is 20-32 pgs., digest-sized, photocopied from ink-jet typeset copy and glue bound with white card cover. The editor says he accepts about 15% of the poetry received. Press run is 200 for 50 subscribers from 3 continents. Single copy: $3 (by airmail); two-year subscription: $12. **Submit 1-7 poems at a time. Previously published poems and simultaneous submissions OK. Cover letter required. "Keep cover letter terse and informative. Please enclose SAE along with**

ALWAYS include a self-addressed, stamped envelope (SASE) when sending a ms or query to a publisher within your own country. When sending material to other countries, include a self-addressed envelope and International Reply Coupons (IRCs), available for purchase at most post offices.

one unattached U.S. (airmail) postage stamp or one IRC for all submissions. **Send only copies of your poems, as I do not return poems with my reply." Always comments on rejections. Reports in 1 month. Pays "a brace of free copies." All rights revert to author.** The Mandrake Press also publishes one perfect-bound collection of poems, averaging 36 pgs., each year. Press runs vary from 60 to 300. "I should at least be familiar with a poet before publishing a book. If he's published poems in magazines and has a modest readership, it certainly helps." **Query first with sample poems and cover letter with brief bio and publication credits. Replies to queries and mss in 1 month. Pays copies. "More copies can be purchased at the cost of production, usually $1.80 a book."** Recently published books: *Henry's Will* by Leonard Cirino, *Prelude To A Dream* by David Castleman, *Grief's Herbs* by Stanislaw Grochowiak and *Swiftly, Deeper* by Stephen Todd Booker. Poets may obtain a sample copy of any of the above titles by sending $3 in unattached US postage stamps or by sending 3 oz. worth of IRCs. The editor says, "My advice to beginners is to understand the mind of a lizard, to possess dark secrets like a gnostic, to cast incantations like a wizard, to see bright sparks like a schizophrenic."

THE MANHATTAN REVIEW (II, IV-Translations), 440 Riverside Dr., Apt. 45, New York NY 10027, phone (212)932-1854, founded 1980, poetry editor Philip Fried, tries **"to publish American and foreign writers, and we choose foreign writers with something valuable to offer the American scene. We like to think of poetry as a powerful discipline engaged with many other fields. We want to see ambitious work. Interested in both lyric and narrative. Not interested in mawkish, sentimental poetry.** We select high-quality work from a number of different countries, including the U.S." They have recently published poetry by Wistawa Szymborska, Baron Wormser, D. Nurkse, Julia Mishkin and Penelope Shuttle. As a sample the editor selected these lines by Adam Zagajewski:

> The shoes of Auschwitz, in pyramids
> high as the sky, groan faintly:
> Alas, we outlived mankind, now
> let us sleep, sleep:
> We have nowhere to go.

The *MR* is now "an annual with ambitions to be semiannual." The magazine is 64 pgs., digest-sized, professionally printed with glossy card cover, photos and graphics. Press run is 500 for 85 subscribers of which 35 are libraries. It is also distributed by Bernhard DeBoer, Inc. and Fine Arts Distributors. They receive about 300 submissions/year, use few ("but I do read everything submitted carefully and with an open mind"). "I return submissions as promptly as possible." Single copy: $5; subscription: $10. **Sample: $6.25 with 6×9 envelope. Submit 3-5 pgs. at a time. No simultaneous submissions. Cover letter with short bio and publications required. Editor sometimes comments "but don't count on it." Reports in 10-12 weeks. Pays copies.** Staff reviews books of poetry. Send books for review consideration. Philip Fried advises, "Don't be swayed by fads. Search for your own voice. Support other poets whose work you respect and enjoy. Be persistent. Keep aware of poetry being written in other countries."

MANKATO POETRY REVIEW (II), Box 53, English Dept., Mankato State, Mankato MN 56001, phone (507)389-5511, founded 1984, editor Roger Sheffer, is a semiannual magazine that is **"open to all forms of poetry. We will look at poems up to 60 lines, any subject matter."** They have published poetry by Edward Micus, Judith Skillman and Walter Griffin. As a sample the editor chose the following lines from a poem by Richard Robbins:

> Sage connects to lava rock mile by mile.
> West of Atomic City, blue flowers
> in the craters of the moon.

The magazine is 5×8, typeset on 60 lb. paper, 30 pgs., saddle-stapled with buff matte card cover printed in one color. It appears usually in May and December and has a circulation of 200. Subscription: $5/year. **Sample postpaid: $2.50. Submit 3-5 poems at a time. However, do not submit mss in summer (May through August). No previously published poems or simultaneous submissions. Cover letter required. Send SASE for guidelines. Reports in about 2 months; "We accept only what we can publish in next issue." Pays 2 copies.** The editor says, "We're interested in looking at longer poems— up to 60 lines, with great depth of detail relating to place (landscape, townscape)."

MANNA; MANNA FORTY, INC. (I, IV-Nature/ecology, religion, psychology/science), Box 548, Rt. 1, Sharon OK 73857, phone (405)254-2660, founded 1986, literary format 1991, editor Richard D. Kahoe. As their "Mission Statement" says: **"***manna*, a quarterly literary-professional journal, advances and publishes interests of manna forty, inc., a not-for-profit corporation. *manna* promotes ideals of a holistic view of truth and beauty, expressed in poetry, appropriate prose and pen sketches. It focuses on nature (natural living, ecology, environmental issues); religion (Christian and ecumenical) and psychology (and related sciences), and especially the interfaces of these areas." **They are open to all styles of poetry up to 50 lines, "but prefer shorter (under 25 lines) and will be publishing no more than 35% free verse."** They want poetry related to religion, nature and psychology. "Prefer integrating two or three of these areas. **No mushy sentimentality, highly obscure verse or doggerel (except possibly in short humorous context)."** They have recently published poetry by C. David Hay, Sheryl L. Nelms and Howard F. Stein. As a sample the editor selected these lines from "Prelude" by Marian Ford Park:

> *I search your face as you prepare to leave . . .*
> *We shall not meet again, this much I know.*
> *Our summer love has ended . . . I perceive*
> *A note of haste about you as you go.*
> *But then across the lake I hear the loon*
> *And understand his melancholy tune.*

manna is 8 pgs., 8½ × 11, desktop-published and professionally printed on 70 lb. recycled stock, with line drawings. Press run is 350 for 75 subscribers of which 6 are libraries, 200 distributed free to community groups. Subscription: free ("donation encouraged"). **Sample available for 1 first-class stamp. "Contributors who can are asked (but not required) to make donation toward costs, generally $7.50-15, depending on length of poem." Previously published poems and simultaneous submissions OK. Cover letter required. "Prefer to receive 2-6 poems on separate pages." Deadlines: February 15, May 15, August 15 and November 15. Publication appears one month later. Usually comments on rejections. Publishes occasional theme issues. Send SASE for guidelines and subscribe for upcoming themes. Themes are announced 1 issue in advance. Reports in 1-4 months. Pays at least 2 copies but for minimal donation pays 5 copies direct to poet, 10 mailed to addresses provided by poet. "If contributor does not make donation, we reserve rights to 50% of subsequent cash income from the writing."** The editor says, "Poets and prose contributors should observe our subject guidelines. Beginners are encouraged, but we prefer poems not to *sound* like beginners."

MANOA: A PACIFIC JOURNAL OF INTERNATIONAL WRITING (II), 1733 Donaghho Rd., Honolulu HI 96822, phone (808)956-3070, founded 1989, poetry editor Frank Stewart, appears twice a year. **"We are a general interest literary magazine, open to all forms and styles. We are not for the beginning writer, no matter what style. We are not interested in Pacific exotica."** They have published poetry by John Updike, Norman Dubie, Walter Pavlich and Eugene Ruggles. It is 200 pgs., 7 × 10, offset, flat-spined using art and graphics. They accept about 2% of 3,000 submissions received/ year. Press run is 2,000 for 700 subscribers of which 30 are libraries, 700 shelf sales. Subscription: $18/ year. **Sample postpaid: $10. Submit 3-5 poems at a time. Send SASE for guidelines. Reports in 6 weeks. Always sends prepublication galleys. Pay "competitive" plus 2 copies. Seldom comments on rejections.** They review current books and chapbooks of poetry. Open to unsolicited reviews. Poets may also send books for review consideration, attn. reviews editor. This magazine, one of the most exciting new journals in recent years, has become well known for the quality and diversity of its verse. It has also received a Design Excellence Award from the American Association of University Presses and Best Journal of the Year Award from the Council of Editors of Learned Journals. Poetry published in *Manoa* has also been selected for inclusion in *The Best American Poetry 1995*. The editor says, "We welcome the opportunity to read poetry submissions from throughout the country. We are not a regional journal, but we do feature work from the Pacific Rim, national and international, especially in our reviews and essays. We are not interested in genre or formalist writing for its own sake, or picturesque impressions of the region."

‡MANUSHI (II), C/202, Lajpat Nagar 1, New Delhi 110024 India, phone 6839158 or 6833022, founded 1978, editor Madhu Kishwar, is a bimonthly "journal about women and society." **They look for "good poetry with social relevance." They do not want poetry "which makes no point."** They have published poetry by Archana Verma, Indu Jain and Amrita Pritam. As a sample the editor selected these lines (poet unidentified):

> *Today, once again*
> *She crumpled a poem,*
> *Lit the fire with it,*
> *And put up the water for tea*

Manushi is 44 pgs., approximately 8 × 10½, offset, saddle-stapled with glossy full-color cover. "We receive a considerable number of poems, accept about 10%." **No previously published poems or simultaneous submissions. Cover letter required. Often comments on rejections. Reports "fairly soon." Pays "as many copies as author requires."**

MARK: A LITERARY JOURNAL (II), 2801 W. Bancroft SU1501, Toledo OH 43606, first appeared 1967-69, then resumed 1978, editors change every 1-2 years, current editor Mike Donnelly, is an annual journal of fiction, poetry, photographs and sketches. **"We're tired of the same old romance/love poems. Give us something with substance. Politically irresponsible work (racist, sexist, heterosexist, anti-choice) has no place with us."** As a sample the editor selected these lines from "flood wall revisited" by Robin Murray:

> *At least you're not a dike, he said.*

> *Did he mean*
> *I couldn't keep the flood of water*
> *from innundating the hems*
> *of my rolled up jeans?*

Mark is 70 pgs., digest-sized, saddle-stapled, professionally printed, with matte card cover. Single copy: $3. **Submit 6 poems at a time. "We appreciate brief cover letters with name, address, date and titles of work submitted. We accept submissions all year round; manuscripts received after January 31 are held for the following year's issue." Editor comments "very rarely." Pays 2 copies. Acquires first serial rights.**

MARYLAND POETRY REVIEW; MARYLAND STATE POETRY AND LITERARY SOCIETY (I, II), P.O. Drawer H, Catonsville MD 21228, founded 1985, edited by Rosemary Klein, "is interested in promoting the literary arts in Maryland as well as nationally and internationally. **We are interested in strong, thoughtful poetry with a slight bias to free verse. All submissions are read carefully. *MPR* is open to good poets who have not published extensively as well as to those who have."** They have published poetry by Celia Brown, Elisabeth Stevens, Enid Shomer and Joseph Somoza. As a sample the editor selected these lines from "The Fool's Dark Lantern" by Michael Fallon:

> *Like a fly that spins*
> *in wounded circles on the sill*
> *his thoughts revolve around a single thought:*
> *there is only so much time*
> *in which to know*

MPR is professionally printed in small type on quality eggshell stock, 7×11, 75 pgs., saddle-stapled with a glossy b&w card cover. It appears twice a year in double issues (Spring/Summer and Fall/Winter). In the past they have done special issues on confessional, Irish, Hispanic and Australian poetry. **Query about possible future special issues.** Subscription and Maryland State Poetry and Literary Society membership is $17 ($12 for students and senior citizens; $20 for member and spouse; $25 for institutions). **Sample postpaid: $7. Submit no more than 5 poems at a time with brief bio. No simultaneous submissions. "We read submissions only in January, April and September but accept all year." Reports in 3-6 months. Pays 1 copy.** Book reviews are generally solicited. Send books for review consideration, attn. Robert Cooperman. MSPLS sponsors the Maryland State Poetry and Literary Society's Annual Poetry and Fiction Contest for poetry of any length and fiction to 2,500 words. Entry fee: $3/poem or four for $10, $3/story. Contest runs from January 1 through May 31. Cash prizes and magazine publication. They also sponsor the Michael Egan Memorial Poetry Contest for poetry of any length. Entry fee: $3/poem. Contest runs from September 1 through October 28. Cash prizes and magazine publication. Send SASE for guidelines.

THE UNIVERSITY OF MASSACHUSETTS PRESS; THE JUNIPER PRIZE (II), P.O. Box 429, Amherst MA 01004-0429, phone (413)545-2217, fax (413)545-1226, founded 1964. The press offers an annual competition for the Juniper Prize, in alternate years to first and subsequent books. In 1996 the prize is for a subsequent book: mss whose authors have had at least one full-length book or chapbook of poetry published or accepted for publication. In 1997 only "first books" will be considered: mss by writers whose poems may have appeared in literary journals and/or anthologies but have not been published, or been accepted for publication, in book form. **Submissions should be approximately 60 pgs. in type-script (generally 50-55 poems). Include paginated contents page. A list of poems published in literary journals and/or anthologies must also accompany the ms. Such poems may be included in the ms and must be identified. "Mss by more than one author, entries of more than one ms simultaneously or within the same year, and translations are not eligible." Entry fee: $10 plus SASE for return of ms or notification. Entries must be postmarked not later than September 30.** The award is announced in April/May and publication is scheduled for the following spring. The amount of the prize is $1,000 and is in lieu of royalties on the first print run. **Send SASE for guidelines and/or further information.**

THE MASSACHUSETTS REVIEW (II), Memorial Hall, University of Massachusetts, Amherst MA 01003, founded 1959, editors Paul Jenkins and Anne Halley. Mostly free verse, all lengths and topics, appears here, with emphasis in recent issues on narrative work. An interesting feature: Editors run poems with long-line lengths in smaller type, to fit on the page without typographical interruption (as in other journals). They have published poetry by Marge Piercy, Michael Benedikt and Eavan Boland. The editors describe this quarterly as offset (some color used in art sections), 6×9. They receive about 2,500 poems a year, use about 50. Press run is 1,600 for 1,100-1,200 subscribers of which 1,000 are libraries, the rest for shelf sales. Subscription: $15 (US), $20 outside US, $17 for libraries. **Sample postpaid: $5.75. No simultaneous submissions or previously published poems. Read submissions October 1 through June 1 only. Send SASE for guidelines. Reports in 6 weeks. Pays minimum of $10, or 35¢/ line, plus 2 copies.** Work published in this review has been included in *The Best American Poetry 1995*.

MATTOID (II), School of Literature & Journalism, Deakin University, Geelong, Victoria, Australia 3217, founded 1977, contact Dr. Brian Edwards, appears 3 times/year. **"No special requirements but interesting complexity, quality, experimentation. No naive rhyming verse."** They have published poetry by Lauris Edmond, Kevin Hart and Judith Rodriguez. It is 200 pgs., flat-spined with 2-color cover. They receive about 800 poems a year, publish 10-15%. Press run is 600 for 400 subscribers of which 10 are libraries, 30-50 shelf sales. **Sample postpaid: $15 overseas. Publishes theme issues. Send SASE (or SAE and IRC) for upcoming themes. Reports in 2-3 months. Pays 2 copies.** Reviews books of poetry in 1,000-2,000 words, single format.

MATURE YEARS (IV-Senior citizen, religious), P.O. Box 801, 201 Eighth Ave. S., Nashville TN 37202, phone (615)749-6292, founded 1954, editor Marvin W. Cropsey, is a quarterly. "The magazine's purpose is to help persons understand and use the resources of Christian faith in dealing with specific opportunities and problems related to aging. **Poems are usually limited to fifteen lines and may, or may not, be overtly religious. Poems should not poke fun at older adults, but may take a humorous look at them. Avoid sentimentality and saccarine. If using rhymes and meter, make sure they are accurate."** As a sample the editor selected these lines by Carole Johnston:

> *What is winter*
> *but a large and cold*
> *secret that somehow*
> *keeps me warm . . . for*
> *I know where sweet*
> *daffodils lie sleeping.*
> *I know the graves of*
> *six brave crocuses*
> *and the tulip colors*
> *of next spring.*

It is 112 pgs., magazine-sized, saddle-stapled, with full-color glossy paper cover. Circulation 70,000. **Sample postpaid: $3.50. Submit season and nature poems for spring during December through February; for summer, March through May; for fall, June through August; and for winter, September through November. Send SASE for guidelines. Reports in 2 months, a year's delay before publication. Pays 50¢-$1/line upon acceptance.**

THE MAVERICK PRESS; SOUTHWEST POETS SERIES ANNUAL CHAPBOOK CONTEST (II, IV-Regional, themes), Rt. 2 Box 4915, Eagle Pass TX 78852, phone (210)773-1836, founded 1991, editor Carol Cullar, publishes a biannual of "outstanding Texas writers and other mavericks whose works represent the contemporary scene. Each issue is individually named (i.e., the April 1995 issue was titled *Wild Turkey*)." They are **looking for "strong, uncluttered figurative language to 100 lines. No diatribes on current events or political posturings, no smut."** They have recently published poetry by Errol Miller, Bayla Winters, Steve Koziolek and Simon Perchik. As a sample the editor selected these lines from "Avis on the Street" by Mauricio Mondragon:

> *. . . she finds them all in place:*
> *the cigarette case, checkbook, lipstick,*
> *treasures that disappear but soon resurface,*
> *having slipped through*
> *the widening cracks of her*
> *extra ordinary preoccupation. . . .*

The editor says it is 74 pgs., 5½×8½, saddle-stapled. Cover is an original block print by the editor, inside illustrations include b&w line drawings or block prints by contributors. They receive 1,000-2,000 poems a year, accept 4-8%. Press run is 250 for 100 subscribers of which 12 are libraries, 120 shelf sales. Subscription: $13.50. **Sample postpaid: $7.50. Submit up to 6 poems at a time. "Author's name and address must appear on every page submitted. Prefer standard size paper and envelopes 6×9 or larger."** No previously published poems; simultaneous submissions OK with notification up front and a phone call if ms is accepted elsewhere. Cover letter with brief bio required. Time between acceptance and publication is a year and a half maximum. **"All entries are sorted into Texans/Non-Texans, then read impartially. Outstanding pieces are reread and resorted later with slight consideration made to Texas writers. Final selections are made after consultation with Rio Bravo Literary Arts Council."** Often comments on rejections. Criticism provided, if requested. Fee negotiated on a job-by-job basis, minimum $25. Publishes one theme issue each year. Send SASE for guidelines and upcoming themes. Theme for November 1995: "Cathedrals/man's gods, fetishes, icons." Reports in 6-8 weeks. Sometimes sends prepublication galleys. Pays 2 copies. All rights retained by authors. They also sponsor the Southwest Poets Series Annual Chapbook Contest, for residents of Arizona, New Mexico, Oklahoma and Texas. Entry fee: $10, includes copy of winning chapbook published in February of following year. Deadline: October 31. Write for details. The editor says, "We are looking for strong, uncluttered, figurative language and prefer free verse, although the exception is considered. I would like to see more poems that 'push the envelope'—test the limits of what is poetic. Main criterion is excellence. Beginners: Presentation is important, but content is paramount."

MAYAPPLE PRESS (III, IV-Regional, women), P.O. Box 5473, Saginaw MI 48603-0473, phone (517)793-2801, founded 1978, publisher/editor Judith Kerman, publishes **"women's poetry, Great Lakes regional poetry"** in chapbooks. **They want "quality contemporary poetry rooted in real experience and strongly crafted. No greeting card verse, sentimental or conventional poetry."** They have published chapbooks by Judith Minty, Evelyn Wexler and Toni Ortner-Zimmerman. **Query with 5-6 samples. Check** *Poets & Writers* **for open times.** "We are not likely to publish unless poet accepts a *primary* role in distribution. Reality is only poets themselves can sell unknown work." **Usually sends prepublication galleys. Pays 5% of run. Publishes on "cooperative" basis.** "Generally poet agrees to purchase most of the run at 50% of cover price." **Editor "sometimes comments (very briefly)" on rejections.** She says, "Poets must create the audience for their work. No small press 'white knight' can make an unknown famous (or even sell more than a few books!)."

‡MEADOWBROOK PRESS (IV-Anthologies, children, humor), 18318 Minnetonka Blvd., Deephaven MN 55391, founded 1975, contact Children's Poetry Editor. Meadowbrook Press publishes one anthology a year as part of a series of funny poetry books for children. **They want humorous poems aimed at children ages 6-12. Length limit: 45 lines. "Poems should be fun, light and refreshing. We're looking for new, hilarious, contemporary voices in children's poetry that kids can relate to."** They have published poetry by Shel Silverstein, Jack Prelutsky, Jeff Moss and Bruce Lansky. As a sample the editor selected "The Burp" (anonymous):

> Pardon me for being so rude.
> It was not me, it was my food.
> It got so lonely down below,
> it just popped up to say hello.

Their first two anthologies are *Kids Pick the Funniest Poems* and *A Bad Case of the Giggles*. Forthcoming will be *Miles of Smiles*. **"Submit your best work." One poem to a page, name and address on each. Previously published poems and simultaneous submissions OK. Cover letter required "just to know where the poet found us."** Time between acceptance and publication is 1-2 years. **Poems are tested in front of grade school students before being published. Send SASE for guidelines and upcoming anthology titles and topics. Pays $75-150 for each poem published.**

‡MEDELA REVIEW (I, II), 2 W. Read St. #108, Baltimore MD 21201, founded 1994, editor Kim LaVigueur, is a semiannual journal devoted to contemporary literary arts. **They welcome submissions of poetry, fiction and camera-ready art, but offer no specifications regarding form, length, subject matter or style of poetry.** The editor says *Medela* is 64-128 pgs., digest-sized. Single copy: $3.50; subscription: $6. **"All mss must be accompanied by a brief biography and a SASE. Please, no simultaneous submissions." Occasionally comments on rejections. Reports in 3-4 months. Pays in copies. Acquires first rights.**

MEDIPHORS (I, II, IV-Specialized: medicine/health-related), P.O. Box 327, Bloomsburg PA 17815, founded 1992, editor Eugene D. Radice, M.D. *Mediphors* is a biannual literary journal of the health professions that publishes literary work in medicine and health, including poetry, short story, humor, essay, drawing, art/photography. **They want "fresh insights into illness and those caregivers with the burden and joy of working in the fields of medicine and health. Optimism in the face of adversity and overwhelming sorrow. The day-to-day feelings of healthcare workers in diverse settings from hospitals in cities to war zones in military hot spots."** As a sample the editor selected these lines from "The Horn of Africa" by Michael H. Lythgoe:

> In the villages, voices long dehydrated,
> Grope to compose lyrical lines,
> Rumors of virtues among the villainy.
> Oral poems trickle as a serum,
> Sustaining drips
> Of life for skin and bones.

Mediphors is 72 pgs., 8½×11, offset and saddle-stapled with color cover and b&w art, graphics and photos throughout. They receive about 1,200 poetry submissions a year, accept approximately 100. Press run is 900 for 275 subscribers of which 20 are libraries, 200 shelf sales. Single copy: $6.50; subscription: $12. **Sample postpaid: $5. Submit "2 copies of each poem that we can keep; 6 poems maximum, 30 lines each. We do not accept previously published poems or simultaneous submissions, and it is upsetting to find out that this has occurred when we accept a poem. We then reject all the poems of that author." Cover letter not required "but helpful."** Time between acceptance and publication is 10-12 months. **Seldom comments on rejections. Send SASE for guidelines. Reports in 1-3 months. Pays 2 copies. "We require authors to sign a very tight contract for first North American serial rights that makes them legally responsible for plagiarism, libel,**

copyright infringement, etc." The editor says, "Our goal is to place in print as many new authors as possible, particularly those working within the health/medical fields (such as doctors, nurses, technologists, therapists, etc.). We encourage unsolicited manuscripts."

THE EDWIN MELLEN PRESS (II), P.O. Box 450, Lewiston NY 14092-0450, phone (716)754-2266, fax (716)754-4056, founded 1973, poetry editor Patricia Schultz, is a scholarly press. "We do not have access to large chain bookstores for distribution, but depend on direct sales and independent bookstores." **They pay 2 copies, no royalties. "We require no author subsidies. However, we encourage our authors to seek grants from Councils for the Arts and other foundations because these add to the reputation of the volume." They want "original integrated work—living unity of poems, preferably unpublished, encompassable in one reading."** They have published poetry by W.R. Elton and Albert Cook. Their books are 64 pgs., 6×9, softcover binding, no graphics. Price: $12.95. **Submit 30-60 sample poems with cover letter including bio and publications. "We do not print until we receive at least 100 prepaid orders. Successful marketing of poetry books depends on the author's active involvement.** We send out up to 15 free review copies to journals or newspapers, the names of which may be suggested by the author. An author may (but is not required to) purchase books to make up the needed 100 prepublication sales." The editor says, "We seek to publish volumes unified in mood, tone, theme."

MEN AS WE ARE (II, IV-Specialized), P.O. Box 150615, Brooklyn NY 11215-0007, e-mail menas weare@aol.com, founded 1991, editor-in-chief Jonathan Running Wind, is a quarterly of fiction, poetry, essays, commentary, art, reviews and photography designed to nurture "self-acceptance and transformation of men. **All forms of poetry welcome. Subject must be some aspect of the male experience, but from any perspective."** They have published poetry by Timothy Walsh and David Thorn. As a sample the editor selected these lines from "The Overthrow of Despair" by Jim Sorcic:

> *Each breath is a rosary*
> *of desire, a prayer*
> *for the overthrow of despair.*
> *There are times*
> *When I breathe, it seems*
> *a small sound, a found voice*
> *erupts, crying for*
> *forgiveness.*

The editor says *Men As We Are* is 40 pgs., 8¼×10⅞, offset, saddle-stitched, self-cover, with lots of art and graphics, 10% ads. They receive about 400 submissions a year, accept approximately 4%. Press run is 1,000 for 200 subscribers, 800 shelf sales. Single copy: $3; subscription: $12. **Sample postpaid: $3.98. Submit 1-5 poems at a time. Previously published poems and simultaneous submissions OK. Cover letter required; include brief bio and "note where you heard about us."** Time between acceptance and publication is 3-6 months. **Sometimes comments on rejections. Send SASE for guidelines and upcoming themes. Reports in 3-6 months. Pays 3-5 copies. Acquires first North American serial or reprint rights and non-exclusive anthology rights.** Reviews books of poetry in 300-500 words. Open to unsolicited reviews. Poets may also send books for review consideration.

MENNONITE PUBLISHING HOUSE; PURPOSE; STORY FRIENDS; ON THE LINE; WITH (IV-Religious, children), 616 Walnut Ave., Scottdale PA 15683-1999, phone (412)887-8500. **Send submissions or queries directly to the editor of the specific magazine at address indicated.** The official publisher for the Mennonite Church in North America seeks also to serve a broad Christian audience. **Each of the magazines listed has different specifications, and the editor of each should be queried for more exact information.** *Purpose*, editor James E. Horsch, a "monthly in weekly parts," circulation 16,000, is **for adults of all ages, its focus: "action oriented, discipleship living."** It is 5⅜×8⅜, with two-color printing throughout. **They buy appropriate poetry up to 12 lines.** *Purpose* uses 3-4 poems/week, receives about 2,000/year of which they use 150, has a 10- to 12-week backlog. **Send SASE for guidelines and free sample. Mss should be typewritten, double-spaced, one side of sheet only. Simultaneous submissions OK. Reports in 6-8 weeks. Pays $5-15/poem plus 2 copies.** *On the Line*, edited by Mary C. Meyer, another "monthly in weekly parts," is **for children 10-14,** a "story paper that reinforces Christian values," circulation 6,500. It is 7×10, saddle-stapled, with 2-color printing on the cover and inside, using art and photos. **Sample free with SASE. Wants poems 3-24 lines. Submit 5 poems at a time, "each typed on a separate 8×11½ sheet." Simultaneous submissions and previously published poems OK. Reports in 1 month. Pays $10-25/poem plus 2 copies.** *Story Friends*, edited by Marjorie Waybill, is for **children 4-9,** a "story paper that reinforces Christian values," also a "monthly in weekly issues," circulation 6,900, uses poems **3-12 lines. Send SASE for guidelines/sample copy. Pays $5-10.** *With*, Editorial Team, Box 347, Newton KS 67114, phone (316)238-5100, is for **"senior highs, ages 15-18,"** focusing on helping "high school youth make a commitment to Christ in the context of the church amidst the complex and conflicting values they encounter in their world," circulation 5,800, uses **poetry dealing with youth in relation to their**

world, nature and light verse. Poems should be 4-50 lines. Pays $10-25.

MERLYN'S PEN: THE NATIONAL MAGAZINES OF STUDENT WRITING, GRADES 6-12 (IV-Students, young adults), Dept. PM, Box 1058, East Greenwich RI 02818, phone (401)885-5175, founded 1985, editor R. Jim Stahl, one for grades 6-9, the other ('senior edition') for grades 9-12. Each edition is 40 pgs., magazine-sized, professionally printed with glossy paper, color cover. Press run is 40,000 for 38,000 subscriptions of which 5,000 are libraries. Subscription: $21. **Sample postpaid: $3. Send SASE for guidelines. Reports in 3 months. Pays 3 copies plus $5-10/piece.**

METAMORPHOUS PRESS (V), P.O. Box 10616, Portland OR 97210-0616, phone (503)228-4972, founded 1982, publishes and distributes books, cassettes and videotapes on **neurolinguistic programming,** health and healing education, business and sales, women's studies, and children's books. **They currently do not accept unsolicited poetry.**

METRO SINGLES LIFESTYLES (I), Box 28203, Kansas City MO 64118, phone (816)436-8424, founded 1984, editor Robert L. Huffstutter. *MSL* is a tabloid publication for women and men of all ages: single, divorced, widowed or never-married. Not a lonely hearts type of publication, but positive and upbeat, it is published 6 times/year and has a circulation of 30,000 (approximately 5,000 subscribers in Kansas City and throughout the USA), newsstand, bookstore sales and limited complimentary copies to clubs, organizations and singles groups. Interested in seeing **"free verse, lite verse, philosophical, romantic, sentimental and Frost-type poetry. All subjects considered."** They have published poetry by Patricia Castle, Milton Kerr and Mary Ann McDonnell. As a sample, the editor selected these lines from "The Women of Cairo" by Phillip Slattery:

> *Eyes made of the Egyptian night*
> *Sparkling like an oasis pool*
> *Skin the color of the endless sand*
> *Beauty of forgotten goddesses lives on.*

Each issue is about 36 pgs. and printed on Webb Offset press. Each issue features at least 12 poems by poets living throughout the USA. "Poets are invited to send a photo and a brief paragraph about their goals, single status and lifestyle. This is optional and does not influence selection of poetry, but does add interest to the publication when space for this extra feature permits." Subscription: $18 for 6 issues. **Sample copy of current issue is $3 postpaid. Ms should be typewritten, double-spaced or written in easy-to-read format. "Prefer to look at original poetry. No simultaneous or previously published work." Reports in 6-8 weeks. Pays from $5/poem or in subscriptions plus complimentary copies.** The editor says, "We do not limit or restrict subject of poems, but insist they convey an emotion, experience or exercise the reader's imagination."

MICHIGAN QUARTERLY REVIEW (III), Dept. PM, 3032 Rackham Bldg., University of Michigan, Ann Arbor MI 48109, phone (313)764-9265, founded 1962, editor-in-chief Laurence Goldstein, is "an interdisciplinary, general interest academic journal that publishes mainly essays and reviews on subjects of cultural and literary interest." They use **all kinds of poetry except light verse. No specifications as to form, length, style, subject matter or purpose.** They have published poetry by Tess Gallagher, Robert Hass, Amy Gerstler and Cathy Song. As a sample the editor selected these lines by Donald Hall:

> *Daylilies go from the hill; asters return; maples redden again*
> *as summer departs for winter's virtuous deprivation.*
> *When we stroll the Pond Road at nightfall, western sun stripes*
> *down through dust raised by a pickup ten minutes ago:*
> *vertical birches, hilly road, sunlight slant and descending.*

The *MQR* is 160 pgs., 6×9, flat-spined, professionally printed with glossy card cover, b&w photos and art. They receive 1,500 submissions/year, use 30, have a 1-year backlog. Circulation is 2,000, with 1,500 subscriptions of which half are libraries. Single copy: $5; subscription: $18. **Sample postpaid: $2.50. They prefer typed mss. No previously published poems or simultaneous submissions. Publishes theme issues. For example, the Fall 1995/Winter 1996 issue will be a double issue on the "100th Anniversary of Motion Pictures." Reports in 4-6 weeks. Always sends prepublication galleys. Pays $8-12/page. Buys first rights only.** Reviews books of poetry. "All reviews are commissioned." Poetry published in the *Michigan Quarterly Review* was also selected for inclusion in the 1992, 1994 and 1995 volumes of *The Best American Poetry.* Laurence Goldstein advises, "There is no substitute for omnivorous reading and careful study of poets past and present, as well as reading in new and old areas of knowledge. Attention to technique, especially to rhythm and patterns of imagery, is vital."

MID-AMERICAN REVIEW; JAMES WRIGHT PRIZE FOR POETRY (II, IV-Translations), Dept. of English, Bowling Green State University, Bowling Green OH 43403, phone (419)372-2725, founded 1980, editor-in-chief George Looney, appears twice a year. **"Poetry should emanate from strong, evocative images; use fresh, interesting language; and have a consistent sense of voice. Each line**

must carry the poem, and an individual vision should be evident. **We encourage new as well as established writers. There is no length limit."** They have recently published poetry by Stephen Dunn, Catherine Sasanov, Albert Goldbarth, Naomi Shihab Nye, Greg Pape, David Baker, Martín Espada and Frankie Paino. As a sample the editor selected these lines from "Conversations With Air" by Al Maginnes:

> . . . *Now we are silent*
> *before those angels, listening*
> *for the rustle of scaled wings, the conversations*
> *with air that all flight, all language*
> *finally is. Between blows of the chisel,*
> *those sculptors listened and were answered.*

The review is 200 pgs., flat-spined, offset printed, using line drawings, laminated card cover. They receive over 1,000 mss a year, use 60-80 poems. Press run is 1,000. Single copy: $7; subscription: $12. **Sample postpaid: $5. Reads submissions September 1 through May 30 only. Send SASE for guidelines. Sometimes sends prepublication galleys. Pays $10/printed page plus 2 copies. Rights revert to authors on publication.** Reviews books of poetry. Open to unsolicited reviews. Poets may also send books to Andrea Van Vorhis, reviews editor, for review consideration. **They also publish chapbooks in translation** and award the James Wright Prize for Poetry to a ms published in regular editions of *MAR*, when funding is available.

MIDDLE EAST REPORT (IV-Regional, ethnic, themes), 1500 Massachusetts Ave. NW, Suite 119, Washington DC 20005, phone (202)223-3677, founded 1971, editor Joe Stork, is "a magazine on contemporary political, economic, cultural and social developments in the Middle East and North Africa and U.S. policy toward the region. We occasionally publish **poetry that addresses political or social issues of Middle Eastern peoples."** They have published poetry by Dan Almagor (Israeli) and Etel Adnan (Lebanese). It is 32 pgs., magazine-sized, saddle-stapled, professionally printed on glossy stock with glossy paper cover, 6 issues/year. "We published 9 poems last year, all solicited." Press run is 7,500. Subscription: $30. **Sample postpaid: $6 domestic; $8 airmail overseas. Simultaneous submissions and previously published poems OK. Editor sometimes comments on submissions. Reports in 6-8 weeks. "We key poetry to the theme of a particular issue. Could be as long as 6 months between acceptance and publication." Pays 3 copies.**

MIDLAND REVIEW (II), English Dept., Morrill Hall, Oklahoma State University, Stillwater OK 74078, phone (405)744-9474, founded 1985, is a literary annual that publishes "poetry, fiction, essays, ethnic, experimental, women's work, contemporary feminist." The editors say, **"style and form are open." They do not want "long or religious poetry."** They have published poetry by Amy Clampitt, William Stafford, Bill Knott, Tom Lux and Richard Kostelanetz. As a sample, the editors selected these lines by James Doyle:

> *The pressured houses squat*
> *beneath a black sky. Smoke*
> *passes back and forth between*
> *them down the street. Gilled*
> *animals swim the thin odors*
> *home, calling themselves planets . . .*

Midland Review is 100-120 pgs., digest-sized, with photography, artwork and ads. Circulation is 500, of which 470 are subscriptions. Single copy: $6. **Sample postpaid: $5. Writers should submit 3-5 poems at a time, typed ms in any form. "We no longer read during the summer (May 1 through August 31)." Reporting time is 3-6 months and time to publication 6-12 months. Pays 1 copy.**

‡MIDMARCH ARTS PRESS; WOMEN ARTISTS NEWS (IV-Women), 300 Riverside Dr., New York NY 10025, founded 1979, editor Sylvia Moore. They have published poetry by Muriel Rukeyser, Eve Merriam and Jane Cooper. *WAN* is a 40-page magazine focusing **on women in the arts**, using some poetry. **Sample postpaid: $3.75. Send SASE for guidelines. Reports in 6 weeks. Pays 5 copies.** Midmarch Arts Press publishes 6 paperbacks/year.

MIDSTREAM: A MONTHLY JEWISH REVIEW (IV-Ethnic), 110 E. 59th St., New York NY 10022, phone (212)339-6040, editor Joel Carmichael, managing editor M.S. Solow, is an international journal appearing monthly except February/March, June/July and August/September, when it is bimonthly. **They want short poems with Jewish themes or atmosphere.** They have published poetry by Yehuda Amichai, James Reiss, Abraham Sutzkever, Liz Rosenberg and John Hollander. The magazine is 48 pgs., approximately 8½ × 11, saddle-stapled with colored card cover. Each issue includes 4 to 5 poems (which tend to be short, lyric and freestyle expressing seminal symbolism of Jewish history and Scripture). They receive about 300 submissions/year, use 5-10%. Circulation: 10,000. Single copy: $3; subscription: $21. **Submit 3 poems at a time. Publishes theme issues. Reports in 3 months. Pays $25/poem. Buys all rights.**

Preserving a Way of Life Through Poetry

As a well-known cowboy poet and a centerpiece for the wildly successful Cowboy Poetry Gathering held annually in Elko, Nevada, Wallace (Wally) McRae is not a poet looking for financial success or even notoriety. Rather, he is looking for a way to preserve his culture and tell the reality of today's cowboy.

Wallace McRae

A third generation rancher with a degree in zoology from Montana State University, McRae runs a cow/calf operation at his home near Colstrip, Montana. His first experience with poetry came at age four when he recited a Christmas poem at a one-room schoolhouse attended by his older sisters. McRae didn't begin writing poetry, however, until after returning home from college and the Navy. "I came back home and looked around and thought, 'There are wonderful stories here, wonderful characters, and the culture has a lot of intriguing facets to it.' One of the ways I could capture some of these was to write them down."

By choosing poetry as his expressive medium, McRae continues the century-old tradition of cowboys passing down their culture and stories through poems. Sitting in a bunkhouse or by the chuck wagon, cowboys shared poems for entertainment. "Cowboy poetry tends to be more of a spoken type of poetry. It's strength is in its recitation," says McRae. "It's a way to preserve the culture and tell our story. Our story has not been told very well. I don't think it was told in the dime cowboy novels or in the B movies of the '40s or in all the television cowboy shows. So who is going to tell our story for us? Who is better qualified than we are?"

McRae writes in meter and rhyme because of the poetry that influenced him growing up and the strong tradition of cowboy poetry being in metered and rhymed verse. "The first introduction people have to poetry is in meter and rhyme. Maybe it's nursery rhymes and maybe it's not the best poetry in the world, but it's those first two or three steps that grow into other kinds of poetry."

He is quick to add that there are also many wonderful free verse poems written by today's cowboy poets. "I don't think the form is all that important. Good writing is good writing. However, there is a growing awareness and acceptance of different types of poetry. The instance of free verse in the cowboy poetry arena is certainly growing."

Working from end to beginning, McRae usually has his poems figured out before sitting down with pad and pencil or at the computer. "I start backwards

"Things of Intrinsic Worth"

Remember that sandrock on Emmels Crick
Where Dad carved his name in 'thirteen?
It's been blasted down into rubble
And interred by their dragline machine.
Where Fadhls lived, at the old Milar Place,
Where us kids stole melons at night?
They 'dozed it up in a funeral pyre
Then torched it. It's gone alright.
The "C" on the hill, and the water tanks
Are now classified "reclaimed land."
They're thinking of building a golf course
Out there, so I understand.
The old Egan Homestead's an ash pond
That they say is eighty feet deep.
The branding corral at the Douglas Camp
Is underneath a spoil heap.
And across the crick is a tipple, now,
Where they load coal onto a train.
The Mae West Rock on Hay Coulee?
Just black-and-white snapshots remain.
There's a railroad loop and a coal storage shed
Where the bison kill site used to be.
The Guy Place is gone; Ambrose's too.
Beulah Farley's a ranch refugee.

But things are booming. We've got this new school
That's envied across the whole state.
When folks up and ask, "How things goin' down there?"
I grin like a fool and say, "Great!"
Great God, how we're doin'! We're rollin' in dough,
As they tear and they ravage The Earth.
And nobody knows . . . or nobody cares . . .
About things of intrinsic worth.

(from *Cowboy Curmudgeon and Other Poems*, 1992, Gibbs Smith, Publisher;
reprinted by permission of the author)

because I know where I want to end. I think about the last impression I want to leave. Once I have that in mind, then I go to the beginning and try to figure out how to get where I want to end up." Of course, as in the case of most writers, McRae's poems don't necessarily end up where he wants them to. They have some control of their own, he says.

Having published four poetry collections (most recently **The Cowboy Curmudgeon and Other Poems**, published by Gibbs Smith, 1992), as well as having numerous poems appear in publications such as **Boots: For Folks With Their Boots On!** and **Dry Crik Review**, McRae does not consider himself a natural poet and believes writing is an acquired art. "They talk about natural musicians, but for most successful, competent musicians it's an exercise in practice, practice, practice. You get better with practice; you hone your skills. I think I have gotten better and that tells me that I wasn't a natural writer. There are very few people who are instantly successful."

McRae contributes his success to just "pure rotten luck." Yet, this "luck" has recently landed McRae's poems in an attractive anthology entitled **Between Earth and Sky** (W.W. Norton & Company, 1995). The anthology also includes work from 11 other cowboy poets.

In addition to his publication credits, McRae has also been a featured performer at the Cowboy Poetry Gathering since its inception in 1985. The event attracts thousands of people every year. "When we go to the cowboy poetry mecca in Elko each January, we have sell-out crowds. We had 10,000 people show up last year and the town is barely that big," he says.

When the gatherings first began they mostly attracted ranchers, now more and more people from urban areas are getting caught up in the excitement of cowboy poetry, says McRae. "I think we are envied a lot of the time because we are misunderstood. People look at us and think, 'Boy, wouldn't I ever like to do that, wouldn't I ever like to be free.' What they don't realize, however, is that we answer to one of the most exacting bosses there ever was, Mother Nature. So many people are dissatisfied with their lives, where they live, what they do, the rat race, the pollution and the stress. Maybe we do lead enviable lives. I know very few of us would trade."

Despite the commercial success of cowboy poetry and the gatherings, McRae avoids using this success as a judge of what is good or bad in poetry. "I draw back from using commercial success as a litmus test. I'm a little uncomfortable with the lengths someone will go to ensure commercial success. It is kind of unsettling to me and tends to dilute the very reason for writing. I don't write poetry hoping for its success. I write to try to get perspective or a point of view across. If somebody buys a book or goes to a gathering looking to be a cowboy for the day, fine. A lot of people want to grab a piece of the dream and cowboy poetry allows them to do just that."

—*Chantelle Bentley*

MIDWEST POETRY REVIEW (II), P.O. Box 20236, Atlanta GA 30325-0236, founded 1980, editor/publisher John K. Ottley, Jr., is a quarterly, with no other support than subscriptions and contest entry fees. **They are looking for "quality accessible verse. Great imagery with powerful adjectives and verbs. Poetry that opens the door to the author's feelings through sensory descriptions.** We are attempting to encourage the cause of poetry by purchasing the best of modern poetry. **No jingly verses or limericks. 40-line limit. Any subject is considered, if handled with skill and taste. No pornography."** They have published poetry by Tom McFadden, John Thomas Baker, B.R. Culbertson, Martin Musick, Nancy Graham and Maude Paro. As a sample the editor selected this poem "Drought," by Kimberly Courtright:

> Each slow and
> snowless month-to-a-minute
> day lies sluggish on
> brittle hills where grass no longer
> grows (the clouds are
> Ebenezer-stingy here).

The digest-sized, saddle-stapled magazine is 40 pgs., professionally printed in Helvetica type, with matte card cover. Contests have entry fees. Send SASE for details. **Subscription: $20 ($25 Canadian, $30 foreign, both in US funds). Submit 5 poems at a time. Send SASE and $1 for guidelines. Reports in 2-3 weeks. Pays $5-20/poem. Buys first rights.** They have quarterly and annual contests plus varied contests in each issue, with prizes ranging from $25-250, with "unbiased, non-staff judges for all competitions." A 20-point Self-Analysis Survey to assist poets in analyzing their own work is offered free to new subscribers.

THE MIDWEST QUARTERLY (II), Pittsburg State University, Pittsburg KS 66762, phone (316)235-4689, e-mail smeats@pittstate.edu, founded 1959, poetry editor Stephen Meats, "publishes articles on any subject of contemporary interest, particularly literary criticism, political science, philosophy, education, biography and sociology, and each issue contains a **section of poetry usually 15 poems in length.** I am interested in **well-crafted, though not necessarily traditional poems that explore the inter-relationship of the human and natural worlds in bold, surrealistic images of a writer's imaginative, mystical experience. 60 lines or less (occasionally longer if exceptional)."** They have recently published poetry by Walter McDonald, David Ray, Rita Signorelli-Pappos, Lyn Lifshin, Jeanne Murray Walker and William Kloefkorn. As a sample the editor selected these lines from "The Ox" by George Eklund:

> Ox, my dying flower,
> my wooden ship with sails ablaze
> my cannon of symphonies
> my destroyer of geometry and the atomic clock.
> Your mind sings in the last famine of the crows
> you have suckled Allah, the Buddah and the Christ
> and the psychopathic generals who squat
> in jungles and in the toilets of Washington.

The magazine is 130 pgs., digest-sized, flat-spined, matte cover, professionally printed. A nice mix of poems appears here, most of it free verse with room for an occasional formal or narrative piece. Circulation is 650, with 600 subscribers of which 500 are libraries. They receive approximately 4,200 poems annually; publish 60. "My plan is to publish all acceptances within 1 year." Subscription: $12. **Sample: $3. Mss should be typed with poet's name on each page, 10 poems or fewer. No previously published poems; simultaneous submissions OK. Publishes theme issues occasionally. Reports in 1 month, usually sooner. "Submissions without SASE cannot be acknowledged." Pays 3 copies. Acquires first serial rights. Editor comments on rejections "if the poet or poems seem particularly promising."** Reviews books of poetry by *MQ* published poets only. He says, "Keep writing; read as much contemporary poetry as you can lay your hands on; don't let the discouragement of rejection keep you from sending your work out to editors."

‡MIDWEST VILLAGES & VOICES (V, IV-Regional), 3220 Tenth Ave. S., Minneapolis MN 55407, founded 1979, is a cultural organization and small press publisher of **Midwestern poetry and prose**. They have published books of poetry by Ethna McKiernan, Florence Chard Dacey, Kevin FitzPatrick and Sue Doro. Forthcoming: a collection of poetry and prose by Irene Paull. As a sample here are lines from Dacey's poem "Necklace":

> Layer upon layer
> of bone, bead,
> wood and stone,
> heavier than your body,
> breathing, sinister,
> raised
> at great cost

> *from the cave below the tree,*
> *as common as your life,*
> *strung that tightly,*
> *as large as a shroud.*

The flat-spined books are generally 48 + pgs., professionally printed with glossy card covers, selling for $5-6. **"We encourage and support Midwestern writers and artists. However, at this time submissions are accepted by invitation only."**

MIDWIFERY TODAY (IV-Specialized: childbirth), P.O. Box 2672, Eugene OR 97402, phone (503)344-7438, founded 1986, editor Jan Tritten, is a quarterly that "provides a voice for midwives and childbirth educators. **We are a midwifery magazine. Subject must be birth or profession related."** **They do not want poetry that is "off subject or puts down the subject."** As a sample the editor selected these lines by Karen Hope Ehrlich:

> *you get to keep the baby*
> *not the midwife*
> *she is a fickle lover*
> *merged and passing*

MT is 52 pgs., approximately 8½ × 11, offset, saddle-stapled, with glossy card cover with b&w photo and b&w photos, artwork and ads inside. They use about 1 poem/issue. Press run is 3,000 for 1,500 subscribers, 1,000 shelf sales. Subscription: $30. **Sample postpaid: $7.50. No previously published poems or simultaneous submissions. Cover letter required.** Time between acceptance and publication is 1-2 years. **Seldom comments on rejections. Publishes theme issues. Send SASE for writer's guidelines and upcoming themes. Reports in 2-6 weeks. Pays 2 copies. Acquires first rights.** The editor says, "With our publication *please* stay on the subject."

MILKWEED EDITIONS (II), 430 First Ave. N., Suite 400, Minneapolis MN 55401, phone (612)332-3192, founded 1979, poetry editor Emilie Buchwald. Three collections published annually. **Unsolicited mss are only accepted from writers who have previously published a book-length collection of poetry or a minimum of 10 poems in commercial or literary journals.** One of the leading literary presses in the country, Milkweed publishes some of the best poets composing today in well-made, attractively designed collections. Published books of poetry include: *The Phoenix Gone*, *The Terrace Empty* by Marilyn Chin; *Firekeeper* by Pattiann Rogers; and *Paul Bunyan's Bearskin* by Patricia Goedicke. **Submit 60- to 200-page ms. Unsolicited mss read in June and January; please include return postage.** Catalog available on request, with $1 in postage.

MIND IN MOTION: A MAGAZINE OF POETRY AND SHORT PROSE (I, II), P.O. Box 1118, Apple Valley CA 92307, phone (619)248-6512, founded 1985, a quarterly, editor Céleste Goyer, wants **poetry "15-60 lines. Explosive, provocative. Images not clichéd but directly conveyant of the point of the poem. Use of free association particularly desired. We encourage free verse, keeping in mind the essential elements of rhythm and rhyme. Traditional forms are acceptable if within length restrictions. Meaning should be implicit, as in the styles of Blake, Poe, Coleridge, Stephen Crane, Emily Dickinson, Leonard Cohen. Not interested in sentimentality, emotionalism, simplistic nature worship, explicit references.** *MIM* is known for thoughtful poetry that explores the timeless themes of philosophy and human nature."** She has recently published poetry by Robert E. Brimhall, Karl Lorenzen, Laurie Calhoun, Michael Swofford and Brent Kinder. As a sample she selected these lines from "Dare Not Ask" (poet unidentified):

> *They christen their children*
> *in your name and still*
> *you ask for more.*
> *More deaths, more poverty,*
> *more idealistic subservience,*
> *more familiarity with conceit*
> *and vain striving and yet*
> *you expect still more.*

MIM is 54 pgs., digest-sized, saddle-stapled, photocopied from photoreduced typescript with a heavy matte cover with b&w drawing. Of approximately 2,400 poems/year she accepts about 200. Press run is 525 for 350 subscribers. Subscription: $14. **Sample postpaid: $3.50 (overseas: $4.50, $18/year). Submit 6 poems at a time. Unpublished works only. Simultaneous submissions OK if notified. "Please have name and address on each poem. We also use dates of composition; it would help if these were provided with submissions."** Editor usually comments on rejected mss. **Send SASE for guidelines. Reports in 1-6 weeks. Pays 1 copy "when financially possible." Magazine is copyrighted; all rights revert to author.** "Please do not submit further material until your last submission has been responded to. Please be patient and don't overwhelm the editor."

MIND MATTERS REVIEW (III), 2040 Polk St., #234, San Francisco CA 94109, founded 1988, editor Carrie Drake, poetry editor Lorraine A. Donfor **(and submissions should be sent directly to her at 2837 Blue Spruce Lane, Silver Spring MD 20906)**, is a **"literary quarterly with emphasis on use of science as a tool for responsible organization of information;** analysis of the role of language in consciousness, knowledge and intelligence; and social criticism particularly of metaphysics. Also includes book reviews, poetry, short stories, art and essays." **They want "short poems for fillers. Would like to see inspirational poetry; but open to satire and contemporary subjects that reflect the struggle between the 'inner voice' and external pressures; poetry on social issues. Rhythm important, but rhyme isn't."** They have published poetry by T.N. Turner. As a sample the editor selected these lines by Barbara Zeolla:

> There is no shelter from their thoughts
> Or the images of faces
> Reflected in the glass.
> They are there and yet
>   not there at all.

MMR is magazine-sized, desktop-published, includes graphics, sketches, b&w photos. Subscription: $15 US, $20 foreign. **Sample postpaid: $3.50. Poets are encouraged to buy a copy before submitting. Submit 3 poems at a time. No simultaneous submissions; previously published poems OK. Cover letter required; include publishing credits and note if submissions have been previously published or accepted for publication elsewhere. Publishes theme issues. Send SASE for guidelines and upcoming themes. Sometimes sends prepublication galleys. Pays 1 copy.** Staff reviews books of poetry. Send books for review consideration to David Castleman, 512 Tamalpais Dr., Mill Valley CA 94941. The editor says, "Poetry should reflect the deeper layers of consciousness, its perceptions, observations, joys and sorrows; should reflect the independence of the individual spirit. Should not be 'trendy' or 'poetic' in a forced way."

THE MINNESOTA REVIEW (II), English Dept., East Carolina University, Greenville NC 27858-4353, phone (919)328-6388, founded 1960, editor Jeffrey Williams, poetry editor Rebecca Wee, is a biannual literary magazine wanting **"poetry which explores some aspect of social or political issues and/or the nature of relationships. No nature poems, and no lyric poetry without the above focus."** As a sample the editors selected the opening lines from "In Historic Perspective" by Charlotte Mayerson:

> Without the women of the Holocaust
> Who saw their children ripped asunder
> I could not go on.
> Without the women
> Of eighteen hundred and five
> Who bore eight children and raised five
> I would go under. . . .

TMR is 200 pgs., digest-sized, flat-spined, with b&w glossy card cover and art. Mostly free verse (lyric and narrative), poems here tend to have strong themes and powerful content, perhaps to coincide with the magazine's subtitle: "a journal of committed writing." Circulation: 2,500 for 1,500 subscribers. Subscription: $12 to individuals, $24 to institutions. **Sample postpaid: $7.50. Address submissions to "Poetry Editor," (not to a specific editor). Cover letter including "brief intro with address" preferred. Publishes theme issues. Send SASE for upcoming themes. Theme for Spring 1996 is "The White Issue." Reports in 2-4 months. Pays 2 copies. Acquires all rights. Returns rights upon request.** Reviews books of poetry in single or multi-book format. Open to unsolicited reviews.

MIORITA: A JOURNAL OF ROMANIAN STUDIES (IV-Ethnic), Dept. of Linguistics, University of Rochester, Rochester NY 14627, phone (716)275-8053, is an irregular scholarly publication, 100 pgs., digest-sized, circulation 200, focusing on **Romanian culture and using some poetry by Romanians or on Romanian themes. Sample: $5. Pays copies.** Reviews books of poetry "occasionally; must be Romanian-connected."

THE MIRACULOUS MEDAL (IV-Religious), 475 E. Chelten Ave., Philadelphia PA 19144-5785, phone (215)848-1010, founded 1928, editor Rev. John W. Gouldrick, C.M., is a religious quarterly. **"Poetry should reflect solid Catholic doctrine and experience. Any subject matter is acceptable, provided it does not contradict the teachings of the Roman Catholic Church. Poetry must have a**

Market categories: (I) Beginning; (II) General; (III) Limited; (IV) Specialized; (V) Closed.

religious theme, preferably about the Blessed Virgin Mary." They have published poetry by Gladys McKee. The editor describes it as 32 pgs., digest-sized, saddle-stapled, 2-color inside and cover, no ads. *The Miraculous Medal* is no longer circulated on a subscription basis. It is used as a promotional piece and is sent to all clients of the Central Association of the Miraculous Medal. Circulation is 340,000. **Sample and guidelines free for postage. Poems should be a maximum of 20 lines, double-spaced. No simultaneous submissions or previously published poems. Reports in 6 months to 3 years. Pays 50¢ and up/line, on acceptance. Buys first North American rights.**

MISSISSIPPI MUD (III), 1505 Drake Ave., Austin TX 78704, phone (512)444-5459, founded 1973, editor Joel Weinstein, is an irregular publication that features fiction, poetry and artwork that "portray life in America at the twilight of the 20th century." As for poetry **they want "lively, contemporary themes and forms, free verse preferred." They do not want "anything stodgy, pathetic or moralistic; the self-consciously pretty or clever; purely formal exercises."** They have published poetry by Ivan Arguelles, Christy Sheffield Sanford and Simon Perchik. *MM* is 52 pgs., 11×17, saddle-stitched, with 4-color glossy paper cover, full-page graphics and display ads. They receive 100-200 poems a year, accept less than 10%. Press run is 1,500 for 150 subscribers of which 16 are libraries, 1,000 shelf sales, about 200 distributed free to galleries, museums and critical media. Subscription: $25 for 4 issues. **Sample postpaid: $6. Submit no more than 6 poems at a time. No previously published poems; simultaneous submissions OK.** Time between acceptance and publication is a year or more. **Seldom comments on rejections. Reports in 4-6 months. Pays $25 and 2 copies. Buys first North American serial rights.**

MISSISSIPPI REVIEW (II), University of Southern Mississippi, Box 5144, Hattiesburg MS 39406-5144, phone (601)266-4321, editor Frederick Barthelme, managing editor Rie Fortenberry. Literary publication for those interested in contemporary literature. Poems differ in style, length and form, but all have craft in common (along with intriguing content). **Sample: $8. Query before submitting. Does not read manuscripts in summer. Pays copies.**

MISSOURI REVIEW (II), 1507 Hillcrest Hall, University of Missouri, Columbia MO 65211, phone (314)882-4474, fax (314)884-4671, founded 1978, poetry editor Greg Michalson, general editor Speer Morgan, is a quality literary journal, 6×9, 208 pgs., which appears 3 times a year, **publishing poetry features only—6-12 pages for each of 3 to 5 poets/issue.** By devoting more editorial space to each poet, *MR* provides a fuller look at the work of some of the best writers composing today. However, the number of poets whose work appears here has decreased significantly, limiting your chances in a prestigious market where competition has become even keener than in the past. **Sample: $6. Submit 6-12 poems at a time. "Poets should submit only unpublished work." No simultaneous submissions. Reports in 8-10 weeks. Sometimes sends prepublication galleys. Pays $125-250/feature. Buys all rights. Returns rights "after publication, without charge, at the request of the authors."** Reviews books of poetry. "Short, inhouse reviews only." Awards the Tom McAfee Discovery Feature once or twice a year to an outstanding young poet who has not yet published a book; poets are selected from regular submissions at the discretion of the editors. Also offers the Editors' Prize Contest in Poetry. Deadline: October 15. $500 first prize and publication. Three finalists named in addition. Write for details. The editors add, "We think we have enhanced the quality of our poetry section and increased our reader interest in this section. We remain dedicated to publishing at least one younger or emerging poet in every issue."

MR. COGITO PRESS; MR. COGITO (II), Pacific University, 2518 NW Savier, Portland OR 97210, founded 1973, poetry editors John M. Gogol and Robert A. Davies. *Mr. Cogito*, published 2-3 times/year, is a tall, skinny ($4\frac{1}{2} \times 11$) magazine, 24-26 pgs. of poetry. The editors want **"no prose put in lines. Yes: wit, heightened language, craft. Open to all schools and subjects and groups of poets."** They have published poetry by Norman Russell, Ann Chandonnet, John Minczeski, Peter Wild and Zbigniew Herbert. As a sample the editors selected these lines from "ghost poem" by Bill Shields:

> *I don't think the country is ever going to forgive us*
> *for throwing up our hands and dying in Vietnam*

They use poems in both English and translation, "preferably representing each poet with several poems." The magazine has a circulation of 400. Subscription for 3 issues: $9. **Sample: $3. Submit 4-5 poems at a time. Simultaneous submissions OK. Reports in 2 weeks to 2 months. Pays copies. Acquires first rights and anthology rights.** Mr. Cogito Press publishes collections by poets they invite from among those who have appeared in the magazine. Send SASE for catalog to buy samples. They also conduct special theme and translation contests with prizes of $50 or $100. The editors advise, "Subscribe to a magazine that seems good. Read ours before you submit. Write, write, write."

‡MOCKINGBIRD; ROBERT FRANCIS MEMORIAL PRIZE (II), P.O. Box 761, Davis CA 95617, founded 1994, co-editors C.G. Macdonald and Joe Aimone (with frequent guest editors as well). *Mockingbird* is a biannual journal of poetry and reviews. **They are looking for "craft and inspira-**

tion; also we value clarity and intensity. We want form, but not witless conformity; innovation, but not convenient ignorance of tradition." They have published poetry by Sandra McPherson, Charles Bukowski, Francisco Alarcon, Alan Williamson and Taylor Graham. As a sample the editors selected "Fox" by Barry Spacks:

> Fox panics his fleas, backing into a river,
> a moss-raft in his teeth. Fleas spray
>
> from tail past tip of snout and away
> on the raft launched off as Fox dunks under,
>
> rid by this wit of his itchy freight . . .
> till tomorrow's fleas accumulate.

Mockingbird is 48 pgs., 5½×8½, photocopied from desktop-published originals and saddle-stapled with matte card cover with b&w art. They receive about 800 poems a year and publish about 50 (not counting a few solicited works). Press run is 150 for 50 subscribers of which 4 are libraries, 20 shelf sales. Subscription: $7.50 for 1 year, $12 for 2 years. **Sample postpaid: $4. Submit no more than 5-6 pages of poetry at a time. No previously published poems or simultaneous submissions. Cover letter preferred. Sometimes comments on rejections. Send SASE for guidelines. Reports usually within 2 months, "3-4 months on acceptances and near misses." Pays 1 copy. Acquires first serial rights. Requests acknowledgement if work is reprinted elsewhere.** Reviews books and chapbooks of poetry as well as other magazines in up to 1,500 words. Open to unsolicited reviews. Poets may also send books for review consideration. They also sponsor the Robert Francis Memorial Prize which awards a total of $150 to one first place winner and two seconds. The contest runs from July 4 to Halloween. Entry fee: $2/poem. An $8 entry includes a one-year subscription. Send SASE for details. The editor says, "We are a unique magazine. Reading a sample copy could be very helpful to submitting poets. We are eclectic but especially interested in formal poetry, West Coast and other marginalized writers, wit, and a flair for the vernacular. We encourage real world referents, especially to the natural, personal, sensual and political worlds."

MODERN BRIDE (IV-Love/romance), 249 W. 17th St., New York NY 10011, phone (212)337-7000, executive editor Mary Ann Cavlin, a slick bimonthly, occasionally buys **poetry pertaining to love and marriage. Pays $30-40 for average short poem.**

MODERN HAIKU; FIVE HIGH SCHOOL SENIOR SCHOLARSHIPS (IV-Form, students), P.O. Box 1752, Madison WI 53701, phone (608)233-2738, founded 1969, poetry editor Robert Spiess, "is the foremost international journal of English language haiku and criticism. We are devoted to publishing only the very best haiku being written and also publish articles on haiku and have the most complete review section of haiku books. Issues average over 100 pages." **They want "contemporary haiku in English (including translations into English) that incorporate the traditional aesthetics of the haiku genre, but which may be innovative as to subject matter, mode of approach or angle of perception, and form of expression. Haiku only. No tanka or other forms."** They have published haiku by Wally Swist, Phyllis Walsh, Paul O. Williams and Elizabeth Lamb. As a sample the editor selected this haiku (poet unidentified):

> a tree with heart rot—
> its one living branch
> laden with ripened wild plum

The digest-sized magazine appears 3 times a year, printed on heavy quality stock with cover illustrations especially painted for each issue by the staff artist. They receive 16,000-18,000 submissions/year, use 800. There are over 260 poems in each issue. Circulation 650. Subscription: $15. **Sample postpaid: $5. Submit on "any size sheets, any number of haiku on a sheet; but name and address on each sheet." No previously published haiku or simultaneous submissions. Send SASE for guidelines. Reports in 2 weeks. Pays $1/haiku (but no contributor's copy). Buys first North American serial rights.** Staff reviews books of haiku in 350-1,000 words, single format. Send books for review consideration. They offer five annual scholarships for the best haiku by high school seniors. Scholarships range from $200-500 (total $1,600). Deadline is in early March. Send SASE for rules. The editor says, "Haiku achieve their effect of felt-depth, insight and intuition through juxtaposition of perceived entities, not through intellective comment or abstract words."

MOKSHA JOURNAL; VAJRA PRINTING & PUBLISHING OF YOGA ANAND ASHRAM (IV-Spiritual), 49 Forrest Pl., Amityville NY 11701, phone/fax (516)691-8475, founded 1984, is a "small press publisher of **spiritual and/or philosophical literature, nonfiction and poetry pertaining to the concept of 'Moksha,'** defined by Monier-Williams as a **'liberation, release' (A Sanskrit-English Dictionary, 1899). Perspectives include, but are not limited to: Yoga, various schools of Buddhism, Sufism, Mystical Christianity, etc."** *Moksha Journal* appears twice a year, regularly using poetry, and is 50-70 pgs., 7¼×9½, offset, litho. Press run is 400-500 for that many subscribers. Subscription:

$8. **Sample: $4. Submit 1-5 poems at a time. Simultaneous submissions OK. Reports in 4-6 weeks. Pays 2 copies.** The press publishes perfect-bound paperbacks, including *Ways of Yoga* by Gurani Anjali. Yoga Anand Ashram is a not-for-profit organization "dedicated singularly to community education through each person's realization of the highest goal of human existence as realized through the practice of Yoga."

MONOCACY VALLEY REVIEW (II), Dept. of English, Mount Saint Mary's College, Emmitsburg MD 21727, phone (301)447-6122, founded 1985, editor William Heath, is an annual literary review. **Submissions should be received by January 15th.** "In general, we cannot publish longer poems; we also publish short stories, nonfiction prose, book reviews and artwork. **We pride ourselves in being a review that is always local but never provincial. If we have a bias, it is in favor of clarity of vision and eloquence of language. We dislike poems that 'hurt the ear and unfit one to continue.' "** *MVR* is 60 pgs., magazine-sized, saddle-stapled, high quality paper. "We reject over 95% of submissions, publish 15-20 poems an issue." Their press run is 500 with 200 subscribers of which 10 are libraries. Subscription: $8. **Sample postpaid: $5. Submit up to 6 poems at a time with a biographical statement of 50 words or less. All submissions are judged anonymously and there is no backlog. If mss are sent in December and early January, response time is 6-8 weeks. Pays $10-25/poem plus 2 copies.** The editor says they "prefer reviews of major writers in the area."

WILLIAM MORROW AND CO. (V), 1350 Avenue of the Americas, New York NY 10019, phone (212)261-6500, publishes poetry on standard royalty contracts **but accepts no unsolicited mss. Queries with samples should be submitted through an agent.**

‡**MOSAIC PRESS (V)**, 358 Oliver Rd., Cincinnati OH 45215, phone (513)761-5977, poetry editor Miriam Irwin. The press publishes fine hardbound small books (under 3″ tall): **"interesting topics beautifully written in very few words—a small collection of short poems on one subject. No haiku." However, the press is currently not accepting poetry submissions.** She has published poetry by Marilyn Francis and Robert Hoeft. The sample miniature book the editor sent is *Water and Windfalls*, by Marilyn Francis, illustrated by Mada Leach. It is ¾×⅞, flat-spined (⅛″ thick), an elegantly printed and bound hardback, with colored endpapers and gold lettering on spine and front cover. The press publishes 1 book/year, average page count 64. **She is "booked up—going to finish existing projects before starting new ones." Query with 3 or more sample poems and "whatever you want to tell me." Simultaneous submissions OK. Payment is in author's copies (5 for a whole collection or book) plus a $50 honorarium. She pays $2.50 plus 1 copy for single poems. "Be prepared to wait patiently; some of our books take 4 years to complete."** The press publishes private editions but does not call it subsidy publishing. Catalog and writers manual free for large SASE with 55¢ postage. The editor advises, "Type neatly, answer letters, return phone calls, include SASE."

MOSTLY MAINE (I, II), P.O. Box 8805, Portland ME 04104, founded 1992, editor Peter McGinn, poetry editor Vera Smetzer, appears bimonthly. **"We are open to all types of poetry. Take creative risks, don't be predictable. Looking for vivid imagery."** They have recently published poetry by Rod Farmer, Helen Peppe and John Tagliabue. As a sample the editor selected these lines from "Reconstructive Criticism" by Michael Smetzer:

> When the Inquisitor comes you will be
> in bed with your poems.
> He will summon you by banging pipes
> in your dreams.
>
> His hands will knead your shoulder like clay,
> and he will speak as a just god.

MM is 40 pgs., digest-sized, photocopied from laser printed original and saddle-stapled, with card stock cover and original artwork. In addition to poetry, fiction and creative nonfiction, it includes a "Feedback File" where readers may comment on material published in previous issues. They currently receive about 240 poems a year, accept 40. Press run is 125 for 40 subscribers, 60 shelf sales. Single copy: $2.50; subscription: $12. **Sample postpaid: $2. Submit 2-5 poems at a time. Previously published poems and simultaneous submissions OK. Include brief bio in cover letter, not just list of publications. Submissions must be legible. Photocopies are fine. Always include SASE. Sometimes comments on rejections. Send SASE for guidelines. Reports generally in 1-2 months. Pays 1 copy to first-time contributors. "We found early on that authors/poets whose work has appeared more than once have wanted to subscribe to help support the magazine. Extra issues are available at a discount." Acquires one-time rights. All rights revert to author upon publication.** Open to unsolicited reviews. The editors say, "Make the poem matter to the reader and we'll print it."

(m)ÖTHÊR TØÑGUÉS PRESS (I, II), 290 Fulford-Ganges Rd., Salt Spring Island, British Columbia V8K 2K6 Canada, founded 1990, editor/publisher Mona Fertig, holds an annual poetry chapbook contest for the best international ms of poetry and the best Canadian ms of poetry. For each category, the winner receives $300 plus publication of a "beautiful limited edition chapbook." **Send 15 pgs. of unpublished poetry with short bio and $20 entry fee. SASE (or SAE with IRCs) must be included. Mss will not be returned. Send SASE (or SAE with IRCs) for details. Deadline: November 30.** Last year's winners were Elizabeth Killer of California and Shannon Bailey of British Columbia, Canada.

MOVING PARTS PRESS (V), 70 Cathedral Dr., Santa Cruz CA 95060, phone (408)427-2271, fax (408)458-2810, founded 1977. Poetry editor Felicia Rice says they are a "fine arts literary publisher using letterpress printing and printmaking to produce handsome and innovative books, broadsides and prints in limited editions." Moving Parts has published books of poetry by Francisco X. Alarcón, Elba Rosario Sánchez and Henri Michaux. As a sample here are the opening lines of "On a Darkening Road" by Robert Lundquist from *Before-the-Rain*:

> *This evening the tide is low,*
> *Ducks walk through bunched beds of kelp*
> *Looking for insects.*

They do not accept unsolicited mss. Pay 10% of the edition in copies. In 1993 the book *De Amor Oscuro/Of Dark Love* received one of 18 international design awards from among the "600 Best Designed Books in the World" exhibit mounted by Stiftung Buchkunst at the Leipzig Book Fair.

MS. MAGAZINE (V), 230 Park Ave., 7th Floor, New York NY 10169, founded 1972, is a bimonthly "feminist source of national and international news, politics, arts, scholarship and book reviews." **They are currently not accepting unsolicited poetry.** They have published poetry by Alice Walker, Maya Angelou and May Swenson. Circulation is 150,000. Single copy: $5.95 (available on newsstands); subscription: $30. They say, "Due to the volume of the material received, we cannot accept, acknowledge or return unsolicited poetry or fiction. We cannot discuss queries on the phone and cannot be held responsible for manuscripts sent to us."

‡MUDDY RIVER POETRY REVIEW (I, II), 89 Longwood Ave., Brookline MA 02146, phone (617)277-5667, founded 1995, editor Zvi A. Sesling, is a semiannual poetry publication seeking a broad range of subjects and styles. **They prefer free verse, one page in length. "No inspirational verse. No pornography or explicit sexual content. Rhyming poetry only if exceptional."** They have recently published poetry by Sam Cornish, Louis Phillips and Jean Hull Herman. They prefer not to provide a sample "so poets are not influenced, misled or intimidated." The editor says *MRPR* is 48-60 pgs., stapled. They receive about 500 poems an issue, accept 10-20%. **No previously published poems; simultaneous submissions OK, if indicated. Cover letter required. Reads submissions February 15 through May 15 and September 15 through November 15. Often comments on rejections. Send SASE for guidelines. Reports in 1 month. Pays 1 copy (20% discount on additionals). Acquires first rights.** The editor says, "First-timers, don't be afraid to submit. Rejection only reflects what the editor is looking for, not your talent!"

MUDFISH; BOX TURTLE PRESS (I, II), 184 Franklin St., New York NY 10013, phone (212)219-9278, founded 1983, editor Jill Hoffman. *Mudfish*, published by Box Turtle Press, is a journal of poetry and art that appears once a year and is looking for **free verse with "energy, intensity, and originality of voice, mastery of style, the presence of passion." Considers sexually explicit material.** They have published poetry by Charles Simic, Gerrit Henry, Nicholas Kolumban, Denise Duhamel and John Ashbery. As a sample the editor selected these lines from "AIDS" by Shelley Stenhouse:

> *I couldn't help thinking about your penis,*
> *that deflated party balloon, that old thin*
> *dachshund hanging behind the dark curtain of*
> *your pants. I knew I should have been thinking*
> *how sad it is I have to lift you into a cab,*
> *wearing a turtleneck in the middle of summer*

Press run is 1,500. Single copy: $10. **Sample copies are available, include $2.50 shipping and handling. Submit 4-6 poems at a time. They will not consider simultaneous submissions or previously published poems. Reports from "immediately to 3 months." Sometimes sends prepublication galleys. Pays 1 copy.**

‡MULBERRY PRESS (I, II), P.O. Box 1236, Harvey LA 70059, phone (504)348-3337, founded 1991, publisher G.M. Frey. This is an arrangement for publishing chapbooks only. mulberry press (they prefer lowercase) will consider **chapbooks (any length) for a $5 reading fee, for which you get 2 sample chapbooks in return if your ms is rejected, 50 copies if accepted (additional copies at cost). Press run 150-200 copies, and additional printings. Poems may be previously published.** They are also open to co-op publishing: Poet pays "a modest fee to cover cost of their copies only and receives 50 copies." They have published chapbooks by Nate Tate, Steve Ullmann, Bob Balo, Richard Swiss, Todd

Moore, Tony Moffeit, Lyn Lifshin and many others. As a sample here is a complete poem, "Communion In Venice," from *White Horse Cafe* by Gina Bergamino:

> he told me time was running out
> so I loved him
> dropping to my knees
>   and walls became clouds
>   the pigeons listened
>   from rooftops

Submit 30 typed poems at a time. Sponsors the annual mulberry press Poetry Prize for unpublished poems. Award: $500. Entry fee: $2/poem. Send SASE for contest rules. They also offer an annual chapbook contest. Entry fee: $5. All entrants receive copy of winning chapbook. Winner receives 100 copies. **Send SASE for guidelines.** mulberry press received a grant from the Puffin Foundation enabling them to publish an anthology entitled *New York Poets*. The editor advises, "Take your art seriously, make it a priority in your life. Be persistent and patient and eventually you will endure and prevail. If you keep on writing, you can only get better."

MUSE PORTFOLIO (II), 25 Tannery Rd., Unit Box 8, Westfield MA 01085, founded 1992, editor Haemi Balgassi, appears 2-4 times a year. *Muse Portfolio* is a "casual magazine for sincere, eloquent, earnest writers who crave forum to share work with others." **They want poetry of "any structure, formal or free, 50 lines maximum. Poetry with writing themes welcome. No forced rhymes, nothing profane.** We also publish short stories and nonfiction, as well as cartoons and art sketches." They have recently published poetry by Paul A. Hanson and James Rocha. As a sample the editor selected these lines from "You Are an Author" by Delma Luben:

> A writer will grow old
> austerely regimenting his
> short allotted days—all
> for a temporary season of
> praise: Author, author.

Muse Portfolio is 40 pgs., 5½×8½, saddle-stapled, printed on 20 lb. paper with heavier stock cover, b&w artwork, occasional ads. They receive about 300 poems/year, accept 5%. Press run is 150 for 100 subscribers. Subscription: $5. **Sample postpaid: $2.50. Submit up to 3 poems at a time. Previously published poems and simultaneous submissions OK. Cover letter required. "Include a biographical paragraph—need not list published credits if author prefers to write something else." Seldom comments on rejections. Send SASE for guidelines. Reports in 2-3 months. Pays 1 copy. Acquires one-time rights.** The editor says, "Remember the three P's: Be professional, persistent and patient."

MUSICWORKS (IV-Themes), 179 Richmond St. W., Toronto, Ontario M5V 1V3 Canada, phone (416)977-3546, founded 1978, editor Gayle Young, is a triannual journal of contemporary music. The editor says, **"The poetry we publish only relates directly to the topics discussed in the magazine or relates to contemporary sound poetry—*usually* it is poetry written by the (music) composer or performers we are featuring."** Poets published include bpnichol, Colin Morton and Jackson Mac Low. The magazine is 64 pgs., 8½×11, with b&w visuals, b&w photography, some illustrative graphics and scores and accompanied by 60-minute cassette. Circulation is 1,600, of which 500 are subscriptions. Price is $5/issue or $10 for the magazine plus CD. **Sample postpaid: $10 for magazine and CD. Considers simultaneous submissions. They report on submissions within 2 months, and there is no backlog before publication. The magazine pays Canadian contributors $20-50/contribution plus 2-3 free copies.**

THE MUSING PLACE (IV-Specialized: poets with a history of mental illness), 2700 N. Lakeview, Chicago IL 60614, phone (312)281-3800, ext. 2465, fax (312)281-8790, founded 1986, editor Linda Krinsky, is a biannual magazine **"written and published by people with a history of mental illness. All kinds and forms of poetry are welcome."** As a sample the editor selected these lines from "Why Must I Be Poor?" by Gracian Vital:

> Wrapped in elegance,
> I was born
> Queenly to behold
> But when you see my
> Pocketbook
> I fold.

The editor says *The Musing Place* is 32 pgs., 8½×11, typeset and stapled with art also produced by people with a history of mental illness. They receive about 100 poems/year, publish about 40. Press run is 1,000. Single copy: $2. **No previously published poems; simultaneous submissions OK. Cover letter required. "Poets must prove and explain their history of mental illness."** Time between acceptance and publication is 6 months to 1 year. **"The board reviews submissions and chooses those that fit into each issue of the publication. All submissions are kept for possible publication in** future issues." Seldom comments on rejections. Reports within 6 months. Pays "negotiable" number of contributor's copies.

MY LEGACY (I); OMNIFIC (I); FELICITY (I, IV-Themes); THE BOTTOM LINE, HC-13, Box 21-AA, Artemas PA 17211-9405, phone (814)458-3102, editor/publisher Kay Weems. *My Legacy* is a quarterly of poetry and short stories using **36-line, sometimes longer, poems, "anything in good taste" with an Editor's Choice small cash award for each issue. No contributor copies.** Subscription: $12/year; $3.50/copy. *Omnific,* a "family-type" quarterly publishes poetry only, **36 lines, sometimes longer; readers vote on favorites, small cash award or copy to favorites. Send SASE for guidelines. No contributor copies.** Subscription: $16/year; $3.50/copy. *Felicity,* founded 1988, is a bimonthly newsletter for contests only, 30-40 pgs. They offer 10 contests/flyer including a bimonthly theme contest, 36 lines. Other contests may be for theme, form, chapbook, etc. Entry fees vary. Send SASE for guidelines and upcoming themes. Payment for contest winners is small cash award and/or publication. No work is returned. They consider simultaneous submissions and previously published poems. All winning entries including honorable mentions are printed in the newsletter which also publishes market and other contest listings. Subscription: $16/year; $2.50/copy. She also publishes an annual **Christmas anthology. Poetry only, published/unpublished, 36 lines maximum, Christmas themes. Address to "Christmas Anthology." Deadline: August 31.** *The Bottom Line,* founded 1988, is a monthly newsletter listing over 50 publications and contests for writers, reproducing guidelines of still others. Information is presented in chronological order by deadline date, and then in alphabetical order. Circulation 200-300. Subscription: $21/year; $2.50/copy.

MYSTERY TIME (I, IV-Mystery); RHYME TIME (IV-Subscribers), P.O. Box 2907, Decatur IL 62524, poetry editor Linda Hutton, founded 1983, is a semiannual containing 3-4 pages of **humorous poems about mysteries and mystery writers** in each issue. As a sample the editor selected the poem "Gut Instinct" by Jessica J. Frasca:

> *"Great Scot!" declared Holmes with a look of surprise.*
> *"It's the cook's fault he's dead?" Disbelief in his eyes.*
> *Watson's head nodded, the cook turned and fled.*
> *"Alimentary, my dear Holmes," was all that he said.*

Mystery Time is 44 pgs., digest-sized, stapled with heavy stock cover. They receive up to 15 submissions a year, use 4-6. Circulation 100. **Sample: $3.50. Submit 3 poems at a time, "typed in proper format with SASE." Previously published poems OK. Does not read mss in December. Guidelines available for #10 SASE. Pays $5 on acceptance.** Hutton's other publication, *Rhyme Time*, is a quarterly newsletter **publishing only the work of subscribers. No length limit or style restriction.** Subscription: $24. **Sample: $4.** Cash prize of $5 awarded to the best poem in each issue. She also sponsors an annual poetry contest that awards a $10 cash prize for the best poem in any style or length. Submit typed poem with SASE. No entry fee; one entry/person. Deadline: November 1.

THE MYTHIC CIRCLE; THE MYTHOPOEIC SOCIETY (II, IV-Fantasy), P.O. Box 6707, Altadena CA 91001, editor Tina Cooper. *The Mythic Circle* is a "writer's workshop in print," appearing 2-3 times a year, publishing fantasy short stories and poems. **They want "poetry, particularly traditional poetry, with a mythic or fairy-tale theme."** They have published poetry by Angelee Anderson and Gwyneth Hood. They receive approximately 100 poetry submissions/year, accept 10%. Press run is 230 for 200 subscribers. Subscription: $18/year for non-members of sponsoring organization, The Mythopoeic Society; $13/year for members. **Sample postpaid: $6.50. No previously published poems or simultaneous submissions.** Time between acceptance and publication is 2 years. **Seldom comments on rejections. Send SASE for guidelines. Reports in 2-4 months. Pays 1 copy for 3 poems.** The editor says, "Subscribers are heavily favored, since they provide the critical review which our authors need in their letters of comment."

NADA PRESS; BIG SCREAM (II, IV-Form/style), 2782 Dixie SW, Grandville MI 49418, phone (616)531-1442, founded 1974, poetry editor David Cope. *Big Scream* appears annually and is **"a brief anthology of mostly 'unknown' poets. We are promoting a continuation of objectivist tradition begun by Williams and Reznikoff. We want objectivist-based short works; some surrealism; basically short, tight work that shows clarity of perception and care in its making."** They have published poetry by Antler, Richard Kostelanetz, Andy Clausen, Allen Ginsberg, John Steinbeck, Jr., Jim Cohn and Marcia Arrieta. *Big Scream* is 35 pgs., magazine-sized, xerograph on 60 lb. paper, side-stapled, "sent gratis to a select group of poets and editors." They receive "several hundred (not sure)" unsolicited submissions/year, use "very few." Press run is 100. Subscription to institutions: $6/year. **Sample postpaid: $6. Submit after July. Send 10 pgs. No cover letter. "If poetry interests me, I will ask the proper questions of the poet." Simultaneous submissions OK. Comments on rejections "if requested and ms warrants it." Reports in 1-14 days. Sometimes sends prepublication galleys. Pays as many copies as requested, within reason.** The editor advises: "Read Pound's essay, 'A Retrospect,' then Reznikoff and Williams; follow through the Beats and NY School, especially Denby

& Berrigan, and you have our approach to writing well in hand. I expect to be publishing *BS* regularly 10 years from now, same basic format."

NASSAU REVIEW (II), English Dept., Nassau Community College, Garden City NY 11530, phone (516)572-7792, founded 1964, managing editor Dr. Paul A. Doyle, is an annual "creative and research vehicle for Nassau College faculty and the faculty of other colleges." **They want "serious, intellectual poetry of any form or style. No light verse or satiric verse." Submissions from adults only. "No college students; graduate students acceptable."** They have published poetry by Patti Tana, Dick Allen, Louis Phillips, David Heyen and Simon Perchik. As a sample the editor selected these lines from "Chekhov, For Beginners" by Barbara Novack:

> Chekhov said
> throw out the first three pages;
> it takes that long
> to get to the beginning.
>
> And I may say
> put aside the first three decades
> sweep away their debris
> cast off versions of the self . . .

NR is about 150 pgs., digest-sized, flat-spined. They receive 500-600 poems/year, use approximately 20-25. Press run is 1,200 for about 1,200 subscribers of which 600 are libraries. **Sample free. Submit only 3 poems at a time. No previously published poems or simultaneous submissions. Reads submissions October 1 through March 1 only. Reports in 3-6 months. Pays copies.** They sponsor occasional contests with $100 or $200 poetry awards, depending on college funding. Well-edited and visually appealing, *Nassau Review* tends to publish free verse emphasizing voice in well-crafted lyric and narrative forms.

THE NATION; "DISCOVERY"/THE NATION POETRY CONTEST (III), 72 Fifth Ave., New York NY 10011, founded 1865, poetry editor Grace Schulman. *The Nation*'s **only requirement for poetry is "excellence,"** which can be inferred from the list of poets they have published: Marianne Moore, Robert Lowell, W.S. Merwin, Maxine Kumin, Donald Justice, James Merrill, Richard Howard, May Swenson, Amy Clampitt, Edward Hirsch and Charles Simic. The editor chose this sample from a poem in *The Nation*, 1939, by W.B. Yeats:

> Like a long-legged fly upon the stream
> His mind moves upon silence.

Pay for poetry is $1/line, not to exceed 35 lines, plus 1 copy. The magazine co-sponsors the Lenore Marshall Prize for Poetry which is an annual award of $10,000 for the outstanding book of poems published in the US in each year. For details, write to the Academy of American Poets, 584 Broadway, #1208, New York NY 10012. They also co-sponsor the "Discovery"/*The Nation* Poetry Contest ($200 each plus a reading at The Poetry Center, 1395 Lexington Ave., New York NY 10128. Deadline: mid-February. Send SASE for application). Poetry published in *The Nation* has been included in the 1993 and 1995 volumes of *The Best American Poetry*.

NATIONAL ENQUIRER (II, IV-Humor), Lantana FL 33464, filler editor Darryl Wrobel, is a weekly tabloid, circulation 4,550,000, which uses **short poems, most of them humorous and traditional rhyming verse. "We want poetry with a message or reflection on the human condition or everyday life. Avoid sending obscure or 'arty' poetry or poetry for art's sake. Also looking for philosophical and inspirational material. Submit seasonal/holiday material at least 3 months in advance. No poetry over 8 lines will be accepted." Submit 1-5 poems at a time. Requires cover letter from first-time submitters; include name, address, social security and phone numbers. "Do not send SASE; filler material will not be returned." Pays $25 after publication; original material only. Buys first rights.**

NATIONAL FORUM: THE PHI KAPPA PHI JOURNAL (III), 129 Quad Center, Mell St., Auburn University AL 36849-5306, phone (334)844-5200, founded 1915, editor James P. Kaetz, is the quarterly of Phi Kappa Phi using **quality poetry.** As a sample the editor selected these lines from "Visiting Hours" by Molly Tamarkin:

> The rip of rip-stop nylon against barbed wire,
> the flash of headlights, and the drifting snow
> suggest it's time. The faint light casts shadows
> with the wintry air of permanence,
> and the fisherman, packing up his tackle,
> appears grossly overshadowed by a cottonwood.

NF is 48 pgs., magazine-sized, professionally printed, saddle-stapled, with full-color paper cover and two-color interior. They publish about 20 poems of 300 received a year. Their press run is 120,000 with

117,000 subscriptions of which 300 are libraries. Subscription: $25. **Submit 3-5 poems, including a biographical sketch with recent publications. Reads submissions approximately every 3 months. Reports about 4 months after submission. Pays 10 copies.**

‡NATURALLY: NUDE RECREATION FOR ALL AGES; EVENTS UNLIMITED PUBLISHING CO. (IV-Specialized), P.O. Box 317, Newfoundland NJ 07435-0317, founded 1981, editor/publisher Bern Loibl. *Naturally* is a quarterly magazine devoted to family nudism and naturism. **They want poetry about the naturalness of the human body and nature, any length.** As a sample the editor selected the opening stanzas of "Why?" by Lois Ann Horowitz:

> *I see you're nude, and so am I.*
> *It feels so good: my pores breathe free.*
> *But others may be asking, why?*
> *While breezes play their games with me.*
>
> *No sandy fabric chafes my skin,*
> *No bands restrict my movement here;*
> *I'm closer to my origin,*
> *And greet the world without veneer.*

Naturally is 48 pgs., 8½×11, printed on glossy paper and saddle-stitched with b&w and full-color photos throughout. They receive about 30 poems a year, use 5-10. Press run is 10,000 for 4,500 subscribers, 4,500 shelf sales. Single copy: $5.95; subscription: $19.95. **Sample postpaid: $6.95. Previously published poems and simultaneous submissions OK. Often comments on rejections. Reports in 2 months. Pay is negotiable. Buys first North American serial or one-time rights.**

NAZARENE INTERNATIONAL HEADQUARTERS; STANDARD; LISTEN; BREAD; TEENS TO-DAY; HERALD OF HOLINESS (IV-Religious, children), 6401 The Paseo, Kansas City MO 64131, phone (816)333-7000. Each of the magazines published by the Nazarenes has a separate editor, focus and audience. *Standard*, circulation 177,000, is a weekly **inspirational "story paper" with Christian leisure reading for adults. Send SASE for free sample and guidelines. Uses a poem each week. Submit maximum of 5, maximum of 50 lines each. Pays 25¢ a line.** For *Listen, Bread, Teens Today* and *Herald of Holiness*, write individually for guidelines and samples.

NEBO: A LITERARY JOURNAL (II), English Dept., Arkansas Tech University, Russellville AR 72801-2222, phone (501)968-0256, founded 1982, poetry editor Michael Ritchie, appears in May and December. Regarding poetry they say, **"We accept all kinds, all styles, all subject matters and will publish a longer poem if it is outstanding. We are especially interested in formal poetry."** They have published poetry by Jack Butler, Turner Cassity, Wyatt Prunty, Charles Martin, Julia Randall and Brenda Hillman. *Nebo* is digest-sized, 50-70 pgs., professionally printed on quality matte stock with matte card cover. Press run "varies." **Sample postpaid: $6. Submit 3-5 poems at a time. Simultaneous submissions OK. "Please no onion skin or offbeat colors." Cover letter with bio material and recent publications required. Do not submit mss between May 1 and August 15. Editor comments on rejections "if the work has merit but requires revision and resubmission; we do all we can to help." Reports at the end of November and February respectively. Pays 1 copy.** Staff reviews books of poetry. Send books for review consideration.

THE NEBRASKA REVIEW; TNR AWARDS (II), University of Nebraska, Omaha NE 68182-0324, phone (402)554-2771, fax (402)554-3436, founded 1973, co-editor Art Homer, is a semiannual literary magazine publishing fiction and poetry with occasional essays. The editor wants **"lyric poetry from 10-200 lines, preference being for under 100 lines. Subject matter is unimportant, as long as it has some. Poets should have mastered form, meaning poems should have form, not simply 'demonstrate' it."** He doesn't want to see "concrete, inspirational, didactic or merely political poetry." They have published poetry by Patricia Goedicke, Mary Swander, Roger Weingarten and Billy Collins. As a sample, he selected these lines from "The Twins Visit a Farm" by Mary Crow:

> *The heavy black bulk of the draft horse*
> *lay in the heat, circled by lime. Too huge*
> *to bury, it was left for flies, night animals.*
> *We walked around the gleaming hill*

Use the General Index to find the page number of a specific publisher. If the publisher you are seeking is not listed, check the " '95-'96 Changes" list at the end of this section.

> *of its flanks, the tulip-blue nostrils,*
> *the tiny terrain of the pink gums,*
> *the belly mushrooming sweetness.*

The magazine is 6×9, nicely printed, 60 pgs., with flat-spined, glossy card cover. It is a publication of the Writer's Workshop at the University of Nebraska. Some of the most exciting, accessible verse is published in this magazine. All styles and forms are welcome here, although relatively few long poems are used. Circulation is 500, of which 380 are subscriptions and 85 go to libraries. Single copy: $5; subscription: $9.50/year. **Sample postpaid: $3. Submit 4-6 poems at a time. "Clean typed copy strongly preferred." Reads submissions August 15 through March 31 only. Reports in 3-4 months.** Time between acceptance and publication is 3-6 months. **Pays 2 copies and 1-year subscription. Acquires first North American serial rights.** The TNR Awards of $500 each in poetry and fiction are published in the spring issue. Entry fee: $9, includes discounted subscription. You can enter as many times as desired. Deadline: November 30. The editor says, "Your first allegiance is to the poem. Publishing will come in time, but it will always be less than you feel you deserve. Therefore, don't look to publication as a reward for writing well; it has no relationship."

NEDGE (II), (formerly *Northeast Journal*), P.O. Box 2321, Providence RI 02906, founded 1969, editor Henry Gould, is a biannual published by The Poetry Mission, a nonprofit arts organization. It includes poetry, fiction, reviews and essays. **They want work that "exhibits originality, talent, sincerity, skill and inspiration."** As a sample the editor selected these lines from "Library Termites" by Pete Lee:

> *the workers*
> *devour Marx*
> *and Steinbeck*
> *swarm over*
> *Upton Sinclair*

The purpose of *Nedge* is "to aim toward a Rhode Island literary standard, both local and international in scope." Circulation is 300. **Sample postpaid: $5. Reports in 2-5 months. Pays 1 copy. Simultaneous submissions OK, if noted. SASE required.**

NEGATIVE CAPABILITY; NEGATIVE CAPABILITY PRESS; EVE OF ST. AGNES COMPETITION (III), 62 Ridgelawn Dr. E., Mobile AL 36608-2465, phone (334)343-6163, fax (334)344-8478, founded 1981, poetry editor Sue Walker. *Negative Capability* is a tri-quarterly of verse, fiction, commentary, music and art. The press publishes broadsides, chapbooks, perfect-bound paperbacks and hardbacks. They want **both contemporary and traditional poetry. "Quality has its own specifications—length and form."** They have recently published poetry by John Brugaletta, Marge Piercy, John Updike, Carolyn Page, Vivian Shipley and Diana Der Hovanessian. As a sample Sue Walker selected these lines from "Flakey Blake" by Dorothy Moseley Sutton:

> *I asked Billy Blake*
> *to come out and play with me*
> *and while we was out there playin'*
> *he said he seen a buncha angels*
> *settin' up in a tree.*
> *There wasn't no angels*
> *settin' up in a tree.*
> *I ain't playin with that flakey Blake no more.*

The editor says, "Reaching irritably after a few facts will not describe *Negative Capability.* Read it to know what quality goes to form creative achievement. Shakespeare had negative capability, do you?" In its short history this journal has indeed achieved a major prominence on our literary scene. It is a flat-spined, elegantly printed, digest-sized format of 130 pgs., glossy card color cover with art, circulation 1,000. About 60 pgs. of each issue are devoted to poetry. They receive about 1,200 unsolicited submissions/year, use 350. Single copy: $5; subscription: $15. **Sample postpaid: $4. Submit 3-5 poems at a time. Reads submissions September 1 through May 30 only. Send SASE for guidelines. Reports in 6-8 weeks. Pays 1 copy. Acquires first rights.** Reviews books of poetry. **For book publication, query with 10-12 samples and "brief letter with major publications, significant contributions, awards. We like to know a person as well as their poem." Replies to queries in 3-4 weeks, to submissions (if invited) in 6-8 weeks. Payment arranged with authors. Editor sometimes comments on rejections.** They offer an annual Eve of St. Agnes Competition with major poets as judges. Send SASE for details.

‡NERVE (I, II), P.O. Box 124578, San Diego CA 92112-4578, founded 1994, editor/publisher Geoffrey N. Young, appears 3 times a year. "We publish about 10 poems per issue along with a couple short stories." **They are "open to anything that is well-crafted. No poem will be rejected on the basis of form alone—all styles welcome."** However, they do not want to see "Hallmark greeting card type verse." They have recently published poetry by Mary Cecile Leary, Scott C. Holstad, Paul Semel and Richard King Perkins II. As a sample the editor selected these lines from "Same Old Story" by Mark Salfi:

> *You teeter uneasily with your female friends*
> *dreading the day they confess their love*
> *because now you must date them*
> *because now you must lose them*
> *playing the insensitive jerk*
> *feeling them up the way you know they hate. . .*

nerve is 32-40 pgs., 5½×8½, photocopied from desktop originals and saddle-stapled with card cover. They receive about 300 poems a year, accept approximately 10%. Press run is 300. Subscription: $5. **Sample postpaid: $2. Make checks payable to Geoffrey N. Young. Submit up to 5 poems at a time, with SASE. No previously published poems or simultaneous submissions. Cover letter not required, but "it never hurts to include one." Seldom comments on rejections. Reports in 2-4 months. Pays 3 copies. Rights return to poet upon publication.** Staff reviews books of poetry, chapbooks and other magazines. Reviews are generally kept to fewer than 200 words. Send books for review consideration. The editor says, "Read a lot. Write a lot. Practice your craft. Research the markets. Above all, always have faith in yourself and your potential to be brilliant."

NEW COLLAGE MAGAZINE (II), 5700 N. Tamiami Trail, Sarasota FL 34243-2197, phone (813)359-5605, founded 1970, poetry editor A. McA. Miller. *New CollAge* provides "a forum for contemporary poets, both known and undiscovered. We are **partial to fresh slants on traditional prosodies and poetry with clear focus and clear imagery. No greeting card verse. We prefer poems shorter than five single-spaced pages. We like a maximum of 3-5 poems per submission."** They have published poetry by Peter Meinke, Yvonne Sapia, Lola Haskins, J.P. White, Peter Klappert, Peter Wild, Stephen Corey and Malcolm Glass. The editor selected these sample lines from "The Palm at the Edge of the Bay" by Daniel Bosch:

> *I would need a ship to moore here, really,*
> *if I were to earn this girth of fibrous hemp,*
> *round-waisted, tall, leaning a head*
> *into the corner a cross-breeze walls itself against . . .*

The magazine appears 3 times a year, 28-32 pgs. of poetry in each issue, circulation 500 with 200 subscriptions of which 30 are libraries. They receive about 5,000 poems/year, use 90. Subscription: $6. **Sample: $2. No simultaneous submissions. Publishes theme issues. Send SASE for upcoming themes. Reports in 6 weeks. Pays 2 copies. Editor sometimes comments on rejections.** "We review books and chapbooks in 1,000-2,000 words." Editor "Mac" Miller advises, "Sending a ms already marked 'copyright' is absurd and unprofessional. Mss may be marked 'first North American serials only,' though this is unnecessary. Also, quality is the only standard. Get a sample issue to see our taste."

THE NEW CRITERION (III), The Foundation for Cultural Review, Inc., 850 Seventh Ave., New York NY 10019, poetry editor Robert Richman, is a monthly (except July and August) review of ideas and the arts, which uses **poetry of high literary quality.** They have published poetry by Donald Justice, Andrew Hudgins, Elizabeth Spires and Herbert Morris. It is 90 pgs., 7×10, flat-spined. Poems here truly are open, with structured free verse and formal works highlighted in the issues we critiqued. Much of it was excellent, and book reviews were insightful. **Sample postpaid: $4.75. Cover letter required with submissions. Reports in 2-3 months. Pays $2.50/line ($75 minimum).** Poetry published in this review was selected for inclusion in the 1992 and 1994 volumes of *The Best American Poetry*. The editor says, "To have an idea of who we are or what we stand for aesthetically, poets should consult back issues."

NEW DELTA REVIEW; THE EYSTER PRIZE (II), English Dept., Louisiana State University, Baton Rouge LA 70803-5001, poetry editor Brook Haley, writes, **"We publish works of quality, many of them by young writers who are building their reputations."** They have published poetry by Robert Brown, Janet Bowdan, Timothy Geiger and Ioanna-Veronika Warwick. As a sample, the editor selected these lines from "Those Tattooed" by Allan Peterson:

> *Bodies are gangs of ourselves;*
> *there is a heap of us in our organs*
> *and the edge of us may hold messages.*
> *Diagnostic spiders and roses come like fish*
> *to the surface, the names of those women*
> *surely wronged have come up on the arms*
> *once around them. . .*

NDR appears twice a year, 6×9, 90-120 pgs., flat-spined, typeset and printed on quality stock with glossy card cover with art. Press run is 500, with 100 subscriptions, 20 of which are from libraries; the rest are for shelf sales. Subscription: $7. **Sample postpaid: $4. No simultaneous submissions or previously published poems. Cover letter with biographical information required. Mss read in summer. Poetry editor sometimes comments on rejections, often suggesting possible revisions. Reports in 1-2 months. Sometimes sends prepublication galleys. Pays 2 copies. Acquires first**

North American serial rights. Reviews books of poetry in no more than 2,000 words, single or multi-book format. Open to unsolicited reviews and interviews. Poets may also send books to poetry editor for review consideration. The Eyster Prize of $50 is awarded to the best story and best poem in each issue. The editor says, "Our only criterion is quality: work that has obviously resulted from much care and respect for the poetic arts. We consider all work that we accept innovative, because even formal verse is an inexhaustible source of new, beautiful poems."

NEW DIRECTIONS PUBLISHING CORPORATION (V, IV-Translations), 80 Eighth Ave., New York NY 10011, phone (212)255-0230, founded 1936, contact poetry editor. New Directions is "a small publisher of 20th-Century literature with an emphasis on the experimental," publishing about 36 paperback and hardback titles each year. **"We are looking for highly unusual, literary, experimental poetry. We can't use traditional poetry, no matter how accomplished. However, we are not accepting submissions at this time."** They have published poetry by William Carlos Williams, Ezra Pound, Denise Levertov, Jerome Rothenberg, Robert Creeley, Michael McClure, Kenneth Rexroth, H.D., Robert Duncan, Stevie Smith, David Antin, Hayden Carruth, George Oppen, Dylan, Thomas, Lawrence Ferlinghetti, Jimmy Santiago Baca, Rosmarie Waldrop and Gary Snyder. **To see samples, try the library or purchase from their catalog (available), local bookstores or their distributor, W.W. Norton.** New Directions advises, "Getting published is not easy, but the best thing to do is to work on being published in the magazines and journals, thus building up an audience. Once the poet has an audience, the publisher will be able to sell the poet's books. Avoid vanity publishers and read a lot of poetry."

NEW EARTH PUBLICATIONS (IV-Spiritual, political, translations), 1921 Ashby Ave., Berkeley CA 94703, phone (510)549-0176, founded 1990, editors Clifton Ross and Dave Karoly, publishes **"books (up to 96 pgs.; query if longer) dealing with the struggle for peace and justice, revolutionary anarchism, quality poetry, prose and translations. Some publications are author subsidized."** They publish 1-2 paperbacks, 2-3 chapbooks/year. **Reports on queries in 2 weeks, on mss in 6 weeks. Sometimes sends prepublication galleys. Pays 10% royalties or 10% of press run.**

NEW ENGLAND REVIEW (II), Middlebury College, Middlebury VT 05753, phone (802)388-3711, ext. 5075, founded 1978, editor Stephen Donadio. *New England Review* is a prestigious literary quarterly, 6×9, 160 pgs., flat-spined, elegant make-up and printing on heavy stock, glossy cover with art. All styles and forms are welcome in this carefully edited publication. Poets published include Toi Derricotte, Albert Goldbarth, Norman Dubie, Philip Booth and Carol Frost. Sample copies or subscriptions may be ordered through the University Press of New England, 23 S. Main St., Hanover NH 03755; (800)421-1561. Subscription: $23. **Sample postpaid: $7. Reads submissions September 1 through June 1 only. Response times can be exceptionally slow here, far exceeding published limits of 6-8 weeks. Always sends prepublication galleys. Pays.** Also features essay-reviews. Publishers may send books for review consideration. Work published in this review was included in the 1992, 1993 and 1994 volumes of *The Best American Poetry.*

NEW ERA MAGAZINE (I, IV-Religious, teen/young adult), 50 E. North Temple St., Salt Lake City UT 84150, phone (801)240-2951, fax (801)240-5997, founded 1971, managing editor Richard M. Romney, appears monthly. *New Era* is an "official publication for youth of The Church of Jesus Christ of Latter-day Saints; it contains feature stories, photo stories, fiction, news, etc." **They want "short verse in any form, particularly traditional—must pertain to teenage LDS audience (religious and teenage themes). No sing-songy doggerel, gushy love poems or forced rhymes."** As a sample the editor selected these lines from "Walls" by Dorothy Karen Patterson:

> All those walls,
> See how they crumble
> At the touch of the hand
> Of love.
>
> Like sandcastles,
> Melted by the kiss of the sea,
> My fortress falls
> With each warm word
> And gentle look.

New Era is 52 pgs., approximately $8 \times 10\frac{1}{2}$, 4-color offset, saddle-stitched, quality stock, top-notch art and graphics, no ads. They receive 200-300 submissions, purchase 2-5%. Press run is 220,000 for 205,000 subscribers, 10,000 shelf sales. Single copy: 75¢; subscription: $8/year. **Sample: 75¢ plus postage. Send no more than 5 poems at one time. No previously published poems or simultaneous submissions.** Time between acceptance and publication is a year or longer. "We publish one poem each month next to our photo of the month." **Sometimes comments on rejections. Publishes 1-2 theme issues each year, one of which is geographically themed (LDS youth in one country). Theme for** the June 1995 issue: The Scriptures; for September 1995: LDS Youth in Canada. Send SASE for writer's guidelines and upcoming themes. Reports in 6-8 weeks. Sometimes sends prepublication galleys. Pays $10 minimum. "LDS church retains rights to publish again in church publications— all other rights returned." They also offer an annual contest—including poetry—for active members of the LDS church between ages 12-23. Poetry entries should consist of one entry of 6-10 different original poems (none of which exceeds 50 lines) reflecting LDS values. Deadline: January. Winners receive either a partial scholarship to BYU or Ricks College or a cash award. Send SASE for rules. The editor says, "Study the magazine before submitting. We're a great market for beginners, but you must understand Mormons to write well for us. Just because a subject is noble or inspirational doesn't mean the poetry automatically is noble or inspirational. Pay attention to the craft of writing. Poetry is more than just writing down your thoughts about an inspirational subject. Poetry needs to communicate easily and be readily understood—it's too easy to mistake esoteric expression for true insight."

NEW HOPE INTERNATIONAL (II), 20 Werneth Ave., Gee Cross, Hyde, Cheshire SK14 5NL United Kingdom, founded 1969, editor Gerald England, includes *"NHI Writing*, **publishing poetry, short fiction, artwork, literary essays and reports. All types of poetry from traditional to avant-garde, from haiku to long poems, including translations (usually with the original).** *NHI Review* **carries reviews of books, magazines, cassettes, CDs, records, PC software, etc. Special Edition Chapbooks with a theme or individual collections also included."** They have recently published poetry by John Brander, Damian Furniss, Jean Jorgensen, Ann Keith, Kenneth C. Steven, Belinda Subraman and Carmen Willcox. As a sample the editor selected these lines from "Lost in Translation" by Tony Charles and Stuart A. Paterson:

> *Yet the metaphors we scribble*
> *Far outweigh linguistic quibble*
> *—it's the* poetry *defines imagination*
> . . . . .
> *I agree, we're getting lost in the translation:*
> *But I'll wager, by and by,*
> *You'll understand me if you try*
> *To look on poetry as* everybody's *nation.*

The digest-sized magazine, 36-40 pgs., is printed offset-litho from computer typesetting, saddle-stapled, color card cover, using b&w artwork. Press run is 600 for 300 subscribers of which 25 are libraries. $30 for 6 issues (*NHI Writing*, *NHI Review* and **S.E. Chapbooks** as published). **Sample postpaid: $5 cash (add $5 to cover bank charges if paying by check; make checks payable to Gerald England). Put name and address on each sheet; not more than 6 at a time; simultaneous submissions** *not* **encouraged. Cover letter required. Translations should include copy of original. Full guidelines available for IRC (3 for airmail). Send 1 IRC for reply if return of mss not required. Reports "usually fairly prompt, but sometimes up to 4 months." Always sends prepublication galleys. Pays 1 copy. Acquires first British serial rights.** Staff reviews books of poetry. Send books for review consideration. **For chapbooks, query first.** The editor advises, "Long lists of previous publications do not impress; perceptive, interesting, fresh writing indicative of a live, thinking person makes this job worthwhile."

NEW HORIZONS POETRY CLUB (II, IV-Membership), Box 5561, Chula Vista CA 91912, phone (619)474-4715, founded 1984, poetry editor Alex Stewart. This organization offers poetry contests of various sorts for experienced writers, publishing winners in an anthology. They also offer newsletters and critiques and publish anthologies of members' poetry. Membership (includes 4 newsletters): $10/ year. They have published poetry by Alice Mackenzie Swaim, Glenna Holloway, Pegasus Buchanan and Thelma Schiller. Prizes in their Annual Poetry Day Contest are "$250 and down. We offer other cash awards, prizes and trophies, and certificates for honorable mentions. 'Mini-manuscript' winners are offered trophies, cash prizes and free anthologies." Entry fees are $5/2 poems, $10/5 poems. **"We expect poets to know technique, to be familiar with traditional forms and to be able to conform to requirements regarding category, style and length and to show originality, imagery and craftsmanship. Nothing amateurish, trite or in poor taste."** Alex Stewart offers critiques at reasonable rates. (Discounts on critiques and books to members.) She says, "Poets need to study technique before *rushing to get published!* (*Where* is what counts!) The current trend seems to be a healthy blend of traditional forms and comprehensible free verse." NHPC publishes 3 books annually, 2 in the NHPC Poets' Series (4 poets/book) and 1 anthology of prizewinning and selected poems from the semiannual contests. (Book list, including *The Poet's Art*, the editor's complete handbook on the craft of poetry writing, available on request.)

THE NEW LAUREL REVIEW (II, IV-Translations), 828 Lesseps St., New Orleans LA 70117, founded 1971, editor Lee Meitzen Grue, "is an annual independent nonprofit literary magazine dedicated to fine art. Each issue contains poetry, translations, literary essays, reviews of small press books, and visual art." They want **"poetry with strong, accurate imagery. We have no particular preference in style.**

We try to be eclectic. No more than 3 poems in a submission." They have published poetry by Jane McClellan, Kalamu Ya Salaam, Melody Davis, Sue Walker and Keith Cartwright. The *Review* is 6×9, laser printed, 115 pgs., original art on cover, accepts 30 poems of 300 mss received. It has a circulation of 500. Single copy: $9. **Sample (back issue) postpaid: $7. No simultaneous submissions. Submit 3-5 poems with SASE and a short note with previous publications. Reads submissions September 1 through May 30 only. Guidelines for SASE. Reports on submissions in 3 months, publishes in 8-10 months. Pays contributor's copies. Acquires first rights.** Reviews books of poetry in 1,000 words, single or multi-book format. The editor advises, "Read our magazine before submitting poetry."

NEW LETTERS; NEW LETTERS POETRY PRIZE (II), University of Missouri-Kansas City, Kansas City MO 64110, phone (816)235-1168, fax (816)235-2611, founded 1934 as *University Review*, became *New Letters* in 1971, managing editor Bob Stewart, editor James McKinley, "is dedicated to publishing the best short fiction, best contemporary poetry, literary articles, photography and artwork by both established writers and new talents." They want **"contemporary writing of all types—free verse poetry preferred, short works are more likely to be accepted than very long ones."** They have published poetry by Joyce Carol Oates, Hayden Carruth, John Frederick Nims, Louise Glück, Louis Simpson, Vassar Miller and John Tagliabue. The flat-spined, professionally printed quarterly, glossy 2-color cover with art, 6×9, uses about 40-45 (of 120) pgs. of poetry in each issue. Circulation 1,845 with 1,520 subscriptions of which about 40% are libraries. They receive about 7,000 submissions/year, use less than 1%, have a 6-month backlog. Poems appear in a variety of styles exhibiting a high degree of craft and universality of theme (rare in many journals). Subscription: $17. **Sample postpaid: $5. Send no more than 6 poems at a time. No previously published poems or simultaneous submissions. Short cover letter preferred. "We strongly prefer original typescripts and we don't read between May 15 and October 15. No query needed." Reports in 4-10 weeks. Pays a small fee plus 2 copies.** Occasionally James McKinley comments on rejections. The New Letters Poetry Prize of $750 is given annually for a group of 3-6 poems, entry fee $10 (check payable to New Letters Literary Awards). Send SASE for entry guidelines. Deadline: May 15. They also publish occasional anthologies, selected and edited by McKinley. Work published in *New Letters* appeared in *The Best American Poetry 1992*.

NEW METHODS: THE JOURNAL OF ANIMAL HEALTH TECHNOLOGY (IV-Specialized: animals), P.O. Box 22605, San Francisco CA 94122-0605, phone (415)664-3469, founded as *Methods* in 1976, poetry editor Ronald S. Lippert, AHT, is an irregular 4-page newsletter, "a networking service in the animal field, active in seeking new avenues of knowledge for our readers, combining animal professionals under one roof." They want poetry which is **"animal related but not cutesy, two pages maximum."** They receive about 50 poems a year, accept 5. Press run is 5,000 for 4,000 subscribers of which 100 are libraries. Subscription: $32. **Sample: $3.20. A listing of all back issues and the topics covered is available for $5, and there is a 20% discount on an order of 12 or more mixed copies. No previously published poems or simultaneous submissions. Dated cover letter required. Everything typed, double-spaced with one-inch margins. Often comments on rejections. Send SASE for guidelines. Reports in 2-4 weeks. Pays negotiable number of copies.** Reviews books of poetry "pertaining to our subject matter."

NEW ORLEANS POETRY JOURNAL PRESS (III), 2131 General Pershing St., New Orleans LA 70115, phone (504)891-3458, founded 1956, publisher/editor Maxine Cassin, co-editor Charles deGravelles. **"We prefer to publish relatively new and/or little-known poets of unusual promise or those inexplicably neglected—'the real thing.' "** They do not want to see **"cliché or doggerel, anything incomprehensible or too derivative, or workshop exercises. First-rate lyric poetry preferred (not necessarily in traditional forms)."** They have published books by Vassar Miller, Everette Maddox, Charles Black, Raeburn Miller and Martha McFerren. Their most recent book is *Illuminated Manuscript* by Malaika Favorite. As a sample the editor selected these lines from "Missing Z and Nola" in *Hanoi Rose* by Ralph Adamo:

> Nobody owns the bright blue dawn for long.
> You can be there day after day, raking it in,
> and still there'll be a palm under your token,
> and the palm won't be yours. And the animal
> you traded power with will contrive to be
> given away. In the barracks where the last
> detachment waits, beauty won't show her face.

Query first. They do not accept unsolicited submissions for chapbooks, which are flat-spined paperbacks. **The editors report on queries in 2-3 months, mss in the same time period, if solicited. Simultaneous submissions will possibly be accepted. Sometimes sends prepublication galleys. Pays copies, usually 50-100.** Ms. Cassin does not subsidy publish at present and does not offer grants or awards. For aspiring poets, she quotes the advice Borges received from his father: "1) Read as much as possible! 2) Write only when you *must*, and 3) Don't rush into print!" As a small press editor and publisher, she urges poets to read instructions in *Poet's Market* listings with utmost care! She says, "No poetry should be sent without querying first! Publishers are concerned about expenses unnecessarily incurred in mailing manuscripts. *Telephoning is not encouraged.*"

NEW ORLEANS REVIEW (II), Box 195, Loyola University, New Orleans LA 70118, phone (504)865-2295 or 865-2286, fax (504)865-2294, e-mail adamo@music.loyno.edu., founded 1968, editor Ralph Adamo. They have recently published poetry by Jimmy Carter, and a special section on the life and work of the late poet Everette Maddox. *New Orleans Review* publishes "**lyric poetry of all types**, fiction that is strongly voiced and essays." It is 100 pgs., perfect-bound, elegantly printed with glossy card cover. Circulation is 750. **Sample postpaid: $10. Submit 3-6 poems at a time. No previously published work. Brief cover letter preferred. Reports in 3 months. Acquires first North American serial rights.**

THE NEW POETS SERIES, INC.; CHESTNUT HILLS PRESS (III); STONEWALL SERIES (IV-Gay/lesbian/bisexual), 541 Piccadilly Rd., Baltimore MD 21204, phone (410)828-0724, founded 1970, editor/director Clarinda Harriss. The New Poets Series, Inc. brings out **first books by promising new poets. Poets who have previously had book-length mss published are not eligible. Prior publication in journals and anthologies is strongly encouraged. They want "excellent, fresh, nontrendy, literate, intelligent poems. Any form (including traditional), any style."** Provides 20 copies to the author, the sales proceeds going back into the corporation to finance the next volume (usual press run: 1,000). "It has been successful in its effort to provide these new writers with a national distribution; in fact, The New Poets Series was named an Outstanding Small Press by the prestigious Pushcart Awards Committee, which judges some 5,000 small press publications annually." Chestnut Hills Press publishes author-subsidized books—"High quality work only, however. CHP has achieved a reputation for prestigious books, printing only the top 10% of mss CHP and NPS receive." CHP authors receive proceeds from sale of their books. The New Poets Series has recently published books by Jan-Mitchell Sherrill, Gail Wronsky, M.S. Montgomery, Michael Carrino, Joel Zizik, Earl Jay Perel and Betty Parry. As a sample we selected these lines from "My Uncles' Cigars, part I" from Richard Fein's *At the Turkish Bath*:

> *I hovered near the card table*
> *where they figured out the deal.*
> *Silver clinked below the gray fumes.*
> *I breathed in that acrid tang, it*
> *swirled up my nose and swarmed in my head*
> *and plunged into my lungs. I envied*
> *the stink of grown men.*

Send a 50- to 55-page ms, $10 reading fee and cover letter giving publication credits and bio. Simultaneous submissions OK. Cover letters should be very brief, businesslike and include an accurate list of recently published work. Editor sometimes comments briefly on rejections. Reports in 6 weeks to 8 months. Mss "are circulated to an editorial board of professional, publishing poets. NPS is backlogged, but the best 10% of the mss it receives are automatically eligible for Chestnut Hills Press consideration," a subsidy arrangement. **Send $5 and a 7 × 10 SASE for a sample volume.** Stonewall Series offers a chapbook contest whose winner is published by NPS. Send 20-25 poems with $20 entry fee. Jim Elledge's *Into the Arms of the Universe* won the 1994 Stonewall Chapbook Competition. Stonewall is for gay, lesbian and bisexual writers.

THE NEW PRESS LITERARY QUARTERLY; THE NEW PRESS POETRY CONTEST (II), 53-35 Hollis Ct. Blvd., Flushing NY 11365, phone (718)229-6782, founded 1984, poetry editors Evie-Ivy and Bob Balogh, is a quarterly magazine using **poems "less than 200 lines, accessible, imaginative. No doggerel, sentimentality."** They have published poetry by Allen Ginsberg, Lawrence Ferlinghetti, Les Bridges and Gina Bergamino. As a sample the editor selected these lines by R. Nikolas Macioci:

> *a conversation he has*
> *with himself as he thinks now*
> *of hinges he must oil*
> *before old doors will open*
> *quietly onto another year's*
> *garden and the scent*
> *of newly spaded soil.*

It is magazine-sized, 40 pgs., desktop-published, with glossy cover, saddle-stapled. They accept about 10% of 700 poems received/year. Press run is 1,600 for 320 subscribers of which 3 are libraries, 1,100 shelf sales. Subscription: $15. **Sample postpaid: $4. Submit 4 poems at a time. "Include name and address on the top of each page." Publishes theme issues. Send SASE for upcoming themes. Reports in 3 months. Always sends prepublication galleys. Pays 3 copies. Acquires first-time rights.** The New Press Poetry Contest is annual, deadline is July 1, entry fee of $5 for up to 3 poems or 200 lines, has prizes of $200, $75 and five 2-year subscriptions. Also sponsors quarterly essay and short story contests. Send 10 and 22 double-spaced pgs. maximum with entry fee of $5 and SASE. Prize is $100. They also sponsor poetry readings in Brooklyn, Queens and Manhattan. Send SASE for details.

THE NEW QUARTERLY (II, IV-Regional), ELPP University of Waterloo, Waterloo, Ontario N2L 3G1 Canada, phone (519)885-1211, ext. 2837, founded 1981, managing editor Mary Merikle, is a "literary quarterly—new directions in Canadian writing." For the poetry they want, the editors have **"no preconceived conception—usually Canadian work, poetry capable of being computer type-set—4½" line length typeset lines. No greeting card verse."** The editor describes it as 120 pgs., flat-spined, $6 \times 8½$, with a photograph on the cover, no graphics or art, some ads. Of 2,000 poems received/year, they use 100. Press run is 600 for 300 subscriptions (10 of them libraries) and additional shelf sales. Subscription: $18 ($23 for US or overseas subscriptions). **Sample postpaid: $5 Canadian, $5 US. Submit no more than 5 poems at a time. Cover letter with short bio required. Send SASE for guidelines. Reports in 3-6 months. Pays $20/poem.**

THE NEW RENAISSANCE (II, IV-Translations, bilingual), 9 Heath Rd., Arlington MA 02174, founded 1968. *the new renaissance* is "intended for the 'renaissance' person, the generalist not the specialist. Publishes the best new writing and translations. Offers a forum for articles of public concern, features established as well as emerging visual artists and writers, and highlights reviews of small press books and other books of merit. **We are open to traditional as well as other types of poetry and usually receive samples of every kind during our submission periods.**" They have recently published poetry by J. Patrick Lewis, Joan Colby, Kai Peronard, Ann Struthers and Marian Steele and translations of Albino Pierro (by Luigi Bonaffini) and Ye Fang (by Jun Wang). As a sample of the poetry they're publishing, the editor selected these lines from "Gems" by Norman Nathan:

> Nirvana is self lost
> in a sapphire soul
> buoyed in passionless peace
>
> so whisper the tormented
> icing their truth
> to match their pallor

tnr is flat-spined, professionally printed on heavy stock, glossy, color cover, 144-186 pgs., using 20-40 pgs. of poetry in each issue. They receive about 750 poetry submissions/year, use 15-20, have about a 2½-year backlog. Usual press run is 1,600 for 710 subscribers of which approximately 132 are libraries. Subscriptions: $20.50/3 issues US, $22 Canada, $24 all others. **"We're an unsponsored, independent small litmag. Contributors are expected to help the magazine by sending in, with their submissions, a check for $10, for which they may receive any combination of the following: 2 back issues or a current issue.** *Exceptions to this rule*: **All current subscribers and all writers who have bought an issue or two since July 1, 1993." Submit 3-6 poems at a time, "unless a long poem—then one."** No previously published poems **"unless magazine's circulation was under 300"; simultaneous submissions OK, if notified. Reads mss in September and October. Send SASE for guidelines. Reports in 3-6 months. Pays $13-20, more for the occasional longer poem, plus 1 copy. Buys all rights. Returns rights provided** *tnr* **retains rights for any** *tnr* **collection, anthology, etc.** Reviews books of poetry. "We believe that poets should not only be readers but lovers of poetry. We're looking for 'literalists of the imagination—imaginary gardens with real toads in them.' **Our range is from traditionalist poetry to post-modern, experimental (the latter only occasionally, though) and street poetry. We also like the occasional 'light' poem and, of course, have an emphasis on translations. We're especially interested in the individual voice. We aren't interested in greeting card verse or prose set in poetic forms. If you're querying us about anything, please include a SASE. We won't answer unless there is one."**

THE NEW REPUBLIC (II), 1220 19th St. NW, Washington DC 20036, phone (202)331-7494, founded 1914, poetry editor Mark Strand. *The New Republic*, a weekly journal of opinion, is magazine-sized, printed on slick paper, 42 pgs., saddle-stapled with 4-color cover. Subscription: $69.97/year. **Back issues available for $3.50 postpaid. Include SASE with submissions. Always sends prepublication galleys. They provide no payment information.** Poetry published in *The New Republic* has also been included in the 1993, 1994 and 1995 volumes of *The Best American Poetry*.

NEW RIVERS PRESS; MINNESOTA VOICES PROJECT, INC. (II, IV-Regional, translations), 420 N. Fifth St., Suite 910, Minneapolis MN 55401, phone (612)339-7114, founded 1968, publishes collections of poetry, translations of contemporary literature, collections of short fiction, and is also involved in publishing **Minnesota regional literary material. Write for free catalog or send SASE for guidelines/inquiries. New and emerging authors living in Iowa, Minnesota, North and South Dakota and Wisconsin are eligible for the Minnesota Voices Project. Book-length mss of poetry,** short fiction, novellas or familiar essays are all accepted. **Send SASE for entry form. Winning**

authors receive a stipend of $500 plus publication by New Rivers. Second and subsequent print-ings of works will allow 15% royalties for author.

NEW VIRGINIA REVIEW (II), 1310 E. Cary St., Richmond VA 23219, phone (804)782-1043, founded 1978, poetry editor Margaret Gibson, appears 3 times a year publishing both fiction and poetry. **They want "seriously written poetry addressing any subject matter, in any variety of styles. No greeting card verse or haiku."** They have published poetry by Mona Van Duyn, Mary Oliver, Philip Booth and Norman Dubie. *NVR* is 160 pgs., 6¾ × 10, offset, perfect-bound, with color cover, no graphics. They receive over 6,000 mss a year, accept approximately 10%. Press run is 2,500 for 1,500 subscribers of which 20% are libraries, 250 shelf sales. Subscription: $15. **Sample postpaid: $6. No previously published poems or simultaneous submissions. Reads submissions September 1 through May 31 only. Seldom comments on rejections. Send SASE for guidelines. Reports in 3-6 weeks. Pays $25/ poem on publication, plus $10 for additional printed pages. Buys first North American serial rights.**

NEW VOICES IN POETRY AND PROSE; NEW VOICES SPRING/FALL COMPETITIONS (I), P.O. Box 52196, Shreveport LA 71135, founded 1990, editor Cheryl White, is a semiannual that publishes new poets and writers and reviews collected works. **"All types of poetry welcome. However, prefer poetry that makes a statement about the emotions of the writer."** The editor says it is 12-16 pgs., 8½ × 11. Press run is approximately 250 for 100 subscribers. Subscription: $8. **Sample postpaid: $5. Submit 5-10 poems at a time. No handwritten submissions. Cover letters are a plus, "especially if they serve to introduce the writer." Seldom comments on rejections. Send SASE for guidelines. Reports in approximately 1 month. Pays 1 copy.** Offers semiannual poetry and short fiction competi-tions. Small entry fees. Cash prizes.

‡NEW WELSH REVIEW (II, IV-Ethnic), Chapter Arts Centre, Market Rd., Cardiff CF5 1QE Wales, United Kingdom, phone 0222-665529, founded 1988, editor Robin Reeves. *NWR* is a literary quarterly publishing articles, short stories and poems. The editor describes it as an average of 88 pgs., glossy paper in three colors, laminated cover, using photographs, graphics and ads. Their press run is 1,100. Subscription: £15. **Sample postpaid: £4.20. Submit poems double-spaced. No simultaneous sub-missions or previously published poems. Reports in 6 weeks. Publication within 1-7 months.** Reviews books of poetry.

NEW WRITER'S MAGAZINE (I, II, IV-Humor, writing), P.O. Box 5976, Sarasota FL 34277, phone (813)953-7903, founded 1986, editor George J. Haborak, is a bimonthly magazine "for aspiring writers, and professional ones as well, to exchange ideas and working experiences." **They are open to free verse, light verse and traditional, 8-20 lines, reflecting upon the writing lifestyle. "Humorous slant on writing life especially welcomed."** They do not want poems about "love, personal problems, abstract ideas or fantasy." *NWM* is 28 pgs., 8½ × 11, offset, saddle-stapled, with glossy paper cover, b&w photos and ads. They receive about 300 poems a year, accept approximately 10%. Press run is 5,000. Subscription: $15 for 1 year, $25 for 2 years. **Sample postpaid: $3. Submit up to 3 poems at a time. No previously published poems or simultaneous submissions.** Time between acceptance and publication is 1 year maximum. **Send SASE for guidelines. Reports in 1-2 months. Pays $5/poem. Buys first North American serial rights.** Each issue of this magazine also includes an interview with a recognized author, articles on writing and the writing life, tips and markets.

NEW YORK QUARTERLY (II), P.O. Box 693, Old Chelsea Station, New York NY 10113, founded 1969, poetry editor William Packard, appears 3 times/year. They seek to publish "a cross-section of the best of contemporary American poetry" and, indeed, **have a record of publishing many of the best and most diverse of poets**, including W.D. Snodgrass, Gregory Corso, James Dickey and Judson Jerome. It appears in a 6 × 9, flat-spined format, thick, elegantly printed, glossy color cover. Subscrip-tion: $15. **Submit 3-5 poems at a time; include SASE. Reports within 2 weeks. Pays copies.**

THE NEW YORKER (III, IV-Translations, humor), 20 W. 43rd St., New York NY 10036, founded 1925, poetry editor Alice Quinn, circulation 640,000, uses **poetry of the highest quality (including translations). Sample: $2.50 (available on newsstands). Mss are not read during the summer. Replies in 6-8 weeks. Pays top rates.** Poems appearing in *The New Yorker* have also been selected for inclusion in the 1992, 1993, 1994 and 1995 volumes of *The Best American Poetry*.

NEWSLETTER INAGO (I), P.O. Box 26244, Tucson AZ 85726-6244, phone (602)294-7031, founded 1979, poetry editor Del Reitz, is a monthly newsletter, 4-5 pgs., corner-stapled. **"Free verse and short narrative poetry preferred although other forms will be read. Rhymed poetry must be truly exceptional (nonforced) for consideration. Due to format, 'epic' and monothematic poetry will not be considered. Cause specific, political or religious poetry stands little chance of consider-ation. A wide range of short poetry, showing the poet's preferably eclectic perspective is best for**

NI. **No haiku, please."** They have recently published poetry by Christopher Woods, Karen Legg, Bob Dial, Lynda S. Silva, Mary Rudbeck Stanko, Fay Green, Stacy Packard, Jennifer Militello, Chocolate Waters and Peter Lewin. The editor says, "Since editorial taste in poetry especially is such a subjective and narrow thing," a short selection cannot be chosen "with any fairness to either that taste or the poet whose material might be quoted." However, as a sample the editor selected these lines by Harriet B. Shatraw:

> *It studies me like an alphabet*
> *then snorts a warning and darts away*
> *though I have made no move*
> *Those sensitive nostrils must have caught*
> *a whiff*
> *of my almost reluctant*
> *humanity*

Their press run is approximately 200 for that many subscriptions. **No price is given for the newsletter, but the editor suggests a donation of $3.50 an issue or $17.50 annually ($3.50 and $20.50 Canada, £5 and £22 UK). Submit 10-15 poems at a time. "Poetry should be submitted in the format in which the poet wants it to appear, and cover letters are always a good idea." They consider simultaneous submissions and previously published poems. Editor sometimes comments on rejections. Send SASE for guidelines. Reports ASAP (usually within 2 weeks). Pays 4 copies.** The first and second audio anthologies of poetry (on audiotapes) are now available. These anthologies present selections from the poetry published in *Newsletter Inago* during the first and second five years, respectively. Write for current price and details.

‡NEXT PHASE; PHANTOM PRESS PUBLICATIONS (II), 5A Green Meadow Dr., Nantucket Island MA 02554, phone (508)325-0411, founded 1989, poetry editor Holly Day and **submissions should go directly to her at 477 S. Hines, #1513, Tampa FL 33611.** *Next Phase* is a fiction magazine that appears 3 times a year and includes poetry, commentary, interviews and book reviews. **They prefer "positive, inspirational work with an emphasis on environmental and social issues." They do not want to see work over two pages long . . . "and please no depressing poetry!"** They have recently published poetry by Allen Ginsberg and John Grey. As a sample the editor selected these lines from "Silences" by Diane Thiel:

> *In a small boat distance changes*
> *the world becomes big and wild again*
> *the weather is more than words*
> *but what you live your life by*
>
> *We who numb ourselves with noise*
> *need to listen for the silences*

Next Phase is 44 pgs., 8½×11, saddle-stitched with a 4-color semi-glossy paper cover; b&w photos, art and graphics inside. They receive about 150 poetry submissions a year, publish about 20. Press run is 1,500 for 400 subscribers, 750 shelf sales. Single copy: $3; subscription: $16 for 2 years. **Sample postpaid: $4. Previously published poems and simultaneous submissions OK. Cover letter required.** Time between acceptance and publication is 1-2 years. **Seldom comments on rejections. Send SASE for guidelines. Reports in 6 weeks. Pays 2 copies. Acquires one-time rights.** "We review small press books only." Send books for review consideration to Charlie Cockett, Box 1239, Torrington WY 82240.

NEXUS (II), WO16A Student Union, Wright State University, Dayton OH 45435, phone (513)873-5533, founded 1967, editor Tara L. Miller. **"*Nexus* is a student operated magazine of mainstream and street poetry; also essays on environmental and political issues. We're looking for truthful, direct poetry. Open to poets anywhere. We look for contemporary, imaginative work."** *Nexus* appears 3 times a year—fall, winter and spring, using about 40 pgs. of poetry (of 80-96) in each issue. They receive 1,000 submissions/year, use 30-50. Circulation 1,000. **For a sample, send a 10×15 SAE with 5 first-class stamps and $5. Submit 4-6 pgs. of poetry, with bio, September through May. Simultaneous submissions OK. Editor sometimes comments on rejections. Send SASE for guidelines. Reports in 10-12 weeks except summer months. Pays 2 copies. Acquires first rights.** The magazine received a Medalist Award from The Columbia Scholastic Press Association in 1994.

NIGHT ROSES (I, IV-Teen/young adult, love/romance, nature, students, women/feminism); MOONSTONE BLUE (I, IV-Anthology, science fiction/fantasy), P.O. Box 393, Prospect Heights IL 60070-0393, phone (708)392-2435, founded 1986, poetry editor Allen T. Billy, appears 2-4 times a year. **"*Moonstone Blue* is a science fiction/fantasy anthology, but we have no set dates of publication. We do an issue every 14-24 months as items, time and funds allow. We look for women/feminism themes for our *Bikini* series."** For *Night Roses* they want **"poems about dance, bells, clocks, nature, ghost images of past or future, romance and flowers (roses, wildflowers, violets,**

etc.). **Do not want poems with raw language."** They have published poetry by Judith Beckett, M. Riesa Clark, Joan Payne Kincaid, Lyn Lifshin and Alice Rogoff. As a sample the editor selected these lines from "Blue Notes" by Cynthia C. Bergen:

> *A funky sax wails*
> *on a violet evening*
> *in the square.*

Night Roses is 44 pgs., saddle-stapled, photocopied from typescript on offset paper with tinted matte card cover. Press run is 200-300. Subscription: $10 for 3 issues. **Sample postpaid: $3.50 for** *Night Roses*, **$3 for** *Moonstone Blue*. **Submit no more than 8 poems at a time. "Desire author's name and address on all sheets of ms. If previously published—an acknowledgment must be provided by author with it." No simultaneous submissions; some previously published poems used. "I prefer submissions between March and September." Reports in 6-12 weeks. "Material is accepted for current issue and 2 in progress." Sometimes sends prepublication galleys. Pays 1 copy. Acquires first or reprint rights.** Staff reviews books of poetry. Send books for review consideration. The editor says, "We are more interested in items that would be of interest to our teen and women readers and to our readership in the fields of dance, art and creative learning. We are interested in positive motives in this area."

NIGHT SONGS (IV-Horror), 4998 Perkins Rd., Baton Rouge LA 70808-3043, founded 1991, editor Gary William Crawford, is a quarterly newsletter that publishes "supernatural horror poetry in the great tradition of supernatural verse. Poems that modernize themes explored in the poetry of Poe, Baudelaire, H.P. Lovecraft." **They want "horror poetry in a variety of forms. However, not interested in strict imitations of such poets as Edgar Allan Poe or H.P. Lovecraft. In general, themes of terror and darkness, madness and death should be present. Poems that explore the underlying horror of civilization."** They have published poetry by Bruce Boston, Lisa Lepovetsky, Keith Allen Daniels and Joey Froehlich. As a sample the editor selected these lines from "The Morning of Interment" by June Miller:

> *The human step creeps closer, almost silent*
> *but at first tread great wings outspread,*
> *three glittering jet projectiles shoot the sky*
> *soaring, arcing over shore and ocean,*
> *black against the sun.*

Night Songs is 6 pgs., 8½×11, neatly photocopied with line drawings and stapled at the corner. They receive about 30 poems/month, use approximately 5. Press run is 75 for 45 subscribers. Subscription: $3/year. **Sample postpaid: $1. Submit 3 poems at a time. No previously published poems or simultaneous submissions. Cover letter required.** Time between acceptance and publication is 6 months. **Often comments on rejections. Reports in 2 weeks. Always sends prepublication galleys. Pays $1/poem. Buys first rights.**

NIGHTSUN (II), Dept. of English, Frostburg State University, Frostburg MD 21532, phone (301)689-4221 or 4208, founded 1981, editor Douglas DeMars, is a literary annual of poetry, fiction and interviews. **They want "highest quality poetry." Subject matter open. Publishes mostly free verse. Prefers poems not much longer than 40 lines. Not interested in the "extremes of sentimental, obvious poetry on the one hand and the subjectless 'great gossamer-winged gnat' school of poetry on the other."** They have recently published poetry by Marge Piercy, Diane Wakoski, Philip Dacey, Walter McDonald, David Citino, Stephen Perry and Robert Cooperman. Interviews include Lucille Clifton, Sharon Olds, Galway Kinnell, Stephen Dobyns, Maxine Kumin and Marvin Bell. As a sample the editor selected these lines from "Skeleton Key" by Dixie Salazan:

> *Darkness gathers in the corners*
> *of my eyes and I hear him*
> *creeping along the baseboards,*
> *dropping pennies in the dust.*
> *When I leave the house*
> *I know he spits in my soup,*
> *sets the canaries loose.*

Nightsun is 68 pgs., 6×9, printed on 100% recycled paper and perfect-bound with card cover, b&w print on front. This attractive journal features well-known poets alongside relative newcomers. Editors take free verse mostly with attention paid to line, stanza and shape of poem. They accept about 1% of poetry received. **Subscription/sample postpaid: $6.50. Submit 3-5 poems at a time. No simultaneous submissions. Do not submit mss during summer months. Reports within 2-3 months. Pays 2 copies. Acquires first rights. "Contributors encouraged to subscribe."**

NIMROD INTERNATIONAL JOURNAL OF CONTEMPORARY POETRY AND FICTION; RUTH G. HARDMAN AWARD: PABLO NERUDA PRIZE FOR POETRY (II), 2210 S. Main St., Tulsa OK 74114, phone (918)584-3333, fax (918)582-2787, founded 1956, editor-in-chief Fran Ringold, "is an active 'little magazine,' part of the movement in American letters which has been essential to the development of modern literature. *Nimrod* publishes 2 issues per year: an awards issue in the fall featuring the prize winners of our national competition and a thematic issue each spring." **They want "vigorous writing that is neither wholly of the academy nor the streets, typed mss."** They have published poetry by Pattiann Rogers, Denise Levertov, Willis Barnstone, Alvin Greenberg, Francois Camoin, Tess Gallagher, Mekeel McBride, Bronislava Volek, Josephine Jacobsen, Lars Gustaffson, William Stafford and Ishmael Reed. The 6×9, flat-spined, 160-page journal, full-color glossy cover, professionally printed on coated stock with b&w photos and art, uses 50-90 pgs. of poetry in each issue. It is an extraordinarily lovely magazine with one of the best designs in the lit world. Poems in non-award issues range from formal to freestyle with several translations. They use about 1% of the 2,000 submissions they receive each year, have a 3- to 6-month backlog. Circulation 3,500, 500 subscriptions of which 100 are public and university libraries. Subscription: $15/year inside USA; $18 outside. **Sample postpaid: $8 for a recent issue, $6.95 for an issue more than 2 years old. Submit 1-10 poems at a time. Theme for Spring 1996 issue is "Borderlands: Ec-centric Writing." Send SASE for upcoming themes. Reports in 3 weeks to 1 month. Pays $5/page up to $25 total/issue. "Poets should be aware that during the months that the Ruth Hardman Awards Competition is being conducted, reporting time on non-contest manuscripts will be longer."** Send business-sized SASE for guidelines and rules for the Ruth G. Hardman Award: Pablo Neruda Prize for Poetry ($1,000 and $500 prizes). Entries accepted January 1 through April 1 each year with $15 entry fee for which you get one copy of *Nimrod*. This annual poetry contest is considered one of the most prestigious in the publishing world, and your material is still considered for publication if you lose in the contest! Poetry published in *Nimrod* has been included in *The Best American Poetry 1995*.

‡96 INC (I, II); BRUCE P. ROSSLEY LITERARY AWARDS (IV-Regional), P.O. Box 15559, Boston MA 02215, founded 1992, editors Julie Anderson, Nancy Mehegan and Andrew Dawson. *96 Inc* is a biannual literary magazine that focuses on new voices, "connecting the beginner to the established, a training center for the process of publication." **They want all forms and styles of poetry, though "shorter is better."** They have recently published poetry by Jean Pedrick, Jean Monahan, David Fedo and Linda Russo. As a sample the editors selected these lines (poet unidentified):

> *We could join in whenever we cared to,*
> *and we didn't care to.*
> *We dredged, built, buttressed,*
> *manned the peep holes, ran the cat walks*
> *nimble-fingered, howled against*
> *the boiled-up ocean's awful onslaught.*
> *We were a wave thrown up at the wave.*
> *We were the Castlemakers.*

96 Inc is 38-50 pgs., 8½×11, saddle-stapled with coated card cover and b&w photos and graphics. They receive "a few hundred" submissions a year, accept 10%. Press run is 3,000 for 400 subscribers of which 50 are libraries, 1,500 shelf sales. Single copy: $4; subscription: $13. **Sample postpaid: $5.50. No previously published poems; simultaneous submissions OK.** Time between acceptance and publication is 1 year. **Poems are circulated to an editorial board. Often comments on rejections. Send SASE for general guidelines. Reports in 6 months. Pays $20-75 (depending on funding) and 4 copies. Copyright reverts to author 2 months after publication.** Occasionally, staff reviews books of poetry. Send books for review consideration, attn: Mark Wagner. The Bruce P. Rossley Literary Awards are given to previously under-recognized writers (of poetry or fiction) in the state of Massachusetts. Writers can be nominated by anyone familiar with their work. Send SASE for further information. The editors add, "*96 Inc* is an artists' collaborative and a local resource. It often provides venues and hosts readings in addition to publishing a magazine."

NINETY-SIX PRESS (V, IV-Regional), Furman University, Greenville SC 29613, founded 1991, editors William Rogers and Gilbert Allen, publishes 1 paperback book of poetry/year. "The name of the press is derived from the old name for the area around Greenville, South Carolina—the Ninety-Six District. The name suggests our interest in the writers, readers and culture of the region. In 1994, we published an anthology of South Carolina poetry, including the work of more than 40 poets. **We currently accept submissions by invitation only. At some point in the future, however, we hope to be able to encourage submissions by widely published poets who live in South Carolina."** They

---

The Subject Index, located before the General Index, can help you narrow down markets for your work. It lists those publishers whose poetry interests are specialized.

have published poetry by William Aarnes and Bennie Lee Sinclair. As a sample the editors selected these lines from "Who Can Show the Child as She Is?" in Aarnes' book, *Learning to Dance*:

> *Truth is, she's just too ridiculous,*
> *my daughter standing naked in her pool,*
> *her swimming suit tossed into the grass,*
> *and over her head the tilted hose spouting*
> *a putto's wing. She commands, imperious:*
> *"Take your shorts off; take them off now!"*

That book is 58 pgs., 6×9, professionally printed and perfect-bound with coated stock cover. **For a sample, send $10.**

9TH ST. LABORATORIES; THE EXPERIODDICIST; THE ELECTRIC EXPERIODDICIST (IV-Form), P.O. Box 3112, Florence AL 35630, e-mail bugsd@aol.com, founded 1986, "front man" Jake Berry. "*9th St. Laboratories* is a noncommercial enterprise publishing *experimental* poetry, fiction, graphics and audio material in broadsheets, booklets, postcards, objects, chapbooks and audiotapes. *The Experioddicist* is a newsletter of poetry, deviant theory and graphics. **The key words are *experiment* and *explore*. Poetry that breaks new ground for the poet personally, that comes from the commitment to a vision. Also graphic poetry. Poetry using devices other than straight linear narrative, that makes use of things otherwise considered nonsensical or absurd." We have begun an electronic version of *The Experioddicist*. Submissions can be through mail or e-mail. The electronic version and print version will contain different material with the electronic version appearing every month and the print version somewhat less frequently.** They have published poetry by Jack Foley, Chris Winkler, Malok, Richard Kostelanetz, Mike Miskowski and John M. Bennett. As a sample the editor selected these lines by Harry Polkinhorn:

> *to challenge your balance drastic yet nuclear ocean*
> *urgent to implement an unwilling shifty murder victim*
> *subject I say a minister question of what she meant*

They use about 10 of 150 submissions received a year. Press run is 100-200. **Sample postpaid: $4. "All checks or money orders should be made out to Jake Berry, not the name of the mag and not to** *9th St. Laboratories*.**" No simultaneous submissions. They use some previously published work. Considers submissions January 1 through October 31 only. They pay 1 copy. They publish chapbooks by invitation only. Pay 15-20 copies. Editor sometimes comments on rejections.** He says, "We publish as much as we can as often as we can, attempting to expand the area of poetic, visionary concentration. Going to the mailbox to find it full of work that ignores conventional limitations and is highly involved with exploring new ideas, provoking unusual insights, is what makes us happy. We would especially like to receive more experimental poetry by women."

‡NO EXIT (II), 52175 Central Ave., South Bend IN 46637-3807, founded 1994, editor Mike Amato, is a quarterly forum "for the experimental as well as traditional excellence." **The editor says he wants "poetry that takes chances in form or content. Form, length, subject matter and style are open. Astonish me." They do not want anything handwritten nor anything on sheets smaller than** 8½×11, **"regardless of how good. No bad rhyme nor poetry that's unsure of why it was written."** They have recently published poetry by Errol Miller, Simon Perchik and Michael Casey. *NE* is 32 pgs., saddle-stapled, digest-sized, card cover with art. They accept 10-15% of the submissions received. Press run is less than 500 for 65 subscribers of which 6 are libraries. Subscription: $12. **Sample postpaid: $4. No previously published poems; simultaneous submissions OK.** Time between acceptance and publication can vary from 1 month to 1 year. **Sometimes comments on rejections, "if the poem strikes me as worth saving." Send SASE for guidelines. Reports in 6-8 weeks. Pays 1 copy plus 4-issue subscription. Acquires first North American serial rights.** Reviews books of poetry. "Also looking for articles, critical in nature, on poetry/poets." Open to unsolicited reviews. Poets may also send books for review consideration. The editor says, "Don't let rejection keep you from submitting again. Presentation means something; namely, that you care about what you do. I'm amazed at the number of submissions I get that don't have the writer's name on them. And it takes a powerful piece of work for me to overlook spelling and other like errors. Don't take criticism, when offered, personally. I'll work with you if I see something solid to focus on."

NOCTURNAL LYRIC, JOURNAL OF THE BIZARRE (I, IV-Horror, science fiction/fantasy), P.O. Box 115, San Pedro CA 90733, phone (310)519-9220, founded 1987, editor Susan Moon, is a quarterly journal "featuring bizarre fiction and poetry, primarily by new writers." **They want "poems dealing with the bizarre: fantasy, death, morbidity, horror, gore, etc. Any length. No 'boring poetry.' "** They have recently published poetry by Kent Gowran and R.E. Hughes. As a sample the editor selected these lines from "Darkness" by Sharon Anderson:

> *I lay, it seemed, an eternity, anticipating release.*
> *The sockets of my eyes painfully dehydrated, throat parched,*
> *bones aching as they strain for freedom, almost piercing my*

skin, they reach for you. Come sweet darkness, come.

NL is 40 pgs., digest-sized, photocopied, saddle-stapled, with trade ads and staff artwork. They receive about 140 poems a year, use approximately 70%. Press run is 250 for 40 subscribers. Subscription: $10. **Sample postpaid: $3, $2 for back issues. "Make checks payable to Susan Moon." Submit up to 6 poems at a time. Previously published poems and simultaneous submissions OK. Seldom comments on rejections. Reports in 3 months. Pays 50¢ "discount on subscription" coupons. Acquires one-time rights.** The editor says, "Please send us something really wild and intense!"

NOMAD'S CHOIR (II), % Meander, P.O. Box 232, Flushing NY 11385-0232, founded 1989, editor Joshua Meander, is a quarterly. **"No curse words in poems, little or no name-dropping, no naming of consumer products, no two-page poems, no humor, no bias writing, no poems untitled. 9-30 lines, poems with hope. Simple words, careful phrasing. Free verse, rhymed poems, sonnets, half-page parables, myths and legends, song lyrics. Subjects wanted: love poems, protest poems, mystical poems, nature poems, poems of humanity, poems with solutions to world problems and inner conflict."** They have published poetry by Brenda Charles, Joseph Gourdji, Dorothy Wheeler and Jeff Swan. As a sample the editor selected these lines from "Love's Giant Piano" by Connie Goodman:

> *Walk a giant piano . . .*
> *Destination, the stars*
> *Along love's entrancing melody;*
> *The night, it is ours.*

Nomad's Choir is 10 pgs., 8½×11, typeset and saddle-stapled with 3 poems/page. They receive 150 poems/year, use about 50. Press run is 400, all distributed free. Subscription $5; **per copy $1.25. Make check payable to Joshua Meander. Reports in 6-8 weeks. Pays one copy.** The editor says, "Stick to your guns; however, keep in mind that an editor may be able to correct a minor flaw in your poem. Accept only minor adjustments. Go to many open poetry readings. Respect the masters. Read and listen to other poets on the current scene. Make pen pals. Start your own poetry journal. Do it all out of pure love."

NOMOS PRESS INC.; NOMOS: STUDIES IN SPONTANEOUS ORDER (IV-Political), 9400 S. Damen, Chicago IL 60620, phone (312)233-8684, poetry editor John Enright. *Nomos* is a quarterly magazine **"dedicated to individual freedom and responsibility."** One page of each issue is devoted to poetry up to 24 lines, **"although longer pieces are considered. Poetry must promote individual freedom and responsibility, skepticism toward government solutions for economic and social ills, and/or celebrate the human condition. Clarity of meaning and direct emotional appeal are paramount; form should contribute to, not detract or distract from these."** They have published poetry by James Henderson and Roger Donway. As a sample John Enright selected these lines of his own:

> *Into the distance*
> *run at full speed.*
> *Something bright glistens—*
> *Something you need.*

"*Nomos*' purpose is to call attention to the erosion of civil and economic rights, much of which erosion has government as its catalyst." The editor describes it as magazine-sized, generally 40 pgs. in length, offset, matte cover occasionally printed 2-color. Ad copy, line art for cover and article illustrations are solicited. It has a circulation of 1,000 with 450 subscribers of which 10 are libraries, 300 sent out to potential subscribers. Subscription: $18. **Sample postpaid: $4.50. Submit poems with name on each page. Reporting time varies, up to 1 year to publication. Pays 3 copies.**

NORTH AMERICAN REVIEW (III), University of Northern Iowa, Cedar Falls IA 50614, phone (319)273-6455, founded 1815, poetry editor Peter Cooley, is a slick magazine-sized bimonthly of general interest, 48 pgs. average, saddle-stapled, professionally printed with glossy full-color paper cover, **publishing poetry of the highest quality.** They have published poetry by Francine Sterle, Cynthia Hogue and Marvin Bell. The editor says they receive 15,000 poems a year, publish 20-30. Press run is 6,400 for 2,200 subscribers of which 1,100 are libraries, some 2,800 newsstand or bookstore sales. Subscription: $18. **Sample postpaid: $4. No simultaneous submissions or previously published poems. Send SASE for guidelines. Reports in 1-2 months, as much as a year between acceptance and publication. Always sends prepublication galleys. Pays 50¢/line and 2 copies.** Work published in the *North American Review* has been included in the 1992 and 1995 volumes of *The Best American Poetry.*

NORTH DAKOTA QUARTERLY (III), Box 7209, University of North Dakota, Grand Forks ND 58202-7209, fax (701)777-3650, founded 1910, poetry editor Jay Meek, is a literary quarterly published by the University of North Dakota that includes material in the arts and humanities—essays, fiction, interviews, poems and visual art. **"We want to see poetry that reflects an understanding not only of the difficulties of the craft, but of the vitality and tact that each poem calls into play."** Poets recently published include Susan Clements, Patricia Goedicke, Edward Kleinschmidt and Rick Lyon. As a sample, the poetry editor selected lines from "Carving Your Future" by Douglas Woodsum:

> . . . *I don't sell knives,*
> *I sell pardons, and relics, and talismans. I sell hope,*
> *belief, faith, self-esteem. I save marriages*
> *and battered kids. I sell knives out of a wooden*
> *booth I've pulled behind my pickup from Fryburg, Maine,*
> *to West Point, Mississippi.*

The poetry editor says *North Dakota Quarterly* is 6×9, about 250 pgs., perfect-bound, professionally designed and often printed with full-color artwork on the white matte card cover. You can find almost every kind of poem here—avant-garde to traditional. Typically the work of about 10 poets is included in each issue. Circulation of the journal is 850, of which 650 are subscriptions. Subscription: $15/year. **Sample postpaid: $5. Submit 5 poems at a time, typed, double-spaced. No previously published poems or simultaneous submissions. Reporting time is 4-6 weeks and time to publication varies. Always sends prepublication galleys. Pays 2 copies and a year's subscription.** Reviews books of poetry in 500-5,000 words, single or multi-book format. The press does not usually publish chapbooks.

THE NORTH; THE POETRY BUSINESS; SMITH/DOORSTOP PUBLISHING (III), The Studio, Byram Arcade, Westgate, Huddersfield HD1 1ND England, phone 01484 434840, fax 01484 426566, founded 1986, editors Peter Sansom and Janet Fisher, is a small press and magazine publisher of contemporary poetry. **"No particular restrictions on form, length, etc. But work must be contemporary, of a high standard, and must speak with the writer's own authentic voice. No copies of traditional poems, echoes of old voices, poems about the death of poet's grandfather, poems which describe how miserable the poet is feeling right now."** They have published poetry by Robert Hershon, Paul Violi, Joan Jobe Smith and John Harvey. As a sample, the editors selected these lines from "Swimming the English Channel" by Susan Bright:

> *I did not intend to be a theater.*
> *I do not like the man in the basement who controls me.*
> *I do not want to be a house, a hotel, a car.*
> *I do not like being exposed!*

The North is "⅔ A4 format, 48-52 pgs., offset litho, graphics, ads, colored card cover, staple-bound." It appears 2 times/year. Press run is 600 for 400 subscriptions. Subscription: £10 (£12 US rate). **Submit up to 6 poems at a time. Poems should be typed with writer's name and address on each page.** "We'll accept poems previously published in the U.S. but not the U.K." **Pays 2 copies.** Smith/Doorstop publishes 6 perfect-bound paperbacks/year. **For book consideration, submit 6 sample poems and brief cover letter with bio and previous publications. Responds to queries in 1 month, to mss in 3 months. Pays 20 copies.** They hold an annual book (perfect-bound, laminated) competition. Write for full details. The editors say, "Read plenty of poetry, contemporary and traditional. Attend workshops, etc., and meet other writers. Keep submitting poems, even if you fail. Build up a track record in magazines before trying to get a book published."

NORTHEAST ARTS MAGAZINE; BOSTON ARTS ORGANIZATION, INC. (III), P.O. Box 6061, J.F.K. Station, Boston MA 02114, founded 1990, editor/president Mr. Leigh Donaldson, is a biannual using **poetry that is "honest, clear, with a love of expression through simple language, under 30 lines. Care for words and craftsmanship are appreciated."** They have recently published poetry by S.P. Lutrell, Eliot Richman, Elizabeth R. Curry and Alisa Aran. As a sample the editor selected these lines by Martina Fischer:

> *This golden necklace dropped*
> *into a Venice canal*
> *will kill a man*
> *in New York City. . .*

It is digest-sized, 32 or more pgs., professionally printed with 1-color coated card cover. They accept 20-25% of submissions. Press run is 500-1,000 for 150 subscribers of which half are libraries, 50 to arts organizations. An updated arts information section and feature articles are included. Subscription: $10. **Sample postpaid: $4.50. Reads submissions September 1 through May 30 only. "A short bio is helpful." Send SASE for guidelines. Reports in 1-2 months. Pays 2 copies. Acquires first North American serial rights.**

NORTHEASTERN UNIVERSITY PRESS; SAMUEL FRENCH MORSE POETRY PRIZE (III), Northeastern University, 360 Huntington Ave., Boston MA 02115. The Samuel French Morse Poetry Prize, % Prof. Guy Rotella, Editor, Morse Poetry Prize, English Dept., 406 Holmes, Northeastern University, Boston MA 02115, for book publication (ms 50-70 pgs.) by Northeastern University Press and an **award of $500. Entry fee: $10. Deadline of August 1 for inquiries, September 15 for single copy of ms. Ms will not be returned. Open to US poets who have published no more than 1 book of poetry.**

THE NORTHERN CENTINEL (II), 115 E. 82nd St., Suite 8B, New York NY 10028-0872, founded 1788, poetry editors Ellen Rachlin and Lucie Aidinoff, is a newspaper appearing 6 times/year focusing on "political/cultural essays and analyses on matters of national interest." **They publish 2 poems each issue.** They have recently published poetry by Molly Peacock, Allen Ginsberg and Martin Tucker. It is 20-24 pgs., 11×17, offset on newsprint, with b&w artwork, photos, engravings, woodcuts, political cartoons and ads. Press run is 20,000. Subscription: $15. **Sample postpaid: $2.50. No previously published poems; simultaneous submissions OK. Cover letter with SASE required.** Time between acceptance and publication is up to a year. **Seldom comments on rejections. Reports within 3 months. Pays $40 plus 1 copy.**

‡NORTHERN PERSPECTIVE (II), Northern Territory University, Darwin NT 0909 Australia, phone (089)466124, fax (089)466151, founded 1977, managing editor Dr. Jim Cameron, appears twice a year. This liberal arts journal is magazine-sized, 115-125 pgs., using a full-color cover, professionally printed. Press run is 700 for 300 subscribers of which 20 are libraries, including university and public libraries in the US, UK, Europe and Africa; 300 shelf sales. **Sample postpaid: $7.50 AUD. Submit 3 poems at a time, in March and September. Editor often comments on rejections. Reports "hopefully within 10 weeks." Pays minimum of $20 AUD/poem.** Reviews books of poetry in 300-500 words. "Review articles are 1,500-2,500 words. *NP* reviews are *not* solicited; review articles, however, may be submitted."

‡NORTHWEST LITERARY FORUM; NORTH LAKE PRESS (II, IV-Form), 3439 NE Sandy Blvd. #143, Portland OR 97232, founded 1992, editors Ce Rosenow and Nancy Hune, is a quarterly publication of poetry, short fiction, short plays and essays. **They are open to all types of poetry (except translations) and even have a special section for haiku and related forms.** They have recently published poetry by Taylor Graham, Michael Dylan Welch and Nasira Alma. As a sample the editors selected these lines from "Braiding/Ribbons of Hope" by Victoria Lena Manyarrows:

> some say treaties are made to be broken
> and braiding is out of fashion
> but i'll still braid your ribbons of hope
> joining those strands of strength & years
> weaving us together as one

NLR is 28 pgs., $5\frac{1}{2} \times 8\frac{1}{2}$, offset printed and saddle-stapled with card cover and b&w cover art. Press run is 120 for 80 subscribers, 20 shelf sales. Single copy: $4; subscription: $15. **Sample postpaid: $3. No previously published poems or simultaneous submissions.** Time between acceptance and publication is 1-6 months. **Seldom comments on rejections. Reports in 1 month. Pays 1 copy. Acquires first North American serial rights.** Does not review books of poetry, but lists publications received with ordering information. Poets may send books for listing consideration.

NORTHWEST REVIEW (II), 369 PLC, University of Oregon, Eugene OR 97403, phone (503)346-3957, founded 1957, poetry editor John Witte. They are "seeking excellence in whatever form we can find it" and use **"all types" of poetry.** They have published poetry by Alan Dugan, Olga Broumas, William Stafford and Richard Eberhart. *NR*, a 6×9, flat-spined magazine, appears 3 times/year and uses 25-40 pgs. of poetry in each issue. They receive 3,500 submissions/year, use 4%, have up to a 4-month backlog. Press run is 1,300 for 1,200 subscribers of which half are libraries. **Sample postpaid: $3. Submit 6-8 poems clearly reproduced. No simultaneous submissions.** The editor comments **"whenever possible" on rejections. Send SASE for guidelines. Reports in 8-10 weeks. Pays 3 copies.** Poetry published in this review has been included in *The Best American Poetry 1994*. The editor advises poets to "persist."

NORTHWOODS PRESS; NORTHWOODS JOURNAL: A MAGAZINE FOR WRITERS; C.A.L. (II), P.O. Box 298, Thomaston ME 04861-0298, phone (207)354-0998, Northwoods Press founded 1972, C.A.L. (Conservatory of American Letters) 1986 and *Northwoods Journal* 1993. *Northwoods Journal* is a quarterly literary magazine. **"The journal is interested in all poets who feel they have something to say and who work to say it well. We have no interest in closet poets, or credit seekers. All poets seeking an audience, working to improve their craft and determined to 'get it right' are welcome here. Please request submission guidelines (with SASE) before submitting."** Subscription: $12/ year, free to C.A.L. members. **Sample: $5. Deadlines are the 1st of April, July, October and January for seasonal publication. Reports within 2 weeks after deadline, sometimes sooner. Pays $5/page, average, on acceptance.** "Northwoods Press is designed for the excellent *working poet* who has a following which is likely to create sales of $3,000 or more. Without at least that much of a following and at least that level of sales, no book can be published. Request 15-point poetry program." **Northwoods Press will pay a minimum of $250 advance on contracting a book.** C.A.L. is a nonprofit taxexempt literary/educational foundation; up to 4 anthologies of poetry and prose are published each year. **There is a $1 (cash—no checks) reading fee for each poetry submission to their anthologies, which goes to readers, not to the publisher. Poets are paid $5/page on acceptance, shorter poems pro-**

rata page rate. "**Payment is advance against 10% royalties on all sales we can attribute to the influence of the author.**" Robert Olmsted regards his efforts as an attempt to face reality and provide a sensible royalty-contract means of publishing many books. He says, "**If you are at the stage of considering book publication, have a large number of poems in print in respected magazines, perhaps previous book publication, and are confident that you have a sufficient following to insure very modest sales, send 8½ × 11 SASE (3 oz. postage) for descriptions of the Northwoods Poetry Program and C.A.L.**" His advice is, "**Poetry must be non-trite, non-didactic. It must never bounce. Rhyme, if used at all, should be subtle. One phrase should tune the ear in preparation for the next. They should flow and create an emotional response.**" **Query with cover letter dealing with publication credits and marketing ideas. Submit "entire ms as desired for final book form." No simultaneous submissions; no previously published poems. Pays 10% royalties.** Bob Olmsted "rarely" comments on rejections, but he offers commentary for a fee, though he says he "strongly recommends *against* it." **Query.** Membership in C.A.L. is $24 a year, **however, membership is not required.** Members receive the quarterly *Northwoods Journal* plus 10% discount on all books and have many services available to them. C.A.L. sponsors an annual writers' conference with no tuition, only a $20 registration fee. The *Northwoods Journal* now sponsors "the only no compromise poetry contest in the country." Unpublished poems only. Send SASE for contest guidelines.

W.W. NORTON & COMPANY, INC. (III), 500 Fifth Ave., New York NY 10110, phone (212)354-5500, founded 1925, poetry editor Jill Bialosky. W.W. Norton is a well-known commercial trade publishing house that publishes only original work in both hardcover and paperback. **They want "quality literary poetry" but no "light or inspirational verse."** They have recently published books by Ellen Bryant Voigt, Marilyn Hacker, Joy Harjo, Martin Espada, Stephen Dunn and Eavan Boland. W.W. Norton publishes approximately 10 books of poetry each year with an average page count of 64. They are published in cloth and flat-spined paperbacks, attractively printed, with two-color glossy card covers. **Unsolicited submissions are accepted, but authors should query first, sending credits and 15 sample poems plus bio. Simultaneous submissions will be considered if the editor is notified. Norton will consider only poets whose work has been published in quality literary magazines. They report on queries in 2-3 weeks and mss in 4 months. Catalog is free on request.** W.W. Norton recently published an anthology of Cowboy poets, entitled *Between Earth and Sky: Poets of the Cowboy West*, edited by Anne Heath Widmark. The antholology showcases the work of 12 well-known cowboy poets, including Buck Ramsey, Wallace McRae, Paul Zarzyski and Sue Wallis.

NOSTALGIA: A SENTIMENTAL STATE OF MIND (II), P.O. Box 2224, Orangeburg SC 29116, founded 1986, poetry editor Connie Lakey Martin, appears spring and fall using "**nostalgic poetry, style open, prefer *non* rhyme, but occasional rhyme OK, relatively short poems, never longer than one page, no profanity, no ballads.**" *Nostalgia* is 24 pgs., digest-sized, saddle-stapled, offset typescript, with matte card cover. Press run is 1,000. **Subscription: $5. Sample postpaid: $3.** "Most poems

"Since this was our fall issue, 'The Ferris Wheel' art conjured images of the county fair and all the nostalgia that engulfs us during autumn," says Connie L. Martin, editor/publisher of the South Carolina-based Nostalgia. *The cover image was specially created for this edition by New Jersey resident Michael Debiak, a "faithful subscriber" whose poetry has also been featured in the magazine. The biannual publication primarily publishes nostalgic poetry. Martin says, "We are interested in modern prose poetry packed with expressive moments-that-happen, images, sounds and messages tucked tightly inside."*

NOSTALGIA

NUMBER 17

The Ferris Wheel
1893 World's Columbian Exposition
Chicago, Illinois

A Sentimental
State of Mind

selected from contest." There are contests in each issue with award of $100 and publication for outstanding poem, publication and 1-year subscription for Honorable Mentions. Entry fee of $3 reserves future edition, covers 3 entries. Deadlines: June 30 and December 31 each year. **"Previously published poems OK *with credits*, but prefer no simultaneous submissions." Guidelines available for SASE. Sometimes sends prepublication galleys. All rights revert to author upon publication.** Reviews books of poetry. Open to unsolicited reviews. Poets may also send books for review consideration. Connie Martin says, "I offer criticism to most rejected poems, but I suggest sampling before submitting. I receive a wide variety of poems but most poets don't seem to take time to read what's really accepted in literary magazines. Many are more interested in publication, rather than sampling for preferred use."

NOSUKUMO (V), GPO Box 994-H, Melbourne, Victoria 3001 Australia, founded 1982, editor Javant Biarujia, publishes 1-2 chapbooks/year. **"We publish language-oriented and experimental poetry, as well as literary and social criticism. We are particularly interested in prose poems. However, our program is fully committed for the foreseeable future."** Their products are characterized by elegant printing on quality paper in sewn chapbooks. Send SASE (or SAE and IRCs if outside Australia) for catalog.

NOW AND THEN (IV-Regional, themes), ETSU, P.O. Box 70556, Johnson City TN 37614-0556, phone (615)929-5348, founded 1984, editor-in-chief Jane Woodside, poetry editor Linda Parsons, is a regional magazine that covers Appalachian issues and culture. **The editor specifically wants poetry related to the region. Previous issues have focused on Appalachian politics, storytelling, the Civil War, education, sports, the Scottish-Appalachian connection, New Writing, media, family and community, tourism, and activism. "We want genuine, well-crafted voices, not sentimentalized stereotypes."** They have published poetry by Fred Chappell, Rita Quillen, Michael Chitwood, Jim Wayne Miller and George Ella Lyon. As a sample the editor selected these lines from "For the Cutover Woods of Dixie" by Errol Miller:

> *O Lord of the Long Nap, something*
> *is moving in my net, fermenting, ruling over me,*
> *something sweet and sour like Dixie's*
> *lingering dreams. There is festering within me*
> *a sense of history, of myself, of the earth, of all*
> *the great structures of commerce boarded up,*
> *that reverse momentum where the wind*
> *sways through the trees for a while before*
> *the workmen come to silence the music.*

Now and Then appears three times a year and is 42 pgs., magazine-sized, saddle-stapled, professionally printed, with matte card cover. Its press run is 2,000 for 900 members of the Center for Appalachian Studies and Services, of which 200 are libraries. They accept 6-10 poems an issue. Center membership is $15; the magazine is one of the membership benefits. **Sample: $4.50 plus $1.50 postage. They will consider simultaneous submissions; they occasionally use previously published poems. Submit up to 5 poems, with SASE and cover letter including "a few lines about yourself for a contributor's note and whether the work has been published or accepted elsewhere." Deadlines: March 1, July 1 and November 1. Publishes theme issues. Send SASE for guidelines and upcoming themes. Reports in 4 months. Sometimes sends prepublication galleys. Pays $10/poem plus 2 copies. Acquires all rights.** Reviews books of poetry in 750 words. Open to unsolicited reviews. Poets may also send books for review consideration to Sandy Ballard, book review editor, Dept. of English, Carson-Newman College, Box 2059, Jefferson City TN 37760.

‡NUTHOUSE; TWIN RIVERS PRESS (I, IV-Humor), P.O. Box 119, Ellenton FL 34222, press founded 1989, magazine founded 1993, editor D.A. White. *Nuthouse*, "amusements by and for delightfully diseased minds," appears every 6 weeks using humor of all kinds, including homespun and political. **They simply want "humorous verse; virtually all genres considered."** They have recently published poetry by Holly Day, Daveed Garstenstein-Ross and Don Webb. The editor says *Nuthouse* is 12 pgs., digest-sized and photocopied from desktop-published originals. They receive about 100 poems a year, usually accept about 25. Press run is 100 for 50 subscribers. Subscription: $5/5 issues. **Sample postpaid: $1. Previously published poems and simultaneous submissions OK.** Time between acceptance and publication is 6-12 month. **Often comments on rejections. Reports within 1 month. Pays 1 copy/poem. Acquires one-time rights.**

‡NV MAGAZINE; HOMELESS PUBLICATIONS (I), 4360 E. Main #242, Ventura CA 93003, phone (805)339-8243, founded 1994, editor Heather Woodward, is a bimonthly magazine "dedicated to publishing unknown talent in the USA. **We like to see good, solid, well thought-out poetry; mostly free verse, all subjects. No rhyme. No greeting card verse. Please don't send anything fashionable or trendy, mundane or mainstream."** The editor says they work mainly with unpublished artists. As a sample she selected these lines (poet unidentified):

> *mirrors reflect the sweat*
> *glistening on fingers*
> *pulling hair biting lips*
> *fingers*
> *thin and dainty*
> *handkerchiefs*

The editor says *NV* is 50-100 pgs., 8 × 11, with 100 lb. glossy color cover, b&w text and lots of graphics and ads. She says, "75% of what we receive is poetry. 40% we accept." Their press run is 1,900. Single copy: $5; subscription: $25. **Sample postpaid: $3.50. No previously published poems or simultaneous submissions. Cover letter required. "No SASE = destruction."** Time between acceptance and publication is 6 months. **Always comments on rejections. Send SASE for guidelines. Reports in 3 months. Pays 5 copies. "We retain all periodical rights to what we publish for one year after publication (at which time they revert to the author), and reprint, electronic and anthology rights for the duration of the copyright."** The editor says, "We are particularly interested in poets who incorporate graphics into their writing. We also like liberal and/or opinionated work. We are hard to offend. The more bizarre, left-wing, right-wing or up in the balcony, the better."

THE OAK (I); THE ACORN (I, IV-Children); THE GRAY SQUIRREL (I, IV-Senior citizens); PHANTASM (I, IV-Fantasy, horror, mystery), 1530 Seventh St., Rock Island IL 61201, phone (309)788-3980, poetry editor Betty Mowery. *The Oak*, founded 1990, is a "publication for writers with poetry and fiction (no more than 500 words)." They want poetry **"no more than 32 lines. No restrictions as to types and style, but no pornography."** *The Oak* appears 6 times/year. They take more than half of about 100 poems received each year. Press run is 250, with 10 going to libraries. Subscription: $10. **Sample: $2. Submit 5 poems at a time. Simultaneous submissions and previously published poems OK. Reports in 1 week.** *"The Oak* **does not pay in dollars or copies but you need not purchase to be published." Acquires first or second rights.** *The Oak* holds an Orange Blossom Poetry Contest February 1 through August 1. *The Acorn*, founded 1988, is a "newsletter for young authors and teachers or anyone else interested in our young authors. **Takes mss from kids K-12th grades. Poetry no more than 32 lines.** It also takes fiction of no more than 500 words." It appears 4 times/year and **"we take well over half of submitted mss."** Press run is 100, with 6 going to libraries. Subscription: $10. **Sample postpaid: $2. Submit 5 poems at a time. Simultaneous submissions and previously published poems OK. Reports in 1 week.** *"The Acorn* **does not pay in dollars or copies but you need not purchase to be published." Acquires first or second rights. Young authors, submitting to** *The Acorn***, should put either age or grade on manuscripts.** Founded 1991, *The Gray Squirrel* appears 6 times/year. **Takes poetry of no more than 20 lines only from poets 60 years of age and up.** Press run is about 100. Six issues: $10. **Sample: $2. Submit 5 poems at a time. Reports in 1 week. Acquires first and second rights.** *The Gray Squirrel* sponsors the Minnie Chezum Memorial Contest December through May. *Phantasm*, founded 1993, appears 4 times/year and publishes **soft horror, fantasy and mystery. They want poetry of no more than 35 lines** and fiction up to 500 words. Take well over half of mss submitted. Press run is 75. Subscription: $5. **Sample: $2. Submit 5 poems at a time. Simultaneous submissions and previously published poems OK. Reports in 1 week.** *"Phantasm* **does not pay in dollars or copies but you do not need to purchase to be published."** Sponsors annual poetry contest. Editor Betty Mowery advises, "Beginning poets should submit again as quickly as possible if rejected. Study the market: don't submit blind. Always include a SASE or rejected manuscripts will not be returned. Please make checks for *all* publications payable to *The Oak*."

‡OASIS BOOKS; OASIS (III), 12 Stevenage Rd., London SW6 6ES England, founded 1969, editor and publisher Ian Robinson. *Oasis* is a bimonthly magazine of short fiction and poetry as well as occasional reviews and other material. **"No preference for style or subject matter; just quality. No long poems;** *Oasis* **is a very short magazine. Also, usually no rhyming poetry."** They have published poetry by John Ash, Lee Harwood, George Evans and Roy Fisher. The editor says *Oasis* is international A5 size, litho, folded sheets. They receive 500-600 poems a year, use about 4 or 5. Press run is 500 for 400 subscribers of which 10 are libraries. **Sample postpaid: $2.50. Submit up to 6 poems at a time. Previously published poems sometimes OK; simultaneous submissions OK "if work comes from outside the U.K." Include SAE and 4 IRCs for surface mail return. Seldom comments on rejections OK "if work comes from outside the U.K." Reports in 1 month. Pays 4 copies.** Staff reviews books of poetry. Send books for review consideration. Oasis Books publishes 2-3 paperbacks and 2-3 chapbooks/year. **Replies to queries and mss in 1 month. For sample books or chapbooks, write for catalog.** Ian Robinson says, "One IRC is not enough to ensure return postage; four will, provided manuscript is not too thick. No return postage will ensure that the ms is junked."

OBLATES (IV-Religious, spirituality/inspirational), Missionary Association of Mary Immaculate, 15 S. 59th St., Belleville IL 62223-4694, phone (618)233-2238, editor Christine Portell, is a magazine circulating free to 500,000 benefactors. **"We use well-written, perceptive traditional verse, average 16 lines. Avoid heavy allusions. Good rhyme and/or rhythm a must. We prefer a reverent, inspira-**

tional tone, but not overly 'sectarian and scriptural' in content. We like to use seasonal material. We like traditional poetry (with meter) and are always on the lookout for good Christmas poetry." They have recently published poetry by Jeanette Land, Kathleen Bergeron and Claire Puneky. *Oblates* is 20 pgs., digest-sized, saddle-stapled, using color inside and on the cover. **Sample and guidelines for SAE and 2 first-class stamps. Submit not more than 2 poems at a time. Considers simultaneous submissions.** Time to publication "is usually within 1 to 2 years." **Editor comments "occasionally, but always when ms 'just missed or when a writer shows promise.' " Reports within 4-6 weeks. Pays $30 plus 3 copies. Buys first North American serial rights.** She says, "We are a small publication very open to mss from authors—beginners and professionals. We do, however, demand professional quality work. Poets need to study our publication, **and to send no more than one or two poems at a time. Content must be relevant to our older audience to inspire and motivate in a positive manner."**

‡OFFERINGS (I, IV-Students), P.O. Box 1667, Lebanon MO 65536, founded 1994, editor Velvet Fackeldey, is a poetry quarterly. **"We accept traditional and free verse from established and new poets, as well as students. Prefer poems of less than 30 lines. No erotica."** They have recently published poetry by Michael Estabrook, Kent Braithwaite, John Binns (England) and Robert Boyce (Australia). As a sample we selected the first stanza of "Lightless for Millenia" by Robert Cooperman:

> My mother called today,
> her oldest friend had just died,
> a heaviness in her sentences
> like a horse struggling
> with an eviction wagon
> through Lower East Side mud
> at the turn of the century.

Offerings is 50-60 pgs., digest-sized, neatly printed (one poem to a page) and saddle-stapled with paper cover. They receive about 500 poems a year, accept approximately 25%. Press run is 60 for 25 subscribers, 25 shelf sales. Single copy: $5; subscription: $16. **Sample postpaid: $3. Submit typed poems with name and address on each page. Students should also include grade level. SASE required. No previously published poems or simultaneous submissions. Seldom comments on rejections. Send SASE for guidelines. Reports in 1 week. Acquires first rights.** The editor says, "We are unable to offer payment at this time (not even copies) but hope to be able to do so in the future. We welcome beginning poets."

OFFICE NUMBER ONE (I, IV-Form), 1708 S. Congress Ave., Austin TX 78704, founded 1988, editor Carlos B. Dingus, appears 2-4 times/year. *ONO* is a "zine of news information and events from parallel and alternate realities." In addition to stories, they want **mostly limericks, but 3-5-3 or 5-7-5 haiku and rhymed/metered quatrains are also acceptable. Poems should be short (2-12 lines) and make a point. No long rambling poetry about suffering and pathos. Need metered poetry that is technically perfect."** As for a sample, the editor says, "No one poem will provide a fair sample of what I accept." *ONO* is 12 pgs., $8\frac{1}{2} \times 11$, computer set in 10 pt. type, saddle-stitched, with graphics and ads. They use about 20 poems a year. Press run is 2,000 for 75 subscribers, 50 shelf sales, 1,600 distributed free locally. Single copy: $1.85; subscription: $8.82/6 issues. **Sample postpaid: $2. Submit up to 5 pgs. of poetry at a time. Previously published poems and simultaneous submissions OK. "Will comment on rejections if comment is requested." Publishes theme issues occasionally. Send SASE for guidelines and upcoming themes. Reports in 1 month. Pays "23¢" and 1 copy. Buys "one-time use, and use in any *ONO* anthology."** The editor says, "Say something that can change a life."

THE OGALALA REVIEW (II), P.O. Box 628, Guymon OK 73942, founded 1990, editors Gordon Grice and Tracy Hiatt Grice, is an annual journal of poetry, fiction, creative nonfiction and translation, **interested in all styles of poetry.** They have published poetry by Enid Shomer and Trent Busch. As a sample the editors selected these lines from " 'Large Bear Deceives Me' " by David Citino:

> He could turn even a song
>
> against you, rearing suddenly
> as you open wide as night
> to life's final surprise,
> the sweet delicate meat of you.

Format for *The Ogalala Review* varies, but the most recent issue we received was 120 pgs., digest-sized, perfect-bound, with glossy cover. They receive about 2,000 poems a year, use about 2%. Subscription: $10. **Sample postpaid: $5. Include name and address on each poem. Simultaneous submissions OK, "but writers must notify us promptly of acceptance elsewhere. We do not normally consider previously published work."** For translations, include written permission from copyright holder or statement that the work is in the public domain. **Publishes theme issues. Send SASE for guidelines and upcoming themes. Reports in 2 months or less. Pays 2 copies. Acquires**

first serial rights only. "We are phasing out our review section, but will list all books received." The editors add, "Because the magazine is under new staff, we suggest people who haven't seen it recently order a sample or a subscription."

THE OHIO POETRY REVIEW; THE BACCHAE PRESS; THE BACCHAE PRESS CHAPBOOK CONTEST (II), 985 Hyde-Shaffer Rd., Bristolville OH 44402, founded 1992, editor/publisher Robert Brown. *The Ohio Poetry Review* (formerly *Oregon Review*) is a nationally distributed biannual magazine of poetry and reviews. **"We're open to all types of poetry. We want poems that surprise and delight us. We'd like to see more good language and experimental poems. No didactic, badly rhymed, overly sentimental poems written by beginners who haven't practiced their craft."** They have published poetry by Robert Wrigley, Heather McHugh, David Citino and Vern Rutsala. As a sample the editor selected these lines from "The Clam Diggers" by E.G. Burrows:

> *What the sea leaves behind are craters,*
> *fragments of sky in sloughs*
>
> *like the kettles where glacial ice*
> *boiled and melted, hollows*
> *like any odd life or country*
> *you might unwarily stumble into.*

The Ohio Poetry Review is 60-80 pgs., digest-sized, professionally printed, flat-spined with heavy matte cover. They receive about 10,000 poems a year, publish approximately 1%. Press run is 500 for 100 subscribers of which 50 are libraries, 300 shelf sales. Subscription: $9. **Sample postpaid: $5. Submit no more than 6 pgs. at a time. Send clean copies of poems with name and address on each. No previously published poems; simultaneous submissions OK. Cover letter preferred.** Time between acceptance and publication is 6 months. **Seldom comments on rejections. Reports in 2 months. Pays 1 copy. Buys first North American serial rights.** Reviews books and chapbooks of poetry. "We usually review books by Ohio poets and *Ohio Poetry Review* contributors." Open to unsolicited reviews. Poets may also send books for review consideration, attn. review editor. The Bacchae Press also publishes 1-3 paperback books of poetry and 3-5 chapbooks each year. **Query first with sample poems and cover letter with brief bio and publication credits. Replies in 6 months. Pays 10% royalties and 10 author's copies. Send $8 for a sample book, $5 for a chapbook.** One of the two chapbooks is selected for publication through an annual contest. Send SASE for information.

THE OHIO REVIEW (II); OHIO REVIEW BOOKS (V), 209C Ellis Hall, Ohio University, Athens OH 45701-2979, phone (614)593-1900, founded 1959, editor Wayne Dodd, attempts "to publish the best in contemporary poetry, fiction and reviews" in the *Review* and in chapbooks, flat-spined paperbacks and hardback books. They use **"all types"** of poetry and have published poems by David Baker, William Matthews, Lynn Emanuel and Robin Behn. As a sample the editor selected these lines from "Alba" by Pamela Kircher:

> *The lovers rise from bed and leave*
> *the fire banked in ashes,*
> *stars dim and disappearing*
> *as night unpins and drops*
> *its faded cloth.*

The Ohio Review appears 3 times/year in a professionally printed, flat-spined format of 140 pgs., matte cover with color and art, circulation 2,000, featuring about 18 poets/issue. One of the respected "credits" in the literary world, this magazine tends to publish mostly lyric and narrative free verse with an emphasis on voice. Content, structure and length seem open, and voices tend to complement each other, evidence of careful editing. Moreover, you'll find top-name writers appearing with relative newcomers. They receive about 3,000 submissions/year, use 1% of them, and have a 6- to 12-month backlog. Subscription: $16. **Sample postpaid: $4.25. Reads submissions September 15 through April 30 only. Editor sometimes comments on rejections. Send SASE for guidelines. Reports in 1 month. Always sends prepublication galleys. Pays $1/line for poems and $5/page for prose plus copies. Buys first North American serial rights.** Reviews books of poetry in 5-10 pgs., single or multi-book format. Send books to Robert Kinsley for review consideration. **They are not presently accepting unsolicited submissions of book mss. Query with publication credits, bio.** Work published in *The*

Market conditions are constantly changing! If you're still using this book and it is 1997 or later, buy the newest edition of Poet's Market *at your favorite bookstore or order directly from* Writer's Digest Books.

Ohio Review has been included in *The Best American Poetry* (1992 and 1993) and *Pushcart Prize* anthologies.

OHIO STATE UNIVERSITY PRESS/THE JOURNAL AWARD IN POETRY (II), 180 Pressey Hall, 1070 Carmack Rd., Columbus OH 43210-1002, phone (614)292-6930, poetry editor David Citino. Each year *The Journal* (see that listing) selects for publication by Ohio State University Press for the Ohio State University Press/Journal Award **one full-length (at least 48 pgs.) book ms submitted during September, typed, double-spaced, $15 handling fee (payable to OSU).** Send SASE for return of ms; self-addressed, stamped postcard for notification of ms receipt. **Some or all of the poems in the collection may have appeared in periodicals, chapbooks or anthologies, but must be identified. Along with publication,** *The Journal* **Award in Poetry pays $1,000 cash prize from the Helen Hooven Santmyer Fund "in addition to the usual royalties."** Each entrant receives a subscription (2 issues) to *The Journal.*

‡OLD CROW REVIEW (III), P.O. Box 662, Amherst MA 01004-0662, e-mail tkelley@ais.smith.edu, founded 1990, editors John Gibney and Tawnya Kelley, is a biannual magazine with mythic concerns, "visions or fragments of visions of a new myth." It includes novel fragments, short stories, poems, essays, interviews, photography and art. **They have no specifications regarding form, length, subject matter or style of poetry.** They have recently published poetry by Simon Perchick, Patricia Martin and Pat Schneider. As a sample the editors selected these lines from "The Density of Her Gaze" by Christopher Jones:

> *I have never seen my mother, but I*
> *can feel sometimes when she goes by,*
> *crouched down in a taxicab.*
>
> *She hides from me, has always hidden.*
> *I know my mother only through blurry spy*
> *photographs and the density of her gaze.*

Old Crow is 100 pgs., digest-sized, neatly printed and perfect-bound with card cover. They receive about 1,000 submissions a year, accept 2-3%. Press run is 500. Subscription: $9/year. **Sample postpaid: $5. (A portion of the sale price from each review goes to Food For All, a nonprofit organization benefiting the hungry and homeless.) Submit 3-6 poems at a time. Previously published poems and simultaneous submissions OK. Cover letter with brief bio (for Contributor's Notes) required. Reads submissions February 1 through July 30 and October 1 through December 15. Poems are screened by editorial assistants then the editorial board then the editor-in-chief (John Gibney). Seldom comments on rejections. Reports in 1 month. Pays 1 copy. Copyright reverts to poet at publication.** Open to unsolicited reviews. The editors say, "Long live the new flesh!"

THE OLD RED KIMONO (I, II), P.O. Box 1864, Rome GA 30162, phone (706)295-6312, founded 1972, poetry editors Valerie Gilreath and Jon Hershey, a publication of the Humanities Division of Floyd College, has the "sole purpose of putting out a magazine of original, high-quality poetry and fiction. *ORK* **is looking for submissions of 3-5 short poems. Poems should be very concise and imagistic. Nothing sentimental or didactic."** They have recently published poetry by Walter McDonald, Peter Huggins, Midred Greear, John C. Morrison, Jack Stewart, Kirsten Fox and Al Braselton. The magazine is an annual, circulation 1,400, 72 pgs., 8½×11, professionally printed on heavy stock with b&w graphics, colored matte cover with art, using approximately 40 pgs. of poetry (usually 1 or 2 poems to the page). They receive 1,000 submissions/year, use 60-70. **Reading period is September 1 through March 1. Reports in 3 months. Pays copies. Acquires first publication rights.**

THE OLIVE PRESS PUBLICATIONS (V), Box 99, Los Olivos CA 93441, phone/fax (805)688-2445, founded 1979, editor Lynne Norris, is a general small press publisher for whom "poetry is an incidental effort at this time. We specialize in local and family history." They have previously published *It Don't Hurt to Laugh*, a collection of cowboy poetry by Jake Copass.

OLYMPIA REVIEW; ZERO CITY PRESS; ORVILLE BABCOCK MEMORIAL POETRY PRIZE (II), 3430 Pacific Ave. SE, Suite A-6254, Olympia WA 98501, founded 1992, editor Michael McNeilley, managing editor Stephanie Brooks, appears at least twice annually, publishing "the best available contemporary writing, without regard for rules, conventions or precedent. **No taboos, beyond reasonably good taste; style and talent, significance and artistry are our only criteria. Seldom use rhyme. Nothing incidental, religious or sentimental. Prefer poems under 50 lines or so."** They have published poetry by Charles Bukowski, Ronald Wallace, Hayley R. Mitchell, Albert Huffstickler, Errol Miller, Virgil Hervey, Antler, Kurt Nimmo, John Forrest Glade, Matt Dennison and Lyn Lifshin. As a sample the editor selected this poem, "I Love You," by Janet Bernichon:

> *say it say it say it*
> *say it 'till it sounds like breathing*

whispered lips apart
hissed through teeth
say it

The editor says *OR* is 60-100 pgs., digest-sized, flat-spined, with 2-color coated card cover, art, graphics, photos and ads. Press run is 750-1,000. Subscription: $12.95 for 4 issues. **Sample postpaid: $4.50. Submit up to 6 poems at a time. Previously published poems ("tell us where") and simultaneous submissions OK. Cover letter and short bio required. Seldom comments on rejections. Send SASE for guidelines. Reports in 1-12 months. Pays 1 copy. Acquires first North American serial or one-time rights.** Reviews books of poetry and magazines in up to 700 words, single or multi-book format. Zero City Press publishes 1-2 chapbooks/year in varied formats; authors selected from those published in *OR*. They also publish a periodic broadside "using work representative of the quality found in the *Olympia Review*." Pays 3 copies. *OR* also sponsors the annual Orville Babcock Memorial Poetry Prize. Maximum 36 lines. Entry fee: $2/poem; 3 poems for $5. Deadline: December 1. Winners receive publication in annual contest issue, free subscription and other prizes. Entries cannot be returned. Send SASE for list of winners. The editor advises poets to "start with the classics, to see where poetry has been. Then read more poetry, and fiction, in the little magazines, where today's writing is found. Develop your own voice, write a clean line, edit mercilessly and you may help determine where poetry is going. We look for poetry, prose and things between that illuminate archetypal hopes, fears, dreams and understandings. We want every issue of *OR* to connect with every reader, in as visceral a way as possible. Read an issue, see firsthand what we're up to, then submit."

‡ON SPEC: THE CANADIAN MAGAZINE OF SPECULATIVE WRITING (IV-Regional, science fiction/fantasy), P.O. Box 4727, Edmonton, Alberta T6E 5G6 Canada, founded 1989, is a quarterly featuring Canadian science fiction writers and artists. **They want work by Canadian poets only and only science fiction/speculative poetry. 100 lines maximum.** They have recently published poetry by Alice Major and Eileen Kernaghan. *On Spec* is 96 pgs., digest-sized, offset printed on recycled paper and perfect-bound with color cover, b&w art and ads inside. They receive about 100 poems a year, accept approximately 5%. Press run is 1,750 for 800 subscribers of which 10 are libraries, 600 shelf sales. Single copy: $4.95; subscription: $19.95 (both in Canadian funds). **Sample postpaid: $6. Submit no more than 5 poems at a time, in "competition format" (author's name should not appear on the ms). No previously published poems or simultaneous submissions. Cover letter with poem titles and 2-sentence bio required.** Time between acceptance and publication is 6 months. **Poems are circulated to an editorial board. Seldom comments on rejections. Send SASE for guidelines. Reports in 5 months maximum. Pays $15/poem and 1 copy. Acquires first North American serial rights.**

ONIONHEAD; ARTS ON THE PARK, INC. (THE LAKELAND CENTER FOR CREATIVE ARTS); WORDART, THE NATIONAL POETS COMPETITION; ESMÉ BRADBERRY CONTEMPORARY POETS PRIZE (II), 115 N. Kentucky Ave., Lakeland FL 33801-5044, phone (813)680-2787. Arts on the Park founded 1979; *Onionhead* founded 1988. *Onionhead* is a literary quarterly. **"Our focus is on provocative political, social and cultural observations and hypotheses. Controversial material is encouraged. International submissions are welcome. We have no taboos, but provocation is secondary to literary excellence. No light verse please."** They have published poetry by Jessica Freeman, Arthur Knight, Lyn Lifshin, B.Z. Niditch and A.D. Winans. As a sample we selected these lines from "Paying Back Karma" by Jo Ann Lordahl:

This bed I made
will haunt me

Until I burn it
bury it, or defuse it.

The magazine is 40-50 pgs., digest-sized, photocopied from typescript, saddle-stapled with glossy card cover. They use 100 of 2,500 submissions received/year. Press run is 250. Complimentary distribution to universities, reviews and libraries worldwide. Subscription: $8 US, $16 other. **Sample postpaid: $3. Submit 3-8 poems at a time, maximum 60 lines each. No previously published poems or simultaneous submissions. Short cover letter preferred. Poet's name and title of poems should appear on the upper right-hand corner of each page. Poem "should be submitted exactly as you intend it to appear if selected for publication." SASE required for return of material.** Editor comments on rejections "rarely." Poems are reviewed by an Editorial Board and **submissions are reported on within 2 months. If accepted, poems will normally appear within one year. Pays 1 copy. Acquires first serial rights.** WORDART, The National Poets Competition, established 1983, is open to all American authors. Cash awards, "including the prestigious Esmé Bradberry Contemporary Poets Prize and chapbook, are announced at a reading and reception during the first part of March." $5 reading fee. For guidelines and specific dates send SASE to the sponsoring organization, Arts on the Park, Inc., at the above address.

ONTARIO REVIEW; ONTARIO REVIEW PRESS (V), 9 Honey Brook Dr., Princeton NJ 08540, founded 1974. *Ontario Review* appears twice a year. They have published poetry by William Heyen, Alicia Ostriker, Albert Goldbarth and Jana Harris. **However, they are currently not accepting unsolicited poetry.** *OR* is 112 pgs., 6×9, offset, flat-spined. Press run is 1,200 for 650 subscribers of which 450 are libraries, 250 shelf sales, 75 direct sales. Subscription: $12. **Sample postpaid: $6.** Poetry published in this review has been included in *The Best American Poetry 1993*. **Ontario Review Press is also not currently considering new poetry mss. They publish 1-2 hardbacks and that many paperbacks/year, paying 10% royalties plus 10 copies.**

ONTHEBUS; BOMBSHELTER PRESS (II), P.O. Box 481270, Bicentennial Station, Los Angeles CA 90048, founded 1975, *ONTHEBUS* editor Jack Grapes, Bombshelter Press poetry editors Jack Grapes and Michael Andrews. *ONTHEBUS* uses **"contemporary mainstream poetry—no more than 6 poems (10 pgs. total) at a time. No rhymed, 19th Century traditional 'verse.' "** They have published poetry by Charles Bukowski, Albert Goldbarth, Ai, Norman Dubie, Kate Braverman, Stephen Dobyns, Allen Ginsberg, David Mura, Richard Jones and Ernesto Cardenal. As a sample Jack Grapes selected these lines from "A Significant Poet" by Michael Andrews:

> Tu Fu knew what I found out—
> a poet that leaves his poems to unborn children
> is planting dandelions on his grave.
> Pissing on your grave won't make the roses grow.
> For all the difference the poem will make
> it is better to dig an honest trench.

ONTHEBUS is a magazine appearing 2 times/year, 275 pgs., offset, flat-spined, with color card cover. Press run is 3,500 for 600 subscribers of which 40 are libraries, 1,200 shelf sales ("500 sold directly at readings"). Subscription: $28 for 3 issues; Issue #8/9, special double issue: $15. **Sample postpaid: $12. Guidelines are printed on the copyright page of each issue. Submit 3-6 poems at a time. Simultaneous submissions and previously published poems OK, "if I am informed where poem has previously appeared and/or where poem is also being submitted. I expect neatly typed, professional looking cover letters with list of poems included plus poet's bio. Sloppiness and unprofessional submissions do not equate with great writing." Do not submit mss between November 1 and March 1 or between June 1 and September 1. Submissions sent during those times will be returned unread. Reports in "anywhere from 2 weeks to 2 years." Pays 1 copy. Acquires one-time rights. No comments on rejections.** Reviews books of poetry in 400 words (chapbooks in 200 words), single format. Open to unsolicited reviews. Poets may also send books for review consideration. This exciting journal seems a cross between *The Paris Review* and *New York Quarterly* with a distinct West Coast flavor that puts it in a league of its own. Editor Jack Grapes jampacks each issue with dozens upon dozens of poems, mostly free verse (lyric, narrative, dramatic)—some tending toward avant-garde and some quite accessible—that manages somehow to reach out and say: "Read Me." Poetry published in *ONTHEBUS* has been included in *The Best American Poetry 1993*. Bombshelter Press publishes 4-6 flat-spined paperbacks and 5 chapbooks/year. **Query first. Primarily interested in Los Angeles poets. "We publish very few unsolicited mss." Reports in 3 months. Pays 50 copies.** Jack Grapes says, "My goal is to publish a democratic range of American poets and insure they are read by striving to circulate the magazine as widely as possible. It's hard work and a financial drain. I hope the mag is healthy for poets and writers, and that they support the endeavor by subscribing as well as submitting."

OPEN HAND PUBLISHING INC. (V), P.O. Box 22048, Seattle WA 98122, phone (206)323-2187, fax (206)323-2188, founded 1981, publisher P. Anna Johnson, is a "literary/political book publisher" bringing out flat-spined paperbacks as well as cloth cover editions about African-American and multicultural issues." They have recently published *Puerto Rican Writers at Home in the USA*, "an anthology of seventeen of the most well-known Puerto Rican writers"; *Where Are the Love Poems for Dictators?* by E. Ethelbert Miller; and *Stone on Stone/Piedra Sobre Piedra*, a bilingual anthology edited by Zoë Anglesey. **They do not consider unsolicited mss. Send SASE for catalog to order samples.**

ORACLE POETRY; ASSOCIATION OF AFRICAN WRITERS; RISING STAR PUBLISHERS (I, IV-Ethnic), 2105 Amherst Rd., Hyattsville MD 20783, phone (301)422-2665, founded 1989, editorial director Obi Harrison Ekwonna. *Oracle Poetry* and *Oracle Story* appear quarterly using works **"mainly of African orientation; must be probing and must have meaning—any style or form. Writers must have the language of discourse and good punctuation. No gay, lesbian or erotic poetry."** As a sample the editor selected these lines from "War of 1968" by Greggette Soto:

> Twenty-three years ago
> A son went off to war
> It wasn't to fight
> Communism in Vietnam

> *But to fight*
> *Racism in his own backyard.*

Membership in the Association of African Writers is $20/year. The editor describes *Oracle Poetry* as digest-sized, saddle-stapled, print run 500. Subscription: $20/year. **No previously published poems or simultaneous submissions. Reports in 4-6 weeks. Pays copies. Acquires first North American serial rights.** Reviews books of poetry. The editor says, "Read widely, write well and punctuate right."

ORBIS: AN INTERNATIONAL QUARTERLY OF POETRY AND PROSE (II); RHYME INTERNATIONAL COMPETITION FOR RHYMING POETRY (IV-Form),

199 The Long Shoot, Nuneaton, Warwickshire CV11 6JQ England, founded 1968, editor Mike Shields, considers **"all poetry so long as it's genuine in feeling and well executed of its type."** They have published poetry by Sir John Betjeman, Ray Bradbury, Seamus Heaney and Naomi Mitchison, as well as a US issue including Bukowski, Levertov, Piercy, Stafford and many others, "but are just as likely to publish absolute unknowns." The quarterly is $6 \times 8\frac{1}{2}$, flat-spined, 64 pgs., professionally printed with glossy card cover. They receive "thousands" of submissions/year, use less than 5%." Circulation 1,000 with 600 subscriptions of which 50 are libraries. Single copy: £3.95 ($6); subscription: £15 ($28). **Sample postpaid: $2 (or £1). Submit one poem/sheet, typed on 1 side only. No bio, no query. Enclose IRCs for reply, not US postage. Reports in 1-2 months. Pays $10 or more/acceptance plus 1 free copy automatically. Each issue carries £50 in prizes paid on basis of reader votes. Editor comments on rejections "occasionally—if we think we can help.** *Orbis* is completely independent and receives no grant-aid from anywhere." They sponsor the Rhyme International Competition for Rhyming Poetry. The competition has 2 categories (open class, any rhyming poem up to 50 lines; strict form class) with prizes averaging £500 in each class each year (at least 60% of fees received); minimum entry fee. They claim to be "the only competition in the world exclusively for rhymed poetry." Write for entry form. Deadline: September 30.

ORCHISES PRESS (II),

P.O. Box 20602, Alexandria VA 22320-1602, founded 1983, poetry editor Roger Lathbury, is a small press publisher of literary and general material in flat-spined paperbacks. **"Although we will consider mss submitted, we prefer to seek out the work of poets who interest us."** Regarding poetry he states: **"No restrictions, really; but it must be technically proficient and deeply felt. I find it increasingly unlikely that I would publish a ms unless a fair proportion of its contents has appeared previously in respected literary journals."** He has recently published poetry by L.S. Asekoff and Greg Kuzma. Asked for a sample, he says, "I find this difficult, but . . ." (from Fred Dings's "Redwing Blackbirds"):

> *Tonight, as I look at the cold sky*
> *and its flock of blue-white scars,*
> *I can't yet turn from Orion's red star*
> *whose trembling red light has traveled for years*
> *to die now into any eyes that will hold it.*

He publishes about 4 flat-spined paperbacks of poetry a year, averaging 96 pgs., and some casebound books. **Submit 5-6 poems at a time. Poems must be typed. When submitting, "tell where poems have previously been published." Brief, polite cover letter preferred. Reports in 1 month. Pays 36% of money earned once Orchises recoups its initial costs.**

ORE (III, IV-Psychic/occult, spirituality/inspirational),

7 The Towers, Stevenage, Hertfordshire SG1 1HE England, founded 1955, editor Eric Ratcliffe, is a magazine that appears 2-3 times/year. They want work that is or relates to **"folk, legend, Celtic, Arthurian, romantic, spiritual, religious. No obscenities or too much materialism."** They have published poetry by Peter Russell, Jay Ramsay and James Kirkup. As a sample the editor selected these lines from "Fishermen in Marusici, Croatia" by Isabel Cortan:

> *pale water strokes the boat*
> *moon washed the night*
> *a shining silk of sea*
> *lit by a gala melon globe*
>
> *a lantern throws soft light*
> *upon bent heads of men*
> *who cast with canny hands*
> *their lines into the sea*

They receive about 1,000 poems/year, accept 5%. **Sample: £2.40 (surface mail) or 6 IRCs. Simultaneous submissions OK. Brief cover letter noting "items forwarded and successes elsewhere" recommended. Editor *always* comments—"no curt rejection slips." Pays 1 copy, others at half price.** Staff reviews books of poetry. Send books for review consideration. Query regarding unsolicited reviews. He advises: "1.) Realize what your type of interest is and your educational and expression limits. 2.) Read lots of poetry consistent with 1. Dwell internally on imagery, etc. 3.) Write poetry when something comes in the head—don't intend to write first. 4.) Put it away for a week and rewrite it."

OREGON EAST (II, IV-Regional), Hoke Center, Eastern Oregon State College, La Grande OR 97850, phone (503)962-3787, founded 1950, editor changes yearly, is the "literary annual of EOSC, 50% of magazine open to off-campus professional writing." Their preferences: **"Eclectic tastes in poetry with the only requirement being literary quality work for off-campus submissions. Chances of publication are better for short poems (one page) than longer ones. Northwest themes welcome. No 'greeting card' verse."** They have published poetry and fiction by Felicia Mitchell, Mark Shadle, Jessica Mills, David Reimer and Kari Sharp Hill. It is flat-spined, book format, typeset, with end papers, 6×9, approximately 100 pgs., using graphics and b&w art. Content tends toward free verse lyrics. Editors try to give readers an overview of art in each issue, from poetry to prose to graphics. "We also publish short one-act plays." Circulation is 1,000 (300 off-campus) with 100 subscribers of which 30-40 are libraries. Single copy: $5. Special 35-year issue available for $9.95 (256 pgs.). "Our 35-year anthology includes work by William Stafford, Ursula K. LeGuin, George Venn and Vern Rutsala." **Submit only 3-5 typed poems at a time. No simultaneous submissions. All submissions must be accompanied by SASE and cover letter with brief bio and phone number. Reads submissions September 1 through March 1 only. Notification by June. Sometimes sends prepublication galleys. Pays 2 copies. Acquires all rights. Returns rights "with condition that *Oregon East* may reprint in any upcoming anthology."** The editor says, "When I read poetry, I look for original images that address the senses in startling new ways. We're always on the lookout for new voices that are exploring the human experience in an inventive fashion."

ORTALDA & ASSOCIATES (V), 1208 Delaware St., Berkeley CA 94702, founded 1985, poetry editor Floyd Salas, director/editor Claire Ortalda, publishes quality flat-spined paperbacks of poetry but **is not accepting submissions at this time.** They have published poetry by Czeslaw Milosz, Robert Hass, Ishmael Reed, Gary Soto, Jack Micheline and Carolyn Kizer. As a sample Claire Ortalda selected these lines by Floyd Salas:

> There is no honor among thieves
> He will bleed me down to serum for his vein
> and pop me into his arm
> He will sell me to the fence
> at the corner grocery store

OSIRIS, AN INTERNATIONAL POETRY JOURNAL/UNE REVUE INTERNATIONALE (II, IV-Translations, bilingual), P.O. Box 297, Deerfield MA 01342-0297, founded 1972, poetry editor Andrea Moorhead, is a 6×9, saddle-stapled, 40-page semiannual that **publishes contemporary poetry in English, French and Italian without translation and in other languages with translation, including Polish, Danish and German.** They also publish graphics and photographs. They want poetry which is **"lyrical, non-narrative, multi-temporal, post modern, well crafted. Also looking for translations from non-IndoEuropean languages."** They have recently published poetry by Richard Jones, Ingrid Swanberg, Louise Dupré (Quebec) and Robert Marteau (France). As a sample the editor selected this poem, "In Memoriam," by Eugenio de Andrade, translated from the Portuguese by Alexis Levitin:

> An open night,
> the moon
> stumbling among the reeds.
> What's it looking for?
> A root of blood?
> A river to sleep in?

There are 15-20 pgs. of poetry in English in each issue of this intriguing publication. They have a print run of 500 and send 50 subscription copies to college and university libraries, including foreign libraries. They receive 200-300 unsolicited submissions/year, use 12. Single copy: $6; subscription: $12. **Sample postpaid: $3. Submit 4-6 poems at a time. Include short bio and SASE with submission. "Translators should include a letter of permission from the poet or publisher as well as copies of the original text." Reports in 1 month. Sometimes sends prepublication galleys. Pays 5 copies.** If you translate poems from other countries or want to gain an international perspective on the art, you should send for a sample copy. Two poems published in *Osiris* have received Honorable Mentions from *The Pushcart Prize*. The editor advises, "It is always best to look at a sample copy of a journal before submitting work, and when you do submit work, do it often and do not get discouraged. Try to read poetry and support other writers."

THE OTHER SIDE MAGAZINE (III, IV-Political, religious, social issues), 300 W. Apsley St., Philadelphia PA 19144, phone (215)849-2178, founded 1965, poetry editor Rod Jellema, is a "magazine (published 6 times a year) concerned with **social justice issues from a Christian perspective. The magazine publishes 1-2 poems per issue. Submissions should be of high quality and must speak to**

and/or reflect the concerns and life experiences of the magazine's readers. We look for fresh insights and creative imagery in a tight, cohesive whole. Be warned that only 0.5% of the poems reviewed are accepted. Seldom does any published poem exceed 40-50 lines. We do not want to see pious religiosity, sentimental schlock or haiku." They have recently published poetry by Kathleen Norris, Paul Ramsey, Carol Hamilton and John Knoepfle. *The Other Side* is magazine-sized, professionally printed on quality pulp stock, 64 pgs., saddle-stapled, with full-color paper cover, circulation 13,000 to that many subscriptions. Subscription: $29.50. **Sample postpaid: $4.50. Submit 3-5 poems at a time. No simultaneous submissions. No previously published poems. Editor "almost never" comments on rejections. Send SASE for guidelines. Pays $15 plus 4 copies and free subscription.**

‡**OTIS RUSH; LITTLE ESTHER BOOKS (III)**, P.O. Box 21, North Adelaide 5006 South Australia, founded 1987, editor Ken Bolton. *Otis Rush*, appearing every 4 to 10 months, is a journal of "new writing, mostly poetry, some prose, plus writing on Australian visual art and occasional literary reviews." **They want "new, self-conscious, stylistically aware poetry."** They have recently published poetry by Harry Mathews, Tony Towle, Jenny Bornholdt and Gregory O'Brien. The editor says *OR* is 120-150 pgs., offset, perfect-bound, with some ads and art. Press run is 500 for about 100 subscribers of which 15 are libraries, 200 shelf sales. Single copy: $15; subscription: $40 Australian, $60 overseas. **Sample postpaid: $14. Submit 3-6 poems at a time. Previously published poems and simultaneous submissions OK. Cover letter required. Often comments on rejections. Send SASE for guidelines. Reports in 2 months. Pays $10/page minimum. Buys first publication rights.** Little Esther Books publishes 1-6 paperbacks/year. **Replies to queries in 1 month, to mss in 3-4 months. Pays 10% royalties and 15 author's copies.**

OTTER (IV-Regional), Parford Cottage, Chagford, Devon TQ13 8JR United Kingdom, founded 1988, editor Christopher Southgate, appears 3 times/year **using poetry by contributors associated with the County of Devon, "poems concerned with local community and issues—social, political, religious—and/or in strict forms."** They have published poetry by Lawrence Sail, Ron Tamplin, Harry Guest and Jane Beeson. As a sample, here are lines from "The Yellow and Green Daughter" by Sandra McBain:

> She dances like a daffodil
> or wind driven forsythia
> like a petal whirled in water

It is digest-sized, 48 pgs., stapled with glossy card cover, professionally printed. They accept about 25% of 400-500 poems/year. Press run is 400 for 70 subscribers of which 5 are libraries. Subscription: £6.50. **Sample postpaid: £2 (or $5 US; dollar checks OK). Submit up to 5 poems at a time. "Those not resident in Devon should indicate in their cover letter their connection with the county." Editor always comments on rejections. Reports within 3 months. Pays 1 copy.**

OUR FAMILY (IV-Religious), Box 249, Battleford, Saskatchewan S0M 0E0 Canada, phone (306)937-7771, fax (306)937-7644, founded 1949, editor Nestor Gregoire, o.m.i., is a monthly religious magazine for Roman Catholic families. **"Any form of poetry is acceptable. In content we look for simplicity and vividness of imagery. The subject matter should center on the human struggle to live out one's relationship with the God of the Bible in the context of our modern world. We do not want to see science fiction poetry, metaphysical speculation poetry, or anything that demeans or belittles the spirit of human beings or degrades the image of God in him/her as it is described in the Bible."** They have published poetry by Nadene Murphy and Arthur Stilwell. *Our Family* is 40 pgs., magazine-sized, glossy color paper cover, using drawings, cartoons, two-color ink. Circulation 10,000 of which 48 are libraries. Single copy: $1.95; subscription: $15.98 Canada/$21.98 US. **Sample postpaid: $2.50. Send SASE or SAE with IRC or personal check (American postage cannot be used in Canada) for writer's guidelines. Will consider poems of 4-30 lines. Simultaneous submissions OK. Reports within 1 month after receipt. Pays 75¢-$1/line.** The editor advises, "The essence of poetry is imagery. The form is less important. Really good poets use both effectively."

OUTERBRIDGE (II), English A324, The College of Staten Island, 2800 Victory Blvd., Staten Island NY 10314, phone (718)982-3640, founded 1975, editor Charlotte Alexander, publishes "the most crafted, professional poetry and short fiction we can find (unsolicited except special features—to date rural, urban and Southern, promoted in standard newsletters such as *Poets & Writers, AWP, Small Press Review*), interested in newer voices. **Anti loose, amateurish, uncrafted poems showing little awareness of the long-established fundamentals of verse; also anti blatant PRO-movement writing when it sacrifices craft for protest and message. Poems usually 1-4 pgs. in length."** They have recently published poetry by Walter McDonald, Thomas Swiss and Naomi Rachel. As a sample the editor selected these lines from "How to Imagine Deafness" by Kim Roberts:

> Darken your ears until the tunnels
> with their intricate clockwork
> are sheathed in pitchy calm.

Hum a little blue, to yourself,

but keep it secret.

The digest-sized, flat-spined annual is 100 pgs., about half poetry, circulation 500-600, 150 subscriptions of which 28 are libraries. They receive 500-700 submissions/year, use about 60. **Sample postpaid: $5. Submit 3-5 poems only, anytime except June and July. Include name and address on each page. "We dislike simultaneous submissions and if a poem accepted by us proves to have already been accepted elsewhere, a poet will be blacklisted as there are many good poets waiting in line." Cover letter with** *brief* **bio preferred. Reports in 2 months. Pays 2 copies (and offers additional copies at half price). Acquires first rights.** The editor says, "As a poet/editor I feel magazines like *Outerbridge* provide an invaluable publication outlet for individual poets (particularly since publishing a book of poetry, respectably, is extremely difficult these days). As in all of the arts, poetry—its traditions, conventions and variations, experiments—should be studied. One current 'trend' I detect is a lot of mutual backscratching which can result in very loose, amateurish writing. Discipline!"

OUTREACH: FOR THE HOUSEBOUND, ELDERLY AND DISABLED (IV-Senior citizens, specialized: disabled, religious), 7 Grayson Close, Stocksbridge, Sheffield S30 5BJ England, editor Mike Brooks, founded 1985, is a quarterly using **"semi-religious poetry and short articles. This is a magazine for the housebound, elderly and disabled who need cheering up, not made more depressed or bored!"** As a sample, here are lines from "Stairs to God" by Helen S. Rice:

Prayers are the stairs
We must climb every day,
If we would reach God
There is no other way.

Outreach is photocopied from typescript on ordinary paper, folded and saddle-stapled.

OUTRIDER PRESS (II, IV-Women, anthology), 1004 E. Steger Rd., Suite C-3, Crete IL 60417, founded 1988, president Phyllis Nelson, publishes 1-2 novels/anthologies/chapbooks annually. **They want "poetry dealing with the terrain of the human heart and plotting inner journeys; growth and grace under pressure. No bag ladies, loves-that-never-were, please."** As a sample the editor selected these lines from "Elegy" in *Listen to the Moon* by Whitney Scott:

He slipped
Away,
Gently as the rustle of silk
He so favored in his shirts.

That chapbook is 16 pgs., digest-sized, photocopied from typescript with matte card cover, $4. **Submit 3-5 poems at a time. Include name, address and phone/fax number on every poem. Simultaneous submissions OK, if specified. Cover letter preferred. Accepting submissions for an anthology of midwestern writers called** *Prairie Hearts*. **For this anthology, "poems should have a definite sense of place." Deadline: December 1995. Responds to queries for other projects in 3 months, to submissions in 6 months. Sometimes sends prepublication galleys. Pay is negotiable.** The editor notes, "Outrider Press published its first original trade paper novel, *Dancing to the End of the Shining Bar*, by Whitney Scott, in January, 1994." The press is affiliated with the Feminist Writers Guild, a 15-year-old organization open to all who support feminist writing.

THE OVERLOOK PRESS; TUSK BOOKS (V), 149 Wooster St., New York NY 10012, phone (212)477-7162, founded 1972, are trade publishers with about 8 poetry titles. They have published *Disappearances* by Paul Auster, *After a Lost Original* by David Shapiro and, most recently, *The Boy in the Well* by Daniel Mark Epstein. Tusk/Overlook Books are distributed by Viking/Penguin. **They publish on standard royalty contracts with author's copies. They "are no longer accepting poetry submissions."**

OVERVIEW LTD. POETRY (I, II), P.O. Box 211, Wood-Ridge NJ 07075, fax (201)778-5111, founded 1990, editor Joseph Lanciotti, is a biannual publication of **"plain good poetry, 10-40 lines."** They have recently published poetry by Diane Wilson and Forrest Woods. As a sample we selected these lines from "Feeling Good" by Joanne L. Emery:

It feels good to be in bed,
Naked and alone
With no one taking all the covers—
Crushing me against the frigid wall.
It feels good to lie between
Clean floral sheets,
Making love to myself tonight,
Resting my mind and
Dreaming—it feels good

To be naked for no one

Overview Ltd. is 24 pgs., digest-sized, professionally printed and saddle-stapled with matte card cover. Press run is 500 for 150 subscribers, 250 shelf sales. **Sample postpaid: $5. Submit 3-4 poems at a time. No previously published poems; simultaneous submissions OK. Cover letter required. Send SASE for guidelines "*before* submitting." Reports in 3 months. Pays 1 copy.** The editor says, "*Overview Ltd.* is published only when a sufficient amount of good poetry has been submitted. It has no board of directors, or committees, or budget. We exist from day to day to supply a base for honest poets. There are unheard voices out there and we know it. Send us a message and we will listen."

‡OWEN WISTER REVIEW (II), Box 4238, University Station, Laramie WY 82071, phone (307)766-3819, fax (307)766-2346, founded 1979, is the biannual literary and art magazine of the University of Wyoming. **They have no specifications regarding form, length, subject matter or style of poetry.** The editor says *OWR* is 76-92 pgs., 6×9, professionally printed and perfect-bound with art on the cover and inside; no ads. They receive more than 500 submissions a year, accept 4-6%. Press run is 500. Single copy: $7.50; subscription: $15. **Sample postpaid: $3.50. No previously published poems; simultaneous submissions OK. Cover letter required. Reads submissions September 1 through March 31 only. Poems are circulated to an editorial board. Often comments on rejections. Send SASE for guidelines. Reports in 2-3 months. Pays 1 copy and 10% discount on additional copies. Acquires first rights.**

OWL CREEK PRESS; OWL CREEK POETRY BOOK AND CHAPBOOK COMPETITIONS (II), 1620 N. 45th St., Seattle WA 98103, founded 1979, poetry editor Rich Ives. "Owl Creek Press is a nonprofit literary publisher. Selections for publication are based solely on literary quality." They publish full-length poetry books, chapbooks, anthologies. **"No subject or length limitations. We look for poetry that will endure."** They have published poetry by Angela Ball, Art Homer and Laurie Blauner. As a sample here are the opening lines of "Ordinance on Returning" by Naomi Lazard:

> We commend you on your courage.
> The place you have chosen to revisit
> is as seductive as ever.
> It has been in that business for centuries.

Owl Creek Press accepts books and chapbooks for publication only through its annual contests for each. The *book* competition selects 1-3 books for publication. Mss should be a minimum of 50 typed pages and should include an acknowledgments page for previous publications. Deadline: February 15; entry fee: $15; winners receive $750 and 10 copies of published book. The *chapbook* competition chooses 1-3 chapbooks for publication. Mss should be under 40 pages and should include an acknowledgments page for previous publications. Deadline: August 15; entry fee: $10; winners receive 5 copies of published chapbook and a cash prize of $500 as an advance against royalties. Additional payment for reprinting. Send SASE for information on Owl Creek Poetry Book and Chapbook Contests. The editor says, "It is clear that many would-be poets do not read enough. A hungry mind is a valuable asset. Feed it."

‡OXFORD MAGAZINE (II), 261 Bachelor Hall, Miami University, Oxford OH 45056, phone (513)529-1954, fax (513)529-1392, founded 1984, appears annually, in the spring. **"We are open in terms of form, content and subject matter. We have eclectic tastes, ranging from New Formalism to Language poetry to Nuyorican poetry."** They have recently published poetry by Eve Shelnutt, Denise Duhamel and Walter McDonald. It is 6×9, 100-120 pgs., flat-spined, professionally printed. Press run is 500. **Sample postpaid: $5. Submit 3-5 poems at a time. No previously published poems. Simultaneous submissions OK, with notification. Cover letter with a short (one or two-line) bio required. The deadline for each issue is January 1. Pays copies. Buys first North American serial rights.**

OXFORD UNIVERSITY PRESS, 198 Madison Ave., New York NY 10016. See listing in Publications Useful to Poets.

‡OXYGEN (II), 535 Geary St. #1010, San Francisco CA 94102, phone (415)776-9681, founded 1991, editor Richard Hack, is a "spirited and independent literary magazine" which appears 3-4 times a year and is designed "to seek and celebrate beauty, truth and justice in well-crafted verse and prose." **They want poetry that is "ambitious, vivid, exploring sensitive areas of life; any form or mode or length (1-20 pgs.); grassroots focus welcome—may be radical, but not mere sloganeering. Dark side welcome. We also like translations, but be sure to include original text. We generally stay away from light verse (unless it's very clever), so-called experimental writing, and post-mod theorizing. Let there be meaning!"** They have recently published poetry by Juan Felipe Herrera, Bill Knott and David Fisher. As a sample the editor selected these lines from "The Beach" by Victor Martinez:

> When finally the black mold of dread
> is burnt away, and a hand on your shoulder

> *smacks of the impending fire,*
> *you know you've been cleansed, and can once again*
> *go home to the open window: the stamp of blue*
> *happiness, that was always there.*

Oxygen is 40 pgs., 8½ × 11, set in Pagemaker and photocopied on 60 lb. vellum, comb-bound with colored card stock cover, 2-3 graphics each issue. They receive about 1,200 poems a year, publish approximately 2%. Press run is 150 for 25 subscribers, 50 shelf sales. Single copy: $2.50; subscription: $14 (libraries $20). **Sample postpaid: $3.50 current issue, $5 back issue. Submit up to 12 poems at a time with 2-4 lines for possible contributor's note. Previously published poems and simultaneous submissions OK, "but let us know." Seldom comments on rejections (but will provide editorial commentary and consultation for a fee: $25 minimum). Send SASE for general writer's guidelines. Reports within 2 months generally, "often 3-4 weeks." Pays 2 copies. All rights revert to contributors.** Occasionally reviews books of poetry or other magazines. Open to unsolicited reviews. Poets may also send books for review consideration. The editor's advice: "Love words and rhythm. Educate yourself as much as possible in literature and experience. Eschew stand-up comedy posing as literature. Avoid easy cynicism and flatness. Develop your spiritual life. Feel gratitude to society, acknowledge interdependence, love sharing."

PABLO LENNIS (I, IV-Science fiction/fantasy), 30 N. 19th St., Lafayette IN 47904, founded 1976, editor John Thiel, appears irregularly, is a **"science fiction and fantasy fanzine preferring poems of an expressive cosmic consciousness or full magical approach. I want poetry that rhymes and scans and I like a good rhythmic structure appropriate to the subject. Shorter poems are much preferred. I want them to exalt the mind, imagination, or perception into a consciousness of the subject. Optimism is usually preferred, and English language perfection eminently preferable. Nothing that is not science fiction or fantasy, or which contains morbid sentiments, or is perverse, or does not rhyme, or contains slang."** They have recently published poetry by Sean McCormack, Don Meyerowitz, Deborah Kolodui, and Davic C. Bryan. As a sample the editor selected these lines from "Wizard's Sestina" by Lynn Tait:

> *A raging war of tides against the night,*
> *Blue, blazing trails no man may ever see,*
> *Irregular distortions of the light*
> *Like lasers bouncing aimlessly and free*
> *Towards an upward plateau where the white*
> *Of wizards flourish, ghosts there guard the key.*

It is 22 pgs., magazine-sized, side-stapled, photocopied from typescript, using fantastic ink drawings and hand-lettering. "I get maybe fifty poems a year and have been using most of them." Press run is "up to 100 copies." Subscription: $12/year. **Sample postpaid: $2. No previously published poems or simultaneous submissions. Send SASE for guidelines. Reports "at once. I generally say something about why the poetry was not used, if it was not. If someone else might like it, I mention an address." Pays 1 copy, 2 if requested.** Reviews books of poetry if they are science fiction or fantasy. Open to unsolicited reviews. Poets may also send books for review consideration. The editor says, "Poetry is magic. I want spells, incantations, sorceries of a rhythmic and rhyming nature, loftily and optimistically expressed, and I think this is what others want. People buy poetry to have something that will affect them, add new things to their lives. If they want something to think about, they get prose. See how much magic you can make. See how well-liked it is."

PAINTBRUSH: A JOURNAL OF CONTEMPORARY MULTICULTURAL LITERATURE (III), Division of Language & Literature, Northeast Missouri State University, Kirksville MO 63501, phone (816)785-4185, founded 1974, editor Ben Bennani. *Paintbrush* appears annually and is 5½ × 8½, 250-300 pgs., using **quality poetry**. Circulation is 500. **Sample: $7. No submissions June, July and August. Send SASE with inquiries and request for samples.** Reviews books of poetry.

PAINTED BRIDE QUARTERLY (II), 230 Vine St., Philadelphia PA 19106, phone (215)925-9914, editors Kathy Volk Miller, Brian Brown and Marion Wrenn, founded 1973, appears quarterly. **"We have no specifications or restrictions. We'll look at anything."** They have published poetry by Robert Bly, Charles Bukowski, S.J. Marks and James Hazen. *"PBQ* aims to be a leader among little magazines published by and for independent poets and writers nationally." The 80-page, perfect-bound, digest-sized magazine uses 40 pgs. of poetry/issue, receiving over 1,000 submissions/year and using under 150. Neatly printed, it has a circulation of 1,000, 850 subscriptions, of which 40 are libraries. Subscription: $16. **Sample postpaid: $6. Submit no more than 6 poems, any length, typed; only original, unpublished work. "Submissions should include a *short* bio." Editors seldom comment on rejections. They have a 6- to 9-month backlog. Pays 1-year subscription and half-priced contributor's copies.** Reviews books of poetry. Poetry published in *PBQ* has been included in *The Best American Poetry 1995*.

PALANQUIN/TDM; PALANQUIN POETRY SERIES (II), Dept. of English, University of South Carolina-Aiken, 171 University Pkwy., Aiken SC 29801, phone (803)648-6851 ext. 3208, founded 1988, editor Phebe Davidson, publishes a pamphlet series 6 times a year featuring one poet/issue. **They do not want "sentimental, religious, consciously academic" poetry.** They have recently published poetry by Dorothy Perry Thompson, Lamont Steptoe and Michelle Hollander. As a sample the editor selected these lines by John Repp:

> He wants that woman so bad he can taste
> the salt behind her knee, relish the bite
> of her next thought and the aroma
> of the last, and don't get him started
> on her hair, etcetera. His brother
> says to get off it, that's bad, that's never-
> turn-back time, which the man knows,
> and says so.

The pamphlet we received, featuring poems by Dorothy Perry Thompson, is professionally printed on heavy recycled paper. Press run is 100 for 50 subscribers. Subscription: $10. **Sample postpaid: $1. Submit 5-10 poems at a time with bio and SASE. No previously published poems. "I read January through March for the following year." Reports in 2-3 months. Pays half of press run.** *Palanquin* also holds a spring chapbook contest for fall publication. Entry fee: $10 (includes subscription). Contest deadline: May 1. Send SASE for further information.

‡PALO ALTO REVIEW (I, II, IV-Themes), 1400 W. Villaret Blvd., San Antonio TX 78224, phone (210)921-5255 or 921-5017, fax (210)921-5115, e-mail eshull@accd.edu, founded 1992, editors Ellen Shull and Bob Richmond, is a biannual publication of Palo Alto college. "We invite writing that investigates the full range of education in its myriad forms. Ideas are what we are after. The *Palo Alto Review* is interested in connecting the college and the community. We would hope that those who attempt these connections will choose startling topics and find interesting angles from which to study the length and breadth of ideas and learning, a lifelong pursuit." The review includes articles, essays, memoirs, interviews, book reviews, fiction and poetry. **They want "poetry which has something to say, literary quality poems, with strong images, up to 50 lines. No inspirational verse, haiku or doggerel."** They have published poetry by Diane Glancy, Wendy Bishop, Lyn Lifshin and Ruth Daigon. As a sample we selected these lines from "A Sentence On Buck Creek" by Barbara Van Noord:

> Buck Creek froze in winter and we skated
> before the snows fell, far, far
> beyond the farmhouse, beyond
> the little vineyard, into no man's land
> further than we had ever gone before,
> brushing aside the past, leaving
> just broken stencils in the nubbly ice,
> white glide lines like a trail of bread crumbs. . .

PAR is 60 pgs., 8½ × 11, professionally printed on recycled paper and saddle-stapled with matte card cover with art; b&w photos, art and graphics inside. They publish about 8 poems in each issue (16 poems/year). Press run is 700 for 400 subscribers of which 10 are libraries, 200 shelf sales. Subscription: $10. **Sample postpaid: $5. Submit 3-5 poems at a time. No previously published poems; simultaneous submissions OK. Poems are read by an advisory board and recommended to editors, who sometimes suggest revisions. Always comments on rejections. "Although we frequently announce a theme, the entire issue will not necessarily be dedicated to the theme." Send SASE for guidelines and upcoming themes. Reports in 1-3 months. Pays 2 copies. Acquires first North American serial rights.** The editors say there are no requirements for submission, "though we recommend the reading (purchase) of a sample copy."

PANCAKE PRESS (V), 163 Galewood Circle, San Francisco CA 94131, phone (415)665-9215, founded 1974, publisher Patrick Smith, a small press publisher of hand-bound paperbacks with sewn signatures. **Currently not accepting unsolicited mss.** The editor publishes **"poetry aware of its own language conventions, tuned to both the ear and eye, attentive to syntax, honest about its desires, clear about something, spoken or written as a member of the species."** He has published books by John Logan, David Ray and Stephen Dunning.

✝ *The double dagger before a listing indicates that the listing is new in this edition. New markets are often the most receptive to submissions.*

THE PANHANDLER (II), Dept. PM, English Dept., University of West Florida, Pensacola FL 32514, phone (904)474-2923, founded 1976, editor Dr. Laurie O'Brien appears twice a year, using **poetry "grounded in experience with strong individual 'voice' and natural language. Any subject, no 'causes.' Length to 200 lines, but prefer 30-100. No self-consciously experimental, unrestrained howling, sophomoric wailings on the human condition."** They have published poetry by Malcolm Glass, Lyn Lifshin, Donald Junkins, David Kirby and Joan Colby. As a sample here is the first stanza of "York, Maine" by Leo Connellan:

> Through the Cutty Sark motel room 21 picture window now
> the gray waves coming into York Beach like
> an invasion of plows pushing snow. Tomorrow
> the sun will scratch its chin and bleed along the skyline
> but today everything is gray poached in a steam of fog.

The handsomely printed magazine is 64 pgs., digest-sized, flat-spined, large type on heavy eggshell stock, matte card cover with art. Circulation is 500 for 100 subscribers of which 10 are libraries and 200 complimentary copies going to the English department and writing program. Subscription: $5. **Sample postpaid: $2. No simultaneous submissions. Submit maximum of 7 poems, typewritten or letter-perfect printout. Reports in 1-2 months.** Time between acceptance and publication is 6-12 months. **Pays 2 copies.** They sponsor a national chapbook competition each year, October 15 through January 15. Submit 24-30 pgs. with $7 reading fee. Send SASE for details. The editor advises: "(1) Take care with ms preparation. Sloppy mss are difficult to evaluate fairly. (2) Send only poems you believe in. Everything you write isn't publishable; send finished work."

‡PANJANDRUM BOOKS; PANJANDRUM POETRY JOURNAL (III, IV-Translations), 6156 Wilkinson Ave., North Hollywood CA 91606, founded 1971, editor Dennis Koran, associate editor David Guss. **The press publishes a distinguished list of avant-garde books. They are interested in translations (especially European) of modern poetry, surrealism, dada and experimental poetry and accept book-length mss only with SASE; query first. Cover letter listing previous publications is required.** *Panjandrum Poetry Journal* is published occasionally. **Submit no more than 10 poems at a time. No simultaneous submissions.** Staff also reviews books of poetry. Send books for review consideration to Dennis Koran.

PANTHEON BOOKS INC., 201 E. 50th St., New York NY 10022. Prefers not to share information.

THE PAPER BAG (I, II), P.O. Box 268805, Chicago IL 60626-8805, founded 1988, editor M. Brownstein, is a quarterly using **poetry "any kind, any style. We look for strong and original imagery. No love poems at the beach, by water, across from candlelight."** As a sample the editor selected this complete poem, "Road Kill," by Michael Scott:

> In the cool light of summer
> morning, the possum seems
> almost alive, no blood or guts
> spilled in the road, white
> fur tipped with gray,
> looking like the dirty
> snow of early spring.

The Paper Bag is 24 pgs., digest-sized, saddle-stapled, photocopied from typescript, with matte card cover. They publish about 30 of 200 poems received/issue. "Our circulation varies from 20-300 and we sell out every issue." Subscription: $12/4-5 issues plus "anything else we publish." **Sample postpaid: $3. Typed mss only, address and phone number on each submission. Cover letter with brief bio required. Editor comments on submissions "always." Send SASE for guidelines. Sometimes sends prepublication galleys. Pays copies.** All checks or money orders should be made out to M. Brownstein. The editor says, "Be persistent. Because we reject one group of submissions does not mean we will reject another batch. Keep trying."

THE PAPER SALAd POETRY JOURNAL (II), P.O. Box 520061, Salt Lake City UT 84152-0061, founded 1990, editor R.L. Moore, is an annual using **"poetry by poets who work rigorously on their poetry, who make every poem an attempt at the 'perfect' poem, and who know that the meaning of a poem is always secondary to the music of the poem." Note:** *PAPER SALAd* **will not be accepting submissions between June 1996 and January 1997.** They have recently published poetry by Richard Cronshey, Lyn Lifshin, Christien Gholson and Gayle Elen Harvey. As a sample the editor selected this untitled poem by Steven B. Edmonds:

> Nature opens above-around-within us
> Green canopy,
> Umbrella hung in the human head,
> Halo of a planet cooled & coddled by a mother of cloud.
> What delicacy there is in this good common sense,

> *One thing threaded to another, and We, quilted tight,*
> *Stitched & centered—the focal eye that is the fabric.*

The editor describes it as 80-110 pgs., flat-spined, digest-sized. Press run is 400. **Sample: $7.25 ("An additional dollar will help with postage, but is optional"). Submit no more than 6 poems at a time, one poem to a page, name and address on each. "Submissions without a SASE get tossed." A $1.50/item coupon toward** *PAPER SALAd* **stuff will be given to each poet who submits work on disk. "All poems in one file, please. IBM compatible, WordPerfect preferred. Please also include a hard copy of each poem." Seldom comments on rejections. Replies within 2 months. Pays 1 copy.** The editor says, "I don't really feel that a poem has to be *about* anything at all. In fact it's often the poem that tries to be *about* something that ends up failing. It starts to feel forced or too intentional. I think it's more important for a poem to draw the reader into a space or situation that is both familiar and yet new. I personally like poetry that has a bit of a surreal edge to it, but that doesn't mean the weirder the better. All poems must arise out of the genuine experience of existence to be of any value. I feel the best poetry helps to draw attention to the tension between the mundane and the ascensional."

PAPIER-MACHE PRESS (IV-Themes, anthologies, women), 135 Aviation Way, #14, Watsonville CA 95076, phone (408)763-1420, fax (408)763-1421, founded 1984, editor Sandra Martz, is a small press publisher of anthologies, poetry and short fiction in perfect-bound and casebound books. **Their anthologies typically "explore a particular aspect of women's experience, such as aging, parental relationships, work or body image."** They have published *Bare As the Trees* and *Another Language* by Sue Saniel Elkind, *Phases of the Moon* by Lynn Kozma, and *Wetlands* by Patti Tana. The following lines are from *Between One Future and the Next* by Ruth Daigon:

> *Women know how to wait.*
> *They smell the dust,*
> *listen to light bulbs dim,*
> *and guard the children*
> *pale with dreaming.*

They publish 1-2 poetry collections each year and one anthology every two years. Poetry collections contain 100-120 poems and are accepted in July and August only. Each anthology contains 30-40 poems, and submissions are accepted only when a particular theme has been announced (watch *Poets & Writers Magazine* **for announcements). Send SASE for guidelines. Simultaneous submissions must be identified as such. Cover letter required; include name, address, phone and fax numbers (if available) as well as length and subject of submission. They report on mss in 3-4 months. Always sends prepublication galleys. Royalties, modest advances and several copies are negotiated for both individual collections and work accepted for anthologies. Send SASE for catalog to buy samples, books typically cost $8-14.** "*Papier-Mache*'s primary objective is to publish anthologies, poetry and fiction books by, for and about midlife and older women and about the art of women and men aging. We select well-written, accessible material on subjects of particular importance to women, develop attractive, high quality book formats and market them to an audience that might not otherwise buy books of poetry. We take particular pride in our reputation for dealing with our contributors in a caring, professional manner."

‡PARABOLA: THE MAGAZINE OF MYTH AND TRADITION (IV-Spirituality, themes), 656 Broadway, New York NY 10012, phone (212)505-9037, fax (212)979-7325, founded 1976, is a quarterly "devoted to the exploration of the quest for meaning as expressed in the myths, symbols, and tales of the world's spiritual traditions. **We very rarely publish poetry, and only use material** *directly* **related to one of our upcoming themes. Please send SASE for current list."** They have published poetry by Jane Yolen, Kenneth Koch, James Laughlin and William Stafford. Almost all of the poetry they have published has been reprints. *Parabola* is 128 pgs., 6½×10, professionally printed and perfect-bound with full-color, semi-glossy paper cover and b&w art and photos inside. More than half the publication contains articles, stories and poetry; the rest is book reviews and ads. They receive 120-150 poetry mss a year, accept 1-2 original poems, 2-4 reprints. Press run is 40,000. Subscription: $20. **Sample postpaid: $6 current issue, $8 back issue. Previously published poems and simultaneous submissions OK. Cover letter required. "State to which theme you are submitting, and please make separate submissions if you have work for more than one theme." Send SASE for general guidelines and upcoming themes. Reports in 3-6 months. Payment varies. Author retains rights.** Reviews nationally available books, including related books of poetry, in 500 words, single format. Open to unsolicited reviews. Poets may also send related books for review consideration, attn: Book Review Editor.

PARADISE PUBLICATIONS (I, IV-Cowboy), P.O. Box 9084, Wichita Falls TX 76310, phone (817)691-1777, founded 1992, editor Leah Galligar, publishes 3-4 perfect-bound paperback books of poetry each year. **"We are looking for cowboy poetry and poetry with an old-fashioned, Western flair."** They have published poetry by D.L. Chance and Sharon Chance. As a sample the editor selected this poem, "TEXAS #2," by D.L. Chance:

The French tourguide became unusually distressed
when the rich Texan gazed at the Eiffel, unimpressed.
"Well, I have to admit it's the BIGGEST I've seen yet,
but what matters, Pierre, is how many BARRELS does she get?"

Query first with 5 sample poems and cover letter with brief bio and publication credits. No previously published poems; simultaneous submissions OK. Replies to queries in 1 month. Pays 10% royalties and 2 author's copies. Send $5 for sample copies of their books.

PARADOX; PARADOX PUBLICATIONS (II), P.O. Box 643, Saranac Lake NY 12983, e-mail zbodah @ocvaxa.cc.oberlin.edu, founded 1991, editor Rev. Dan Bodah, appears 1-2 times/year. *"Paradox* thrives on diversity and raw electricity. *Paradox* is exempt from stopping at railroad crossings. **I like poetry with** *power,* **no matter which genre. However, I wish to see no light verse. From now on, all issues will be theme issues."** They have published poetry by Maurice Kenny, John M. Bennett, Rochelle Owens and Susan Smith Nash. As a sample the editor selected these lines from "Resurgence" by Jake Berry:

Suddenly I'm nauseous and run for the door.
Outside and vomiting I see frogs like
crucifixes rising out of the ground, drifting
toward the sun where they explode in a
sweet crimson rain of mother horns.

The editor says *Paradox* varies between digest-sized and magazine-sized and is photocopied, hand-assembled, and often individually decorated. "Audiotapes are included with #3 onwards." Press run is 200 for 3 subscribers, 25-50 shelf sales. Single copy: $5; subscription: $15 for 4 issues. **Sample postpaid: $4. No previously published poems; simultaneous submissions OK.** Time between acceptance and publication is 6-12 months. **Seldom comments on rejections. Send SASE for upcoming themes. Reports in 2-8 weeks. Pays 1-2 copies. Acquires first rights.** Paradox Publications **also publishes 1 chapbook/year. "I can only be swayed to publish unsolicited book mss if they are really good and I feel I can do them justice and/or handle the project. Poets can feel free to send an entire ms without a prior query." Replies in 2-4 weeks. Pays royalties and 10 author's copies. For sample chapbook, send $3.**

PARAGON HOUSE PUBLISHERS (III), Dept. PM, 370 Lexington Ave., Suite 1700, New York NY 10017, phone (212)953-5950, founded 1983, has published books of poetry by Louis Simpson and Leo Connellan.

‡PARAMOUR MAGAZINE (I, II, IV-Erotica), P.O. Box 949, Cambridge MA 02140-0008, phone/fax (617)499-0069, founded 1993, poetry editor John Mulrooney, publisher/editor Amelia Copeland, is a quarterly devoted to "literary and artistic erotica," including short fiction, poetry, photography, illustration and reviews. **They want erotic poetry—"crude, humorous, sweet, all OK. Nothing navel-contemplative."** They have recently published poetry by Lyn Lifshin, Corwin Ericson, John Cantey Knight and Cheryl Townsend. *Paramour* is 36 pgs., 9×12, printed 2-color on recycled paper and saddle-stapled with paper cover and b&w photos throughout. Much of the content is sexually explicit. They receive 400-500 poems a year, accept approximately 10%. Press run is 12,000 for 250 subscribers, about 8,000 shelf sales. Single copy: $4.95; subscription: $18. **Sample postpaid: $6. Submit no more than 10 poems each quarter. Include name, address and phone number on every page. Previously published poems OK, "only if published in obscure publications." Simultaneous submissions OK, "but you must inform us of which publications." Written work will not be returned. Send SASE for guidelines. Reports in 4 months. Pays 3 copies plus a 1-year subscription. Acquires first or second rights.**

THE PARIS REVIEW; BERNARD F. CONNORS PRIZE (III), 45-39 171 Pl., Flushing NY 11358, phone (718)539-7085, founded 1952, poetry editor Richard Howard. **(Submissions should go to him at 541 E. 72nd St., New York NY 10021).** This distinguished quarterly (circulation 10,000, digest-sized, 200 pgs.) has published many of the major poets writing in English. Though form, content and length seem open, free verse—some structured, some experimental—tends to dominate recent issues. Because the journal is considered one of the most prestigious in the world, competition is keen and response times can lag. **Sample: $10. Study publication before submitting.** The Bernard F. Connors prize of $1,000 is awarded annually for the best previously unpublished long poem (over 200 lines). **All submissions must be sent to the 541 E. 72nd St., New York NY 10021 address.** Poetry published in *The Paris Review* was selected for inclusion in the 1992, 1993, 1994 and 1995 volumes of *The Best American Poetry.*

PARNASSUS LITERARY JOURNAL (I, II), P.O. Box 1384, Forest Park GA 30051, phone (404)366-3177, founded 1975, edited by Denver Stull: "Our sole purpose is to promote poetry and to offer an outlet where poets may be heard. **We are open to all poets and all forms of poetry, including**

Oriental, 24-line limit, maximum 3 poems." They have recently published poetry by Alice Mackenzie Swaim, Diana Kwiatkowski Rubin, Ruth Schuler, T.K. Splake, William J. Vernon and H.F. Noyes. As a sample the editor selected "Shadings" by Gloris H. Procsal:

> *Don't begrudge Monet*
> *his waterlillies, the way*
> *they drip in rosy blobs*
> *from every paintbrush.*
> *They each have a*
> *difference, you know.*

PLJ is 84 pgs., saddled-stapled, photocopied from typescript, with an occasional drawing. They receive about 1,500 submissions/year, of which they use 350. Currently have about a 1-year backlog. The magazine comes out 3 times a year with a print run of 300 copies. Subscribers presently number 200 (5 libraries). Circulation includes Japan, England, Greece, India, Korea, Germany and Netherlands. **Sample: $4.50** (regularly $5.25/copy, $15/subscription US, $16.50 Canada, $22.50 overseas). **Make checks or money orders payable to Denver Stull. Include name and address on each page of ms. "I am dismayed at the haphazard manner in which work is often submitted. I have a number of poems in my file containing no name and/or address. Simply placing your name and address on your envelope is not enough." Previously published poems OK; no simultaneous submissions. Cover letter including something about the writer preferred. "Definitely" comments on rejections. "We do not respond to submissions or queries not accompanied by SASE." Reports within 1 week. Pays 1 copy. Acquires all rights. Returns rights.** Readers vote on best of each issue. Also conducts a contest periodically. Staff reviews books of poetry by subscribers only. The editor advises: "Write about what you know. Study what you have written. Does it make sense? A poem should not leave the reader wondering what you are trying to say. Improve your writings by studying the work of others. Be professional."

PARNASSUS: POETRY IN REVIEW; POETRY IN REVIEW FOUNDATION (V), 41 Union Square W., Room 804, New York NY 10003, phone (212)463-0889, founded 1972, poetry editor Herbert Leibowitz, provides "comprehensive and in-depth coverage of new books of poetry, including translations from foreign poetry. **We publish poems and translations on occasion, but we solicit all poetry. Poets invited to submit are given all the space they wish; the only stipulation is that the style be non-academic."** They have published work by Alice Fulton, Eavan Boland, Ross Feld, Debora Greger, William Logan, Tess Gallagher, Seamus Heaney and Rodney Jones. They do consider unsolicited essays. In fact, this is an exceptionally rich market for thoughtful, insightful, technical essay-reviews of contemporary collections. However, it is strongly recommended that writers study the magazine before submitting. **Multiple submissions disliked. Cover letter required. Send SASE for upcoming themes. Reports on essay submissions within 4-10 weeks (response takes longer during the summer). Pays $25-250 plus 2 gift subscriptions—contributors can also take one themselves. Acquires all rights. Editor comments on rejections—from 1 paragraph to 2 pages.** Send for a sample copy (prices of individual issues can vary) to get a feel for the critical acumen needed to place here. Subscriptions are $23/year, $46/year for libraries; they have 1,100 subscribers, of which 550 are libraries. The editor comments, "Contributors should be urged to subscribe to at least one literary magazine. There is a pervasive ignorance of the cost of putting out a magazine and no sense of responsibility for supporting one."

PARTING GIFTS; MARCH STREET PRESS (II), 3413 Wilshire, Greensboro NC 27408, founded 1987, editor Robert Bixby. **"I want to see everything**. I'm a big fan of Jim Harrison, C.K. Williams, Amy Hempel and Janet Kauffman. If you write like them, you'll almost certainly be published. But that's pretty useless advice unless you're one of those people." He has published poetry by Eric Torgersen, Lyn Lifshin, Elizabeth Kerlikowske and Russell Thorburn. *PG* is 72 pgs., digest-sized, photocopied, with colored matte card cover, appearing twice a year. Press run is 200. Subscription: $8. **Sample postpaid: $4. Submit in groups of 3-10 with SASE. No previously published poems, but simultaneous submissions OK. "I like a cover letter because it makes the transaction more human. Best time to submit mss is early in the year." Send SASE for guidelines. Reports in 1-2 weeks.** Sometimes sends prepublication galleys. **Pays 1 copy.** March Street Press **publishes chapbooks; $10 reading fee.**

PARTISAN REVIEW (II, IV-Translations, themes), Dept. PM, 236 Bay State Rd., Boston MA 02215, phone (617)353-4260, founded 1934, editor William Phillips, is a distinguished quarterly literary journal (6×9, 160 pgs., flat-spined, circulation 8,200 for 6,000 subscriptions and shelf sales), using poetry of high quality. "Our poetry section is very small and highly selective. We are open to fresh, quality translations but submissions must include poem in original language as well as translation. We occasionally have special poetry sections on specified themes." They have recently published poetry by John Hollander, Czeshaw Milosz, Donald Revell and Rosanna Warren. **Sample postpaid: $7.50. Submit maximum of 6 poems at a time. No simultaneous submissions. Reports in**

2 months. Pays $50 and 50% discount on copies. Work published in this review has also been selected for inclusion in *The Best American Poetry 1995*.

PASQUE PETALS; SOUTH DAKOTA STATE POETRY SOCIETY, INC. (I, IV-Regional, subscribers), 909 E. 34th St., Sioux Falls SD 57105, phone (605)338-9156, founded 1926, editor Barbara Stevens. This is the official poetry magazine for the South Dakota State Poetry Society, Inc., but it is open to non-members. **Those not residents of SD are required to subscribe when (or before) submitting. They use "all forms. 44-line limit, 50-character lines. Count titles and spaces. Lean toward SD and Midwest themes. No rough language or porno—magazine goes into SD schools and libraries."** As a sample the editor chose her poem "The Errol Flynn Look-Alike":

> His tongue was as smooth as honey on a spoon.
> Went from job to job,
> Fooled everyone at first meeting
>   talked great projects completed by others.
> Fooled his wife all the time,
> she grew fat and comfortable
>   He left her
>   for a size five.

PP appears 10 times a year (no August or November issues) and is 16-20 pgs., digest-sized, using small b&w sketches. Circulation is 250 to members/subscribers (16 to libraries). Subscription: $20/year. **Sample postpaid: $2. Submit 3 poems at a time, 1 poem (or 2 haiku)/page, seasonal material 3 months ahead. Editor "always" comments on rejections. Send SASE for guidelines. Reports in 3 months. Has a 2- to 3-month backlog. Pays non-members only 1 copy. Acquires first rights.** Reviews books of poetry by members only. Offers $5 prize for the best poem in every issue. They also sponsor a yearly contest with 10 categories. Entry fees vary. Prizes total $600. Send SASE for details.

PASSAGER: A JOURNAL OF REMEMBRANCE AND DISCOVERY (I, II, IV-Senior citizen, themes), School of Communications Design, University of Baltimore, 1420 N. Charles St., Baltimore MD 21201-5779, phone (410)837-6026, founded 1989, editors Kendra Kopelke, Mary Azrael and Ebby Malmgren. *Passager* is published quarterly and publishes fiction, poetry and interviews that give voice to human experience. **"We seek powerful images of remembrance and discovery from writers of all ages. One of our missions is to provide exposure for new older writers; another is to function as a literary community for writers across the country who are not connected to academic institutions or other organized groups."** The journal is 32 pgs., 8×8, printed on white linen and saddle-stitched. Includes photos of writers. **Submit 3-5 poems at a time, each 30 lines maximum; fiction, 3,000 words maximum. "We like clean, readable typed copy with name, address and phone number on each page." Simultaneous submissions acceptable if notified. No reprints. "We prefer cover sheets because it makes it personal. However, we hate pushy cover letters, 'I'm sure you'll find your readers will love my story.' " Does not read mss June-August. Occasionally does special issues. Send SASE for guidelines and upcoming themes. Reports in 2 months. Pays 1 year's subscription.** They sponsor an annual spring poetry contest for new poets over 50 years old, with 1st, 2nd and 3rd prizes; honorable mentions; and publication in *Passager*.

PASSAGES NORTH (II), Kalamazoo College, 1200 Academy St., Kalamazoo MI 49006-3295, phone (616)337-7331, founded 1979, editor Michael Barrett, poetry editor Conrad Hillberry, is a semiannual magazine containing fiction, poetry, essays, interviews and visual art. **"The magazine publishes quality work by established and emerging writers."** They have recently published poetry by William Matthews, Thomas Lux, Jo Anne Rawson, Michael Collier, Lisa Sewell, Nancy Willard, Mark Halliday, Nancy Eimers and John Rybicki. As a sample the editor selected these lines from "Totally" by Tony Hoagland:

> For example, it is autumn here.
> The defoliated trees look frightened
> at the edge of town,
>
> as if the train they missed
> had taken all their clothes.
> The whole world in unison is turning
> toward a zone of nakedness and cold.
>
> But me, I have this strange conviction
> that I am going to be born.

Passages North is 100 pgs., perfect-bound. Circulation is at 1,000 "and growing." Single copy: $6; subscription: $10 for 1 year, $18 for 2 years, add $10 for international mail. **Prefers groups of 4-6 poems, typed single-spaced. Simultaneous submissions OK, if writer agrees to telephone *Passages North* immediately when work accepted elsewhere. Reads submissions September through May** only. Reports in 6-8 weeks, delay to publication is 6 months. Pays copies.

PATH PRESS, INC. (IV-Ethnic), 53 W. Jackson Blvd., Suite 724, Chicago IL 60604, phone (312)663-0167, fax (312)663-5318, founded 1969, president Bennett J. Johnson, executive vice president and poetry editor Herman C. Gilbert, is a small publisher of books and poetry primarily **"by, for and about African-American and Third World people."** The press is open to all types of poetic forms except **"poor quality."** **Submissions should be typewritten in manuscript format. Writers should send sample poems, credits and bio.** The books are "hardback and quality paperbacks."

THE PEACE FARM ADVOCATE (IV-Social issues), HCR 2 Box 25, Panhandle TX 79068, phone (806)335-1715, founded 1986, editor Mavis Belisle, is a quarterly which promotes peacemaking through information, commentary and reflection. **"We consider only poetry related to peace, environmental and social justice issues."** As a sample the editor selected these lines from "Packing for Saudi Arabia" by Mary Carter Rak:

> *I stare at the empty green bag*
> *I must fill in the next fifteen minutes*
> *with things most important*
> *to you. Underwear, T-shirts,*
> *your St. Christopher medal*
> *wrapped in tissue.*

The Peace Farm Advocate is 40 pgs., 8½ × 11, printed on recycled paper. Press run is 1,000 for 800 paid subscribers. The rest are distributed free. Subscription: $5. **Previously published poems and simultaneous submissions OK.** Time between acceptance and publication is 3-6 months. **Reports in 6 months. "We do not pay for published poems."** Open to unsolicited reviews. Poets may also send books for review consideration. The editor says, "Because of downsizing, opportunity will be very limited; we do not expect to be able to accept more than 1-2 short to medium-length poems per issue."

"This van represents the freedom expressed in the '60s," says Linda James, editor of the California-based Peace Magazine. **"The decorations on the van were typical of the era and the peace sign sun added an artistic element that just made the cover."** The quarterly magazine includes articles, interviews, reprints, personal essays, photos and letters all about the '60s. They also publish one to two poems in every issue. **"We look for very simple poetry that expresses an idea of the '60s, either then or now—looking back and reflecting on that time."** The cover artwork is by Phil Kano.

‡PEACE MAGAZINE (IV-Specialized: the 1960s), P.O. Box 902404, Palmdale CA 93590-2404, founded 1994, editor Linda James, is a quarterly designed "to inform, reminisce and update the 60s generation with the 60s. This magazine is written by and for those who were there and those who wished they were." **They want "poetry related to the 1960s—political, humorous, beat style or Brautigan-like."** As a sample the editor selected these lines from "Bill" by Tom Shadley:

> *Whatever happened to good ol' Bill,*
> *his head was on so straight.*
>
> *Whoever thought the evil disease*
> *would be poor Billy's fate.*
>
> *The beard and pony tail are gone,*
> *no more listening to the Dead.*
>
> *Talk radio's his drug of choice*
> *and stock quotes fill his head. . . .*

Peace is 40 pgs., 8½ × 11, attractively designed, printed on coated stock and saddle-stitched with b&w illustration on the cover and b&w photos inside. They accept 2 poems each issue. Press run is 5,000. Single copy: $3.95; subscription: $14. **Sample postpaid: $4. Previously published poems OK: no simultaneous submissions. "All poems are reviewed by the editor and head hippie." Often comments on rejections. Send SASE for guidelines. Reports within 2 months. Pays 5¢/word and 1 copy. Buys one-time rights.** The editor says, "We are a new magazine looking for new material, new thoughts, fresh ideas. We want to bring part of the '60s back, or at least the sense of the '60s now when the world needs it."

PEARL; PEARL CHAPBOOK CONTEST (II), 3030 E. Second St., Long Beach CA 90803, phone (310)434-4523 or (714)968-7530, founded 1974, poetry editors Joan Jobe Smith, Marilyn Johnson and Barbara Hauk, is a literary magazine appearing three times a year. **"We are interested in accessible, humanistic poetry that communicates and is related to real life. Humor and wit are welcome, along with the ironic and serious. No taboos stylistically or subject-wise. Prefer poems up to 35 lines, with lines no longer than 10 words. We don't want to see sentimental, obscure, predictable, abstract or cliché-ridden poetry. Our purpose is to provide a forum for lively, readable poetry, the direct, outspoken type, variously known as 'neo-pop' or 'stand-up,' that reflects a wide variety of contemporary voices, viewpoints and experiences—that speaks to *real* people about *real* life in direct, living language, profane or sublime."** They have recently published poetry by Edward Field, Lisa Glatt, Ron Koertge, Suzanne Lummis, Laurel Speer and Fred Voss. As a sample they selected these lines from "Craving" by Donna Hilbert:

> *I ate the skin*
> *from the tips of my fingers,*
> *from the tops of my toes*
> *until they bled.*
> *I didn't know then*
> *what was bitter,*
> *as my life spilled out around me,*
> *fine powder from a dark brown tin.*

Pearl is digest-sized, 96 pgs., perfect-bound, offset, with laminated cover. Their press run is 600 with 100 subscriptions of which 7 are libraries. Subscription: $15/year. **Sample postpaid: $6. Submit 3-5 poems at a time. "Handwritten submissions and unreadable dot-matrix print-outs are not acceptable." No previously published poems; simultaneous submissions OK. "Cover letters appreciated." Guidelines available for SASE. Reports in 6-8 weeks. Sometimes sends prepublication galleys. Pays 2 copies. Acquires first serial rights.** Each issue contains the work of 60-70 different poets and a special 10- to 15-page section that showcases the work of a single poet. Staff reviews books of poetry. Send books for review consideration to Marilyn Johnson. "We sponsor an annual chapbook contest, judged by one of our more well-known contributors. Winner receives publication, $200 and 50 copies. Entries accepted during the months of May and June. There is a $10 entry fee, which includes a copy of the winning chapbook." Send SASE for complete rules and guidelines. Recent chapbooks include *The Wave He Caught* by Rick Noguchi, *Reflections of a White Bear* by Carolyn E. Campbell, *The Old Mongoose and Other Poems* by Gerald Locklin and *Das 1st Alles: Charles Bukowski Recollected*, edited by Joan Jobe Smith. The editors add, "Advice for beginning poets? Just write from your own experience, using images that are as concrete and sensory as possible. Keep these images fresh and objective, and always listen to the music. . . ."

PECKERWOOD (II), 1475 King St. West, Apt. C-3, Toronto, Ontario M6K 1J4 Canada, phone (416)531-4262, founded 1987, editors Ernie Ourique and Yuki Hayashi, appears 3 or 4 times/year. **"It could be any style you wish, any length. Haiku—yes. Rhymes—yes. Beauty—yes. Ugliness—yes. No clones of good poets, creative writing class crap or poems written by television housewives."** They have recently published poetry by Chris Wood, Charles Bukowski, Allen Ginsberg, Pablo Garcia and Michael Fraser. As a sample the editor selected these lines from "bottles" by Coral Hull:

> *and how his dog branto used to dive down to the rivers centre and bring up fresh water*
> *mussels*
> *cracking them between his canine teeth in his frenzy to please*
> *i would feel the black edge of mussel shells between my toes . . .*

It is 30-40 pgs., saddle-stapled, photocopied from typescript with matte card cover. They accept about 30% of poems received. Press run is 450 for 160 shelf sales. **Sample: $2 cash. Editors sometimes provide comments on rejections. Pays 5 copies.** Staff reviews books of poetry. Send books for review consideration. Ernie Ourique says, "The poems should have tongues and hearts. No one can teach you how to write poetry. Don't accept the 'masters' of poetry (Pound, Eliot, Yeats) as the greatest. Explore poetry from all over the world. This means reading more than writing. Also get a job that doesn't involve brains: construction, washing toilets. You'll meet the greatest and worst human beings in the working class. Never insult people."

PEGASUS (II), 525 Ave. B, Boulder City NV 89005, founded 1986, editor M.E. Hildebrand, is a poetry quarterly "for serious poets who have something to say and know how to say it using sensory imagery." **Submit 3-5 poems, 3-40 lines. Avoid "religious, political, pornographic themes."** They have recently published poetry by John Grey, Stan Moseley, Gayle Elen Harvey, Robert K. Johnson and Elizabeth Perry, who provides the opening lines of "The Meeting Hour" as a sample:

> *Before Dawn drops*
> *her luminous petals*
> *I wake and listen*
> *for your muted voice*
> *to break the silence*
> *of our worlds*
> *like rustlings*
> *in the deep woods.*

Pegasus is 32 pgs., digest-sized, saddle-stapled, offset from typescript with colored paper cover. Publishes 10-15% of the work received. Circulation 200. Subscription: $12.50. **Sample postpaid: $4.50. Previously published poems OK, provided poet retains rights, but no simultaneous submissions. Send SASE for guidelines. Reports in 2 weeks. Publication is payment. Acquires first or one-time rights.**

THE PEGASUS REVIEW (I, II, IV-Themes), P.O. Box 88, Henderson MD 21640-0088, phone (410)482-6736, founded 1980, is a 14-page (counting cover) pamphlet entirely in calligraphy, illustrated on high-quality paper, some color overlays. Editor Art Bounds says, "This magazine is a bimonthly, **based on specific themes. Those for 1996 are: January/February—Language; March/ April—Animals; May/June—Childhood; July/August—America; September/October—Old Age; and November/December—Ideas. Because of the calligraphic format, open to all styles, but brevity is the key. Uses poetry not more than 24 lines (the shorter the better); fiction that is short short (about 2½ pages would be ideal); essays and cartoons. All material must pertain to indicated themes only. Would like to see various forms rather than just free verse."** Poets recently published include C. David Hay, Thelma Schiller, Ella Cavis and M.J. Vassallo. As a sample the editor selected these lines from "Art" by L.A. Evans:

> *Next to the ruddy glow*
> *of the eternal fire*
> *I place my small lump of coal*
> *inside is my heart.*

Press run is 160 for 150 subscribers, of which 4 are libraries. Subscription: $10. **Sample: $2. Submit 3-5 poems with name and address on each page. "Previously published poems OK, if there is no conflict or violation of rights agreement. Simultaneous submissions OK, but author must notify proper parties once specific material is accepted. Brief cover letter with specifics as they relate to one's writing background welcome." Query if additional information is needed. Reports within a month, often with a personal response. Pays 2 copies.** Occasional book awards throughout the year. Also issues a writer's calendar—in calligraphy—with motivational sayings and writing advice ($8 plus $2.50 p&h). The editor advises, "Follow all published guidelines carefully and accurately. Try to become familiar with most of the publications through a sample copy, a library copy or, possibly, a subscription. Many small presses are falling to the wayside. But new ones appear to come up. Overall they need support of both their subscribers as well as contributors. I urge each and every writer to either join or start a writers group. The benefits can be most rewarding. Above all, market your work and study your markets through such publications as *Poet's Market*, *International Directory of Small Presses and Literary Magazines* and the numerous writing magazines available. It pays to do your homework."

‡THE PEKING DUCK; O PATO, INC. (II), P.O. Box 331661, Corpus Christi TX 78463, founded 1993, editor Edward Cossette, appears 3 times a year. *The Peking Duck* (and its variant form, *O Pato!*) is "a mendicant publication with the aim of promoting experimental or other 'offbeat' forms of writing." **They have no specific guidelines regarding form, length, subject matter or style of poetry—"good work is good work."** They have recently published poetry by B.Z. Niditch, Lyn Lifshin, Arlene Mandrell and Errol Miller. As a sample we selected these lines from "A Different Kind of Surrender" by William J. Vernon:

> *This morning, fog breaking, I pause*
> *at windows, watching pine boughs*
> *droop with cones. Out there like dreams,*
>
> *the world makes designs,*
> *leaving patterns in lines*
> *so distinct, I imagine,*
> *tracing them to their source.*

The Peking Duck is 12 pgs., 8½ × 11, offset printed in 2 colors on 70 lb. glossy paper, saddle-stapled, drawings and graphics throughout. They receive 200-300 poems a year, accept approximately 5%. Press run is 400 for 100 subscribers of which 10 are libraries, 150 shelf sales. Single copy: $1-2; subscription: $6. **Sample postpaid: $2. Submit no more than 5 poems at a time. Previously published poems and simultaneous submissions OK. Seldom comments on rejections. Send SASE for guidelines. Reports in 1-3 months. Pays 5 copies.** The editor says, "Read an issue first! Much perfectly 'good' work gets passed over because it doesn't mesh with our outlook/style. Published poets are relentless: submitting often, writing always."

PELICAN PUBLISHING COMPANY (V, IV-Children, regional), Box 3110, Gretna LA 70054, founded 1926, editor Nina Kooij, is a "moderate-sized publisher of cookbooks, travel guides, regional books and inspirational/motivational books," which accepts **poetry for "hardcover children's books *only*, preferably with a Southern focus. However, our needs for this are very limited; we do fewer than 5 juvenile titles per year, and most of these are prose, not poetry."** They have recently published *Santa's Christmas Surprise*, by Robert Bernardini. As a sample the editor selected these lines from *Gaston Goes to the Kentucky Derby* by James Rice:

> The gallant Cajun steed
>   had nothing if not class.
> He politely stepped aside
>   and let the filly pass.

They are currently not accepting unsolicited mss. Query first with sample poems and cover letter including "work and writing backgrounds, plot summary and promotional connections." No previously published poems or simultaneous submissions. Reports on queries in 1 month, on mss (if invited) in 3 months. Always sends prepublication galleys. Pays royalties. Buys all rights. Returns rights upon termination of contract. These are 32-page, large-format (magazine-sized) books with illustrations. Two of their popular series are prose books about Gaston the Green-Nosed Alligator by James Rice and Clovis Crawfish by Mary Alice Fontenot. They have a variety of books based on "The Night Before Christmas" adapted to regional settings such as Cajun, prairie, and Texas. Typically their books sell for $14.95. **Write for catalog to buy samples.** The editor says, "We try to avoid rhyme altogether, especially predictable rhyme. Monotonous rhythm can also be a problem."

PEMBROKE MAGAZINE (II), Box 60, Pembroke State University, 1 University Dr., Pembroke NC 28372-1510, founded 1969 by Norman Macleod, edited by Shelby Stephenson, is a heavy (252 pgs., 6×9), flat-spined, quality literary annual which has published poetry by Fred Chappell, Stephen Sandy, A.R. Ammons, Barbara Guest and Betty Adcock. Press run is 500 for 125 subscribers of which 100 are libraries. **Sample postpaid: $5. Sometimes comments on rejections. Reports within 3 months. Pays copies.** Stephenson advises, "Publication will come if you write. Writing is all."

PEMMICAN (II); PEMMICAN PRESS (V), P.O. Box 16374, St. Paul MN 55116, phone (612)698-7710, founded 1992, editor Robert Edwards, is an annual magazine designed to publish "the best poetry of imagery, imagination and political commitment we can find." **They want "political poetry and poetry of imagery and imagination. No workshop minimalist, right wing or fundamentalist poetry; no greeting card verse. Poets familiar with the work of Thomas McGrath, Meridel LeSeuer and Don Gordon should have no problem understanding what it is we're looking for."** They have published poetry by Adrian C. Louis, Margaret Randall and Patrick Stanhope. As a sample the editor selected these lines from "Little Big Man" by Sherman Alexie:

> I got eyes, Jack, that can see
> an ant moving along the horizon
> can pull four bottles shattering
> down from the sky and recognize
> the eyes of a blind man

Pemmican is 40 pgs., 7×8½, saddle-stitched, card stock cover with original art. They receive 200-300 submissions a year, use less than 10%. Press run is 300 for 50 subscribers of which 15 are libraries, 100 shelf sales. Single copy: $3.50. **Sample postpaid: $2. Submit 6 poems at a time. No previously published poems; simultaneous submissions OK, "but *Pemmican* expects to be notified if a poem has been accepted elsewhere." Cover letter required. "Make sure postage on SASE is adequate for full return of submitted materials." Seldom comments on rejections. Send SASE for guidelines. Reports in 1 week to 6 months. Pays 1 copy. Acquires first North American serial rights.** The editor says, "There are no requirements—however, I hope poets realize the importance of the small presses and put their money where their mouth is. Advice for beginners? Keep writing. Read everything. Don't write to please an editor or to get published. Follow your own voice."

‡PEN AND INK MAGAZINE (I, II), P.O. Box 130574, Ann Arbor MI 48113-0574, founded 1994, editor Peter D. MacKay, is a semiannual magazine designed "to provide a forum for both new and established poets. *Pen and Ink* is interested in all forms of poetry, including free verse, experimental, and traditional styles. We prefer short to moderate length poems. Diversity is the key—many

styles, forms and subjects from many writers." They have recently published poetry by Junette Fabian, Winnie E. Fitzpatrick, Eric Bernreuter, Helen E. Rilling, T.N. Turner, Jane Taylor Overton, Todd Weiss, Bruce E. Massis, M.Q. Thorburn and Taylor Reese. As a sample the editor selected this complete poem, "Hibernation," by Joy Hewitt Mann:

> *My need to write is dormant*
> *as I sleep between my winter words,*
> *praying spring will come to melt*
> *the ice that seals this unlit cave.*

Pen and Ink is 40-52 pgs., digest-sized, neatly printed and saddle-stapled with light card stock cover. They accept 10-15% of the poetry received. Press run is 100-150. Subscription: $9. **Sample postpaid: $5. Include name, address and phone number on every page of submission. No previously published poems or simultaneous submissions. A SASE (or SAE and IRCs) must be included for response. Send SASE for guidelines. Reports in 1-3 months. Pays 1 copy. Acquires first rights.**

‡**PENNINE INK (I, II)**, % Mid Pennine Arts, MP The Gallery, Yorke St., Burnley BB11 3JJ Great Britain, founded 1985, appears annually ("hopefully more frequently") using mainly poems, a few short prose items and a few b&w illustrations. They want **"poetry up to 40 lines maximum. Consider all kinds."** As a sample the editor selected these lines from "Bandit Player" by Derek Woodcock:

> *Racy lights moved the bar wall*
> *as the girl, all high-tech poise,*
> *switched on menus, shot coins down chutes,*
> *her face, I imagined, warmed by coals,*
> *sweetened by a line of grapes.*
> *The black-eyed Cleopatra flaunted tokens,*
> *played for time, sipped the final snakebite.*

The editor says it is 48 pgs., A5, with b&w illustrated cover, a few small local ads and 3 or 4 b&w graphics. They receive about 400 items a year, use approximately 40. Press run is 350. **Sample postpaid: £1.50 sterling. Submit up to 6 poems at a time. Previously published poems and simultaneous submissions OK. Cover letter preferred. Seldom comments on rejections. "Contributors whose works are accepted receive one free copy if 2 IRCs sent."** Reviews small press poetry books in about 200 words.

PENNINE PLATFORM (II), Ingmanthorpe Hall Farm Cottage, Wetherby, W. Yorkshire LS22 5EQ England, phone 0937-584674, founded 1973, poetry editor Brian Merrikin Hill, appears 3 times a year. The editor wants **any kind of poetry but concrete ("lack of facilities for reproduction"). No specifications of length, but poems of less than 40 lines have a better chance. "All styles—effort is to find things good of their kind. Preference for religious or sociopolitical awareness of an acute, not conventional kind."** They have published poetry by Elizabeth Bartlett, Anna Adams, John Ward, Ian Caws, John Latham and Geoffrey Holloway. As a sample the editor selected these lines from "A Vision of Cabez De Vaca" by Cal Clothier:

> *Blanched to a skin manned by bones,*
> *we have blood and our breathing*
> *to prove we are men, and the hungry light*
> *jerking our eyes. We are down to mercy,*
> *gratitude, love, down to humanity.*

The 6×8, 48-page journal is photocopied from typescript, saddle-stapled, with matte card cover with graphics, circulation 400, 300 subscriptions of which 16 are libraries. They receive about 300 submissions/year, use about 30, have about a 6-month backlog. Subscription: £7 for 3 issues (£10 abroad; £25 if not in sterling). **Sample postpaid: £2. Submit 1-6 poems, typed. Reports in about a month. No pay. Acquires first serial rights. Editor occasionally comments on rejections.** Reviews books of poetry in 2,500 words, multi-book format. Open to unsolicited reviews. Poets may also send books for review consideration. They would like to see more sociopolitical themes in traditional forms, less free verse. Brian Hill comments, "It is time to avoid the paradigm-magazine-poem and reject establishments—ancient, modern or allegedly contemporary. Small magazines and presses often publish superior material to the commercial hyped publishers."

ALWAYS include a self-addressed, stamped envelope (SASE) when sending a ms or query to a publisher within your own country. When sending material to other countries, include a self-addressed envelope and International Reply Coupons (IRCs), available for purchase at most post offices.

PENNSYLVANIA ENGLISH (II), Penn State-Erie, Erie PA 16563, phone (814)824-2000, founded 1988 (first issue in March, 1989), poetry editor John Coleman, is "a journal sponsored by the Pennsylvania College English Association." They want poetry of **"any length, any style."** The journal is magazine-sized, saddle-stapled, and appears twice a year. Press run is 300. Subscription: $15, which includes membership in PCEA. **Submit 4-5 typed poems at a time. Do not submit mss in the summer. They consider simultaneous submissions but not previously published poems. Reports in 1 month. Pays 2 copies.**

THE PENNSYLVANIA REVIEW (II), English Dept., 526 CL, University of Pittsburgh, Pittsburgh PA 15260, phone (412)624-0026, founded 1985, editor Rick Sides. This ambitious semiannual journal is most noted for "gathering the works of writers of varying cultural and stylistic orientations. We are not afraid to publish fresh, strange voices." **There are no restrictions on subject matter, style or length, although they do not want to see "light verse or greeting card verse." They would like to receive more work by "non-mainstream writers (African-American, Latino/a, etc.)."** They have published poetry by Nance Van Winckel, Jim Daniels, Sharon Doubiago, Lawrence Joseph and Sonia Sanchez. As a sample the editor selected these lines from "Ontological" by Maggie Anderson:

> This is going to cost you.
> If you really want to hear a
> country fiddle, you have to listen
> hard, high up in its twang and needle.
> You can't be running off like this,
> all knotted up with yearning. . .

PR is changing to a tabloid format (in the style of *American Poetry Review* and *The Threepenny Review*). Circulation is approximately 1,000 with 350 subscriptions. Subscription: $7 for 2 issues. **Sample postpaid: $4. Writers should submit 3-6 poems, typewritten only. Cover letter with brief 3-line bio (publishable if work is accepted) required. Do not submit mss between May 1 and September 1. Publishes theme issues occasionally. Reports in 2-3 months. Pays 2 copies.** Staff reviews books of poetry and fiction. Send books for review consideration.

THE PENUMBRA PRESS (II), 920 S. 38th St., Omaha NE 68105, phone (402)346-7344, founded 1972, poetry editors Bonnie O'Connell and George O'Connell, publishes "contemporary literature and graphics in the tradition of fine arts printing." Their books are "designed, illustrated (unless otherwise indicated), hand printed from hand-set type, and bound by the proprietor," Bonnie O'Connell. All are limited editions, including hard and soft cover books, chapbooks, postcards and theme anthologies. They have published poetry by David St. John, Sam Pereira, Brenda Hillman, Debora Greger, Peter Everwine, Laura Jensen, Norman Dubie and Rita Dove. As a sample the editor selected these lines from "Cool Dark Ode" by Donald Justice:

> When the long planed table that served as a desk
> was recalling the quiet of the woods
> when the books, older, were thinking farther back,
> to the same essential stillness . . .

Query with 5-6 samples, some personal background and publication credits. Simultaneous submissions OK. Editor sometimes comments on rejections. Send SASE for catalog to order samples or inquire at university libraries (special collection) or through the distributor, Nebraska Book Arts Center, 124 Fine Arts Bldg., University of Nebraska-Omaha, Omaha NE 68182.

PEOPLENET (I, IV-Specialized: disabled people, love/romance), P.O. Box 897, Levittown NY 11756-0911, phone (516)579-4043, e-mail rmauro@delphi.com, founded 1987, editor/publisher Robert Mauro, is a newsletter **for disabled people focusing on dating, love and relationships.** The editor wants **"poetry on relationships, love and romance only. The length should remain 10 lines or less. We publish beginners, new poets. Prefer free verse, a lot of good imagery—and very little rhyme."** As a sample the editor selected these lines from his poem "When All That Blooms Are Roses":

> Mornings are not mornings
> when all that blooms are roses:
> dewy petals opening, blushing
> in the wind; a hand
> plucks a flower, a finger
> touches a bud that didn't
> bloom and never will.

Peoplenet appears 3 times a year and is 12-16 pgs., magazine-sized, offset, using graphics and ads. Press run is about 200, with that many subscriptions. Subscription: $25. **Sample copy: $3. Submit 3 poems at a time. Poems should be neatly typed, double-spaced, with name and address on each page. No simultaneous submissions. Editor comments on good but rejected mss. Reports "immediately." Pays tearsheets only. Acquires first rights.** (Copies of the newsletter, which contains personal ads, go to subscribers only. Free brochure available.) **He says, "We want to publish poems** that express the importance of love, acceptance, inner beauty, the need for love and relationship, and the joy of loving and being loved."

PEP PUBLISHING; LOVING MORE (I, IV-Specialized: "ethical multiple relationships"), P.O. Box 6306, Ocean View HI 96737, fax (808)929-9831, founded 1984, editor Ryam Nearing. *Loving More* is a quarterly that "publishes articles, letters, poems, drawings and reviews related to polyfidelity, group marriage and multiple *intimacy.*" They use "relatively short poems, though a quality piece of length would be considered, but topic relevance is essential. Please no swinger or porno pieces. Group marriage should not be equated with group sex." It is 40 pgs., magazine-sized, few ads. Circulation 1,000. Subscription: $49 a year. **Sample: $6 to poets. Submit up to 10 poems at a time. Ms should be "readable." Considers simultaneous submissions.** Time between acceptance and publication is 2-6 months. **Editor comments on rejections "sometimes—if requested." Publishes theme issues. Send SASE for upcoming themes. Responds "ASAP." Pays 1 copy.** Open to unsolicited reviews. Poets may also send books for review consideration. The editor says, "Writers should read our publication before submitting, and I emphasize no swinger or porno pieces will be published."

PEQUOD: A JOURNAL OF CONTEMPORARY LITERATURE AND LITERARY CRITICISM (III), Dept. of English, New York University, 19 University Place, Room 200, New York NY 10003, contact poetry editor, is a semiannual literary review publishing **quality poetry, fiction, essays and translations**. They have published poetry by Sam Hamill, Donald Hall and John Updike. It is professionally printed, digest-sized, 200 pgs., flat-spined with glossy card cover. Subscription: $12. **Sample postpaid: $5. Reads submissions September 15 through April 15 only. Always sends prepublication galleys.** Poetry published in *Pequod* has also been included in the 1993 and 1995 volumes of *The Best American Poetry*.

PERIVALE PRESS; PERIVALE POETRY CHAPBOOKS; PERIVALE TRANSLATION SERIES (II, IV-Translations, anthology), 13830 Erwin St., Van Nuys CA 91401-2914, phone (818)785-4671, founded 1968, editor Lawrence P. Spingarn, publishes **Perivale Poetry Chapbooks, Perivale Translation Series**, anthologies. The collections by individuals are usually translations, but here are some lines by R.L. Barth from "Da Nang Nights: Liberty Song" in *Forced-Marching to the Styx*:

> *In sudden light we choose*
> *Lust by lust our bar:*
> *And whatever else we lose,*
> *We also lose the war.*

They publish an average of one 20-page saddle-stapled chapbook, one perfect-bound (20-70 pgs.) collection, one anthology per year, all quality print jobs. Send SASE for catalog. Perivale publishes both on **straight royalty basis (10%, 10 author's copies) usually grant supported, and by subsidy, the author paying 100%, being repaid from profits, if any.** "Payment for chapbooks accepted is 100 free copies of press run. Authors should agree to promote books via readings, talk shows, orders and signings with local bookshops. **Contributors are encouraged to buy samples of chapbooks, etc., for clues to editor's tastes." Samples of previous poetry chapbooks: $5.75 postpaid.** (Barth title out of print.) Latest title: *Going Home* (chapbook) by Sheryl St. Germain. **To submit, query first, with sample of 5 poems, cover letter, bio, previous books. Do not submit mss from June 15 to September 1. Reports in 6 weeks. Always sends prepublication galleys.** Spingarn, a well-known, widely published poet, offers criticism for a fee, the amount dependent on length of book. Sponsors a poetry chapbook contest. Winner receives $100 plus 60 copies of chapbook. Reading fee: $12. Send SASE for details. The editor advises, "Contributors should read samples and guidelines thoroughly before submitting. Also, we would like to see poems with less self-involvement (fewer poems that open with 'I') and a wider world view."

PERMAFROST: A LITERARY JOURNAL; MIDNIGHT SUN CHAPBOOK CONTEST (II, IV-Regional), %English Dept., 203 Fine Arts Complex, University of Alaska Fairbanks, Fairbanks AK 99775, is an annual publication founded 1977. *Permafrost* publishes poems, short stories, creative nonfiction and b&w drawings, photographs and prints. "We survive on both new and established writers, and hope and expect to see your best work. **We publish any style of poetry provided it is conceived, written and revised with care.** While we encourage submissions about Alaska and by Alaskans, we also encourage and welcome poems about anywhere and from anywhere. We have published work by Wendy Bishop, John Haines, Naomi Shihab Nye, Peggy Shumaker, Leslie Fields, John Morgan and Patricia Monaghan." The journal is 100-125 pgs., 4×6, flat-spined, professionally printed, with b&w graphics and photos. Subscription: $7. **Sample postpaid: $5. Submit 3-10 poems, typed, single or double-spaced, and formatted as they should appear. Considers simultaneous submissions. Deadline: March 15. Does not accept submissions between April 1 and August 1.** Editors comment only on mss that have made the final round. Send SASE for further guidelines. Return time is 1-3 months. Journal is distributed in late summer/early fall. **Pays 2 copies; reduced contributor rate on additional copies.** *Permafrost* also sponsors the Midnight Sun Poetry Chapbook

Contest. Chapbook should be approximately 20-25 pages in length. Contest entry fee: $10, includes a subscription to the journal. Deadline: March 15. Winner receives 25 copies. Recent winners include Laurie O'Brien and Kevin Griffith.

PERMEABLE PRESS; PUCK: THE UNOFFICIAL JOURNAL OF THE IRREPRESSIBLE (III), 47 Noe St. #4, San Francisco CA 94114-1017, phone (415)648-2175, founded 1984, editor Brian Clark, associate editor Stan Henry. *Puck* is a triannual designed to "provoke thought, dialog. Contents: reviews, stories, essays, poems." **As for poetry they want "radical reinterpretations of the 'accepted.' No restrictions as to style, length, etc. No love poems."** They have published poetry by B. Subraman and Hugh Fox. As a sample they selected these lines from "Tarot of Nature" by Susan Luzarro:

> *Yesterday the queen of wands came to me. She was painted with honey-colored locks*
> *to perpetuate the myth that nature, like christ, was blonde.* Lay me down, *she said.*
> Do not reverse me & I will offer you this sunflower, beneath it—a promise—the
> bud of an unknown flower. I spit on the solace of nature, *I said,* give me a happy life.

The editors describe *Puck* as 80 pgs., 8½ × 11, offset and saddle-stapled with color covers. They accept 1% or less of poetry received. Press run is 2,000 for 200 subscribers of which 4 are libraries, 1,000 shelf sales. Single copy: $6.50; subscription: $17/3 issues. **Previously published poems OK; no simultaneous submissions. Cover letter required. "SASE must be big enough to accommodate return of all material submitted." Send SASE for guidelines. Reports in 1-4 weeks. Pays 2 copies. Acquires first North American serial or reprint rights. "Subsequent publication should mention** *Puck.*" They add, "Current issue contains 30 (out of 80) pages of reviews. We review anything, everything." Permeable Press also publishes 6 paperbacks and **3 chapbooks/year. Query first with sample poems and cover letter with brief bio and publication credits. Replies to queries in 1 month, to mss in 1-2 months. Pays 50 author's copies for chapbooks.**

PERSEA BOOKS (V), 60 Madison Ave., New York NY 10010, phone (212)779-7668, editor Michael Braziller, publishes books of **"serious" poetry.** They have published poetry by Thylias Moss, Paul Blackburn and Wayne Koestenbaum. They publish 1-2 books of poetry/year. **However, they are not reading unsolicited mss until November 1996. "We are committed to future books of poets we are already publishing."**

PETERLOO POETS (II), 2 Kelly Gardens, Calstock, Cornwall PL18 9SA Great Britain, founded 1977, poetry editor Harry Chambers. They publish collections of "well-made" poetry (rhyming and free verse) under the Peterloo Poets imprint: flat-spined paperbacks, hardbacks and poetry cassettes. They have recently published poetry by U.A. Fanthorpe, John Levett, John Whitworth and Maurice Rutherford. As a sample we selected these lines from "In the Pub" as published in *Masterclass* by Brian Waltham:

> *Out here the two of us yell*
> *Above the yell above the jukebox.*
> *We need words that reach, but the*
> *Words we need make no sense*
> *Unless they're said quietly*
> *Or said by needful arms or*
> *By a hand tracing the*
> *Curve of a cheek.*

Query with 10 sample poems, bio and list of publications. Considers simultaneous submissions and previously published poems if they have not been in book form. Always sends prepublication galleys. Pays 10% royalties, $100 advance (for first volume, $200 for subsequent volumes) and 12 copies. Editor "normally, briefly" comments on rejections. Sponsors an annual open poetry competition. First prize: £3,000 sterling; second prize: £1,000 sterling; four other prizes totaling £1,100 sterling. Send IRC for entry form and rules.

‡PETRONIUM PRESS (V, IV-Regional), 1255 Nuuanu Ave., 1813, Honolulu HI 96817, founded 1975, editor Frank Stewart. Petronium is a small press publisher of poetry, fiction, essays and art— **"primarily interested in writers in and from Hawaii, but will publish others under special circumstances.** Interested in fine printing, fine typography and design in limited editions." They publish chapbooks, trade books, limited editions, broadsides and "other ephemera," but they **are not accepting unsolicited material at this time."** They publish 3-6 poetry chapbooks/year, with an average page count of 32, flat-spined paperbacks. The editor says, **"Query letters are welcome, with SASE." He replies to queries within 3 weeks and reports on mss in the same amount of time. He has "no special requirements," but will not accept photocopied mss or discs. "Payment of authors is negotiated differently for each book." Buys all rights. Returns rights by request. The editor does not comment on rejections "unless the material is exceptionally good."** He says, "We are not really for beginners nor, in general, for people outside the Pacific region. We are not strict regionalists, but believe in nurturing first the writers around us. Beginning writers might do well to look for publishers with this same philosophy in their own cities and states rather than flinging their work to the wind, to unknown editors or to large publishing houses. All writers should consider supporting quality publishing in their own region first." Some of Petronium's books are distributed by the University of Hawaii Press (2840 Kolowalu St., Honolulu HI 96822) and may be obtained from them; "send for their literature catalog or ask for our titles specifically."

PHASE AND CYCLE (II); PHASE AND CYCLE PRESS (V), 3537 E. Prospect, Fort Collins CO 80525, phone (303)482-7573, founded 1988, poetry editor Loy Banks. *Phase and Cycle* is a poetry magazine published semiannually. **"We look for short to moderate-length poems of all kinds, especially those that set out 'the long perspectives open at each instance' (Larkin). We are looking for poetry that will pass technical inspection in the academic community. Also, we prefer poetry that is largely accessible rather than deliberately 'difficult'."** They have recently published poetry by Theresa Arceneaux, Diane Webster, David Starkey, Rhina Espaillat and Rod Farmer. As a sample the editor selected these lines from "Hiroshima Maidens" by Daniel James Sundahl:

> *Hiroshima,*
> *our barren city,*
> *where the one red leaf,*
> *there,*
> *upon the bough,*
> *churns*
> *in blind delirium.*

The magazine is 48 pgs., digest-sized, saddle-stapled. **Sample postpaid: $1. Submit 4-7 poems at a time. "A brief bio note may accompany poems." No simultaneous submissions or previously published poems. Editor sometimes comments on rejections. Send SASE for guidelines. Reports in 5-10 weeks. Pays 2 copies. Acquires first rights only.** Poets may send books for review consideration. Phase and Cycle Press has published two poetry chapbooks, *Breathing In The World* by Bruce Holland Rogers and Holly Arrow and *Out of Darkness* by Mary Balazs. **"At present we accept inquiries only. No book manuscripts."**

‡PHILOMEL; PHILOMATHEAN SOCIETY (II), Box 7, College Hall, University of Pennsylvania, Philadelphia PA 19104, phone (215)898-8907, e-mail philo@dolphin.upenn.edu, founded in 1813, editor Mr. E.C. Morales. *Philomel* is a literary annual using **"any kind of poetry, no more than 300 words or 3 pgs. per poem."** They also use stories, essays and "witty recipes." As a sample, they selected these lines from "Epitaph" by Jennifer Dozio:

> *You are the sign I leave.*
> *One contribution of the million that could have been.*
> *Thus the Father meant to say to the Daughter:*
> *I gave you life inadvertantly.*
> *I left flesh behind me*
> *as I was flesh.*

Philomel comes out each spring. It is 64 pgs., 6×9, flat-spined, with matte card cover. Poems are selected by a committee of the Philomathean Society. Press run is 1,500 for 20 subscribers of which 3 are libraries, 1,400 distributed free to the university community. **Sample postpaid: $3. Submit up to 3 poems at a time. Deadline for submissions: February 1, annually.**

PHILOMEL BOOKS (III), 200 Madison Ave., New York NY 10016, phone (212)951-8700, an imprint founded in 1980, editorial director Patricia Gauch. Philomel Books publishes 2-3 paperbacks, 25-30 hardbacks and 5-7 chapbooks/year. They say, "Since we're a children's book imprint, **we are open to individual poem submissions—anything suitable for a picture book. However, publication of poetry collections is usually done on a project basis—we acquire from outside through permissions, etc. Don't usually use unpublished material."** They have published poetry by Edna St. Vincent Millay and Walt Whitman. **Query first with 3 sample poems and cover letter including publishing history. Previously published poems and simultaneous submissions OK. Replies to queries in 1 month, to mss in 2. Pay is negotiable.**

‡THE PHLEBAS PRESS (V), 2 The Stables, High Park, Oxenholme, Kendal, Cumbria LA9 7RE United Kingdom, founded 1990, publishes **up to 3 chapbooks/year.** They publish **"poems that take an independent or imaginative view of the human condition and human spirit. No middle-class sentimentality or poems that could double as adverts."** They have published chapbooks of poetry by A.C. Evans and Martin A. Hibbert. As a sample the editor selected these lines from "Vertical Time" in *In the Absence of a Summit* by Norman Jope:

> *Every dome of crystal, however distantly, reflects a*
> *murder. White and red, the tissues line the spotless aisles*
> *of supermarkets. Muzak 'happens'— a theme from Offenbach,*
> *played digitally, asserts the act of liquidation.*

> *Now, we work to work, we live to live, and only*
> *cheque-cards hold us to our promises . . .*

"Unfortunately we cannot accept any submissions at present. Unsolicited mss will be burned. Recommended poets are asked for submissions." Phlebas normally expects authors to buy back, and distribute, most of the print run.

PHOEBE (IV-Women/feminism), Women's Studies Dept., S.U.N.Y. College at Oneonta, Oneonta NY 13820, phone (607)436-2014, founded 1988, editor Kathleen O'Mara, is a biannual feminist journal containing scholarly articles, short fiction and poetry, book reviews and occasional artwork. **As for poetry, they have "no specifications vis-a-vis form, length, etc. Seek material describing, either directly or vaguely, women's experiences/realities. Nothing sexist, racist or homophobic."** They have recently published poetry by Lyn Lifshin, B.A. St. Andrews, Edith Pearlman, Patti Tana and Kyoko Mori. As a sample the editor selected these lines from "Girlfriends" by Wanda Coleman:

> *we are faced with the irrefutable analyses*
> *no one's gonna pay us for what's left of*
> *our gal youth and out lady beauty*
>
> *a connection in New York, London or the Vatican*
> *is worth the expense of self-transmission as in*
> *send bio demo-tape shoe size and lock of hair*

Phoebe is 120 pgs., approximately 7×9, professionally printed and perfect-bound, coated card cover with artwork. They receive about 220 poems a year, use approximately 18-20%. Press run is 500 for 200 subscribers of which 15% are libraries, 100 shelf sales. Single copy: $7.50; subscription: $15. **Sample postpaid: $5. Previously published poems OK; no simultaneous submissions. Submissions preferred August 15 through April 15. Seldom comments on rejections. Send SASE for guidelines. Reports within 3 months. Pays 2 copies.** Reviews books of poetry in 500-2,000 words.

PHOEBE (II), George Mason University, 4400 University Dr., Fairfax VA 22030, phone (703)993-2915, founded 1970, poetry editors Jean Donnelly and Kaki Cuzts, is a literary biannual **"looking for imagery that will make your thumbs sweat when you touch it."** They have published poetry by C.K. Williams, Mark Doty, Cornelius Eady, Carolyn Forché, Thomas Lux and Bill Knott. As a sample the editor selected these lines from "Semantics of Longing" by Leslie Bumstead:

> *Was he superb in speech*
> *class? Even at parties with women dangling*
> *hunger on their brilliant clavicles, he must*
> *forever look for the just and longest*
> *word (it's Samson through the trees*
> *of high heels) . . .*

Circulation 3,000, with 30-35 pgs. of poetry in each issue. Subscription: $8/year; $4/single issue. *Phoebe* receives 4,000 submissions/year. **Submit up to 5 poems at a time; submission should be accompanied by SASE and a short bio. No simultaneous submissions. Reports in 2-3 months. Pays copies.** Work published in *Phoebe* was selected for inclusion in *The Best American Poetry 1993*.

PIG IRON; KENNETH PATCHEN COMPETITION (II, IV-Themes), Dept. PM, P.O. Box 237, Youngstown OH 44501, phone (216)747-6932, founded 1975, poetry editor Jim Villani, is a literary annual devoted to special themes. They want **poetry "up to 300 lines; free verse and experimental; write for current themes."** Forthcoming themes: The Family: Tradition & Possibility and Jazz Tradition. **They do *not* want to see "traditional" poetry.** They have published poetry by Wayne Hogan, Laurel Speer, Louis McKee, Lloyd Mills, Marian Steele, Hugh Fox and John Pyros. As a sample the editor selected these lines by Joan Kincaid:

> *I'm yelling my goose call*
> *bahonk bahonk*
> *to make her laugh*
> *because there are no geese*
> *when we're surprised*
> *by an eerie screech-purr*
> *echoing across the dark water*
> *I bahonk again*
> *and a white swan launches*
> *into the night a song*
> *I've never heard.*

Pig Iron is 128 pgs., magazine-sized, flat-spined, typeset on good stock with glossy card cover using b&w graphics and art, no ads, circulation 1,000. They have 200 subscriptions of which 50 are libraries. Single copy: $10.95. Subscription: $9/1 year, $16/2 years. **Sample postpaid: $4. No simultaneous submissions. Send SASE for guidelines. Reports in 3 months.** Time between acceptance and publication is 12-18 months. **Pays $5/poem plus 2 copies. Buys one-time rights.** They sponsor the annual Kenneth Patchen Competition. Send SASE for details. The editor says, "We want tomorrow's poetry, not yesterday's."

THE PIKESTAFF FORUM; PIKESTAFF PUBLICATIONS, INC.; THE PIKESTAFF PRESS; PIKE-STAFF POETRY CHAPBOOKS (II, IV-Children, teens), P.O. Box 127, Normal IL 61761, phone (309)452-4831, founded 1977, poetry editors Robert D. Sutherland, James R. Scrimgeour and James McGowan, is "a not-for-profit literary press. Publishes a magazine of national distribution, *The Pikestaff Forum*, and a poetry chapbook series." They want **"substantial, well-crafted poems; vivid, memorable, based in lived experience—*Not*: self-indulgent early drafts, 'private' poems, five finger exercises, warmed over workshop pieces, vague abstractions, philosophical woolgathering, 'journal entries,' inspirational uplift. The shorter the better, though long poems are no problem; we are eclectic; welcome traditional or experimental work. We won't publish pornography or racist/sexist material."** They have published poetry by Gayl Teller, J.W. Rivers, Lucia Cordell Getsi, Frannie Lindsay and Fritz Hamilton. *The Pikestaff Forum* is an annual newsprint tabloid, 40 pgs., "handsome, open layout. Trying to set a standard in tabloid design. Special features: poetry, fiction, commentary, reviews, young writers (7-17 in a special section), editors' profiles (other magazines), The Forum (space for anyone to speak out on matters of literary/publishing concern)." Circulation 1,100 with 200 subscriptions of which 5 are libraries. They receive 2,000-3,000 submissions/year, use 2%, have a year's backlog. Subscription: $12/6 issues. **Sample postpaid: $3. "Each poem should be on a separate sheet, with author's name and address. We prefer no simultaneous submissions—but if it is, we expect to be informed of it." No more than 6 poems/submission. Send SASE for guidelines. Reports within 3 months. Pays 3 copies.** Reviews books of poetry if published by small presses or self-published. Open to unsolicited reviews. This is a lively publication and editors typically comment on rejected work that has merit. All forms and styles appear here, but published verse usually displays a high degree of craft that somehow enhances content (always insightful or unusual). **Query with samples and brief bio for chapbook publication. Replies to queries in 2 weeks, to submission (if invited) in 3 months. Always sends prepublication galleys for chapbooks. Pays 20% of press run.** They advise, "For beginners: Don't be in a hurry to publish; work toward becoming your own best editor and critic; when submitting, send only what you think is your very best work; avoid indulging yourself at the expense of your readers; have something to say that's worth your readers' life-time to read; before submitting, ask yourself, 'Why should *any* reader be asked to read this?'; regard publishing as conferring a responsibility."

PIKEVILLE REVIEW (II), Humanities Dept., Pikeville College, Pikeville KY 41501, phone (606)432-9234, founded 1987, editor James Alan Riley, who says: **"There's no editorial bias though we recognize and appreciate style and control in each piece. No emotional gushing."** *PR* appears once yearly, accepting about 10% of poetry received. Press run is 500. **Sample postpaid: $3. No simultaneous submissions or previously published poetry. Editor sometimes comments on rejections. Send SASE for guidelines. Pays 5 copies.** They also sponsor contests.

PINCHGUT PRESS (V), 6 Oaks Ave., Cremorne, Sydney, NSW 2090 Australia, founded 1948, publishes **Australian poetry but is not currently accepting poetry submissions. Send SASE for catalog to order samples.**

THE PINEHURST JOURNAL; PINEHURST PRESS (I, II), P.O. Box 360747, Milpitas CA 95036, phone (510)440-9259, founded 1990, editor Michael K. McNamara, is a quarterly. **"Generally open, 24-line limit. Some sort of rhyme, meter, assonance, consonance or alliteration is a plus as well as good haiku. No religious, porno or dire despair. Work should be original, no reprints."** They have recently published poetry by Pearl Bloch Segall, Daniel Greer and Wilma Elizabeth McDaniel. As a sample the editor selected "Waiting" by Barbara Kinsey Sable:

> There's sun of my sinning
> And lie-a-weep, too.
> And love of my living
> And bide-a-sleep, do.
> You're gain and a-goning
> And humming shall fly.
> I'm lone and a-homing
> And worrying why.
> So come to my waiting
> Come to my near.
> Compassion and clearing,
> Come, come to my dear.

It is 44 pgs., magazine-sized, offset from typescript, saddle-stapled. Of 800 poems/year received they use 120. Press run is 250 for 100 subscribers of which 1 is a library. Subscription: $18. **Sample** postpaid: **$5. Submit no more than 6 poems at a time. "We feel a cover letter is an asset/vehicle of introduction for all contributors and should be employed. It is not a requirement, however." Send SASE for guidelines. Reports in 6-8 weeks. Pays 1 copy. Acquires one-time rights.** Staff reviews books of poetry. Send books for review consideration.

THE PIPE SMOKER'S EPHEMERIS (I, IV-Specialized), 20-37 120th St., College Point NY 11356, editor/publisher Tom Dunn, who says, "The *Ephemeris* is a limited edition, irregular quarterly **for pipe smokers and anyone else who is interested in its varied contents.** Publication costs are absorbed by the editor/publisher, assisted by any contributions—financial or otherwise—that readers might wish to make." **They want poetry with themes related to pipes and pipe smoking.** Issues range from 76-96 pgs., offset from photoreduced typed copy, colored paper covers, with illustrations, saddle-stitched. The editor has also published collections covering the first and second 15 years of the *Ephemeris*. **Cover letter required with submissions; include any credits.** Staff also reviews books of poetry. Send books for review consideration.

PIRATE WRITINGS; PIRATE WRITINGS PUBLISHING (I, II, IV-Science fiction/fantasy, mystery), 53 Whitman Ave., Islip NY 11751, founded 1992, editor and publisher Edward J. McFadden. *Pirate Writings* is a quarterly magazine "filled with fiction, poetry, art and reviews by top name professionals and tomorrow's rising stars." **They want all forms and styles of poetry "within our genres—literary (humorous or straight), fantasy, science fiction, mystery/suspense and adventure. Best chance is 20 lines or less. No crude language or excessive violence. No pornography, horror, western or romance. Poems should be typed with exact capitalization and punctuation suited to your creative needs."** They have recently published poetry by Warren Lapine, G.O. Clark, John Grey and C. David Hay. As a sample the editor selected these lines from "The Long Cellar" by Jane Yolen:

> *Jack Dogherty knew a merrow*
> *could drink any man of Ennis*
> *under the pub table*
> *and still find strength*
> *to crawl back to the sea.*

Pirate Writings is 72 pgs., magazine-sized and saddle-stapled with a full-color cover and b&w art throughout. They receive about 150 poetry submissions a year, use approximately 15-25 poems. Press run is 5,000. Subscription: $15 for 4 issues. **Sample postpaid: $4.99. Simultaneous submissions OK. Cover letter required; include credits, if applicable. Often comments on rejections. Send SASE for guidelines. Reports in 1-2 months. Pays 1-2 copies. Acquires first North American serial rights. Also "reserves the right to print in anthology."** Query regarding reviews of chapbooks. Pirate Writings Publishing **publishes chapbooks through various arrangements.** They have recently published *Moorhaven Fair* by Richard Novak. **Query first. Replies to queries in 1 month, to mss in 2 months. Poets may have to share publication costs. For sample chapbooks, write for flier.** Pirate Writings Publishing has also published *The Poe Pulpit*, stories and poems in the Poe tradition, and *Thoughts of Christmas*.

PITT POETRY SERIES; UNIVERSITY OF PITTSBURGH PRESS; AGNES LYNCH STARRETT POETRY PRIZE (II), 127 N. Bellefield Ave., Pittsburgh PA 15260, founded 1968, poetry editor Ed Ochester, publishes **"poetry of the highest quality; otherwise, no restrictions—book mss minimum of 48 pages." Poets who have previously published books should query. Simultaneous submissions OK. Always sends prepublication galleys.** They have published books of poetry by Richard Garcia, Larry Levis, Sharon Doubiago, Robley Wilson and Liz Rosenberg. Their booklist also features such poets as Peter Meinke, Leonard Nathan, Sharon Olds, Ronald Wallace, David Wojahn and Belle Waring. **"Poets who have not previously published a book should send SASE for rules of the Starrett competition ($12.50 handling fee), the *only* vehicle through which we publish first books of poetry."** The Starrett Prize consists of cash award of $2,500 and book publication.

THE PITTSBURGH QUARTERLY; THE SARA HENDERSON HAY PRIZE (II), 36 Haberman Ave., Pittsburgh PA 15211-2144, phone (412)431-8885, founded 1990, editor Frank Correnti, who says, **"Our first criterion is good writing with the variety of content that is common to a broad community interest. Generally, writing with narrative and real-life elements. We don't want doggerel or most rhyme."** They have published poetry by Marc Jampole, Ellen Smith, Kristin Kovacic, Robert Cooperman and Lynne Hugo de Courcy. As a sample the editor selected these lines from "Tender Meat" by June Hopper Hymas:

> *. . . the sounds and the smells of the lives of the poet*
> *and the poet's ancestors. I haven't thought*
>
> *to ask my children if they talk to janitors or sometimes feel*
> *like sawdust: null brown bits, cellulose without form.*

> *Tonight is a hot night; when you hung up on me,*
> *I did not call you back. I am reclaiming myself.*

It is 76 pgs., digest-sized, professionally printed, saddle-stapled with matte card cover. Press run is 700 for 250 subscribers of which 10 are libraries, 300 shelf sales. Subscription: $12 ($14 Canadian). **Sample postpaid: $5. "We will reply by letter to queries." Editor often comments on submissions. Reports in 3-4 months. Pays 2 copies. Acquires first North American serial rights.** Published books are reviewed as space is available, 1-2/issue. Accepts reviews of 4-6 pages, double-spaced. Send books for review consideration. "We are responding in part to the network of writers whose crafted creativity made the magazine possible, but we also are attempting to provide a readership that will connect more strongly to the community of poets and writers through this quarterly." *The Pittsburgh Quarterly* now sponsors an annual prize for poetry: The Sara Henderson Hay Prize. Entry requires current subscription or renewal and is limited to 3 poems up to 100 lines each. Deadline: July 1. Winner receives a cash award and publication of the winning poem in the fall issue.

PIVOT (II), 250 Riverside Dr., #23, New York NY 10025, phone (212)222-1408, founded 1951, editor Martin Mitchell, is a poetry annual that has published poetry by Philip Appleman, William Matthews, Eugene McCarthy, Craig Raine, W.D. Snodgrass and Robert Wrigley. As a sample the editor selected "January Thaw" by X.J. Kennedy:

> *Beware. This seamless inverness of ice*
> *Cloaking the brick walk and the treacherous street*
> *Might, in a plot that sweeps you off your feet,*
> *Induce paralysis.*
>
> *Some gray, malignant growth, it lies immune*
> *To clouded skies till, slicing through the cold,*
> *One ray of sun, inserted, breaks its hold*
> *Like a good scalpel freeing up a brain.*

Pivot is a handsome, 6×9, flat-spined, professionally printed magazine with glossy card cover. Press run is 1,200. Single copy: $5. **Submit 3-7 poems at a time. Brief cover letter preferred. Reads submissions January 1 through June 1 only. Reports in 2-4 weeks. Sometimes sends prepublication galleys. Pays 2 copies.**

THE PLACE IN THE WOODS; READ, AMERICA! (I, IV-Children), 3900 Glenwood Ave., Golden Valley MN 55422, phone (612)374-2120, founded 1980, editor and publisher Roger A. Hammer, publishes *Read, America!*, a quarterly newsletter for reading coordinators. They want **"poems for children that are understandable, under 500 words, unusual views of life. Also, foreign-language poems with English translation. Nothing vague, self-indulgent, erotic. No navel introspection."** As a sample we selected these lines from "Circus" by Eugene C. Baggott:

> *Did you ever watch the bareback riders*
> *As they lovingly groomed their steeds?*
> *Or the trapeze artist practice his catch*
> *While hanging by his knees?*

Read, America! is 8 pgs., magazine-sized, professionally printed on yellow paper. "Pages 1-4 are distributed free to some 10,000 programs. Four additional pages go only to readers who support us as subscribers." Most poems appear in the "Subscribers only" insert but poets do not have to be subscribers to submit. Subscription: $20. **No previously published poems; simultaneous submissions OK. Cover letter "optional and appreciated for insight into poet's background and interests or goals." Always comments on rejections. Pays $10 on publication. Buys all rights.**

PLAINSONG (I, II), Box 8245, Western Kentucky University, Bowling Green KY 42101, phone (502)745-5708, founded 1979, poetry editors Frank Steele, Elizabeth Oakes and Peggy Steele, is an occasional poetry journal. "Our purpose is to print the best work we can get, from known and unknown writers. This means, of course, that we print what we like: poems about places, objects, people, moods, politics, experiences. **We like straightforward, conversational language, short poems in which the marriage of thinking and feeling doesn't break up because of spouse-abuse (the poem in which ideas wrestle feeling into the ground or in which feeling sings alone—and boringly—at the edge of a desert). Prefer poems under 20 lines in free verse—brief, understated lyrics that depend on the image combined with an intimate, conversational voice. No limits on subject matter, though we like to think of ourselves as humane, interested in the environment, in peace (we're anti-nuclear), in the possibility that the human race may have a future."** They have recently published poetry by Robert Bly, Ted Kooser, Judy Kronenfeld, Laurie Lamon, David Till and Angie Estes. The magazine is 48-56 pgs., 6×9, professionally printed, flat-spined, color matte card cover with photos and graphics. They use about 100 of the 2,000 submissions received each year. Press run is 600 with 250 subscriptions of which 65 are libraries. Subscription: $7. **Sample postpaid: $3.50. Submit 5-6 poems at a time. "We prefer poems typed, double-spaced. Simultaneous submissions can, of course, get people into**

trouble, at times." Publishes theme issues occasionally. Send SASE for guidelines. Reports "within a month, usually." Pays copies. Staff reviews books of poetry. Send books for review consideration to Frank Steele. The editor says, "We receive too many poems in 'the schoolroom voice'—full of language that's really prose. We'd like to see more poems with a voice that feels something without being sentimental or melodramatic."

PLAINSONGS (II), Dept. of English, Hastings College, Hastings NE 68902-0269, phone (402)463-2402, founded 1980, editor Dwight C. Marsh, a poetry magazine that **"accepts manuscripts from anyone, considering poems on any subject in any style but free verse preferred. Regional poems encouraged."** They have recently published poetry by Chet Corey, Pam Greenberg, Susanne Kort, Stephen Paling and Michael Robbins. As a sample the editor selected these lines from "The Winter Chair" by George Eklund:

> From my winter chair I might hear a bell
> straining up through an acre of white trees
> or feel myself suddenly closer
> to the silence that surrounds a bell,
> a winter loosened under the skin,
> she and the town dancing in my sleep.

Plainsongs is 40 pgs., digest-sized, saddle-stapled, set on laser in Times font, printed on thin paper with one-color matte card cover with generic black logo. The magazine is supported by the English Dept. of Hastings College and financed primarily by subscriptions, which cost $9 for 3 issues/year. The name suggests not only its location on the Great Plains, but its preference for the living language, whether in free or formal verse. It is committed to poems only, to make space without visual graphics, bio or critical positions. **Sample copies: $3. Submit 1-6 poems at a time with name and address on each page. Ms deadlines are August 15 for fall issue; November 15 for winter; March 15 for spring. Notification is mailed about 5 weeks after deadlines. Pay is 2 copies and a year's subscription, with 3 award poems in each issue receiving small monetary recognition (currently $25). "A short essay in appreciation accompanies each award poem." Acquires first-time rights.**

PLANET: THE WELSH INTERNATIONALIST (III), P.O. Box 44, Aberystwyth, Dyfed, Wales, phone 01970-611255, fax 01970-623311, founded 1970, editor John Barnie, is a bimonthly cultural magazine, "centered on Wales, but with broader interests in arts, sociology, politics, history and science." **They want "good poetry in a wide variety of styles. No limitations as to subject matter; length can be a problem."** They have published poetry by Les Murray and R.S. Thomas. As a sample we selected this poem, "The Mating Behaviour of Human Beings," by J.K. Gill:

> Puzzled by her hedgehog spikes
> his paws uncurl her to
> her softest.

Planet is 120 pgs., A5 size, professionally printed and perfect-bound with glossy color card cover. They receive about 300 submissions a year, accept approximately 5%. Press run is 1,400 for 1,150 subscribers of which about 10% are libraries, 200 shelf sales. Single copy: £2.50; subscription: £12 (overseas: £13). **Sample postpaid: £3.56. No previously published poems or simultaneous submissions.** Time between acceptance and publication is 6-10 months. **Seldom comments on rejections. Send SASE (or SAE and IRCs if outside UK) for guidelines. Reports within a month or so. Pays £25 minimum. Buys first serial rights only.** Reviews books of poetry in 700 words, single and multi-book format. Open to unsolicited reviews. Poets may also send books for review consideration.

PLANTAGENET PRODUCTIONS (V), Westridge, Highclere, Nr. Newbury, Royal Berkshire RG 15 9 PJ England, founded 1964, director of productions Miss Dorothy Rose Gribble. Plantagenet issues cassette recordings of poetry, philosophy and narrative (although they have issued nothing new since 1980). Miss Gribble says, "Our public likes classical work . . . We **have published a few living poets, but this is not very popular with our listeners, and we shall issue no more.**" They have issued cassettes by Oscar Wilde, Chaucer and Pope, as well as Charles Graves, Elizabeth Jennings, Leonard Clark and Alice V. Stuart. The recordings are issued privately and are obtainable only direct from Plantagenet Productions; write for list. Miss Gribble's advice to poets is: "If intended for a listening public, let the meaning be clear. If possible, let the music of the words sing."

THE PLASTIC TOWER (II), P.O. Box 702, Bowie MD 20718, founded 1989, editors Carol Dyer and Roger Kyle-Keith, is a quarterly using **"everything from iambic pentameter to silly limericks, modern free verse, haiku, rhymed couplets—we like it all! Only restriction is length—under 40 lines preferred. So send us poems that are cool or wild, funny or tragic—but especially those closest to your soul."** They have published poetry by "more than 400 different poets." As a sample we selected these lines from "the realist" by W. Gregory Stewart:

> . . . says
> that his cup is half-full

> *if he has been filling it,*
> *and that it is half-empty*
> *if he has been drinking from it.*
> *he knows*
> *the difference between*
> *politics and government,*
> *and does not confuse*
> *truth with fact.*

It is digest-sized, 38-54 pgs., saddle-stapled; "variety of typefaces and b&w graphics on cheap photocopy paper." Press run is 200. Subscription: $8/year. Copy of current issue: $2.50. **"We'll send a back issue free for a *large* (at least 6 × 9) SAE with 75¢ postage attached." Submit no more than 10 poems at a time. Previously published poems and simultaneous submissions OK. Editors comment on submissions "often." Send SASE for guidelines. Reports in approximately 3 months. Pays 1-3 copies.** Open to unsolicited reviews. Poets may also send books for review consideration. Roger Kyle-Keith says, "*PT* is an unpretentious little rag dedicated to enjoying verse and making poetry accessible to the general public as well as fellow poets. We don't claim to be the best, but we try to be the nicest and most personal. And we really, genuinely love poetry—just like you! And always remember (never forget?) your poems are important. Rejection and acceptance slips aren't. Don't let those cruddy pieces of paper define your life. Most, ours included, aren't worth the paper on which they're printed. So sing and shout and laugh and cry and stop on by *The Plastic Tower.*"

‡THE PLAZA (II, IV-Bilingual), U-Kan, Inc., Yoyogi 2-32-1, Shibuya-ku, Tokyo 151, Japan, phone 81-3-3379-3881, fax 81-3-3379-3882, founded 1985, poetry editors Roger Lakhani and Mari Tochiya, is a quarterly which "represents a borderless forum for contemporary writers and artists" and includes poetry, fiction and essays published simultaneously in English and Japanese. **They want "highly artistic poetry dealing with being human and interculturally related. Nothing stressing political, national, religious or racial differences. *The Plaza* is edited with a global view of mankind."** They have recently published poetry by Morgan Gibson, Sharon Scholl and Catherine Buckaway. As a sample the editors selected "One Breath" by Antler:

> *One of your breaths contains*
> *all the air*
> *a Mayfly breathes*
> *in its life.*

The Plaza is 48 pgs., A5, professionally printed and saddle-stapled with card cover. Submissions (and its covers) are illustrated with artistic b&w drawings. They receive about 2,500 poems a year, accept approximately 4%. Press run is 7,000 for 4,800 subscribers of which 460 are libraries (including 160 overseas), 1,500 shelf sales. Single copy: 380 yen; subscription: 1,500 yen. **Sample available for 5 IRCs (for overseas airmail). No previously published poems; simultaneous submissions OK. Cover letter required.** "Please include telephone and fax numbers with submissions. As *The Plaza* is a bilingual publication in English and Japanese, it is sometimes necessary, for translation purposes, to contact authors. Japanese translations are prepared by the editorial staff." **Seldom comments on rejections. Reports within 1 month. Pays 10 copies.** Reviews books of poetry, usually in less than 500 words. Open to unsolicited reviews. Poets may also send books for review consideration. Roger Lakhani says, "*The Plaza* focuses not on human beings but humans being human in the borderless world. It is not international, but intercultural. And it is circulated all over the world—in the American continents, Oceania, Asia, the Middle East, Europe and Africa."

‡PLAZM MAGAZINE; PLAZM MEDIA (I, II), P.O. Box 2863, Portland OR 97208-2863, phone (503)234-8289, fax (503)235-9666, founded 1991. *Plazm Magazine* is published 3 times a year by Plazm Media, "a nonprofit cooperative dedicated to free expression." **They want experimental poetry. Nothing "rudimentary."** They have recently published poetry by Dan Raphael, Jay Marvin and Bill Shields. As a sample the editor selected these lines by Laura Winter:

> *rolled*
> *up tight*
> *as a potato bug*
> *the fiddle head*
> *is edible*
> *and*
> *won't*
> *run away*

The editor says *Plazm* is 9 × 12, printed offset litho and saddle-stitched, with "much art and design." Press run is 7,500 for 250 subscribers of which 10 are libraries, most shelf sales. Single copy: $4.49; subscription: $12 for 3 issues. **Sample postpaid: $6. Previously published poems OK (but not preferred). Simultaneous submissions also OK. SASE and biographical statement required. Poems are circulated to an editorial board. Often comments on rejections. Send SASE for guide-**

lines. **Reports in 3-4 months. Pays 3 copies and a subscription.** Reviews books of poetry in 25-250 words. Open to unsolicited reviews. Poets may also send books for review consideration.

PLOUGHSHARES (III), Emerson College, 100 Beacon St., Boston MA 02116, phone (617)578-8753, founded 1971. **The magazine is "a journal of new writing edited on a revolving basis by professional poets and writers to reflect different and contrasting points of view."** Editors have included Carolyn Forché, Gerald Stern, Rita Dove, Chase Twichell and M.L. Rosenthal. They have published poetry by Donald Hall, Li-Young Lee, Robert Pinsky, Brenda Hillman and Thylias Moss. The triquarterly is 5½×8½, 250 pgs., circulation 6,000. They receive approximately 2,500 poetry submissions/year. Since this influential magazine features different editors with each issue, content varies. The issue edited by Carolyn Forché, for example, displays a variety of styles and forms with strong voices and messages. As always with prestigious journals, competition is keen. Response times can be slow because submissions are logged inhouse and sent to outside guest editors. Subscription: $19 domestic; $24 foreign. **Sample postpaid: $8.95 current issue, $6 back issue. "We suggest you read a few issues and send a #10 SASE for writer's guidelines before submitting." Simultaneous submissions acceptable. Do not submit mss from April 1 to July 31. Reports in 3-5 months. Always sends prepublication galleys. Pays $40 minimum per poem, $20/printed page per poem, plus 2 contributor copies and a subscription.** Work published in *Ploughshares* appears in the 1992, 1993, 1994 and 1995 volumes of *The Best American Poetry*.

THE PLOWMAN (I, II), Box 414, Whitby, Ontario L1N 5S4 Canada, phone (905)668-7803, founded 1988, editor Tony Scavetta, appears 3 times/year using **"didactic, eclectic poetry; all forms. We will also take most religious poetry except satanic and evil."** As a sample the editor selected these lines from his own poetry:

> *The Word of God*
> *Sharper than a two edged sword*
> *Rip and tear*
> *The eyes of your children*
> *Like a fish-hook*
> *Same Holy Spirit*
> *Gives you everlasting Life*
> *Through Jesus Christ*
> *My Lord and Saviour*

The Plowman is a 56-page, newsprint tabloid which accepts 70% of the poetry received. Press run is 15,000 for 1,200 subscribers of which 500 are libraries. Single copy: $7.50; subscription: $10. **Sample free. Previously published poems and simultaneous submissions OK. Cover letter required. No SASE necessary. Always comments on rejections. Guidelines available free. Reports in 1 week. Always sends prepublication galleys.** Reviews books of poetry. They offer monthly poetry contests. Entry fee: $2/poem. 1st prize: 50% of the proceeds; 2nd: 25%; 3rd: 10%. The top poems are published. "Balance of the poems will be used for anthologies." **They also publish 125 chapbooks/year. Replies to queries and mss in 1 week. Requires $25 reading fee/book. Pays 20% royalties.**

THE PLUM REVIEW (II), P.O. Box 1347, Philadelphia PA 19105-1347, founded 1990, editors Mike Hammer and Christina Daub, managing editor Karen Faul, appears twice a year. **"We are open to original, high quality poetry of all forms, lengths, styles and subject matters. Our only criterion is excellence."** They have recently published poetry by Robert Bly, Donald Hall, David Ignatow, Linda Pastan, Elizabeth Spires, Diane Wakoski, Sherod Santos and Books Haxton. As a sample the editor selected these lines from "Hospital Parking Lot Rendezvous" by John Yau:

> *Yes, I believe in charcoal dust and secret hand signals,*
> *but I don't know any characters or assassins,*
> *only the empty raisin boxes they've left behind.*
> *Would you like me to read your calm?*
> *You were the dog and I was the drooping fence*
> *you ran beside. . . .*

It is approximately 100 pgs., flat-spined, professionally printed, 6×9. Editors seem to favor well-made free verse, emphasizing voice and line. Press run is 1,000. **Sample postpaid: $7. Submit 1-5 poems at a time. "Absolutely no simultaneous submissions. Include a brief bio indicating previous publications and/or awards." Sometimes comments on rejections. Reports in 1-2 months. Pays 1 copy.** They welcome unsolicited reviews (up to 15 pgs., single or multi-book format) of recently published

---

Market categories: (I) Beginning; (II) General; (III) Limited; (IV) Specialized; (V) Closed.

books of poetry and interviews with prominent poets. Poets may also send books for review consideration. They sponsor a reading series and creative writing workshops for the elderly and the handicapped. *The Plum Review* also has an annual poetry competition which awards $500 to the best poem(s). Deadline: February 28, 1996. Submit up to 3 poems with SASE and $5 entry fee. All entries will be considered for publication. No simultaneous submissions. No previously published poems. This magazine says that it is "so delicious"—a takeoff on William Carlos Williams' famous lyric "This Is Just To Say"?—and it is, too, featuring the best work of top-name poets and relative newcomers. In addition, *The Plum Review* was awarded a grant from the Council of Literary Magazines and Presses for outstanding content and design.

POCAHONTAS PRESS, INC.; MANUSCRIPT MEMORIES (V), P.O. Drawer F, Blacksburg VA 24063-1020, phone (540)951-0467, e-mail mchollim@vtvmi.vt.edu, founded 1984, president Mary C. Holliman, publishes chapbook collections of poetry, but is temporarily not considering new mss "because I am trying to finish those already accepted." Inquire before submitting. **Prefers Appalachian-related themes. "Most of the poetry books I have published have been subsidized to some extent by the author. So far one of those authors' books has sold enough copies that the author has received a significant reimbursement for his investment. We continue to market all of our books as aggressively as possible. The idea is to make a profit for both of us (though we have yet to do so)."** She has published books by Leslie Mellichamp, Lynn Kozma, Mildred Nash, Preston Newman and Elaine Emans. As a sample the editor selected these lines by Cecil J. Mullins:

> *In the East, time has been divorced*
> *From things. No clocks hem the hours*
> *In, and time, not being firmly forced,*
> *Slops around.*

Submit 8-10 poems at a time. Always sends prepublication galleys. Pays 10% royalties on all sales receipts, 10 free copies of book, and any number of copies at 50% for resale or "whatever use author wishes. If author helps with printing costs, then an additional percentage of receipts will be paid." She offers editorial critiques for $40/hour. Mary Holliman adds, "There's much more good poetry being written than is getting published, and I only wish I could publish more of it. We are planning to try a new marketing technique—single-fold notecards with one poem from a collection per card, perhaps 3 poem/cards (2 each in a set of 6). The full collection and how to order will be given on the back of each card."

POEM; HUNTSVILLE LITERARY ASSOCIATION (II), English Dept., University of Alabama at Huntsville, Huntsville AL 35899, founded 1967, poetry editor Nancy Frey Dillard, appears twice a year, consisting entirely of poetry. **"We are particularly open to traditional as well as non-traditional forms, but we favor work with the expected compression and intensity of good lyric poetry and a high degree of verbal and dramatic tension. We welcome equally submissions from established poets as well as from less known and beginning poets. We do not accept translations, previously published works or simultaneous submissions. We prefer to see a sample of 3-5 poems at a submission, with SASE. We generally respond within a month. We are a nonprofit organization and can pay only in copy to contributors. Sample copies are available at $5."** They have published poetry by Robert Cooperman, Andrew Dillon and Scott Travis Hutchison. As a sample the editor selected these lines from "Mister Varsey" by Sally Jo Sorensen:

> *With the myths*
> *his methods excelled:*
> *The Odyssey, for instance,*
> *became more than just the same old song*
> *about some guy who'd left his wife and kid*
> *for the guys. Mr. Varsey fetched a bow*
> *out of his great, fabled closet*
> *and asked the gentlemen of the class—*
> *as he called them—to see who might be*
> *Penelope's true suitor. None could*
> *match the task, so he exclaimed*
> *blind Homer walks again!*
> *until I raised my hand*

Poem is a flat-spined, 4⅜ × 7¼, 90-page journal that contains more than 60 poems (mostly lyric free verse under 50 lines) generally featured one to a page on good stock paper with a clean design and a classy matte cover. Circulation is 400 (all subscriptions of which 90 are libraries). Overall, it's a good market for beginners and experienced poets who pay attention to craft.

POEMS & PLAYS; THE TENNESSEE CHAPBOOK PRIZE (II), English Dept., Middle Tennessee State University, Murfreesboro TN 37132, phone (615)898-2712, founded 1993, editor Gay Brewer, is an annual "eclectic publication for poems and short plays," published in April/May. **They have no**

restrictions on style or content of poetry. They have recently published poetry by Ray Bradbury, Charles Bukowski, Steven Sater, David Citino and Vivian Shipley. As a sample the editor selected these lines from "Wash Silver" by Mike Burwell:

> Some nights with a hooked fish slapping down river
> and the brush trilling with birds, I'd see the whole scene wash silver,
> see these slicing fish hurtle like errant moons through the late, deep light.
> And I drank the thick bright milk of it, all of it.

Poems & Plays is 88 pgs., 6×9, professionally printed and perfect-bound with coated color card cover and art. "We received 1,550 poems for our second issue (Spring/Summer 1995, published 35." Press run is 550. Subscription: $10 (2 issues). **Sample postpaid: $6. No previously published poems or simultaneous submissions (except for chapbook submissions). Reads submissions October 1 through January 15 only. "Work is circulated among advisory editors for comments and preferences. All accepted material is published in the following issue." Usually comments on rejections. Reports in 1-2 months. Pays 1 copy. Acquires first publication rights only.** "We accept chapbook manuscripts (of poems or plays) of 24 pages for The Tennessee Chapbook Prize. The winner is printed as an interior chapbook in *Poems & Plays* and receives 50 copies of the issue. SASE and $10 fee (for one copy of the issue) required. Dates for contest entry are the same as for the magazine (October 1 through January 15). The 1995 chapbook competition drew 90 manuscripts from 29 states, Japan, New Zealand and Guam."

POEMS FOR A LIVABLE PLANET (I, IV-Nature/ecology, translations), 1235½ N. Larrabee St., Los Angeles CA 90069, founded 1990, editor Jeffrey Dellin, publishes **"poems dealing with the beauty/peril of the Earth & Her Creatures. Any form, language given equal consideration; length limit 50 lines. Non-English should include translation."** The ecology theme of this publication is one of the most important of our time. The poetry is insightful and, overall, well-executed; craft does not suffer because of politics. *PFLP* is 26 pgs., digest-sized, neatly printed with 1 poem/page, saddle-stitched with glossy cover. **Sample postpaid: $3.75. Submit up to 3 poems at a time. No previously published poems. Does not read submissions between September and April. "May take as long as 6 months to reply." Pays 1 copy.**

POET LORE; JOHN WILLIAMS ANDREWS NARRATIVE POETRY COMPETITION (II), The Writer's Center, 4508 Walsh St., Bethesda MD 20815, phone (301)654-8664, founded 1889, managing editor Sunil Freeman, executive editors Philip Jason and Geraldine Connolly, is a quarterly dedicated "to the best in American and world poetry and objective and timely reviews and commentary. We look for **fresh uses of traditional form and devices, but any kind of excellence is welcome. The editors encourage narrative poetry and original translations of works by contemporary world poets."** They have published poetry by Sharon Olds, John Balaban, William Heyen, Walter McDonald, Reginald Gibbons and Howard Nemerov. *Poet Lore* is 6×9, 80 pgs., perfect-bound, professionally printed with matte card cover. Circulation includes 600 subscriptions of which 200 are libraries. Editors are open to all styles (as long as the work is well-crafted and insightful), leaning toward lyric and narrative free verse with an emphasis on voice. They receive about 3,000 poems/year, use about 125. Single copy: $4.50 plus $1 postage. Subscription: $15. **Sample postpaid: $4. Submit typed poems, author's name and address on each page. Reports in 3 months. Pays 2 copies.** Reviews books of poetry. Open to unsolicited reviews. Poets may also send books for review consideration. Sponsors the John Williams Andrews Narrative Poetry Competition for unpublished poems of 100 lines or more. The annual competition awards $350 and publication in *Poet Lore*. Deadline: November 30. Send SASE for entry form and guidelines. Poetry published in *Poet Lore* has also been selected for inclusion in *The Best American Poetry 1994*.

POET MAGAZINE; COOPER HOUSE PUBLISHING INC.; JOHN DAVID JOHNSON MEMORIAL POETRY AWARDS; IVA MARY WILLIAMS INSPIRATIONAL POETRY AWARDS; AMERICAN CHAPBOOK AWARDS; AMERICAN COLLEGE & UNIVERSITY POETRY AWARDS; AMERICAN HIGH SCHOOL POETRY AWARDS; THE AMERICAN LITERARY MAGAZINE AWARDS (II), P.O. Box 54947, Oklahoma City OK 73154, founded 1984, managing editor Peggy Cooper, editor Joy Hall, poetry editor Michael Hall. "*Poet* is one of the largest commercial publishers of poetry in the U.S. and is **open to submissions from writers at all levels of experience."** Michael Hall says, **"I look for poems that display wit, knowledge and skill . . . verse that employs arresting images, poems that make the reader think or smile or even sometimes cry."** They have published poetry by Lewis Turco and H.R. Coursen. As a sample the editor selected the opening stanzas of "Marshwind Song" by Patricia A. Lawrence:

> The music of the marsh has my heart pinned
> To tidal flats and skittle dancing crabs.
> A hanging gull is tossed on beats of wind.
>
> Her lonely mewing, plaintive, swordlike, stabs

> *Each note that wells to fullness like a tide*
> *Until she streaks the sky. A talon grabs*
>
> *Another note that haunts me . . .*

Poet is magazine-sized, professionally printed, 56-80 pgs. with glossy cover, saddle-stitched. Of about 7,000-10,000 submissions, they use a little fewer than 5%. Subscription: $20/year. Subscribers receive free the giant "Forms of Poetry" poster. **Sample copy of *Poet*, postpaid: $5.50 or "call your bookstore where you can purchase it for $4.50 ($5.50 Canada) if it's in stock. If it's not in stock, ask them to order it through Fine Print Distributors." For guidelines, send 3 loose first-class stamps with request. Submit 5 poems at a time. Previously published poems and simultaneous submissions OK. Editor sometimes comments on rejections. Reports within 3-6 months. Pays 1 copy.** Reviews books of poetry. Open to unsolicited reviews. Poets may also send books for review consideration to Joy Hall, P.O. Box 22047, Alexandria VA 22304. They sponsor annual chapbook awards (up to 48 pgs., $30 entry fee, grand prize: publication in book form and 50 free copies). John David Johnson Memorial Poetry Awards (prizes of $100, $50, $25, special merit and honorable mention awards, award certificates, publication and a copy of the magazine in which the winning poems appear to all winners. Entry fee: $5/poem. March 1 and September 1 deadlines). Iva Mary Williams Inspirational Poetry Awards (prizes of $100, $50, $25, special merit and honorable mention awards, award certificates, publication and a copy of the magazine in which the winning poems appear to all winners. Entry fee: $5/poem. February 1 and August 1 deadlines). American College & University Poetry Awards (prizes of $100, $50, $25, each divided equally between winning student and teacher, special merit and honorable mention awards, award certificates, publication and copy of the magazine in which the winning poems appear to all winners. No entry fee. Rules and official entry forms may be requested with 4 loose first-class stamps). American High School Poetry Awards (prizes of $100, $50, $25, each divided equally between winning student and teacher, special merit and honorable mention awards, award certificates, publication and copy of the magazine in which the winning poems appear to all winners. No entry fee. Rules and official entry forms may be requested with 4 loose first-class stamps). The American Literary Magazine Awards are engraved plaques, award certificate and free advertising in *Poet Magazine*. All contestants receive a gift. $30 entry fee/title. Deadline: December 31. Send 2 loose first-class stamps with request for rules and entry form.

POETIC ELOQUENCE (I), Route 5, Box 181-N, Elgin TX 78621, phone (512)281-2222, e-mail 76500.3106@compuserve, founded 1992, editor/publisher Doris F. Rodriguez, is a quarterly poetry journal published at the end of February, May, August and November. **They want "any subject (except holiday), any style, 40 lines maximum, 12-24 lines preferred. No profanity or sexually graphic material nor anything that puts crime in a positive light. Each issue highlights two sestinas and one page of tanka and/or haiku."** They have published poetry by Marian Ford Park, Phil Eisenberg, Kathleen Wheeler-Bramer and Nancy Watson-Dodrill. The editor says *Poetic Eloquence* is 50-60 pgs., 8½ × 11, typeset and perfect-bound with colored card cover. It includes a featured poet section, a poetry book review column and a biographical section. **"We also feature three writing challenges per issue to stimulate, encourage and awaken the poetic muse sleeping inside us all.** Seeing how others respond to the same challenge is a valuable tool in helping poets stretch beyond their usual style and voice." They publish approximately 75% of the poetry received. Single copy: $7; subscription: $28. **Sample postpaid: $6. Submit up to 10 poems, typed, with name, address and phone number in the top righthand corner of each page. Previously published poems OK; no simultaneous submissions. Include brief (50-word) bio. Poems will not be returned.** Time between acceptance and publication is 3-6 months. **Sometimes comments on rejections. Send SASE for guidelines. Reports within 3-6 weeks. Pays 1 copy to first-time contributors. Acquires one-time rights.** Offers Reader's Choice awards of $25 each to the top three poems in each issue. Also offers $10 to the top poem for each writing challenge. Promotes books and chapbooks of poetry in 50-100 words. Send one copy of the book you want promoted. Books will not be returned. The editor says, "Subscriptions are encouraged but not required for publication. We welcome poets who employ knowledge of the craft, skill and imagination in just the right combination to create a poem that displays vivid imagery, powerful feelings and outstanding craftsmanship . . . a poem that fairly dances across the page or transports its reader to another place and time by the skillful use of concise words and creative phrases to create fresh insight into old themes."

THE POETIC KNIGHT: A FANTASY ROMANCE MAGAZINE (I, IV-Fantasy, romance), 300½ Park Ave., East Palestine OH 44413-1567, founded 1990, editor Michael While, appears 4 times/year. **They want "fantasy poetry that exemplifies the classical romantic in all of us. Accept poetry from haiku to ballad length as well as fiction under 5,000 words. Prefer traditional, but will look at all forms. No profanity or explicit sex. Like to see work based on very human characters. Looking for more poetry with action bent to it and something that tells a specific story."** They have published poetry by Carl Heffley and William Robertson. As a sample the editor selected these lines from "The Ocean Tryst" by Jessica Amanda Salmonson:

> *There standing in the gate or crack*
> *A damsel clad in green and black*
> *Her eyes half shut, her hair adrift-*
> *Around her brilliant rainbows shift.*

It is 40-52 pgs., magazine-sized, laser set with full color cover, saddle-stapled. They accept on a "30 to 1 ratio and we get 50-60 submissions a week." Press run is 300 for 100 subscribers of which 10 are libraries, 150 shelf sales. Subscription: $20/4 issues. **Sample postpaid: $5. Submit 2-3 poems at a time, with cover letter. No simultaneous submissions. Send SASE for guidelines. Pays 1 copy. Acquires first North American serial rights. Editor "tries to comment on all submissions and make everyone who writes to us feel at home."**

POETIC PAGE (I,II); OPUS LITERARY REVIEW (II), P.O. Box 71192, Madison Heights MI 48071-0192, *Poetic Page* founded 1989, *Opus Literary Review* founded 1993, editor Denise Martinson. *Poetic Page* appears bimonthly. **Each issue has a contest, $1/poem fee, prizes of $30, $20, $10 and $5. About 90% of the poetry published is that of contest winners, and the rest is invitational only. "All forms are used except explicit sex, violence and crude. 30 lines."** They have recently published poetry by Billy Ray Cyrus, MacDonald Carey, Alice Mackenzie Swaim, T.N. Turner, T. Kilgore Splake, Glenna Holloway and John Grey. As a sample the editor selected the ending to "Infected" by Corrine DeWinter:

> *There is nothing*
> * I could have done*
> *to pull the arrow*
> *from its target.*
> *But now I can tell*
> *you and you and you*
> * almost how it feels*
> *to be a vine*
> *clinging*
> *to something solid.*

Poetic Page is 32-36 pgs., magazine-sized, enamel cover, desktop-published. Press run is 250-350, sent to libraries, universities, editors and subscribers. Subscription: $15. **Sample postpaid: $3. Simultaneous submissions and previously published poems OK. Prefers cover letter. Send SASE for guidelines. Nonsubscribers receive 1 copy.** The editor says, "We look for poetry that has something to say. No trite rhyme. Only the very best poems are selected each issue. First place is featured on its own page. We now use more articles, tidbits, poet interactions and fillers. We pay copies for articles and cover art, but must be of the highest quality. We ask poets to send us copies of their poetry books for our 'Review' section. Just because we are listed under the **I** category, does not mean that we are an easy magazine to be published in. We want poetry that is well written, poetry that demands to be read. Send your best." *Opus Literary Review* is a biannual. **No specifications as to form, length, style, subject matter or purpose.** They have published poetry by Rudy Zenker, Leonard Cirino, Laurel Speer, Robert S. King, Lyn Lifshin, Pearl Bloch Segall, John Grey and Patricia A. Lawrence. As a sample, the editor selected these lines from "A Moment of Rest for a Drag-line Operator" by Janice L. Braud:

> *Bury him with hardhat, steel-toed shoes.*
> *He'll need them again*
> *perhaps to scoop out habitation space*
> *in airless asteroid millennia away*
> *or fence the flow of milky way debris*
> *to power man-made turbine stars with*
> *Big-Bang energy.*
> * Dig him a hole he would be proud of.*

Opus Literary Review is desktop-published with matte cover. Subscription: $10. **Sample postpaid: $5. No previously published poems or simultaneous submissions "unless of exceptional quality." Cover letter required. Editor often comments on rejections. Send SASE for guidelines. All accepted poets receive one copy and are listed with bio. Acquires first rights.** The editor says: "We want poetry that will last the ages. Poetry that is intelligent, well thought out. If you want to write a poem about a flower, go ahead. But make that flower unique—surprise us. Give us your best work. But beginners beware, no trite rhyme here. However, we will publish a well-written rhyme if the rhyme is the poem, not the word endings. Free verse is what we prefer."

POETIC SPACE: POETRY & FICTION (I), P.O. Box 11157, Eugene OR 97440, founded 1983, editor Don Hildenbrand, is a literary magazine with emphasis on contemporary poetry, fiction, reviews (including film and drama), interviews, market news and translations (Chinese and Spanish). Accepts poetry and fiction that is **"well-crafted and takes risks. We like poetry with guts. Would like to see some poetry on social and political issues. We would also like to see gay/lesbian poetry and poetry on women's issues. Erotic and experimental OK."** They have recently published poetry by Crawdad

Nelson, Ed Meek, Kell Robertson, Ray Barker, Kit Knight and Lynda S. Silva. As a sample the editor selected these lines by Olga Browmas and T. Begley:

> *As in Heaven*
> *women care for fresh game*
> *we pick up the nude sounds*
>
> *what can heart do to splash on their bodies*
> *what do these things that I am feeling mean*
> *whose hand is holding on*

The magazine is 8½ × 11, saddle-stapled, 20-24 pgs., offset from typescript and sometimes photoreduced. It is published twice a year. They use about 25% of the 200-300 poems received/year. Press run is 800-1,000 with 50 subscriptions of which 12 are libraries. Single copy: $5; subscription: $8/one year, $15/two years. **Send SASE for list of available back issues ($4). Simultaneous submissions and previously published poems OK. Ms should be typed, double-spaced, clean, name/address on each page. "Submissions without SASE will not be considered." Editor provides some critical comments. Guidelines for SASE. Reports in 2-4 months. Pays 1 copy, but more can be ordered by sending SASE and postage.** Reviews books of poetry in 500-1,000 words. Open to unsolicited reviews. Poets may also submit books for review consideration. They have published an *Anthology: 1987-1991 Best of Poetic Space*, $5. Also publishes one chapbook each spring. Their first chapbook is *Truth Rides to Work & Good Girls*, poetry by Crawdad Nelson and fiction by Louise A. Blum ($5 plus $1.50 p&h). Don Hildenbrand says, "We like poetry that takes risks—original writing that gives us a new, different perspective."

POETPOURRI; COMSTOCK WRITERS' GROUP INC.; SUMMER SIZZLER CONTEST (II), 907 Comstock Ave., Syracuse NY 13210, phone (315)475-0339, founded 1987, published by the Comstock Writers' Group, Inc., co-editors Jennifer B. MacPherson and Kathleen Bryce Niles, appears biannually. **They use "work that is clear and understandable to a general readership, that deals with issues, ideas, feelings and beliefs common to us all—well-written free and traditional verse. No obscene, obscure, patently religious or greeting card verse."** They have recently published poetry by Gayle Elen Harvey, Katharyn Howd Machan, Robert Cooperman, Robert Edwards and Susan A. Manchester. As a sample they selected these lines from "Photograph of a Horse" by Sarah Patton:

> *Here, the black hills*
> *pull like Clydesdales*
> *along the horizon,*
> *lightless and obscure,*
> *great haunches,*
> *bellies and withers*
> *strained against the sky.*

Poetpourri is 100 pgs., digest-sized, professionally printed, perfect-bound, raised cover. Circulation 550. Subscription: $8. **Sample postpaid: $4. Poems may be submitted anytime for possible publication, 3-6 at a time, name and address on each page, unpublished poems only. Cover letter with short bio of poet preferred. Return time is about 6 weeks. Editors usually comment on returned submissions. Pays copies. Acquires first North American serial rights.** They offer a yearly Summer Sizzler contest with over $400 in prizes, $2/poem fee, 30-line limit.

POETRY; THE MODERN POETRY ASSOCIATION; BESS HOKIN PRIZE; LEVINSON PRIZE; OSCAR BLUMENTHAL PRIZE; EUNICE TIETJENS MEMORIAL PRIZE; FREDERICK BOCK PRIZE; GEORGE KENT PRIZE; UNION LEAGUE PRIZE; J. HOWARD AND BARBARA M.J. WOOD PRIZE; RUTH LILLY POETRY PRIZE (III), 60 W. Walton St., Chicago IL 60610, founded 1912, editor Joseph Parisi, "is the oldest and most distinguished monthly magazine devoted entirely to verse," according to their literature. "Founded in Chicago in 1912, it immediately became the international showcase that it has remained ever since, publishing in its earliest years—and often for the first time—such giants as Ezra Pound, Robert Frost, T.S. Eliot, Marianne Moore and Wallace Stevens. *Poetry* has continued to print the major voices of our time and to discover new talent, establishing an unprecedented record. There is virtually no important contemporary poet in our language who has not at a crucial stage in his career depended on *Poetry* to find a public for him: John Ashbery, Dylan Thomas, Edna St. Vincent Millay, James Merrill, Anne Sexton, Sylvia Plath, James Dickey, Thom Gunn, David Wagoner—only a partial list to suggest how *Poetry* has represented, without affiliation with any movements or schools, what Stephen Spender has described as 'the best, and simply the best' poetry being written." Although its offices have always been in Chicago, *Poetry*'s influence and scope extend far beyond, throughout the US and in over 45 countries around the world. Asked to select 4 lines of poetry "which represent the taste and quality you want in your publication" Joseph Parisi selected the opening lines of "The Love Song of J. Alfred Prufrock" by T.S. Eliot, which first appeared in *Poetry* in 1915:

> *Let us go then, you and I,*

> *When the evening is spread out against the sky*
> *Like a patient etherized upon a table;*
> *Let us go, through certain half-deserted streets . . .*

Poetry is an elegantly printed, flat-spined, 5½×9 magazine. They receive over 75,000 submissions/year, use 300-350, have a 9-month backlog. Circulation 7,500, 6,000 subscriptions of which 53% are libraries. Single copy: $2.50; subscription: $25, $27 for institutions. **Sample postpaid: $3.50. Submit no more than 4 poems at a time. Send SASE for guidelines. Reports in 2-3 months—longer for mss submitted during the summer. Pays $2 a line. Buys all rights. Returns rights "upon written request."** Reviews books of poetry in 750-1,000 words, multi-book format. Open to unsolicited reviews. Poets may also send books to Stephen Young, associate editor, for review consideration. This is probably the most prestigious poetry credit in the publishing business. Consequently, competition here is extraordinarily keen with more poems received in a year than there are people in some cities in your state. Yet Joseph Parisi is one of the most efficient (and discerning) editors around, and he does much to promote poetry. This is a magazine that you can buy straight off the newsstand to get a feel for the pulse of poetry each month. Eight prizes (named in heading) ranging from $100 to $1,000 are awarded annually to poets whose work has appeared in the magazine that year. *Only verse already published in* **Poetry** *is eligible for consideration and no formal application is necessary.* **Poetry** also sponsors the Ruth Lilly Poetry Prize, an annual award of $75,000, and the Ruth Lilly Collegiate Poetry Fellowship, an annual award of $15,000 to undergraduates to support their further studies in poetry/creative writing. Work published in ***Poetry*** was also selected for inclusion in the 1992, 1993, 1994 and 1995 volumes of *The Best American Poetry*.

POETRY & AUDIENCE (I, II), School of English, University of Leeds, Leeds, West Yorkshire LS2 9JT England, fax 01132331751, e-mail engmt@arts.o1.novell.leeds.ac.uk., founded 1953, editors Alex Goody and Mark Tranter. *P&A* appears 2 times/year and accepts work from new and established poets. **"We do not discriminate against any form of poetry although there is a general move towards a more lyrical style. This said, we have and will continue to publish even the most obscure poetic forms."** They have recently published poetry by Carol Ann Duffy, Geoffrey Hill and Tony Harrison. As a sample the editors selected these lines from "Palm Reading" by Sonya Ardan:

> *I fill time—write to you*
> *Of Spain in the full fever*
> *Of its Easter, how it divides*
> *Its cities by color (the suffering*
> *Of a blue Virgin against the bitterness*
> *Of White) and how there's silence*

Press run is 200-300 for 50 subscribers of which 10 are libraries. Subscription: £10 (overseas). **Sample: £1.50. Submit 4 poems at a time. "Please double or at least use 1.5 spacing for all lines with triple-line spacing of stanzas. Please give birth date and place in any correspondence as well as previous publications, if applicable. We require work to be previously unpublished and not simultaneously submitted. We will often try to include constructive comments in the event of a rejection." Replies in 2 months. Pays 1 copy.** Open to unsolicited reviews. Poets may also send books for review consideration.

POETRY EAST (II), Dept. of English, DePaul University, 802 W. Belden Ave., Chicago IL 60614, phone (312)325-7487, founded 1980, editor Richard Jones, "is a biannual international magazine publishing poetry, translations and reviews. We suggest that authors look through back issues of the magazine before making submissions. **No constraints or specifications; we are open to both traditional forms and free verse.**" They have published poetry by Tom Crawford, Thomas McGrath, Denise Levertov, Galway Kinnell, Sharon Olds and Amiri Baraka. The digest-sized, flat-spined journal is 100 pgs., professionally printed with glossy color card cover. They use 60-80 pgs. of poetry in each issue. They receive approximately 4,000 submissions/year, use 10%, have a 4-month backlog. Circulation 1,200, 250 subscriptions of which 80 are libraries. Single copy: $8; subscription: $12. **Sample postpaid: $5. Reports in 4 months. Pays copies. Editors sometimes comment on rejections.** Open to unsolicited reviews. Poets may also send books for review consideration. This is one of the best-edited and designed magazines being published today. Award-winning editor Richard Jones assembles an exciting array of accessible poems, leaning toward lyric free verse with room for narrative and otherwise well-structured poems in all traditions. He occasionally schedules theme issues and selects poems accordingly. Because competition is keen, response times can exceed stated limits, particularly in the spring. Work published in ***Poetry East*** has been included in *The Best American Poetry 1993*.

THE POETRY EXPLOSION NEWSLETTER (THE PEN) (I), P.O. Box 2648, Newport News VA 23609-0648, phone (804)599-3399, founded 1984, editor Arthur C. Ford, is a "quarterly newsletter dedicated to the preservation of poetry." Arthur Ford wants **"poetry—40 lines maximum, no minimum. All forms and subject matter with the use of good imagery, symbolism and honesty. Rhyme and non-**

rhyme. No vulgarity." He has published poetry by Veona Thomas and Rose Robaldo. *The Pen* is 12-16 pgs., saddle-stitched, mimeographed on both sides. He accepts about 80 of 300 poems received. Press run is 450 for 350 subscribers of which 5 are libraries. Subscription: $15. **Send $4 for sample copy and more information. Submit maximum of 5 poems at a time. Include $1 reading fee. Simultaneous submissions and previously published poems OK. Editor comments on rejections "sometimes, but not obligated." Pays 1 copy.** He will criticize poetry for 15¢ a word. Open to unsolicited reviews. Poets may also send books for review consideration. The editor comments: "Even though free verse is more popular today, we try to stay versatile."

POETRY FORUM (I); THE JOURNAL (IV-Subscription); HEALTHY BODY-HEALTHY MINDS (IV-Specialized), 5713 Larchmont Dr., Erie PA 16509, phone (814)866-2543 (also fax: 8-10 a.m. or 5-8 p.m.), e-mail 75562.670@compuserve.com, editor Gunvor Skogsholm. *Poetry Forum* appears 3 times a year. **"We are open to any style and form. We believe new forms ought to develop from intuition. Length up to 50 lines accepted. Would like to encourage long themes. No porn or blasphemy, but open to all religious persuasions."** As a sample the editor selected these lines (poet unidentified):

> *Is it anger I see in your eyes*
> *When they look at mine?*
> *Because I see no smile or happiness*
> *there—merely a blank stare.*
> > *Is it anger I see*
> > *Or is it Longing for me?*

The magazine is $7 \times 8\frac{1}{2}$, 38 pgs., saddle-stapled with card cover, photocopied from photoreduced typescript. **Sample postpaid: $3. They will consider simultaneous submissions and previously published poems. Editor comments on poems "if asked, but respects the poetic freedom of the artist." Publishes theme issues. Send SASE for guidelines and upcoming themes. Sometimes sends prepublication galleys. Gives awards of $25, $15, $10 and 3 honorable mentions for the best poems in each issue. Acquires one-time rights.** Reviews books of poetry in 250 words maximum. Open to unsolicited reviews. Poets may also send books for review consideration. *The Journal*, which appears twice a year, accepts **experimental poetry of any length from subscribers only. Sample: $3.** *Healthy Body-Healthy Minds* is a biannual publication concerned with health issues. **They accept essays, poetry, articles and short-shorts on health, fitness, mind and soul. Send SASE for details.** They offer a poetry chapbook contest. Entry fee: $9. Prize is publication and 20 copies. Send SASE for information. The editor says, "I believe today's poets should experiment more and not feel stuck in the forms that were in vogue 300 years ago. I would like to see more experimentalism—new forms will prove that poetry is alive and well in the mind and spirit of the people."

POETRY HARBOR; NORTH COAST REVIEW (I, II, IV-Regional), P.O. Box 103, Duluth MN 55801-0103, phone (218)728-3728, founded 1989, director Patrick McKinnon. Poetry Harbor is a "nonprofit, tax-exempt organization dedicated to fostering literary creativity through public readings, publications, radio and television broadcasts, and other artistic and educational means." Its main publication, *North Coast Review*, is a regional magazine appearing 3 times a year with **poetry and prose poems by and about Upper Midwest people, including those from Minnesota, Wisconsin, North and South Dakota, and the upper peninsula of Michigan. "No form/style/content specifications, though we are inclined toward narrative, imagist poetry. We do not want to see anything from outside our region, not because it isn't good, but because we can't publish it due to geographics."** They have recently published poetry by Mark Vinz, Joe Paddock, Susan Hauser and Barton Sutter. As a sample the editor selected these lines from "Rolling Up Sidewalks" by William Borden:

> *I imagine the sidewalks rolled to each corner*
> *like sardine can lids*
> *each evening at sundown by old men*
> *underpaid but loyal, in blue uniforms*
> *a bit shabby and threadbare. They start at one corner*
> *and wiggle their calloused fingers into the crack*
> *between curb and cement. No one tries it, so no one knows it's easy.*

NCR is 56 pgs., $7 \times 8\frac{1}{2}$, offset and saddle-stapled, paper cover with various b&w art, ads at back. They receive about 500 submissions a year, use 100-150. Press run is 1,000 for 200 subscribers of which 20 are libraries, 300 shelf sales. Two-year subscription: $19.50. **Sample postpaid: $3.50. Submit 3-5 pgs. of poetry, typed single-spaced, with name and address on each page. Previously published poems and simultaneous submissions OK, if noted. Cover letter with brief bio ("writer's credits") required. "We read three times a year, but our deadlines change from time to time. Write to us for current deadlines for our various projects." Send SASE for guidelines. Reports in 1-5 months. Pays $10 plus copies. Buys one-time rights.** Poetry Harbor also publishes 1 perfect-bound paperback of poetry and 4-8 chapbooks each year. One chapbook is selected through an annual contest; send SASE for guidelines. "Others are selected by our editorial board from the pool of poets we have published in

CLOSE-UP

Community Sets Poetry in Motion

poems are magic carpets
that sing while they fly
& you ride them free
like space is a subway
& you go as many stops as you will
no end of the line on this baby
ride em if ya got em

(from "poetry should be read in the dark," in *Out Past the Chainlinks of Time* by
Patrick McKinnon, 1994. Reprinted by permission of Poetry Harbor)

©Jeff Frey & Associates Photography

Patrick McKinnon

Look no further for ideas on making poetry a community affair. Meet Patrick McKinnon, a California
native who, after spending years performing odd
jobs, "ended up in Duluth, Minnesota, of all
places." But he's not complaining: It's there he has
made a home and founded a poetry empire. You can call it fortuitous. In Northern
Minnesota, however, they call it Poetry Harbor.

After establishing his own small journal, *Poetry Motel*, in 1984, McKinnon
embarked on making poetry more participatory. Along with his wife Andrea,
friends Elle Schoenfeld and Kelly Green, McKinnon started Poetry Harbor in
1989. "There weren't regular readings north of Minneapolis so we decided to
hold one. We distributed fliers, and—surprisingly—23 people came just to read.
And, believe it or not, there were 100 people in the audience," he says.

Readings were held in a local tavern until members were ousted after two
months—they filled lots of space but spent no money. The group then moved
to an old, privately-owned building. "They put us in this basement in mid-winter.
Poets read with coats, hats and gloves on. Still, 100 people came, regardless of
the cold!" Northern Minnesota craved poetry; Poetry Harbor fed it.

They're still nourishing the Lake Superior region, while also letting regional
poets feed themselves. "Our format features a selected reader for a half hour,
and then an open mike for ten people who each read for up to ten minutes,"
says McKinnon. This approach works well, giving audience members the opportunity to see poets they're interested in, hear poets they don't recognize, or even
read their own work.

When McKinnon says, "there are just so many positive things about Poetry
Harbor," he's not exaggerating. In addition to publishing the *North Coast Review*
and numerous chapbooks, and conducting readings, Poetry Harbor manages a
number of projects involving the community. "We do many one-time events
with local organizations," says McKinnon. "We get regular calls from people
wanting poets for readings, interviews or workshops. Callers aren't sure which

poet is best suited for what, so we make a match for the appropriate function."

For example, McKinnon once found himself reading poetry to the mayor of Duluth at a Kiwanis Club breakfast. Poetry Harbor members also have made trips to the local health center where they helped AIDS patients write poems, and eventually compiled the work into a book called *We Are All Living with AIDS*. A special reading featuring such poems drew 250 people.

These one-time functions are only part of Poetry Harbor's community involvement. Each poetry reading is videotaped and aired on cable television, with the best performances compiled for an "Encore Series," which is aired throughout the region. Poetry Harbor also airs 20 to 30 radio broadcasts throughout the year on various regional FM stations.

As if this weren't enough, the organization sponsors what's termed "poetry outreach." Take Poetry Furlough, a workshop held at the Duluth federal prison. Each month a poet reads his or her work, and then inmates read their work and get feedback. Eight to fifteen inmates participate, a few of whom have been published. And Poetry Harbor launched "The Small Press Food Shelf," a small press free-distribution service. "We fill boxes with books, magazines and journals and make them available to people who might not otherwise be interested in reading. There are enough libraries; we don't need to create another. Why archive what we can share with the public?"

The outreach program doesn't limit itself to Duluth. "We're serving poetry. We're concerned with audience development. When we look around, that's what is lacking. We're not short on the number or quality of poems, the diversity of visions and voices, but the number of people who pick up a poetry book and read it," he says. "Poets need an audience. We make sure they get one. If there's no poetry in Buhl, Minnesota, and there's a poet in Buhl, then we want an audience for poetry in Buhl. We want to get out into the region as much as we can, because we bring something special."

Special indeed. And the communities know it. Every book Poetry Harbor publishes sells out. Recent successes include their anthologies: *Poets Who Haven't Moved to Minnesota*, *Poets Who Haven't Moved to St. Paul*, and *Days of Obsidian, Days of Grace*, a Native American anthology which sold out its first press run of 1,500 copies in two months.

Considering the paucity of the poetic climate the last 20 years, Poetry Harbor has accomplished what many would have deemed impossible: establishing poetic venues. "At Poetry Harbor, we're into poetry that is written for oneself *and* for a body of strangers," says McKinnon. "We create venues for those wanting poetry. And we've proven people sure want it!"

Creating venues isn't the only trick to establishing an audience. While television and radio shows help, as do the "outreach" programs, what really makes Poetry Harbor survive is its egalitarian approach. "We stand for no bars on anybody's vision. Together all visions are larger than any one. We have no ideology, except to promote poetry. We offer and receive a great cross-section of styles, voices and subject matter. We embrace all poets in all forms."

Such egalitarianism has worked well for Poetry Harbor, and McKinnon thinks it can work anywhere. "You just have to let people know you're here and they're welcome," he says. "People know they can come to us and we'll go to them. That's why we're successful."

—*Don Prues*

North Coast Review or have worked with in our other projects. **We suggest you send a submission to North Coast Review first. We almost always print chapbooks and anthologies by poets we've previously published or hired for readings."** Recent anthologies include *Poets Who Haven't Moved to St. Paul* and *Days of Obsidian, Days of Grace*, selected poetry and prose by four Native American writers. Send SASE for complete publications list. Poetry Harbor also sponsors a monthly reading series ("poets are paid to perform"), a weekly TV program (3 different cable networks regionally), various radio programming, a prison workshop series and other special events. They say, "Poetry Harbor is extremely committed to cultivating a literary community and an appreciation for our region's literature within the Upper Midwest. There was a vacuum up here when it came to poetry reaching this community. Poetry Harbor projects are in place to change that. Poets are now OK to people up here, and literature is thriving. The general public is proving to us that they *do* like poetry if you give them some that is both readable and rooted in the lives of the community."

‡POETRY IN MOTION; NATIONAL POET'S ASSOCIATION (I, IV-Membership), P.O. Box 173, Dept. PM, Bayport MN 55003-0173, e-mail diananaiad@aol.com, founded 1992, editor Nadia Giordana. *Poetry in Motion* is a bimonthly publication "dedicated to providing a platform for new and emerging poets and writers and to providing those writers with the kind of up-to-date and valuable information they need to perfect their craft." Each issue includes poetry, short stories, cartoons, artwork, book reviews and articles. **"Approximately 60% of the material published is by members of the National Poet's Association; 40% is written by nonmembers. Nonmembers must pay a $1 per page reading fee."** They are open to all kinds of poetry, including humorous poems and haiku, 32 lines maximum. They have recently published poetry by Clyde Wallin Jr., James S. McLellan, Sara L. Holt and Nancy S. Young. As a sample we selected these lines from "Clavicle" by Sharon F. Suer:

> *Fractured—and an oddly pleasant discomfort,*
> *like the wet sponge inside your head with a cold*
> *or the unrest in every muscle with the flu,*
> *so that you just want to stretch your limbs*
> *in a whole-body yawn. Or the fatigue so intense*
> *that it hurts, every cell trying hard to lie down.*

Poetry in Motion is 40 pgs., digest-sized, desktop-published and saddle-stapled with light card stock cover and b&w art, graphics and numerous ads. Press run is 300. Membership/subscription: $15.99. **Sample postpaid: $3.50. Submit work typed single-spaced, 1 poem (or 3 haiku) to a page, name and address on each. Cover letter (with "interesting information about yourself") required. Nonmembers must include reading fee. Send large SASE for guidelines. "We may keep material for up to three months if it is being seriously considered for publication." Pays copies.** Reviews books of poetry. Send books for review consideration. They also publish chapbooks, calendars with poetry and illustrations, and an occasional full-sized anthology. Send SASE for details. The editor says, "Membership does not insure publication. All material submitted by members and nonmembers alike is judged and chosen solely on its own merit. Since we publish poetry and stories on a wide variety of subjects, it is always a good idea to review a sample copy to get an idea of what is likely to get published. Please, nothing excessively profane or violent."

‡POETRY IRELAND REVIEW (II, IV-Regional), Bermingham Tower, Upper Yard, Dublin Castle, Dublin 2, Ireland, phone 353.1.6714632, fax 353.1.6714634, founded 1979, administrator Niamh Morris, the magazine of Ireland's national poetry organization "provides an outlet for **Irish poets; submissions from abroad also considered. No specific style or subject matter is prescribed. We strongly dislike sexism and racism."** They have recently published poetry by Allen Ginsberg, Carol Ann Duffy, Sharon Olds, John Montague and Eavan Boland. Occasionally publishes special issues. The 6×8 quarterly uses 60 pgs. of poetry in each issue, circulation 1,200, with 800 subscriptions of which 120 are libraries. They receive about 1,000 submissions/year, use 10%, have a 2-month backlog. Single copy: IR£4; subscriptions: IR£16. **Sample postpaid: $10. Submit 5-8 poems at a time. No previously published poems or simultaneous submissions.** Time between acceptance and publication is 1-3 months. **Seldom comments on rejections. Send SASE (or SAE with IRCs) for guidelines. Reports in 6-8 weeks. Pays IR£10/poem or 1 year subscription.** Reviews books of poetry in 500-1,000 words. They offer a bimonthly newsletter giving news, details of readings, competitions, etc. for IR£6/year. They also sponsor an annual poetry competition. Send SASE (or SAE with IRCs) for details. The editors advise, "Keep submitting: good work will get through."

POETRY KANTO (V), Kanto Gakuin University, Kamariya-cho, Kanazawa-Ku, Yokohama 236, Japan, founded 1984, editor William I. Elliott. *Poetry Kanto* is a literary annual published by the Kanto Poetry Center, which sponsors an annual poetry conference. It publishes **well-crafted original poems in English and in Japanese.** The magazine publishes **"anything except pornography, English haiku and tanka, and tends to publish poems under 30 lines." They are not reading mss until further notice, however, as "special numbers are planned."** They have published work by A.D. Hope, Peter

Robinson, Naomi Shihab Nye, Nuala Ni Ohomhnaill and Kudō Naoko. As a sample the editor selected these lines by Chris Wallace-Crabbe:

> *But here, in the serene glass,*
> *hairy tussocks are wearing rhinestones*
> *and the sun appears hunched*

> *behind a strip of pewter cloudbank*
> *while the big moon-face*
> *sits on an old rooftree, hoping to set.*

The magazine is digest-sized, nicely printed (the English poems occupy the first half of the issue, the Japanese poems the second), 60 pgs., saddle-stapled, matte card cover. Circulation is 700, of which 400 are complimentary copies sent to schools, poets and presses; it is also distributed at poetry seminars. The magazine is unpriced. **Pay is 3-5 copies.** The editor advises, "Read a lot. Get feedback from poets and/or workshops. Be neat, clean, legible and polite in submissions. *SAE with International Reply Coupons absolutely necessary when requesting sample copy.*"

‡**THE POETRY MISCELLANY (II)**, English Dept., University of Tennessee at Chattanooga, Chattanooga TN 37403, phone (615)755-4629, founded 1971 (in North Adams, MA), poetry editor Richard Jackson. "We publish new and established writers—poems, interviews, essays, translations. We are truly a miscellany: **we look at all schools, types, etc.**" They have recently published poetry by William Matthews, Marvin Bell, Paula Rankin, Tomaž Šalamun and Donald Justice. As a sample the editor selected these lines from "Elvis Poem" by Regina Wilkins:

> *But the big things come into your life*
> *only through the little things that give you identity.*
> *That's when things like Love become real.*
> *We spent a lot of the fifty dollars in the Snack Bar.*
> *We spent a little more at the souvenir shop.*
> *The preacher at grandfather's funeral said he could*
> *explain the Bible as plainly as if he had spoken*
> *to Paul himself. I knew when Janis turned down*
> *the Elvis impersonator he'd hit on me. So everything was*
> *back to normal. The world wasn't ending.*
> *And we had ten dollars left, which was enough.*

The 16-page tabloid appears annually, professionally printed, with black ink on grey paper. Circulation is 750 for 400 subscriptions of which 100 are libraries. They receive about 10,000 submissions/year, use 20, have a 6-12 month backlog. Subscription: $5. **Sample postpaid: $2.50. Send 3-4 clear copies/submission. Reports in 3-4 months. Pays 2 copies. Send SASE for guidelines. Editor "rarely" comments on rejections. Also publishes chapbooks.** Sometimes holds contests "when grants allow."

POETRY MOTEL; SUBURBAN WILDERNESS PRESS BROADSIDES (I, II), 1619 Jefferson, Duluth MN 55812, founded 1984, editors Patrick McKinnon, Bud Backen, Ed Gooder and Ellen Seitz-Ryan aim **"to keep the rooms clean and available for these poor ragged poems to crash in once they are through driving or committing adultery." They want "poems that took longer than 10 minutes to author." No other specifications.** They have recently published poetry by Adrian C. Louis, Robert Peters, Hayley Mitchell, Albert Huffstickler, Carolyn Stoloff, Tony Moffeit and Todd Moore. As a sample they selected this poem, "Family Traditions," by Will Lahti:

> *when great-grandfather was 4 years old*
> *he and his brothers would play funeral.*

> *since matti was the youngest*
> *he had to be the corpse.*

> *he played this role so well that*
> *one day his brothers buried him alive.*

Poetry Motel appears "every 260 days" as a 7 × 8½ digest, with wallpaper cover, circulation 1,000 (to 600 subscribers), 52 pgs. of poetry, prose, essays, literary memoirs and reviews. They receive about 1,500 submissions/year, take 150, have a 3- to 24-month backlog. **Sample: $5.95. Submit 3-5 pgs. of poetry at a time, with SASE. Simultaneous submissions OK. Informal cover letter with bio credits required. Reports in 1-10 weeks. Sometimes sends prepublication galleys. Pay varies.** Reviews books of poetry. Open to unsolicited reviews. Poets may also send books for review consideration. They advise, "Poets should read as much poetry as they can lay their hands on. And they should realize that although poetry is no fraternal club, poets are responsible for its survival, both financially and emotionally. Join us out here—this is where the edge meets the vision. We are very open to work from 'beginners.'"

POETRY NEW YORK: A JOURNAL OF POETRY AND TRANSLATION (II, IV-Translations, themes), P.O. Box 3184, Church Street Station, New York NY 10008, founded 1985, editors Burt Kimmelman, Todd Thilleman and Emmy Hunter, is an annual. They have published poetry by Wanda Coleman, Jerome Rothenberg, Enid Dame, Amiel Alcalay and Ann Lauterbach, and translations of Mallarme, Hesiod and Makoto Ooka. As a sample the editors selected these lines from "The Second Month of Separation" by Corinne Robins:

> I don't hear or see,
> an ocean and your drugs are
> in between.
> The beautiful garbage birds fly the island ferry,
> and ocean planes criss-cross
> while I dream you grow beyond closed doors.

The editors describe it as 6×9, perfect-bound, 80 pgs. They accept about 20% of "blind submissions." Press run is 500 for 300 shelf sales. **Some issues are on themes. "Query us first to see whether we are currently reading manuscripts. If so, send no more than five poems per submission." Editor comments on submissions "at times." Reports in 3-4 months. Pays 1 copy.** They sometimes sponsor readings. Work published in *Poetry New York* has been included in the 1993 and 1994 volumes of *The Best American Poetry*.

POETRY NORTHWEST (II), University of Washington, 4045 Brooklyn Ave. NE, JA-15, Seattle WA 98105, phone (206)685-4750, founded 1959, editor David Wagoner, is a quarterly. The magazine is 48 pgs., 5½×8½, professionally printed with color card cover. It features all styles and forms. For instance, in two recent issues, lyric and narrative free verse was included alongside a sonnet sequence, minimalist sonnets and stanza patterns—all accessible and lively. They receive 10,000 poems/year, use 160, have a 3-month backlog. Circulation 1,500. Subscription: $15. **Sample postpaid: $4. Occasionally comments on rejections. Reports in 1 month maximum. Pays 2 copies. Awards prizes of $500, $100, $50 and $50 yearly, judged by the editors.**

POETRY OF THE PEOPLE (I, IV-Humor, love, nature, fantasy, themes), P.O. Box 13077, Gainesville FL 32604, founded 1986, poetry editor Paul Cohen. *Poetry of the People* is a leaflet that appears 3 times a year. **"We take all forms of poetry but we like humorous poetry, love poetry, nature poetry and fantasy. No racist or highly ethnocentric poetry will be accepted. I do not like poetry that lacks images or is too personal or contains rhyme to the point that the poem has been destroyed."** The format for *Poetry of the People* varies from 8-32 pgs., 5½×8 to 5½×4⅛, stapled, sometimes on colored paper. Issues are usually theme oriented. It has a circulation between 300 and 2,300. Copies are distributed to Gainesville residents for 25¢ each. **Samples: $4 for 11 pamphlets. "Please send donations, the magazine bank account is overdrawn. Suggested donation: $2." Submit 1-10 poems at a time. Cover letter with biographical information required with submissions. "I feel autobiographical information is important in understanding the poetry." Poems returned within 3 months. Editor comments on rejections "often." Send SASE for upcoming themes. Takes suggestions for theme issues. Sometimes sends prepublication galleys. Pays 5 copies. Acquires first rights.** He advises, "Be creative; there is a lot of competition out there."

POETRY PLUS MAGAZINE; GERMAN PUBLICATIONS (I), Route 1, Box 52, Pulaski IL 62976, founded 1987, publisher/editor Helen D. German. *PPM* is a quarterly with articles on writing and getting published. "We also publish a variety of thought provoking, stimulating poems, articles on business information, health information and recipes. **We accept all styles of poetry. Length should be no more than one page. Poets can write on any subject that offers a meaningful message. Poems must be in good taste. We do *not* want any holiday poems."** As a sample the editor selected these lines from "Tacit Time" by Charles E. Chessa:

> Time an element of space
> Rather or not it has gone
> As the past of yesterday
> Or even light years beyond

PPM is magazine-sized, 25-35 pgs., photocopied from typescript, bound with tape, paper cover. Subscription: $12/year. Sample postpaid: $3. **"Please submit at least 5 poems for consideration."** No previously published poems or simultaneous submissions. Send SASE for guidelines. "We feature

---

Use the General Index to find the page number of a specific publisher. If the publisher you are seeking is not listed, check the " '95-'96 Changes" list at the end of this section.

a 'Poem of the Month' that pays $10 to the poem we deem written the best." Offers critique service for $5/poem—limit 1 page. Sponsors an annual poetry contest. $2 reading fee/poem. Prizes are $50 for first, $35 for second, $25 for third. They also publish a yearly anthology. Submit 5 poems for consideration. Write for details. The editor says, *"Poetry Plus* is a fresh magazine that offers poets and writers the opportunity to see their poems in print. We want poems that are written to stimulate the deeper side of the reader. Rhymed or unrhymed, poems should offer a message that is meaningful. They should leave a memorable impression. Always send a large SASE with sufficient postage to return your unused poems. We publish both the work of our subscribers and nonsubscribers."

POETRY WALES; SEREN PRESS (II, IV-Ethnic), 2 Wyndham St., First Floor, Bridgend, Mid-Glamorgan CF31 1EF Wales, founded 1965. *Poetry Wales*, a 72-page, 253×185mm quarterly, circulation 1,000, has a primary interest in **Welsh and Anglo-Welsh poets but also considers submissions internationally. Send submissions (with SAE and IRC) to Richard Poole, editor, Glan-y-Werydd, Llandanwg, Harlech LL46 2SD Wales.** Overseas subscription: £18/year. **Sample: £2.50. Submit 6 poems at a time. No previously published poems. One-page cover letter required; include name, address and previous publications. SASE or SAE with IRC must be included for reply. Publishes theme issues. Send SASE (or SAE and IRC) for upcoming themes. Theme for September 1995 was narrative poetry. Pays.** Staff reviews books of poetry. Send books for review consideration to Amy L. Wack, reviews editor, Wyndham Street address. Seren Press publishes books of **primarily Welsh and Anglo-Welsh poetry**, also biography, critical works and some fiction, distributed by Dufour Editions, Inc., Box 449, Chester Springs PA 19425. They have received several Welsh Arts Council "Book of the Year" Prizes. The editor says, "We would like to see more formal poetry."

POETRY WLU (I, II), Dept. of English, Wilfrid Laurier University, Waterloo, Ontario N2L 3C5 Canada, phone (519)884-1970, ext. 3308, founded 1979, editorial contact E. Jewinski, is an annual literary magazine (published every March) "with emphasis on *all* poetry and *all* prose *under* 1,000 words. **20-30 lines are ideal; but all kinds and lengths considered.**" As a sample the editor selected the opening lines from "Katherine's Eye" by Bruce Bond:

> *It's the faithfulness that fools us,*
> *how its fine red vein*
> *slips under the living seam*
>
> *When Katherine lost her glass eye*
> *in the deep-end of her uncle's pool,*
> *her brothers scouted the blue*

Poetry WLU is $6\frac{1}{2} \times 8$, saddle-stapled, typeset, with matte card cover using b&w art. They receive about 100-120 submissions a year, use approximately 15-20%. Press run is 300. **Sample postpaid: $5. Submit 5 poems at a time. "We strongly discourage simultaneous submissions." Cover letter preferred. Reads submissions September 1 through January 30 only. "When the editorial board has time, comments are made." Reports in 6-8 months. Pays 1 copy.** Staff reviews books of poetry.

POETS AT WORK (I, IV-Subscribers), VAMC 325 New Castle Rd., Box 113, Butler PA 16001, founded 1985, editor/publisher Jessee Poet, **all contributors are expected to subscribe.** Jessee Poet says, **"Every poet who writes within the dictates of good taste and within my twenty-line limit will be published in each issue. I accept all forms and themes of poetry, including seasonal and holiday, but no porn, no profanity."** He has recently published poetry by Jaye Giammarion, Katherine Krebs, James Webb, Phil Eisenberg and Ralph Hammond. As a sample he selected his poem "An Old Romance":

> *I almost loved you . . . did you know?*
> *Sometimes you still disturb my dreams.*
> *A summer romance long ago*
> *I almost loved you . . . did you know?*
> *We danced to music soft and low*
> *Just yesterday . . . or so it seems*
> *I almost loved you . . . did you know?*
> *Sometimes you still disturb my dreams.*

Poets at Work, a bimonthly, is generally 36-40 pgs., magazine-sized, saddle-stapled, photocopied from typescript with colored paper cover. Subscription: $18. **Sample: $3. Submit 5-10 poems at a time. Simultaneous submissions and previously published poems OK. Reports within 2 weeks. Pays nothing, not even a copy.** "Because I publish hundreds of poets, I cannot afford to pay or give free issues. Every subscriber, of course, gets an issue. Subscribers also have many opportunities to regain their subscription money in the numerous contests offered in each issue. Send SASE for flyer for my separate monthly and special contests." He also publishes chapbooks. Send SASE for details. Jessee Poet says, "These days even the best poets tell me that it is difficult to get published. I am here for the novice as well as the experienced poet. I consider *Poets at Work* to be a hotbed for poets where each one can stretch and grow at his or her own pace. Each of us learns from the other, and we do not criticize one another. The door for poets is always open, so please stop by; we probably will like each other immediately.''

POET'S FANTASY (I, IV-Fantasy), Dept. PM, 227 Hatten Ave., Rice Lake WI 54868, founded 1991, publisher/editor Gloria Stoeckel, is a bimonthly designed "to help the striving poet see his/her work in print." **They want sonnets, haiku and humorous free verse, 4-16 lines. "I accept good, clean poetry. Looking for poems of fantasy, but not exclusively. No profanity or sexual use of words."** They have recently published poetry by earl jay perel and Gary Michael Lawson. As a sample we selected these lines from "Speechio" by Jane Stuart:

> *You unblinking told me I was curtains*
> *and the rabbit jumped again against*
> *the mirror.*
>
> *The nothingness of being isn't anything*
> *to write home about*
> *and my heart rings with less than true*
> *de facto.*

Poet's Fantasy is 36 pgs., digest-sized, computer-generated dot-matrix, photocopied and saddle-stapled with colored paper cover, graphics and ads. They receive approximately 200 poems a year, accept about 90%. Press run is 300 for 250 subscribers. Subscription: $15/year; foreign $18/year. **Sample postpaid: $3. Submit 3-5 poems at a time. No previously published poems or simultaneous submissions. Often comments on rejections. Send SASE for guidelines. Reports within 2 weeks. Pays coupon for $3 off subscription price or greeting card order. (Poets must purchase copy their work is in.) Acquires first North American serial rights.** "I do book reviews if poet sends a complimentary copy of the book and a $3 reading fee. Reviews are approximately 200 to 300 words in length." She holds contests in each issue and also creates greeting cards for poets. "They use verse they wrote and can design their own cover." Send SASE for details.

POETS ON: (II, IV-Themes), 29 Loring Ave., Mill Valley CA 94941, phone (415)381-2824, founded 1976, poetry editor Ruth Daigon, is a poetry semiannual, **each issue on an announced theme (such as** *Poets On: Regrets*). **"We want well-crafted, humanistic, accessible poetry. We don't want to see sentimental rhymed verse. Length preferably 40 lines or less, or at the very most 80 lines (2-page poems)."** They have published poetry by Marge Piercy, Charles Edward Eaton, Walter Pavlich, Barbara Crooker and Lyn Lifshin. As a sample the editor selected these lines from "A Way of Saying" by Robert Funge in *Poets On: Remembrance*:

> *So we have named the Wind, that we may have*
> *a way of saying what it is that moves*
> *between us, as between all things that move*
> *and through all that are still. And this we call*
> *Touch, this thing like wind that we can know*
> *only by what it moves. And we have named ourselves*
> *Man and Woman, to have soft words to call*
> *each other, who like the wind are known*
> *more by how we move the things we touch.*

Poets On: is 48 pgs., digest-sized, professionally printed, matte card cover with b&w graphics. They use about 5% of the 800 submissions they receive each year, have a 2- to 3-month backlog. Daigon tends to accept strong and well-structured lyric free verse, although you are apt to find any style or form with exciting or insightful content. Circulation is 450, 350 subscriptions of which 125 are libraries. Subscription: $8. **Sample postpaid: $5. Query with SASE for upcoming themes and deadlines. Submit 1-4 poems (40 lines or less). No previously published poems; simultaneous submissions OK, if "notified well in advance whether poem is accepted elsewhere." No handwritten mss. Include short bio with writing background. "It's a good idea to read the magazine before submitting poetry." Submit only September 1 through December 1 or February 1 through May 1. Reports in 2-3 months. Pays 1 copy. Editor sometimes comments on rejections.** She has designed a rejection slip that has several categories explaining why your work didn't make it into the magazine, and yet she'll often add a comment to encourage good work. Daigon says, "We are not interested in poetry that is declamatory, sloganeering, bathetic or opaque. Nor are we concerned with poetry as mere word-games or technical exercises."

POETS. PAINTERS. COMPOSERS; COLIN'S MAGAZINE (II), 10254 35th Ave. SW, Seattle WA 98146, phone (206)937-8155, founded 1984, editor Joseph Keppler, who says *"Poets. Painters. Composers.* is an avant-garde arts journal which appears once or twice a year and publishes poetry, drawings, scores, criticism, essays, reviews, photographs and original art. **If poetry, music or art is submitted, the work should be somehow extraordinary, not what other magazines already have published**

too much of." The journal is magazine-sized, 86 pgs. Each cover has an original painting on it. Mr. Keppler says, "each odd-numbered issue appears in an 8½×11 format; each even-numbered issue changes format: No. 2, for example, is published as posters; No. 4 appears on cassettes. No. 6 has incorporated an exhibition, a gallery and a series of sculptures as part of its content. No. 7 will be a print issue featuring poetry, art and criticism. No. 8 will be a radio issue involving art specifically for radio communication." Circulation is 300, no subscriptions. Each issue of the magazine carries an individual price tag. A copy of *Poets. Painters. Composers.* **No. 5 is $50. Sample of No. 3 available for $21.50 postpaid. "Contributors' poetry receives great care. All material is returned right away unless (a) it's being painstakingly examined for acceptance into the journal or (b) it's being considered as right for some other way of publishing it or (c) we died." Contributors receive 1 copy. Acquires one-time rights.** "We prefer short (500-800 word) reviews unless we already have asked for a longer piece from a poet/reviewer because of his or her interest in the book."

POET'S REVIEW (I, IV-Subscribers); THEME POETRY (IV-Themes), P.O. Box I, 806 Kings Row, Varnell GA 30756, phone (706)694-8441, founded 1988, publisher Bob Riemke, is a monthly booklet, using **poetry by subscribers** and making cash awards monthly and annually on basis of votes by subscribers. **"Prefer rhyme. Short poems, 44 lines or less. Open to limericks and humor. Any subject. No porn! No foreign languages."** They have published poetry by Helen Webb, Ashley Anders and J. Alvin Speers. *PR* is 28 pgs., digest-sized, photocopied from typescript with paper cover. Subscription: $36. **Sample postpaid: $4. Submit 1 typed poem at a time. "Subscribers are sent a ballot along with their monthly booklet to vote for the poems they believe to be the best." Monthly prizes are $75, $50 and $25, plus 7 honorable mentions. "All $75 winners are presented to the subscribers again at the end of the year and compete for a $500, $250 and $100 prize."** 30-50 poems are printed each month along with the names of winners for the previous month. They also publish *Theme Poetry*, "a monthly magazine for poems with a theme." **They want poems under 40 lines dealing with the specific theme for the month. "No porn or foreign languages." Themes for October 1995, November 1995 and December 1995 are Halloween, fall, harvest; Thanksgiving and Christmas, respectively. Send SASE for guidelines and upcoming themes.**

POETS' ROUNDTABLE; POETS' STUDY CLUB OF TERRE HAUTE; POETS' STUDY CLUB INTER-NATIONAL CONTEST (I, IV-Membership), 826 S. Center St., Terre Haute IN 47807, phone (812)234-0819, founded in 1939, president/editor Esther Alman. Poets' Study Club is one of the oldest associations of amateur poets. It publishes, every other month, *Poets' Roundtable*, a newsletter of market and contest information and news of the publications and activities of its members in a mimeographed, 10-page bulletin (magazine-sized, stapled at the corner), circulation 2,000. They have also published an occasional chapbook-anthology of poetry by members "but do not often do so." **Dues: $6/year. Sample free for SASE. Uses short poems by members only. Simultaneous submissions and previously published poems OK.** They offer an annual Poets' Study Club International Contest, open to all, with no fees and cash prizes—a $25 and $15 award in 3 categories: traditional haiku, serious poetry, light verse. Deadline: February 1. Also contests for members only each two months. "We have scheduled criticism programs for members only."

THE POINTED CIRCLE (II), 705 N. Killingsworth, Portland OR 97217, phone (503)978-5230, fax (503)240-5370, e-mail rstevens@pcc.edu, founded 1980, advisor Rachel Stevens, is an annual. **They want poems "under 60 lines, mostly shorter. One-page poems on any topic of any form."** They have recently published poetry by Judith Barrington, Lyn Lifshin and Barbara Drake. As a sample the editor selected this poem, "Solitary Cheating," by Anne Ellsworth:

> *Alone at night,*
> *my mother would play solitaire,*
> *believing if she won the game,*
> *her cheating husband would return,*
> *manipulating hearts and spades,*
> *drinking wine and shuffling cards,*
> *cheating.*

It is 80 pgs., flat-spined, with b&w glossy card cover, professionally printed. Press run is 200. **Sample postpaid: $3.50. No simultaneous submissions. Cover letter required. Submit mss from December 1 through February 15 only. "Place name, address, etc., on cover sheet only, listing titles of submissions. Limit 6 poems/poet. All submissions are read anonymously by student editorial staff; notification about June 1 for submissions received by February 15." Send SASE for guidelines. Pays 1 copy. Acquires one-time rights.**

POLYPHONIES (III, IV-Translations), 85, rue de pa Santé, 75073 Paris, France, founded 1985, editor Pascal Culerrier. Editorial committee: Laurence Breysse, Emmanuelle Dagnaud, Jean-Yves Masson and Alexis Pelletier. Appears twice a year. **"Every case is a special one. We want to discover the new important voices of the world to open French literature to the major international productions.**

For example, we published Brodsky in French when he was not known in our country and had not yet the Nobel Prize. No vocal poetry, no typographic effects." They have published poetry by Mario Luzi (Italy), Jeremy Reed (Great Britain), Octavio Paz (Mexico) and Claude Michel Cluny (France). It is about 110 pgs., 6½×9½, flat-spined, with glossy card cover, printed completely in French. Press run is 850 for 300 subscribers. **Uses translations of previously published poems. Pays 2 copies.** The editor says, "Our review is still at the beginning. We are in touch with many French editors. Our purpose is to publish together, side-by-side, poets of today and of yesterday."

PORTABLE WALL (V), 215 Burlington, Billings MT 59101, phone (406)256-3588, founded 1977, publisher Daniel Struckman. He publishes, as Ezra Pound described, **"words that throw the object on to the visual imagination and that induce emotional correlations by the sound and rhythm of the speech."** He has published poetry by Dave Thomas and Joe Salerno. As a sample he selected these lines by Kathleen Taylor:

> Lightning rams down
> a cloud-clotted sky;
> the red moon is wasted.

PW is published irregularly. It is 60 pgs., saddle-stapled, on heavy tinted stock with 2-color matte card cover. Press run is 400. Subscription: $18 for 4 issues. **Sample postpaid: $6.50. Currently not accepting poetry submissions.** The editor says, "I have more poetry than I can print."

PORTLAND REVIEW (II), Box 751-SD, Portland State University, Portland OR 97207, phone (503)725-4533, founded 1954, is a literary annual published by Portland State University 3 times a year. **"Experimental poetry welcomed. No poems over 3 pages. No rhyming poetry."** The annual is magazine-sized, about 128 pgs. They accept about 30 of 300 poems received each year. Press run is 500 for 100 subscribers of which 10 are libraries. **Sample: $5. Simultaneous submissions OK. Send SASE for guidelines. Pays 1 copy.**

POST-INDUSTRIAL PRESS (III), P.O. Box 265, Greensboro PA 15338, founded 1989, publishes 1-3 paperbacks/year. They have published poetry by Georges Perec and Johannes Poethen. **No simultaneous submissions. Replies to queries in 1 month.**

POTATO EYES; NIGHTSHADE PRESS (II), P.O. Box 76, Troy ME 04987-0076, phone (207)948-3427, founded 1988, editors Roy Zarucchi and Carolyn Page, is a semiannual literary arts journal **"with a focus on writers who write about the land and/or quality of life close to the earth. We now accept submissions from throughout the U.S. and Canada, although much of our poetry is from Appalachian states."** They have recently published poetry by Linda L. Harper, Barbara Presnell, Jack Coulehan, Julie Kate Howard and Craig Czury. As a sample the editors selected these lines from "You Never Get To The Horizon" by Ava Leavell Haymon, published in her chapbook *Built in Fear of Heat*:

> In the delta, you're ringed by horizons.
> The great plowed land is flat as Holland
> and all the trees were cut down with the Indians.
> The taste of dust in your mouth there
> is flavored always by cotton poison.
> The air must have tasted like that
> in Berlin, between the wars.

PE is 5½×8½, 100 pgs., flat-spined, professionally printed, with block cut matte paper cover. Circulation is 800. Subscription: $11 ($14 Canadian). **Sample postpaid: $6 (back issue $5), or $7 Canadian.** The editors say, "those who submit receive a handwritten rejection/acceptance. We are open to any form other than rhymed, in batches of 3-5, but we tend to favor poetry with concrete visual imagery, solid intensity and compression. We respect word courage and risk-taking, along with thoughtful lineation. We prefer rebellious to complacent poetry. We prefer a cover letter with brief bio along with SASE. We occasionally have a guest editor. However, submissions should still be sent to the Maine address." Reports in 1-2 months. Pays 1 copy. Acquires first North American serial rights.** Reviews books of poetry. Open to unsolicited reviews. Poets may also send books for review consideration. Nightshade Press is the imprint under which they publish about 10 chapbooks/year, each 24-48 pgs., "usually with block print or pen-and-ink covers, endsheets and recycled 60 lb. text, 80 lb. covers. **Chapbooks are selected from competitions, mainly, but a few may be from poets who appear first in our magazine."** Send SASE for catalog and information and/or send $5 for sample chapbook.** They advise, "Beginning poets should devour as much good poetry as possible in order to delineate their own style and voice. Look for a match between substance and sound."

POTES & POETS PRESS, INC.; ABACUS (III), 181 Edgemont Ave., Elmwood CT 06110, phone (203)233-2023, press founded in 1981, magazine in 1984, editor Peter Ganick. The press publishes avant-garde poetry in magazine form under the *Abacus* imprint, one writer per issue. The P+Pinc books are perfect-bound and range from 80-120 pgs. in trade editions. **In addition to avant-garde,**

they want experimental or language-oriented poetry, not too much concrete poetry. No *"New Yorker* magazine, *Ploughshares* magazine, mainstream poetry."* They have published poetry by Ron Silliman, Jackson Mac Low, Charles Bernstein, Leslie Scalapino, Carla Harryman and Rachel Blau Du Plessis. *Abacus* is 12-18 pgs., magazine-sized, photocopied, no graphics; it appears every 6 weeks. Circulation is 150, of which 40 are subscriptions and 10 go to libraries. Price per issue is $4; subscription: $26/year. **Sample postpaid: $4.50. Simultaneous submissions are OK. Pay is 10 copies. Unsolicited submissions are accepted for book publication. Writers should "just send the manuscript."** *However, they rarely accept mss from authors new to the press.* The press publishes 2 flat-spined paperback books of poetry/year with an average page count of 100.

POTPOURRI (II), P.O. Box 8278, Prairie Village KS 66208, phone (913)642-1503, fax (913)642-3128, founded 1989, poetry editors Pat Anthony and Terry Hoyland, haiku editor Carl Bettis, is a monthly magazine "to publish works of writers, **including new and unpublished writers. We want strongly voiced original poems in either free verse or traditional. Traditional work must represent the best of the craft. No religious, confessional, racial, political, erotic, abusive or sexual preference materials unless fictional and necessary to plot or characterization. No concrete/visual poetry (because of format)."** They have recently published poetry by David Ray, Richard Moore, Pattiann Rogers and Tess Gallagher. As a sample the editors selected these lines from "Polar Realities" by Bernard E. Morris:

> *Extend your hand across the valley, sweep*
> *away the fog and watch the eddies curl*
> *around the treetops. We'll address the deep,*
> *abiding earth by living on it, whirl*
> *across the lake, and wriggle through the wood.*

It is 80 pgs. Press run is 2,000 for 550 subscribers. "Over 500 distributed to other publications through *Potpourri*'s networking program." Subscription: $15. **Sample postpaid: $4.95. Submit no more than 3 poems at a time, one to a page, length to 75 lines (approximately 30 preferred). Submit seasonal themes 6 months in advance. Address haiku and related forms to Carl Bettis.** "*Potpourri* publishes reprints of exceptional materials only from submissions by other magazines." **Send SASE for guidelines. Reports in 8-10 weeks at most. Pays 1 copy. Acquires first North American serial rights.** The David Ray Poetry Award ($100 or more, depending upon grant monies) is given annually for best of volume. A new annual award will be sponsored by the Council on National Literatures and offers $100 and publication in *Potpourri* for selected poem or short story; alternating years (1996 fiction). Send SASE for official guidelines. Deadline: June 30, 1996. They also publish a line of *Potpourri Petites*, 50-54 pgs., 4×8. "At present, we do not accept unsolicited submissions for *Petites*. New poets can establish themselves for consideration by solid acceptances in *Potpourri* and through other credits." *Potpourri* received the 1994 Governor's Arts Award sponsored by the Kansas Arts Commission in recognition of its "outstanding contribution to the excellence of literary arts in Kansas." The editors advise, "Keep your new poems around long enough to become friends with them before parting. Let them ripen, and, above all, learn to be your own best editor. Read them aloud, boldly, to see how they ripple the air and echo what you mean to say. Unrequited love, favorite pets and description that seems to be written for its own sake find little chance here."

‡POULTRY, A MAGAZINE OF VOICE (IV-Humor), P.O. Box 4413, Springfield MA 01101, founded 1979, editors Jack Flavin, Brendan Galvin and George Garrett, is a tabloid (2-3 times a year) of **"parody, satire, humor and wit, particularly of the modern literary scene." They do not want to see "serious" poetry.** They have recently published poetry by R.S. Gwynn, Louis Phillips, Bruce Boehrer, Jennifer Horne and R.H.W. Dillard. As a sample the editors selected these lines from "Leaning Against the Bar" by Peter Makuck:

> *A drunk drifts through the door, looking for home.*
> *I have wasted my life.*

The 11½×17 tabloid, 8 pgs., unstapled, professionally printed on newsprint, uses b&w photos, graphics, drawings. Press run is 500 for 250 subscribers of which 35 are libraries. Subscription: $6. **Sample postpaid: $3. Submit 5-6 poems at a time. Simultaneous submissions OK, "rarely" uses previously published poems. Pays 10 copies. Acquires first rights.** Jack Flavin calls for "a little more humor and light, please, in the deadly serious (and oftentimes deadly) business of being a poet, a writer and getting published. Beginning poet? Get it down while it's hot, let it cool and consider it with a cold eye a bit later. Learn to write by doing it, if you're lucky, under the watchful eye and with encouragement from a good critic."

PRAIRIE DOG: A QUARTERLY FOR THE SOMEWHAT ECCENTRIC (II), (formerly *Infinity Limited*), P.O. Box 470757, Aurora CO 80047-0757, phone (303)696-0490, founded 1988, editor-in-chief John R. Hart, is an illustrated "literary quarterly dedicated to presenting emerging and established talent. Staff artists illustrate some of our work, but we encourage submissions from writer-artists, artists and photographers as well." They want poetry that **"traffics in delight as well as agony, that deals**

both with the 'foul rag and bone shop of the heart,' and 'the sovereign floating of joy.' " They have recently published poetry by William Nesbit, Norman Kraeft, Norman Kirk, Mary De Maine and Kenneth Johnson. As a sample the editor selected the final stanza of a poem by Simon Perchik:

> —you are allowed two spoons
> and everywhere you open windows
> open doors, the small spoons
> opened, pressed against the sweetness
> that lasts and your mouth.

Prairie Dog is magazine-sized, "printed on 60 lb. bond with parchment cover (2-3 color)" and appears "more or less quarterly, 4 times a year. We receive about 40 submissions per week, use about 25 poems per issue." Press run is 1,000 for 250 subscribers. Subscription: $14. **Sample $4.95 plus $1 p&h and 9 × 12 SAE. Submit 2-10 poems at a time. Simultaneous submissions OK, if noted. Cover letter with "bio info is helpful if work accepted." Send SASE for guidelines. Reports within 6 months, "but we read everything." Editor comments on submissions "if writing or art shows promise." Pays 2 copies. Acquires one-time or first reprint rights.** Open to unsolicited reviews. Poets may also send books for review consideration. The editor says, "Because we just acquired *Infinity Limited* in March 1995, please be patient. We read everything and will respond if you provide a SASE. We accept double-sided and photocopied manuscripts (save the trees) but will not read faint dot-matrix manuscripts. We would like to feature one "youthful new voice" (under 25, just beginning to be published) per issue, but our standards are high. Mass submissions based on class assignments are sure to be rejected."

PRAIRIE FIRE (III), 100 Arthur St., Room 423, Winnipeg, Manitoba R3B 1H3 Canada, phone (204)943-9066, fax (204)942-1555, founded 1978, editor Andris Taskans, is a quarterly magazine of new writing including fiction, poetry and reviews. **They want "poetry that articulates a connection between language and ethics, an aesthetic of writing 'from the body,' and open to the nuances of orality, ethnic and racial differences and feminism. No haiku, sonnets or other rhyming forms, nor political or religious treatises in verse form."** They have recently published poetry by Di Brandt, Katharine Bitney and Kristjana Gunnars. As a sample the editor selected these lines from "talking 3 a.m." by Patrick Friesen:

> it's 3 a.m. and I remember the fall of white silk from my love's shoulders
> the mole on her left arm her slender thighs
> remembering again and again what matters losing the rest in small
> blowouts of the brain and the radio's noise
> I want to say something about love how it's flesh only for a while how
> it's words for a long time

Prairie Fire is 128 pgs., 6 × 9, offset, perfect-bound, glossy card cover, illustrations and ads. They receive 400-500 submissions (average 6 poems each), accept approximately 2%. Press run is 1,600 for 1,200 subscribers of which 100 are libraries, 150 shelf sales. Single copy: $8.95; subscription: $24 Canadian, $28 US. **Sample postpaid: $9 Canadian. Submissions should be typed, double-spaced, one poem to a page, name and address on each page, no more than 6 poems at a time. No previously published poems or simultaneous submissions. Cover letter required. Include other publications, brief biographical information, list of poems submitted, name, address and phone number. Reads submissions September 1 through June 30 only.** Time between acceptance and publication is 1 year. Seldom comments on rejections. Publishes theme issues. **Send SASE (or SAE and IRC) for guidelines and upcoming themes. Reports in 3-4 months. Pays $30 for first page, $25 for each additional page, plus 1 copy. Buys first Canadian serial rights only.** Staff reviews books of poetry in 500-2,000 words, single or multi-book format. Send books for review consideration. The editor says, "Be patient!"

THE PRAIRIE JOURNAL (II); PRAIRIE JOURNAL PRESS (IV-Regional, themes), P.O. Box 61203, Brentwood Post Office, 217-3630 Brentwood Rd. NW, Calgary, Alberta T2L 2K6 Canada, founded 1983, editor A. Burke, who wants to see **poetry of "any length, free verse, contemporary themes (feminist, nature, urban, non-political), aesthetic value, a poet's poetry." Does not want to see "most rhymed verse, sentimentality, egotistical ravings. No cowboys or sage brush."** They have published poetry by Mick Burrs, Lorna Crozier, Mary Melfi, Art Cuelho and John Hicks. *Prairie Journal* is 7 × 8½, 40-60 pgs., offset, saddle-stitched with card cover, b&w drawings and ads, appearing twice a year. They accept about 4% of the 500 or so poems they receive a year. Press run is 600 per issue, 200 subscriptions of which 50% are libraries. Subscription: $6 for individuals, $12 for libraries. **Sample postpaid: $6 ("Use postal money order"). No simultaneous submissions or previously published poems. Guidelines available for postage (but "no U.S. stamps, please"—get IRCs from the Post Office). "We will not be reading submissions until such time as an issue is in preparation (twice yearly), so be patient and we will acknowledge, accept for publication or return work at that time." Sometimes sends prepublication galleys. Pays $10-50 plus 1 copy. Acquires first North American serial rights.** Reviews books of poetry "but must be assigned by editor. Query first." **For**

chapbook publication, Canadian poets only (preferably from the region) should query with 5 samples, bio, publications. Responds to queries in 2 months, to mss in 6 months. Payment in modest honoraria. They have published *Voices From Earth*, selected poems by Ronald Kurt and Mark McCawley. "We also publish anthologies on themes when material is available." A. Burke advises, "Read recent poets! Experiment with line length, images, metaphors. Innovate."

THE PRAIRIE PUBLISHING COMPANY (III, IV-Regional), Dept. PM, Box 2997, Winnipeg, Manitoba R3C 4B5 Canada, phone (204)885-6496, founded 1963, publisher Ralph E. Watkins, is a "small press catering to regional market, local history, fantasy, poetry and nonfiction," with flat-spined paperbacks. They want **"basically well-crafted poems of reasonable length" and do not want to see "the work of rank amateurs and tentative and time-consuming effort."** They have published collections of poetry by Brian Richardson and Brian MacKinnon. Their books are 6×9, handsomely produced, using b&w photos and art along with the poems, glossy card covers. They publish about 1 a year, 68 pgs. **Samples available at a 20% discount—send SASE or SAE and IRC for catalog. Query with samples. Simultaneous submissions OK. Do not submit mss during summer. Responds to queries in 6 weeks.** Nancy Watkins notes, "Robert E. Pletta's point that most poets need to do more reading is well taken. We would endorse this suggestion."

PRAIRIE SCHOONER; STROUSSE PRIZE; SLOTE PRIZE; FAULKNER AWARD; STANLEY AWARD; READERS' CHOICE AWARDS (II), 201 Andrews, University of Nebraska, Lincoln NE 68588-0334, phone (402)472-0911, founded 1927, editor Hilda Raz; "one of the oldest literary quarterlies in continuous publication; publishes poetry, fiction, personal essays, interviews and reviews." **They want "poems that fulfill the expectations they set up." No specifications as to form, length, style, subject matter or purpose. No simultaneous submissions.** They have recently published poetry by Albert Goldbarth, Rafael Campo, Toi Derricotte, Alicia Ostriker, Dave Smith and Marcia Southwick. As a sample the editor selected these lines from "How to Get in the Best Magazines" by Eleanor Wilner:

> it is time to write
> the acceptable poem—
> ice and glass, with its splinter
> of bone, its pit
> of an olive,
> the dregs
> of the cup of abundance,
> useless spill of gold
> from the thresher, the dust
> of it filling the sunlight, the chum
> broadcast on the black waters
> and the fish
>   —the beautiful, ravenous fish—
> refusing to rise.

The magazine is 6×9, flat-spined, 176 pgs. and uses 70-80 pgs. of poetry in each issue. They receive about 4,800 mss (of all types)/year from which they choose 300 pgs. of poetry. Press run is 3,100. Subscription: $20/year; $6.45/copy. **Sample postpaid: $3.50. Submit 5-7 poems at a time. "Clear copy appreciated." Considers mss from September through May only. Publishes theme issues. Send SASE for guidelines. Reports in 2-3 months; "sooner if possible." Always sends prepublication galleys. Pays copies. Acquires all rights. Returns rights upon request without fee.** Reviews books of poetry. Open to unsolicited reviews. Poets may also send books for review consideration. One of the most influential magazines being published today (often named as such in independent surveys of creative writers), this publication is genuinely open to excellent work in any form: lyric, narrative, dramatic, traditional, etc. Send only your best work, as competition is keen. Brief reviews are an excellent way to break into the journal. Editor Hilda Raz also promotes poets whose work has appeared in her pages by listing their continued accomplishments in a special section (even when their work does not concurrently appear in the magazine). The $500 Strousse Prize is awarded to the best poetry published in the magazine each year. The Slote Prize for beginning writers ($500), the Stanley Award for Poetry ($300) and six other *PS* prizes are also awarded, as well as the Faulkner Award for Excellence in Writing ($1,000). Also, each year 5-10 Readers' Choice Awards ($250 each) are given for poetry, fiction and nonfiction. Editors serve as judges. Hilda Raz comments, "*Prairie Schooner* receives a large number of poetry submissions; we're not unusual. We don't have time to comment on mss, but the magazine's reputation is evidence of our careful reading. We've been dedicated to the publication of good poems for a very long time and have published work early in the career of many successful poets."

PRAIRIE WINDS (II), Box 536, Dakota Wesleyan University, 1200 W. University Ave., Mitchell SD 57301, editor Howard F. Gunston, is an annual of poetry, fiction, short essays, photos and art. **They are open to all forms, lengths, styles and subjects of poetry except pornographic.** They have published poetry by Simon Perchik, Aaron Kramer, David Ignatow and Henry Hughes. The editor says *PW* is 50-60 pgs., 7½×9¼, offset, bound, gloss litho, no ads. They accept approximately 25% of the poetry received each year. Press run is 500 for 50 subscribers of which 10 are libraries. The rest are distributed free to professors and students. **Sample postpaid: $2. Submit 5-10 poems at a time. No previously published poems; simultaneous submissions OK. Cover letter required. "We are an annual, published in spring. All submissions must arrive by January 4." Reads submissions January 4 through 31 only. Seldom comments on rejections. Send SASE for guidelines. Reports by end of February. Pays 1 copy.**

PRAKALPANA LITERATURE; KOBISENA (I, IV-Bilingual, form), P-40 Nandana Park, Calcutta 700034, West Bengal, India, phone (91)(033)478-2347, *Kobisena* founded 1972, *Prakalpana Litera-ture* press founded 1974, magazine 1977, editor Vattacharja Chandan, who says, "We are small maga-zines which publish only *Prakalpana* (a mixed form of prose and poetry), Sarbangin (whole) poetry, experimental b&w art and photographs, essays on Prakalpana movement and Sarbangin poetry move-ment, letters, literary news and very few books on Prakalpana and Sarbangin literature. **Purpose and form: for advancement of poetry in the super-space age, the poetry must be really experimental and avant-garde using mathematical signs and symbols and visualizing the pictures inherent in the alphabet (within typography) with sonorous effect accessible to people. That is Sarbangin poetry. Length: within 30 lines (up to 4 poems). Prakalpana is a mixed form of prose, poetry, essay, novel, story, play with visual effect and it is not at all short story as it is often misunderstood. Better send 6 IRCs to read *Prakalpana Literature* first and then submit. Length: within 16 pages (up to 2 prakalpanas) at a time. Subject matter: society, nature, cosmos, humanity, love, peace, etc. Style: own. We do not want to see traditional, conventional, academic, religious, mainstream and poetry of prevailing norms and forms."** They have recently published poetry by Dilip Gupta, Susan Smith Nash, John M. Bennett and Bisweswar Ray. As a sample the editor chose these lines by Utpal:

> *Emerging from Nought*
> *and fading into Nought 0 ◊ 0*
> *Or Biography can be written as =*
> *walking backwards from one Nought*
> *to another = 0 ◊ 0*

Prakalpana Literature, an annual, is 120 pgs., 7×4½, saddle-stapled, printed on thin stock with matte card cover. *Kobisena*, which appears once a year, is 16 pgs., digest-sized, a newsletter format with no cover. Both are hand composed and printed by letterpress. Both use both English and Bengali. They use about 10% of some 400 poems received/year. The press run is 1,000 for each, and each has about 450 subscriptions of which 50 are libraries. **Samples: 15 rupees for *Prakalpana*, 4 rupees for *Kobisena*. Overseas: 6 IRCs and 3 IRCs respectively or exchange of avant-garde magazines. Submit 4 poems at a time. Simultaneous submissions OK. Previously published poetry OK. Cover letter with short bio and small photo/sketch of poet/writer/artist required; camera-ready copy (4×6½) preferred.** Publication within a year. **After being published in the magazines, poets may be included in future anthologies with translations into Bengali/English if and when necessary. "Joining with us is welcome but not a pre-condition." Editor comments on rejections "if wanted." Send SAE with IRC for guidelines. No reporting time given. Sometimes sends prepublication galleys. Pays 1 copy.** Reviews books of poetry, fiction and art, "but preferably experimental books." Open to unsolicited reviews. Poets, writers and artists may also send books for review consideration. He says, "We believe that only through poetry, fiction and art, the deepest feelings of humanity as well as nature and the cosmos can be best expressed and conveyed to the peoples of the ages to come. And only poetry can fill up the gap in the peaceless hearts of dispirited peoples, resulted from the retreat of god and religion with the advancement of hi-tech. So, in an attempt, since the inception of Prakalpana Movement in 1969, to reach that goal in the avant-garde and experimental way we stand for Sarbangin poetry. And to poets and all concerned with poetry we wave the white handkerchief saying (in the words of Vattacharja Chandan) 'We want them who want us.' "

THE PRESBYTERIAN RECORD (IV-Inspirational, religious), 50 Wynford Dr., North York, Ontario M3C 1J7 Canada, phone (416)441-1111, founded 1876, is "the national magazine that serves the membership of The Presbyterian Church in Canada (and many who are not Canadian Presbyterians). We seek to stimulate, inform, inspire, to provide an 'apologetic' and a critique of our church and

---

The Subject Index, located before the General Index, can help you narrow down markets for your work. It lists those publishers whose poetry interests are specialized.

the world (not necessarily in that order!)." **They want poetry which is "inspirational, Christian, thoughtful, even satiric but *not* maudlin. No 'sympathy card' type verse a la Edgar Guest or Francis Gay. It would take a *very* exceptional poem of epic length for us to use it. Shorter poems, 10-30 lines, preferred. Blank verse OK (if it's not just rearranged prose). 'Found' poems. Subject matter should have some Christian import (however subtle)."** They have recently published poetry by Margaret Avison, Jeanne Davis, Joan Stortz, Marlow C. Dickson, Charles Cooper and J.R. Dickey. The magazine comes out 11 times a year. Press run is 64,000. Subscription: $13. **Submit 3-6 poems at a time; seasonal work 6 weeks before month of publication. Simultaneous submissions OK; rarely accepts previously published poems. Poems should be typed, double-spaced. Pays $20-50/poem. Buys one-time rights.** Staff reviews books of poetry. Send books for review consideration. *The Presbyterian Record* has won several Canadian Church Press Awards.

PRESCOTT STREET PRESS (V, IV-Regional), Box 40312, Portland OR 97240-0312, founded 1974, poetry editor Vi Gale: **"Poetry and fine print from the Northwest."** Vi Gale says, "Our books and cards are the product of many hands from poet, artist, printer, designer, typesetter to bookstore and distributor. Somewhere along the line the editor/publisher [herself] arranges to pay one and all in the same way. Sometimes we have had grant help from the NEA and also from state and metropolitan arts organizations. But most of our help has come from readers, friends and the poets and artists themselves. Everyone has worked very hard. And we are immodestly pleased with our labors! **We are not a strictly regional press, although the poets I take on are connected with the Northwest in some way when we bring out the books. We are chronically overstocked with poetry."** Vi Gale publishes a series of postcards, notecards, paperback and hardback books of poetry in various artistic formats with illustrations by nationally known artists. Send SASE for catalog to order copies. As a sample, here are lines by Rolf Aggestam from a postcard:

> *muttering. cold*
>> *hands split fresh kindling*
>>> *damn*
>> *what a life. you are far away.*
>>> *in the darkness we used to call*
>>> *each other forth*
>>>> *with fingers and a few small words.*
>> *we created a little border*
>>> *between darkness and darkness.*

Considers simultaneous submissions. Sometimes sends prepublication galleys. "We pay all of our poets. A modest sum, perhaps, but we pay everyone something."

‡PRESS GANG PUBLISHERS (III, IV-Regional, women), #101-225 E. 17th Ave., Vancouver, British Columbia V5V 1A6 Canada, phone (604)876-7787, fax (604)876-7892, founded 1975, managing editor Barbara Kuhne, publishes 1 perfect-bound paperback book of poetry a year. **"We give priority to Canadian women's work. Nothing sexist, racist, homophobic."** They have published books of poetry by Chrystos and Joanne Arnott. As a sample the editor selected these lines from Chrystos's poem "Savage Eloquence":

> *Big Mountain*
> *you old story you old*
> *thing you fighting over nothing everything*
> *how they work us*
> *against one another   They mean to kill us*
> *all   Vanishing is no joke   they mean it*

Query first with sample poems and cover letter with brief bio and publication credits. Previously published poems and simultaneous submissions OK. "U.S. postage cannot be used to return manuscripts from Canada. Send international postal coupons." Time between acceptance and publication is 9-12 months. **Seldom comments on rejections. Replies to queries in 1 month, to mss (if invited) in 4-6 months. Pays 8-10% royalties and 20 author's copies.** To see what type of work Press Gang publishes, "ask your local bookstore to order books from Inland Book Co., our U.S. distributor."

‡PRESS HERE (IV-Form), P.O. Box 4014, Foster City CA 94404, phone (415)571-9428, e-mail WelchM@aol.com, founded 1989, editor/publisher Michael Dylan Welch, publishes 3 chapbooks a year. "Press Here was founded to publish fine books of haiku and related forms. Its goal is to present new and established voices through a variety of high quality publications. Available books include informative interviews with established haiku poets, individual poetry collections and broad-ranging anthologies. **I wish to see manuscripts of poetry, or essays and interviews, related to haiku, senryu or tanka. I am also interested in concrete poetry."** They have recently published work by William J. Higginson, Penny Harter, Lee Gurga and Virginia Brady Young. As a sample the editor selected these lines of his own:

a snail has left
its delicate silver trail
on my book of love poems
left out on your porch
overnight

Query first with sample poems and cover letter with brief bio and publication credits. Previously published poems OK; no simultaneous submissions. Always comments on rejections. Replies to queries in 1 month, to mss (if invited) in 6-9 months. Pays author's copies. For sample books, write for catalog.

THE PRESS OF MACDONALD & REINECKE (II); PADRE PRODUCTIONS (I), P.O. Box 840, Arroyo Grande CA 93421-0840, phone/fax (805)473-1947, founded 1974, poetry editor Lachlan P. MacDonald. Padre Productions prints books on a fee basis, as a book packager. MacDonald & Reinecke **requires the poet to "purchase 200 copies of an edition (at liberal discounts)" but they do not consider themselves subsidy publishers. They publish under the M&R imprint only work they consider of merit and in which they, like the poet, must invest.** "The press is a division of Padre Productions bringing together under one imprint drama, fiction, literary nonfiction and poetry. We publish poetry in paperback and hardcover. We are looking for **poetry of literary merit and also poetry suitable for travel and nature photo books. We are averse to tightly rhymed conventional poetry unless designed to appeal to the general humor market.**" They have published Terre Ouwehand's *Voices from the Well*, Steven Schmidt's *Avigation and Other Poems* and Phyllis K. Collier's *Daughters of Cain*. **Query with 5-6 samples, publication credits, bio. The editor also wants to know "do they give readings or have marketing opportunities? Some authors distribute fliers to build up prepublication orders sufficient to justify the print order." Replies to queries in 2-4 weeks, to submissions (if invited) in 2-6 months. Simultaneous submissions OK. Ms should be double-spaced. Pays minimum of 4% royalties, 6 copies. The editor "frequently makes brief comments" on rejections. Send 6×9 SASE for catalog.** The editor advises, "Poets who have not published 10 or 20 poems in literary magazines are unlikely to have developed the craft we require. We also prefer books with a unifying theme rather than a sampling reflecting the author's virtuosity."

THE PRESS OF THE NIGHTOWL (V), 320 Snapfinger Dr., Athens GA 30605, phone (706)353-7719, founded 1965, owner Dwight Agner, publishes 1-2 paperbacks and 1-2 hardbacks each year. They have published poetry by Paul Zimmer, Stephen Corey, Mary Anne Coleman and C.K. Williams. **However, they are currently not accepting unsolicited poetry submissions. Pays author's copies. Sample books may be ordered directly from the publisher or located through bookstores.**

THE PRESS OF THE THIRD MIND (IV-Form), 65 E. Scott St., Loft 6P, Chicago IL 60610, phone (312)337-3122, founded 1985, poetry editor "Badly Steamed Lard (anagram of Bradley Lastname)", is a small press publisher of artist books, poetry and fiction. **"We are especially interested in found poems, Dada, surrealism, written table-scraps left on the floors of lunatic asylums by incurable psychotics, etc."** They have recently published poetry by Anthony Stark, Jorn Barger, Tom Vaultonberg, Kevin Riordan and Eric Forsburg. As a sample the editor selected these lines from "Blind Trail With Wings (for Phillip Lamantia)" by Paul Grillo:

An unidentified heart explodes packed with lava
With blood of violins and undersea brambles
I see the beautiful Swimmer unfolding himself
Weighted down with Death's dark sequins
His wide skirts billowing over the arches
Embracing the angels of empty subways
Who scratch the opposite side of the pearl into song

They have a press run of 500-1,000 with books often going into a second or third printing. **Sample postpaid: $5. For book publication submit up to 20 sample poems. Simultaneous submissions OK, if noted. "Cover letter is good, but we don't need to know everything you published since you were age 9 in single-spaced detail." Send SASE for upcoming themes. "Authors are paid as the publication transcends the break-even benchmark."** In March 1995, the press released an 80-page anthology entitled *Empty Calories*. In the summer of 1995, they published a deconstructivist novel about the repetition complusion called *The Squeaky Fromme Gets the Grease*.

PRIMAVERA (II, IV-Women), P.O. Box #37-7547, Chicago IL 60637, phone (312)324-5920, founded 1975, co-editor Ruth Young, is "an irregularly published but approximately annual magazine of poetry and fiction reflecting **the experiences of women. We look for strong, original voice and imagery, generally prefer free verse, fairly short length, related, even tangentially, to women's experience.**" They have recently published poetry by Lynne Hugo de Courcy, Sagaree Sengupta, Anita N. Feng and Denise Dumars. As a sample the editors selected these lines by Diane Seuss Brakeman:

Unfasten your belt. Let your stomach out.

> *Let it lower. Let it grow. Unbraid the braid.*
> *Shake your hair out. Blow your nose. Spit.*

The elegantly printed publication, flat-spined, generously illustrated with photos and graphics, uses 30-35 pgs. of poetry in each issue. They receive over 1,000 submissions of poetry/year, use 32. Circulation is 1,000. Single copy: $9. **Sample postpaid: $5. Submit no more than 6 poems anytime, no queries. No simultaneous submissions. Editors comment on rejections "when requested or inspired." Send SASE for guidelines. Reports in 1-2 months. Pays 2 copies. Acquires first-time rights.**

PRINCETON UNIVERSITY PRESS; LOCKERT LIBRARY OF POETRY IN TRANSLATION (IV-Translations, bilingual), 41 William St., Princeton NJ 08540, phone (609)258-4900. "In the Lockert Library series, we publish simultaneous cloth and paperback (flat-spine) editions for each poet. Cloth-bound editions are on acid-free paper, and binding materials are chosen for strength and durability. Each book is given individual design treatment rather than stamped into a series mold. We have published a wide range of poets from other cultures, including well-known writers such as Hölderlin and Cavafy, and those who have not yet had their due in English translation, such as Ingeborg Bachmann and Faiz Ahmed Faiz. Manuscripts are judged with several criteria in mind: the ability of the translation to stand on its own as poetry in English; fidelity to the tone and spirit of the original, rather than literal accuracy; and the importance of the translated poet to the literature of his or her time and country." The editor says, "All our books in this series are heavily subsidized to break even. We have internal funds to cover deficits of publishing costs. We do not, however, publish books chosen and subsidized by other agencies, such as AWP." **Simultaneous submissions OK if you tell them. Cover letter required. Send mss only during respective reading periods stated in guidelines. Send SASE for guidelines to submit. Reports in 2-3 months.**

PRISM INTERNATIONAL (II), Dept. of Creative Writing, University of British Columbia, Vancouver, British Columbia V6T 1Z1 Canada, phone (604)822-2514, fax (604)822-3616, founded 1959, executive editors Leah Postman and Andrew Gray. "*Prism* is an international quarterly that publishes poetry, drama, short fiction, imaginative nonfiction and translation into English in all genres. We have no thematic or stylistic allegiances: Excellence is our main criterion for acceptance of mss. **We want poetry that shows an awareness of the tradition while reiterating its themes in a fresh and distinctive way. We read everything.**" They have recently published poetry by Daphne Marlatt, Al Purdy, Diana Hartog, Roo Borson and Lorna Crozier. As a sample the editors selected these lines from "In The Time of The Dying of Mothers" by Jane Southwell Munro:

> *The black cat has crept up to lie between our waists. I am not*
> *sleeping and feel her warm against my hip. She is licking her paws,*
> *between the claws. I can tell by the way her back shifts and the*
> *snuffling noises she makes. She has lived with you longer than I*
> *have. Billie, because she is black and she is beautiful.*

Prism is elegantly printed in a flat-spined, 6×9 format, 80 pgs., original color artwork on the glossy card cover, circulation to 1,000 subscribers of which 200 are libraries. They receive 1,000 submissions/year, use 80, have a 2- to 4-month backlog. Subscription: $16. **Sample postpaid: $5. Submit a maximum of 6 poems at a time, any print so long as it's typed. No previously published poems or simultaneous submissions. Cover letter with brief introduction and previous publications required. Send Canadian SASE or SAE with IRCs for guidelines. Reports in 2-4 months ("or we write to poets to tell them we're holding onto their work for a while"). Pays $20/printed page plus subscription. Editors sometimes comment on rejections.** *Prism International* is known in literary circles as one of the top journals in Canada. The editors say, "While we don't automatically discount any kind of poetry, we prefer to publish work that challenges the writer as much as it does the reader. We are particularly looking for poetry in translation."

PRISONERS OF THE NIGHT; MKASHEF ENTERPRISES (IV-Psychic/occult, science fiction/fantasy, horror, erotica), P.O. Box 688, Yucca Valley CA 92286-0688, poetry editor Alayne Gelfand. *Prisoners of the Night*, founded 1987, **focusing on vampire erotica, uses poetry that is "erotic, unique, less horrific and more romantic, non-pornographic, original visions of the vampire."** Poets who have appeared recently in *POTN* include Karen Verba, Charlee Jacob, Ann K. Schwader and John Grey. As a sample the editor selected these lines from "The Vampire Cathedral" by Wendy Rathbone:

> *My love who leaves*
> *widows in his wake,*
> *who moves like water,*
> *who hunts backwards*
> *toward death,*
> *the infants womb-dream. . .*

The intent of *POTN* is "to show the erotic, the romantic, rather than the horrific aspects of the vampire." It is 70-90 pgs., magazine-sized, perfect-bound, with color cover, produced by high-speed photocopying. Most poems are illustrated. It appears annually, usually in August. Of over 300 poems received/year they use between 10 and 20. It has an initial press run of 3,000, but each issue is kept in print. **Sample postpaid: $15 each (for #1-4), $12 (#5), $9.95 each (#6-8). Send SASE for guidelines. No more than 6 poems/submission. No simultaneous submissions or previously published poems, "unless they've only appeared in your own chapbook." Reading schedule: "The past two issues filled to quota by December. The earlier you submit, the better your chance of appearing in an issue. Reading for issue #10 will begin September 15, 1995 and will end March 31, 1996." Editor sometimes comments on rejections. Reports "within 3 months." Pays $5/poem plus 1 copy. Buys first serial rights.** *POTN* wants unusual visions of the vampire, not stereotypical characterizations. The editor says, "I'm *not* looking for clichés or the 'traditional' count or countess. The gothic loner in his run-down castle is the exact image I *do not* want. Expand the stereotype, find new visions, new ways of approaching the theme of the vampire. I'm looking for the unique, the fresh, the startling. Also, I *strongly* discourage rhyme and structured poetry."

‡THE PROLIFIC WRITER'S MAGAZINE (I, II), P.O. Box 554, Oradell NJ 07649, phone/fax (201)262-3277, founded 1992, editor Brian S. Konradt, appears 4-6 times a year including poetry and short stories in addition to how-to articles, interviews, profiles, reviews and market news to help aspiring and professional freelance writers. **They want all types of poetry, up to 500 words. "Especially considers themes of feelings and human values. No science fiction or fantasy."** They have recently published poetry by Merry Harris, Kim Tobias, Christine Knox Wood and Stephen Gill. As a sample we selected these lines from "Myself" by Pandora Deichert:

> *I am my own*
> *and will make*
> *my tomorrows*
> *my magic*
> *my life*
> *out of bits and pieces,*
> *scraps and remnants*
> *and it will be worthy*
> *of the glories of the sky.*

The Prolific Writer's Magazine is 38 pgs., 8½ × 11, web offset printed and saddle-stapled with an 80 lb. glossy paper cover, b&w art, graphics and ads throughout. They accept about 50% of the poetry received. Press run is 4,000 for about 2,000 subscribers, about 2,000 shelf sales. Subscription: $16. **Sample postpaid: $4. Make checks or money orders payable to BSK Communications & Associates. No previously published poems; simultaneous submissions OK. Cover letter, including brief bio, required.** Time between acceptance and publication is 4-12 months. **Often comments on rejections. Send SASE for guidelines. Reports in 4-6 weeks. Pays 1-2 copies. Acquires first North American (or occasionally second) serial rights.** Reviews books and chapbooks of poetry and other magazines in up to 1,000 words. Open to unsolicited reviews. Poets may also send books for review consideration. "In addition, we encourage poets to do profile pieces on other poets and submit them to us for possible publication." The editor adds, "Advice? Write with a lot of passion, thought and feeling. Make readers react to your poetry."

PROOF ROCK PRESS; PROOF ROCK (I, II, IV-Humor), Box 607, Halifax VA 24558, founded 1982, poetry editors Don R. Conner and Serena Fusek. "We try to wake up a passive readership. We challenge our writers to search for something new under the sun and improve on the old." **They want "adventure, contemporary, humor/satire, fantasy and experimental poetry. Avoid overt sentimentality. Poems up to 32 lines. All subjects considered if well done."** The digest-sized magazine appears 2-3 times/year, is offset from typescript copy, colored matte card cover, with 30-40 pgs. in each issue. They receive 800-1,000 submissions/year, use 120-150, have a 3- to 6-month backlog. Press run is 300 for 100 subscribers of which 8-10 are libraries. Subscription: $4. **Sample postpaid: $2.50. Submit no more than 6 pieces, year round. No query needed, though some issues are on announced themes. Simultaneous submissions OK. Send SASE for guidelines. Reports "usually within 1 month." Pays 1 copy.** Proof Rock Press publishes an occasional anthology and collections by individuals. **Query with 8-10 samples, bio and publishing credits. Replies to queries in 1 month, to submissions (if invited) in 1-3 months. Simultaneous submissions OK. Pays copies. Send $3.50 for a sample. Editor sometimes comments on rejections.** His advice is, "Be introspective. Accept the challenge of looking within and write from experience."

PROPHETIC VOICES (II); HERITAGE TRAILS PRESS (V), 94 Santa Maria Dr., Novato CA 94947, founded 1982, poetry editors Ruth Wildes Schuler, Goldie L. Morales and Jeanne Leigh Schuler. "Our goal is to share thoughts on an international level. We see the poet's role as that of prophet, who points the way to a higher realm of existence." They publish *Prophetic Voices* twice a year and chapbooks. They want **"poetry of social commentary that deals with the important issues of our time. Poetry with beauty that has an international appeal. Do not want religious poetry or that with a limited**

scope. **Open to any kind of excellent poetry, but publish mostly free verse. Limited number of long poems accepted due to lack of space."** They have published Jack Brooks, Hazel F. Goddard, A. Manoussos, B.Z. Niditch, H.F. Noyes, Gloria H. Procsal and Bo Yang. *Prophetic Voices* is digest-sized, 144 pgs., perfect-bound, offset from typescript with matte card cover, colored stock with graphics. They have 100 pgs. of poetry in each issue, circulation to 400 subscribers of which 10 are libraries. They receive 4,000 submissions/year, use 800, have a 5-year backlog. Single copy: $7; subscription: $14; $16 to libraries. **Sample postpaid: $5. Submit 4 poems or less. Reports in 1-8 weeks. Pays 1 copy. "Due to our excessive backlog, Heritage Trails can no longer read unsolicited mss."** The editors advise, "Be aware of what is going on in the world around you. Even the personal poem should have universal appeal if it is to survive the test of time."

THE PROSE POEM (II, IV-Form), 1004 Sycamore, San Marcos TX 78666, phone (512)353-4998, founded 1990, editor Steve Wilson, is an annual using **prose poems only. "I hope and pray the author knows what prose poetry is before submitting to me. For me 'prose poems' run from margin to margin, with no line breaks, and use intense, compact language."** They have published poetry by Linda Nemec Foster, Barry Silesky, Ray Gonzalez, Tom Whalen, Harriet Zinnes, Robert Bly and George Myers, Jr. The editor describes *TPP* as 60 pgs., professionally printed with card stock cover, saddle-stapled. Most selections are one paragraph or a few small ones, each about (or under) 200 words. Press run is 200. **Sample postpaid: $3. Publishes theme issues. Send SASE for upcoming themes and reading periods. Reports by 1 month after deadline. Pays 1 copy. Acquires first North American serial rights.** Staff reviews books of poetry. Send books for review consideration. The editor says, "*TPP* is a journal focusing on one particular genre and publishing only the best work done in that genre. This does not mean an author cannot experiment. I encourage it. It also does not mean I don't want to see work from new writers. Please send, but only your best. I publish this magazine with my own money, so sales are very important. If you think prose poetry matters and like the idea of a journal dedicated to it, please help me keep it going by sending great work and subscribing."

PROSETRY: NEWSLETTER FOR, BY AND ABOUT WRITERS (I), The Write Place, P.O. Box 117727, Burlingame CA 94011, phone (415)347-7613, editor P.D. Steele, founded 1985. *Prosetry* is a monthly newsletter featuring "new and newly published poets and prose writers with a 'guest writer' column each month. Includes original poetry, new markets, contests, seminars, workshops and **general poetry potpourri gleaned from our subscribers." 50% freelance. Sample for 55¢ postage. Invites new writers. Send up to 3 poems, no more than 20 lines, English only. No profanity. Requires 2-line bio plus latest credits ("tell us if you've never been published"). Publishes theme issues. Send SASE for guidelines and upcoming themes. Themes for February, May and December are Love, Spring and Holidays, respectively. "All deadlines are first of month." Reports in less than 1 month. Pays one-year subscription. Acquires one-time rights; release required.** Reviews books of poetry in 150 words. Open to unsolicited reviews. "For 'guest writer' column we would prefer information relevant to the beginning or newly published writer/poet." Also publishes "How-to" *CLIPS*© for writers, $2.50 each. Free list for SASE. The editor says, "I'd like to receive less morose poetry and more humor."

PROVINCETOWN ARTS; PROVINCETOWN ARTS PRESS (II), 650 Commercial St., Provincetown MA 02657, phone (508)487-3167, founded 1985, editor Christopher Busa, is an elegant annual using quality poetry. "*Provincetown Arts* focuses broadly on the artists and writers who inhabit or visit the tip of Cape Cod and seeks to stimulate creative activity and enhance public awareness of the cultural life of the nation's oldest continuous art colony. Drawing upon a century-long tradition rich in visual art, literature and theater, *Provincetown Arts* publishes material with a view towards demonstrating that the artists' colony, functioning outside the urban centers, is a utopian dream with an ongoing vitality." They have published poetry by Bruce Smith, Franz Wright, Sandra McPherson and Cyrus Cassells. As a sample the editor selected these lines from "Sky of Clouds" by Susan Mitchell:

> And after heavy rains, when the egrets
> settle on the gardens, cramming
> their beaks with the shrill
> cries of the frogs, I think
> I could do that too, I could be gorgeous and cruel.

PA is 170 pgs., flat-spined with full-color glossy cover. Press run is 10,000 for 500 subscribers of which 20 are libraries, 6,000 shelf sales. **Sample postpaid: $10. Submit 1-3 typed poems at a time. "We discourage simultaneous submissions." Send SASE for guidelines. Reads submissions September 1 through March 1. Reports in 2-3 months. Sometimes sends prepublication galleys. Pays $25-100/poem plus 2 copies. Buys first rights.** Reviews books of poetry in 500-3,000 words, single or multi-book format. Open to unsolicited reviews. Poets may also send books for review consideration. The Provincetown Arts Press has published 4 volumes of poetry. The Provincetown Poets Series includes *Rival Heavens* by Keith Althaus and *1990* by Michael Klein which won a 1994 Lambda Literary Award. *Provincetown Arts* has also had work published in *Pushcart Prize XVIII* and in *The Best American Poetry* (1991 and 1993, respectively).

PSYCHOPOETICA (II, IV-Specialized: psychologically-based), Dept. of Psychology, University of Hull, Hull HU6 7RX England, founded 1979, editor Dr. Geoff Lowe, uses **"psychologically-based poetry."** That is not a very narrow category, though many of the poems in *Psychopoetica* are explicitly about psychology or psychological treatment. But most good poetry is in some sense "psychologically based," as the editor seems to recognize in these comments (from his guidelines): **"I prefer short, experimental, rhymed and unrhymed, light verse, haiku, etc., (and visual poems). I will read and consider any style, any length, providing it's within the arena of 'psychologically-based' poetry. I'm not too keen on self-indulgent therapeutic poetry (unless it's good and original), nor sweetly inspirational stuff. I like poetry that has some (or all!) of the following: humor, vivid imagery, powerful feelings, guts and substance, originality, creative style, punch or twist, word-play, good craftsmanship, etc."** Published poets include Sheila E. Murphy, Wes Magee, R. Nikolas Macioci, Allen Renfro, Vi Vi Hlavsa and John Brander. The magazine appears 3 times/year, circulating to "several hundred and increasing." It is A4, perfect-bound. **Sample: £1.50 ($3). Submit a maximum of 6 poems at a time. Previously published poems ("state where and when") and simultaneous submissions OK. Publishes theme issues. Send SASE for guidelines and upcoming themes. Theme for the Winter 1995/1996 issue is Introducing Poetry (brief introductions to accompany each poem). Editor usually comments on rejections. Pays 1 copy.** Occasionally reviews books of poetry in 25 words, single format. Open to unsolicited reviews. Poets may also send books for review consideration. He says, "Careful presentation of work is most important. But I continue to be impressed by the rich variety of submissions, especially work that shifts boundaries. Also, we now welcome interesting juxtapositions of words and graphics."

THE PUCKERBRUSH PRESS; THE PUCKERBRUSH REVIEW (I, IV-Regional), 76 Main St., Orono ME 04473, phone (207)866-4868, press founded 1971, *Review* founded 1978, poetry editor Constance Hunting, is a "small press publisher of a literary, twice-a-year magazine focused on Maine and of flat-spined paperbacks of literary quality." The editor **looks for freshness and simplicity, but does not want to see "confessional, religious, sentimental, dull, feminist, incompetent, derivative" poetry.** They have published poetry by Amy Clampitt, and the editor selected these sample lines from "Not a Navigable River" by Muska Nagel:

> *flow seaward, seaward*
> *my river, filled to the brink—*
> *(but no king's horses, no more*
> *will ever come to drink).*

For the review, submit 5 poems at a time. For book publication, query with 10 samples. Prefers no simultaneous submissions. Offers criticism for a fee: $100 is usual. Pays 10% royalties plus 10 copies.

PUDDING HOUSE PUBLICATIONS; PUDDING MAGAZINE: THE INTERNATIONAL JOURNAL OF APPLIED POETRY; PUDDING HOUSE WRITING COMPETITIONS; PUDDING HOUSE BED & BREAKFAST FOR WRITERS; OHIO POETRY THERAPY CENTER & LIBRARY (II, IV-Political, social issues, popular culture), 60 N. Main St., Johnstown OH 43031, phone (614)967-6060, founded 1979, editor Jennifer Bosveld, provides "a sociological looking glass through poems that provide 'felt experience' and share intense human situations. Speaks for the difficulties and the solutions. Additionally a forum for poems and articles by people who take poetry arts into the schools and the human services." They publish *Pudding* every several months, also chapbooks, anthologies, broadsides. They **"want experimental and contemporary poetry—what hasn't been said before. Speak the unspeakable. Don't want preachments or sentimentality. Don't want obvious traditional forms without fresh approach. Long poems happily considered too, as long as they aren't windy. Interested in receiving poetry on popular culture and rich brief narratives, i.e. 'virtual journalism.' "** They have published poetry by Lowell Jaeger, Edward Boccia and Jane Elsdon. The editor selected these sample lines from "Dustbowl Prophet" by Wilma Elizabeth McDaniel:

> *Like all the men in the Meade family*
> *Uncle John's hands were farmer rough and big as shovels.*

Pudding **is a literary journal with an emphasis on poetry arts in human service.** They use about 80 pgs. of poetry in each issue—5½ × 8½, 80 pgs., offset composed on IBM 1st choice, circulation 1,500, 1,400 subscriptions of which 50 are libraries. Subscription (3 issues): $15.75. **Sample postpaid: $6.75. Submit 4-10 poems. No simultaneous submissions. Previously published submissions** *respected* **but include credits. Likes cover letter. Sometimes publishes theme issues. Send SASE for guidelines and upcoming projects. Reports on same day (unless traveling). Pays 1 copy—to featured poet $10 and 4 copies. Returns rights "with** *Pudding* **permitted to reprint."** Staff reviews books of poetry. Send books for review consideration. **For chapbook publication, no query. $5 reading fee. Send complete ms and cover letter with publication credits and bio. Editor often comments, will critique on request for $3/page of poetry or $50 an hour in person.** Jennifer Bosveld shares, "Editors have pet peeves. I won't respond to postcards or on them. I require envelopes, not postcards. Don't individually-fold rather than group-fold poems. I don't like cover letters that state the obvious."

The Pudding Writing Competitions are for single poems (deadline September 30, fee $2/poem) and for chapbook publication (deadline June 30, $9 entry fee). Pudding House Bed & Breakfast for Writers offers "luxurious rooms with desk and all the free paper you can use" as well as free breakfast in large comfortable home ½ block from post office. Location of the Ohio Poetry Therapy Center and Library. $65 single or double/night, discounts available. Reservations recommended far in advance. Send SASE for details.

PUEBLO POETRY PROJECT (IV-Regional), Dept. PM, 1501 E. Seventh St., Pueblo CO 81001, phone (719)584-3401, founded 1979, director Tony Moffeit, **publishes poets from the Pueblo area only. If you qualify, inquire.**

"Poetry is a significant part of Puerto del Sol, in importance, if not pages," says Poetry Editor Kathleene West. About 30 percent of the biannual is devoted to poetry. The rest is filled with fiction, essays, reviews and photos. The magazine, celebrating its 30th anniversary with this issue, is published by New Mexico State University and seeks quality poetry of any style, from anywhere, but is especially open to work about the Southwest. "This cover represents the Southwest origin of the magazine and acknowledges the scope of the material which reaches far beyond the Southwest. Our contributors range from the never before published to poets of national and international reputation," West says. Cover illustration: Louis Ocepek.

PUERTO DEL SOL (II, IV-Translations, regional), Box 3E, New Mexico State University, Las Cruces NM 88003, phone (505)646-2345, fax (505)646-7725, founded 1972 (in present format), poetry editor Kathleene West. "We publish a literary magazine twice per year. Interested in poems, fiction, essays, photos, originals and translations from the Spanish. Also (generally solicited) reviews and dialogues between writers. We want **top quality poetry, any style, from anywhere. We are sympathetic to Southwestern work, to those who *know* the area. Excellent poetry of any kind, any form."** They have recently published poetry by Judith Sornbergen, Colette Inez, Marilyn Hacker and Pieter Weslowski. The 6 × 9, flat-spined, professionally printed magazine, matte card cover with art, has a circulation of 1,250, 300 subscriptions of which 25-30 are libraries. 40-50 pgs. are devoted to poetry in each 150-page issue, which also includes quite a lot of prose. They use about 50 of the 800 submissions (about 4,000 poems) received each year to fill up the 90 pgs. of poetry two issues encompass. "Generally no backlog." You won't find many literary journals as attractive as this one. It has an award-caliber design (from the selection of fonts to the use of rules and type-size to enhance content). Furthermore, the journal features readable, thought invoking verse in all styles including translations. It's an exceptional publication. One-year subscription (2 issues): $10. **Sample copy: $7. Submit 3-6 poems at a time, 1 poem to a page. Simultaneous submissions OK. Cover letter welcome. Offers editorial comments on most mss. Reports in 3 months. Sometimes sends prepublication galleys. Pays copies.** In the past this publication was awarded a NEA Literary Magazine Grant. The editor says, "We're looking for poems that take risks, especially in language and form."

PURDUE UNIVERSITY PRESS; VERNA EMERY POETRY PRIZE (II), 1532 S. Campus Courts-E, West Lafayette IN 47907-1532, phone (317)494-8428, founded 1960. They select 1 book/year to publish through the Verna Emery Poetry Prize. They have published poetry by Jim Barnes, editor of *Chariton Review*, and Fleda Brown Jackson, whose book, *Fishing With Blood*, won the GLCA New Writers Award. **There is a reading fee. Those interested are urged to send SASE for guidelines as particulars vary from year to year.**

THE PURPLE MONKEY (II), 200 E. Redbud Rd., Knoxville TN 37920, founded 1993, editors "and zoo keepers" W. Brian Ellis and Scott Gilbert, appears 4 times/year "juxtaposing seasoned and fledgling poets, creating a publication of well-crafted material." **They want "challenging work that is dynamic and colorful with a creative emphasis toward style and craft. No pretentious, self-righteous, bad examples of poetic movements or art without craft. We want poetry with teeth, poetry that has been agonized over."** They have recently published poetry by Linda Parsons and Ted Kooser. As a sample the editors selected these lines from "Poem About Weird Boats" by Keith Woodruff:

> *Beached in his backyard,*
> *an old wooden rowboat*
>
> *painted white & filled*
> *to the oar-locks with black dirt,*
>
> *springs leaks of iris, daisy*
> *& rose, while slow as clock hands*
>
> *it sinks into his lawn.*

tpm is 30-40 pgs., 5½ × 8½, professionally printed and saddle-stapled with card stock cover, some art and graphics, no ads. Interestingly, in the issue we received, unusual animal names were used instead of page numbers, and the last page included definitions of these terms (everything from addax to zibet). Their press run is 100 for 20 subscribers (2 libraries), 50 shelf sales. Subscription: $8/year. **Sample postpaid: $2.50. Submit 3-5 typed poems at a time. Simultaneous submissions OK, if noted. Cover letter with brief bio required. "Mss without SASE are ignored."** Time between acceptance and publication is 1-5 months. **Seldom comments on rejections. Reports within 2 months. Pays 1 copy. Acquires one-time rights.** The editors add, "Poetry is not for the common man. We pay particular attention to craft and skillful editing. Unpolished journal entries are not poetry."

PYGMY FOREST PRESS (II), P.O. Box 591, Albion CA 95410, phone (707)937-2347, founded 1987, editor/publisher Leonard Cirino, publishes flat-spined paperbacks. **"Forms of any kind/length to 96 pgs., subject matter open; especially ecology, prison, asylum, Third World, anarchist to far right. Prefer Stevens to Williams. I like Berryman, Roethke, Jorie Graham; dislike most 'Beats.' Open to anything I consider 'good.' Open to traditional rhyme, meter, but must be modern in subject matter. Also open to translations."** He has recently published *From Beirut* by Mahmoud Darwish, translated by Stephen Kessler; *Pagan Fishing & Other Poems* by Walt McLaughlin; *Where the Four Winds Blow* (including epitaphs) by Phillipe Soupault, translated by Pat Nolan; *The Circle & The Line* by Victoria Bouroncle; *Lessons of A Radical Finitude* by Michael McIrwin; and *Inside the Boar's Circle* by Stephen Miller. As a sample the editor selected these lines from "Exile" by John P. Freeman, published in his book *Illusion on the Louisiana Side*:

> *Then everything is once more as it always was,*
> *standing you in a field to watch a flight*
> *of geese calling in a dialect*
> *only your blood can know.*

Submit 10-15 poems with bio, acknowledgements, publications. Simultaneous submissions and previously published material OK. Reports on queries in 1-3 weeks, submissions in 2-4 weeks. Sometimes sends prepublication galleys. Pays 10% of run—about 30-50 copies. Buys first rights. He comments on **"almost every" ms.** Leonard Cirino says, "I am basically an anarchist. Belong to no 'school.' I fund myself. Receive no grants or private funding. Generally politically left, but no mainline Stalinist or Marxist. Plan to publish 3-8 books yearly."

‡PYX PRESS; MAGIC REALISM (II, IV-Fantasy); SHILLELAGH (II, IV-Horror, fantasy); WRITER'S KEEPER (I, II, IV-Writing), P.O. Box 922648, Sylmar CA 91392, founded 1990, editor C. Darren Butler. *Magic Realism* appears 2-3 times/year using poetry of **"depth and imagination. *Magic Realism* subverts reality by shaping it into a human mold, bringing it closer to the imagination and to the subconscious. Inner reality becomes empirical reality. We always need good short poems of 3-12 lines."** It is typeset, offset or xerographically printed, digest-sized, 80 pgs. with card cover using b&w art. They use 5-15 poems/issue. Press run is 600-800. **Sample postpaid: $5.95. Previously published poems and simultaneous submissions OK. Send #10 SASE for guidelines. Reports in 2-6 months. Always sends prepublication galleys. Pays $3/magazine page for poetry and 1 copy. Buys first North American serial or one-time rights and nonexclusive reprint rights; also needs worldwide Spanish language rights for translation which appears 1-2 years after English edition. Editor rarely comments.** The editor says, "I am looking for literary work based in exaggerated realism. Fantasy should permeate the reality, give it luster. My needs are somewhat flexible. For example, I occasionally publish genre work, or glib fantasy of the sort found in folktales and fables." *Shillelagh* appears irregularly (perhaps 1-2 times/year) using **"bizarre, horrific short-shorts and poetry. We are most interested in dreamy, surreal, decadent poetry; intensely imaginative and bizarre works. We try to publish material in any form or category that promotes a sense of**

wonder or terror or awe, work that transforms the mind and the experience of living. Horror and comedy are closely related. For this reason, we also accept comedic or absurd work when they fit thematically with the magazine." No obscene, gory, gratuitous, pornographic or trite poetry. The editor says *Shillelagh* is 48 pgs., digest-sized, xerographically printed, saddle-stapled with b&w cover and art, ads also included. They use approximately 20 poems/issue. Press run is 400 for 50 subscribers. Subscription: $10.95 for 3 issues. **Sample postpaid: $4.50. Previously published poems and simultaneous submissions OK. Send SASE for guidelines. Reports in 2-6 months. Pays 1 copy. Acquires first North American serial rights; reprint rights optional.** *Writer's Keeper* is a quarterly publishing poetry, fiction and nonfiction **pertaining to writing. Accepts poetry to 30 lines, any style. "Humorous works especially needed."** *WK* is 2-6 pgs., 8½ × 11, photocopied, corner-stapled. They receive 500-700 submissions a year, accept approximately 2%. Press run 800-1,000 for 40 subscribers, 80% are distributed free. Subscription: $5. **Sample postpaid: $1.25 or free for #10 SASE. Previously published poems and simultaneous submissions OK. Send SASE for guidelines. Reports in 3 months, "occasionally longer, often sooner." Pays $1 plus contributor's copy and 3-issue subscription. Acquires first North American serial rights.** All three magazines review books of poetry, chapbooks and magazines in ¼ to ½ page as space permits. Poets may send books for review consideration. Pyx Press publishes books and chapbooks. "Generally poets we publish first appear in *Magic Realism* or *Shillelagh*." Send SASE for catalog.

THE QUARTERLY (II), 650 Madison Ave., Suite 2600, New York NY 10022, phone (212)888-4769, founded 1987, editor Gordon Lish, is a literary quarterly publishing poetry, fiction, essays and humor. **They want poetry of the "highest standards."** They have published poetry by Sharon Olds, Bruce Beasley, Jack Gilbert and Thomas Lynch. It is 256 pgs., digest-sized, flat-spined, with matte cover. Circulation: 15,000. Subscription: $30. **"Do not submit a batch of poems folded separately!" Sends prepublication galleys. Pays contributor's copies.** The editor says, "Don't apply unless your work is worth your life."

QUARTERLY REVIEW OF LITERATURE POETRY SERIES; QRL PRIZE AWARDS (II, IV-Subscription, translation), 26 Haslet Ave., Princeton NJ 08540, phone (609)258-4703, fax (609)258-2230, founded 1943, poetry editors T. Weiss and R. Weiss. After more than 35 years as one of the most distinguished literary journals in the country, *QRL* now appears as the *QRL Poetry Series*, in which 4-6 books, chosen in open competition, are combined in one annual volume, each of the 4-6 poets receiving $1,000 and 100 copies. The resulting 300- to 400-page volumes are printed in editions of 3,000-5,000, selling in paperback for $10, in hardback for $20. Subscription—2 paperback volumes containing 10 books: $20. **Manuscripts may be sent for reading during the months of November and May only. The collection need not be a first book. It should be 50-80 pgs. if it is a group of connected poems, a selection of miscellaneous poems, a poetic play or a work of poetry translation, or it can be a single long poem of 30 pgs. or more. Some of the individual poems may have had magazine publication. Also considers simultaneous submissions. Manuscripts in English or translated into English are also invited from outside the US. Only one ms may be submitted per reading period and must include a SASE. They always send prepublication galleys.** "Since poetry as a thriving art must depend partly upon the enthusiasm and willingness of those directly involved to join in its support, the editors require that **each ms be accompanied by a subscription to the series.**"

QUARTERLY WEST (II), 317 Olpin Union, University of Utah, Salt Lake City UT 84112, phone/fax (801)581-3938, founded 1976, co-editors M.L. Williams and Lawrence Coates, poetry editors Sally Thomas and Margot Schilpp. *Quarterly West* is a semiannual literary magazine that **seeks "original and accomplished literary verse—free or formal. No greeting card or sentimental poetry." Also publishes translations.** They have recently published poetry by Stephen Dunn, Robert Pinsky and Eavan Boland. *QW* is 220 pgs., 6 × 9, offset with 4-color cover art. They receive 750-1,000 submissions a year, accept less than 1%. Press run is 1,100 for 500 subscribers of which 300-400 are libraries. Subscription: $11 for 1 year, $20 for 2 years. **Sample postpaid: $6.50. Submit 3-5 poems at a time. No previously published poems; simultaneous submissions OK, with notification. Seldom comments on rejections. Send SASE for guidelines. Reports in 1-6 months. Pays $15-100. Buys all rights. Returns rights with acknowledgement and right to reprint.** Reviews books of poetry in 1,000-3,000 words. Open to unsolicited reviews. Poets may also send books for review consideration.

QUEEN OF ALL HEARTS (IV-Religious), 26 S. Saxon Ave., Bay Shore NY 11706, phone (516)665-0726, founded 1950, poetry editor Joseph Tusiani, is a magazine-sized bimonthly that uses **poetry "dealing with Mary, the Mother of Jesus—inspirational poetry. Not too long."** They have published poetry by Fernando Sembiante and Alberta Schumacher. The professionally printed magazine, 48 pgs., heavy stock, various colors of ink and paper, liberal use of graphics and photos, has approximately 5,000 subscriptions at $15/year. Single copy: $2.50. **Sample postpaid: $3.** They receive 40-50 submissions of poetry/year, use 2/issue. **Submit double-spaced mss. Reports within 3-4 weeks. Pays 6 copies (sometimes more) and complimentary subscription. Sometimes editor comments on**

rejections. His advice: "Try and try again! Inspiration is not automatic!"

ELLERY QUEEN'S MYSTERY MAGAZINE (IV-Mystery), 1540 Broadway, New York NY 10036, fax (212)782-8309, founded 1941, appears 13 times a year, primarily using short stories of mystery, crime or suspense. **"We also publish short limericks and verse pertaining to the mystery field."** As a sample the editor selected these lines from "Loud Mouf Mary" by Katherine H. Brooks:

> *I stufft it up wif mortar, brick,*
> *an Mary Ellen also.*
> *And when I heered a dreffle sound*
> *a comin' thoo the floorin',*
> *I worrit sum afore I found*
> *my dawg had took to snorin'.*

EQMM is 160 pgs., 5×7¾, professionally printed newsprint, flat-spined with glossy paper cover. Subscription: $31. **Sample: $2.50 (available on newsstands). No previously published poems; simultaneous submissions OK. Reports in 3 months. Pays $5-50.**

QUEEN'S QUARTERLY: A CANADIAN REVIEW (II, IV-Regional), Queen's University, Kingston, Ontario K7L 3N6 Canada, phone (613)545-2667, founded 1893, editor Boris Castel, is "a general interest intellectual review featuring articles on science, politics, humanities, arts and letters, extensive book reviews, some poetry and fiction. **We are especially interested in poetry by Canadian writers. Shorter poems preferred."** They have published poetry by Evelyn Lau, Sue Nevill and Raymond Souster. There are about 12 pgs. of poetry in each issue, 6×9, 224 pgs., circulation 3,500. They receive about 400 submissions of poetry/year, use 40. Subscription: $20 Canadian $25 US for US and foreign subscribers. **Sample postpaid: $6.50 US. Submit no more than 6 poems at a time. No simultaneous submissions. Reports in 1 month. Pays usually $50 (Canadian)/poem, "but it varies,"** plus 2 copies.

RADCLIFFE QUARTERLY (IV-Specialized: alumnae), 10 Garden St., Cambridge MA 02138, phone (617)495-8608, editor Diane Sherlock, is an alumnae quarterly that **publishes alumnae and college-related poets**. *RQ* is magazine-sized, with glossy full-color paper cover. They receive about 50 poems/year, use 3 poems/issue. Press run is 31,000 for 30,500 subscribers. **Samples free to anyone. No pay.** Reviews books of poetry in 250 words, single format. The Dean's office sponsors a contest for poets, winners printed in the quarterly. Must be a Radcliffe student to enter.

RADIANCE: THE MAGAZINE FOR LARGE WOMEN (I, IV-Women), P.O. Box 30246, Oakland CA 94604, phone/fax (510)482-0680, founded 1984, publisher/editor Alice Ansfield, appears quarterly. **"Keeping in mind that our magazine is geared toward large women, we look for poetry from women of any size and men who don't accept society's stereotypical standards of beauty and weight—but who celebrate women's bodies, sexuality, search for self-esteem and personal growth."** As a sample she quotes "Homage to My Hips" by Lucille Clifton:

> *these hips are big hips*
> *they need space to*
> *move around in.*
> *they don't fit into little*
> *petty places. these hips*
> *are free hips.*
> *they don't like to be held back.*
> *these hips have never been enslaved,*
> *they go where they want to go*
> *they do what they want to do.*
> *these hips are mighty hips.*
> *these hips are magic hips.*
> *i have known them*
> *to put a spell on a man and*
> *spin him like a top!*

Radiance is 60 pgs., magazine-sized, professionally printed on glossy stock with full-color paper cover, saddle-stapled, 2-color graphics, photos and ads, circulation 10,000 to 4,000 subscriptions, 2,500 selling on newsstands or in bookstores, 1,000 sent as complimentary copies to media and clothing stores for large women. Subscription: $20/year. **Sample postpaid: $3.50. Submit double-spaced, typed ms. Editor usually comments on rejections. Send SASE for guidelines. Reports in 4-6 months. Pays $10-30. Buys one-time rights.** Reviews related books of poetry in 500-800 words.

RAG MAG; BLACK HAT PRESS (I, II), P.O. Box 12, Goodhue MN 55027, phone (612)923-4590, founded 1982, poetry editor Beverly Voldseth, accepts **poetry of "any length or style. No pornographic SM violent crap."** They have recently published poetry by Bill Keith, James Lineberger, Lee

Walker Bock and Pierre Garnier. As a sample the editor selected these lines from "Poem For The Woman I Am Missing" by Sara Pust:

> If there were something to write back,
> *a way to hand you the vision of*
> *trail blueberries crushed like smoke on linen*
> *in the palm, a manner of tethering myself*
> *from mountain to valley; if there were a*
> *space, a clearing, an empty page to fill*
> *without shame or stutter, these would be my*
> *offering to you. . . .*

Rag Mag, appearing twice a year, is 80-112 pgs., perfect-bound, 6×9, professionally printed in dark type with ads for books, matte colored card cover. The editor says she accepts about 10% of poetry received. Press run is 250 for 80 subscriptions of which 8 are libraries. Subscription: $10. **Sample postpaid: $6. "Send 3-9 of your best with brief bio and SASE. Something that tells a story, creates images, speaks to the heart." Name and address on each page. Brief cover letter preferred. "Please don't explain your writing to me." Send SASE for guidelines and upcoming themes. Pays 1 copy.** Reviews books of poetry. Open to unsolicited reviews. Poets may also send books for review consideration. **They may publish chapbook or paperback collections of poetry under the imprint of Black Hat Press. Query first. Simultaneous submissions and previously printed material OK. Reports in 6 weeks. Detailed comments provided "sometimes." Financial arrangements for book publication vary.** They have published Riki Kölbl Nelson's English/German poems about living in 2 worlds/2 languages, *Borders/Grenzen*, 128 pages plus the author's artwork. In addition, they published *The Book of Hearts*, poems by Karen Herseth Wee, which was a nominee in the Minnesota Book Awards.

RANGER RICK MAGAZINE (III, IV-Children, nature/ecology), 8925 Leesburg Pike, Vienna VA 22184, founded 1967, senior editor Deborah Churchman, is a monthly nature magazine for children aged 6-12. **They want "short, funny verses for children about nature and the environment. Must be accurate. No religious, preachy or difficult poetry."** They have published poetry by John Ciardi and Charles Ghigna. *RR* is 48 pgs., 8×10, saddle-stitched, glossy paper with numerous full color photos. They receive 100-200 submissions/year, "may accept one." Press run is 900,000. Subscription: $15. **Sample postpaid: $2. Submit up to 5 poems at a time. Previously published poems OK; no simultaneous submissions.** Time between acceptance and publication is 2-5 years. **Seldom comments on rejections. Publishes theme issues. Send SASE for guidelines and upcoming themes. Reports in 2 months. Always sends prepublication galleys. Pays $5/line plus 2 copies. Buys all rights. Return is "negotiable."** The editor says, "Think: Will kids understand these words? Will it hook them? Will an 8-year-old want to read this instead of playing Nintendo?"

RANT (IV-Form/style), P.O. Box 6872, New York NY 10128-0017, founded 1992, editor Alfred Vitale. *Rant*, which appears 3 times/year, is "a journal of fiction, poetry and nonfiction rants, a hybrid of a literary zine and a literary journal, offering real voice, real thought, real humor." **They want "ranting verse, raw, powerful, unpretentious, sharp, witty, radical, political and poignant. Nothing over three pages, no Romanticism, no technically crafted academic poems, nothing vague, inane, harmless or PC. *Rant* seeks to publish poetry that relays a sharp opinion on the state of things . . . whatever those things may be."** They have recently published poetry by Charles Bukowski, Tuli Kupferberg, Mary Panza, Robert Anton Wilson, Sparrow and Tsaurah Litzky. As a sample the editor selected these lines from "Meat/Hate/War" by J. Donnelly:

> *He eats food already fouling de com pos ing*
> *I see it when I'm out among the dumpsters*
> *he says I hate the homeless scum*
> *but I feel the scum he swallows when it runs down the cloth of my workpants*
> *through a break in the plastic bag*
> *I think of him saying hate*

Rant is 80 pgs., 5½×8½, perfect-bound, with card cover, b&w graphics and ads. They receive about 3,000 poems a year, publish approximately 60. Press run is 1,000 for 60 subscribers, 430 shelf sales. Single copy: $3.95; subscription: $16 (4 issues). **Sample postpaid: $5. Submit 6 poems at a time.**

Previously published poems and simultaneous submissions OK. Often comments on rejections. Send SASE for guidelines. Reports in 2 weeks to 3 months. Pays 1 or 2 copies. Includes small staff-written zine reviews and listings. The editor says, "Please don't tell me where you have been published and where you studied. I am unimpressed by degrees, awards, fellowships, residencies, grants or published work. In fact, I lean towards work that points out the superfluous nature of academic training. But don't take my word for it, just read the pretentious crap in some of the larger journals and you'll know what I'm talking about."

RARACH PRESS (V), 1005 Oakland Dr., Kalamazoo MI 49008, phone (616)388-5631, founded 1981, owner Ladislav Hanka, is a "small bibliophilic press specializing in hand-printing, hand-binding with original artwork. The material is either in Czech or, if English, dealing with environmentalist subject matter." He has printed books of poetry by Richard Neugebauer, Ben Mitchell and Rainer Maria Rilke. As a sample the editor selected these lines from "Wildness" by Jim Armstrong:

> *We were far from the road, and in those places*
> *where silence grew like a root: anonymous flowers*
> *opened themselves. Deer tracks marked off absence.*
> *A stump crumbled. A caddis fly clung to a stone.*
> *It was routine—but a kind of organization*
> *unlike our own, and we yearned for it.*

The editor says, "Authors tend to be friends, acquaintances or dead. They are given a portion of the books or a portion of sales after the fact. **I do not care to receive unsolicited mss.** I pity the lot of you. I fully expect most of my books to eventually be taken apart and sold for the artwork when they pass from the present collector of bibliophilia to some philistine. This means the poetry will be lost . . . I really sell my books for the price of the binding and artwork."

RARITAN QUARTERLY (III), Dept. PM, 31 Mine St., New Brunswick NJ 08903, phone (908)932-7887, founded 1982, editor Richard Poirier. **"We publish very little poetry. We publish *almost* no unsolicited poetry, so it would be misleading to encourage submissions."** They have published poetry by J.D. McClatchy, James Merrill, Richard Howard and Robert Pinsky. It is 150 pgs., 6×9, flat-spined, with matte card cover, professionally printed. The few poems appearing here (including sequences and translations) tend toward free verse. Press run is 4,000 for 3,500 subscribers of which 800 are libraries. Subscription: $16. **Sample postpaid: $5. Pays $100/submission if accepted.** Reviews recent poetry books and chapbooks. Poetry published in this quarterly was included in *The Best American Poetry 1992*.

RASHI (IV-Ethnic), Box 1198, Hamilton, New Zealand, founded 1985, editor Norman Simms, uses poetry on **"Jewish topics in English or any Jewish language such as Hebrew, Yiddish, Ladino, etc."** They do not want poetry that is **"pompous, self-indulgent nonsense."** They have published poems by Anne Ranasinghe and Simon Lichman. *Rashi* is the literary quarterly of the *New Zealand Chronicle*. They accept about 25 of 40 poems received/year. Circulation is over 2,000. Subscription: $20. **Sample postpaid: $7. Subscription "recommended, but not necessary." Cover letter with some background on the author required. Reports in 1 month. Pays 1 copy. Editor comments on rejections for $5/page.** Open to unsolicited reviews. Poets may also send books for review consideration. He says, "This is a special part of our overall projects. We would like to see multilingualism develop, reinterpretation of ancient and medieval traditions."

RAW DOG PRESS; POST POEMS (II, IV-Humor), 151 S. West St., Doylestown PA 18901-4134, phone (215)345-6838, founded 1977, poetry editor R. Gerry Fabian, "publishes Post Poems annual—a postcard series. **We want short poetry (3-7 lines) on any subject. The positive poem or the poem of understated humor always has an inside track. No taboos, however. All styles considered. Anything with rhyme had better be immortal."** They have recently published poetry by Charles Rossiter, Lyn Lifshin, John Grey, Glen G. Coats and the editor, R. Gerry Fabian, who selected his poem, "Arc Welder," as a sample:

> *After years of burning*
> *he pressed his lips against hers*
> *and sealed out any doubt.*

Submit 3-5 poems at a time. Send SASE for catalog to buy samples. The editor "always" comments on rejections. Pays copies. Acquires all rights. Returns rights on mention of first publication. Sometimes reviews books of poetry. He says he will offer criticism for a fee; "if someone is desperate to publish and is willing to pay, we will use our vast knowledge to help steer the ms in the right direction. We will advise against it, but as P.T. Barnum said . . . . Raw Dog Press welcomes new poets and detests second-rate poems from 'name' poets. We exist because we are dumb like a fox, but even a fox takes care of its own."

REACH MAGAZINE (I, IV-Subscribers), P.O. Box 134, Drawer 194, Pearl Harbor HI 96860-5181, founded March 1993, publisher/editor Jessie Porter. *REACH Magazine* (successor to *Breakthrough!*)

is a quarterly **subscribers-only publication** designed to provide a place for "new writers around the world who would otherwise be overlooked by larger publishers. **Range, format and style of poetry is unlimited. No vulgar, sexually lewd and/or hate poems nor poems without social or literary value."** They have published poetry by Li Min Hua, Neal E. Desch and Allison Grayhurst. As a sample the editor selected these lines from "Humble Servant" by Barry Elisofon:

> *Do me a great endeavor,*
> *and sanctify my soul,*
> *let me worship in your spirit,*
> *in an exalted and priestly role,*
> *baptize me in your aura,*
> *surround me with holy air,*
> *train me in your rituals,*
> *be the object of my prayer*

REACH is at least 20 pgs., 8½ × 11, typeset and saddle-stitched with card stock cover and b&w graphics. About 30% of the submissions they receive are poetry and "we accept about 29%." Press run is 600 for 400 subscribers. Single copy: $3; subscription: $11. **Sample postpaid: $2. "Priority is given to our subscribers for publication." Previously published poems OK; no simultaneous submissions. Cover letter required. A 1-page biography is also required for new subscribers. Always comments on rejections. "We provide one-on-one critiques." Send SASE for guidelines. Reports within 2 weeks. Pays 2 copies. Acquires first North American serial or one-time rights.** Staff reviews books of poetry. Send books for review consideration with $10 reading fee. The editor says, "1)Do not insist on sending material which is unacceptable for publication. 2) Be original. Practice the art of rewriting if something does not fit. 3)Write to inspire, not so much gloom."

REAL (RE ARTS & LETTERS) (II, IV-Bilingual, translations, humor), Dept. PM, Box 13007, Stephen F. Austin State University, Nacogdoches TX 75962, phone (409)468-2028, founded 1968, editor Lee Schultz, is a "Liberal Arts Forum" using short fiction, drama, reviews and interviews; contains editorial notes and personalized "Contributors' Notes"; printed in the winter and summer. They "hope to use from 15 to 35 pages of poetry per issue, one poem per page (typeset in editor's office). Last two issues had submissions from thirty-eight states, Great Britain, Italy and Israel." **They receive between 10-35 poems/week. "We presently do not receive enough formal or witty/ironic pieces. We need a better balance between open and generic forms. We're also interested in critical writings on poems or writing poetry and translations with a bilingual format (permissions from original author)."** As a sample the editor selected these lines from "Within the Womb of This Mountain" by Jenna Fedock:

> *We will not see him again,*
> *"Lord have mercy,"*
> *but only in the black box wedged in an aisle,*
> *heavy lid crushing our heads. We chant*
> *"Vichnaya pamyat, Vichnaya pamyat, Vichnaya pamyat,"*
> *trying to cast it off—but cannot.*

It is handsomely printed, "reserved format," perfect-bound with line drawings and photos. Simply one of the most readable literary magazines published today, *REAL* welcomes all styles and forms that display craft, insight and accessibility. Circulation approximately 400, "more than half of which are major college libraries." Subscriptions also in Great Britain, Ireland, Italy, Holland, Puerto Rico, Brazil and Canada. **Sample postpaid: $5. Submit original and copy. "Editors prefer a statement that ms is not being simultaneously submitted; however, this fact is taken for granted when we receive a ms." Writer's guidelines for SASE. They acknowledge receipt of submissions and strive for a 1-month decision. Submissions during summer semesters may take longer. "We will return poems rather than tie them up for more than a one-issue backlog (6-9 months)." Pays copies.** Reviews are assigned, but queries about doing reviews are welcome.

REALITY STREET EDITIONS (V), 4 Howard Court, Peckham Rye, London SE15 3PH United Kingdom, is the joint imprint of Reality Studios and Street Editions, editors Ken Edwards and Wendy Mulford. They publish 4 paperbacks/year. They have recently published books of poetry by Allen Fisher, Tom Raworth and Fanny Howe, but **they currently do not accept unsolicited mss.** Their US distributor is Small Press Distribution, 1814 San Pablo Ave., Berkeley CA 94302.

THE RED CANDLE PRESS; CANDELABRUM (II), 9 Milner Rd., Wisbech PE13 2LR England, phone 01945-581067, founded 1970, editor M.L. McCarthy, M.A., administrative editor Helen Gordon, B.A., was "founded to encourage poets working in **traditional-type verse, metrical unrhymed or metrical rhymed**. We're more interested in poems than poets: that is, we're interested in what sort of poems an author produces, not in his or her personality." They publish the magazine, *Candelabrum*, twice yearly (April and October), occasional postcards, paperbound staple-spined chapbooks and occasional poetry leaflets. For all of these they want **"good-quality metrical verse, with rhymed verse specially**

wanted. **Elegantly cadenced free verse is acceptable. No weak stuff (moons and Junes, loves and doves, etc.) No chopped-up prose pretending to be free verse. Any length up to about 50 lines for** *Candelabrum*, **any subject, including eroticism (but not porn)—satire, love poems, nature lyrics, philosophical—any subject, but nothing racist or sexist."** They have recently published poetry by Virginia Black, Roger Taylor, Sheila Sullivan, Peter Russell, Thomas Land and Janine Rosenberg. The editors offer these lines by David Horowitz as a sample:

> The night-time air is cool, and warms the mind.
> The blossoms fountain trees that ring the square,
> And irrigate with scent the city air.
> Refreshed by springtime's vital beauty, I
> Release my sorrow to the star-spread sky,
> At once prepared for pain, yet unresigned.

The digest-sized magazine, staple-spined, small type, exemplifies their intent to "pack in as much as possible, wasting no space, and try to keep a neat appearance with the minimum expense." They get in about 44 pgs. (some 60 poems) in each issue. They receive about 2,000 submissions/year, use approximately 5% of those, sometimes holding over poems for the next year or longer. Circulation: 900 with 700 subscriptions of which 22 are libraries. **Sample: $4 in bills only; checks not accepted. "Submit anytime. IRCs essential if return wished, and please check the weight. Each poem on a separate sheet please, neat typescripts or neat** *legible* **manuscripts.** *Please* **no dark, oily photostats, no colored ink (only black or blue). Author's name and address on each sheet, please."** No simultaneous submissions. **Reports in about 2 months. Pays 1 contributor's copy.** Staff occasionally reviews books of poetry in 500 words, single format. Send books for review consideration. They occasionally publish poetry pamphlets of 12-24 pgs. **"at our invitation to the poet, and at our expense. We pay the author a small royalty-advance, but he/she keeps the copyright."** The editor comments, "Traditional-type poetry is much more popular here in Britain, and we think also in the United States, now than it was in 1970, when we founded *Candelabrum*. We **always welcome new poets, especially traditionalists, and we like to hear from the U.S.A. as well as from here at home**. General tip: Study the various outlets at the library, or buy a copy of *Candelabrum*, or borrow a copy from a subscriber, before you go to the expense of submitting your work. The Red Candle Press regrets that, because of bank charges, it is unable to accept dollar cheques for under $100. However, it is always happy to accept U.S. and Canadian dollar bills."

RED CEDAR REVIEW (II), 17C Morrill Hall, Dept. of English, Michigan State University, East Lansing MI 48824, editor Laura Klynstra, founded 1963, is a literary biannual which uses poetry—**"any subject, form, length; the only requirement is originality and vision." The editor encourages work "that shows careful thought and unification of imagery."** They have published poetry by Margaret Atwood, Jim Harrison and Stuart Dybek. As a sample the editor selected these lines from "The Moon Slides Her Pointed Slipper Into the Darkening Sky" by Diane Wakoski:

> Gambler, I'm a gambler / this stack of poker chips
> is moonlight, and the poker hand comes,
> the cards click click clicking
> like the toenails of a friend's bull terrior on marbled floors
> of Viennese palaces and cafes—

The review is 120 pgs., digest-sized. They receive about 500 submissions/year, use 20. Press run is 400 for 200 subscribers of which 100 are libraries. Subscription: $10. **Sample postpaid: $2.50. Current issue: $5. Submit up to 4 poems at a time. Submit only previously unpublished works.** Simultaneous submissions are discouraged. **Reports in 1-4 months. Pays 2 copies.** Editor sometimes comments on rejections. **Send SASE for submission guidelines.**

RED DANCEFLOOR (V); RED DANCEFLOOR PRESS (III), P.O. Box 4974, Lancaster CA 93539-4974, founded 1989, editor David Goldschlag, publishes poetry, fiction, interviews, profiles, reviews, photos and art. **"No restrictions on form, length or subject matter. We want poetry that is well thought out—not a first draft. If you send us rhyme it should have a specific purpose and work; would consider a good sestina."** They have published poetry by Michael C Ford, David Lake, Mario René Padilla and Charles Webb. As a sample the editor selected the poem "(Avalanche)" by Laurel Ann Bogen:

> (my secret name)
>
> frozen tundra glistens
> in moonlight
> as precise
>   as this
>   icicle
> while growing
> faultlines loom craggy

> *in* these *mountains*
> *like the Gestapo*
> *outside the window*
> *in the snow*
> *with their dogs*

> *(will you say it?)*

He says, **"The magazine will be suspending publication until further notice."** Current issue postpaid: $6.50. **Sample postpaid: $4.50.** Red Dancefloor Press publishes full-length books, chapbooks and poetry audiotapes. "The author may want to get a copy of a book, chap or tape before submitting. (Send SAE with first-class stamp for catalog.) **"We openly accept submissions for books, chaps and tapes, but *please* query first with 10 samples and a cover letter explaining which area of our press you are interested in. Listing credits in a cover letter is fine, but don't go crazy."**

RED HERRING POETS; MATRIX; RED HERRING PRESS; RED HERRING CHAPBOOK SERIES; CHANNING-MURRAY FOUNDATION (IV-Membership), 1209 W. Oregon St., Urbana IL 61801, phone (217)344-1176, founded 1975, director of Red Herring Poets Ruth S. Walker. The Red Herring Poets is a workshop that publishes its members' work, after they have attended at least 5 meetings, in their annual magazine, *Matrix*, and, for those who have been members for at least 2 years and given 2 public readings, one chapbook/year.

RED RAMPAN' PRESS; RED RAMPAN' REVIEW; RED RAMPAN' BROADSIDE SERIES (V), 4707 Fielder St., Midland TX 79707-2817, phone (915)697-7689, founded 1981, poetry editor Larry D. Griffin. *RRR* is an "eclectic review quarterly." The editor says it is 6 × 9, 48-60 pgs., with a press run of 300, **"presently not accepting poetry** and only using staff-written reviews."

THE REDNECK REVIEW OF LITERATURE (II, IV-Regional), 1556 S. Second Ave., Pocatello ID 83201, phone (208)232-4263, founded 1975, editor Penelope Reedy, is a semiannual magazine publishing poetry, fiction, drama and essays **dealing with the contemporary West. The editor wants to see "any form, length or style." She does not want "ethereal ditties about nothing; obscure."** She has recently published poetry by Charlie Mehrhoff, Charles Potts, Laurel Speer and Lawson Inada. As a sample the editor selected these lines by Kristina Youso:

> *I've lived at the bottom and*
> *when you're down nobody*
> *gives you instructions*
> *no one tells you what up is like or*
> *where it is or*
> *even how it sits in time*

The magazine, which appears in the spring and fall each year, is magazine-sized, offset, perfect-bound, some advertising. Circulation is 500, of which 200 are subscriptions and 100-150 are newsstand sales. **Sample postpaid: $7. Writers should submit "3 poems at a time, letter quality—don't like simultaneous submissions. Please send SASE with *enough* postage to return mss."** Criticism is sometimes given. Rejected mss are reported on in 3 months, and no accepted mss are held beyond 3 issues. Publishes theme issues. Send SASE for upcoming themes. Pays 1 copy. Reviews books of poetry. The editor says, "Rethink what 'the West' means to American culture—as a concept rather than merely a geographical area. Lighten up—share your poems and write a new one tomorrow."

‡REDOUBT (II), Faculty of Communication, University of Canberra, P.O. Box 1, Belconnen, ACT 2616, Australia, phone 06-201-5090, fax 06-201-5300, founded 1988, managing editor Ruth Sless, is a biannual literary magazine of fiction, poetry, reviews, articles and graphics which publishes new and established writers. **In poetry, they want "the immediate image, the fresh metaphor. Work preferably under 25 lines. No doggerel, long narrative, limerick or other light entertainment."** They have published poetry by Charles Bukowski, Coral Hull and David Linwood. As a sample the editor selected these lines from "Sylvia Plath in a Bikini," a 17-line poem by Kevin Densley:

> *"Sylvia Plath in a Bikini"*
> *—I've had this title in my mind*
> *for a long time now.*
> *I got it from a picture*
> *of (no surprises here!) Sylvia Plath in a bikini,*
> *a picture I saw whilst flicking through*
> *a book about her life.*

Redoubt is about 130 pgs., approximately 7 × 10, professionally printed and perfect-bound with coated card cover with b&w photo and b&w photos and illustrations inside. They receive about 500 poetry submissions a year, accept about 10%. Press run is 300-400 for 150 subscribers of which 20 are libraries, 50 shelf sales. Single copy: A$8.50; subscription: A$16 posted in Australia, A$20 abroad.

Sample postpaid: A$8. No previously published poems; simultaneous submissions OK. Name on every page. Cover letter with brief bio required. Reads submissions March 1 through November 30 only. Seldom comments on rejections. Send SASE for guidelines; SAE and IRCs if outside Australia. Reports anywhere from 2 weeks to 6 months. Pays $10 Australian and 1 copy. Reviews books of poetry in about 500 words. Open to unsolicited reviews. Poets may also send books for review consideration. The editor says, "Keep it short. Aim for a single image. Don't try to be funny unless you are very experienced at humour. Don't send originals and keep copies of everything."

REFLECT (IV-Form/style), 3306 Argonne Ave., Norfolk VA 23509, phone (804)858-4097, founded 1979, poetry editor W.S. Kennedy. They use **"spiral poetry: featuring an inner-directed concern with sound (euphony), mystical references or overtones, and objectivity—rather than personal and emotional poems. No love poems, pornography, far left propaganda; nothing overly senti- mental."** They have published poetry by B.Z. Niditch, Joe Malone, Ruth Wildes Schuler and Stan Proper. As a sample the editor selected these lines from "Euphonies" by Marikay Brown:

> *The spring wind is a silver flute*
> *Piping lilac-hyacinth*
> *Passionatos of perfume.*
> *The summer wind—a green guitar*
> *Of fluttering leaves and grasses*
> *Strummed on fretted sunlight gold . . .*

The quarterly is digest-sized, 48 pgs., saddle-stapled, typescript. Subscription: $8. **Sample postpaid: $2. Submit 4 or 5 poems at a time. All submissions are** *single-spaced* **and should fit on one typed page. No previously published poems or simultaneous submissions. Editor sometimes comments on rejections. Guidelines available for SASE. Reports within a month. No backlog. Pays 1 copy. Acquires first rights.** Occasionally reviews books of poetry in 50 words or more.

RENDITIONS: A CHINESE-ENGLISH TRANSLATION MAGAZINE (IV-Translations), Research Center for Translation, CUHK, Shatin, NT, Hong Kong, editor Dr. Eva Hung, appears twice a year. **"Contents exclusively translations from Chinese, ancient and modern."** They also publish a paper- back series of Chinese literature in English translation. They have published translations of the poetry of Gu Cheng, Shu Ting, Mang Ke and Bei Dao. *Renditions* is magazine-sized, 180 pgs., flat-spined, elegantly printed, all poetry with side-by-side Chinese and English texts, using some b&w and color drawings and photos, with glossy card cover. Annual subscription: $20; 2 years: $36; 3 years: $50 (US). **Sample postpaid: $13. Publishes theme issues. Reports in 2 months. Pays "honorarium" plus 2 copies. Use British spelling. They "will consider" book mss, for which they would like a query with sample translations. Books pay 10% royalties plus 10 copies. Mss usually not returned. Editor sometimes comments on rejections.**

RENEGADE (II), P.O. Box 314, Bloomfield Hills MI 48303, phone (313)972-5580, founded 1988, editors Miriam Jones and Michael Nowicki, appears twice a year using stories, essays and poems. **"We are an eclectic publication. There is no preference for form or style; we simply wish to see polished work of good quality. Poems are generally of a length no more than 200 lines, no less than 10 lines. We try to avoid anything that is anarchistic, antifeminist or of a derogatory nature to any group of persons or individuals."** They have published poetry by John Sinclair, M.L. Liebler, Linda Nemec Foster, Laurence Pike, S.S. Waters, Mary Rudbeck Stanko and Lyn Lifshin. As a sample the editors selected "Day After Tomorrow" by Kainoa Koeninger:

> *i'm gonna get up*
> *& dance,*
> *just rise like a phoenix dancing a resurrection dance. . .*
>
> *With every one watching,*
> *i'm gonna dance like a bright phoenix,*
>
> > *burning a hole in the night*

Renegade is 32 pgs., digest-sized, laser-printed, with matte card cover, b&w drawings and graphics. Ads welcome. They accept about 5% of 300 mss of 5 poems or less. Press run is 200 for 20 subscribers, free to libraries and editors of other literary journals, 50 shelf sales. Subscription: $9.90. **Sample postpaid: $5. Editor comments on submissions "often." Reports in 3-6 months. Sometimes sends prepublication galleys. Pays 1 copy, 2 on request. Acquires all rights. Returns rights to author free of charge.** Reviews books of poetry. Open to unsolicited reviews. Poets may also send books for review consideration to the attention of Larry Snell. "We put together Warlords of the Subculture Poetry Contest. People interested should inquire first." They add, "We want poems in any form that speak clearly, metaphorically and imagistically to the reader about pain, or joy."

‡REPORT TO HELL (I), P.O. Box 44089, Calabash NC 28467, founded 1993, co-editors P. Saur and M. O'Shaughnessy, appears every 2-3 months and features poetry, stories and essays **"on discontent,**

misery and angst (plus the occasional glimmer of hope)." **They want poetry that is "dark but not necessarily morbid; thoughtful without clichés. Nothing flowery or bland."** They have recently published poetry by R.W. Howington, M. Estabrook, John Grey and John Bennett. As a sample the editors selected these lines from "deal" by Michael O'Shaughnessy:

> *i wished for wings*
> *and awoke with two, both broken.*
> *and bleeding gills.*

The editors say *RTH* is 40-60 pgs., digest-sized, simple type, photocopied and staple-bound with graphics included. They accept "much" of the poetry received. Press run is 100 for 20 subscribers. Subscription: $5 for 4 issues. **Sample postpaid: $1.50. Previously published poems and simultaneous submissions OK. Cover letter with brief bio required. Often comments on rejections. Reports ASAP. Pays 1 copy.** Reviews books of poetry in 100 words or less. Open to unsolicited reviews. Poets may also send books for review consideration. The editors hope to also publish chapbooks in the future.

RESPONSE (IV-Ethnic, students), 27 W. 20th St., Ninth Floor, New York NY 10011, phone (212)620-0350, fax (212)929-3459, e-mail response@panix.com, founded 1966, poetry editor Yigal Schleifer, is a "contemporary Jewish review publishing poetry, fiction and essays **by students and young adult authors." The only specification for poetry is that it be on a Jewish theme and have some significant Jewish content.** They have published poetry by Sharon Kessler, Sue Saniel Elkind and Shulamith Bat-Yisrael. As a sample the editor chose these lines from "Old Nazis Don't Die (They Move To South America)" by Sylvia Warsh:

> *The jungles of Brazil teem*
> *with a new strain of*
> *European animal, serpents of*
> *such camouflage that their own*
> *Bavarian mothers would not*
> *recognize them,*
> *insects that thrust hard*
> *consonants into a victim's*
> *heart and suck him dry,*
> *then use his shell*
> *for a livingroom.*

They look for "creative, challenging and chutzapadik writing" from young writers. The quarterly is 64 pgs., 6×9, professionally printed on heavy stock, flat-spined, with a glossy "varnished" cover with artwork. Circulation 1,600 with 600 subscribers of which 30% are libraries. 1,000 distributed through bookstores and newsstands. Subscription: $20 ($12 for students); $25 for institutions. **Sample postpaid: $4. Cover letter with bio and previous publications required with submissions.** Time between acceptance and publication is 6 months. **Reports in about 2 months. Pays 2 copies/poem published. Acquires all rights.** Occasionally reviews books of Jewish poetry. Open to unsolicited reviews. Poets may also send books for review consideration.

REVIEW: LATIN AMERICAN LITERATURE AND ARTS (IV-Ethnic, regional, translations), Dept. PM, 680 Park Ave., New York NY 10021, phone (212)249-8950 ext. 366, founded 1967, managing editor Daniel Shapiro, is a biannual magazine which serves as a "major forum for Latin American literature in English translation and articles on Latin American visual and performing arts." **They want contemporary Latin American poetry.** They have published poetry by Jose A. Mazzotti, Mateo Rosas de Oquendo and Gregorio de Matos. As a sample the editor selected these lines from "The Forest" by Mariela Dreyfus, translated from the Spanish by Alfred J. MacAdam:

> *Dark, I wander amid the uncertain*
> *I avoid the traces of the human*
> *silence is the king in this forest*
> *here, where only your breath protects me in winter.*

It is 100 pgs., 8½×11, with b&w photos of Latin American art. They receive 50-100 submissions, accept the work of 1-2 poets. Press run is 10,000 for 6,000 subscribers of which 500 are libraries. Subscription: $18 for individuals, $25 for institutions. **Sample postpaid: $9. Query before submitting work. Previously published poems and simultaneous submissions OK. Cover letter required. Reports in 2-3 months. Pays $100-300.** Reviews books of poetry by Latin Americans. The *Review* is published by the Americas Society, a not-for-profit organization.

RFD: A COUNTRY JOURNAL FOR GAY MEN EVERYWHERE (I, IV-Gay), P.O. Box 68, Liberty TN 37095, founded 1974, poetry editor Steven Riel. *RFD* "is a quarterly for gay men with emphasis on lifestyles outside of the gay mainstream—poetry, politics, profiles, letters." **They want poetry with "personal, creative use of language and image, relevant to journal themes, political themes. We try to publish as many poets as we can so tend to publish shorter poems and avoid epics."** They have published poetry by Antler, James Broughton, Gregory Woods and Winthrop Smith. *RFD* has a circulation of 3,800 for 1,300 subscriptions. Single copy: $5.50; subscription: $30 first class, $20 second class. **Sample postpaid: $6. Submit up to 5 poems at a time. Simultaneous submissions OK. Send SASE for guidelines. Editor sometimes comments on rejections. Reports in 6-9 months. Pays copies.** Open to unsolicited reviews. The editor says, "*RFD* looks for interesting thoughts, succinct use of language and imagery evocative of nature and gay men and love in natural settings."

RHINO (I), 8403 W. Normal, Niles IL 60714 or 1808 N. Larrabee, Chicago IL 60614, founded 1976, editors Kay Meier and Don Hoffman, "is an annually published poetry journal. **We seek well-crafted work with fresh insights and authentic emotion by known or new writers, poems which show careful attention to form and contain surprise. Poems no longer than 3 pgs. double-spaced.**" They have published poetry by John Dickson, Marcellus Leonard and Robert Edwards. The editors chose as a sample the opening lines of "Grandma and the Latch-Key Child" by Carol L. Gloor:

> *In 1916 my Irish grandma clutches*
> *her needlepoint satchel on the heaving*
> *ferry from Ellis Island. She has escaped*
> *the starched convent, and the wheeling*
> *seagull air screams fish, sweat and hope.*
> *She doesn't know in four years she will marry*
> *the Midwest and a man*
> *she doesn't love.*

Rhino is a 96-page journal, digest-sized, matte card cover with art, offset from typescript on high-quality paper. They receive 1,000 submissions a year, use 50-70. Press run is 300 for 200 subscribers of which 10 are libraries. **Sample: $6 plus $1.15 postage. Submit 3-5 double-spaced poems with $3 reading fee. Submissions are accepted year-round. Decisions are made in late December. Pays 1 copy. Acquires first rights only.**

THE RIALTO (II), 32 Grosvenor Rd., Norwich, Norfolk NR2 2PZ England, founded 1984, poetry editors John Wakeman and Michael Mackmin, want **"poetry of intelligence, wit, compassion, skill, excellence, written by humans. We seek poetry that works in its own terms, regardless of form or subject. Potential contributors are strongly advised to read *The Rialto* before submitting."** They have recently published poetry by Carol Ann Duffy, Simon Armitage, Les Murray, Miroslav Holub, U.A. Fanthorpe and Peter Portev. As a sample the editors selected "Nothing More" by Jan Twardowski, translated by Iain Higgins and Bogdan Czaykowski:

> *He wrote "My God" but crossed it out, since he thought*
> *God is mine only in so far as I am selfish*
> *he wrote "God of humanity" but bit his tongue, since he recalled*
> *that there were still angels*
> *and stones resembling rabbits in the snow*
> *finally he wrote just "God". Nothing more*
> *But he still wrote too much*

The Rialto, which appears 3 times a year, is 48 pgs., magazine-sized, saddle-stapled, beautifully printed on glossy stock with glossy b&w card cover, using b&w drawings. "U.S.A. subscription is now £16. **Single issue to U.S.A. is £6 sterling. Payment in sterling only."** Submit up to 6 poems with SAE and IRCs. No simultaneous submissions or previously printed poetry. Editor "only rarely" comments on rejections. Reports within 3 months. Pays £10/poem.** *The Rialto* has been called "the poets' choice" among U.K. literary magazines and has received a special grant for "excellence" from the Arts Council of Great Britain. The editors add, "We would like to receive more poetry that confronts contemporary political issues with compassion and art, without hysteria."

RIDGE REVIEW MAGAZINE; RIDGE TIMES PRESS (IV-Regional), Dept. PM, Box 90, Mendocino CA 95460, phone (707)964-8465, founded 1981, poetry editor Nancy Kay Webb, is a "bio-regional quarterly looking at economic, political and social phenomena of the area" which uses **only poets from Northern California.** They have published poetry by Michael Sykes and Judith Tannenbaum. The 7 × 10 magazine is 50 pgs., saddle-stapled with linen card cover containing art, photos and ads with text. Circulation is 3,500 for 1,000 subscriptions, uses about 1 page of poetry/issue. Subscription: $10. **Sample postpaid: $3.85. Considers simultaneous submissions. Reports in about a week. Usually pays $10/poem.**

RIO GRANDE PRESS; SE LA VIE WRITER'S JOURNAL (I, IV-Themes), P.O. Box 71745, Las Vegas NV 89170, founded 1987, editor Rosalie Avara. *Se La Vie Writer's Journal* is a quarterly journal with articles and cartoons about poetry and writing and monthly contests in poetry and quarterly contests in poetry, essays and short stories. Prizes are $5-25 for poems, entry fee $5 for 3 poems. Publishes 70% of mss received/quarter, **"dedicated to encouraging novice writers, poets and artists; we are interested in original, unpublished mss that reflect the 'life' theme (La Vie). Poems are judged on originality, clarity of thought and ability to evoke emotional response."** They have published poetry by Marian

Ford Park, Phil Eisenberg and Doris Benson. *SLVWJ* is 64 pgs., digest-sized, photocopied from typescript, with blue cover, saddle-stapled. **Sample postpaid: $4. Publishes theme issues. Send SASE for guidelines and upcoming themes.** Staff reviews books of poetry. Send books for review consideration. Also publishes several poetry/short story anthologies annually. "No fee or purchase necessary to enter contests and be published." Cash prizes. Send SASE for guidelines.

‡**RIVELIN GRAPHEME PRESS (II)**, The Annexe Kennet House, 19 High St., Hungerford, Berkshire RG170NL England, founded 1984, poetry editor Snowdon Barnett, publishes **only poetry. Query first with biographical information, previous publications and a photo, if possible. If invited, send book-length manuscript, typed, double-spaced, photocopy OK. Payment is 20 copies of first printing up to 2,000, then 5% royalties on subsequent printings.**

RIVER CITY; HOHENBERG AWARD (II), English Dept., Memphis State University, Memphis TN 38152, phone (901)678-2651, founded 1980, editor Dr. Paul Naylor. *River City* publishes fiction, poetry, interviews and essays. Contributors have included John Updike, Marvin Bell, Philip Levine, Maxine Kumin, Robert Penn Warren, W.D. Snodgrass, Mary Oliver, Fred Busch, Beth Bentley, Mona Van Duyn and Peter Porter. The biannual is 100 pgs., 6×9, perfect-bound, professionally printed with two-color matte cover. Publishes 40-50 pgs. of poetry in each issue. Circulation 1,000. Subscription: $9. **Sample postpaid: $5. Submit no more than 5 poems at a time. Does not send mss June through August. Reports in 2-12 weeks. Pays 2 copies (and cash when grant funds available).** $100 Hohenberg Award is given annually to best fiction or poetry selected by the staff.

RIVER STYX MAGAZINE; BIG RIVER ASSOCIATION (II), 3207 Washington Ave., St. Louis MO 63103-1218, phone (314)533-4541, founded 1975, senior editors Michael Castro and Quincy Troupe, managing editor Richard Newman, is "an international, multicultural journal publishing both award-winning and relatively undiscovered writers. We feature fine art, photography, interviews, poetry and short prose." They want **"excellent poetry—thoughtful."** They have published work by Diane Wakoski, Marge Piercy, Simon Ortiz, Toni Morrison, Gary Snyder and John Brandi. As a sample the editor selected these lines from "Unsent Letter 2" by Carol Muskie-Duke:

> You say you don't know who you are. I take
> the plate of the homeless man and fill it
> with macaroni and salad. Does he know who he is?
> The next man comes up and I say "Would you like
> a roll?" and he says "In the sand?" and laughs.

River Styx appears 3 times a year. The editor describes it as 70-100 pgs., digest-sized with b&w cover. They accept less than 10% of 1,000 mss received a year. **Sample postpaid: $7. Submit 3-5 poems at a time, "legible copies with name and address on each page." Reading period is September 1 through October 31. Guidelines available for SASE. Editor sometimes comments on rejections. Reports in 1 week to 2 months, publication within a year. Pays 2 copies. Buys one-time rights.** Poetry published in *River Styx* has been selected for inclusion in *The Best American Poetry 1994*.

RIVERRUN (II), Glen Oaks Community College, Centreville MI 49032-9719, founded 1974, poetry editor David Bainbridge, is a literary biannual, using **30-40 magazine-sized pages of poetry in each issue—"no prejudices. We try to give each issue its own distinct, admittedly subjective personality. Best bet is to see the attitude and themes portrayed in the most recent guidelines."** As a sample the editor selected these opening lines from "One That Will Do to Swell a Progress" by Robert R. Hentz:

> Our game over, we were ready to go
> When he said, "It's discouraging to know
> That you are mediocre and will never do
> Anything of extraordinary value
> Like the composer who knows in his heart
> He is no Beethoven or Mozart."

They receive 1,000 poems/month, use up to 240/year. Press run is 850. **Sample postpaid: $5. Submit 3-6 poems at a time. Previously published poems and simultaneous submissions OK. Publishes theme issues. Send SASE for upcoming themes. Reports ASAP (usually 2 weeks to 1 month). Pays 1 copy.** The editor says, "We proudly publish an extremely broad range of individuals well-known to small press circles and beyond (for instance, t. Winter-Damon, Bruce Boston, Stuart Friebert, Tom Riley, Lyn Lifshin and Denise Dumars), but we also pride ourselves on devoting occasional space to local poets and as-yet-unpublished poets."

RIVERSIDE QUARTERLY (II, IV-Science fiction/fantasy), Box 958, Big Sandy TX 75755, phone (903)845-2280, founded 1964, editor Leland Sapiro, poetry editor Sheryl Smith **(and submissions should go directly to her at 515 Saratoga #2, Santa Clara CA 95050).** *Riverside Quarterly* is **"aimed at the literate reader of science fiction and fantasy.** If you've been reared on 'Startrek,' then *RQ* is not for you. **We have no specific subject matter or style preferences. Length: 50 lines maximum. No didactic or 'uplifting' verse.**" They have published poetry by George Gott, Sue Saniel Elkind, Julia Thomas, Edward Mycue and Denise Dumars. As a sample the editor selected these lines from "Ymir's Mirror/Eiseley's Glass" by Ace Pilkington:

> From the skull in the stone
> Eye sockets scrape the sky:
> Both are wayward worlds
> Aglint with stars.
> Black, bleak caverns
> Where the lightning grows

RQ is 68 pgs., approximately 5×8, offset, saddle-stapled with paper cover and b&w art. They receive about 1,100 poems a year, accept approximately 3%. Press run is 1,200 for 550 subscribers of which 200 are libraries. Subscription: $8. **Sample postpaid: $2.50. No previously published poems or simultaneous submissions. Cover letter recommended.** Time between acceptance and publication is 15 months. **Usually comments on rejections. Reports in 10 days. Always sends prepublication galleys. Pays 4 copies. Acquires all rights; rights released to contributor after publication.** "We print reviews of books, movies and magazines—no maximum length." They say, "We advise all contributors (of poetry or prose) to read a copy or two (available at any major public or college library) before sending a ms."

‡RIVERSTONE, A PRESS FOR POETRY (II), 1184A MacPherson Dr., West Chester PA 19380, founded 1992, publishes 1 or 2 chapbooks a year through an annual contest. They have published chapbooks by Gia Hansbury, Jefferson Carter and, most recently, Marcia Hurlow. As a sample we selected these lines from Hurlow's "Milin an Elorn":

> We have lived here long enough
> to plant our own trees, to see them
> flower their first sudden spring.
> The birches, two orderly rows
> above the mill stream banks,
> were planted so long ago
> no one knows the name
> of the gardener's children . . .

That's from the chapbook *Dangers of Travel*, which won the 1994 Riverstone Poetry Chapbook Award. It is 32 pgs., digest-sized, attractively printed on cream-colored paper and hand-sewn with endleaves and a light card stock cover. **To be considered for the contest, submit $8 reading fee and chapbook ms of 20-24 pgs., "including poems in their proposed arrangement, title page, contents and acknowledgements." Previously published poems OK. Include 6×9 SASE for notification and copy of the winning chapbook. Send SASE for guidelines. Contest deadline: June 30 postmark. Winner receives publication, author's copies and a cash prize when possible (in 1995 it was $100).** Sample chapbooks can be ordered from the press for $5 postpaid.

RIVERWIND (II, IV-Regional), General Studies, Hocking College, Nelsonville OH 45764, phone (614)753-3591, ext. 2375, founded 1982, poetry editor J.A. Fuller, is a literary annual publishing **mainly writers from Appalachia.** They want **"work from serious writers. We are most open to work with serious content, though humor may be the vehicle. Do not want to see poetry from those who view it as a 'hobby.' We have not published limericks."** They have published poetry by Naton Leslie, Gloria Ruth, Charles Semones, Walter McDonald, John Haines, John Aber, James Riley and Greg Anderson. *Riverwind* is 7×7, flat-spined, 80-120 pgs., offset, with 2-color semiglossy card cover. Of 500 poems received they accept approximately 60. Press run is 500. Single copy: $2.50. **Sample back issue postpaid: $1. Submit batches of 3-5, no previously published poems, no simultaneous submissions. Reads submissions September 15 through June 15 only. Submissions received after June 15 will be considered for the following year.** Editor comments "particularly if we would like to see more of that person's work." **Reports in 1-4 months. Response slow during summer months. Pays 2 copies.** Reviews books of poetry. They hope to begin publishing chapbook collections.

ROANOKE REVIEW (II), English Dept., Roanoke College, Salem VA 24153, founded 1968, poetry editor Robert R. Walter, is a semiannual literary review which uses **poetry that is "conventional; we have not used much experimental or highly abstract poetry."** They have published poetry by Peter Thomas, Norman Russell, Alan Seaburg, Mary Balazs and Irene Dayton. *RR* is 52 pgs., 6×9, professionally printed with matte card cover with decorative typography. They use 25-30 pgs. of poetry in each issue. Circulation is 250-300 for 150 subscriptions of which 50 are libraries. They receive 400-500 submissions of poetry/year, use 40-60, have a 3- to 6-month backlog. Subscription: $5.50. **Sample postpaid: $3. Submit original typed mss, no photocopies. Reports in 8-10 weeks. No pay.** The editor advises, "There is a lot of careless or sloppy writing going on. We suggest careful proofreading and study of punctuation rules."

ROCK FALLS REVIEW; AUTHOR'S INK (I), P.O. Box 104, Stamford NE 68977, phone (308)868-3545, founded 1989, editor Diana L. Lambson. *Rock Falls Review* is a quarterly that "started as a learning tool for our writer's group. We try to maintain a learning atmosphere. Much of what we publish is by new writers but we still insist on quality work submitted in a professional manner." They **"prefer shorter poems—under 100 lines. Inspirational poetry is okay. No 'doomsday' or 'preachy' verse, though. Also okay: fantasy and science fiction, free verse, humor and traditional forms. No obscure, far out, experimental or pornographic verse. No horror or dark image. No violence. *No obscene language!* Concrete or shaped verse is nearly impossible for us to use."** They have recently published poetry by John Grey, Lyn Lifshin, Mary Winters, Terry Thomas and Barbara Crooker. As a sample the editor selected these lines from "Waking Up" by Noel Smith:

> *Headfirst*
> *I drift down a silken thread*
> *Arms folded like wings.*
>
> *Voices of grand—*
> *Mothers and children who cannot follow*
> *Echo*
> *From far back at the beginning.*

RFR is 35-60 pgs., 8½ × 11, photocopied typescript, side-stapled with colored paper cover, clip art and original b&w line art and ads inside. They receive about 300-400 poems a year, use 150-200. Press run is 120 for 50 subscribers. Single copy postpaid: $3.50 US, $6 foreign; subscription: $12.50 US, $24 foreign. **Submit no more than 3-5 poems at a time, one poem/page. Previously published poems OK with release and proper credits. Simultaneous submissions also OK. "While we do not require a cover letter it is nice to know something about the person submitting." Often comments on rejections. Send SASE for guidelines. Reports in 6-12 weeks "usually." Pays 1 copy.** Reviews books of poetry. Open to unsolicited reviews. Poets may also send books for review consideration; "one of our group will review." The editor says, "We do not require purchase or subscription. However, because of space and funding restrictions, members of Author's Ink or the Great Plains Writers Club and subscribers will be given first consideration. This should not discourage anyone, however, as more than 80% of our accepted submissions are non-subscribers. We prefer poetry that is *not* obscure. In order for most people to read and enjoy poetry, it should be understandable: something they can relate to."

ROCKET PRESS (I, II), (formerly *Rocket Literary Quarterly*), P.O. Box 672, Water Mill NY 11976-0672, e-mail rocketusa@peconic.com (don't send poems by e-mail), founded 1993, editor Darren Johnson, features "styles and forms definitely for the 21st century." **The editor wants "experimental and eccentric poetry and original ideas expressed in 'a true voice.' I don't want to see hero worship-type poems that drop names. Don't use the words 'poem,' 'love' or 'ode.'"** They have published poetry by Leslie Scalapino, Lyn Lifshin and Ana Christy. As a sample we selected these lines from "The Holiday Season Falls" by Cheryl A. Townsend:

> *like the stock market sending*
> *mass hysteria and emotional*
> *duress out like children to recess*
> *hurry get your shopping done*
> *while the druggers quietly await*
> *in the dark by your car for any*
> *money not already spent . . .*

Rocket Press is 20 pgs., photocopied, saddle-stapled with colored card cover, cartoons and ads for almost anything. (Sometimes *Rocket* is printed as a newspaper tabloid, professionally, with a circulation over 1,000.) They receive about 400 poems a year, accept approximately 3%. Press run is 500 for 200 subscribers of which 2 are libraries, 100 shelf sales. Subscription: $6. **Sample postpaid: $2 (checks payable to D. Johnson). Submit 3 poems at a time. No previously published poems; simultaneous submissions OK.** Time between acceptance and publication is 3 months to 1 year. **Often comments on rejections. "Subscribers get fuller critiques." Reports in less than 3 months. Pays 1 copy. Acquires one-time rights.** Editor includes his own blurb reviews "of anything cool." Send books for review consideration. They also sponsor an annual poetry competition. Submit 3 poems with SASE and $1 reading fee. Deadline: September 1. The editor says poets published by *Rocket* get full support through community fliers with samples and mailings of interest. His advice: "Write whatever you want! But if you send me a form letter, I'll send a form rejection right back!"

THE ROCKFORD REVIEW (I, II), P.O. Box 858, Rockford IL 61105, founded 1971, editor David Ross, is a quarterly publication of the Rockford Writers Guild, **publishing their poetry and prose, that of other writers throughout the country and contributors from other countries. "We look for the magical power of the words themselves, a playfulness with language in the creation of images and fresh insights on old themes, whether it be poetry, satire or fiction."** They have published poetry by

Russell King, David Koenig and Christine Swanberg. As a sample the editor selected these lines by Olivia Diamond:

> The chill will nip us all in the end
> even fragile stems we brace in vases.
> The tips of petals curl in and bend
> toward the ground in stiff embraces.

TRR is 50 pgs., digest-sized, flat-spined, glossy cover with b&w photos. Circulation 1,000. Single copy: $5; subscription: $15 (4 issues). **Considers simultaneous submissions. Reports in 4-6 weeks. Pays 1 copy. Acquires first North American serial rights.** They offer Editor's Choice Prizes of $25 for prose, $25 for poetry each issue.

ROCKY MOUNTAIN REVIEW OF LANGUAGE AND LITERATURE (IV-Membership, transla-tions), Boise State University English Dept., Boise ID 83725, phone (208)385-1233, fax (208)385-4373, e-mail aaswidma@idbsu.idbsu.edu, founded 1947, editor Jan Widmayer, poetry editor Marcia Southwick **(and submissions should go directly to her at English Dept., University of Nebraska, Lincoln NE 68588-0333). Contributors to the literary quarterly must be members of Rocky Mountain Modern Language Association. Poetry should be "generally relatively short" and may be in English or other modern languages.** The review has recently published poetry by Scott P. Sanders, David Faldet and translations of Antonio Cisneros, David Huerta and Viktor Bokov. As a sample we selected these lines from "Bitches on the Bright Side" by Constance Merritt:

> Say what you will, there's something to be said
> For desperate calls unanswered, meals alone,
> Keeping corners, and lying late in bed.
>
> For bodies over-full but seldom nourished,
> For cold and rain that's carried in the bone.
> Say what you will, there's something to be said

The 6×9, 224-page, flat-spined semiannual publishes work of interest to college and university teach-ers of literature and language. Circulation of the review is 1,100-1,200, all membership subscriptions. They accept a few ads from other journals and publishers. **Contributors are not paid and do not receive extra copies; contributors must be RMMLA members. Poets should submit 2 copies, *without author's name*.** They report on submissions in 1-2 months and publish usually within 6 months but no more than 1 year after acceptance.

THE ROMANTIST (IV-Fantasy), Saracinesca House, 3610 Meadowbrook Ave., Nashville TN 37205, phone (615)226-1890, poetry editor Steve Eng, founded 1977, is an "irregular literary magazine of nonfiction articles on fantasy, imaginative and romantic literature, using **lyrical poetry—prefer fan-tasy content. No homespun, gushy, trite verse with forced rhyme.**" They have published poetry by Donald Sidney-Fryer, Joey Froehlich, Stephanie Stearns and Margo Skinner. The editor says *The Romantist* is 100-152 pgs., or magazine-sized, letterpress or offset, perfect-bound with b&w illustra-tions and ads. Press run is 300 numbered copies for 150 subscriptions of which 30 are libraries. **Sample postpaid: $15. Submit no more than 3 poems at a time, double-spaced. No previously published poems or simultaneous submissions. Cover letter required.** Time between acceptance and publica-tion may be as long as 2-3 years. **Editor sometimes comments on rejections. Reports in 1 month. Contributors may purchase a copy for 50% of its price. Acquires all rights.** Open to unsolicited reviews. Poets may also send books for review consideration. The editor says, "Too much contempo-rary poetry is easy to write and hard to read. We resist the depressed, carefully jaded tone so often fashionable. We prefer lyric verse that reflects some knowledge of traditions of poetry, though we do not require the slavish adherence to any school."

RONSDALE PRESS (II, IV-Regional), (formerly Cacanadadada Press), 3350 W. 21st Ave., Vancouver, British Columbia V6S 1G7 Canada, founded 1988, director Ronald B. Hatch, publishes 3 flat-spined paperbacks of poetry/year—**by Canadian poets only—classical to experimental.** They have recently published *Phantoms in the Ark* by A.F. Moritz, *The East Wind Blows West* by George Jonas, and *Burning Stone* by Zoë Landale. As a sample the editor selected the opening lines from "To Richard Cicci-marra" in *Popping Fuchsias* by Robin Skelton:

> Ouspensky would have understood your reading him
> holed up in your box of an apartment,
> face a mask, eyes bloodshot, elegance gone,
> having reached a time discounting time,
> having pared away all mortal lendings
> till mankind had become no more than shadows . . .

Query first, with sample poems and cover letter with brief bio and publication credits. Previously published poems and simultaneous submissions OK. Often comments on rejections. Replies to queries in 2 weeks, to mss in 2 months. Pays 10% royalties and 10 author's copies. Write for

catalog to purchase sample books. The director adds, "Confessional poetry or even first-person poetry is very difficult to write well."

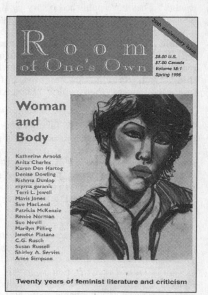

Canada's oldest feminist literary journal, **Room of One's Own**, *is a quarterly published by members of the Growing Room Collective. The cover for its Spring 1995 edition spotlights the publication's overall focus of work by, for and about women. "We chose this cover because of the kindness and sympathy that it speaks from," says collective member Verna Feehan. The journal publishes poems, short stories, reviews and commentary. "Now celebrating our 20th anniversary,* **Room** *strives to be a forum in which women can share their unique perspectives on the world, each other, and themselves." The cover art is by Vancouver-based artist Felicity Don. Cover design: Wendy Putnam.*

ROOM OF ONE'S OWN (II, IV-Women), P.O. Box 46160 Station D, Vancouver, British Columbia V6J 5G5 Canada, founded 1975, is a quarterly using **"poetry by and about women, written from a feminist perspective. Nothing simplistic, clichéd. Short fiction also accepted."** It is 128 pgs., digest-sized. Press run is 1,000 for 420 subscribers of which 50-100 are libraries, 350 shelf sales. Subscription: $20 ($30 US or foreign). **Sample: $7 plus postage or IRCs. "We prefer to receive 5-6 poems at a time, so we can select a pair or group." Include bio note. No simultaneous submissions. The mss are circulated to a collective, which "takes time." Publishes theme issues. Send SASE or SAE with 1 IRC for guidelines and upcoming themes. Reports in 6 months. Pays honorarium plus 2 copies. Buys first North American serial rights.** "We solicit reviews." Send books for review consideration, attn. book review editor.

‡ROSEBUD (II, IV-Themes), P.O. Box 459, Cambridge WI 53523, phone (608)423-9690, founded 1993, editor Rod Clark, is an attractive quarterly "for people who enjoy writing." The editor says it is "a writer's feast for the eye, ear and heart" which has rotating themes/departments. **They want contemporary poetry with "strong images, real emotion, authentic voice; well crafted, literary quality. No inspirational verse."** As a sample we selected these lines from "Silk" by Anne Giles Rimbey:

> I would write a letter to a lover today
> on apricot paper with a cream fountain pen.
> I pretend I am curled in a quilt of dark wool
> and lean against the window. Raindrops like moonstones
> leak down the pane. I tell a tale in velvet lines
> of yellow flames and turquoise silk scarves, sandalwood
> and drums. For you, I dance soft dances on skin rugs.

Rosebud is 128 pgs., 7×10, offset printed and perfect-bound with duotone coated card cover, art, graphics and ads. They receive about 700 poems a year, accept approximately 10%. Press run is 6,000 for 1,500 subscribers of which 300 are libraries, 4,000 shelf sales. Subscription: $18. **Sample postpaid: $5.50. Submit 3-5 poems at a time. Previously published poems and simultaneous submissions OK. Often comments on rejections. Send SASE for guidelines and explanation of themes/departments. Reports in 10 weeks. Pays $45/piece and 2 copies. Buys one-time rights.** Each year they also award 3 prizes of $150 for work published in the magazine. The editor says, "We are seeking stories, articles, profiles and poems of love, alienation, travel, humor, nostalgia and unexpected revelation. And something has to 'happen' in the pieces we choose."

THE ROUND TABLE: A JOURNAL OF POETRY AND FICTION (II), P.O. Box 18673, Rochester NY 14618, phone (716)244-0623, founded 1984, poetry editors Alan Lupack and Barbara Lupack. "We publish a journal of poetry and fiction. Currently, one issue a year. **Few restrictions on poetry—except**

high quality. **We like forms if finely crafted. Very long poems must be exceptional. We are tending to focus more on Arthurian poetry and prose and to publish almost exclusively material on this theme."** They have published poetry by Kathleene West, John Tagliabue, Wendy Mnookin and Paul Scott. *The Round Table* is 64 pgs., digest-sized, perfect-bound, professionally printed (offset) with matte card cover. Circulation is 125 for 75 subscribers of which 3 are libraries. Subscription: $7.50. Sample postpaid: $5. **"We like to see about 5 poems at a time (but we read whatever is submitted)." Cover letter required. Simultaneous submissions OK. "But we expect to be notified if a poem submitted to us is accepted elsewhere. Quality of poetry, not format, is most important thing. We try to report in 3 months, but—especially for poems under serious consideration—it may take longer." Pays copies.** "Some years we will publish a volume of Arthurian poetry by one author."

‡RUBY (II), P.O. Box 5915, Takoma Park MD 20913, founded 1993, poetry editor Dana Hoffman, fiction editor Abby Bardi, is an annual journal publishing "poetry, short fiction, vignettes and odysseys, art, photographs and sophisticated cartoons. **We like strong, accessible, intelligent, heartfelt, but not sentimental, work—poems of any length**, prose to 1,300 words. (We'd love to see prose under 500 words.) **No erotica, purely political or religious work, poems about poetry, art, museums or music."** They have recently published poetry by Reed Whittemore, Linda Pastan, Lyn Lifshin and Martin Galvin. As a sample, Dana Hoffman selected these lines from "Listening for Wings" by Maxine Combs:

> And last night in my dream
> an Etruscan soothsayer, a haruspex,
> poked my entrails with a stick, and predicted
> from my shrivelled and ravaged liver
> the end of civilization.

Ruby is 32 pgs., 11⅜ × 14½, saddle-stitched, printed on 50 lb. white offset paper, with color on its cover and center pages. They receive about 600 poems a year, use approximately 100. Press run is 3,000 of which 1,500 are distributed free and 1,500 are shelf sales and subscriptions. Copies are automatically mailed to *Ruby* Supporters ($15), Patrons ($50) and Benefactors ($100), and advertisers. Single copy: $4; subscription: $5. **Sample postpaid: $3. Submit up to 8 typed poems** or 3 stories **with name and address on each page** and **"short cover letter with bio note (not publication history), 4 lines maximum, including books and/or awards." No previously published poems. Will consider simultaneous submissions ("please indicate"). Seldom comments on rejections. Reports in 1 month. Pays 2 copies and occasional monetary Editors' Award for exceptional submission(s). "Publication in *Ruby* means possible inclusion in future anthologies."** Dana Hoffman says, "*Ruby* is designed to entertain and inform and to touch the seams, visible and invisible, where we become one. Send only your best work. And read, read, read the best, the best, the best."

THE RUNAWAY SPOON PRESS (V, IV-Form), Box 3621, Port Charlotte FL 33949, phone (813)629-8045, founded 1987, editor Bob Grumman, is a "photocopy publisher of chapbooks of otherstream poetry & illumagery." He publishes **"visual poetry, textual poetry mixed with visual matter, verbo-visual collages, burning poodle poetry—or anything insane. No work in which politics is more important than aesthetics. Plaintext poetry is way too traditional for my press."** He has recently published poetry by Bill Keith, John Martone and Irving Weiss. As a sample the editor selected this poem by Guy R. Beining:

> blue-prints of a dream
> in red
> for the insomniac

The books are usually about 4 × 5½, printed on good stock with matte card covers. He prints about 10 a year averaging 48 pgs. **"Backlog too great for me to accept new work in 1995." Query for 1996. Simultaneous submissions and previously published poems OK. Editor comments on submissions "always." Sometimes sends prepublication galleys. Pays 25% of first edition of 100. Acquires all rights. Releases rights to author(s) upon publication. Sample books available for $3 apiece.** The editor advises, "Don't let anti-intellectuals convince you the brain is less important than the heart in poetry."

RURAL HERITAGE (I, IV-Rural, humor), 281 Dean Ridge Lane, Gainesboro TN 38562-5039, phone (615)268-0655, founded 1975, editor Gail Damerow, **uses poetry related to draft animal power,**

✝ *The double dagger before a listing indicates that the listing is new in this edition. New markets are often the most receptive to submissions.*

livestock, rural living, Americana. "**Traditional meter and rhyme only. Poems must have touch of humor or other twist. Please, no comparisons between country and city life and no religious, political or issues-oriented material.**" As a sample the editor selected this poem, "He Should've Bought a Horse," by John M. Floyd:

> *An old Kansas farmer named Ben*
> *Had a mule kick him square in the chin.*
> *As he whipped out his gun,*
> *He saw three mules, not one,*
> *And the middle one kicked him again.*

RH is magazine-sized, bimonthly, using b&w photos, graphics and ads, 4-6 poems/issue. Circulation 3,000. Subscription: $19. **Sample postpaid: $6. Submit no more than 3 poems at a time, one/page. "Previously published poems are OK if we are told where and when. Simultaneous submissions must be withdrawn before we publish."** Time between acceptance and publication is 4-6 months. "We often group poems by theme, for example gardening, quilting, and so forth according to season. Verse is also coupled with an article of similar theme such as maple sugaring, mule teams, etc." **Send SASE for guidelines. Reports ASAP. Pays on publication, $5 and up (depending on length) and 2 copies.** The editor says, "We receive too much modern poetry, not enough traditional, not enough humor. We get too much image poetry (we prefer action) and most poems are too long—we prefer 12 lines or less."

SACHEM PRESS (II, IV-Translations, bilingual), P.O. Box 9, Old Chatham NY 12136, founded 1980, editor Louis Hammer, a small press publisher of poetry and fiction, both hardcover and flat-spined paperbacks. **No new submissions, only statements of projects, until January 1996. Submit mss January through March.** The editor wants to see "**strong, compelling, even visionary work, English-language or translations.**" He has published poetry by Cesar Vallejo, Yannis Ritsos, 24 leading poets of Spain (in an anthology), Miltos Sahtouris and himself. As a sample, he selected the following lines from his book *Poetry at the End of the Mind*:

> *If the only paper you had*
> *was the flesh on your back*
> *between your shoulder blades*
> *what would you write*
> *with the motion of your body?*

The paperbacks average 120 pgs. and the anthology of Spanish poetry contains 340 pgs. Each poem is printed in both Spanish and English, and there are biographical notes about the authors. The small books cost $6.95 and the anthology $11.95. **Royalties are 10% maximum, after expenses are recovered, plus 50 author's copies. Rights are negotiable.** Book catalog is free "when available," and poets can purchase books from Sachem "by writing to us, 33⅓% discount."

ST. ANDREW PRESS (IV-Religious), P.O. Box 329, Big Island VA 24526, fax (804)299-5949, founded 1986, poetry editor Ray Buchanan, is a "small press publisher of religious material (worship materials, lyrics and music, etc.), **specializing in meditations, lifestyle, church renewal, spirituality, hunger, peace and justice issues." Any form or style up to 64 lines on subjects listed. "No profanity for shock value only; no sickeningly sweet idealism."** They say they will publish 1-2 chapbooks and flat-spined paperbacks, averaging 64 pgs., each year. **Submit 4-6 samples, bio, other publications. Simultaneous submissions and previously published poems OK. Reports in 2-4 weeks. Payment is usually $10 minimum, averages more.** The editor says, "We are looking forward to doing more with poetry in the next couple of years. The amount we do will be largely determined by quality of submissions we receive. Poetry is not accepted if it is too 'sing-song' with trite rhymes, if it could be rewritten in paragraphs as prose, or if it is so 'stream-of-consciousness' that no one could possibly follow the thought or get any meaning from it."

ST. ANTHONY MESSENGER (IV-Religious), 1615 Republic St., Cincinnati OH 45210-1298, phone (513)241-5615, is a monthly 56-page magazine, circulation 325,000, for Catholic families, mostly with children in grade school, high school or college. In some issues, they have a **poetry page which uses poems appropriate for their readership. Their poetry needs are limited but poetry submissions are always welcomed.** As a sample here is "A Valentine for Darby" by Jean M. Syed:

> *Why do I love you, my potbellied love?*
> *Not for your pregnant form or shiny pate.*
> *Were these on tender those decades ago,*
> *would I have been so indiscriminate*
> *as to let you win my heart? No princess*
> *from passion ever took a frog to mate.*

"**Submit seasonal poetry (Christmas/Easter/nature poems) several months in advance. Submit a few poems at a time; do not send us your entire collection of poetry. We seek to publish accessible poetry of high quality.**" Send regular SASE for guidelines and 9 × 12 SASE for free sample. Pays

$2/line on acceptance. Buys first North American serial rights. *St. Anthony Messenger* poetry occasionally receives awards from the Catholic Press Association Annual Competition.

ST. JOSEPH MESSENGER AND ADVOCATE OF THE BLIND (I, IV-Religious), 541 Pavonia Ave., P.O. Box 288, Jersey City NJ 07303, phone (201)798-4141, founded 1898, poetry editor Sister Ursula Maphet, C.S.J.P., is a quarterly (16 pgs., 8 × 11). They want **"brief but thought-filled poetry; do not want lengthy and issue-filled."** Most of the poets they have used are previously unpublished. They receive 400-500 submissions/year, use 50. There are about 2 pgs. of poetry in each issue. Circulation 20,000. Subscription: $5. **Editor sometimes comments on rejections. Publishes theme issues. Send SASE for guidelines, free sample and upcoming themes. Reports within 2 weeks. Pays $5-20/ poem.**

ST. MARTIN'S PRESS, 175 Fifth Ave., New York NY 10010. Prefers not to share information.

SALMON RUN PRESS (III), P.O. Box 231081, Anchorage AK 99523-1081, founded 1991, editor/ publisher John E. Smelcer, publishes 2-3 books/year. They want **"quality poetry by established poets, any subject, any style. No poetry that is not representative of the highest achievement in the art."** They have recently published John Daniel, Ursula K. Le Guin, X.J. Kennedy, John Haines, Molly Peacock, Joy Harjo and Denise Duhamel. As a sample the editor selected these lines from Haines's "Shepherd's Purse":

> *November like a tax collector*
> *will come to the poor,*
> *the cut and the shaken,*
>
> *with nothing to save*
> *but their paper mittens*
> *and a straw whistle.*

Their books are flat-spined and printed on heavy, natural-colored paper. **Query first with sample poems and cover letter with brief bio. Previously published poems and simultaneous submissions OK. Usually comments on rejections. Replies to queries within 1-3 weeks, to mss in 1-2 months. Pays 10% royalties, sometimes advances and a negotiable number of author's copies.** They also sponsor a pamphlet series and an annual poetry contest for book-length mss of 48-96 pgs. $15 reading fee and SASE required. Entries must be postmarked by December 30. The winning ms will be published in book form, nationally distributed and all contestants will receive a copy of the winning book.

‡SALON ARTS MAGAZINE (II), 1508 13th Place S., Birmingham AL 35205, founded 1993, editor Leisha Hultgren, is a bimonthly magazine **designed to showcase contemporary artists, "especially those who take some kind of risk." They welcome both traditional and experimental poetry—no particular specifications.** They have recently published poetry by R.T. Smith, Will Palmer and Georgette Norman. The editor says *Salon Arts* is 24 pgs., 8½ × 12½, web press printed and staple-bound. Press run is 10,000, distributed free to retail stores. **Sample available for the cost of postage: $1.50/ issue. Previously published poems and simultaneous submissions OK. Poems are reviewed by editorial staff. Seldom comments on rejections. Send SASE for guidelines. Reports in 1 month. Pays 2 copies.**

SALT LICK; SALT LICK FOUNDATION, INC.; SALT LICK PRESS; SALT LICK SAMPLERS; LUCKY HEART BOOKS (II), 2107 NE Multnomah St., Portland OR 97232-2119, phone (503)249-1014, founded 1969, editor James Haining, publishes "new literature and graphic arts in their various forms." They have published poetry by Robert Creeley, Charles Olson, Michael Lally, David Searcy, Julie Siegel, Paul Shuttleworth, Wm. Hart, Robert Slater, Gerald Burns and Sheila Murphy. The magazine-sized journal, 100 pgs., saddle-stapled, matte cover, experimental graphics throughout, appears irregularly. They receive 400-600 poems/year, use 1-2%. Press run is 1,000. **Sample postpaid: $6. Reports in 1-6 weeks. Pays copies. To submit for book publication under the Lucky Heart Books imprint, send 20 samples, cover letter "open." Simultaneous submissions OK. Always sends prepublication galleys. Pays copies.**

‡SAMSARA (I, IV-Specialized: Suffering/healing), P.O. Box 367, College Park MD 20741-0367, founded 1993, editor R. David Fulcher, is a biannual publication of poetry and fiction dealing with suffering. **"All subject matter should deal with suffering/healing."** They have recently published poetry by John Grey and Corrine DeWinter. As a sample we selected these lines from DeWinter's "Glissando":

> *All that separates the living*
> *and the grey cloaked director is one*
> *hand, one heart, one move.*
> *Rolling them into one you found*

easier said than done.

Samsara is 80 pgs., 8½ × 11, neatly typeset and stapled down the side with a colored card stock cover and b&w art. They receive about 150 poems a year, accept approximately 7%. Press run is 200 for 35 subscribers. Single copy: $6.50; subscription: $12. **Sample postpaid: $5. No previously published poems; simultaneous submissions OK, but "if it is a simultaneous submission, a cover letter should be provided explaining this status." Seldom comments on rejections. Send SASE for guidelines. Reports in 1-2 months. Pays 1 copy. Acquires first North American serial rights.** The editor says, "Make me feel anguish, pain and loss—and then some hope—and you'll probably get into *Samsara*."

SAN DIEGO POET'S PRESS; LA JOLLA POET'S PRESS; AMERICAN BOOK SERIES (II), P.O. Box 8638, La Jolla CA 92038. San Diego Poet's Press, a nonprofit press founded 1981 by editor/publisher Kathleen Iddings, has published collections and anthologies that include Galway Kinnell, Carolyn Kizer, Allen Ginsberg, Carolyn Forche, Tess Gallagher and Robert Pinsky, among others. Iddings began publishing individual poets in 1985 and has published approximately 25 poets to date. In 1989, she originated the "American Book Series" wherein she awards the winner $500 and publishes his/her first book of poetry. Past winners include Joan LaBombard, Regina McBride, Charles Atkinson and Michael Cleary. As a sample she selected these lines from "The Pond Near Crematorium Four" in Kevin Griffith's *Someone Had To Live*:

> *Now, our guide's red dress flaps*
> *as she leads us through*
> *cautioning fields, each long blade*
> *wind bent. She stops, slips*
> *her arm in pond's shallows,*
> *and lifts the bone chips*
> *into my hand*
> *light and delicate as wasps.*

Sample of any winning book, postpaid: $11.50. Watch the *Small Press Review* or *Poets & Writers* for contest information.

SAN FERNANDO POETRY JOURNAL; KENT PUBLICATIONS, INC. (I, IV-Social issues), 18301 Halsted St., Northridge CA 91325, founded 1978, poetry editors Richard Cloke, Shirley Rodecker and Lori Smith. *San Fernando Poetry Journal* uses **poetry of social protest.** According to Richard Cloke, "Poetry, for us, should be *didactic* **in the Brechtian sense. It must say something, must inform, in the tenor of our time.** We follow Hart Crane's definition of poetry as architectural in essence, building upon the past but incorporating the newest of this age also, including science, machinery, sub-atomic and cosmic physical phenomena as well as the social convulsions wrenching the very roots of our present world." **Send SASE for guidelines which explain this more fully.** For example, we quote this passage for its general usefulness for poets: "In some, the end-line rhyming is too insistent, seeming *forced;* in others the words are not vibrant enough to give the content an arresting framework. Others do not have any beat (cadence) at all and some are simply not well thought out—often like first drafts, or seem like prose statements. Please try reworking again to get some energy in your statement. If your poetry is to succeed in impelling the reader to act, it must electrify, or at least command interest and attention." **They welcome new and unpublished poets.** As a sample the editor selected this poem, "Paradise Lost," by Marian Steele:

> *Adam trod the earth enraptured*
> *When he was nearly alone on a younger land.*
> *His name was Muir . . . Bartram . . . Burroughs . . .*
> *Audubon.*
> *It was not so long ago.*
> *We have seen to it;*
> *Whether in Saudi desert,*
> *Flaming Brazilian rain forest,*
> *In Detroit's blighted back streets*
> *Or South Bronx alleyways,*
> *In the belches from redbrick smokestack,*
> *Recoilless rifle, naval Big Gun,*
> *Or even Three-Mile-Island-Chernobyl—*
> *We have remodeled our planet*
> *In our own image.*

The flat-spined quarterly, photocopied from typescript, uses 100 pgs. of poetry in each issue. They use about 300 of the 1,000 submissions (the editor rightly prefers to call them "contributions") each year. Press run is 400 for 350 subscribers of which 45 are libraries. **Sample postpaid: $2.50. No specifications for ms form. Simultaneous submissions OK. Reports in 1 week. Pays copies.** The press, under its various imprints, also publishes a few collections by individuals. **Query with 5-6 pgs. of samples.**

SAN JOSE STUDIES; CASEY MEMORIAL AWARD (II), San Jose State University, San Jose CA 95192-0090, phone (408)924-4476, founded 1975, poetry editor John Engell. This "journal of general and scholarly interest, featuring critical, creative and informative writing in the arts, business, humanities, science and social sciences" uses poetry of **"excellent quality—with a focus on Bay Area and California cultures. Tend to like poems with something to say, however indirectly it may be communicated. Usually publish 7-12 pgs. of verse in each issue. We like to publish several poems by one poet—better exposure for the poet, more interest for the reader."** They have published poetry by Leonard Nathan and James Sutherland-Smith. As a sample the editor chose these lines from "Mountain Woman" by Virginia de Araújo:

> . . . But place in her is deep root:
> hand, brain, nerve, tooth. Planted, she will
> spill upward in fern fronds, tight buds and fists.
> Overhead, winter and summer secretly will move,
> and she remain planted in true place.

SJS appears thrice yearly in a 6×9, flat-spined, 100-page format, professionally printed, matte card cover, using b&w photos, circulation of 500-600 of which 70-75 are libraries. They receive about 200 submissions/year, use 8-10 authors, have a 1-year backlog. Subscription: $12 individuals, $18 institutions. **Sample postpaid: $5. No simultaneous submissions. Reports in 2-3 months. Pays 2 copies. Annual award of a year's subscription for best poetry printed that year and a Casey Memorial Award of $100 for the best contribution in prose or poetry.** Editor Emeritus O.C. Williams comments, "Poetry is both an art and a craft; we are not interested in submissions unless the writer has mastered the craft and is actually practicing the art."

SANDBERRY PRESS; DEBROSSE, REDMAN, BLACK & CO. LTD. (IV-Ethnic/nationality, regional, children), P.O. Box 507, Kingston 10, Jamaica, West Indies, fax (809)968-4067, founded 1986, managing director Pamela Mordecai, publishes 8 paperbacks and 5 hardbacks/year. "We concentrate on producing first collections by well-regarded or especially promising Caribbean poets." **They want to see work from "poets born in the Caribbean or naturalized citizens of a Caribbean country or poets who have lived most of their lives in the region. Nothing racist, sexist or pornographic. Also interested in poetry for children."** They have published collections by Judith Hamilton, Elaine Savory and Jane King. As a sample they selected these lines from "Dirge for Abu Bakr" in King's collection, *Fellow Traveller*:

> They won't pay poets, for, they say, they find
> we're fiddling while the Caribbean burns.
> Fickle, frail, purple flowers have burst out on the hills
> after the long drought. But the people's minds
> are still dry.

Submit 15-25 poems at a time. "Previously published poems may form part of a ms submission" but no simultaneous submissions. Cover letter required "to know whether, what and where the author has previously published. Also a brief bio note." Often comments on rejections. Also publishes themed collections. Send SASE (or SAE and IRCs) for upcoming themes. Replies to queries in 2 months, to mss in 6 months. Always sends prepublication galleys. Pays 10% royalties on net receipts, $200 (US) advance and 6 author's copies. Inquire about sample books. Their book, *Fellow Traveller* by Jane King, won the 1994 James Rodway Memorial Prize, a $1,200 prize which is awarded annually. The editor says, "We would like to receive more humorous verse."

SANDPIPER PRESS (V), P.O. Box 286, Brookings OR 97415, phone (503)469-5588, founded 1979, is a small press publisher of large print books. They have published *Poems from the Oregon Sea Coast*; *Unicorns for Everyone*, which includes some poetry; and *Walk With Me*, a book of prayers and meditations. However, **they currently do not accept unsolicited poetry.**

SANSKRIT (I), Cone Center, UNCC, Charlotte NC 28223, phone (704)547-2326, founded 1965, editor Scott Hubbard, is a literary annual using **poetry. "No restrictions as to form or genre, but we do look for maturity and sincerity in submissions. Nothing trite or sentimental."** They have published poetry by Kimberleigh Luke-Stallings, Stella Hastie and Makyo. As a sample the editor selected these lines by Christy Beatty:

> If your father's taking lithium and your nana
> won't let the shades up and the caterpillars
> in your backyard are ablaze at some slight
> fault of your own, if there exists urban
> atrocity and decay that don't quite touch you
> yet infect your daily media intake
> Fight back.
> Change your name.

Their purpose is "to encourage and promote beginning and established artists and writers." It is 60-65 pgs., 9×12, flat-spined, printed on quality matte paper with heavy matte card cover. Press run is 3,500 for about 100 subscriptions of which 2 are libraries. **Sample postpaid: $6. Submit no more than 5 poems at a time. Simultaneous submissions OK. Cover letter with biographical information and past publications required. Reads submissions September through October only. Editor comments on submissions "infrequently." Reports in 6-8 weeks. Pays 1 copy.**

‡**SANTA BARBARA REVIEW (II)**, 104 La Vereda Lane, Santa Barbara CA 93108, founded 1993, editor Patricia Stockton Leddy, is a literary arts journal appearing 3 times a year publishing poetry, fiction and essays, including essays on poetry. **They want poetry with "lively, concrete imagery. Show us connections between things we had previously thought disparate. Nothing self-indulgent. No therapeutic diatribes, doggerel or epics. We're also not interested in abstract explanations of what life is about."** They have recently published poetry by Tess Gallagher, Chana Bloch, Stephen Ratcliffe, Marilyn Chandler and John Sanford. As a sample we selected these lines from "Tea" by Peter Munro:

> We sipped chamomile, murmured in the dark.
> The wet bench beneath us soaked through our clothes;
> we didn't care. You smoked. I poured. Steam rose.
> Your dog galloped through the empty park,
> startling mallards. The lights across the lake flowed
> in the ripples. Hot tea soothed my tongue. The swell
> of your hips filled my mind . . .

SBR is 160 pgs., 6×9, professionally printed and perfect-bound with b&w coated card cover and b&w illustrations inside. They use 12-18 poems each issue. Press run is 1,000 for 200 subscribers of which 10 are libraries, 75% shelf sales. Single copy: $6; subscription: $10. **Sample postpaid: $4. Submit 3-5 poems at a time. Previously published poems OK; no simultaneous submissions. Cover letter required. Reads submissions September 1 through June 30 only. Often comments on rejections. Send SASE for guidelines. Reports in 2-3 months. Pays 2 copies. Acquires one-time rights.** The editor says, "The first thing we look for in any submission, whether it is a photograph, essay, poem or story, is voice. Other than a desire to avoid topics for their news value or political correctness, we have no taboo relative to subject matter. So far as length is concerned, make every image, word or trope count."

SANTA MONICA REVIEW (III), Santa Monica College, 1900 Pico Blvd., Santa Monica CA 90405, founded 1988, editor Lee Montgomery, appears twice a year publishing fiction and poetry, but is **not interested in traditional forms**. They have recently published poetry by David Trinidad, Marc Cohen, Tom Clark, Alicia Ostriker, Maureen Owen and Eileen Myles. Single copy: $7; subscription: $12/year. **No submission information provided.** Poetry published in this review has been included in *The Best American Poetry 1993*.

SANTA SUSANA PRESS (V), CSU Libraries, 18111 Nordhoff St., Northridge CA 91330, phone (818)885-2271, founded 1973, a small press publisher of limited edition fine print books, history, literature and art, some poetry, all hardcover editions. **They do not accept unsolicited submissions of poetry. Poets should query first, and queries will be answered in 2 weeks. Honorariums paid depend on grant money.** The press has published books by George Elliott, Ward Ritchie and Ray Bradbury. Book catalog is free on request; prices are high. For instance, *Reaching: Poems by George P. Elliott*, illustrated, is published in an edition of 350 numbered copies at $35 and 26 lettered copies at $60.

‡**SARABANDE BOOKS, INC.; THE KATHRYN A. MORTON PRIZE IN POETRY (II)**, 2234 Dundee Rd., Suite 200, Louisville KY 40205, phone (502)458-4028, fax (502)458-4065, founded 1994, editor-in-chief Sarah Gorham, publishes books of poetry and short fiction. **They want "poetry of superior artistic quality. Otherwise no restraints or specifications." Query with 10 sample poems during the month of September only. Previously published poems OK if acknowledged as such. Simultaneous submissions OK "if notified immediately of acceptance elsewhere." Seldom comments on rejections. Replies to queries in 3 months, to mss (if invited) in 6 months. Pays 10% royalties and author's copies.** The Kathryn A. Morton Prize in Poetry is awarded to a book-length ms submitted between January 1 and February 15. $15 handling fee and entry form required. Send SASE for guidelines beginning in November. Winner receives a $2,000 cash award, publication and a standard royalty contract.

SATURDAY EVENING POST (IV-Humor), 1100 Waterway Blvd., Indianapolis IN 46202, phone (317)636-8881, founded 1728 as the *Pennsylvania Gazette*, since 1821 as *The Saturday Evening Post*, Post Scripts editor Steve Pettinga, P.O. Box 567, Indianapolis IN 46206. *SEP* is a general interest, mass circulation monthly with emphasis on preventive medicine, using *"humorous light verse only.* **No more than 100 words per poem. Stay away from four-letter words and sexually graphic subject**

matter. No experimental verse (haiku, etc.). Morally, the *Post* is an anachronism of the early 50s; most of its readers are elderly. Other than that, anything goes, as long as it's in good taste." Subscription: $13.97. **Payment is $15 for all rights.**

SATURDAY PRESS, INC.; EILEEN W. BARNES AWARD SERIES; INVITED POETS SERIES (V, IV-Women), Box 884, Upper Montclair NJ 07043, phone (201)256-5053, founded 1975, poetry editor Charlotte Mandel with contest guest editors; these have included Maxine Kumin, Colette Inez, Sandra M. Gilbert, Geraldine C. Little and Rachel Hadas. "Saturday Press, Inc., is a nonprofit literary organization. The press has a **special—though not exclusive—commitment to women's poetry, and by sponsoring the Eileen W. Barnes Award Competition for first books by women over 40 seeks to offer opportunity for new poets who have delayed their writing careers. Selection is by means of open competition or, in alternate years, by editorial board decision. Query for current information.** Not an annual event, the contest is widely posted when announced. The Invited Poets Series offers publication to established or less-known poets. We want **authoritative craft, strong, fresh imagery, sense of imagination and a good ear for syntax, sounds and rhythms. Language should lead the reader to experience a sense of discovery. Any form, content or style, but do not want polemic, jingles or conventional inspiration."** They have published books of poetry by Janice Thaddeus, Jean Hollander, Anne Carpenter, Anneliese Wagner and Doris Radin. As a sample the editor selected these lines from "A Well-Tuned Harp" by Geraldine C. Little:

> I wonder tonight as an owl sinks to the top
> of the pine tree, signing with fingery wingtips
> against the moon, fall earth savory
> as risen bread, creature sounds in the night
> immense and holy in the hearing,
> in the hearing, the hearing.

"We are fully committed at present." Query first. Enclose 1-3 samples and minimum summary of publications. Replies to queries in 2 weeks. If invited, book ms may be photocopied; simultaneous submissions OK. "Prefer no binder, simple folder or paper clip." Always sends prepublication galleys. Pays 50 copies and possible honorarium ("depends on grants"). Send SASE for catalog to buy samples.

‡SCARP (II); FIVE ISLANDS PRESS (IV-Regional), School of Creative Arts, University of Wollongong, Locked Mail Bag 8844, South Coast Mail Centre 2521 Australia, fax (042)213301, founded 1981, editor Ron Pretty. *Scarp*, which appears twice a year, is a publication of poetry, prose fiction and new art. It also contains articles and reviews. Both new and established writers are encouraged to contribute. **"Not restricted by genre or form or subject matter or style or purpose, however we would prefer not to publish anything of an epic length."** They have recently published poetry by Opal Palmer Adisa, Graham Rowlands, Andy Kissane and Charlotte Clutterbuck. As a sample the editor selected these lines from "Birthdays" by Deb Westbury:

> Champagne corks could break windows
> and dent the ceiling,
> they could make a great noise
> and come all over the carpet.
>
> Now I hold the bottle
> between my knees and make a face;
> and gently ease it out
> anticipating a small, discreet
> explosion in my palm.

Scarp is 72-84 pgs., A4 landscape format, perfect-bound, color card cover, b&w art and photography, some (mainly local) ads. There's a different flavor to poetry down under, but it is still mostly free verse bordering sometimes on what US poets would call the avant garde. Other poems are well-crafted and accessible, and the magazine is an odd rectangular shape but handsome and artistically designed. "*Scarp 25* received about 1,500 poems from 200 contributors. We published 17 poems from these." Press run is 1,000 for approximately 650 subscribers of which 100 are libraries. **Sample postpaid: $A7.50. Submit no more than 5 poems at a time. No previously published poems or simultaneous submissions. Reads submissions February through April (June issue) and July through August (October issue). Seldom comments on rejections. Send SASE for guidelines. Reports in 1-4 months.** "Material that is clearly unsuitable we send back within a month; but material that has some chance of inclusion is kept to be considered after entries close at the beginning of May and September each year. The best way to avoid delays is to submit in March and/or August each year." **Pays "at least" $A40 plus subscription. However, overseas contributors receive 2 copies plus a 2-year subscription. Buys first Australian rights only.** Staff reviews books of poetry in 300-1,000 words, single or multi-book format. Five Islands Press publishes poetry by Australian poets only. However, "We publish poetry from all over the world in *Scarp*." The editor says, "We're looking for poetry and prose that leaps off the page at you, and that usually means there's a lot of life in the language."

SCAVENGER'S NEWSLETTER; KILLER FROG CONTEST (IV-Science fiction/fantasy, horror, mystery, writing), 519 Ellinwood, Osage City KS 66523-1329, phone (913)528-3538, may seem an odd place to publish poems, but its editor, Janet Fox, uses 1-2 every month. The *Newsletter* is a **booklet packed with news about science fiction and horror publications. Janet prefers science fiction/ fantasy, horror and mystery poetry and will read anything that is offbeat or bizarre. Writing-oriented poetry is occasionally accepted but "poems on writing must present fresh ideas and viewpoints. Poetry is used as filler so it must be 10 lines or under. I like poems with sharp images and careful craftsmanship."** Recently published poets include R. Monk Habjan, Lorraine Brown, Joey Froehlich and Steve Sneyd. As a sample she selected this poem by Herb Kauderer:

> *left*
> *orbiting garbage*
> *plastic & metal gravestones*
> *of forsaken dreams*

Scavenger's Newsletter is 28 pgs., printed at a quick printing shop for 950 subscribers. Subscription: $15.50/year; $7.75/6 months. **Sample copy plus guidelines for $2; guidelines alone for SASE. Submit 3-6 poems at a time. Previously published poems and simultaneous submissions OK (if informed)—reprints if credit is given. At last report was "accepting about 1 out of 20 poems submitted. I have changed my policy of closing from September to April due to overstock to staying open even when I have somewhat of a backlog. I am currently reading selectively. I put the notice 'reading selectively due to overstock' on my guidelines, so writers will realize that I will be accepting very little during this period." Reports in 1 month or less. Pays $2 on acceptance plus one copy. Buys one-time rights.** Staff reviews science fiction/fantasy/horror and mystery chapbooks, books and magazines only. Send materials for review to either: Jim Lee, 801 - 26th St., Windber PA 15963 or Steve Sawicki, 186 Woodruff Ave., Watertown CT 06795. "I hold an annual 'Killer Frog Contest' for horror so bad or outrageous it becomes funny. There is a category for horror poetry. Has been opening April 1, closing July 1 of each year. Prizes are $25 each in four categories: poetry, art, short stories and short short stories, plus the 'coveted' Froggie statuette." The last contest had no entry fee but entrants wanting the anthology pay $3.50 (postpaid). Winners list available for SASE.

SCIENCE FICTION POETRY ASSOCIATION; STAR*LINE (IV-Science fiction, horror); THE RHYSLING ANTHOLOGY (V), 1412 NE 35th St., Ocala FL 34479, founded 1978, editor Margaret Simon, the Association publishes *Star*Line*, a bimonthly newsletter and poetry magazine. The Association also publishes *The Rhysling Anthology*, a yearly collection of nominations from the membership "for the best science fiction/fantasy long and short poetry of the preceding year." The magazine has published poetry by Bruce Boston, Thomas Disch, Denise Dumars, John M. Ford, Robert Frazier and Steve Rasnic Tem. As a sample we selected these lines from "Threshold-Haunting" by Karen Verba:

> *atoms virulently mobilized, screaming hindrance*
> *shattered like proverbs on the periphery of matter.*
> *feeling pain, an illusion of solidity—*
> *fearfully pacified by those sins*
> *we possessively clutch to ourselves*
> *in imagined conflict between the mystical & the mundane.*

The digest-sized magazines and anthologies are saddle-stapled, photocopied, with numerous illustrations and decorations. They have 250 subscribers (1 library) paying $13 for 6 issues/year. **Sample postpaid: $2. Submissions to *Star*Line* only.** They receive 200-300 submissions/year and use about 80—**mostly short (under 50 lines).** They are **"open to all forms—free verse, traditional forms, light verse—so long as your poetry shows skilled use of the language and makes a good use of science fiction, science, fantasy, horror or speculative motifs." Send 3-5 poems/submission, typed. Best time to submit is November. Brief cover letter preferred. No simultaneous submissions, no queries. Publishes theme issues. They have one all-horror issue each year. Send SASE for upcoming themes. Reports in a month. Pays 5¢/line plus 1¢/word and a copy. Buys first North American serial rights.** Reviews books of poetry "within the science fiction/fantasy field" in 50-500 words. Open to unsolicited reviews. Poets may also send books for review consideration to Todd Earl Rhodes, 735 Queensbury Loop, Winter Garden FL 34787-5808. A copy of *The Rhysling Anthology* is $3.

SCOP PUBLICATIONS, INC. (II, IV-Regional), Box 376, College Park MD 20740, phone (301)422-1930, founded 1977, president Stacy Tuthill, publishes approximately 2 paperbacks/year as well as an occasional anthology. They want **"book-length regional manuscripts. No restrictions as to length or form but want well-crafted modern poetry with vivid imagery and skillful use of language with regard to sense impressions and fresh insights."** They have published poetry by Ann Darr, Barbara Lefcowitz and Elisavietta Ritchie. **For sample book, send $5.** Interested poets should **query with sample poems. Previously published poems and simultaneous submissions OK. Cover letter**

should include a short biography and recent credits. Seldom comments on rejections. Replies to queries in 6 weeks, to mss in 2-3 months. Pays copies.

SCORE MAGAZINE; SCORE CHAPBOOKS AND BOOKLETS (II, IV-Form), 812 SW Cityview St., Pullman WA 99163, phone (509)332-1120, poetry editors Crag Hill and Laurie Schneider, is a small press publisher of **visual poetry** in the magazine *Score*, booklets, postcards and broadsides. They want "**poetry which melds language and the visual arts such as concrete poetry; experimental use of language, words and letters—forms. The appearance of the poem should have as much to say as the text. Poems on any subject; conceptual poetry; poems which use experimental, non-traditional methods to communicate their meanings.**" They don't want "**traditional verse of any kind—be it free verse or rhymed.**" They have recently published poetry by Stephen-Paul Martin, Dan Davidson, Jonathan Brannen, Larry Eigner and Bern Porter. They say that it is impossible to quote a sample because "some of our poems consist of only a single word—or in some cases no recognizable words." **We strongly advise looking at a sample copy before submitting if you are not familiar with visual poetry.** *Score* is 18-40 pgs., magazine-sized, offset, saddle-stapled, using b&w graphics, 2-color matte card cover, appearing once a year. Press run is 200 for 25 subscriptions (6 of them libraries) and about 40 shelf sales. **Sample postpaid: $6. No simultaneous submissions. Previously published poems OK "if noted." Send SASE for guidelines. Pays 2 copies.** Open to unsolicited reviews. Poets may also send books for review consideration. **For chapbook consideration send entire ms. No simultaneous submissions. Almost always comments on rejections. Pays 8-16 copies of the chapbook.** They subsidy publish "if author requests it."

SCREAM PRESS; WHISPER; ETHEREAL DANCES, P.O. Box 2354, Rohnert Park CA 94927, founded 1987, editor of *Whisper* Anthony Boyd, editor of *Ethereal Dances* Sara Hyatt Boyd. All are "publications promoting new and established literary thinkers. **Interested in any poetry well done, 40 lines or less, free verse, villanelles, haiku, etc. No 'guy' poems about beer, bars, hookers, etc. For *Whisper*, we would like to see more traditional forms and more humorous verse.**" They have recently published poetry by Lyn Lifshin, Sam Vargo and Michael Estabrook. As a sample the editors selected these lines from "It Looks Like Rain" by Graham Duncan (published in *Whisper*):

> *the flimsy words we mutter,*
> *mere hints of all that's falling,*
> *that, voiceless, passes through us*
> *and roots us to the ground.*

and these lines from "war paint" by Jenifer Bartels (published in *Ethereal Dances*):

> *Earth's paint splatters and splashes*
> > *drips and dribbles*
> > *and the Artist made a wonderful mistake*
> *when he spilled the ocean blue into your eyes.*

Whisper is a quarterly publication, 20 pgs., 8×11, web offset, saddle-stapled, with art, ads. *Ethereal Dances* is a triannual, 20 pgs., 5½×8½, laser printed, saddle-stapled, color paper, cover artwork. Anthony Boyd says he receives about 500 submissions a year for *Whisper*. He accepts approximately 9%. Sara Boyd receives about 300 poems from 75 poets for *Ethereal Dances*. She accepts approximately 15%. Press run for *Whisper* is 1000. Subscription: $10. **Sample postpaid: $2 (for *Whisper* and *Ethereal Dances*). Submit 1 poem to a page. Previously published poems OK if noted; no simultaneous submissions. Often comments on rejections. Send SASE for guidelines. Reports in 1 month. Pays 1-2 copies. Acquires first or one-time rights (printed and electronic).** Anthony Boyd reviews books of poetry in *Whisper*. Send books for review consideration to his attention. They say, "Anyone can send anything, but the acceptance rate for those who have seen a sample of our publications is double the rate for those who have not. *Whisper* is also available on the World Wide Web. Point your Web browser to: ftp://ftp.crl.com/ftp/users/ro/whisper/sphome.html."

SCRIVENER (II), 853 Sherbrooke St. W., Montreal, Quebec H3A 2T6 Canada, founded 1980, is an annual review of contemporary literature and art published by students at McGill University. With a circulation throughout North America, *Scrivener* publishes the best of new Canadian and American poetry, short fiction, criticism, essays, reviews and interviews. "*Scrivener* is committed to publishing the work of new and unpublished writers." *Scrivener* uses about 50 of 1,000 submissions received each year. It is a book-sized review, 120 pgs., printed on natural recycled paper and bound with a flat spine and one color matte card cover; all graphics and ads are black and white. Subscription: $10/2 years. **Sample postpaid: $5. January 31 deadline for submissions for April 1st publication; contributors encouraged to submit in early fall. Send 5-10 poems, one poem/page; be sure that each poem be identified separately, with titles, numbers, etc.... Editors comment individually on each submission. Reports in 6 months. Pays 2 copies or 2-year subscription.**

SEATTLE REVIEW (II), Padelford Hall GN-30, University of Washington, Seattle WA 98195, phone (206)543-9865, founded 1978, poetry editor Colleen McElroy, appears in the fall and spring using

"contemporary and traditional" poetry. They have published poetry by William Stafford, Tess Gallagher, Marvin Bell and Walter McDonald. As a sample the editor selected these lines from "Car Mechanic Blues" by Jan Wallace:

> He lords his wrench over me like
> a magic wand. His ease with grease, the way
> he calms the speeding idle should convince
> me, this man's got the power. He wants
> to show me how the sparks fire. I say,
> No thanks, I'll get the book.

The review is 110 pgs., professionally printed, flat-spined, with glossy card cover. Press run is 800 for 250 subscribers of which 50 are libraries, 400 shelf sales. Single copy: $5; subscription: $9. **Sample postpaid: $3. Reads submissions September 1 through May 31 only. Send SASE for guidelines. Reports in 2-6 months. Pay "varies, but we do pay" plus 2 copies.** The editors offer these "practical suggestions: Cover letters with submissions do help. A cover letter provides something about the author and tells where and for what s/he is submitting. And don't let those rejection letters be cause for discouragement. Rejections can often be a matter of timing. The journal in question may be publishing a special issue with a certain theme (we've done a number of themes—'all-fiction,' 'all-poetry,' 'Asian-American,' 'Northwest,' 'science fiction,' etc.). Also, editorial boards do change, and new editors bring their individual opinions and tastes in writing. Good poetry will eventually be published if it is circulated."

SECOND AEON PUBLICATIONS (V), 19 Southminster Rd., Roath, Cardiff CF2 S4T Wales, phone 01222-493093, founded 1966, poetry editor Peter Finch, is a "small press concerned in the main with **experimental literary works."** He has published poetry by Bob Cobbing and himself. **Does not accept unsolicited mss. Pays copies.** Reviews poetry as a freelancer for a broad range of publications.

SEEMS (II), P.O. Box 359, Lakeland College, Sheboygan WI 53082-0359, founded 1971, published irregularly (30 issues in 23 years). This is a handsomely printed, nearly square ($7 \times 8\frac{1}{4}$) magazine, saddle-stapled, generous with white space on heavy paper. Two of the issues are considered chapbooks, and the editor, Karl Elder, suggests that a way **to get acquainted would be to order *Seems #14, What Is The Future Of Poetry?* for $5**, consisting of essays by 22 contemporary poets, and "If you don't like it, return it and we'll return your $5." ***Explain That You Live: Mark Strand with Karl Elder*** (#29) is available for $3. There are usually about 20 pgs. of poetry/issue. Elder has recently used poetry by Albert Huffstickler, Philip Hughes, Joan Payne Kincaid, Louis McKee, Ronald Moran and Gerald Williams. He said it was "impossible" to select four illustrative lines. The magazine has a print run of 350 for 200 subscriptions (20 libraries) and sells for $4 an issue (or $16 for a subscription—four issues). There is a **1- to 2-year backlog. Reports in 1-3 months. Pays copies. Acquires North American serial rights. Returns rights upon publication.** The editor says, "We'd like to consider more prose poems, especially those with a narrative quality."

SEGUE FOUNDATION; ROOF BOOKS; SEGUE BOOKS (V), 303 E. Eighth St., New York NY 10009, phone (212)674-0199, fax (212)254-4145, president James Sherry, is a small press publisher of poetry, literary criticism, and film and performance texts. Most of their books are flat-spined paperbacks, some hardcover. They have published books by Jackson MacLow, Charles Bernstein, Ron Silliman and Diane Ward, but **they do not consider unsolicited mss. Query first**.

SENECA REVIEW (II, IV-Translations), Hobart and William Smith Colleges, Geneva NY 14456-3397, phone (315)781-3349, founded 1970, editor Deborah Tall. **They want "serious poetry of any form, including translations. No light verse. Also essays on contemporary poetry."** They have published poetry by Seamus Heaney, Rita Dove, Denise Levertov, Stephen Dunn and Hayden Carruth. *Seneca Review* is 100 pgs., 6×9, flat-spined, professionally printed on quality stock with matte card cover, appearing twice a year. You'll find plenty of free verse here—some accessible and some leaning toward experimental—with the emphasis on voice, image and diction. All in all, poems and translations complement each other and create a distinct editorial mood each issue. Of 3,000-4,000 poems received

---

ALWAYS include a self-addressed, stamped envelope (SASE) when sending a ms or query to a publisher within your own country. When sending material to other countries, include a self-addressed envelope and International Reply Coupons (IRCs), available for purchase at most post offices.

they accept approximately 100. Press run is 1,000 for 500 subscribers of which half are libraries, about 250 shelf sales. Subscription: $8/year, $15/2 years. **Sample postpaid: $5. Submit 3-5 poems at a time. No simultaneous submissions or previously published poems. Reads submissions September 1 through May 1 only. Reports in 6-12 weeks. Pays 2 copies.** Poetry published in *Seneca Review* has also been included in *The Best American Poetry 1994*.

SENSATIONS MAGAZINE (I, IV-Membership/subscription, themes), 2 Radio Ave., A5, Secaucus NJ 07094, founded 1987, founder David Messineo. **Subscription required before submission of material, but this is among the top 10 paying poetry markets in the US.** *Sensations* is an unusual mix of contemporary poetry, contemporary fiction and historical research. **"We encourage diversity: Buy back issue, see types and themes of published poems, and send something different."** As a sample, the founder selected these lines from "The Pearl Eater" by Melanie Pimont:

> *Night creatures shiver in their burrows*
> *as darkness flies over the earth. A raven croaks.*
> *Its wings beat above and my ears feel*
> *the weight of its passage. Even the shadows*
> *have fled. Hurry, light the round lanterns.*
> *Hang paper moons from tree branches. Shoot*
> *fireworks high into the sky. Scare the sky dragon.*
> *Make it loose light upon this world again.*

Sensations is "desktop-published with elegance and respect for the written word." Subscription: $20 for 110 pg. back issue (includes 5 full-color pages). **"We send SASE for your poetry submission once you have subscribed, so don't send poetry until *after* you have subscribed. Check (or International Money Order) must be made payable to David Messineo. If you send material without a SASE, you will receive no response." Previously published poems OK. Theme for March 1996 issue is "almost anything goes, 120 lines or less (no profanity)." Deadline: December 30, 1995. Pays $125/poem. Acquires one-time publication rights.** The founder says, "Funds raised go into costs of publication and research—editors are unpaid volunteers. Have doubts? Name five independent, non-grant-funded publications you submitted to back in 1987 that are still around. We have beaten the odds of failure and are looking forward to our Fifteenth Anniversary Issue in 2002 (we even advance planned all issues, deadlines, and themes between now and then). *Sensations Magazine* is unlike any other literary magazine you've seen. We will treat you with respect and remarkable courtesy, and ask your professionalism in return by following our submission requirements in full. For those of you who tried us before, we strongly encourage you to revisit. Why not prepare a SASE right now and send it to the address above, while we're on your mind? We look forward to hearing from you, and will respond within a week or two of your inquiry."

SEQUOIA (II), Storke Publications Building, Stanford University, Stanford CA 94305, founded 1892, poetry editor Carlos Rodriguez, appears twice a year. They have published poetry by Susan Howe, Seamus Heaney, Adrienne Rich, Rita Dove and James Merrill. As a sample the editor selected these lines from "The Amish Visit Pella, Iowa" by Keith Ratzlaff:

> *to be healed of themselves,*
> *the curves their bones take.*
> *They come because the chiropractor*
> *works in the open the way they do:*
> *hard and with his hands.*

Sequoia is 80-100 pgs., 6×9, professionally printed, flat-spined, with matte card cover with art. They publish a small percentage of hundreds of unsolicited submissions. Their press run is 500 with 200 subscriptions, of which half are libraries. Subscription: $10. **Sample postpaid: $5. Submit up to 9 typed poems at a time. They do not consider simultaneous submissions or previously published poems. Reads submissions September 15 through June 1. Reports in "2 months or more." Pays 2 copies.**

SERPENT & EAGLE PRESS (V), RD#1, Box 29B, Laurens NY 13796, phone (607)432-2990, founded 1981, poetry editor Jo Mish. "Our aim is to print fine limited letterpress editions of titles worth printing in all subject areas." Their chapbooks are elegantly designed and printed on handmade paper with hand-sewn wrappers. **However, they are currently not accepting poetry submissions.**

SEVEN BUFFALOES PRESS; AZOREAN EXPRESS; BLACK JACK; VALLEY GRAPEVINE; HILL AND HOLLER ANTHOLOGY SERIES (IV-Rural, regional, anthologies), Box 249, Big Timber MT 59011, founded 1973, editor Art Cuelho, who writes, "I've always thought that rural and working class writers, poets and artists deserve the same tribute given to country singers." These publications all express that interest. For all of them Art Cuelho wants **poetry oriented toward rural and working people, "a poem that tells a story, preferably free verse, not longer than 50-100 lines, poems with strong lyric and metaphor, not romantical, poetry of the heart as much as the head, not poems**

written like grocery lists or the first thing that comes from a poet's mind, no ivory tower, and half my contributors are women." He has published poetry by R.T. Smith, James Goode, Leo Connellan and Wendell Berry. *The Azorean Express* is 35 pgs., 5½×8½, side-stapled. It appears twice a year. Circulation 200. **Sample postpaid: $6.75. Submit 4-8 poems at a time. No simultaneous submissions. Reports in 1-2 weeks. Pays 1 copy.** *Black Jack* is an anthology series on Rural America that uses rural material from anywhere, especially the American West; *Valley Grapevine* is an anthology on central California, circulation 750, that uses rural material from central California; *Hill and Holler*, Southern Appalachian Mountain series, takes in rural mountain lifestyle and folkways. **Sample of any postpaid: $6.75. Seven Buffaloes Press does not accept unsolicited mss but publishes books solicited from writers who have appeared in the above magazines.** Art Cuelho advises, "Don't tell the editor how great you are. This one happens to be a poet and novelist who has been writing for 30 years. Your writing should not only be fused with what you know from the head, but also from what you know within your heart. Most of what we call life may be some kind of gift of an unknown river within us. The secret to be learned is to live with ease in the darkness, because there are too many things of the night in this world. But the important clue to remember is that there are many worlds within us."

SEVENTEEN (V), 850 Third Ave., New York NY 10022, phone (212)407-9700, founded 1944, contact poetry/voice editor, is a slick monthly for teenage girls, circulation 1,750,000. They publish **"all styles of poetry up to 40 lines by writers 21 and under. However, due to a large backlog, *Seventeen* can no longer accept poetry submissions."** Purchase sample ($1.75) at newsstands.

THE SEWANEE REVIEW; AIKEN TAYLOR AWARD FOR MODERN POETRY (III), University of the South, Sewanee TN 37375, phone (615)598-1000, founded 1892, thus being our nation's oldest continuously published literary quarterly, editor George Core. Fiction, criticism and poetry are invariably of the **highest establishment standards. Most of our major poets appear here from time to time.** They have published poetry by William Logan, Howard Nemerov and Barry Spacks. Each issue is a hefty paperback of nearly 200 pgs., conservatively bound in matte paper, always of the same typography. Truly a magazine open to all styles and forms, issues we critiqued featured formal sequences, metered verse, structured free verse, sonnets, and lyric and narrative forms—all accessible and intelligent. Circulation: 3,200. **Sample: $5.75. Reports in 1-4 weeks. Pays 70¢/line.** Also includes brief, standard and essay-reviews. The Aiken Taylor Award for Modern Poetry is awarded by *The Sewanee Review* and its publisher, the University of the South in Sewanee, TN, "for the work of a substantial and distinguished career." Poetry published in *The Sewanee Review* was also selected for inclusion in *The Best American Poetry 1992*.

SHAMAL BOOKS (IV-Ethnic, anthologies), Dept. PM, GPO Box 16, New York NY 10116, phone (718)622-4426, founded 1976, editor Louis Reyes Rivera. Shamal Books is a small press whose purpose is **"to promote the literary efforts of African-American and Caribbean writers, particularly those who would not otherwise be able to establish their literary credentials as their concerns as artists are with the people."** The press publishes individual and "anthological" books and chapbooks, mostly flat-spined paper texts. They have published poetry by SeKou Sundiata, Sandra Maria Esteves and Rashidah Ismaili. The editor wants to see **"poetry that clearly demonstrates an understanding of craft, content and intent as the scriptural source of the word guiding and encouraging the intellect of the people." He does not consider unsolicited submissions of individual mss, but will look at work only while anthologies are open. Submit 2 sample poems. Mss should be "neat and single-spaced." Cover letter "leaning toward personal goals and poetic principles" required. Replies to queries within 2 months. Royalties for book authors are 15%.** The editor says that he will subsidy publish "delicately—depends on resources and interest in work." His projects include "an international anthology; drama; prison anthology; books on language as a weapon; a collectivized publisher's catalog of Third World presses working out of NYC." His advice to poets: "Certainly to study the craft more and to research more into the historical role that has been the hallmark of poetry across class and caste conscious lines that limit younger perspectives. Not to be as quick to publish as to be in serious study, then while looking to publish, looking as well into collective ventures with other poets for publication and distribution. Above all, *read*!"

SHARING THE VICTORY (IV-Spirituality/inspirational, sports), 8701 Leeds Rd., Kansas City MO 64129, phone (816)921-0909, founded 1959, editor John Dodderidge, assistant editor Robyne Baker, managing editor Don Hilkemeier. This monthly magazine is published September through May by the Fellowship of Christian Athletes. **They want free verse on themes of interest to Christian athletes (high school and college, male and female).** As a sample they selected these lines by Aileen L. Myers:

> I am more than
> skill and conditioning
> More because
> I am a child of a loving God,

> *who created me in His spiritual image,*
> *loves me for myself*
> *and promises me the eternal Victory.*

They use 2-3 poems/year. Press run is 50,000. **Sample available for $1 with 8½ × 11 SASE (first-class stamps for 3 ozs.). Reads submissions July 1 through March 1 only.** Time between acceptance and publication averages 3-4 months. **Guidelines available free. Reports in 2 weeks. Pays $25-50. Buys first or second rights.**

SHATTERED WIG REVIEW (II), 2407 Maryland Ave., #1, Baltimore MD 21218, phone (410)243-6888, founded 1988, contact Fred Engels, is a semiannual using **"liquid, messy poetry, oozing the stuff of life. No frustrated English professor poetry."** They have published poetry by John M. Bennett, Eel Leonard, Lyn Lifshin and Dan Raphael. As a sample the editor selected these lines by Chris Toll:

> *A 10,000-year-old white man rules the world*
> *when he needs a new heart,*
> *he murders a 16-year-old boy*
> *His tanks may rumble through the cities*
> *My crack dealers will fight back to back with my crystal healers*
> *Every cell in my body knows the new world is coming*

SHW is approximately 70 pgs., 8½ × 8½, photocopied, side-stapled with card stock covers with original artwork, art and graphics also inside. They receive about 10 submissions/week, accept about 20%. Press run is 300 for 100 subscribers of which 10 are libraries, 100 shelf sales. Subscription: $9 for 2 issues. **Sample postpaid: $4. Previously published poems and simultaneous submissions OK. Seldom comments on rejections. Reports within a month. Pays 1 copy. Acquires one-time rights.** Occasionally reviews books of poetry in 100 words. Open to unsolicited reviews. Poets may also send books for review consideration. The editor says there are no requirements for contributors except "that the contributor include us in their nightly prayers."

HAROLD SHAW PUBLISHERS; WHEATON LITERARY SERIES (V), P.O. Box 567, Wheaton IL 60189, phone (708)665-6700, founded 1967, managing editor Joan Guest, is "small publisher of the Wheaton Literary Series and Northcote Books, **works of Christian and literary merit** including fiction, poetry, literary criticism and original prose" in flat-spined paperback and hardback books. They have published poetry by Madeleine L'Engle, John Leax, Sister Maura Eichner and Luci Shaw. **They publish on a 10/5% royalty basis plus 10 author's copies.** They publish a volume of poetry approximately every 2 years. "Our work reflects **a Christian evangelical world-view**, though this need not be explicit. In the future we may publish an anthology, rather than single poets." **However, they are currently still not accepting poetry submissions.**

‡SHAWNEE SILHOUETTE (I), Shawnee State University, 940 Second St., Portsmouth OH 45662, phone (614)354-3205, founded 1985, editor Judith Allen, appears 3 times/year (fall, winter and spring) publishing poetry, artwork and photography, and occasionally sponsoring a poetry contest. **They want "any subject done in good taste; blank and free verse conventional forms; 28 lines including spaces. We will also be publishing Special Issues."** They have recently published poetry by Harding Stedler, Lena Nevison, Dexter Wolfe, Homer Bailey and Mabel Massie. As a sample the editor selected these lines by Sue Lonny:

> *In the Dark*
> *One night I woke to hear a poem*
> *shaken loose in sleep,*
> *I copied words in darkness*
> *I later could not read.*
> *Perhaps because the piece was lost*
> *It was my finest work,*
> *and I will spend a poet's life*
> *remembering the words.*

Shawnee Silhouette is 44 pgs., digest-sized, offset from WordPerfect 6.0 with Laser writer Plus, utilizing a variety of typestyles, with b&w drawings and photographs, saddle-stapled, matte card cover with b&w photo. Single copy: $2; subscription: $5/year. **Send 3 poems at a time, typed double-spaced. No simultaneous submissions.** Time between acceptance and publication is 6 months. **Reports in 3 months. Pays 1 copy.** The editor says, "We are interested only in quality material and try to provide a diversity of styles and topics in each issue."

SHEILA-NA-GIG (II), 23106 Kent Ave., Torrance CA 90505, founded 1990, editor Hayley R. Mitchell. *Sheila-na-gig* appears once a year as a large general issue using **"all forms (particularly free verse), styles and subject matter—length, I generally don't publish poems over three pages (don't ramble!). No religious or ultra traditional verse, please."** They have recently published work by Lyn

Lifshin, Gerald Locklin, Arthur G. Gottlieb, Robert Headley, Michael McNeilley, Ioanna-Veronica Warwick and Charles Webb. As a sample the editor selected these lines by Terry Wolverton:

> *My lover, steering wheel in hand,*
> *stared into narrow streets*
> *with the eyes of a dark bird,*
> *"Which way," she cawed, "which way?"*
> *But mine glowed with the blankness*
> *of a woman swaying from a noose, . . .*

Sheila-na-gig is digest-sized, flat-spined, 100-150 pgs., photocopied from laser prints with matte card cover. Subscription: $7 yearly, $12 for two years. **Sample postpaid: $7 for current issue ($5/$3 for older back issues). Cover letter preferred with submissions. Include SASE, brief bio and note stating whether poems are previously published or simultaneous submissions. 1996 Deadline: May 31. "Work received before April will be returned unread. I'll begin reading submissions on June 1, and will report in 6-8 weeks. Submit up to 5 poems,** and/or short stories (1-10 pgs.), and/or b&w artwork (5×7 and easy to reproduce)." **Send SASE for upcoming themes. Pays copies. Acquires first rights.** For the 4th Annual Poetry Contest: Submit 3 poems. Include SASE and $5 entry fee. $50 first prize, copies, and publication of runners-up. Deadline: June 1. Work in *Sheila-na-gig* has been nominated for inclusion in *Pushcart Prize XIX: Best of the Small Presses (1994-95 edition)*. The editor says, "I encourage new poets with new styles and a strong voice, and look especially for poets not afraid to speak out on issues of sexuality, politics, human rights and feminist issues. Looking for poetry on the edge. If in doubt, order a back issue. Please make all checks payable to Hayley R. Mitchell. Thank you for your interest in and support of *Sheila-na-gig.*"

SHENANDOAH (II), Box 722, Lexington VA 24450, phone (703)463-8765, founded 1950, editor Dabney Stuart, managing editor Lynn Williams. Published at Washington and Lee University, it is a quarterly literary magazine which has published poetry by Conrad Hilberry, Martha McFerren, Robert B. Shaw, Cathy Song and Jeanne Walker. As a sample the editor chose these lines from "The Lake of the Unconscious" by Geraldine Connolly:

> *and everything was still,*
> *the deer frozen between two pines*
>
> *the way the child was caught*
> *between the two worlds, the air*
>
> *and the bottom of the lake*
> *bobbing there, amazed*

The magazine is 100 pgs., 6×9, perfect-bound, professionally printed with full-color cover. Generally, it is open to all styles and forms but leans toward lyric and narrative free verse with an emphasis on voice. Circulation: 1,700. **Sample postpaid: $3.50. All submissions should be typed on one side of the paper only. Your name and address must be clearly written on the upper right corner of the ms. Include SASE. Reads submissions September 1 through May 30. Reports in 3 months. Payment includes a check, one-year subscription and one copy. Buys first publication rights.** Staff reviews books of poetry in 7-10 pages, multi-book format. Send books for review consideration. Some reviews are solicited. Poetry published in *Shenandoah* has been included in *The Best American Poetry 1993*.

SHIP OF FOOLS (II); SHIP OF FOOLS PRESS (V), Box 1028, University of Rio Grande, Rio Grande OH 45674, phone (614)245-5351, founded 1983, editor Gina Pellegrino-Pines, assistant editor Jack Hart, review editor James Doubleday, is "more or less quarterly." They want **"coherent, well-written, traditional or modern, myth, archetype, love, odd and/or whimsical poetry—most types. No concrete, incoherent or greeting card poetry."** They have published poetry by Rhina Espaillat, Carolyn Page, Denver Stull and T. Kilgore Splake. As a sample the editors selected these lines from "Following the Reaper" by Nancy Haas:

> *I am here again;*
> *Gathering the heads*
> *With their wide astonished eyes*
> *And the hands*
> *With their silent fluttering fingers.*

They describe *Ship of Fools* as digest-sized, saddle-stapled, offset printed with cover art and graphics. Press run is 275 for 36 subscribers of which 6 are libraries. Subscription: $7 for 4 issues. **Sample postpaid: $2. No previously published poems or simultaneous submissions. Cover letter preferred. Often comments on rejections. Reports in 2-4 weeks. "If longer than six weeks, write and ask why." Pays 1 copy.** Reviews books of poetry. Ship of Fools Press publishes chapbooks but does not accept unsolicited mss.

SHOFAR (IV-Children, ethnic, religious), 43 Northcote Dr., Melville NY 11747, phone/fax (516)643-4598, founded 1984, publisher/editor Gerald H. Grayson, is a magazine **for Jewish children 8-13**, appearing monthly October through May (double issues December/January and April/May). It is 32 pgs., magazine-sized, professionally printed, with color paper cover. Their press run is 17,000 with 16,000 subscriptions of which 1,000 are libraries. Subscription: $14.95. **Sample: $1.01 postage and SAE. They will consider simultaneous submissions and "maybe" previously published poems. Send SASE for guidelines. Submit holiday theme poems at least 4 months in advance. Reports in 6-8 weeks. Pays $25-50/poem. Buys North American serial rights.**

‡SIDESADDLE (IV-Cowgirl, regional, women), 500 W. Seventh, Suite 1750, Fort Worth TX 79045, founded 1979, is the annual publication of the National Cowgirl Hall of Fame and Western Heritage Center and is designed to honor cowgirls and Western women. **"All poetry must be cowgirl or Western poetry."** They have recently published poetry by Keith Avery, Georgie Sicking and Betty Solt. *SideSaddle* is 92 pgs., 8½×11, professionally printed on slick stock and saddle-stitched with a laminated full-color cover. Inside it features Western women and includes both b&w and full-color art and photos. **Sample postpaid: $6. Previously published poems and simultaneous submissions OK. Cover letter required. Poems are circulated to an editorial board. Always comments on rejections. Reports "ASAP."** Includes related book features/reviews within each issue. Open to unsolicited reviews. Poets may also send related books for review consideration.

SIERRA NEVADA COLLEGE REVIEW (I), P.O. Box 4269, Incline Village NV 89450, founded 1990, editor June Sylvester, is an annual literary magazine featuring poetry and short fiction by new writers. They want **"high quality, image-oriented poems that suggest or surprise; no limit on length, style, etc. No light verse, sloppy sentiment, purposeful obscurity, clichés or cuteness."** They have recently published poetry by Marisella Veiga, Ivanov Y. Reyez, Collen O'Brien and B.Z. Nidith. As a sample the editor selected these lines from "The Book of Ruth" by Margaret Almon:

> I must not dream of anger.
> Placing a kernel
> in the bend of his knee,
> willing it to sprout into tangles
> around his throat—
> tangles like the ones in my hair
> that break the comb.
> Placing a sheaf beneath his bed,
> his body becoming a field of bruises.

The editor says *SNCR* is approximately 75 pgs., with cover art only. "We receive approximately 500 poems a year and accept approximately 50." Press run is 500. Subscription: $5/year. **Sample postpaid: $2.50. Submit 5 poems at a time. No previously published poems; simultaneous submissions OK. Include brief bio. Reads submissions September 1 through April 1. Often comments on rejections. Reports in 3 weeks to 3 months. Pays 2 copies.** The editor says, "We delight in publishing the unpublished or underpublished writer. We look specifically for subtlety and skill."

THE SIGNPOST PRESS; THE BELLINGHAM REVIEW; 49TH PARALLEL POETRY CONTEST (II), English Dept., Western Washington University, Bellingham WA 98225, founded 1975, editor Knute Skinner, publishes *The Bellingham Review* twice a year, runs an annual poetry competition and publishes other books and chapbooks of poetry occasionally. **"We want well-crafted poetry but are open to all styles,"** no specifications as to form. Poets they have published recently include James Bertolino, Katharyn Howd Machan, Kalo Clarke, John Doorty, Richard Martin and Sheila Farr. As a sample, the editor selected these lines by Paul Gillie:

> Dark hills walled off winds and one end of the world,
> but now that I've climbed beyond them
> they were closer all the time to Japan or London than the school
> four football fields and a bus ride away.

The *Review* is digest-sized, saddle-stapled, typeset, with art and glossy cover. Each issue has about 38 pgs. of poetry. They have a circulation of 700 with 500 subscriptions. **Sample postpaid: $2. Submit 1-10 poems at a time. Simultaneous submissions OK. Reads submissions September 1 through March 1 only. Reports in 1-4 months. Pays 1 copy plus a year's subscription. Acquires first North American rights.** Staff reviews books of poetry in 500-1,000 words, single or multi-book format. Send books for review consideration also between September 1 and March 1. Send SASE for rules for the next 49th Parallel Poetry Contest and query regarding book publication.

SILVER APPLES PRESS (V), P.O. Box 292, Hainesport NJ 08036, phone (609)267-2758, founded 1982, poetry editor Geraldine Little. "We're a very small press with very limited funds. Published our first chapbook in 1988; open contest for same. We plan to publish randomly, as things turn us on and as funds permit—pamphlets, chapbooks, a set of postcards. **We are over-committed at present. Not**

currently accepting unsolicited poetry submissions. Watch *Poets & Writers* for announcements." They publish **"first-class poetry by experienced poets. No greeting card verse, soupy sentimental verse or blatantly religious verse."** They have published *Contrasts in Keening: Ireland* by Geraldine C. Little, *Abandoned House* by Susan Fawcett and *The Verb to Love* by Barbara Horton. As a sample the editor selected these lines from *Keeping Him Alive* by Charlotte Mandel:

> We do not cut it down.
> In winter,
> within the bitter scrabble
> of bared, practiced branches,
> the dead tree, too, promises.

SILVER WINGS (IV-Religious, spirituality/inspirational), P.O. Box 1000, Pearblossom CA 93553-1000, phone (805)264-3726, founded 1983, published by Poetry on Wings, Inc., poetry editor Jackson Wilcox. "As a committed Christian service we produce and publish *Silver Wings*, a quarterly poetry magazine. We want **poems with a Christian perspective, reflecting a vital personal faith and a love for God and man. Will consider poems from 3-20 lines. Quite open in regard to meter and rhyme**." They have published poetry by Elva McAllaster, Mary Ann Henn, Sigmund Weiss and C. David Hay. As a sample the editor selected this poem, "A Song of Recognition," by Dorothy Holley:

> On a clear moonlit night
> with sparkles on the snow
> like diamonds in the sky
> I ask as did the Psalmist
> long ago, "What is man
> that Thou art mindful of him?"
> You answer with a breath
> of air and I say: "I know!"

The magazine is 32 pgs., digest-sized, offset from typescript with hand-lettered titles on tinted paper with cartoon-like art. They receive 1,500 submissions/year, use 260. Circulation is 450 with 300 subscribers, 50 shelf sales. Subscription: $7. **Sample postpaid: $2. Submit typed ms, double-spaced. No previously published poems; simultaneous submissions OK. Send SASE for guidelines. Reports in 3 weeks, providing SASE is supplied;** time to publication can be up to 2 years. **Pays subscription. "We occasionally offer a $50 award to a poem we consider outstanding and most closely in the spirit of what** *Silver Wings* **seeks to accomplish." Acquires first rights.** The editor says, "We have felt that the state of secular poetry today is thrashing in a stagnant pond out of which it cannot extract itself. We want to lift our poetry to a high road where God's sunlight is shining. We even encourage poets with little ability but having an upward mobil commitment."

SILVERFISH REVIEW; SILVERFISH REVIEW PRESS (II), P.O. Box 3541, Eugene OR 97403, phone (503)344-5060, founded 1979, poetry editor Rodger Moody, is a semiannual literary magazine. **"The only criterion for selection of poetry is quality. In future issues** *Silverfish Review* **also wants to showcase the short short story."** They have published poetry by Chelsey Minnis, Denise Duhamel, Dick Allen, Ivan Arguelles, D.M. Wallace, Robert Gregory, Ralph Salisbury, Richard Jones, Floyd Skloot and Susan Cobin. As a sample the editor selected these lines by Lauren Mesa:

> This one, the tall boy with brown hair,
> the wicker creel's strap slung
> across his crest, is Great-Uncle Mickey,
> Michelangelo Cipolla, the uncle
> who dressed as Santa the years
> my mother was a child.

The magazine is 48 pgs., digest-sized, professionally printed in dark type on quality stock, matte card cover with art. There are 36-48 pgs. of poetry in each issue. They receive about 1,000 submissions of poetry/year, use 20, have a 6- to 12-month backlog. Circulation 750. Subscription for institutions: $15; for individuals: $12. **Sample: $4, single copy orders should include $2 for p&h. Submit at least 5 poems to editor. No simultaneous submissions. Reports in about 2-6 months. Pays 2 copies and one-year subscription, plus small honorarium when grant support permits.** Reviews books of poetry. Open to unsolicited reviews. Poets may also send books for review consideration. **Silverfish Review Press will consider mss for poetry chapbook publication and conducts an annual chapbook competition with an award of $100 and 25 copies (with a press run of 750). Send SASE for rules.**

SING HEAVENLY MUSE! (IV-Feminist), Box 13320, Minneapolis MN 55414, founded 1977, editor Sue Ann Martinson, fosters "the work of women poets, fiction writers and artists. The magazine is **feminist in an open, generous sense: We encourage women to range freely, honestly and imaginatively over all subjects, philosophies and styles. We do not wish to confine women to women's subjects,** whether these are defined traditionally, in terms of femininity and domesticity, or modernly,

CLOSE-UP

Research Makes Your Writing Count

"Backbones in the Sand"

Two Ethiopians tried
To hold themselves
On a spike of sand:
A baby boy attached himself
To the shoulders of his mother
As if he were a flame
And she, a candle.
Life flickered in his face
Until a gust of death blew it out.
The candle toppled.
Vultures leave behind
The wick of a human being.

(reprinted by permission of *Pudding Magazine*)

Timothy Hodor

Although many poets trying to break into publica-
tion are convinced they need contacts to get published, Timothy Hodor is proof
that it isn't always who you know but what you write that counts—if you direct
your work to the proper market.

An American who lives and works in Vienna, Austria, Hodor has more than
120 publications to his credit, including **Blue Unicorn**, **Commonweal**, **Negative
Capability** and **The Northern Centinel**. "Submitting from Vienna for more than
ten years, I can say that I've never met an editor or even talked with one. I have
no connections, no editors, no writers to facilitate publication. However, I do
believe editors and publishers are people who've had a love affair going on their
whole lives with books and the written word. This love leads them to select the
best work that comes their way, the work that best fits into their pages and best
suits their readership."

Born in 1955, in East Chicago, Indiana, Hodor began writing poetry at age
16, when a student a grade higher committed suicide after failing a test. "I was
devastated and felt there was no one I could communicate this to verbally, so I
put my feelings down on paper. I started writing poetry because it was one way
I could cry, penning mental tears." He continues to write poetry during periods
of discontentment and emotional upheaval, drawing ideas from the world around
him, human nature, his travels and metaphysics. "I try not to write formulaic
poetry, and I believe in expanding yourself by venturing into new thematic
territory."

While attending the university of Rutgers, Hodor started submitting poetry to
the campus publication to ease the sense of loneliness created by keeping his

work to himself. "I seek publication because it involves people. I want to be alone when I conceive a poem, but I want to be with other people when I finish it." In 1980, he fulfilled a dream of settling in Europe by moving to Vienna where he teaches English as a second language at an international language school. His work mainly consists of one-on-one teaching, and his students come from several countries and all walks of life.

Most of Hodor's writing is done on streetcars or trains while traveling between lessons, or in coffeehouses after work. "I don't write poetry every day, however, or even every season. My poetical soul needs to hibernate or to estivate so that it can wake to a world of fresh words." Because he does a lot of traveling and seeks sights "off the beaten track," Hodor's poetry shows variety. He has written poetry on subjects ranging from Napoléon's residence on Elba to Cochise's stronghold in Arizona to an African village in Kenya.

He believes editors who want to be creative look for poetry with interesting content, poems about other countries for instance. "Poems about unique places have interest to readers. It's a matter of arousing curiosity." Yet, he says, "I strive for universal themes which appeal to the human in all of us. And I think universality is important when submitting poetry because a poet should be, or want to become, a citizen of the world."

While Hodor currently submits his work to both American and European publications, he applies a standard submission technique to all markets. "It's important to mention that following the guidelines in *Poet's Market* is one of the finest ways to approach editors. I am the perfect example of a person who has followed the submission procedures and succeeded. Done with love, respect, professionalism, enthusiasm and dedication, you *can* find a readership."

Hodor learns about publications outside Austria from market directories and by asking visitors to Vienna to bring information from wherever they reside. He also looks for magazines in the bookstores of cities he visits. "London is a great city for discovering U.K. publications," he says. "You can go bookstore hopping and come across all kinds of finds."

Believing "guidelines don't tell you much about the style of poetry that appears in a publication," Hodor prefers to read the magazines he's interested in and obtains sample copies at bookstores and libraries or by ordering them directly from publishers—sometimes requesting an older sample, "simply because it's cheaper." Hodor also suggests poets seek out the journals their favorite poets have appeared in. These journals may be receptive to your work, if it's in a similar style.

When submitting to American markets, Hodor denies having an advantage over other poets outside the U.S. "Being an American doesn't help me write better for American markets; it helps me aim a specific poem at the right target. Although, living on European soil has taught me that the markets here are more receptive to poetry some editors in the U.S. would label as bleak or too political." Lately, Hodor has been submitting more poetry to markets in the United Kingdom. "It has something more human to it, a kinder, more gentle market."

After having sent out more than 1,000 poetry submissions, Hodor believes all his work has been given serious consideration. "I have received very few form rejections, except from those long-standing category III publications in *Poet's Market*. Submitting to some of these is like panning for literary gold. It is better to be realistic and to appreciate and accept your status as a category I and II poet. I'm proud of every publication I appear in."

Asked to offer advice for "beginners," Hodor says, "At the start of every poem I am a beginner. Somehow we are all beginners." He then adds, "Poets need to read poetry from the beginning of time to today. Read words everywhere. You write at the level you read. Learn where words come from, love etymology. Learn a few languages. Know the names of things. Train your senses. Look at things from all angles. See how nature and people affect them. Close your eyes and listen.

"Jack Lemmon once said, 'Actors can call themselves actors when they're able to stand on stage, take their clothes off, and turn slowly and patiently in front of an audience.' Poets have to do this undressing and rotating with their souls. Don't let anyone kill your dream of being a poet. Only you can commit this suicide."

—Chantelle Bentley

66Poems about unique places have interest to readers. It's a matter of arousing curiosity. 99

—Timothy Hodor

from a sometimes narrow polemical perspective. We look for explorations, questions that do not come with ready-made answers, emotionally or intellectually." For poetry they have **"no limitations except women's writing or men's writing that reflects awareness of women's consciousness."** They have published poetry by Alexis Rotella, Jill Breckenridge and Amirh Bahati. The editor selected these sample lines from "Sons of Soweto" by June Jordan:

> *Words live in the spirit of her face*
> *and that sound will no longer yield . . .*
> *she will stand under the sun!*
> *She will stay!*

The magazine appears once a year in a 6×9, flat-spined, 125-page format, offset from typescript on heavy stock, b&w art, glossy card color cover. They receive 1,500 submissions/year, use 50-60. Press run is 1,000 for 275 subscribers of which 50 are libraries. Single copy: $8 plus $2 p&h; subscription: $15 for 2 issues, $20 for 3 issues ($16 low income), $38 for 6 issues. **Sample postpaid: $4. "Copies are also available in bookstores nationwide that carry small press women's literature." Submit 3-5 poems at a time, name and address on each page. No simultaneous submissions. Editors sometimes comment on rejections. Send SASE for guidelines, information about upcoming reading periods and themes. Reports in 4-5 months. Pays "usually $25 plus 2 copies."**

SINGULAR SPEECH PRESS (V), 10 Hilltop Dr., Canton CT 06019, phone (203)693-6059, fax (203)693-6338, founded 1976, editor Don D. Wilson. "Singular Speech Press presents examples of our many real poets—probably our most unsupported artists. **And so we publish at least 6 mss per annum, 40-96 pages. We have few biases, are enamored of both free and formal verse, are gladdened by unknown and well-known poets; we cannot stomach prosaic or confessional poetry."** They have recently published William Burns, Ivan Radoev, Michael Cadnum, Stephen Smith and Geraldine Little. As a sample here are six lines from "Smelting" in **Impossible Mirrors** by Christopher Millis:

> *Ovid omitted the story of smelts,*
> *how a boy who saw no reflection in a stream's running*
> *water worried that he wasn't there. His eye caught on a small fish,*
> *threading darkness and impossible mirrors.*
> *When he stood up the stars leaped out of his eyes.*
> *Now men net them at night with flashlights, standing in water.*

The press is currently not encouraging poetry submissions—booked up for next 2½ years.

SISTER VISION PRESS (IV-Ethnic, women), P.O. Box 217, Station E, Toronto, Ontario M6H 4E2 Canada, phone (416)595-5033, founded 1985, managing editor Makeda Silvera, publishes 8-10 paperbacks/year. They want **"poetry that reflects our lives as women of color; not restricted by form or length."** They have published poetry by ahdri zhina mandiela and Ramabai Espinet. As a sample the editor selected these lines from "Crebo" in Espinet's book *Nuclear Seasons*:

> *My hands had wrinkles*
> *But rims grew around my eyes*
> *My skin became ebony and rose*
> *And my tongue grew long beyond words*

Submit a sample of work, to a maximum of 10 pages. Previously published poems and simultaneous submissions OK. Cover letter required. Replies to queries in 1 month, to mss (if invited) in 2 months. Pays 10% royalties and 10 author's copies. Write for samples. They say, "Know the publisher you are submitting mss to. This saves the poet and publisher time, money and energy."

SISTERS TODAY (II, IV-Spirituality/inspirational), The Liturgical Press, Collegeville MN 56321; send submissions to: 1884 Randolph, St. Paul MN 55105, poetry editor Sister Mary Virginia Micka, C.S.J. *Sisters Today* has been published for about 60 years. Though it is a Roman Catholic magazine, **poetry may be on any topic, but "should clearly be *poems*, not simply *statements* or *prayers*." They want "short poems (not over 25 lines) using clean, fresh images and appealing to the reader's feelings in a compelling way." They do not want poetry that depends "heavily on rhyme and on 'tricks' such as excessive capitalization, manipulation of spacing, etc."** *ST*, appearing 6 times/year, is 80 pgs., 6×9, saddle-stapled, professionally printed with matte card cover. They receive about 50 poems/month, accept about 6. Press run is 9,000 for 8,500 subscribers. Subscription: $16 US; $18 foreign. **Sample postpaid: $3 (Send to: Sister Mary Anthony Wagner, O.S.B., Editor, *Sisters Today*, St. Benedict's Convent, St. Joseph MN 56374). Submit 3-5 poems at a time. No simultaneous submissions. Original poems much preferred. They require "each poem typed on a separate standard-size typing sheet, and each page must carry complete legal name, address and social security number typed in the upper right corner." Send SASE to poetry editor at St. Paul, MN address (above) for guidelines. Reports within 1-2 months, 6-12 months until publication. Pays $10/poem and 2 copies. Buys first rights.**

SIVULLINEN (II), Kaarelantie 86 B 28, 00420 Helsinki, Finland, founded 1985, editor Jouni Waarakangas, is a biannual publication of drawings, graphics, poems and short stories—**open to all kinds of poetry.** They have published poetry by Bob Z, Belinda Subraman and Paul Weinman. As a sample we selected these lines from "written with a short sword" by C. Ra McGuirt:

> *i didn't come here*
> *to kill your*
> *god.*
>
> *i only brought you*
> *his suicide*
> *note.*
>
> *try to kill*
> *the messenger*
>
> *if you*
> *can.*

The editor says *Sivullinen* is offset and varies between 32-40 pgs., A4 size and 28 pgs., A5 size. They accept about 20% of poetry received. Press run is 500. **Sample postpaid: $2-3. Submit 3-5 poems at a time. Previously published poems and simultaneous submissions OK.** Time between acceptance and publication is 3 months to a year. **Reports in 3-10 weeks. Pays 1 copy.**

SKYLARK (I, II, IV-Themes), Purdue University Calumet, 2200 169th St., Hammond IN 46323, phone (219)989-2262, founded 1972, editor Pamela Hunter, is "a fine arts annual, **one section (about 25 pages) of which is devoted to a special theme.**" They are looking for **"fresh voices, original images, concise presentation and honesty; poems up to 30 lines; narrative poems to 75 lines. No horror, nothing extremely religious, no pornography."** They have recently published poetry by Mary Blinn, Amy England, Edward Lynskey and Michael Skau. As a sample the editor selected these lines from "Physics" by Francine Witte:

> *On one of those nights that gives loneliness*
> *its name, even the rain is confused,*
> *runs wrong down a one-way street.*
> *No one is saying what it might have done*
> *different.*

Skylark is 100 pgs., magazine-sized, professionally printed, with matte card cover. Press run is 500-800 for 50 subscriptions of which 12 are libraries. Single copy: $7. **Sample postpaid: $5. Submit 3-5 poems at a time. "Typed or computer printout manuscripts OK. No simultaneous submissions. Inquire (with SASE) as to annual theme for special section." The theme for 1996 is "Anniversaries." Do not submit mss between June 1 and November 1. Reports in 4 months. Pays 1 copy. Acquires first rights. Editor may encourage rejected but promising writers.** She says she would like to receive "poems with better editing, greater coordination of form and content, and sharper, more original imagery."

SLANT: A JOURNAL OF POETRY (II), Box 5063, University of Central Arkansas, Conway AR 72035, phone (501)450-5107, founded 1987, editor James Fowler, is an annual using *only* poetry. They use **"traditional and 'modern' poetry, even experimental, moderate length, any subject on approval of Board of Readers; purpose is to publish a journal of fine poetry from all regions of the United States. No haiku, no translations."** They have recently published poetry by Michael Carrino, John McKernan and Natalie Safir. As a sample the editor selected these lines from "At the Laurel & Hardy Festival" by Sherman Pearl:

> *Murder was the first sight gag—*
> *a club swung at flies, an innocent head*
> *batted across the cave.*
> *Some feast-fattened genius must have*
> *seen through the blood, found*
> *something funny in the victim's*
> *startled expression.*

Slant is 125 pgs., professionally printed on quality stock, flat-spined, with matte card cover. They publish about 70-80 poems of the 1,400 received each year. Press run is 250 for 70-100 subscribers. **Sample postpaid: $10. Submit no more than 5 poems of moderate length. "Put name and address top of each page." No simultaneous submissions or previously published poems. Editor comments on rejections "on occasion." Allow 3-4 months from November 15 deadline for response. Pays 1 copy.** The editor says, "I would like to see more formal verse."

‡THE SLATE (II), P.O. Box 581189, Minneapolis MN 55458-1189, founded 1994, first issue published in April of 1995, appears 3 times/year and is designed "to promote the written word as an art form."

The editors have no restrictions regarding form, length or subject of poetry. They say *The Slate* is 100 pgs., 6×9, perfect-bound. Press run is 1,500. No simultaneous submissions. All four editors read everything and then discuss it. Often comments on rejections. Send SASE for guidelines. Pays 2 copies. Acquires all rights. Returns rights "when our next issue comes out."

SLATE & STYLE (IV-Specialized: blind writers), Dept. PM, 2704 Beach Dr., Merrick NY 11566, phone (516)868-8718, fax (516)868-9076, editor Loraine Stayer, is a **quarterly for blind writers available on cassette, in large print and Braille,** "including articles of interest to blind writers, resources for blind writers. Membership/subscription $5 per year, all formats. Division of the National Federation of the Blind." **Poems may be "5-35 lines. Prefer contributors to be blind writers, or at least writers by profession or inclination, but prefer poems *not* about blindness. No obscenities. Will consider all forms of poetry including haiku. Interested in new talent."** They have published poetry by Stephanie Pieck, Louise Hope Bristow, Janet Wolff and Ken Volonte. As a sample we selected these lines from "Milkshakes" by Nancy Scott:

> *I count the calories;*
> *discount that I am forty.*
> *When I was twenty, I wanted*
> *January's hot chocolate.*
> *Now there is July fire*
> *that can only be quenched*
> *by the cold.*

The print version is magazine-sized, 28-32 pgs., stapled, with a fiction and poetry section. Press run is 200 for 160 subscribers of which 4-5 are libraries. Subscription: $5/year. **Sample postpaid: $2.50. No simultaneous submissions or previously published poems. Submit 3 poems once or twice a year. Cover letter preferred. "On occasion we receive poems in Braille. I prefer print, since Braille slows me down. Typed is best." Do not submit mss in July. Editor comments on rejections "if requested." Send SASE for guidelines. Reports in "2 weeks if I like it." Pays 1 copy.** Reviews books of poetry. Open to unsolicited reviews. Poets may also send books for review consideration. They offer an annual poetry contest. Entry fee: $5/poem. Deadline: May 1. Write for details. Loraine Stayer says, "Poetry is one of the toughest ways to express oneself, yet ought to be the easiest to read. Anything that looks simple is the result of much work."

SLIGHTLY WEST (I), CAB 320, The Evergreen State College, Olympia WA 98505, phone (206)866-6000, ext. 6879, e-mail west@elwha.evergreen.edu, founded 1985, coordinators Ethan Salter and Brian Nadal, is a biannual designed "to give a boost to new or struggling writers and to promote art throughout the community." **They are open to all types, forms and styles of poetry. "No fluff. We are taking only the upper crust of submissions."** They have recently published poetry by Errol Miller, Douglas S. Johnson, Martin Kitch and Mahdy Y. Khaiyat. As a sample the editors selected these lines from "Early July 5th" by Gay Brewer:

> *Mosquitoes*
> *big as quarters*
> *rise from*
> *the marsh grass*
>
> *The air smells*
> *of sulfur*
>
> *Today slouches*
> *toward*
> *a short week*
>
> *At the door*
> *your arms*
> *decorated in blood*

The editors say *SW* is 50-60 pgs., 7¼×10½, saddle-stitched with cover and inside artwork. They receive 700-1,000 submissions a year, accept approximately 15%. Press run is 1,500 for 55 subscribers of which 5 are libraries; 1,000 distributed free to local community. Subscription: $5. **Sample postpaid: $2.50. Submit 3 poems at a time. Previously published poems and simultaneous submissions OK. Cover letter required. "They allow the poet to become more recognizable, not just a poem but a person behind the words." Reads submissions September 10 through June 17 only. "We have a selections board of 5-10 poets and writers who critique and comment on submissions." Often comments on rejections. Send SASE for guidelines. Reports in 2-3 months. Pays 1 copy. Acquires one-time rights.** The editors say, "We have been established for 10 years as just a 'school' magazine. Currently we are upgrading our requirements for poetry submissions. We encourage beginners to send poetry. We will return manuscripts with comments only if SASE enclosed."

SLIPSTREAM; SLIPSTREAM AUDIO CASSETTES (II, IV-Themes), Box 2071, New Market Station, Niagara Falls NY 14301, phone (716)282-2616 (after 5pm, EST), founded 1980, poetry editors Dan Sicoli, Robert Borgatti and Livio Farallo. *Slipstream* is a "small press literary mag, that is about 90% poetry and 10% prose, some artwork. The editors like **new work with contemporary urban flavor. Writing must have a cutting edge to get our attention. We like to keep an open forum, any length, subject, style. Best to see a sample to get a feel. Like city stuff as opposed to country. Like poetry that springs from the gut, screams from dark alleys, inspired by experience.**" No "**pastoral, religious, traditional, rhyming**" **poetry.** They have recently published poetry by Fred Voss, Peter Pereira, Gerald Locklin, Alan Catlin, Charles Bukowski, Paul Dilsaver, Jennifer Olds, Marael Johnson, Denise Duhamel and M. Scott Douglass. As a sample the editors selected these lines from "If Walt Whitman Were Homeless Today" by Frank Van Zant:

> *He would become the bag-prophet from Forest Park,*
> *the chatterbeard who hangs out in front of our building on Metropolitan,*
> *who leans on the light post amid the oils and smells of summer,*
> *who coughs oysters, spits on the* Newsday *machine, and speaks to us all,*
> *all* baffled, exiled, ragged, gaunt.

Slipstream appears 1-2 times a year in a $7 \times 8\frac{1}{2}$ format, 128 pgs., professionally printed, saddle-stapled, using b&w photos and graphics. It contains mostly free verse, some stanza patterns. They receive over 2,500 submissions of poetry/year, use less than 10%. Press run is 300 for 200 subscribers of which 10 are libraries. Subscription: $8.50/2 issues. **Sample postpaid: $5. Editor sometimes comments on rejections. Publishes theme issues. "Reading for an issue on 'Black and Blue' through 1995." Send SASE for guidelines and upcoming themes. Reports in 2-8 weeks, "if SASE included." Pays copies. Also produces an audio cassette series that unfortunately will be inactive through 1996. Query for current needs.** Annual chapbook contest has December 1 deadline. Reading fee: $10. Submit up to 40 pgs. of poetry, any style, previously published work OK with acknowledgments. Winner receives $500 and 50 copies. All entrants receive copy of winning chapbook and an issue of the magazine. Past winners have included Gerald Locklin, Serena Fusek, Robert Cooperman, Kurt Nimmo, David Chorlton, Richard Amidon and Sherman Alexie. Dan Sicoli advises, "Do not waste time submitting your work 'blindly.' Sample issues from the small press first to determine which ones would be most receptive to your work."

SMALL POND MAGAZINE OF LITERATURE (II), P.O. Box 664, Stratford CT 06497, phone (203)378-4066, founded 1964, editor Napoleon St. Cyr, a literary triquarterly that features poetry . . . "and anything else the editor feels is original, important." Poetry can be **"any style, form, topic, except haiku, so long as it is deemed good, but limit of about 100 lines." Napoleon St. Cyr wants "nothing about cats, pets, flowers, butterflies, etc. Generally nothing under 8 lines."** Although he calls it name-dropping, he "reluctantly" provided the names of Marvin Soloman, Marilyn Johnson, Richard Kostelanetz, Fritz Hamilton and Emilie Glen as poets published. The magazine is digest-sized, offset from typescript on off-white paper, 40 pgs. with matte card cover, saddle-stapled, artwork both on cover and inside. Circulation is 300, of which about a third go to libraries. Subscription: $9 (for 3 issues). **Sample postpaid: $2.50 for a random selection, $3 current. Guidelines are available in each issue. The editor says he doesn't want 60 pages of anything; "dozen pages of poems max." Name and address on each page. No previously published poems or simultaneous submissions. Brief cover letter preferred. He reports on submissions in 10-45 days (longer in summer), and publication is within 3-18 months. Pays 2 copies. Acquires all rights. Returns rights with written request including stated use. "One-time use per request."** Staff reviews books of poetry. Send books for review consideration. All styles and forms are welcome here. The editor usually responds quickly, often with comments to guide poets whose work interests him. He says, "I would like to receive more good surreal verse."

‡SMELLFEAST (I), 2644 N. Maroa #B, Fresno CA 93704, founded 1994, editors Mark Begley and Staven Bruce, is a poetry publication appearing 3 times a year. **"No specifications as to form, length or style. We'll look at just about anything. Narrative free verse with a personal feel seems to work well for us. But experimental, Dada, surreal, concrete or something new will be considered as well. Nothing blatantly anti-religious. No rhyme. No erotica. Sex poems are usually only interesting to the poet!"** They have recently published poetry by Steve Richmond, Gerald Locklin, Judson Crews and Dan Nielsen as well as "many great newcomers." *smellfeast* is 40-50 pgs., $5\frac{1}{2} \times 8\frac{1}{2}$, typeset on Pagemaker and saddle-stapled with linen finish cover stock and b&w art. Press run is 200 for 20 subscribers, 20 shelf sales. Subscription: $7.50. **Sample postpaid: $3 (guidelines inside). Make**

Market categories: (I) Beginning; (II) General; (III) Limited; (IV) Specialized; (V) Closed.

checks payable to Mark Begley. Submit 3-5 poems at a time. No previously published poems or simultaneous submissions. "A cover letter is not required but is looked upon with much gratitude." Often comments on rejections. Reports in up to 6 months, usually sooner. Pays 1 copy. Acquires first North American serial rights. They plan to also publish occasional chapbooks as issues of the magazine. Chapbooks and any broadsides will be published by invitation only. The editors' advice? "Deluge the scene with your work. Send everywhere, as much as possible. Discover who seems supportive and/or genuine. Lit mags are a dime-a-dozen; choose ones to support that seem to be devoted to craft, not to schools. We'd like to see those poems that the writer loves but can't get accepted elsewhere."

GIBBS SMITH, PUBLISHER; PEREGRINE SMITH POETRY COMPETITION (II), P.O. Box 667, Layton UT 84041, founded 1971, poetry series established 1988, poetry editor Dawn Valentine Hadlock. **They want "serious, contemporary poetry of merit."** They have published books of poetry by David Huddle and Carol Frost. Books are selected for publication through competition for the Peregrine Smith Poetry Prize of $500 plus publication. **Entries are received in April only and require a $15 reading fee and SASE. Mss should be 48-64 typewritten pgs. Send SASE for complete guidelines.** The winner of the 1994 contest was Angie Estes's *The Uses of Passion*. The judge and general editor for the series is Christopher Merrill.

THE SMITH; THE GENERALIST PAPERS (II), 69 Joralemon St., Brooklyn NY 11201, founded 1964, editor Harry Smith, publishes 3 to 5 books yearly. They have published poetry by Menke Katz, Lloyd Van Brunt, Richard Nason, Glenna Luschei and Karen Swenson. As a sample the editor selected these lines from "Hawk Forever in Mid-Dive" in Lance Lee's *Wrestling with the Angel*:

> Her feet on the patio are leaves blown
> over flagstones. Aimed at her head,
> beak thrust out wings angled severely
> a hawk hangs frozen in mid-air,
> fanned to permanent fire in her sky.

"Send 3-6 poem sampling with query. No jingles, no standard academic verse. The decision process is relatively slow—about three months—as many mss are offered. Readers' reports are often passed along and the editor often comments." Always sends prepublication galleys. Pays 15% royalties, $500 advance, 10 copies. Write for catalog (free) or send $2 for a "slightly irregular" book ("with bumped corners or a little dust"). *The Generalist Papers*, appearing 6 times/year, consists of lively critical commentaries on contemporary writing—more candor than you will find in most reviews. Subscription: $12. **Sample postpaid: $2.** Harry Smith received the 1992 Poor Richard Award, a lifetime achievement award for distinguished contribution to small press publishing from the Small Press Center. He advises, "Revert to earlier models. *Avoid* university wordshops where there are standard recent models leading to standard mod verse. A close reading of *The Pearl Poet* will be more nourishing than all the asparagus of John Ashbery or Robert Bly."

SMITHS KNOLL (I, II), 49 Church Rd., Little Glemham, Woodbridge, Suffolk IP13 0BJ England, founded 1991, co-editors Roy Blackman and Michael Laskey, is a magazine appearing 3 times a year. They look for **poetry with honesty, depth of feeling, lucidity and craft.** As a sample the editors selected this poem by James Keery:

> Mum was in two minds, but in the end she didn't go
> To the Peace Movement demonstration outside BNFL
> About plutonium waste going to the states for missiles,
> Because she was afraid of embarrassing Dad—
> Though according to him she should have gone ahead—
> He reckoned he might have got his early retirement.

The editors say it is 60 pgs., A5, offset-litho, perfect-bound, with card cover. They receive 3,500-4,000 poems a year, "accept about one in twenty-four." Press run is 400 for 250 subscribers. Single copy: £3.50; subscription: £9 for 3 issues (outside UK). **Submit 5 poems at a time. "We would consider poems previously published in magazines outside the U.K." No simultaneous submissions. Poems only. Doesn't commission work. "Cover letters should be brief: name, address, date, number of poems sent (or titles). We don't want life histories or complete publishing successes or what the poems are about. Constructive criticism of rejections where possible."** Tries to report within 1 month (outside UK). Pays £5 plus 1 copy/poem.

SNAKE NATION REVIEW; SNAKE NATION PRESS (II), 110 W. Force St., #2, Valdosta GA 31601, phone (912)249-8334, founded 1989, editor Roberta George, appears 4 times a year (2 contest issues, 2 noncontest issues). **"Any form, length of 60 lines or less."** They have recently published poetry by Hunt Hawkins, Penelope Schott and David Kirby. The handsome magazine is 100 pgs., 6×9, flat-spined with matte card cover. Press run is 1,500 for 300 subscribers of which 25 are libraries. Subscription: $20. **Sample postpaid: $6. Sometimes comments on submissions. Send SASE for guidelines.**

Reports in 3 months. Pays $10 plus 2 copies. Deadlines: January 1 and June 1. Acquires first rights. The review sponsors biannual contests with prizes of $100, $75 and $50 for the top three winners. Others published in contest issues receive $10. Entry fee: $1/poem. Deadlines: April 1 and September 1. Poets published in noncontest issues are eligible for the Editor's Choice Award. Prize of $100 is given to the top poem. Snake Nation Press publishes books of poetry. Submit 60-page ms with SASE. The press also sponsors the Violet Reed Haas Poetry Prize which awards $500, 50 copies and distribution to the winning book ms. For contest consideration, submit 75-page ms with $10 entry fee. Deadline: April 15, 1996.

SNAKE RIVER REFLECTIONS (II), 1863 Bitterroot Dr., Twin Falls ID 83301, phone (208)734-0746, e-mail wjan@aol.com, appears 10 times a year using **short poems, up to 30 lines, any topic.** As a sample we selected these lines from "The Wall" by C. David Hay:

> *Could tears but wash the pain away*
> *And heal a nation's scar,*
> *That men may find a better way*
> *Than futile acts of war.*
>
> *Pray their death was not in vain—*
> *A lesson to recall;*
> *A future world without the need*
> *Of names upon a Wall.*

It is 12 pgs., stapled on the side. Press run is 100-300. Subscription: $9.50/10 issues. **Sample postpaid: 30¢. Submit 20-25 poems maximum at a time. No previously published poems or simultaneous submissions. Cover letter encouraged. Send SASE for guidelines. Pays 1 copy. Acquires first North American serial rights.** Reviews books of poetry. Send books for review consideration to editor William White.

SNOWY EGRET (II, IV-Nature), P.O. Box 9, Bowling Green IN 47833, founded 1922 by Humphrey A. Olsen, editor Philip Repp. **They want poetry that is "nature-oriented: poetry that celebrates the abundance and beauty of nature or explores the interconnections between nature and the human psyche."** As a sample of published poetry they selected the opening lines of "In a Climax Forest" by Conrad Hilberry:

> *The wooden past grows larger, I grow less*
> *and less convincing in this sullen air*
> *that wants a wind to stir its emptiness.*

Snowy Egret appears twice a year in a 48-page, magazine-sized format, offset, saddle-stapled, with original graphics. Of 500 poems received they accept about 20. Their press run is 800 for 500 subscribers of which 50 are libraries. **Sample postpaid: $8. Send #10 SASE for writer's guidelines. Reports in 1 month. Always sends prepublication galleys. Pays $4/poem or $4/page plus 2 copies. Buys first North American or reprint rights.** Open to unsolicited reviews. Poets may also send books for review consideration.

SOCIAL ANARCHISM (IV-Political, social issues, women/feminism), 2743 Maryland Ave., Baltimore MD 21218, phone (410)243-6987, founded (Vacant Lots Press) 1980, poetry editor Howard J. Ehrlich, is a biannual using about 6 pgs. of poetry in each issue which **"represents a political or social commentary that is congruent with a nonviolent anarchist, antiauthoritarian and feminist perspective."** They have published poetry by Earl Coleman, John Sokol, E.C. Archibeque, Richard Ballon, Barbara F. Stout, Deirdre V. Lovecky, Joel Lewis and Steven Hill. As a sample we selected these lines from "The Painted Soldier" by Lynn Olson:

> *He lay flat on the dirt road*
> *flat where the thick, wide tires of our trucks*
> *had pressed him out thin against the dirt road*
> *flat where the wide treads of our tanks*
> *had pressed him out thinner on the dirt road. . . .*

SA is 112 pgs., digest-sized. Print run is 1,500. **Sample postpaid: $4. Submit up to 5 poems at a time. Considers simultaneous submissions. Cover letter with short (3-sentence) bio required. Reports in 4-6 weeks. Pays 3 copies.** Query regarding book reviews.

THE SOCIETY OF AMERICAN POETS (SOAP); IN HIS STEPS PUBLISHING COMPANY; THE POET'S PEN (I, IV-Religious, membership), P.O. Box 85, Tifton GA 31793, phone (912)382-5377, founded 1984, editor Dr. Charles E. Cravey. *The Poet's Pen* is a literary quarterly of poetry and short stories. In His Steps publishes religious and other books and publishes music for the commercial record market. **"Open to all styles of poetry and prose—both religious and secular. No gross or 'X-rated' poetry without taste or character."** They have published poetry by Carlton Cook, Lessie Perry and Joann Saulino. As a sample the editor selected these lines from "Grapevine" by Carol Ann Lindsay:

The withered winter vine
of naked, knotted branches
nailed to man-made fences,
chains the cursing crosses to stolid, silent rows
that betray the bitter sip
of hollow human ways.

The Poet's Pen uses **poetry primarily by members and subscribers.** (Membership: $20/year.) **Submit 3 poems at a time, include name and address on each page. "Submissions or inquiries will not be responded to without a SASE. We do stress originality and have each new poet and/or subscriber sign a waiver form verifying originality." Simultaneous submissions OK; previously published poems OK, if permission from previous publisher is included. Publishes seasonal/theme issues. Send SASE for upcoming themes. Sometimes sends prepublication galleys. Query for book publication. 60/40 split of pay. Editor "most certainly" comments on rejections.** Sponsors several contests each quarter which total $250-500 in cash awards. Editor's Choice Awards each quarter, prizes $25, $15 and $10. President's Award for Superior Choice has a prize of $50; deadline is November 1. They also publish a quarterly anthology that has poetry competitions in several categories with prizes of $25-100. The editor says, "We're looking for poets who wish to unite in fellowship with our growing family of poets nationwide. We currently have over 850 poets and are one of the nation's largest societies, yet small enough and family operated to give each of our poets individual attention and pointers."

SOJOURNERS (IV-Religious, political), 2401 15th St. NW, Washington DC 20009, phone (202)328-8842, fax (202)328-8757, founded 1975, poetry editor Rose Berger, appears 6 times/year, "with approximately 40,000 subscribers. **We focus on faith, politics and culture from a radical Christian perspective. We publish 1-3 poems/month depending on length. All poems must be original and unpublished. We look for seasoned, well-crafted poetry that reflects the issues and perspectives covered in our magazine. Poetry using non-inclusive language (any racist, sexist, homophobic poetry) will not be accepted."** As a sample the editor selected these lines by David Abrams:

An eagle against a clear sky,
A snake coming off a rock,
A skiff in the center of a lake,
And the Spirit slipping into bodies.

The editor describes *Sojourners* as 52 pgs., offset printing. It appears monthly except that there is one issue for August/September and February/March. Of 400 poems received/year, they publish 8-10. Press run is 50,000 for 40,000 subscribers of which 500 are libraries, 2,000 shelf sales. Subscription: $30. **Sample postpaid: $3.95. Submit no more than 3 poems at a time. Cover letter with brief bio required. Editor comments on submissions "sometimes." Publishes theme issues. Send SASE for guidelines and upcoming themes. Reports in 4-6 weeks. Pays $15-25/poem plus 5 copies. "We assume permission to grant reprints unless the author requests otherwise."** Staff reviews books of poetry in 600 words, single or multi-book format.

SOLEIL PRESS (IV-Ethnic), Box 452, RFD 1, Lisbon Falls ME 04252, phone (207)353-5454, founded 1988, contact Denis Ledoux, publishes and distributes **writing by and about Franco-Americans (Americans of French-Canadian and Acadian descent)** in chapbooks and paperbacks. **Not interested in the continental French experience. Submit sample poems with cover letter noting how the material is Franco-North American. Pays copies.**

SOLO FLYER; SPARE CHANGE POETRY PRESS (IV-Regional), 2115 Clearview NE, Massillon OH 44646, Spare Change Poetry Press founded 1979, editor David B. McCoy. *Solo Flyer* is a 4-page flyer appearing 2-5 times/year featuring the work of a single poet in each issue. **"Submissions limited to Ohio poets."** They want **poetry using punctuation and capitalization. "Like to see poems with a common theme."** As a sample the editor selected "Absences" by Ruth V. Tams-Fuquen:

Wordless
we walked that hotel's midnight garden.
The blossom you laid on my palm

spoke
for the song you hummed,

suggested
the words you chose
not to sing.

The flyers are folded 8½×11 sheets of colored paper. **Sample free with #10 SASE. Previously published material OK. Pays 20-25 copies.** The editor says, "Submissions without SASE are not read."

‡**SONOMA MANDALA (II)**, c/o English Dept., Sonoma State University, Rohnert Park CA 94928, phone (707)664-3902, e-mail Elizabeth.Herron@sonoma.edu, founded 1973, faculty advisor Elizabeth Herron, is an annual literary review that publishes poetry, short fiction and some artwork. They are **"open to all styles. Preferably not over two pages."** They have published poetry by Lucille Clifton, Stephen Torre, Lyn Lifshin, Simon Perchik, Etheridge Knight and Maureen Hurley. As a sample the editor selected these lines (poet unidentified):

> *There are people who are combustible, people that is*
> *who spontaneously burst into flames. We know this by*
> *their remains, the manner in which the body has been*
> *consumed. Always there is a small blackened area*

She says *Sonoma Mandala* is 140 pgs., typeset, perfect-bound, no ads. They receive over 600 mss a year, accept approximately 10-15%. Press run is 500 for 10 subscribers of which 6 are libraries, 300 shelf sales. Subscription: $6. **Sample postpaid: $3. No previously published poems; simultaneous submissions OK. "Brief bio helps." Reads submissions August 1 through November 15 only. Comments on rejections "whenever possible." Send SASE for guidelines. Reports in 4-6 months. Pays 2 copies. Acquires first North American serial rights.** Elizabeth Herron says, "We are open to all schools of thought/poetics and seek fresh, original writing with life-affirming values."

SONORA REVIEW (II), Dept. of English, University of Arizona, Tucson AZ 85721, phone (602)626-8383 or 621-1836, founded 1980, address all work to Poetry Editor, is a semiannual literary journal that publishes "non-genre" fiction and poetry. **The editors want "quality poetry, literary concerns. Translations welcome. No dull, well-crafted but passionless poetry or swooping and universal sentiment. Experimental work welcome."** They have published poetry by Jane Miller, Christopher Davis, Barbara Cully and Rosmarie Waldrop. As a sample, the editors chose the following lines by Joshua Clover:

> *Across the tracks her scalp took on the feel*
> *of a cigarette foil's papered side. Snow*
> *hair & boots. The most wasted man around*
> *would persuade his lover to waste him even more*
> *in the pause I woke into.*

Sonora Review is a handsome magazine, 130 pgs., 6×9, professionally printed on heavy off-white stock, flat-spined, with 2-color glossy card cover. Recent issues have tended to include lyric and narrative free·verse, with some metered poetry, translations and sequences rounding out selections. Circulation is 650, of which 250 are subscriptions and 45 go to libraries. Subscription: $12/year, $20/2 years. **Back issue available for $5 postpaid. Poets should submit typed copy; simultaneous submissions OK. "Brief cover letter helpful but optional." Publishes theme issues. Send SASE for upcoming themes. Reporting time is 2 months and time to publication 6 months. Sometimes sends prepublication galleys. Pays 2 copies.** Send books for review consideration. The magazine also sponsors annual poetry awards. Send #10 SASE for deadlines and guidelines. In the past, contributors to *Sonora Review* have been listed in *Best of the West*, *Pushcart Prize*, *O. Henry* and *Best American Poetry* anthologies.

SOPHOMORE JINX (I, II), P.O. Box 770728, Woodside NY 11377-0728, phone (718)507-8360, e-mail sophjinx@aol.com, founded 1993, editors Anne-Marie Mooney and Anthony Rutella, Jr., is a quarterly poetry publication especially open to beginners. **"We would like to see traditional forms as well as free verse and conventional subjects as well as experimental material. Nothing more than 60 lines. No vulgarity."** As for a sample, they say, "We do not feel that any one of our poems/poets exemplifies what we are looking for at *Sophomore Jinx*. We have published poems ranging from very serious to humorous and free verse to traditional forms." *SJ* is about 80 pgs., 5½×8½, desktop-published and saddle-stapled with paper cover. Subscription: $15 for 1 year, $25 for 2 years. **Sample postpaid: $5. Please submit no more than 3 poems at a time." No previously published poems; simultaneous submissions OK. Cover letter required. No handwritten submissions.** Time between acceptance and publication is 3-6 months. **Send SASE for guidelines. Reports within 1 month. Each issue the authors of the top 3 poems (chosen by the editors) are awarded 1 copy and prizes of $20, $15 and $10, respectively. Other contributors must order a copy/subscription if they would like to see their work in print.** Sponsors the Beginner's Luck contest for unpublished poems of 14 lines or less (including space between lines and stanzas). $3 entry fee includes copy of contest issue. Top 3 winners receive $50, $30 and $20, respectively. Write for details. The editors add, "We encourage our submitters to tell us about themselves in their cover letter. We don't mean a formal bio—we want to know who you are so that we can see where you're coming from. And we like to be personal in our replies."

SOUNDINGS EAST (II), Salem State College, Salem MA 01970, phone (508)741-6000 ext. 2403 or 741-6270, founded 1978, "*SE* is published by the students of Salem State College. We accept short fiction and **contemporary poetry.** Purpose is to promote poetry and fiction in the college and beyond its environs. Although our standards are extremely high, **we publish both established and previously unpublished writers and artists. All forms of poetry welcome."** *SE* appears twice a year, 64 pgs., digest-sized, flat-spined, b&w drawings and photos, glossy card cover with b&w photo. They receive about 500 submissions/year, use 40-50. Press run is 2,000 for 120 subscribers of which 35 are libraries. Subscription: $6/year. **Sample postpaid: $3. Submit 5 poems at a time. Simultaneous submissions OK. When submitting simultaneous submissions, write a cover letter informing the editors. Be prompt when notifying *SE* that the work(s) was accepted elsewhere. Reads submissions September 1 through April 20 only. Fall deadline: November 20; spring: April 20. Reports within 1-4 months. Pays 2 copies. Rights revert to author upon publication.** "We occasionally, when funding allows, publish an extra spring issue which features only poetry, fiction and artwork by Salem State College students."

SOUTH ASH PRESS (I, II), 2311 E. Indian School Rd., Phoenix AZ 85016, founded 1991, publisher Chuck Hadd Jr., is a monthly poetry magazine sustained and distributed by community advertisers. **They want "well-crafted poems by beginning and established poets. 75 lines maximum."** They have published poetry by Denis Johnson. As a sample the publisher selected these lines from "Traveling Between Storms" by Albino Carrillo:

> *Thunder is what wakes us all,*
> *the taste like salt and meat*
> *lingering as we pull on our clothes.*
> *And just before the evening's spent*
> *to wander with the gray constellations.*
> *To know this blackness, to know it well.*

South Ash Press is 12 pgs., magazine-sized, saddle-stapled with card cover with b&w photo, numerous ads on same pages as poems. They receive about 1,500 poems a year, publish about 250. Each issue includes a number of poems by a "Featured Poet." Press run is 2,000, distributed free through advertisers. Subscription: $20/year. **Sample postpaid: $2. Submit 1-5 poems at a time. One poem to a page including name and address. No previously published poems; simultaneous submissions OK. "Three people select submissions. An acceptance by any one of them gets poem included. While we are glad to see work by beginners, we do not provide critiques and/or advice." Reports in 3-4 months. Pays 1 copy. Acquires first rights.**

SOUTH CAROLINA REVIEW (II), English Dept., Clemson University, Clemson SC 29634-1503, phone (803)656-5404 or 656-3457, fax (803)656-1345, founded 1968, managing editor Elizabeth Boleman-Herring, is a biannual literary magazine "recognized by the *New York Quarterly* as one of the top 20 of this type." They will consider **"any kind of poetry as long as it's good. No stale metaphors, uncertain rhythms or lack of line integrity. Interested in seeing more traditional forms. Format should be according to new MLA Stylesheet."** They have published poetry by Pattiann Rogers, J.W. Rivers and Claire Bateman. It is 200 pgs., 6×9, flat-spined, professionally printed and uses about 8-10 pgs. of poetry in each issue. Reviews of recent issues back up editorial claims that all styles and forms are welcome; moreover, poems were accessible and well-executed, too. Circulation is 600, for 400 subscribers of which 250 are libraries. They receive about 1,000 unsolicited submissions of poetry/year, use 10, have a 2-year backlog. **Sample postpaid: $10. Submit 3-10 poems at a time in an "8×10 manila envelope so poems aren't creased." No previously published poems or simultaneous submissions. "Editor prefers a chatty, personal cover letter plus a list of publishing credits." Do not submit during June, July, August or December. Publishes theme issues. Themes for Fall 1995 and Spring 1996 are a women's issue and Virginia Woolf, respectively. Send SASE for upcoming themes. Reports in 6-9 months. Pays copies.** Staff reviews books of poetry.

SOUTH DAKOTA REVIEW (II, IV-Regional, themes), University of South Dakota, Vermillion SD 57069, phone (605)677-5229 or 677-5966, founded 1963, editor John R. Milton, is a "literary quarterly publishing poetry, fiction, criticism, essays. **When material warrants, an emphasis on the American West; writers from the West; Western places or subjects; frequent issues with no geographical emphasis; periodic special issues on one theme, or one place or one writer. Looking for originality, some kind of sophistication, significance, craft—i.e., professional work. Nothing confessional, purely descriptive, too filled with self-importance."** They use 6-10 poems/issue, "receive tons, it seems." Press run is 650-900 for 450 subscribers of which half are libraries. Subscription: $15/year, $25/2 years. **Sample postpaid: $4. Editor comments on submissions "rarely." Reports in 1-12 weeks. Pays 1 copy/page. Acquires first and reprint rights.** They have a distinct bias against personal or confessional poems, and generally publish free verse with a strong sense of place, a strong voice and a universal theme. Read the magazine—it's attractive and well-edited—to get a feel for the type of poetry that succeeds here. Milton advises, "Find universal meaning in the regional. Avoid constant 'I' personal experiences that are not of interest to anyone else. Learn to be less self-centered and more objective."

‡**SOUTH HEAD PRESS; POETRY AUSTRALIA (II)**, Market Place, Berrima, NSW 2577 Australia, founded 1964, poetry editor John Millett. "We have published 132 issues of *Poetry Australia* (5-6 per year), minimum of 80 pgs. per issue, and many books of poetry." 30-50 poets appear in each issue of *PA*. As a sample here are the first two (of 8) stanzas of "Right Winger" by David Ray:

> *1*
>
> *On planes*
> *he always sat*
> *over the right wing.*
> *2*
> *When he went hunting*
> *he always shot*
> *the duck in the left wing.*

PA is 6×9¾, professionally printed, flat-spined with glossy card cover. Single copy: $10. They invite **"unpublished verse in English from writers in Australia and abroad. Mss should be typed double-spaced on one side of paper with name and address on reverse side. Overseas contributors are advised that sufficient money for return postage should accompany poems. Stamps of one country are not legal tender in another." Pays $10 or 1 year's subscription. Overseas poets are paid in copies. South Head Press will consider submissions for book publication. Query with 3 samples. They pay advance and copies. Editor sometimes comments on rejections.** There is a list of books of poetry they have published in *Poetry Australia*, which serves as their catalog. The editor advises, "Read all you can of the best that has been published in the last 20 years. Include *PA, Hudson Review*, etc."

THE SOUTHERN CALIFORNIA ANTHOLOGY; ANN STANFORD POETRY PRIZES (III), c/o Master of Professional Writing Program, WPH 404, University of Southern California, Los Angeles CA 90089-4034, phone (213)740-3252, founded 1983, is an "annual literary review of serious contemporary poetry and fiction. **Very open to all subject matters except pornography. Any form, style OK."** They have published poetry by Robert Bly, John Updike, Denise Levertov and Peter Viereck. As a sample the editor selected these lines from "The Rivers of Paris" by James Ragan:

> *The boulevards are the rivers wind owes*
> *to the eyes' reflections, light*
> *to the panes transparent*
> *in the domes of air wind weaves along Sacre Coeur*

The anthology is 144 pgs., digest-sized, perfect-bound, with a semi-glossy color cover featuring one art piece. A fine selection of poems distinguish this journal, and it has an excellent reputation, well-deserved. The downside, if it has one, concerns limited space for newcomers. Circulation is 1,500, 50% going to subscribers of which 50% are libraries. 30% are for shelf sales. **Sample postpaid: $5.95. No simultaneous submissions or previously published poems. Submit 3-5 poems between September 1 and January 1. All decisions made by mid-February. Send SASE for guidelines. Reports in 4 months. Pays 3 copies. Acquires all rights.** The Ann Stanford Poetry Prizes ($750, $250 and $100) have an April 15 deadline, $10 fee (5 poem limit), for unpublished poems. Include cover sheet with name, address and titles and SASE for contest results. All entries are considered for publication, and all entrants receive a copy of *SCA*.

SOUTHERN HUMANITIES REVIEW; THEODORE CHRISTIAN HOEPFNER AWARD (II, IV-Translations), 9088 Haley Center, Auburn University AL 36849, co-editors Dan Latimer and R.T. Smith, founded 1967, is a 6×9 literary quarterly, 100 pgs., circulation 700. **Interested in poems of any length, subject, genre. Space is limited, and brief poems are more likely to be accepted. "Translations welcome."** This journal continues to gain influence and prestige in the literary world by publishing a wide variety of verse that displays careful attention to image, theme, craft and voice. They have recently published poetry by Eamon Grennan, Donald Hall, Brendan Galvin, Mary Ruefle, Hayden Carruth, Robert Morgan and Fred Chappell. Subscription: $15/year. **Sample: $5. "Send 3-5 poems in a business-sized envelope. Avoid sending faint computer printout." No previously published poems or simultaneous submissions. Responds in 1-2 months, possibly longer in summer. Always sends prepublication galleys. Pays 2 copies and $50 for the best poem published during the year. Copyright reverts to author upon publication.** Reviews books of poetry in approximately 750-1,000 words. Send books for review consideration. Sponsors the Theodore Christian Hoepfner Award. A $50 award selected from works published in a given volume of *SHR*. The editors advise, "For beginners we'd recommend study and wide reading in English and classical literature, and, of course, American literature—the old works, not just the new. We also recommend study of or exposure to a foreign language and a foreign culture. Poets need the reactions of others to their work: criticism, suggestions, discussion. A good creative writing teacher would be desirable here, and perhaps some course work too. And then submission of work, attendance at workshops. And again, the reading: history, biography, verse, essays—all of it. We want to see poems that have gone beyond the language of slippage and easy attitudes."

SOUTHERN POETRY REVIEW; GUY OWEN POETRY PRIZE (II), English Dept., University of North Carolina, Charlotte NC 28223, phone (704)547-4309, editor Ken McLaurin, founded 1958, a semiannual literary magazine "with emphasis on effective poetry. **There are no restrictions on form, style or content of poetry; length subject to limitations of space.**" They have published work by Linda Pastan, Judith Ortiz Cofer, David Ray, Stephen Sandy, Betty Adcock and Walter McDonald. As a sample the editor selected these lines from "The Last Image" by Heather Burns:

> I hold onto it with dissolving hands.
> The bed is wet from nightsweating.
> A vapor has entered the room.
> It smells like ocean foam and salt.
> It is warm, like another skin.
> Whose face have I touched besides my own?

Southern Poetry Review is 78 pgs., 6×9, handsomely printed on buff stock, flat-spined with textured, one-color matte card cover. Circulation is 1,000. Subscription: $8/year. **Sample postpaid: $2. Queries answered with SASE. Submit no more than 3-5 poems at a time. Reads submissions September 1 through May 31 only. Pays 1 copy. Acquires first-time rights.** Staff reviews books of poetry. Send books for review consideration. This is the type of literary magazine to settle back with in a chair and read, particularly during dry creative spells, to inspire one's muse. It is recommended as a market for that reason. It's a tough sell, though. Work is read closely and the magazine reports in a timely manner. There is a yearly contest, the Guy Owen Poetry Prize of $500, to which the entry fee is a subscription; submission must be postmarked in April.

THE SOUTHERN REVIEW (II), 43 Allen Hall, Louisiana State University, Baton Rouge LA 70803, phone (504)388-5108, founded 1935 (original series), 1965 (new series), poetry editors James Olney and Dave Smith, "is a literary quarterly which publishes fiction, poetry, critical essays and book reviews, with emphasis on contemporary literature in the U.S. and abroad, and with special interest in Southern culture and history. Selections are made with careful attention to craftsmanship and technique and to the seriousness of the subject matter." By general agreement this is one of the most distinguished of literary journals. Joyce Carol Oates, for instance, says, "Over the years I have continued to be impressed with the consistent high quality of *SR*'s publications and its general 'aura,' which bespeaks careful editing, adventuresome tastes and a sense of thematic unity. *SR* is characterized by a refreshing openness to new work, placed side by side with that of older, more established, and in many cases highly distinguished writers." The editors say, **"We are interested in any formal varieties of poetry, traditional or modern, that are well crafted, though we cannot normally accommodate excessively long poems (say 10 pgs. and over)."** They have published poetry by Norman Dubie, Margaret Gibson, Susan Ludvigson and Peter Schmitt. The editors selected these sample lines by Mary Oliver:

> The story about Jesus in the cave
>   is a good one,
>   but when is it ever like that
>
>   as sharp as lightning,
>   or even the way the green sea does everything—
>   quickly,
>   and with such grace?

The beautifully printed quarterly is massive: 6¾×10, 240 pgs., flat-spined, matte card cover. They receive about 2,000 submissions of poetry, use 10%. All styles and forms seem welcome, although accessible lyric and narrative free verse appear most often in recent issues. Press run is 3,100 for 2,100 subscribers of which 70% are libraries. Subscription: $20. **Sample postpaid: $6. "We do not require a cover letter but we prefer one giving information about the author and previous publications." Prefers submissions of 1-4 pgs. Send SASE for guidelines. Reports in 2 months. Pays $20/printed page plus 2 copies. Buys first North American rights.** Staff reviews books of poetry in 3,000 words, multi-book format. Send books for review consideration. Work published in this review has been included in *The Best American Poetry 1995*.

SOUTHWEST REVIEW; ELIZABETH MATCHETT STOVER MEMORIAL AWARD (II), 307 Fondren Library West, Box 374, Southern Methodist University, Dallas TX 75275, phone (214)768-1037, founded 1915, editor Willard Spiegelman. *Southwest Review* is a literary quarterly that publishes fiction, essays, poetry and interviews. "It is hard to describe our preference for poetry in a few words. We always suggest that potential contributors read several issues of the magazine to see for themselves what we like. But some things may be said: We demand **very high quality in our poems; we accept both traditional and experimental writing, but avoid unnecessary obscurity and private symbolism; we place no arbitrary limits on length but find shorter poems easier to fit into our format than longer ones. We have no specific limitations as to theme.**" They have recently published poetry by Adrienne Rich, Amy Clampitt, Albert Goldbarth, John Ashbery, Molly Peacock and Charles Wright. The journal is 6×9, 144 pgs., perfect-bound, professionally printed, with matte text stock cover. They receive about 1,000 unsolicited submissions of poetry/year, use 32. Poems tend to be lyric and narrative free verse combining a strong voice with powerful topics or situations. Diction is accessible and content often conveys a strong sense of place. Circulation is 1,500 with 1,000 subscriptions of which 600 are libraries. Subscription: $20. **Sample postpaid: $5. No simultaneous submissions or previously published work. Publishes theme issues. Send SASE for guidelines. Reports within a month. Always sends prepublication galleys. Pays cash plus copies.** The $150 Elizabeth Matchett Stover Memorial Prize is awarded annually for the best poem, chosen by editors, published in the preceding year. Poetry published in *Southwest Review* has been included in the 1993, 1994 and 1995 volumes of *The Best American Poetry*.

SOU'WESTER (II), Box 1438, Southern Illinois University, Edwardsville IL 62026, phone (618)692-3190, founded 1960, managing editor Fred W. Robbins, poetry editor Nancy Avdoian, appears 3 times a year. **"We like poetry with imagery and figurative language that has strong associations and don't care for abstract poetry. We have no particular preference for form or length."** They have published poetry by Marnie Bullock, Susan Swartwont and Bruce Guernsey. As a sample the editor selected the final stanzas of "The Gleaners" by William Jolliff:

> And even when their too-large coats are soaked
> with winter rains, I envy those children,
> the birds we were, kicking their buckles
>
> through the muddy dark. It would be a fair trade,
> a fair swap, for the work we turn to now,
> each grey and brittle season, seeking, digging,
>
> kicking the stalks for a blessing.

There are 25-30 pgs. of poetry in each 6×9, 80-page issue. The magazine is professionally printed, flat-spined, with textured matte card cover, circulation 300, 110 subscriptions of which 50 are libraries. They receive some 2,000 poems (from 600 poets) each year, use 36-40, have a 4-month backlog. Subscription: $10 (3 issues). **Sample postpaid: $5. Simultaneous submissions OK. Rejections usually within 4 months. Pays 2 copies. Acquires all rights. Returns rights. Editor comments on rejections "usually, in the case of those that we almost accept."** He says, "Read poetry past and present. Have something to say and say it in your own voice. Poetry is a very personal thing for many editors. When all else fails, we may rely on gut reactions, so take whatever hints you're given to improve your poetry, and keep submitting."

THE SOW'S EAR POETRY REVIEW (II), 19535 Pleasant View Dr., Abingdon VA 24211-6827, phone (703)628-2651, founded 1988, managing editor Larry Richman, graphics editor Mary Calhoun, is a quarterly. **"We are open to many forms and styles, and have no limitations on length. We try to be interesting visually, and we use graphics to complement the poems. Though we publish some work from our local community of poets, we are interested in poems from all over. We publish a few by school-age and previously unpublished poets."** They have recently published poetry by Patricia Goedicke, George Ella Lyon and Bill Morgan. As a sample the editors selected these lines from "Ice Water" by C.G. MacDonald:

> As familiar and beyond us as sleep—the water
> welling up to drench our stairs
> and signposts. Is this, perhaps, what we
> wanted, why we built our towns
> then cities, by chipping surf,
> by corded, seething rivers?

TSE is 32 pgs., $8\frac{1}{2} \times 11$, saddle-stapled, with matte card cover, professionally printed. They accept about 100 of 2,000 poems submitted. Press run is 800 for 700 subscribers of which 15 are libraries. Shelf sales: 20-40. Subscription: $10. **Sample postpaid: $3.50. Submit 1-5 poems at a time. No previously published poems; simultaneous submissions OK if you tell them promptly when work is accepted elsewhere. Enclose brief bio. Reports in 3-6 months. Pays 1 copy. Buys first publication rights.** Most prose (reviews, interviews, features) is commissioned. They offer an annual contest for unpublished poems, with fee of $2/poem, prizes of $500, $100 and $50, and publication for 15-20 finalists. For contest, submit poems in September/October, with name and address on back of each poem. Submissions of 5 poems/$10 receive a subscription. Include SASE for notification. 1994 Judge: David Huddle. They also sponsor a chapbook contest in March/April with $10 fee, $500 prize and publication; second and third prizes of $100. Send SASE for chapbook contest guidelines.

SPARROW: THE SONNET YEARBOOK (IV-Form), 103 Waldron St., West Lafayette IN 47906, editor and publisher Felix Stefanile, publishes "as material permits. **We are noted for our devotion to the publication of formal, contemporary sonnets. We occasionally publish other types of structured verse, but only rarely, and only when the poem seems to compel us to take it. No subject**

restrictions. We don't publish poems in poor taste." They have recently published poetry by Gabriella Mirollo and Robert Mezey. As a sample the editor selected these lines from "Six Lines Probably in F-Minor" by Miller Williams:

> *Though we have found some comfort in how the whole*
> *as always more than its parts—read spleen and liver—*
> *seems to make an argument for the soul*
>
> *still we could be nothing but star-stuff*
> *recycling itself atom by atom forever.*
> *The question may be why that is not enough.*

The editor says *Sparrow* is 9×12, using occasional graphics only by invitation. Their 1995 issue was 100 pgs. They receive about 1,000 pieces a year, use less than 1%. Press run is 750 for about 450 subscribers of which about 100 are libraries, 300 shelf sales. Single copy: $5.50. **Sample back issue postpaid: $5. Submit 4-5 poems at a time, typed on $8\frac{1}{2} \times 11$ bond paper. "We consider previously published poems only now and then." No simultaneous submissions. No material returned without SASE. "We have a very cynical attitude toward long cover letters." Seldom comments on rejections. "We are not in the business of offering criticism or advice." Send SASE with all queries. Reports "usually in a week." Sometimes sends prepublication galleys. Pays $3 a sonnet plus 1 copy. Buys first and non-exclusive reprint rights. "We also offer a $25 prize for the best sonnet each issue."** Staff reviews books of poetry. Send books for review consideration. The editor says, "We are now essentially a 'new' magazine with a fine, old name. We pride ourselves on our liveliness and our currency. We also publish scores of musical settings for sonnets, by special arrangement with the composer. We are really not a market for beginners and the MFA degree does not impress us."

SPECTRUM (II), Anna Maria College, Box 72-D, Paxton MA 01612, phone (508)849-3450, founded 1985, editor Robert H. Goepfert, is a "multidisciplinary national publication with liberal arts emphasis," presenting 6-8 poems in each 64-page issue: **"poems of crisp images, precise language, which have something of value to say and say it in an authentic voice. Not the self-conscious, the 'workshop poem,' the cliché, the self-righteous."** They have published poetry by William Stafford. *Spectrum* appears twice a year in a 6×9, flat-spined format, professionally printed on quality stock with 2-color matte card cover, using b&w photos and art. Press run is 1,000 for 650 subscriptions (200 of them to libraries). Single copy: $4; subscription: $7 for 1 year, $13 for 2 years. **Sample: $3. Submit 3-5 poems at a time. No previously published poems or simultaneous submissions. Reads submissions September 1 through May 15 only. Editor "occasionally" comments on rejections. Mss returned only with SASE. Reports in 2 months. Always sends prepublication galleys. Pays $20/poem plus 2 copies. Buys first North American serial rights.**

SPINDRIFT (II), Shoreline Community College, 16101 Greenwood Ave., Seattle WA 98133, founded 1962, faculty advisor varies each year, currently Carol Orlock, is **open to all varieties of poetry except greeting card style.** They have published poetry by James Bertolino, Edward Harkness and Richard West. *Spindrift*, an annual, is 125 pgs., handsomely printed in an 8″ square, flat-spined. Circulation 500. Single copy: $6.50. **Sample postpaid: $5. "Submit 2 copies of each poem, 6 maximum. Include cover letter with biographical information. We accept submissions until February 1—report back in March."** Send SASE for guidelines. **Pays 1 copy. Acquires first serial rights.** The editors advise, "Read what the major contemporary poets are writing. Read what local poets are writing. Be distinctive, love the language, avoid sentiment."

‡SPINNING JENNY (II), P.O. Box 356, Cooper Station, New York NY 10276-0356, phone (212)802-9919, fax (212)463-0310, founded 1994, first issue Fall 1995, editor C.E. Harrison, appears twice a year. **"We are especially devoted to the work of emerging writers, and welcome the opportunity to review poetry of all shapes, sizes, flavors, persuasions, and schools."** As a sample the editor selected these lines from "Insomnia" by Michael Loncar:

> *It starts, inevitably*
> *as something small;*
> *the suicide of a friend,*
> *your team's loss in*
> *the World Series a*
> *chipped tooth.*

The editor says *SJ* is approximately 40 pgs., $5\frac{1}{2} \times 8\frac{1}{2}$, web printed and flat-spined with heavy card stock cover, contains ads, no artwork. "We accept approximately 5% of unsolicited submissions." Press run is 2,000. Single copy: $4; subscription: $8/year. **Sample postpaid: $5. No previously published poems; simultaneous submissions OK. Seldom comments on rejections. Send SASE for guidelines. Reports within 1 month. Pays contributor copies. Authors retain rights.** "We will review books and chapbooks, though not in every issue. Reviews should be approximately 200 words in length." Open to unsolicited reviews. Poets may also send books for review consideration (Attn: Book Review Editor).

THE SPIRIT THAT MOVES US; THE SPIRIT THAT MOVES US PRESS (II); EDITOR'S CHOICE (IV-Anthology), P.O. Box 720820-PM, Jackson Heights, Queens NY 11372-0820, phone (718)426-8788, founded 1974, poetry editor Morty Sklar. *"The Spirit That Moves Us* will be continuing its *Editor's Choice* series biennially and publishing regular issues only occasionally. *Editor's Choice* consists of reprints from other literary magazines and small presses, where our selections are made from nominations by the editors of those magazines and presses." They have published poetry by Susan Montez, Darryl Holmes, Yala Korwin, Rhina Espaillat and Rita Dove. As a sample the editor selected these lines from "Just Off The Queen Elizabeth, New York City, 1948" by Joan Dobbie:

> *"I called out the only two words*
> *I could think of in English,*
> *'GO AWAY!'*
> *I meant for the children to come,*
> *I was longing to touch them."*

They offer *Patchwork of Dreams: Voices from the Heart of the New America*, an anthology in which the above poem appears, as a sample for $8 plus $1 postage (regularly $11 plus $1.50 postage). **Publishes theme issues. Send SASE for upcoming themes and time frames. Sometimes sends prepublication galleys.** The editor's advice: "Write what you would like to write, in a style (or styles) which is/are best for your own expression. Don't worry about acceptance, though you may be concerned about it. Don't just send work which you think editors would like to see, though take that into consideration. Think of the relationship between poem, poet and editor as personal. You may send good poems to editors who simply do not like them, whereas other editors might."

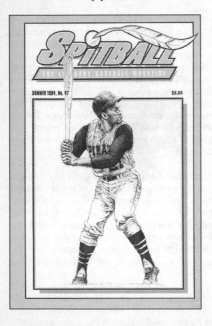

"We have decided to use realistic illustrations of players in action on every cover to convey the baseball emphasis of the magazine, rather than the literary aspect," says Mike Shannon, editor-in-chief of Spitball, a quarterly publication based in Cincinnati, Ohio. *"Roberto Clemente, an immortal of baseball, was chosen for the Summer 1994 issue. We'd never had him on the cover before, so the honor was overdue."* Although SB began as a baseball poetry magazine, it now includes fiction and book reviews also exclusively about baseball. However, Shannon says poetry remains key to the magazine's mission. Spitball *is always looking for fresh talent and is very open to beginners who know the subject. The cover art is by Donnie Pollard, a computer artist/designer for Logo Athletic in Indianapolis, Indiana.*

SPITBALL; CASEY AWARD (IV-Sports), 5560 Fox Rd., Cincinnati OH 45239, phone (513)385-2268, founded 1981, poetry editor William J. McGill, is "a unique literary magazine devoted to poetry, fiction and book reviews *exclusively* about baseball. Newcomers are very welcome, but remember that you have to know the subject. We do and our readers do. Perhaps a good place to start for beginners is one's personal reactions to the game, *a* game, a player, etc. and take it from there." The digest-sized, 96-page quarterly is computer typeset and perfect-bound. They receive about 1,000 submissions/year, use 40—very small backlog. "Many times we are able to publish accepted work almost immediately." Circulation is 1,000, 750 subscriptions of which 25 are libraries. Subscription: $16. **Sample postpaid: $5. "We are not very concerned with the technical details of submitting, but we do prefer a cover letter with some bio info. We also like batches of poems and prefer to use several of same poet in an issue rather than a single poem." Publishes theme issues. Send SASE for upcoming themes. Pays 2 copies.** "We encourage anyone interested to submit to *Spitball*. We are always looking for fresh talent. Those who have never written 'baseball poetry' before should read some first probably before submitting. Not necessarily ours. We sponsor the Casey Award (for best baseball book of the year) and hold the Casey Awards Banquet every January. Any chapbook of baseball poetry should be sent to us for consideration for the 'Casey' plaque that we award to the winner each year."

THE SPOON RIVER POETRY REVIEW (III, IV-Regional, translations); EDITORS' PRIZE CONTEST (II), 4240/English Dept., Illinois State University, Normal IL 61790-4240, phone (309)438-7906, founded 1976, poetry editor Lucia Getsi, is a "poetry magazine that features newer and well-known poets from around the country and world." Also features **one Illinois poet/issue** at length for the magazine's Illinois Poet Series. **"We want interesting and compelling poetry that operates beyond the ho-hum, so-what level, in any form or style about anything; language that is fresh, energetic, committed, filled with a strong voice that grabs the reader in the first line and never lets go. Do not want to see insipid, dull, boring poems, especially those that I cannot ascertain why they're in lines and not paragraphs; poetry which, if you were to put it into paragraphs, would become bad prose." They also use translations of poetry.** They have recently published poetry by Frankie Paino, Margaret Gibson, Kurt Leland, Tim Seibles, Dave Smith, Elaine Terranova, Roger Mitchell and Katharine Soniat. As a sample Lucia Getsi selected these lines by Kay Murphy:

> This is as close as I can come to make what she says true:
> Inside, my uncle has his hand inside my aunt's blue dress.
> The fields are burning with a want I don't yet understand.
> The orchard has simply given up, as my cousin has.

SRPR has moved to a twice a year, double issue format. It is digest-sized, laser set with card cover using photos, ads. They accept about 2% of 1,000 poems received/month. Press run is 800 for 400 subscriptions (100 of them libraries) and shelf sales. Subscription: $12. **Sample: $8.** "No simultaneous submissions unless we are notified immediately if a submission is accepted elsewhere. Include name and address on every poem." Do not submit mss May 1 through September 1. Editor comments on rejections "many times, if a poet is promising." Reports in 2 months. Pays a year's subscription. Acquires first North American serial rights only.** Staff reviews books of poetry. Send books for review consideration. Sponsors the Editor's Prize Contest for previously unpublished work. One poem will be awarded $500 and published in the fall issue of *SRPR*, and two finalists will receive $50 each and publication in the fall issue. Entry fee: $15, including 1-year subscription. Write for details. *The Spoon River Poetry Review* has received several Illinois Arts Council Awards and is one of the best reads in the poetry-publishing world. Editor Lucia Cordell Getsi jampacks the journal with poems of varied styles and presents them in a handsome, perfect-bound product. You'll want to order a sample issue to get a feel for this fine publication. Work published in this review has also been included in *The Best American Poetry 1993*.

‡SPRING: THE JOURNAL OF THE E.E. CUMMINGS SOCIETY (IV-Specialized), 33-54 164th St., Flushing NY 11358-1442, phone (718)353-3631, editor Norman Friedman, is an annual publication designed "to maintain and broaden the audience for Cummings and to explore various facets of his life and art." **They want poems in the spirit of Cummings, primarily poems of one page or less. Nothing "amateurish."** They have recently published poetry by John Tagliabue, Ruth Whitman, M.L. Rosenthal, William Jay Smith and Theodore Weiss. As a sample the editor selected these lines from "The Whip" by Robert Creeley:

> I spent a night turning in bed,
> my love was a feather, a flat
>
> sleeping thing. She was
> very white
>
> and quiet, and above us on
> the roof, there was another woman . . .

Spring is 100-120 pgs., 5½ × 8½, offset and perfect-bound with light card stock cover. Press run is 500 for 200 subscribers of which 15 are libraries, 300 shelf sales. Subscription or **sample postpaid: $15. Some previously published poems OK; no simultaneous submissions. Cover letter required. Reads submissions March through May. Seldom comments on rejections. Reports in 6 months. Pays 1 copy.** "Contributors are encouraged to subscribe."

STAND MAGAZINE; NORTHERN HOUSE (I, II, IV-Translations), 179 Wingrove Rd., Newcastle on Tyne NE4 9DA England. US Editors: Daniel Schenker and Amanda Kay, 122 Morris Rd., Lacey's

---

Use the General Index to find the page number of a specific publisher. If the publisher you are seeking is not listed, check the " '95-'96 Changes" list at the end of this section.

Spring AL 35754. *Stand*, founded by editor Jon Silkin in 1952, is a highly esteemed literary quarterly. Jon Silkin seeks more subscriptions from US readers and also hopes "that the magazine **would be seriously treated as an alternative platform to American literary journals." He wants "verse that tries to explore forms. No formulaic verse."** They have published poems by such poets as Peter Redgrove, Elizabeth Jennings and Barry Spacks. *Library Journal* calls *Stand* "one of England's best, liveliest and truly imaginative little magazines." Among better-known American poets whose work has appeared here are Robert Bly, William Stafford, Michael Mott, Angela Ball and Naomi Wallace. Poet Donald Hall says of it, "among essential magazines, there is Jon Silkin's *Stand*, politically left, with reviews, poems and much translation from continental literature." In its current format it is 6×8, flat-spined, 84 pgs., professionally printed in 2 columns, small type, on thin stock with glossy cover, using ads. Circulation is 4,500 with 2,800 subscriptions of which 600 are libraries. Subscription: $25. **Sample postpaid: $7. Cover letter required with submissions, "assuring us that work is not also being offered elsewhere." Publishes theme issues. Always sends prepublication galleys. Pays £30/poem (unless under 6 lines) and 1 copy (⅓ off additional copies). Buys first world serial rights for 3 months after publication. If work(s) appear elsewhere *Stand*/Northern House must be credited.** Reviews books of poetry in 3,000-4,000 words, multi-book format. Open to unsolicited reviews. Poets may also send books for review consideration. Northern House (13 Queen's Terrace, Newcastle on Tyne NE2 2PJ England) "publishes mostly small collections of poetry by new or established poets. The pamphlets often contain a group of poems written to one theme. Occasionally larger volumes are published, such as the full-length collection by Sorley Maclean, translated by Iain Crichton Smith."

STAPLE (II), Gilderoy East, Upperwood Rd., Matlock, Bath DE4 3PD United Kingdom, phone 0629-583867 and 0629-582764, founded 1982, co-editor Bob Windsor. This literary magazine appears 4 times a year including supplements. **"Nothing barred: Evidence of craft, but both traditional and modernist accepted; no totally esoteric or concrete poetry."** They have recently published poetry by Donna Hilbert, Jennifer Olds, Michael Daugherty, Paul Munden and Vuyelwa Carlin. As a sample they selected these lines from "Flint" by Kenneth C. Steven:

> . . . *Where drums of high water roll the rocks*
> *Shining things are skipped up dancing*
> *Grey as wolves.*

> . . . *Men chipped arrowtips, fine and perfect*
> *As a wren's beak, so thin you could see the sky*
> *Through the milky tip.*

Staple is professionally printed, flat-spined, 80 pgs., with card cover. Of 10,000 poems received/year they accept about 2%. Their press run is up to 800 with 350 subscriptions. Subscription: £15 (sterling only). **Sample postpaid: £3. Submit 6 poems at a time. They do not consider simultaneous submissions or previously published poems. Cover letter preferred. Editors sometimes comment on rejections. Submission deadlines are end of February, June and November. Response in up to 3 months. Sometimes sends prepublication galleys. Pays overseas writers complimentary copies.** Send SASE (or SAE with IRC) for rules for their open biennial competitions (£1,200 in prizes) and for *Staple First Editions* monographs (sample postpaid: $10). Recently published monographs include *An Extra Half-Acre* by Jennifer Olds. They also produce (to order) poetry postcards of poetry *published* in the magazine. The editor says, "We get too many short minimalist pieces from America. More developed pieces of around 40 lines preferred."

STATE STREET PRESS (II), P.O. Box 278, Brockport NY 14420, phone (716)637-0023, founded 1981, poetry editor Judith Kitchen, "publishes **chapbooks of poetry (20-24 pgs.) usually chosen in an anonymous competition**. State Street Press hopes to publish emerging writers with solid first collections and to offer a format for established writers who have a collection of poems that work together as a chapbook. We have also established a full-length publication—for those of our authors who are beginning to have a national reputation. We want **serious traditional and free verse. We are not usually interested in the language school of poets or what would be termed 'beat.' We are quite frankly middle-of-the-road. We ask only that the poems work as a collection, that the chapbook be more than an aggregate of poems—that they work together."** They have recently published poetry by Naomi Shihab Nye, Dionisio Martinez, Diane Swan, Patricia Hooper and Joe Survant. As a sample the editor selected these lines from "Botany" by Kathleen Wakefield:

> *Each day I watch the blossoms close,*
> *then open skyward, as if aspiring to something.*
> *By night, the moth mullein, named*
> *for beast and flower, practices its cool white deceit*
> *by which its stationary blooms in darkness*
> *endlessly repeat.*

Chapbooks are beautifully designed and printed, 6×9, 30 pgs., with textured matte wrapper with art. **Send SASE for guidelines and chapbook contest rules. There is a $10 entry fee, for which you** receive one of the chapbooks already published. **Simultaneous submissions encouraged. Always sends prepublication galleys. Pays copies and small honorarium. Authors buy additional copies at cost, sell at readings and keep the profits.** Judith Kitchen comments, "State Street Press believes that the magazines are doing a good job of publishing beginning poets and we hope to present published and unpublished work in a more permanent format, so we do reflect the current market and tastes. We expect our writers to have published individual poems and to be considering a larger body of work that in some way forms a 'book.' We have been cited as a press that prints poetry that is accessible to the general reader."

THE STEELHEAD SPECIAL (I), P.O. Box 219, Bayside CA 95524, phone (707)445-1907, founded 1991, editor Crawdad Nelson, is a bimonthly "Northwest working-class cultural and literary review." They want **"fresh, working-class, rugged, bold poetry. Nothing weepy, clichéd, sentimental."** They have published poetry by Joe Smith, Sharon Doubiago and John Colburn. As a sample the editor selected these lines from "The Throat" by L.J. Cirino:

> This morning, walking down the ridge,
> the throat of the river, beautifully
> bloody, washed out and purpled the sea . . .

It is 40 pgs., 8½ × 11, newsprint, saddle-stapled, with art and graphics. They receive 500-600 poems a year, accept 10-20/issue. Press run is 3,500 for 200 subscribers, rest distributed free to the general public and fishermen. Single copy: $1; subscription: $12. **Sample postpaid: $2. Submit 6 poems at a time. Previously published poems and simultaneous submissions OK. Often comments on rejections. Publishes theme issues. Reports in 1-8 weeks. Sometimes sends prepublication galleys. Pays 1-2 copies; "discounts to poets on larger orders."** Open to unsolicited reviews. Poets may also send books for review consideration. Crawdad Nelson says, "We see lots of good poetry. Hope to see more. Nothing bogged down in bourgeois ennui, please. Vitality helps, but stay alert. We need more *lyrical*, less broken prose. Subscriptions encouraged."

STERLING HOUSE PUBLISHER (I), (formerly Guyasuta Publisher), The Sterling Building, 440 Friday Rd., Pittsburgh PA 15209, phone (412)821-6211, fax (412)821-6099, founded 1988, owner Cynthia Shore-Sterling. **"Sterling House offers both straight and co-op publishing. We publish approximately 25 collections of poetry each year, poetry in all its variety of styles and forms.** As a sample the owner selected these lines from Sheila Fiscus's poem "Thoughts From The Throne" from her book *Just A Housewife*:

> As I sit naked on the porcelain throne,
> My life files by, a procession of household care products.
> But what of my heart, my soul, my joy of living?
> Are they to be flushed into the sewer
> By consummate daily tasks?

They will consider simultaneous submissions and unsolicited mss of 25-60 poems throughout the year. For further information, send SASE for catalog and guidelines. Sample: $5.95 (includes shipping). They are presently developing the Sterling Foundation.

‡THE STEVAN COMPANY; SOCIETY OF ETHICAL AND PROFESSIONAL PUBLISHERS OF LITERATURE (III, IV-Translations), 911 Bridge Rd., #F, Charleston WV 25314, founded 1980, publisher Kathryn Stewart-McDonald. **"If you read *The New Yorker, The Atlantic*, and have read textbooks such as Voice Great Within Us, the major Mentor book of poems, e.e. cummings, R.H. Blyth, Li Po, William Blake, you're on track. Well-read poets usually write well. Our readers are very well read and read between 175-210 small press books per year. We prefer to work with experienced writers."** They have published poetry by Jack Terahata (Japan), Nat Scammacca (Italy) and Dong Jiping (China). In addition to anthologies, they publish collections by individuals. **Query with no more than 5 samples, bio, publication credits. "No lengthy cover letter; please do not inundate us with all 900 poems you have written. We prefer no previously published poems and usually not simultaneous submissions. No phone calls. Not necessary to subscribe or join SEPPL." Reading period June through August. Reports in 6-8 weeks.** Time between acceptance and publication is 1-2 years. **Pays copies. "We comment on rejections occasionally if requested. We will also accept foreign language poems with English translations."** Kathryn McDonald says, "We are not a vanity press, sometimes try to solicit grants, will accept money from foundations. The Society of Ethical Publishers agrees to maintain a code of ethics, can make legal referrals, sometimes offers mechanical advice to poets and publishers. This is a private club of like-minded publishers who wish to continue traditions and facilitate rapport between publisher and writer. Board members share mailing lists, copyright attorney and networking information. Members receive free samples, parties and share trade information (i.e., grants available, distributors, printers information, etc.) All members have excellent references, personal and professional. Many can translate and all are committed to their craft."

THE WALLACE STEVENS JOURNAL (II, IV-Specialized), Liberal Studies, Clarkson University, Box 5750, Potsdam NY 13699-5750, e-mail duemer@craft.camp.clarkson.edu, founded 1977, poetry editor Prof. Joseph Duemer, appears biannually using **"poems about or in the spirit of Wallace Stevens or having some relation to his work. No bad parodies of Stevens' anthology pieces."** They have published poetry by Elizabeth Spires, Jorie Graham, Charles Wright, X.J. Kennedy and Robert Creeley. As a sample the editor selected these lines from "A World Without Desire" by Michael G. Gessner:

> Occurred tonight for an hour only,
> An hour spent around the back porch
> Where I was sent from the family, exiled
> From myself. It was a world of order,
> Order and presence, the final meaning
> Of forms conversing through the night
> As large as all thought must be
> This house a ragged piece of locale
> Torn adrift in the space of a dark mind.

The editor describes it as 80-120 pgs., 6×9, typeset, flat-spined, with cover art on glossy stock. They accept 10-15 poems of 150-200 received. Press run is 900 for 600 subscribers of which 200 are libraries. Subscription: $15. **Sample postpaid: $4. Submit 3-5 poems at a time. "We like to receive clean, readable copy. We generally do not publish previously published material, though we have made a few exceptions to this rule." Reports in 4-10 weeks. Always sends prepublication galleys. Pays 2 copies. Acquires all rights. Returns rights with permission and acknowledgment.** Staff reviews books of poetry. Send books for review consideration "only if there is some clear connection to Stevens." *The Wallace Stevens Journal* is published by the Wallace Stevens Society. The editor says, "Brief cover letters are fine, even encouraged. Please don't submit to *WSJ* if you have not read Stevens. We like parodies, but they must *add* a new angle of perception. Most of the poems we publish are not parodies but meditations on themes related to Wallace Stevens and those poets he has influenced. Those wishing to contribute might wish especially to examine the Spring 1993 issue, devoted to prose and poetry by American poets."

STICKS; STICKS PRESS (III, IV-Form), P.O. Box 399, Maplesville AL 36750-0399, press founded 1989, journal 1991, editor/publisher Mary Veazey. *Sticks*, appearing irregularly, **publishes "the best short poems of experienced/established poets. All styles, subjects. Preferred length: 10 lines or less; width: 50 spaces per line."** She has published poetry by X.J. Kennedy and Richard Kostelanetz. As a sample the editor selected this poem, "Eros" by Gary Aspenberg:

> white raindrop
> spilling
> > over
> the rosepetal's
> curled lip. . .

The magazine is a $4\frac{1}{4} \times 5\frac{1}{2}$, saddle-stapled or saddle-sewn booklet, professionally printed on acid-free paper, 32 pgs. Press run is 500. Permanent mailing list in lieu of subscriptions. **Sample issue $1; sewn binding by request. Submit 1-3 poems at a time. "No guidelines, just be a master of the short poem." Does not comment on rejections. Reports in 3 months or less. Pays 2 copies. Acquires first North American serial rights.** The editor says, "*Sticks* will appear *only* when money for printing and a number of excellent small poems converge. *The Oxford Book of Short Poems* is the touchstone here; write the poem that will outlast us all; historically many such poems have been brief."

STILL WATERS PRESS (II, IV-Women), 112 W. Duerer St., Galloway NJ 08201-9402, phone (609)652-1790, founded 1989, editor Shirley Warren, is a "small press publisher of poetry chapbooks and poet's handbooks (contemporary craft). Especially interested in **works by, for and about women. We prefer poetry firmly planted in the real world, but equally mindful of poetry as art. The transformation from pain to perseverance, from ordinary to extraordinary, from defeat to triumph, pleases us. But we reject Pollyanna poetry immediately. Nothing sexist, in either direction, nothing sexually erotic. No rhymed poetry unless you're a master of form who can meticulously avoid strange manipulations of syntax simply to achieve end-rhyme. No patriarchal religious verse. Preferred length: 4 lines to 2 pages per poem. Form: no restrictions—we expect content to dictate the form."** They have published poetry by Linda Milstein and Susan Cavanaugh. The press publishes 4-8 chapbooks a year, averaging 28 pgs. Sample chapbooks: $5; writer's guide booklets: $3. **Send SASE for guidelines, then query. Simultaneous submissions and previously published poems OK. Always sends prepublication galleys. Pays 10% of the press run. Royalties on 2nd and subsequent press runs. Acquires first or reprint rights.** They hold 2 annual contests, each with $10 reading fee; send SASE for detailed guidelines. The editor says, "Read other poets, contemporary and traditional. Attend workshops, establish rapport with your local peers, attend readings. Keep your best work in circulation. Someone out there is looking for you."

STONE SOUP, THE MAGAZINE BY YOUNG WRITERS AND ARTISTS; THE CHILDREN'S ART FOUNDATION (IV-Children), P.O. Box 83, Santa Cruz CA 95063, phone (408)426-5557, fax (408)426-1161, founded 1973, editor Ms. Gerry Mandel. *Stone Soup* publishes **writing and art by children through age 13; they want to see free verse poetry but no rhyming poetry, haiku or cinquain.** As a sample the editor selected this poem, "Nightfall," by 7-year-old Jaiva Larsen:

> *When the blackberry moon rises*
> *And the sky flies by like ocean waves*
> *And the chill of the evening*
> *Flies through your heart*
> *Run home*
> *Run home*

Stone Soup, published 5 times a year, is a handsome 6 × 8¾ magazine, professionally printed on heavy stock with 4 full-color art reproductions inside and a full-color illustration on the coated cover, saddle-stapled. A membership in the Children's Art Foundation at $24/year includes a subscription to the magazine, each issue of which contains an Activity Guide. The editor receives 5,000 poetry submissions/year and only uses 20. There are 4 pgs. of poetry in each issue. Circulation is 20,000; 13,000 in subscriptions, 5,000 to bookstores, 2,000 other. **Sample postpaid: $4.50. Submissions can be any number of pages, any format, but not simultaneous. Criticism will be given when requested. Guidelines are available for SASE. Reports in 1 month. Pays $10 and 2 copies plus discounts. Buys all rights. Returns rights upon request.** Open to reviews by children. Children through age 13 may also send books for review consideration. *Stone Soup* has received both Parents' Choice and Edpress Golden Lamp Honor Awards.

STONEVALE PRESS (II), P.O. Box 484, Burkittsville MD 21718, phone (301)834-9380, founded 1991, editor Helen Vo-Dinh, publishes 2 paperbacks and 1 chapbook/year. **No specifications as to form, length, subject matter, style or purpose, "except no 'inspirational' verse or pornography."** They have published books of poetry by Mary Azrael and Kendra Kopelke. As a sample the editor selected these lines from "Girl Asleep At A Table" in Kopelke's book *Eager Street*:

> *You see she is asleep*
> *so you want to turn away, embarrassed*
> *yet you feel*
>
> *strangely welcome, as if you*
> *are the subject of her inner gaze*
> *the stone that holds the plum . . .*

That book is about 80 pgs., 5½ × 9, flat-spined with matte card cover, $8.95. **Query first with 10-15 pgs. of typed material and a cover letter with brief bio and publication credits. Previously published poems and simultaneous submissions OK, if indicated. Replies to queries in 1 month, to mss (if invited) in 2-3 months.** Time between acceptance and publication is 6-12 months. **Occasionally comments on rejections. Pays 10% royalties after expenses and 25 author's copies. Co-op publishing is also an option. Sample book: $7.**

STORMLINE PRESS, INC. (V), Box 593, Urbana IL 61801, phone (217)328-2665, founded 1985, publisher Ray Bial, is an independent press publishing fiction, poetry and photography, **with emphasis upon the rural Midwest. They accept submissions "only by invitation. Do not send unsolicited manuscripts. Query in November and December only with SASE. We publish both established and new poets, but in the latter case prefer to publish those poets who have been working some years to master their craft."** The press publishes 1-2 books each year with an average page count of 48-64. They are 6 × 9, some flat-spined paperbacks and some hardcover.

STORY LINE PRESS (V); NICHOLAS ROERICH POETRY PRIZE FOR FIRST BOOK OF POETRY (II), Three Oaks Farm, 27006 Gap Road, Brownsville OR 97327-9718, phone (503)466-5352, Story Line Press founded 1985, poetry editor Robert McDowell. Story Line Press publishes each year the winner of the Nicholas Roerich Poetry Prize for a First Book of Poetry ($1,000 plus publication and a paid reading at the Roerich Museum in New York City; a runner-up receives a full Story Line Press Scholarship to the Wesleyan Writers Conference in Middletown, CT [see listing in Conferences and Workshops section]; $15 entry and handling fee). Deadline for submissions: October 15. Send SASE for complete guidelines. The press also publishes books about poetry and has published collections by such poets as Colette Inez, Rita Dove, Bruce Bawer and George Keithley. **They consider unsolicited mss only for the Nicholas Roerich Poetry Prize competition. Always sends prepublication galleys.**

STRAIGHT; STANDARD PUBLISHING CO. (IV-Religious, teens), 8121 Hamilton Ave., Cincinnati OH 45231, editor Carla J. Crane. Standard is a large religious publishing company. *Straight* is a weekly take-home publication (digest-sized, 12 pgs., color newsprint) **for teens. Poetry is *by* teenagers, any**

style, religious or inspirational in nature. No adult-written poetry. As a sample the editor selected "Our Savior's Love" by Rustie Hill:

> I know the anger locked in you is wear-
>   ing out your heart.
> I know you hit because you hurt and
>   need a brand new start.
> Despite the fact you hurt me, I still love
>   you even now;
> My Lord said, "Love thy neighbor," and
>   His love has shown me how.

Teen author must include birthdate. Submit 1-5 poems at a time. Simultaneous submissions OK. Time between acceptance and publication is 9-12 months. Publishes theme issues. Guidelines and upcoming themes available for SASE. Reports in 4-6 weeks. Pays $10/poem plus 5 copies. Buys first or reprint rights. The editor says, "Many teenagers write poetry in their English classes at school. If you've written a poem on an inspirational topic, and your teacher's given you an 'A' on it, you've got a very good chance of having it published in *Straight*."

THE STRAIN (II), P.O. Box 330507, Houston TX 77233-0507, poetry editor Michael Bond, editor Norman C. Stewart, Jr. *The Strain* is a monthly magazine using **"experimental or traditional poetry of very high quality."** They do not include sample lines of poetry here as they "prefer not to limit style of submissions." **Simultaneous submissions and previously published poems OK. Guidelines issue: $5 and 8 first-class stamps. Pays "no less than $5. We would prefer you submit before obtaining the guidelines issue which mostly explains upcoming collections and collaborations."** Send books for review consideration.

STREET PRESS (V), P.O. Box 772, Sound Beach NY 11789-0772, founded 1974, editor Graham Everett. Street Press publishes an occasional limited edition book of poetry. Recent publications: *Minus Green Plus* by Graham Everett, *Limousine to Nowhere* by Jim Tyack and *Endless Staircase* by Sandy McIntosh. **They are currently not accepting poetry submissions.** Send SASE for a list of available titles.

STRIDE PUBLICATIONS (II), 11 Sylvan Rd., Exeter, Devon EX4 6EW England, founded 1980, editor R.M. Loydell. Stride Publications publishes poetry, poetry sequences, prose and novels, and an occasional arts magazine. **The editor wants to see any poetry that is "new, inventive, nothing self-oriented, emotional, no narrative or fantasy."** He has published work by Peter Redgrove, Alexis Lykiard, Sheila E. Murphy and David Miller. Stride Publications publishes paperbacks 60-100 pgs. of poetry, plus a few novels and anthologies. **Unsolicited submissions for book publication are accepted. Authors should query first, sending sample poems with return postage. Cover letter required with bio, summary and review quotes. Queries will be answered in 6 weeks and mss reported on in 3 months or more. Pays author's copies.** Magazine reviews books and tapes of poetry in 100-200 words, multi-book format. Send books etc. for review consideration.

STRUGGLE: A MAGAZINE OF PROLETARIAN REVOLUTIONARY LITERATURE (I, II, IV-Political, science fiction/fantasy, workers' social issues, women/feminism), P.O. Box 13261, Detroit MI 48213-0261, phone (313)441-1204, founded 1985, editor Tim Hall, is a "literary quarterly, content: the struggle of the working people and all oppressed against the rich. Issues such as: racism, poverty, aggressive wars, workers' struggle for jobs and job security, the overall struggle for a non-exploitative society, a genuine socialism." The **poetry and songs they use are "generally short, any style, subject matter must criticize or fight against the rule of the billionaires. We welcome experimentation devoted to furthering such content."** They have recently published poetry by Elizabeth Glass, Kimberly Sonnich, Michelle Leasure, Mark A. Reece, Lee Dennard and Chloe L. Brown. As a sample the editor selected this excerpt from "Pulpit Bullies" by Ray Pence:

> Pulpit bullies
> breathing fascist fire
> stoked by racist brimstone,
> fanning the flames
> of intolerant ideology
> with flag-draped rhetoric,
> striving to divide the working class
> like so many loaves and fishes.

Struggle is 36 pgs., digest-sized, printed by photo offset using drawings, occasional photos of artwork, short stories and short plays as well as poetry and songs. Subscription: $10 for 4 issues. **Sample postpaid: $2.50. Submit 8 poems at a time. Checks must be payable to "Tim Hall—Special Account."** Accepted work usually appears in the next issue. Editor tries to provide criticism "with every submission." **Tries to report in 3-4 months. Pays 2 copies.** Tim Hall says, "Show passion and fire. Formal experiments, traditional forms both welcome. Especially favor: works reflecting rebellion by the working people against the rich; works against racism, sexism, militarism, imperialism; works critical of our exploitative culture; works showing a desire for—or fantasy of—a nonexploitative society; works attacking the Republican New Stone Age and the Democrats' surrender to it."

STUDENT LEADERSHIP JOURNAL (IV-Students, religious), Dept. PM, P.O. Box 7895, Madison WI 53707-7895, phone (608)274-9001, editor Jeff Yourison, is a **"magazine for Christian student leaders on secular campuses. We accept a wide variety of poetry. Do not want to see trite poetry. Also, we accept little rhymed poetry; it must be very, very good."** As a sample the editor selected the last stanzas of "A bird in the church" by Luci Shaw:

> *and high and low and up again, through the sun's*
> *transfixing shafts, her wings test gravity*
> *in a bewilderment of interior air, opening*
> *and closing on her feathered restlessness*
> *until, as though coming home, she settles*
>
> *on the arm of the crucifix. Having found*
> *a nesting tree (even thine altars, O Lord!),*
> *she lodges at last, at the angle*
> *where vertex and horizon meet, resting*
> *in the steady pain of Christ's left eye.*

Student Leadership is a quarterly, 32 pgs., magazine-sized, 2-color inside, 2-color covers, with no advertising, 70% editorial, 30% graphics/art. Press run is 8,000 going to college students in the US and Canada. Subscription: $16. **Sample postpaid: $3. No simultaneous submissions. Previously published poems OK. "Would-be contributors should read us to be familiar with what we publish."** Best time to submit mss is March through July ("We set our year's editorial plan"). Editor "occasionally" comments on rejections. Send SASE for guidelines. Reports in 2-3 months. Time between acceptance and publication is 1-24 months. **Pays $25-50/poem plus 2 copies. Buys first or reprint rights.** He says, "Try to express feelings through images and metaphor. Religious poetry should not be overly didactic, and it should never moralize!"

STUDIO, A JOURNAL OF CHRISTIANS WRITING (II, IV-Religious, spirituality), 727 Peel St., Albury, New South Wales 2640 Australia, founded 1980, publisher Paul Grover, is a small press literary quarterly "with contents **focusing upon the Christian striving for excellence in poetry,** prose and occasional articles relating Christian views of literary ideas." **In poetry, the editors want "shorter pieces but with no specification as to form or length (necessarily less than 3-4 pages), subject matter, style or purpose. People who send material should be comfortable being published under this banner: *Studio, A Journal of Christians Writing*."** They have published poetry by John Foulcher and other Australian poets. *Studio* is 36 pgs., digest-sized, professionally printed on high-quality recycled paper, saddle-stapled, matte card cover, with graphics and line drawings. Circulation is 300, all subscriptions. Subscription: $40 (Aud) for overseas members. **Sample available (airmail from US) for $8 (Aud). Submissions may be "double-spaced, typed copy or simultaneous." Name and address must appear on the reverse side of each page submitted. Cover letter required; include brief details of previous publishing history, if any. Reporting time is 2 months and time to publication is 9 months. Pays 1 copy. Acquires first Australian rights.** Reviews books of poetry in 250 words, single format. Open to unsolicited reviews. Poets may also send books for review consideration. The magazine conducts a biannual poetry and short story contest. The editor says, "Trend in Australia is for imagist poetry and poetry exploring the land and the self. Reading the magazine gives the best indication of style and standard, so send a few dollars for a sample copy before sending your poetry. Keep writing, and we look forward to hearing from you."

STUDIO ONE (II), P.O. Box 1558, St. Joseph MN 56374, founded 1976, editor changes yearly. *Studio One* is an annual literary visual arts magazine designed as a forum for local, regional and national poets/ writers. **They have no specifications regarding form, subject matter or style of poetry submitted. However, poetry no more than 2 pages stands a better chance of publication.** They have recently published poetry by Larry Schug. As a sample the editor selected these lines from "my son the religious jew" by Jonathan Levant:

> *i making love am more important than*
> *my parents trying to sarah another man*
> *son using sharp knife as a chisel pierces*
> *the bottom of his orange juice sniffer glass*

The editor says *Studio One* is 50-80 pgs., soft cover, typeset. It includes 1-3 short stories, 22-30 poems and 10-13 visual art representations. They receive 250-400 submissions a year, accept about 30-40. Submit not more than 10 poems at a time. **Previously published poems and simultaneous submis-**

sions OK. **Deadline: February 24 for spring publication. Seldom comments on rejections. Send SASE if you want material returned.** *Studio One* received the 1994 Medalist Award from The Columbia Scholastic Press Association, Columbia University.

SUB-TERRAIN; ANVIL PRESS (II, IV-Social issues, political, form/style), P.O. Box 1575, Bentall Centre, Vancouver, British Columbia V6C 2P7 Canada, phone (604)876-8710, founded 1988, poetry editor Paul Pitre. Anvil Press is an "alternate small press publishing *Sub-Terrain*—a socially conscious literary quarterly whose aim is to produce a reading source that will stand in contrast to the trite and pandered—as well as broadsheets, chapbooks and the occasional monograph." They want **"work that has a point-of-view; work that has some passion behind it and is exploring issues that are of pressing importance (particularly that with an urban slant); work that challenges conventional notions of what poetry is or should be; work with a social conscience. No bland, flowery, uninventive poetry that says nothing in style or content."** As a sample the editor selected these lines from "Skin Dogs" by Helen Baker:

> The bodies are buried, but
> not the images:
> the school girl left
> squirming in a trash bag, a
> two-year-old cut open
> with the top of a tin
>
> Skin dogs; skinners
> other cons call them. . . .

Sub-Terrain is 40 pgs., 7½ × 10½, offset, with a press run of 3,000. Subscription: $15. **Sample postpaid: $4. Submit 4-6 poems at a time. They will consider simultaneous submissions, but not previously published poems. Reports in 8-10 weeks. Pays money only for solicited work; for other work, 4-issue subscription. Acquires one-time rights for magazine. "If chapbook contract, we retain right to publish subsequent printings unless we let a title lapse out-of-print for more than 1 year."** Staff occasionally reviews small press poetry chapbooks. Sponsors Last Poems Poetry Contest for "poetry that encapsulates North American experience at the close of the 20th Century"; information for SASE (or SAE and IRC). **For chapbook or book publication submit 4 sample poems and bio, no simultaneous submissions. "We are willing to consider mss. But I must stress that we are a co-op, depending on support from an interested audience. New titles will be undertaken with caution. We are not subsidized at this point and do not want to give authors false hopes—but if something is important and should be in print, we will do our best." Editor provides brief comment and more extensive comments for fees.** He says, "Poetry, in our opinion, should be a distillation of emotion and experience that is being given back to the world. Pretty words and fancy syntax are just that. Where are the modern day writers who are willing to risk it all, put it all on the line? Young, new writers: Show it all. The last thing the world needs is soppy, sentimental fluff that gives nothing and says nothing."

SULFUR MAGAZINE (II, IV-Translations), %Dept. of English, Eastern Michigan University, Ypsilanti MI 48197, phone (313)483-9787, founded 1981, poetry editor Clayton Eshleman, is a physically gorgeous and hefty (250 pgs., 6×9, flat-spined, glossy card cover, elegant graphics and printing on quality stock) biannual that has earned a distinguished reputation. They have published poetry by John Ashbery, Ed Sanders, Gary Snyder, Jackson MacLow, Paul Blackburn and the editor (one of our better-known poets). As a sample the editor selected "Irish" by Paul Celan, translated by Pierre Joris:

> Give me the right of way
> across the grain ladder of your sleep,
> the right of way
> across the sleep trail,
> The right, for me to cut peat
> along the heart's hillside,
> tomorrow.

Published at EMU, *Sulfur* has a circulation of 2,000, using approximately 100 pgs. of poetry in each issue. They use 15-20 of 600-700 submissions received/year. Free verse dominates here, much of it leaning toward the experimental. Subscription: $14. **Sample postpaid: $7. "We urge would-be contributors to *read* the magazine and send us material only if it seems to be appropriate." Editor comments "sometimes, if the material is interesting." Reports in 2-3 weeks. Pays $35-45/ contributor.** Reviews 10-20 poetry books/issue. Open to unsolicited reviews. Poets may also send books for review consideration. Clayton Eshleman says, "Most unsolicited material is of the 'I am sensitive and have practiced my sensitivity' school—with little attention to language as such, or incorporation of materials that lead the poem into more ample contexts than 'personal' experience. I fear too many young writers today spend more time on themselves, without deeply engaging their *selves*, in a serious psychological way—and too little time breaking their heads against the Blakes, Stevens and

Vallejos of the world. That is, writing has replaced reading. I believe that writing is a form of reading and vice versa. Of course, it is the quality and wildness of imagination that finally counts—but this 'quality' is a composite considerably dependent on assimilative reading (and translating, too)."

SULPHUR RIVER LITERARY REVIEW (II), P.O. Box 402087, Austin TX 78704-5578, founded 1978, reestablished 1987, editor/publisher James Michael Robbins, is a semiannual of poetry, prose and artwork. They have **"no restrictions except quality." They do not want poetry that is "trite or religious or verse that does not incite thought."** They have published poetry by Walt McDonald, Lyn Lifshin, Laurel Speer, Albert Huffstickler and Gerald Burns. As a sample the editor selected these lines from "The Small Credo" by Harland Ristau:

> *living*
> *is believing*
> *what we did*
> *what is not done.*
> *believing wrapped*
> *with ribbons of hope,*
> *the dream we wake from,*
> *living is believing*
> *spirit will mend,*
> *mend all things,*
> *bandaged by mercy,*
> *with time moored*
> *to a heart knowing*
> *when to come home.*

SRLR is digest-sized, perfect-bound, with glossy cover. They receive about 500 poems a year, accept about 10%. Press run is 400 for 200 subscribers, 100 shelf sales. Subscription: $8. **Sample postpaid: $4.50. No previously published poems or simultaneous submissions. Often comments on rejections. Reports in 1 month. Sometimes sends prepublication galleys. Pays 2 copies.** The editor says, "Poetry is, for me, the essential art, the ultimate art, and any effort to reach the effect of the successful poem deserves some comment other than 'sorry.' This is why I try to comment as much as possible on submissions, though by doing so I risk my own special absurdity. So be it. However, there can be no compromise of quality if the poem is to be successful or essential art."

SUMMER STREAM PRESS (II), P.O. Box 6056, Santa Barbara CA 93160-6056, phone (805)962-6540, founded 1978, poetry editor David D. Frost, publishes a series of books (Box Cars) in hardcover and softcover, each presenting 6 poets, averaging 70 text pgs. for each poet. "The mix of poets represents many parts of the country and many approaches to poetry. The poets previously selected have been published, but that is no requirement. We welcome traditional poets in the mix and thus offer them a chance for publication in this world of free-versers. **The six poets share a 15% royalty. We require rights for our editions worldwide and share 50-50 with authors for translation rights and for republication of our editions by another publisher. Otherwise all rights remain with the authors."** They have published poetry by Virginia E. Smith, Sandra Russell, Jennifer MacPherson, Nancy Berg, Lois Shapley Bassen and Nancy J. Wallace. To be considered for future volumes in this series, **query with about 12 sample poems, no cover letter. Replies to query in 3 months, to submission (if invited) in 1 year. Previously published poetry and simultaneous submissions OK. Editor usually comments on rejections. Always sends prepublication galleys.** He says, "We welcome both traditional poetry and free verse. However, we find we must reject almost all the traditional poetry received simply because the poets exhibit little or no knowledge of the structure and rules of traditional forms. Much of it is rhymed free verse."

THE SUN (II), 107 N. Roberson St., Chapel Hill NC 27516, phone (919)942-5282, founded 1974, editor Sy Safransky, is "a monthly magazine of ideas. Noted for honest, personal work. that's not too obscure or academic. **We avoid traditional, rhyming poetry, as well as limericks, haiku and religious poetry. We're open to almost anything else: free verse, prose poems, short and long poems."** They have recently published poetry by Alison Luterman, David Budhill, Carolyn Acree, Lyn Lifshin, Robert Bly and Lou Lipsitz. *The Sun* is magazine-sized, 40 pgs., printed on 50 lb. offset, saddle-stapled, with b&w photos and graphics, circulation 27,000, 25,000 subscriptions of which 50 are libraries. They receive 3,000 submissions of poetry/year, use 36, have a 1- to 3-month backlog. Subscription: $32. **Sample postpaid: $3.50. Submit no more than 6 poems. Poems should be typed and accompanied by a cover letter. Previously published poems and simultaneous submissions OK, but should be noted. Send SASE for guidelines. Reports within 3-5 months. Pays $25 on publication and in copies and subscription. Buys first serial or one-time rights.** *The Sun* received an *Utne Reader* Award for General Excellence.

SUN DOG: THE SOUTHEAST REVIEW (II), 406 Williams Bldg., English Dept., Florida State University, Tallahassee FL 32306, phone (904)644-4230, founded 1979, poetry editor Ron Wiginton. "The journal has a small student staff. We publish two magazines per year of poetry, short fiction and essays. As a norm, we usually accept about 12 poems per issue. **We accept poetry of the highest caliber, looking for the most 'whole' works. A poet may submit any length, but because of space, poems over 2 pages are impractical. Excellent formal verse highly regarded.**" They have published poetry by David Bottoms, David Kirby, Peter Meinke and Leon Stokesbury. *SD* is 100 pgs., 6×9, flat-spined with a glossy card cover, usually including half-tones, line drawings and color art when budget allows. Press run is 1,250. Subscription: $8 for 2 issues. **Sample postpaid: $4. Submit 2-5 poems at a time, typed, single-spaced. If simultaneous submission, say so. No previously published poems. Editor will comment briefly on most poems, especially those which come close to being accepted. Send SASE for guidelines. Reports in 3 months. Pays 2 copies. Acquires first North American serial rights.** *SD* sponsors the Richard Eberhart Prize in Poetry. This is an annual award given to the best unpublished poem of no fewer than 30 lines and no more than 100. The winner receives $300 and publication in *Sun Dog*. Submit 1 poem only and SASE for results to the Richard Eberhart Prize at the above address. No entry fee or form is requierd. Submission deadline: September 15. Winner will be announced on December 31.

‡SUNSTONE (II), 331 S. Rio Grande St., Suite 206, Salt Lake City UT 84101, founded 1974, poetry editor M. Shayne Bell, appears 8 times a year. *Sunstone* publishes "scholarly articles of interest to a liberal, Mormon audience; personal essays; fiction; and, of course, poetry." **They want "poetry dealing with life in or the landscape of the American West; poetry of the religious experience, including doubt and disbelief; any poem on any subject that uses the language with confidence and beauty. No didactic poetry, know-it-all poetry or sing-song rhymes."** They have recently published poetry by Dixie Partridge, Niranjan Mohanty, Rosemary A. Klein and Virginia Ellen Baker. As a sample the editor selected these lines from "A Trip to the Sea" by Philip White:

> At our backs the sun burned,
> and the gulls crossed it, hung
> trembling on the wind, turned,
> crossed again, their bodies
> on crooked wings falling and falling
> into the circle of flames.

Sunstone is 96 pgs., 8½×11, professionally printed and saddle-stapled with a semi-glossy paper cover. They receive more than 300 poems a year, accept 20-30. Press run is 10,000 for 8,000 subscribers of which 300 are libraries, 700 shelf sales. Subscription: $32 for 8 issues. **Sample postpaid: $4.95. No previously published poems or simultaneous submissions.** Time between acceptance and publication is a year or less. **Seldom comments on rejections. Send SASE for guidelines. Reports in 5 months. Pays 3 copies. Acquires first North American serial rights.** Reviews books of poetry. Open to unsolicited reviews. Poets may also send books for review consideration. The editor says, "Poetry does not have to be Mormon related at all. Most of it is not. The poetry we've published has covered all kinds of topics—from gay coming-out experiences to excommunication courts, to poems from India about life there, to the coming of spring in the Utah desert."

‡SURPRISE ME (I, IV-Spirituality), P.O. Box 1762, Claremore OK 74018, founded 1994, editor Lynda Nicolls, is a biannual. "*Surprise Me* is founded on the hope of providing a home for those souls who believe life's purpose is to serve Truth and Beauty. Our main interests are religion, mysticism, nature, art, literature, music, dance, relationships, love and peace. **We are open on form, length and style to all kinds of poetry. Profanity, intolerance and pro-violence are not welcome.**" They have recently published poetry by Jane Stuart and Paul Truttman. As a sample the editor selected these lines from "Prayer" by Phil Eisenberg:

> Muffle our strident conflicts,
> blunt the spikes of our wrath,
> disperse the god of hatred
> that palls the meteor's path;
> ease the writhing of earth
> and tune its discords of fear. . .

Surprise Me is 16-20 pgs., 8½×11, professionally printed by offset lithography on colored paper with b&w artwork and saddle-stapled. They receive about 1,000 poems a year, use approximately 10%. Press run is 150. Most copies distributed free to friends, contributors, libraries, universities and prisoners. Subscription: $8 individual in US; $10 institution in US; $10 Canada and Mexico; $12 overseas. **Sample postpaid: $4. Submit no more than 6 double-spaced pages at a time, name and address at the top of each page. Previously published poems and simultaneous submissions OK. Cover letter with brief bio required. "Submissions without cover letters (or at least a note) are too impersonal for me.**" Submissions without SASE or IRCs will usually not receive a response." Time between acceptance and publication is usually 6-12 months. **Seldom comments on rejections. Send SASE for**

guidelines. Reports ASAP. Pays 1 copy. Acquires one-time rights. "We may review contributors' books and magazines in the future. Please query before sending books for review consideration." Open to unsolicited reviews. The editor says, "I don't like much of what is being currently published, because it lacks spirituality and often has shock value as its motive. I'm glad to see that rhyming poetry is making a comeback. I would advise beginners to read a lot—perhaps Yeats, Jeffers, Frost, Eliot, Whitman and Dickinson—and to remember that editorial comments (bad or good) are only one person's opinion. If one editor thinks your work is garbage, another editor may call it a treasure."

‡SURREAL (II), P.O. Box 2105, Detroit MI 48231-2105, phone (313)567-1904, fax (313)567-1887, founded 1992, assistant editor Vince Cousino, is a quarterly "underground entertainment" magazine designed to "celebrate writers, artists and performers with unique talents who deserve broader exposure." It includes reviews, articles, poetry and stories. **They want "well-crafted poetry—strong visuals a plus. No political poetry for the sake of complaining. No light verse."** As a sample the editor selected these lines from "Lavender Blue," by Errol Miller:

> *And I was alone*
> *among the factory workers of the south,*
> *oily mechanics, greasing the grinding noisy gears*
> *of a shrouded universe, their mangy dogs*
> *whimpering, howling for rain.*

Surreal is 44 pgs., 8½ × 11, professionally printed and saddle-stapled with full-color glossy paper cover and glossy inside with b&w photos, art and ads throughout. The issue we received contained 3 poems. Their press run is 3,000 for 300 subscribers of which 50 are libraries, 2,000 shelf sales. Subscription: $11.33/year. **Sample postpaid: $3.95. Submit up to 5 poems at a time. No previously published poems; simultaneous submissions OK. Seldom comments on rejections. Send SASE for guidelines. Reports in 2 months. Pays 3 copies. Acquires first North American serial rights.** Reviews books of poetry. "Length varies—up to a page and a half as an unwritten rule. Both single and multibook format, though concentration is on single." Open to unsolicited reviews. Poets may also send books for review consideration. *Surreal* assigns artists to illustrate the poetry published within its pages. Artist Greg Carter won the "Best of Illustration" category, as recognized in the December 1994 issue of *Aldus Magazine*, for his illustration for "The Confessions of the Phoenix," a poem by M. DeCarteret.

SYCAMORE REVIEW (II), Dept. of English, Purdue University, West Lafayette IN 47907, phone (317)494-3783, founded 1988 (first issue May, 1989), editor-in-chief M.S. Manley, poetry editor changes each year; submit to Poetry Editor. "We accept personal essays, short fiction, translations and **quality poetry in any form. We aim to publish many diverse styles of poetry from formalist to prose poems, narrative and lyric."** They have recently published poetry by Elizabeth Dodd, Stuart Friebert, Lee Upton, Brigit Pegeen Kelly, Donald Hall, Gregory Orr and Colette Inez. As a sample the editors selected these lines from "The Gift Clock" by Jane Flanders:

> *I have written a few words and crossed them out.*
> *I have nicked myself and bled. ("Tsk tsk.")*
> *I have loved the world and the world's odd gifts.*
> *And I have remembered to turn the key that raises*
> *lead weights. For many days, my darlings,*
> *they will descend. I promise you, they will fall.*

The magazine is semiannual in a digest-sized format, 150 pgs., flat-spined, professionally printed, with glossy, color cover. Press run is 900 for 400 subscribers of which 50 are libraries. Subscription: $9; $11 outside US. **Sample postpaid: $5. Submit 3-6 poems at a time. Name and address on each page. No previously published poems except translations; simultaneous submissions OK, if notified immediately of acceptance elsewhere. Cover letters not required but invited; include phone number, short bio and previous publications, if any. "We read September 1 through May 1." Guidelines available for SASE. Reports in 4 months. Pays 2 copies.** Staff reviews books of poetry. Send books to editor-in-chief for review consideration. The editor says, "Poets who do not include SASE do not receive a response."

TAK TAK TAK (V, IV-Themes), BCM Tak, London WC1N 3XX England, founded 1986, editors Andrew and Tim Brown, appears occasionally in print and on cassettes. **"No restrictions on form or style. However, we are currently not accepting poetry submissions. Each issue of the magazine is on a theme (e.g., 'Mother Country/Fatherland,' 'Postcards from Paradise'), and *all* contributions must be relevant. If a contribution is long it is going to be more difficult to fit in than something shorter. Write for details of subject(s), etc., of forthcoming issue(s)."** They have published poetry by Michael Horovitz, Karl Blake, Keith Jafrate, Ramona Fotiade and Paul Buck. The editors describe it as "100 pgs., A5, photolithographed, board cover, line drawings and photographs, plus cassette of spoken word, music, sounds." Press run is 1,000. **Sample postpaid to US: £7.06 airmail (without cassette), £8.11 airmail (with cassette).** The editors say, "Poetry is just one of the many creative forms our contributions take. We are equally interested in prose and in visual and sound media."

TALISMAN: A JOURNAL OF CONTEMPORARY POETRY AND POETICS (III), P.O. Box 3157, Jersey City NJ 07303-3157, phone (201)938-0698, founded 1988, editor Edward Foster, appears twice a year. "Each issue centers on the poetry and poetics of a *major* contemporary poet and includes a selection of new work by other important contemporary writers. **We are particularly interested in poetry in alternative (*not* academic) traditions. We don't want traditional poetry.**" They have published poetry by William Bronk, Robert Creeley, Ron Padgett, Anne Waldman, Alice Notley, Edouard Roditi and Rosmarie Waldrop. As a sample the editor selected the following lines from "Opening Day" by Ann Lauterbach:

> *Locally a firm disavowal within the drift.*
> *Shaman of discourse said*
> *Or could have said*
> *These logics go teasingly forward*
> *Into capacities, and then the then.*

Talisman is 268 pgs., digest-sized, flat-spined, photocopied from computer printed Baskerville type, with matte card cover. "We are inundated with submissions and lost track of the number long ago." Their press run is 1,000 with "substantial" subscriptions of which many are libraries. Subscription: $11 individual; $15 institution. **Sample postpaid: $6. Reports in 2 months. Always sends prepublication galleys. Pays 1 copy. Acquires first North American serial rights.** Reviews books of poetry in 500-1,000 words, single format.

TAMAQUA (II, IV-Themes), C120, Parkland College, 2400 W. Bradley Ave., Champaign IL 61821-1899, phone (217)351-2380, founded 1989, editor-in-chief Bruce Morgan, is a biannual literary/arts journal **"of *high* quality. No restrictions on poetry, but it must be intelligently and professionally done."** They have recently published poetry by Gloria Bird, Ray Young Bear and Lida Aronne Amestoy. As a sample the editor selected these lines from "Meeting, at a Party, a Woman with an Artificial Larynx" by Conrad Hilberry:

> *"How do you do," she said, her lips and tongue*
> *shaping the words but the voice flat, metallic,*
> *a wire on which the other voices hung*
> *like laundry flapping. I thought I heard a click*
> *where a thought ended.*

Tamaqua is 160-256 pgs., digest-sized, offset and perfect-bound with 4-color coated card cover, b&w (and occasional color) art and photos inside. They receive 2,000-3,000 poems/year, accept approximately 50. Press run is 1,500 for 400 subscribers of which 50 are libraries, 750 shelf sales. Subscription: $10/year. **Sample postpaid: $6. Submit 3-7 poems at a time. Prefers poems typed on bonded paper. No previously published poems; simultaneous submissions OK, "if noted in cover letter and contacted immediately if accepted elsewhere." Cover letter required. "All submissions are juried anonymously; only managing editor knows identity of writer before selection." Seldom comments on rejections. Publishes theme issues. Send SASE for guidelines.** Theme for Winter 1996 issue is "European Voices." **Deadline: November 15, 1995. Reports in 4 months. Pays $10-20 plus copies. Acquires first North American serial rights.** Reviews books of poetry in both single and multi-book format, no minimum length. Open to unsolicited reviews, but prefers "meditative review." Poets may also send books for review consideration, attn. Sue Kuykendall. The editor says, "Nothing replaces knowledge of your market; hence *study Tamaqua* and similar magazines to discern the difference between good, solid, intelligent literature/art and that which is not."

TAMPA REVIEW (III), Dept. PM, University of Tampa, 401 W. Kennedy Blvd., Tampa FL 33606-1490, phone (813)253-3333, ext. 6266, founded 1964 as *UT Poetry Review,* became *Tampa Review* in 1988, editor Richard Mathews, poetry editors Kathryn Van Spanckeren and Donald Morrill, is an elegant semiannual of fiction, nonfiction, poetry and art (not limited to US authors) wanting **"original and well-crafted poetry written with intelligence and spirit. We do accept translations, but no greeting card or inspirational verse."** They have published poetry by Alberto Rios, Paul Mariani, Mark Halliday, Denise Levertov and Stephen Dunn. As a sample, the editors selected these lines from "The Psalm of the Pallbearers" by Nancy J. Wiegel:

> *We thought of those men buried centuries*

The Subject Index, located before the General Index, can help you narrow down markets for your work. It lists those publishers whose poetry interests are specialized.

> *ago with their banners and armour.*
> *Your weight, though, was different. It was more*
> *like a star's. It was more like a star,*
> *collapsed totally inward, whose gravity*
> *not even light could escape.*

TR is 78-96 pgs., flat-spined, 7½ × 10½ with a matte card color cover. They accept about 50-60 of 2,000 poems received a year. Their press run is 500 with 175 subscriptions of which 20 are libraries. **Sample postpaid: $5. Submit 3-7 poems at a time. No previously published poems or simultaneous submissions. Unsolicited mss are read between September and December. Reports by mid-February. Sometimes sends prepublication galleys. Pays $10/printed page plus 1 copy and 40% discount on additional copies. Buys first North American serial rights.** This review received the 1994 Phoenix Award for "Significant Editorial Achievement" from the Council of Editors of Learned Journals and poetry published in *Tampa Review* has been included in *The Best American Poetry 1995*.

TANGRAM PRESS (III), Dept. PM, P.O. Box 2249, Granbury TX 76048, phone (817)579-1777, contact Karee Gallaway. This very small press would like to publish more books such as their handsome coffee-table volume, 12 × 12, hardback, *Where Rainbows Wait for Rain: The Big Bend Country*, combining poems by Sandra Lynn and b&w photographs by Richard Fenker Jr., but "we have a limited staff. **While we do not discourage submissions, we cannot guarantee comments on same. We are not your standard poetry publisher. Send SASE with submission if you want it returned."**

TANTRA PRESS (I, II), P.O. Box 4334, Parkersburg WV 26104, phone (304)422-3112, founded 1993, editors David B. Prather and David W. Carvell, is a biannual journal of poetic verse. **"We want to see all work—no restrictions, but we do look for detailed imagery and a sensitivity to language. We stay away from singsong and work with little substance."** They have published poetry by Susan Sheppard and Kenneth Pobo. As a sample the editors selected these lines from "Ollala: A Meditation on a Name" by Jane Somerville:

> *She lifts a fleshy finger*
> *and makes a room,*
> *her own, accoutered in gold*
> *and looped in blue*
> *and every line of all that loot*
> *laid out to follow her body.*

Tantra Press is 60 pgs., 5½ × 8½, saddle-stapled with colored card cover with art. They receive 300-500 poems a year, accept 20-30%. Press run is 200. Subscription: $9. **Sample postpaid: $4. No previously published poems; simultaneous submissions OK. Cover letter required. "Please include biographical information. We read all year long with deadlines for submissions on May 15 and November 15."** Time between acceptance and publication is 3-6 months. **Seldom comments on rejections. Reports within 2 months. Pays 1 copy. All rights revert to authors.**

TAPJOE: THE ANAPROCRUSTEAN POETRY JOURNAL OF ENUMCLAW (II, IV-Nature/rural/ecology, political), P.O. Box 632, Leavenworth WA 98826, founded 1987, contact editor, is a biannual. **"We try to be very open-minded but have a definite preference for free verse poems, 10-50 lines, which links humans with the natural world while encompassing some thought or insight."** They have recently published poetry by Noah Farnsworth, Sean Brendan Brown, Marlene Muller and Joan Hue. As a sample the editor selected these lines from "Answers" by Glenda Cassutt:

> *You who love land*
> *long for forest,*
> *distrust the jumbled waves,*
> *the distance from seawall*
> *and lighthouse.*

The magazine is 40 pgs., digest-sized, saddle-stapled, offset from desktop with matte card cover. Accepts about 60 poems/year with 1,000 submissions. Press run is 200 for 60 subscribers. Subscription: $10 for 4 issues. **Sample postpaid: $3. No simultaneous submissions or previously published poems. "Cover letters appreciated but not necessary."** Final selections may take 6 months or so. **Often comments on rejections. Send SASE for guidelines. Reports in 1-4 months, "often longer."** **Pays 1 copy for each accepted poem.** They say, "Submissions are circulated among several editors living hundreds of miles apart and working hectic jobs; sometimes this makes our responses very slow but we do the best we can. We appreciate purchases of our magazine—but mostly we enjoy receiving submissions of 'good' poetry! We publish poetry that connects the human and natural worlds; that is, poems which explore the ways in which those worlds coexist and form a whole."

TAPROOT LITERARY REVIEW (I), 302 Park Rd., Ambridge PA 15003, phone (412)266-8476, founded 1986, editor Tikvah Feinstein, is an annual contest publication, open to beginners. In addition to contest, each year guest poets are selected; payment in copies. Writers recently published include

Robert Johnson, George Kalamaras, Elizabeth Cappo, Mary Pogge and B.Z. Niditch. As a sample the editor selected these lines from "Children's Transport" by Lyn Lifshin:

> *in post partum*
> *fever her husband*
> *can't tell her the*
> *other daughter's*
> *gone. Only the*
> *infant screams*

The review is approximately 95 pgs., printed by offset on white stock with one-color glossy cover, art and no ads. Circulation is 500, sold at bookstores, readings and through the mail. Single copy: $5.50. **Sample postpaid: $5. There is a $10 entry fee for up to 5 poems, "no longer than 30 lines each." Nothing previously published or pending publication will be accepted. Cover letter with general information required. "We cannot answer without a SASE." Submissions accepted between September 1 and December 31. Publishes theme issues. Send SASE for upcoming themes. Sometimes sends prepublication galleys. All entrants receive a copy of** *Taproot***; enclose $2 for p&h.** Send books for review consideration. The editor says, "We publish the best poetry we can in a variety of styles and subjects, so long as its literary quality and speaks to us."

TAR RIVER POETRY (II), English Dept., East Carolina University, Greenville NC 27858-4353, phone (919)752-6041, founded 1960, editor Peter Makuck, associate editor Luke Whisnant. **"We are not interested in sentimental, flat-statement poetry. What we would like to see is skillful use of figurative language."** They have published poetry by William Matthews, William Stafford, Susan Ludvigson, Susan Elizabeth Howe, A.R. Ammons, Naomi Shihab Nye, Peter Davison, Margaret Gibson, Brendan Galvin and Sharon Bryan. As a sample the editors selected these lines from "Poem for Dizzy" by Betty Adcock:

> *Sweet and sly, you were all business when that bent-skyward*
> *old horn went up. Sometimes it went up like a rocket,*
> *sometimes like a gentle-turning lark*
> *high in a summer day. Or like an island wind*
> *snapping a line of red and yellow clothes*
> *hard against blue . . . .*

Tar River appears twice yearly and is 60 pgs., digest-sized, professionally printed on salmon stock, some decorative line drawings, matte card cover with photo. They receive 6,000-8,000 submissions/ year, use 150-200. Press run is 900 for 500 subscribers of which 125 are libraries. Subscription: $10. **Sample: $5.50. Submit 3-6 poems at a time. "We do not consider previously published poems or simultaneous submissions. Double or single-spaced OK. Name and address on each page. We do not consider mss during summer months." Reads submissions September 1 through April 15 only. Send SASE for guidelines. Reports in 4-6 weeks. Pays copies. Acquires first rights. Editors will comment "if slight revision will do the trick."** Reviews books of poetry in 4,000 words maximum, single or multi-book format. This is an especially good market for intelligent, concisely written book reviews. Poets may also send books for review consideration. *Tar River* is an "all-poetry" magazine that accepts dozens of poems in each issue, providing the talented beginner and experienced writer with an excellent forum that features all styles and forms of verse. Frequently contributors' works are included in the *Anthology of Magazine Verse & Yearbook of American Poetry*. Poetry published in *Tar River* was also selected for inclusion in *The Best American Poetry 1994*. The editors advise, "Read, read, read. Saul Bellow says the writer is primarily a reader moved to emulation. Read the poetry column in *Writer's Digest*. Read the books recommended therein. Do your homework."

"TEAK" ROUNDUP (I, IV-Subscribers); AARDVARK ENTERPRISES (I), A Division of Speers Investments Ltd., 204 Millbank Dr. SW, Calgary, Alberta T2Y 2H9 Canada, phone (403)256-4639, founded 1962, editor J. Alvin Speers. *"Teak" Roundup* **is an international quarterly open to the work of subscribers only.** They publish work from authors, poets and cartoonists across North America and beyond. Aardvark **publishes chapbooks on subsidy arrangements.** They have recently published *Down Lundy's Memory Lane* by W. Ray Lundy and *Fallen Soldiers* by J. Alvin Speers. As a sample the editor selected these lines from his poem "Fallen Soldiers":

> *We think of fallen soldiers,*
> *Remembering their goal*
> *To uphold lofty principles*
> *And elevate the soul.*

TR publishes poetry, prose, articles, essays, reviews and illustrations from **subscribers only. "We strongly prefer rhyme, but clarity of meaning is also important."** Subscription: $17, $24 overseas. **Sample: $5, $8 overseas. Submit 3-5 poems at a time. Simultaneous submissions OK, if notified. Cover letter preferred. SASE (or SAE with IRC) required for response. Send SASE for guidelines and upcoming themes. No payment.** "It is our goal to become a paying market when circulation makes it feasible." For subsidized chapbook publication, query with 3-5 samples, bio, previous

publications. "We publish for hire—quoting price with full particulars. We do not market these except by special arrangement. Prefer poet does that. We strongly recommend seeing our books first. Send SASE (or SAE with IRC) for catalog to buy book samples. **Please note US stamps cannot be used in Canada.**"

TEARS IN THE FENCE (II), 38 Hodview, Stourpaine, Nr. Blandford Forum, Dorset DT11 8TN England, phone 01258-456803, founded 1984, general editor David Caddy, poetry editor Sarah Hopkins, is a "small press magazine of poetry, fiction, interviews, articles, reviews and graphics. **We are open to a wide variety of poetic styles. Work of a social, political, ecological and feminist awareness will be close to our purpose. However, we like to publish a balanced variety of work." The editors do not want to see "didactic rhyming poems."** They have recently published poetry by Joan Jobe Smith, Martin Stannard, Ann Born and Catherine Swanson. As a sample, they selected the following lines from "From a Gloucestershire Window" by Brian Hinton:

> Look, the manor house blazes red, its complex windows on fire
> with history, blind mirrors in which we disappear, over wrought
> gates that we can never enter. My mother, orphaned here, inspired
> me with tales of forced church on Sunday, bowing to the court

Tears in the Fence appears 3 times/year. It is 64 pgs., A5, desktop-published on 90 gms. paper with b&w art and graphics and matte card cover. It has a press run of 400, of which 223 go to subscribers. Subscription: $15 for 3 issues. **Sample: $5. Writers should submit 6 typed poems with IRCs. Cover letter with brief bio required. Publishes theme issues. Send SASE (or SAE and IRC) for upcoming themes. Reports in 3 months.** Time to publication is 8-10 months "but can be much less." **Pays 1 copy.** Reviews books of poetry in 2,000-3,000 words, single or multi-book format. Open to unsolicited reviews. Poets may also send books for review consideration. The magazine is informally connected with the East Street Poets literary promotions, workshops and publications. They also sponsor an annual pamphlet competition open to poets from around the world. The editor says, "I think it helps to subscribe to several magazines in order to study the market and develop an understanding of what type of poetry is published. Use the review sections and send off to magazines that are new to you."

‡THE TENNESSEE QUARTERLY (II), Dept. of Literature and Language, Belmont University, 1900 Belmont Blvd., Nashville TN 37212-3757, first issue Spring 1994, co-editor Anthony Lombardy, appears 3 times/year (in the fall, winter and spring). "*The Tennessee Quarterly* publishes poems, short fiction, essays of general interest as well as of broad literary-critical and theoretical reach, translations, and articles of art theory and criticism." **They want poetry of "any form, subject or style, but we favor language highly marked whether by metrical form or rhetorical figure."** They have recently published poetry by Peter Russell, Emily Grosholz and Richard Moore and a translation by Dana Gioia. As a sample the editor selected the last stanza of "In the Shield of Athena" by Greg Williamson:

> And so envision shrouds of grief, the gem
> Of naked beauty, and the knucklebone
> Of hate; such things as on the face of them
> Would blind the eye or turn the heart to stone.

The Tennessee Quarterly is 60-100 pgs., 6×9, professionally printed on quality stock and flat-spined with light matte card cover. They receive 4,000-5,000 poems a year, accept about 50. Press run is 500 for 200 subscribers, 100 shelf sales. Subscription: $15/year. **Sample postpaid: $5. No previously published poems or simultaneous submissions. Reads submissions September 1-June 15 only.** Time between acceptance and publication is 6 months. **Seldom comments on rejections. Reports usually within a month. Pays 2 copies. Acquires first North American serial rights.** Reviews books of poetry in up to 2,000 words. Open to unsolicited reviews. Poets may also send books for review consideration.

TESSERA (IV-Women, regional, bilingual, themes, translations), 350 Stong, York University, 4700 Keele St., North York, Ontario M3J 1P3 Canada, founded 1984, revived 1988, appears twice a year: **"feminist literary theory and experimental writing by women in French and English, preference to Canadians."** It is 94 pgs., digest-sized, professionally printed, with glossy card cover. Subscription: $18. **Sample postpaid: $10. Submit 4 poems at a time. Simultaneous submissions and previously published poems ("sometimes") OK. Editor comments on submissions "sometimes." Publishes theme issues. Themes for Volume 20 and Volume 21 are "Non-literary genres—comics, graffiti, etc." (deadline December 31, 1995) and "Symbolic Violence and the Avant Garde" (deadline May 31, 1995), respectively. Pays $10/page.** The editor says, "I appreciate a cover letter introducing the poetic project the poems come out of. I also appreciate poets who have done a bit of research and are familiar with the kinds of texts we publish."

TESSERACT PUBLICATIONS (I), P.O. Box 505, Hudson SD 57034-0505, phone (605)987-5070, fax (605)987-5071, founded 1981, publisher Janet Leih. **"All my books are subsidized publications. Payment is ⅓ in advance, ⅓ when book goes to printer, balance when book is complete. I help my**

poets with copyright, bar codes, listings and whatever publicity I can get for them. I have a number of mailing lists and will prepare special mailings for them, work with competent proofreaders, artists and a capable reviewer." Sometimes sends prepublication galleys. They have helped publish books of poetry by Helen Eikamp, Gertrude Johnson, Fern Stuefen, Wanda Todd and Ellis Ovesen. As a sample Janet Leih selected these lines by Lois Bogue:

> Last night northern lights
> shimmered in silent glory
> across starry spaces.
> Suddenly I was a child
> sky-watching with my father.

They also hold occasional contests. Send SASE for information. Janet Leih adds, "I publish a catalog of books by South Dakota writers and take their books on consignment to fill orders. The catalog is new and modest at this time but the hope is to expand to a larger catalog and distribute it more widely."

TEXAS TECH UNIVERSITY PRESS (III, IV-Series), P.O. Box 41037, Lubbock TX 79409-1037, phone (806)742-2982, founded 1971, editor Judith Keeling, considers volumes of poetry in 3 categories only: **First-Book Poetry Series**: "Winning and finalist mss in an annual competition conducted by Poetry Editor Walter McDonald, who surveys some 20 literary journals throughout the year and invites up to 12 poets to submit mss for consideration in the competition"; **Invited Poets Series**: "Collections invited from established poets whose work continues to appear in distinguished journals"; and **TTUP Contemporary Poetry Series**: "Winning and finalist works in current national competitions." **Mss for the TTUP Contemporary Poetry Series should be submitted with cover letters and attachments to verify eligibility. Editors never comment on rejections. Books published on royalty contracts.**

‡TEXTURE; TEXTURE PRESS (II, IV-Form/style), 3760 Cedar Ridge Dr., Norman OK 73072, fax (405)364-3627, founded 1989, editor Susan Smith Nash, is an annual ("approximately") of experimental and innovative writing: poetry, criticism, fiction and reviews. **They want "innovative or experimental poetry which openly addresses difficult philosophical, theoretical or linguistic issues. No dull, sterile, derivative work."** They have recently published poetry by Robert Kelly, Rochelle Owens, Cydney Chadwick, Valerie Fox and Douglas Messerli. As a sample the editor selected these lines from "Prime Sway: A Transduction of Sor Juana's Primero Suento, 1692" by John M. Bennett:

> PYRAMID, wall, furnace tears
> nascent slumber, Ah Ceiling walking
> vanes and obelisks pumped the thigh . . .

texture is 100 pgs., 8½ × 11, offset and perfect-bound with colored matte card cover. They receive 1,000 poems a year, accept approximately 20%. Press run is 1,000 for 300 subscribers of which 15 are libraries. Single copy: $8; subscription: $10 for 2 issues. **Sample postpaid: $6. No previously published poems or simultaneous submissions. Cover letter required. Reads submissions October 1 through May 15 only. Poems are circulated to an editorial board. Seldom comments on rejections. Reports in 3-6 months. Pays 1 copy. Acquires first rights.** Includes book briefs of 50 words and reviews of 250-500 words. Open to unsolicited reviews. Poets may also send books for review consideration. texture press also publishes books, chapbooks and miniatures. **"Query first and explain the critical grounding of the work. texture likes to publish a critical accompaniment to help readers locate the text within the current literary scene and understand how to read it." Replies to queries in 2 months, to mss (if invited) in 6 months. Payment is negotiated.** The editor says, "Feel free to experiment, to mangle text, and to ironize the cultural verities by juxtaposing them with the words of sages, philosophers, or your favorite great aunt."

THALIA: STUDIES IN LITERARY HUMOR (I, IV-Subscribers, humor), Dept. of English, University of Ottawa, Ottawa, Ontario K1N 6N5 Canada, editor Dr. J. Tavernier-Courbin, appears twice a year using **"humor (literary, mostly). Poems submitted must actually be literary parodies."** The editor describes it as 7 × 8½, flat-spined, "with illustrated cover." Press run is 500 for 475 subscribers. Subscription: $20 for individuals, $22 for libraries. **Sample postpaid: $8 up to volume 11, $15 and $20 for volumes 12 and 13 respectively (double issues). Contributors must subscribe. Simultaneous submissions OK but *Thalia* must have copyright. Will authorize reprints. Editor comments on submissions.** Reviews books of poetry. "Send queries to the editor concerning specific books."

THEMA (II, IV-Themes), Thema Literary Society, P.O. Box 74109, Metairie LA 70033-4109, founded 1988, editor Virginia Howard, is a triannual literary magazine **using poetry related to specific themes. "Each issue is based on an unusual premise. Please, please send SASE for guidelines before submitting poetry to find out the upcoming themes. Upcoming themes (and submission deadlines) include: 'Jogging on ice' (11-1-95), 'A Visit from the imp' (3-1-96), 'I know who you are!' (7-1-96) and 'Too proud to ask' (11-1-96). No scatologic language, alternate life-style, explicit love poetry."** They have recently published poetry by Kristina Simms, David Alpaugh, Judith Saunders and Kaye Bache-Snyder. As a sample the editor selected these lines by William Sheldon:

> *Holding him at the mirror,*
> *I watch my son,*
> *his brother lost at birth,*
> *reach this first time*
> *for his own hand.*

Thema is digest-sized, 200 pgs., professionally printed, with matte card cover. They accept about 8% of 400 poems received/year. Press run is 500 for 270 subscribers of which 30 are libraries. Subscription: $16. **Sample postpaid: $8. Submit only 1-3 poems at a time. All submissions should be typewritten and on standard 8½ × 11 paper. Submissions are accepted all year, but evaluated after specified deadlines. Editor comments on submissions. Pays $10/poem plus 1 copy. Buys one-time rights only.**

‡THE THIRD ALTERNATIVE (II, IV-Science fiction/fantasy, horror); ZENE: THE SMALL PRESS GUIDE, 5 Martins Lane, Witcham, Ely, Cambridgeshire CB6 2LB England, phone 01353-777931, founded 1994, editor Andy Cox. *The Third Alternative* is a quarterly of **"cutting-edge horror, dark fantasy and science fiction, often transcending such genres to explore the slipstream, the interface of genre and mainstream writing." They want "well-crafted, literary, powerful poems, usually 40 lines maximum, from imaginative to disturbing. Translations welcome. Not keen on rhyming poetry or haiku."** They have recently published poetry by Sheila E. Murphy, Bruce Boston, Andrew Darlington and Steve Sneyd. As a sample the editor selected these lines from "The Birth of Hierony-mous Bosch" by David Chorlton:

> *A bell drips*
> *from a shivering tower. The leading*
> *melts in coloured windows*
>
> *and glass*
> *rains onto the silky wings*
> *of bats circling in crepuscular panic.*

The Third Alternative is 52 pgs., A5, litho printed on coated paper and saddle-stitched with b&w coated card cover and b&w graphics. They accept less than 10% of the poetry received. Press run is 300 for 150 subscribers ("and rising"). Subscription: £9, $22 USA. **Sample postpaid: £2.50, $6 USA. Previously published poems OK; no simultaneous submissions. Cover letter required.** Time between acceptance and publication is 2-3 issues. **Always comments on rejections. Reports in 1 month. Pays 1 copy. Acquires first British serial rights.** Andy Cox is also the editor of *Zene: The Small Press Guide*, a quarterly which lists "detailed contributor's guidelines of small press, independent and semi-pro markets worldwide, plus articles, news, views, interviews and reviews. Every issue carries a number of reviews of poetry publications, plus articles on various types of poetry." Poets may send books for review consideration to the above address. *Zene* is 36 pgs., A5, litho printed on coated paper and saddle-stitched. Single copy: £1.95, $4.50 USA; subscription: £7, $16.60 USA.

THE THIRD HALF LITERARY MAGAZINE; K.T. PUBLICATIONS (I, II), 16, Fane Close, Stamford, Lincolnshire PE9 1HG England, founded 1987, editor Mr. Kevin Troop. *TTH* appears "as often as possible each year." K.T. Publications also publishes up to 6 other books, with a Minibooks Series, for use in the classroom. The editor wants **"meaningful, human and humane, funny poems up to 40 lines. Work which actually *says* something without being obscene."** They have published poetry by Lee Bridges (Holland), Ann Keith (Amsterdam), Toby Litt (Prague) and Edmund Harwood, Michael Newman, Louise Rogers and Steve Sneyd (Britain). As a sample the editor selected this poem, "Fly," by Esther Gress (Denmark):

> *Like a butterfly*
> *we often fly in vain*
> *against the window pane*
> *and see not*
> *like the butterfly*
> *the open door*
> *to the sky*

TTH is 44 pgs., A5, printed on white paper with glossy cover. Press run is about 200. Individual booklets vary in length and use colored paper and card covers. **Submit 6 poems at a time. No simultaneous submissions. Cover letter and suitable SAE required. Reports ASAP. Pays 1 copy.** "Procedure for the publication of books is explained to each author; each case is different. *The Third Half* is priced at £2.25 each; two subsequent issues for £4.25 and three issues for £6.25 plus suitable SAEs, including postage and handling."

13TH MOON (II, IV-Women), English Dept., SUNY-Albany, 1400 Washington Ave., Albany NY 12222, phone (518)442-4181, founded 1973, editor Judith Johnson, is a feminist literary magazine appearing yearly (one double issue) in a 6 × 9, flat-spined, handsomely printed format with glossy card

Discover the Value in Chapbook Publishing

"Today the Jays"

Today the Jays came early,
to gossip, and crack the heavy seeds.
I hear them talk of Sartre, and Kierkegaard
. . . they laugh
and leave the millet begging in the bowl.
. . . I laugh.
What can they possibly know about Sartre,
or Kierkegaard?
. . . they were certainly wrong
about Nietzsche.

Photo by Jeffrey Hawkins

Laurence F. Hawkins

Laurence F. Hawkins's passion for poetry goes far beyond just writing it. He reads submissions. Chooses poetry. Types. Prints. Folds. And trims the uneven paper edges of everything he produces.

"It's a one-person endeavor," says Hawkins about Trout Creek Press, the name under which he publishes chapbooks and the semiannual *Dog River Review*.

Although there's the constant dilemma of not having enough time and money to publish as much as he would like, there's also a great satisfaction in publishing, particularly with chapbooks. "I enjoy holding them in my hands when I'm through—they're tangible products that I've produced in conjunction with the poets. We have something to show for our efforts."

In the past 12 years, Hawkins has published about 24 chapbooks. He hasn't profited from any of them, but then, making money isn't his goal in publishing poets' work. "The people I publish have something to say," he says.

About 15 years ago, Hawkins, a third generation printer, bought a 1947 offset press. Wanting to communicate with writers, he began publishing *Dog River Review* in 1982 and, two years later, published his first chapbook. Trout Creek Press—named after the creek that runs behind his Parkdale, Oregon, house—was a logical outgrowth of the magazine, he says. It enables him to publish additional poems by poets he especially likes.

For poets, the chapbook format provides a more economical way of getting a collection published—a bridge between having poems published in a review and having a commercial or university press publish a volume of poetry.

At Trout Creek Press, chapbooks come in many sizes, from the more standard journal-size (5¼×8¼ inches), to pocket-size (4×5¼) and elongated formats (4¼×10½), to accommodate longer verses. Some poets sign and sell their chapbooks at readings. (At $2.50 to $5 per copy, they're more affordable for interested readers than volumes from university and commercial presses.)

The cost of producing a chapbook can be considerable, though, for the publisher. Hawkins provides the paper, ink and labor and, since his press broke down last year, rents time on a job-printer's press to do the printing. Poets provide manuscripts, goodwill and promises to help promote the chapbooks.

For the poet, a collection demands careful planning, Hawkins says. "Collections have to have underlying themes that tie them together—whether that's from characters or events in the poems or whether it's just a feeling or type of poetry."

He has also found that the arrangement of the poems can enhance or detract from a collection. Like any poetry volume, the chapbook must be balanced so there are high and low points. "They have to have some kind of logical order or arrangement and have to lead somewhere from point A to point B, however sinuous that path may be."

Of course, collections begin with individual poems. Get a poem on paper, Hawkins advises, and then consider its essence and what detracts from it. "Emotions have to come first before the brain takes over to whip the poem into shape."

Know personally and be involved with your subject and, also, go one step beyond—"feeling and understanding what it is you want to say. To me, the poem has to have some sort of inner music, the lyric, some kind of a harmony," says Hawkins. "Sometimes the poem is so unbalanced that it's hard to read."

One of the best ways to hear the inner melody is to read the poem aloud and in various ways. Hawkins tape-records the reading of his own poems. Rehearing the poem helps him analyze the line breaks and know if the breaks are in the right places. In reading other poets' submissions, Hawkins finds that word choice will immediately attract his attention. Sometimes the words just aren't right, he says. "There's a clash between either lines or stanzas. It's not cohesive enough."

As editor and publisher, he likes poems that "tend toward nature and toward the basic human emotions. I look for poems that express, in an imaginative way, universal feelings and yet cause the readers to ruminate on what they've read. I shy away from verse that is more pedantic or analytical. I like something that has a visceral feel to it so readers can get emotionally involved."

What makes a good poem? It's difficult to pinpoint, Hawkins admits—except that a good poem is well-crafted. For an editor, a group of poems is like a museum full of paintings. Why a person is drawn to one painting instead of others is difficult to say, he muses. Perhaps that's the attraction of art and poetry.

Once you have a collection of well-crafted poems that are linked in some way, you're ready to consider chapbook publication. In selecting a publisher, read a wide range of chapbooks. Target publishers which publish the types of poems you write. Also, look for a track record and a standard of quality work, says Hawkins.

With desktop-publishing equipment, anyone can publish a chapbook, but not everyone has a publisher's objectivity and printer's know-how. "It doesn't cost extra money to put out a clean, balanced-looking product, and I strive in that direction," Hawkins says.

All Trout Creek volumes reflect this goal. And Hawkins's love for poetry and printing. Pleasing, unobtrusive typefaces. Heavy matte paper. Pen-and-ink drawings on the covers. As the publisher says, "I look for things that are exciting, brilliant, sharp and clear."

—*Paula Deimling*

cover, using photographs and line art, ads at $200/page. Beyond a doubt, a real selection of forms and styles is featured here. For instance, in recent issues free verse has appeared with formal work, concrete poems, long poems, stanza patterns, prose poems, a crown of sonnets and more. Press run is 2,000 for 690 subscribers of which 61 are libraries, 700 shelf sales. Subscription: $10. **Sample postpaid: $8. Submit 3-5 poems at a time. No previously published work or simultaneous submissions. Reads submissions September 1 through May 30 only. Publishes theme issues. Send SASE for guidelines and upcoming themes.** Themes include "special issues on women's poetics, one focusing on poetry, one on narrative forms." **Pays 2 copies. Acquires first North American serial rights.** Staff reviews books of poetry in 1,500 words "more or less." Send books to Sue Shaferzak, review editor, for review consideration.

THIS: A SERIAL REVIEW (II), 6600 Clough Pike, Cincinnati OH 45224-4090, founded 1993, editor (Mr.) Robin Yale Bergstrom, poetry editor Paul Aharon Cagle, appears 3 times/year "to give voice to underdogs and established writers and artists. We enjoy writers and artists taking risks—whether in poetry, fiction, prose, artistry or photography. **We seek strong, effective poetry as well as today's ground-breaking styles of craft. No trite rhyme, sentimental or inspirational poetry.**" The editor says *This* is about 120 pgs., 8 × 8, perfect-bound, with 2-color cover, art and graphics and exchange ads. Press run is 2,000. Subscription: $27 (3 issues). **Sample postpaid: $7. Submit no more than 10 poems at a time. Previously published poems and simultaneous submissions OK, if notified. Cover letter required.** Time between acceptance and publication is 4-6 months. **Seldom comments on rejections. Send SASE for guidelines. Reports in 2-3 months. Pays 2 copies. Acquires one-time rights.** Reviews books of poetry. Open to unsolicited reviews. Poets may also send books for review consideration. The editor says, "Our publication seeks what is definitive in *today's* poetic craft. We encourage all poets to add their voice. Advice for beginners? Read, read, and read some more."

THISTLEDOWN PRESS LTD. (IV-Regional), 633 Main St., Saskatoon, Saskatchewan S7H 0J8 Canada, phone (306)244-1722, fax (306)244-1762, founded 1975, editor-in-chief Patrick O'Rourke, is "a literary press that specializes in **quality books of contemporary poetry by Canadian authors. Only the best of contemporary poetry that amply demonstrates an understanding of craft with a distinctive use of voice and language. Only interested in full-length poetry mss with 53-71 pgs. minimum.**" They have recently published books of poetry by Glen Sorestad, Rhona McAdam, Doug Beardsley, John Clark, Anne Campbell and John V. Hicks. **Do not submit unsolicited mss.** Canadian poets must **query first with letter, bio and publication credits. Poetry ms submission guidelines available upon request. Replies to queries in 2-3 weeks, to submissions (if invited) in 3 months. No authors outside Canada. No simultaneous submissions. "Please submit quality dot-matrix, laser-printed or photocopied material." Always sends prepublication galleys. Contract is for 10% royalty plus 10 copies.** They comment, "Poets submitting mss to Thistledown Press for possible publication should think in 'book' terms in every facet of the organization and presentation of the mss: Poets presenting mss that *read* like good books of poetry will have greatly enhanced their possibilities of being published. We strongly suggest that poets familiarize themselves with some of our poetry books before submitting a query letter."

THORNTREE PRESS (II), 547 Hawthorn Lane, Winnetka IL 60093, founded 1986, contact Eloise Bradley Fink. This not-for-profit press publishes professionally printed, digest-sized, flat-spined paperbacks, 96 pgs., selected through competition January 1 through February 14 in odd-numbered years only. **Sample postpaid: $7.95.** "Included in our 18 books are 27 poets." From *Troika V* Lydia Webster writes:

> "*I sing to you my . . . goodbyography . . . and flatten myself like a*
> *map across your knee. I rent a room . . . . the stare of*
> *strangers who have slept in my room and try to*
> *pull me on like a sweater. I smell snow on the*
> *tip of God's tongue . . . . I become a raven, knife into the*
> *canyon . . . . Ravens touch nothing for luck but sky;*
> *only we know where we're going, like an ember knows*
> *to burn out.*"

Submit a stapled group of 10 pages of original, unpublished poetry, single or double-spaced, photocopied, with a $4 reader's fee. Mss will not be returned. (A SASE for winners' names may be included.) "The top fifteen finalists will be invited to submit a 30-page manuscript for possible publication in *Troika VII.*" Recent winners include Glen Brown, Martin Marcus and Lydia Webster. They have also published *Your Neighborhood of Poems*, a special 1994-95 anthology of 160 pgs., including 73 poets.

THOUGHTS FOR ALL SEASONS: THE MAGAZINE OF EPIGRAMS (IV-Form, humor), % editor Prof. Em. Michel Paul Richard, 478 NE 56th St., Miami FL 33137-2621, founded 1976, "is an irregular serial: **designed to preserve the epigram as a literary form; satirical.** All issues are commemorative." **Rhyming poetry and nonsense verse with good imagery will be considered although most modern epigrams are prose.** Prof. Richard has published poetry by Jack Hart and offers this sample:

> *Beware a cause: it is our fate*
> *To turn into the things we hate*

TFAS is 84 pgs., offset from typescript with full-page illustrations, card cover, saddle-stapled. The editor accepts about 20% of material submitted. Press run is 500-1,000. There are several library subscriptions but most distribution is through direct mail or local bookstores and newsstand sales. Single copy: $4.75 plus $1.50 postage. **Submit at least one full page of poems at a time, with SASE. Simultaneous submissions OK, but not previously published epigrams "unless a thought is appended which alters it." Editor comments on rejections. Publishes one section devoted to a theme. Send SASE for guidelines. Reports in 1 month. Pays 1 copy.**

THREE CONTINENTS PRESS INC. (III, IV-Ethnic, translations), P.O. Box 38009, Colorado Springs CO 80937-8009, phone (719)579-0977, fax (719)576-4689, founded 1973, poetry editor Donald Herdeck. **"Published poets only welcomed and only non-European and non-American poets . . . We publish literature by creative writers from the non-western world (Africa, the Middle East, the Caribbean and Asia/Pacific)—poetry** *only* **by non-western writers or good translations of such poetry if original language is Arabic, French, African vernacular, etc."** They have published poetry by Derek Walcott, Khalil Hawi, Mahmud Darwish, Julia Fields, Hilary Tham, Houda Naamani and Nizar Kabbani. They also publish anthologies and criticisms focused on relevant themes. As a sample the editor selected these lines from "Fear," published in *Fan of Swords* by Muhammad al-Maghut:

> *On these cloudy days*
> *I am afraid to awaken one morning and find no birds left,*
> *no single flower tucked into a braid,*
> *no friend in any coffee house.*
> *I fear being chained to the wash-stand*
> *or chimney*
> *being sprayed by bullets*
> *while the toothbrush is still in my mouth.*
> *Hurry up, Mother, ask the bedouins*
> *for a leatherbound charm or special weed*
> *to protect me from this fear.*

Query with 4-5 samples, bio, publication credits. Replies to queries in 5-10 weeks, to submissions (if invited) in 4-5 weeks. Sometimes sends prepublication galleys. Offers 10% royalty contract (5% for translator) with $100-200 advance plus 10 copies. Buys worldwide English rights. Send SASE for catalog to buy samples.

THE THREEPENNY REVIEW (II), P.O. Box 9131, Berkeley CA 94709, phone (510)849-4545, fax (510)849-4551, founded 1980, poetry editor Wendy Lesser, "is a quarterly review of literature, performing and visual arts, and social articles aimed at the intelligent, well-read, but not necessarily academic reader. Nationwide circulation. **Want: formal, narrative, short poems (and others); do not want: confessional, no punctuation, no capital letters. Prefer under 50 lines but not necessary. No bias** *against* **formal poetry, in fact a slight bias in favor of it."** They have published poetry by Thom Gunn, Frank Bidart, Seamus Heaney, Czeslaw Milosz and Louise Glück. There are about 9-10 poems in each 36-page tabloid issue. They receive about 4,500 submissions of poetry/year, use 12. Press run is 10,000 for 8,000 subscribers of which 300 are libraries. Subscription: $16. **Sample: $6. Send 5 poems or fewer/submission. Do not submit mss June-September. Send SASE for guidelines. Reports in 2-8 weeks. Pays $100/poem. Buys first serial rights.** Open to unsolicited reviews. "Send for review guidelines (SASE required)." Work published in this review has also been included in the 1993, 1994 and 1995 volumes of *The Best American Poetry*.

THRESHOLD BOOKS (IV-Spirituality, translations), RD #4, Box 600, Dusty Ridge Rd., Putney VT 05346, phone (802)254-8300, fax (802)257-2779, founded 1981, poetry editor Edmund Helminski, is "a small press dedicated to the publication of quality works in metaphysics, poetry in translation and literature with some spiritual impact. **We would like to see poetry in translation of high literary merit with spiritual qualities, or original work by established authors. We specialize in publication of poetry with Sufi tradition."** Published books of poetry include *Love Is A Stranger* by Rumi

---

✝ *The double dagger before a listing indicates that the listing is new in this edition. New markets are often the most receptive to submissions.*

and ***Doorkeeper Of The Heart*** by Rabia. As a sample the editor selected these lines by Jelaluddin Rumi, translated by John Moyne and Coleman Barks:

> *We've given up making a living.*
> *It's all this crazy love poetry now.*
>
> *It's everywhere. Our eyes and our feelings*
> *Focus together, with our words*

That comes from a collection, ***Open Secret, Versions of Rumi***, published in a beautifully printed, flat-spined, digest-sized paperback, glossy color card cover, 96 pgs. Per copy: $9. **Query with 10 poems, bio, publication credits and SASE. Previously published poems and simultaneous submissions OK; disks compatible with IBM and hard copy preferred. Replies to queries and submissions (if invited) in 1-2 months. Publishes on 7% contract plus 10 copies (and 50% discount on additional copies). Send SASE for catalog to buy samples.**

THUMBPRINTS (I, IV-Writing, regional), 928 Gibbs, Caro MI 48723, phone (517)673-5563, founded 1984, editor Janet Ihle, is the monthly 8-page Thumb Area Writers' Club newsletter. They want **poetry about writers and writing, nothing "vulgar." Maximum 32 lines.** As a sample, the editor selected her poem "Time to Eat?":

> *Thoughts were roaming all through her head,*
> *She wanted to write them before going to bed.*
> *So she opened a can and dotted an i,*
> *Wrote a few words and started to fry.*
> *The words kept coming, the food did simmer*
> *and the poem was done long before dinner.*

Press run is 45 for 30 subscribers. **Sample postpaid: 75¢. Submit 1-10 poems at a time. Simultaneous submissions and previously published poems OK. Send SASE for guidelines and upcoming themes. Editor comments on submissions "sometimes." Reports in 3-6 months. Pays 1 copy.** They also sponsor seasonal contests for Michigan amateur writers. The editor says, "I'd like to send all entries back, but can't afford postage for those who neglect to send a SASE."

TIA CHUCHA PRESS (II), P.O. Box 476969, Chicago IL 60647, phone (312)252-5321, fax (312)252-5388, founded 1989, president Luis J. Rodriguez. They publish 2-4 paperbacks a year, **"multicultural, lyrical, engaging, passionate works informed by social, racial, class experience. Evocative. Poets should be knowledgeable of contemporary and traditional poetry, even if experimenting."** They have recently published poetry by Marvin Tate, Lisa Buscani and Andres Rodriguez. As a sample the editor selected these lines from "Poem for the Unnamed" from ***Crossing With the Light*** by Dwight Okita:

> *They say if you don't*
> *name a child when it is born,*
> *it will start crawling north,*
> *unable to be pulled back*
> *by the string of its name.*

Submit complete ms of 48 pages or more with SASE ("unless you don't want the manuscript returned"). Simultaneous submissions OK, if notified. Only original, unpublished work in book form. "Although, we like to have poems that have been published in magazines and/or chapbooks." Deadline: June 30. Reads submissions during the summer months. They say, "We are known for publishing the best of what is usually spoken word or oral presentations of poetry. However, we like to publish poems that best work on the page. Yet, we are not limited to that. Our authors come from a diversity of ethnic, racial and gender backgrounds. Our main thrust is openness, in forms as well as content. We are cross-cultural, but we don't see this as a prison. The openness and inclusiveness is a foundation to include a broader democratic notion of what poetry should be in this country."

TICKLED BY THUNDER: WRITER'S NEWS & ROUNDTABLE (I, II, IV-Subscribers), 7385 129th St., Surrey, British Columbia V3W 7B8 Canada, fax (604)591-6095, founded 1990, publisher/editor Larry Lindner, appears 3 times/year, using poems about **"fantasy particularly, about writing or whatever. Prefer original images and thoughts. Keep them short (up to 40 lines)—not interested in long, long poems. Nothing pornographic, childish, unimaginative. Welcome humor and inspirational verse."** They have published poetry by Stephen Gill, Helen Singh, Victoria Collins and John Grey. As a sample the editor selected these lines (poet unidentified):

> *So she put a monkee in his tea*
> *marshmallows on the side . . .*

It is 16-20 pgs., digest-sized, published on Macintosh. Press run is 150 for 100 subscribers. Subscription: $12 for 4 issues. **Sample postpaid: $2.50. Send SASE (or SAE and IRC) for guidelines. Include 3-5 samples of writing with queries. Cover letter required with submissions; include "a few facts about yourself and brief list of publishing credits." Reports in 2-3 months. Pays 5¢/line** to $2 maximum. Buys first rights. Editor comments on rejections "99% of the time." Reviews books of poetry in up to 300 words. Open to unsolicited reviews. Poets may also send books for review consideration. They also offer a poetry contest 3-4 times/year. Deadlines: the 15th of February, May, August and October. Entry fee: $2 for 3 poems; free for subscribers. Prize: cash, publication and subscription. Send SASE (or SAE and IRC) for details.

TIGHT; TIGHT PRESS (II), P.O. Box 1591, Guerneville CA 95446, founded 1990, editor Ann Erickson, appears 5 times/year. *"tight* uses immediate, experimental poems, including, 'language,' sound-based and surrealist."** They have recently published poetry by Ben Baxter, Guy R. Beining, Ed Mycue, John M. Bennett, Pat Nolan, Sheila E. Murphy, Spencer Selby, John Perlman, Jim Leftwich, Charlene Mary-Cath Smith, Noelle Kocot and Melissa Kwasny. As a sample the editor selected these lines from "Grief" by Sean Brendan-Brown:

> The woman with a mouth like a circle of firelight
> sets the table of faro,
> spreads her fortune on the slap
> of casekeeper buttons as the shiny cards snap.

tight is 72 pgs., 7 × 8½, photocopied from typescript. Press run is 150 for 25 subscribers, 25 shelf sales. **Sample postpaid: $4.50. Checks must be payable to Ann Erickson. Submit 5 poems at a time for 1996. Simultaneous submission OK, if notified. Reports in 2 months. Pays 1 copy. Acquires one-time rights. Under tight Press the editor has published 2 chapbooks,** *The Principal of Things* by Michael H. Brownstein and *untitled selfknowledge* by Peter Ganick.

TIGHTROPE (II); SWAMP PRESS (V), 323 Pelham Rd., Amherst MA 01002, founded 1977, chief editor Ed Rayher. Swamp Press is a small press publisher of poetry and graphic art in limited edition, letterpress chapbooks. *Tightrope*, appearing 1-2 times a year, is a literary magazine of varying format, circulation 300, 150 subscriptions of which 25 are libraries. Subscription: $10 for 2 issues. **Sample of** *Tightrope* **postpaid: $6. Submit 3-6 poems at a time. No simultaneous submissions. Sometimes comments on rejections. Send SASE for guidelines. Reports in 2 months, 6-12 months until publication. Pays "sometimes" and provides 2 contributor's copies. Acquires first rights.** Reviews books of poetry in one paragraph, single format. Swamp Press has published books by Edward Kaplan, editor Ed Rayher, Alexis Rotella (miniature, 3 × 3, containing 6 haiku), Sandra Dutton (a 4 foot long poem), Frannie Lindsay (a 10 × 13 format containing 3 poems), Andrew Glaze, Tom Haxo, Carole Stone and Steven Ruhl. **Not presently accepting unsolicited submissions for chapbook publication but when he publishes chapbooks he pays 5-10% of press run and, if there is grant money available, an honorarium (about $50).** Send SASE for catalog.

TIMBER CREEK REVIEW (II, IV-Humor); WORDS OF WISDOM (I, IV-Humor), 612 Front St. East, Glendora NJ 08029-1133, founded 1981, editor J.M. Freiermuth. Both magazines appear quarterly using **"primarily short stories, but occasionally short, pithy poetry. The stuff that brings a smile to the reader's face on the first reading. No blank verse or blank thought. No religious."** *Words of Wisdom* **is more open to work by beginning writers.** The editor has recently published poetry by Richard Davignon, Mary Winters, Jay Liveson and Lois Greene Stone. *TCR* and *WOW* are similar in format. They are 60-84 pgs., 5½ × 8½, photocopied, saddle-stapled with color paper covers and some graphics. They publish 20% of the 500-600 submissions received. Press runs are 130-150 for 70-120 subscribers. For either magazine a subscription is $12. **Sample postpaid: $3. Make checks payable to J.M. Freiermuth. Previously published poems and simultaneous submissions OK. Cover letter required; "include names of lit mags author subscribes to." No submissions accepted December 1 through January 31. Seldom comments on rejections. Reports in 1-3 months. Pays 1 copy. Acquires one-time rights.** The editor says, "Stop watching TV and read a book of poetry."

TIMBERLINE PRESS (V), 6281 Red Bud, Fulton MO 65251, phone (314)642-5035, founded 1975, poetry editor Clarence Wolfshohl. "We do limited letterpress editions with the goal of blending strong poetry with well-crafted and designed printing. We lean toward **natural history or strongly imagistic nature poetry but will look at any good work. Also, good humorous poetry. Currently, still not accepting submissions because we have a good backlog of mss to publish—enough for the next 2-3 years."** They have recently published the books *Pigeons in the Chandeliers* by Judy Ray and *Blowing Reeds* by Wally Swist. As a sample the editor selected these lines from "Morning News" published in Ray's *Pigeons in the Chandeliers* (1993):

> Trees obscured the thunderheads
> so yesterday's bolt came from
> sunshine, flinging racquets from
> startled tennis grip,
>   whipcrack
> breaking sky-blue china.

Sample copies may be obtained by sending $5 requesting sample copy and noting you saw the listing in *Poet's Market*. **Reports in under 1 month. Pays "50-50 split with author after Timberline Press has recovered its expenses."

TIME OF SINGING, A MAGAZINE OF CHRISTIAN POETRY (I, IV-Religious, themes), P.O. Box 211, Cambridge Springs PA 16403, founded 1958-1965, revived 1980, editor Charles A. Waugaman, managing editor Lora Hill. "The viewpoint is **unblushingly Christian—but in its widest and most inclusive meaning**. Moreover, it is believed that the vital message of Christian poems, as well as inspiring the general reader, will give pastors, teachers, and devotional leaders rich current sources of inspiring material to aid them in their ministries. We tend to have a Fall/Christmas issue, a Lent/Easter one, and a Summer one. But **we do have themes quite often. We tend to value content, rather than form; prefer short poems for practical reasons.**" They have published poetry by Elva McAllaster, Ralph Seager, Ken Siegelman, Frances P. Reid, Tony Cosier, Mary Balazs, Edith Lovejoy Pierce and Nancy James. As a sample the editor selected these lines from "Wrestlers" by H. Edgar Hix:

> *Our God is a wrestler who throws us to our knees*
> *again and again. He is a bruised and bruising God*
> *with strong, quick hands; a Master who understands*
> *how we must wrestle, who gives us purple knees*
> *and strengthened souls.*

The triquarterly is 40 pgs., digest-sized, offset from typescript with decorative line drawings scattered throughout. They receive over 500 submissions/year, use about 210. Circulation is 350 with 150 subscriptions. Single copy: $6; subscription: $12. **Sample: $3. Prefers about 5 poems at a time, double-spaced. No simultaneous submissions; previously published poems OK, but not encouraged.** Time between acceptance and publication is 6 months to 1 year. **Editor frequently comments with suggestions for improvement for publication. Send SASE for guidelines and upcoming themes. Reports in 1-2 months. Pays 1 copy plus 25¢/line ($1 minimum to $4 maximum/poem). Reserves right to reprint poems in other formats. "We tend to be traditional. We like poems that are aware of grammar. Collections of uneven lines, series of phrases, preachy statements, unstructured 'prayers,' and trite sing-song rhymes usually get returned. We look for poems that 'show' rather than 'tell.' "** They also publish chapbooks of poets of the editor's selection and offer contests, "generally one for each issue on a given subject related to our theme. Send SASE for rules."

‡TIMES LITERARY SUPPLEMENT (II), Priory House, St. John's Lane, London EC1M 4BX England, founded 1902, is a weekly of book reviews which also accepts **poetry of all kinds ("shortness a virtue").** They have published poetry by Seamus Heaney, Thom Gunn, Joseph Brodsky and Paul Muldoon. It is 32 pgs., newsprint, folded with color cover, color and b&w illustrations, display and classified advertising. They receive about 5,000 poems a year, use approximately 2%. Press run is 30,000 for 20,000 subscribers, 10,000 shelf sales. Single copy: £1.90; subscription: £75 ($120 US). **Submit no more than 5 poems at a time. No previously published poems or simultaneous submissions.** Time between acceptance and publication averages 1 month. **Reports in "1 day to 5 months." Pays £2.15/line. Buys first world rights.** "New poetry books reviewed constantly, mainly singly, in 300-3,000 words." Send books to F. Mount, editor, for review consideration.

TOAD HIGHWAY (II), 178 E. Main St. B, Lansdale PA 19446, founded 1988, editor Grant Clauser. *Toad Highway* is a small magazine appearing irregularly using "all types of artwork, poetry and reviews. **We want poetry which proves that the poet is obsessed by each sound, each stress, each image, each line. No 'happy poems' or work which shows that the poet has not studied contemporary poetry.**" They have published work by Peter Wild, Harry Humes, William Heyen and Simon Perchik. As a sample the editor selected these lines from "Hubbel Trading Post" by Robert Edwards:

> *The first time was the dust,*
> *bolts of calico and velvet,*
> *and Hopi and Pima baskets hanging*
> *by a shadow from the rafters.*
> *There were Navajo rugs of Ganado red,*
> *like flexible iron, on the floor,*
> *and the smell of dark leather*
> *glossed on the salt of many hands.*

TH is a 52-page pamphlet, saddle-stapled. "We accept about one in every 100 poems received." Their press run is 250 with 20 subscriptions. **Single copy: $2. Make checks payable to Grant Clauser. Submit maximum of 5 poems at a time, single-spaced. Simultaneous submissions OK. Editor "seldom" comments on rejections. Responds to submissions "when I get to it." Pays 1 copy (discount on others).** "We will review books sent to us." He says, "We want to see strong imagistic narrative or descriptive meditation. Nothing experimental just for the sake of being different. No L.A. type poems. The poem must say something real, not just sit there and wet itself. *Toad Highway* aims to be an outlet for quality contemporary poetry at a low budget. I sometimes like to print short prose bits by the authors about their poetry."

TOMORROW MAGAZINE (II), P.O. Box 148486, Chicago IL 60614, e-mail 74264.3245@compuser ve.com, founded 1982, editor Tim W. Brown, is a biannual magazine appearing in January and July. "We focus roughly half on poets from Chicago, half from elsewhere. We prefer work that falls between the 'academic' and 'saloon' extremes of the literary spectrum." **They want "free verse strong in image and emotion. No formalist and academic poetry, Hallmark verse, or religious poetry."** They have recently published poetry by Richard Kostelanetz, Lyn Lifshin, Hugh Fox and Antler. As a sample, the editor selected these lines from "Poem" by Jim Tyack:

> . . . *Who else could live in those eyes*
> *they are quite unhouse-like and I plod and sweep fluttering*
> *insects and leaves off the water's shimmering surface*
> *as you drift away somewhere praying to the snow-covered*
>
> *Andes or a tree in the backyard where you become an expert*
> *at divining deeper meaning from the common place.*

TM is 32 pgs., 8½×11, custom-bound, with card stock cover, b&w cover photo. They receive about 300 mss/year, usually accept 10-12%. Press run is 300 for 200 shelf sales. **Sample postpaid: $5. Send no more than 5-6 poems at one time. No previously published poems; simultaneous submissions OK. Cover letter with brief bio welcome.** Time between acceptance and publication is 6-9 months. **Seldom comments on rejections. Send SASE for guidelines. Reports in 3 weeks to 3 months. Pays 1 copy. Acquires first rights. Requests acknowledgment when reprinting in anthologies or collections.** The editor says, "There are too many tribes in poetry. At *Tomorrow* we like to think we have a pluralistic outlook."

TOUCH (IV-Religious, teens, themes), P.O. Box 7259, Grand Rapids MI 49510, phone (616)241-5616, founded 1970, poetry editor Carol Smith: "Our magazine is a 24-page edition written **for girls 7-14 to show them how God is at work in their lives and in the world around them.** *Touch* **is theme-orientated. We like our poetry to fit the theme of each issue. We send out a theme update biannually to all our listed freelancers. We prefer short poems with a Christian emphasis that can show girls how God works in their lives."** They have published poetry by Janet Shafer Boyanton and Iris Alderson. As a sample we selected "Shall I Compare Myself to Others?" by May Richstone:

> *Better not. Such comparisons*
> *Most likely would become a strain—*
> *My betters could make me envious,*
> *The lesser tend to make me vain.*
>
> *Much better compare*
> *Yesterday's me*
> *With the tomorrow's*
> *I hope to be.*

Touch is published 10 times a year, magazine-sized. Circulation is 15,800 for 15,500 subscribers. They receive 150-200 freelance submissions of poetry/year, use 2 poems in each issue, have a 6-month backlog. Subscription: $11.50 US, $14 Canada, $20 foreign. **Sample and guidelines free with 8×10 SASE. Poems must not be longer than 20 lines—prefer much shorter. Simultaneous submissions OK. Query with SASE for theme update. Reports in 2 months. Pays $10-15 and copies.**

TOUCHSTONE (I, II), Viterbo College, La Crosse WI 54601, phone (608)791-0271, fax (608)791-0367, e-mail eng_ruppel@viterbo.edu, founded 1950, moderator Richard Ruppel, is a literary quarterly publishing poetry, short stories and artwork. As a sample the editor selected these lines from "Out-bound" by Kate Larkin:

> *Beware of the Park Street exit*
> *Where corners cross*
> *And weepy people*
> *Stare, pasty-faced.*

The magazine is digest-sized, 48 pgs., saddle-stapled, with semi-glossy card cover. Press run is 800 for 100 subscribers of which 25 are libraries. Subscription: $5. **Sample postpaid: $2.50. Cover letter required; include "a note of origination" (i.e. that the work is original). Reads submissions August 1 through March 1 only. Send SASE for guidelines. Reports in 2 months. Best poem gets $20. All get 1 copy.**

TOUCHSTONE LITERARY JOURNAL; TOUCHSTONE PRESS (III, IV-Translations), P.O. Box 8308, Spring TX 77387-8308, founded 1975, poetry editor William Laufer, is an annual publishing **"experimental or well-crafted traditional form, including sonnets, and translations. No light**

verse or doggerel." They have recently published poetry by Walter Griffin, Thomas Amherst Perry, Paul Ramsey and Janice Whittington. As a sample the editor selected these lines from "Blue Prefect" by John Marvin:

> *We had spoken of stance in circumstance*
> *soul on ice rowan martin pueblo tet*
> *like the semblance of an image*
> *nature can't betray what it hasn't promised*
> *mccarthy johnson king kennedy*
> *of notion ocean of estimation nation*
> *robinson hair columbia*
> *grant that we would stand*
> *in stony silence gazing forth*
> *tool in hand prepared for the new day*

Touchstone is digest-sized, flat-spined, 100 pgs., professionally printed in small, dark type with glossy card cover. Subscription: $7. **Sample postpaid: $4. Submit 5 poems at a time. "Cover letter telling something about the poet piques our interest and makes the submission seem less like a mass mailing." Sometimes sends prepublication galleys. Pays 1 copy.** Reviews books of poetry. Open to unsolicited reviews. Poets may also send books for review consideration, to Review Editor. Touchstone Press also **publishes an occasional chapbook. Send SASE for chapbook submission guidelines.** "Last year we published a book-length epic, *Kingdom of the Leopard: An Epic of Old Benin* by Nigerian poet chi chi layor. We are open to new projects. Query first, with SASE. Absolutely no mail is answered without SASE."

TOWER POETRY SOCIETY; PINE TREE SERIES; TOWER (II), Dundas Public Library, 18 Ogilvie St., Dundas, Ontario L9H 2S2 Canada, founded 1951, editor-in-chief Joanna Lawson. "The Tower Poetry Society was started by a few members of McMaster University faculty to promote interest in poetry. We publish *Tower* twice a year and a few chapbooks. We want **rhymed or free verse, traditional or modern, but not prose chopped into short lines, maximum 40 lines in length, any subject, any comprehensible style."** They have published poetry by June Walker and Helen Fitzgerald Dougher. The editor selected these sample lines by Tony Cosier:

> *From forging brass he took to forging soul,*
> *gave up plowing soil to plow his skull,*
> *ripped open the eye that never closed again*
> *and took for tongue the howl of the beast in pain.*

Tower is 40 pgs., digest-sized. Circulation is 250 for 60 subscribers of which 8 are libraries. They receive about 400 unsolicited submissions of poetry/year, use 30, no backlog. Subscription: $6 including postage; $7.50 abroad. **Sample postpaid: $2. Submit no more than 4 poems at a time. Reads submissions during February or August. Reports in 2 months. Pays 1 copy.** The editor advises, "Read a lot of poetry before you try to write it."

TOWNSHIPS SUN (IV-Rural/ecological, regional), 7 Conley St., P.O. Box 28, Lennoxville, Quebec J1M 1Z3 Canada, phone (819)566-7424, founded 1972, editor Patricia Ball, is a monthly newspaper in English "concerned with **history of townships, English community, agriculture and ecology and using poetry on these themes. Only poems about the area and people of Quebec ever accepted. Others need not submit."** The tabloid has a press run of 1,500 for 1,200 subscribers of which 20 are libraries, and 280 shelf sales. Subscription: $15/year Canada, $20/year outside Canada. **Sample postpaid: $2. Pays $10-30 plus 1 copy. "Will publish poems specifically about townships, townshippers, or of specific interest to townshippers."** Staff reviews books of poetry.

TRADESWOMEN MAGAZINE (IV-Women, specialized), P.O. Box 2622, Berkeley CA 94702, founded 1982, poetry editor Sue Doro, editor Roberta Tracy, is a national bimonthly **"particular to women in blue collar non-traditional work"** and uses poetry **"pertaining to women in trades, tradeswomen as mothers, family and co-worker relationships."** Subscription: $35. **Sample postpaid: $2. Guidelines available for SASE. They consider simultaneous submissions and previously published poems. Cover letter with short bio—particularly about work history—required. Reports in 1 month. No backlog.** Open to unsolicited reviews. Poets may also send books for review consideration.

TRANSNATIONAL PERSPECTIVES (III), CP161, 1211 Geneva 16 Switzerland, fax 33 50 047452, founded 1975, editor René Wadlow, is a "journal of world politics with some emphasis on culture that crosses frontiers." Uses 4-6 poems/issue, usually illustrated by drawing or photo. They want **"poems stressing harmony of nature, human potential, understanding of other cultures—relatively short. No humor, nationalistic themes, nothing 'overly' subjective."** They have published poetry by Verona Bratesch and Janet Pehr. As a sample the editor selected these lines from "1989, A Pivot Year" by Brian Walker:

> *This year, all bets are off.*
> *Unpredictable chances,*
> *expectations jilted;*
> *adepts will learn new dances.*
> *Watch old system hiccough,*
> *welcome new solutions*
> *in native phrase unstilted:*
> *in apt thoughts, revolutions.*

TP appears 3 times a year; it "is oriented toward making policy suggestions in international organizations, especially in the United Nations." It is 48 pgs., handsomely produced, magazine-sized, saddle-stapled with coated color paper cover. They receive about 100 poems/year, use 16. Press run is 5,000 for 4,000 subscribers of which half are libraries. **Sample back issue free on request. Simultaneous submissions OK. No previously published poems. Editor comments "rarely on quality, only why not for *TP*." Reports in 1 month. Pays 5 copies, more if desired.** René Wadlow says, "Poems in *TP* come from many countries, especially Eastern Europe, Scandinavia and India, often translated into English, usually 'upbeat' since most articles are on political and economic difficulties of the world."

TRESTLE CREEK REVIEW (II,IV-Regional), 1000 West Garden, Coeur d'Alene ID 83814, phone (208)769-3300, ext. 384, founded 1982-83, poetry editor Chad Klinger et al, is a "2-year college creative writing program production. Purposes: (1) expand the range of publishing/editing experience for our small band of writers; (2) expose them to editing experience; (3) create another outlet for serious, beginning writers. **We're fairly eclectic but prefer poetry on the Northwest region, particularly the innermountain West (Idaho, Montana, etc.). We favor poetry strong on image and sound, and country vs. city; spare us the romantic, rhymed clichés. We can't publish much if it's long (more than 2 pgs.).**" They have recently published poetry by Jesse Bier, Lowell Jaeger, Thomas Kretz, Susan Linehan and Errol Miller. As a sample Chad Klinger selected these lines by Ron McFarland:

> *All around you the furious mines are closing*
> *like angry fists,*
> *their galvanized shells rusting too slowly*
> *to be a tourist attraction.*
> *Outside town a black bronze miner drills the sky.*

TCR is a digest-sized, 57-page annual, professionally printed on heavy buff stock, perfect-bound, matte cover with art, circulation 500, 6 subscriptions of which 4 are libraries. This publication is well-designed and features both free and formal verse by relative newcomers. The editors receive unsolicited poetry submissions from about 100 persons/year, use 30. **Sample: $4. Submit before March 1 (for May publication), no more than 5 pgs. No simultaneous submissions or previously published poems. Reports by March 30. Pays 2 copies.** The editor advises, "Be neat; be precise; don't romanticize or cry in your beer; strike the surprising, universal note. Know the names of things."

TRIQUARTERLY MAGAZINE (II), 2020 Ridge Ave., Evanston IL 60208, phone (708)491-7614, founded 1964, editors Reginald Gibbons and Susan Hahn, is one of the most respected and visually appealing journals produced in the United States. Editors accept a wide range of verse forms and styles of verse (long poems, sequences, etc.) **with the emphasis solely on excellence,** and some issues are published as books on specific themes. They have published poetry by Tom Sleigh, Albert Goldbarth, Linda McCarriston, Pattiann Rogers and Theodore Weiss. *TriQuarterly*'s three issues per year are 200 pgs., 6×9, flat-spined, professionally printed with b&w photography, graphics, glossy card cover. There are about 40 or more pgs. of poetry in each issue. They receive about 3,000 unsolicited submissions of poetry/year, use 60, have about a year backlog. Press run is 4,500 for 2,000 subscribers of which 35% are libraries. Single copy: $9.95; subscription: $24; **Sample postpaid: $5. No simultaneous submissions. Reads submissions October 1 through March 31 only. Sometimes works with poets, inviting rewrites of interesting work. Reports in 3 months. Always sends prepublication galleys. Payment varies. Acquires first North American serial rights. "We *suggest* prospective contributors examine sample copy before submitting."** Reviews books of poetry "at times." Send books for review consideration. Work appearing in *TriQuarterly* has been included in *The Best American Poetry* (1993, 1994 and 1995) and the *Pushcart Prize* anthology.

TROUT CREEK PRESS; DOG RIVER REVIEW; DOG RIVER REVIEW POETRY SERIES; BACK-POCKET POETS (II), 5976 Billings Rd., Parkdale OR 97041-9610, phone (503)352-6494, e-mail LFH42@aol.com, founded 1981, poetry editor Laurence F. Hawkins, prefers **"visceral poetry with cerebral undertones or vice versa. Shorter poems (to 30 lines) but will consider longer. Will also consider book or chapbook pubication. No restrictions on form or content. No pornography or religious verse."** They have recently published poetry by Judson Crews, Gerald Locklin, Arthur Winfield Knight, Wilma Elizabeth McDaniel, Nathaniel Tarn and Sam Silva. As a sample the editor selected these lines from "Toccata" by Elvira Bennet:

> *What I am touched by*

> *heals me of wounds I*
> *hardly knew I had.*
> *What you touch you heal.*
> *In our sensitive*
> *carapace, sealing*
> *in, turning out, we*
> *are all wounds, all cures.*

Dog River Review is a semiannual, 64 pgs., digest-sized, saddle-stapled, offset from computer typescript with b&w graphics. They receive about 500 submissions of poetry/year, use 40-50. Press run is 300 for 50 subscribers of which 7 are libraries. Single copy: $4; subscription: $8. **Sample postpaid: $3. Submit 4-6 poems at a time. Send SASE for guidelines. Reports in 1 week to 3 months. Pays in copies. Acquires first North American serial rights.** *Dog River Review* is open to unsolicited reviews. Poets may also send books for review consideration. Backpocket Poets is a series of 4×5¼ chapbooks, professionally printed, 26-32 pgs., saddle-stapled or perfect-bound with matte card cover, selling for $2.50-4 each, a drawing or photo of the author on the back. The Dog River Review Poetry Series consists of digest-sized, professionally printed, saddle-stapled chapbooks up to 56 pgs. with matte card covers, selling for $3-6. **For book publication by Trout Creek Press, submit complete ms of up to 44 pgs. Replies to queries immediately, to submissions in 1-2 months. No simultaneous submissions. Editor sometimes comments on rejections. Always sends prepublication galleys for chapbooks. No payment until "material costs recovered. We also publish individual authors on cassette tape."** Send SASE for catalog to buy samples.

TUCUMCARI LITERARY REVIEW (II), 3108 W. Bellevue Ave., Los Angeles CA 90026, founded 1988, editor Troxey Kemper, assistant editor Neoma Reed, appears every other month. **"Prefer rhyming and established forms, 2-100 lines, but the primary goal is to publish good work. No talking animals. No haiku. The quest here is for poetry that will be just as welcome many years later as it is now. A good example is Jimmy Carter's book,** *Always a Reckoning and Other Poems*. **Preference is for readable, understandable writing of literary and lasting quality."** They have recently published poetry by John Sokol, Harvey Stanbrough, Dan Kaderli, David Offutt, Jim Dunlap, Patricia Higginbotham, Andy Peterson, Wilma Elizabeth McDaniel and Ken MacDonnell. As a sample the editor selected a triolet, "Mulberry Morning" by Fontaine Falkoff:

> *Held in the damp arms of my tree,*
> *I choose ripe berries, wet and sweet.*
> *The dawn is cool and kind to me,*
> *Held in the damp arms of my tree.*
> *Last night's rainfall graciously*
> *Washed away the muggy heat.*
> *Held in the damp arms of my tree,*
> *I choose ripe berries, wet and sweet.*

The magazine is digest-sized, 48 pgs., saddle-stapled, photocopied from typescript, with card cover. Their press run is 150-200. Subscription: $12, $20 for overseas. **Sample: $2, $4 for overseas. Submit no more than 4 poems at a time. Considers simultaneous submissions and previously published poems. Send SASE for guidelines. Reports within 1 month. Pays 1 copy. Acquires one-time rights.** This magazine is inexpensively produced but contains some good formal poems. If you're looking to place a particular sonnet or villanelle, try Troxey Kemper's magazine. He reports quickly, by the way, and may comment on rejections.

TURKEY PRESS (V), 6746 Sueno Rd., Isla Vista CA 93117, founded 1974, poetry editor Harry Reese along with his wife, Sandra Reese, "is involved with publishing contemporary literature, producing traditional and experimental book art, one-of-a-kind commissioned projects and collaborations with various artists and writers. **We do not encourage solicitations of any kind to the press. We seek out and develop projects on our own."** They have published poetry by Thomas Merton, James Laughlin, Sam Hamill, Edwin Honig, Glenna Luschei, Tom Clark, Michael Hannon, Keith Waldrop, David Ossman, Peter Whigham, Jack Curtis, Kirk Robertson and Anne E. Edge.

TURNSTILE (II), 175 Fifth Ave., Suite 2348, New York NY 10010, founded 1988, is a biannual literary magazine publishing poetry, fiction, essays, art, interviews, novel excerpts and plays. **They want poetry that is "well-crafted, with a strong sense of line, form and sound."** They have published poetry by James Applewhite, Kevin Pilkington, Robert Morgan and Dabney Stuart. The editors describe it as 128 pgs., 6×9, 55 lb. paper. Circulation: 1,500. Subscription: $12. **Sample postpaid: $6.50. "Send no more than 4 poems at one time. Refer to the guidelines in the front of our magazine." Often comments on rejections. Reports in 2-3 months. Pays 5 copies.**

TURNSTONE PRESS (II, IV-Regional), 607-100 Arthur St., Winnipeg, Manitoba R3B 1H3 Canada, phone (204)947-1555, managing editor James Hutchison, founded 1975, is a "literary press publishing quality contemporary fiction, nonfiction, poetry and criticism by **Canadian citizens and permanent residents of Canada"** in flat-spined books (8/year). They want **"writing based on contemporary poetics, but otherwise wide-ranging. Welcome experimental, graphic, long poems, the unusual. Nothing overly concerned with traditional rhyme and meter."** They have published poetry by Di Brandt, Maara Haas and Kristjana Gunnars. **Submit complete ms with cover letter including bio and other publications. Poems previously published in magazines OK. Reports in 2-3 months. Pays $100-200 advance, 10% royalties and 10 copies. Editor comments on rejections "if we believe it has promise." Send 9 × 12 SASE (or, from the US, SAE with IRCs) for catalog to buy samples.**

TWISTED (IV-Horror, fantasy), P.O. Box 1249, Palmetto GA 30268-1249, phone (404)463-1458, founded 1985, editor/publisher Christine Hoard, uses **poetry of "horror/dark fantasy; humor OK. Form and style open. Not more than 1 page long."** They have published poetry by John Grey, Lisa Lepovetsky and Jeffery Lewis. As a sample the editor selected these lines by Jana Hakes:

> As a child takes
> to puddles of mud
> for play,
> I prefer puddles
> of blood
> every day;
> horror that stains
> the mind,
> never washes away.

Christine Hoard describes *Twisted* as "150 pgs., magazine-sized, offset, vellum bristol cover, much art, some ads, 60 lb. matte paper. I receive a lot of poetry submissions, use 30-50 per issue." Press run is 300 for single-copy sales. **Sample postpaid: $6, payable to Christine Hoard. "Don't submit more than four poems at a time. You should see a sample copy to get a 'feel' for what we publish." No simultaneous submissions, but previously published poems are sometimes accepted. Editor often comments on rejections. Send SASE for guidelines. Reports within 3 months. "We sometimes close when we are preparing next issue or are overstocked." Pays 1 copy.** She says, "Poets of science fiction, horror, fantasy will be pleased to know there are several markets in the small press and some organizations are available to offer support and market information."

TWISTED NIPPLES; WORLD'S TOO HEAVY PRESS (I), P.O. Box 237, Corvallis OR 97339, phone (503)753-8439, e-mail yedwelsh@csos.orst.edu, founded 1993, editor Mark Hadley, is a monthly publication designed "to give creative curmudgeons a chance to see their work in print without hassle." **He wants poetry that is "humorous, raw, dark, observational. *TN*'s motto is 'Frustration with a smile.' No simple rhyme, epic death poetry, Rush Limbaugh/Geraldo-type logic, racist/sexist or violent crap. You can only override these guidelines using parody.** All contributors are real people who have a creative bent." As a sample the editor selected these lines from "Passion," a poem from his own collection:

> They say a baby's cry is involuntary,
> merely a reaction to the sudden change
> from liquid to air.
> I've always wondered myself,
> if it wasn't the seed of dissatisfaction. . .
> taking root in our young heart.

TN is 24 pgs., 7 × 8½, typeset, photocopied and saddle-stapled, b&w drawings, collages and computer-generated graphics. He receives more than 50 pieces each month, uses approximately 90%. Press run is 250 for 25 subscribers, 50-75 shelf sales. "Most are given away locally." Subscription: $20. **Sample postpaid: $2 or send SAE with 2 stamps for a free sample copy and guidelines. Submit 5 poems at a time. Previously published poems and simultaneous submissions OK. "Typewritten copies with your name and address on every page. Pay is 1 copy "only if you include a SAE with 2 stamps for each piece submitted." All mail must be addressed to World's Too Heavy Press! Rights revert to authors.** The editor says, "If you have a collection of poems that frightens your mother, confuses your father, speaks from the heart and soul of creative frustration, send it. I want to see the stuff written late at night, when no one was looking—poetry, articles, rants, cartoons, drawings—that had to be let out or kill you—because they will. I don't have rules . . . but simple poems and spot drawings are best suited for other publications . . . don't send 7,000 lines either. I love to laugh. and so do regular readers of *TN*. If you can make me smile, wince or groan, you'll be a regular contributor. Be bold, raw, scabby-kneed and unsure."

2 AM MAGAZINE; 2 AM PUBLICATIONS (IV-Science fiction/fantasy, horror), P.O. Box 6754, Rockford IL 61125-1754, e-mail p.anderson2/@genie.geis.com, founded 1986, editor Gretta McCombs Anderson, is a quarterly that wants **"fantasy, science fiction, heroic fantasy, horror, weird; any form, any style; preferred length is 1-2 pgs. We want poetry that leaves an after-image in the mind of the**

reader." They have published poetry by Mark Rich, G.N. Gabbard, Bruce Boston and Robert Frazier. The editor describes it as 68 pgs., magazine-sized, offset on 60 lb. stock, cover printed on glossy stock, illustrations "by leading fantasy artists" and ads. Circulation 2,000 with 350 subscriptions. Single copy: $4.95; subscription: $19/year. **Sample postpaid: $5.95. Submit no more than 5 poems at a time. "Prefer original poems no more than 2 pages in length. Please type all manuscripts." Editor "sometimes" comments on rejections. Send SASE for guidelines. Reports in 2 months, 6-12 months to publication. Always sends prepublication galleys. Pays 5¢/line or $1 minimum plus 1 copy, 40% discount for more. Buys one-time rights.** Reviews books of poetry in 250 words, single format. Open to unsolicited reviews. Poets may also send books for review consideration, attn. Irwin Chapman. Gretta M. Anderson advises, "Read widely, be aware of what's already been done. Short poems stand a good chance with us. Looking for mood-generating poetry of a cosmic nature, poems with extended imagery that work on multiple levels. Not interested in self-indulgent poetry."

TYRO PUBLISHING (I, II), 194 Carlbert St., Sault Ste. Marie, Ontario P6A 5E1 Canada, phone (705)253-6402, founded 1984, editor Stan Gordon. They only consider full-length mss for book publication. Published works include: *The Book of Cries* by Bruce Bedell, *On a Mound a Sleeping Leopard* by Anna Livig, and *Insight Into Mind of a Schizophrenic Friend* by Gordon Stone and Joan Neimi. **Query first with at least 6 sample poems. Mss should be in standard format. Send SASE for guidelines and further information. Always sends prepublication galleys.**

UGLY PUBLICATIONS; UGLY REVIEW (I, II), P.O. Box 4853, Richmond VA 23220, founded 1992, editors Max and Patrick. The *Ugly Review* is a quarterly tabloid. "We publish enough writing by each writer to express personality and voice. **Rather than publishing 50 poems by 50 poets, we publish 8 or 9 pieces from each writer. We also accept anything that goes on a piece of paper."** They have published poetry by Bill Sheilds, Dave McCord and Dave Saulnier. Press run is 5,000, all distributed free. **Sample available for "stamps." Submit at least 8 poems at a time. Previously published poems and simultaneous submissions OK. Cover letter required.** Time between acceptance and publication is included in acceptance letter. **Often comments on rejections. Send SASE for guidelines. Reports in 1 month. Pays copies.** "We review mags, chapbooks and books." Open to unsolicited reviews. Poets may also send books for review consideration. Ugly Publications also publishes 2 paperbacks and 5 chapbooks of poetry/year. **Query first with sample poems and cover letter with brief bio and publication credits. Replies to queries in 1 week, to mss in 1 month. Pays author's copies.**

ULTRAMARINE PUBLISHING CO., INC. (II), P.O. Box 303, Hastings-on-Hudson NY 10706, founded 1974, editor C.P. Stephens, who says, "We mostly distribute books for authors who had a title dropped by a major publisher—the author is usually able to purchase copies very cheaply. We use existing copies purchased by the author from the publisher when the title is being dropped." Ultramarine's list includes 250 titles, 90% of them cloth bound, one-third of them science fiction and 10% poetry. **The press pays 10% royalties. "Distributor terms are on a book-by-book basis, but is a rough split." Authors should query before making submissions; queries will be answered in 1 week. Simultaneous submissions OK, but no disks.**

‡THE UNFORGETTABLE FIRE (IV-Women/feminism), 530 Riverside Dr. #5G, New York NY 10027, founded 1991, editor Jordan O'Neill, is a biannual publication of poetry, short short stories, reviews and "activist activities" **written by, for and about women. They want relatively short poetry that is "women oriented, activist oriented. Nothing book-length. No haiku nor any poetry which advocates violence, racism, sexism or homophobia."** They have recently published poetry by Lyn Lifshin, Elisavietta Ritchie, Linda Wasmer Smith and Mary Sue Koeppel. As a sample the editor selected these lines from "the flower woman" by Cara Andrichak:

> saw her today
> silent on the staircase.
> The flower woman,
> on her arm

ALWAYS include a self-addressed, stamped envelope (SASE) when sending a ms or query to a publisher within your own country. When sending material to other countries, include a self-addressed envelope and International Reply Coupons (IRCs), available for purchase at most post offices.

the purple appeared again
as bright as the petunias
she's growing on her windowsill.

The editor says *The Unforgettable Fire* is 30-40 pgs., 8½ × 11, with art, graphics and ads. They receive 200-300 poems a year, accept 50-60%. Press run is 3,000 for 1,200 subscribers of which 15 are libraries. Subscription: $10. **Sample back issue postpaid: $5. Previously published poems and simultaneous submissions OK. Include short bio, "about author and work." Often comments on rejections. Send SASE for guidelines. Reports in 1-2 months. Pays 1-2 copies.** Reviews related books and magazines, usually in 500 words or less. Open to unsolicited reviews. Poets may also send books for review consideration. They hope to sponsor a poetry contest in 1996. Send SASE for details. The editor says, "I believe it's important to read, read, read what is out there. Big and small publications are incredibly valuable to writers, and writers should read publications (including *The Unforgettable Fire*) before submitting to them. Also read guidelines carefully."

UNITED METHODIST REPORTER; NATIONAL CHRISTIAN REPORTER; UNITED METHODIST REVIEW; UNITED METHODIST RECORD (IV-Religious), P.O. Box 660275, Dallas TX 75266-0275, phone (214)630-6495, founded "about 1840." *UMR* is a weekly broadsheet newspaper, circulation 400,000, "aimed at United Methodists primarily, ecumenical slant secondarily." They use at most one poem a week. **The poetry "must make a religious point—United Methodist or ecumenical theology; short and concise; concrete imagery; unobtrusive rhyme preferred; literary quality in freshness and imagery; not trite but easy to understand. Do not want to see poems by 'my 13-year-old niece,' poems dominated by 'I' or rhyme; poems that are too long, too vague or too general; poems without religious slant or point."** Editor John A. Lovelace says they use fewer than 50 of 1,000 poems received/year. Poems may appear in all publications. **No previously published poems. Send no more than 3-4 poems at a time.** Time to publication can be a year or more. **Editor comments on rejection "if it is promising." Send SASE for guidelines. Pays $2/poem and 1 copy.**

UNITY; DAILY WORD (IV-Religious), Unity School of Christianity, Unity Village MO 64065, founded 1889. "Unity periodicals are devoted to spreading the truth of practical Christianity, the everyday use of Christ's principles. The material used in them is constructive, friendly, unbiased as regards creed or sect, and positive and inspirational in tone. We suggest that prospective contributors study carefully the various publications before submitting material. **Sample copies are sent on request. Complimentary copies are sent to writers on publication. We accept mss only with the understanding that they are original and previously unpublished. Mss should be typewritten in double space. Unity School pays on acceptance, buying first North American serial rights.** *Unity Magazine* is a monthly journal that publishes "articles and **poems that give a clear message of Truth and provide practical, positive help in meeting human needs for healing, supply and harmony. Only 1 or 2 poems are published each month. We pay a $30 minimum."** *Daily Word* is a "monthly manual of daily studies" which "buys a limited number of short devotional articles and poems. **We pay a $30 minimum for poetry and $30 a page for prose.**

UNMUZZLED OX (IV-Themes, bilingual/foreign language), 105 Hudson St., New York NY 10013, phone (212)226-7170, or Box 550, Kingston, Ontario K7L 4W5 Canada, founded 1971, poetry editor Michael Andre, is a tabloid literary biannual. **Each edition is built around a theme or specific project.** The editor says, "The chances of an unsolicited poem being accepted are slight since I always have specific ideas in mind." Contributors have been Allen Ginsberg, Robert Creeley and Denise Levertov. As a sample the editor selected these lines from "CL" by Daniel Berrigan:

Let's be grandiose, it's a game
Let's climb a balcony
Let's issue a manifesto

Why, we're turning things on their head
we're making history
we're—

Harmless.

He is assembling material for issues titled *Poems to the Tune*, "simply poems to old tunes, a buncha contemporary *Beggar's Opera*. The other is tentatively called *The Unmuzzled Ox Book of Erotic Verse*. **Only unpublished work will be considered, but works may be in French as well as English."** Subscription: $20.

UNSILENCED VOICE (I), (formerly *Outside Lining Death Batch*), 9333 N. Lombard, #29, Portland OR 97203, founded 1990, editor Clint C. Wilkinson, is a monthly of "politically left (anarchist) and experimental art/literature." **They want "anarchist, humorous, weird free verse poetry of one page**

or less. **Nothing else."** They have published poetry by Jon Brann. As a sample the editor selected these lines (poet unidentified):

> *Single raindrop falls*
> *from a cloudless blue heaven*
> *maybe it was spit*

The editor says *UV* is 16-pgs. and photocopied. They receive about 5 poems/issue, accept 1-2. Press run is for 8 subscribers. Subscription: $10/year. No single copy sales. **Submit 3 poems at a time. Previously published poems and simultaneous submissions OK. "Write a great cover letter (funny, poignant, angry, interesting) and I'll include it with poems when published." Often comments on rejections. Send SASE for guidelines. Reports in 1 month. Pays 1 copy. Acquires one-time rights.** The editor says, "Put your guts into your work and throw them at the universe. If it's good, it'll stick. One sure way to know what I want is to read us for a while. If you hate Newt Gingrich and love Fantasy Man, then by all means, *UV* is for you."

‡THE URBANITE; URBAN LEGEND PRESS (II, IV-Fantasy, themes), P.O. Box 4737, Davenport IA 52808, founded 1991, editor Mark McLaughlin, appears 3 times a year "to promote literate, character-oriented and entertaining fiction and poetry in the genre of surrealism." **Each issue is based on a particular theme. Send SASE for details. They want contemporary fantasy/surrealism (maximum 2 pages/poem). No "slice-of-life, sentimental, gore, porn, Western, haiku or rambling rants against society."** They have recently published poetry by Marni Griffin, Don Webb and Michelle Demers. As a sample the editor selected these lines from "Rock Babies" by Joy Golisch:

> *friends tumbling together*
> *through birthing stone*
> *the kick inside*
> *I'm kicking inside*
> *a heavy soft spot*
> *the rolling ball*
> *I play soccer inside*
> *I win every time*

The Urbanite is 60-90 pgs., 8½ × 11, saddle-stitched with 2-color coated card cover. They receive about 500 poems a year, accept less than 10%. Press run is 500. Subscription: $13.50 for 3 issues. **Sample postpaid: $5. Submit only 3 poems at a time. No previously published poems or simultaneous submissions. Cover letter required. Seldom comments on rejections. Send SASE for guidelines. Reports within 4 months, sometimes longer. Pays $10/poem and 2 copies. Buys first North American serial rights and nonexclusive rights for public readings.** ("We hold readings of the magazine at libraries and other venues.") **Print rights revert to the writer after publication.** In addition to the magazine, Urban Legend Press **publishes 1 chapbook a year. Interested poets should "submit to the magazine first, to establish a relationship with our readers. Also, we do tend to prefer poets who are widely published, or who have a 'following.' For example, Joy Golisch has many fans because she performs her work at poetry readings."** A copy of Golisch's chapbook, *Surfing with Monkeys and Other Diversions*, is available from the press for $4. The editor says, "Don't write because you want to see your name in print. Write because you have a message."

URBANUS MAGAZINE; URBANUS PRESS (III), P.O. Box 192921, San Francisco CA 94119-2921, founded 1987, editor Peter Drizhal, which appears 3 times/year, is a journal of fiction, poetry, features and art—with an urban emphasis. **"Seeks post-modernist, experimental and mainstream poetry—with a social slant."** They have recently published poetry by Yusef Komunyakaa, Isabel Nathaniel, Clarence Major, Charles Fort, Anna Enquist and Denise Duhamel. As a sample the editors selected these lines from "And What Do You Get" by Heather McHugh (also appears in *The Best American Poetry 1995*):

> *Excise the er from exercise. Or from*
> *example, take the ex out: now it's bigger;*
> *to be lonely, take the amp out*
> *and replace it with an I. Take am or me*
> *away from name*
> *and suddenly there's not*
> *much left, the name's one of many names*

The digest-sized, 64-page, perfect-bound magazine uses approximately 40 of the 3,000 submissions they receive annually. Circulation is 1,200. Subscription: $12 ($15 institutions). **Sample postpaid: $5. Submit 3-5 poems (under 40 lines each) at a time. No previously published poems or simultaneous submissions.** "We have **limited open reading periods**, so unless a reading frame has been announced in a writer's periodical, please QUERY before sending mss." Reports in 3-12 weeks. Time between acceptance and publication is 4-18 months. **Pays 2 copies.** Poetry published in *Urbanus* has been selected for inclusion in the 1994 and 1995 volumes of *The Best American Poetry*. The editor says, "We do not actively seek haiku (though a humorous 'feature' appears in a recent issue), *very rarely* accept rhymed verse, and with few exceptions, would rather not see conversational narrative poetry—or for that matter, the 'classic' chopped prose poem (though we *are* guilty of having published this sort, and will, without apologies, publish it again; suffice to say, this approach doesn't very often hold our interest . . .); we also have a bias against poetry littered with similes ('it is like this/it is like that'). *Urbanus Magazine* solicits much of its writing, and generally speaking, we are a very difficult market to break into; but talented newcomers are always welcome."

US1 WORKSHEETS; US1 POETS' COOPERATIVE (II), %Postings, P.O. Box 1, Ringoes NJ 08551-0001, founded 1973, is a literary annual, 20-25 pgs., 11½ × 17, circulation 500, which uses **high quality poetry and fiction. "We use a rotating board of editors; it's wisest to query when we're next reading before submitting. A self-addressed, stamped postcard to the secretary will get our next reading period dates."** They have published poetry by Alicia Ostriker, Toi Derricotte, Elizabeth Anne Socolow, Jean Hollander, Grace Cavalieri, Geraldine C. Little and David Keller. **"We read a lot but take very few. Prefer complex, well-written work." Sample: $5. Submit 5 poems at a time. Include name, address and phone number in upper right hand corner. No simultaneous submissions; rarely accepts previously published poems. Requests for sample copies, subscriptions, queries, information about reading periods and all manuscripts should be addressed to the secretary, % POSTINGS (address at beginning of listing). Sometimes sends prepublication galleys.**

UTAH STATE UNIVERSITY PRESS (V), Logan UT 84322-7800, phone (801)797-1362, founded 1972, editor John R. Alley, publishes poetry but is **not open for submissions.**

VEGETARIAN JOURNAL; THE VEGETARIAN RESOURCE GROUP (IV-Specialized, children/ teens), P.O. Box 1463, Baltimore MD 21203, founded 1982. The Vegetarian Resource Group is a small press publisher of nonfiction, sometimes incorporating poetry. *VJ* is a bimonthly, 36 pgs., 8½ × 11, saddle-stapled and professionally printed with glossy card cover. Circulation is 20,000. **Sample: $3.** The Vegetarian Resource Group offers an annual contest for ages 18 and under, $50 savings bond in 3 age categories for the best contribution on any aspect of vegetarianism. "Most entries are essay, but we would accept poetry with enthusiasm." Deadline: May 1 postmark. Send SASE for details.

VEHICULE PRESS; SIGNAL EDITIONS (III, IV-Regional), Box 125 Station Place du Parc, Montreal, Quebec H2W 2M9 Canada, phone (514)844-6073, fax (514)844-7543, poetry editor Michael Harris, publisher Simon Dardick, is a "literary press with poetry series, Signal Editions, **publishing the work of Canadian poets only.**" They publish flat-spined paperbacks and hardbacks. Among the poets they have published are Peter Dale Scott, Don Coles, David Solway, Susan Glickman and Jan Conn. As a sample they selected these lines by Gérald Godin:

> *"What, you've forgotten my telephone number?"*
> *"Listen, old friend, I think you know*
> *they removed a tumour from my brain*
> *as big as a mandarine orange*
> *and I'm afraid*
> *your telephone number was in it . . . "*

They publish Canadian poetry which is **"first-rate, original, content-conscious." However, they are booked until 1998."**

VERSE (III), English Dept., College of William and Mary, P.O. Box 8795, Williamsburg VA 23187-8795, founded 1984, editors Henry Hart, Nancy Schoenberger and Brian Henry, is "a poetry journal which also publishes interviews with poets, articles about poetry and book reviews." They **want "no specific kind; we only look for high quality poetry. Our focus is not only on American poetry, but on all poetry written in English, as well as translations."** They have published poetry by A.R. Ammons, James Merrill, James Dickey, Galway Kinnell, Richard Kenney, Sharon Olds, Charles Wright, Robert Pinsky, Charles Simic and Wendell Berry. *Verse* is published 3 times/year. It is 128-256 pgs., digest-sized, professionally printed using small type, perfect-bound with card cover. They accept about 100 of 3,000 poems received. Press run is 1,000 for 600 subscribers of which 150 are libraries, 100 shelf sales. Subscription: $15 for individuals, $21 for institutions. **Sample postpaid: $5. Submit up to 5 poems at a time. No previously published poems; simultaneous submissions OK. Cover letter required. Reports in 2 months, usually 4-5 months to publication. Often comments on rejections. Sometimes sends prepublication galleys. Pays 2 copies.** Open to unsolicited reviews. Poets may also send books for review consideration. Poetry published in this journal has appeared in *The Best American Poetry 1992*. The editor says, "We would like to receive more translations of contemporary poetry."

VERVE (II, IV-Themes), P.O. Box 3205, Simi Valley CA 93093, founded 1989, editor/publisher Ron Reichick, editor Marilyn Hochheiser, associate editors Virginia Anderson and Margie Davidson, is now published twice a year and is **"open to contemporary poetry of any form which fits the theme of the**

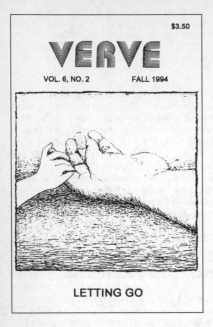

$3.50

VERVE

VOL. 6, NO. 2   FALL 1994

LETTING GO

"This cover depicts both the pain and emotional release of 'Letting Go' which is the theme of the issue," says Ron Reichick, editor/publisher of Verve. *The California-based biannual devotes at least 80 percent of its pages to poetry; the remainder contains short fiction.* Verve *looks for contemporary poetry of any form which fits into each edition's theme. "We look for our writers to expand our themes with fresh metaphor, unique ideas, and language and imagery that informs," says Reichick. The cover art is by Charles DePaul, an Illinois artist whose work has been featured on* Verve *covers since 1990.*

issue; we look for fresh metaphor, unique ideas and language and vivid imagery that informs." They have published poetry by Marge Piercy, Carol Muske, Denise Levertov, Alberto Rios and Quincy Troupe. As a sample the editors selected these lines from "A Glass of Sea Water Or A Pinch of Salt" by Philip Levine:

> *In the city at the end of the world*
> *everyone goes about in finery.*
> *Our mothers flash their shoulders and breasts*
> *at all hours, our fathers make their music,*
> *the long moaning notes of the sea at rest.*
> *Beyond the viaduct, I could be the sea spume*
> *riding toward shore, you could be the hum*
> *of the clouds at play, if only there were time.*

Verve is digest-sized, approximately 40 pgs., saddle-stitched, using bios of each contributor. Press run is 750 for 100 subscribers of which 3 are libraries. **Sample postpaid: $3.50. Submit up to 5 poems, 2 pgs. maximum/poem; "36 lines or less has best chance." Simultaneous submissions, if noted, OK. Publishes theme issues. Send SASE for guidelines and upcoming themes. Sometimes sends prepublication galleys. Pays 1 copy. Acquires first rights.** Staff reviews books of poetry in 250 words, single format. Send books for review consideration. They also sponsor 2 annual contests, each having prizes of $100, $50 and $25. Entry fee: $2/poem. Deadlines: April 1 and October 1. The editor advises, "Read a copy of *Verve* before you submit. Read good contemporary poetry—then write. Listen to criticism, but follow your instinct *and* the poem. *Then*—keep submitting."

VIET NAM GENERATION; BURNING CITIES PRESS (II, IV-Themes), 18 Center Rd., Woodbridge CT 06525, phone (203)387-6882, fax (203)389-6104, e-mail kalital@minerva.cis.yale.edu, founded 1988, editor Kali Tal, is a quarterly that publishes "the best current fiction, poetry and nonfiction dealing with the Viet Nam War generation." **"We publish honest, uncompromising poetry. We place more emphasis on the 'message' of a poem than on its form." Poetry should deal with issues of interest to the Viet Nam War generation. "No POW/MIA poems, unless written by POWs. No racist or sexist poetry."** They have published poetry by W.D. Ehrhart, Maggie Jaffe, Gerald McCarthy and Jon Forrest Glade. As a sample the editor selected "Motherfucker" by Elliot Richman:

> *It was a real mess. Only a white guy survived.*
> *He sat in a puddle near a burning truck*
> *clutching the torso of a black trooper.*
> *"You motherfucker," he whispered. "You motherfucker,"*
> *like it was the tenderest word in the language.*

The editor says it is approximately 200 pgs., 8½ × 11, perfect-bound, with photos and graphics, no ads. They receive 200-300 submissions a year, accept about 60. Press run is 1,000 for 400 subscribers of which 200 are libraries. Subscription: $40. **Sample postpaid: $20 for double issues. Submit 4-6** poems at a time. Cover letter always welcome. Previously published poems and simultaneous submissions OK; please notify if accepted elsewhere. Usually comments on rejections. Send SASE for upcoming themes. Reports within 3-4 months. Pays 2 copies. Acquires "reprint rights for our own publications." The Burning Cities Press publishes 6 paperbacks and **4 chapbooks/year.** They have recently published: David Connolly's *Lost in America*, Gerry McCarthy's *Throwing The Headlines* and Joe Amato's *Symptoms of a Finer Age*. Query first with sample poems and a cover letter with brief bio and publication credits. Replies to queries and submitted mss in 6-8 weeks. Pays 10% of press run. Sample book or chapbook: $12.

VIGIL; AMMONITE; VIGIL PUBLICATIONS (II), 12 Priory Mead, Bruton, Somerset BA10 ODZ England, founded 1979, poetry editor John Howard Greaves. *Vigil* appears 3 times a year. **They want "poetry with a high level of emotional force or intensity of observation. Poems should normally be no longer than 35 lines. Color, imagery and appeal to the senses should be important features. No whining self-indulgent, neurotic soul-baring poetry."** They have published poetry by Claudette Bass, Bettie Anne Doebler, Joseph Farley, Mario Petrucci, Patrick Cauchi and Tom Farbman. As a sample we selected the poem "Night's Colours" by Hilary Mellon:

> You make me dress
> and leave this naked darkness
> before green shades of day
> can wake your fears
>
> though knowing that for you
> I'll wear night's colours
> my stockings shiny as tears

The digest-sized magazine is 40 pgs., saddle-stapled, photoreduced typescript, with colored matte card cover. They accept about 60 of 200 submissions received. Press run is 250 for 85 subscriptions of which 6 are libraries. Subscription: £4.50. **Sample postpaid: £2. Submit no more than 6 poems at a time. Send SASE (or SAE and IRC) for upcoming themes. Sometimes sends prepublication galleys. Pays 2 copies. Editor sometimes comments on rejections.** *Ammonite* appears twice a year with **"myth, image and word towards the secondary millenium ... a seedbed of mythology for our future, potently embryonic."** Single copy: £1.75 (UK), £2.50 (overseas); subscription: £3.50 (UK), £5 (overseas). **Query regarding book publication by Vigil Publications.** The editor offers "appraisal" for £7.50 for a sample of a maximum of 12 poems.

VIKING PENGUIN, 375 Hudson St., New York NY 10014. Prefers not to share information.

THE VILLAGER (II), Dept. PM, 135 Midland Ave., Bronxville NY 10708-1800, phone (914)337-3252, founded 1928, editor Amy Murphy, poetry editor Mae Aiello, a publication of the Bronxville Women's Club for club members and families, professional people and advertisers, circulation 750, in 9 monthly issues, October through June. **Sample postpaid: $1.25. Submit 1 poem at a time, "unless it is very short."** They use one page or more of poetry/issue, prefer poems less than 20 lines, "in good taste only," seasonal (Thanksgiving, Christmas, Easter) 3 months in advance. SASE required. Pays 2 copies. They copyright material but will release it to author on request.

THE VINCENT BROTHERS REVIEW (II, IV-Themes), 4566 Northern Circle, Riverside OH 45424-5733, founded 1988, editor Kimberly A. Willardson, is a journal appearing 3 times a year. **"We look for well-crafted, thoughtful poems that shoot bolts of electricity into the reader's mind, stimulating a powerful response. We also welcome light verse and are thrilled by unusual, innovative themes/ styles. We do not accept previously published poems, simultaneous submissions or any type of bigoted propaganda. Sloppy mss containing typos and/or unintentional misspellings are automatically rejected.** *TVBR* publishes 2 theme issues/year—**poets should send us a SASE to receive details about our upcoming themes."** They have recently published poetry by Anselm Brocki, John Marvin and Gary Pacernick. As a sample the editor selected these lines from "The Wolf Man" by Matthew J. Spireng:

> and nothing lurked in the hall. Outdoors
> beneath the hot full moon the child recalled
> what it was that brought the wolf man out,
> but found his hands were smooth, his teeth
> unchanged, and nothing came to claim
> his life, not the wolf man or the bullet.

TVBR is 80 pgs., digest-sized, perfect-bound, professionally printed with matte card cover. Press run is 350. "We have 200 subscribers, 10 of which are libraries." Subscription: $12. **Sample postpaid: $6. Submit no more than 6 poems at a time, name and address on each page. Cover letter preferred; include recent publication credits and note "where author read or heard about *TVBR*. We do not read in December." Editor "often" comments on rejections. Send SASE for guidelines. Reports in**

3-4 months (after readings by editor and 2 associate editors). **Always sends prepublication galleys. Pays 2 copies for poems printed inside the journal. Pays $5 for each poem printed on "Page Left" (the back page). "For 'Page Left,' we look for the unusual—concrete poems, wordplay, avant-garde pieces, etc." Acquires one-time rights.** Reviews books of poetry in 3,500 words maximum, single or multi-book format. Open to unsolicited reviews. Poets may also send books for review consideration. The editor advises, "*Don't* send your poetry to a magazine you haven't read. Subscribe to the little magazines you respect—they contain the work of your peers and competitors. Proofread your poetry carefully and read it aloud before sending it out."

VIOLETTA BOOKS (I, IV-Anthologies), P.O. Box 15191, Springfield MA 01115, founded 1983, editor Kathleen Gilbert, seeks poems of a spiritual, not religious, nature for an anthology to be published in mid 1996. The editor notes, "I generally look for understandable writing, unordinary insights into daily life and mystical feeling rising from everyday experiences. In this anthology, especially, I seek **poems about such things as guardian angels, insights from vivid dreams and a feeling of approaching the Deity or universal mind, all in a positive vein." She does not want poetry that is "cutely sentimental, trite, tightly rhymed or overly negative."** The editor has recently published poetry by Teresa Burleson, Laurence F. O'Brien and Elaine Thomas. As a sample she selected these lines from "The Garden of Night" by Laurie Lessen:

> *Luminous and radiant*
> *The moonbeams warm our desperate*
> *Souls, white stairways*
> *To our vast and blinding*
> *Dreams of other worlds.*

The anthology is digest-sized, 35-40 pgs., offset from typescript, with matte card cover. **Sample postpaid: $3.50. (Make checks payable to Kathleen Gilbert.) Submit 5-10 poems of up to 40 lines each. Reading fee: $2/poem. Send 1 copy of each poem with name and address. Previously published poems OK, as long as poet holds rights; simultaneous submissions also OK. Pays 1 copy/each poem used; "additional copies will be available for purchase." Acquires one-time rights.** Kathleen Gilbert says, "I seek good, accessible work that offers the reader the benefits all good art offers its perceptors—hope, strength, renewal. My purpose in publishing poetry is to encourage poets of all ability levels to write accessible and yet individualistic poetry. I also offer how-to books on poetry marketing and independent publishing. Send SASE for details."

VIRGIN MEAT (IV-Horror), 2325 West Ave. K-15, Lancaster CA 93536, phone (805)722-1758, e-mail belalagosi@aol.com, founded 1986. *VM* is a computerized, interactive magazine of gothic horror. Prints fiction, poetry, art, .SND Sound and .MooV Quick Time movies. **Guidelines are available by request from e-mail or for a SASE. Sample postpaid: $5 (Macintosh only). Simultaneous and previously published poems OK.** Submissions without a SASE or to the e-mail address will not be read. **Reports in 4 months. Pays 1 copy. Reviews anything with a cover price.**

THE VIRGINIA QUARTERLY REVIEW; EMILY CLARK BALCH PRIZE (III), 1 West Range, Charlottesville VA 22903, founded 1925, is one of the oldest and most distinguished literary journals in the country. **It uses about 15 pgs. of poetry in each issue, no length or subject restrictions.** Recent issues largely include lyric and narrative free verse, most of which features a strong message or powerful voice. The review is 220 pgs., digest-sized, flat-spined, circulation 4,000. **Pays $1/line.** They also sponsor the Emily Clark Balch Prize, an annual prize of $500 given to the best poem published in the review during the year. Poetry published here has been included in *The Best American Poetry 1993*.

VIRTUE: THE CHRISTIAN MAGAZINE FOR WOMEN (IV-Religious), P.O. Box 36630, Colorado Springs CO 80936-3663, founded 1978, editor Nancie Carmichael, managing editor Jeanette Thomason, is a Christian magazine, appearing 6 times a year, to **"encourage and integrate biblical truth with daily living." As for poetry, they look for "rhythmic control and metric effects, whether free or patterned stanzas; use of simile and metaphor; sensory perceptions, aptly recorded; and implicit rather than explicit spiritual tone."** As a sample the editor selected these lines from "Bending" by Barbara Seaman:

> *Down on my knees again, Lord*
> *and undignified as ever,*
> *(how to mop mud with grace?)*
> *attempting to confine the exuberance*
> *of yesterday's rain to the kitchen only . . .*

Virtue is 80 pgs., magazine-sized, saddle-stapled, with full-color pages inside as well as on its paper cover. Press run is 150,000. Single copy: $2.95; subscription: $16.95. **Sample postpaid: $3. Submit "no more than 3 poems, each on separate sheet, typewritten; notify if simultaneous submission."** Time between acceptance and publication is 3-9 months. **Send SASE for guidelines. Reports in approximately 2 months. Pays $20-40/poem and 1 copy. Buys first rights.**

VOICES (II), (formerly *The Review*), P.O. Box 3331, Montebello CA 90640, founded 1992, editor Paul Quintero, is now an annual journal which **"accepts all poetry; open to length, subject matter and style."** They have recently published poetry by Adam P. Donovan, B.A. Cantwell and Carol Frith. As a sample the editor selected these lines from "Appalachian Night" by Mark Jackley:

> In a kitchen window,
> The silhouette of an enormous man who thinks,
> Gazing at the train
> He could love anyone on board.

The editor says *Voices* is about 30 pgs., desktop-published. Subscription: $6. **Sample postpaid: $6. Make checks or money orders payable to the editor. Submit 3-5 poems at a time, typed one to a page. Previously published poems OK; "please state when and where."** No simultaneous submissions. **Reports in 1 month. Pays 1 copy. Acquires one-time rights. Rights revert to authors upon publication.** The editor says, "I would really like to see more poetry in the styles of Leonard Cohen and Stephen Crane. Also, please submit with a SASE; I still have authors submitting without one, and I won't be nice by returning material to them as I have in the past."

VOICES INTERNATIONAL (II), 1115 Gillette Dr., Little Rock AR 72207, phone (501)225-0166, editor Clovita Rice, is a quarterly poetry journal. **"We look for poetry with a new focus, memorable detail and phrasing, and significant and haunting statement climax, all of which impel the reader to reread the poem and return to it for future pleasure and reference."** As a sample the editor selected "And the Gulf Pulls" by Ella Cavis:

> me like a magnet that never lets go,
> as she once clutched Masefield.
> I must see the white flounces of her frock,
> jewelry of shells she wears and casts off,
> flight of pelicans above
> emulating her smoothness on windless days,
> and people playing in her precinct,
> bathers huddling close to shore,
> as if they know they are specks
> in sweeping water.

It is 32-40 pgs., 6×9, saddle-stapled, professionally printed with b&w matte card cover. Subscription: $10/year. **Sample postpaid (always a back issue): $2. Prefers free verse but accepts high quality traditional. Limit submissions to batches of 5, double-spaced, 3-40 lines (will consider longer if good). No simultaneous submissions. Cover letter preferred; include personal data.** Publishes an average of 18 months after acceptance. **Send SASE for guidelines. Pays copies.** The editor says, "Too many poets submit poetry without studying a copy to become familiar with what we are publishing. Our guidelines help poets polish their poems before submission."

VOICES ISRAEL (I, IV-Anthology); REUBEN ROSE POETRY COMPETITION (I); MONTHLY POET'S VOICE (IV-Members), P.O. Box 5780, 46157 Herzlia Israel, founded 1972, *Voices Israel* editor Mark L. Levinson, with an editorial board of 7, is an annual anthology of poetry in English coming from all over the world. **You have to buy a copy to see your work in print. Submit all kinds of poetry (up to 4 poems), each no longer than 40 lines, in seven copies.** They have published poetry by Yehuda Amichai, Eugene Dubnov, Alan Sillitoe and Gad Yaacobi. As a sample the editor selected this poem "Commentary," by Moshe-Ben-Zvi:

> I listen to my heart
> playing jokes on itself.
> My life depends
> on each punch line.

The annual *Voices Israel* is 6½×9⅛, offset from laser output on ordinary paper, approximately 121 pgs., flat-spined with varying cover. Circulation 350. Subscription: $15. **Sample back copy postpaid: $10. Contributor's copy: $15 airmail. Previously published poems OK, "but please include details and assurance that copyright problems do not exist." No simultaneous submissions. Cover letter with brief biographical details required with submissions. Deadline end of February each year. Reports in fall.** Sponsors the annual Reuben Rose Poetry Competition. Send poems of up to 40 lines each, plus $5/poem to P.O. Box 236, Kiriat Ata, Israel. Poet's name and address should be on a separate sheet with titles of poems. *The Monthly Poet's Voice*, a broadside edited by Ezra Ben-Meir, **is sent only to members of the Voices Group of Poets in English.** The *Voices Israel* editor advises, "We would like to see more humorous but well constructed poetry. We like to be surprised."

‡VOICES OF YOUTH (IV-Teens, students), P.O. Box 1869, Sonoma CA 95476, phone (707)938-8314, fax (707)996-1738, founded 1990, is a national magazine "dedicated to supporting and encouraging creative work by teenagers." **They are open to any subject and style of poetry but all work must be written by high school students.** The magazine is 40-48 pgs., 8½×11, neatly printed and saddle-stitched with color coated card cover and b&w art and photos inside (all by students). It is published 4 times during the academic year. Subscription: $16.95. **Sample postpaid: $5.25. Submissions must include writer's name, address, phone number and grade in school as well as the school's name, address and phone number. No previously published poems; simultaneous submissions OK. Send SASE for guidelines. Pays 1 copy. Acquires first serial rights.**

VOL. NO. MAGAZINE (II, IV-Themes), 24721 Newhall Ave., Newhall CA 91321, phone (805)254-0851, founded 1983, poetry editors Richard Weekley, Jerry Danielsen, Tina Landrum and Don McLeod. "*Vol. No.* publishes lively and concise works. Vivid connections. **Each issue has a theme. Theme for August, 1996, is Epicenter (when emotional, philosophical or actual foundations crumble before your very eyes). Send SASE for details. No trivial, clichéd or unthoughtout work. Work that penetrates the ozone within. One-page poems have the best chance.**" They have published poetry by Octavio Paz, Anne Marple, Jane Hirshfield and Julian Pulley. The editors selected these sample lines by William Stafford:

> *We stand for hours where sunlight tells us*
> *it forgives. A golden shaft pours down.*
> *The air waits. A cardinal sings and sings.*
> *We stand for hours.*

Vol. No. is a digest-sized, saddle-stapled, 32-page annual, circulation 300. They receive about 600 unsolicited submissions of poetry/year, use 60, have a 6-month backlog. Subscription: $10 (2 issues). **Sample postpaid: $5. Submit limit of 6 poems. Simultaneous submissions OK. Reports in 1-5 months. Pays 2 copies.**

THE VOYANT; HOLLOW MAN PUBLISHING (II), Box 414, 20384 Fraser Highway, Langley, British Columbia V3A 4G1 Canada, e-mail petrus@mpersandsfu.ca, founded 1994, editors Robert Ivins and Jamie Scott, appears annually. "*The Voyant* (formerly *Tyrannosaurus Poetry Machine*) is unearthing stones in search of the sublime, the grotesque, and the beautiful, and is seeking poets unafraid to confront whatever might slither out." **They do not want "badly-written love poems or overtly sexual material. We are always looking for vitality, freshness and surprise. We favour surrealism, but are seeking poetry that goes beyond categorical boundaries. We are open to innovative work of any kind and encourage submissions on a variety of mediums other than paper."** As each issue will be in a different format, there are no subscription rates. **Query for cost of sample. Submit up to 10 poems at a time. Cover letter "appreciated." Previously published poems and simultaneous submissions OK. Comments on rejections "where time and merit allow." Send SASE (or SAE and IRC) for guidelines. Reports "as soon as humanly possible." Usually pays in copies. Acquires first North American serial or one-time rights.** Hollow Man Publishing (formerly Impoverished Poets Press) may, in the future, publish chapbooks of outstanding material. Robert Ivins says, "The Voyant embodies the spirit of revolution and discovery. He induces madness in himself in order to bring to his people knowledge of the unknown, and this is what we are attempting to do with *The Voyant*. We retain a strong interest in poets of the West Coast and Canada, but will publish material from anywhere in the world. We publish innovative work whether in form or content, but not experimental for experiment's sake."

W.I.M. PUBLICATIONS (WOMAN IN THE MOON); THE SPIRIT; 2 CROW'S MAGIC (I, IV-Gay/lesbian, women/feminism), Dept. PM, P.O. Box 2087, Cupertino CA 95015-2087, phone/fax (408)738-4623, e-mail 5602701@mercuryfhda.edu., founded 1979, poetry editor Dr. SDiane Bogus, who says, "We are a small press with trade press ambitions. We publish poetry, New Age and reference books. **We pay royalties. We prefer a query and a modest track record.**" She wants poetry by **"gay, black, women, prison poets, enlightened others—contemporary narrative or lyric work, free verse OK, but not too experimental for cognition. We prefer poems to be a page or less if not part of long narrative. No obviously self-indulgent exercises in the psychology of the poet. No sexual abuse themes. No gross sexual references. No hate poems."** In addition to her own work, she has recently published poetry by Merilene M. Murphy and I. Lillian Randolph. As a sample she selected these lines from "His Life" in *The Book of Lives* by Sherrylynn Poscy:

> *I had 4 maybe 5 lovers*
> *in my life*
> *one of them*
> *lied to me*

Dr. Bogus publishes 2-4 chapbooks and flat-spined paperbacks a year each averaging 48-100 pages. Press run is 250-1,000. **Submit 6 sample poems, typed, 1 to a page. Include cover letter with statement of "vision and poetics, theme selection of the work, poetic mentors, track record and $20 reading fee. New poets must take poetry test ($10 plus free critique). Submit between January 1 and April 30 each year. We acknowledge submissions upon receipt. Send 2 first-class stamps or 78¢ for guidelines/catalog. We report at end of reading season, July through August 7. Simultaneous submissions and previously published poems OK. Authors are asked to assist in promo and** sales by providing list of prospective readers and promotional photos. To established authors we pay 7-10% royalties after costs; others 5-8%. We may take advanced orders. We will accept subscriptions for a book in production at retail price. We fill orders author has provided and others our promo has prompted." W.I.M. subsidy publishes under the imprint 2 Crow's Magic. Write for details. They also publish the quarterly newsletter, *The Spirit*. It features reviews, poetry, stories, news from the press and winner announcements. Subscription: $22. They sponsor 3 poetry contests/year: The T. Nelson Gilbert Poetry Prize (January 1 through May 31), Pat Parker Memorial Poetry Award (March 1 through May 31) and the Poetry Lottery (one poet wins every 3 months; submissions are good for two chances). Write for guidelines. W.I.M. also offers a self-publishing and consultation criticism service for a fee. Bogus says, "W.I.M. promotes readings for its poets and encourages each poet who submits with a personal letter which discusses her or his strengths and weaknesses. Often we allow repeat submissions. Also, we welcome a tape of the poet reading from the submitted manuscript."

WARTHOG PRESS (II), 29 S. Valley Rd., West Orange NJ 07052, phone (201)731-9269, founded 1979, poetry editor Patricia Fillingham, publishes books of poetry **"that are understandable, poetic."** They have published poetry by Barbara A. Holland, Penny Harter and Marta Fenyves. **Query with 5 samples, cover letter "saying what the author is looking for" and SASE. Simultaneous submissions OK. Ms should be "readable." Comments on rejections, "if asked for. People really don't want criticism." Pays copies, but "I would like to get my costs back."** Patricia Fillingham feels, "The best way to sell poetry still seems to be from poet to listener."

WASCANA REVIEW (II), Dept. of English, University of Regina, Regina, Saskatchewan S4S 0A2 Canada, phone (306)585-4311, fax (306)585-4827, founded 1966, editor Kathleen Wall, appears twice a year publishing contemporary poetry and short fiction along with critical articles on modern and post-modern literature. **"We look for high-quality literary poetry of all forms, including translations. No haiku or doggerel. No long poems. No concrete poetry."** They have published poetry by Stephen Heighton, Robert Cooperman, Cornelia Hoogland and Eugene Dubnov. The editor says *WR* is a trade-sized paperback, 75-100 pgs., no art/graphics, no ads. They receive about 200-300 submissions a year, accept under 10%. Press run is 400 for 192 subscribers of which 134 are libraries, 100 shelf sales. Subscription: $7/year, $8 outside Canada. **Sample postpaid: $4. No previously published poems or simultaneous submissions. Cover letter required. SASE or SAE and IRCs necessary for return of mss. "Poems are read by at least two individuals who make comments and/or recommendations. Poetry editor chooses poems based on these comments." Often comments on rejections. Reports within 6 months. Pays $10/page and 2 copies. Buys all rights; does not return them.** Reviews books of poetry in both single and multi-book format. The editor says, "*WR* will be featuring special issues from time to time. Poets should watch for news of these in upcoming editions."

WASHINGTON REVIEW; FRIENDS OF THE WASHINGTON REVIEW OF THE ARTS, INC. (II), P.O. Box 50132, Washington DC 20091-0132, phone (202)638-0515, founded 1974, literary editor Joe Ross, is a bimonthly journal of arts and literature published by the Friends of the Washington Review of the Arts, Inc., a nonprofit, tax-exempt educational organization. **They publish local Washington metropolitan area poets as well as poets from across the US and abroad. "We have eclectic tastes but lean with more favor toward experimental work."** *WR* is tabloid-sized, using 2 of the large pgs. each issue for poetry, saddle-stapled on high-quality newsprint, circulation 2,000 with 700 subscribers of which 10 are libraries. **Sample postpaid: $2.50. Cover letter with brief bio required with submissions. Pays 5 copies.** Reviews books of poetry in 1,000-1,500 words, single format—multi-book "on occasion." Open to unsolicited reviews. Poets may also send books for review consideration.

WASHINGTON WRITERS' PUBLISHING HOUSE (IV-Regional), P.O. Box 15271, Washington DC 20003, phone (202)543-1905, founded 1975. An editorial board is elected annually from the collective. "We are a poetry publishing collective that publishes outstanding poetry collections in flat-spined paperbacks by **individual authors living in the greater Washington, DC area (60-mile radius, excluding Baltimore) on the basis of competitions held once a year.**" They have published poetry by Myra Sklarew, Ann Darr, Barbara Lefcowitz, Maxine Clair, Ann Knox, Nan Fry and Naomi Thiers. The editors chose this sample from "The Kidnapping of Science" in *From the Red Eye of Jupiter* by Patricia Garfinkel:

> Conception had been a quiet event, not
> the harsh strike of steel to flint,
> but an easing into fertile corners,
> patient as bacteria for the right conditions.

Send SASE for guidelines and a brochure of published poets to: Barri Armitage, Secretary, 13904 North Gate Dr., Silver Spring MD 20906. Pays copies. Poets become working members of the collective.

WATER MARK PRESS (V), 138 Duane St., New York NY 10013, founded 1978, editor Coco Gordon, proposes "to publish regardless of form in archival editions with handmade paper and hand done elements in sewn, bound books, broadsides, chapbooks and artworks. **I use only avant-garde material." Currently they do not accept any unsolicited poetry.** They have recently published poetry by Carolyne Wright and Alison Knowles. The editor selected this sample from "After Eden" by Michael Blumenthal:

> *Once again the invasion of purpose*
> *into gesture: the stem towards the vase,*
> *the hands towards the dreaded morning music*
> *of predictability, Indian paintbrush fades*

That's from a collection of his poetry, *Sympathetic Magic*, published in 1980, 96 pgs., flat-spined, with art by Theo Fried, printed on archival, matte card cover with colored art, $9; hardbound $40. **Note: Please do not confuse Water Mark Press with the imprint Watermark Press, used by other businesses.**

WATERWAYS: POETRY IN THE MAINSTREAM (I, IV-Themes); TEN PENNY PLAYERS (IV-Children/teen/young adult); BARD PRESS (V), 393 St. Paul's Ave., Staten Island NY 10304, phone (718)442-7429, fax (718)442-4978, founded 1977, poetry editors Barbara Fisher and Richard Spiegel, "publishes **poetry by adult poets in a magazine that is published 11 times a year. We do theme issues** and are trying to increase an audience for poetry and the printed and performed word. The project produces performance readings in public spaces and is in residence year round at our local library with workshops and readings. We publish the magazine, *Waterways*; anthologies and chapbooks. **We are not fond of haiku or rhyming poetry; never use material of an explicit sexual nature.** We are open to reading material from people we have never published, writing in traditional and experimental poetry forms. While we do 'themes,' sometimes an idea for a future magazine is inspired by a submission so we try to remain open to poets' inspirations. Poets should be guided however by the fact that we are children's and animal rights advocates and are a NYC press." They have recently published poetry by Ida Fasel, Joan Payne Kincaid, Terry Thomas and Joanne Seltzer. As a sample, the editors chose these lines from "The Way of Art" by Albert Huffstickler:

> *It seems to me that,*
> *paralleling the paths of action, devotion, etc.,*
> *there is a path called Art*
> *and that the sages of the East would have recognized*
> *Faulkner, Edward Hopper, Beethoven, William Carlos Williams,*
> *and addressed them as equals.*

Waterways is published in a 40-page, 4¼×7 format, saddle-stapled, photocopied from various type styles, using b&w drawings, matte card cover. They use 60% of poems submitted. Circulation 150 with 58 subscriptions of which 12 are libraries. Subscription: $20. **Sample postpaid: $2.60. Submit less than 10 poems for first submission. Simultaneous submissions OK. Send SASE for guidelines for approaching themes.** "Since we've taken the time to be very specific in our response, writers should take seriously our comments and not waste their emotional energy and our time sending material that isn't within our area of interest. Sending for our theme sheet and for a sample issue and then objectively thinking about the writer's own work is practical and wise. Without meaning to sound 'precious' or unfriendly, the writer should understand that small press publishers doing limited editions and all production work inhouse are working from their personal artistic vision and know exactly what notes will harmonize, effectively counterpoint and meld. Many excellent poems are sent back to the writers by *Waterways* because they don't relate to what we are trying to create in a given month or months. Some poets get printed regularly in *Waterways*; others will probably never be published by us, not because the poet doesn't write well (although that too is sometimes the case) but only because we are artists with opinions and we exercise them in building each issue. Manuscripts that arrive without a return envelope are not sent back." **Reports in less than a month. Pays 1 copy. Acquires one-time publication rights. Editors sometimes comment on rejections.** They hold contests for children only. **Chapbooks published by Ten Penny Players are "by children and young adults only—and not by submission; they come through our workshops in the library and schools. Adult poets are published by us through our Bard Press imprint, by invitation only. Books evolve from the relationship we develop with writers who we publish in *Waterways* and whom we would like to give more exposure."** The editors advise, "We suggest that poets attend book fairs. It's a fast way to find out what we are all publishing."

WAYNE STATE UNIVERSITY PRESS (V), 4809 Woodward Ave., Detroit MI 48201-1309, phone (313)577-4606, fax (313)577-6131, founded 1941, director Arthur B. Evans, publishes 1 paperback

---

Market categories: (I) Beginning; (II) General; (III) Limited;
(IV) Specialized; (V) Closed.

book of poetry/year. They have published poetry by Ruth Whitman and Jim Daniels. **However, they are currently not accepting unsolicited submissions. Query first with sample poems and cover letter with brief bio and publication credits. Previously published poems OK; no simultaneous submissions.** They currently have a 2- to 3-year backlog. **"Two peer reviews are required. If favorable, the project is recommended to an edit board, which must approve all books published."** Seldom comments on rejections. Replies to queries in 1 week, to mss (if invited) in 2 months. Pays 6-10% royalties and 6 author's copies.

WEBSTER REVIEW (II, IV-Translations), English Dept., St. Louis Community College—Meramec, 11333 Big Bend Rd., St. Louis MO 63122, founded 1974, poetry editors Robert Boyd and Greg Marshall, is a literary annual. They want **"no beginners. We are especially interested in translations of foreign contemporary poetry."** They have published poetry by Georgi Belev, Antony Oldknow, Bruce Bond, Jane Schapiro and Ernest Kroll. As a sample the editor selected these lines from "That Day I Died" by James Finnegan:

> *This is my story of how I died and didn't.*
> *My body paralyzed suddenly*
> *while swimming in the Black River,*
> *you can find it on any map of Missouri,*
> *I sank on my back to the riverbed. Eyes open*
> *awash with all of the world above and around me, . . .*

Webster Review is 128 pgs., digest-sized, flat-spined, professionally printed with glossy card cover. They receive about 1,500 poems/year, use 90. Press run is 1,000 with 500 subscribers of which 200 are libraries. Single copy/subscription: $5. **Sample free for SASE. Submit 3-6 poems at a time. No previously published poems, simultaneous submissions OK, but not encouraged. Editors comment on rejections "if time permits." Reports "within a month, usually." Contributors receive 2 copies.**

WELTER (I, II), English Dept., University of Baltimore, 1420 N. Charles St., Baltimore MD 21201, founded 1963, is a literary annual **"extremely interested in beginners and lesser known writers. Let us know if you're a student."** It is flat-spined, digest-sized. Press run is 500. **Sample postpaid: $3. Submit 10 poems no more than 40 lines each. Neatly typewritten pages with name and address on each page. No simultaneous submissions. Reads submissions September through January only; makes decisions in February through March. Send SASE for guidelines. Pays 2 copies. Acquires first-time rights.** The editor says, "Please get a copy of submission guidelines and note our acceptance, reading and notification schedules before you inundate us with 'where are my poems' postcards."

THE WESLEYAN ADVOCATE (IV-Religious), P.O. Box 50434, Indianapolis IN 46250-0434, phone (317)595-4156, founded 1843, contact Jerry Bricheisen, is a monthly magazine using **"short religious poetry only; no long free verse or secular."** The editor describes it as 36 pgs., magazine-sized, offset, saddle-stapled, with 4-color cover. They use 10-15% of 100-200 poems received/year. Press run is 20,000 with "some" subscriptions of which 50 are libraries, no shelf sales (so it must be distributed free). Subscription: $12.50. **Sample: $2. Reports in 2 weeks. Pays $5-10 plus 4 copies on request. Buys first and/or one-time rights.**

WESLEYAN UNIVERSITY PRESS (III), 110 Mt. Vernon, Middletown CT 06459, phone (203)344-7918, founded 1957, editor Suzanna Tamminen, is one of the major publishers of poetry in the nation. They publish 4-6 titles/year. They have published poetry by James Dickey, Joy Harjo, James Tate and Yusef Komunyakaa. **Send query and SASE. Considers simultaneous submissions. Send SASE for guidelines. Responds to queries in 6-8 weeks, to mss in 2-4 months. Pays royalties plus 10 copies.** Poetry publications from Wesleyan tend to get widely (and respectfully) reviewed.

WEST BRANCH (II), Bucknell Hall, Bucknell University, Lewisburg PA 17837, founded 1977, is a literary biannual, using **quality poetry.** Free verse is the dominant form—lyric, narrative and dramatic—occasionally longer than one page, much of it accessible with the emphasis on voice and/or powerful content. They have published poetry by D. Nurkse, Deborah Burnham, Jim Daniels, Anneliese Wagner, Betsy Sholl, David Citino, Barbara Crooker and David Brooks. It is 100-120 pgs., digest-sized, circulation 500. One-year subscription: $7. Two years (4 issues): $11. **Sample: $3. "We do not consider simultaneous submissions. Each poem is judged on its own merits, regardless of subject or form. We strive to publish the best work being written today." Reports in 6-8 weeks. Pays copies and subscription to the magazine. Acquires first rights.** Reviews books and chapbooks of poetry but only those by writers who have been published in *West Branch*.

WEST COAST LINE (II, IV-Regional), 2027 EAA, Simon Fraser University, Burnaby, British Columbia V5A 1S6 Canada, phone (604)291-4287, editor Roy Miki, founded 1965. *West Coast Line* is published 3 times a year and **"favors work by both new and established Canadian writers, but it**

observes no borders in encouraging original creativity. Our focus is on contemporary poetry, short fiction, criticism and reviews of books." They have recently published poetry by Monty Reid, Daphne Marlatt, Erin Mouré, Bruce Andrews, Gerry Shikatani and Hiromi Goto. The editor chose these sample lines from "*Flesh, Song*(e) et Promenade" by Nicole Brossard, translated by Lola Lemire Tostevin:

revocable words
culture caught red-handed
this truly biographical nuance
of shoulders and knees
amidst the arguments
in a yes the lightning *I*

The magazine is handsomely printed on glossy paper, 6×9, flat-spined, 144 pgs. They accept about 20 of the 500-600 poetry mss received each year. Approximately 26 pages of poetry/issue. Press run is 800 for 500 subscriptions of which 350 are libraries, 150 shelf sales. Subscription: $20. Single copy: $10. **No simultaneous submissions or previously published poetry.** Time between acceptance and publication is 2-8 months. **Publishes theme issues. They published a double issue entitled "Colour—An Issue," on race in Canada. Send SASE for guidelines. Reports in 6-8 weeks. Sends prepublication galleys on request. Pays approximately $8 (Canadian)/printed page plus a one-year subscription. Mss returned only if accompanied by sufficient Canadian postage or IRC.** The editor says, "We have a special concern for contemporary writers who are experimenting with, or expanding the boundaries of, conventional forms of poetry, fiction and criticism. That is, poetry should be formally innovative."

WEST END PRESS (IV-Social issues, ethnic/nationality, women), P.O. Box 27334, Albuquerque NM 87125, founded 1976, publisher John Crawford, publishes 6 paperbacks/year. **They want "political or personal experience, any style. Nothing self-indulgent, racist, sexist, elitist, etc. Normally we publish literature of a progressive political orientation. This includes working class literature, literature with political themes and multicultural literature. A majority of our books are written by women. We have also published bilingual books."** They have recently published poetry by Margaret Randall, Adrian Louis, Russell Leong and Luis Alberto Urrea. As a sample the editor selected these lines from "The Great Pat Smith American Dreampoem" by Pat Smith:

One day my customer is Busby Berkeley
He leans on my counter, lights his cigar
likes what he sees
and says in a wise voice
Girlie, can you swim?

Submit 3-6 poems at a time. "Prefer cover letter giving an idea of previous work and reason for interest in the press." Editor often comments on rejections. "Reporting time 3 months, no panel review, at least a year backlog." Pays maximum of 6% royalties, but payment is usually in copies, 10% of press run. West End Press's book, *The Fever of Being* by Luis Alberto Urrea, won the 1994 Western States Book Award for poetry. The editor says, "Do not simply send us narrative or autobiographical pieces. The work must have a social edge."

WEST OF BOSTON; MENKE KATZ POETRY AWARDS (II), Box 2, Cochituate Station, Wayland MA 01778, phone (508)653-7241, press founded 1983, poetry editor Norman Andrew Kirk, wants to see **"poetry of power, compassion, originality and wit—and talent, too. Poetry that reveals the nature of life from the religious to the sensual, from personal exposures to universal truths. No subject is taboo so long as it is authentic and/or passionate."** They have published poetry by Mary K. Leen, R. Nikolas Macioci, Errol Miller, Lyn Lifshin and Barry Spacks. As a sample the editor selected these lines from "Leaves of an Autumn Past" by Lynda S. Silva:

you remember . . .

we had that old
painted-lady house
with a bathroom
red tile and chrome,

an Indian woman, nude,
touched with silver, . . .

They are now accepting submissions for a new publication of previously unpublished poems, also called *West of Boston*. Depending on submissions, it will be an annual or semiannual, perfect-bound on high quality paper. **Submit no more than 10 poems at a time. Include a brief bio and SASE with submission. All contributors will receive 1 copy.** Subscription available for $10/issue. **For book or chapbook submission, query with 5-10 sample poems, credits and bio. Simultaneous submissions and previously published poems OK. Editor "sometimes" comments on rejected mss. Sometimes sends prepublication galleys. Pays 10% of press run.** Sponsors the Menke Katz Poetry Awards for a poem of merit by a poet who has not had a volume of poetry published and a poem of merit by a poet with at least 1 published book. Each poet will receive a $250 award. All submissions will be eligible. Some poets will be invited to submit their work. Only subscribers will receive cash awards. Non-subscribers will receive 10 issues when their poem is selected.

WEST WIND REVIEW (II, IV-Anthology), English Dept., Southern Oregon State College, Ashland OR 97520, phone (503)552-6181, founded 1982, is an annual **"looking for sensitive but strong verse that celebrates all aspects of men's and women's experiences, both exalted and tragic. We are looking to print material that reflects ethnic and social diversity."** As a sample the editor selected these lines by Eve Sutton:

> *Soft mud, gray clay*
> *Pressed in my hands on a whim*
> *Inspired by Michelangelo,*
> *Sculpts itself, becomes surprisingly familiar*
> *All right, mother, now that you've dared me . . .*

WWR is 140-160 pgs., digest-sized, handsomely printed, flat-spined, appearing each spring. They receive about 200 submissions/year, publish 40-50 poems and 10 short stories. Press run is 500. **Sample "at current year's price. We take submissions—limit of 5 poems not exceeding 50 lines. Manuscripts should have poet's name and address on each page."** No previously published poems or simultaneous submissions. Cover letter required; include brief bio and publication credits. Deadline: January 1 for publication in late May or early June. Send SASE for guidelines. Reports in 2-3 months after deadline. Pays 1 copy.** Offers awards for each category.

WESTERLY; PATRICIA HACKETT PRIZE (II), Centre for Studies in Australian Literature, University of Western Australia, Nedlands 6009, Australia, phone (09) 380-2101, fax (09)380-1030, e-mail westerly@uniwa.uwa.edu.au, founded 1956, editors Dennis Haskell and Delys Bird. *Westerly* is a literary and cultural quarterly publishing quality short fiction, poetry, literary critical, socio-historical articles and book reviews. **"No restrictions on creative material. Our only criterion [for poetry] is literary quality. We don't dictate to writers on rhyme, style, experimentation, or anything else. We are willing to publish short or long poems. We do assume a reasonably well read, intelligent audience. Past issues of *Westerly* provide the best guides. Not consciously an academic magazine."** They have published work by Edwin Thumboo, Jean Kent, Diane Fahey, Brian Turner and Kirpal Singh. The quarterly magazine is 7×10, "electronically printed," 96 pgs., with some photos and graphics. Press run is 1,000. Single copy: $6 (Aus.) plus overseas postage via surface mail; subscription: $24 (Aus.)/year or $10 by e-mail. **Sample: $7 (Aus.) surface mail, $8 (Aus.) airmail. Submit 1-6 poems at a time. "Please do not send simultaneous submissions. Covering letters should be brief and nonconfessional." Publishes occasional theme issues. Theme for December 1995 is war. Reporting time is 2-3 months and time to publication approximately 3 months. Minimum pay for poetry is $30 plus 1 copy. Buys first publication rights; requests acknowledgement on reprints.** Reviews books of poetry in 500-1,000 words. Open to unsolicited reviews. Poets may also send books to Reviews Editor for review consideration. The Patricia Hackett Prize (value approx. $500) is awarded in March for the best contribution published in *Westerly* during the previous calendar year. The advice of the editors is: "Be sensible. Write what matters for you but think about the reader. Don't spell out the meanings of the poems and the attitudes to be taken to the subject matter—i.e. trust the reader. Don't be swayed by literary fashion. Read the magazine if possible before sending submissions. Read, read, read literature of all kinds and periods."

WESTERN HUMANITIES REVIEW (II), Dept. of English, 341 OSH, University of Utah, Salt Lake City UT 84112, phone (801)581-6168, fax (801)585-5167, founded 1947, managing editor Amanda Pecor, is a quarterly of poetry, fiction and a small selection of nonfiction. **They want "quality poetry of any form, including translations."** They have recently published poetry by Philip Levine, Bin Ramke, Lucie Brock-Broido, Timothy Liu and Rachel Wetzsteon. As a sample we selected these lines from "Storm on Fishing Bay" by John Drury:

> *What's hard to explain*
> *darkens the prospect of happiness—*
> *like wind picking up off shore*
> *where four people retreat, separately.*
>
> *Darkened, the prospect of happiness*
> *falls back to a hunting lodge*
> *where four people retreat, separately*
> *latching shutters, brewing coffee, gazing.*

WHR is 96-125 pgs., 6×9, professionally printed on quality stock and perfect-bound with coated card cover. They receive about 700 submissions a year, accept less than 10%, publish approximately 60 poets. Press run is 1,100 for 1,000 subscribers of which 900 are libraries. Subscription: $20 to individuals in the US. **Sample postpaid: $6. "We do not publish writer's guidelines because we think that the magazine itself conveys an accurate picture of our requirements." No previously published poems; simultaneous submissions OK. Reads submissions September 1 through May 31 only.** Time between acceptance and publication is 1-3 issues. **Managing editor Dawn Corrigan makes an initial cut ("eliminating only a few submissions"), then Richard Howard, the poetry editor, makes the final selections. Seldom comments on rejections. Occasionally publishes special issues. Reports in 1-6 months. Pays $50/poem and 2 copies. Acquires first serial rights.** They also offer an annual spring contest for Utah poets. Prize is $250. Poetry published in this review has been selected for inclusion in the 1992, 1993 and 1995 volumes of *The Best American Poetry.*

WESTERN PRODUCER PUBLICATIONS; WESTERN PEOPLE (IV-Regional), P.O. Box 2500, Saskatoon, Saskatchewan S7K 2C4 Canada, phone (306)665-3500, founded 1923, managing editor Michael Gillgannon. *Western People* is a magazine supplement to *The Western Producer*, a weekly newspaper, circulation 100,000, which uses **"poetry about the people, interests and environment of rural Western Canada."** As a sample the editor selected the entire poem "sky so heavy and low" by Marilyn Cay:

> it is November in Saskatchewan
> the sky so heavy and low
> I can feel the weight of it
> on my chest
> the days so short and getting shorter
> I can touch the sides of them
> at midday

The magazine-sized supplement is 16 pgs., newsprint, with color and b&w photography and graphics. They receive about 300 submissions of poetry/year, use 40-50. **Sample free for postage (2 oz.)—and ask for guidelines. One poem/page, maximum of 3 poems/submission. Name, address and telephone number in upper left corner of each page. Reports within 2 weeks. Pays $15-50/poem.** The editor comments, "It is difficult for someone from outside Western Canada to catch the flavor of this region; almost all the poems we purchase are written by Western Canadians."

WESTVIEW: A JOURNAL OF WESTERN OKLAHOMA (II), 100 Campus Dr., SOSU, Weatherford OK 73096, phone (405)774-3168, founded 1981, editor Fred Alsberg, is a quarterly that is **"particularly interested in writers from the Southwest; however, we are open to work of quality by poets from elsewhere. We publish free verse and formal poetry."** They have recently published poetry by Mark Sanders, Michael McKinney, Alicia Ostriker and James Whitehead. As a sample the editor selected these lines from "Learning from Mother" by Holly Hunt:

> I will tell you that my mother was smart,
> a wire-cutting wit that could snap everything
> midair and bring pause to all voices there.
> And in that pause would form a certain space
> in every thought, when she would say something
> so accurate that all ears would leap,
> heads tilted to the Common Philosophy Lady

Westview is 44 pgs., magazine-sized, saddle-stapled, with glossy card cover in full-color. They use about 25% of 100 poems received/year. Press run is 1,000 for 500 subscribers of which about 25 are libraries, 150 shelf sales. Subscription: $10. **Sample postpaid: $4. Submit 5 poems at a time. Cover letter including biographical data for contributor's note required with submissions. "Poems on computer disk are welcome so long as they are accompanied by the hard copy and the SASE has the appropriate postage." Editor comments on submissions "when close." "Mss are circulated to an editorial board; we usually respond within 2-3 months." Pays 1 copy.**

WEYFARERS; GUILDFORD POETS PRESS (II), 9, White Rose Lane, Woking, Surrey GU22 7JA United Kingdom, phone (0483)762614, founded 1972, administrative editor Margaret Pain, poetry editors Margaret Pain, Martin Jones and Jeffery Wheatley. They say, "We publish *Weyfarers* magazine three times a year. All our editors are themselves poets and give their spare time free to help other poets." They describe their needs as **"all types of poetry, serious and humorous, free verse and rhymed/metered, but mostly 'mainstream' modern. Excellence is the main consideration. NO hard porn, graphics, way-out experimental. Any subject publishable, from religious to satire. Not more than 40 lines."** They have recently published poetry by Anthony Walstorm, Linda Chase, Joseph M. Farley and Thomas Michael McDade. As a sample the editors chose this extract from "Walking Ackling Dyke" by Edmund Harwood:

> . . . . A swirl of swifts explodes like living flak
> to meet the hobby falcon, out to kill,
> approaching with the bright sun at her back.

Despite the raptor's aerobatic skill,
The swifts confuse her aim and all escape.
I walk on past a cornfield, up the hill

between some yellow fields of oil-seed rape. . .
The digest-sized, saddle-stapled format contains about 28 pgs. of poetry (of a total of 32 pgs.). They use about 125 of 1,200-1,500 submissions received each year. The magazine has a circulation of "about 300," including about 200 subscribers of which 5 are libraries. **Sample (current issue) postpaid: $5 in cash USA or £1.60 UK. Submit no more than 6 poems, one poem/sheet. No previously published or simultaneous submissions. Closing dates for submissions are end of January, May and September. Sometimes comments briefly, if requested, on rejections. Pays 1 copy.** Staff reviews books of poetry briefly, in newsletter sent to subscribers. "We are associated with Surrey Poetry Center, which has an annual Open Poetry Competition. The prize-winners are published in *Weyfarers*." Their advice to poets is, "Always read a magazine before submitting. And read plenty of modern poetry."

WHETSTONE; WHETSTONE PRIZE (II), P.O. Box 1266, Barrington IL 60011, phone (708)382-5626, editors Sandra Berris, Marsha Portnoy, Jean Tolle and Julie Fleenor, is an annual. **"We emphasize quality more than category and favor the concrete over the abstract, the accessible over the obscure. We like poets who use words in ways that transform them and us."** They have published poetry by Jackie Bartley, Nancy Cherry, Bruce Guernsey, Peyton Houston and Louis Phillips. As a sample an editor selected these lines by Helen Reed:

I know the corpse inside.
It has my face,
as did each of the others
before it.
It is 96 pgs., digest-sized, professionally printed, flat-spined with matte card cover. Press run is 600 for 100 subscribers of which 5 are libraries, 350 shelf sales. **Sample postpaid: $3. Reports in 1-4 months. Always sends prepublication galleys. Buys first North American serial rights. Pay varies**, with Whetstone Prize of $500 awarded for best poetry or fiction in each issue, and additional prizes as well.

‡WHISKEY ISLAND MAGAZINE (II), English Dept., Cleveland State University, Cleveland OH 44115, phone (216)687-2056, founded 1978, editor Patricia Harusame Leebove, is a biannual magazine publishing poetry, fiction and an interview with a poet/writer each issue. **They want "advanced writing; political/ethnic poetry welcome. Nothing very conservative or very traditional."** They have recently published poetry by Vivian Shipley, Kathleene West, Claudia Rankine, Nuala Archer and Patricia Smith. As a sample the editor selected these lines from "Looking for Judas" by Adrian C. Louis:

They say we killed the Deer People,
we told them their spirits
would live in our flesh.
We used bows of ash, no spotlights, no rifles,
and their holy blood became ours.
Or something like that.
Whiskey Island Magazine is 86-104 pgs., 6×9, professionally printed and perfect-bound with light card stock cover and b&w photos. They receive 1,000-1,500 poetry mss a year, accept approximately 6%. Press run is 1,200 for 200 subscribers of which 20 are libraries, about 120 shelf sales. Subscription: $10. **Sample postpaid: $6. Submit no more than 10 pgs. of poetry at a time. Include name, address and phone number on each page. No previously published poems or simultaneous submissions. Cover letter with brief bio required. Poems are circulated to an editorial committee. Send SASE for guidelines. Reports within 3 months. Pays 2 copies.** Staff reviews books of poetry in 500-700 words. Send books for review consideration. In 1995, they held a contest for both poetry and fiction. Query regarding contest for 1996. The editor says, "Always type everything. Don't send ridiculous, long, effusive letters about yourself. Always include SASEs and your name and address for contact. Keep trying. Rejection, like acceptance, is subjective and often arbitrary."

WHITE EAGLE COFFEE STORE PRESS (II); FRESH GROUND (II, IV-Anthology), P.O. Box 383, Fox River Grove IL 60021-0383, phone (708)639-9200, founded 1992, is a small press publishing 5-6 chapbooks/year. **"Alternate chapbooks are published by invitation and by competition. Author published by invitation becomes judge for next competition."** They are **"open to any kind of poetry. No censorship at this press. Literary values are the only standard. Generally not interested in sentimental or didactic writing."** They have recently published poetry by Annie Davidovicz, Peter Blair, Martha Vertreace, James Plath, Leilani Wright and Jill Peláez Baumgaertner. As a sample the editor selected these lines from "Hot Saws" by Paul Andrew E. Smith:

It's a metallic taste she has, sweet,

> *my teeth are numb, my cheek bones.*
> *Yes, by God in the treetops,*
> *I'm beginning to see how these are*
> *necessary skills, this lumberjacking.*

Sample postpaid: $5.95. Submit complete chapbook ms (20-24 pgs.) with a brief bio, 125-word statement that introduces your writing and $10 reading fee. Previously published poems and simultaneous submissions OK, with notice. Competition deadlines: March 30 for spring contest; September 30 for fall contest. Send SASE for guidelines. "Each competition is judged by the author of the most recent chapbook published by invitation." **Seldom comments on rejections. Reports 3 months after deadline. All entrants will receive a copy of the winning chapbook. Winner receives $150 and 25 copies.** *Fresh Ground* is an annual anthology that features "some of the best work of emerging poets. **We're looking for edgy, crafted poetry.** *Fresh Ground* is published in September. Poems for this annual are accepted during May through June." They say, "Poetry is about a passion for language. That's what we're about. We'd like to provide an opportunity for poets of any age who are fairly early in their careers to publish something substantial. We're excited by the enthusiasm shown for this new press and by the extraordinary quality of the writing we've received."

WHITE PINE PRESS (V); THE WHITE PINE POETRY PRIZE (II), 10 Village Square, Suite 28, Fredonia NY 14063, phone (716)672-5743, founded 1973, editor Dennis Maloney, managing director Elaine LaMattina. White Pine Press publishes poetry, fiction, literature in translation, essays—perfect-bound paperbacks. **"At present we are accepting unsolicited mss only for our annual competition, The White Pine Poetry Prize. This competition awards $500 plus publication to a book-length collection of poems by a US author. Entry fee: $15. Deadline: December 1. Send SASE for details."** They have published poetry by William Kloefkorn, Marjorie Agosin, Miguel Hernandez, Peter Blue Cloud, Basho, Pablo Neruda, Maurice Kenny and James Wright. **Send $1 for catalog to buy samples.**

JAMES WHITE REVIEW: A GAY MEN'S LITERARY QUARTERLY (IV-Gay), Box 3356, Butler Quarter Station, Minneapolis MN 55403, phone (612)339-8317, founded 1983, poetry editor Clif Mayhood, **uses all kinds of poetry by gay men.** They have published poetry by Robert Peters, Jonathan Bracker and Joel Zizik. They receive about 1,400 submissions/year, use 100, have a 6-week backlog. Press run is 4,000 for 1,500 subscribers of which 50 are libraries. Subscription: $12/year (US). **Sample postpaid: $3. Submit a limit of 8 poems or 250 lines. A poem can exceed 250 lines, but it "better be very good." Send SASE for guidelines. Reports in 4 months. Pays $10/poem.** Reviews books of poetry.

WHITE WALL REVIEW (I), 63 Gould St., Toronto, Ontario M5B 1E9 Canada, phone (416)977-1045, founded 1976, editors change every year, is an annual using **"interesting, preferably spare art. No style is unacceptable. Should poetry serve a purpose beyond being poetry and communicating a poet's idea? Nothing boring, self-satisfied, gratuitously sexual, violent or indulgent."** They have recently published poetry by John Alan Douglas and Terry Watada. As a sample the editor selected this poem, "Buddhist Barbie," by Denise Duhamel:

> *(for Nick)*
>
> *In the 5th century B.C.*
> *an Indian philosopher Gautama*
> *teaches 'All is emptiness'*
> *and 'There is no self.'*
> *In the 20th century A.D.*
> *Barbie agrees, but wonders how a man*
> *with such a belly could pose,*
> *smiling, and without a shirt.*

WWR is between 144-160 pgs., digest-sized, professionally printed, perfect-bound, with glossy card cover, using b&w photos and illustrations. Press run is 500. Subscription: $9 in Canada, $9.50 in US and elsewhere. **Sample postpaid: $8. Submit up to 5 poems at a time with a $5 reading fee. "Please do not submit between January and August of a given year." Cover letter required; include short bio. Reports "as soon as we can (usually in April or May). We comment on all mss, accepted or not." Pays 1 copy.** They say, "We are known for publishing first-time or little-known poets as well as sending constructive criticism back to the writer on all work. Poets should send what they consider *their best work*, not everything they've got."

WHOLE NOTES; WHOLE NOTES PRESS (I, II, IV-Children, translations), P.O. Box 1374, Las Cruces NM 88004, phone (505)382-7446, *WN* founded 1984, Whole Notes Press founded 1988, editor Nancy Peters Hastings. *WN* appears twice a year. Whole Notes Press publishes 1 chapbook/year by a single poet. *WN* **tends toward close observation of the natural world, the beauty of nature and a**

poetry which affirms the human spirit. "**All forms will be considered.**" They have recently published poetry by Stuart Friebert, David Garrison and Timothy Monaghan. As a sample the editor selected these lines from "The Dead Kingbird" (in memory of Bill Stafford) by Don Welch:

> *Long ago I picked up*
> *a flower with wings*
> *and carried it home.*
>
> *A breath of decay*
> *was slowly circling*
> *its body.*

WN is 32 pgs., digest-sized, "nicely printed," staple bound, with a "linen 'fine arts' cover." They accept about 10% of some 800 submissions/year. Press run is 400 for 200 subscriptions of which 10 are libraries. Subscription: $6. **Sample postpaid: $3. Submit 4 poems at a time. Some previously published poems used; no simultaneous submissions. Reports in 2-3 weeks. Pays 2 copies. For 20-page chapbook consideration, submit 3-15 samples with bio and list of other publications. Pays 25 copies of chapbook. Editor sometimes comments on rejections.** The editor says, "In the fall of each even-numbered year I edit a special issue of *WN* that features writing by young people (under 21). Overall, we'd like to see more translations and more poems about rural experiences."

THE WICAZO SA REVIEW (IV-Ethnic), 3755 Blake Court N., Rapid City SD 57701-4716, phone (605)341-3228, founded 1985, poetry editor Elizabeth Cook-Lynn, is a "scholarly magazine, appearing twice a year, devoted to the developing of Native American Studies as an academic discipline and using **poetry of exceptional quality.**" They have published poetry by Simon Ortiz, Joy Harjo, Gray Cohoe and Earle Thompson. As a sample the editor chose these lines by Ray Young Bear:

> *With the Community's great "registered" Cottonwood*
> *Smoldering under an overcast sky*
> *no one will believe we are here*
> *in the middle & deepest part*
> *of the flood*

TWSR is magazine-sized, 80-120 pgs., saddle-stapled, professionally printed on heavy glossy stock with b&w glossy card cover, press run 600, using only 3-4 poems/issue. Once in a while they "feature" an exceptional poet. **Sample postpaid: $10. Cover letter required including credits and tribal enrollment affiliation. Pays 3 copies.** Reviews books of poetry. Open to unsolicited reviews and literary criticism essays. Poets may also send books for review consideration.

WICKED MYSTIC (IV-Horror), Dept. WD, P.O. Box 3087, Astoria NY 11103-0087, phone (718)545-6713, founded 1990, editor Andre Scheluchin, is a quarterly of hardcore horror poetry and short stories. **They want "psychological horror, splatter-gore, erotic, death, gothic themes, etc. No safe, conventional, conservative poetry."** They have published poetry by Michael A. Arnzen, John Grey and James S. Dorr. As a sample the editor selected this poem, "Alcohol," by Jonathan Yungkans:

> *In a giant glass vat, a man*
> *hangs by his ankles, drinks beer*
> *into his lungs. A child watches,*
> *walled in a block of ice*
> *stabbed many times, the reddened*
> *pieces dropped into the vat*
> *to keep the man's drink cold.*

Wicked Mystic is 100 pgs., magazine-sized, perfect-bound, with heavy stock colored cover and display ads. They receive about 1,000 poems a year, use approximately 5%. Press run is 2,000 for 1,000 subscribers of which 50 are libraries. Subscription: $24 for 4 issues. **Sample postpaid: $6.50 made payable to Andre Scheluchin. Submit typed poems, no longer than 30 lines. No previously published poems or simultaneous submissions. Cover letter required. Often comments on rejections. Reports within 2-8 weeks. Pays 1 copy. Acquires first North American serial rights.**

WILDE OAKS (I, IV-Gay/lesbian/bisexual), 175 Stockton Ave., San Jose CA 95126, phone (408)293-2429, founded 1992, editor Bill Olver, is a biannual publication of the Billy DeFrank Lesbian and Gay Community Center. *Wilde Oaks* publishes "**lesbian/gay/bisexual/transgender material only—open to all forms, themes, styles and tones. We get a lot of free verse, but do not want to see 'greeting card verse.'** " They have published poetry by Lisa Vice, Shelley Adler and Louie Crew. As a sample the editor selected these lines from "Headless Chickens" by Mark Hallman:

> *The woman who chops off*
> *chickens' heads is my favorite*
> *Joan Didion character,*
> *not because I have anything*
> *against chickens, but because*

CLOSE-UP

Reclaiming the Power of Oral Tradition

When asked what she views as the most difficult tasks for poets, especially women poets, Ayanna Black points to challenges that will seem familiar to most: breaking into the canons of the publishing industry, economic survival, finding a good publisher, and getting your first book published.

But when she is asked about the most difficult tasks faced by minority poets, Black touches the pulse of her own work as a poet and an editor. "For minority poets, especially Caribbean poets living in Canada, [the greatest difficulty] is the validation of our writing traditions, and the complexities of that tradition historically, socially, culturally and aesthetically. How do we coin this into art that publishers view as good literature?" The answer, suggests Black, is a new consideration of the communicative power of oral literature.

Ayanna Black

©Photo by Jim Dawson - Fotowork

Much of Black's work has been tied to reclaiming the oral tradition of her African ancestors, which has largely been obliterated in Western literature. Now residing in Toronto, Ontario, Black was born in Jamaica and lived in England prior to immigrating to Canada in 1964. Growing up without her biological father, who left Jamaica before she was born, Black began writing stories to invent her father, and to create a voice for herself about father-daughter relationships. "Being the only child, with lots of constructed secrets, writing was the one form that I discovered where I was able to eliminate some of my fears, my anger. It gave me buckets filled with pleasure, and assisted me with clarifying my thoughts and my feelings as a teenager—it was like my best friend."

Black's first publication came in 1975 in *One Out of Many* (WACACRO Productions), a collection of writings from 21 previously unpublished black women in Ontario, Canada. Since then she has authored the poetry collection *No Contingencies* (Williams-Wallace, 1986); co-authored *Linked Alive* (Èditions Trois, 1990), a collection of renga (linked verse by two or more people); and edited *Voices* (HarperPerennial, 1992) and *Fiery Spirits* (HarperPerennial, 1994), two collections of poetry and short fiction by Canadian writers of African descent. Her writings have been anthologized in various books, including *Other Voices*, *Women & Words* and the first volume of *The Best Writing on Writing*, and she is currently at work on a new collection of poetry, to be called *Invoking the Spirits*.

Though Black has seen much of her work reach publication, she views the

"A Pretty Baby Girl in a da Nursery"

Mi 'ave a baby girl
She dah weight six pounds two oz
Mi dah com' out a hospital pon thursday
Mi nuh 'ave no place to go
And only 'a dolla' to mi name

Mi dah call de pickney father
'im sey
Him comin to see mi
Mi nuh se 'im yet

One whole 'ear now
Mi dah go together
Yu no mis
'im left and' go married Doris two mont' now
'ere mi a lay

With only a dolla' to mi name
With only a dolla' to mi name
'nd a pretty baby girl
In a di nursery
'nd a pretty baby girl
In a di nursery

(from *No Contingencies*, 1986, Williams-Wallace; reprinted by permission of the author)

writing of her first poem in the Jamaican vernacular in 1985 as a major turning point in her career. She says this move represented a "reclaiming and validation" for her, and admits that, while the experience of reading it aloud made her extremely nervous, "it felt great . . . and totally liberating." She recalls that when such "dub" poetry (poetry that combines English and African language) first appeared in Canada, publishers didn't understand it, and didn't view it as poetry. "Even some middle-class Caribbean people, especially Jamaicans here, turned their noses up," she says.

Acknowledging the ever-present challenge of finding acceptance for the African oral tradition in Western culture, Black looks to African writer Ata Ama Aidoo for a possible solution. "I think that Aidoo speaks of this very eloquently when she suggests 'the need for a kind of redefinition of poetry—the whole idea that poetry has to conform to certain accepted Western standards.' Aidoo indicated that not all literature has to be written."

Upholding this philosophy, Black avoids pigeonholing her work and doesn't write a particular type of poetry. Instead she allows the creative process to dictate the style or the form. "I've discovered that the deeper I dig into my interior landscape, it seems I'm constructing a part of myself that is deeply encased. But I'm aware that my poetry has a lyrical tone and a narrative form, and that I write mostly in verses. I'm a poet who writes from the interior landscape." She tries to write daily, and revises her poems "until I feel satisfied—anywhere from three to eight drafts. As a matter of fact, even after the work is published, I can find ways to improve it. So for me, revising or editing is a continuous process."

Editing the work of other writers has been another important aspect of Black's experience as a poet. In 1990, while curating an author reading series for Canadian Artists' Network: Black Artists in Action (CAN:BAIA), in cooperation with the Art Gallery of Ontario, she was contacted by two major publishers who were interested in the authors featured in the series. "[The publishers] asked me to send them a proposal based on my curatorial statements. I decided to go with HarperCollins here [the parent company of HarperPerennial]. Consequently, *Voices* was birthed, and then *Fiery Spirits*."

The contributors to both books include recent immigrants from the Caribbean and Africa, as well as more established African-Canadians. "For both collections, I had specific writers in mind, especially with *Voices*," she says. "I knew most of the 15 writers' works well. For *Fiery Spirits*, I invited 47 writers and selected 20. I included unpublished pieces that reflected the experience of Africans in a changing Canadian landscape—that was my priority. I included diverse styles and the best writings, and also simply what I liked."

As a poet and an editor, Black has acquired a sensible perspective on poetry submission and publication. She encourages all poets to wait to submit their work until they are sure that it's the best they can do. With her own submissions, she says she uses some of the techniques used in job searches: prior research to familiarize oneself with editorial policies, presenting only one's best work, and always following up. "Remember," she says, "this is a job." And as painful as it may be, "rejection is part of the turf." The key is not to let it paralyze you. "It's not that the work isn't good. It's quite possible that it isn't appropriate, or that they just have too much material already."

Black approaches networking as a part of doing business, and suggests it is essential for minority writers facing limited outlets for their work. She often attends authors' conferences, festivals and readings as a way of meeting other writers and people in the publishing industry. "My friends call me 'The Queen of Networking,' " she says. "For me, networking is like Fort Knox—it's very important, in terms of anyone from the margin [that is, anyone outside the mainstream literary tradition]. We need people who are active in the African communities and the literary community."

But beyond the mechanics of getting published, and regardless of the tradition that one writes in, Black reminds beginning poets to remember the significance of craft. "I think craft is crucial in poetry as with any job, be it the job of an accountant, a musician, or a potter," she says. "The whole process of writing is interlaced with craft. And that requires a lot of writing, determination and practice as we anticipate perfection or our very best."

—*Roseann S. Biederman*

> *this well-bred lady swings*
> *her axe without a flinch . . .*

Wilde Oaks is 108-120 pgs., 5½ × 8½, perfect-bound with b&w or 3-color cover and b&w interior art, photos and cartoons. They receive 150-200 poems a year, accept approximately 50%. Press run is 300 for 20 subscribers. Single copy: $7.95; subscription: $15/year. **Sample postpaid: $8. Previously published poems OK with notation of where published. No simultaneous submissions. Cover letter with brief bio required. "Submissions on 3.5 (non-returnable) Macintosh format diskettes are greatly appreciated." Deadlines are May 1 and November 1. Often comments on rejections. Send SASE for guidelines. Reports within 1 month of deadlines. Pays 1 copy. Acquires one-time rights.** They also publish a bimonthly newsletter of "news, reviews and items of interest." It is free to subscribers and contributors. Poets may send books for review consideration. The editor says, "Our writers in the San Jose area are encouraged to attend our workshops and parties. Others can send a nice note or Christmas card. We really do like to hear from people. We would particularly like to see more work from people of color, of different backgrounds and ability. However, even if you are God's gift to poetry, please refrain from identifying yourself as such. Remember, the editors are poets, too, and God has probably saved the receipt. As for new writers, be sincere, be honest and be diligent and eventually you will be brilliant."

WILDERNESS (II, IV-Nature/rural/ecology), 23030 W. Sheffler Rd., Elmira OR 97437 (poetry submissions only should be sent to this address), founded 1935, poetry editor John Daniel, is a quarterly magazine of "The Wilderness Society, one of the oldest and largest American conservation organizations." Requests for sample and subscriptions should go to *Wilderness*, 900 17th St. NW, Washington DC 20006. They want **"poetry related to the natural world. Shorter poems stand a better chance than longer, but all will be read. Poetry in any form or style is welcome."** They have recently published poetry by Mary Oliver, Jody Gladding, Robert Bly, Deborah Miller, David Wagoner and E.G. Burrows. The magazine is published on slick stock, full-color, professionally printed, with full-color paper cover, saddle-stapled, 76 pgs. Their press run is 260,000 with 255,000 subscriptions. Subscription: $15. **Sample postpaid: $3.50. Submit up to 6 poems at a time. No simultaneous submissions or previously published material. Prefers cover letter with submissions indicating that "a human being has sent the poems." Editor comments on rejections "occasionally. Please understand that we have room for only about 15 poems a year." Responds in 2 months. Always sends prepublication galleys. Pays $100 plus 2 copies on publication. "We buy one-time rights and the right to anthologize the poem without further compensation."**

WILDWOOD JOURNAL (IV-Specialized: college affiliation); THE WILDWOOD PRIZE IN POETRY (II), T.H.S. Wallace, Arts 213, 1 HACC Dr., Harrisburg PA 17110-2999, phone (717)780-2487. *Wildwood Journal*, an annual, is **open only to students, alumni and faculty of Harrisburg Area Community College. Sample copy: $5.** The Wildwood Prize, however, is open to any poet, $500 annually, $5 reading fee made payable to HACC. Final selection for the prize is made by a distinguished poet (in 1995: Karen Blomain) who usually remains anonymous until the winner is announced. Poems are accepted between October 15 and November 30. Rules available for SASE.

‡WILLAMETTE RIVER BOOKS (II), P.O. Box 605, Troutdale OR 97060, founded 1990, publishes 2 chapbooks annually. "We are open to fresh new voices as well as established ones. We hope to publish chapbooks of newer poets who may not yet have published a chapbook but who have a publication history in magazines and small press. **Quality is our sole criterion."** They have recently published books by Dennis Saleh and Martin Anderson. **No unsolicited mss. Query first with samples. Cover letter including "publishing history and a little about the author" required. Payment for publication arranged with author.**

THE WILLIAM AND MARY REVIEW (II), Campus Center, College of William and Mary, P.O. Box 8795, Williamsburg VA 23187-8795, phone (804)221-3290, fax (804)221-3451, founded 1962, editor Laura Sims, poetry editors Telisha Moore and Forrest Pritchard, is a 112-page annual, **"dedicated to publishing new work by established poets as well as work by new and vital voices."** They have published poetry by Dana Gioia, Robert Morgan, Cornelius Eady, Amy Clampitt, Elizabeth Alexander, Robert Hershon, Diane Ackerman, Agha Shahid Ali, Bruce Weigl, Judson Jerome and Phyllis Janowitz. They accept 15-20 of about 5,000 poems submitted/year. Press run is 3,500. They have 250 library

---

Use the General Index to find the page number of a specific publisher. If the publisher you are seeking is not listed, check the " '95-'96 Changes" list at the end of this section.

subscriptions, about 500 shelf sales. **Sample postpaid: $5.50. Submit 1 poem/page, batches of no more than 6 poems. Cover letter required; include address, phone number, past publishing history and brief bio note. Reads submissions September 15 through February 15 only. Reports in approximately 4 months. Always sends prepublication galleys. Pays 5 copies.** Open to unsolicited reviews. Poets may also send books to poetry editors for review consideration.

WILLOW REVIEW; COLLEGE OF LAKE COUNTY READING SERIES (II), College of Lake County, 19351 W. Washington St., Grayslake IL 60030-1198, phone (708)223-6601, ext. 2956, fax (708)223-9371, founded 1969, edited by Paulette Roeske. **"We are interested in poetry and fiction of high quality with no preferences as to form, style or subject."** They have recently published poetry by Lisel Mueller, Lucien Stryk, David Ray and Garrett Hongo and interviews with Gregory Orr and Diane Ackerman. As a sample the editor selected these lines from "The Remedy" by Richard Jones:

> *I pour my bowl of soup,*
> *and recite this poem,*
> *this magic,*
> *this incantation cleaving sickness from*
> *health. I fold the two knives of my hands*
> *in prayer and say grace,*
> *asking to live*
> *a while longer in this body,*
> *which I bless at every meal,*
> *crossing it with one hand*
> *and feeding it with another.*

The review is an 88-page, flat-spined annual, 6×9, professionally printed with a 4-color cover featuring work by an Illinois artist. Editors are open to all styles, free verse to form, as long as each poem stands on its own as art and communicates ideas. Circulation is 1,000, with distribution to bookstores nationwide. Subscription: $13 for 3 issues, $20 for 5 issues. **Sample back issue: $4. Submit up to 5 poems or short fiction/creative nonfiction up to 4,000 words. Simultaneous submissions OK. Cover letter required; include name, address, Social Security number, and information for contributor's notes. "We read year round but response is slower in the summer months." Sometimes sends prepublication galleys. Pays 2 copies. Acquires first North American serial rights. Prizes of $100 are awarded to the best poetry and fiction/creative nonfiction in each issue, with additional prizes totaling $350.** The reading series, 4-7 readings/academic year, has included Angela Jackson, Ellen Bryant Voigt, Thomas Lux, Charles Simic, Gloria Naylor, David Mura, Galway Kinnell, Lisel Mueller, Amiri Baraka, Stephen Dobyns, Heather McHugh, Linda Pastan, Katha Pollitt, Tobias Wolff, William Stafford and others. One reading is for contributors to *Willow Review*. Readings are usually held on Thursday evenings, for audiences of about 150 students and faculty of the College of Lake County and other area colleges and residents of local communities. They are widely publicized in Chicago and suburban newspapers.

WILLOW SPRINGS (II, IV-Translations), 526 Fifth St., MS-1, Eastern Washington University, Cheney WA 99004-2431, phone (509)458-6429, founded 1977. "We publish quality poetry and fiction that is imaginative, intelligent, and has a concern and care for language. **We are especially interested in translations from any language or period."** They have published poetry by Denise Levertov, Carolyn Kizer, Michael Burkard, Russell Edson, Dara Wier, Thomas Lux, Madeline DeFrees, Hayden Carruth, Al Young, Odysseas Elytis, W.S. Merwin, Olga Broumas, Kay Boyle and Lisel Mueller. *Willow Springs*, a semiannual, is one of the most visually appealing journals being published. It is 128 pgs., 6×9, flat-spined, professionally printed, with glossy 4-color card cover with art. Circulation is 1,000 for 500 subscribers of which 30% are libraries. They use 1-2% of some 4,000 unsolicited poems received each year. Editors seem to prefer free verse with varying degrees of accessibility (although an occasional formal poem has appeared in recent issues). Subscription: $10.50/year, $20/2 years. **Sample postpaid: $5.50. Submit September 15 through May 15 only. "We do not read in the summer months." Include name on every page, address on first page of each poem. Brief cover letter saying how many poems on how many pages preferred. No simultaneous submissions. Send SASE for guidelines. Reports in 1-3 months. Pays 2 copies, others at half price, and cash when funds available. Acquires all rights. Returns rights on release.** Reviews books of poetry and short fiction in 200-500 words. Open to unsolicited reviews. Poets may also send books for review consideration. They have annual poetry and fiction awards ($100 and $250 respectively) for work published in the journal.

WIND PUBLICATIONS; WIND MAGAZINE (II), P.O. Box 24548, Lexington KY 40524, phone (606)885-5342, *Wind Magazine* founded in 1971, editors/publishers Steven R. Cope and Charlie G. Hughes. "Although we publish poets of national repute, we are friendly toward beginners who have something to say and do so effectively and interestingly. **No taboos, no preferred school, form, style, etc. Our interests are inclusive.** Competition is keen; send only your best." *Wind* appears twice a year and is about 100 pgs., digest-sized, perfect-bound, containing approximately 40% poetry, also short fiction, essays and reviews ("Editor's Choice"). "We accept about 1% of submissions." Subscription: $10/year. **Sample postpaid: $3.50. Submit no more than 5 poems. No simultaneous submissions. "Cover letter optional; short bio desirable." Editor comments on submissions which are near misses. Reports in 6-8 weeks, publication within 1 year.** Sometimes sends prepublication galleys. **Pays 1 contributor's copy plus discount on extras. "Your submission is understood to guarantee Wind Publications first North American serial rights and anthology reprint rights only."** Wind Publications sponsors a yearly chapbook competition. Reading fee: $10. Send SASE for chapbook guidelines. Also publishes periodic anthologies; the *Best of Wind* anthology is $11.95 plus $1.50 p&h, $8 plus $1.50 p&h to subscribers.

THE WINDLESS ORCHARD; THE WINDLESS ORCHARD CHAPBOOKS (II), English Dept., Indiana University, Fort Wayne IN 46805, phone (219)483-6845, founded 1970, poetry editor Robert Novak, is a "shoestring labor of love—chapbooks only from frequent contributors to magazine. Sometimes publish calendars." They say they want **"heuristic, excited, valid non-xian religious exercises. Our muse is interested only in the beautiful, the erotic and the sacred."** *The Windless Orchard* appears irregularly, 50 pgs., digest-sized, offset from typescript, saddle-stapled, with matte card cover with b&w photos. There are about 35 pgs. of poetry in each issue (**with a regular section of autobiographical poems on being age 17**). They receive about 3,000 submissions of poetry/year, use 200, have a 6-month backlog . The editors say they have 100 subscribers of which 25 are libraries, a press run of 300, total circulation: 280. Subscription: $10. **Sample postpaid: $4. Submit 3-7 pgs. of poetry at a time. Considers simultaneous submissions. Reports in 1 day to 4 months. Pays 2 copies. Chapbook submissions by invitation only to contributors to the magazine. Poets pay costs for 300 copies, of which The Windless Orchard Chapbook Series receives 100 for its expenses. Sample: $4. Editors sometimes comment on rejections.** They advise, "Memorize a poem a day, do translations for the education."

WINDSOR REVIEW (II), English Dept., University of Windsor, Windsor, Ontario N9B 3P4 Canada, phone (519)253-4232, ext. 2332, fax (519)973-7050, e-mail uwrevu@uwindsor.ca, founded 1966, poetry editor John Ditsky, appears twice a year. **"Open to all poetry but epic length."** They have published poetry by Ben Bennani, Walter McDonald, Larry Rubin and Lyn Lifshin. As a sample the editor selected these lines (poet unidentified):

> *talking to white wolves*
> *talking to the first*
> *white wolves ever*
> *telling of how things are*
> *in his world.*

It is professionally printed, 100 pgs., digest-sized. They accept about 15% of 500 poems received/year. Press run is 400. Subscription: $19.95 (+7% GST) individuals, $29.95 (+7% GST) institutions (Canadian); $19.95 individuals, $29.95 institutions (US). **Sample postpaid: $10. Submit 5-10 poems at a time. Reports in 6 weeks.**

WISCONSIN ACADEMY REVIEW (IV-Regional), 1922 University Ave., Madison WI 53705, phone (608)263-1692, founded 1954, poetry editor Faith B. Miracle, "distributes information on scientific and cultural life of Wisconsin and provides a forum for **Wisconsin (or Wisconsin background) artists and authors.**" They want **"good lyric poetry; traditional meters acceptable if content is fresh. No poem over 65 lines."** They have published poetry by Credo Enriquez, Jean Feraca, Felix Pollak, Ron Wallace, Sara Rath and Lorine Niedecker. As a sample we selected these lines from "J L Jones" by Art Madson:

> *Running before the wind*
> *on canvas wings,*
> *on lifting hands, empty spirits,*
> *I try, like flying fish*
> *sailing the Pacific,*
> *to transcend my element.*

Wisconsin Academy Review is a 52-page quarterly, magazine-sized, professionally printed on glossy stock, glossy card color cover. Press run is 1,700 for 1,300 subscribers of which 109 are libraries. They use 3-6 pgs. of poetry/issue. Of over 150 submissions of poetry/year, they use about 24, have a 6- to 12-month backlog. **Sample postpaid: $3. Submit 5 pgs. maximum, double-spaced, with SASE. Must include Wisconsin connection if not Wisconsin return address. Editor sometimes comments on rejections. Reports in 4-6 weeks. Always sends prepublication printouts. Pays 3 copies.** Staff reviews books of poetry with Wisconsin connection only. Send related books for review consideration. The editor says, "We would like to receive good traditional forms—not sentimental rhymes."

UNIVERSITY OF WISCONSIN PRESS; BRITTINGHAM PRIZE IN POETRY; FELIX POLLAK PRIZE IN POETRY (II), 114 N. Murray St., Madison WI 53715-1199, Brittingham Prize inaugurated in 1985, poetry editor Ronald Wallace. The University of Wisconsin Press publishes primarily scholarly works, but they offer the annual **Brittingham Prize and now the Felix Pollak Prize, both $1,000 plus publication. These prizes are the only way in which this press publishes poetry. Send SASE for rules. For both prizes, submit between September 1 and October 1, unbound ms volume of 50-80 pgs., with name, address and telephone number on title page. No translations. Poems must be previously unpublished in book form. Poems published in journals, chapbooks and anthologies may be included but must be acknowledged. There is a non-refundable $15 reading fee which must accompany the ms. (Checks to University of Wisconsin Press.) Mss will *not* be returned. Enclose SASE for contest results.** Qualified readers will screen all mss. Winners will be selected by "a distinguished poet who will remain anonymous until the winners are announced in mid-February." Past judges include C.K. Williams, Maxine Kumin, Mona Van Duyn, Charles Wright, Gerald Stern, Mary Oliver, Donald Finkel, Donald Justice, Lisel Mueller and Henry Taylor. Winners include Jim Daniels, Patricia Dobler, David Kirby, Lisa Zeidner, Stefanie Marlis, Judith Vollmer, Renée A. Ashley, Tony Hoagland, Stephanie Strickland, Lisa Lewis and David Clewell. The editor says, "**Each submission is considered for both prizes (one entry fee only).**"

WISCONSIN REVIEW; WISCONSIN REVIEW PRESS (II), Box 158, Radford Hall, University of Wisconsin-Oshkosh, Oshkosh WI 54901, phone (414)424-2267, founded 1966, editor Philip Krause, is published 3 times/year. **"In poetry we publish mostly free verse with strong images and fresh approaches. We want new turns of phrase."** They have published poetry by Laurel Mills, Joseph Bruchac, Kenneth Frost, Paul Marion, Dionisio Martinez, Stephen Perry, Margaret Randall, David Steingass, Brian Swann and Peter Wild. As a sample the editor selected these lines from "Early Morning of Another World" by Tom McKeown:

> After squid and cool white wine there is
> no sleep. The long tentacles uncurl
> out of the dark with all that was left behind.
> Promises expand promises. A frayed mouth
> loses its color in the dawn.

The *Review* is 48-64 pgs., 6×9, elegantly printed on quality white stock, glossy card cover with color art, b&w art inside. They receive about 1,500 poetry submissions/year, use about 75. They use 30-40 pgs. of poetry in each issue. Press run is 2,000, for 50 subscribers, 30 of which are libraries. Single copy: $3; subscription: $8. **Sample postpaid: $2. Submit mss September 15 through May 15. Offices checked bimonthly during summer. Editor requests no more than 4 poems/submission, one poem/page, single-spaced with name and address of writer on each page. Simultaneous submissions OK, but previously unsubmitted works preferable. Cover letter also preferred; include brief bio. Send SASE for guidelines. Reports within 1-4 months. Pays 2 copies.**

‡THE WISHING WELL (IV-Membership, women/feminism, lesbian/bisexual), P.O. Box 713090, Santee CA 92072-3090, phone (619)443-4818, founded 1974, editor/publisher Laddie Hosler, is a "contact magazine for **gay and bisexual women** the world over; members' descriptions, photos, some letters and poetry published with their permission only; resources, etc., listed. I publish writings only for and by members so membership is required." 1-2 pgs. in each issue are devoted to **poetry, "which can be 6″ to full page—depending upon acceptance by editor, 3″ width column."** It is 7×8½ offset press from typescript, with soft matte card cover. It appears bimonthly and goes to 800 members. **A sample is available for $5. Membership in** *Wishing Well* **is $35 for 3-5 months, $60 for 5-7 months, $120 for 15 months. Membership includes the right to publish poetry, a self description (exactly as you write it), and to have responses forwarded to you, and other privileges.** Reviews books of poetry. Personal classifieds section just begun, members and/or nonmembers, $1/word.

WITHOUT HALOS; OCEAN COUNTY POETS COLLECTIVE (II), P.O. Box 1342, Point Pleasant Beach NJ 08742, founded 1983, editor-in-chief Frank Finale, is an annual publication of the Ocean County Poets Collective; it prints "good contemporary poetry." The magazine **"accepts all genres, though no obscenity. Prefers poetry no longer than 2 pages. Wants to see strong, lucid images ground in experience." They do not want** "religious verse or greeting card lyrics." They have recently published poetry by Robert Cooperman, Geraldine C. Little, Alan Britt, John Dickson, Marvin Solomon and Nancy Westerfield. "Issue XII features Toi Derricotte with several poems and an essay about her work." As a sample, the editor selected these lines from "The Literary Life" by Harold Witt:

> What is it about the literary life
> especially in this U.S. of A.
> that's dangerous, that kills so many off
> when they're yet hardly even turning grey?

Without Halos is 120 pgs., digest-sized, handsomely printed with b&w artwork inside and on the glossy card cover, flat-spined. Circulation is 1,000, of which 100 are subscriptions and 100 are sold on newsstands; other distribution is at cultural events, readings, workshops, etc. Single copy: $6. **Sample** (back issue) postpaid: $5. The editors "prefer letter-quality printing, single or double-spaced, no more than 5 poems. Name and address should appear on each page. Reads submissions January 1 through June 30 only. No manuscript returned without proper SASE. Sloppiness tossed back." Reports in 2-4 months and all acceptances are printed in the next annual issue, which appears in the winter. Sends prepublication galleys only if requested by the featured poet. Pays 1 copy; discount on extras. Acquires first North American serial rights. For the last eight years, *Without Halos* has received modest grants from the New Jersey State Council on the Arts. The editor says, "We would like to receive more poems with some humor."

‡WITNESS (II, IV-Themes), Oakland Community College, Orchard Ridge Campus, 27055 Orchard Lake Rd., Farmington Hills MI 48334, phone (810)471-7740, founded 1987, editor Peter Stine, is a biannual journal of poetry, fiction and essays which often publishes special issues centered around themes. **They want "poetry that highlights the role of the writer as witness to his/her times. No real specifications, except nothing concrete or wildly experimental."** They have recently published poetry by John Balaban, Mary Oliver, Alicia Ostriker and Mark Doty. As a sample we selected the opening lines of "Omaha" by Steve Langan, published in the special issue on American cities:

> City no one's said it best about;
> city that ignores its river,
> its young, its elderly, its myths.
>
> I sat in its taverns for five years,
> my pledge not to miss a day —
> that pledge got me nowhere . . .

Witness is 192 pgs., 6×9, professionally printed and perfect-bound with coated card cover with full-color photo and b&w photos inside. They receive about 500 poems a year, accept approximately 5%. Press run is 2,800 for 400 subscribers of which 60 are libraries, 1,200 distributed to bookstores. Subscription: $12/year. **Sample postpaid: $7; upcoming special issues are announced inside. No previously published poems; simultaneous submissions OK. Cover letter required. Seldom comments on rejections. Reports in 2-3 months. Pays $10/page. Buys first serial rights.** Poetry published here has also been included in the 1992, 1994 and 1995 volumes of *The Best American Poetry*.

WOLSAK AND WYNN PUBLISHERS LTD. (II), Box 316, Don Mills Post Office, Don Mills, Ontario M3C 2S7 Canada, phone (416)222-4690, founded 1982, poetry editors Heather Cadsby and Maria Jacobs, publishes 5 flat-spined literary paperbacks/year (56-100 pgs.). They have recently published collections of poetry by Richard Harrison and Polly Fleck. Here is a sample from *Cantos From A Small Room* by Robert Hilles:

> Some mornings I wake to an opera on the radio
> and I think of her hand raised to me
> and how small I was as I kissed it and she
> smiled and I knew that her defeat was mine too that
> there is little that the living can share with the dying.

The books are handsomely printed. **Sample: $10 US or $12 Canadian. Send sample poems with query, bio, publications. No simultaneous submissions. Reports on queries in 4 months. Always sends prepublication galleys. Pays 10% royalties. Buys first rights.** Maria Jacobs says, "W&W prefers not to prescribe. We are open to *good* writing of any kind."

‡WOMAN'S WAY: THE PATH OF EMPOWERMENT (I, II, IV-Women/feminism, themes), P.O. Box 19614, Boulder CO 80308-2614, phone (303)530-7617, e-mail womansway@aol.com, founded 1993, is a quarterly publication of self-discovery and creativity by and for women. **Each issue is centered around a theme, and they want personal poetry (under 500 words) about women's issues/social issues and women's spirituality.** As a sample the editor selected these lines from "Waiting to Tell You" by Cynthy Kaufman:

> I caught them with my teeth
> a small, speckled eggshell
> and a jewel
> afraid speaking them
> would crush them
> and all you would hear is dust.

Woman's Way is 28-36 pgs., approximately 8×10½, printed 2-color and saddle-stitched with semi-glossy paper cover and art, graphics and ads inside. They receive 200-300 poems a year, accept about 25. Press run is 2,000 for 300 subscribers, 700 shelf sales. Single copy: $3.50; subscription: $14. **Sample postpaid: $3. Previously published poems and simultaneous submissions OK.** Time between acceptance and publication is 6 months. **Seldom comments on rejections. Send SASE for guidelines. Reports in 1-6 months. Pays 1 copy. Acquires one-time rights.** Reviews related books of poetry in 500 words. Open to unsolicited reviews. Poets may also send books for review consideration.

WOMEN'S EDUCATION DES FEMMES (IV-Regional, women/feminism), 47 Main St., Toronto, Ontario M4E 2V6 Canada, phone (416)699-1909, fax (416)699-2145, founded 1982, editor Christina Starr, is a quarterly using **"feminist poetry, about women, written by Canadian women only."** They have recently published poetry by Sue Nevill and Annette LeBox. As a sample the editor selected these lines by Catherine Lake:

> walking on Saturday, i glanced a tree shedding chestnuts
> upon that same cement
> but all weekend; recalled the hurtful words
> then sunday night i dreamt that
> i kissed you lightly on the nose
> and smiled back at you.

The editor describes it as 48 pgs., magazine-sized, web offset, saddle-stapled, with one-color cover. Subscription: $17 individual, $30 institution. **Sample postpaid: $2.50. Submit 3-6 poems at a time. Publishes theme issues. Send SASE for upcoming themes. Reports in 2-3 months. Pays $25/poem plus 2 copies.** Occasionally reviews books of poetry. Open to unsolicited reviews.

WOMEN'S PRESS (CANADA) (IV-Women/feminism, lesbian, regional), 517 College St., #233, Toronto, Ontario M6G 4A2 Canada, founded 1972, co-managing editors Ann Decter and Martha Ayim, publishes **"minimum ms 48 pgs. Women of colour, feminist, political content, lesbian, modern or post-modern form. No haiku. Prefer Canadian authors."** They have published poetry by Carmen Rodríguez, Betsy Warland, Cherríe Moraga and Lillian Allen. As a sample the editor selected these lines by Dionne Brand:

> this is you girl, this is the poem no woman
> ever write for a woman because she 'fraid to touch

They publish 1 flat-spined paperback/year. **Query first with cover letter and sample poems. Reports in 6 months. Always sends prepublication galleys. Pays 10% royalties, $150 advance, 6 copies.**

WOMEN'S STUDIES QUARTERLY; THE FEMINIST PRESS AT CUNY (V, IV-Women, feminist, bilingual), Dept. PM, 311 E. 94th St., New York NY 10128, phone (212)360-5790. *Women's Studies Quarterly*, founded 1972, publisher Florence Howe, is a nonfiction quarterly publishing **"poetry that focuses on current issues of importance to women; emphasis on education or activism preferable."** They have published poetry by Mila Aguilar. The editor describes it as $5\frac{1}{2} \times 8\frac{1}{2}$, 150-200 pgs. Their press run is 1,500. **Sample postpaid: $13. "Although poetry is included in each issue, the poems are chosen by the guest editor. No unsolicited submissions are accepted."** The Feminist Press publishes primarily both historical and contemporary fiction and nonfiction (12-15 titles/year), but it also publishes some poetry, such as the series, *The Defiant Muse,* bilingual volumes (Hispanic, French, Italian and German) of poetry by women from the Middle Ages to the present.

WOMENWISE (III, IV-Women/feminism, specialized: health issues), 38 S. Main St., Concord NH 03301, phone (603)225-2739, founded 1978, run by an editorial committee, is "a quarterly newspaper that deals specifically with issues relating to women's health—research, education, and politics." They want **"poetry reflecting status of women in society, relating specifically to women's health issues." They do not want** "poetry that doesn't include women or is written by men; poetry that degrades women or is anti-choice." As a sample we selected these lines from "Two Days Before My Stroke" by Margaret Robison:

> Whatever happens, we'll always have this, *I said,*
> *wondering at the melodrama of my words.*
> *We stood at the boat rail, eyes filled with ocean.*
> *Neither of us understood the dream that had waked her*
> *in the night, with a voice that said:* Tell Margaret
> to feel the energy that spirals through you, into her
> and back again. This will be only for a little while . . .

WomenWise is a tabloid newspaper, 12 pgs., printed on quality stock with b&w art and graphics. Press run is 3,000. Subscription: $10/year. **Sample: $2.95. Submissions should be typed double-spaced. Reads submissions March, June, September and December only. Reporting time and time to publication varies. Pays 1-year subscription. Acquires first North American serial rights.** Staff reviews books of poetry in "any word count," single format. They say they often receive mss with no SASE. "We throw them away. Please remember that we are a nonprofit organization with limited resources." The editor adds, "We receive a great deal of badly written free verse. We would appreciate receiving more poetry in traditional form, as well as more poetry in free verse written with skill and care."

WOODLEY MEMORIAL PRESS; THE ROBERT GROSS MEMORIAL PRIZE FOR POETRY (IV-Regional), English Dept., Washburn University, Topeka KS 66621, phone (913)231-1010, ext. 1448, founded 1980, editor Robert Lawson, publishes 1-2 flat-spined paperbacks a year, **collections of poets**

from Kansas or with Kansas connections, "terms individually arranged with author on acceptance of ms." They have published poetry by Craig Goad, Michael L. Johnson, Bruce Bond and Harley Elliott. As a sample the editor selected these lines from "In the Old House" by William Stafford:

> *Inside our Victrola a tin voice, faint*
> *but somehow both fragile and powerful, soared*
> *and could be only Caruso, all the way from*
> *Rome: I traced my fingers on the gold letters*
> *and listened my way deeper and deeper*

Samples may be individually ordered from the press for $5. "We charge $5 reading fee for unsolicited mss." Replies to queries in 2 weeks, to mss in 2 months. Time between acceptance and publication is 1 year. Send SASE for guidelines for Robert Gross Memorial Poetry and Fiction Prize ($100 and publication).

‡WOODNOTES; TWO AUTUMNS PRESS; HAIKU POETS OF NORTHERN CALIFORNIA (I, IV-Form, membership/subscription), 248 Beach Park Blvd., Foster City CA 94404, e-mail Welch-M@aol.com, founded 1988, editor Michael Dylan Welch (who is also editor/publisher of Press Here). *Woodnotes* is the quarterly publication of the Haiku Poets of Northern California (HPNC) and **you must be a member/subscriber to submit. "We want to see striking and engaging haiku, senryu, tanka and haibun. We don't want to see unrelated forms."** They have recently published work by Garry Gay, Paul O. Williams, Alexis Rotella and Pat Shelley. As a sample the editor selected this piece of his own:

> *spring breeze—*
> *the pull of her hand*
> *as we near the pet store*

The editor says *Woodnotes* is 44 pgs., 5½ × 8½, offset printed and saddle-stapled with cover art and some interior illustrations. They receive about 3,600 poems a year, accept approximately 12%. Press run is 300 for 220 subscribers of which 6 are libraries. Subscription (which includes membership in HPNC): $12. **Sample postpaid: $4. Note: Requests for samples/subscriptions (checks payable to HPNC) should be sent to Pat Gallagher, HPNC Secretary, 864 Elmira Dr., Sunnyvale CA 94087. "We accept no more than two poems from each subscriber per issue." No previously published poems or simultaneous submissions. Cover letter preferred. Often comments on rejections. Reports usually in 1-2 weeks. Acquires first North American serial rights. There is no payment, other than the best poem in each issue (chosen by the editors) receives $10.** They review haiku-related poetry books in anywhere from 100 to 1,000 words. Reviews are usually assigned or done by the editors, but they are open to unsolicited reviews. Poets may also send books for review consideration. HPNC also sponsors annual contests for haiku, senryu and tanka, as well as other events, and also publishes anthologies of members' work (and haiku books by members) under the Two Autumns Press imprint. The editor says, "Haiku in English is a brief, one-breath form of poetry using objective words to convey heightened subjective feeling about nature and human nature. Read William J. Higginson's *Haiku Handbook*, Cor van den Heuvel's *The Haiku Anthology* and Bruce Ross's *Haiku Moment* for a good introduction to haiku and examples in English. Although HPNC is a membership organization based in the San Francisco area, membership and subscriptions are open to anyone anywhere."

WORCESTER REVIEW; WORCESTER COUNTY POETRY ASSOCIATION, INC. (II, IV-Regional), 6 Chatham St., Worcester MA 01609, phone (508)797-4770, founded 1973, managing editor Rodger Martin. *WR* appears annually with emphasis on poetry. **New England writers are encouraged to submit, though work by other poets is used also. They want "work that is crafted, intuitively honest and empathetic, not work that shows the poet little respects his work or his readers."** They have published poetry by Kathleen Spivack, William Stafford and Walter McDonald. As a sample the editor selected these lines from "At the Conservatory of Flowers" by Chris Gompert:

> *In the snug greenhouse air, water drips down leaves*
> *of* Quisqualis Indicia—*Rangoon Creeper vine*
> *that rambles overhead. Lapping at my feet*
> *are heart-shaped Brazilian Prayer Plants. I stop,*
> (To be a real flower, you must be a sunflower) . . .

WR is 6 × 9, flat-spined, 160 pgs., professionally printed in dark type on quality stock with glossy card cover. Press run is 1,000 for 300 subscriptions (50 of them libraries) and 300 shelf sales. Subscription: $15 (includes membership in WCPA). **Sample postpaid: $4. Submit maximum of 5 poems at a time. "I recommend 3 or less for most favorable readings." Simultaneous submissions OK "if indicated." Previously published poems "only on special occasions." Editor comments on rejections "if ms warrants a response." Send SASE for guidelines. Reports in 4-6 months. Pays 2 copies. Buys first rights.** They have an annual contest for poets who live, work, or in some way (past/present) have a Worcester County connection. The editor advises, "Read some. Listen a lot."

WORDSONG; BOYDS MILLS PRESS (IV-Children), 815 Church St., Honesdale PA 18431, phone (800)949-7777), founded 1990, editor-in-chief Dr. Bernice E. Cullinan, is the imprint under which Boyds Mills Press (a *Highlights for Children* company) publishes books of poetry for children of all ages. **"Wordsong encourages quality poetry which reflects childhood fun, moral standards and multiculturalism. We are not interested in poetry for adults or that which includes violence or sexuality or promotes hatred."** They have recently published poetry by Isaac Olaleye and Sam Holbrook. As a sample the editor selected these lines from "The Distant Talking Drum" by Olaleye:

> From deep in the rain forest
> The sound of the distant talking drum I hear—
> Far away, far away.
> For me it calls.
> Clearly it calls
> For me to dance. . .

"Wordsong prefers original work but will consider anthologies and previously published collections. We ask poets to send collections of 30-50 poems with a common theme; please send complete book manuscripts, not single poems. We buy all rights to collections and publish on an advance-and-royalty basis. Wordsong guarantees a response from editors within one month of our receiving submissions or the poet may call us toll free to inquire. Please direct submissions to Beth Troop, manuscript coordinator." Always sends prepublication galleys. Wordsong's *Inner Chimes* received the International Reading Association Teachers' Choice Award. Dr. Cullinan says, "Poetry lies at the heart of the elementary school literature and reading program. In fact, poetry lies right at the heart of children's language learning. Poetry speaks to the heart of a child. We are anxious to find poetry that deals with imagination, wonder, seeing the world in a new way, family relationships, friends, school, nature and growing up."

WORKS MAGAZINE (IV-Science fiction), 12 Blakestones Rd., Slaithwaite, Huddersfield, Yorks HD7 5UQ United Kingdom, founded 1989, editor Dave W. Hughes, is a biannual using "speculative and imaginative fiction and poetry favoring science fiction." They want **"surreal/science fiction poetry. Nothing more than 50 lines. No romance or general work."** They have published poetry by Andy Darlington, Steve Sneyd, Paul Weinman and Brian Aldiss. The editor says *Works* is 40 pgs., A4, stitched with glossy cover. They receive about 150 poems/year, use 36. Press run is 400 for 200 subscribers of which 4 are libraries, 50 shelf sales. Single copy: £2 (£4.50 for US); 4-issue subscription: £7.50 (£14 US). **No simultaneous submissions. Cover letter required. Disk submissions acceptable: IBM (5¼ or 3½-inch) or Atari 520ST (3½-inch); ASCII files only. Seldom comments on rejections. Send SASE (or SAE and IRC) for guidelines. Reports within a month. Pays 1 copy.** The editor says, "Study the market."

WoRM fEASt!; TAPE WoRM; VIDEO WoRM; KNIGHTMAYOR PRODUCTIONS (III, IV-Horror, occult), P.O. Box 519, Westminster MD 21158-0519, *WoRM fEASt!*, an underground monthly, founded 1989, editor Llori Steinberg. *Tape WoRM* is an audio magazine with music, poetry, comedy and more. *Video WoRM* is a video endeavor with movies, visual art, music videos, news events and more. Send SASE for details. For *Wf* they want **"as strange as humanoids can get; no traditional verse, no rhyme (unless it's way off the keister), no haiku, no love poems unless one-sided and morbid/dark and unusually sickening; and no Christian poetry."** They have published poetry by Gregory K.H. Bryant, Robert Howington, C.F. Roberts, Bill Shields and Vinnie Van Leer. The editor says *Wf* is usually 32 pgs., saddle-stitched, format size varies, with artwork and photos (from subscribers). Press run is 500. "The digest is different colors every time." Subscription: $25 for *Tape WoRM;* $20 for *WoRM fEASt!*, when available. **Sample postpaid: $5 (make all checks and any other forms of payment to Llori Steinberg). Submit 1 poem at a time. Previously published poems OK. Cover letter with SASE required;** "don't have to be professional, just state the facts and why you're interested in submitting; include a picture please." **Always comments on rejections. Publishes theme issues. Send SASE for guidelines and upcoming themes. "We report as quickly as we can." Sometimes sends prepublication galleys. Pays 1 copy of *WoRM fEASt!* No payment on *Tape WoRM;* contact for submission guidelines.** Reviews books of poetry. Open to unsolicited reviews. Send books to Llori Steinberg for review consideration. "Sometimes we publish chapbooks for poets' personal use. They buy and they sell." Cost is $100 for 100 chapbooks of under 40 pgs. each. Sponsors contests. Send SASE for details. The editor says, "We want weird, shock therapy art and literature; politics, drugs, insanity. Your writing must show depth, must shock us into a coma."

WORMWOOD REVIEW PRESS; THE WORMWOOD REVIEW; THE WORMWOOD AWARD (II), P.O. Box 4698, Stockton CA 95204-0698, phone (209)466-8231, founded 1959, poetry editor Marvin Malone. "The philosophy behind *Wormwood:* (i) avoid publishing oneself and personal friends, (ii) avoid being a 'local' magazine and strive for a national and international audience, (iii) seek unknown talents rather than establishment or fashionable authors, (iv) encourage originality by working with and promoting authors capable of extending the existing patterns of Amerenglish literature, (v) avoid all cults and allegiances and the you-scratch-my-back-and-I-will-scratch-yours approach to publishing, (vi) accept the fact that magazine content is more important than format in the long run, (vii) presume a literate audience and try to make the mag readable from the first page to the last, (viii) restrict the number of pages to no more than 40 per issue since only the insensitive and the masochistic can handle more pages at one sitting, (ix) pay bills on time and don't expect special favors in honor of the muse, and lastly and most importantly (x) don't become too serious and righteous." They want **"poetry and prose poetry that communicate the temper and range of human experience in contemporary society; don't want religious poetry and work that descends into bathos; don't want imitative sweet verse. Must be original; any style or school from traditional to ultra experimental, but *must* communicate; 3-600 lines."** They have published poetry by Ron Koertge, Gerald Locklin, Charles Bukowski and Edward Field. As a sample the editor selected these lines from "Shaker House" by Lyn Lifshin:

> they know what to leave out
> like back packers who know you
> must get rid of what you
> don't need or it can kill you

Wormwood is a digest-sized quarterly, offset from photoreduced typescript, saddle-stapled. Yellow pages in the center of each issue feature "one poet or one idea." Press run is 700 for 500 subscribers of which 210 are libraries. Subscription: $12. **Sample postpaid: $4. Submit 2-10 poems on as many pages. No previously published poems or simultaneous submissions. Send SASE for guidelines. Reports in 2-8 weeks. Pays 2-10 copies of the magazine or cash equivalent ($6-30). Acquires all rights. Returns rights on written request, without cost, provided the magazine is acknowledged whenever reprinted.** Reviews books of poetry. **For chapbook publication, no query; send 40-60 poems. "Covering letter not necessary—decisions are made solely on merit of submitted work." Reports in 1-2 months. Pays 35 copies or cash equivalent ($105). Send $4 for samples or check libraries.** They offer the Wormwood Award to the Most Overlooked Book of Worth (poetry or prose) for a calendar year, judged by Marvin Malone. Comments on rejections if the work has merit. The editor advises, "Have something to say. Read the past and modern 'master' poets. Absorb what they've done, but then write as effectively as you can in your own style. If you can say it in 40 words, do *not* use 400 or 4,000 words."

THE WRITER; POET TO POET (I, II), 120 Boylston St., Boston MA 02116-4615, founded 1887. This monthly magazine for writers has a quarterly instructional column, "Poet to Poet," to which poets may submit work for possible publication and comment. Subscription: $27 (introductory offer: 5 issues for $10). Single copy: $3. **Submit no more than 3 poems, no longer than 30 lines each, not on onion skin or erasable bond, name and address on each page, one poem to a page. Send SASE for guidelines. There is no pay and mss are not acknowledged or returned. Acquires first North American serial rights.**

WRITERS' CENTER PRESS; THE FLYING ISLAND; WRITERS' CENTER OF INDIANAPOLIS (II, IV-Regional), P.O. Box 88386, Indianapolis IN 46208, phone (317)929-0625, founded 1979, executive director Jim Powell. Writers' Center Press publishes *The Flying Island*, a biannual of fiction, poetry, reviews and literary commentary by those **living in or connected to Indiana. They want poetry of high literary quality; no stylistic or thematic restrictions.** They have published poetry by Jared Carter, Alice Friman, Yusef Komunyakaa and Roger Mitchell. As a sample the editor selected these lines from "Snapshot: Father Washing the Dog" by Karen I. Jaquish:

> The reek of Sergeant's Flea Soap stings.
> Our dog is lathered into placid acceptance.
> You glance up, toss that famous grin
> given to stangers and Kodak cameras.

TFI, a 24-page tabloid, includes artwork, graphics and photography. They receive about 1,000 poems a year, accept approximately 5%. Press run is 1,000 for 500 subscribers. **Submit 3 poems at a time. Previously published poems OK, but not encouraged. Simultaneous submissions OK, if so advised. Brief bio required. Often comments on rejections. Send SASE for guidelines. Reports in 3-6 months. Pays $5 minimum for previously unpublished work. Buys first North American serial rights.** Staff reviews books of poetry. Send books for review consideration. The center sponsors frequent contests for members through its quarterly newsletter and open readings. They advise, "Balance solitary writing time by getting involved in a writing community. We frequently recommend rejected writers join a poetry workshop."

WRITER'S DIGEST (IV-Writing, humor); WRITER'S DIGEST WRITING COMPETITION (II), 1507 Dana Ave., Cincinnati OH 45207, phone (513)531-2222, founded 1921, associate editor Paul Singer, is a monthly magazine for writers—fiction, nonfiction, poetry and drama. "All editorial copy is aimed at helping writers to write better and become more successful. **Poetry is included in 'The Writing Life' section of *Writer's Digest* only. Preference is given to short, light verse concerning 'the writing**

life'—the foibles, frenzies, delights and distractions inherent in being a writer. Serious verse is acceptable; however, no poetry unrelated to writing. We're looking for more serious poems on the joys and foibles of the writing life, but avoid the trite or maudlin." **Preferred length: 4-20 lines.** The magazine has published poetry by Charles Ghigna. As a sample, the editors selected this poem, "Mixed Messages," by Lois McBride Terry:

> *"As a poet, you're no Poe."*
> *"At prose, you're certainly not a pro."*
> *"Your movie script is nondescript.*
> *(And sadder still, your comic strip.)"*
> *The only line they don't reject:*
> *"Enclosed is my subscription check."*

They use a maximum of 2 short poems/issue, about 15/year of the 1,500 submitted. *Writer's Digest* has a circulation of 240,000. Subscription: $27. **Sample postpaid: $3.50. Do not submit to Michael Bugeja, poetry columnist for the magazine. Submit to Paul Singer, associate editor, each poem on a separate page, no more than 8/submission. Previously published poems and simultaneous submissions OK if acknowledged in cover letter. Editor comments on rejections "when we want to encourage or explain decision." Send SASE for guidelines and/or reply. Reports in 3-6 weeks. Always sends prepublication galleys. Pays $15-50/poem.** Poetry up to 32 lines on any theme is eligible for the annual Writer's Digest Writing Competition. Watch magazine for information, or send a SASE for a copy of the contest's rules. Deadline: May 31. (Also see Writer's Digest Books under Publications Useful to Poets.)

WRITER'S EXCHANGE; R.S.V.P. PRESS (I), Box 394, Society Hill SC 29593, phone (803)378-4556, founded 1983, editor Gene Boone, is a quarterly newsletter of articles on any aspect of writing, poetry and artwork with a special emphasis on beginners. He wants **"poetry to 24 lines, any subject or style. I also consider short poems such as haiku, tanka, senryu and other fixed forms. I like writing that is upbeat, positive, enlightening or inspiring, especially humorous poetry. I will not consider material that is anti-religious, racist or obscene."** He has published poetry by Victor Chapman, Winnie E. Fitzpatrick, Violet Wilcox and Mary Ann Henn. As a sample he selected these lines (poet unidentified):

> *A hurried world, spinning too fast*
> *Modern technology replaces dreams*
> *With skyscraper nightmares*
> *God watches as we dance at Satan's feet.*

WE is 12-20 pgs., digest-sized, saddle-stitched, with a colored paper cover. He accepts about half or more of the poetry received. Press run is 250. Subscription: $10. **Sample postpaid: $2. Submit 3-10 poems at a time. "I prefer typed mss, one poem per page, readable. Poets should always proofread mss before sending them out. Errors can cause rejection." No simultaneous submissions. Previously published poetry OK. Cover letter required; list "prior credits, if any, and other details of writing background."** Time between acceptance and publication is 4 months. **Send SASE for guidelines. Reports in 2-4 weeks. Pays 1 copy. Acquires one-time rights.** Staff reviews books of poetry. Send books for review consideration. They offer cash awards for quarterly contests sponsored through the magazine. Send SASE for current rules. The editor says he comments on rejections, "if I feel it will benefit the poet in the long run, never anything too harsh or overly discouraging." His advice to poets: "Support the small press publications you read and enjoy. Without your support these publications will cease to exist. The small press has given many poets their start. In essence, the small press is where poetry lives!"

WRITERS' FORUM (II, IV-Regional), Dept. PM, University of Colorado, Colorado Springs CO 80933-7150, founded 1974, poetry editor Victoria McCabe. *Writers' Forum*, an annual, publishes both beginning and well-known writers, giving **"some emphasis to contemporary Western literature**, that is, to representation of living experience west of the 100th meridian in relation to place and culture. We collaborate with authors in the process of revision, reconsider and frequently publish revised work. We are open to **solidly crafted imaginative work that is verbally interesting and reveals authentic voice. We would like to see more formal work, nicely executed."** They have published poems by William Stafford, David Ray, Kenneth Fields, Harold Witt and Judson Crews. The annual is digest-sized, 225 pgs., flat-spined, professionally printed with matte card cover, using 40-50 pgs. of poetry in each issue. They use about 25 of 500 submissions of poetry/year. Circulation 800 with 100 subscriptions of which 25 are libraries. **The list price is $8.95 but they offer it at $5.95 to readers of *Writer's Digest*. Submit 3-5 poems at a time with SASE. No previously published poems; simultaneous submissions OK, if acknowledged. Reads submissions September 1 through March 15. Reports in 3 months. Pays 1 copy. Acquires all rights; returns rights.**

WRITERS FORUM; AND; KROKLOK (IV-Form), 89A Petherton Rd., London N5 2QT England, phone (0171)226-2657, founded 1963, editor Bob Cobbing, is a small press publisher of experimental work including sound and visual poetry in cards, leaflets, chapbooks, occasional paperbacks and magazines. **"Explorations of 'the limits of poetry' including 'graphic' displays, notations for sound and performance, as well as semantic and syntactic developments, not to mention fun."** They have recently published poetry by Paul Dutton, Pierre Garnier, Bill Keith, Arrigo Lora-Totino, Hiroshi Tanabu and Eric Mottram. As a sample the editor selected these lines by Sheila Murphy:

> *preen unisonly craft in satchels plummeting*
> *to ward off gravity (earth's facing*
> *east again supremely hot caked to the*
> *nines for southerly appreciative and temperature*
> *(psychic is as psychic*
> *buzz*

The magazines are published "irregularly" and use "very little unsolicited poetry; practically none." Press run "varies." **Submit 6 poems at a time. "We normally don't publish previously published work." Work should generally be submitted camera-ready. Payment is "by arrangement."** Under the imprint Writers Forum they publish 12-18 books a year averaging 28 pgs. **Samples and listing: $5. For book publication, query with 6 samples, bio, publications. Pays "by arrangement with author."** The editor says, "We publish only that which surprises and excites us; poets who have a very individual voice and style."

WRITER'S JOURNAL (I, II), incorporating *Minnesota Ink*, 3585 N. Lexington Ave., Suite 328, Arden Hills MN 55126, phone (612)486-7818, *Writer's Journal* founded 1980, poetry editor Esther M. Leiper. *Writer's Journal* is a bimonthly magazine "for writers and poets that offers advice and guidance, motivation, inspiration, to the more serious and published writers and poets." Esther Leiper has 2 columns: "Esther Comments," which specifically critiques poems sent in by readers, and "Every Day with Poetry," which discusses a wide range of poetry topics, often—but not always—including readers' work. She says, **"I enjoy a variety of poetry: free verse, strict forms, concrete, Oriental. But we take nothing vulgar, preachy or sloppily written. Since we appeal to those of different skill levels, some poems are more sophisticated than others, but those accepted must move, intrigue or otherwise positively capture me.** 'Esther Comments' is never used as a negative force to put a poem or a poet down. Indeed, I focus on the best part of a given work and seek to suggest means of improvement on weaker aspects. **Short is best: 25-line limit, though** *very* **occasionally we use longer. 3-4 poems at a time is just right."** They have published poetry by Lawrence Schug, Diana Sutliff and Eugene E. Grollmes. As a sample the editor selected these lines from "an unidentified author we'd love to hear from":

> *I am with Haysie again on God's ranch,*
> *It is not yet dawn; we ride west*
> *over the mountains. His face is in shadow*
> *but I know it is Haysie because*
> *I have loved his shadow so.*

Writer's Journal is magazine-sized, professionally printed, 60 pgs. (including paper cover), using 4-5 pgs. of poetry in each issue, including columns. Circulation is 51,000. They receive about 400 submissions/year of which they use 30-40 (including those used in Esther's column). **Sample postpaid: $4. No query. Reports in 4-5 months. Pays 25¢/line.** The section *Minnesota Ink* began as a separate magazine in 1987. "We are **open to style, prefer light-hearted pieces and of good taste."** Payment varies. *Writer's Journal* has quarterly poetry contests for previously unpublished poetry. Deadlines: February 28, April 15, August 15 and November 30. Reading fee for each contest: $2 first poem, $1 each poem thereafter.

WRITER'S LIFELINE (I), P.O. Box 1641, Cornwall, Ontario K6H 5V6 Canada, phone (613)932-2135, fax (613)932-7735, founded 1974, editor Stephen Gill, published 3 times a year, containing articles and information useful to writers, **poetry** and book reviews. **"We prefer poems on social concerns. We avoid sex."** As a sample the editor selected these lines from his poem, "Bigotry":

> *It grows*
> *on the babel of confusion*
> *in the lap of*
> *the blinding dust of vanity*
> *by the arrogant prince of ignorance.*

WL is 36-40 pgs., digest-sized, saddle-stitched with 2-color paper cover, printed in small type, poems sometimes in bold or italics. Circulation is 1,500. Subscription: $18. **Sample postpaid: $3. Publishes theme issues. Send SASE for guidelines and upcoming themes. Responds in 1 month. Pays 3 copies. Acquires first North American serial rights.** Reviews books of poetry in 500-1,500 words. "We need book reviews." Query if interested.

WRITER'S WORLD; MAR-JON PUBLICATIONS (III), 204 E. 19th St., Big Stone Gap VA 24219, phone/fax (703)523-0830, founded 1990, editor Gainelle Murray, poetry editor Diane L. Krueger (submissions should go directly to her at 17 Oswego Ave., Rockaway NJ 07866, phone (201)627-0439, fax (201)627-3314). *Writer's World* is a bimonthly literary publication presenting poetry, articles and columns on writing. **They want "avant-garde, free verse, light verse, traditional, 12-16 lines. No erotica nor anything mentioning violence, abortion or drug abuse."** They have published poetry by Joyce Carbone, Denise Martinson, William J. White and Arthur C. Ford. As a sample the editor selected the opening lines of "The Poet" by Linda J. Crider:

> Bits of memory
> Ideas and dreams,
> Running in sunlight
> Dancing in moonbeams
> Floating through tomorrow
> On gossamer wings.

WW is 20 pgs., 8½×11, typeset and saddle-stapled with glossy paper cover, clip art and ads. They receive 300-500 poems a year, accept approximately 15%. Press run is 3,600 for 3,100 subscribers of which 2% are libraries. Single copy: $4.50; subscription: $15. **Sample: $3.50 and 9×12 SAE with $1.01 postage. Submit 3-5 poems, none untitled. Previously published poems OK; no simultaneous submissions. Cover letter required. "Submissions without name and address on each page and a SASE will not be read or returned."** Time between acceptance and publication is 6-12 months. **Often comments on rejections. Send SASE for guidelines and upcoming themes. Reports in 2 months. Pays $5 for poetry used on the front cover; all others receive 2 copies. Buys one-time rights.** The editor says, "We have a critique service with subscribers given reduced rates. Write for more information."

WRITING FOR OUR LIVES; RUNNING DEER PRESS (I, II, IV-Women), 647 N. Santa Cruz Ave., The Annex, Los Gatos CA 95030, founded 1991, editor/publisher Janet McEwan, appears twice a year. "*Writing For Our Lives* serves as a vessel for poems, short fiction, stories, letters, autobiographies and journal excerpts from the life stories, experiences and spiritual journeys of women." They want **poetry that is "personal, women's real life, life-saving, autobiographical, serious—but don't forget humorous, silence-breaking, many styles, many voices. Women writers only, please."** They have recently published poetry by Michele Aranguiz, Vesna Dye, Cora Greenhill, Minal Hajratwala and Lian Njo. As a sample the editor selected these lines from "Afterwards" by Leonne Gould:

> Grief blesses the small of my back,
> laps at my feet
> and settles me like fog.
> She enlarges my pores
> and spreads through my rooms
> like incense.

Writing For Our Lives is 80 pgs., 5¼×8¼, printed on recycled paper and perfect-bound with matte card cover. They receive about 400 poems a year, accept approximately 5%. Press run is 1,000. Subscription: $11.50 individuals, $14 institutions. **Sample postpaid: $7. Submit 1-5 typed poems with name and phone number at top of each page. Previously published poems ("sometimes") and simultaneous submissions OK. Include a self-addressed, stamped postcard "so I can promptly acknowledge receipt of your work." A SASE should also be included for reply and return of ms. Closing dates are February 15 and August 15. "I read, make selections and send notification letters as soon as possible after the closing dates." Seldom comments on rejections. Send SASE for guidelines. Pays 2 copies, discount on additional copies and discount on 1-year subscription. Acquires first world-wide English language serial (or one-time reprint) rights.** "Our contributors and circulation are international."

‡WRITING WORKS (I, IV-Students), P.O. Box 338, Columbus NE 68602-0338, phone/fax (402)564-5295, founded 1993, editor Jeanne K. Schieffer, is a quarterly publication for secondary students and teachers of writing. *Writing Works* is designed "to encourage young writers to publish outside the classroom, to provide a network for young authors, and to offer a realistic tool for teachers to use in their classrooms." **They want "poems of positive impact, whether in topic or in promoting critical thought. Nothing profane, pro self-destruction or very negative."** They have published poetry by both teachers and students. As a sample the editor selected these lines from "Thursday Afternoon," written by student Shevaun Johnson:

> Each Thursday afternoon Brian sits
> across from me at the short, blue table
> and laboriously pulls from me
> bits of a shattered paragraph
> or pieces of a broken equation.
> He smiles softly and reads sections of
> James Joyce aloud to me.

Writing Works is a 12- to 20-page newsprint tabloid appearing in August, November, February and

May (in conjunction with the school year). They receive 800-1,000 poems a year, accept approximately 75%. Press run starts at 1,200. Subscription: $20. **Sample postpaid: $5. Submit no more than 3 poems at a time. Include writer's name and grade and the name and address of the school attended/currently teaching. Previously published poems and simultaneous submissions OK. Always comments on rejections. Send SASE for guidelines. Reports within 3 months.** They also sponsor occasional contests. The editor says, "Young authors need to remember that uniqueness and originality are essential to good poetry. Too often we receive poems written on topics such as friends, lost loves and graduating."

‡**WYRD (IV-Psychic/occult)**, P.O. Box 624, Monroeville PA 15146-0624, founded 1986, "editrix" Goldie Brown, is a quarterly using news, articles, music and poetry related to the Magickal/Pagan community. They want **poetry about magick, the occult, nature or spirituality—no longer than 50 lines.** They have published poetry by Fletcher de Wolf, Victor Anderson, Ken McDonnell and Ken Deigh. As a sample the editor selected these lines from "Rainbow Eclipse" by jon Eric:

> *Temple of the Golden Sun*
> *Silver Moon, Brazen Twin*
> *Garden of the Emerald Earth*
> *Turquoise Sea, Indigo Sky*
> *Chalice of the Violet Flame*
> *Ruby Blood, Umbar Flesh*

WYRD is 16 pgs., 8½ × 11, side stapled, with art, graphics and ads. They receive about 100 poems a year, use approximately 10%. Press run is 150 for 100 subscribers. Subscription: $16. **Sample postpaid: $4. Submit 2 poems at a time. No previously published poems; simultaneous submissions OK. Cover letter required. Reports in 2 months. Pays 1 copy—more (up to 3), if requested.** Reviews related books of poetry in 150-200 words, single format.

XANADU; POETIMES; LONG ISLAND POETRY COLLECTIVE (II), % LIPC, P.O. Box 773, Huntington NY 11743, founded 1979, editors Lois V. Walker, Mildred Jeffrey, Sue Kain and Weslea Sidon, is an annual publishing "serious poems and an occasional, adventuresome essay on contemporary poetry or critical theory." They want **"well-crafted quality poems. Nothing inspirational, obscene or from beginners."** They have recently published poetry by Philip Dacey, Diana Chang, Simon Perchik, Louis David Brodsky and Ioanna-Veronika Warwick. As a sample the editors selected these lines from "Sex, Genetics, The Sea" by Charles Entrekin:

> *Like falling backwards in time*
> *toward something I don't comprehend,*
> *if I run forward, if I stand still,*
> *what I see has no name,*
> *slouches away if I look at it,*
> *yet feel in the touch of bones . . .*

The editors describe the journal as 55-65 pgs., no ads, no graphics. Press run is 300 for 100 subscribers of which 5 are libraries. **Sample postpaid: $7. No previously published poems; simultaneous submissions OK. Poems must be typed. Seldom comments on rejections. Send #10 SASE for guidelines. Reports in 2 weeks to 4 months. Pays 1 copy. Acquires first North American serial rights.** The Long Island Poetry Collective also publishes *Poetimes*, a bimonthly newsletter that includes an extensive calendar of poetry events on Long Island, contests, market listings and poetry by its members. Subscription: $18/year, includes membership in LIPC and subscription to *Xanadu*. They say, "We would be glad to look at more quality post-modernist and formalist poetry."

XAVIER REVIEW (II), Box 110C, Xavier University, New Orleans LA 70125, phone (504)486-7411, founded 1961, editor Thomas Bonner, Jr., is a biannual that publishes poetry, fiction, nonfiction and reviews (contemporary literature) for professional writers, libraries, colleges and universities. Press run is 500. **No submission information provided.**

XIB; XIB PUBLICATIONS (II), P.O. Box 262112, San Diego CA 92126, phone (619)298-4927, fax (619)278-5101, founded 1990, editor tolek, appears irregularly, usually annually, publishing poetry, short fiction and b&w artwork and photos. **They want poetry of any form, length, subject, style or purpose. "Prefer 'quirky' things, however."** They have recently published poetry by Christine C. Brown, Sheila E. Murphy and Judson Crews. As a sample the editor selected these lines from "Scarecrow" by Arthur G. Gottleib:

> *My fingers tremble on the bolt,*
> *but if I let him in, the ravens*
> *will eat my eyes in revenge.*

xib is 60 pgs., 6½ × 8½, photocopied on heavy bond, saddle-stapled, 12 pt. gloss mimeo cover, 80% illustrated with art and photos, some ads. They receive about 3,000 poems a year, use approximately 3%. Press run is 500 for 50 subscribers of which a third are libraries, 350 shelf sales. Subscription: $10 for 2 issues and a chapbook. **Sample postpaid: $5, back issues $4; make checks payable to tolek. Submit 5-7 poems at a time. Previously published poems and simultaneous submissions OK. Cover letter preferred. "Work sent without a cover letter will be read but may be returned without comment." Seldom comments on rejections. "Guidelines, broadsides and tearsheets available for SASE." Reports in 3-5 weeks. Pays 1 copy. Acquires one-time rights.** xib publications **publishes 1-2 chapbooks/year, "irregularly and arbitrarily. Please do not query or submit with chapbook intent. Most chaps form out of friendly joint-efforts."** Press run for chapbooks is about 75-100. Authors receive half; the rest goes to subscribers, reviewers and trades. The editor says, "Cover letters tell me by their content how formal/informal the submission is, and how I respond to it. People show their personality, I show mine. Previously published and simultaneous submissions indicate two things: My periodical isn't as special as others and the writer doesn't produce very much. But, I publish poems, not famous names (for the sake of the name)."

THE YALE REVIEW (II), Yale University, P.O. Box 208243, New Haven CT 06520-8243, phone (203)432-0499, founded 1911, editor J.D. McClatchy, is a "quarterly general magazine of intellectual distinction and literary excellence." It is known for publishing all forms and styles of poetry, and issues reviewed verify that fact. Both formal and free verse, marked by excellence, seems welcome. They have published poetry by John Ashbery, W.S. Merwin and Amy Clampitt. Press run is 6,000 for 2,000 subscribers of which 1,000 are libraries. Single copy: $8; subscription: $23.50. **No previously published poems or simultaneous submissions. Reads submissions September 1 through June 30 only.** Time between acceptance and publication is 9 months to 1 year. **Seldom comments on rejections. Reports within 2 months. Always sends prepublication galleys. Pays $100-300.** "Volumes of poetry reviewed in a regular essay." Send books for review consideration. Poetry published in *The Yale Review* was also selected for inclusion in the 1992, 1993, 1994 and 1995 volumes of *The Best American Poetry*.

YALE UNIVERSITY PRESS; THE YALE SERIES OF YOUNGER POETS COMPETITION (III), P.O. Box 209040, New Haven CT 06520-9040, phone (203)432-0900, founded 1908, poetry editor (Yale University Press) Richard Miller. The Yale Series of Younger Poets Competition is **open to poets under 40 who have not had a book previously published. Submit ms of 48-64 pgs. in February. Entry fee: $15. Send SASE for rules and guidelines.** Poets are not disqualified by previous publication of limited editions of no more than 300 copies or previously published poems in newspapers and periodicals, which may be used in the book ms if so identified. Previous winners include Richard Kenney, Carolyn Forché and Robert Hass.

YANKEE MAGAZINE; YANKEE ANNUAL POETRY CONTEST (II), P.O. Box 520, Dublin NH 03444-0520, phone (603)563-8111, founded in 1935, poetry editor (since 1955) Jean Burden. Though it has a New England emphasis, the poetry is not necessarily about New England or by New Englanders, and it has a national distribution of more than a million subscribers. They want to see **"high quality contemporary poems in either free verse or traditional form. Does not have to be regional in theme. Any subject acceptable, provided it is in good taste. We look for originality in thought, imagery, insight—as well as technical control." They do not want poetry that is "cliché-ridden, banal verse."** They have published poetry by Maxine Kumin, Liz Rosenberg, Josephine Jacobsen, Nancy Willard, Linda Pastan, Paul Zimmer and Hayden Carruth. As a sample the editor selected these lines from "Waking" by Joan LaBombard:

> But blood's in thrall to the world
> and the body's bound
> by its clocks and invisible pulleys—
> sun plucking at bedclothes,
> a mockingbird's ultimatum.
> I reenter the world's cage, the house
> of my daylight body.
> My blood discovers its old riverbed,
> and my name remembers me.

The monthly is 6 × 9, 170 pgs., saddle-stapled, professionally printed, using full-color and b&w ads and illustrations, with full-color glossy paper cover. They receive over 30,000 submissions a year, accept about 50-60 poems, use 4-5 poems/monthly issue. Subscription: $22. **Submit no more than 6 poems up to 30 lines each, free verse or traditional. No simultaneous submissions or previously published poems. "Cover letters are interesting if they include previous publication information."** Submissions without SASE "are tossed." Editor comments on rejections "only if poem has so many good qualities it only needs minor revisions." **Reports in 2-3 weeks. Approximately 18-month backlog. Pays $50/poem, all rights; $35, first magazine rights.** Sponsors an annual poetry contest judged by a prominent New England poet and published in the February issue, with awards of $150, $100 and $50 for the best 3 poems in the preceding year. Jean Burden advises, "Study previous issues of *Yankee* to determine the kind of poetry we want. Get involved in poetry workshops at home. Read the best contemporary poetry you can find."

YARROW, A JOURNAL OF POETRY (II), English Dept., Lytle Hall, Kutztown State University, Kutztown PA 19530, founded 1981, editor Harry Humes, appears twice a year. They have published poetry by Gibbons Ruark, Jared Carter, William Pitt Root and Fleda Brown Jackson. It is 40 pgs., 6 × 9, offset. Press run is 350. Subscription: $5/2 years. **Reports in 1-2 months. Pays 2 copies plus 1-year subscription.** Poetry published in *Yarrow* was also selected for inclusion in a *Pushcart Prize* anthology.

YEFIEF (II), P.O. Box 8505, Santa Fe NM 87504, founded 1993, editor Ann Racuya-Robbins, is an annual designed "to construct a narrative of culture at the end of the century." **They want "innovative visionary work of all kinds."** They have recently published poetry by Michael Palmer, Simon Perchik and Carla Harryman. As a sample the editor selected these lines from "Tendons, Paragraphs and Milky Way" by Nicole Brossard, translated by Susanne de Lotbiniere-Harwood:

> *Everything was within range of the gaze, autumn, the century and the narrative. Truth alone*
> *was missing.*

Yefief is 176 pgs., 7 × 9, offset and perfect-bound with color coated card cover and b&w photos, art and graphics inside. Press run is 1,000. Single copy: $7.95. **Submit 3-6 poems at a time. Previously published poems and simultaneous submissions OK. Reports in 6-8 weeks. Pays 2-3 copies.** Open to unsolicited reviews. Poets may also send books for review consideration.

YELLOW SILK: JOURNAL OF EROTIC ARTS, Verygraphics, P.O. Box 6374, Albany CA 94706. "We currently receive far more poetry than we need and cannot afford to add to it."

YESTERDAY'S MAGAZETTE (I, IV-Senior citizens), Independent Publishing Co., P.O. Box 15126, Sarasota FL 34277, editor and publisher Ned Burke, founded 1973. This bimonthly magazine is for **"all nostalgia lovers.** *YM* believes that everyone has a yesterday and everyone has a memory to share. Nothing fancy here . . . just 'plain folks' relating their individual life experiences. **We are always seeking new and innovative writers with imagination and promise, and we would like to see more 40s, 50s and 60s pieces."** As a sample here are lines from "The Backyard Pump" by J.E. Coulbourn:

> *With two small hands you'd*
> *grasp the monster's tail*
> *And try to pump the water in the pail,*
> *But if his darned esophagus got dry*
> *No water came no matter how you'd try.*

YM is 28 pgs., magazine-sized, saddle-stapled, professionally printed on good stock with glossy color cover. A year's subscription is $15 or 2 years for $25. **Sample: $3. Submissions for "Quills, Quips, & Quotes" (their poetry page) should be "thoughtful, amusing, or just plain interesting for our 'plain folks' readers. No SASE is required as short items are generally not returned nor acknowledged, unless requested by the contributor." Pays copies.**

THE YOUNG CRUSADER (IV-Children), National Woman's Christian Temperance Union, 1730 Chicago Ave., Evanston IL 60201, is a bimonthly publication for **children of about 6-12 years. They want "short poems offering character-building subjects, high moral values and nature themes, for a young audience."** It is a 16-page, digest-sized leaflet. Submit 1-5 poems at a time. **Pays 10¢/line.**

YOUNG VOICES MAGAZINE (V, IV-Children), P.O. Box 2321, Olympia WA 98507, phone (206)357-4683, founded 1988, founder/publisher Steve Charak, editor Char Simons, is "a magazine of **creative work of elementary through high school students. The age limit is rigid."** It appears every other month. Press run is 2,000 for 1,000 subscribers of which 100 are libraries. Subscription: $15 for 1 year, $28 for 2. **Sample postpaid: $4. Query first. No longer accepting unsolicited poetry submissions.** Steve Charak says, "Revise. Remember that in a poem, every word counts. Forget about the need to rhyme. Instead, put feeling into each word."

ZEITGEIST (II), P.O. Box 1006, Kalispell MT 59903, fax (406)296-3198, founded 1990, publisher/editor John S. Slack, appears 4 times/year. For poetry, **"best is 1 page or less dealing with personal relationships to world and others. Focused ideas. Disturbing or provocative imagery welcomed. No same old love-death-suicide stuff, graphic sex and/or gratuitous profanity. No blatantly didactic stuff. We want poems that contain truth."** They have recently published poetry by Paul Hadella, Thomasine Reed and Lyn Lifshin. As a sample the editor selected these lines from "Border Town" by Jill Buckner:

> *She is seamless, shameless*
> *and will roll you*
> *on a bed so coarse welts form*
> *on the skin, Guatemalan blankets*

whirling around and around.

Zeitgeist is 20-28 pgs., 8½ × 11, photocopied, edge-stapled. They accept about 10% of poems submitted. Press run is 50 for 40 subscribers of which 3 are libraries. Subscription: $12. **Sample postpaid: $3.50. Submit up to 10 poems at a time. Previously published poems and simultaneous submissions OK. Cover letter with 3-4 publishing credits preferred. "A 3-line bio would help us get a feel of who you are." Editor often comments on rejections. Send SASE for guidelines. Reports in 1-6 months. Pays "each issue in which poet appears."** Open to unsolicited reviews. The editor says, "Keep your eyes, ears and nose open, along with your mind. Don't take rejection personally. Sometimes it takes a while to find your audience. Strive for truth, write lots and send the best."

ZEPHYR PRESS (III, IV-Translations), 13 Robinson St., Somerville MA 02145, founded 1980, editors Ed Hogan and Leora Zeitlin. **"We are now publishing very little poetry, and only Russian and Eastern European poetry in translation."** An example publication is *The Complete Poems of Anna Akhmatova*, translations by Judith Hemschemeyer. Their catalog lists books of poetry by Sue Standing, Anne Valley Fox and Miriam Sagan. **Query with 5 sample poems. Simultaneous submissions OK. "We will respond only if interested." Pays 10% of press run or by royalty, depending upon the particular project.**

‡ZERO ONE; DANCING PATCH MAGAZINE (V), 39 Minford Gardens, West Kensington, London W14 OAP England, phone 01602-9142, poetry editor and publisher Arthur Moyse. *Zero One* is an anarchist oriented publication appearing twice a year "with luck." He describes *Dancing Patch Magazine* as a "literary quarterly, anarchist oriented, egotistical, clichés. **To avoid disappointments we do not seek submissions for we operate on the 'old pals act' style."** He has published poems by Cunliffe, Woods and Gould. As a sample he selected these lines from "On the Death of the American Poet George Montgomery" by Jim Burns:

Reading about your death
I started to look back at the 1960s
and the little magazines
that used to arrive every day, ...

DPM appears 3-4 times a year. The editor describes it as magazine-sized. He says he receives "too much poetry, takes hardly any." He advises, "Just write it and send it off off off. Give up waiting for editorial acceptance or rejection. Just write and post."

ZOLAND BOOKS INC. (III), 384 Huron Ave., Cambridge MA 02138, phone (617)864-6252, founded 1987, publisher Roland Pease, is a "literary press: fiction, poetry, photography, gift books, books of literary interest." They want **"high-quality" poetry, not sentimental.** They have recently published poetry by James Laughlin, William Corbett, Karen Fiser, Marge Piercy, Patricia Smith, Sam Cornish and Kim Vaeth. They publish 8-10 books/year, flat-spined, averaging 104 pgs. **Query with 5-10 sample poems, bio, publications and SASE. Editor does not comment on submissions. Sometimes sends prepublication galleys. Pays 5-10% royalties plus 5 copies. Buys all rights.** Zoland's *An Altogether Different Language* by Anne Porter was a 1994 National Book Award Finalist.

ZUZU'S PETALS ANNUAL (II), (formerly *Zuzu's Petals Quarterly*), P.O. Box 4476, Allentown PA 18105, phone (610)821-1324, (fax available/call ahead), founded 1992, editor T. Dunn. "We publish high quality fiction, essays, poetry and reviews. As an anthology of both the written and visual arts, we provide a home for outstanding works of postmodern creativity. **Free verse, blank verse, experimental, visually sensual poetry, etc. are all welcome here. We're looking for a freshness of language, new ideas and original expression. No 'June, moon and spoon' rhymed poetry. No light verse. I'm open to considering more feminist, ethnic, alternative poetry."** They have recently published poetry by Max Greenberg, Gayle Elen Harvey, Timothy Russell and Sandra Nelson. As a sample the editor selected these lines from Jean-Paul DeVellard:

Now I must learn to draw
all over again
struggle to lay claim
to the perfect and last
for all time depiction
of your soft and faithful
universal mouth

ZPA is 170-200 pgs., 8½ × 11, perfect-bound, matte card cover, b&w graphics and artwork throughout. They receive about 2,000 poems a year, accept approximately 10%. Press run is 300. Subscription: $17 US, $25 international. "We've greatly expanded our format for the coming year. **Samples of the previous incarnation of *ZPA*, *Zuzu's Petals Quarterly*, are available for $5." Submit up to 5 poems at a time. Previously published poems and simultaneous submissions OK. "Cover letters are not necessary. The work should speak for itself." Electronic submissions in ASCII (DOS IBM) format on 3½ or 5¼ disks OK. Seldom comments on rejections. Send SASE for guidelines. Reports in 2**

weeks to 2 months. Pays 1 copy. Acquires one-time rights. Staff reviews books of poetry and audiotapes of poetry readings in approximately 200 words. Send books or galleys for review consideration. They also sponsor twice-yearly poetry contests. Entry fee: $2/poem, any style, length or subject. Deadlines are the first of March and September. 40% of proceeds goes to prize winners: 25% to first prize, 10% to second, 5% to third. Free critiques to honorable mentions. The remaining 60% of proceeds goes towards the anthology and keeps it ad-free. The editor says, "Read as much poetry as you can. Support the literary arts: Go to poetry readings, read chapbooks and collections of verse. Eat poetry for breakfast, cultivate a love of language, then write!"

ZYZZYVA, 41 Sutter St., Suite 1400, San Francisco CA 94104. Prefers not to share information.

Publishers of Poetry/'95-'96 Changes

Each year we contact all the publishers listed in *Poet's Market* to request updated information for our next edition. The following magazine and book publishers were listed in the 1995 edition of *Poet's Market* but are not in the 1996 edition because they did not respond to our request to update their listing (these names appear without further explanation) *or* their listing was deleted for the reason indicated in parentheses.

While many of these publishers have ceased operation, the reasons some of them are not included this year are temporary (e.g., overstocked, temporarily suspending publication, etc.). If you're interested in any of the following, first research the publisher and then write a brief letter inquiring as to whether they are now interested in receiving submissions. Remember to always enclose a SASE with any inquiry.

The American Voice (requested deletion)
Anima: The Journal of Human Experience (ceasing publication)
Arc
Asking the Question (ceased publication)
Asylum (ceased publication)
Attitude Problem (no longer publishes poetry)
Bad Attitude (responded too late)
Bad Haircut (out of business)
Baker Street Publications
Bare Wire (unable to contact)
Bear Tribe's Publishing (future uncertain)
Beggar's Press
Bellflower Press
Berkeley Poets Cooperative (suspended until further notice)
Big Head Press (suspending publication indefinitely)
Bird Watcher's Digest (overstocked)
Black River Review
Black Sparrow Press (overstocked)
Branch Redd Books
Brussels Sprout (future uncertain)
Carleton Arts Review
Carpenter Press
The Carrefour Press
Catalyst
Cat's Ear
Cencrastus
Charlotte Magazine (no longer publishes poetry)
Chips Off the Writer's Block
The Christian Way (ceased publication)

Co-Laborer Magazine
Columbia University Translation Center (closed down)
Cornfield Review (no outside submissions)
Council for Indian Education (overstocked)
Cowboy Magazine
Creeping Bent (suspended publication)
Cyphers
DAM (Disability Arts Magazine)
The Dead Rebel News
Diehard
A Different Drummer
Djinni
Duckabush Journal (ceased publication)
Duende Press (seeking financial contributions)
The Eagle
The Eleventh Muse (short handed)
Equilibrium[10]
Family Earth (ceased publication)
First Time (responded too late)
FishDrum (responded too late)
Five Fingers Review
Four Quarters (suspended publication)
Fredrickson-Kloepfel Publishing Co. (out of business)
Gaia: A Journal of Literary & Environmental Arts
Gain Publications
Galaxy Press (no outside submissions)
Giorno Poetry Systems Records
Good Housekeeping (no longer publishes poetry)
Great River Review (requested deletion)

Gypsy (requested deletion)
Hangman Books
Hanson's Symposium
Heresies
Holmgangers Press (suspended publication)
Hopewell Review
House of Moonlight (ceased publication)
Icon (no outside submissions)
Innisfree Magazine (going out of business)
Insight Press
Intrepid (out of business)
Jacaranda Review (ceased publication)
Journeymen
Kaldron (suspended publication)
Kennesaw Review (suspended publication)
Kingfisher
L'Apache: An International Journal of Literature & Art
Legend: An International "Robin of Sherwood" Fanzine
L'Epervier Press
Linwood Publishers
Lips
Literary Focus Poetry Publications
Literary Olympics, Inc. (future uncertain)
Living Poets Society (unable to contact)
The Lizard's Eyelid
LMNO Press (unable to contact)
London Magazine
M.A.F. Press (ceased publication)
Manna
Matrix (unable to contact)
Minority Literary Expo
Minotaur Press

Mirrors (ceased publication)
Misnomer
Mississippi Valley Review (out of business)
University of Missouri Press (no longer publishes poetry)
Mixed Media (ceased publication)
Mobius
The Montana Poet Magazine
The Moody Street Review
Moving Out: A Feminist Literary and Arts Journal
Nashville House
NCASA Journal
Night Owl's Newsletter (overstocked)
Obsidian II: Black Literature in Review
Odradek (no outside submissions)
Old Hickory Review (ceased publication)
Once Upon a World
One Earth: The Findhorn Foundation & Community Magazine
Oriel Bookshop
Oxalis (ceased publication)
Page 5
Painted Hills Review (out of business)
Paisley Moon Press
Paris/Atlantic, International Magazine of Creative Work
Peace and Freedom
Peacemaking for Children (suspended publication)
The Penny Dreadful Review
Perceptions
Peregrine: The Journal of Amherst Writers & Artists
Phoenix Broadsheets
Phoenix Press
PIE (Poetry Imagery and Expression)
Piedmont Literary Review
Plains Poetry Journal (suspended publication)

Pleiades Magazine (unable to contact)
Poem Train
Poetic License
Poetical Histories
Poetry Break (ceased publication)
Poetry Durham (ceased publication)
Poetry London Newsletter
Poetry Nottingham
Poetry: USA
Poets Pen Quarterly
Point Judith Light
The Prospect Review (out of business)
Purple Patch
Quarry Magazine
Quartos Magazine
Rackham Journal of the Arts and Humanities (suspended publication)
Raddle Moon
Rambunctious Press
Ranger International Productions (requested deletion)
Raven Chronicles
Reconstructionist (no longer publishes poetry)
Rose Shell Press (out of business)
The Rugging Room
Salmagundi (overstocked)
San Miguel Writer
Scat! (ceased publication)
Scratch
Shades of Gray (out of business)
Shooting Star Review
Singing Horse Press
Sinister Wisdom
Slippery When Wet
Small Press Genre Association
Soundings: A Newsletter for Survivors of Childhood Sexual Abuse
South Coast Poetry Journal (ceased publication)
Southeastern Front

Southern Review (Australia)
Spectacular Diseases
The Squib (ceased publication)
Star Books, Inc. (out of business)
Starmist Books
The Sucarnochee Review (ceased publication)
Superintendent's Profile & Pocket Equipment Directory (under new ownership)
Tails of Wonder (ceased publication)
10th Muse
Textile Bridge Press (ceasing publication)
Thematic Poetry Quarterly (ceased publication)
Tidepool (ceased publication)
Timberlines
Tin Wreath
Turbulence
Underpass (on hiatus for 2-3 years)
The Vanitas Press
Verandah
Vivo (suspended publication)
Wake Forest University Press
Wayne Literary Review
West Anglia Publications (ceased publication)
Whetstone (Canada)
White Sands Poetry Review
Tahana Whitecrow Foundation
The Wind-Mill
Wineberry Press
The Wisconsin Restaurateur
The Wise Woman (overstocked)
The Word Works
Writ (ceasing publication)
The Write Way
Writer's Guidelines: A Roundtable for Writers and Editors
Xenophilia (out of business)
Xiquan Publishing House

Market conditions are constantly changing! If you're still using this book and it is 1997 or later, buy the newest edition of Poet's Market *at your favorite bookstore or order directly from* Writer's Digest Books.

Contests and Awards

Though considerably smaller than Publishers of Poetry, this section of *Poet's Market* also contains "markets" for your work. Here you will find various contests and awards whose offerings may include publication of your poetry in addition to their monetary prizes. And even if publication is not included, the publicity generated upon winning some of these contests can make your name more familiar to editors.

Of the 129 listings in this section, two dozen are new to this edition. Included are a wide range of competitions—everything from contests with modest prizes sponsored by state poetry societies, colleges or even cities to prestigious awards offered by private foundations. What you will not find, however, is any contest or award associated with publishers or organizations listed elsewhere in this directory. For those, you should refer to the list of Additional Contests and Awards at the end of this section and consult the listings mentioned there for details.

Selecting contests

Whether you're reading the listings in this section or referring to those in other sections, you should never submit to contests and awards blindly. Since many contests require entry fees, blind submissions will just waste your money. As in the Publishers of Poetry section, each listing here contains one or more Roman numerals in its heading. These "codes" will not only help you narrow the list of contests and awards, but they can also help you evaluate your chances of winning (and recouping your expenses).

The **I** code, for instance, is given to contests that are very open to beginners. While these contests may require small fees, or membership in the sponsoring organization, they typically are not exploitive of poets, beginning or otherwise. Keep in mind, however, that if a contest charges a $5 entry fee and offers $75 in prizes, then the organizers only need 15 entries to cover the prizes. Even though fees may also go toward providing a small honorarium for the judge, 100 entries will surely net the organizers a tidy profit—at the expense of the participating poets. Be careful when deciding which of these contests are worth your money.

The **II** code follows the name of general literary contests, usually for poets with some experience. This code may also follow awards for recently published collections, such as The Poets' Prize and the Kingsley Tufts Poetry Award, or fellowships designed for poets of "demonstrated ability," such as the Guggenheims. If you're just beginning, start building a reputation by having your work accepted by periodicals, then try your hand at these competitions.

Of all the codes, however, perhaps the most useful is **IV**, which designates specialized contests and awards. That is, you—or your poetry—must meet certain criteria to be eligible. Some contests are regional, so only poets from a certain area can enter. For example, fellowships and grants offered by state and provincial arts councils are only open to residents of the particular state or province. Some of these programs are detailed here. For those not found, see the list of State and Provincial Grants at the end of this section.

Other contests are limited to certain groups, such as women or students. For instance, the Andreas-Gryphius-Preis (which is new to this edition) is open only to German-speaking authors. A few contests are for translations only. Still others are limited to poets writing in certain forms. If you write sonnets, for example, consider the Salmon Arm Sonnet Contest. One award limited to a certain subject is the Boardman Tasker Award, which only considers work that deals with the mountain environment. Competitions that primarily consider themselves specialized are often open to both beginning and established poets.

While most of the contests and awards in this section are open to entries, there are a few to which you cannot apply. These are coded **V**, indicating that the winners are chosen by nomination—often by an anonymous committee. See the listing for The Whiting Writers' Awards, for example. We include such awards because winning one is a very high honor and it is not only helpful to know that these awards exist, but it is also important to know that you should not attempt to apply for them.

Once you've narrowed down the contests and awards you want to enter, treat the submission process just as you would if you were submitting to a magazine: Always send a SASE for more information. Many contests want you to submit work along with their specific entry form or application. Others offer guidelines that detail exactly how they want poetry submitted. Also, deadlines for entries are often subject to change and if your work arrives after the deadline date, it may automatically be disqualified.

Finally, request a list of recent winning entries for any contest you are considering. This will give you a good idea of the kind of work the judges appreciate. However, this may not apply if the judges change each year. In either case, we wish you the best of luck!

AAA ANNUAL NATIONAL LITERARY CONTEST; ARIZONA LITERARY MAGAZINE (I), 3509 Shea Blvd., Suite 117-PM, Phoenix AZ 85028-3339, sponsoring organization Arizona Authors' Association, award director Iva Martin. 42 lines maximum, $5 entry fee, submit between January 1 and July 29. Prizes are $125, $75, $40, 6 honorable mentions $10 each. Include SASE with entry for contest results; no material will be returned. Winners are announced and prizes awarded in October. Winning entries are published in a special edition of *Arizona Literary Magazine*. Entries must be typed, double-spaced on 8½×11 paper. Write for more information and entry rules; enclose SASE.

MILTON ACORN POETRY AWARD; PRINCE EDWARD ISLAND LITERARY AWARDS (IV-Regional), The Prince Edward Island Council of the Arts, P.O. Box 2234, Charlottetown, Prince Edward Island C1A 8B9 Canada. Awards are given annually for poetry. Writers must have been resident at least 6 of the 12 months before the contest. Submit November 28 through February 15. For the Milton Acorn Poetry Award, participants may submit as many entries as they wish, each of no more than 10 pgs. Entry fee: $5. Prizes: A trip for 2 via Air Nova to Montreal or Ottawa, first prize; $200 and $100, second and third prizes.

THE AIR CANADA AWARD (IV-Regional), % Canadian Authors Association, 275 Slater St., Suite 500, Ottawa, Ontario K1P 5H9 Canada. The Air Canada Award is an annual award of two tickets to any Air Canada destination, to a Canadian author, published or unpublished, under 30 who shows the most promise. Nominations are made before April 30 by Canadian Authors Association branches or other writers' organizations and the award is given at the CAA banquet in June.

AMERICAN-SCANDINAVIAN FOUNDATION TRANSLATION PRIZE; SCANDINAVIAN REVIEW (IV-Translation), 725 Park Ave., New York NY 10021, for the best translation into English of a work (which may be poetry) of a Scandinavian author after 1800; $2,000, publication in the *Scandinavian Review*, and a bronze medallion. To enter, first request rules. Deadline: June 1.

‡ANDREAS-GRYPHIUS-PREIS; NIKOLAUS-LENAU-PREIS (II, IV-Foreign Language), Die Künstlergilde e.V., Hafenmarkt 2, D-73728, Esslingen a.N., Germany, phone 0711/3969 01-0. "The prize is given annually to German-speaking authors who are dealing with the particular problems of the German culture in eastern Europe. The prize is given to the best published literary works (which may be poems) that promote understanding between Germans and eastern Europeans." Prizes awarded: 1 Grand Prize of DM 15,000; 3 prizes of DM 7,000. Submissions judged by an 8-member jury. They also sponsor the Nikolaus-Lenau-Preis for German-speaking poets. The prize is named in honor of Nikolaus Lenau, "a poet who facilitated understanding with the people of eastern Europe." The prize of DM 12,000 is awarded in 3 parts. Only 3 unpublished poems/entrant. Write for details.

ARIZONA STATE POETRY SOCIETY ANNUAL CONTEST (I, II, IV), 317 Hackney Ave., Globe AZ 85501, co-directors Audrey Opitz and Pat Blanco. Contest for various poetry forms and subjects. Prizes range from $10-75; first, second and third place winners are published in the winter edition of *The Sandcutters*, the group's quarterly publication, and names are listed for honorable mention winners. Contest information available for SASE. Fees vary. Deadline: August 31.

ARKANSAS POETRY DAY CONTEST; POETS' ROUNDTABLE OF ARKANSAS (I), over 25 categories, many open to all poets. Brochure available in June; deadline in September; awards given in October. For copy send SASE to Verna Lee Hinegardner, 605 Higdon, Apt. 109, Hot Springs AR 71913.

ARTIST TRUST; ARTIST TRUST GAP GRANTS; ARTIST TRUST FELLOWSHIPS (IV-Regional), 1402 Third Ave., Suite 404, Seattle WA 98101, phone (206)467-8734. Artist Trust is a nonprofit arts organization that provides grants to artists (including poets) who are residents of the state. It also publishes, three times a year, a 16-page journal of news about arts opportunities and cultural issues.

‡ARTS RECOGNITION AND TALENT SEARCH (ARTS) (II, IV-Students), National Foundation for Advancement in the Arts, 800 Brickell Ave., Suite 500, Miami FL 33131, phone (305)377-1140, president Dr. William H. Banchs. "ARTS is a national program designed to identify, recognize and encourage young people who demonstrate excellence in Dance, Music, Music/Jazz, Music/Voice, Theater, Visual Arts, Photography and Writing." Offers annual awards of $3,000 (Level 1), $1,500 (Level 2), $1,000 (Level 3), $500 (Level 4) and $100 (Level 5). Submit up to 6 poems in up to but not more than 10 pgs. Open to high school seniors and young people aged 17 or 18 by December 1 of the award year. Send SASE for entry form and guidelines. Entry fee: $25 (June 1 early application deadline), $35 (October 1 regular application deadline).

ARVON INTERNATIONAL POETRY COMPETITION (I, II), Kilnhurst, Kilnhurst Rd., Todmorden, Lancashire OL14 6AX England, phone 01706 816582, fax 01706 816359, jointly sponsored by Duncan Lawrie Limited and *The Observer*. Poems (which may be of any length and previously unpublished) must be in English. First prize is £5,000 ($8,425), and other cash prizes. The competition is biennial. Distinguished poets serve as judges. Though the contest (which raises funds by entry fees) may be better known internationally, the major function of the Arvon Foundation is to offer writing courses at three retreats: at Totleight Barton, Sheepwash, Beaworthy, Devon EX21 5NS, phone 01409 231338; at Lumb Bank, Hebden Bridge, West Yorkshire HX7 6DF, phone (01422) 843714; and at Moniack Mhor, Teavarran, Kiltarlity, Beauly, Inverness-shire 1V4 7HT, phone (01463) 741675. These are residential programs at attractive country retreats, offered by established writers in subjects such as poetry, playwriting, short fiction, radio drama, and words and music. The tuition is £260 for, typically, 5 days, which includes tuition, food and accommodations, and there is scholarship available from the foundation for those who cannot otherwise afford to attend.

‡B.C.L.A. TRANSLATION COMPETITION (I, IV-Translations), British Comparative Literature Association, St. John's College, Oxford OX1 3JP England, phone 0865-277381, award director Dr. N.J. Crowe, offers annual awards of £350 1st prize and £150 2nd prize, plus other prizes in special restricted categories. Submissions must be unpublished. Submit 25 typed pgs., any subject, any form. Submit SASE (or SAE and IRCs) for entry form and guidelines. Entry fee £3/entry. Deadline: January 15, 1996. "Winning translations are guaranteed publication in U.K., as well as prize. The competition enjoys worldwide prestige."

‡BARNARD NEW WOMEN POETS PRIZE; WOMEN POETS AT BARNARD; BARNARD NEW WOMEN POETS SERIES; BEACON PRESS (IV-Women), Barnard College of Columbia University, 3009 Broadway, New York NY 10027-6598. Women Poets at Barnard holds open competition and annual series. The winner receives an award of $1,000 and publication in the Barnard New Women Poets Series, Beacon Press. The competition is open to any woman poet with a book-length ms who has not yet published a book (exclusive of chapbooks). Deadline: October 1. Send SASE for guidelines.

‡BAVARIAN ACADEMY OF FINE ARTS LITERATURE PRIZE (V), Max Joseph-Platz 3, 80539 Munich, Germany. An award of DM 30,000 given annually to an author in the German language, to honor a distinguished literary career—**by nomination only**.

GEORGE BENNETT FELLOWSHIP (II), Phillips Exeter Academy, 20 Main St., Exeter NH 03833-2460, provides a $5,000 fellowship plus room and board to a writer with a ms in progress. The Fellow's only official duties are to be in residence while the academy is in session and to be available to students interested in writing. The committee favors writers who have not yet published a book-length work with a major publisher. Send SASE for application materials. Telephone calls strongly discouraged. Deadline: December 1.

‡THE BOARDMAN TASKER AWARD (IV-Specialized: mountain literature), The Boardman Tasker Memorial Trust, 14 Pine Lodge, Dairyground Rd., Bramhall, Stockport, Cheshire SK7 2HS United Kingdom, secretary Dorothy Boardman, offers prize of £2,000 to "the author or authors of the best literary work, whether fiction, nonfiction, drama or poetry, the central theme of which is concerned with the mountain environment. Entries for consideration may have been written by authors of any nationality but the work must be published or distributed in the United Kingdom between November 1, 1995 and October 31, 1996. The work must be written or have been translated into the English language." Submit ms in book format. "In a collection of essays or articles by a single author, the inclusion of some material previously published but now in book form for the first time will be acceptable." Submissions accepted from the publisher only. Four copies of entry must be submitted with application. Deadline: August 1, 1996.

BOLLINGEN PRIZE (V), Beinecke Rare Book and Manuscript Library, Yale University, New Haven CT 06520, prize of $25,000 to an American poet for the best poetry collection published during the previous two years, or for a body of poetry written over several years. **By nomination only.** Judges change biennially. Announcements in February of odd-numbered years.

BUCKNELL SEMINAR FOR YOUNGER POETS; STADLER SEMESTER FOR YOUNGER POETS (IV-Students), Bucknell University, Lewisburg PA 17837, phone (717)524-1853, director John Wheatcroft, includes the Stadler Semester for Younger Poets, the Seminar for Younger Poets and the Poet-in-Residence Series. The Stadler Semester is distinctive in allowing undergraduate poets almost four months of concentrated work centered in poetry. Guided by practicing poets, the apprentice will write and read poetry and will receive critical response. The two Fellows selected will work with Bucknell's writing faculty. The visiting Poet-in-Residence also will participate in the program. Fellows will earn a semester of academic credit by taking four units of study: a tutorial or individual project with a mentor poet, a poetry-writing workshop, a literature course, and an elective. Undergraduates from four-year colleges with at least one course in poetry writing are eligible to apply; most applicants will be second-semester juniors. Send a 10- to 12-page portfolio and a letter of presentation (a brief autobiography that expresses commitment to writing poetry, cites relevant courses and lists any publications). Also include a transcript, two recommendations (at least one from a poetry-writing instructor), and a letter from the academic dean granting permission for the student to attend Bucknell for a semester. Application deadline for the Stadler Semester is November 1. Students chosen for the fellowships will be notified by November 25. The Bucknell Seminar For Younger Poets is not a contest for poems but for 10 fellowships to the Bucknell Seminar, held for 4 weeks in June every year. Seniors and juniors from American colleges are eligible to compete for the 10 fellowships, which consist of tuition, room, board, and spaces for writing. Application deadline for each year's seminar is March 1. Students chosen for fellowships will be notified by April 8. Please write for details.

THE BUNTING FELLOWSHIP PROGRAM (IV-Women), Radcliffe College, 34 Concord Ave., Cambridge MA 02138, phone (617)495-8212, supports women of exceptional promise and demonstrated accomplishment who want to pursue independent study in the creative arts (among other things). The stipend is $33,000 for a fellowship fulltime September 15 through August 15, requiring residence in the Boston area. Awards 6-10 fellowships. Applicants in creative arts should be at the equivalent stage in their careers as women who have received doctorates two years before applying. Deadline is early October.

CALIFORNIA WRITERS' ROUNDTABLE POETRY CONTEST (I), under the auspices of the Los Angeles Chapter, Women's National Book Association, Lou Carter Keay, chairman, 11684 Ventura Blvd., Suite 807, Studio City CA 91614-2652. Annual contest with $50, $25 and $10 cash prizes for unpublished poems on any subject, in various forms, not more than 42 lines in length. WNBA members may submit free; nonmembers pay $3/poem entry fee. Send SASE for guidelines. Deadline: September 30.

CANADIAN AUTHORS ASSOCIATION LITERARY AWARDS; CANADIAN AUTHORS ASSOCIATION (IV-Regional), 275 Slater St., Suite 500, Ottawa, Ontario K1P 5H9 Canada, $5,000 in each of 4 categories (fiction, poetry, nonfiction, drama) to Canadian writers, for a published book in the year of publication (or, in the case of drama, first produced), deadline December 15. Nominations may be made by authors, publishers, agents or others. (Also see The Air Canada Award in this section.)

CAPRICORN POETRY AWARD (II); OPEN VOICE AWARDS (I, II); THE WRITER'S VOICE, Writer's Voice, 5 W. 63rd St., New York NY 10023. Capricorn Poetry Award, a cash prize of $1,000 and a reading at The Writer's Voice, limited to writers over 40. $15 entry fee. Deadline: December 31. Send SASE for application guidelines. Open Voice Awards, annual awards, $500 honorarium and a reading at The Writer's Voice, open to both published and unpublished poets who have not previously read at The Writer's Voice. $10 entry fee. Deadline: December 31. Send SASE for application form. The Writer's

Voice is a literary center sponsoring weekly readings, writing workshops, writing awards and other activities.

CINTAS FELLOWSHIP PROGRAM (IV-Regional), Arts International, Institute of International Education, 809 United Nations Plaza, New York NY 10017, makes awards of $10,000 to young professional writers and artists of Cuban lineage living outside of Cuba. Call (212)984-5370, ext. 5588, for applications and guidelines. Deadline for applications: March 1.

CLARK COLLEGE POETRY CONTEST (I), % Arlene Paul, 4312 NE 40th St., Vancouver WA 98661, jointly sponsored by Clark College, The Oregon State Poetry Association and Washington Poetry Association. $3/poem entry fee (checks payable to Clark College Foundation), prizes of $50, $75 and $100, for poems up to 25 lines, unpublished, not having won another contest. Entries in triplicate, not identified. Type name, address and phone number on a 3 × 5 card, include title and first line on card. May purchase book of winners' poems for $3 plus $1 postage. Deadline: February 10. (For information about The Oregon State Poetry Association, see listing in Organizations Useful to Poets.)

INA COOLBRITH CIRCLE ANNUAL POETRY CONTEST (IV-Regional), Audrey Allison, Treasurer, 2712 Oak Rd., #54, Walnut Creek CA 94596, has prizes of $10-50 in each of several categories for California residents and out-of-state members only. Three poems per contestant, but no more than 1 poem in any one category. Poems submitted in 2 copies, include name, address, phone number and member status on 1 copy only. Enclose a 3 × 5 card with name, address, phone number, category, title, first line of poem and status as member or nonmember. Members of the Ina Coolbrith Circle pay no fee; others pay $5 for 3 poems (limit 3). Send SASE for details. Deadline is August.

ABBIE M. COPPS POETRY COMPETITION; GARFIELD LAKE REVIEW (I, II), contest chairperson Linda Jo Scott, Dept. of Humanities, Olivet College, Olivet MI 49076, phone (616)749-7683. Annual contest awarding $150 prize and publication in the *Garfield Lake Review*. $2/poem entry fee for unpublished poem up to 100 lines. Submit unsigned, typed poem, entrance fee, and name, address and phone number in a sealed envelope with the first line of the poem on the outside. Judge to be announced. Deadline: February 15.

COUNCIL FOR WISCONSIN WRITERS, INC. (IV-Regional), Box 55322, Madison WI 53705. Offers annual awards of $500 or more for a book of poetry by a Wisconsin resident, published within the awards year (preceding the January 13 deadline). Entry form and entry fee ($10 for members of the Council, $25 for others) required.

HART CRANE AWARD (II), English Dept., Kent State University, Trumbull Campus, 4314 Mahoning Ave. NW, Warren OH 44483, phone (216)847-0571, founded 1966, contact Dr. Robert Brown, is an annual poetry award of $100 given in March. Submit no more than 3 poems with SASE. Do not query. Judging is done by a committee of English professors. Deadline: February 1.

CREATIVE ARTIST PROGRAM (IV-Regional), Cultural Arts Council of Houston/Harris County, 1964 West Gray, Suite 224, Houston TX 77019-4808, phone (713)527-9330. Offers annual awards of $5,000 to Houston visual artists, writers, choreographers and composers selected through an annual competition. The program also offers Artist Project grants. Deadline for entry is in the fall. Write for application forms and guidelines.

‡CREATIVE WRITING FELLOWSHIPS IN POETRY (II, IV-Regional), Arizona Commission on the Arts, 417 W. Roosevelt St., Phoenix AZ 85003, phone (602)255-5882, literature director Tonda Gorton, offers biennial prizes of $5,000-7,500. Next poetry fellowships awarded in 1997. Submissions can be previously published or unpublished, and can be entered in other contests. Submit 10 pgs. maximum on any subject. Open to Arizona residents over 18 years old. Send SASE for entry form. Entry deadline is tentatively set for September 1996.

DALY CITY POETRY AND SHORT STORY CONTEST (I), Serramonte Library, 40 Wembley Dr., Daly City CA 94015. Contest held annually, awarding prizes of $35, $25, $20, $15 and $10 in various categories and $5 for honorable mention. Entry fee of $1/poem or $2/story. Stories must be unpublished. Send SASE for rules; attn: Ruth Hoppin, coordinator. Contest opens September 1. Postmark deadline: January 4.

BILLEE MURRAY DENNY POETRY AWARD (II), % Janet Overton, Lincoln College, 300 Keokuk St., Lincoln IL 62656. Annual award with prizes of $1,000, $500 and $250. Open to poets who have not previously published a book of poetry with a commercial or university press (except for chapbooks with a circulation of less than 250). Enter up to 3 poems, 100 lines/poem or less at $10/poem. Poems may be on any subject, using any style, but may not contain "any vulgar, obscene, suggestive or offensive word or phrase." Entry form and fees payable to Poetry Contest, Lincoln College. Winning poems are published in *The Denny Poems*, a biennial anthology, available for $4 from Lincoln College. Send SASE for entry form. Deadline: May 31 postmark.

MILTON DORFMAN NATIONAL POETRY PRIZE (II), % Rome Art & Community Center, 308 W. Bloomfield St., Rome NY 13440. Annual award for unpublished poetry. Winners for 1994: Carolyne Wright, first place; Tony Barnstone, second place; and Joyce Le Mers, third place. Judge for 1994 was Bruce Berlind. Prizes: $500, $200 and $100. Entry fee $3/poem (American funds only; $10 returned check penalty); checks made payable to: Rome Art & Community Center. Include name, address and phone number on each entry. Poems are printed in Center's Newsletter. Contest opens July 1. Deadline: November 1. Winners are notified by December 1. Send SASE for results.

‡FLORIDA INDIVIDUAL ARTIST FELLOWSHIPS (II, IV-Regional), Florida Division of Cultural Affairs, Dept. of State, The Capitol, Tallahassee FL 32399-0250, phone (904)487-2980, annually offers an undetermined number of fellowships in the amount of $5,000 each. "The Individual Artist Fellowship Program is designed to recognize practicing professional creative artists residing in Florida through monetary fellowship awards. The program provides support for artists of exceptional talent and demonstrated ability to improve their artistic skills and enhance their careers. Fellowships may be awarded in the following discipline categories: dance, folk-arts, interdisciplinary, literature, media arts, music, theatre and visual arts and crafts." Submissions can be previously published or unpublished. Submit 3-5 representative poems, single or double-spaced. "Reproductions of published work may not be submitted in published format. Open to Florida residents of at least 18 years of age who are not matriculated undergraduate or graduate students. Seven copies of the work sample, with Indentification Sheet and Artist's Statement attached to the front of each copy, must be included with 7 copies of the application form. Write for entry form and guidelines. Deadline: January 25.

FOSTER CITY WRITERS' CONTEST (II), F.C. Arts & Culture Committee, 650 Shell Blvd., Foster City CA 94404, phone (415)345-5731. Yearly competition for previously unpublished work. $10 entry fee, $250 prize. Send SASE for instructions. Deadline: November 1. Awards announced January 15.

FRIENDS OF DOG WATCH OPEN POETRY COMPETITION (I), 267 Hillbury Rd., Warlingham, Surrey CR6 9TL England, phone 01883-622121, contact Michaela Edridge. Annual competition for poems up to 40 lines. Cash prizes. Entry fees: £2/poem. Contest information available for SASE (or SAE and IRCs). Deadline: January 1.

ROBERT FROST CHAPTER: CALIFORNIA FEDERATION OF CHAPARRAL POETS ANNUAL POETRY COMPETITION (I, IV-Students), % Vivian Moody, 342 S. Redwood Ave., San Jose CA 95128. This annual contest has 6 categories with annual changes as to form or fee, limited to 2 entries per category. Prizes are $25, $15 and $10 in each category. Entry fee $2, plus $1/poem for nonmembers. Submissions may be previously published. Award poems not eligible. Open to residents of Canada and US. Deadline first half of August. The parent federation also sponsors monthly contests listed in the Chapter's *Frostorial N/L* published since 1963. Affiliation through the chapter includes state activities with yearly convention/award banquet in which the Golden Pegasus is awarded, terminating competitions since 1940.

GEORGIA STATE POETRY SOCIETY, INC.; BYRON HERBERT REECE AND EDWARD DAVIN VICKERS INTERNATIONAL AWARDS; THE REACH OF SONG ANNUAL ANTHOLOGY; GEORGIA STATE POETRY SOCIETY NEWSLETTER (I, IV-Anthologies, form), P.O. Box 120, Epworth GA 30541-0120. The society sponsors a number of contests open to all poets, described in its quarterly newsletter (membership $20/year). Sponsors an annual anthology, *The Reach of Song*. The Byron Herbert Reece and the Edward Davin Vickers International Awards have prizes of $250, $100, $50, $25, $15 and $10. Entry fee: $5 first poem, $1 each additional. Deadline: January 31, Reece Awards; July 31, Vickers Awards. Send SASE for guidelines. Sample newsletter: $2; *Reach of Song:* $10.

JOHN GLASSCO TRANSLATION PRIZE (IV-Translation, regional), Literary Translators' Association of Canada, 3492, avenue Laval, Montreal, Quebec H2X 3C8 Canada. $1,000 awarded annually for a translator's first book-length literary translation into French or English, published in Canada during the previous calendar year. The translator must be a Canadian citizen or landed immigrant. Eligible genres include fiction, creative nonfiction, poetry, published plays and children's books. Write for application form. Deadline: February 15.

GREEN RIVERS WRITERS' CONTESTS (I, IV-Themes, forms), Contest Chairman, 1043 Thornfield Lane, Cincinnati OH 45224, offers 6 contests for poetry on various themes and in various forms. Send SASE for rules. Entry fee $3/poem for nonmembers, prizes from $5-75. Deadline: October 31.

GROLIER POETRY PRIZE; ELLEN LA FORGE MEMORIAL POETRY FOUNDATION, INC. (II, IV-Themes), 6 Plympton St., Cambridge MA 02138, phone (617)547-4648, award director Louisa Solano. The Grolier Poetry Prize is open to all poets who have not published either a vanity, small press, trade or chapbook of poetry. Two poets receive an honorarium of $150 each. Up to 4 poems by each winner and 1-2 by each of 4 runners-up are chosen for publication in the *Grolier Poetry Prize Annual*. Opens January 15 of each year; deadline May 1. Submit up to 5 poems, not more than 10 double-spaced pages. Submit one ms in duplicate, without name of poet. On a separate sheet give name, address, phone number and titles of poems. Only 1 submission/contestant; mss are not returned. $6 entry fee includes copy of *Annual*, checks payable to the Ellen La Forge Memorial Poetry Foundation, Inc. Enclose self-addressed stamped postcard if acknowledgement of receipt is required. For update of rules, send SASE to Ellen La Forge Memorial Poetry Foundation before submitting mss. The Ellen La Forge Memorial Poetry Foundation sponsors intercollegiate poetry readings and a reading series, generally 10/semester, held on the grounds of Harvard University. These are generally poets who have new collections of poetry available for sale at the Grolier Poetry Book Shop, Inc., which donates money toward costs (such as rental of the auditorium). They pay poets honoraria from $100-400 and occasionally provide overnight accommodations (but not transportation). Such poets as Mark Strand, Philip Levine, Robin Becker, Donald Hall and Brigit Pegeen Kelly have given readings under their auspices. The small foundation depends upon private gifts and support for its activities.

GUGGENHEIM FELLOWSHIPS (II), John Simon Guggenheim Memorial Foundation, 90 Park Ave., New York NY 10016. Approximately 152 Guggenheims are awarded each year to persons who have already demonstrated exceptional capacity for productive scholarship or exceptional creative ability in the arts. The amounts of the grants vary. The average grant is about $28,000. Application deadline: October 1.

HACKNEY LITERARY AWARDS; BIRMINGHAM-SOUTHERN COLLEGE WRITER'S CONFERENCE (II), Birmingham-Southern College, Box A-3, Birmingham AL 35254. This competition, sponsored by the Cecil Hackney family since 1969, offers $4,000 in prizes for novels, poetry and short stories as part of the annual Birmingham-Southern Writer's Conference. Novels postmarked by September 30. Poems and short stories must be postmarked by December 31. Send SASE for Hackney guidelines. Winners are announced at the conference, which is held in the spring. (Also see Writing Today in Conferences and Workshops.)

THE HODDER FELLOWSHIP (II), The Council of the Humanities, 122 E. Pyne, Princeton University, Princeton NJ 08544, is awarded for the pursuit of independent work in the humanities. The recipient is usually a writer or scholar in the early stages of his or her career, a person "with more than ordinary learning" and with "much more than ordinary intellectual and literary gifts." Traditionally, the Hodder Fellow has been a humanist outside of academia. **Candidates for the Ph.D. are not eligible.** The Hodder Fellow spends an academic year in residence at Princeton working independently. He or she may choose to present a lecture to students and faculty in the humanities. Applicants must submit a résumé, sample of previous work (10 pgs. maximum, not returnable), a project proposal of 2 to 3 pgs., and a SASE. The announcement of the Hodder Fellow is made in February by the President of Princeton University. Deadline: November 15.

HENRY HOYNS FELLOWSHIPS (II), Dept. of English, University of Virginia, Charlottesville VA 22903, are fellowships in poetry and fiction of varying amounts for candidates for the M.F.A. in creative writing. Sample poems/prose required with application. Deadline: February 1.

IRISH AMERICAN CULTURAL INSTITUTE LITERARY AWARDS (IV-Ethnic, foreign language), Mail #5026, 2115 Summit Ave., St. Paul MN 55105, for Irish writers who write in Irish or English, **resident in Ireland,** with published work. A total of $10,000 in prizes awarded every year.

JOHANN-HEINRICH-VOSS PRIZE FOR TRANSLATION (V), German Academy for Language and Literature, Alexandraweg 23, 64287 Darmstadt, Germany, is an annual award of DM 20,000 for outstanding lifetime achievement for translating into German, **by nomination only**. 1993: Roswitha Matwin-Büschmann. 1994: Werner von Koppenfels. 1995: Rosemarie Tietze.

THE CHESTER H. JONES FOUNDATION NATIONAL POETRY COMPETITION (II), P.O. Box 498, Chardon OH 44024, an annual competition for persons in the USA, Canadian and American citizens living abroad. Prizes: $1,000, $750, $500, $250, and $50 honorable mentions. Winning poems plus others called "commendations" are published in a chapbook available for $3.50 from the foundation. Entry fee $2 for the first poem, $1 each for others, no more than 10 entries, no more than 32 lines each. Distinguished poets serve as judges. Deadline: March 31.

‡KENTUCKY ARTISTS FELLOWSHIPS (II, IV-Regional), Kentucky Arts Council, 31 Fountain Place, Frankfort KY 40601, award director Irwin Pickett, offers biennial fellowships of $5,000 to "encourage excellence and assist Kentucky artists in the professional development of their various art forms and careers." Fellowship recipients will be selected by a panel of out-of-state professional artists in a "blind jurying" process. Submit 15 pgs. of poetry maximum, 1 poem/page. Open to Kentucky residents who have lived in the state one year immediately prior to the fellowship application deadline. Send SASE for entry form. Deadline: September 15, 1996.

LAMPMAN AWARD (IV-Regional); OTTAWA INDEPENDENT WRITERS, 265 Elderberry Terrace, Orleans, Ontario K1E 1Z2 Canada, phone (613)841-0572, is a $400 award for a published book of English-language poetry by writers in the National Capital region. Submit 3 copies of each title by February 28. Membership in Ottawa Independent Writers is $60/year, and offers their newsletter, programs, an entry in the OIW Directory and registration at reduced fees for workshops.

‡LATINO LITERATURE PRIZE (IV-Ethnic/Nationality), Latin American Writers Institute, Hostos Community College, 500 Grand Concourse, Bronx NY 10451, phone (718)518-4195, award director Isaac Goldemberg, offers annual prize of $1,000. Submissions must be previously published and can be entered in other contests. Only open to books by Latino authors living in the US—in English or Spanish. Send SASE for guidelines. Deadline: February 28. The Institute also publishes *Brújula/Compass*, a bilingual journal devoted to Latino writing in the US.

THE STEPHEN LEACOCK MEDAL FOR HUMOUR (IV-Humor, regional), award chairman, Mrs. Jean Bradley Dickson, Stephen Leacock Associates, P.O. Box 854, Orillia, Ontario L3V 3P4 Canada, phone (705)325-6546, for a book of humor in prose, verse, drama or any book form—by a Canadian citizen. Submit 10 copies of book, 8×10 b&w photo, bio and $25 entry fee. Prize: Silver Leacock Medal for Humour and Manulife Bank cash award of $5,000. Deadline: December 31. The committee also publishes *The Newspacket* 3 times/year.

THE LEAGUE OF MINNESOTA POETS CONTEST (I, IV-Students), % Robert Temple, 1011 Cottage Place, St. Paul MN 55126. Offers 20 different contests in a variety of categories and prizes of $5-75 for poems up to 55 lines, fees of $3 to enter all categories for members and $1/category for nonmembers. There is one category for students in grades 7 through 12 and one category for elementary students through grade 6. Deadline: July 31. Winners are not published. Write for details.

LETRAS DE ORO SPANISH LITERARY PRIZES (IV-Foreign language), Iberian Studies Institute, North-South Center, University of Miami, P.O. Box 248123, Coral Gables FL 33124, fax (305)284-4406. Awards include a general prize of $2,500 and publication of the book-length entry. For creative excellence in poetry written in the Spanish language. Write for guidelines. Deadline: October 12.

AMY LOWELL POETRY TRAVELLING SCHOLARSHIP (II), Trust u/w/o Amy Lowell, Exchange Place, 34th Floor, Choate, Hall & Stewart, Boston MA 02109-2891, award director F. Davis Dassori, Jr., Trustee, is an annual award of $29,000 (more-or-less: the amount varies annually), to an American-born "advanced" poet who agrees to live outside of North America for the year of the grant. Deadline for application: October 15. Requests for applications must be received by October 1.

‡MACARTHUR FELLOWS (V), John D. and Catherine T. MacArthur Foundation, 140 S. Dearborn St., Suite 1100, Chicago IL 60603. "The MacArthur Fellows Program provides unique, unrestricted fellowships to exceptionally talented and promising individuals who have given evidence of originality, dedication to creative pursuits, and capacity for self-direction. MacArthur Fellows receive an income in quarterly installments over five years so that they may have the time and freedom to fulfill their promise by devoting themselves to their own endeavors at their own pace. The fellowships are intended to support individuals, not projects." **Fellows are selected by an anonymous group of 100 nominators from across the country. Applications and informal nominations are not accepted.** Fellowships range from $30,000-75,000 annually plus comprehensive health insurance.

MASSACHUSETTS STATE POETRY SOCIETY, INC.; ANNUAL NATIONAL POETRY DAY CONTEST; ANNUAL GERTRUDE DOLE MEMORIAL CONTEST (I), %Jeanette C. Maes, President, 64 Harrison Ave., Lynn MA 01905, both contests are open to all poets. The National Poetry Day Contest, with a August 1 deadline, offers prizes of $25, $15 and $10 (or higher) for each of 25 or more categories; $3 fee for entire contest. The Gertrude Dole Memorial Contest, deadline March 1, offers prizes of $25, $15 and $10; $1 entry fee, one prize/poet. Send SASE for contest flyer.

FREDERIC G. MELCHER BOOK AWARD (V, IV-Religious), 25 Beacon St., Boston MA 02108, is an annual $1,000 prize for a book making a significant contribution to religious liberalism. **Books are nominated by Melcher judges.**

‡MID-LIST PRESS FIRST POETRY SERIES AWARD (I), Mid-List Press, 4324 12th Ave. S., Minneapolis MN 55407-3218, phone (612)822-3733, senior editor Lane Stiles. "Our First Poetry Series Award is an annual contest we sponsor for poets who have never published a book of poetry. The award includes publication and an advance against royalties. The award winner is the only poetry we publish." Individual poems within the book manuscript can be previously published and can be entered in other contests. Submit at least 65 single-spaced pages. "Other than length we have no restrictions, but poets are encouraged to read previous award winners we have published." Recent award winners include Jeff Worley, Neil Shepard, Douglas Gray, Stephen Behrendt and Mary Logue. Submissions are circulated to an editorial board. Send SASE for guidelines. Entry fee: $10. Accepts submissions November 1 through February 1. "The First Series Award contest is highly competitive. We are looking for poets who have produced a significant body of work, but have never published a book-length collection. (A chapbook is not considered a 'book' of poetry.)"

MILFORD FINE ARTS COUNCIL NATIONAL POETRY CONTEST (I, II), 40 Railroad Ave. S., Milford CT 06460, contest chairperson Emma J. Blanch, offers an annual award open to adults in the US. Submissions must be unpublished and have not received any other awards. Submit no more than 5 typed poems, single spaced. The contest awards 3 prizes of $50, $30 and $20 plus publication in *High Tide*, an annual literary magazine published by the Milford Fine Arts Council. Winners will receive a complimentary copy. Send SASE for rules. Entry fee: $2 for the first entry, $1 for each additional. Open to entries September 15 through January 31.

MISSISSIPPI VALLEY POETRY CONTEST (I, II, IV), sponsored by North American Literary Escadrille, P.O. Box 3188, Rock Island IL 61204, director S. Katz, annually offers prizes of approximately $1,400 for unpublished poems in categories for students (elementary, junior and senior high), adults, Mississippi Valley, senior citizens, jazz, religious, humorous, rhyming, haiku, ethnic and history. Fee: $5 for 1-5 poems; 50 lines/poem limit. Fee for children: $3 for 1-5 poems. Professional readers read winning poems before a reception at an award evening in May. Deadline: April 1.

‡MISSOURI WRITERS' BIENNIAL AWARD (II, IV-Regional), Missouri Arts Council, 111 N. Seventh St., Suite 105, St. Louis MO 63101, phone (314)340-6845, award director Michael Hunt, offers biennial award of $5,000 plus publication in an anthology. Submissions must be unpublished. Submit 12 typed pgs. Open to Missouri residents over 21 years old. Send SASE for guidelines. Deadline: August 1997.

MONEY FOR WOMEN (IV-Women/feminism), Barbara Deming Memorial Fund, Inc., Box 40-1043, Brooklyn NY 11240-1043, fund administrator Pam McAllister, provides small grants to feminists in the arts. Subjects include women, peace, justice issues. Send SASE for application form. Applicants must be citizens of US or Canada. Deadlines: December 31 and June 30.

MONTANA ARTS FOUNDATION POETRY CONTEST; MARY BRENNEN CLAPP MEMORIAL AWARD (IV-Regional), P.O. Box 1872, Bozeman MT 59771, annual contest with a September 15 deadline. Open to Montana poets only, for 3 unpublished poems up to 100 lines total. Mary Brennen Clapp Memorial Award of $50 and prizes of $40, $30 and $20. Must submit 3 poems and cover letter. Send SASE for guidelines.

JENNY MCKEAN MOORE FUND FOR WRITERS (II), Dept. of English, George Washington University, Washington DC 20052, provides for a visiting lecturer in creative writing for about $40,000 for 2 semesters. Apply by November 15 with résumé and writing sample of 25 pgs. or less. Awarded to poets and fiction writers in alternating years.

‡NATIONAL BOOK AWARD (II), National Book Foundation, 260 Fifth Ave., Room 904, New York NY 10001, phone (212)685-0261, award directors Neil Baldwin, Meg Kearney and Kevin LaFollette, offers annual grand prize of $10,000 plus 4 finalist awards of $1,000. Submissions must be previously published and **must be entered by the publisher**. Send SASE for entry form and guidelines. Entry fee $100/title. Deadline: July 15.

NATIONAL ENDOWMENT FOR THE ARTS; FELLOWSHIPS FOR CREATIVE WRITERS; FELLOWSHIPS FOR TRANSLATORS (II), Literature Program, Room 722, Nancy Hanks Center, 1100 Pennsylvania Ave. NW, Washington DC 20506, phone (202)682-5451. Fellowships for Creative Writers is the largest program of individual grants for American writers of poetry, fiction and creative nonfiction. Awards of $20,000 are made each year to published writers. Applications are reviewed and recommendations for funding are made by an advisory panel composed of experts from the literature field. In reviewing applications, advisory panelists consider solely the literary quality of the manuscripts submitted. To be eligible, a poet must have in publication a volume of at least 48 pages, or 20 or more poems or pages of poetry in five or more literary publications in the last 10 years. A limited number of $10,000 fellowship grants are awarded to published translators of creative literature for translation projects from other languages into English. Matching grants are also available to nonprofit organizations for publishing and audience development projects, residencies and reading series, and services to writers and literary organizations. Phone or write for guidelines and application for ms for 1997. Anticipated deadlines: January 1996 for 1997 translation fellowships; March 1996 for 1997 poetry fellowships.

‡NATIONAL POETRY SERIES ANNUAL OPEN COMPETITION (II), P.O. Box G, Hopewell NJ 08525, between January 1 and February 15 considers book-length (approximately 48-64 pgs.) mss. Entry fee $25. Manuscripts will not be returned. The 5 winners receive $1,000 each and are published by participating small press, university press and trade publishers. Send SASE for complete submissions procedures.

NATIONAL WRITERS ASSOCIATION ANNUAL POETRY CONTEST (I), 1450 S. Havana, Suite 424, Aurora CO 80012, award director Sandy Whelchel, an annual contest with prizes of $100, $50 and $25. Entry fee $8/poem; additional fee charged if poem is longer than 40 lines. All subjects and forms are acceptable. Deadline: October 1.

NATIONAL WRITERS UNION ANNUAL NATIONAL POETRY COMPETITION (II), P.O. Box 2409, Aptos CA 95001, phone (408)457-7488. See National Writers Union listing under Organizations Useful to Poets. The Santa Cruz/Monterey Local 7 chapter at this address sponsors an annual competition with entry fee: $3/poem; prizes of $200, $100 and $50, with prominent poets as judges. Send SASE for rules beginning in April.

THE NATIONAL WRITTEN & ILLUSTRATED BY . . . AWARDS CONTEST FOR STUDENTS; LANDMARK EDITIONS (IV-Students), P.O. Box 4469, Kansas City MO 64127, award director David Melton, is an annual contest for unpublished work for a book written and illustrated by a student. Three books published, one from each of 3 age categories (6-9; 10-13; 14-19). Send #10 SAE with 60¢ postage for rules.

NEUSTADT INTERNATIONAL PRIZE FOR LITERATURE; WORLD LITERATURE TODAY (V), University of Oklahoma, 110 Monnet Hall, 630 Parrington Oval, Norman OK 73019-0375. Award of $40,000 given every other year in recognition of life achievement or to a writer whose work is still in progress; **nominations from an international jury only**.

‡NEW JERSEY STATE COUNCIL ON THE ARTS FELLOWSHIP PROGRAM (II, IV-Regional), CN 306, 20 W. State St., Trenton NJ 08625, phone (609)292-6130, award director Steven R. Runk, offers annual fellowship grants that currently range between $5,000-12,000. Submissions can be previously published or unpublished and can be entered in other contests. Submit 7 pgs. maximum; any subject, any style. Open to New Jersey residents, except matriculated undergraduate and graduate students. Send SASE for entry form and guidelines. Deadline is mid-December of each year.

NEW YORK FOUNDATION FOR THE ARTS (IV-Regional), 155 Avenue of Americas, 14th Floor, New York NY 10013, phone (212)366-6900, ext. 217, offers fellowships of $7,000 every other year for poets who are at least 18 and have resided in New York State for 2 years prior to application. Submit up to 10 pages of poetry (at least 2 poems), 3 copies of a 1-page résumé, and an application form. Call for application form in June. Deadline is October.

NORDMANNS-FORBUNDET TRANSLATION GRANT (IV-Translation), NORLA, Bygdoy Allé 21, 0262 Oslo, Norway. In its desire to make Norwegian culture known abroad, the Nordmanns-Forbundet awards an annual grant (maximum 15,000 Norwegian crowns) to one or more publishing houses introducing Norwegian fiction or poetry in translation (preferably contemporary). Applications should be sent to NORLA (The Office for Norwegian Literature Abroad), and future decisions will be made by NORLA's Literary Advisory Board. Mark the application "Nordmanns-Forbundet's translation grant." Deadline: December 15.

THE NORTH CAROLINA POETRY SOCIETY ZOE KINCAID BROCKMAN MEMORIAL BOOK AWARD CONTEST (IV-Regional), % Sharon Sharp, P.O. Box 3345, Boone NC 28607, is an annual contest for a book of poetry (over 20 pages) by a North Carolina poet (native-born or current resident for 3 years). Send SASE for details. $100 cash prize and a Revere-style bowl awarded.

OHIOANA BOOK AWARDS; OHIOANA KROUT MEMORIAL AWARD FOR POETRY; OHIOANA QUARTERLY; OHIOANA LIBRARY ASSOCIATION (IV-Regional), Ohioana Library Association, 65 S. Front St., Suite 1105, Columbus OH 43215. Ohioana Book Awards given yearly to outstanding books published each year. Up to 6 awards may be given for books (including books of poetry) by authors born in Ohio or who have lived in Ohio for at least 5 years. The Ohioana Poetry Award of $1,000 (with the same residence requirements), made possible by a bequest of Helen Krout, is given yearly "to an individual whose body of work has made, and continues to make, a significant contribution to the poetry of Ohio, and through whose work as a writer, teacher, administrator, or in community service, interest in poetry has been developed." Nominations to be received by December 31. *Ohioana Quarterly* regularly reviews Ohio magazines and books by Ohio authors. It is available through membership in Ohioana Library Association ($20/year).

NATALIE ORNISH POETRY AWARD (IV-Regional); SOEURETTE DIEHL FRASER TRANSLATION AWARD (IV-Translations, regional); TEXAS INSTITUTE OF LETTERS, % James Hoggard, T.I.L., P.O. Box 9032, Wichita Falls TX 76308-9032. The Texas Institute of Letters gives annual awards for books by Texas authors in 8 categories, including the Natalie Ornish Poetry Award, a $1,000 award for best volume of poetry. Books must have been first published in the year in question, and entries may be made by authors or by their publishers. Deadline is January 4 of the following year. One copy of each entry must be mailed to each of three judges, with "information showing an author's Texas association . . . if it is not otherwise obvious." Poets must have lived in Texas for at least two consecutive years at some time or their work must reflect a notable concern with matters associated with the state. Soeurette Diehl Fraser Translation Award ($1,000) is given for best translation of a work into English. Same rules as those for Natalie Ornish poetry award. Write during the fall for complete instructions.

PACIFIC NORTHWEST WRITERS CONFERENCE ADULT LITERARY CONTEST (I), 2033 Sixth Ave., Suite 804, Seattle WA 98121, phone (206)443-3807. For information, please request a contest brochure. Complete entry form must accompany entry.

PANHANDLE PROFESSIONAL WRITERS (I), % Contest Chairman, P.O. Box 19303, Amarillo TX 79114, open to all poets, any subject or form, 50 lines maximum, limit of 2 poems/entry, awards of $25, $20 and $15, fee $7.50 for 2 poems. Send SASE for contest rules. Deadline: on or before June 15.

PAUMANOK POETRY AWARD COMPETITION; THE VISITING WRITERS PROGRAM (II), SUNY College of Technology, Farmingdale NY 11735, phone (516)420-2031, director Dr. Charles Fishman. The Paumanok Poetry Award Competition offers a prize of $750 plus expenses for a reading in their 1996-97 series. They will also award two runner-up prizes of $300 plus expenses. Submit cover letter, 1-paragraph bio, 5-7 poems, published or unpublished, and $10 entry fee by September 15. Check payable to SUNY Farmingdale Visiting Writers Program (VWP). Poets who have read in their series include Hayden Carruth, Allen Ginsberg, Linda Pastan, Marge Piercy, Joyce Carol Oates, Louis Simpson and David Ignatow. The series changes each year, so entries in the 1995 competition will be considered for the 1996-97 series, entries in 1996 for the 1997-98 series, and so on.

PENNSYLVANIA POETRY SOCIETY ANNUAL CONTEST; PEGASUS CONTEST FOR STUDENTS, 801 Spruce St., West Reading PA 19611-1448, phone (610)374-5848, newsletter editor and recording secretary Ann Gasser. The deadline for the society's annual contest, which has 12 categories open to nonmembers and 4 to members only, is January 15. Grand prize category awards 3 prizes of $100, $50, $25 and three poems may be entered at $2 each for members and nonmembers alike. All other categories award three prizes of $25, $15 and $10 and permit one poem in each category. Twelve categories are open to all poets; nonmembers pay $1.50 per category 2-12. PPS members pay $2.50 total for entries in categories 2-16. For information about the annual contest send a SASE to Lillian Tweedy, contest chairman, 2488 New Franklin Rd., Chambersburg, PA 17201. For information about the Pegasus Contest for Students, write to Anne Pierre Spangler, contest chairman, 1685 Christian Dr., R.D. #2, Lebanon PA 17042. Deadline for the Pegasus contest is March 1. The Pennsylvania Poetry Society publishes a quarterly newsletter and an annual *Prize Poems* soft cover book, containing prize-winning and honorable mention award poems. Prize poems in the Pegasus contest are published in a booklet for the schools which enter. PPS membership dues are $15/year. Make check payable to PPS, Inc. and mail to Richard R. Gasser, Treasurer, at the above address.

‡PENUMBRA POETRY COMPETITION (I, IV-Form), Tallahassee Writers' Association, P.O. Box 15995, Tallahassee FL 32317-5995, poetry chairperson Barbara Hogan, offers annual prizes of $50, $20 and $10 in each category, plus publication in chapbook. Submission must be unpublished. No simultaneous submissions. Two categories: (1) poetry of about 30 lines and (2) 3-line haiku. "Poems on 8½ × 11 paper; haiku on 3 × 5 cards. Please send two copies of each entry. On the back of one copy only, write author's name, full address, telephone number, and source of contest information." Send SASE for details. Entry fee: $4/30-line poem, $2/haiku. Deadline: June 30.

THE RICHARD PHILLIPS POETRY PRIZE (II), The Phillips Publishing Co., P.O. Box 121, Watts OK 74964, award director Richard Phillips, Jr. Annual award of $1,000 open to all poets. Submit 40-page ms, published or unpublished poems, any subject, any form. Include $10 reading fee/ms, payable to Richard Phillips Poetry Prize. Postmark deadline: September 5. "Winner will be announced and check for $1,000 presented October 15." Publication is the following year. Mss are not returned. Send SASE for guidelines.

POETRY OF HOPE AWARD (II, IV-Themes, young adult), P.O. Box 21077, Piedmont CA 94620, awarded annually, $200 first prize ($100 for junior division) for a poem up to 100 lines expressing "the spirit of hope" using inspirational themes. Themes should speak to the "healing" of social problems (i.e., war/peace, self-transformation, human rights, the homeless, the earth/ecology, etc.), hope for the highest good for all of creation. Application needed. No fee. Send SASE. Deadline: December 30.

POETRY SOCIETY OF MICHIGAN ANNUAL CONTESTS; THE PSM OPEN; SCHNEIDER MEMORIAL NARRATIVE; MARGARET DRAKE ELLIOTT CONTEST; EDWARD VAN LEISHOUT MEMORIAL CONTEST; KENNETH HEAFIELD CONTEST FOR YOUNG ADULTS (I, IV-Children), 1051 Fox Hills Dr., East Lansing MI 48823, contest coordinator Ben Bohnhorst. Sponsors 5 annual contests open to nonmembers: The PSM Open, any subject, form or length; Schneider Memorial Narrative, any form or length; Margaret Drake Elliott Contest, poetry for children, 20-line limit; Edward Van Leishout Memorial Contest, for poets age 16-25, 30-line limit; Kenneth Heafield Contest, for college students age 18-24, any subject or form, 60-line limit. Various entry fees. Prizes range from $5-100, some include publication. Also sponsors 10 contests for PSM members only. Send SASE for guidelines on all contests and membership information. Deadline for all contests is November 15.

POETS CLUB OF CHICAGO INTERNATIONAL SHAKESPEAREAN/PETRARCHAN SONNET CONTEST (II, IV-Form), chairman LaVone Holt, 130 Windsor Park Dr., C-323, Carol Stream IL 60188. Write for rules, include SASE, not earlier than March. No entry fee. Prizes of $50, $35 and $15. Deadline: September 1 postmark.

POETS' DINNER CONTEST (IV-Regional), 2214 Derby St., Berkeley CA 94705, (510)841-1217. Since 1926 there has been an annual awards banquet sponsored by the ad hoc Poets' Dinner Committee, usually at Spenger's Fish Grotto (a Berkeley Landmark). Three typed copies of original, unpublished poems in not more than 3 of the 8 categories are submitted anonymously without fee, and the winning poems (grand prize, 1st, 2nd, 3rd) are read at the banquet and honorable mentions awarded. **Contestant must be present to win.** Cash prizes awarded; honorable mention, books. The event is nonprofit. Deadline: January 25.

POETS OF THE VINEYARD CONTEST (I), P.O. Box 12154, Santa Rosa CA 95406, an annual contest sponsored by the Sonoma County Chapter (PofV) of the California Federation of Chaparral Poets with entries in 7 categories. These include traditional forms, free verse, haiku/senryu and tanka and a themed category on grapes, vineyards, wine, viticulture. For a copy of the current contest rules send SASE. Prizes in each category are $20, $15 and $10, with a grand prize chosen from category winners ($50). Entry fee $2/poem. Prize winning poems will be published in the annual anthology, *Vintage*. Every winning poet will receive a complimentary copy of the anthology in which his/her poem appears. Deadline: March 1.

THE POETS' PRIZE (II), The Poets' Prize Committee, % the Nicholas Roerich Museum, 319 W. 107th St., New York NY 10025, phone (212)864-7752, award directors Robert McDowell, Frederick Morgan and Louis Simpson. Annual cash award of $3,000 given for a book of verse by an American poet published in the previous year. The poet must be an American citizen. Poets making inquiries will receive an explanation of procedures. Books may be sent to the committee members. A list of the members and their addresses will be sent upon request with SASE.

POETS RENDEZVOUS CONTEST; INDIANA STATE FEDERATION OF POETRY CLUBS (I), % Dottie Mack, 14915 Gemini Dr., Huntertown IN 46748. The Poets Rendezvous Contest offers $1,200 in prizes for poems in 29 categories, $5 fee covers 29 categories in different forms and subjects, September 1 deadline. The Indiana State Federation of Poetry Clubs also has contests with January 15 and June 15 deadlines for poems no longer than 1 page, $1/poem fee, prizes of $25, $15 and $10 with 3 honorable mentions. Write for details.

PRESIDIO LA BAHIA AWARD; SUMMERFIELD G. ROBERTS AWARD (IV-Regional), Sons of the Republic of Texas, 5942 Abrams Rd., Suite 222, Dallas TX 75231, phone (214)343-2145. Both may be awarded for poetry. The Presidio La Bahia Award is an annual award or awards (depending upon the number and quality of entries) for writing that promotes research into and preservation of the Spanish Colonial influence on Texas culture. $2,000 is available, with a minimum first prize of $1,200. Entries must be in quadruplicate and will not be returned. Deadline: September 30. The Summerfield G. Roberts Award, available to US citizens, is an annual award of $2,500 for a book or manuscript depicting or representing the Republic of Texas (1836-46), written or published during the calendar year for which the award is given. Entries must be submitted in quintuplicate and will not be returned. Deadline: January 15.

PRO DOGS CREATIVE WRITING & PHOTOGRAPHIC COMPETITION (I), PRO Dogs National Charity, 4 New Road, Ditton, Kent ME20 6AD England, phone 01732 848499, award director Michaela Edridge. Annual contest for poems up to 32 lines with prize of £250. Contest information available for SASE (or SAE and IRCs). Fees: £3 for first entry; £1.50 for subsequent entries, or £2 first entry for members of the Charity. Deadline: October 1.

PULITZER PRIZE IN LETTERS (II), % The Pulitzer Prize Board, 702 Journalism, Columbia University, New York NY 10027, phone (212)854-3841, offers 5 prizes of $3,000 each year, including 1 in poetry, for books published in the calendar year preceding the award. Submit 4 copies of published books (or galley proofs if book is being published after November), photo, bio, entry form and $20 entry fee. July 1 deadline for books published between January 1 and June 30; November 1 deadline for books published between July 1 and December 31.

‡QUINCY WRITERS GUILD WRITING CONTEST (I), P.O. Box 433, Quincy IL 62306, offers annual award for original, unpublished poetry, fiction and nonfiction. Cash prizes based on dollar amount of entries. 1st, 2nd and 3rd place will be awarded in all categories. Send SASE for guidelines. Entry fee $2/poem; $4/nonfiction or fiction piece. Entries accepted from January 1 through April 15.

REDWOOD ACRES FAIR POETRY CONTEST (I), P.O. Box 6576, Eureka CA 95502, offers an annual contest with various categories for both juniors and seniors with entry fee of 50¢/poem for the junior contests and $1/poem for the senior contests. Deadline: May 31.

REGIONAL ARTISTS' PROJECTS GRANT (I, IV-Regional), Randolph Street Gallery, 756 N. Milwaukee Ave., Chicago IL 60622, phone (312)666-7737, RAP coordinator Kapra Fleming. Offers grants up to $4,000 maximum for regional artists working in interdisciplinary or innovative ways. Must be 1-year resident of Indiana, Illinois, Ohio, Missouri or Michigan. Application available for SASE. Deadline: May 15.

MARY ROBERTS RINEHART FOUNDATION AWARD (V), Mail Stop Number 3E4, The Mary Roberts Rinehart Award, English Dept., George Mason University, 4400 University Dr., Fairfax VA 22030-4444. Two grants are made annually to writers who need financial assistance "to complete work definitely projected." The amount of the award depends upon income the fund generates; in the past the amount was approximately $900 in each category. Poets and fiction writers should submit work in odd numbered years, e.g., 1995, 1997. **A writer's work must be nominated by an established author or editor**; no written recommendations are necessary. Nominations must be accompanied by a sample of the nominee's work, up to 25 pgs. of poetry and 30 pgs. of fiction. Deadline: November 30.

ANNA DAVIDSON ROSENBERG AWARD (IV-Ethnic), Judah L. Magnes Museum, 2911 Russell St., Berkeley CA 94705, offers prizes of $100, $50 and $25, as well as honorable mentions, for up to 10 pgs. of 1-3 unpublished poems (in English) on the Jewish Experience. There is also a Youth Commendation for poets under 19, a Senior Award if 65 or over and a New/Emerging Poet Award. Do not send poems without entry form; write between April 1 and July 15 for form and guidelines (enclose SASE). Deadline: August 31.

SALMON ARM SONNET CONTEST (IV-Form), Salmon Arm & Dist. Chamber of Commerce, Box 1270, Salmon Arm, British Columbia V1E 4P4 Canada. An annual contest for unpublished sonnets. Prizes: $100-500 and books. Entry fee: $6/poem. Limit 2 entries. New juvenile category for 18 and under, entry fee: $2/poem plus $6 to enter the main contest. Deadline: June 1. Copies of winning entries will be sent to all entrants.

SAN FRANCISCO FOUNDATION; JOSEPH HENRY JACKSON AWARD; JAMES D. PHELAN AWARD (IV-Regional), % Intersection for the Arts, 446 Valencia St., San Francisco CA 94103. The Jackson Award ($2,000) will be made to the author of an unpublished work-in-progress in the form of fiction (novel or short stories), non-fictional prose, or poetry. Applicants must be residents of northern California or Nevada for three consecutive years immediately prior to the deadline date of January 31, and must be between the ages of 20 and 35 as of the deadline. The Phelan Award ($2,000) will be made to the author of an unpublished work-in-progress in the form of fiction (novel or short stories), non-fictional prose, poetry or drama. Applicants must be California-born (although they may now reside outside of the state), and must be between the ages of 20 and 35 as of the January 31 deadline. Mss for both awards must be accompanied by an application form, which may be obtained by sending a SASE to the above address. Entries accepted November 15 through January 31.

‡**SAN MATEO COUNTY FAIR FINE ARTS COMPETITION (I)**, P.O. Box 1027, San Mateo CA 94403-0627, phone (415)574-3247, for unpublished poetry. Adult and youth divisions. Write or call for entry form and additional information. Adult Division awards of $100, $50, and $25; fee $10 for each poem. Youth Division awards of $50, $25 and $15; no fee. Limit 2 entries per division. July 7 deadline for poems.

CARL SANDBURG AWARDS (IV-Regional), sponsored by Friends of the Chicago Public Library, 400 S. State St., 10S-7, Chicago IL 60605, are given annually to native-born Chicago authors or present Chicago-area writers for new books in 4 categories, including poetry. Each author receives $1,000. Publisher or authors should submit 2 copies of books published between June 1 of one year and May 31 of the next. Deadline: August 1.

‡**SCOTTISH INTERNATIONAL OPEN POETRY COMPETITION; THE AYRSHIRE WRITERS' & ARTISTS' SOCIETY (I)**, 42 Tollerton Dr., Irvine, Ayrshire, Scotland. Open to all poets. Inaugurated in 1972 it is the longest running poetry competition in the U.K. Entries are free, restricted to two per person and should be accompanied by SASE (or SAE and IRCs). December deadline. Special award ceremony March. First prize, U.K. Section, MacDiarmid Trophy and $100. First prize, International Section, The International Trophy. Scots Section, The Clement Wilson Cup. Diplomas are awarded to runners up. Competition opens September each year.

SOCIETY OF MIDLAND AUTHORS AWARD (IV-Regional), % Phyllis Ford-Choyke, 29 E. Division St., Chicago IL 60610, is for authors from Midland states: IL, IN, IA, KS, MI, MN, MO, NE, ND, SD, OH, WI. It is an annual cash award and a plaque given at a dinner. Books in each calendar year are eligible, not self-published. Deadline January 15 of award year. Send SASE for entry form; books must be submitted to each of 3 judges, not to Phyllis Ford-Choyke. The Society of Midland Authors provides camaraderie and encouragement to writers practicing their art in the heartland. Membership is by invitation only and restricted to authors of books "demonstrating literary style and published by a recognized publisher," and published or professionally produced plays. However, as a public service, their monthly meetings are open to anyone who wants to attend.

SOUTH DAKOTA POETRY SOCIETY CONTESTS (I), Present Chairman of S.D. State Poetry Society Contests Myra Osterberg, P.O. Box 613, Salem SD 57058, 10 categories. Deadline: August 31.

SPARROWGRASS POETRY FORUM (I), Dept. HM, 203 Diamond St., Box 193, Sistersville WV 26175, offers 6 annual free contests, each of which has $1,000 in prizes, including a $500 grand prize. Entrants are solicited to buy an anthology, but you do not have to buy the anthology to win. Send 1 original poem, no longer than 20 lines. Name and address at the top of the page. Any style, any subject. Contest deadlines are the last day of every other month.

SPRINGFEST AND WINTERFEST POETRY CONTESTS; MILE HIGH POETRY SOCIETY (I), P.O. Box 21116, Denver CO 80221, phone (303)657-8461, award director Jane C. Schaul. Each spring and fall they offer a contest with $300 1st prize, $100 2nd prize, and two 3rd prizes of $50 each for maximum 36-line poems. Entry fee $3/poem. Deadlines: June 30 and December 31. Send SASE for details.

WALLACE E. STEGNER FELLOWSHIPS (II), Creative Writing Program, Stanford University, Stanford CA 94305, 5 in poetry, $13,000 plus tuition of $4,800, for promising writers who can benefit from 2 years instruction and criticism at the Writing Center. Previous publication not required, though it can strengthen one's application. Deadline: Postmarked by the first working day after January 1.

‡**TOWSON STATE UNIVERSITY PRIZE FOR LITERATURE (II, IV-Regional)**, Towson State University, College of Liberal Arts, Towson MD 21204-7097, phone (410)830-2128, award director Dean of the College of Liberal Arts, offers annual prize of $1,000 "for a single book or book-length manuscript of fiction, poetry, drama or imaginative nonfiction by a young Maryland writer. The prize is granted on the basis of literary and aesthetic excellence as determined by a panel of distinguished judges appointed by the university. The first award, made in the fall of 1980, went to novelist Anne Tyler." The work must have been published within the three years prior to the year of nomination or must be scheduled for publication within the year in which nominated. Open to Maryland residents under 40 years of age. Submit 5 copies of work in bound form or in typewritten, double-spaced ms form. Send SASE for entry form and guidelines. Deadline: May 15.

TRILLIUM BOOK AWARD; PRIX TRILLIUM (IV-Regional), Ministry of Culture, Tourism and Recreation, Libraries Branch, 77 Bloor St. W, 3rd Floor, Toronto, Ontario M7A 2R9 Canada, is given annually for a book by an Ontario author. Submissions of published books are by publishers. Winning author receives $12,000; publisher of winning book receives $2,500. Award given in April. Deadline: December 31.

KINGSLEY TUFTS POETRY AWARD; KATE TUFTS DISCOVERY AWARD FOR POETRY (II), The Claremont Graduate School, 160 E. Tenth St., Claremont CA 91711, phone (909)621-8068, award director Murray M. Schwartz. The Kingsley Tufts Poetry Award is a $50,000 prize awarded annually to a book-length ms that has been published during the previous year. Unpublished book-length mss created during the previous year are also acceptable, if poet has publication credits. Subject and form are open. No translations. Submit 3 copies with entry form. Entry form must accompany submission. Deadline: December 15. The Kate Tufts Discovery Award for Poetry is an annual $5,000 prize awarded to "first books" only. Submission requirements and deadline are the same as Kingsley Tufts Poetry Award. Both awards are presented at a ceremony in April. Entrants to the Kingsley Tufts Award must "agree to reproduction rights, be present at the award ceremony and spend a week in residence at the Claremont Graduate School." Send SASE for rules and entry forms.

‡UTAH ORIGINAL WRITING COMPETITION (II, IV-Regional), Utah Arts Council Literary Program, 617 E. South Temple, Salt Lake City UT 84102-1177, award director G. Barnes, offers annual awards in 7 categories: novel, nonfiction book, book-length collection of poetry, juvenile book, poetry, short story and personal essay. Prizes range from $200-1,000 and a $5,000 publication prize is awarded to one of the book-length first place winners from the previous year's competition. Open to Utah residents only. "Submit work in standard publishing ms style." Write for entry form. Deadline: mid-June.

LAURA BOWER VAN NUYS CREATIVE WRITING CONTEST (I, II), Black Hills Writers Group, P.O. Box 1539, Rapid City SD 57709-1539. **"We will be holding the contest in even-numbered years only."** Professional and nonprofessional categories in fiction, articles and poetry. Guidelines available after January 1 of contest year.

‡THE VICTORIAN FELLOWSHIP OF AUSTRALIAN WRITERS; FAW AWARDS (IV-Regional), FAW (Vic) Inc., P.O. Box 528, Camberwell 3124, Australia, all awards for Australian authors. The FAW Anne Elder Poetry Award (prizes of $1,000 and $500) is for a first published book of poetry. The FAW Christopher Brennan Award is a bronze plaque to honor an Australian poet who has written work of sustained quality and distinction (entries not required; award by committee). The FAW John Shaw Neilson Poetry Award (prizes of $500 and $250) is for an unpublished poem of at least 14 lines. The FAW Fedora Anderson Young Writers' Poetry Award ($150 and $75) is for unpublished poems by Australian writers 15-20 years old. The FAW C.J. Dennis Young Writers' Poetry Award (prizes of $100 and $50) is for unpublished poems by Australian writers 10-14 years old. The FAW Mavis Thorpe Clark Young Writers' Award gives 2 prizes of $150 each to Australian postprimary students. "One of the prizes will be awarded for an individual submission and the other is for a group entry by students attending the same postprimary school."

THE W.D. WEATHERFORD AWARD (IV-Regional), Berea College, CPO 2336, Berea KY 40404, contact chairman, for the published work (including poetry) which "best illuminates the problems, personalities, and unique qualities of the Appalachian South." Work is nominated by its publisher, by a member of the award committee or by any reader. The award is for $500 and sometimes there are special awards of $200 each. Deadline: December 31 of the year work was published.

WEST HAVEN COUNCIL OF THE ARTS, P.O. Box 17594, West Haven CT 06516. An annual national poetry contest open April 15 to September 15. Entry fee: $2 for the first poem, $1 each additional to a maximum of $5. Prizes of $50, $25 and $15 will be awarded plus publication in the annual poetry anthology, *Sound and Waves of West Haven*. Send SASE for guidelines.

WESTERN STATES BOOK AWARDS; WESTERN STATES ARTS FEDERATION (IV-Regional), Dept. PM, 236 Montezuma Ave., Santa Fe NM 87501, presents annual book awards to outstanding authors and publishers. The awards include cash prizes of $5,000 which are divided between writers and their respective publishers. Mss must be written by an author living in Alaska, Arizona, California, Colorado, Idaho, Montana, Nevada, New Mexico, Oregon, Utah, Washington or Wyoming. Award given to books to be published in fall of 1996. Work must already have been accepted for publication by a publisher in one of these states. Work must be submitted by the publisher, submitted in ms form (not previously published in book form). Publisher must have published at least 3 books. Write for more information.

WFNB ANNUAL LITERARY CONTEST; THE ALFRED G. BAILEY AWARD; WRITERS' FEDERATION OF NEW BRUNSWICK (IV-Regional), P.O. Box 37, Station A, Fredericton, New Brunswick E3B 4Y2 Canada, offers prizes of $200, $100, $30, for unpublished poems of up to 100 lines (typed, double-spaced). Open to New Brunswick residents only. The Alfred G. Bailey Award is a $400 prize given annually for poetry mss of 48 pgs. or more. May include some individual poems that have been published. Entry fee: $10 for members, $15 for nonmembers. Send SASE for guidelines. Deadline: February 14.

WHITE RABBIT POETRY CONTEST; THE HARBINGER (II), P.O. Box U-1030 USAL, Mobile AL 36688, is an annual, the winners and honorable mentions being virtually the only poetry published by *The Harbinger*. Awards are $100, $50 and $25. Entry fee: $5 for the first poem, $2 each additional. Send SASE for entry form, which must accompany submisssions (2 copies, author's name on 1 only). Deadline: March 31.

WHITING WRITERS' AWARDS; MRS. GILES WHITING FOUNDATION (V), 1133 Avenue of the Americas, 22nd Floor, New York NY 10036-6710, director Gerald Freund. The Foundation makes awards of $30,000 each to up to 10 writers of fiction, nonfiction, poetry and plays chosen by a selection committee drawn from a list of recognized writers, literary scholars and editors. Recipients of the award are selected from nominations made by writers, educators and editors from communities across the country whose experience and vocations bring them in contact with individuals of unusual talent. The nominators and selectors are appointed by the foundation and serve anonymously. **Direct applications and informal nominations are not accepted by the foundation.**

OSCAR WILLIAMS & GENE DERWOOD AWARD (V), Community Funds, Inc., 2 Park Ave., New York NY 10016, is an award given annually to nominees of the selection committee "to help needy or worthy artists or poets." **Selection Committee for the award does not accept nominations.** Amount varies from year to year.

‡WISCONSIN ARTS BOARD FELLOWSHIPS (II, IV-Regional), Wisconsin Arts Board, 101 E. Wilson St., First Floor, Madison WI 53703, phone (608)266-0190, award director Elizabeth Malner, offers fellowships of $5,000. Submission can be previously published or unpublished. Submit 15 pgs. maximum. Open to Wisconsin residents only. Write for entry form and guidelines. Deadline: September ("call for exact date").

WORLD ORDER OF NARRATIVE AND FORMALIST POETS (II, IV-Subscription, form), P.O. Box 174, Station A, Flushing NY 11358, contest chairman Dr. Alfred Dorn. This organization sponsors contests in at least 15 categories of traditional and contemporary poetic forms, including the sonnet, blank verse, ballade, villanelle, free verse and new forms created by Alfred Dorn. Prizes total at least $5,000 and range from $20 to $300. Only subscribers to *The Formalist* will be eligible for the competition, as explained in the complete guidelines available from the contest chairman. "We look for originality of thought, phrase and image, combined with masterful craftsmanship. Trite, trivial or technically inept work stands no chance." Postmark deadline for entries: December 8, 1995.

WORLD'S WORST POETRY CONTEST (IV-Regional), Pismo Beach Hardware and Nursery, 930 Price St., Pismo Beach CA 93449, phone (805)773-NAIL, fax (805)773-6772, award directors "Pismo Bob" Pringle and Rudy Natoli. Contest for "bad" poetry that mentions Pismo Beach. The contest is simple to enter. Just send a poem or poems to "Pismo Bob" Pringle, originator of the contest. The poems must include the word "Pismo," but aside from that there are no literary requirements. "In addition to the sheer pride of being the world's worst bard, the Chosen One will also win a free round trip to the wonderful shores of Pismo Beach, California." Deadline: September 30.

‡WRITERS AT WORK FELLOWSHIP COMPETITION (II), Writers at Work, P.O. Box 1146, Centerville UT 84103, phone (801)292-9285, award director Shelly Hunt-Camoin, offers annual awards of $1,500 and $500 plus publication in *Quarterly West* (first place only) and *The Best of Writers at Work Anthology*. Submissions must be unpublished and can be entered in other contests, "but must be withdrawn if they win another contest." Submit 6 poems, 10 pgs. maximum, subject and form open. Entry must include 2 copies of ms, 2 #10 SASEs and cover letter stating name, address, phone number, genre and title of ms. "No names on mss." Mss will not be returned. Open to any writer who has not published a book-length volume of original work. Entry fee: $12/entry (make check payable to Writers at Work). Postmark deadline: March 15. "Selected finalists will be published with the winners in *The Best of Writers at Work Anthology*."

WRITERS' GUILD OF ALBERTA BOOK AWARD (IV-Regional), Writer's Guild, 10523 100th Ave., Edmonton, Alberta T5J 0A8 Canada, phone (403)426-5892, awarded in six categories, including poetry. Eligible books will have been published anywhere in the world between January 1 and December 31. Their authors will have been resident in Alberta for at least 12 of the 18 months prior to December 31. Contact the WGA head office for registry forms. Unpublished manuscripts are not eligible. Except in the drama category, anthologies are not eligible. Four copies of each book to be considered must be mailed to the WGA office no later than December 31. Submissions postmarked after this date will not be accepted. Exceptions will be made for any books published between the 15th and 31st of December. These may be submitted by January 15. Three copies will go to the three judges in that category; one will remain in the WGA library. Works may be submitted by authors, publishers, or any interested parties.

WRITERS UNLIMITED (I), %Voncile Ros, 4709 New Hope Ave., Pascagoula MS 39581-3040, offers an annual literary competition, deadline September 1. There are up to 20 categories with cash prizes up to $50 and other prizes. Do not use the same poem for more than one category. $5 entry fee covers entries in all categories up to 20. Send SASE for contest rules.

‡WYOMING ARTS COUNCIL FELLOWSHIP COMPETITION (II, IV-Regional), 2320 Capitol Ave., Cheyenne WY 82002, phone (307)777-7742, award director Guy Lebeda, offers annual award of $2,000. Submissions can be entered in other contests. Submit 10 pgs. maximum. Open to poets residing in Wyoming for 1 year prior to award. "No name should appear on manuscript." Send SASE for entry form and guidelines. Deadline: July 1.

Additional Contests and Awards

The following listings also contain information about contests and awards. See the General Index for page numbers, then read the listings and send SASEs for specific details about their offerings.

Abiko Quarterly
Academy of American Poets, The
Advocate, The
African Voices
Aguilar Expression, The
Albatross
Alicejamesbooks
Alms House Press
Amelia
America
American Poetry Review
American Tolkien Society
Analecta
Anhinga Press
Appalachia
Appalachian Heritage
Appalachian Writers' Association
    Conference
Apropos
Arkansas Press, The University of
Arkansas Writers' Conference
Associated Writing
    Programs
Bay Area Poets Coalition (BAPC)
Bell's Letters Poet
Beloit Poetry Journal, The
Blue Unicorn, A Triquarterly of
    Poetry
Bohemian Chronicle
BOOG Literature
Borderlands: Texas Poetry
    Review
Bread Loaf Writers' Conference
Button Magazine
Calapooya Collage
Canada Council, The
Canadian Writer's Journal
Cape Rock, The
Carolina Quarterly, The
Center Press
Chelsea
Chiron Review
Cincinnati Poetry Review
Cleveland State University Poetry
    Center
Climbing Art, The
Cochran's Corner

Connecticut River Review
Copper Canyon Press
Country Woman
Cover Magazine
CQ (California State Poetry
    Quarterly)
Craft of Writing
Crazyhorse
Cream City Review
Creativity Unlimited Press
Cricket
Crucible
Cumberland Poetry Review
Cutbank
Deep South Writers Conference
Defined Providence
Devil's Millhopper Press, The
Dialogue: A Journal of Mormon
    Thought
Dream Shop, The
Echoes Magazine
1812
Eighth Mountain Press, The
Elk River Review
Embers
En Plein Air
Envoi
Epoch
Equinox Press
Excursus Literary Arts Journal
Explorations
Explorer Magazine
Expressions
Expressions Forum Review
Fauquier Poetry Journal
Federation of British Columbia
    Writers
Feelings: America's Beautiful
    Poetry Magazine
Fine Madness
Flume Press
Folio: A Literary Journal
Footwork: The Paterson Literary
    Review
Formalist, The
Freedom Rag Magazine
Frogmore Papers

Frogpond: Quarterly Haiku
    Journal
Fudge Cake, The
Gentle Survivalist, The
Georgetown Review
Geppo Haiku Worksheet
Glass Cherry Press, The
Golden Isis Magazine
Grain
Greensboro Review, The
Haiku Headlines: A Monthly
    Newsletter of Haiku and
    Senryu
Half Tones to Jubilee
Harp-Strings
Heartlands Today, The
Heaven Bone Magazine
Helicon Nine Editions
Hellas: A Journal of Poetry and
    the Humanities
Hippopotamus Press
Hob-Nob
Home Planet News
Housewife-Writer's Forum
Hubbub
Hudson Review, The
Hyacinth House Publications
Imago: New Writing
International Black Writers
Iowa Press, University of
Iowa Woman
Jackson's Arm
Kalliope, a journal of women's art
Kansas Quarterly
Keystrokes
Kinesis
League of Canadian Poets, The
Ledge Poetry and Fiction
    Magazine, The
Light and Life Magazine
Lines n' Rhymes
Lite Magazine: The Journal of
    Satire and Creativity
Literal Latté
Literature and Belief
Loft, The
Long Island Quarterly

State and Provincial Grants

Arts councils in the United States and Canada provide assistance to artists (including poets) in the form of fellowships or grants. These grants can be substantial and confer prestige upon recipients; however, **only state or province residents are eligible**. Because deadlines and available support vary annually, query first (with a SASE).

United States Art Agencies

Alabama State Council on the Arts
Becky Mullens, Manager
Performing Arts Program
1 Dexter Ave.
Montgomery AL 36130
(205)242-4076

Alaska State Council on the Arts
Jean Palmer, Grants Officer
411 W. Fourth Ave., Suite 1-E
Anchorage AK 99501
(907)269-6610

Arizona Commission on the Arts
Tonda Gorton, Public Information Officer
417 W. Roosevelt
Phoenix AZ 85003
(602)255-5882

Arkansas Arts Council
Sally Williams, Artists Program Coordinator
1500 Tower Bldg., 323 Center St.
Little Rock AR 72201
(501)324-9150

California Arts Council
Carol Shiffman, Individual Fellowships
2411 Alhambra Blvd.
Sacramento CA 95817
(916)227-2550

Colorado Council on the Arts and Humanities
Daniel Salazar, Director
Individual Artists Program
750 Pennsylvania St.
Denver CO 80203-3699
(303)894-2619

Connecticut Commission on the Arts
Linda Dente, Grants Information
227 Lawrence St.
Hartford CT 06106
(203)566-7076

Delaware State Arts Council
Barbara King, Coordinator
Individual Artist Fellowships
State Office Building, 820 N. French St.
Wilmington DE 19801
(302)577-3540

District of Columbia Commission on the Arts and Humanities
Carlos Arrien, Program Coordinator
Stables Art Center, Fifth Floor
410 Eighth St. NW
Washington DC 20004
(202)724-5613

Florida Arts Council
Valerie Ohlsson, Arts Consultant
Division of Cultural Affairs
Florida Dept. of State, The Capitol
Tallahassee FL 32399-0250
(904)487-2980

Georgia Council for the Arts
Ann Davis, Program Manager
Community Arts Development
530 Means St. NW, Suite 115
Atlanta GA 30318
(404)651-7920

Hawaii State Foundation on Culture & Arts
Hinano Campton, Artist Grant Coordinator
44 Merchant St.
Honolulu HI 96813
(808)586-0300

Idaho Commission on the Arts
Diane Josephy Peavey, Literature Director
P.O. Box 83720
Boise ID 83720-0008
(208)334-2119

Illinois Arts Council
Richard Gage, Director
Communication Arts
100 W. Randolph, Suite 10-500
Chicago IL 60601
(312)814-6750

Indiana Arts Commission
Robert Burnett, Interim Artist Manager
402 W. Washington St., Room 072
Indianapolis IN 46204-2741
(317)232-1268

Iowa Arts Council
Julie Bailey, Grants Coordinator
Capitol Complex, 600 E. Locust
Des Moines IA 50319
(515)281-4451

Kansas Arts Commission
Tom Klocke, Program Coordinator
Jay Hawk Tower

700 Jackson, Suite 1004
Topeka KS 66603
(913)296-3335

Kentucky Arts Council
Al Smith, Fellowship Program
Irwin Pickett, Program Branch Manager
31 Fountain Place
Frankfort KY 40601
(502)564-3757

Louisiana State Arts Council
James Border, Program Director
1051 N. Third St., Room 420
Baton Rouge LA 70802
(504)342-8180

Maine State Arts Commission
Alden C. Wilson, Director
State House, Station 25
55 Capitol St.
Augusta ME 04333-0025
(207)287-2724

Maryland State Arts Council
Charles Camp, Grants Officer
601 N. Howard St.
Baltimore MD 21201
(410)333-8232

Massachusetts Cultural Council
Lisa Sasier, Public Information
80 Boylston St., Tenth Floor
Boston MA 02116
(617)727-3668

Arts Foundation of Michigan
Kim Adams, Executive Director
645 Griswold, Suite 2164
Detroit MI 48226
(313)964-2244

Minnesota State Arts Board
Karen Mueller, Program Associate
432 Summit Ave.
St. Paul MN 55102-2624
(612)297-2603

Mississippi Arts Commission
Cindy Harper, Program Director
239 N. Lamar St., Suite 207
Jackson MS 39201
(601)359-6030

Missouri Arts Council
Michael Hunt, Program Administrator
Wainwright State Office Complex
111 N. Seventh St., Suite 105
St. Louis MO 63101
(314)340-6845

Montana Arts Council
Fran Morrow, Dir. of Art Services/Progs.
316 N. Park Ave., Suite 252
Helena MT 59620
(406)444-6430

Nebraska Arts Council
Nancy Quinn, Grants Officer
3838 Davenport
Omaha NE 68131-2329
(402)595-2122

Nevada State Council on the Arts
Susan Bofkoff, Executive Director
602 N. Curry

Carson City NV 89710
(702)687-6680

New Hampshire State Council on the Arts
Audrey Sylvester, Artists Services Coordinator
Phoenix Hall, 40 N. Main St.
Concord NH 03301
(603)271-2789

New Jersey State Council on the Arts
Steve Runk, Grants Coordinator
CN 306, Third Floor, Roebling Bldg.
Trenton NJ 08625
(609)292-6130

New Mexico Arts Division
Eleanor Broh-Kahn, Administrative Secretary
228 E. Palace Ave.
Santa Fe NM 87501
(505)827-6490

New York State Council on the Arts
Jewelle Gomez, Director, Literature Program
915 Broadway
New York NY 10010
(212)387-7020

North Carolina Arts Council
Deborah McGill, Literature Director
Department of Cultural Resources
221 E. Lane St.
Raleigh NC 27601-2807
(919)733-2111

North Dakota Council on the Arts
John Carroll, Assistant Director
418 E. Broadway, Suite 70
Bismark ND 58501-4086
(701)328-3954

Ohio Arts Council
Bob Fox, Literature Coordinator
727 E. Main St.
Columbus OH 43205
(614)466-2613

State Arts Council of Oklahoma
Betty Price, Executive Director
P.O. Box 52001-2001
Oklahoma City OK 73152-2001
(405)521-2931

Oregon Arts Commission
Vincent Dunn, Assistant Director
775 Summer St. NE
Salem OR 97310
(503)986-0082

Pennsylvania Council on the Arts
Marsha Salvatore, Literature Program Director
Finance Bldg., Room 216
Harrisburg PA 17120
(717)787-6883

Institute of Puerto Rican Culture
Sandra Rodriguez, Assistant Director
P.O. Box 4184
San Juan PR 00905
(809)724-0700

Rhode Island State Council on the Arts
Sheila Haggerty, Director,
Individual Artist Program
95 Cedar St., Suite 103
Providence RI 02903
(401)277-3880

South Carolina Arts Commission
Steve Lewis, Literary Arts Director
1800 Gervais St.
Columbia SC 29201
(803)734-8696

South Dakota Arts Council
Dennis Holub, Director
230 S. Phillips Ave., Suite 204
Sioux Falls SD 57102
(605)367-5678

Tennessee Arts Commission
Alice Swanson, Director of Literary Arts
404 James Robertson Pkwy., Suite 160
Nashville TN 37243-0780
(615)741-1701

Texas Commission on the Arts
Rita Starpattern, Program Director
Visual and Communication Arts
P.O. Box 13406
Austin TX 78711-3406
(512)463-5535

Utah Arts Council
Amanda Pahnke, Assistant Director
617 E. South Temple
Salt Lake City UT 84102
(801)533-5895

Vermont Council on the Arts
Cornelia Carey, Grants Officer
136 State St., Drawer 33
Montpelier VT 05633-6001
(802)828-3291

Virgin Islands Council on the Arts
Marie Daniel, Grants Officer
41-42 Norre Gada
St. Thomas VI 00802
(809)774-5984

Virginia Commission for the Arts
Susan FitzPatrick, Program Coordinator
223 Governor St.
Richmond VA 23219
(804)225-3132

Washington State Arts Commission
Artist Fellowship
Marschel Paul, Executive Director
1402 Third Ave., Suite 415
Seattle WA 98101-2118
(206)753-3860

West Virginia Arts and Humanities Division
Jill Ellis, Grants Coordinator
1900 Kanawha Blvd. E.
Charleston WV 23505
(304)558-0220

Wisconsin Arts Board
Beth Malner, Individual Artists Program Dir.
101 E. Wilson St., First Floor
Madison WI 53702
(608)266-0190

Wyoming Council on the Arts
Guy Lebeda, Literary Arts Coordinator
2320 Capitol Ave.
Cheyenne WY 82002
(307)777-7742

Canadian Provinces Art Agencies

Alberta Arts and Cultural Industries Branch
Clive Padfield, Director
10158 - 103 St., Third Floor
Edmonton, Alberta T5J 0X6
(403)427-6315

British Columbia Arts Council
Cultural Services Branch
Walter Quan, Coord. of Arts Awards Prog.
800 Johnson St., Fifth Floor
Victoria, British Columbia V8V 1X4
(604)356-1728

Manitoba Arts Council
Pat Sanders, Writing/Publishing Off.
525 - 93 Lombard Ave.
Winnipeg, Manitoba R3B 3B1
(204)945-0422

New Brunswick Department of Tourism, Recreation and Heritage
Arts Branch, % Bruce Dennis
P.O. Box 6000
Fredericton, New Brunswick E3B 5H1
(506)453-2555

Newfoundland Department of Municipal and Provincial Affairs
Cultural Affairs, % Elizabeth Channing
P.O. Box 1854
St. John's, Newfoundland A1C 5P9
(709)729-3650

Nova Scotia Department of Tourism and Culture
Cultural Affairs, % Peggy Walt
P.O. Box 578
Halifax, Nova Scotia B3J 2S9
(902)424-5000

The Canada Council
General Information Officer
P.O. Box 1047, 350 Albert St.
Ottawa, Ontario K1P 5V8
(613)566-4365

Ontario Arts Council
Lorraine Filyer, Literature Officer
151 Bloor St. W., Suite 600
Toronto, Ontario M5S 1T6
(416)961-1660

Prince Edward Island Council of the Arts
Judy McDonald, Executive Director
P.O. Box 2234
Charlottetown, Prince Edward Island C1A 8B9
(902)368-4410

Saskatchewan Arts Board
Gail Paul Armstrong, Arts Consultant
3475 Albert St.
Regina, Saskatchewan S4S 6X6
(306)787-4056

Government of Yukon Arts Branch
Laurel Parry, Arts Consultant
P.O. Box 2703
Whitehorse, Yukon Y1A 2C6
(403)667-5264

Resources

Conferences and Workshops

Conferences and workshops are valuable resources for many poets, especially beginners. A conference or workshop serves as an opportunity to learn about specific aspects of the craft, gather feedback from other poets and writers, listen to submission tips from editors, and revel in a creative atmosphere that may stimulate one's muse.

In this section you'll find listings for 61 conferences and workshops—more than a dozen of which are new to this edition. Some, such as the White River Writers' Workshop in Batesville, Arkansas, are specifically geared to poets. Most, however, are more general conferences with offerings for a variety of writers, including poets.

A "typical" conference may have a number of workshop sessions, keynote speakers and perhaps even a panel or two. Topics may include everything from writing fiction, poetry, and books for children to marketing one's work. Often a theme, which may change from year to year, will be the connecting factor. Other conferences and workshops cover a number of topics but have an overriding focus. For example, you'll find two gatherings for Appalachian writers. There are also events geared to women writers and Christian writers. And the Writing Workshop in Lexington, Kentucky, is specifically designed to aid adults ages 55 or older.

Despite different themes or focuses, each listing in this section details the offerings available for poets. Each also includes information about other workshops, speakers and panels of interest. It is important to note, however, that conference and workshop directors were still in the organizing stages when contacted. Consequently, some listings include information from last year's events simply to provide an idea of what to expect this year. For more up-to-date details, including current costs, send a SASE to the director in question a few months before the date(s) listed.

Benefiting from conferences

Without a doubt, attending conferences and workshops is beneficial. First, these events provide opportunities to learn more about the poetic craft. Some even feature individual sessions with workshop leaders, allowing you to specifically discuss your work with others. If these one-on-one sessions include critiques (generally for an additional fee), we've included this information.

Besides learning from workshop leaders, you can also benefit from conversations with other attendees. Writers on all levels often enjoy talking to and sharing insights with others. A conversation over lunch can reveal a new market for your work, or a casual chat while waiting for a session to begin can acquaint you with a new resource. If a conference or workshop includes time for open readings and you choose to participate, you may gain feedback from both workshop leaders and others.

Another reason conferences and workshops are worthwhile is the opportunity they provide to meet editors and publishers who often have tips about marketing work. The availability of these folks, however, does not necessarily mean they will want to read your latest collection of poems (unless, of course, they are workshop leaders and you have an individual meeting scheduled with them). Though editors and publishers are glad to meet poets and writers, and occasionally discuss work in general terms, they cannot give personal attention to everyone they meet.

Selecting a conference or workshop

When selecting a conference or workshop to attend, keep your goals in mind. If you want to learn how to improve your craft, for example, consider one of the events entirely devoted to poetry or locate a more general conference where one-on-one critique sessions are offered. If you're looking for more informal feedback, choose an event which includes open readings. If marketing your work seems like an ominous task, register for a conference that includes a session with editors. And if you also have an interest in other forms of writing, an event with a wide range of workshops is a good bet.

Of course, also take your resources into consideration. If both your time and funds are limited, search for a conference or workshop within your area. Many events are held during weekends and may be close enough for you to commute. On the other hand, if you want to combine your vacation with time spent meeting other writers and working on your craft, consider workshops such as those sponsored by The Writers' Center at Chautauqua. In either case, it is important to at least consider the conference location and be aware of activities to enjoy in the area.

Still other factors may influence your decision. Events that sponsor contests, for instance, may allow you to gain recognition and recoup some of your expenses. Similarly, some conferences and workshops have financial assistance or scholarships available. Finally, many are associated with colleges or universities and offer continuing education credits. You will find all of these options included here. Again, send a SASE for more details.

For other conferences and workshops, see *The Guide to Writers Conferences* (Shaw-Guides, Inc., P.O. Box 1295, New York NY 10023) or the May issue of *Writer's Digest* magazine (available on newsstands or directly from the publisher at 1507 Dana Ave., Cincinnati OH 45207).

AMERICAN CHRISTIAN WRITERS CONFERENCES, P.O. Box 5168, Phoenix AZ 85010, phone (800)21-WRITE, director Reg Forder. Annual 3-day events founded in 1981. Held throughout the year in cities such as Houston, Dallas/Ft. Worth, Boston, Minneapolis, New York, St. Louis, Detroit, Pittsburgh, Atlanta, Miami and Phoenix. Usually located at a major hotel chain like Holiday Inn. Average attendance is 300. **Open to anyone. Conferences cover fiction, poetry, writing for children.** Cost is $119, extra for beginning writers day; participants are responsible for their own meals. Accommodations include special rates at host hotel. Send SASE for brochures and registration forms.

ANTIOCH WRITERS' WORKSHOP, P.O. Box 494, Yellow Springs OH 45387, phone (513)767-7068, director Judy DaPolito. Annual 7-day event founded in 1986. Usually held in July at Antioch College in the village of Yellow Springs. "The campus is quiet, shady, relaxed. The village is unusual for its size: a hotbed of artists, writers and creative people." Average attendance is 70. **Open to everyone. "We create an intense community of writers and cover fiction, poetry and writing for children plus playwriting, screenwriting and mystery. Also talks by editors, agents, and others in the industry."** Offerings specifically available for poets include an introductory class in writing poetry, an intensive seminar, night sessions for participants to share poetry, and critiquing. Speakers for the 1995 conference included Sue Grafton, who also taught a class in novel writing and read mss. Cost for 1995 conference was $450; scholarships and some work-study fellowships are available (including the Judson Jerome Scholarship sponsored by *Writer's Digest* magazine). Both graduate and undergraduate credit is available for an additional fee. Campus dining room meal ticket is $105 (for 20 meals); must be purchased in advance. Transportation from airport is provided. Information on overnight accommodations is available and includes housing in campus dorms. Individual critiques are also available. Submit work for critique in advance with $60 fee for poetry; $60 fee for story, book or script. Send SASE for brochures and registration forms. Antioch Writers' Workshop is supported in part by Poets & Writers, Inc.

APPALACHIAN WRITERS' ASSOCIATION CONFERENCE, Dept. of English, WCU, Cullowhee NC 28723, phone (704)227-7264, program chair Steve Eberly. Annual 3-day event founded in 1980. 1996 dates: July 12-14. Location: Madison Dorm and Conference Center on the campus of Western Carolina University. Average attendance is 65 members. **Open to Appalachian writers, "including any interested writers in Kentucky, Tennessee, Georgia, South Carolina, North Carolina, Virginia, West Virginia and other kindred spirits." The conference is designed "to share readings, workshops, marketing tips and skills relating to poetry, fiction and essays; to celebrate the successes, common bonds and concerns of writers in the Appalachian region."** Special features include "Readings by the Creek," a picnic and open readings, at WCU picnic grounds. Cost for conference ranges from $100-130, including room (2 nights), meals and registration. Local accommodations on campus are arranged by AWA. A list of other accommodations is available on request. Poetry, fiction and essay contests are sponsored as part of the conference. Entry requirements: $15/year membership fee, $5/year for students. Judges are published regional writers. Send SASE for brochures and registration forms.

APPALACHIAN WRITERS WORKSHOP, P.O. Box 844, Hindman KY 41822, phone (606)785-5475, director Mike Mullins. Annual 5-day event founded 1977. Usually held at the end of July or beginning of August. Location: Campus of Hindman Settlement School in Knott County, KY. "The campus is hilly and access for housing is limited for physically impaired, but workshop facilities are accessible." Average attendance is 60-70. **Open to "anyone regardless of sex, age or race." Conference is designed to promote writers and writing of the Appalachian region. It covers fiction, poetry, writing for children, dramatic work and nonfiction.** Offerings specifically available for poets include daily sessions on poetry, individual critique sessions and readings. All of the staff for 1995 were featured readers, including James Still, Jeff Daniel Marion, Jim W. Miller, George Ella Lyon, Lisa Koger, Bobbie Ann Mason and Barbara Smith. Cost for workshop is approximately $350 for room, board and tuition. Information on overnight accommodations is available for registrants. Accommodations may include special rates at area hotels "once our facilities are filled." Submit mss for individual critiques in advance. Send SASE for brochures and registration forms. They have published *A Gathering At The Forks*, an anthology "of the best of the past 15 workshops." Write for information.

ARKANSAS WRITERS' CONFERENCE, 1115 Gillette Dr., Little Rock AR 72207, phone (501)225-0166, director Clovita Rice. Annual 2-day event founded 1944. "In 1994 we celebrated our 50th anniversary." Always 1st weekend of June at the Holiday Inn West in Little Rock. Average attendance is 200. **Open to all writers. The conference is designed to "appeal both to beginning and already active writers with a varied program on improving their writing skills and marketing their work."** Offerings specifically available for poets include poetry contests and sessions with poetry editors. In 1995, the guest speakers were Linda Nommer, former associate editor of *Redbook*, and Beth Brickell, award-winning actress and scriptwriter. Other special features include an awards luncheon (door prizes such as *Writer's Market* and *Poet's Market*) and banquet, and the announcement of the person selected for Arkansas Writers' Hall of Fame. Cost for 1995 conference was $10 registration for 2 days, $5 for 1 day. Five dollar fee to cover entry to 36 contests. Limousine service from airport to Holiday Inn West is provided. Accommodations include special rates at host hotel. Individual critiques are available. Thirty-six contests (4 require attendance and 8 are limited to Arkansas residents) are sponsored as part of the conference. Each contest has a chairman who will judge or secure a judge. Send SASE for brochures and registration forms after February 1 each year. Clovita Rice, conference director, is editor of *Voices International* (see listing in the Publishers of Poetry section).

AUSTIN WRITERS' LEAGUE SPRING AND FALL WORKSHOPS, 1501 W. Fifth St., Suite E-2, Austin TX 78703, phone (512)499-8914, executive director Angela Smith. Biannual workshops founded 1982. "Each workshop series has 12-18 workshops. Workshops are usually 3- or 6-hour sessions." Usually held weekends in March, April, May and September, October, November. Location: St. Edward's University Moody Hall. Average attendance is 15 to 200 per workshop. **Open to all writers, beginners and advanced. Workshops cover fiction, poetry, writing for children, nonfiction, screenwriting, book promotion and marketing, working with agents and publishers, journal writing, special interest writing, creativity, grantwriting, copyright law and taxes for writers.** Offerings specifically available for poets include at least 2 workshops during each series. Poetry presenters have included Lorenzo Thomas, Laurel Ann Bogen, Bobby Byrd and Benjamin Saenz. Past speakers have included Sandra Scofield, Sue Grafton, Peter Mehlman, Gregg Levoy, Lee Merrill Byrd and several New York agents and editors. "Occasionally, presenters agree to do private consults with participants. Also, workshops sometimes incorporate hands-on practice and critique." Cost is $35-75. Members get discount. Cost includes continental breakfast and refreshments for breaks. Meals not included. Arrangements can be made in advance for airport transportation. Information on overnight accommodations is available for registrants. Accommodations include special rates at area hotels.

Requirements for critiques are posted in workshop brochure. Send SASE for brochures and registration forms. The Austin Writers' League publishes *Poetography*, an anthology of poems selected by jury, and *The Austin Writer*, a monthly publication of poetry selected from submissions each month. These poems are eligible for six $100 Word Is Art awards presented in December of each year. Poetry guidelines for other publications, awards and grants programs, and market listings are available through the League library.

AUTUMN AUTHORS' AFFAIR, 1507 Burnham Ave., Calumet City IL 60409, phone (708)862-9797, president Nancy McCann. Annual 3-day event founded 1983. The 1995 conference will be held October 6, 7 and 8 at the Hyatt Lisle in Lisle, IL. Average attendance is 200-275. **Open to anyone. Conference covers fiction, but Professor Charles Tinkham of Purdue University-Calumet, called "the poet of the people," usually gives a poetry workshop "covering the entire realm" of writing poetry. "We have between 40-75 published authors and qualified speakers at the conference each year."** Saturday-only and weekend packages, including most meals, are available. Information on overnight accommodations is also available. Send SASE for brochures and registration forms which include the cost of each package, special hotel rates and itinerary.

BAY AREA WRITERS WORKSHOP, % Poetry Flash, P.O. Box 4172, Berkeley CA 94704, phone (510)525-5476, fax (510)540-1057, co-directors Katy Kennedy and Jennifer Rodrique. Annual 2-day events founded in 1988. Usually held 4-5 summer weekends at various workshop settings. Average attendance is 15 for workshops. **Open to literary writers. Workshops cover poetry, novel and short story.** In 1994 the weekend intensive workshops were led by Brenda Hillman, Yusef Komunyakaa, James Salter and Dorothy Allison. Cost for workshop is $250; participants are responsible for their own meals. Full scholarships are awarded to 10-15% of participants. Information on overnight accommodations and transportation is available for participants. Workshop evaluations are included. All participants receive manuscripts prior to weekend. Bay Area Writers also sponsor a biennial 1-day literary publishing conference for 300 participants. Send SASE for brochures and registration forms.

‡**BENNINGTON SUMMER WRITING WORKSHOPS**, Bennington College, Bennington VT 05201, phone (802)442-5401 ext. 160, fax (802)442-6164, assistant director Priscilla Hodgkins. Annual 2-4 week event founded 1977. Usually held in July. Located at Bennington College Campus. "A 550-acre site in the Green Mountains of southwestern Vermont." Average attendance is 80-90 students/session, 12/workshop. **Open to everyone over 18 years of age. Conference is designed to provide small classes and tutorials with distinguished faculty in fiction, nonfiction and poetry. There is time to write and revise while in residence at Bennington College."** Offerings specifically available for poets include readings and workshops. "Student readings are held several times each week and offer all students valuable experience of reading before an audience." In 1995, guest speakers included David Broza who puts modern poetry to song (e.g., "One Art" by Elizabeth Bishop), Ann Quinn, Nan Graham, Peter Stitt, Alexander Taylor, Fiona McCrae, Judith Doyle and Elizabeth Gaffney. Cost for 1995 was $1,380 for 2-week tuition including room and board; $2,280 for 4-week tuition including room and board. "Participants may take room and board at the college or a list of local motels, inns, B&Bs is available." On-site accommodations include single rooms in college houses. Linens are supplied. Cost is $495 for 2 weeks; $870 for 4 weeks. Includes meals. "Students may take meal plan without staying on campus. Those who do stay on campus are automatically enrolled in meal plan. All prospective participants must submit a writing sample with their application. This is reviewed by an admissions panel. This or another writing sample (12 pages of poetry) is critiqued by faculty in workshop and in tutorial. Students also critique each other's work." Call or write for brochures and registration forms. Affiliated with Associated Writing Programs and Writers Conferences and Festivals.

BREAD LOAF WRITERS' CONFERENCE, Middlebury College, Middlebury VT 05753, phone (802)388-3711, ext. 5286, administrative coordinator Carol Knauss. Annual 12-day event founded 1926. Usually held in mid-August. Average attendance is 230. **Conference is designed to promote dialogue among writers and provide professional critiques for students. Conference usually covers fiction, nonfiction and poetry.** Cost for 1995 conference was $1,585, including tuition, room and board. Fellowships and scholarships for the conference are available. "Candidates for fellowships must have a book published. Candidates for scholarships must have published in major literary periodicals or newspapers. A letter of recommendation, application and supporting materials due by April 1. Awards are announced in June for the conference in August." Taxis to and from the airport or bus station are available. Individual critiques are also available. Send for brochures and application forms.

‡**BROCKPORT WRITERS FORUM SUMMER WORKSHOPS**, Lathrop Hall, SUNY-Brockport, Brockport NY 14420, phone (716)395-5713, fax (716)395-2391, director Dr. Stan Rubin. Annual 7-day event founded 1980. Usually held the second week in July. Average attendance is 60-75. **Open to all writers, "advanced beginners through published authors." Workshop covers fiction, poetry, creative nonfiction, journals/autobiography and fantasy/science fiction.** Panels for 1996 are on

publishing, craft and on individual genre. Offerings specifically available for poets include poetry workshop with 2 nationally known leaders. Guest speaker at the last conference was Peter Stitt, editor of *The Gettysburg Review*. Other special features include individual conferences (critiques) for all participants, access to the Brockport Writers Forum videotape library and readings by faculty and participants. "Up to 3 college credits—graduate or undergraduate—can be earned." Cost for conference is approximately $400, lodging is extra. "Some meals are included, such as a workshop dinner with special guest." Transportation to and from the event is provided as required. Accommodations available in on-site conference center. Send SASE for brochures and registration forms. "We publish occasional broadsides and pamphlets of participant and faculty work."

CAPE COD WRITERS CONFERENCE OF CAPE COD WRITERS' CENTER, c/o Cape Cod Conservatory, Rte. 132, West Barnstable MA 02668, phone (508)375-0516, director Marion Vuilleumier. Annual week-long event founded in 1963. Usually held the third week of August at the Tabernacle, Craigville Conference Center. Average attendance is 150. **Open to everyone. Conference covers poetry, fiction, nonfiction, mystery/suspense and writing for children.** In 1995 the poetry teacher was Liz Rosenberg. Cost is $80 registration, $90 each course (full time); $25 registration, $25 each course (one day); 4 scholarships available. Participants are responsible for their own meals. "It is recommended that participants stay at the Craigville Conference Center (early registration necessary)." Other housing information available from Bed & Breakfast Cape Cod. Manuscript evaluations ($60) and personal conferences ($30) are also available. Send SASE for brochures and registration forms.

CAPE WRITING WORKSHOPS OF CAPE COD WRITERS' CENTER, c/o Cape Cod Conservatory, Rte. 132, West Barnstable MA 02668, phone (508)375-0516, director Marion Vuilleumier. Annual week-long event founded 1985. Usually held the 2nd week of August at the Parish House, St. Mary's Church, Barnstable. Average attendance is 10/workshop. **Open to everyone. Workshops usually cover poetry, fiction, scriptwriting, travel, science fiction, magazine article writing and children's book writing and illustration.** Cost is $410; participants are responsible for meals although "plentiful snack spreads" are included. "Twenty hours of practically individual attention is given, including one personal critique." Private transportation recommended. Contact Bed & Breakfast Cape Cod for housing information. Send SASE for brochures and registration forms.

CHARLESTON WRITERS' CONFERENCE, Lightsey Conference Center, College of Charleston, Charleston SC 29424-0001, phone (803)953-5822, fax (803)953-1454, director Paul Allen. Annual 4-day event founded 1989. Usually held in March at the College of Charleston, founded 1770, in historic downtown Charleston, South Carolina, "a setting renowned for its beauty, history and intimacy." Average attendance is 150. **Open to everyone. Conference covers fiction, poetry and nonfiction.** Past offerings have included a panel discussion on issues in writing and workshops covering various genres. Speakers at previous conferences have included Jill McCorkle, Bret Lott, Kelly Cherry and Sydney Lea. Cost for 1995 conference was $110 ($75 for students); participants are responsible for their own meals. Information on overnight accommodations is available for registrants. Accommodations include special rates at hotels within walking distance of conference. Individual critiques are also available. Submit up to 3 poems, not to exceed 7 pgs., typed and single-spaced with $40 ms evaluation fee. Send SASE for brochures and registration forms or call Judy Sawyer at phone number above.

‡**CHRISTIAN WRITERS WEEKEND**, Cedar Hills Conference Center, 5811 Vrooman Rd., Painesville OH 44077, phone (216)352-6363, coordinator Lea Leever Oldham. Held mid-June from dinner Friday through Sunday afternoon. Founded 1995. Weekend includes seminars on various subjects including poetry as well as one-on-one sessions for published authors. Cost is approximately $125 for conference, room and board.

COOS BAY WRITERS WORKSHOP, P.O. Box 4022, Coos Bay OR 97420, phone (503)756-7906, director Mary Scheirman. Annual 4-day event founded 1987. Usually held the last Thursday through Sunday in August. Location: University of Oregon Biological Research Station at Charleston Harbor on the beach. Average attendance is 40. **Open to everyone. Workshop usually covers poetry and prose.** Special features include a " 'walking workshop'—an 8-mile hike on wilderness beach with two practicing writers who lead exercises and discussions along the way." Cost for conference is $275, including room, board, tuition and meals. Information on overnight accommodations is available for registrants. Individual critiques are also available. "Submit ms with registration prior to the workshop." Send SASE for brochures and registration forms.

‡**CRAFT OF WRITING**, University of Texas at Dallas, Center for Continuing Education, Box 830688, Mail Station CN1.1, Richardson TX 75081, phone (214)883-2204, fax (214)883-2995, director of continuing education Janet Harris. Annual 2-day event founded 1983. 1995 dates were September 22 & 23. Location: Omni Richardson Hotel. Average attendance is 175. **Open to all writers. Conference covers the creative, technical and business aspects of writing.** Offerings specifically available for

poets include workshops and critique sessions. Speakers at the 1995 conference included Millard Lampell, Fran Vick, Diana Gabaldon and A.W. Gray. Other special features include 28 workshops covering all facets of a writer's world, discussion sessions conducted by editors and agents, and tips for marketing yourself and your writing. Cost for 1996 conference is $195, includes 1 lunch and 1 banquet. Accommodations include special rates at the Omni Richardson where conference is held. Group critiques are available. Bring 3- to 8-page ms with you and sign up at registration desk. Contest sponsored as part of conference. You must be registered for the conference by July 21 to enter contest. Manuscript must be sent with registration. Write for brochures and registration forms.

‡**DEEP SOUTH WRITERS CONFERENCE**, %English Dept., USL Box 44691, Lafayette LA 70504, phone (318)482-6918, director John Fiero. Annual 3-day event founded 1960. Usually held the third week in September at the University of Southwestern Louisiana in Lafayette, LA. Average attendance is 200. **Open to anyone. "The conference emphasis is on adult writing. Within workshops, we cover poetry, fiction and scriptwriting. We have also had children's literary workshops."** Speakers for last conference included Ernest G. Gaines and Wendell Mayo. Cost for 1995 conference was $50 registration for readings and craft lectures. Includes one catered reception. Special fee for workshops. Information on overnight accommodations is available for registrants. Accommodations include special rates at area hotels. Individual critiques are also available. "Supplement fee is required plus sample of work." Contest sponsored as part of conference. Submit $10 entry fee and up to 3 poems. Send SASE for contest rules and registration forms. Sponsors the Spring Literary Festival and the biennial Miller Prize. They also publish an anthology of prize-winning work, *The Chapbook*.

FESTIVAL OF POETRY, Robert Frost Place, Franconia NH 03580, phone (603)823-5510, executive director Donald Sheehan. Annual week-long event founded in 1978. Usually held first week of August at Robert Frost's mountain farm (house and barn), made into a center for poetry and the arts. Average attendance is 50-55. **Open to poets only.** Recent faculty included Luci Topahonzo, William W. Cook, Molly Peacock, Martin Espada, Dana Gioia and Ellen Bryant Voigt.. Cost is $375-395 tuition, plus a $25 reading fee. "Room and board available locally; information sent upon acceptance to program." Application should be accompanied by 3 sample pages of your work. Send SASE for brochures and registration forms.

FESTIVAL OF POETS AND POETRY AT ST. MARY'S; EBENEZER COOKE POETRY FESTIVAL, St. Mary's College of Maryland, St. Mary's City MD 20686, phone (301)862-0239. An annual event held during the last two weekends in May. Approximately 18 guest poets and artists participate in and lead workshops, seminars and readings. Concurrent with the festival, St. Mary's College offers a 2-week intensive poetry writing workshop and a 10-day writer's community retreat. **The poetry workshop engages the participants in structured poetry writing experiences. Intended for anyone with a serious interest in writing poetry**, it offers four college credits or may be taken as a non-credit course. **The retreat, designed for the serious writer, offers individual plans for writing alone or in conjunction with other participants.** Three 90-minute workshop sessions are organized for participants. There is also a 12-day fiction writing workshop offered during the festival. For applications or more information on these workshops or the festival, please write to Michael S. Glazer at the above address. The Ebenezer Cooke Poetry Festival is a biennial event in August of even numbered years, held in the name of the first Poet Laureate of Maryland. Poets from Maryland and the surrounding areas are invited to give 5-minute readings, enjoy a crab feast and otherwise celebrate together.

THE FLIGHT OF THE MIND, WOMEN'S WRITING WORKSHOPS, 622 SE 29th Ave., Portland OR 97214, phone (503)236-9862, director Judith Barrington. Annual events founded 1983. Usually held at the end of June, beginning of July. Two workshops in summer for 7 days each at "a rustic retreat center (Dominican owned) right on the wild McKenzie River in the foothills of the Oregon Cascades." Average attendance is 65 women/workshop in 5 different classes. **Open to women writers. Workshops cover fiction, poetry, essays, screenwriting, special-topic classes (e.g. "landscape and memory") with a feminist philosophy.** In 1995 workshop leaders included Ursula K. Le Guin, Naomi Shihab Nye and Grace Paley. Cost for workshop (including tuition, all meals and room) was $635 and up depending on accommodations chosen. Scholarships available. Transportation to and from the event is provided. Participants are selected on the basis of work submitted. Peer critique groups form at workshop. "Competition is discouraged." Send first-class stamp for brochures and registration forms.

‡**FLORIDA CENTER FOR WRITERS' WEEKEND WORKSHOP**, Dept. of English, University of South Florida, Tampa FL 33620, phone (813)974-1711, fax (813)974-2270, director Steve Rubin. Annual 3½-day event founded 1995. Usually held in April at the University of South Florida, Tampa campus. Average attendance is 75-80. **"Open to all writers, beginning and advanced. Workshop covers poetry, fiction and nonfiction."** Offerings specifically available for poets include poetry workshop and readings. Speakers at last conference were Tobias Wolff, Dannie Abse and Peter Meinke. Other special features include intensive small-group seminars, guest speakers and a banquet. Cost for

conference is $225, includes ms evaluation and banquet. Transportation to and from the event is provided. Information on overnight accommodations is available for registrants. Accommodations include special rates at area hotels. Manuscript evaluation available for each participant. Send SASE for brochures and registration forms.

‡**FLORIDA SUNCOAST WRITERS' CONFERENCE**, Dept. of English, University of South Florida, Tampa FL 33620, phone (813)974-1711, fax (813)974-2270, directors Steve Rubin and Edgar Hirshberg. Annual 3-day event founded 1970. 1996 dates: February 1-3. Location: University of South Florida, St. Petersburg campus. Average attendance is 350. **"Open to students, teachers, established and aspiring writers. Conference covers all areas—fiction, poetry, nonfiction, children's, mystery/ detective, romance, etc."** Offerings specifically available for poets included seminars, workshops, poetry readings and ms evaluation. Speakers at past conferences included Peter Meinke, Sharon Olds, Nikki Giovanni, Yeugency Yevtushenko, Maxine Kumin, Michael Dennis Brown and Toi Derricotte. Cost for 1996 conference is $115; $95 for students and teachers. Information on overnight accommodations is available for registrants. Accommodations include special rates at area hotels. Manuscript evaluation available at extra cost. Send SASE for brochures and registration forms. They also publish *Sunscripts*, an anthology of writing from Florida Suncoast Writers' Conference. All participants eligible to submit.

‡**HARVARD SUMMER WRITING CENTER**, 51 Brattle St., Dept 733, Cambridge MA 02138, phone (617)495-4024, fax (617)495-9176, director David Gewanter. Annual 8-week event. 1995 dates were June 26-August 18. Location: Harvard University. Average attendance is approximately 300. **"Open to everyone. Conference covers fiction, nonfiction, poetry, creative and expository writing, technical writing, journalism, etc.** Offerings specifically available for poets included beginning poetry, intermediate poetry and advanced poetry courses. Other special features included small classes, one-on-one conferences, instructors who are writers themselves and faculty members of Harvard University and others. Cost for 1995 conference was $1,325/course (2 courses is considered full-time), plus $2,175 for room and board. Dormitory accommodations available. "Critiques available during class." Send SASE for brochures and registration forms. They publish a journal at the end of the 8-week session. "Work submitted is not always included."

HAYSTACK WRITING PROGRAM, School of Extended Studies, Portland State University, P.O. Box 1491, Portland OR 97207, phone (503)725-4186, fax (503)725-4840, contact Maggie Herrington. Annual summer program founded 1968. One-week courses over the six weeks of the program. 1995 dates: June 26-August 4. "Classes are held in the local school of this small coastal community; some evening lectures and other activities." Average attendance is 10-15/class; 350 total. **Open to all writers. One-week workshops cover fiction, poetry, mystery, radio essay and nonfiction.** Cost for workshop is $305-350; participants pay for their own lodging and meals. Accommodation options range from camping to luxury hotels. Write for brochures and registration forms (no SASE necessary).

‡**THE HEIGHTS WRITER'S CONFERENCE**, Writer's World Press, P.O. Box 24684, Cleveland OH 44124, phone (216)481-1974, fax (216)481-2057, conference coordinator Lavern Hall. Annual 1-day event founded 1991. Usually held the third Saturday in May. "The conference is held at the Marriott hotel in Beachwood, OH. Conference rooms are centrally located and handicapped accessible. Lunch is served in the ballroom." Average attendance is 100. **"Open to all writers who are interested in learning about the craft and business of writing and networking with professionals. We cover a variety of genres including poetry, fiction, science fiction, romance, mystery, travel, etc.** We don't have themes; however, each year two intensive hands-on workshops will vary. In 1995, the workshops were in children's literature and writing fiction. These workshops are teaching workshops limited to 25 students who must pre-register on a first come, first serve basis." Offerings specifically available for poets include a seminar conducted by a published poet. The 1995 poetry seminar leader was Kate Kilbane who talked about "Making Poems—Readings, Resources, Approaches To Writing." Guest speaker for the last conference was well-known mystery writer Les Roberts, who spoke on "Putting Yourself On The Page." "Our format is unique. We have four major sessions (two in the morning and two in the afternoon) with three concurrent one-hour seminars. In addition, we offer two 2½-hour teaching workshops, one in the morning, the other in the afternoon. The genre teaching workshops will vary each year." Cost for 1995 conference was $59 preregistration; $70 late registration. "All activities are included: continental breakfast, seminars/workshops, lunch with guest speaker program, networking reception and author autographing at conclusion of day. In addition there are many free handouts and The Writer's Book Shop offers a selection of writing-related books. We provide accommodation information upon request for those arriving the day before." Critiques are handled through the speaker directly. Send SASE for brochures and registration forms. Information on local poetry readings and poetry publishers soliciting work available.

‡**HIGHLAND SUMMER WORKSHOP**, P.O. Box 7014, Radford University, Radford VA 24142, phone (703)831-5366, director Grace Toney Edwards. Annual 2-week event founded 1978. Usually held the

last 2 weeks in June. Location: Radford University campus. Average attendance is 20-25. **Open to everyone. "The conference, a lecture-seminar-workshop combination, is conducted by well-known guest writers and offers the opportunity to study and practice creative and expository writing within the context of regional culture." Topics covered vary from year to year. Poetry, fiction and essays (prose) are generally covered each year.** In 1995, offerings specifically available for poets included workshops taught by Appalachian poet and fiction writer, Jim Wayne Miller. Speakers at the last conference were Anndrena Belcher, Dori Sanders and Ron Rash. Other special features included evening readings by each of the speakers and a workshop offered for 3 semester credit hours. Cost for 1995 conference ranged from $406-925 plus $15/day for meals. Individual meals may also be purchased. On-site housing costs range from $16-26/night. On-site accommodations are available at Norwood Hall. Accommodations are also available at local motels. Send SASE for brochures and registration forms.

HOFSTRA UNIVERSITY SUMMER WRITERS' CONFERENCE, 110 Hofstra University, Hempstead NY 11550, phone (516)463-5997, fax (516)463-4833, director Lewis Shena. Annual 10-day event founded 1972. Usually starts the Monday after July 4th. Location: Hofstra University. Average attendance is 50-60. **Open to all writers. Conference covers fiction, nonfiction, poetry, children's writing, stage/screenwriting and, on occasion, one other area (science fiction, mystery, etc.).** Guest speakers (other than the workshop leaders) "usually come from the world of publishing." There are also "readings galore and various special presentations." Cost for 1995 conference was $625 (noncredit). Additional fee of $350 for air-conditioned dorm room, one dinner and coffee/tea on a daily basis. For those seeking credit, other fees apply. Individual critiques are also available. "Each writer gets a half hour one-on-one with each workshop leader." They do not sponsor a contest, but "we submit exceptional work to various progams sponsored by Writers Conferences and Festivals." Write for brochures and registration forms (available as of April).

IOWA SUMMER WRITING FESTIVAL, University of Iowa, 116 International Center, Iowa City IA 52242-1802, phone (319)335-2534, fax (319)335-2740, coordinators Amy Margolis and Peggy Houston. Annual event founded in 1987. Held each summer in June and July for six weeks, includes one-week and weekend workshops at the University of Iowa campus. Average attendance is 125/week. **Open to "all adults who have a desire to write." Conference offers courses in most all writing forms. In 1995, offerings available for poets included 15 poetry classes for all levels.** Speakers were Elizabeth McCracken, Diane Glancy, Beth Nugent, Stephen Greenleaf, Michael Dennis Browne and Donald Justice. Cost for 1995 conference was $150 for a weekend course, $335-360 for a week course and $485-510 for a week through weekend course. Participants are responsible for their own meals. Accommodations available at the Iowa House and the Holiday Inn. Housing in residence hall costs about $25/night. Participants in week-long workshops will have private conference/critique with workshop leader. Send for brochures and registration forms.

THE IWWG SUMMER CONFERENCE, The International Women's Writing Guild, P.O. Box 810, Gracie Station, New York NY 10028, phone (212)737-7536, executive director Hannelore Hahn. Annual week-long event founded 1978. Usually begins on the second Friday in August and runs through following Friday. Location: Skidmore College in Saratoga Springs, NY. Average attendance is 400. **Open to all women. Fifty-six workshops offered. "At least four poetry workshops offered for full week."** Cost is $600 for conference program and room and board. "Critiquing available throughout the week." Send SASE for brochures and registration forms. The International Women's Writing Guild's bimonthly newsletter publishes and features hundreds of outlets for poets. See listing in Organizations Useful to Poets.

LIGONIER VALLEY WRITERS CONFERENCE, Box 8, RR 4, Ligonier PA 15658, phone (412)238-5749, fax (412)238-5190, president E. Kay Myers. Annual 3-day event founded 1986. 1996 dates: July 12-14. "This is a relaxing, educational, inspirational conference in a scenic, small town." Average attendance is 80. **Open to anyone interested in writing. Conference covers fiction, creative nonfiction, poetry, writing for children and screenwriting.** Poetry workshops each day. 1995 workshops conducted by Margaret Gibson. Cost for conference is approximately $200, including some meals and picnic. Participants are responsible for their own dinner and lodging. Information on overnight accommodations is available for registrants. Individual critiques are also available. Must send samples in advance. Send SASE for brochures and registration forms. "We also publish *The Loyalhanna Review*, a literary journal, which is open to participants."

‡MARITIME WRITERS' WORKSHOP, UNB Dept. of Extension, Box 4400, Fredericton, New Brunswick E3B 5A3 Canada, phone (506)454-9153, fax (506)453-3572, coordinator Glenda Turner. Annual 1-week event founded 1976. Usually held the first week in July. Location: University of New Brunswick campus. Average attendance is 50. **Open to all writers. Workshop covers fiction, nonfiction, poetry and writing for children.** Offerings specifically available for poets included a daily workshop group for poets, limited to 10 participants, and individual conferences arranged with instructors. Speakers at last conference were Elisabeth Harvor and Steven Heighton (fiction); Richard Lemm and Lesley-Anne Bourne (poetry); Sharon Butala (nonfiction); Joan Clark (writing for children). Other special features included readings. Cost for 1995 conference was $300 plus $250 for room and board. Scholarships are available. Information on overnight accommodations is available for registrants. "All participants must submit a manuscript which is then 'workshopped' during the week." Write for brochures and registration forms.

MIDLAND WRITERS CONFERENCE, Grace A. Dow Memorial Library, 1710 W. St. Andrews, Midland MI 48640, phone (517)835-7151, fax (517)835-9791, conference co-chairs Margaret Allen, Eileen Finzel and Barbara Brennan. Annual 1-day event founded 1979. Usually held the second weekend in June at the Grace A. Dow Memorial Library in Midland, MI. Average attendance is 100. **Open to any writer, published or unpublished. Conference usually includes six sessions that vary in content. "We always have one session on poetry and one session on writing for children. The other four sessions cover other subjects of interest to writers."** In 1995, Nick Bozanic of Interlocken Fine Arts Academy conducted a 2-hour poetry workshop, and the keynote speaker was Dave Barry. "We always have a well-known keynoter. In the past we have had Judith Viorst, Kurt Vonnegut, Mary Higgins Clark, David McCullough, P.J. O'Rourke." Cost for 1995 conference was $45 until 2 weeks prior to the event ($55 after that). For students, senior citizens and handicapped participants, cost was $35 until 2 weeks prior to the event ($45 after that). Information on overnight accommodations is available for registrants. Send for brochures and registration forms.

MIDWEST WRITERS' CONFERENCE, 6000 Frank Ave. NW, Canton OH 44720-7599, phone (216)499-9600, fax (216)494-6121, coordinator of continuing studies Debbie Ruhe. Annual weekend event founded 1968. 1996 dates: October 4-5. Location: Kent State University Stark Campus in Canton, Ohio. Average attendance is 350. **Open to aspiring writers in any category, but the writing contest is directed toward fiction, nonfiction, juvenile literature and poetry. "The conference provides an atmosphere in which aspiring writers can meet with and learn from experienced, established writers through lectures, workshops, competitive contests, personal interviews and informal group discussions."** Offerings specifically available for poets include a lecture session in the poetry area and a contest. Past panelists have included Joyce Carol Oates, Edward Albee, Kurt Vonnegut and John Updike. One special feature of the conference is an all day book fair which includes several Ohio small presses. Cost for 1995 conference was $65, including conference registration, workshops, keynote address, lunch and ms entry fee. Contest entry fee exclusively: $40 for two mss and $10 for each additional ms. Participants are responsible for other meals. Information on overnight accommodations is available for registrants. Special conference rates are available through the Sheraton Inn, and there is a special shuttle between the university and the hotel. Individual critiques are also available in the areas of poetry, fiction, nonfiction and juvenile literature. Submit one individual poem up to 200 lines. Contest sponsored as part of conference. "Work must be original, unpublished and not a winner in any contest at the time of entry." Judging is performed by local professionals in their appropriate categories. Send SASE for brochures and registration forms. Kent State University offers submissions to the annual publication of *Canto*. For more information, call (216)499-9600. Co-sponsor of the Midwest Writers' Conference is the Greater Canton Writers' Guild, 919 Clinton Ave. SW, Canton OH 44706-5196.

MISSISSIPPI VALLEY WRITERS CONFERENCE, 3403 - 45th St., Moline IL 61265, phone (309)762-8985, founder/director David R. Collins. Annual week-long event founded in 1973. Usually held the second week in June at the Liberal Arts College of Augustana College. Average attendance is 80. **Open to all writers, "beginning beginners to polished professionals." Conference provides a general professional writing focus on many genres of writing. Offers week-long workshop in poetry.** Evening programs as well as daily workshops are included. Cost for 1995 conference was $25 registration, $40 one workshop, $70 two workshops, $30 each additional workshop. Conferees may stay on campus or off. Board and room accommodations are available at Westerlin Hall on Augustana campus, 15 meals and 6 nights lodging approximately $200. Individual critiques are also available. Submit up to 10 poems. Awards presented by workshop leaders. Send SASE for brochures and registration forms.

MOUNT HERMON CHRISTIAN WRITERS CONFERENCE, P.O. Box 413, Mount Hermon CA 95041, phone (408)335-4466, fax (408)335-9218, director of specialized programs David R. Talbott. Annual 5-day event founded 1970. Always held Friday through Tuesday over Palm Sunday weekend. 1996 dates: March 29-April 2. Location: Full hotel-service-style conference center in the heart of the California redwoods. Average attendance is 150-200. **Open to "anyone interested in the Christian writing market." Conference is very broad-based. Always covers poetry, fiction, article writing, writing for children, plus an advanced track for published authors.** In 1995, offerings specifically available for poets included a 4-day, 8-hour track on "Writing the Published Poem," plus individual one-hour workshops on poetry. "We had 34 teaching faculty for 1995—will be similar for 1996. Faculty was made up of publishing reps of leading Christian book and magazine publishers, plus selected freelancers." Other special features included an advance critique service (no extra fee); residential conference, with meals taken family-style with faculty; private appointments with faculty; and an autograph party. "High spiritual impact." Cost for 1995 conference was $650 deluxe; $545 standard; $465 economy; including 13 meals, snacks, housing and $285 tuition fee. No-housing fee: $435. All housing on grounds. $15 airport, Greyhound or Amtrack shuttle from San Jose, CA. Send SASE for brochures and registration forms.

NAPA VALLEY WRITERS' CONFERENCE, Napa Valley College, 1088 College Ave., St. Helena CA 94574, phone (707)967-2900, managing director Sherri Hallgren. Annual week-long event founded 1981. Usually held the last week in July or first week in August at Napa Valley College's new facility in the historic town of St. Helena, 30 minutes north of Napa in the heart of the valley's wine growing community. Average attendance is 36 in poetry and 36 in fiction. **"The conference has maintained its emphases on process and craft, featuring a faculty as renowned for the quality of their teaching as for their work. It has also remained small and personal, fostering an unusual rapport between faculty writers and conference participants. The poetry session provides the opportunity to work both on generating new poems and on revising previously written ones. Participants spend time with each of the staff poets in daily workshops that emphasize writing new poems—taking risks with new material and forms, pushing boundaries in the poetic process."** The 1995 poetry staff was Stephen Dunn, Kathleen Fraser, Brenda Hillman and Marie Howe. "Participants register for either the poetry or the fiction workshops, but panels and craft talks are open to all writers attending. Evenings feature readings by the faculty that are open to the public and hosted by Napa Valley wineries." Cost is $450, not including meals or housing. There are some limited partial scholarships, depending on donations. A list of valley accommodations is mailed to applicants on acceptance and includes at least one reduced-rate package. "Through the generosity of Napa residents, limited accommodations in local homes are available on a first-come, first-served basis." All applicants are asked to submit a qualifying ms with their registration (no more than 5 pgs. of poetry or 10-15 pgs. of fiction) as well as a brief description of their background as a writer. Application deadline: June 1. Send SASE for brochures and registration forms.

THE NAROPA INSTITUTE WRITING & POETICS SUMMER PROGRAM, 2130 Arapahoe Ave., Boulder CO 80302, phone (303)444-0202, director of writing & poetics Anne Waldman, assistant director Andrew Schelling. Annual month-long summer program founded in 1974. Held from mid-June to mid-July, participants may attend from 1-4 weeks. "We are located on 3.7 acres in the center of Boulder, Colorado. The campus houses a performing arts center, meditation hall, classrooms, offices and library. Many of the summer lectures are held under a huge tent on our back lawn." Average attendance is 100-120. **Open to anyone; students attending for credit must obtain department's permission. "It is a convocation of students, scholars, fiction writers, poets and translators. In dialogue with renown practitioners of verbal arts, students confront the composition of poetry and prose."** Theme for 1994 was Beat Reunion, "a tribute to Allen Ginsberg." The 1995 summer program included emphasis in these areas: "Dharma/Ecopoetics, International Writers, The Oral Tradition and Experimental/Wild Forms." Offerings specifically available for poets include lectures, readings (both student and faculty), workshops and one-on-one interviews with guest faculty. Conference speakers have included Allen Ginsberg, Anselm Hollo, Bobbie Louise Hawkins, Jack Collom, Bernadette Mayer, Michael McClure, Ron Silliman, Michael Ondaatje, Nathaniel Mackey and Eagle Cruz. Cost for 1 week is $375 (non credit), for 2 weeks $630 (non credit) and $750 (BA credit). Cost of 4 weeks is $1,260 (non credit), $1,500 (BA credit) and $2,000 (MFA credit). Lab fees are $10/week. Four scholarships are available for minority students. Participants are responsible for their own meals. "Student services can help find places to stay." Work to be critiqued does not need to be sent in advance. "During the weekly workshops and personal interviews, every writer will have a chance to be critiqued by professional poets/fiction writers." Write for brochures and registration forms. "We also sponsor student readings and have an informal summer magazine and a school sponsored magazine, *Bombay Gin*."

‡NEBRASKA WRITERS' GUILD CONFERENCE, 941 "O" St., Suite 728, Lincoln NE 68508, phone (402)475-1123, fax (402)475-1123, president Linda Dageforde. Biannual 1-day event founded 1925. Usually held in April and October at various locations statewide. Average attendance is 50-75. **"Open to members and any writers. Conference covers all areas of writing, publishing and marketing."** Guest speaker at the last conference was poet Roy Scheele. Other special features included a book fair and book exchange. Cost for conference was $35/member, $40/nonmember. Information on overnight accommodations is available for registrants. Send SASE for brochures and registration forms.

OZARK CREATIVE WRITERS CONFERENCE, 6817 Gingerbread Lane, Little Rock AR 72204, phone (501)565-8889, conference counselor Peggy Vining. Annual 3-day event. Usually held in October at the Inn of the Ozarks in Eureka Springs, Arkansas. 1995 dates were October 12-14. **Open to all writers.** Registration fee is $35 prior to September 1. Various writing contests sponsored as part of conference.

Awards of $25, $15 and $10 ("some higher"). Deadline for entry is August 31 postmark. Send #10 SASE for brochure after April 1.

‡**POETRY RENDEZVOUS**, 1409 Williams, Great Bend KS 67530, phone (316)792-2409, fax (316)793-7260, director of public relations Terri Nye. Annual 2-day event founded 1988. 1996 dates: August 3 and 4. Location: Great Bend Public Library (handicapped accessible). Average attendance is 200. **"Open to anyone interested in poetry. Concentration is on all forms of poetry. Our purpose is to draw poetry lovers together to share talent and information. Open readings allow the general public an opportunity to experience poetry presented by the poet.** We try to allow everyone who wants to read a chance to read their work." Offers a variety of workshops, usually 4 in all. One workshop is presented by the featured poet. "In 1994, we started 'Poets Round Table,' an opportunity for poets to discuss issues of interest to them in an informal forum." Workshops are held on Saturday. Public readings are Sunday afternoon. Featured poet for 1995 was Joan Jobe Smith. Past featured poets include Tony Moffeit, Lyn Lifshin, Rochelle Lynn Holt, Ruth Moon Kempher, Gerald Locklin and Todd Moore. Cost for workshops is $10-15 each. "Sunday's readings are free and open to the public. Lunch is provided at a small charge. Dinner followed by poetry readings and music costs $5 (in 1995). (These two are Saturday.)" Information on overnight accommodations is available upon request. Send SASE for brochures and registration forms. They publish an anthology of work from poets who attend the Rendezvous. Submit poems in advance. Michael Hathaway, editor of *Chiron Review*, is a sponsor of the Poetry Rendezvous.

PORT TOWNSEND WRITERS' CONFERENCE, c/o Centrum, P.O. Box 1158, Port Townsend WA 98368, phone (360)385-3102, fax (360)385-2470, director Carol Jane Bangs. Annual 10-day event founded 1974. Usually held the second week in July at a 400-acre state park at the entrance to Puget Sound. Average attendance is 160. **Open to "all serious writers who pass our preliminary manuscript screening." Conference usually covers fiction (no genre fiction), poetry, creative nonfiction, and writing for children.** Offerings specifically available for poets include "three limited-enrollment workshops, private manuscript conference, open-mike readings, faculty readings and technique classes." Speakers at the last conference were Richard Kenney, Carolyn Kizer, Agha Shahid Ali, Janice Eidus, Pam Houston, Craig Lesley, Christopher Merrill, Jane Yolen, Bruce Coville, Omar Castañeda and David Rigsbee. Cost for the 1995 conference was $400 tuition including workshop, ms conference, classes, readings, lectures; $290 tuition without workshop or ms conference; plus $315 optional for dormitory housing and 3 meals per day. Information on overnight accommodations is available for registrants. Individual critiques are also available, however "you must be enrolled in a manuscript workshop." Send SASE for brochures and registration forms.

ST. DAVIDS CHRISTIAN WRITERS CONFERENCE, 1775 Eden Rd., Lancaster PA 17601-3523, phone (717)394-6758, address Registrar. Annual 5-day event founded 1957. Usually held in June at the campus of Eastern College in St. Davids, PA. Average attendance is 100-120. **Open to "anyone interested in writing." Conference is designed to "train and develop skills of writers for Christian and secular markets."** Offerings include a series of advanced classes that require prior acceptance to attend. Cost for conference is $400-500, including classes, room and board. Price varies according to choice of study packages. Transportation to and from the conference includes a commercial airport shuttle plus pickup from St. Davids train station. Housing in on-site facilities costs $200-230. Individual critiques are also available. "Must have a body of work to submit." Contest sponsored as part of conference. "Must be a conference attendee. Faculty members judge contest." Send SASE for brochures and registration forms.

SANTA BARBARA WRITERS' CONFERENCE, P.O. Box 304, Carpinteria CA 93014, phone (805)684-2250, fax (805)684-7003, conference director Barnaby Conrad. Annual week-long event founded in 1973. Held the last Friday to Friday in June at the Miramar Hotel in Montecito. Average attendance is 350 people. **Open to everyone. Covers all genres of writing.** Workshops in poetry offered. Past speakers have included Ray Bradbury, Phillip Levine, Gore Vidal and Willian Styron. Cost for 1995 conference, including all workshops and lectures, 2 al fresco dinners and room (no board), was $1,010 single, $740 double occupancy, $350 day students. Individual critiques are also available. Submit 1 ms of no more than 3,000 words in advance with SASE. Competitions with awards sponsored as part of conference. Send SASE for brochures and registration forms.

SEWANEE WRITERS' CONFERENCE, 310 St. Luke's Hall, Sewanee TN 37383-1000, phone (615)598-1141, fax (615)598-1145, conference administrator Cheri B. Peters. Annual 12-day event founded 1990. Usually held the last 2 weeks in July at The University of the South ("dormitories for housing, Women's Center for public events, classrooms for workshops, student union building for dining, etc."). Attendance is about 105. **Open to poets, fiction writers and playwrights who submit their work for review in a competitive admissions process. "Genre, rather than thematic, workshops are offered in each of the three areas."** In 1995, faculty members were fiction writers Russell

Banks, James Gordon Bennett, John Casey, Ellen Douglas, Ann Hood, Alice McDermott; Francine Prose and Stephen Wright; poets Anthony Hecht, John Hollander, Charles Martin and Mary Jo Salter; and playwrights Kent Brown and Horton Foote. Other speakers included editors, agents and additional writers. Cost for 1995 conference was $1,150, including room and board. Each year scholarships and fellowships based on merit are available on a competitive basis. "We provide bus transportation from the Nashville airport on the opening day of the conference and back to the airport on the closing day at no additional cost." Individual critiques are also available. "All writers admitted to the conference will have an individual session with a member of the faculty." A ms should be sent in advance after admission to the conference. Write for brochure and application forms. No SASE necessary.

SINIPEE WRITERS WORKSHOP, P.O. Box 902, Dubuque IA 52004-0902, phone (319)556-0366, director John Tigges. Annual 1-day event founded 1986. Usually held the 3rd or 4th Saturday in April on the campus of Clarke College, Dubuque, Iowa. Average attendance is 50-100. **Open to anyone, "professional or neophyte," who is interested in writing. Conference covers fiction, poetry and nonfiction.** Speakers for 1995 included best-selling novelist Thomas Gifford, best-selliing nonfiction author Robert Byrne, Emmy award winner and novelist Ben Logan, western author Paul Adams and Pam Schuster, who gave her dissertation on poetry in rhyme. Cost for 1995 workshop was $60 pre-registration, $65 at the door. Scholarships covering half of the cost are traditionally available to senior citizens and to full-time students, both college and high school. Cost included handouts, coffee and donut break, lunch, snacks in afternoon and book fair with authors in attendance available to autograph their books. Information on overnight accommodations is available for out-of-town registrants. Annual contest for nonfiction, fiction and poetry sponsored as part of workshop. There is a $5 reading fee for each entry (article/essay of 1,500 words, short story of 1,500 words or poetry of 40 lines). First prize in each category is $100 plus publication, second prize $50 and third prize $25. Entrants in the contest may also ask for a written critique by a professional writer. The cost for critique is $15/entry. Send SASE for brochures and registration forms.

‡SOCIETY OF THE MUSE OF THE SOUTHWEST (SOMOS), P.O. Box 3225, Taos NM 87571, phone/fax (505)758-0081, office manager Beth Enson. Founded 1983. "We offer workshops at different times during the year, at least one during the summer." Length of workshops vary. Held at various sites from the University of New Mexico-Taos campus to a bed & breakfast in New Buffalo. Average attendance is 10-50. **Open to anyone. "We offer workshops in various genres—fiction, poetry, nature writing, etc."** In 1995 they offered poetry workshop by Robin Becker. Other special features include writing in nature/nature walks and beautiful surroundings in a historic writer's region. Cost for workshops range from $50-175, excluding room and board. Transportation to and from the events is provided. "With advance notice, we will pick up people in Taos and bring them to New Buffalo, if they take the Greyhound from Albuquerque." Information on overnight accommodations is available. "We reserve rooms at New Buffalo (special group rate of $25/day for shared rooms), which must be paid 45 days in advance." Individual critiques are also available. Submit 5 poems in advance. Send SASE for brochures and registration forms. "We're affiliated with Blinking Yellow Books in Taos, which publishes local authors including poets."

SOUTHWEST FLORIDA WRITERS' CONFERENCE, P.O. Box 60210, Ft. Myers FL 33906-6210, phone (813)489-9226, fax (813)489-9051, director Joanne Hartke. Annual event founded 1980. Usually held the 4th Friday and Saturday in February on the campus of Edison Community College. Average attendance is 150-200. **Open to anyone interested in writing, including full-time high school and college students. "We cover many areas; in 1995 our offerings included poetry and writing for children. Sessions are usually varied to provide something for both beginning and published writers."** The 1995 poetry session was with Rochelle Holt. Cost for the 1995 Friday sessions was $25; the Saturday conference was $49, including a continental breakfast and lunch. Limited scholarships are usually available and full-time students can attend the conference for only $15. Information on overnight accommodations available for registrants. An annual contest (including poetry) is sponsored as part of the conference. Judges are published authors and writers in the Ft. Myers community. Send SASE for brochures and registration forms.

STATE OF MAINE WRITERS' CONFERENCE, P.O. Box 146, Ocean Park ME 04063, phone (207)934-5034, fax (207)934-2823 (summer), phone (413)596-6734, fax (413)782-1746 (winter), director Dick Burns. Annual August event founded 1941. Usually runs from Tuesday evening to Friday noon. 1996 dates: August 20-23. Average attendance is 50-75. **Open to any interested person. Conference is "very eclectic, covers writing to publishing."** Every year there is a poetry tournament including a poetry booklet, Poems to be Put on Trees Contest and Beach Inspiration Poetry. "In 1995, there was a Haiku Workshop. Something similar is expected to be continued annually." Cost is $75. Those 21 and under may attend at half price. Information on overnight accommodations is available for registrants. "Local accommodations are reasonable." There are many contests, 15-20/year. Separate contest announcement is available in advance to registrants. Send SASE for brochures and registration forms.

TRENTON STATE COLLEGE WRITERS CONFERENCE, Trenton State College, Hillwood Lakes CN 4700, Trenton NJ 08650-4700, phone (609)771-3254, director Jean Hollander. Annual 1-day event founded 1981. Usually held the beginning of April at Trenton State College Campus. Average attendance is about 800. **Open to anyone. Conference covers all genres of writing. "We usually have a special presentation on breaking into print." 12-15 separate poetry and fiction workshops as well as readings are offered.** In 1995 the speakers were Kurt Vonnegut and Molly Peacock. Cost in 1995 was $40 for day session; additional cost for workshops and evening session. Discounts available for students. Information on overnight accommodations is available for registrants. Poets and fiction writers may submit ms to be critiqued in writing by workshop leaders. Poetry and short story contest sponsored as part of conference. 1st prize: $100; 2nd prize: $50. Judges are workshop leaders and a special panel from the English Dept. Write or call for brochures and registration forms.

‡UNIVERSITY OF WISCONSIN-MADISON'S SCHOOL OF THE ARTS AT RHINELANDER, 726 Lowell Hall, 610 Langdon St., Madison WI 53703, administrative coordinator Kathy Berigan. Annual 5-day event founded 1964. Usually held the third or fourth week in July. Held at a local junior high school. Average attendance is 300. **Open to all levels and ages.** Offerings specifically available for poets include poetry workshops. Guest speakers at last workshop was Jerry Apps, *Writing Your Life Story*. Cost for 1995 workshop ranged from $125-205. Information on overnight accommodations is available for registrants. Write for brochures and registration forms.

‡WESLEYAN WRITERS CONFERENCE, Wesleyan University, Middletown CT 06457, phone (203)685-3604, fax; (203)347-3996, director Anne Greene. Annual 5-day event founded 1956. Usually held the last week in June, on the campus of Wesleyan University. The campus is located "in the hills overlooking the Connecticut River, a brief drive from the Connecticut shore. Wesleyan's outstanding library, poetry reading room, and other university facilities are open to participants." Average attendance is 100. **"Open to both experienced and new writers. The participants are an international group. The conference covers the novel, short story, fiction techniques, fiction-and-film, poetry, literary journalism and memoir."** Themes for 1995 were "How Poets Make a Living," "Writing a First Novel," "Investigative Journalism" "Publishing," "Translation" and "Readings of New Fiction." Offerings specifically available for poets included seminars and ms consultations with Henry Taylor and discussion sessions with Dana Gioia, Molly Peacock, George Garrett, David Slavitt and Michael Lind. Speakers at last conference were Zhang Jie (China's foremost woman writer), Robert Stone, Peter Maas, Amy Bloom, Tom Drury and Richard Bausch. Cost for 1995 conference was $620 plus $105 for room and board, includes all meals. "Wesleyan has special scholarships for journalists who are interested in poetry and fiction techniques. Request brochure for application information." Information on overnight accommodations is available. "Conference participants may stay in university dormitories or off campus in local hotels." Individual critiques are also available. Registration for critiques must be made before the conference. Send SASE for brochures and registration forms.

WESTERN RESERVE WRITERS AND FREELANCE CONFERENCE, 34200 Ridge Rd., #110, Willoughby OH 44094, phone (216)943-3047, coordinator Lea Leever Oldham. Annual 1-day event founded 1983. Usually held the second Saturday in September. Average attendance is 150. **Open to "writers, published and aspiring." Conference usually covers fiction; nonfiction; poetry; articles; books; sometimes photography and other freelance subjects; copyright; writing for children; etc.** "We always include a presentation specifically for poetry." Cost for conference is about $49, including lunch. Participants can make arrangements one-on-one for possible time with guest speakers. Send SASE for brochures and registration forms.

WESTERN RESERVE WRITERS MINI CONFERENCE, 34200 Ridge Rd., #110, Willoughby OH 44094, phone (216)943-3047, coordinator Lea Leever Oldham. Annual ½-day conference founded 1991. Usually held the last Saturday in March. Average attendance is 100. **Open to "published and aspiring writers." Conference usually covers fiction, nonfiction, poetry, writing for children, articles and romance writing.** "We always have a session with a published poet." Cost for conference is $25, including morning refreshments. Attendees can make their own arrangements with presenters for possible critiques. Send SASE for brochures and registration forms.

‡WHITE RIVER WRITERS' WORKSHOP, Lyon College, P.O. Box 2317, Batesville AR 72503-2317, phone (501)793-1766, fax (501)698-4622, director Andrea Hollander Budy. Annual 7-day event founded 1995. Usually held the third week of June at the "campus of Lyon College on the banks of the White River in the foothills of the Arkansas Ozarks. This workshop offers a beautiful setting, rich with opportunities to experience the natural and cultural attractions of this region." Limited to 50 participants. **Open to poets. "Workshop is designed as an intensive for poets in poetry, translation and**

presentation. Serious poets are invited to work on new poems and/or translations. All are also invited to work on oral presentation." Speakers at last workshop were Lola Haskins, Dana Gioia, Linda Gregg, Susan Ludvigson, Ted Kooser and Lee Potts. Special features included panels, craft lectures and readings. Also, all faculty and fellows available for one-on-one guidance. Cost for 1995 workshop was $375 plus $300 for room and board. "Five scholarships and five fellowships are awarded each summer. The scholarships (which cover tuition costs only) are available to poets who have not yet published a first full-length book but who have published individual poems in established and reputable literary journals. Fellowships (which cover tuition and room and board) are awarded to poets who have published at least one, but no more than two, full-length poetry collections. Applications for scholarships and fellowships are due by April 1." Transportation to and from the event is available. "A van or taxi will be available for a reasonable fee." All participants are expected to live on campus during the week-long event. Write for brochures and application forms. Applications are read and evaluated as they are received. There is no deadline, but once the workshop is filled all other applications will be returned. Early application is suggested.

WILDACRES WRITERS WORKSHOP, c/o 233 S. Elm St., Greensboro NC 27401, phone/fax (910)273-4044, director Judith Hill. Annual week-long event founded 1983. Usually held the 2nd week in July at "a beautiful retreat facility in the Blue Ridge Mountains of North Carolina." Average attendance is 100. **Open to all "serious adult writers."** Conference covers fiction, poetry, screen and play writing, and nonfiction. **"We have two poetry workshops with a limit of twelve to a class.** In total, we have eleven writers on staff who read and give programs. Plus we have an agent in residence." Cost is approximately $360, including a double room, all meals and ms critique. Van transportation to and from the Asheville Airport is provided. Send SASE for brochures and registration forms. Some years they also publish *The Wildacres Review.*

WISCONSIN REGIONAL WRITERS' ASSOCIATION, 912 Cass St., Portage WI 53901, phone (608)742-2410, president Elayne Clipper Hanson. Biannual conferences founded in 1948. Usually held first Saturday in May and last weekend in September at various hotel-conference centers around the state. Average attendance is 100-130. **Open to all writers, "aspiring, amateur or professional." All forms of writing/marketing rotated between conferences. "The purpose is to keep writers informed and prepared to express and market their writing in a proper format." Poetry covered once a year.** In 1995, spring speakers included Rev. Williams Heins, publisher, Heins Publications; Jonis Agee, novelist; Bill Nelson, Wisconsin journalist; and Diane Clancy, teacher of Native American Literature and Creative Writing at Macalester College, St. Paul MN. A book fair is held at both conferences where members can sell their published works. A banquet is held at the fall conference where writing contest winners receive awards. Spring conference is approximately $30-35, fall conference approximately $35-40. Spring conference includes coffee and sweet rolls, lunch and hors d'oeuvres at book fair. Fall conference also includes dinner and entertainment. Information about overnight accommodations is available for registrants. "Our organization 'blocks' rooms at a reduced rate." Sponsors 3 writing contests/year. Membership and small fee are required. Send SASE for brochures and registration forms. "We are affiliated with the Wisconsin Fellowship of Poets, the Wisconsin Authors and Publishers Alliance and the Council of Wisconsin Writers. We also publish a newsletter four times a year for members."

THE WRITERS' CENTER AT CHAUTAUQUA, Box 408, Chautauqua NY 14722, phone (716)357-2445 (June-August) or (717)872-8337, director Mary Jean Irion. Annual event founded 1988. Usually held 9 weeks in summer from late June to late August. Participants may attend for one week or more. "We are an independent, cooperative association of writers located on the grounds of Chautauqua Institution." Average attendance is 30 for readings and speeches, 12 for workshops. **Readings and speeches are open to anyone; workshops are open to writers (or auditors). The purpose is "to make creative writing one of the serious arts in progress at Chautauqua; to provide a vacation opportunity for skilled artists and their guests (one each); and to help learning writers improve their skills and vision."** Workshops are available all nine weeks. Poetry Works meets two hours each day offering one hour of class for every hour of workshop. In 1995, leaders included Michael Waters, Geraldine Connolly, Stephen Corey and Margaret Gibson. Prose Works offers two hours a day in fiction and nonfiction, writing for children and Young Writers' Workshops. Poets are welcome to explore other fields. Other special features include two speeches a week and one reading, usually done by the Writers-In-Residence. Cost is $60/week. Participants are responsible for gate fees, housing and meals and "may bring family; sports, concerts, activities for all ages. A week's gate ticket to Chautauqua is $155/adult (less if ordered early); housing cost varies widely, but is not cheap; meals vary widely depending on accommodations—from fine restaurants to cooking in a shared kitchen." Access is best by car or plane to Jamestown, NY, where a limousine service is available for the 14 miles to Chautauqua ($18). Phone number for Accommodations Directory Service is available for registrants. Individual critiques are also usually available. Information published in spring mailing. Send SASE for brochures and registration forms.

WRITERS' FORUM, Community Education Dept., Pasadena City College, 1570 E. Colorado, Pasadena CA 91106-2003, phone (818)445-0704, contact Meredith Brucker. Annual 1-day event founded 1954. Usually held all day Saturday in mid-March at Pasadena City College. Average attendance is 200. **Open to all. Conference covers a wide variety of topics and always includes one poet.** Recent speakers have included poet Ron Koertge, *ONTHEBUS* editor Jack Grapes, Philomene Long speaking on "Poetry for Non-poets," and Myra Cohn Livingston describing "Poem Making" for children. Cost for the 1995 conference was $75, including lunch. Write for brochures and registration forms. No SASE necessary.

WRITING TODAY, BSC A-3, Birmingham AL 35254, phone (205)226-4921, fax (205)226-4931, director of special events Martha Andrews. Annual 2-day event founded 1978. 1996 dates: April 12-13. Location: Birmingham-Southern College campus. Average attendance is 400-500. **Open to "everyone interested in writing—beginners, professionals and students. Conference topics vary year to year depending on who is part of the faculty."** In 1995, Ray Bradbury was the major speaker and Master Award recipient. Other speakers at the last conference were Mark Childress, Peter Hellman, and Mavis Jukes. Cost for 1995 conference was $85 before deadline ($90 after deadline), including lunches and reception. Cost for a single day's events was $45, including luncheon. Either day's luncheon was only $20. $10 cancellation fee. Information on overnight accommodations is available for registrants. Accommodations include special rates at area hotels. Individual critiques are also available. In addition, the Hackney Literary Awards competition is sponsored as part of the conference. The competition, open to writers nationwide, offers $2,000 in prizes for poetry and short stories and a $2,000 award for the novel category. Entry requirements for poetry include: Poems not to exceed 50 lines/entry. More than 1 poem may be submitted, but all poems together must not exceed the 50-line limit. Postmark deadline: December 31. Fee: $5/entry. Send SASE to Hackney Literary Awards at above address for complete guidelines. Also send SASE for conference brochures and registration forms.

WRITING WORKSHOP, (formerly Writing Workshop for People Over 57), % Donovan Scholars Program, University of Kentucky, Ligon House, 658 S. Limestone St., Lexington KY 40506-0442, phone (606)257-2657, fax (606)323-4940. Annual event founded 1966. Usually held in June, the workshop runs from Sunday afternoon to Friday afternoon. Location: Gratz Park Inn. Average attendance is 35-50 (maximum). **Open to "adults aged 55 or older who share an interest in writing and wish to learn more about how to express their thoughts in the written form. We offer classes in fiction, nonfiction, children's literature/juvenile novel and poetry."** Offerings specifically available for poets include "classes instructed by established writers in the field of poetry, whether local or elsewhere." Cost is $320/person, includes classes, meals and double occupancy room. Writers may register as full-student status, which requires a ms to be submitted for critique, or as auditor status, which does not require a ms. Send SASE for brochures and registration forms. *Second Spring*, their yearly publication, contains the written work of past workshop participants.

YELLOW BAY WRITERS' WORKSHOP, Center for Continuing Education, The University of Montana, Missoula MT 59812, phone (406)243-6486, fax (406)243-2047, program officer Nancy J. Harte. Annual week-long event founded 1988. Usually held mid-August at the University of Montana's biological research station which includes informal educational facilities and rustic cabin living on Flathead Lake in western Montana. Average attendance is 60. **Open to all writers. Conference offers two workshops in fiction, one in nonfiction and one in poetry.** In 1995, workshop faculty included Andrea Barrett (fiction), Robert Hass (poetry), William Kittredge (essay/nonfiction) and Melanie Rae Thon (fiction). Elizabeth Grossman, a literary agent with Sterling Lord Literistic in New York, joined editors of regional literary journals for a forum on publishing. Cost for 1995 workshop was $425, commuter fee; $725, tuition and single-occupancy cabin/meals; $695, tuition and double-occupancy cabin/meals. Round-trip shuttle from Missoula to Yellow Bay (85 miles) is available for $40. Applicants must send a writing sample. Full and partial scholarships are available. Send SASE for brochures and registration forms.

Writing Colonies

Writing colonies are places for writers (including poets) to find solitude and spend concentrated time focusing on their work. While a residency at a writing colony may offer participation in seminars, critiques or readings, the atmosphere of a colony or retreat is much more relaxed than that of a conference or workshop. Also, a writer's stay at a colony is typically anywhere from one to twelve weeks (sometimes longer), while time spent at a conference may only run from one to fourteen days.

Like conferences and workshops, however, writing colonies and retreats span a wide range. Yaddo, perhaps the most well-known colony, limits its residencies to writers "who have already achieved some recognition in their field and have new work under way," whereas Walker Woods (which is new to this edition) offers residencies to writers completing their first books. Hedgebrook (also new to this edition) is limited as well. It only offers residencies to women writers. The Dobie-Paisano Project, on the other hand, limits its fellowships and residencies to writers with an identifiable Texas connection. And, in addition to listings for colonies across the United States, this section contains listings for residencies in Canada, France, Ireland, and the Italian Alps.

Despite different focuses and locations, all writing colonies and retreats have one thing in common: They are places where you may work undisturbed, usually in very nature-oriented and secluded settings. A colony serves as a place for rejuvenation, a place where you may find new ideas for poems, rework old ones, or put the finishing touches to a collection.

Selecting a writing colony

When selecting a colony or retreat, the primary consideration for many writers is cost, and you'll discover that arrangements vary greatly. The Millay Colony for the Arts, Inc., for instance, has no fee. Other colonies provide residencies as well as stipends for personal expenses. Some suggest donations of a certain amount. Still others offer residencies for tidy sums but have financial assistance available.

When investigating the various options, consider meal and housing arrangements and your family obligations. Some colonies provide meals for residents, while others require residents to pay for meals. Some colonies house writers in one main building; others provide separate cottages. (In both cases, you are given private work space, although you must usually bring along your own reference materials and typewriter or personal computer.) A few writing colonies have provisions for spouses and families. Others prohibit families altogether.

Overall, residencies at writing colonies and retreats are competitive. Since only a handful of spots are available at each place, you must often apply months in advance for the time period you desire. A number of locations are open year-round, and you may find that planning to go during the "off-season" lessens your competition. Other colonies, however, are only available during certain months. In any case, be prepared to include a sample of your best work with your application. Also, know what project you'll work on while in residence and have alternative projects in mind in case the first one doesn't work out once you're there.

Each listing in this section details fee requirements, meal and housing arrangements, and space and time availability, as well as the retreat or colony's surroundings, facilities and special activities. Of course, before making a final decision, send a SASE to the colonies or retreats that interest you to receive the most up-to-date details. Costs, application requirements and deadlines are particularly subject to change.

For other listings of writing colonies, see *The Guide to Writers Conferences* (available from ShawGuides, Inc., P.O. Box 1295, New York NY 10023), which not only provides information about conferences, workshops and seminars but also residencies, retreats and organizations. Another resource is *Havens for Creatives*, available from ACTS Institute, Inc. The Institute has also published a compilation of works produced by artists while in residence at eight different colonies. For more information, write to ACTS Institute, Inc., P.O. Box 30854, Palm Beach Gardens FL 33420.

THE EDWARD F. ALBEE FOUNDATION, INC.; THE WILLIAM FLANAGAN MEMORIAL CREATIVE PERSONS CENTER ("THE BARN"), 14 Harrison St., New York NY 10013, phone (212)226-2020, for information and application forms. The Albee Foundation maintains the center (better known as "The Barn") in Montauk, on Long Island, offering 1-month residencies for writers, painters, sculptors and composers, open June 1 through October 1, accommodating 6 persons at a time. Applications accepted at the above address by regular mail only January 1 through April 1. Fellowship announcements by May 15. "Located approximately 2 miles from the center of Montauk and the Atlantic Ocean, 'The Barn' rests in a secluded knoll that offers privacy and a peaceful atmosphere. The foundation expects all those accepted for residence to work seriously and to conduct themselves in such a manner as to aid fellow residents in their endeavors. The environment is simple and communal. Residents are expected to do their share in maintaining the condition of 'The Barn' as well as its peaceful environment."

ATLANTIC CENTER FOR THE ARTS, 1414 Art Center Ave., New Smyrna Beach FL 32168, phone (904)427-6975. The center was founded in 1979 by sculptor and painter Doris Leeper, who secured a seed grant from The Rockefeller Foundation. That same year the center was chartered by the state of Florida and building began on a 10-acre site. The facility now covers 67 acres. The center was officially opened in 1982. Since 1982, 61 Master Artists-in-Residence sessions have been held. At each of the 3-week sessions, internationally known artists from different disciplines conduct interdisciplinary workshops and lectures and critique works in progress. They also give readings and recitals, exhibit their work and develop projects with their "associates"—mid-career artists who come from all over the US to work with them. The center is run by an advisory council which chooses Master Artists for residencies, helps set policies and guides the center in its growth. The process of becoming an associate is different for each Master Artist. Recent poets in residence at the center include Robert Creeley (November 1994), Rachel Hadas (January 1995) and Sonia Sanchez (May 1995). Ntozake Shange is scheduled to be at the center in May 1996.

BANFF CENTRE FOR THE ARTS WRITING STUDIO, Box 1020, 107 Tunnel Mountain Dr., Banff, Alberta T0L 0C0 Canada, offers 4-6 weeks of residence between October 23 and November 24 to writers "who already have a body of work (some of it preferably, but not necesssarily, published) attesting to their commitment and talent. Applicant should have a project in progress . . . . Enrollment is limited to 20 participants—10 in poetry, 10 in prose. Artists may receive awards up to 80% of cost of program fee, room and board." Located in an inspirational mountain setting, The Banff Centre for the Arts is a unique Canadian institution. Participants are housed in single rooms that also serve as their private work spaces. Application deadline: April 30.

BELLAGIO STUDY AND CONFERENCE CENTER, The Rockefeller Foundation, 420 Fifth Ave., New York NY 10018-2702, manager Susan Garfield. Offers 1-month individual or parallel residencies from February 1 through December 15 for artists, scholars, scientists, policy makers and practitioners with significant and substantial publications, compositions, exhibitions, productions or other accomplishments. Applications are considered 4 times/year on a competitive basis. Approximately 140 residencies are awarded annually. The Center is located on Lake Como in the Italian Alps. Room available for spouses. Residents must pay their own travel costs. Write for application and guidelines.

CENTRUM, Residency Program, P.O. Box 1158, Port Townsend WA 98368, offers 1-month residencies, September through May, for architects, writers, musicians and printmakers. Centrum provides individual cottages, a stipend of $75/week and solitude. Families welcome. Located in Fort Worden State Park on the Strait of Juan de Fuca. Also sponsors the Port Townsend Writers' Conference (See Conferences and Workshops) and other seminars. Contact Carol Jane Bangs, Literature Program Manager, for more information on these programs.

CHATEAU DE LESVAULT, Onlay, 58370 Villapourçon, France, phone/fax (33)86-84-32-91. This French country residence is located in the national park "Le Morvan" of western Burgundy, halfway between Nevers and Autun and is surrounded by green hills and forests. The chateau accommodates 5 residents at a time in 5 large rooms with private baths, fully furnished and equipped for working. The facilities of the chateau are at the disposal of residents, including the salon, library and grounds. Requests for residencies from October through April should be made at least 3 months in advance. The cost is 4,500 FF per month for room, board (5 days a week) and utilities.

THE CLEARING, Box 65, Ellison Bay WI 54210, phone (414)854-4088, resident managers Donald and Louise Buchholz, "is first a school, then a place of self-discovery." Made up of cabins and lodges in a rustic setting overlooking Green Bay, it offers a variety of courses, including courses in writing and poetry, May through October. Fees include tuition, room (dormitory or twin-bedded room) and board.

DOBIE-PAISANO PROJECT, Attn: Audrey N. Slate, Main Building 101, The University of Texas, Austin TX 78712. Offers two annual fellowships of $7,200 and 6-month residency at Frank Dobie's ranch, Paisano, for Texans, Texas residents or writers with published works about Texas. Write for application and guidelines. Application deadline: January 26, 1996.

DORLAND MOUNTAIN ARTS COLONY, P.O. Box 6, Temecula CA 92593, established 1979. A 300-acre nature preserve which offers 1-month residences for writers, visual artists and composers in a rustic environment with no elecricity, propane appliances (refrigerator, water heater, cooking stove, some lights) and oil lamps. Residents provide their own meals. A donation of $150/month is requested. Send SASE for application form and guidelines. Deadlines are the first of September and March.

DORSET COLONY HOUSE RESIDENCIES; AMERICAN THEATRE WORKS, INC., P.O. Box 519, Dorset VT 05251, director John Nassivera. Residencies available to writers fall and spring for periods of 1 week to 2 months for intensive work. Requested fee of $90/week, but ability to pay is not a criterion in awarding residencies.

‡FAIRVIEW SUMMIT MOUNTAIN TOP RETREAT, 10800 Mt. Fairview Rd. SE, Cumberland MD 21502, phone (301)724-6842, director Petrina Aubol, founded 1992. Offers unlimited weekly or week-end residencies on a year-round basis for "anyone seeking the ultimate getaway," including writers and artists. The retreat is a remodeled 100-year-old farmhouse situated in secluded Fairview Summit. "A world with no street lights, no burglar alarms, no pollution. The woodlands, the gardens, the dramatic vistas combine to shake off impositions of the modern world." Accommodates 20 residents at a time in single, double or dormitory rooms with shared baths; country kitchen, living room with TV/VCR and meeting room also available. Activities include a biannual workshop and local writers group meetings. Cost is $25/day, fee negotiable for long-term residency; additional cost for meals. Send SASE for application forms and guidelines. When reserving space, 25% deposit required. "Note: Ideal use of our retreat is for groups of writers/poets to schedule their own private meeting. (We only have one group at a time.)"

FINE ARTS WORK CENTER IN PROVINCETOWN, 24 Pearl St., Provincetown MA 02657, provides monthly stipends of $375 and studio/living quarters for 7 uninterrupted months for 20 young artists and writers (10 of each) who have completed their formal training and are capable of working independently. The center arranges readings and slide presentations and visits from other distinguished writers and artists. Sessions run from October 1 through May 1. Applications, accompanied by a $35 processing fee, must be received by February 1. To receive an application and program brochure, send a SASE to Writing Fellowship. Unlike the winter residency, the Summer Program offers open-enrollment workshops with "an outstanding faculty in the visual arts and writing." The 10-week program consists of 40 one-week workshops in poetry, fiction, nonfiction, painting, sculpture, installation, printmaking and photography. Write for catalog of course descriptions and registration materials.

‡GELL WRITERS CENTER OF THE FINGER LAKES, %Writers & Books, 740 University Ave., Rochester NY 14607, phone (716)473-2590, fax (716)729-0982, director Joseph Flaherty. Offers 1-week to 1-month residencies on a year-round basis for writers and readers who "seek a quiet and restorative time away from their usual routine. The center is located at the southern end of Canandaigua Lake, in the center of New York State's famous Finger Lakes region. Rich in natural diversity, the area contains one of the world's great grape-growing regions, as well as many fine cultural and recreational attractions. Visitors stay in The Gell House, a completely furnished hillside home surrounded by a beautifully landscaped yard and 23 acres of woodlands." Accommodates 2 writers at a time in single rooms with private baths and shared kitchen facilities; private desks and an extensive library available. Activities include workshops, lectures and readings at a nearby literary center. Cost is $25/day for members of Writers & Books; $35/day for nonmembers. Memberships are available. Participants are responsible for own meals. Send SASE for application forms, guidelines and membership information for Writers & Books. A 5- to 10-page work sample must accompany application.

GREEN RIVER WRITERS RETREAT, Shelbyville Campus, University of Louisville, Green River Writers, 403 S. Sixth St., Ironton OH 45638, secretary D.H. Spears, phone (614)533-1081, provides a 3-day workshop, then 5-day retreat. Rooms are available at the conference center per night stayed plus registration fee. Beginning writers are furnished with advisors. Details available for SASE.

THE TYRONE GUTHRIE CENTRE, Annaghmakerrig, Newbliss, Co. Monaghan, Ireland, phone (353)47-54003, fax (353)47-54380, resident director Bernard Loughlin. Offers residencies, normally 3 weeks to 3 months, for artists, including poets. "Each resident has a private apartment within the house . . . and all the centrally heated comfort an Irish Big House can afford. It is set on a wooded estate of 400 acres and overlooks a large lake. The house is surrounded by gardens and a working dairy farm. Couples or small groups of artists may stay for up to a year in Maggie's Farm, a cottage on the estate, and have use of studios at the Big House. Five newly built, self-contained farmyard cottages are also available for individuals and couples for longer stays. To qualify for residence it is necessary to show evidence of a significant level of achievement in the relevant field. Once accepted, Irish artists are asked to contribute what they can afford toward the cost of their stay. Overseas artists are expected to pay the whole cost of a residency."

HAMBIDGE CENTER FOR CREATIVE ARTS AND SCIENCES, P.O. Box 339, Rabun Gap GA 30568, phone (706)746-5718. The Center is located on 650 acres of unspoiled wooded slopes, mountain meadows and streams, near Dillard, Georgia. It is listed on the National Register of Historic Places. Resident Fellowships of 2 weeks to 2 months are awarded to individuals engaged in all artistic disciplines for the purpose of solitude and the pursuit of creative excellence. Those accepted are given a private cottage equipped with a kitchen, living and studio/work space. Center is open from May through October with limited winter fellowships available. For more information and application forms send SASE. Deadline: January 31. Application review begins in March.

HAWK, I'M YOUR SISTER; WOMEN'S WILDERNESS CANOE TRIPS; WRITING RETREATS, Beverly Antaeus, P.O. Box 9109, Santa Fe NM 87504-9109. This organization offers wilderness retreats for women, many of them with writing themes, including A Writing Retreat with Sharon Olds in Montana and A Writing Retreat with Deena Metzger in Baja California, Mexico. The canoe trips are held all over North America and typically last 8-10 days with fees of $895-1,895. Write for annual listing of specific trips.

‡HAWTHORNDEN CASTLE INTERNATIONAL RETREAT FOR WRITERS, Hawthornden Castle, Lasswade, Midlothian EH18 1EG Scotland, phone (0131)440-2180, contact administrator, founded 1982. Offers 8 four-week sessions from February through July and September through December for dramatists, novelists, poets or other creative writers who have published one piece of work. Located in a "remotely situated castle amid wild romantic scenery, a 30-minute bus ride to Edinburgh." Accommodates 5 writers at a time in study bedrooms with communal breakfasts and evening meals; desks, typewriters for hire, and limited reference materials available. Board and lodging are free. Write for application forms and guidelines. Application deadline is the end of September for upcoming year.

‡HEDGEBROOK, 2197 E. Millman Rd., Langley WA 98260, phone (360)321-4786, founded 1988. Offers 1-week to 3-month individual residencies from early January through May and mid-June through early December for "women writers of all ages and from all cultural backgrounds. The Hedgebrook community, on 30 acres of farmland and woods located on Whidbey Island in Washington State, seeks to balance human needs with those of the earth while providing a nurturing environment in which creativity can thrive." Accommodates 6 writers at a time. "Each writer has her own cottage with writing space, living room, sleeping loft, small kitchen, bathroom, electricity and a woodstove. Writers gather for dinner in the farmhouse every evening and may read in the living room/library afterwards. A bathhouse serves all six cottages." Public libraries with excellent interlibrary loan located within 2-6 miles. Computers available for rent. Activities include occasional cultural celebrations and field trips. Free room and board. Limited, need-based travel scholarships are available. Send SASE for application forms and guidelines. When sending application, include writing sample. Application deadlines: April 1 for residencies from mid-June to mid-December; September 30 for mid-January through May.

‡KALANI HONUA OCEANSIDE ECO-RESORT, RR2, Box 4500, Pahoa HI 96778, phone (808)965-7828 or (800)800-6886, fax (808)965-9613 (call first), director Richard Koob, founded 1980. Offers 2-week to 2-month residencies on a year-round basis for visual, literary, folk and performing artists. "Kalani Honua is situated near Kalapana on the big island of Hawaii on 20 acres of secluded forest and dramatic coastline, 45 minutes from the city of Hilo and one hour from Hawaii Volcanoes National Park. Visitors stay in four two-story wooden lodges and four private cottage units that provide simple but comfortable accommodations." Accommodates 100 (generally about 5 artists-in-residence) at a time in private rooms with full meal service plus optional kitchen facilities and shared or private baths; private desks and access to computers, typewriters and reference material available. Activities include a variety of dance, drawing, fitness and mind/body classes; also available are an olympic pool, sauna, volleyball, tennis, basketball and fitness room. Cost ranges from $28/night (multiple occupancy) to $85/night (private cottage); plus $25/day for meals. Stipends are most available in the periods of May through July and September through December. Stipends provide for 50% of lodging costs; balance is responsibility of the artist (stipends may *not* be applied toward dorm lodging or camping, or reduction in food or transportation costs). Send SASE for application forms and guidelines. When sending application, include $10 fee.

THE MACDOWELL COLONY, 100 High St., Peterborough NH 03458, founded 1907, offers residencies to established and emerging writers, composers, visual artists, filmmakers, architects and interdisciplinary artists. Over 3,000 artists have stayed here, many of them producing major works. Apply about 8 months before desired residency. Application deadlines: January 15 for May through August; April 15 for September through December; September 15 for January through April. Private studio, room and meals provided. Accepted artists are asked to contribute toward residency costs. Ability to pay is not considered in the application process. Current application form is necessary; write address above or call (603)924-3886. Average residency is 6 weeks. Professional work samples required with application.

THE MILLAY COLONY FOR THE ARTS, INC., P.O. Box 3, Austerlitz NY 12017-0003, founded in 1974, assistant director Gail Giles. Provides work space, meals and sleeping accommodations at no cost for a period of 1 month. Send SASE for brochure and application forms and apply with samples of your work before February 1 for June through September; before May 1 for October through January; before September 1 for February through May.

MONTALVO CENTER FOR THE ARTS; MONTALVO BIENNIAL POETRY COMPETITION (IV-Regional), Box 158, Saratoga CA 95071, presents theatre, musical events and other artistic activities. They have an Artist Residency program which has 5 apartments available for artists (including poets) for maximum 3-month periods. (No children or pets.) Limited financial assistance available. Deadlines: March 1 and September 1 of every year. They offer a biennial poetry competition open to residents of Oregon, Nevada, Washington and California, with a prominent judge, with a first prize of $1,000 (and artist residency), other prizes of $500, $300 and 8 honorable mentions. Submit 3 poems in duplicate with $5 entry fee. Deadline: October 2, 1995. Send SASE for rules.

‡**MY RETREAT**, P.O. Box 1077, South Fallsburg NY 12779, phone (914)436-7455, owner Cora T. Schwartz, founded 1993. Offers weekend, weekly or monthly residencies on a year-round basis for writers, poets and "artists of life." Located in the foothills of the Catskill Mountains, My Retreat is approximately 90 miles northwest of New York City. The writers' colony consists of a main house and two cottages across the road. The two 1950-style cottages (open May through October) have seven furnished bedrooms, three kitchens and four bathrooms. The main house, with five bedrooms, is available year-round. There are six screened and open porches, and a cool library is in the basement of one of the cottages. There is also a separate suite with a private entrance, comprised of a bedroom, kitchen and bath. Accommodates 5-12 writers/artists at a time in single or double rooms with shared and private baths and kitchens; private desks, use of computer in main house, extensive library and bookshop available. Activities include ongoing monthly workshops and informal readings. "If one wishes to take a break, there is a park with a lake for row boating and a pool for swimming nearby, along with riding stables, canoeing facilities, art galleries, a famous ashram and museums." Cost per person starts at $85 for the weekend and $185 for one week, including continental-style breakfast. There is a two night minimum. Residents are responsible for the remainder of their meals. Special rates available on longer stays of 1 week or more. Send SASE for information.

‡**THE NEW YORK MILLS ARTS RETREAT**, 24 N. Main Ave., Box 246, New York Mills MN 56567, phone (218)385-3339, fax (218)385-3366, coordinator Kent Scheer. Offers 1- to 4-week residencies on a year-round basis for emerging artists and writers of demonstrated quality and commitment. "The retreat is a 15-acre retired farmstead located three miles outside the small town of New York Mills. Loft space is provided in the upstairs of the old dairy barn while the original farm home serves as shared living quarters." Accommodates one writer/artist at a time in a single room with shared bath and kitchen. Work space and supplies are simple and minimal. A private loft is available for concentrated work. "All residencies in our program are supported by the Jerome Foundation. In this way we can provide stipends for 5 to 7 visiting artists annually. Beyond this, we will do all the necessary coordination for any artists interested in funding themselves for a personal retreat within our community. Artists and writers selected for our program receive up to $1,500 as a stipend. The criteria are artistic excellence as demonstrated by work samples, commitment to the arts as demonstrated by the résumé and a creative proposal for interaction with the community of New York Mills." Send SASE for application forms and

guidelines. When sending application, include a résumé, artist's statement and a retreat proposal. Application deadlines: June 1 and January 1.

THE NORTHWOOD UNIVERSITY ALDEN B. DOW CREATIVITY CENTER, 3225 Cook Rd., Midland MI 48640-2398, phone (517)837-4478, fax (517)837-4468, founded 1979, director Carol Coppage. Offers fellowships for 2-month summer residencies at the Northwood University Campus. Travel, room and board plus $750 stipend for personal expenses and/or project materials. No families/pets. Applicants can be undergraduates, graduates, or those without any academic or institutional affiliation, including citizens of other countries (if they can communicate in written and spoken English). Projects may be in any field, but must be new and innovative. Write for application. Annual deadline is December 31 for the following summer.

PUDDING HOUSE PUBLICATIONS, 60 N. Main St., Johnstown OH 43031. See listing in Publishers of Poetry section.

RAGDALE FOUNDATION, 1260 N. Green Bay Rd., Lake Forest IL 60045, founded 1976, director Michael Wilkerson, provides a peaceful place and uninterrupted time for 12 writers, composers and artists. Meals, linen and laundry facilities are provided. Each resident is assigned private work space and sleeping accommodations. Couples are accepted if each qualifies independently. Residents may come for 2 weeks to 2 months. The fee is $84/week. Some full and partial fee waivers available. The foundation also sponsors poetry readings, concerts, workshops and seminars in writing. Ragdale is open year-round except for two weeks in the late spring and at Christmas. Send SAE for application. Apply by January 15 for residencies in June through December and June 1 for January through May. Application fee: $20.

SPLIT ROCK ARTS PROGRAM, University of Minnesota, 306 Wesbrook Hall, 77 Pleasant St. SE, Minneapolis MN 55455. The program is a summer series of week-long workshops in the visual and literary arts and in the nature and applications of creativity, on the Duluth campus of UM "in the green hills overlooking Lake Superior." The 1995 faculty included Christina Baldwin, Sandra Benitez, Carol Bly, Michael Dennis Browne, Sharon Doubiago, Kate Green, Phebe Hanson, Alexs Pate, Jane Resh Thomas, Dan Coffey (Dr. Science of NPR), Jane Hirshfield, Alice Koller, Myrna Kostash, Mary La Chapelle and Gayle Pemberton. Tuition is $346-366 with an additional charge for graduate credit. Housing ranges from $168-246, depending on type of accommodation. Most students choose single or double rooms in 2-bedroom apartments on campus. Other housing options also available. Meals are in UMD's cafeteria, cooked by participants in their apartments, or in Duluth restaurants. Complete catalog available in March by mail or phone: (612)624-6800.

UCROSS FOUNDATION RESIDENCY PROGRAM, 2836 US Hwy. 14-16, Clearmont WY 82835, phone (307)737-2291, executive director Elizabeth Guheen. There are 8 concurrent positions open in various disciplines, including poetry, each extending from 2 weeks to 2 months. No charge for room, board or studio space, and they do not expect services or products from guests. Send SASE for information and application guidelines. Residents are selected from a rotating panel of professionals in the arts and humanities. Semiannual application deadlines are March 1 and October 1.

VERMONT STUDIO CENTER; VISUAL ARTISTS AND WRITERS RESIDENCIES, P.O. Box 613NW, Johnson VT 05656, phone (802)635-2727, founded 1984. Offers 2-week Writing Studio Sessions led by prominent writers/teachers focusing on the craft of writing. Independent Writers' Retreats for 2, 4 or more weeks are also available year-round for those wishing more solitude. Room, working studio and meals are included in all programs. Generous work-exchange Fellowships are available. Write or call for more information and application.

VIRGINIA CENTER FOR THE CREATIVE ARTS, Mt. San Angelo, Sweet Briar VA 24595, director William Smart. Provides residencies for 12 writers (and 9 visual artists and 3 composers) for 2 weeks to 2 months at the 450-acre Mt. San Angelo estate. All accommodations provided. The normal fee is $30/day. Financial assistance is available.

‡WALKER WOODS, 1397 La Vista Rd. NE, Atlanta GA 30324, phone/fax (404)634-3309, founder Dalian Moore, founded 1993. Offers 1- to 6-month residencies to "writers completing their first book (novels, short story collections, nonfiction, poetry, etc.) and also to foreign authors writing or translating a first book in the English language." Located on 1½ acres in North Atlanta, Walker Woods, the home of the late Reuters foreign correspondent Richard Leigh Walker, "features a waterfall into a pond stocked with colorful coy fish, a stone-lined stream (a tributary of the Chattahoochee River), hot tub, inspiration garden, and a three-story tree house currently in design. Writers may share a room or have one of their own, and all meals are taken communally—with residents cooking for each other."

Accommodates 8 writers at a time in three private suites (two with bathrooms), shared and convertible rooms. Kitchen and library are also shared. A computer system with laser printer is available on a reservation basis, but writers are encouraged to bring their own computers (laptops best). A fax machine and other office features are also available. Activities at Walker Woods include a public introduction of writers in residence. "A party is held in each writer's honor, with a full public relations campaign that introduces them nationally. Each night writers also have the opportunity to share new work and offer shared critique, and many nights patrons and community arts leaders join in for dinner and readings. Writers in residence are also listed with speakers bureaus in the immediate area and included in radio, television and public appearances made by Dalian Moore. They are also included in cultural programs at the symphony, ballet, museums and other institutions." Cost ranges from $300-600/month depending on accommodation and needs. "Residents selected for support live at Walker Woods free, but pay for their food, phone calls and office time (if they do not bring their own equipment). Everyone in residence takes up small projects on the property (be it planting a tree or flower bed) or assisting with general upkeep of the property—we live as a family." Full or partial scholarships are available on a competitive basis. Requirements for consideration are submission of 2 chapters of a novel or nonfiction book, 2 short stories or 20 poems for a collection in progress. Send SASE for application forms and guidelines. Application deadlines for scholarships are quarterly, and there is a onetime $20 application fee.

THE WRITERS COMMUNITY OF THE WRITER'S VOICE, West Side YMCA, 5 W. 63rd St., New York NY 10023, phone (212)875-4124. Offers a residency to an established poet in the fall and spring of each year. Honorarium: $7,500. The poet selects and teaches a 3-month master-level workshop and gives a public reading. Previous writers-in-residence include: Thomas Lux, Ntozake Shange, John Yau, Charles Simic, Jayne Cortez and Mary Stewart Hammond. Send SASE for application forms and guidelines. Recommendation must accompany application. The 3-month master-level workshop in poetry is held October through December and March through May (application deadline mid-September, mid-February), working with the writer-in-residence. Applicants should be within commuting distance of New York City. Tuition: $110. Submit cover letter and a maximum of 10 pgs. of poetry, which may be published material. All material should be typed or printed and copies should be retained. Mss cannot be returned. Call for application deadlines for the residency and workshop. (Also see the listing for the Capricorn Poetry Award in the Contests and Awards section.)

THE HELENE WURLITZER FOUNDATION OF NEW MEXICO, Box 545, Taos NM 87571. Offers residencies to creative, *not* interpretive, artists in all media, for varying periods of time, usually 3 months, from April 1 through September 30, annually. Rent free and utilities free. Residents are responsible for their food. No families. No deadlines on application.

YADDO, Box 395, Saratoga Springs NY 12866-0395, phone (518)584-0746, founded 1900, offers residencies to writers, visual artists, composers, choreographers, film/video artists and performance artists who have already achieved some recognition in their field and have new work under way. During the summer 35 guests can be accommodated at a time, 14 during the winter, approximately 200/year. The hours 9-4 are a quiet period reserved for work. There is no fixed charge for a guest stay, but voluntary payment in the suggested amount of $20/day to help defray costs of the program is accepted. However, no qualified artist is denied admission based on inability to pay. Write for applications to: Admissions, Yaddo, address above; enclose SASE. Application deadlines are January 15 and August 1. A $20 application fee is required.

Organizations Useful to Poets

The organizations listed in this section offer encouragement and support to poets and other writers through a wide variety of services. They may sponsor contests and awards, hold regular workshops or open readings, or release publications with details about new opportunities and area events. Many of these groups provide a combination of these services to both members and nonmembers.

The PEN American Center, for instance, holds public events, sponsors literary awards, and offers grants and loans to writers in need. Poets seeking financial assistance should also refer to the listing for the Authors League Fund or contact the arts council in their state or province (see State and Provincial Grants on pages 473-475).

Many organizations provide opportunities to meet and discuss work with others. Those with access to computers and modems can connect with poets around the world through computer online services like GEnie. The National Federation of State Poetry Societies, Inc. and the Canadian Poetry Association are both national organizations with smaller affiliated groups which may meet in your state or province. And for those seeking gatherings more local or regional in focus, there are organizations such as the Bergen Poets, the Dakota Cowboy & Western Poets Association, and the Philadelphia Writers Organization (all of which are new to this edition).

For organizations even closer to home, check for information at the library or contact the English department at a nearby college. Better yet, if you are unable to find a local writer's group, start one by placing an ad in your community newspaper or posting a notice on the library bulletin board. There are sure to be others in your area who would welcome the support, and the library might even have space for your group to meet on a regular basis.

To locate some of the larger organizations (or representative samples of smaller groups) read through the listings that follow. Then send a SASE to those groups that interest you to receive more details about their services and membership fees. Also refer to the list of Additional Organizations Useful to Poets at the end of this section.

THE ACADEMY OF AMERICAN POETS; FELLOWSHIP OF THE ACADEMY OF AMERICAN POETS; WALT WHITMAN AWARD; THE LAMONT POETRY SELECTION; HAROLD MORTON LANDON TRANSLATION AWARD; THE LENORE MARSHALL POETRY PRIZE, 584 Broadway, Suite 1208, New York NY 10012-3250, founded 1934, executive director William Wadsworth. Robert Penn Warren wrote in *Introduction to Fifty Years of American Poetry*, an anthology published in 1984 containing one poem from each of the 126 Chancellors, Fellows and Award Winners of the Academy: "What does the Academy do? According to its certificate of incorporation, its purpose is 'To encourage, stimulate and foster the production of American poetry. . . .' The responsibility for its activities lies with the Board of Directors and the Board of 12 Chancellors, which has included, over the years, such figures as Louise Bogan, W.H. Auden, Witter Bynner, Randall Jarrell, Robert Lowell, Robinson Jeffers, Marianne Moore, James Merrill, Robert Fitzgerald, F.O. Matthiessen and Archibald MacLeish." They award fellowships, currently of $20,000 each, to distinguished American poets (no applications taken)—60 to date—and other annual awards. The Walt Whitman Award pays $5,000 plus publication of a poet's first book by a major publisher. Mss of 50-100 pgs. must be submitted between September 15 and November 15 with a $20 entry fee. Entry form required. Send SASE. The James Laughlin Award (formerly The Lamont Poetry Selection), for a poet's second book, is also a prize of $5,000. Submissions must be made by a publisher, in ms form, prior to publication. The Academy distributes 3,000 copies to its members. Poets entering either contest must be American citizens. The Harold

Morton Landon Translation Award is for translation of a book-length poem, a collection of poems or a verse-drama translated into English from any language. One award of $1,000 each year to a US citizen. Only publishers may submit the book. Write for guidelines. The Lenore Marshall Poetry Prize is a $10,000 award for the most outstanding book of poems published in the US in the preceding year. The contest is open to books by living American poets published in a standard edition (40 pgs. or more in length with 500 or more copies). Self-published books are not eligible. Publishers may enter as many books as they wish. Deadline: June 1. Write for guidelines. *Poetry Pilot* is an informative periodical sent to those who contribute $25 or more/year or who are members. Membership: $45/year. The Academy sponsors a national series of poetry readings and panel discussions.

‡**ADIRONDACK LAKES CENTER FOR THE ARTS**, P.O. Box 205, Rte. 28, Blue Mountain Lake NY 12812, phone (518)352-7715, fax (518)352-7333, director Tina Thompson Pine. An independent, private, nonprofit educational organization founded in 1967 to promote "visual and performing arts through programs and services, to serve established professional and aspiring artists and the region through educational programs and activities of general interest." Open to everyone. Currently has 1,300 members. Levels of membership available are individual, family and business. Offerings available for poets include workshops for adults and children, reading performances, discussions and lectures. Offers a "comfortable, cozy performance space—coffeehouse setting with tables, candles, etc." Computers available for members and artists. Publishes a triannual newsletter/schedule that contains news, articles, photos and a schedule of events. "All members are automatically sent the schedule and others may request a copy." Sponsors a few readings each year. "These are usually given by the instructor of our writing workshops. There is no set fee for membership, a gift of any size makes you a member." Members meet each July. Send SASE for additional information.

ASSOCIATED WRITING PROGRAMS; AWP CHRONICLE; THE AWP AWARD SERIES, Tallwood House, MS 1E3, George Mason University, Fairfax VA 22030, founded 1967. Offers a variety of services to the writing community, including information, job placement assistance, publishing opportunities, literary arts advocacy and forums. Annual individual membership is $45; placement service extra. For $18 you can subscribe to the *AWP Chronicle* (published 6 times/year), containing information about grants and awards, publishing opportunities, fellowships, and writing programs. They have a directory, *The Official Guide to Writing Programs*, of over 250 college and university writing programs for $23.95 (includes shipping). The AWP Award Series selects a volume of poetry (48 pg. minimum) each year ($10 entry fee for members; $15 for nonmembers) with an award of $2,000 and publication. Deadline: February 28. Send SASE for submission guidelines. Query after November. Their placement service helps writers find jobs in teaching, editing and other related fields.

THE AUTHORS GUILD, INC., 330 W. 42nd St., New York NY 10036, phone (212) 563-5904, executive director Robin Davis Miller, "is an association of professional writers which focuses its efforts on the legal and business concerns of published authors in the areas of publishing contract terms, copyright, taxation and freedom of expression. We do not work in the area of marketing mss to publishers nor do we sponsor or participate in awards or prize selections." Send SASE for information on membership.

AUTHORS LEAGUE FUND, 234 W. 44th St., New York NY 10036. Makes interest-free loans to published authors in need of temporary help because of illness or an emergency. No grants.

‡**BERGEN POETS**, 180-G1 Summit Ave., Summit NJ 07901, phone (908)277-6245, fax (908)277-2171, president Ms. Roberta L. Greening, founded in 1969 to "bring together poets and friends of poetry in our area, help the individual in writing and appreciation of poetry, and add to the cultural life of the community." Open to anyone in the community interested in poetry. "Our base is in Bergen County, New Jersey. However, our members extend from New York to Florida." Currently has 66 members. Offerings available to poets include workshops on craft, discussions of individual poets and readings at area facilities. "Our meetings are held at various public libraries and local bookstores." Publishes a quarterly newsletter at an annual cost of $5 to new members. Sponsors open-mike readings following featured members' readings. Membership dues are $5 to receive newsletter and meeting announcements. Members meet a minimum of 4 times/year. Send SASE for additional information. "Bergen Poets is one of the oldest poetry organizations in the state of New Jersey."

BEYOND BAROQUE LITERARY/ARTS CENTER, 681 Venice Blvd., Venice CA 90291, phone (310)822-3006, director Tosh Berman. A nonprofit arts center established in 1968 that has been funded by the NEA, state and city arts councils and corporate donations. Members get a calendar of events, discounts on regularly scheduled programs, discounts in the bookstore, and borrowing privileges in the small press library of 3,000 volumes of poetry, fiction and reference materials, including audiotapes of Beyond Baroque readings. Beyond Baroque contains a bookstore open 5 days a week, including Friday evenings to coincide with regular weekly readings and performances. About 130 writers are invited to read each year; there are also open readings and poetry and fiction workshops.

BLACK CULTURAL CENTRE FOR NOVA SCOTIA, 1149 Main St., Dartmouth, Nova Scotia B2Z 1A8 Canada, phone (902)434-6223, or (800)465-0767, fax (902)434-2306. Founded in 1977 "to create among members of the black communities an awareness of their past, their heritage and their identity; to provide programs and activities for the general public to explore, learn about, understand and appreciate black history, black achievements and black experiences in the broad context of Canadian life. The centre houses a museum, reference library, small auditorium and workshops."

BURNABY WRITERS' SOCIETY, 6584 Deer Lake Ave., Burnaby, British Columbia V5G 2J3 Canada, contact person Eileen Kernaghan. Corresponding membership in the society, including a newsletter subscription, is open to anyone, anywhere. Yearly dues are $20. Sample newsletter in return for SASE with Canadian stamp. The society holds monthly meetings at The Burnaby Arts Centre (address at beginning of listing), with a business meeting at 7:30 followed by a writing workshop or speaker. Members of the society stage regular public readings of their own work.

THE WITTER BYNNER FOUNDATION FOR POETRY, INC., P.O. Box 10169, Santa Fe NM 87504, phone (505)988-3251, fax (505)986-8222. The foundation awards grants exclusively to nonprofit organizations for the support of poetry-related projects in the area of: 1) support of individual poets through existing nonprofit institutions; 2) developing the poetry audience; 3) poetry translation and the process of poetry translation; and 4) uses of poetry. The foundation "may consider the support of other creative and innovative projects in poetry." Grant applications are accepted annually from January 1 through February 1; requests for application forms should be submitted to Steven Schwartz, executive director, at the address above.

THE CANADA COUNCIL; GOVERNOR GENERAL'S LITERARY AWARDS; INTERNATIONAL LITERARY PRIZES, P.O. Box 1047, 350 Albert St., Ottawa, Ontario K1P 5V8 Canada, phone (613)566-4376. Established by Parliament in 1957, it "provides a wide range of grants and services to professional Canadian artists and art organizations in dance, media arts, music, opera, theater, writing, publishing and the visual arts." The Governor General's Literary Awards, valued at $10,000 (Canadian) each, are given annually for the best English-language and best French-language work in each of seven categories, including poetry. Books must be first-edition trade books written, translated or illustrated by Canadian citizens or permanent residents of Canada and published in Canada or abroad during the previous year (September 1 through September 30). In the case of translation, the original work must also be a Canadian-authored title. Books must be submitted by publishers with a Publisher's Submission Form, which is available from the Writing and Publishing Section. All entries (books and galleys) must be received at the Canada Council by August 31. If the submission is in the form of a bound galley, the actual book must be published and received at the Canada Council no later than September 30. The Canada Council administers three International Literary Prizes (Canada-Australia, Canada-French Community of Belgium, Canada-Switzerland) of $2,500-3,500 (Canadian) and the Canada-Japan Book Award worth $10,000 (Canadian). Winners are selected by juries. Except for the Canada-Japan Book Award, applications are not accepted.

CANADIAN CONFERENCE OF THE ARTS (CCA), 189 Laurier Ave. E., Ottawa, Ontario K1N 6P1 Canada, phone (613)238-3561, fax (613)238-4849, is a national, non-governmental, not-for-profit arts service organization dedicated to the growth and vitality of the arts and cultural industries in Canada. The CCA represents all Canadian artists, cultural workers and arts supporters, and works with all levels of government, the corporate sector and voluntary organizations to enhance appreciation for the role of culture in Canadian life. Each year, the CCA presents awards for contribution to the arts. Regular meetings held across the country ensure that members' views on urgent and ongoing issues are heard and considered in organizing advocacy efforts and forming Board policies. Members stay informed and up-to-date through *Proscenium*, a news magazine, which is published 5 times a year, and receive discounts on conference fees and on all other publications. Membership is $30 (plus GST) for Canadian individual members, $35 for US members and $45 for international members.

CANADIAN POETRY ASSOCIATION; POEMATA, 340 Station B, London, Ontario N6A 4W1 Canada, e-mail lurc.lspc@onlinesys.com (cpa Library); also wayne.ray@onlinesys.com (National Coordinator Wayne Ray). A broad based umbrella organization that aims to promote the reading, writing, publishing, purchasing and preservation of poetry in Canada through the individual and combined efforts of its members; to promote and encourage all forms and styles of poetry; to promote communication among poets, publishers and the general public; to promote the establishment and maintenance of poetry libraries and archives in educational institutions across Canada; and to develop an international connection for Canadian poets through *Poemata,* its bimonthly newsletter, and events organized by independent, locally-run chapters. Through its 6 autonomous local chapters, CPA organizes poetry readings, literary and social events, and runs a book club. Membership is open to anyone with an interest in poetry, including other literary organizations, for $20/year. *Poemata* publishes articles, book reviews and essays related to writing. Sample newsletter: $3.

CANADIAN SOCIETY OF CHILDREN'S AUTHORS, ILLUSTRATORS & PERFORMERS, 542 Mount Pleasant Rd., #103, Toronto, Ontario M4S 2M7 Canada, is a "society of professionals in the field of children's culture. Puts people into contact with publishers, offers advice to beginners, and generally provides a visible profile for members; 365 professional members and over 1,000 associates who are termed 'friends.' An annual conference in Toronto the last week of October provides workshops to people interested in writing, illustrating, and performing for children." Membership is $60 for professional members (and a free copy of the Membership Directory); $25 for associates/year. Both include a subscription to the quarterly *CANSCAIP News*.

COSMEP, THE INTERNATIONAL ASSOCIATION OF INDEPENDENT PUBLISHERS; COSMEP NEWSLETTER, P.O. Box 420703, San Francisco CA 94142-0703, phone (800)546-3303. If you are starting a small press or magazine or are embarking on self-publication, you should know about the advantages of membership in COSMEP. Write for information. It is the largest trade association for small press in the US. Included among membership benefits is the monthly *COSMEP Newsletter*, which prints news and commentary for small publishers. It also sponsors publishing conferences, stages exhibits at booksellers' and librarians' conventions and has insurance and cooperative advertising programs.

COUNCIL OF LITERARY MAGAZINES AND PRESSES, Suite 3-C, 154 Christopher St., New York NY 10014-2839. Compiles an annual directory useful to writers: The *Directory of Literary Magazines*, which has detailed descriptions of over 500 literary magazines, including type of work published, payment to contributors and circulation. The directory is $15 postage paid and may be ordered by sending a check to CLMP.

COWBOY POETRY GATHERING; WESTERN FOLKLIFE ROUNDUP; WESTERN FOLKLIFE CENTER, 501 Railroad St., Elko NV 89801. Both of these gatherings are sponsored by Western Folklife Center, Box 888, Elko NV 89803, phone (702)738-7508, fax (702)738-2900. There is an annual 6-day January gathering of cowboy poets in Elko. The Western Folklife Roundup is held annually the last weekend in August. The Western Folklife Center publishes and distributes books and tapes of cowboy poetry and songs as well as other cowboy memorabilia. The well-established tradition of cowboy poetry is enjoying a renaissance, and thousands of cowboy poets participate in these activities.

‡DAKOTA COWBOY & WESTERN POETS ASSOCIATION, RR 1, Box 171, Spearfish SD 57783, phone (605)642-0779, president Ken Rost, founded in 1989 to promote "the Western Heritage of this part of the country and to give cowboy poets a forum for their work. It is an organization for internal support and constructive criticism." Regional organization open to "anyone who writes poetry that rhymes and is related to ranching and the cowboy way of life both past and present." Currently has 18 members. "We generally put on several small cowboy poet gatherings for the association each year as a place for people to try out their new stuff. We also keep members informed on cowboy poet gatherings around the U.S. and Canada." Members and/or nationally known writers give readings that are open to the public. They also sponsor open-mike readings. Membership dues are $10/year. Members meet about every 2 months. Send SASE for additional information. "All poetry must be free of profanity, have rhyme and meter, and relate to some aspect of cowboy or pioneer life, past or present from either a male or a female perspective."

FEDERATION OF BRITISH COLUMBIA WRITERS, M.P.O. Box 2206, Vancouver, British Columbia V6B 3W2 Canada, manager Corey Van't Haaff. The federation "is a nonprofit organization of professional and emerging writers in all genres." They publish a newsletter of markets, political reports, awards and federation news; act as "a network centre for various other provincial writer's organizations; host, promote and organize workshops, readings, literary competitions and social activities; publish directories which are distributed to schools, businesses, and organizations which may request the services of writers; and represent writers' interests to other professionally related organizations."

GENIE SERVICE; WRITERS' INK, 401 N. Washington St., Rockville MD 20850, phone (800)638-9636, provides news, research information and entertainment to individuals throughout the US, Canada and numerous foreign countries. "There are dozens of areas of interest to poets, from workshops to an electronic encyclopedia. The heart of the writing community on GEnie is Writers' Ink, an electronic association of poets, authors, illustrators, screenwriters and others interested in all aspects of writing for enjoyment and/or publication. Members 'meet' using their computer and a modem (for most, it's a local phone call). The Writers' Ink Bulletin Board is filled with discussions and information on a wide variety of subjects—from publishing your first poem to working with imagery. Writers' Ink conducts frequent electronic meetings where people from all over the world can gather and discuss poetry and writing. There are also weekly online poetry readings where members share and discuss their work. Poets will find the Writers' Ink Libraries full of useful software, helpful articles and interviews as well as poems and stories by members. Poets can even find market information as well as tips for dealing with editors." Cost is $8.95 for 4 hours of standard time; then cost us $3/hour. This fee includes electronic mail, an encyclopedia and access to many bulletin boards (including Writers' Ink).

INTERNATIONAL WOMEN'S WRITING GUILD, P.O. Box 810, Gracie Station, New York NY 10028, phone (212)737-7536, founded 1976, "a network for the personal and professional empowerment of women through writing." The Guild publishes a bimonthly 32-page newsletter which includes members' needs, achievements, contests, and publishing information. A manuscript referral service introduces members to literary agents. Other activities are 13 annual national and regional events, including a summer conference at Skidmore College (see listing under Conferences and Workshops); "regional clusters" (independent regional groups); job referrals; round robin manuscript exchanges; sponsorship of the "Artist of Life" award; and group health insurance. Membership in the nonprofit Guild costs $35/year in the US and $45/year foreign.

JUST BUFFALO LITERARY CENTER, 493 Franklin St., Suite 209, Buffalo NY 14202, phone (716)881-3211, fax (716)881-3552, founded 1975 by executive director Debora Ott, has one full-time program coordinator, executive assistant, coordinator of community resources, a coordinator of marketing and administration, and a radio producer and interdisciplinary program consultant. They offer readings, workshops, master classes, residencies, an annual Western New York Writers-in-Residence competition, an annual Labor-in-Literature competition open to WNY union members, Spoken Arts Radio broadcasts on National Public Radio affiliate WBFO, and Writers-in-Education for school-age populations. Just Buffalo acts as a clearinghouse for literary events in the Greater Buffalo area and offers diverse services to writers and to the WNY region. "Although we are not accepting submissions for publication at this time, we will review works for possible readings."

THE LEAGUE OF CANADIAN POETS; WHEN IS A POEM; WHO'S WHO IN THE LEAGUE OF CANADIAN POETS; HERE IS A POEM; POETRY MARKETS FOR CANADIANS; NATIONAL POETRY CONTEST; GERALD LAMPERT AWARD; PAT LOWTHER AWARD, 3rd Floor, 54 Wolseley, Toronto, Ontario M5T 1A5 Canada, phone (416)504-1657, founded 1966, contact Edita Petrauskaite. The league's aims are the advancement of poetry in Canada and promotion of the interests of professional, Canadian poets. Information on full and associate membership can be obtained by writing for the brochure, League of Canadian Poets: Services and Membership. The league publishes a biannual *Museletter* (30 pgs., magazine-sized) plus six newsletters; *When is a Poem*, on teaching poetry to children; a directory called *Who's Who in The League of Canadian Poets* that contains 1 page of information, including a picture, bio, publications and "what critics say" about each of the members; *Here is a Poem*, a companion anthology to *When is a Poem*, featuring the work of Canadian poets; and *Poetry Markets for Canadians* which covers contracts, markets, agents and more. The league's members go on reading tours, and the league encourages them to speak on any facet of Canadian literature at schools and universities, libraries or organizations. The league has arranged "thousands of readings in every part of Canada"; they are now arranging exchange visits featuring the leading poets of such countries as Great Britain, Germany and the US. The league sponsors a National Poetry Contest with prizes of $1,000, $750 and $500; the best 50 poems published in a book. Deadline: January 31. Entry fee: $6/poem. Poems should be unpublished, under 75 lines and typed. Names and addresses should *not* appear on poems but on a separate covering sheet. Please send SASE for complete rules, info on judges, etc. Open to Canadian citizens or landed immigrants only. The Gerald Lampert Award of $1,000 is for a first book of poetry written by a Canadian, published professionally. The Pat Lowther Award of $1,000 is for a book of poetry written by a Canadian woman and published professionally. Write for entry forms.

THE LOFT; LOFT-MCKNIGHT AWARDS; THE NATIONAL POETRY PRIZE, Pratt Community Center, 66 Malcolm Ave. SE, Minneapolis MN 55414, phone (612)379-0754, founded 1974, executive director Linda Myers. The Loft was started by a group of poets looking for a place to give readings and conduct workshops and has evolved into a sophisticated hub of activity for creative writing in all genres managed by an 19-member board of directors and staff of 12. This past year 2,300 members contributed $35/year to the Loft; it was further supported by tuition from creative writing classes, fees from readings, and grants from individuals, corporations and the government. The Loft offers over 75 6- and 12-week courses each year, in addition to 30 workshops and panels. Its publication readings and emerging voices readings are meant for Minnesota writers whereas the Mentor Series and Creative Non-fiction residency feature nationally known writers. The Loft publishes a monthly newsletter called *A View from the Loft*. The Loft-McKnight Awards are offered annually to Minnesota writers: 8 awards of $7,500 each, 3 in poetry, 5 in creative prose; 2 Awards of Distinction, $10,500 each. The National Poetry Prize is a $1,000 award given annually to 1 poet. The winning poem is also published in the *Michigan Quarterly Review* (see listing in the Publishers of Poetry section).

MAINE WRITERS & PUBLISHERS ALLIANCE; MAINE IN PRINT; MAINE WRITERS CENTER, 12 Pleasant St., Brunswick ME 04011-2201, phone (207)729-6333, founded 1975, outreach coordinator

Cate DiMarzio. This organization is "a nonprofit organization dedicated to promoting all aspects of writing, publishing, and the book arts. Our membership currently includes over 1,500 writers, publishers, librarians, teachers, booksellers and readers from across Maine and the nation. For an individual contribution of $25 per year members receive a range of benefits including *Maine in Print*, a monthly compilation of calendar events, updated markets, book reviews, grant information, interviews with Maine authors and publishers, articles about writing and more. The alliance distributes selected books about Maine and by Maine authors and publishers, and it maintains a bookstore, reference library, performance space and word processing station at the Maine Writers Center in Brunswick. MWPA regularly invites writers to conduct Saturday workshops." Reviews books of poetry only by Maine-based presses and poets. "We also have extensive ongoing workshops in fiction and poetry and offer an annual fall writing retreat."

NATIONAL FEDERATION OF STATE POETRY SOCIETIES, INC. Membership Chairperson: Barbara Stevens, 909 E. 34th St., Sioux Falls SD 57105; Contest Chairperson: Amy Jo Zook, 3520 State Route 56, Mechanicsburg OH 43044. "NFSPS is a nonprofit organization exclusively educational and literary. Its purpose is to recognize the importance of poetry with respect to national cultural heritage. It is dedicated solely to the furtherance of poetry on the national level and serves to unite poets in the bonds of fellowship and understanding." Any poetry group located in a state not already affiliated but interested in affiliating with NFSPS may contact the membership chairperson. Canadian groups may also apply. "In a state where no valid group exists, help may also be obtained by individuals interested in organizing a poetry group for affiliation." Most reputable state poetry societies are members of the National Federation and advertise their various poetry contests through the quarterly bulletin, *Strophes*, available for SASE and $1, editor Kay Kinnaman, Route 3, Box 348, Alexandria IN 46001. Beware of organizations calling themselves state poetry societies (however named) that are not members of NFSPS, as such labels are sometimes used by vanity schemes trying to sound respectable. Others, such as the Oregon State Poetry Association, are quite reputable, but they don't belong to NFSPS. NFSPS holds an annual meeting in a different city each year with a large awards banquet, addressed by an honorary chairperson. They sponsor 50 national contests in various categories each year, including the NFSPS Prize of $1,500 for first place; $500, second; $250, third; with entry fees ($3 for the entire contest for members, $5 for NFSPS Award; $1/poem for nonmembers and $5 for NFSPS Award, up to 4 poems/entry). All poems winning over $10 are published in an anthology. Rules for all contests are given in a brochure available from Kay Kinnaman at *Strophes* or Amy Jo Zook at the address above; you can also write for the address of your state poetry society. Scholarship information is available from Pj Doyle, 4242 Stevens Ave., Minneapolis MN 55409.

THE NATIONAL POETRY FOUNDATION; SAGETRIEB; PAIDEUMA, University of Maine, 5752 Neville Hall, Room 302, Orono ME 04469-5752, publications coordinator Marie M. Alpert. "The NPF is a nonprofit organization concerned with publishing scholarship on the work of 20th century poets, particularly Ezra Pound and those in the Imagist/Objectivist tradition. We publish *Paideuma*, a journal devoted to Ezra Pound scholarship, and *Sagetrieb*, a journal devoted to poets in the imagist/objectivist tradition, as well as one other journal of contemporary poetry and comment. NPF conducts a conference each summer and celebrates the centennial of an individual 20th century poet." Sample copies: $8.95 for *Paideuma* or *Sagetrieb*.

NATIONAL WRITERS UNION, 873 Broadway, Room 203, New York NY 10003. Offers members such services as a grievance committee, contract guidelines, health insurance, press credentials, car rental discounts, and caucuses and trade groups for exchange of information about special markets. Members receive *The American Writer*, the organization's newsletter. Membership is $75 for those earning less than $5,000/year; $125 for those earning $5,000-25,000; and $170 for those earning more than $25,000.

‡NEW ENGLAND POETRY CLUB, 2 Farrar St., Cambridge MA 02138, president Diana Der-Hovanessian, founded in 1915 by Amy Lowell, Robert Frost and Conrad Aiken to "bring the best poets to the area and foster fellowship among writers." National organization open to beginning poets, professional poets and teachers of poetry. Currently has 500 members. Offerings available for poets include a newsletter with poetry information, free admission to readings and contests and free participation in workshops. Nationally known writers regularly give readings that are open to the public. Sponsors open-mike readings for members only. Membership dues are $20. Readings and workshops are held monthly. Of the 12 contests they sponsor, 9 are open to nonmembers for an entry fee of $2/poem. Entries must be original, unpublished poems in English. Send SASE for details.

NORTH CAROLINA WRITERS' NETWORK; THE NETWORK NEWS; HARPERPRINTS POETRY CHAPBOOK COMPETITION; THE RANDALL JARRELL POETRY PRIZE, P.O. Box 954, Carrboro NC 27510, established 1985. Supports the work of writers, writers' organizations, independent bookstores, little magazines and small presses, and literary programming statewide. A $35 donation annually brings members *The Network News*, a 24-page bimonthly newsletter containing organizational news, national market information and other literary material of interest to writers, and access to the Resource Center, other writers, workshops, conferences, readings and competitions, and a critiquing service. 1,600 members nationwide. Annual fall conference features nationally-known writers, publishers and editors. It is held in a different North Carolina location each year in November. Also sponsors competitions in short fiction, one-act plays and nonfiction essays for North Carolinians and members.

THE OREGON STATE POETRY ASSOCIATION, % Linda Smith, 471 NW Hemlock, Corvallis OR 97330, phone (503)753-3335; newsletter editor Elizabeth Bolton, P.O. Box 219006, Portland OR 97225. Founded for "the promotion and creation of poetry," the association has over 200 members, $12 dues, publishes a quarterly *OSPA Newsletter*, and sponsors contests twice yearly, October and April, with total cash prizes of $300 each (no entry fee to members, $2/poem for nonmembers; out of state entries welcome). Themes and categories vary. For details write to OSPA, P.O. Box 219006, Portland OR 97225 after August 1 and February 15 each year. The association sponsors workshops, readings and seminars around the state.

PEN AMERICAN CENTER; PEN WRITERS FUND; PEN TRANSLATION PRIZE; GRANTS AND AWARDS, 568 Broadway, New York NY 10012, phone (212)334-1660, "is the largest of more than 100 centers which comprise International PEN, founded in London in 1921 by John Galsworthy to foster understanding among men and women of letters in all countries. Members of PEN work for freedom of expression wherever it has been endangered, and International PEN is the only worldwide organization of writers and the chief voice of the literary community." Its total membership on all continents is approximately 10,000. The 2,700 members of the American Center include poets, playwrights, essayists, editors, novelists (for the original letters in the acronym PEN), as well as translators and those editors and agents who have made a substantial contribution to the literary community. Membership in American PEN includes reciprocal privileges in foreign centers for those traveling abroad. Branch offices are located in Cambridge, Chicago, Portland/Seattle, Baton Rouge and San Francisco. Among PEN's various activities are public events and symposia, literary awards, assistance to writers in prison and to American writers in need (grants and loans up to $1,000 from PEN Writers Fund). Medical insurance for writers is available to members. The quarterly *PEN Newsletter* is sent to all members and is available to nonmembers by subscription. The PEN Translation Prize is sponsored by the Book-of-the-Month Club, 1 prize each year of $3,000 for works published in the current calendar year. They publish *Grants and Awards* biennially, containing guidelines, deadlines, eligibility requirements and other information about hundreds of grants, awards and competitions for poets and other writers: $10 postpaid. Send SASE for booklet describing their activities and listing their publications, some of them available free.

‡PHILADELPHIA WRITERS ORGANIZATION, P.O. Box 42497, Philadelphia PA 19101, phone (610)649-8918, president Bill Wartman. Founded in 1982 to promote "educational and social programs for writers." Regional organization open to all writers. Currently has 200 members. Levels of membership available are full (published writers) and associate (unpublished writers). Offerings available for poets include monthly meetings with speakers, social events, a monthly newsletter, job bank and group health insurance. Membership dues are $50/year. Members meet monthly. Send SASE for additional information.

PITTSBURGH POETRY EXCHANGE, P.O. Box 4279, Pittsburgh PA 15203, phone (412)481-POEM. Founded in 1974 as a community-based organization for local poets, it functions as a service organization and information exchange, conducting ongoing workshops, readings, forums and other special events. No dues or fees. "Any monetary contributions are voluntary, often from outside sources. We've managed not to let our reach exceed our grasp." Their reading programs are primarily committed to local and area poets, with honorariums of $25-60. They sponsor a minimum of three major events each year in addition to a monthly workshop. Some of these have been reading programs in conjunction with community arts festivals, such as the October South Side Poetry Smorgasbord—a series of readings throughout the evening at different shops (galleries, bookstores). Poets from out of town may contact the exchange for assistance in setting up readings at bookstores to help sell their books. Contact Michael Wurster at the above address or phone number.

THE POETRY COMMITTEE OF THE GREATER WASHINGTON AREA, % The Folger Shakespeare Library, 201 E. Capitol St. SE, Washington DC 20003, phone (202)544-7077, executive director Saskia Hamilton. An independent, nonprofit group, the membership (by invitation) consists of about 60 people who represent major and minor poetry organizations in the metropolitan area. Annual sponsors of Celebration of Washington Poetry, a reading and book sale highlighting area poets and presses, the Columbia Book Award for best book of poetry by Washington area poet within the past calendar year and the Columbia Merit Award for service to area poetry.

THE POETRY PROJECT AT ST. MARK'S CHURCH-IN-THE-BOWERY, 131 E. 10th St., New York NY 10003, phone (212)674-0910, was established in 1966 by the US Dept. of H.E.W. in an effort to help wayward youths in the East Village. It is now funded by a variety of government and private sources. Artistic Director: Ed Friedman. Program Coordinator: JoAnn Wasserman. From October through May the project offers workshops, talks, staged readings, performance poetry, lectures, an annual 4-day symposium, literary magazines and a series of featured writers who bring their books to sell at the readings. If the reading is a publication party, the publisher handles the sales.

POETRY RESOURCE CENTER OF MICHIGAN, %English Dept., Wayne State University, 51 W. Warren, Detroit MI 48202, phone (810)754-9645, president Cindi St. Germain, "is a nonprofit organization which exists through the generosity of poets, writers, teachers, publishers, printers, librarians and others dedicated to the reading and enjoyment of poetry in Michigan." The *PRC Newsletter*, which includes a calendar of events, is available by mail quarterly for an annual membership donation of $20 or more ($10 for students and seniors), and is distributed free of charge at locations throughout the state. To obtain copies for distribution at poetry functions, contact the president or any member of the PRC Board of Trustees.

POETRY SOCIETY OF AMERICA; POETRY SOCIETY OF AMERICA AWARDS, 15 Gramercy Park, New York NY 10003, phone (212)254-9628, is a nonprofit cultural organization in support of poetry and poets, member and nonmember, young and established, which sponsors readings, lectures and workshops both in New York City and around the country. Their Peer Group Workshop is open to all members and meets on a weekly basis. They publish a newsletter of their activities and sponsor a wide range of contests. The following are open to members only: Gordon Barber Memorial Award ($200); Gertrude B. Claytor Award ($250); Mary Carolyn Davies Memorial Award ($250); Alice Fay Di Castagnola Award ($1,000); *Writer Magazine*/Emily Dickinson Award ($100); Consuelo Ford Award ($250); Cecil Hemley Memorial Award ($300); Lucille Medwick Memorial Award ($500). Nonmembers may enter as many of the following contests as they wish, no more than 1 entry for each, for a $5 fee: Elias Lieberman Student Poetry Award, $100 for students in grades 9-12; John Masefield Memorial Award for a narrative poem in English up to 300 lines, $500, translations ineligible; Celia B. Wagner Award, $250 any form or length; George Bogin Memorial Award, $500 for a selection of 4 to 5 poems which take a stand against oppression; Robert H. Winner Memorial Award, $2,500 for a poem written by a poet over 40, still unpublished or with one book. (All have a deadline of December 22; awards are made at a ceremony and banquet in late spring.) The Society also has 3 book contests open to works submitted by publishers only. They must obtain an entry form, and there is a $10 fee for each book entered. Book awards are: Melville Cane Award, $500 in even-numbered years awarded to a book of poems, in odd years to prose work on poetry; Norma Farber Award, $1,000 for a first book; William Carlos Williams Award, $1,000 for a book of poetry published by a small, nonprofit or university press, by a permanent resident of the US—translations not eligible. The Shelley Memorial Award of $2,000-6,000 is by nomination only. For necessary rules and guidelines for their various contests send #10 SASE between October 1 and December 22. Rules and awards are subject to change. Membership: $40.

POETS & WRITERS, INC., See listing under Publications Useful to Poets.

POETS' CORNER, THE CATHEDRAL CHURCH OF ST. JOHN THE DIVINE, Cathedral Heights, 1047 Amsterdam Ave. at 112 St., New York NY 10025, initiated in 1984 with memorials for Emily Dickinson, Walt Whitman, Washington Irving, Robert Frost, Herman Melville, Nathaniel Hawthorne, Edgar Allan Poe, Henry James, Henry David Thoreau, Mark Twain, Ralph Waldo Emerson, William Faulkner, Wallace Stevens, Willa Cather, T.S. Eliot, Marianne Moore, Henry Wadsworth Longfellow, Stephen Crane, Edwin Arlington Robinson, Anne Bradstreet and Hart Crane. It is similar in concept to the British Poets' Corner in Westminster Abbey, and was established and dedicated to memorialize this country's greatest writers. A Board of Electors comprised of thirteen eminent poets and writers chooses two deceased authors each year for inclusion in The Poets' Corner.

POETS HOUSE: THE REED FOUNDATION LIBRARY; THE POETRY PUBLICATION SHOWCASE; DIRECTORY OF AMERICAN POETRY BOOKS; NYC POETRY TEACHER OF THE YEAR, 72 Spring St., New York NY 10012, phone (212)431-7920, founded 1985, executive director Lee Ellen Briccetti. Poets House is a 30,000-volume (noncirculating) poetry library of books, tapes and literary journals, with reading and writing space, and this comfortably furnished literary center is open to the public. Over 25 annual public events include 1) poetic programs of cross-cultural and interdisciplinary exchange, 2) readings in which distinguished poets discuss and share the work of other poets, 3) an annual $1,000 award for NYC Poetry Teacher of the Year, 4) conferences for high school teachers of poetry, and 5) inhouse workshops for students. In addition, each fall Poets House hosts the Poetry Publication Showcase—a comprehensive exhibit of the year's new poetry releases from commercial, university, independent, and micro presses across the country. Related Showcase events include receptions, panel discussions, and a contributor's poetry reading, which is open to the public and of special interest to poets, publishers, booksellers, distributers and reviewers. (Note: Poets House is not a publisher.) Following each Showcase, copies of new titles are added to the library collection and an updated edition of the *Directory of American Poetry Books*—edited by Poets House—is compiled. Membership levels begin at $40/year, and each member receives a free copy of the directory.

POETS THEATRE, RD 2, Box 155, Cohocton NY 14826, director Beatrice Obrien, founded 1981. Sponsors readings and performances with limited funding from Poets & Writers. For a mostly conservative, rural audience. A featured poet, followed by open reading, monthly.

POETS-IN-THE-SCHOOLS. Most states have PITS programs that send published poets into classrooms to teach students poetry writing. If you have published poetry widely and have a proven commitment to children, contact your state arts council, Arts-in-Education Dept., to see whether you qualify. Three of the biggest programs are Teachers & Writers Collaborative, Inc., 5 Union Square W., Seventh Floor, New York NY 10003, phone (212)691-6590; California Poets-in-the-Schools, 870 Market St., Suite 1148, San Francisco CA 94102, phone (415)399-1565; and COMPAS, 304 Landmark Center, 75 W. Fifth St., St. Paul MN 55102, phone (612)292-3249, which includes both writers and artists in their program.

SCOTTISH POETRY LIBRARY; SCHOOL OF POETS; CRITICAL SERVICE, Tweeddale Court, 14 High St., Edinburgh EH1 1TE Scotland, phone (031)557-2876, director Tessa Ransford, librarian Penny Duce. It is a central information source and free lending library, also lending by post. The library has a computerized catalogue allowing subject-based searches. The collection has over 14,000 items and consists of Scottish and international poetry. The School of Poets is open to anyone; "at meetings members divide into small groups in which each participant reads a poem which is then analyzed and discussed." Meetings normally take place at 7:30 p.m. on the first Tuesday of each month at the library. They also offer a Critical Service in which groups of up to 6 poems, not exceeding 200 lines in all, are given critical comment by members of the School: £15 for each critique (with SAE).

SONGWRITERS AND POETS CRITIQUE, 11599 Coontz Rd., Orient OH 43146, phone (614)877-1727, founded in 1985 by Ellis Cordle. A nonprofit association whose purpose is to serve songwriters, poets and musicians in their area. The president of the organization says, "We have over 200 members from over 16 states at several levels of ability from novice to advanced, and try to help and support each other with the craft and the business of poetry and songs. We have published writers and recorded artists. We share information about how to pitch, send and package a demo and who to send it to. We also have a songwriting contest for member writers." Annual dues are $25.

SOUTHERN POETRY ASSOCIATION; THE POET'S VOICE, P.O. Box 524, Pass Christian MS 39571, founded 1986, poetry editor Mildred Klyce. SPA offers networking, publishing, free critique service for members through Round Robin Groups and assistance in publishing chapbooks. $10 annual membership fee includes *The Poet's Voice* quarterly newsletter. The association sponsors a number of contests, including Voices of the South, Yarn Spinner, Poetry in Motion, Special People; some are for members only; some, such as the Voices of the South Contest, are open to all. Prizes total $200 with $3 entry fee/poem (28-line limit). June 1 deadline. High scoring poems are published in an anthology (which the poet is not required to purchase). Send #10 SAE with 64¢ postage for details. *The Poet's Voice* contains poetry book reviews, articles on great poets of the past, current activities, input from SPA members and contest winning poems.

THE THURBER HOUSE; JAMES THURBER WRITER-IN-RESIDENCE, 77 Jefferson Ave., Columbus OH 43215, phone (614)464-1032, officially opened in 1984. It is "one of the most diversely active of all restored writer's homes." The Thurber House has a staff of 8, over 50 volunteers and 22 board members. Its budget comes from state, local and national arts councils; foundations; corporate, business and individual sponsors; and sales. Listed on the National Register of Historic Places, The Thurber House is a literary center, bookstore and museum of Thurber materials. Programs include writing classes, author readings, Thurber celebrations, events for children and an art gallery. The Thurber House sponsors a writer-in-residence program where 2 journalists, a playwright, a poet and a fiction writer are invited to spend a season living and writing in The Thurber House while teaching a course at The Ohio State University. Each writer will receive a $5,000 stipend and housing in the third-floor apartment of Thurber's boyhood home. Please call or write to The Thurber House for application information.

THE UNTERBERG POETRY CENTER OF THE 92ND STREET Y; "DISCOVERY"/THE NATION POETRY CONTEST, 1395 Lexington Ave., New York NY 10128, phone (212)415-5760. Offers annual series of readings by major literary figures (36 readings September through May), writing workshops, master classes in fiction and poetry, and lectures. Also co-sponsors the "Discovery"/*The Nation* Poetry Contest. Deadline early February. Send SASE for information.

‡**WELFARE STATE INTERNATIONAL**, The Ellers, Ulverston, Cumbria LA12 0AA England, phone 01229-581127, fax 01229 581232, founded 1968, artistic director John Fox, is a "celebratory arts company of national and international status creating functional poetry both visual and verbal, for ceremonial occasions. Commissions range from small-scale domestic celebrations to city-scale spectaculars." They publish poster poems in limited editions, dramatic songs and interludes for performance works, and poetic masques.

WALT WHITMAN CULTURAL ARTS CENTER; CAMDEN POETRY AWARD, 2nd and Cooper St., Camden NJ 08102, executive director René L. Huggins, program coordinator J. Daniel Johnson, phone (609)964-8300. A writers' center, founded 1975, it offers a variety of programs such as Notable Poets and Writers Series, Walt Whitman Poetry Series, school programs, adult and children's theater, musical presentations, Fine Art Exhibitions and the Camden Poetry Award. Their regular season runs September through June. During the summer months they provide a 1-month Creativity Camp and a children's theater series entitled "10 Fridays of Fun."

WOODLAND PATTERN, P.O. Box 92081, 720 E. Locust St., Milwaukee WI 53202, phone (414)263-5001. Executive director Anne Kingsbury calls it "a semi-glamorous literary and arts center." Kingsbury regards the center as a neighborhood organization; it includes a bookstore that concentrates on contemporary literature, much of it small press, much of it poetry, and also on multicultural children's literature. It also incorporates a multipurpose gallery/performance/reading space, where exhibitions, readings, a lecture series, musical programs and a reading and study group are held. The *Woodland Pattern Newsletter*, mailed free to 2,500 people, contains an annotated calendar and pieces about visiting writers.

‡**WORDS—THE ARKANSAS LITERARY SOCIETY**, P.O. Box 174, Little Rock AR 72203, phone (501)661-9389, e-mail 71044.3371@compuserve.com, president H.K. Stewart, founded in 1984 to "help support literature and literary activities in the state of Arkansas. WORDS is a statewide group of people who love the language and encourage its use and celebration by Arkansans. Some of us are writers; some of us are readers. All hope, together, to accomplish good things for our state." Currently has over 200 members. Offerings available for poets include an annual contest and workshops, periodic readings and a quarterly newsletter. The annual literary contest awards a $250 prize in three categories: poetry, fiction and nonfiction. Deadline: early June. Workshops also are offered each spring in poetry, fiction and nonfiction. The annual gala reading is for members only, but they offer support to other in-state readings. They also support the Porter Fund Award, an annual state award for literary excellence. The quarterly newsletter, *Words from WORDS*, is "a desktop-published slick magazine announcing contests, readings, events, submission information, reviews, workshops, in-state conferences and other items of interest for members. It is not generally distributed to nonmembers. WORDS helps support different literary readings—some by members and some by nationally known writers. Some of the readings offer open mike time." Membership dues are $20/year for an individual or family, $10/year for students and senior citizens. Board meetings are held quarterly and are open to anyone. Send SASE for additional information. "WORDS always welcomes suggestions, ideas, and volunteers to help support and nurture the literary community in Arkansas."

WORLD-WIDE WRITERS SERVICE, INC.; WRITERS INK; WRITERS INK PRESS; WRITERS UNLIMITED AGENCY, INC., P.O. Box 698, Centereach NY 11720-0698, phone (516)736-6439, founded in 1976, Writers Ink Press founded 1978, director Dr. David B. Axelrod. "World-wide Writers Service is a literary and speakers' booking agency. With its not-for-profit affiliate, Writers Unlimited Agency, Inc., it presents literary workshops and performances, conferences and other literary services, and publishes through Writers Ink Press, chapbooks and small flat-spined books as well as arts editions. **We publish only by our specific invitation at this time.**" *Writers Ink* is "a sometimes newsletter of events on Long Island, now including programs of our conferences. We welcome news of other presses and poets' activities. Review books of poetry. We fund raise for nonprofit projects and are associates of Westhampton Writers Festival and Jeanne Voege Poetry Awards. Arts Editions are profit productions employing hand-made papers, bindings, etc. We have editorial services available at small fees ($50 minimum), but only after inquiry and if appropriate. We are currently concentrating on works in translation, particularly Chinese."

THE WRITER'S CENTER; WRITER'S CAROUSEL; POET LORE, 4508 Walsh St., Bethesda MD 20815, phone (301)654-8664, founder and artistic director Allan Lefcowitz, director Jane Fox. This is an outstanding resource for writers not only in Washington DC but in the wider area ranging from southern Pennsylvania to North Carolina and West Virginia. The Center offers 200 multi-meeting workshops each year in writing, word processing, and graphic arts, and provides a research library. It is open 7 days a week, 10 hours a day. Some 2,300 members support the center with $30 annual donations, which allows for 5 paid staff members. There is a book gallery at which publications of small presses are displayed and sold. The center's publication, *Writer's Carousel*, is a 24-page magazine that comes out 6 times a year. They also sponsor 80 annual performance events, which include presentations in poetry, fiction and theater. The Center is publisher of *Poet Lore*—100 years old in 1989 (see listing in the Publishers of Poetry section). Reviews books of poetry. This year the Center also has a computer on-line service with news and information about the Washington metropolitan literary community. The number to connect with the service via modem is (301)656-1638 or 1639.

THE WRITERS ROOM, 153 Waverly Pl., 5th Floor, New York NY 10014, phone (212)807-9519, provides a "home away from home" for any writer "with a serious commitment to writing," who needs a place to work. It is open 24 hours a day, 7 days a week, offering desks, storage space and "an alternative to isolation" for up to 150 writers. Space is allotted on a quarterly basis (which may be extended indefinitely) and costs $165/quarter. "We now offer in-house scholarships for one-quarter year to writers in financial need." It is supported by the National Endowment for the Arts, the New York State Council on the Arts and other public and private sources, and it encourages applications. The Writers Room also offers monthly readings and workshops for its residents and has occasional exhibits on "writerly" subjects, such as revision.

Additional Organizations Useful to Poets

The following listings also contain information about organizations useful to poets. See the General Index for page numbers.

Air Canada Award, The
Arkansas Poetry Day Contest
Bay Area Poets Coalition (BAPC)
California Writers' Roundtable
  Poetry Contest
Canadian Author
Canadian Authors Association
  Literary Awards
Capricorn Poetry Award
Coastal Forest Review
Connecticut River Review
Coolbrith Circle Annual Poetry
  Contest, Ina
Council for Wisconsin Writers,
  Inc.
CQ (California State Poetry
  Quarterly)
Dream Shop, The
Equinox Press
Fairbanks Arts Association
Frogpond: Quarterly Haiku
  Journal

Frost Chapter: California
  Federation of Chaparral Poets
  Annual Poetry Competition,
  Robert
Georgia State Poetry Society, Inc.
Grolier Poetry Prize
Intro
IWWG Summer Conference, The
Jewish Women's Literary Annual
Keystrokes
Kwibidi Publisher
Lampman Award
Lines Review
Maryland Poetry Review
Midwest Villages & Voices
Onionhead
Oracle Poetry
Outrider Press
Pasque Petals
Pennsylvania Poetry Society
  Annual Contest
Philomel

Poem
Poetpourri
Poetry
Poetry Harbor
Poetry Society of Michigan
  Annual Contests
Pudding House Publications
Science Fiction Poetry
  Association
Society of American Poets, The
Stevan Company, The
Tesseract Publications
Washington Review
Washington Writers' Publishing
  House
Weyfarers
WFNB Annual Literary Contest
Without Halos
Woodnotes
Worcester Review

Publications
Useful to Poets

The publications in this section are designed to help poets with all aspects of writing and publishing poetry. While few are actual markets, many detail new publishing opportunities in addition to providing information on craft, advice on marketing, or interviews with poets and writers.

Poets & Writers Magazine, in fact, is one of the most useful resources for both poets and fiction writers. In addition to informative articles and interviews, it includes calls for submissions and contests and awards. *Writer's Digest*, on the other hand, covers the entire field of writing and features market listings as well as a monthly poetry column by Michael J. Bugeja, author of *The Art and Craft of Poetry* (Writer's Digest Books).

Other publications, such as *Dusty Dog Reviews*, *Small Press Review* (see Dustbooks) and *Literary Magazine Review*, include reviews of poetry books and chapbooks or reviews of small press magazines. These reviews provide further insight into the different markets.

Finally, for those interested in various publishing opportunities, this section also includes information about other market directories as well as materials on self-publishing. And, in addition to the listings that follow, you will find other useful publications, such as *Canadian Author* and *New Writer's Magazine*, under Additional Publications Useful to Poets at the end of this section.

To determine which of these publications may be most useful to you, read sample issues. Many of these books and periodicals may be found in your local library or located on newsstands or in bookstores. If you are unable to locate a certain magazine, order a copy directly from the publisher. For books, send a SASE with a request for the publisher's current catalog or order information.

R.R. BOWKER; LITERARY MARKET PLACE; BOOKS IN PRINT, 121 Chanlon Rd., New Providence NJ 07974, phone (908)464-6800. *LMP* is the major trade directory of publishers and people involved in publishing books. It is available in most libraries, or individual copies may be purchased (published in September each year; standing order price: $157). *BIP* is another standard reference available in most libraries and bookstores. Bowker publishes a wide range of reference books pertaining to publishing. Write for their catalog.

CANADIAN POETRY, English Dept., University of Western Ontario, London, Ontario N6A 3K7 Canada, phone (519)661-3403, founded 1977, editor Prof. D.M.R. Bentley. A biannual journal of critical articles, reviews and historical documents (such as interviews). It is a professionally printed, scholarly edited, flat-spined, 100-page journal which pays contributors in copies. Subscription: $15. **Sample: $7.50. Note that they publish no poetry except as quotations in articles.**

DUSTBOOKS; INTERNATIONAL DIRECTORY OF LITTLE MAGAZINES AND SMALL PRESSES; DIRECTORY OF POETRY PUBLISHERS; SMALL PRESS REVIEW; SMALL MAGAZINE REVIEW, P.O. Box 100, Paradise CA 95967. Dustbooks publishes a number of books useful to writers. Send SASE for catalog. Among their regular publications, *International Directory* is an annual directory of small presses and literary magazines, over 6,000 entries, a third being magazines, half being book publishers, and the rest being both. There is very detailed information about what these presses and magazines report to be their policies in regard to payment, copyright, format and publishing schedules. *Directory of Poetry Publishers* has similar information for over 2,000 publishers of poetry. *Small Press Review* is a monthly magazine, newsprint, carrying current updating of listings in *ID*, small press needs, news, announcements and reviews—a valuable way to stay abreast of the literary marketplace. *Small Magazine Review*, which began publication in June, 1993, is included within *Small Press Review* and covers small press magazines in a similar fashion.

DUSTY DOG REVIEWS, 1904-A Gladden, Gallup NM 87301, phone (505)863-2398, founded 1990, editor/publisher John Pierce. *Dusty Dog Reviews* is a review magazine appearing 4 times/year, reviewing small press poetry books and chapbooks, 20-30/issue, average length 200 words. Subscription: $4.50. Sample: $1.50. Open to unsolicited reviews. Poets may also send books for review consideration to Dave Castleman, 512 Tamalpais Dr., Mill Valley CA 94941. "All editors and publishers whose poetry books/chapbooks get reviewed will receive one copy of the issue in which the review appears." The editor advises, "Become very familiar with *Poet's Market* and what is said at the beginning of the book. The small press magazines are often one-person staff and work very hard for you, the poet. Be patient with them, and support the magazines you like. If poets don't subscribe to the magazines that publish them, it is very hard for the magazines to continue publishing."

FAIRBANKS ARTS ASSOCIATION; FAIRBANKS ARTS, P.O. Box 72786, Fairbanks AK 99707, phone (907)456-6485, fax (907)456-4112, editor Heather Robertson. FAA publishes a bimonthly magazine, *Fairbanks Arts*, which covers interior Alaskan arts and cultural events, organizations and people (artists, writers, musicians, actors, etc.), plus provides how-to information, market tips for Alaskan writers, humor and personal experiences pertaining to writing, marketing and lifestyles. They also accept quality short stories, nonfiction, essays on art, philosophy, literature and quality art and photos. Articles run 800-1,300 words. **Accepts all forms of poetry; limit submissions to 3 poems with maximum 40 lines each. Pays 5 contributor copies.** Subscription: $15. **Sample and guidelines free.** FAA also sponsors a Community Reading Series for Alaskan and visiting writers.

LAUGHING BEAR NEWSLETTER; LAUGHING BEAR PRESS, P.O. Box 36159, Denver CO 80236, phone (303)744-3624, founded 1976, editor Tom Person. *LBN* is a monthly publication of small press information for writers and publishers containing articles, news and reviews. Cost: $12/year. Send SASE for sample copy. *LBN* is interested in short (200- to 300-word) articles on self-publishing and small press. Pays copies.

THE LETTER EXCHANGE, published by The Readers' League, % Stephen Sikora, P.O. Box 6218, Albany CA 94706-0218. Published 3 times each year, *The Letter Exchange* is a digest-sized magazine, 36 pgs., that publishes 4 types of listings: regular (which are rather like personal classifieds); ghost letters, which contain lines like "Send news of the Entwives!"; amateur magazines, which publicizes readers' own publishing ventures; and sketch ads, in which readers who would rather draw than write can communicate in their chosen mode. All ads are coded, and readers respond through the code numbers. Subscription to *The Letter Exchange* is $20/year, and sample copies are $9 postpaid for current issue. Poets who are so inclined often exchange poems and criticism with each other through this medium.

LITERARY MAGAZINE REVIEW, English Dept., Kansas State University, Manhattan KS 66506, founded 1981, editor G.W. Clift. A quarterly magazine (digest-sized, perfect-bound, about 60 pgs.) that publishes critiques, 2-5 pgs. long, of various literary magazines, plus shorter "reviews" (about ½ page), directories of literary magazines (such as British publications) and descriptive listings of new journals during a particular year. Single copies are available for $5 or subscriptions for $12.50 year.

‡OHIO WRITER, P.O. Box 528, Willoughby OH 44094, editor Linda Rome, is a bimonthly newsletter for Ohio writers or those connected with Ohio. It is 16 pgs., professionally printed in colored ink on off-white stock, containing news and reviews of Ohio writing events, publications and regional opportunities to publish. Subscription: $12/year, $18 for institutions.

OPEN HORIZONS, P.O. Box 205, Fairfield IA 52556-0205, phone (515)472-6130, publisher John Kremer, publishes how-to books about book publishing and self-publishing, such as *1001 Ways to Market Your Books*, *Directory of Book Printers*, and *Book Publishing Resource Guide* (also available on IBM PC or Macintosh disk as a database). Send SASE for catalog.

OXFORD UNIVERSITY PRESS, 198 Madison Ave., New York NY 10016, phone (212)679-7300, founded 1478, literature editor Elizabeth Maguire (NY), is a large university press publishing academic, trade and college books in a wide variety of fields. **Not accepting poetry mss.** "Our list includes editions of English and American poets for classroom use, thematically-oriented anthologies and critical studies of poets and their work for general readers. Unfortunately, we do not publish new poetry by contemporary writers."

PARA PUBLISHING, Box 2206-880, Santa Barbara CA 93118-2206, phone (805)968-7277, orders (800)727-2782, fax (805)968-1379. Author/publisher Dan Poynter publishes how-to books on book publishing and self-publishing. *Is There a Book Inside You?* shows you how to get your book out. *The Self-Publishing Manual, How to Write, Print and Sell Your Own Book* is all about book promotion. *Publishing Short-Run Books* shows you how to typeset and lay out your own book. Poynter also publishes *Publishing Contracts on Disk, Book Fairs* and 19 Special Reports on various aspects of book production, promotion, marketing and distribution. *Free* book publishing information kit. Newly available through Para Publishing is a 24-hour fax service called Fax-On-Demand. This service enables you to obtain free documents on book writing and publishing; and lists of workshops and presentations offered by Dan Poynter. Call (805)968-8947 from your fax machine handset, then follow the voice prompts to hear a list of documents and to order. The fax machine will retrieve the documents and print them instantly. This is a good way to sample Para Publishing's offerings.

PERSONAL POEMS, (formerly Personal Poets United), %Jean Hesse, Villa B-7, 16591 Perdido Key Dr., Pensacola FL 32507, phone (904)492-7909. Jean Hesse started a business in 1980 writing poems for individuals for a fee (for greetings, special occasions, etc.). Others started similar businesses, after she began instructing them in the process, especially through a cassette tape training program and other training materials. Send SASE for free brochure or $25 plus $4.50 p&h (make checks payable to F. Jean Hesse) for training manual, *How to Make Your Poems Pay*.

POETRY BOOK SOCIETY, Book House, 45 East Hill, London SW18 2QZ England. A book club with an annual subscription rate of £37, which covers 4 books of new poetry, the *PBS Bulletin*, a premium offer (for new members) and free surface postage and packing to anywhere in the world. The selectors also recommend other books of special merit, which are obtainable at a discount of 25%. The Poetry Book Society is subsidized by the Arts Council of England. Please write for details or phone 081-877-1615 (24-hour fax/answer service).

THE POETRY CONNECTION, 13455 SW 16 Court #F-405-PM, Pembroke Pines FL 33027, phone (305)431-3016, editor/publisher Sylvia Shichman. *The Poetry Connection* provides information in flyer format. Poets, writers and songwriters receive information on how to sell their poetry/books, poetry and musical publications and contests, and obtain assistance in getting poetry published. *TPC* has information on writing for greeting card companies, poetry and songwriting publications, and greeting card directories. Sample issue: $5 plus $2 postage. Send SASE for more information.

POETRY EXCHANGE, P.O. Box 85477, Seattle WA 98145-1477. A monthly newsletter, circulation 1,600, $12/year, to which you may subscribe or in which you can buy ads. It has listings of workshops, "manuscripts wanted," and a calendar of regional poetic events. It is 4 to 8 magazine-sized pages.

POETS & WRITERS, INC.; A DIRECTORY OF AMERICAN POETS AND FICTION WRITERS; WRITER'S GUIDE TO COPYRIGHT; AUTHOR & AUDIENCE; LITERARY AGENTS; LITERARY BOOKSTORES; POETS & WRITERS MAGAZINE, 72 Spring St., New York NY 10012, phone (212)226-3586 or (800)666-2268 (California only), is a major support organization. Its many helpful publications include *Poets & Writers Magazine*, which appears 6 times a year ($18 or $3.95 for a single copy), magazine-sized, 88 pgs., offset, has been called *The Wall Street Journal* of our profession, and it is there that one most readily finds out about resources, current needs of magazines and presses, contests, awards, jobs and retreats for writers, and discussions of business, legal and other issues affecting writers. P&W also publishes a number of valuable directories such as its biennial *A Directory of American Poets and Fiction Writers* ($24.95 paperback), which editors, publishers, agents and sponsors of readings and workshops use to locate over 7,000 active writers in the country. (You may qualify for a listing if you have a number of publications.) They also publish *A Writer's Guide to Copyright*; *Author & Audience*, a list of over 400 organizations which sponsor readings and workshops involving poets and fiction writers, including a section on how to organize and present a reading or workshop; *Literary Agents: A Writer's Guide*; *Literary Bookstores: A Cross-Country Guide*, for people who travel; a series of eight chapbooks, "Into Print: Guides to the Writing Life," that includes *Out of the Slush Pile and Into Print*; *Contracts and Royalties: Negotiating Your Own*; *On Cloud Nine: Writers' Colonies, Retreats, Ranches, Residencies, and Sanctuaries*; and *Helping Writers Help Themselves: A National Guide to Writers' Resources*; and a list of literary resources for writers in all 8 regions of the country. The chapbooks and resource lists are available from P&W for $6 each plus p&h.

POETS' AUDIO CENTER; THE WATERSHED FOUNDATION, P.O. Box 50145, Washington DC 20091. This is an international clearinghouse for ordering any poetry recording available, from both commercial and noncommercial producers. Catalog available free ("an introduction to our collection"); they stock over 500 titles. **Foundation not accepting applications at this time.**

BERN PORTER INTERNATIONAL, 22 Salmond Rd., Belfast ME 04915, founded 1911. A monthly journal that both reviews books of poetry and publishes poetry. Also provides sleeping bag space for poets and writers May 1 through November 1 for the cost or freewill contribution.

PUSHCART PRESS, P.O. Box 380, Wainscott NY 11975. Publishes a number of books useful to writers, including the Pushcart Prize Series—annual anthologies representing the best small press publications, according to the judges; The Editors' Book Award Series, "to encourage the writing of distinguished books of uncertain financial value"; *The Original Publish-It-Yourself Handbook*; and the Literary Companion Series. Send SASE for catalog.

SIPAPU; KONOCTI BOOKS, 23311 County Rd. 88, Winters CA 95694, phone (916)662-3364, founded 1970, editor/publisher Noel Peattie. *Sipapu* consists of reviews of small press publications, interviews and conference news, but publishes no new poetry. Konocti Books has published poetry but is now publishing by invitation only.

THE WASHINGTON INTERNATIONAL ARTS LETTER, P.O. Box 12010, Des Moines IA 50312-9401. Appears 4 times/year, 6- to 8-page newsletter on grants and other forms of assistance for the arts and humanities—mostly lists various programs of support to artists, including many for poets. Reviews books of poetry. Subscription: $124 full rate; $55 for individuals; $82 for institutions. Send all orders and requests for information to the address above, or call (800)364-6484.

WRITER'S DIGEST BOOKS; WRITER'S DIGEST, 1507 Dana Ave., Cincinnati OH 45207, phone (800)289-0963 or (513)531-2690. Writer's Digest Books publishes an array of books useful to all types of writers. In addition to *Poet's Market*, books for poets include *The Poet's Handbook* by Judson Jerome, *Creating Poetry* by John Drury and *The Art and Craft of Poetry* by Michael J. Bugeja. Call or write for a complete catalog. *Writer's Digest* is a monthly magazine about writing with a regular poetry column and frequent market news. See the listing in the Publishers of Poetry section.

‡THE WRITING SELF, P.O. Box 245, Lenox Hill Station, New York NY 10021, managing editor Scot Nourok, founded 1990, is a quarterly publication "devoted to the act of writing. We are looking for manuscripts that will stimulate our readers to keep on writing." Each issue features personal essays; short columns, such as "Coping with Isolation" and "Gaining Confidence"; book and magazine reviews; and interviews. They also publish 1 poem in each issue. It is approximately 16 pgs., 8½×11, offset litho with photo on cover and some art. Subscription: $10. Sample postpaid: $3.

Additional Publications Useful to Poets

The following listings also contain information about publications useful to poets. See the General Index for page numbers.

Glossary

A3, A4, A5. Metric equivalents of $11\frac{3}{4} \times 16\frac{1}{2}$, $8\frac{1}{4} \times 11\frac{3}{4}$ and $5\frac{7}{8} \times 8\frac{1}{4}$ respectively.

Bio. A short biographical paragraph often requested with a submission; it is commonly called a "bio." In your bio, publishers may ask you to note your most recent and noteworthy publication credits.

Chapbook. A small book of approximately 20-25 pages of poetry. Such a book is less expensive to produce than a full-length book collection, though it is seldom noted by reviewers.

Cover letter. Letter accompanying a submission; it usually lists titles of poems and gives a brief account of publishing credits and biographical information.

Digest-sized. Approximately $5\frac{1}{2} \times 8\frac{1}{2}$, the size of a folded sheet of conventional typing paper.

Flat-spined. What many publishers call "perfect-bound," glued with a flat edge (usually permitting readable type on the spine).

Galleys. Typeset copies of your poem(s). You should proofread and correct any mistakes and return galleys to editors within 48 hours of receipt.

IRC. International Reply Coupon, postage for return of submissions from another country. One IRC is sufficient for one ounce by *surface mail*. If you want an airmail return, you need one IRC for each half-ounce. Do not send checks or cash for postage to other countries: The exchange rates are so high it is not worth the bother it causes editors. (Exception: Many Canadian editors do not object to U.S. dollars; use IRCs the first time and inquire.)

Magazine-sized. Approximately $8\frac{1}{2} \times 11$, the size of conventional typing paper unfolded.

ms, mss. Manuscript, manuscripts.

Multi-book review. Also known as an omnibus or essay review. A review of several books by the same author or by several authors, such as a review of four or five political poetry books.

Multiple submission. Submission of more than one poem at a time; most poetry publishers *prefer* multiple submissions and specify how many poems should be in a packet. Some say a multiple submission means the poet has sent another manuscript to the same publication before receiving word on the first submission. This type of multiple submission is generally discouraged.

p. Abbreviation for pence.

pg., pgs. Page, pages.

Perfect-bound. See Flat-spined.

Query letter. Letter written to a publisher to elicit interest in a manuscript or to determine if submissions are acceptable.

Rights. First North American serial rights means the publisher is acquiring the right to publish your poem first in a U.S. or Canadian periodical. All rights means the publisher is buying the poem outright. Selling all rights usually requires that you obtain permission to reprint your work, even in a book-length collection.

Saddle-stapled. What many publishers call "saddle-stitched," folded and stapled along the fold.

SAE. Self-addressed envelope.

SASE. Self-addressed, stamped envelope. *Every* publisher requires, with any submission, query or request for information, a self-addressed, stamped envelope. This requirement is so basic it is repeated in bold type at the bottom of a number of pages throughout this book. The return envelope (usually folded for inclusion) should be large enough to hold the material submitted or requested, and the postage provided—stamps if the submission is within your own country, IRCs if it is to another country—should be sufficient for its return.

Simultaneous submission. Submission of the same manuscript to more than one publisher at a time. Most magazine editors *refuse to accept* simultaneous submissions. Some book and chapbook publishers do not object to simultaneous submissions. In all cases, notify them that the manuscript is being simultaneously submitted if that is what you are doing.

Slush pile. The stack of unsolicited manuscripts received by an editor or publisher.

Status. The current situation concerning a particular manuscript: 1) The manuscript was never received. 2) We received the manuscript but cannot locate it. 3) We received and rejected said manuscript. 4) We are still considering it. 5) We are in the process of accepting your manuscript.

Subsidy press. See Vanity press.

Tabloid-sized. 11×15 or larger, the size of an ordinary newspaper folded and turned sideways.

Vanity press. A slang term for a publisher that requires the writer to pay publishing costs, especially one that flatters an author to generate business. These presses often use the term "subsidy" to describe themselves. Some presses, however, derive subsidies from other sources, such as government grants, and do not require author payment. These are not considered vanity presses.

Visual poetry. A combination of text and graphics usually only reproduced photographically.

Indexes

Chapbook Publishers

A chapbook is a slim volume of a poet's work, usually 20-25 pages (although page requirements vary greatly). Given the high cost of printing, a publisher is more apt to accept a chapbook than an entire book from an unproven poet.

Some chapbooks are published as inserts in magazines. Others are separate volumes. Whenever possible, request submission guidelines and samples to determine the quality of the product.

You'll find many presses charge reading fees. Avoid any over $10. (Some folks go as high as $15 for book-length manuscripts, but chapbooks are easier to process.)

If your chapbook is published, by the way, you may still participate in "first-book" competitions. For more information about both chapbook and book publishing, read Charting Your Path to Poetry Publication, beginning on page 11. Also, for an in-depth look at a chapbook publisher, see the interview with Laurence F. Hawkins on pages 404-405.

Following are publishers who consider chapbook manuscripts. See the General Index for the page numbers of their market listings.

Flume Press
French Broad Press

G

Generator
Global Tapestry Journal
Golden Isis Magazine
Gotta Write Network Litmag
Greenhouse Review Press
Green's Magazine

H

Hartland Poetry Quarterly,
The
Heartlands Today, The
Heaven Bone Magazine
Hellas: A Journal of Poetry
and the Humanities
High/Coo Press
Hippopotamus Press
Hunted News, The
Hyacinth House Publica-
tions

I

Illinois Review, The
Implosion Press
Insects Are People Too
Intercultural Writer's
Review, The
International Black Writers
International Poets
Academy
Inverted-A, Inc.

J

Jackson Harbor Press
Jackson's Arm
Janus
Jones Foundation National
Poetry Competition, The
Chester H.

L

Lake Shore Publishing
Ledge Poetry and Fiction
Magazine, The
Lilliput Review
Limberlost Press
Limited Editions Press
Lone Willow Press
Longhouse
Lucidity

Luna Bisonte Prods

M

Mad River Press
Maverick Press, The
Mayapple Press
Mid-American Review
(m)öthêr TØñgués Press
mulberry press

N

Negative Capability
New Hope International
New Orleans Poetry Journal
Press
New Poets Series, Inc., The
Nosukumo

O

Oasis Books
Ohio Poetry Review, The
Ohio Review, The
Olympia Review
ONTHEBUS
Outrider Press
Owl Creek Press

P

Palanquin/TDM
Panhandler, The
Paradox
Parting Gifts
Pearl
Penumbra Press, The
Perivale Press
Permafrost
Permeable Press
Petronium Press
Phase and Cycle
Phlebas Press, The
Pikestaff Forum, The
Pirate Writings
Plowman, The
Poems & Plays
Poet Magazine
Poetic Space: Poetry &
Fiction
Poetry Forum
Poetry Harbor
Poetry in Motion
Poetry Miscellany, The
Poets at Work
Poets' Roundtable

Potato Eyes
Prairie Journal, The
Press Here
Press of MacDonald &
Reinecke, The
Proof Rock Press
Prophetic Voices
Pudding House Publications
PYX Press

R

Rag Mag
Red Candle Press, The
Red Dancefloor
Red Herring Poets
Riverstone, A Press for
Poetry
Runaway Spoon Press, The

S

St. Andrew Press
Score Magazine
Serpent & Eagle Press
Shamal Books
Ship of Fools
Signpost Press, The
Silver Apples Press
Silverfish Review
Slipstream
smellfeast
Soleil Press
Southern Poetry Association
Sow's Ear Poetry Review,
The
Stand Magazine
State Street Press
Stevan Company, The
Still Waters Press
Stonevale Press
Sub-Terrain

T

Tak Tak Tak
"Teak" Roundup
texture
Third Half Literary Maga-
zine, The
Tightrope
Time of Singing, A Maga-
zine of Christian Poetry
Touchstone Literary Journal
Tower Poetry Society

Geographical Index

Use this index to locate small presses and magazines in your region. Much of the poetry published today reflects regional interests. In addition, publishers often favor poets (and work) from their own areas. Also, keep your neighboring areas in mind for other publishing opportunities.

Here you will find the names of U.S. publishers arranged alphabetically within their state or territory. Following them are lists of publishers in Canada, the United Kingdom, and other countries. See the General Index for the page numbers of their corresponding listings. And, remember to always include a SAE and IRCs for replies from countries outside your own.

Alabama
Alabama Literary Review
Aura Literary/Arts Review
Birmingham Poetry Review
Black Warrior Review, The
Catamount Press
Dreams and Nightmares
Elk River Review
Fighting Woman News
Laureate Letter, The
Livingston University Press
National Forum: The Phi Kappa Phi Journal
Negative Capability
9th St. Laboratories
Poem
Salon Arts Magazine
Southern Humanities Review
Sticks

Alaska
Alaska Quarterly Review
Explorations
Intertext
Permafrost
Salmon Run Press

Arizona
Bangtale International
Bilingual Review Press
Coyote Chronicles: Notes from the Southwest
Forever Alive
Hayden's Ferry Review
Newsletter Inago

Sonora Review
South Ash Press

Arkansas
Arkansas Press, The University of
Bloodreams: A Magazine of Vampires & Werewolves
Crazyhorse
Graffiti Off the Asylum Walls
Hyacinth House Publications
Lucidity
Nebo: A Literary Journal
Slant: A Journal of Poetry
Voices International

California
Acorn, The
Advocacy Press
Amelia
Anthology of Magazine Verse & Yearbook of American Poetry
Anything That Moves: Beyond The Myths of Bisexuality
Applezaba Press
Arshile
Arundel Press
Athena Incognito Magazine
Bakunin
Bay Area Poets Coalition (BAPC)
Berkeley Poetry Review

Bishop Publishing Co.
Black Scholar, The
Black Sheets
Blowfish Catalog, The
Blue Unicorn, A Triquarterly of Poetry
Bottomfish
Cadmus Editions
Cat Fancy
Caveat Lector
Center Press
Christian Poet
City Lights Books
Clutch
College & Career Publishing
CQ (California State Poetry Quarterly)
Crazyquilt Quarterly
Creative With Words Publications (C.W.W.)
Creativity Unlimited Press
Daniel and Company, Publisher, John
Dragon's Teeth Press
Dreambuilding Crusade, The
DreamGirls With Shaman
Dry Crik Review
El Tecolote
Epicenter
Epigrammatist, The
1st & Hope
Flume Press
Free Lunch
Fritz
Fudge Cake, The

Geppo Haiku Worksheet
GLB Publishers
Green Fuse
Greenhouse Review Press
Haight Ashbury Literary
    Journal
Haiku Headlines: A
    Monthly Newsletter of
    Haiku and Senryu
Harcourt Brace & Company
Hard Row to Hoe
Healing Journal
Indefinite Space
India Currents
Insomnia & Poetry
Intercultural Writer's Re-
    view
International Olympic Lifter
    (IOL)
Jewish Spectator
Juggler's World
Kuumba
Lamp-Post, The
Left Curve
Liberty Hill Poetry Review
Libra Publishers, Inc.
Lynx, A Journal for Linking
    Poets
Lynx Eye
Mind in Motion: A Maga-
    zine of Poetry and Short
    Prose
Mind Matters Review
Mockingbird
Moving Parts Press
Mythic Circle, The
nerve
New Earth Publications
New Horizons Poetry Club
New Methods: The Journal
    of Animal Health Tech-
    nology
Nocturnal Lyric, Journal of
    the Bizarre
NV Magazine
Olive Press Publications,
    The
ONTHEBUS
Ortalda & Associates
Oxygen
Pancake Press
Panjandrum Books
Papier-Mache Press

Peace Magazine
Pearl
Perivale Press
Permeable Press
Pinehurst Journal, The
Poems for a Livable Planet
Poets On:
Press Here
Press of MacDonald &
    Reinecke, The
Prisoners of the Night
Prophetic Voices
Prosetry: Newsletter For, By
    and About Writers
Pygmy Forest Press
PYX Press
Radiance The Magazine For
    Radiance: The Magazine
    for Large Women
Red Dancefloor
Ridge Review Magazine
San Diego Poet's Press
San Fernando Poetry Journal
San Jose Studies
Santa Barbara Review
Santa Monica Review
Santa Susana Press
Scream Press
Sequoia
Sheila-na-gig
Silver Wings
smellfeast
Sonoma Mandala
Southern California Anthol-
    ogy, The
Steelhead Special, The
Stone Soup, The Magazine
    by Young Writers and
    Artists
Summer Stream Press
Threepenny Review, The
tight
Tradeswomen Magazine
Tucumcari Literary Review
Turkey Press
Urbanus/Magazine
Verve
Virgin Meat
Voices
Voices of Youth
Vol. No. Magazine
W.I.M. Publications
    (Woman in the Moon)

Wilde Oaks
Wishing Well, The
Woodnotes
Wormwood Review Press
Writing For Our Lives
xib
Yellow Silk: Journal of
    Erotic Arts
Zyzzyva

Colorado
Arjuna Library Press
Atlantean Press Review, The
Blue Mountain Arts, Inc.
Climbing Art, The
Cloud Ridge Press
Coffeehouse
Colorado Review
Communities: Journal of
    Cooperative Living
Denver Quarterly
Dry Creek Review, The
High Plains Literary Review
Phase and Cycle
Prairie Dog: A Quarterly for
    the Somewhat Eccentric
Pueblo Poetry Project
Three Continents Press Inc.
Virtue: The Christian Maga-
    zine for Women
Woman's Way: The Path of
    Empowerment
Writers' Forum

Connecticut
Broken Streets
Chicory Blue Press
Connecticut Poetry Review
Connecticut River Review
Country Journal
Embers
Potes & Poets Press, Inc.
Singular Speech Press
Small Pond Magazine of
    Literature
Viet Nam Generation
Wesleyan University Press
Yale Review, The
Yale University Press

District of Columbia
Aerial
American Scholar, The

Poetry
Poetry East
Poetry Plus Magazine
Press of the Third Mind, The
Primavera
Red Herring Poets
Rhino
Rockford Review, The
Shaw Publishers, Harold
Sou'Wester
Spoon River Poetry Review
Stormline Press, Inc.
Tamaqua
Thorntree Press
Tia Chucha Press
Tomorrow Magazine
TriQuarterly Magazine
2 AM Magazine
Whetstone
White Eagle Coffee Store
   Press
Willow Review
Young Crusader, The

Indiana
African American Review
Barnwood Press
Children's Better Health
   Institute
Electric Consumer
Explorer Magazine
Formalist, The
Indiana Review
Light and Life Magazine
Lines n' Rhymes
No Exit
Pablo Lennis
Poets' Roundtable
Purdue University Press
Saturday Evening Post
Skylark
Snowy Egret
Sparrow: The Sonnet
   Yearbook
Sycamore Review
Wesleyan Advocate, The
Windless Orchard, The
Writers' Center Press

Iowa
Ansuda Publications
BEgiNNer's MIND press
Blue Light Press

Briar Cliff Review, The
Coe Review, The
Common Lives/Lesbian
   Lives
Flyway
Iowa Press, University of
Iowa Review, The
Iowa Woman
North American Review
Urbanite, The

Kansas
Capper's
Chiron Review
Cottonwood
De Young Press
Double-Entendre
Kansas Quarterly
Midwest Quarterly, The
Potpourri
Scavenger's Newsletter
Woodley Memorial Press

Kentucky
Appalachian Heritage
Cincinnati Poets' Collective
Disability Rag & Resource
Georgetown Review
Licking River Review
Limestone: A Literary
   Journal
Louisville Review, The
Pikeville Review
Plainsong
Sarabande Books, Inc.
Wind Publications

Louisiana
Cripes!
Exquisite Corpse
Far Gone
Louisiana Literature
Louisiana State University
   Press
mulberry press
New Delta Review
New Laurel Review, The
New Orleans Poetry Journal
   Press
New Orleans Review
New Voices in Poetry and
   Prose
Night Songs

Pelican Publishing Com-
   pany
Southern Review, The
Thema
Xavier Review

Maine
Alicejamesbooks
Beloit Poetry Journal, The
Café Review, The
Full-Time Dads
Mostly Maine
Northwoods Press
Potato Eyes
Puckerbrush Press, The
Soleil Press

Maryland
Abbey
Antietam Review
Cochran's Corner
Dancing Shadow Press
Dolphin-Moon Press
Expressions Forum Review
Feminist Studies
Gut Punch Press
Jewish Vegetarians News-
   letter
Johns Hopkins University
   Press, The
Lite Magazine: The Journal
   of Satire and Creativity
Maryland Poetry Review
Medela Review
Monocacy Valley Review
New Poets Series, Inc., The
Nightsun
Oracle Poetry
Passager: A Journal of Re-
   membrance and Discov-
   ery
Pegasus Review, The
Plastic Tower, The
Poet Lore
Ruby
Samsara
Scop Publications, Inc.
Shattered Wig Review
Social Anarchism
Stonevale Press
Vegetarian Journal
Welter
WoRM fEASt!

River Styx Magazine
Sharing the Victory
Timberline Press
Unity
Webster Review

Montana
Corona
Cutbank
Kinesis
Portable Wall
Seven Buffaloes Press
Zeitgeist

Nebraska
Lone Willow Press
Nebraska Review, The
Penumbra Press, The
Plainsongs
Prairie Schooner
Rock Falls Review
Writing Works

Nevada
Drop Forge
Interim
Limited Editions Press
Pegasus
Rio Grande Press
Sierra Nevada College
Review

New Hampshire
Bauhan, Publisher,
William L.
Bone & Flesh Publications
Color Wheel
Womenwise
Yankee Magazine

New Jersey
Africa World Press
Ararat
black bough
Chantry Press
Coastal Forest Review
Companion in Zeor, A
Delaware Valley Poets, Inc.
Ever Dancing Muse, The
Exit 13
Fellowship in Prayer
First Hand

Footwork: The Paterson
Literary Review
Janus
Journal of New Jersey Poets
Just About Horses
Kelsey Review
Lactuca
Lincoln Springs Press
Literary Review: An Inter-
national Journal of Con-
temporary Writing, The
Long Shot
Naturally: Nude Recreation
for All Ages
Ontario Review
Overview Ltd. Poetry
Princeton University Press
Prolific Writer's Magazine
Quarterly Review of Litera-
ture Poetry Series
Raritan Quarterly
St. Joseph Messenger and
Advocate of the Blind
Saturday Press, Inc.
Sensations Magazine
Silver Apples Press
Still Waters Press
Talisman: A Journal of Con-
temporary Poetry and
Poetics
Timber Creek Review
US1 Worksheets
Warthog Press
Without Halos

New Mexico
Atom Mind
Blue Mesa Review
Katydid Books
Puerto Del Sol
West End Press
Whole Notes
Yefief

New York
Adrift
Advocate, The
African Voices
Alms House Press
America
Amicus Journal, The
Antipodes
Aphrodite Gone Berserk: A

Journal of Erotic Art
Art Times: A Literary Jour-
nal and Resource for All
the Arts
Asian Pacific American
Journal
Bacon Press, The
Bad Henry Review, The
Bank Street Press, The
Bantam Doubleday Dell
Publishing Group
Belhue Press
Blind Beggar Press
Blueline
Boa Editions, Ltd.
Bomb Magazine
Bong
BOOG Literature
Braziller, Inc., George
Brooklyn Review
Buffalo Spree Magazine
C.L.A.S.S. Magazine
Camellia
Chelsea
Columbia: A Magazine of
Poetry & Prose
Commonweal
Confrontation Magazine
Conjunctions
Cosmopolitan
Cover Magazine
Cross-Cultural Communi-
cations
CWM
dbqp
Earth's Daughters: A Femi-
nist Arts Periodical
1812
11th St. Ruse
ELF: Eclectic Literary Fo-
rum
Epoch
Essence
Excursus Literary Arts
Journal
Farrar, Straus & Giroux/
Books for Young Readers
Feh! A Journal of Odious
Poetry
Firebrand Books
Free Focus
Frogpond: Quarterly Haiku
Journal

North Carolina

North Dakota

North Dakota Quarterly

Ohio

Amateur Writers Journal/
   Four Seasons Poetry
   Club Magazine
Anathema Review
Antioch Review, The
Artful Dodge
Ashland Poetry Press, The
Barham Publishing, E.W.
Bits Press
Byron Poetry Works
Cincinnati Poetry Review
Cleveland State University
   Poetry Center
Confluence
Dream Shop, The
Evil Dog
Field
Fifty Something Magazine
Generator
Heartlands Today, The
Hiram Poetry Review
Hopscotch: The Magazine
   For Girls
Implosion Press
Inkslinger
Journal, The
Kaleidoscope: International
   Magazine of Literature,
   Fine Arts, and Disability
Kenyon Review, The
Luna Bisonte Prods
Luna Negra
Mark: A Literary Journal
Mid-American Review
Mosaic Press
Nexus
Ohio Poetry Review, The
Ohio Review, The
Ohio State University Press/
   The Journal Award in
   Poetry
Oxford Magazine
Pig Iron
Poetic Knight: A Fantasy
   Romance Magazine: The
Pudding House Publications
Riverwind
St. Anthony Messenger
Shawnee Silhouette

Ship of Fools
Solo Flyer
Spitball
Straight
This: A Serial Review
Vincent Brothers Review,
   The
Whiskey Island Magazine
Writer's Digest

Oklahoma

Byline Magazine
Cimarron Review
Eagle's Flight
manna
Midland Review
Nimrod International Jour-
   nal of Contemporary
   Poetry and Fiction
Ogalala Review, The
Poet Magazine
Surprise Me
texture
Westview: A Journal of
   Western Oklahoma

Oregon

Beacon
Calapooya Collage
Calyx, A Journal of Art &
   Literature by Women
Eighth Mountain Press, The
Fireweed: Poetry of Western
   Oregon
Furry Chiclets: A Lawpoets
   Creation
Hubbub
Literary Fragments
Metamorphous Press
Midwifery Today
Mr. Cogito Press
Northwest Literary Forum
Northwest Review
Oregon East
Plazm Magazine
Poetic Space: Poetry &
   Fiction
Pointed Circle, The
Portland Review
Prescott Street Press
Salt Lick
Sandpiper Press
Silverfish Review

Story Line Press
Trout Creek Press
Twisted Nipples
Unsilenced Voice
West Wind Review
Wilderness
Willamette River Books

Pennsylvania

Aguilar Expression, The
Allegheny Review
Alpha Beat Soup
Alternative Arts & Litera-
   ture Magazine
American Poetry Review
American Writing: A Maga-
   zine
Apropos
Black Bear Publications
Bouillabaisse
Boulevard
Carnegie Mellon Magazine
Cokefish
Collages & Bricolages, The
   Journal of International
   Writing
Dust (From the Ego Trip)
Dwan
Echoes Magazine
Fat Tuesday
Feelings: America's Beauti-
   ful Poetry Magazine
5 AM
Flipside
Friends Journal
Gettysburg Review, The
Ginger Hill
Hellas: A Journal of Poetry
   and the Humanities
Highlights for Children
Hob-Nob
Idiot, The
Journal of Asian Martial
   Arts
Lilliput Review
Mediphors
Mennonite Publishing
   House
Miraculous Medal, The
My Legacy
Other Side Magazine, The
Painted Bride Quarterly
Pennsylvania English

Brunswick Publishing
  Corporation
Callaloo
Chronicle of the Horse, The
Chrysalis Reader, The
Conservative Review
Dolphin Log
Dominion Review, The
Fauquier Poetry Journal
5th Gear
Hollins Critic, The
Intro
Iris: A Journal About
  Women
Lintel
Lyric, The
New Virginia Review
Orchises Press
Phoebe
Pocahontas Press, Inc.
Poetry Explosion Newsletter
Proof Rock Press
Ranger Rick Magazine
Reflect
Roanoke Review
St. Andrew Press
Shenandoah
Sow's Ear Poetry Review,
  The
Ugly Publications
Verse
Virginia Quarterly Review
William and Mary Review
Writer's World

Washington
Ag-Pilot International
  Magazine
Arnazella
Bellowing Ark Press
Cleaning Business Maga-
  zine
Copper Canyon Press
Crab Creek Review
Fine Madness
Frontiers: A Journal of
  Women Studies
IHCUT
Lighthouse Publications
Olympia Review
Open Hand Publishing Inc.
Owl Creek Press
Poetry Northwest

Poets. Painters. Composers.
Score Magazine
Seattle Review
Signpost Press, The
Slightly West
Spindrift
Tapjoe: The Anaprocrustean
  Poetry Journal of Enum-
  claw
Willow Springs
Young Voices Magazine

West Virginia
Aegina Press, Inc.
Stevan Company, The
Tantra Press

Wisconsin
Abraxas Magazine
Acorn Whistle
Blank Gun Silencer
Block's Poetry Collection
Caxton Ltd., Wm
Country Woman
Cream City Review
Fox Cry
Glass Cherry Press, The
Jackson Harbor Press
Juniper Press
Madison Review, The
Magazine of Speculative
  Poetry, The
Modern Haiku
Poet's Fantasy
Rosebud
Seems
Student Leadership Journal
Touchstone
Wisconsin Academy Re-
  view
Wisconsin Press, University
  of
Wisconsin Review

Wyoming
High Plains Press
Housewife-Writer's Forum
Owen Wister Review

Canada
Afterthoughts
Amber
Anjou

Antigonish Review, The
Ariel, A Review of Interna-
  tional English Literature
Arsenal Pulp Press
Atlantis: A Women's Studies
  Journal
Beach Holme Publishers
Beneath the Surface
Borealis Press
Canadian Author
Canadian Dimension: The
  Magazine for People
  Who Want to Change the
  World
Canadian Literature
Canadian Writer's Journal
Capers Aweigh Magazine
Capilano Review, The
Chickadee Magazine
Church-Wellesley Review
Claremont Review, The
Coach House Press
Compenions
Cosmic Trend
Coteau Books
Dalhousie Review, The
Dance Connection
Dandelion
Descant
Ekstasis Editions
Ellipse
Event
Fiddlehead, The
Filling Station
Fireweed: A Feminist
  Quarterly
Goose Lane Editions
Grain
Green's Magazine
Guernica Editions Inc.
Herspectives Magazine
Indigo Magazine: The Span-
  ish-Canadian Presence in
  the Arts
Inkstone: A Magazine of
  Haiku
McGill Street Magazine
Malahat Review, The
(m)öthêr TØñgués Press
Musicworks
New Quarterly, The
On Spec: The Canadian

Poetry Kanto (Japan)
Polyphonies (France)
Prakalpana Literature (India)
Rashi (New Zealand)
Redoubt (Australia)
Renditions: A Chinese-
English Translation Magazine (Hong Kong)
Sandberry Press (West Indies)
Scarp (Australia)
Sivullinen (Finland)
South Head Press (Australia)
Studio, A Journal of Christians Writing (Australia)
Transnational Perspectives (Switzerland)
Voices Israel
Westerly (Australia)

Subject Index

Use this index to save time in your search for the best markets for your poetry. The categories are listed alphabetically and contain the magazines, publishers, contests and awards that buy or accept poetry dealing with specific subjects. Most of these markets are coded **IV** in their listings.

Check through the index first to see what subjects are represented. Then look at the listings in the categories you're interested in. For example, if you're seeking a magazine or contest for your poem about a "personal awakening," look at the titles under **Spirituality/Inspirational**. After you've selected a possible market, refer to the General Index for the page number. Then read the listing *carefully* for details on submission requirements.

Under **Themes**, you will find those book and magazine publishers that regularly publish anthologies or issues on announced themes (if interested, send a SASE to these publishers for details on upcoming topics). **Regional** includes those outlets which publish poetry about or by poets from a certain geographic area; and the category **Form/Style** contains those magazines and presses that seek particular poetic forms or styles, such as haiku or sonnets or experimental work. Finally, those publishers listed under **Specialized** are very narrow in their interests—too narrow, in fact, to be listed in one of our other categories.

We do not recommend you use this index exclusively in your search for a market. Most magazines, publishers and contests listed in *Poet's Market* have wide-ranging poetry preferences and don't choose to be listed by category. Also, many of those who specialize in one subject are often open to others as well. Reading *all* the listings is still your best marketing strategy.

Anthology

Anthology of Magazine Verse & Yearbook of American Poetry
Ashland Poetry Press, The
Beer & Pub Poetry
Blind Beggar Press
Catamount Press
Crab Creek Review
Crescent Moon Publishing
Cross-Cultural Communications
Delaware Valley Poets, Inc.
Georgia State Poetry Society, Inc.
Geppo Haiku Worksheet
Guild Press
Helicon Nine Editions
Hen's Teeth
Illinois Press, University of

Intercultural Writer's Review, The
Kawabata Press
Kitchen Table: Women of Color Press
Lake Shore Publishing
Meadowbrook Press
Nada Press
New Horizons Poetry Club
Night Roses
Northwoods Press
Outrider Press
Papier-Mache Press
Penumbra Press, The
Perivale Press
Plowman, The
Poetic Knight: A Fantasy Romance Magazine, The
Prairie Journal, The
Pudding House Publications
Science Fiction Poetry

Association
Seven Buffaloes Press
Shamal Books
Society of American Poets, The
Spirit That Moves Us, The
Three Continents Press Inc.
Violetta Books
Voices Israel
Waterways: Poetry in the Mainstream
West Wind Review
White Eagle Coffee Store Press
Wind Publications

Bilingual/Foreign Language

Andreas-Gryphius-Preis (German)
Bilingual Review Press

(Spanish)
Cross-Cultural Communications
Doc(k)s (French)
Ediciones Universal (Spanish)
Ellipse (French)
Footwork: The Paterson Literary Review (Spanish)
Gairm (Scottish Gaelic)
Indigo Magazine: The Spanish-Canadian Presence in the Arts
Irish American Cultural Institute Literary Awards
Italica Press (Italian)
Language Bridges Quarterly (Polish)
Letras De Oro Spanish Literary Prizes
M.I.P. Company (Russian)
New Renaissance, The
Osiris, An International Poetry Journal/Une Revue Internationale (Danish, French, German, Italian and Polish)
Plaza, The (Japanese)
Prakalpana Literature (Bengali)
Princeton University Press
REAL (Re Arts & Letters)
Sachem Press (Spanish)
Tessera (French)
Unmuzzled Ox (French)
Women's Studies Quarterly (French, German, Italian and Spanish)

Children/Teen/ Young Adult

Advocacy Press
Alive Now
Blind Beggar Press
Cat Fancy
Chickadee Magazine
Children's Better Health Institute
Claremont Review, The
Clubhouse
College & Career Publishing
Communications Publishing Group

Coteau Books
Creative With Words Publications (C.W.W.)
Cricket
Dolphin Log
Farrar, Straus & Giroux/ Books for Young Readers
Fudge Cake, The
Gospel Publishing House
Hanging Loose Press
Hartland Poetry Quarterly, The
Highlights for Children
Holiday House, Inc.
Hopscotch: The Magazine For Girls
Kwibidi Publisher
Lighthouse Publications
Lodestar Books
Louisville Review, The
Meadowbrook Press
Mennonite Publishing House
Merlyn's Pen: The National Magazines of Student Writing, Grades 6-12
Nazarene International Headquarters
New Era Magazine
Night Roses
Oak, The
Pelican Publishing Company
Pikestaff Forum, The
Place in the Woods, The
Poetry of Hope Award
Poetry Society of Michigan Annual Contests
Ranger Rick Magazine
Salmon Arm Sonnet Contest
Sandberry Press
Seventeen
Shofar
Stone Soup, The Magazine by Young Writers and Artists
Straight
Touch
Vegetarian Journal
Voices of Youth
Waterways: Poetry in the Mainstream
Whole Notes

Wordsong
Young Crusader, The
Young Voices Magazine

Cowboy

American Cowboy Poet Magazine, The Boots: For Folks With Their Boots On!
Dry Crik Review
Paradise Publications
SideSaddle

Ethnic/Nationality

Adrift (Irish, Irish-American)
Africa World Press (Africans, African-American, Caribbean, Latin American)
African American Review
African Voices
Afro-Hispanic Review
Aim Magazine
Alicejamesbooks (poets of color)
Ararat (Armenian)
Asian Pacific American Journal
Bilingual Review Press (Hispanic)
Black Books Bulletin
Black Scholar, The
Blind Beggar Press
C.L.A.S.S. Magazine (Caribbean/American/ African Third World)
Callaloo (North, South and Central American; European; African; Caribbean)
Carn (Celtic)
Carolina Wren Press (minorities)
Chapman (Scottish)
Communications Publishing Group (African-American, Asian-American, Hispanic, Native American)
Ediciones Universal (Spanish, Cuban)
El Barrio (Latino)

Press Here (haiku, senryu, tanka)
Press of the Third Mind, The (Dada, surrealistic)
Prose Poem, The
Rant
Red Candle Press, The
Reflect (spiral)
Runaway Spoon Press, The (visual, textual)
Salmon Arm Sonnet Contest
Score Magazine (visual, concrete, experimental)
Sparrow: The Sonnet Yearbook
Sticks (10 lines or less)
Sub-Terrain
texture (innovative, experimental)
Thoughts for All Seasons: The Magazine of Epigrams
Woodnotes (haiku, senryu, tanka, haibun)
World Order of Narrative and Formalist Poets
Writers Forum (England) (experimental, sound, visual)

Gay/Lesbian/ Bisexual

Anything That Moves: Beyond The Myths of Bisexuality
Asian Pacific American Journal
Bay Windows
Belhue Press
Calyx, A Journal of Art & Literature by Women
Carolina Wren Press
Church-Wellesley Review, The
Common Lives/Lesbian Lives
Crescent Moon Publishing
Dwan
Evergreen Chronicles, The
Firebrand Books
First Hand
GLB Publishers
Ice Cold Watermelon

Kitchen Table: Women of Color Press
Kuumba
Libido: The Journal of Sex and Sexuality
New Poets Series, Inc., The
RFD: A Country Journal For Gay Men Everywhere
W.I.M. Publications (Woman in the Moon)
White Review: A Gay Men's Literary Quarterly, James
Wilde Oaks
Wishing Well, The
Women's Press

Horror

Dagger of the Mind
Dead of Night Publications
Deathrealm
Grue Magazine
Haunts
Night Songs
Nocturnal Lyric, Journal of the Bizarre
Oak, The
Prisoners of the Night
PYX Press
Scavenger's Newsletter
Science Fiction Poetry Association
Third Alternative, The
Twisted
2 AM Magazine
Virgin Meat
Wicked Mystic
WoRM fEASt!

Humor

Bits Press
Capper's
Country Woman
Feh! A Journal of Odious Poetry
Graffiti Off the Asylum Walls
Housewife-Writer's Forum
Idiot, The
Krax
Latest Jokes Newsletter
Leacock Medal for Humour, The Stephen

Libido: The Journal of Sex and Sexuality
Meadowbrook Press
Mississippi Valley Poetry Contest
Mystery Time
National Enquirer
New Writer's Magazine
New Yorker, The
Nuthouse
Poetry of the People
Poultry, A Magazine of Voice
Proof Rock Press
Raw Dog Press
REAL (Re Arts & Letters)
Rural Heritage
Saturday Evening Post
Thalia: Studies in Literary Humor
Thoughts for All Seasons: The Magazine of Epigrams
Timber Creek Review
Writer's Digest

Love/Romance/ Erotica

Aphrodite Gone Berserk: A Journal of Erotic Art
Art-Core!
Black Sheets
Blowfish Catalog, The
Cosmic Trend
Crescent Moon Publishing
DreamGirls With Shaman
Eidos Magazine: Sexual Freedom & Erotic Entertainment for Women, Men & Couples
Expedition Press
Explorer Magazine
Graffiti Off the Asylum Walls
Ice Cold Watermelon
Implosion Press
Libido: The Journal of Sex and Sexuality
M.I.P. Company
Modern Bride
Night Roses
Paramour Magazine
Peoplenet

Broadsheet Magazine (New Zealand)

Byron Poetry Works (IN, KY, MI, OH, PA, WV)

C.L.A.S.S. Magazine (Caribbean, American, African Third World)

Canadian Authors Association Literary Awards

Canadian Literature

Capers Aweigh Magazine (Cape Bretoners)

Caribbean Writer, The

Caxton Ltd., Wm (northern Midwest)

Chaminade Literary Review (HI)

Cincinnati Poetry Review

Cintas Fellowship Program (Cuba)

Coach House Press (Canada)

Coastal Forest Review (NJ)

Concho River Review (TX)

Confluence Press (Northwestern US)

Coolbrith Circle Annual Poetry Contest, Ina (CA)

Coteau Books (Canada)

Cottonwood (KS, Midwest)

Council for Wisconsin Writers, Inc.

Coyote Chronicles: Notes from the Southwest

Creative Artist Program (Houston)

Creative Writing Fellowships in Poetry (AZ)

Cross Roads: A Journal of Southern Culture

Dandelion (Alberta, Canada)

Descant (Canada)

Dolphin-Moon Press (MD)

Eastern Caribbean Institute

Ediciones Universal (Cuba)

El Barrio (SW Detroit)

Emerald Coast Review (Gulf Coast)

Farmer's Market (Midwest)

Fiddlehead, The (Canada, Atlantic)

Fireweed: Poetry of Western Oregon

Fleeting Monolith Enterprises (London, England)

Florida Individual Artist Fellowships

Footwork: The Paterson Literary Review (Passaic County, NJ)

Georgia Journal

Glassco Translation Prize, John (Canada)

Goose Lane Editions (Canada)

Guernica Editions Inc. (Italy, Canada, US)

Heartlands Today, The (Midwest)

High Plains Press (WY, US West)

HU (Northern Ireland)

Imago: New Writing (Queensland, Australia)

India Currents

Journal of New Jersey Poets

Kaimana: Literary Arts Hawaii (Pacific)

Kansas Quarterly

Kelsey Review (Mercer County, NJ)

Kentucky Artists Fellowships

Lampman Award (Ottawa)

Leacock Medal for Humour, The Stephen (Canada)

Lines Review (Scotland)

Long Island Quarterly

Loonfeather (MN)

Louisiana Literature

Maverick Press, The (TX)

Mayapple Press (Great Lakes)

Middle East Report

Midwest Villages & Voices

Mississippi Valley Poetry Contest

Missouri Writers' Biennial Award

Montana Arts Foundation Poetry Contest

New Jersey State Council on the Arts Fellowship Program

New Quarterly, The (Canada)

New Rivers Press (IA, MN, ND, SD, WI)

New York Foundation for the Arts

96 Inc (MA)

Ninety-Six Press (SC)

North Carolina Poetry Society Zoe Kincaid Brockman Memorial Book Award Contest, The

Now and Then (Appalachia)

Ohioana Book Awards

On Spec: The Canadian Magazine of Speculative Writing

Oregon East

Ornish Poetry Award, Natalie (TX)

Otter (Devon, England)

Pasque Petals (SD)

Pelican Publishing Company (Southern US)

Permafrost (AK)

Petronium Press (HI)

Pinchgut Press (Australia)

Poetry Harbor (upper Midwest)

Poetry Ireland Review

Poets' Dinner Contest

Potato Eyes (Appalachia)

Prairie Journal, The (Canada)

Prairie Publishing Company, The (Manitoba, Canada)

Prescott Street Press (Northwestern US)

Presidio La Bahia Award (TX)

Press Gang Publishers (Canada)

Puckerbrush Press, The (ME)

Pueblo Poetry Project

Puerto Del Sol (Southwest US)

Queen's Quarterly: A Canadian Review

Redneck Review of Literature, The (US West)

Regional Artists' Projects

Religious

Science Fiction/ Fantasy

DreamGirls With Shaman
Dreams and Nightmares
Gotta Write Network Litmag
Haunts
Hilltop Press
Leading Edge, The
Magazine of Speculative
    Poetry, The
Mythic Circle, The
Night Roses
Oak, The
On Spec: The Canadian
    Magazine of Speculative
    Writing
Pablo Lennis
Pirate Writings
Poetic Knight: A Fantasy
    Romance Magazine, The
Poetry of the People
Poet's Fantasy
Prisoners of the Night
PYX Press
Riverside Quarterly
Scavenger's Newsletter
Science Fiction Poetry
    Association
Struggle: A Magazine of
    Proletarian Revolution-
    ary Literature
Third Alternative, The
Twisted
2 AM Magazine
Urbanite, The
Works Magazine

Senior Citizen

Baptist Sunday School
    Board
Chicory Blue Press
Creative With Words Publi-
    cations (C.W.W.)
Fifty Something Magazine
Mature Years
Mississippi Valley Poetry
    Contest
Oak, The
Outreach: For The House-
    bound, Elderly and Disa-
    bled
Passager: A Journal of Re-
    membrance and Discov-
    ery
Yesterday's Magazette

Social Issues

Aim Magazine
Black Bear Publications
Carolina Wren Press
Christian Century, The
Collages & Bricolages, The
    Journal of International
    Writing
Daughters of Sarah
Green Fuse
Haight Ashbury Literary
    Journal
Implosion Press
Left Curve
Other Side Magazine, The
Peace Farm Advocate, The
Pudding House Publications
San Fernando Poetry Journal
Social Anarchism
Struggle: A Magazine of
    Proletarian Revolution-
    ary Literature
Sub-Terrain
West End Press

Specialized

Ag-Pilot International Mag-
    azine (crop dusting; air
    tanker pilots)
American Atheist Press
American Tolkien Society
Atlantean Press Review, The
    (romantic poetry)
Beer & Pub Poetry
Bloodreams: A Magazine of
    Vampires & Werewolves
Blue Mountain Arts, Inc.
    (greeting cards)
Boardman Tasker Award,
    The (mountain literature)
Carnegie Mellon Magazine
    (university affiliation)
Cat Fancy
Cats Magazine
Chronicle of the Horse, The
Classical Outlook, The
Cleaning Business Maga-
    zine
Climbing Art, The (moun-
    taineering)
Communities: Journal of
    Cooperative Living
Dance Connection

Disability Rag & Resource,
    The
Dream International Quar-
    terly
Dust (From the Ego Trip)
Exit 13 (geography/travel)
Expressions (people with
    disabilities/ongoing
    health problems)
Fighting Woman News
    (martial arts)
Forever Alive (physical
    immortality)
Friends Journal (Quakerism)
Full-Time Dads
Futurific Magazine
Harvard Advocate, The
    (university affiliation)
Healing Journal
Insects Are People Too
International Olympic Lifter
    (IOL)
Jewish Vegetarians News-
    letter
Journal of Asian Martial
    Arts
Journal of Poetry Therapy
Journal of the American
    Medical Association
    (JAMA)
Juggler's World
Just About Horses
Kaleidoscope: International
    Magazine of Literature,
    Fine Arts, and Disability
Mediphors (medicine/
    health-related)
Men As We Are
Midwifery Today (child-
    birth)
Musing Place, The (poets
    with a history of mental
    illness)
Naturally: Nude Recreation
    for All Ages
New Methods: The Journal
    of Animal Health Tech-
    nology (animals)
Outreach: For The House-
    bound, Elderly and Disa-
    bled
Peace Magazine (the 1960s)
Peoplenet (disabled people)

Pep Publishing ("ethical
multiple relationships")
Pipe Smoker's Ephemeris,
The
Poetry Forum
Psychopoetica (psychologi-
cally-based)
Radcliffe Quarterly (alum-
nae)
Samsara (suffering/healing)
Slate & Style (blind writers)
Spring: The Journal of the
E.E. Cummings Society
Stevens Journal, The Wal-
lace
Tradeswomen Magazine
Vegetarian Journal
Wildwood Journal (college
affiliation)
Womenwise (health issues)

Spirituality/
Inspirational
Alive Now
Capper's
Chrysalis Reader, The
Color Wheel
Crescent Moon Publishing
Dreambuilding Crusade,
The
Explorer Magazine
Gentle Survivalist, The
Heaven Bone Magazine
Intercultural Writer's Re-
view, The
Moksha Journal
New Earth Publications
Oblates
Ore
Parabola: The Magazine of
Myth and Tradition
Presbyterian Record, The
Sharing the Victory
Silver Wings
Sisters Today
Studio, A Journal of Christ-
ians Writing
Surprise Me
Threshold Books

Sports
Aethlon: The Journal of
Sport Literature

Sharing the Victory
Spitball

Students
Allegheny Review
Analecta
Arts Recognition and Talent
Search
Bucknell Seminar for
Younger Poets
College & Career Publishing
Dream Shop, The
Fiddlehead, The
Frost Chapter: California
Federation of Chaparral
Poets Annual Poetry
Competition, Robert
Hanging Loose Press
Intro
League of Minnesota Poets
Contest, The
Lyric, The
Merlyn's Pen: The National
Magazines of Student
Writing, Grades 6-12
Mississippi Valley Poetry
Contest
Modern Haiku
National Written & Illus-
trated By ... Awards
Contest for Students, The
Night Roses
Offerings
Pennsylvania Poetry Society
Annual Contest
Response
Student Leadership Journal
Voices of Youth
Writing Works

Themes (as
announced)
Alive Now
American Tolkien Society
Anything That Moves:
Beyond The Myths of
Bisexuality
Apalachee Quarterly
Art-Core!
Ashland Poetry Press, The
Asian Pacific American
Journal

Baptist Sunday School
Board
Bishop Publishing Co.
Black Sheets
Blue Mesa Review
Boots: For Folks With Their
Boots On!
Chicago Review
Chrysalis Reader, The
Collages & Bricolages, The
Journal of International
Writing
Colorado Review
Communications Publishing
Group
Cosmic Trend
Crab Creek Review
Creative With Words Publi-
cations (C.W.W.)
Creative Woman, The
CWM
Daughters of Sarah
Dolphin Log
Earth's Daughters: A Femi-
nist Arts Periodical
Event
Furry Chiclets: A Lawpoets
Creation
Green Rivers Writers'
Contests
Grolier Poetry Prize
Haight Ashbury Literary
Journal
Hartland Poetry Quarterly,
The
Heartlands Today, The
Indigo Magazine: The Span-
ish-Canadian Presence in
the Arts
Journal of the American
Medical Association
(JAMA)
Kalliope, a journal of
women's art
Kansas Quarterly
Magic Changes
Maverick Press, The
Middle East Report
Musicworks
My Legacy
Now and Then
Palo Alto Review
Papier-Mache Press

Parabola: The Magazine of Myth and Tradition
Partisan Review
Passager: A Journal of Remembrance and Discovery
Pegasus Review, The
Penumbra Press, The
Pig Iron
Poetry New York: A Journal of Poetry and Translation
Poetry of the People
Poetry of Hope Award
Poets On:
Prairie Journal, The
Rio Grande Press
Rosebud
Sensations Magazine
Skylark
Slipstream
South Carolina Review
South Dakota Review
Tak Tak Tak
Tamaqua
Tessera
Thema
Time of Singing, A Magazine of Christian Poetry
Touch
Unmuzzled Ox
Urbanite, The
Verve
Viet Nam Generation
Vincent Brothers Review, The
Vol. No. Magazine
Waterways: Poetry in the Mainstream
Witness
Woman's Way: The Path of Empowerment

Translations

Abiko Quarterly
American-Scandinavian Foundation Translation Prize
Artful Dodge
Atlantean Press Review, The
B.C.L.A. Translation Competition
Birmingham Poetry Review
Black Buzzard Press

Blue Unicorn, A Triquarterly of Poetry
Chants
Chelsea
Chicago Review
Classical Outlook, The
Collages & Bricolages, The Journal of International Writing
Colorado Review
Cross-Cultural Communications
Cumberland Poetry Review
Dwan
Eagle's Flight
Edinburgh Review
Ellipse
En Plein Air
Epigrammatist, The
Equinox Press
Field
Forest Books
Formalist, The
Frank: An International Journal of Contemporary Writing and Art
Frogpond: Quarterly Haiku Journal
G.W. Review
Glassco Translation Prize, John
Graham House Review
Guernica Editions Inc.
Hawai'i Review
Illinois Review, The
Indigo Magazine: The Spanish-Canadian Presence in the Arts
International Poetry Review
International Quarterly
Intertext
Iris: A Journal About Women
Jackson's Arm
Johann-Heinrich-Voss Prize for Translation
Kalliope, a journal of women's art
Lactuca
Lang Publishing, Inc., Peter
Lines Review
Manhattan Review, The
Mid-American Review

Mr. Cogito Press
New Directions Publishing Corporation
New Earth Publications
New Laurel Review, The
New Renaissance, The
New Rivers Press
New Yorker, The
Nordmanns-Forbundet Translation Grant
Ogalala Review, The
Ornish Poetry Award, Natalie
Osiris, An International Poetry Journal/Une Revue Internationale
Panjandrum Books
Partisan Review
Perivale Press
Poems for a Livable Planet
Poetic Space: Poetry & Fiction
Poetry New York: A Journal of Poetry and Translation
Polyphonies
Princeton University Press
Puerto Del Sol
Quarterly Review of Literature Poetry Series
REAL (Re Arts & Letters)
Renditions: A Chinese-English Translation Magazine
Review: Latin American Literature and Arts
Rocky Mountain Review of Language and Literature
Sachem Press
Seneca Review
Sonora Review
Southern Humanities Review
Spoon River Poetry Review, The
Stand Magazine
Stevan Company, The
Sulfur Magazine
Tampa Review
Tessera
Three Continents Press Inc.
Threshold Books
Touchstone Literary Journal
Wascana Review

General Index

Can't find a poetry publisher's listing? Check Publishers of Poetry/'95-'96 Changes on pages 453-454 for information about other publishers.

Can't find a poetry publisher's listing? Check Publishers of Poetry/'95-'96 Changes on pages 453-454 for information about other publishers.

Can't find a poetry publisher's listing? Check Publishers of Poetry/'95-'96 Changes on pages 453-454 for information about other publishers.

Can't find a poetry publisher's listing? Check Publishers of Poetry/'95-'96 Changes on pages 453-454 for information about other publishers.

Can't find a poetry publisher's listing? Check Publishers of Poetry/'95-'96 Changes on pages 453-454 for information about other publishers.

Can't find a poetry publisher's listing? Check Publishers of Poetry/'95-'96 Changes on pages 453-454 for information about other publishers.

Can't find a poetry publisher's listing? Check Publishers of Poetry/'95-'96 Changes on pages 453-454 for information about other publishers.

M

Can't find a poetry publisher's listing? Check Publishers of Poetry/'95-'96 Changes on pages 453-454 for information about other publishers.

Can't find a poetry publisher's listing? Check Publishers of Poetry/'95-'96 Changes on pages 453-454 for information about other publishers.

Can't find a poetry publisher's listing? Check Publishers of Poetry/'95-'96 Changes on pages 453-454 for information about other publishers.

Can't find a poetry publisher's listing? Check Publishers of Poetry/'95-'96 Changes on pages 453-454 for information about other publishers.

Can't find a poetry publisher's listing? Check Publishers of Poetry/'95-'96 Changes on pages 453-454 for information about other publishers.

Can't find a poetry publisher's listing? Check Publishers of Poetry/'95-'96 Changes on pages 453-454 for information about other publishers.

Can't find a poetry publisher's listing? Check Publishers of Poetry/'95-'96 Changes on pages 453-454 for information about other publishers.

**Can't find a poetry publisher's listing? Check Publishers of Poetry/'95-'96 Changes
on pages 453-454 for information about other publishers.**

More Great Books for Poets!

The Poetry Dictionary—This comprehensive book unravels the rich and complex language of poetry with clear, working definitions. Drury uses classic and contemporary examples to illustrate how poets have put theories to work. In many cases, several different poems are used to demonstrate the evolution of the form, making *The Poetry Dictionary* a unique anthology. It's a guide to the poetry of today and yesterday, with intriguing hints as to what tomorrow holds. *#48007/$18.99/336 pages*

The Art and Craft of Poetry—Find help from the masters of the past and present in fostering your own poetry writing skills, from generating ideas to constructing the poem. Through exercises you'll first learn how to develop observation and discovery skills; then focus on the craft itself: voice, line, stanza, meter and rhyme; and finish up with the modes and methods of expression—from narrative, lyric and dramatic verse to fixed, free and sequence styles. *#10392/$19.99/352 pages*

Creating Poetry—Designed to encourage budding poets to explore and practice poetry writing skills, Drury's nuts-and-bolts instruction addresses all elements of creating poetry. Each chapter offers an overview of each element discussed, a definition of terms, poetry examples, plus hands-on exercises. *#10209/$18.99/224 pages*

The Poet's Handbook—Here's expert instruction on how to use figurative language, symbols, and concrete images; how to tune the ear to sound relationships; the requirements for lyric, narrative, dramatic, didactic and satirical poetry and more. *#01836/$12.99/224 pages/paperback*

Idea Catcher—This spirited journal will help you open your eyes to the creative possibilities in your everyday world. You'll find something on every page of this journal to stimulate your senses and spark your imagination. *Idea Catcher* will teach you to use rich, surprising sources of inspiration through several writing "prompts." Plus, you'll find insightful quotes from well-known writers and short anecdotes about how authors "caught" the ideas that became great works of literature. *#48011/$14.99/160 pages*

The Best Writing on Writing—The collection of memorable essays, book excerpts and lectures on fiction, nonfiction, poetry, screenwriting and the writing life, all from 1994, features such luminaries as Joyce Carol Oates, Margaret Atwood, Justin Kaplan, Charles Baxter and Maxine Kumin to name a few. *#48013/$16.99/ 224 pages/paperback*

Roget's Superthesaurus—For whenever you need just the right word! You'll find "vocabulary builder" words with pronunciation keys and sample sentences, quotations that double as synonyms, plus the only word-find reverse dictionary in any thesaurus—all in an easy alphabetical format! *#10424/$22.99/624 pages*

The Complete Guide to Self-Publishing—Discover how to make the publishing industry work for you! You'll get step-by-step guidance on every aspect of publishing from cover design and production tips to sales letters and publicity strategies. *#10444/$18.99/432 pages/paperback*

How to Write Fast (While Writing Well)—Learn step-by-step how to cut wasted time and effort by planning interviews for maximum results, beating writer's block with effective plotting, getting the most information from traditional library research and online computer bases, and much more! *#10473/$15.99/208 pages/paperback*

Writing and Illustrating Children's Books for Publication—Create a good, publishable manuscript in eight weeks with the help of this self-taught writing course which covers ideas and getting started, format, theme, setting, plot and characters, writing and polishing, and much more! *#10448/$24.95/128 pages/200 b&w illus./16-page color insert*

Writer's Market—Let this completely revised and updated edition help you realize your writing dreams. This edition contains information on 4,000 writing opportunities. You'll find all the facts vital to the success of your writing career, including an up-to-date listing of buyers of books, articles and stories; listings of contests and awards; plus articles and interviews with top professionals. *#10432/$27.99/1008 pages*

Editors Share More Views ———

"To save postage, we see multiple poems on one sheet, and two-sided pages. This can cause problems. We almost published the first part of a two-sided poem. Perhaps it should have ended there." —Ron Reichick, **Verve**

"We love cover letters. We like to know who we are publishing, and we want to build a community of writers not just a magazine. Although time is something we don't have a lot of, we want to stay in touch with people we publish after the issue has gone to press."
  —W. Brian Ellis, **The Purple Monkey**

"I feel that the inclusion of a cover letter, with a brief three-line bio in case the work is accepted, is essential. This is not because we give increased attention to those who have been widely published, but because it streamlines the production process greatly."
—Rick Sides, **The Pennsylvania Review**

"I value the poet who takes the time to write a cover letter and uses the standard format for submitting poetry. It's aggravating reviewing poetry without even the basic information about the poet on each page. I seldom respond to those who continuously ignore enclosing a SASE. The beginner may not know better, the established poet has no excuse. . . ."
  —Denise Fleischer, **Gotta Write Network**

"We request, nay, demand that poets tell us whether their submissions are disposable. There are far too many postage-due submissions arriving—and far too many SASEs with incorrect postage. I've got one with 13¢ in postage. To what planet shall I mail this?"   —Shannon Frach, **Hyacinth House**